Praise for *Under t... ...ader*

"*Under the Loving Care of the Fatherly Leader* is, from all I have read, simply the best book ever written about North Korea. . . . Martin portrays North Korean life with a clarity that is stunning."
— Nicholas Kristof, *The New York Review of Books*

"Successfully combines history, society, travel writing, and political analysis in a way that makes it totally readable. . . . Must be the most comprehensive single-volume English-language book ever written on North Korea. . . . Overall, Bradley Martin has written a truly remarkable book, one that should be read by anyone even remotely interested in North Korea."
— Yoel Sano, *Asia Times*

"An excellent book, well researched and lucidly written. It is especially refreshing to find someone showing serious interest in North Korean propaganda instead of merely hooting at it."
— B. R. Myers, *The Atlantic Monthly*

"Rich with revealing detail . . . Given the appalling risks of military action, we should give the type of positive engagement that Martin proposes a serious try."
— Mike Mochizuki, *The Washington Post Book World*

"Cracking the cocoon of secrecy and propaganda surrounding North Korea is not a job for the faint of heart. Yet somehow Martin, a former *Newsweek* bureau chief, has pulled it off, presenting a scrupulously detailed, intimate portrait of the Kims, the world's only communist dynasty. He deconstructs the mythologized biographies of the father-and-son leaders, taking us inside their family feuds, harems, and fortified villas."
— Christian Caryl, *Newsweek*

"Fascinating . . . may be the best and most comprehensive English-language history of North Korea ever written."
— Jacob Margolies, *The Daily Yomiuri* (Tokyo)

"Of course no one is really certain what goes on in North Korea. . . . [T]here has been very little human intelligence of value over the last fifty years or so. . . . Bradley K. Martin has stepped into this breach. . . . Martin's massive book provides as useful a set of insights into life in North Korea as can be found anywhere."
— Warren I. Cohen, *Los Angeles Times Book Review*

"The most comprehensive and detailed look yet at the nation-sized theme park of Kim World is Bradley Martin's *Under the Loving Care of the Fatherly Leader*. Mr. Martin paints a portrait of a national horror show demonstrating how ruthless, effective, and evil men can oppress their neighbors. . . . It reads like a medieval court, the Ottoman sultanate, or imperial China. . . . [T]he book paints a vast canvas of what must be as close as possible to hell on earth, other than in the very midst of war."
— Doug Bandow, *The Washington Times*

"*Under the Loving Care of the Fatherly Leader* is a rich and rewarding book that anyone interested in this strange Leninist vestige should read. The sensational extravagance of the leadership; the dreadful sufferings of the common people; the ludicrous personality cults thrown up by both Kims; Kim Jong-il's need for nuclear weapons and ballistic missiles (his possession of the latter is certain, of the former highly probable); the systematic destruction of normal life and language in North Korea—all this is laid out here for inspection. If I may be permitted a book reviewer's cliché: I couldn't put it down. . . . By sheer relentless accumulation of detail, Martin succeeds here in giving us a full portrait of the Kims and their filthy little tyranny."
— John Derbyshire, *National Review*

"Like Orville Schell's penetrating studies of China under Mao, *Under the Loving Care of the Fatherly Leader* is destined to become a classic of Asian studies."
— Derek Pell, *DingBat Magazine*

"A page-turner with footnotes as interesting as the narrative."
— *Get Lost Books*

"Bradley Martin . . . portrays North Korea as a failed state with a dangerous weapon, but he explores as well the mentality of Mr. Kim and of his father, Kim Il-sung, whose leadership from 1948 to 1994 did so much to seal North Korea's fate. Kim Il-sung, Mr. Martin reminds us, once wrote: 'One is pleased to see the bugs die in a fire even though one's house is burned down.' "
— Gordon G. Chang, *The Wall Street Journal*

"A detailed account of the world's most remote kingdom and its leaders, Kim Il-sung and ruling son Kim Jong-il. Martin's analysis illustrates that North Korea is a traditional more than a revolutionary society"
— Robert A. Scalapino, *JoongAng Daily*

"It is often said that North Korea is the most puzzling country in the world. It is a difficult place to visit. The few journalists who make it there don't have the freedom to interview anyone they want. Its archives are not open to scholars. This does not mean, however, that no information is available on North Korea. It just requires a little bit more digging and interpreting. For the last three decades, veteran journalist Bradley Martin has been compiling his notes drawn from four trips to North Korea, patient scrutiny of official publications, and interviews with numerous defectors. His book *Under the Loving Care of the Fatherly Leader*, an immense and detailed examination of North Korean history and politics, integrates much of the recent scholarship on the country and adds some new pieces to the puzzle. . . . The picture of North Korean society that emerges from the narrative is far more thorough and detailed than the usual monochromatic depiction of a monolithic state."
—John Feffer, *Korean Quarterly*

" 'Axis of evil' member North Korea is not on the tourist map for most Western travelers, so its people and what their lives are like are mostly out of reach. Bradley K. Martin . . . moves North Korea within sight in this detailed account."

—Dan R. Barber, *Dallas Morning News*

"Under different circumstances, North Korea could be the subject of a Marx Brothers satire, with the elements of a pompous, ego-driven patriarch, a worshipful population, and a general aura of fantasy and illusion. But North Korea has a superbly equipped million-man army and an expanding nuclear weapons program. So this comprehensive examination of this totalitarian society and the two men who have dominated it is often terrifying. For a quarter century, Martin has covered North Korea while working for the *Baltimore Sun*, the *Asian Wall Street Journal*, and *Newsweek*. Using newly available material from Russian and Chinese sources, Martin offers surprising insights into the career and character of both Kim Il-sung and his son, Kim Jong-il."
—*Booklist*

"This massive study of North Korea embraces its political and economic history over the last seventy years; the lives of its leaders, Kim Il-sung and Kim Jong-il; its diplomatic relations with South Korea, Japan, China, and the United States since 1945; its current crises regarding nuclear weapons and food shortages. . . . Martin, a former bureau chief for the *Baltimore Sun*, the *Asian Wall Street Journal*, and *Newsweek*, has much to offer."
—John F. Riddick, *Library Journal*

"A sharp-eyed look at a cold and hungry outpost of the Axis of Evil. Former *Newsweek* bureau chief Martin first traveled to North Korea in 1979, and what he found was a near-religious cult of personality centered on the person of Kim Il-sung, known variously as the Great Leader, Fatherly Leader, Respected and Beloved Leader, and so on, a partial listing of whose reputed achievements 'would have aroused the envy of a Leonardo da Vinci or Thomas Jefferson.'"
　　　　　　　　　　　　　　　　　　　　　　　　　　　　—*Kirkus Reviews*

"As a result of North Korea's isolation, it's been extremely difficult to get any information about what goes on inside the country, apart from the testimonies of defectors. That's why Bradley Martin's book, *Under the Loving Care of the Fatherly Leader: North Korea and the Kim Dynasty,* is so valuable . . . perhaps the most comprehensive look at the country yet."
　　　　　　　　　　　　　　　　　　　　—Lisa Katayama, *Mother Jones*

"The top U.S. envoy to North Korea is reading a book about the personality cult surrounding the leadership of the North, the world's most impenetrable state. When U.S. Assistant Secretary of State Christopher Hill arrived at a South Korean airport on Saturday for talks on Pyongyang's nuclear weapons program, he was seen holding a book titled *Under the Loving Care of the Fatherly Leader: North Korea and the Kim Dynasty.*"
　　　　　　　—Yonhap news agency, "U.S. nuclear negotiator reading book on
　　　　　　　　　　　　North Korean leaders," *Korea Herald,* May 16, 2005

"Bradley K. Martin has been watching North Korea for a quarter of a century, and his important new book proves just how much it is possible to learn about that closed and secretive country through careful observation and analysis. *Under the Loving Care of the Fatherly Leader* will immediately become an indispensable source for anyone trying to make sense of the modern North Korean state. This is journalism at its best—nothing so comprehensive and authoritative has been written about North Korea for thirty years. It is frankly amazing that a non-Korean could produce such a work."
　　　　　　　　　　　—Nicholas Eberstadt, American Enterprise Institute,
　　　　　　　　　　　　　　　　　　　　author of *The End of North Korea*

"The book is an absolute marvel of new information. . . . A wonderful contribution to the limited information available about North Korea and should be read by both professionals and the general public."
　　　　　　　　　　　　　　　　　—Steven A. Leibo, The Sage Colleges

"*Under the Loving Care of the Fatherly Leader* is terrific. Vastly informative, compulsively readable, it is without doubt the single best book ever written on North Korea."

—Mike Chinoy, senior Asia correspondent, CNN

"Scrupulously checks facts and cross-references stories . . . to find out what it's like to live in North Korea, to raise a family, work in a factory, be a policeman, go to a prison camp. . . . Lively and well done. . . . Easily the most comprehensive accessible account of North Korea."

—Bruce Cumings, *London Review of Books*

"A careful, penetrating analysis of North Korea. Given the levels of secrecy which surround the Pyongyang regime and the danger it poses to its neighbors, Brad Martin has rendered a considerable public service to us all."

—David Halberstam

"As copious an account of Kim Jong-il's ghastliness as one could desire. North Korea may be an ontological crime—but it's still there, and to change it we first have to understand it. Martin forgives the Kims nothing while elucidating much. . . . Exceptionally good."

—Aidan Foster-Carter, Leeds University

"The book is terrific. Bradley Martin has solidly and vividly reconstructed North Korea from the inside, through his extensive interviews with refugees, much as Mike Oksenberg, Doak Barnett, and Ezra Vogel did with China during the Cultural Revolution."

—Yoichi Funabashi, *Asahi Shimbun* columnist

"Thoughtful and informed account . . . Korea specialists will find valuable information and insights in this thick volume that is not exclusively a historical study, but also an oral history, a personal memoir, and a sensational exposé . . . excels in presenting new details about the background, personality, and political maneuvers of Kim Jong-il."

—James I. Matray, *Korean Studies*

"The assumption is that very little is known about what life is like for ordinary people within the country. But Martin's research shows that a surprising amount is out there if you look for it."

—Kerry Brown, *The Asian Review of Books*

"A terrific new book on North Korea, *Under the Loving Care of the Fatherly Leader* by Bradley Martin, underscores how those few glimpses that North Koreans have had of the outside world — by working in logging camps in Russia or sneaking trips to China — have helped undermine Mr. Kim's rule."
— Nicholas Kristof, *The New York Times*

"Martin has put together what is probably the best available description of day-to-day existence for flesh and blood individuals and families in North Korea. They are all there: labor-camp prisoners; exiles banished from the cities to remote, starving rural hamlets; soldiers; farmers; academics and students; bureaucrats; traders and hustlers; generals; scientists; party officials; entertainers; and the two quasi deities themselves."
— Bill James, *News Weekly*

"The best recent book on North Korea's cult of personality."
— *The Chosun Journal*

"A remarkable book and probably the most important on North Korea for many years . . . a mine of insights that are both fascinating and alarming."
— Howard Winn, *Finance Asia*

"So, it's been confirmed. North Korea has nuclear weapons. . . . The hawks versus doves debate won't help us much. What might help us, though, is reading the best book ever published about North Korea."
— *Eamonn Fitzgerald's Rainy Day*

"The mother lode. Ferociously detailed, lengthy account of the world's only communist dynasty."
— *blogjam*

"Gives more details about Kims's lives than any other, and these two Byzantine figures are the most mysterious of any national rulers anywhere. And as Kim the younger could be, at least in theory, the next man to drop a nuclear bomb on the world, he is worth knowing about."
— Christopher Reed, *Counterpunch*

UNDER

THE

LOVING CARE

OF THE

FATHERLY LEADER

NORTH KOREA AND
THE KIM DYNASTY

BRADLEY K. MARTIN

Thomas Dunne Books
St. Martin's Griffin ≋ *New York*

THOMAS DUNNE BOOKS.
An imprint of St. Martin's Press.

UNDER THE LOVING CARE OF THE FATHERLY LEADER. Copyright © 2004, 2006 by Bradley
K. Martin. All rights reserved. Printed in the United States of America. For information,
address St. Martin's Press, 175 Fifth Avenue, New York, N.Y. 10010.

www.stmartins.com

Library of Congress Cataloging-in-Publication Data

Martin, Bradley K.
Under the loving care of the fatherly leader : North Korea and the Kim dynasty /
Bradley K. Martin.
p. cm.
ISBN 0-312-32221-6 (hc)
ISBN 0-312-32322-0 (pbk)
EAN 978-0-312-32322-6
1. Kim, Chong-il, 1942–   2. Kim, Il-song, 1912–   3. Kim family.   4. Heads of state—
Korean (North)—Biography.   5. Korea (North)—Politics and government.   I. Title.

DS934.6.K44 M37 2004
951.9304'3'0922—dc22
[B]
2004056158

20 19 18 17 16 15 14 13 12 11

This book is dedicated to the memory of my parents,
Bradley K. Martin Sr. and Christine Logan Martin.
For them, loving care never became a propaganda slogan.

CONTENTS

PROLOGUE

Here and there among the greenery were palace-like buildings. . . .
"Communism," said I to myself. . . . There were no hedges, no signs
of proprietary rights, no agriculture. . . . The shop, the advertise-
ment, traffic, all that commerce which constitutes the body of our
world, was gone. It was natural on that golden evening that I should
jump at the idea of a social paradise.

—H. G. WELLS, *THE TIME MACHINE*

Alas, as Wells's time traveler soon discovered, man "had not remained one
species, but had differentiated into two distinct animals." The first Eloi spec-
imen he encountered was "indescribably frail. His flushed face reminded me
of the more beautiful kind of consumptive."

The Eloi were a gentle, childlike people who stood "perhaps four feet
high." In their eyes the traveler detected "a certain lack of the interest I
might have expected in them. . . . The question had come into my mind
abruptly: were these creatures fools? . . . You see, I had always anticipated
that the people of the year Eight Hundred and Two Thousand—odd would be
incredibly in front of us in knowledge, art, everything. Then one of them
suddenly asked me a question that showed him to be on the intellectual level
of one of our five-year-old children."

The Eloi proved to be descendants of the wealthier classes of humans.
However, "all the activity, all the traditions, the complex organizations, the
nations, languages, literatures, aspirations, even the mere memory of Man as
I knew him, had been swept out of existence. Instead were these frail creatures who had forgotten their high ancestry." Still, "[h]owever great their

intellectual degradation, the Eloi had kept too much of the human form not to claim my sympathy, and to make me perforce a sharer in their degradation and their Fear."

The dominant species, the Morlocks, had evolved from the working class. Morlocks lived and worked underground, where they kept the machinery that gave them their power. Clever, they treated the Eloi like domesticated herds and lived off them. They were carnivorous, nocturnal. "Beneath my feet then the earth must be tunneled enormously, and these tunnelings were the habitat of the New Race."[1]

In Wells's imagination it had taken 800 millennia for humanity to change so drastically. In North Korea a remarkably similar evolution took only a half-century. The North Korean changes, not likely to be reversed quickly or easily, were largely the work of two men: Kim Il-sung and his son Kim Jong-il (whose gigantic personal movie library no doubt includes both the 1960 and 2002 Hollywood versions of Wells's classic).

This is the story of how they did it.

UNDER THE LOVING CARE OF

THE FATHERLY LEADER

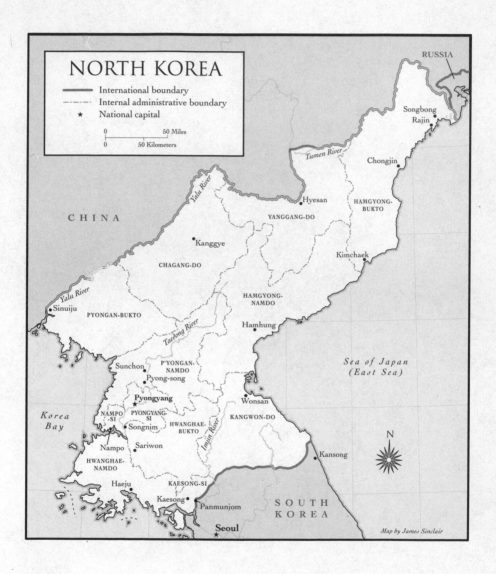

NORTH KOREA

— International boundary
—·—·— Internal administrative boundary
★ National capital

0   50 Miles
0   50 Kilometers

RUSSIA

CHINA

Tumen River

Yalu River

Songbong
Rajin

Chongjin

Hyesan

YANGGANG-DO

HAMGYONG-
BUKTO

Kanggye

CHAGANG-DO

Kimchaek

Yalu River

HAMGYONG-
NAMDO

Sinuiju

PYONGAN-BUKTO

Taedong River

Hamhung

*Sea of Japan
(East Sea)*

Sunchon

P'YONGAN-
NAMDO

Pyong-song

Pyongyang

Wonsan

*Korea
Bay*

NAMPO
-SI

PYONGYANG-
SI

HWANGHAE-
BUKTO

KANGWON-DO

Songnim

Imjin River

N

Nampo

Sariwon

Kansong

HWANGHAE-
NAMDO

Haeju

KAESONG-SI

Kaesong

Panmunjom

SOUTH
KOREA

Seoul

Map by James Sinclair

ONE

To the City of the God-King

Reading about the personality cult of the North Korean leader had not fully prepared me for what I found when I arrived in Pyongyang in April 1979, as a member of the first large contingent of Americans to visit since the Korean War. As I was encountering an economy and society almost unimaginably different from any I had known, the stay was full of surprises. But next to the astonishing all-pervasiveness of leader-worship the rest seemed mere detail.

Everyone sprinkled his speech with straight-faced references to "our Respected and Beloved Leader," "our Great Leader," "our Fatherly Leader." Everyone wore a portrait of the round-faced, unsmiling Kim Il-sung on a gold-framed, enameled badge pinned to the left breast. Larger portraits and statues of the Leader were everywhere.

It gradually became apparent that this was a religion. To North Koreans, Kim Il-sung was more than just a leader. He showered his people with fatherly love. If I could believe what my ears were hearing he might even be immortal, able to provide his followers eternal life. The realization grew during my first few days in Pyongyang. It crystallized as I sat in the Mansudae Art Theater watching a performance of *Song of Paradise*, a musical drama lavishly staged on the scale of a grand opera or Broadway musical.

The curtain rises to reveal a nighttime view of downtown Pyongyang. Holiday crowds enjoy themselves as neon signs and fireworks light up the city's impressive skyline of tall buildings and monuments. Son-hui, a journalist played by a buxom soprano, is about to depart on a trip around the country to gather material for a series of articles on the glories of the workers' paradise. She is unaware that the Great Leader, meanwhile, has commissioned a search for the orphaned daughter of a Korean War hero. The crowd-chorus, overcome with joy at the wonders of social- ist construction, unleashes a mighty, soaring, swelling hymn worthy of the Mor- mon Tabernacle Choir: "With the Leader who unfolded this paradise, we shall live for generations to come."

Paradise? To a first-time visitor, North Korea seemed to be providing its people the basic necessities of life. But there was little sign of opulence and I never saw anyone cutting loose and having a really good time. Even on the May Day holiday, people seemed to be working—as actors, posing as merry- makers and subway passengers for the benefit of foreign visitors. A group of little boys in the uniform of the children's corps sat cross-legged in a circle on the ground in a park, playing a game. A couple of hours later they still sat in the same position, playing the same game, confounding the collective wisdom of the outside world regarding attention spans of unsupervised eight-year-olds.

In the deeply dug, sparkling-clean Pyongyang Metro, with its glittering chandeliers and its imposing murals honoring Kim Il-sung, I saw "passen- gers" exit the station via the escalator and then turn around and go back in for another ride—their repetitive all-day assignment, I supposed.[1] Trains com- posed of only two cars each stopped for several minutes at each station, and the tracks showed enough rust to suggest that impressing visitors was a more important consideration than transporting people in a city where buses could glide quickly through nearly empty streets.

Still, who could be more qualified to unfold a paradise than Kim Il- sung? A partial listing of his talents would have aroused the envy of a Leonardo da Vinci or Thomas Jefferson. Kim was the country's leading nov- elist, philosopher, historian, educator, designer, literary critic, architect, in- dustrial management specialist, general, table tennis trainer (the Americans were in town for the world championship)—and agriculture experimenter. "Our Great Leader," said my government-assigned interpreter, Han Yong, "has a small plot at his residence where he tests planting for a year or two."

One officially propagated "legend" about Kim Il-sung's days as an anti- Japanese guerrilla fighter in the 1930s and '40s described him as a mighty gen- eral astride a white horse, "carrying an enormous sword, cutting a big tree down as if slicing soft bean curd." Another had him walking on water: "Great Leader Comrade Kim Il-sung turned pine cones into bullets and grains of sand into rice, and crossed a large river riding on fallen leaves." To hear the North Koreans talk, Kim must have made himself heir to the ancient Taoist magi- cians' secrets for transcending time and space.

Now he was paying more than lip service to pursuing the goal of living with his people "for generations to come." Kim by 1979 was girding up for a contest with the mortality tables. He celebrated, lavishly, his sixty-seventh birthday on April 15 of that year. During his more than three decades at the helm of the country, he had focused his considerable abilities and enormous power on ensuring that he would outlive his rivals one way or another.

The president smoked heavily and a large if nonmalignant tumor protruded from his neck, both negative signs for one who sought immortality. With little fanfare, however (I learned of this many years later), his government had established a longevity research institute in 1972 on the occasion of his sixtieth birthday. Researchers there were hard at work to make sure Kim would see his seventieth birthday and his eightieth.

Son-hui joins factory girls who are making merry in a Pyongyang park on their day off. They sing of "our happy life, which is always in a festive mood." The heroine's adoptive mother, who heads a work team on a farm, comes to the park and chants her gratitude to the Fatherly Leader, who has brought up the orphaned Son-hui to be a reporter. The two women sing a duet: "Under the Loving Care of the Fatherly Leader."

Solicitude toward war orphans was an important aspect of the image of himself that Kim projected. A quarter of North Korea's 1950 population of 10 million died in the Korean War.[2] Afterward, Pyongyang said, the state raised youngsters who had lost their parents, teaching them to think of Kim Il-sung as their father, themselves as his children. Some of those, like the fictitious Son-hui, had grown up to become members of the elite corps of officials and intellectuals.

On a night train trip[3] to the city of Kaesong, I shared a bottle of whiskey with a man who introduced himself as Bai Song-chul, an official of the Committee for Cultural Relations with Foreign Countries.[4] While other North Koreans I had met sounded totally rehearsed, Bai spoke spontaneously and directly through thin lips that often turned downward in a frown or into a sardonic smile. There was intelligence in his eyes, which seemed to try to peer over his dark-rimmed spectacles. Thick hair (black, of course) surmounted a high forehead and an oval yet strong-jawed face. At thirty-nine years old, he obviously was an up-and-coming member of the elite. Not very tall, he carried himself with something akin to a swagger. His forthrightness bespoke a confidence born of position and access to high levels. As the conversation progressed, I felt emboldened to tell him frankly that I could not help finding the Kim Il-sung cult ludicrous. Bai frowned and replied that such a reaction from an American, new to his country, did not surprise him—"but we feel bad when you talk that way."

Bai said all North Koreans had personal experiences that inspired respect and affection for the Great Leader. Bai himself had been orphaned in the Korean War, he told me. "Kim Il-sung came to our village and asked how many orphans there were. He called us together and said: 'You can stay here or you can go to orphans' school. It's up to you.' We went to the orphans' school. At New Year's, Kim Il-sung came and told us: 'You have no parents, so think of me as your father.'" Bai told his story with force and feeling. It seemed to come from the heart, and I saw no reason to doubt that the filial love he expressed for Kim Il-sung was genuine.

The reporter Son-hui, visiting an orchard, recalls the Great Leader's 1958 teaching that fruit trees should be planted on the hillsides. "Wherever you go in my homeland, the flowers of His great love are blooming," she sings. "We shall live forever in this land of bliss, with His love and care in our hearts."

Dancing farm women take up the theme and sing: "Let's spread the pollen of love. . . . The flowers bloom in the Leader's sunlight."

In North Korea, not just the arias and choruses in *Song of Paradise* but nearly all the songs we heard were about Kim Il-sung. Usually singers sang about him tenderly, with that sense of exultant yet exquisitely agonizing groping upward toward the ineffable that marks the high-church Christian musical tradition. Television documentaries showed the president out among the people, giving "on-the-spot guidance" to farmers. Sweet, sad instrumental music began playing when his face became visible. A television news program showed a foreign visitor picking up a book from a display. The camera moved in for a close-up of the volume, which was one of many works by the Respected and Beloved Leader. Sweet, sad music played as the image lingered on the screen.

People, at least the ones foreign visitors could talk with, spoke about the Leader the same way they sang about him: solemnly but lovingly. Their eyes showed their sincerity, and there was no outward sign of cynicism.

The deputy manager of the fruit farm recalls the days when he fought alongside a soon-to-die Korean War hero—the man for whose orphaned daughter Kim Il-sung has now commissioned a search. As the scene shifts to a realistic-looking wartime battle, the farm leader and other war veterans sing: "For three years and three months I have been under arms. My song echoes home from the trenches when I smash U.S. invaders seeking to rob us of our happiness."

Contrary to the understanding of most of the rest of the world, North Koreans generally believed that the South Koreans had invaded the North to start the Korean War and that North Korea then had gone on to win the war. They believed it as an article of faith because Kim Il-sung told them so. The regime worked successfully to keep at white-hot intensity the people's hatred of American and South Korean invaders and Japanese imperialists. Those outsiders, described as forever hatching new schemes to undermine and attack the North, got the blame for any problems at home. Thus, there was no need for Kim's subjects even to consider the heretical thought that the Great Leader and his system might have something to do with their problems.

Son-hui and the women of a fishing village welcome the fishermen back from a voyage. "Let us enhance our honor as proud fishermen of our Leader," the fishermen sing. "Let us gladden our Leader, our Fatherly Leader. O graceful sea, under His loving care, sway your elegant waves forever! Korea's happy, thriving sea, sing in praise of our Leader's kindness."

Hearing of the fishermen's return from the deep sea, the Great Leader has instructed that they and their families be sent to vacation at scenic Mount Kumgang. The announcement moves the fishermen to tears and the audience to applause. "Oh, this is kindly love, a love much deeper than the deepest sea," sings the fishermen's chorus. "Our hearts throbbed with emotion profound when He hugged us still damp from the sea. By our Fatherly Leader's love . . . even the waters are touched, and quiver. We dedicate our youth to repaying His kindness. The boundless love of our Leader will last forever, like the sea."

People were constantly telling me stories about Kim Il-sung's benevolence. For example, he supposedly sent a team of doctors with medicine "worth the cost of a small factory" aboard his personal airplane when he heard that a resident of the mountains was critically ill.[5]

Even writing off 99 percent to propaganda, it was clear that Kim possessed considerable political genius. In his ability to make North Koreans feel close to him and personally indebted to him, Kim operated much like a successful old-time American big-city boss. Whatever anybody got in the way of goodies came in Kim's name, as a "gift." Instead of Christmas, North Koreans celebrated Kim's birthday—and he sent a present to each child, just like Santa Claus. The Great Leader seemed to get out of the capital a lot, offer his "on-the-spot guidance" and let the people see him.[6] Bai Song-chul told me that Kim was accustomed to spending very little time in Pyongyang. Thus, many people around the country had been in his presence.

Bai said that every North Korean voluntarily wore a badge with Kim's picture. Even if someone happened not to be wearing a badge on a particular day, that did not mean he or she failed to respect the Great Leader. The person simply had forgotten—perhaps had failed to switch the badge while changing clothes.

Son-hui departs for scenic Mount Kumgang, where working people on vacation admire the magnificent view of Nine-Dragon Falls. They chant praises of their country, its beautiful mountains and limpid streams. They extol their Leader. "We shall live with Him forevermore," they sing. "The garden of bliss blooms in His sunlight." Son-hui joins vacationers in singing: "Our happiness blooms in our Leader's care. How glorious to live in our socialist paradise. Let us sing of our socialist nation, of our earthly paradise free from oppression."

Vacationing teachers laud the school system: "As soon as you are born you are received by a nursery, then led through a flowery gate to eleven-year education."

Indeed, officials told me, mothers were entitled to seventy-seven days of maternity leave before turning their babies over to public day nurseries, or in some cases full-time nurseries. "Home education has an important meaning in a society where private ownership of the means of production is predominant," Kim Il-sung had said in a 1968 speech. "But it has no important meaning in a different, socialist society."[7] The state, taking over much of the parental role, had been training youngsters to worship Kim. "Our Great Leader is the Supreme Leader of revolution, its heart and the only center," said one official policy statement. "We have to inculcate in our future generations the absolute authority of the Leader, the indisputable thoughts and instructions of the Leader, so that they may accept them as faith and the law of the land."[8]

Schoolbooks portrayed Kim in his heroic roles. Their illustrations were drawings in the style of children's biblical literature in the United States. Some pictured Kim's exploits, whether real or imagined, as a child and as a young guerrilla commander. Others depicted a mature Kim, sometimes surrounded by children in tableaux reminiscent of the Sunday-school pictures that illustrate the words of Jesus, "Suffer the little children to come unto me." A sort of aura or halo was affixed to the Great Leader's head in those pictures.

The training and peer pressure that reinforced such images had intensified over the years. Thus, the young people I met struck me as more fanatical than North Koreans aged forty or older, whose indoctrination had not been as thoroughgoing.

I was suspicious of the notion of total unanimity and said as much to Bai. "Of course, we have people who dissent; that's why we have police," he replied with his characteristic bluntness—and with a trace of what may have been irritation that I had put him on the spot. But Bai insisted that simple disagreement with policy didn't equate to punishable dissent. For example, he said, when office workers met to decide whether to help out on farms or in factories, voices against the idea could be heard—but once the group decided to volunteer, everyone in the unit had to go along.

I had heard repeatedly during my stay of measures to guard against "impure elements." On a night drive from the east coast, for example, my driver pulled up at a floodlit guard post. When I asked for whom the guards were searching, the answer was "impure elements." Nobody would tell me just what these impure elements were. "*You* know," said one North Korean, peering at me like a disciplinarian schoolteacher waiting for me to confess my guilt. "*You* know who they are." Actually I did not know. When I pestered Bai, he finally grew impatient enough to spit out an unadorned definition. Impure elements, he said, "are spies, people trying to destroy the system. We shoot them." It seemed, then, that "impure elements" were South Korean or American agents, including the saboteurs against whom rifle-toting soldiers were posted at highway and railway bridges.

"We are free from exploitation," the happy vacationers sing, "free from tax or levy, completely free from care for food or clothing. Our socialist system, which our Great Leader has built, is the best in the world."

Although rather severe food shortages had affected at least some parts of the country since the mid-1970s, North Koreans evidently believed that much of what they had was indeed the best in the world. Kim Il-sung told them so, and few had any basis for comparison. Almost none traveled outside the country. Those who did were trusted officials. The foreign news North Koreans got was carefully selected, with little from the industrialized West. Radios were built so they could be tuned only to the official frequency. "Newspapers" were propaganda sheets that filled their pages with Kim Il-sung's speeches. Articles told of foreigners gathering abroad to celebrate the brilliance of Kim, who had "wonderfully adorned human history in the twentieth century"⁹—and whose ideas clearly were the answers to the problems of the underdeveloped world.¹⁰

Son-hui and a photographer tour Mount Paektu, "the holy mountain of revolution," and the battlefields of Kim Il-sung's anti-Japanese struggle. They sing of Kim's feats in "repulsing the one-million-strong Japanese army. Each tree and flower seems to relate the days of struggle against the Japanese. On long marches through blizzards He mapped out today's paradise . . . our blissful land of today."

An image of Mangyongdae, the president's humble ancestral home, appears in the background. A red sun, another symbol of Kim Il-sung, is projected onto the image. The Korean audience applauds as women soldiers onstage remove their hats and bow to the image.

Kim Il-sung could legitimately claim a genuine guerrilla background. He had fought hard against the Japanese colonialists. That gave him impeccable nationalist credentials in a country where it had been all too common for capable and ambitious people to serve the Japanese masters. With that starting point, his publicists over the decades of his reign had inflated his image. North Koreans did not credit the U.S.-led Allied defeat of the Japanese in the Pacific for their national liberation. All young North Koreans had learned that it was Kim Il-sung and his anti-Japanese guerrillas (with help from the Soviet Army, in some versions—but in other versions with no acknowledged help at all) who had liberated Korea from the Japanese. The Americans got only blame, for spoiling the liberation by occupying the South and dividing the country.

Son-hui visits Kangson, an iron-and-steel center, and gathers reporting materials on "the proud life of the smelters, who are performing miracles." The shop manager, played by a full-throated bass, exhorts his workers: "Comrades! Let's fulfill our quota ahead of time!"

The "miracles" at the Kangson complex had begun in 1956, my guide told me. That year Kim Il-sung visited a Kangson rolling mill that was considered to have a capacity of 60,000 tons a year. The country needed 10,000 additional tons, the Great Leader said. The managers replied that such an increase would be "very difficult"—which, in Korean terms, means just about impossible. Kim appealed directly to the workers, who assured him there was no need to limit the improvement to 10,000 tons; they would produce 30,000 extra tons for a total output of 90,000 tons the following year. Indeed, my guide said, the workers responded so enthusiastically to Kim's exhortations that their output doubled in 1957 to 120,000 tons.

Son-hui hears steelworkers sing a rousing number reminiscent of the "Anvil Chorus": "In His warm loving care we are blessed. . . . We are highly cultured under the new policy."

The regime had produced literature, museums and public art aplenty, under the policy that North Korean culture "must not depart from the party

line and its purpose of benefiting the revolution," as Kim Il-sung had instructed one group of artists and writers.[11] In practice that meant that, regarding books, for example, a North Korean could read anything he or she
wished as long as it glorified Kim Il-sung.

Many of the museums showcased nothing but gifts the Great Leader had
sent for the edification of the masses. Some of those were objects that might
better have been used instead of displayed, such as overhead projectors and
pencil sharpeners proudly shown to visitors in a shrinelike room at a
Pyongyang primary school. Others, however, were true relics—stuffed birds
and animals and pickled fish, trophies from the Fatherly Leader's hunting
and fishing trips. Kim Il-sung University showed off a hunting dog sent by
the Respected and Beloved Leader. It, too, was stuffed. Reportedly it had
died a natural death.

As for publicly displayed art and sculpture, most of what I saw depicted
Kim Il-sung. A Japanese newsman, in Pyongyang to cover the table tennis
tournament, was sent home early after he filed an article reporting that the
gold coating on a sixty-five-foot (twenty-meter) bronze statue of the Great
Leader had been removed. His article cited a rumor among foreign residents
in Pyongyang that Deng Xiaoping, during a visit not long before, had suggested to President Kim that a golden statue might be a bit too extravagant a
display for a socialist country seeking Chinese economic aid.

*Son-hui arrives at the village where, following her wartime rescue from a
burning house, she spent her childhood. She is deeply moved to see the village now
becoming a model cooperative farm. It is harvest time, and "the rice stacks rise
mountain-high," the farmers sing. "Let us boast of our bumper harvest to the
whole world." The farmers are grateful to the Great Leader: "For many miles
around He gave us water and sent us machines to ease our heavy toil. Let us sing,
let us dance, let us sing of our Leader's favors for thousands of years."*

*Bowing deeply, the farmers sing: "Heaven and earth the Wise Leader tamed,
repelled the cold front and brought in the best harvest."*

After a couple of weeks in North Korea, believe it or not, a visitor could
catch himself starting to get used to such extravagant tributes. Outside observers had long remarked the romantic propensity of Koreans, north or south,
for excess. Besides, one could reason, the extreme reverence for Kim Il-sung no
doubt reflected Korean history. Like China, North Korea had married traditional Confucianism—patriarchal and authoritarian—to Stalinist dictatorship.

Prior to 1910, native dynasties fashioned more or less on the ancient
Chinese model had ruled the country. Then, during the 1910–1945 colonial
period, Koreans had been Japanese subjects, required to worship the emperor in Tokyo pretty much as North Koreans later came to worship their
Great Leader.[12] *"Mansei!"* (Long life!)—the Korean equivalent of the Japanese *"Banzai!"*—was the cry I heard issuing from the throats of thousands of
North Koreans who assembled on May Day, 1979, in downtown Pyongyang's

Kim Il-sung Square, to praise Kim for having built a workers' paradise.

My guide, Kim Yon-shik, gave every appearance of sincerity when he explained to me that the people had suffered for so long under "flunkeyism"—meaning subordination to surrounding great powers Japan, China, Russia and the United States—that they were grateful to Kim Il-sung for bringing them out of it.

That might have seemed a plausible account of how Kim Il-sung became a god. However, around the same time such explanations started to come easily to the mind, so did a small voice suggesting that it was about time to end the visit—before I might start giving thanks to the Great Leader at the beginning of each meal, as North Koreans were taught from nursery school to do. Any day now I might forget that this was 1979, with just five years to go before the end of the current seven-year economic plan and . . . *1984.*

The voice urging me to flee grew particularly strong on a day when the American reporters were taken to the Demilitarized Zone. The DMZ, as it was abbreviated, divided north from south. We arrived at a visitors' parking area adjoining the truce village of Panmunjom. As I was stepping out of the car that had brought me down from the city of Kaesong, I took care to remove my passport from my bag and place it in my pocket—just in case I should feel the need to make a break. Hit by a fit of temporary madness such as sometimes possesses Western visitors to the Earthly Paradise, I briefly visualized myself sprinting across the DMZ. At the moment we were not yet within sight of the border, but I had visited Panmunjom several times from the Seoul direction and thus had a clear mental picture of the layout. I could visualize the rifle-toting North Korean and American soldiers facing each other just a few feet apart. If I made a dash to the other side, I fantasized, I could then produce the passport as my admission ticket to the considerably Freer World.

However, when I got to the truce village I looked across at the outsized GIs, soldiers handpicked for their ability to project an intimidating presence. I saw that they were glaring, with looks of unbridled ferocity, at me and at my fellow Western correspondents. To look menacing and unwelcoming was their job, of course, but they did it so well that the moment of madness instantly passed and with it my fantasy of leaving North Korea by other than orthodox means.

Finale in Pyongyang: The people dance, joyously singing of their happiness. The searchers have learned that the reporter Son-hui is the dead soldier's daughter, and she has received her father's hero medal from the Great Leader. She joins the crowd in facing the red sun to sing a powerful, ecstatic, spine-tingling hymn of praise and faith: "Oh, unbounded is His love. We shall live forever in His kind care. His grateful love has given us eternal life. . . . We shall relate His everlasting love age after age. Oh, we shall be loyal to Marshal Kim Il-sung, our Leader, our Great, Fatherly Leader."

When I asked what the country would do after the death of the president,

a party member replied: "If he dies—I mean, when he dies—we'll find another leader." Kim Il-sung's choice for the job was his son, Kim Jong-il, then
a chubby thirty-seven and running the secretariat of the Workers' Party. The
younger Kim had disappeared from the public view in the late 1970s. Rumors
had said he was dead, or had been injured in an automobile collision and was
a "vegetable." By 1979, it was known that he was alive and healthy, but still
his name was hardly mentioned publicly. Rather, he was referred to by the
code term "the Party Center" or, often, "the Glorious Party Center."

Many Pyongyang-watchers figured that his curious anonymity had to do
with efforts to buy time in which to get rid of elements opposed to such a reactionary phenomenon as a hereditary succession, unknown elsewhere in
the communist world. A Soviet newsman stationed in Pyongyang told me the
opponents included military men. But the Russian added that Kim Jong-il
"has power in the party. He's a strong man, groomed for power and pushing
to take over."

Indeed, the younger Kim's days in the political wilderness, if such they
had been, appeared to be ending. In September 1978, he had made one highly
visible appearance, at the celebration of the thirtieth anniversary of the
founding of the North Korean republic, where he had met foreign guests. By
1979, a visitor could see his likeness alongside that of his father in a few of the
portraits of the Great Leader that decorated entrances to buildings. Watching
television one night I saw a film of the elder Kim, in wide-brimmed felt hat,
giving "on-the-spot guidance" to peasants and factory workers. The Glorious
Party Center was along, too, and several times the camera focused on him.

Curtain. Standing ovation. Flowers for the prima donna playing Son-hui.

My guide, Kim Yon-shik, was an official whose regular job was arranging North Korean participation in international sporting events. One of the
few North Koreans permitted to travel abroad, he had been in Guyana in the
fall of 1978 around the time of the notorious Jonestown massacre, in which
members of an American religious cult died in a gruesome murder-suicide
spectacle. Kim Yon-shik asked me what Americans thought of the incident. I
could not resist framing my reply in terms that might strike very close to the
bone for him. "Most Americans see Jonestown as a case of fanaticism," I told
him blandly, "people blindly following one leader."

Kim Yon-shik was in his forties, old enough that he would not have been
brought up completely in the current system, and he usually demonstrated a
good sense of humor. Yet he showed no sign of appreciating the irony in my
reply.

"Does the People's Temple sect still survive?" he asked me.

"It's hard," I replied, "for a cult like that to continue for long after its
charismatic leader has died."

Kim Yon-shik still showed no sign of recognizing the barb. "Don't you
think the CIA was involved in that incident?" he asked me.

TWO

Fighters and Psalmists

Concocting a mythology around the nation's founding father is by no means a North Korean monopoly. Think of George Washington's fictional confession to having chopped down his father's cherry tree: "I cannot tell a lie." But while Americans and Europeans in the second half of the twentieth century moved in the opposite direction, gleefully felling the mighty, North Korea's official hagiographers carried to previously unknown heights the art of building up the leader.

Western and South Korean historians have despaired of being able to separate historical truth from the Pyongyang regime's innumerable distortions and fabrications about Kim Il-sung's life, especially his childhood and youth. Lacking verifiable facts beyond the most basic, they have tended to dispose of Kim's first two decades with a few sparse paragraphs before moving along quickly to the events of his adult life—for which, at least, there are sources such as contemporary newspaper accounts and the records of foreign governments.

However, in the years immediately preceding his death in 1994, Kim produced several volumes of memoirs that offer a somewhat franker, more down-to-earth account than his sycophantic writers had provided in earlier official biographies.

To be sure, many exaggerations and distortions remain even in the newer volumes. For example, whatever quantity of disbelief the reader has managed to suspend may come crashing down at an account of bandits capturing Kim's father and two companions. While the bandits smoked opium in their camp, Kim wrote, one captive put out the lamp and helped the other two escape before "attacking the rascals, some ten in all, with skillful boxing. Then he made off from the den of the bandits." It was, enthused Kim, "a truly dramatic sight, resembling a fight scene in a movie."

Indeed. No doubt it *is* a fight scene in at least one of the countless North Korean movies glorifying Kim and his family. Hwang Jang-yop, a leading North Korean intellectual who defected to South Korea in 1997, reported that Kim's autobiography had been "created by artists who had been writing scenarios for revolutionary novels and films. Thus, it made for very interesting reading. When Part I was published it was a huge hit. This was only natural, since its contents were literally scenes straight out of the movies that had been made for the same purpose, and its plot was as interesting as any novel or film." Hwang termed the series a "masterpiece of historical fabrication."[1]

But there is gold among the dross in the memoirs. Some passages can be checked against the recollections of contemporaries—and those passages are found to offer more truthful portrayals than we had been accustomed to getting from Pyongyang.[2] Of course that does not provide the elusive verification for other passages dealing with different phases of Kim's youth. But at least it suggests that Kim, as he worked with his writing staff to produce those memoirs in his seventies, had some notion of straightening out his story in the time remaining to him.

Combining what was previously known of Kim's formative years with a careful reading of the memoirs, tossing out the preposterous, tentatively accepting the plausible while intuitively making allowance for exaggerations, adding in the testimony of contemporaries where available, it is possible now to see a picture that is reasonably complex and believable.

Parts of this picture show Kim as the regime had sketched him—but on a more human scale. Toning down some of the official claims has enhanced their credibility. Thus, we can see in Kim Il-sung a youngster genuinely consumed by patriotic anti-colonialism who, while still in his teens, embraced communism as the key to independence and justice for Koreans.

Other parts of the picture were only recently uncovered. Who, for example, would have imagined that the man whose rule wiped out nearly every trace of religion in North Korea—except worship of himself—had been until his late teens not only a churchgoer but, moreover, a church organist? The young Kim was both. Experience in church-related activities played a considerable role in training one of the most successful mass leaders and propagandists in the history of the world, not to mention providing a model for his own eventual elevation to divine status.[3]

❈   ❈   ❈

The Great Leader–to-be was born Kim Song-ju on April 15, 1912, at the home of his maternal grandfather in the village of Chilgol. The nearby house of his paternal grandparents at Mangyongdae, where he spent several years of his childhood, is his recognized family home. Mangyongdae has since been incorporated into nearby Pyongyang, the provincial capital that became the capital of Kim's Democratic People's Republic of Korea.

Kim's regime enshrined the mud-walled, thatched-roofed Mangyongdae farmhouse as Korea's answer to the manger in Bethlehem or Abe Lincoln's log cabin. I visited there in 1979 and found the parking lot and the pedestrian paths packed with thousands of visitors, mostly Korean. A guide said that Kim's paternal forebears had lived at Mangyongdae since the time of his great-grandfather, a poor tenant farmer who worked as a graves-keeper for the landlord. The name Mangyongdae means a place blessed with countless scenic views. As Kim said in his memoirs, "Rich people and government officials vied with one another in buying hills in the Mangyongdae area as burial plots because they were attracted by the beautiful scenery."[4]

The river Taedong runs past Mangyongdae. Nearly half a century before Kim's birth, that river had been the scene of an ugly incident that represents the unhappy beginning of Korean-American relations. In the context of a push by confident and condescending Americans of the period to open far-flung "heathen" nations to Christian proselytizing and trade, an armed merchant ship in 1866 intruded into the forbidden waters of the Taedong. The *General Sherman,* aptly named for the American Civil War commander who had laid waste to much of Georgia, headed upriver for Pyongyang, firing its guns, capturing one local Korean official and stopping to permit a missionary— who was aboard as the expedition's interpreter—to preach and distribute leaflets.

Then the American captain of the *General Sherman* made the mistake of running aground. An incensed mob of local people descended on the ship, tore it apart and hacked the intruding foreigners to pieces. Kim Il-sung was to claim after taking power that his great-grandfather had been a leader of the people who attacked the ship.[5] Whether that is true or not, there is no denying that the *Sherman* incident lived on in the memories of Korean nationalists. Although Korean scholarship suggests the *Sherman* expedition was an act of piracy by known tomb robbers, the incident led to a more heavily armed intrusion in 1871 in which Americans massacred some 250 Koreans. By 1882, Korean rulers saw that the better part of valor was to accede to a treaty with the United States, arranged by China, which ended the centuries-old isolation of the "hermit kingdom."[6]

Kim Il-sung's father, Kim Hyong-jik, managed enough upward mobility to rise out of the peasant class into which he had been born. He attended—but did not finish—middle school, and he married the daughter of a schoolmaster. He worked first as an elementary school teacher and later as a traditional herbal doctor. While those accomplishments translated into some social cachet, they did not put extra food on the table. Clearly the family was never affluent.

Kim Hyong-jik married at fifteen to a bride, Kang Pan-sok, who was two years older. The Chilgol Kangs were educated people who included Christian clerics and church elders in addition to teachers and schoolmasters. According to Kang Myong-do, who defected to the South in 1994 and described himself as a member of the Chilgol Kang clan, the Kangs felt the marriage was an unequal one in view of the groom's father's work as a graves-keeper and the fact he owned only a little over two acres of reclaimed farmland. But one thing the families had in common was that they were Christian churchgoers.[7]

Kim Hyong-jik entered middle school at sixteen and fathered the future Great Leader at seventeen, still living in his parents' home. The whole family worked at extra jobs to pay the teenager's school fees.[8] Hyong-jik's mother— Kim Il-sung's paternal grandmother—arose before dawn to make breakfast so she could be sure her son would not be late for classes. The North Korean president wrote in his memoirs that his grandmother on occasion awoke far too early. Preparing the meal in the middle of the night, she then stared for hours out the eastern window of the house, waiting for signs of sunrise so she would know when to rouse the student and send him off. A clock was a luxury then; Kim's family did not have one but the neighbor family behind their house did. The grandmother sometimes sent her young daughter-in-law, Kim's mother, to check the time at the neighbors' house. Kang Pan-sok "would squat outside the fence waiting for the clock to strike the hours. Then she would return and tell grandmother the time."[9]

Despite the family's incessant hard work, "such things as fruit and meat were beyond our means," Kim recalled. "Once I had a sore throat and grandmother obtained some pork for me. I ate it and my throat got better. After that, whenever I felt like eating pork I wished I had a sore throat again."[10] He remembered his father's younger brother, Hyong-gwon, then eleven or twelve years old, throwing a tantrum over food. Hyong-gwon could not control his disgust with the coarse gruel, made of millet and uncleaned sorghum, that was the Kim family's regular fare. He banged his head against the bowl, bloodying his head and sending the bowl flying across the room. The future president sympathized. The gruel always tasted bad and, to add injury to insult, the cereal's coarse husks pricked the throat as they went down.[11]

More significant in shaping Kim Il-sung's thinking than the family's poverty was the timing of his birth, less than two years after Korea's annexation by Japan. Heirs to a proud civilization, Koreans for centuries had condescended to Japan as a cultural Johnny-come-lately. The many Japanese borrowings from Korea had ranged from ceramics and architecture to religion. Patriotic Koreans after 1910 observed as National Humiliation Day the August 29 anniversary of the ignominious Japanese takeover.

Independence from Japan was the ardent desire of most Koreans in those days.[12] Kim recalled that it was a consuming passion for members of his family. His father and two uncles were all jailed at different times for pro-independence activities. Kim himself was a patriot long before he became a communist. "No feeling in the world is greater, more ennobling and more sacred than patriotism," he explained.[13]

For his family as well as other Koreans, patriotism meant implacable hatred of Japan. Kim recalled that his own patriotic consciousness had caught fire before his seventh birthday, during the momentous March 1, 1919, uprising against Japanese rule. Joining his family, among tens of thousands of demonstrators who thronged Pyongyang in the mistaken belief that U.S. President Woodrow Wilson would champion their cause, "I shouted for independence standing on tiptoe squeezed in between the adults."[14] From then on, the determination someday to take on the foreign aggressors guided even his play, by Kim's account. The assertion has been enshrined in the official mythology. When I visited Mangyongdae the guide identified a sand pile surrounded by a manicured hedge as the site where the Great Leader–to-be had wrestled older children to practice for his life's work.

The patriotism of Kim's family members, like that of many other Koreans, was linked with Christianity. Protestant and, to a lesser extent, Catholic churches flourished in Korean communities following the 1882 treaty with the United States. Pyongyang, in particular, was such fertile ground for American mission work that the city became known as Korea's Jerusalem.[15]

Following Korea's annexation, the Japanese authorities distrusted Christians. There was some irony in this, since missionaries often were prepared to render unto Caesar and ignore politics if only they could continue with their religious activities. The American missionaries' own government had connived in the Japanese advance into Korea in exchange for Japanese recognition of U.S. interests in the Philippines.[16] But Japanese authorities repressed Korean believers, squandering what might otherwise have been an advantage.[17] A number of Christians became identified with the independence movement. Christians were involved in planning the March 1 uprising.

Kim's Il-sung's own religious training and background represent a side of his early life that he had been reluctant to recall—and finally acknowledged in his memoirs only with considerable hedging about. For example, although both his parents were churchgoers, Kim was intent on assigning them the role of atheistic holy family of the Korean revolution. He insisted that both had been nonbelievers. While some sources have described his mother as a devout woman who served as a deaconess,[18] her son claimed she had gone to church only to relax from her exhausting workaday toil, dozing during the service.[19]

Kim's father attended Sungsil Middle School, founded in 1900 by American Presbyterian missionaries in Pyongyang. But Kim said his father had enrolled there only out of the desire to have a "modern education" in a school where he would not be required to memorize the very difficult Nine Chinese Classics, which were taught at old-fashioned Confucian schools.[20] Kim described his father as a young man consumed by patriotism who exhorted schoolmates: "Believe in a Korean God, if you believe in one!"[21] After the family moved to Manchuria, his father went to every service at a local chapel and sometimes led the singing and played the organ, teaching his son to play also. But this, insisted Kim, was just a chance to spread anti-Japanese propaganda.[22]

Acknowledging his exposure to Christianity, Kim said he rejected its doctrines while still young. "Some miserable people thought they would go to 'Heaven' after death if they believed in Jesus Christ," he wrote. At first "I, too, was interested in church." Later, though, "I became tired of the tedious religious ceremony and the monotonous preaching of the minister, so I seldom went."[23] Kim maintained he was "not affected by religion" despite his youthful connections with the church. Nevertheless, "I received a great deal of humanitarian assistance from Christians, and in return I had an ideological influence on them."[24]

At age seven Kim moved with his family across the Chinese border to Manchuria. A wrenching move for the youngster, in the larger picture that was part of an exodus that eventually planted Korean communities around the globe, from Tashkent to Osaka to Los Angeles. The Korean diaspora came almost to rival those of the Jews and the overseas Chinese.[25]

Since the latter half of the nineteenth century, waves of Koreans had emigrated in search of better lives. Many had gone to Hawaii and North America. There, Kim said, "they were treated as barbarians and hired as servants in restaurants and rich men's houses or were worked hard on plantations under the scorching sun."[26] Others had gone to the relatively wide-open frontier spaces of the Russian Maritime Province and Chinese-ruled Manchuria. Oppression by the Korean rulers of the time propelled the first wave of Korean migrants to those places, around 1860. A famine in northern Korea a decade later accelerated the trend. In the first decade of the twentieth century, Japan's move to absorb Korea as part of the expansion of its Northeast Asia empire triggered another wave of emigration.[27]

Manchuria once had been reserved as the sparsely populated homeland of the last Chinese imperial dynasty and its nomadic Manchu clansmen. As the dynasty weakened and migratory pressures built, however, China had opened vast stretches of the region to settlers. Koreans could become no more than tenant farmers in most of Manchuria. The Japanese, though, in 1909—the year before they completed their conquest of Korea—extracted from a Chinese government in its death throes a very favorable treaty. Among other things it enabled Koreans to own land in Manchuria's Jiandao Province, immediately adjoining the Korean border. Hundreds of thousands of Koreans made the move to Manchuria before Kim's family did so. The majority went to Jiandao, where the Korean settlers far outnumbered the Chinese.

Economic betterment was an important incentive for those early-twentieth-century emigrants. Considering conditions back at Mangyongdae, it could well have been a factor luring Kim's father to Manchuria. As in the 1860s, though, there were settlers whose motives for fleeing across the border were political. Hoping to continue their struggle against oppressive Japanese rule, some determined Korean patriots found sanctuary in Manchuria.[28] The region's mountainous areas, in particular, were relatively lawless and freewheeling places. Chinese warlords, Korean independence fighters, agents of the new Soviet regime in Moscow and assorted bandits all competed for spoils and influence against the encroaching Japanese. Kim described his family as among the political exiles who were driven from their homeland and left to drift "like fallen leaves to the desolate wilderness of Manchuria."[29]

Kim's father had become a medical practitioner by reading "a few books on medicine" and obtaining a diploma from a friend in Pyongyang.[30] While working for the independence movement in Manchuria, the elder Kim supported his family by treating patients with traditional herbal medicine. Kim said he often went on errands for his father—but in connection not so much with the medical work as with pro-independence activities. He took food and clothing to some jailed Korean patriots on one occasion, he wrote, and often went to the post office to pick up his father's newspapers and magazines from Korea.[31]

He told of having been the leader of a group of mischievous children in the Manchurian town of Badaogou. One playmate belonged to a family of "patriotic merchants." The family's storage shed was full of weapons and clothing awaiting shipment to Korean independence fighters. One day that boy injured himself when a detonation cap exploded while he was playing with it. The victim's brother wrapped him in a blanket and carried him to Kim's father's home dispensary for treatment, Kim recalled.[32]

An ordeal that Kim looked back on as a rite of passage to manhood came shortly before his eleventh birthday. His father sent him from Manchuria back to Korea, alone, he said. He had been attending local Chinese schools and learning the Chinese language as spoken in Manchuria.[33] Now, though, the elder Kim instructed him that "a man born in Korea must have a good knowledge of Korea." Kim rode trains for parts of the journey but walked much of the 250-mile distance, carrying a map his father had drawn with a list of places to stop overnight, he recalled.

His father had taken some precautions, telegraphing innkeeper acquaintances to alert them that the boy would be arriving. Kim described those innkeepers as "under the guidance and influence of my father"[34]—a claim in keeping with what outside biographers describe as a massive effort to depict Kim Hyong-jik as a leading light of the independence movement rather than the minor figure they believe he actually was.[35] Whatever the father's importance in the movement, it does seem that he had many friends. Kim Il-sung said he learned from his father "the ethics of comradeship."[36] It appears that as his career progressed he made assiduous use of both his family connections and his father's example of cultivating friendships.

Kim's anecdotal recollections of his "one-thousand-*ri* [250-mile] journey for learning" dwell, understandably, on sore feet and hospitable innkeepers. At the foot of Mount Oga, "I fortunately met an old man who cured my blisters by burning them with matches." An inn in Kaechon offered a mattress and two blankets for 50 *chon*. The night was cold, but to save money Kim asked for only one blanket; the kindly innkeeper gave him two blankets anyhow. At Kanggye, Kim's instructions from his father said to wire home. The telegraph fee increased after the first six characters, so he kept his message to just six: *"kang gye mu sa do chak"*—"Arrived safely in Kanggye."[37]

Back in his home district in Korea after his two-week journey, Kim stayed with his maternal grandparents, the Kangs. One of their sons, Kang Jin-sok, was in prison for anti-Japanese activities. (He eventually died there after thirteen years' imprisonment.[38]) Police surveillance of the family was strict and burdensome, Kim recalled. The boy attended Changdok School, where his grandfather was schoolmaster. A memory of those days is that Grandfather Kang taught him a poem by a Korean warrior who had so distinguished himself against invaders as to be named minister of the army at age twenty:

> *Grinding my sword wears down Mount Paektu's rock;*
> *My horse gulps and dries the Tumen River.*
> *Should a man at twenty fail to subdue the land,*
> *Who will in later years call him a man of caliber?*[39]

Kim's teacher was another relative, Kang Ryang-uk, a Methodist minister. In later years Kang Ryang-uk was to head North Korea's token "opposition" Korean Democratic Party and serve as figurehead vice-president of the

country under Kim. The teacher was a strong nationalist who taught his
pupils patriotic songs. Kim said he remembered the songs and sang them
later while fighting the Japanese.[40]

Like other Korean schools of the time, Changdok School taught the
Japanese language but not Korean. The authorities were trying to integrate
the Korean colony into Greater Japan. To that end they sought to relegate Korean to the status of a regional dialect and replace it with Japanese, which
they referred to as the "national language" or "mother tongue." Later, they
would even demand that Koreans adopt Japanese names. As Kim was to tell
it later, he was shocked when his grandfather gave him his fifth-grade textbooks. "I asked my grandfather why the Japanese language book was titled
Mother-tongue Reader. He merely heaved a sigh." Kim claimed he then took a
pocketknife, resolutely scratched the word "Mother-tongue" from the book's
title and wrote "Japanese" to replace it, making the title *Japanese Reader*.[41]
The anecdote may sound a bit too good to be true, but—as with many of
Kim's claims—no witness is alive to refute his account.

The Kangs had little to share with the grandson who had come to live
with them. They were so poor that one of his uncles had to hire out as a
carter to make ends meet. But like many Korean families the Kangs combined pride with endless respect for formal education. The family "did not
reveal any signs of poverty in my presence and supported me wholeheartedly
while I attended school," Kim recalled. "They provided me with a separate
room furnished with a kerosene lamp and fine floor mats."[42] Their poverty
was only typical of what most Koreans experienced during that period. Even
among the one hundred thousand residents of Pyongyang, Kim said, "only a
small number of Japanese and Americans were living well." Koreans had to
settle for "slum dwellings with straw-mat doors and board roofing."[43]

Hearing the news of the Tokyo area's great earthquake of 1923, Kim was
outraged by reports that Japanese had killed hundreds of Korean émigré
residents. Inflammatory rumors had spread in Japan, accusing Korean residents of plotting to rise up and take advantage of their masters' misfortune,
even of poisoning the wells. Kim realized that Japanese "despised Korean
people, treating them worse than beasts." He said he responded by planting
a board with a nail sticking from it in the road, hoping it would puncture the
bicycle tires of any passing policeman.

His growing awareness of his people's "miseries" made him aspire to a
new sort of society. It would blend productive pride and joy with the characteristic Korean feeling called *han*—a prickly combination of pessimism,
vengefulness and xenophobia that had evolved over centuries, in response to
the frustration aroused by the country's status as a small nation bullied by
bigger and more powerful neighbors. In the new society, Kim dreamed, "the
toiling masses could live happily and harbor a bitter hatred for the Japanese
imperialist aggressors, landlords and capitalists."[44]

* * *

After two years in Korea, Kim returned to Manchuria. The family moved to the town of Fusong. There Kim's father, long in poor health, died at age thirty-two. Now fourteen years old, the boy was sent off to Huadian, another Manchurian town, where he enrolled in a military school founded by nationalists in the Korean independence movement.

Arriving in Huadian he went for supper at the home of one of his father's friends, who offered him his first drink of liquor. "There was a bottle of alcohol made from cereal at one edge of the round table. I thought that Kim Si-u had put it there to drink with his meal. But he poured some into a glass and offered it to me, much to my surprise. I felt so awkward that I flapped my hands." Kim found this first drink potent with symbolism of his coming of age: "Although the glass was so small that it could be hidden in the palm of one's hand, it was loaded with inestimable weight. At that table where Kim Si-u treated me as an adult, I solemnly felt that I should behave like a grown-up," he recalled.[45]

Relations between Korean communists and conservative nationalists, including those in Manchuria, alternated between bitter enmity and a wary alliance against the common foe. As in the case of the Chinese communists and nationalists, the two groupings agreed on little more than the goal of independence from Japan.

Kim had been developing socialist leanings, according to his account. He had read some pamphlets, and he had heard rumors about developments in the Soviet Union since the October Revolution less than a decade before.[46] But he had not yet become a fully committed communist, so he found no contradiction at first in attending the nationalist Huadian School. Becoming more radical as he learned more about communism, Kim criticized the school's prohibition against reading Marxist-Leninist books. His argument, as he recalled it later: "If a man does not read the books he wants to because he has been prohibited from doing so, how can he undertake a great cause?"[47]

Eventually, Kim said, he became thoroughly dissatisfied with the nationalist military school and the bourgeois movement for which it was training soldiers. The movement's volunteer soldiers wore cumbersome traditional robes and broad-brimmed hats, he related. They were armed with little more than swords, spears and flintlock guns. Their minds filled with old-fashioned notions that they had taken from "the nobility's ethics and Buddhist precepts," they were no match for the well-trained Japanese troops armed with modern cannon and machine guns. Besides, Kim noted disapprovingly, "some young students at the school still believed in dynastic rule."[48] In his view, Korea's former royalty had "bled the people white and beheaded or banished loyal subjects who spoke the truth."[49]

In a student debate, Kim asked what type of society Korea should build after winning its independence. Another student replied, "Our nation lost its country to the Japanese because our feudal rulers idled their time away reciting poems while other countries advanced along the road to capitalism. We should build a capitalist society and thus avoid a repeat of the past."[50] Kim recalled delivering a ringing rejection of capitalist and feudal societies, where "people with money lead a luxurious life by exploiting the working people."[51]

The young Kim and his idealistic friends were indignant when national-ist leaders and even fellow cadets at the school behaved just like those earlier feudal rulers, squeezing "contributions" from the local Koreans and then putting the money to personal use. One commander used such contributions to finance his own wedding. He "spent the money like water in order to treat all his neighbors to food and drink over several days," Kim said. "In the bright society we have now, the army and the people would have gathered public support and taken him to court or tried the case among themselves to force him to break this bad habit." At the time, though, adults failed to stop the abuses. Kim said he and some school friends formed an organization called Down-with-Imperialism Union, and the group circulated a letter protesting the newlywed commander's actions.[52]

After only six months at the nationalist school, Kim said, he quit and moved to Jilin, capital of the Manchurian province of the same name. Close to Jiandao with its Korean-majority population, "Jilin was the haunt of many Korean independence fighters and communists who were fleeing from the Japanese army and police," he wrote in his memoirs. This made the city "a theater and a center of political activities for Koreans."[53] But although the Japanese did not have complete control over the city, they had a very strong presence. Japanese agents, claiming authority over citizens of their Korean colony, were able to influence the Chinese warlords and the warlords' police. A friend of his father's took the newly arrived young Kim to meet anti-Japanese activists who gathered in the Sanfeng Hotel, situated within one hundred yards of the Japanese consulate. Since the consulate was the virtual headquarters of the Japanese police agents in Jilin, it seemed risky to use the hotel as the gathering place for independence fighters. "But they came there all the same, saying, 'The darkest place is below the candlestick.'" In-deed, reported Kim, there were no arrests there.[54]

One thing about Jilin that delighted him was the vigorous clash of opin-ions expressed in the city's Beishan Park, Kim said. In that local equivalent of London's Hyde Park, "enlightenment champions from different professions coming from various places, brandishing their fists, delivered fervent speeches on patriotism, morals, the defense of law, aesthetics, unemployment, physical culture, hygiene and other subjects. This was a splendid spectacle, the like of which could not be seen elsewhere."[55]

Kim enrolled in Yuwen Middle School, a Chinese private school described as the most "progressive" in the city. I visited the school in 1982 and found a large statue of Kim in the courtyard. A slogan on the school building proclaimed: "Long Live Sino-Korean Friendship." Strangely, the marble tablets on Kim's statue were blank. I wonder whether the Chinese had erased them— perhaps during the Cultural Revolution of the 1960s and '70s, when the Red Guards criticized Kim harshly, or during the subsequent movement led by Deng Xiaoping and other reformers to stamp out signs of the discredited personality cult built around China's own Mao Zedong. Or could it have been the North Koreans who chose to leave the tablets blank—because it was not then considered politic, from the standpoint of Korean nationalism, to advertise that Kim had been educated in a foreign language? When he chose a Chinese school after leaving the Korean Huadian School, he did have a choice, as there were Korean schools in Jilin.[56]

Simply to continue his studies was an economic struggle for Kim. His mother had remained in Manchuria with her other two sons following her husband's death. While Kim attended Yuwen Middle School, she sent money from her meager earnings as a laundress and seamstress,[57] he recalled later. His poverty is one of the points on which witnesses offer basic corroboration of his account. A younger friend from that period, in a letter that he wrote to me when he was in his eighties and living in the United States, recalled Kim: "Although he was in a neat and tidy school uniform, I could see his family was not well-to-do, for he was boarding at the dormitory belonging to the Methodist Church. That dormitory charged less than others."[58] Kim wrote that he went barefoot much of the time to conserve his single pair of canvas shoes for wearing to school. Jilin "gave off the stink of a class society," he complained in his memoirs. He and his friends "asked ourselves how it was that there were people who rode in a rickshaw while there were others who had to pull it, and why it was that certain people were living in luxury in palatial mansions while others had to wander the streets begging."

Money was so tight that he could not afford to buy books other than his textbooks. He persuaded friends from rich families to buy the books he wanted to read, or so he claimed later. (I have not seen much independent evidence that Kim really was a bookworm, and his later life does not by any means suggest he was an intellectual. But to political activists of that time and place books were weapons, so perhaps there is something to this.) According to his recollections, Kim got involved with some friends in organizing a reading circle and a private one-room library in a rented room. Their library offered love stories as a come-on to attract new members but concentrated on revolutionary works, which he says the group kept on a "secret bookshelf." A bookish older friend who was reading *Das Kapital* in Japanese explained Marx's thinking to him, and Kim said later that this was the period when "I began to realize my class position."[59]

Kim threw himself into organizational work among students and other young people in Jilin, helping to start a Korean Children's Association and to radicalize an already existing group of Korean students.[60] Such activities, especially when he worked with younger children, allowed him to show and to develop his considerable leadership qualities.

The younger friend of Kim's whom I quoted above, a former member of the Jilin Korean Children's Association, recalled that the group occupied its time with patriotic songfests, debates, discussions and speeches on how to regain Korean independence. Their more active pastimes included sports, searches for quartz crystals in Beishan Park, games of hide-and-seek and patriotic play to prepare them for overthrowing the Japanese imperialists. "Very often we played war games," that friend remembered. "One team played outside of the fence and the other team remained inside the fence. The outside-fence team was to invade and the inside team was to defend their citadel."

A communist teacher at Yuwen Middle School became mentor to the future North Korean leader. Shang Yue, a twenty-six-year-old Beijing University graduate, Chinese Communist Party member and aspiring novelist, arrived to teach literature and the Chinese language shortly before Kim's sixteenth birthday in 1928. Hearing from the lad of his zeal to oppose the Japanese imperialists, Shang opened his considerable library to him. Kim in his memoirs ecstatically recalled frequent discussions with Shang, in and out of class, centering on books ranging from the Chinese classic *Dream of the Red Chamber* to such Russian authors as Gorky to the teachings of Lenin and the memoirs of a founder of the Chinese Communist Party.[61] Removed from his teaching post after only six months on account of his views, Shang went on to become one of China's leading historians before his death in 1982. The teacher's daughter told an interviewer from the Reuters news agency in 1994 that her late father had remembered Kim as a star pupil in Jilin, "diligent, putting good questions both inside and outside the class."[62]

Great as his interest in communism had become, patriotism still took first place in Kim's heart, as he illustrated in an anecdote. The English teacher at Yuwen Middle School "worshipped the West" and spoke contemptuously of East Asian customs, including the habit of slurping noodles loudly. Students one day prepared noodles for all the teachers. "The hall was loud with sucking sounds. The English teacher, too, was sucking his noodles down. The students roared with laughter at him."[63]

Kim recalled that he and his communist-leaning friends argued a great deal over a question of priorities. Marxist-Leninist classics, as he understood them, taught that the working class's emancipation would come before the national liberation of colonial peoples. But would it not be better for the Koreans to throw off the yoke of Japanese imperialism *before* reaching the stage of class struggle? Kim said he chafed at the "scientific" answer that Korea's revolution must await revolution in Japan, the colonial power.[64] Actually, Lenin had long since revised that doctrine, placing first priority on national liberation for Koreans as early as 1920, when Kim was eight years old.[65] As this example suggests, there were definite limits to the extent of Kim's serious study of Marxism-Leninism during his school days, when, by his own account, he was still leading younger pupils in soldier games on a riverbank.[66]

Stoking Kim's hatred of the Japanese were stories such as one he said an elderly independence fighter told him, a story that could fit right into the list of complaints by Japan-bashing American trade hawks of the 1980s. A Korean-owned factory produced matches, under the "Monkey" brand, which were so popular that a Japanese factory was unable to compete. So Japanese competitors bought up tens of thousands of boxes of Monkey matches, soaked them in water, dried them and sold them at the market. When they failed to light, customers switched to the Japanese competition; the Korean-owned match factory went bankrupt. Kim said the old man's story could not be confirmed decades later when he was writing his memoirs, but "it was very valuable in understanding Japanese imperialism."[67]

Kim joined his predominantly Chinese and leftist fellow students in 1928 for demonstrations against Japanese military aggression in China. "Reactionary teachers labeled our activities as communist propaganda and thus created a pretext for repression," he said. The teachers went through the library seizing "progressive" books. That censorship inspired a student strike, which succeeded in getting the offending teachers dismissed.[68]

Besides right-wing Chinese teachers and their warlord backers, Kim recalled finding fault with moderate Korean reformists who argued that Korea needed time to develop its economic muscle and to "perfect its national character." Only then would the colony be ready for independence. An article by an influential reformist infuriated Kim, he said, because "the author regarded the Korean nation as inferior." Korea had become backward, Kim acknowledged—but its overall history was so glorious as to give the lie to any notion of inferiority. "Koreans form a civilized and resourceful nation that was the first to build armored ships and produce metallic type," he noted.

An Chang-ho, a prominent reformist, gave a lecture in Jilin when Kim was not quite fifteen. The youngster spoke out, sharply questioning the famous man's view that Koreans were at a low level of "spiritual cultivation" and would be able to restore independence and sovereignty only after refining themselves to the level of the British or Americans. As An Chang-ho wound up his lecture and started to leave the hall, police burst in and arrested him along with hundreds of those who had come to hear him speak. The arrest had nothing to do with the questions Kim had asked, but he felt guilty nonetheless.[69]

Even more than had been the case before Kim moved to Jilin, the older generation of Korean nationalist independence "fighters" disappointed and even disgusted him. Instead of uniting to smite the enemy in battle, they carried on factional struggles among themselves. The various factions gathered to drink, play chess and plot against each other in the Sanfeng Hotel, where they would "spend the whole night in a drunken frenzy, getting up only at noon the next day." Instead of going off to fight the Japanese, the supposed commanders of the resistance "gathered their weapons and hid them in an arsenal; then they spent their time doing nothing. When we visited them they pretended to be doing some work with something like an account book open in front of them. They did so because they did not like to appear to young people as loafers. Sometimes they used extremely foul language against one another while banging the table either with their fists or with wooden pillows."[70]

One visitor to Jilin was a man who had been designated "minister of finance" in a Shanghai-based Korean "provisional government-in-exile." When some of the youngsters criticized his group as composed of factionalists and parasites, the man flew into a rage. In his choler, the eminent nationalist flung off his clothing and threatened to rush into the street naked. "Are you against me?" he shouted. "Well, let all of us, me and you, bring disgrace upon ourselves!" Fearing that he would indeed bring shame upon the independence movement and Koreans in general, Kim and the other youths "managed to soothe and dress him. On our way home that day, we determined never to deal with such people again."[71]

Someone Kim remained very happy to deal with was the Reverend Sohn Jong-do, a Methodist clergyman and Korean independence activist. Formerly pastor of the Jongdong Methodist Church in Seoul, he had been elected chairman of the assembly of the Shanghai Provisional Government before going to Jilin. Sohn was about ten years older than Kim's father but had known Kim Hyong-jik as a fellow Sungsil Middle School alumnus and independence fighter.[72] In Jilin, the pastor helped to pay Kim's school fees and acted as a surrogate father. On holidays, Sohn's wife invited the youngster to dine on such Korean delicacies as bean-curd-and-rabbit stew and herbed rice cakes.[73]

Sohn's youngest son, Won-tai, who grew up to become a pathologist practicing in Omaha, Nebraska, recalled the family's frequent visitor as a tall lad who smiled a lot. Kim "said little of what was unnecessary and light," Dr. Sohn remembered, but "he was very enthusiastic on political and social problems." Won-tai, small, slender and two years younger, followed Kim as he would an elder brother. "Though he was not much older than we, he always looked conspicuous," Dr. Sohn wrote in a 1995 letter to me. "Of imposing stature, he had well-balanced features. He was a charmingly handsome man with a dimple on his left cheek. A future leader, he had able leadership already in those days. So, whenever he was among us children, he was prominent like a 'crane in a flock of pheasants.' "[74]

Kim frequented the chapel, overseeing skit rehearsals by what he later referred to as a propaganda troupe.[75] He played the church's pump organ "very well," said Dr. Sohn, who recalled that the Jilin Korean Children's Association used the chapel for meetings. The association also "availed itself of the religious ceremonies held there." Kim "offered prayer with many members of our Children's Association who believed in religion," said Dr. Sohn. "In those days he stressed that we children should not fall prey to religion with a blind faith, but fight for independence [but] for all that, he was not strongly opposed to the Christian faith, I think." Of two plays that Kim and a youth group associated with him staged, Dr. Sohn remembered, one was a Christmas story and the other was about Korean patriots who captured a Korean traitor and set out to "make him a conscientious man."[76]

In telling of those days Kim described himself as taking a tougher stance against religion than Sohn remembered. Kim said he used the chapel for his political activities even though he had long since rejected religion. In what may have been a wishful attempt to square his admiration for Pastor Sohn with his own dim view of Christianity, he suggested that the clergyman's religious work had been to some extent a "guise" to cover work for Korean independence.[77] Sohn's son disagreed, but acknowledged that his father had devoted more time to the independence movement than to religious work. With few other places available for gatherings, he recalled, "many independence fighters availed themselves of religious places and ceremonies." The pastor was not a communist himself, and he was not fully aware of Kim's communist leanings, but he supported "any organization actively working for independence." Dr. Sohn said his father was disposed to support Kim in his activities because the patriotic youngster was his friend's son and—more important—Kim "was expected for his intelligence to shoulder the future of Korea."[78]

While trying to radicalize Jilin's young people, the group Kim belonged to campaigned against religious belief, according to his account. The goal was not so much to eradicate religion as to prevent turn-the-other-cheek nonviolence from leaving young Koreans "weak-minded and enervated." The revolution needed "fighters who sang of decisive battles more than religious believers who sang psalms."

Many of the pupils in the children's association came from Christian families. Kim said he was at pains to try to disabuse them of their religious beliefs. "However hard we explained to them that there was no God and that it was absurd to believe in one, it was useless because they were under such strong influence of their parents," he wrote. Kim said a primary school teacher sympathetic to the movement took her pupils to church and had them pray for rice cakes and bread. When no food appeared, the teacher took them to a wheat field that had just been harvested. They gleaned the field and the teacher threshed the gleanings and made bread. Eating it, the pupils "learned that it was better to earn bread by working than by praying to God for it."[79]

While rejecting Christian beliefs and agreeing generally with Marx that religion is the opiate of the masses, Kim evidently retained some level of belief in or acknowledgment of the East Asian's traditional duty to propitiate the restless spirits of the dead. Grieving as a teenager over the deaths both of his father and of Pastor Sohn, who died several years after his father, he "made a firm pledge to liberate the country, come what may, in order to safeguard their souls and take vengeance on the enemy. I believed that liberating the country would repay my benefactors' kindness, relieve them of their suffering and break the people's shackles."[80] And he ended the preface to his memoirs with the following words: "Praying for the souls of the departed revolutionaries."

As the decade of the 1920s neared its end, Kim was a junior founding member of a communist youth group. He wrote later that the league's charter members, meeting secretly in the cellar of a shrine in Jilin's Beishan Park, "sang the *Internationale* side by side."[81] During that period he directly involved himself in pro-Soviet activity. Anti-communist Chinese warlords angered Moscow by seizing Manchurian railways that had been under joint Chinese and Soviet management. Kim and his friends distributed handbills supporting the Soviet position. "Some politically ignorant young Chinese gave us a wide berth, vilifying us as evil people who were helping the 'trespassers,'" Kim recalled. For him, though, it seemed only natural that he and his friends viewed the world's first socialist system as a "beacon of hope" and "considered it our solemn internationalist obligation as communists to fight in its defense."

Police got wind of the communist youth group and arrested and interrogated its members, including Kim. The authorities used finger-breaking torture to try to force them to testify about the group's organization and activities in the city and about "the men behind the scenes," according to Kim's account. The young communists stonewalled, insisting that they had done nothing beyond reading some leftist books. Sent to Jilin prison in the autumn of 1929 pending disposition of his case, Kim occupied a cell on the sunless north side, cold and musty even in autumn and so cold when winter came that the walls were white with frost.[82]

The family of Pastor Sohn looked after him, collecting food, clothing and bedding and sending it to him in the care of a daughter, Sohn In-sil, a member of the Jilin Korean Children's Association. In turn, according to his account, Kim used kindness to win over the prison warders and gain better treatment for the jailed activists—even getting his friends outside to provide the items that one impoverished warder needed for his wedding. Still not convicted of any crime but facing the prospect the warlord authorities would turn them over to the Japanese, the young communist prisoners finally resorted to a hunger strike to win their release. Pastor Sohn supplemented this persuasion by offering a bribe to authorities. Kim was released in May of 1930, after what he later recalled as a time for thinking and planning. He walked out through the arched gate of the prison with a heart "full of confidence and enthusiasm."[83]

THREE

On Long Marches Through Blizzards

Much has been made of the fact that the man who became known as Kim Il-sung had been named Kim Song-ju at birth. Kim Il-sung was his nom de guerre, acquired in the 1930s. Some reports suggested that other anti-Japanese figures before him might have called themselves Kim Il-sung, and that something of a guerrilla legend had grown up around the name.[1] On that basis, critics in South Korea and elsewhere charged that the man who ruled North Korea for just under half a century was a mere impostor who had never been a guerrilla hero at all. The skepticism thus engendered abroad tended to apply indiscriminately to all his achievements, real and imagined.

Kim's propagandists played into his critics' hands when they embellished and falsified aspects of his life story to such an extreme that they invited disbelief and laughter. But Kim himself deserves the larger part of the blame. One aspect of his personality that comes through with absolute clarity is that he was ready to lie about matters big or small whenever he thought it might encourage other people to look up to him.

The trait showed itself as early as his late teens, when Kim pretended to be considerably older. He had left school in the eighth grade, near the end of the middle-school course. He rejected friends' urgings that he return and graduate. "I can teach myself," he recalled asserting. He had chosen instead the path of the "career revolutionary."[2] Several months after his release from prison, he said, he set out to revive some communist youth organizations. "In the daytime I dressed in Chinese clothes and spoke Chinese when calling on my comrades, and at night I restored the organizations clad in Korean dress and speaking Korean."[3] Although he was only eighteen at the time, he admitted, he told people he was twenty-three or twenty-four years old in order to get a little more respect from young and old alike.[4]

The change from his birth name, Song-ju, seems to have served a similar purpose. Kim said he was still in his teens when his comrades nicknamed him Il-sung. Previously they had called him Han-byol, meaning "one star." The first version of Il-sung used characters that also mean "one star," but later the characters were changed to the present Il-sung, which means "become the sun." Just before Kim's release from prison, a press report in Manchuria had mentioned the death of someone named Kim Il-sung, a man connected with the communist movement there.[5] Although Kim nowhere acknowledged any previous bearers of the name, he claimed to have felt unworthy nonetheless. He said he protested that comparing him to a star or the sun did not befit such a young man — "but my comrades would not listen to me, no matter how sternly I rebuked them."[6] Like those comrades, we may well brush aside Kim's objections to their laying of the first building block in what was to become his personality cult.

His tendency to self-promotion and prevarication aside, though, independent scholars have established beyond any doubt that Kim as a young man was, in the most important sense, the genuine article: a Korean patriot of unusual determination and resiliency.[7] Whether or not he borrowed the name Kim Il-sung is irrelevant to an assessment of his accomplishments, since it was he who went on to give the name the considerable luster it acquired in the 1930s. He rose quickly as a guerrilla fighter to become a partisan commander in a losing but gallant campaign against Japanese colonialism. While the charge that he was an impostor had a life of its own, appearing in Western news media with some frequency, the evidence to the contrary became clear enough that even South Korean government-sponsored studies granted Kim a role in the struggle for Korean independence.[8]

No separate Korean communist party existed when Kim came of age, despite several attempts over a number of years to start one. The Japanese police had rooted out each fledgling Korean party so thoroughly and ruthlessly that few people remained inside Korea who were willing and able to carry on the communist cause, as Robert A. Scalapino and Chong-sik Lee explain in their trailblazing work *Communism in Korea*.[9] Furthermore, factionalism was and is a deeply rooted problem in the Korean political culture, all across the ideological spectrum.[10] Factional conflicts had proven viciously destructive in Korean communist groupings both at home and abroad.

Lenin in 1919 had established Moscow's Third Communist International, called Comintern for short. Its word was law in the international communist movement. Finally fed up with the squabbling among Korean communists, the body made new rules that eliminated Korean communist parties outside Korea proper. Korean exiles—who comprised the great majority of Koreans seeking to become communists in that period—were directed to join local parties. For Koreans in Manchuria that meant the Moscow-backed Chinese Communist Party.[11]

Kim joined the Chinese Communist Party in 1931.[12] According to his account, he soon won a Comintern appointment as a youth organizer in the heavily Korean eastern part of Manchuria's Jilin Province. Traveling north to the Russian-influenced Manchurian city of Harbin to meet representatives of Moscow, he stayed in a luxury hotel. However, his expense allowance was so modest he had to dine on cornmeal pancakes bought from street vendors. "The first day I entered the hotel, a Russian female attendant accompanied me to my room and offered to attend to my nails," he recalled. "I said I had already done it, for I had no money to pay her. Another attendant came in after her and asked what I wanted to order for my meal. I was obliged to say that I had already eaten at my friend's house."[13]

In the spring of 1931 Kim moved for a time to Manchuria's mountainous Antu County, where his mother and younger brothers lived.[14] It was there, according to his memoirs, that he decided to join the guerrilla warfare against Japan, which that year had completed its occupation of Manchuria. At one meeting of activists late in 1931, skeptics asked how a mere partisan force could expect to beat a Japanese army of several million men armed with tanks, artillery and warplanes. They pointed out that Manchuria-based Korean guerrillas did not have even the advantage of fighting in their home country.[15] According to Kim, he won them over with a lengthy argument.

By the time he was twenty the war games of Kim's boyhood became deadly real as he took up arms in the guerrilla struggle. In his version, he formed with some comrades a Korean guerrilla unit of which he was the commander although he agreed to take orders from a Chinese nationalist commander operating in the area.[16] While he mentioned no transition from ordinary soldier to battlefield leader, some historians say he actually followed various guerrilla bands for a time before qualifying to command his own unit.[17]

In the spring of 1932, according to his account, Kim and his small unit engaged the enemy for the first time. The guerrillas ambushed a convoy of supplies and weapons guarded by soldiers of the puppet government that the Japanese had installed to run "Manchukuo," as they had renamed Manchuria. "I was so tense and excited that I could feel my heart beating," Kim remembered later. His inexperienced unit had planned a night ambush without realizing that darkness makes it difficult to tell friend from foe.

Luckily there was a full moon. The guerrillas prevailed after about ten minutes' firing and captured the goods, he said.[18]

A little later came Kim's first battle with an actual Japanese unit, made up of more professional and seasoned soldiers than those of the Manchukuo army. According to his claim, in that engagement his unit nearly wiped out the enemy but lost several of its own men: "After burying our dead comrades on the nameless hill, we held a funeral ceremony before their graves. As I looked at the sobbing soldiers, with their caps in their hands, I made a farewell address in a trembling voice. I can't remember what I said. I only remember that when I raised my head after my speech I saw the men's shoulders heaving up and down violently."[19]

Kim's headquarters was in a different part of the county from the home of his mother, who was ill with an undiagnosed ailment that he later came to believe was stomach cancer. Kim said his mother rejected his attempts to help her around the house and urged him instead to stick to his revolutionary work. He took her at her word, and seldom visited her as her illness progressed. When he did visit, he carried grain for her and his younger brothers. Arriving for one long-delayed visit, Kim felt uneasy to see no smoke rising from the chimney. Entering the house "feeling such fear and tension that the blood in my heart seemed to freeze," Kim found his mother's bed empty and his brothers sobbing.

Kim related an affecting anecdote. As his bedridden mother's death approached, it had been difficult to keep her hair clean. A neighbor woman who was caring for her had cut Kang Pan-sok's hair to stop her scalp from itching. Hearing about that after his arrival was "tearing me apart inside," Kim recalled. "I had nothing to say, even if I was to blame for being an undutiful son."[20] Kim confessed to confusion about his duty as a son (a confession that contrasted with the self-assurance reflected in most of his reminiscences). Confucian notions of filial piety clearly retained a tenacious hold on his mind. On the other hand, "it was much in vogue among the young people who were my revolutionary companions to think that a man who had stepped out on the road to struggle should naturally forget his family," he wrote. "It was my view of filial piety in those days that earnest devotion to the revolution represented the supreme love for one's family." Nonetheless, "I had no clear, established view of how a revolutionary devoted to the revolution should love his family."[21]

Kim found in Korean history some justification for the course he took. After Japan imposed on Korea a treaty of "protection" in 1905, a militant patriotic band calling itself the Righteous Volunteer Force tried to abrogate the treaty. The Righteous Volunteers were closing in on the capital when the commander, Li Rin-yong, received word that his father had died. Li turned over command to another man and went home, as Kim related the story. Combined with other reverses, Li's departure demoralized the men and led to the collapse of the army. Kim said that while he was studying in Jilin, some of his fellow students spoke up to defend Li. "In those days, he who was devoted only to his parents was considered a dutiful son," Kim explained. But he said he argued that Li should have fought first, fulfilling his duty to the nation, before going to pay homage at his father's grave.[22]

Kim's family members had suffered considerably for the cause of independence, and their suffering was far from over. Kim left his younger brothers behind to be looked after by neighbors or to fend for themselves. Then he joined the other Chinese and Korean troops in a retreat from Antu, where the Japanese were stepping up their countermeasures. The sixteen-year-old middle brother, Chol-ju, wanted to join the guerrillas and fight, but Kim told him to wait a few years. It was the last time they met. Chol-ju later did take up combat, as part of another Chinese-led unit, and was killed in battle three years later, Kim said.[23]

After Chol-ju's death, Kim said, his youngest brother, Kim Yong-ju, wandered from place to place, eking out a living babysitting and running errands, eventually getting a job in a brewery. On a visit to Korea, Kim Il-sung wrote, Yong-ju "turned up in Mangyongdae wearing a black suit and white shoes. His appearance was so dashing that our grandfather even wondered if his youngest grandson had got a high public post and made his fortune."[24] That, however, was to come much later, when President Kim Il-sung promoted his kid brother to top-level positions in the North Korean leadership.

Kim's hot-tempered uncle Hyong-gwon, the same young uncle who had smashed the gruel bowl with his head, had continued as an adult to vent his spleen—but learned to channel his anger against the Japanese. Kim Hyong-gwon and three accomplices shot and killed a Japanese policeman during a 1930 foray into Korea from Manchuria. Kim Il-sung related his surprise at learning that an erstwhile family friend, after hiding the men in his yard, had betrayed their hiding place to the authorities. It turned out that the informer had been serving as a secret agent of the Japanese. This was a lesson for Kim. "Even now I say that it is good to believe in people but that it is mistaken to harbor illusions about them," he wrote.[25]

Hyong-gwon, "stubborn as a mule," died in prison in 1936 at the age of thirty-one, Kim said. The Mangyongdae house, home to two such notorious outlaws as Kim Il-sung and his uncle, attracted considerable attention from the authorities, he recalled. Police sat in the shade of some ash trees in front of his grandparents' home, watching the house and harassing the family. To deprive them of the shade, the older of his father's brothers "went out with an axe and cut down one of the ash trees," Kim wrote.[26] Alone among all the households in the village, he claimed, his family held out against adopting Japanese names as the colonial authorities demanded in the 1930s, although police beat his elder uncle for his refusal to do so.[27]

"The misfortune and distress of our family is the epitome of the misfortune and distress that befell our people after they lost their country," Kim wrote in his memoirs. "Under the inhuman rule of Japanese imperialism millions of Koreans lost their lives—dying of starvation, of the cold, from burning or from flogging."

The 1932 retreat from Antu eventually took Kim and his anti-Japanese fighters to the Manchurian-Soviet border area. Japanese pressure intensified. Chinese and Korean nationalist elements fled across the border or switched to banditry. Kim said that left him and his seventeen teenaged Korean communists isolated in a bleak, wild territory called Luozigou. All their provisions were exhausted, their clothes in tatters, he said. "In the sky airplanes were flying around, dropping leaflets urging us to surrender, and on the ground hordes of Japanese soldiers mobilized for a 'punitive expedition' were closing in on us from all directions."

Choi Jin-sok, who joined the unit about that time, said he enlisted after the Japanese punitive forces had killed his two brothers. Choi's formal induction occurred on a snow-covered ginseng field, where the hungry guerrillas were digging up ginseng roots to eat. "I asked Kim Il-sung to accept me in his unit, and he embraced me, holding my shoulders, and told me to do a good job," Choi told a South Korean reporter more than six decades later.[28]

The Koreans considered abandoning their weapons and giving up guerrilla warfare. "Not only I but our whole group wavered," Kim admitted. In a rare instance of public self-mockery, he recalled that "when we were moving about in Jilin, writing leaflets and making speeches, we had all been heroes and great men. But here in this place we were all beginners." Fortunately, an old man named Ma appeared and helped save the day. Ma hid the guerrillas in a mountain hut and fed them while they regained their strength and their will, according to Kim's account. He added, though, that what really pulled them through this crisis was his sense of destiny. "If I had thought there would be people to save Korea after we had died, we would have been buried under the snow."[29]

Rested, the young warriors marched off in the spring of 1933 to mountainous Wangqing County in Manchuria's Jiandao Province. Communism had been displacing nationalist ideology among local Koreans who worked as slash-and-burn farmers, lumberjacks and raftsmen. Moscow's line, as transmitted through the Chinese Communist Party, was to establish guerrilla zones in Manchuria. Communists had killed or otherwise removed the local representatives of the ruling class and redistributed their land to the peasants.[30] The revolutionary governments, Kim wrote later, were establishing ideal societies. Education and medical care were free. "For the first time in history, everyone enjoyed equality." He waxed rhapsodic when recalling happy peasants who "danced to the beat of the gongs as they drove in the stakes to mark off their plots of the land distributed by the people's revolutionary government."[31]

Kim's memories became less rosy as he described Japanese encirclement of the communist enclaves. While communist guerrilla warfare in Manchuria was but a sideshow compared with the struggle of the main Chinese communist forces to the south, led by Mao Zedong, Tokyo nevertheless sensed a significant threat to its plans and sent troops on "punitive operations" against the Manchuria guerrillas. The year before Kim's arrival in the district, such a Japanese operation had "drowned the fields and mountains of Wangqing in a bloodbath," Kim wrote. "The guts of dead people drifted down the rivers." The Japanese "did not hesitate to destroy a whole village in order to kill one communist." Their policy was "killing everyone, burning everything and plundering everything." Survivors of those scorched-earth tactics had to move from their isolated villages to towns where the authorities could control them. (As Kim noted, the Americans later borrowed and refined this approach in Vietnam, where they took village people from Viet Cong areas and concentrated them in "strategic hamlets."[32])

Kim's band joined communist guerrillas whose mission was to defend some one thousand of the Wangqing people, who had evaded the 1932 punitive campaign. They fled deeper into the mountains, to heavily forested Xiaowangqing. Feeding the refugees was the immediate problem. The small patches of arable land in the area could not grow enough for them. Guerrilla attacks on the enemy yielded only small amounts of supplies. The inhabitants ate gruel made of beans ground with a millstone. When even that was unavailable the revolutionaries had to forage for roots and herbs. In their desperation they made cakes of pine bark that had been boiled in caustic soda water and pounded.[33]

His time in the guerrilla zones was a major formative influence on Kim. In later life he was to recall incessantly those days and the lessons he had learned then. Several lessons arose from his dissatisfaction with the leaders of the guerrilla bases. Like the nationalist buffoons he had so despised in his student days, those communists postured instead of confronting problems directly. "The cadres busied themselves with nothing in particular, simply creating a lot of fuss and shouting 'Revolution! Revolution!' They seldom fought outside the guerrilla zone, but spent day after day mouthing empty slogans about establishing a proletarian dictatorship."

When the guerrillas returned from victorious battles, "the people shouted hurrah, and waved flags." However, there were few major battles. Kim recalled arguing that too few soldiers and arms were available to defend such a large area and to undertake, at the same time, offensive operations. But "weak-kneed officials" rejected his argument. Those officials designated all the people living outside the area as reactionaries, needlessly minimizing the pool of people from whom converts and recruits could be drawn. For any would-be soldiers who met the residential requirements, they set unrealistic standards of class background and ideological development.[34]

Kim told of one young man whose father owned a little over three hectares (7.4 acres) of poor land on a hillside. Three hectares was the cutoff point. No member of a farming household owning more land could qualify as a "poor peasant." Thus the young man flunked the guerrilla district's strict class-background test for military recruits. Turned down several times, the young man finally arranged to sell the land—without his parents' knowledge. He used the proceeds to buy a box of Browning pistols and presented the weapons to the district's defense force. Now that he qualified as a poor peasant, he was accepted. "He was glad that he had become a guerrilla, but his family was at a loss, left without any means of livelihood," Kim wrote.[35]

Kim and others of like mind moved to establish a buffer area surrounding the guerrilla zone. The communists would not fully control the buffer area as they did the heavily protected guerrilla zone. But they could draw from it material support and reserve forces. The buffer area "would be governed by the enemy during daylight, but would come under our control at night." Although opponents attacked his group as "rightist deviationists," Kim's side turned out to be correct, as he recounted the story. By the mid-1930s the guerrilla zone itself proved too big a target. The communists had to disband it. However, the underground revolutionary organizations they had established in enemy-ruled buffer areas continued to function.[36]

Military weakness was not the worst of the problems afflicting the guerrilla districts when Kim arrived at Wangqing in 1933. Radical social changes, dictated from Moscow via the Chinese Communist Party, had disillusioned the people. Many had left in disgust.[37] "Everything was communalized, from land and provisions to the farming tools and implements such as sickles, hoes and pitchforks that had belonged to individual peasants." Life, labor and distribution were all communal. Kim had little problem with the measures themselves; more than a decade later, as leader of North Korea, he adopted many of them himself. Rather, he disagreed with the timing: "This policy amounted to sending kindergarten children to university without giving them primary and secondary education."

The revolutionaries' term for the governing body of a Manchurian guerrilla zone was "soviet," meaning an elected communist government. Local people, however, had no idea what the foreign term meant, as applied to their districts, and the communists had not taken the trouble to educate them. In various districts, as Kim eventually learned, the people had mistaken the term for *soksaepo*, the Korean word for an automatic gun, or *soebochi*, a tin pail. One villager advised people to look closely at the soviet and see whether it was large or small. "Some other villagers were said to have gone out with baskets to gather wild vegetables, because they had nothing special to offer the soviet, an important guest." Even propagandists for the soviet had no clear idea of what it was. To cover their confusion they tossed around additional loanwords such as *kommuna*.

One old man, the father of a guerrilla commander, told Kim that the last straw for him had come when officials collected the people's spoons and chopsticks for use in a new, communal dining hall. The old man spat at them. "If you are going to create a hell and call it a *kommuna*," he told them, "do it yourselves, young men. We are already out of breath and can't keep up with you any longer." The old man likewise was disgusted by mass meetings at which daughters-in-law criticized their husbands' overbearing parents, who in traditional fashion ruled the extended-family households.

The authorities expropriated large and small landholdings alike, taking the owners' cattle, horses and provisions. When a female baby was born in a Chinese household, it had been the custom for her family to prepare flower-patterned shoes for her future children and put them away in a chest. In purges of Chinese landowners the revolutionaries took even those shoes.

Although Kim in his memoirs related such affecting anecdotes, it was not sentiment that made him disapprove of the communalization campaign in the guerrilla zones. Rather, the campaign cut off valuable support the guerrilla armies had been receiving from landowners. The landowners were predominantly patriotic Chinese, opposed to the Japanese colonialists. Alienating them revived old antagonisms on the part of Manchuria's Chinese inhabitants toward Koreans, who made up the vast majority of both Jiandao's population as a whole and the province's communists. The result was a split in the anti-Japanese movement.

Kim blamed the problems on higher-ups who, "in ignorance of specific circumstances, aped the ill-digested principles of the classics"—the Marxist-Leninist classics, that is. The people in charge locally had their orders, handed down from Moscow's Comintern, and they refused to change the policy. Some revolutionaries could see that the directives had failed in practice—but they imagined that the way to correct the situation would be to go to the Soviet Union and study the way the revolution's mother country carried them out.

The North Korean system that Kim constructed in his later life appears so extreme that it may be difficult to picture him as the scourge of overzealous communist radicals. Nevertheless he asserted that for six decades following those days in the guerrilla zones of the 1930s he tirelessly combated "leftist" evils and bureaucratic tendencies.

Some of his 1930s experiences seem to have reinforced a personal bent to authoritarianism. Kim devoted a lengthy section of his memoirs to decrying "ultra-democracy"—another "leftist" tendency—in the commands of some anti-Japanese guerrilla forces in Manchuria.[38] The leftists "advocated absolute equality for every soldier, irrespective of his rank." Officers had to do menial work just like the men. Still more damaging was a rule that, even in the heat of combat, everything had to be decided collectively through majority rule. In practice that meant endless series of meetings.

Kim told of one case in which Japanese surrounded thirteen guerrillas in a house at night. Experienced military men in the house could see that the best hope for escaping was to judge the enemy's weak point, strike quickly and fight their way through the encircling force. However, the company commander had no right to make a decision, and a veteran guerrilla who knew what should be done was not entitled to any special respect merely on account of his seniority. The soldiers argued on and on about whether to try for a breakthrough or simply to stand and fight. They did not stop arguing and start fighting until the enemy commenced firing. All thirteen guerrillas were shot, most fatally. One wounded guerrilla managed to escape to tell the tale. "Ever since then I have shuddered at the mention of ultra-democracy in military affairs, and never tolerated the slightest tendency towards it in our ranks," Kim said. An army in which subordinates speak impolitely to their superiors, dispute their orders and instructions or fail to salute them "is no longer an army. It is a rabble."[39]

During his time in Manchuria's Wangqing guerrilla zone, Kim claimed, people started to see him as a potential Korean version of Vietnam's famed revolutionary leader Ho Chi Minh. A representative of the Comintern known as Inspector Pan came calling in April of 1933, the month Kim turned twenty-one. Kim asked the visitor why Moscow did not permit Koreans to have their own communist party. The Indochinese, after all, had a party of their own despite their own history of factional abuses. Inspector Pan explained the real reason for the distinction: None other than Ho Chi Minh had been representing the Indochinese communists in the Comintern. The Korean communists, on the other hand, had no such outstanding leader who could compel respect from Moscow. Inspector Pan stayed and talked for some days, according to Kim's account, and when he finally left, his parting words to his host were: "Please be Korea's Ho Chi Minh."[40]

❖ ❖ ❖

Whatever his disagreements with party policy, it was Kim's job as a soldier to help defend the Xaiowangqing guerrilla district. He and his fellow communist insurgents in East Manchuria were more than an irritant to Tokyo. They limited Japanese control of that territory and may have impeded further imperial expansion into China proper. Japan assigned a division of its crack Kwantung Army and beefed up the police to rein in the guerrillas. The authorities sent armed Japanese reserve soldiers to establish themselves as colonists. They set up associations "for the maintenance of public peace" all over Manchuria. The associations had instructions to root out insurgents and pacify the populace. Spies for the Japanese infiltrated the commumist-held areas. Undercover agents had authority to execute rebels on the spot.[41]

A major test, Kim related, was a three-month battle with Japanese punitive forces that started in November 1933. He said five thousand enemy troops attacked an area defended by only two companies of guerrillas. The guerrillas used surprise attacks, sniping, ambush, night warfare and feints, luring the enemy into a defense zone of their own choosing. One successful tactic was burying a bomb in the bonfire just before abandoning a guerrilla campsite. Enemy troops moving into the abandoned position warmed themselves at the fire—for the last time. Ho Chi Minh would have approved. The enemy forces, however, accepted their losses and mounted a siege, determined to outlast the poorly provisioned communists. Kim said he took half the guerrillas and sneaked through the line of siege, then attacked and harassed the enemy from the rear. Finally, the Japanese lifted the siege and withdrew.

Kim's explanation of why outside historians knew nothing of this battle was that it was overshadowed by European news as Hitler took office in Germany while Moscow and Washington established diplomatic relations.[42] Other battles did not escape notice, however. From Wangqing and other bases, Kim subsequently conducted many more small-scale military operations, usually in Manchuria but occasionally across the border in Korea. His record in guerrilla warfare proved him a worthy bearer of the illustrious Kim Il-sung name. Press reports in the mid- to late 1930s are sprinkled with references to the exploits of the Kim Il-sung unit.[43] A report to the Comintern in December 1935 described him as "trusted and respected" within the anti-Japanese movement.[44]

Most significant in building his reputation both with the Japanese foe and among fellow Koreans was a battle on June 4, 1937. The twenty-five-year-old Kim and about two hundred of his men crossed into Korea and attacked the border village of Pochonbo at night, killing some Japanese policemen. They then made off with supplies and money seized from local landlords. When a Japanese punitive expedition followed them back across to Manchuria, Kim had his men conceal themselves among the rocks on a mountain. "He told us never to fire until the enemies were close at hand," Choi Jin-sok recalled. To conserve his unit's scarce ammunition, Kim had his men push rocks down upon the attacking Japanese. "Rocks rolled down with a thundering noise," according to Choi. As the Japanese fled, the Koreans captured enough weapons for each guerrilla to be armed with an up-to-date rifle.[45]

Most of the men serving under Kim were Korean, and later he wished to be remembered as commander of a body he referred to as the Korean People's Revolutionary Army. Outside historians, however, know the "KPRA" as the Second Army Corps of a Chinese communist-led force that was called at first the Northeast People's Revolutionary Army. From 1936, it was known as the Northeast Anti-Japanese United Army. (The Chinese referred to Manchuria as Northeast China.) A 1936 declaration of the NEAJUA explained that "every Chinese with passion and brains knows that there is no way for survival other than fighting the Japanese." It added a welcome to "all the oppressed peoples, the Koreans, Mongolians, Taiwanese and their organizations," to join the army.[46]

Kim led at the company and battalion levels and handled political commissar duties for the party. His Chinese education helped him advance quickly as he gained experience—and as his Chinese and Korean seniors were killed, captured or lured into cooperation with the enemy. While still in his mid-twenties he commanded a division. From around 1938, he commanded the entire Second Directional Army Corps within the NEAJUA's First Route Army. The units he actually led in battle were much smaller than such inflated titles might suggest, never much exceeding three hundred soldiers at a time. Nonetheless, by the late 1930s Kim Il-sung's exploits were widely known. Among Koreans he had become one of the recognized heroes of the anti-Japanese struggle.

"He fought the Japanese expeditionary forces at great odds," as biographer Dae-Sook Suh of the University of Hawaii wrote. "He suffered many defeats but he also scored some impressive victories and made a name for himself—indeed, he became the most wanted guerrilla leader in Manchuria. He persisted in the hopeless fight without much support, but he endured and did not surrender or submit to the Japanese."[47]

The Japanese called Kim and his men "bandits," and some other partisan units in fact were known to have degenerated into simple banditry. Sometimes, as in the case of Pochonbo, Kim's unit raided towns and other outposts of civilization to confiscate supplies. According to Kim's own account he operated strictly according to political principles, taking from the rich to help the poor. "Contribute guns if you have guns, money if you have money," he demanded.

The guerrillas could be brutal. In a letter, one Second Army unit warned landlord families that they would begin receiving first the ears and then the heads of their hostage relatives if they failed to deliver 150 sets of underwear as previously demanded.[48] Press reports of the time, influenced by the Japanese authorities, paint an unflattering picture of Kim's activities.[49]

But in portraying himself as a Robin Hood, Kim got in the last word — almost by default. Describing in his memoirs an expedition to North Manchuria in 1934, he wrote that he had no "comrades-in-arms now alive" who could recall it.[50] That passage was written before ex–machine gunner Choi Jin-sok resurfaced to be interviewed for a South Korean magazine, after living in Russia for five decades. Choi backed Kim's version, claiming that when the young commander had to depend on poor villagers to feed and shelter the unit, he paid cash "even if money was short." However, the single example Choi gave was a time when Kim's unit billeted itself at Choi's parents' home.[51]

Few details of Kim's personal life during his guerrilla period are available, but in his account and those of others he comes across as both a man's man — brave, loyal in his friendships — and a ladies' man. Clearly he enjoyed female companionship. "Young communists loved the other sex while they worked for the revolution," Kim recalled later. "Some people say that communists are devoid of human feelings and know neither life nor love that is worthy of human beings. But such people are totally ignorant of what communists are like. Many of us loved while fighting for the revolution. . . ."[52] Indeed. Among the Pyongyang elite it was whispered later that Kim himself had various female companions during his guerrilla years, including both guerrilla comrades and entertainers, and had children by some of those women.

Kim was vague about just whom he himself loved in his early years. But he did recall with affection several young female comrades. One, named Han Yong-ae, accompanied him to Harbin for his meeting with the Comintern representative, shared meals with him (but not, he insisted, his hotel room) and helped disguise him as a Chinese to keep the police at bay. In his memoirs he said that as an old man he still gazed at her picture — but he observed primly that "all the services she did me were the result of a pure, unselfish comradeship transcending feelings of love."[53]

Kim claimed to have pulled off, a bit later, a heroic horseback rescue of Hong Hye-song, whom he described as a "pretty woman political worker" who was using traditional herbal medicine to treat scabies victims in the Wangqing guerrilla zone. In one of a number of passages showing the movie scenarists' touch, Kim related that he was riding a white horse when he heard gunfire and discovered Hong Hye-song caught in an enemy ambush. "I spurred my horse on towards her where, on the brink of being taken prisoner, she was returning the enemy fire, and picked her up instantly. The horse, sensing my intention, shot off like an arrow and galloped for a couple of miles." Kim failed to make clear what his relationship with Hong was but he wrote that, if she had not been killed in a later battle, she "would now be gratefully sharing with me in my recollections of the white horse."[54]

Choe Kum-suk, Wangqing County party committee member for women's work, "was as magnanimous as a man and warm-hearted; and at the same time, she was a woman of principle, faithful to the revolution. She would have hauled a boat over a sandy beach if I had asked her to do it." Choe sympathized with Kim for having lost his parents, and treated him as a younger brother. She nursed him through a severe bout of typhus. "She would visit me before anybody else when I returned from the battlefield, slipping into my hands something she felt I needed. Sometimes she would sew up tears in my clothes and knit wool into underwear for me." Kim mimicked her "funny" Hamgyong Province accent and teased her about being pretty — although actually, with her cherubic face, "she was not a woman of great beauty. But to me, women such as Choe Kum-suk in the guerrilla zone were much nobler and prettier than the girls and ladies in the big towns." Choe died in the enemy's siege of Xaiowangqing in the winter of 1933–1934, Kim related.

Communists in China, including Korean communists, had welcomed women to join the struggle, supposedly on an equal basis.[55] Many did join, not only as fighters but in other capacities. Kim's guerrilla command included female detachments in charge of sewing and cooking. The cooks numbered around thirty women and girls, Choi Jin-sok recalled. The seamstresses made the guerrillas' uniforms and knapsacks, using cotton cloth soaked in a dye obtained from boiling the bark of oak trees. They were the same yellowish khaki color as the Japanese army uniforms, with red stars on the caps instead of the yellow stars the Japanese wore.[56]

With their mixed-gender units, the communists acquired a reputation for promoting free love. Kim told of a Chinese nationalist commander who remarked that he had heard how "communists, men and women alike, all sleep under one quilt." Kim said he replied that this was a Japanese-concocted lie: "There are many woman soldiers in our guerrilla unit, but such a thing never occurs. If they fall in love, they get married. Our discipline between men and women is very strict."[57]

If that made him sound old-fashioned, Kim revealed a contrasting mentality when he wrote approvingly about a "modern" woman of the previous generation. A friend of Kim's father, Li Gwan-rin was a beautiful revolutionary, the "flower" of the nationalist fighting force. In times past, Kim wrote, "whenever a foreign enemy invaded the country and murdered and harassed our people, the women would conceal themselves deep in the mountains or in temples so as to avoid violation." Li Gwan-rin was different, however. Still unmarried in her late twenties, she lived in a man's world where men constantly pursued her while other Korean women were marrying at half her age. Li Gwan-rin did not fit the Confucian notion that chastity is a woman's top priority, Kim said. She was "attractive, bold and of firm character. The like of her was rarely found in Korea in those days." He gave no details of any specific liaisons Li might have enjoyed, but quoted her as lamenting that Kim's father's death had left her gloomy.[58]

A young woman named Kim Jong-suk headed the seamstress detachment of Kim Il-sung's guerrilla unit.[59] Five years his junior, she met him in 1935 when she was seventeen and sometimes worked as a member of his bodyguard detachment[60] besides sewing and cooking. Some accounts say that it was in 1940 that she became his wife[61]—without benefit of a wedding ceremony.[62] In 1942, she gave birth to the first of his acknowledged children, Kim Jong-il.

Various sources say Kim Il-sung already had been married at least once before his marriage to Kim Jong-suk. An earlier marriage is not mentioned in either his memoirs or official North Korean histories, but in those days teenaged Koreans were considered of marriageable age. "A young man over twenty was regarded as an old bachelor," Kim himself said[63]—although he also recalled predicting that he himself might marry late.[64]

Japanese police reported capturing, on April 6, 1940, a woman partisan who called herself Kim Hye-suk and who said she was Kim Il-sung's wife.[65] Various sources maintain that the woman gave a false name to confuse the police but that she was indeed Kim Il-sung's wife (presumably common-law as in the case of Kim Jong-suk) and her real name was Han Song-hui. Han had been chief of the women's department of Kim's partisan band. To win her release from custody, she had to agree to sever all contact with the anti-Japanese movement, change her name and remarry.[66] A Han Song-hui does make a walk-on appearance in Kim's memoirs, in connection with events in the Manchurian guerrilla zones in the autumn of 1934, but he provided no details of her role with the partisan band or of her relationship with him.[67]

Besides liking women, Kim Il-sung wrote of his "great pleasure"[68] in being with children. One entire chapter of his memoirs is devoted to a pair of tap dancers who arrived in the guerrilla zones. There they worked in a children's entertainment corps, whose activities seem to have occupied much of Kim's time when he was not off fighting battles. Kim said he was close to tears when he heard the life story of the older of the girls, Kim Ok-sun. Her father had promised her to a landlord's son when she was only nine. The young man, more than twenty years old and thus over the hill as a marriage partner, "was apparently a dimwit or cripple, with no hopes of getting married by fair and just means," Kim related. The prospective groom's parents had invited the girl's peasant father for a drinking bout and there had paid him a substantial sum for his agreement to marry Ok-sun to their son once she reached fifteen. The girl's father had considered it a good bargain until he had his "class consciousness aroused"—whereupon he had sent Ok-sun, by then thirteen, to the guerrilla zone. Kim Ok-sun rose after liberation to become chair of the Democratic Women's Union of Korea. Her husband, partisan Choe Gwang, became chief of the Korean People's Army general staff.

The younger of the two tap dancers, nine-year-old Kim Kum-sun, rested her head on Kim Il-sung's lap and cried when she heard that her parents had been killed, he wrote. Later the little girl made such a moving speech that one of his fellow guerrillas "took her to his room, set her on his lap and put earrings and bracelets on her ears and wrists." Kim said Japanese police captured Kum-sun, tortured her and then hanged her when she refused to give information about the communists. (Making it unnecessary for us to speculate about whether this Joan of Arc story has any connection with Pyongyang's version of Hollywood, he wrote that "a novel and film depicting Kum-sun have been produced recently.")[69] After a boy orderly who had slept "with his arm around my neck" was killed, Kim dissuaded his comrades from breaking the frozen ground to bury him "because I felt as if he would come to life again and snuggle into my bosom."[70]

By 1935, the Japanese had targeted Kim individually, he said. Writing of one occasion when a Japanese officer and his Chinese troops were on his trail, he recalled that "we had to exchange fire with the pursuing enemy four or five times every day. When we marched, the enemy marched. And when we camped, the enemy camped. They stuck to us like leeches until our tongues were lolling out of our heads from the chase."[71] Japanese pacification teams arrested guerrillas' relatives to gain information about the insurgents. Then they either used the information to capture the rebels or held their relatives hostage to persuade the rebels to surrender. When guerrillas surrendered or were captured, the authorities forced them to cooperate in hunting down their old comrades.

Ex-guerrilla Choi Jin-sok recalled that, in response to such psychological warfare, many of his comrades ran away from the unit. "There were some who even attempted to kill Kim Il-sung. A large reward was offered for his head. Leaflets were issued in the name of a Japanese commander which announced whoever captured Kim Il-sung alive would be given half the entire Korean territory." Choi himself was captured in 1940 and forced to join in the anti–Kim Il-sung efforts. This betrayal brought him a ten-year prison sentence after Kim and the communists took power in 1945. Choi afterward lived in exile in the Soviet Union. Nonetheless, in 1993 he said of Kim Il-sung: "I respected him before 1940 and am proud of him even now."[72]

Eventually most other anti-Japanese fighters succumbed to enemy bullets or were captured. Kim credited his own survival to a sense of destiny tinged with nationalism — and with the Confucian filial piety that his regime by the 1990s was seeking to encourage as part of the scheme to have Kim's son succeed him. "History had not yet given us the right to die," he said. "If we became a handful of dirt without fulfilling our duty to history and the times, we would be unfilial sons not only to our families but also to the nation that gave us birth and brought us up."[73]

He also acknowledged that he and his men had some crucial help from others along the way. "Old man Ma" at Luozigou had appeared and provided needed help in 1933 when his men were thinking of abandoning their struggle. Likewise another old man, this one a timber mill employee named Kim, helped him and his men outwit and escape their Japanese-led pursuers in 1935, he said. "It was strange that whenever my life was in danger benefactors such as old man Kim would appear before me and save me at the critical moment." While some might call this luck, "others regard it as fate. They do not consider it luck when benefactors appear to help patriots who devote their all to the country and the people."[74]

In his memoirs, Kim boasted: "We could defeat the strong enemy who was armed to the teeth, fighting against him in the severe cold of up to forty degrees below zero in Manchuria for over fifteen years,"[75] Fifteen years would mean right up to the 1945 Japanese surrender, for which Kim claimed credit. In fact, though, he did not stay on in Manchuria until 1945. The weight of available evidence suggests he managed to continue fighting there only until the latter part of 1940 or early 1941. By then, the Japanese campaign had succeeded to the point that it was next to impossible for him and what remained of the guerrilla force to continue fighting in company-size units as before. Guerrillas had agreed to scatter and pursue "small-unit" action instead.[76] Finally, for Kim, the better part of valor was to flee, taking refuge across the border in the Soviet Union to await more favorable circumstances for the struggle.

Regardless of the facts, perhaps Kim believed that Koreans deserved to achieve liberation on their own. Perhaps he eventually came to believe that they deserved to imagine that it had happened that way, even though in the end the Allies had done it for them. It is possible that as the events of those years faded into history—and however much he knowingly exaggerated his part in those events—he really came to feel deeply that his patriotism, his determination and his many sacrifices earned him the role of father of the country. "My patriotic spirit made me as a teenager cry out against Japan on the streets of Jilin and carry on a risky underground struggle dodging the enemy's pursuit. Under the banner of anti-Japanese struggle I had to endure hardships going hungry and sleeping outdoors in the deep forests of Mount Paektu, push my way through endless snowstorms and wage long bloody battles convinced of national liberation, fighting against the formidable enemy scores of times stronger than our forlorn force."[77]

To some extent, Kim Il-sung as a young independence fighter deserves to be evaluated on his own terms. Brave and tough, surviving and thriving as an exile, he never gave in. Meanwhile, the Japanese pacification campaigns achieved such success that most other Koreans in his situation, if they were not killed, ultimately accommodated themselves to a future in which Japanese rule seemed impregnable. But Kim did not. "It is his persistence and obstinate will, characteristics of many successful revolutionaries, that deserve recognition," observes biographer Suh.[78]

Kim comes across as a young man who matured fast to become an effective and shrewd leader. If he was not the unfailingly benevolent, all-wise figure he later cast himself to be, at least he showed considerable intelligence and common sense. In many or even most cases, the ideological and policy stands he claimed to have taken in his guerrilla years represented rational — even inspired — choices, given his communist and anti-Japanese orientation.

As his personality cult expanded in later decades, Kim claimed that he had been recognized as the heart of the Korean resistance movement even as early as 1935. (Never mind that he still had been commanding at the battalion level then, with not only Chinese but also Korean generals above him.) "The enemy believed," he wrote, "that without Kim Il-sung the Korean communist army and its resistance to Manchukuo and Japan would collapse."[79] His own men had the same belief, he said. Typical of his recollections was a 1935 scene when he said he awoke from a raging fever to find a tearful subordinate crying, "Comrade Commander, if you die, Korea will be hopeless."

The difficulty of sifting through the many extravagant claims that he and his followers put forth over the decades, to discover what is true and what is false, constitutes the main impediment to reading Kim Il-sung's true character. That very problem, however, gives us a fix on one basic in Kim's personality: his enormous self-regard. Large egos were the rule among the young revolutionaries of his time, by Kim's own account: "Everyone was his own master. Everyone thought of himself as a genius, a hero and a great man."[80] Although he affected an ironic tone in writing those words, the man who bore the proud name Kim Il-sung developed very early a preference for the company of people who acknowledged him as a genius, hero and great man.

Of one guerrilla subordinate he tellingly wrote: "Just as Ko Po-bae followed and respected me unconditionally, so I trusted and loved him absolutely."[81] He related fond memories of Jo Taek-ju, one of those ubiquitous old men who were forever saving him. Jo's family hid Kim from the enemy in 1935 and nursed him through his fever. Kim wrote that when he finally came to, he thanked the old man for having saved his life. "Don't mention it," he quoted Jo as having replied. "God gave birth to you, General Kim, and you have been saved in this log cabin by God's will." Kim claimed he then protested that this was laying it on a bit too thick — but the old man merely chided him for being "too modest."[82]

FOUR

❋

Heaven and Earth the Wise Leader Tamed

Somewhat paradoxically having made of himself in the 1930s a genuine Korean national hero under Chinese Communist command, Kim Il-sung in the 1940s added another sponsor. He survived the Japanese campaign against him by living in the Soviet Union under Soviet protection. He wore a Soviet Army uniform. After Japan's 1945 defeat, he went on to gain political power with backing from many fellow Koreans but also—a more important factor— from the Soviet generals in charge of the occupation of northern Korea.

It was a profitable bargain for both sides. In the process, however, Kim compromised his nationalist credentials to some extent, in his own mind and in the minds of some fellow Koreans. Rather than nationalism, Kim preferred to describe his stance as "socialist patriotism." Regardless of the terminology, taking Moscow's orders required him to subordinate strictly Korean interests to communist internationalism whether he liked it or not. Especially hard for him to swallow was the fact that the triumph over Japanese colonialism was not of his own doing. By no means were all of his official positions and actions his own, even after he had been installed as the most powerful Korean in the northern half of the peninsula.

Kim saw any flaw in his Korea-first image as a threat to his power. He grew determined to redeem his damaged nationalist credentials. Thus, he reworked his life story to suppress the truth about his life in the Soviet Union during the first half of the 1940s. Then, even while carrying out the Soviet program for North Korea, he watched for opportunities to prove that no other Korean was his peer as a patriot. His determination in that regard formed a major strand in the tangled history that led him to plan the invasion of the South, an action that he hoped—based on serious misjudgments, which may have arisen partly from excessive enthusiasm and self-confidence— would reunify Korea and turn it into a powerful country able to withstand the incursions of larger neighbors.[1]

Some time after they fled across the border into the Soviet Union, Kim and his men were inducted into the Soviet Army and sent to a camp at the village of Boyazk, about fifty miles northwest of Khabarovsk in the Russian Maritime Province. There they joined a secret international reconnaissance unit of the Soviet Army. Officially named the Eighty-eighth Special Independent Sniper Brigade, its mission was reconnaissance rather than fighting. The commander of the Eighty-eighth was Zhou Baozhong, a Chinese guerrilla general from the Northeast Anti-Japanese United Army, who had been commissioned as a Soviet Army senior colonel. Kim Il-sung, who had worked with Zhou in Manchuria, became a Soviet Army captain commanding the Eighty-eighth's First Battalion. The approximately two hundred soldiers in Kim's battalion included Chinese and Koreans as well as Soviet citizens of Korean ancestry.[2]

One of Kim's first assignments after he went to the Soviet Union was to write a history of the NEAJUA's First Route Army—of whose top command he was the only surviving member who had not been captured. His Chinese-language chronicle has survived in Beijing's archives.[3]

According to Kim, since his youth in Manchuria he had scoffed at those Koreans who believed foreign powers held the key to their country's liberation. The young Kim's subordination to the Comintern and the Chinese Communist Party, and then to the Soviet Army, may raise doubts about the strength of any such early belief. But if the sentiment was in part an afterthought, inspired by the tactical requirements of his later struggles with political rivals in Korea, it had resonance for Kim nonetheless. He demonstrated that with his longtime refusal to level with the North Korean people about his Soviet sojourn; instead he developed, and stuck to, a claim that he had continued his struggle in Manchuria and Korea until he succeeded in liberating his homeland in 1945.[4]

In fact Kim's escape to the USSR permitted him to wait—wisely, as it turned out—while the Allies dealt with Japan. Meanwhile he could enjoy the comforts of settled life while recovering from health problems that had plagued him during his years of living on the run. Most important, he remained alive, a viable player, in position to take advantage of the Allied victory whenever it might occur.

Focused on defending itself against Hitler, the USSR was still more than three years away from declaring war on Japan—but it already had begun its preparations. The immediate mission of the Soviet Army's Eighty-eighth Brigade was to infiltrate soldiers into Manchuria and Korea to spy on Japanese troops. Training emphasized marksmanship, radio communications and parachuting. A longer-term role of the men of the Eighty-eighth Brigade was to help set up communist regimes in Korea and China following the Japanese empire's collapse. To this end, they underwent heavy communist political indoctrination.[5]

Kim Il-sung quickly impressed his Soviet mentors—thanks to brains, not brawn. Some reports say he was sent on trips to Moscow in 1943 and 1944, probably in the company of his commander, Zhou.[6] Yu Song-chol, a third-generation Soviet citizen of Korean ancestry, was assigned as Kim's Russian-language interpreter in September of 1943. Yu recalled that period in interviews with South Korean researcher Chay Pyung-gil nearly five decades later. Kim was "lean and weak, and his mouth was always open," perhaps due to blockage in his nasal passages, said Yu. Kim led troops back across the border on only one actual reconnaissance mission that Yu knew of. Even during ski training he became so exhausted that he had to tie himself to a subordinate with ropes in order to move. Despite his physical shortcomings, Kim "was regarded as being exceptionally smart and possessive of leadership qualities," Yu said. "I believe this is why he was liked by the Soviets."[7]

As for Kim's subordinates in the Eighty-eighth, their relationship with their commander depended to a great extent on whether they had fought alongside him earlier. He already held considerable authority among the two dozen Korean guerrillas from Manchuria who joined him in the Eighty-eighth Brigade. The ex-partisans "were united with one another based on affection and comradeship that only they themselves shared," according to Yu's recollections. Unlike them, Yu and other ethnic Koreans in the Eighty-eighth who had been reared in the Soviet Union "could only face Kim Il-sung with unemotional, calm, feelings."[8] Perhaps partly for that reason, Yu did not see in Kim the unfailingly benevolent figure portrayed in the North Korean regime's subsequent propaganda. Kim was "stern and cold" to subordinates and he expected unquestioning obedience, Yu remembered.

On the other hand, Kim was "obedient and ardent toward Brigade Commander Zhou Baozhong and the Soviet officers,"[9] said Yu. That characterization rings true. Kim's memoirs make clear that the fatherless young revolutionary, from the beginning of his middle-school days in Huadian, appealed to the paternal instincts of elders and superiors who were eager to help him on his way up. For more than a decade after liberation, Kim was to play for his Russian mentors the role of the consummate company man, flattering them and carrying out their instructions as they rewarded him by granting him more and more power and autonomy.

* * *

The Americans, meanwhile, were working on two plans for the final defeat of the Japanese. The atomic bomb would be the ace in the hole—if the top-secret project could reach fruition in time. Otherwise, a massive invasion of Japan's home islands could cost as many as a million American lives. At a strategy conference at Yalta in the Russian Crimea in February 1945, President Franklin D. Roosevelt pressed Stalin to enter the war. A Soviet attack on Manchuria would keep the Japanese from shifting their troops from China and Manchuria back to the home islands to join the defense. That second front would reduce the invaders' casualties by an estimated two hundred thousand. Moscow agreed to make such an attack, within two or three months following Germany's surrender, in exchange for some Japanese territory— southern Sakhalin and the Kurile Islands—and a grant of postwar "pre-eminence" in Manchuria. The Russians were thus committed to "share the cost in blood of defeating Japan."[10]

The A-bombing of Hiroshima of August 6 showed that there would be no need to invade Japan with infantry and, thus, no military need for Soviet intervention. Nevertheless, sticking to the letter of its agreement, Moscow entered the war two days later. In the less than one week remaining before Tokyo's surrender, Soviet troops attacked the dispirited Japanese in Manchuria and Korea and routed them, suffering fewer than five thousand casualties in the process. In Korea the only real battle may have been the struggle for the northeastern port of Chongjin, where naval units carried the major burden of attack.[11]

The Soviet military occupied the portion of Korea north of the 38th parallel, under a hastily reached agreement that called for the United States to occupy the more populous southern part of the peninsula. Although both victorious allies wanted to maximize their respective spheres of influence in the postwar world, the Americans did not have troops available to go to Korea immediately. Fearing that Soviet troops would press on all the way to the southern tip of the peninsula and present a fait accompli, Washington proposed the demarcation line. Two colonels in the War Department, Dean Rusk (who would become secretary of state during the Vietnam War period) and Charles Bonesteel, took a quick look at a map to come up with the proposed placement of the line. Dividing the country at the 38th parallel left in the southern zone the current capital, Seoul, as well as an ancient capital, Kaesong, which was still an important city. The USSR got control of the northern Korean ports of Chongjin and Wonsan. Moscow had wanted the war to last longer so it could grab more of Japan's territory—but figured this division was the best bargain it could drive, under the circumstances of the unexpectedly quick Japanese collapse.[12]

While carving up the peninsula, neither Washington nor Moscow gave thought to the fact that the line would slice though Korea's major veins and arteries. Once the military occupations began, though, the Americans quickly realized that both halves of Korea were now crippled in terms of resources. Cutting off trade at the artificial demarcation line deprived the South of the coal and electricity that were produced in the North, even as it kept from the relatively infertile North the rice produced in abundance by the South. The realization came too late. The American occupation chief, Gen. John R. Hodge, tried fruitlessly to negotiate a system that would restore the pre-liberation economic flow across the 38th parallel. Balking at even discussing the matter for a time, the Soviet occupation authorities began enforcing North Korea's isolation from South Korea and the capitalist world.[13] The administrative line soon became a fortified barrier.

Some Soviet officials evidently thought of Kim Il-sung as a promising candidate for an important position in a new Korean regime. They could expect to make use of the fame he had achieved among Koreans during his guerrilla-fighting days. But they gave him no chance to polish his reputation further by taking an actual military role in the final defeat of the Japanese. Although Koreans of the Eighty-eighth Brigade expected to join in the fighting to liberate their homeland, it was all over before they could see action.[14] The Soviet Army disbanded the Eighty-eighth and, a month after the surrender, sent its Korean and Soviet-Korean members to North Korea under Kim's command.[15]

By the time the contingent arrived on Korean soil, more than a month had passed since the surrender. The band of returnees first tried to enter Korea via Manchuria and the border city of Sinuiju. Hearing that the Russian invaders had blown up the Yalu River bridges, they returned to Soviet territory and tried again, the second time by ship. They disembarked from the Soviet naval ship *Pugachov* at the Korean east-coast port of Wonsan on September 19, 1945. Reportedly, Kim when he landed still wore the uniform of a Soviet Army captain.

Judging from Yu Song-chol's account, even at that moment Kim was attempting to revise history. Privately, he instructed his comrades that, if anyone should ask, they must say that Kim Il-sung was not among the party that had landed at Wonsan but had traveled separately. Yu figured that Kim, thinking of his reputation as a fighter, "wanted to hide the truth of his shabby, humble return to Korea."[16]

In the division of Korea the American occupation zone got not only the capital but most of the prominent Korean politicians, as well. In the Soviet zone, the scarcity of high-visibility Korean leaders boosted Kim Il-sung's prospects. The commander of the military government in North Korea, Gen.

Ivan M. Chistiakov, showed the Soviets' deep interest in Kim by traveling from Pyongyang to meet him after his arrival at Wonsan.

The occupation leaders assigned members of Kim's group to key public-security posts or, in the case of some Soviet-born ethnic Koreans, jobs as interpreters for the Soviet generals. According to Yu's account, they gave Kim no immediate assignment; they were reserving him for something even bigger than the job of Pyongyang police chief, which they had tentatively mentioned in discussions back in the Eighty-eighth Brigade's camp. (Yu said that job went instead to O Jin-u, who eventually became the top military man in North Korea and held that post until his death in February 1995.[17] O had followed Kim around as an admiring teenager in the Manchurian guerrilla zones, toying with the Mauser pistol in the older man's holster before being permitted to join the guerrilla unit in the mid-'30s.)[18]

In his early days in Pyongyang, Kim conferred frequently with Soviet generals as they puzzled over their choice of an indigenous leadership that would carry out occupation policies for governing the Northern zone. For the time being the Soviet authorities wanted to work through a coalition that would include Northern noncommunist nationalist elements. As their first choice for nominal leader they settled upon the widely respected nationalist Cho Man-sik.

Before liberation Cho had been a leader of the nonviolent reformist movement, influenced by Gandhi and Tolstoy. Instead of attempting fruitlessly to overthrow the iron rule of the Japanese, those reformists had argued, Koreans should focus their energies on education and the development of a self-sufficient economy to prepare for eventual independence. For many years the Presbyterian deacon Cho had costumed himself for his role, dressing in *hanbok*, the traditional Korean cotton suit, and in a Korean overcoat and shoes. Even Cho's name cards, Kim Il-sung himself noted, were printed on homemade paper as "a symbol of his patronage of Korean products."[19]

As the leader of North Korean communists who had served in the Soviet Union under Soviet military orders, the newly arrived Kim Il-sung conferred with Soviet officers over lavish dinners in *kisaeng* — Korean geisha — houses (with Cho Man-sik also present on one such occasion). Soon Kim emerged as an obvious candidate for a high-profile role of his own.[20] On October 14, 1945, less than a month after his arrival in North Korea, the people of Pyongyang were invited to a Soviet-organized rally billed as a "reception for the triumphant return of General Kim Il-sung." Preceded both by his reputation and by an introductory speech that Soviet officers had persuaded a reluctant Cho to deliver, Kim took the rostrum to the crowd's roars of "Long live General Kim Il-sung!"

Kim read a speech drafted by Soviet occupation officials. During the speech, rumors began flashing through the crowd that he was a fake and a Soviet stooge.[21] Koreans had been brought up to respect age and seniority.

Until that moment they had imagined Kim Il-sung as a grizzled veteran. Only thirty-three and looking even younger with a blue suit too small for him and what an unfriendly onlooker described as "a haircut like a Chinese waiter," the speaker hardly seemed the man behind the legend.[22]

Soviet officials polled the audience after the speech and were dismayed by the reaction. According to one report the Russians had been leaning toward making Kim defense minister—the strong man's post—in a regime to be headed nominally by Cho Man-sik.[23] But it would not do to have the Korean populace believe the Russian occupiers were installing a stooge.

The answer was a propaganda offensive to shore up Kim's image. That campaign sought to turn his youth into a virtue. As an official biography later expressed the formula, a promise of "everlasting prosperity to the people" is delivered convincingly not by "an old man given to reminiscing on past glories but a young man who looks to the distant future."[24] By most accounts Kim, during that period, displayed a modest, unassuming demeanor. His Soviet handlers thus had a fairly easy time of it as they worked to correct the initial image problems of the attractive young leader. Here is a description by an apparently dazzled reporter for a South Korean newspaper who interviewed him in December 1945:

> A dimpled smile, gentle eyes and the light of genius glittering in them. . . . Let me present the appearance of the General in detail. Sunburnt brown complexion, short, modern-style hair, gentle, double-lidded eyes, dimples appearing when he smiles—he is a perfectly handsome youth. His height is probably about five feet six and he is not so plump. Generous, open and cheerful character and modest, yet clear-cut attitude make people feel as if they have been his friends for a long time. It is difficult to guess where his ambitious spirit and daring are hidden. . . . The General uses simple and clear expressions. He is modesty itself, and when asked if he had any intention of becoming a statesman, he answered that he is not fitted for such a name. When youthful people or students call him General, he replies: "I am not a General, but your friend. Please call me *dongmoo* [comrade]." . . . He loves the masses of people; above all, young people he loves deeply; he meets everyone with good grace, listens to them with sincerity, and answers their questions with kindness. General Kim is now among our people as a simple citizen. How his youthful wisdom and courage will reflect themselves in the development of our nation must be a great matter of concern of Korea.[25]

The Soviet authorities' initial plans ran into a roadblock when Cho Man-sik showed that he would be no pliant figurehead. He complained that Soviet occupation troops had confiscated grain needed by the hungry Koreans.[26] That same issue in November 1945 inspired student-led riots in Sinuiju, which ushered in several months of often-violent struggle.[27]

More significantly, Cho refused to compromise his demands for immediate independence in favor of a "trusteeship" plan for Korea. Actually put forth first by the Americans, that plan called for up to five years of tutelage by four Allied powers—the United States, the Soviet Union, Britain and Nationalist-ruled China. During that time the Koreans would learn to govern themselves. The American proposal responded to concern over the resource imbalances and other ill effects of dividing Korea into exclusive American and Soviet zones. Trusteeship offered unity for the country and its economy under a single government.[28]

Many Koreans, however, felt insulted and outraged by the notion that they needed tutelage. In the South, opposition from such right-wing nationalists as Rhee Syngman and Kim Ku was ferocious. American occupation officials—including some who had been suspicious of the idea to begin with—quickly sought to distance themselves from the hot-potato trusteeship proposal. In the North, Cho Man-sik had put behind him his longtime advocacy of nonresistance and national self-improvement. With the Japanese defeated, it was time for independence. Cho was not the least bit interested in exchanging Japanese rulers for new foreign masters under the rubric of "trusteeship."

Moscow, however, refused to budge from its public stance. The USSR's position was curious. The Soviet occupation for its first few months otherwise gets generally high marks for responsiveness to Korean aspirations—especially when compared with an often overbearing American occupation in the South. And analysts in the USSR could see clearly that trusteeship would dilute Moscow's control in North Korea, to the benefit of the United States and the other two noncommunist Allies.

How, then, and why did the Soviet authorities get themselves and their Korean communist allies into the unpopular position of appearing to champion "trusteeship"? One theory is that the communists, needing time to strengthen their political forces in the South, saw a trusteeship of several years as in their interests.[29] Dutch scholar Erik van Ree puts forth a different argument, based on Soviet documents made available after the USSR's collapse. Moscow did not really want trusteeship, van Ree asserts; its supposed support of the concept was merely camouflage and a delaying tactic while it pursued its true aim: planting a satellite regime in the North. "Moscow was not anxious to reunify Korea," he says. The Americans, on the other hand, initially favored unification out of the belief that, since they controlled Seoul and two-thirds of the population, "they would profit more from unification than the Russians."[30]

As the Cold War loomed, it is clear, both the Soviet Union and the

United States gave priority to ensuring ideological compatibility in the respective zones they occupied in Korea, at whatever expense to Koreans' yearning for independence and reunification. The country, north and south, was "a shrimp crushed in a battle of the whales," in the words of an old Korean proverb.[31]

The Soviet authorities in January of 1946 placed Cho Man-sik in custody, dispensing with all but a semblance of coalition politics. Cho's precise fate is unknown, but it is thought that authorities killed him later, around the time of the Korean War.[32] The Soviet generals moved to place Korean administrative organizations and political parties in the hands of the communists — a group of Koreans largely willing to swallow nationalistic objections to the trusteeship concept, once Moscow cracked the whip.

Several prominent communist, anti-Japanese figures were available to choose among. Moscow ruled out one group as being too close to the Chinese communists.[33] Pak Hon-yong led another group, the "domestic" communists. Pak's problem was that, like most other leading politicians of all stripes, he was based in the capital, Seoul, and thus in the American occupation zone. Pak headed a single communist party, headquartered in Seoul, which sought to speak for both halves of Korea. He was also involved in an ambitious united-front scheme to draw nationalists from all across the ideological spectrum into a "Korean People's Republic" that claimed legitimacy throughout the peninsula. Moscow withheld support, out of concern about dilution of Soviet control in the North in case the Korean People's Republic or any other Seoul-based pan-Korean government should come into being.[34]

For his part, Kim Il-sung actively attacked the Korean People's Republic's pretensions to Korea-wide governance. It was in the *northern* part of Korea, he argued, that "favorable conditions have been created for building a new country."[35] He did not mention the likelihood that this would mean a new country in which the leading role would go to Kim Il-sung, not Pak Hon-yong.

Kim also attacked Cho Man-sik and Cho's followers for joining with "reactionary strata of the United States" to oppose the agreement on trusteeship.[36] As he wrote in his memoirs, Kim since his student days had despised the reformists — precisely on account of their submission to foreign rule during what they viewed as a period of "preparation" for independence. He purportedly hated the implication that Korea was an "inferior" nation. But now the Japanese were defeated and Soviet generals were in charge of deciding which Koreans would achieve power in Pyongyang. By supporting trusteeship, Kim could be seen as having traded places on this key nationalist issue with the doomed Cho Man-sik.

Stated baldly, Kim was opposing both immediate unification (under the Seoul-based People's Republic, which Pak Hon-yong supported) and immediate independence (which Cho had demanded). There apparently is no record of any pangs that these stands may have caused his patriot's heart to suffer. Perhaps he reasoned that the Soviet Union, having supported Korean liberation for decades, had earned the right to his deference.[37] In any case it is possible to see much of his subsequent career as a conscious, decades-long effort to redeem the nationalist credentials he had soiled by taking orders from Moscow on the People's Republic, trusteeship and other issues. From this point it is not always easy to distinguish actions Kim took out of genuine nationalist convictions from ploys he intended first and foremost to help consolidate and expand his own power.

Kim Il-sung had become chairman of the North Korean branch of the Korean Communist Party in December of 1945. On February 8, 1946, with heavy backing from the Soviet authorities, he became chairman of the Interim People's Committee. That made him the top Korean administrative leader in the North.[38] He was to remain in power until his death on July 8, 1994, forty-eight years and five months later. Thus to an extraordinary extent, as Dae-Sook Suh observes, the study of Kim and his rule "is the study of North Korea."[39]

Kim's Interim People's Committee quickly proclaimed the equality of the sexes, nationalized major industries and, most significantly, launched a drastic land reform. Although those measures all represented Soviet policy as handed down by Stalin, there is little reason to believe Kim harbored major reservations about carrying out the 1946 reforms.[40] Certainly they benefited him politically. Farmland owned by Japanese and Korean landlords went to hundreds of thousands of peasants, the majority of whom had been tenants or mere farm laborers. The redistribution instantly created a devoted popular following for the new regime. "Is this land going to be ours forever?" a former tenant farmer asked Kim when he visited the man's village. The new leader's reported reply: "It was to give this land back to you that the anti-Japanese fighters shed much blood."[41]

The haves resisted the handover of their property to the have-nots, and anti-Soviet Korean patriots opposed Kim Il-sung as Moscow's "puppet." One Russian general reported that rioting and terrorism around that time reminded him of the civil war in his homeland. Some of the violence came perilously close to Kim. Four days *before* the land reform decree of March 5, 1946, a would-be assassin threw a grenade at the platform where Kim, with other North Korean officials and Soviet officers, watched a celebration of the anniversary of 1919's March 1 uprising. A Russian security guard who caught the grenade was seriously injured. A few days later, assassins struck the home of Kim's relative and former teacher, Methodist pastor Kang Ryang-uk, chief secretary of the provisional government. Kang's son and daughter and a visiting cleric died in the attack. Soon, however, the authorities captured most of the conspirators and put down other rebellious Northerners.[42]

Meanwhile, a great many disgruntled citizens voted with their feet. Land reform and nationalization of industry drove away a very large percentage of wealthy and educated people who resented the communist program and who could have been expected to put up further resistance if they had stayed. An estimated one million people migrated to the capitalist South.[43] American historian Bruce Cumings has argued that the radical reforms achieved an overnight revolution in the class structure of North Korea: Most Koreans who had prospered by collaborating with Japan were gone now, living in the South—or, if they remained in the North, were shorn of their wealth and power. Families that had occupied the lower strata for generations now found themselves in the upper ranks of society.[44]

Another way of looking at the exodus of the well-off and better educated, however, is that it created a vacuum of qualified technical and administrative personnel that the former lower classes simply were not prepared to fill, regardless of their upward social mobility. Evidence from the former Soviet Union shows that the USSR filled that vacuum for many years by sending Soviet personnel who called many of the shots in the economy, the government and the party. Historian Kathryn Weathersby has found that a large part of the archival record of Soviet–North Korean relations during the period consists of messages from Pyongyang—often from Kim Il-sung himself—asking Moscow to send specialists.[45]

As the state took over some 90 percent of industry in 1946, it outlawed many of the labor abuses of the past. A new law set standard working hours and mandated sexual equality in pay levels. Kim's government proceeded with Soviet-style economic planning from 1947. Soviet assistance poured in. The regime called upon the hard work and enthusiasm of those subjects who felt grateful for the end of the old order and the dawn of the new. Stakhanovite campaigns urged industrial workers to sacrifice for productivity. One highly publicized group of locomotive factory workers marched off as "storm-troopers" and reopened an abandoned coal mine, to cope with a coal shortage that was keeping trains from running. A campaign exhorted farmers to turn over portions of their rice harvests for "patriotic" use in emulation of a farmer named Kim Je-won; he supposedly had been so moved by land reform that he donated thirty bales out of his rice harvest, leaving only enough to feed his family for the following year.[46]

Kim Il-sung traveled far and wide to give "on-the-spot guidance" to his subjects. Visiting a mountain village in the spring of 1947, he explained that even poor land could be made to yield crops if heavily fertilized with manure. Urging that steep land be cultivated, he exhorted his listeners: "Reap golden ears from all mountains." (Wherever he may have come up with that idea, to the extent it did not involve effective terracing the policy—which he continued for decades—was foolish. Ultimately it proved disastrous for North Korean agriculture.) At a 1947 firing ceremony in Hwanghae for a coking furnace, which the spiteful Japanese had put out of commission at the time of their defeat, Kim urged workers to redouble their efforts and get a critically important blast furnace back into operation, as well. "The Korean people can do anything that they attempt," he proclaimed. He advised the managers to deal with shortfalls in the workers' living standards by creating a fishing fleet and vegetable gardens.[47]

Efforts to increase productivity through attitude changes worked, to some extent, and North Korea managed a burst of economic development in 1947 and 1948, particularly in heavy industry. The Hwanghae blast furnace, for example, reportedly was restored within four months, even though the Japanese supposedly had said it could not be put back into operation even in ten years.

It was not that the phenomenon was unique to North Korea. The Soviet Union's new Eastern European satellites at the time were enjoying similarly impressive advances—as had the USSR itself in the early, enthusiastic years of communist rule. But a special factor in the North's favor was the way it was blessed with the lion's share of the peninsula's mineral resources. Reflecting that, several cities on its east coast had formed the hub of Korean industry that the Japanese colonialists developed.[48]

Worth noting also is that, in this period, many elements of capital were still privately held. While the state officially owned title to the farmland following the land reform, the redistribution had placed it in the possession of the individual tillers—supposedly for their lifetimes.[49] Although Korean communists wanted full collectivization of farming, the Soviet advisors had restrained them, insisting that the country was not yet ready.

Shortly after liberation Northerners had survived serious food shortages.[50] For 1948, however, the regime boasted of a grain harvest of 1.78 million tons—more than 10 percent larger than the biggest ever recorded during the Japanese period.[51] Farm mechanization got much of the official credit. For farmers, however, gaining land they could call their own may well have stimulated greater effort and output.[52]

A nationwide literacy campaign contributed to economic development even as it raised citizen morale. By March of 1949, North Korea claimed to be the first Asian country to have eliminated illiteracy completely. The country had dispensed with complex Chinese characters in favor of sole reliance on the indigenous, simple and phonetically precise *hangul* writing system.[53] The state built schools both for children and for adults. The northern half of Korea had been without colleges and universities under Japanese rule. When the Northern regime founded Kim Il-sung University in Pyongyang in October 1946, it was over the objections of "unsound elements," who complained that the country had not yet built proper foundations upon which to erect a structure of higher education. By the time the North started to introduce compulsory elementary education, in 1950, it had an additional thirteen colleges.[54]

The pride many North Koreans felt in the transformation of their society was very real, as outsiders who spent some time in the North testified. London *Observer* correspondent Philip Deane, captured in 1950 in the early days of the Korean War, remained a prisoner in the North almost for the duration of the conflict. He later sprinkled his memoirs of confinement with quotations from North Koreans expressing their pride in the new, classless and, from their viewpoint, far more just society. North Korea, "under the guidance of our great leader and teacher Stalin, and in accordance with the orders of General Kim Il-sung, has emancipated women," an interpreter in Pyongyang boasted in one such exchange. "Everybody is learning to read—young and old."[55]

While many factors actually combined to produce early successes, Kim was happy to take all the credit and many of his followers were eager to give it. By 1947, he had became the center of a personality cult, modeled on Stalin's, in which he was pictured as wise, strong, compassionate—and energetic enough to involve himself in virtually every significant decision. He was reported to have supervised closely even the composition of the national anthem. Perhaps calling upon his experience as a church organist, he urged the committee involved to insert a refrain between the verses, to "improve the rhythm and harmony of the music [and] add to the solemnity of the song as a whole, and inspire the singer with national pride and self-confidence." According to an official biography, "none of the poets and composers assembled there had thought of this until he pointed it out."[56]

At celebrations staged all across the country, Kim received direct, personal credit and thanks for the land reform.[57] A letter supposedly written by villagers in North Hamgyong Province praised him for liberating the country from the Japanese and then, without even stopping to rest, solving the country's land problems. "Give us whatever are your orders without hesitation," the villagers said. "We will never fail to achieve what you order us to do."

Stories the regime disseminated included one about a visit to a village, at the time of land reform, when Kim peeled hot, boiled potatoes and offered one to an old man. "Old Pak Jang-ban, given the first potato, held it in his hands, sobbing, and bowed his white-haired head deeply. Suddenly he buried his head on the Leader's chest and began to cry loudly." All his life the old man "had been treated like a slave and used like a horse or bullock. Now he was treated for the first time like a human being—by no other person than General Kim Il-sung, the great, Respected and Beloved Leader!" As Kim departed, he used a brush to write Pak's name on the gatepost of the best house in the village, making the old man the new owner of the former landlord's residence. Afterward, Pak "would tell everyone he met: 'Since the creation of the world, has there ever been anyone like General Kim Il-sung?'"[58]

This was heady stuff for a leader still in his thirties. Photographs from the period show the slim, boyishly handsome guerrilla hero gradually expanding in waist and jowl as his power and accompanying perquisites expanded. Meanwhile some people watching him closely saw signs that power was affecting the young ruler's personality.[59] Coming to the fore were the hungers for absolute obedience and lavish praise.

Some analysts have seen in those needs the signs of an inferiority complex rooted in Kim's failure to finish even middle school—so contrary to the Confucian-ingrained Korean worship of formal education as a good in itself and a virtual necessity for a leader. Korean revolutionaries whom Kim had beaten out for the top job were senior to him in years, and not inferior in their own records of dedication to the anti-Japanese struggle. Several were his superiors by far in education and reportedly were not shy about playing up that fact. But while this factor may well have had an intensifying effect, we should recall that a deep craving for deference already had become visible as early as Kim's days as a guerrilla and Soviet Army officer. And Kim was by no means unique in that regard. Regardless of educational attainments, it would have been difficult to find a genuine democrat among the men in either the North or the South who sought to lead Korea after its liberation. Autocratic personalities were the rule in a country lacking any tradition of liberalism or democracy.[60]

Although North Korea quickly had put into place the apparatus of the police state,[61] Kim's personal power still was far from absolute. Within the regime, several strong figures remained. But he had to content himself with that situation only for a time. In a 1946 meeting to merge his Korean Communist Party with another leftist party to create the Workers' Party, one sycophant rose to remark that Kim Il-sung was "the only leader" for Korea and that any opposition to him amounted to reaction and treason.[62] Kim himself said the new party needed unity and iron discipline, which required "a merciless struggle against all with opposing inclinations."[63] By the fall of 1948 he had methodically undercut his rivals, removing them entirely or shunting them aside to secondary posts. For the first time, he had no peers.[64]

South Korean rightists had seized the nationalist high ground by opposing trusteeship, portraying Kim and his fellow communists as tools of Moscow. His taking office with Soviet backing had tended to confirm the unflattering portrait. That had to have been an unaccustomed and extremely unwelcome role for Kim.

Aspiring to recognition as Korea's chief patriot, Kim counterattacked. He highlighted the backgrounds of some South Korean leaders who had collaborated with the Japanese before liberation. Collaborating with the Americans this time, they had reduced the South Korean people to a ragged and hungry population of slaves, he charged in a June 1946 speech.[65] In another speech in August 1946, he referred to right-wing Southern leaders as pro-Japanese, reactionary country-sellers who put patriots in prison while *kisaeng* houses increased in number daily.[66]

Often during this period Kim spoke of the need to expand his provisional government into a Korea-wide "democratic people's republic," which he defined as a leftist regime, different from the capitalist-parliamentary model seen in the South.[67] Once rid of the anti-communist, and to his mind unpatriotic, leaders in the South and their American protectors, Korea must be reunited. Expanding his rule to cover the entire peninsula was to remain Kim's unchanging goal, second only to consolidating and maintaining power in the North, until the final days of the long life and career of this supremely determined and stubborn man.

Communist and other leftist efforts to take over South Korea from within seemed to make headway in 1946 but the U.S. occupation authorities soon clamped down, arresting key figures. By 1948, the Southern communists had gone underground, resorting to guerrilla warfare while seeking to subvert the South's military and police force. The North gave military training to more than two thousand Southerners and sent them south as guerrillas.[68] Meanwhile the rapidly intensifying Cold War dashed hopes for a negotiated reunification of the Soviet-occupied North and American-occupied South — hopes that probably had been unrealistic from the start, given the attitudes on both sides.[69]

While negotiators talked merger, both sides prepared to set up de facto separate Korean regimes. Loath to be seen as responsible for the country's division, Kim vowed never to move first.[70] In April of 1948, he played host to several Southern politicians, who had accepted his invitation to a joint conference opposing the proclamation of separate regimes.[71]

In the end, the South did take formal action first. At Washington's urging, the United Nations dispatched a commission to look into the possibility of Korea-wide elections. Dismissing the United Nations (and not without cause) as an American tool, the North refused to admit its observers. The UN mission then observed the voting in the South alone.[72] Rhee won and his government proclaimed the Republic of Korea on August 15, 1948.

The North was ready. In February of that year, with support from the Soviet Union and the help of his old guerrilla colleagues, Kim had officially formed the Korean People's Army. Long before that — almost immediately after liberation — he had begun under Soviet auspices the actual development of a Northern fighting force. He had done that despite criticism from "factional elements" — a category that seems to have included any communists who did not agree 100 percent with Kim — that there was no need for an army "when North and South are not yet unified." The way Kim's propagandists saw it, in forming the People's Army "the Korean people grew from a bullied and despised people . . . into a strong and dignified people whom no one could slight."[73]

On September 10, 1948, less than a month after the formal proclamation of the Republic of Korea in Seoul, the Northerners established the Democratic People's Republic of Korea, with Kim Il-sung as premier. The DPRK's legislative body, the Supreme People's Assembly, included seats filled by "representatives" of South Korea—showing the intent eventually to consolidate the South into the DPRK.

Political means having failed to reunify the country, Kim built his army into "the strongest of the world's revolutionary forces," in the words of Yu Song-chol, who served as commander of the army's operations bureau in the late 1940s and early '50s. Thanks to Soviet help and domestic economic advancement, it was a far more formidably armed force than South Korea's military. Kim developed the Korean People's Army on a base of commanders who were experienced, as he was, in the anti-Japanese struggle. Those leaders envied the Chinese Communists their 1949 victory over Chiang Kai-shek's Nationalists. They lusted to reunify Korea through a similar victory over the South's Rhee.[74]

In Seoul, Rhee was issuing his own threats against the North, despite Washington's determination to restrain him from mounting an invasion. "We shall respond to the cries of our brothers in distress," he proclaimed on March 1, 1950, "even though some of our friends across the sea tell us that we must not cherish thoughts of attacking the foreign puppet who stifles the liberties of our people in the north."[75] Rhee was as eager as Kim to unify the country, by force if necessary. Indeed, it would have been hard to find any Korean who doubted that the divided country would reunite, eventually, under one system or the other. It was natural enough that both Kim and Rhee saw a zero-sum game in which one system and set of leaders would win totally, while the other would lose just as totally.[76]

A big difference, however, was that Kim prepared his invasion with the encouragement and help of Moscow, in whose view extending communist rule to the South came to be seen as a worthwhile policy goal[77]—while Rhee, hobbled and stymied as he was by his Washington protectors, blustered. Rhee's threats amounted to little more than bravado, in view of the South's comparatively poor state of military preparedness. The Americans had denied the South Koreans heavy weaponry, aircraft and even a large supply of ammunition, precisely in order to discourage them from mounting a northward invasion.[78] Nevertheless, armed border clashes broke out sporadically.[79]

Kim Il-sung long since had begun pitching to Stalin his own proposal to invade South Korea. In Moscow in March of 1949, Kim raised the prospect of Korean reunification through a military campaign. Kim told Stalin that North Koreans wanted to "touch the South with the point of a bayonet," Nikita Khrushchev recalled. "After the first impulse from North Korea, there would be an internal explosion and the people's power would be established."[80] Stalin rejected the proposal then, Soviet documents show. Attacking the South was "not necessary," the Soviet leader said. The only circumstances in which the North Korean army should cross the 38th parallel would be to counter a South Korean attack.

In August and September of that year, Kim sent word to Stalin that the South Koreans were about to attack the North. Once more he asked the Soviet leader to approve a southward attack. It would be done only if the South attacked first, as a roughly equivalent counterattack, Kim promised. However, he assured the Soviet leader that the North Koreans could take the whole peninsula "if the international situation permits"—perhaps a reference to the question of whether the United States would intervene or not.

The Soviet leadership on September 24 withheld approval for the time being, saying the North Korean military was not strong enough yet and insufficient groundwork had been done to enlist Southerners in the overthrow of their government. Besides further buildup of the North Korean forces, the Soviet politburo called for maximum effort for "the development of the partisan movement, the creation of liberated regions and the preparation of a general armed uprising in South Korea in order to overthrow the reactionary regime."

Kim tried again on January 19, 1950, arguing that partisan fighting would not suffice. He pleaded to be permitted to emulate the Chinese Communists, who had just won their civil war on the mainland. Rhee was not giving him the excuse he needed for a counterattack, Kim complained. He wanted permission to unleash his own army offensively. Kim asserted that his own nationalist credentials were at stake: "Lately I do not sleep at night, thinking about how to resolve the question of the unification of the whole country. If the matter of the liberation of the people of the southern portion of Korea and the unification of the country is drawn out, then I can lose the trust of the people of Korea." Stalin, noting that such an effort "needs large preparation" and insisting that it "be organized so that there would not be too great a risk," replied on January 30 that he would be willing to receive Kim to discuss the matter.[81]

Kim did go to Moscow in late March, staying into April.[82] Khrushchev recorded in his diary an account of a dinner he attended that Stalin hosted at his dacha for Kim. There, the North Korean leader held forth on the theme that Korean unification was essential because of the natural economic fit of North and South. Despite the North's advantage in mineral resources, four-fifths of its territory consisted of mountains and highlands and its farmland was mainly dry fields. The South possessed most of the wet-paddy rice-growing land and the better climate for farming, not to mention bountiful fisheries. Putting the North and the South together again, Kim asserted, was the recipe for building a strong country.[83]

During that visit, Stalin—taking account of the "changed international situation"—approved the invasion in principle. A message from Stalin to Mao Zedong, confirming this policy, does not mention which changes in the international situation had affected Stalin's thinking.[84] One obvious candidate is a new policy Washington had developed.

Coming out of World War II, the United States downsized its military rapidly—too rapidly, as many would think later. Upwards of twelve million Americans were in uniform in the various armed services on the day of Japan's surrender. Their families quickly demanded that Washington "bring the boys home." Heeding those cries, and seeking budget cuts, Congress pushed for enormous reductions that produced a standing military only a small fraction of the size of the wartime force. As the cuts proceeded, military planners scratched their heads to figure where they most needed to station the few remaining troops. Since their main concern was another global war, this time against the Soviet Union and other communist countries, Europe was high on the list. But the approximately forty thousand American troops in Korea offered more potential for embarrassment than for strategic advantage in a third world war, as they might be easily overrun or be forced to abandon the country in ignominy.

In 1948, the Soviet Union—confident that the North Korean People's Army had been well trained—announced that it would withdraw all its troops that year. Despite warnings that the United States was planning for the wrong war, and must leave some of its troops to deter a North Korean invasion,[85] all U.S. combat troops likewise were out of Korea by the end of June 1949. "We seemed to want no part of the country, and yet we had planted the flag," as David Halberstam has written. "The American century was about to begin, but clearly no one wanted to pay for it."[86]

U.S. officials the following January enunciated a policy of declining (both publicly and privately) to guarantee the American defense of either South Korea or Taiwan. In a news conference on January 5, 1950, Harry S. Truman said there would be, "at this time," no American defense of Taiwan. The remark had considerable impact—and not only on the Chinese nationalists and their communist foes. Russian scholar Sergei N. Goncharov saw in the Russian archives an intelligence report on a secret meeting of the South Korean cabinet the day after the Truman press conference. The report quoted worried South Korean officials expressing the opinion that the United States, as in the case of Taiwan and China, would stay out of the fight if North Korea invaded South Korea. Goncharov believes that this Soviet intelligence report was "the triggering information" that persuaded Stalin to unleash Kim Il-sung.[87]

The question is whether Pyongyang and Moscow failed to read all of Washington's signals. Understanding the professional soldiers' reluctance to get bogged down in Korea, did they miss some other, ultimately stronger currents in Washington thinking—such as the view promoted by the State Department as early as 1947 that Soviet domination of Korea would amount to "an extremely serious political and military threat" to U.S. interests in Japan and elsewhere in the region? Indeed, considerable evidence indicates that Washington really did not intend to let South Korea fall into hostile hands, and was in fact prepared to lead an international coalition to prevent such an outcome in case of an invasion.[88]

The policy of "containment"—blocking the advance of communism beyond existing borders—had been gaining ground. In his ambitious two-volume work on the origins of the Korean War, Bruce Cumings shows that the logic for applying containment to Korea followed from a pair of premises. First, Washington wanted to maintain the prestige of its commitments. The United States had, after all, encouraged the formation of a noncommunist government in South Korea; abandoning that government would signal allies elsewhere not to put their trust in America. Second, Washington in response to the onset of the Cold War had decided to stop punishing Japan's wartime leaders and encourage them to rebuild their country's economy as the engine of growth for noncommunist economies in Asia. Historians now call that the "reverse course." A total revival of the Greater East Asia Co-Prosperity Sphere was, of course, out of the question. But American planners believed that Japan, to take on its assigned role, did need at least an industrial hinterland and military buffer just across the straits in southern Korea.

Containment was the State Department's policy for Korea, and remained the policy even after the removal of U.S. troops.[89] Moreover, in June 1949, as the troops were leaving, the Pentagon in a top-secret study reluctantly agreed that the response to a full-scale North Korean invasion of the South might include returning—with a military task force under the aegis of the United Nations—if "all else fails."[90]

However, in a speech on January 12, 1950, at the Washington National Press Club, Secretary of State Dean Acheson described the American "defense perimeter" in the Asia-Pacific region as running from the Aleutian Islands to Japan, Okinawa and the Philippines. Generations of commentators have wondered since then: Why did he not mention Korea? The best answer now available is that Acheson wanted to keep secret the American commitment to Korea's defense, to avoid revealing Washington's cards not only to Moscow but also to South Korean President Rhee. He feared that Rhee, if he knew, would take advantage of that guarantee of protection to charge off into the very military struggle with the Northern communists that Washington wanted to avoid.

Historians continue to debate whether some on the communist side took the Acheson speech as a signal that the coast was clear for an invasion. Even taking into account Acheson's wish to keep Rhee guessing, if deterrence was his goal it would seem strange for so skilled and experienced a diplomat not to make Moscow understand that the United States would not sit still for an invasion of South Korea. If what happened was indeed such a failure of deterrence, it may have been one of the most expensive cases of crossed signals in the history of warfare.[91]

On the other hand, revisionist historians starting with I. F. Stone suggested that elements in the United States and some of their allies in Asia *wanted* a war, somewhere in the world—as a means of rallying the American people for active opposition to communism—and were happy to maneuver the other side into striking first. That way, Americans would feel they were fighting a just war. Acheson, if in tune with such an effort, would have wanted Moscow to misjudge American intent. That theory came with even less hard evidence to back it than the similar and persistent minority view that the Franklin D. Roosevelt administration intentionally maneuvered Japan into attacking first at Pearl Harbor.[92]

One report does say the Acheson speech persuaded Kim Il-sung that Washington would not be eager to protect the Rhee government. Whether Kim actually believed it or not, he may well have pressed that interpretation upon Stalin while trying to persuade the Soviet leader to come to his aid.[93] Mao Zedong, too, following the Acheson speech, said in a message to Stalin that he doubted the United States would defend South Korea from a North Korean attack.[94]

That brings up another important change in the international situation that may have affected Stalin's thinking. The Soviet leader was in the process of trying to tie newly communist-controlled China firmly to the anti-Western camp—as Goncharov and colleagues John W. Lewis and Xue Litai have shown by marshaling important Russian and Chinese documentary evidence and interviews with key surviving figures. "By 'drawing the line' in Asia, Stalin was carrying out his ideas on how to prepare for a third world war," they argue.[95] It would help that process along to create a situation pushing Mao to take sides with Kim Il-sung militarily against the American-backed Rhee regime.

In fact, as a condition for granting his approval of the invasion, Stalin insisted that Kim get Mao's backing. Kim visited Mao in May of 1950. Mao was inwardly reluctant, since his real priority was an invasion of Taiwan to reunify his own country. It would be impractical to try to invade Taiwan while simultaneously sending troops to help Kim—which Mao would have expected to do should the Korean invasion lead to American intervention.

But with China's Soviet aid at stake, Mao signed on. Only then did Stalin give his final approval.[96]

Stalin showed diplomatic deftness in maneuvering China into taking big risks while the USSR stood in the background, but he was not the only clever one. Kim Il-sung also got what he wanted at the time (not knowing then that the war he wanted would prove to be a disaster far beyond anything he could handle on his own). Kim "was able to use Stalin's trust for his own aims even as Stalin was using him," say Goncharov and his coauthors. The North Korean leader "managed to make Moscow see the situation on the peninsula through his own eyes." He persuaded Stalin that a Southern invasion of the North was imminent and would overthrow the communist regime—but that if Kim invaded first, large numbers of South Korean leftists would greet his troops by rising to overthrow the Southern leaders.[97]

Soon after the 1950 Stalin-Kim meetings, Tom Connally, chairman of the Senate Armed Services Committee, improved Kim's case by saying the United States would "abandon" South Korea. The Soviet Union "can just overrun Korea just like she probably will overrun Formosa," he said. South Koreans, understandably, were in shock. Rhee accused Connally of issuing the communists "an open invitation" to invade.[98]

Although Acheson declined to take issue publicly with Connally's remarks,[99] in the end the secretary of state could assert that his own press club speech had provided a fairly straightforward description of just what American policy makers intended. While not mentioning Korea specifically in the speech, he spoke of areas that he had not enumerated as part of the "perimeter" and said that no one could guarantee those areas against attack. However:

> Should such an attack occur . . . the initial reliance must be on the people attacked to resist it and then upon the commitments of the entire civilized world under the Charter of the United Nations, which so far has not proved a weak reed to lean on by any people who are determined to protect their independence against outside aggression.

As late as June 19, 1950, less than a week before the North Korean invasion, Acheson's representative, John Foster Dulles, reminded the South Korean National Assembly that the United States already had intervened "with armed might" twice in the twentieth century "in defense of freedom when it was hard pressed by unprovoked military aggression. We were not bound by any treaty to do this."[100]

Presumably Stalin and Kim Il-sung were aware of the warnings implicit in such comments. One explanation as to why they would ignore them comes in Yu Song-chol's recollection that Kim, in Moscow in the spring of 1950, convinced Stalin that the North Koreans had the elements of military superiority, surprise and speed on their side—to the extent that Washington would be unable to intervene before the North had occupied the entire peninsula.[101]

Yu was no mind-reader, and we need not accept his conclusion that Kim's argument was what really convinced Stalin. The Soviet leader could very well have been lulled more by the efforts he himself had made to ensure that it would be the Chinese, not the Soviets, who would join the fight if the Americans intervened.[102]

As for Kim Il-sung's thinking, if Kim himself really believed the argument Yu quotes him as having delivered, all the old questions about U.S. *intentions*, tied to the Truman press conference, the Acheson speech, the Connally interview and so on, decline in relative importance as factors in the decision to invade. A roughly equivalent or perhaps even more important factor becomes the matter of *capability*: the North Korean leader's judgment that Washington might wish to respond but would be too late. It is not yet known precisely how Kim Il-sung might have arrived at such a conclusion. After the June 1949 withdrawal of American troops from Korea, did Kim's intelligence apparatus fail him regarding the U.S. capability to return in force—because, perhaps, of lack of access and familiarity, the wages of that isolation from the West that Moscow had engineered and the Cold War perpetuated? Or was this, rather, a simple matter of Kim's ambition and desperation overcoming facts and reason—"adventurism" and "reckless war-making of the worst kind," as Goncharov, Lewis and Xue phrase it?

A secret now, the answer may emerge if and when the doors to the North Korean archives swing open someday.[103]

FIVE

Iron-Willed Brilliant Commander

In May of 1950, while preparing its army for the invasion, Pyongyang publicly called on the South to join in peaceful unification, urging that a unified national assembly be established by the time of the August anniversary of liberation from Japan. It was a totally cynical proposal. Kim Il-sung harbored no expectation that the wary Southerners would accept the North's terms. As planned, the propaganda offensive helped disguise the North's intentions.

That same month the Soviet Union started sending new military advisors to North Korea: "individuals with extensive combat experience," as Yu Song-chol described them. The new Soviet advisors drew up a draft of a "preemptive strike invasion plan." The assignment to translate and refine the plan went to Yu and three other ethnically Korean officers who, like him, had grown up speaking Russian in the Soviet Union. After preparing troop movements disguised as training exercises, the plan called for mounting an invasion all along the 38th parallel. Blocking any Southern advance, the Korean People's Army would move on to take the Southern capital of Seoul in four days.

Moscow also set in motion shipments of the needed military equipment. Once everything had been shipped and the North Korean forces readied to launch their invasion, the North had twice as much manpower and artillery as the South and at least a six-to-one advantage in aircraft and tanks, according to Soviet estimates.

In the plan, the invasion was referred to as a "counteroffensive." Trying to avoid being branded the aggressor, Pyongyang for decades to come would

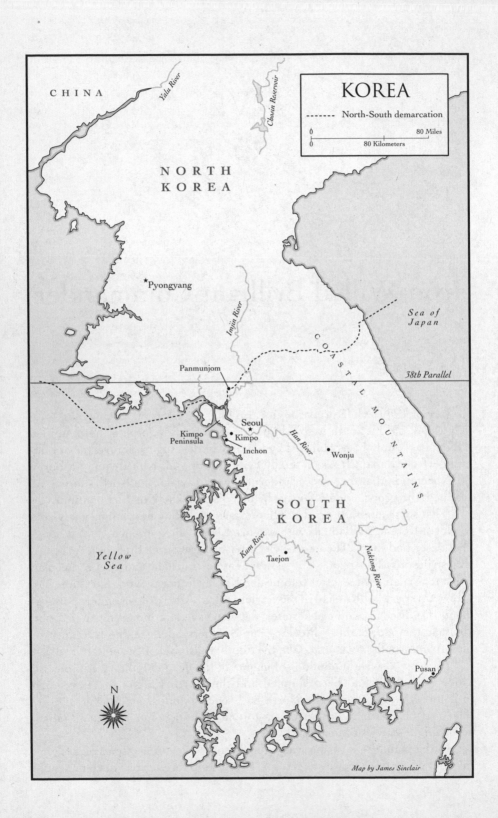

KOREA

----- North-South demarcation

0   80 Miles
0   80 Kilometers

CHINA

Yalu River

Chosin Reservoir

NORTH
KOREA

*Pyongyang

Imjin River

Sea of
Japan

C
O
A
S
T
A
L

M
O
U
N
T
A
I
N
S

38th Parallel

Panmunjom

Seoul
*
Kimpo
Peninsula   •Kimpo
          •Inchon

Han River
•Wonju

SOUTH
KOREA

Yellow
Sea

Kum River
•Taejon

Naktong River

•Pusan

N

Map by James Sinclair

maintain consistently—for both external and internal consumption—that the South had invaded first and the North had merely responded.

Yu Song-chol said he passed the invasion plan up to Kim Il-sung. Kim then signed off on the plan, writing "Concur."[1] On June 25 at 4 A.M., the North Korean forces opened fire. The official propaganda over the years that followed repeated ceaselessly the outright lie that Kim "never for a moment relaxed his struggle to prevent war and achieve national unification peacefully" while South Korea and the United States answered him by launching "a cursed, criminal, aggressive war, for which they had long been preparing."[2]

In Seoul, it was not as if an attack were totally unexpected. "We knew better than almost anywhere in the world that the Communists planned to invade," said Harold Noble, an American diplomat based in Seoul. "But it had been coming since 1946." The passage of time had lulled both Koreans and Americans in the city. Like people living on the edge of a volcano, "we knew it would explode some day, but as day after day, month after month, and year after year passed and it did not blow up, we could hardly believe that tomorrow would be any different."[3] Thus, when the shooting started on that Sunday morning of June 25, the Southern forces had their guard down just as the invasion planners had hoped. Many soldiers were away on weekend passes,[4] and others were sleeping when the all-out Northern artillery and tank attack hit them.

Receiving situation reports in a natural cave near Pyongyang that they had turned into their command post, Maj. Gen. Yu Song-chol and other North Korean military brass were astonished at how easily the Southern forces collapsed. The Korean People's Army's 150 Soviet-made T-34 tanks frightened Southern soldiers, who fell back in helpless confusion as seven Northern divisions surged down to Seoul.

Yu recalled just a couple of lapses at that stage in the otherwise highly successful invasion plan. One tank unit was delayed traversing mountain terrain more rugged than the planners had counted on. (The planners after all were not locals but hailed, one and all, from the Soviet Union.) The KPA First Division's communications system broke down and a weapons storage facility blew up, likewise causing delays. A furious Kim Il-sung ordered the First replaced by the Fourth Division and decreed death by firing squad for the First Division commander, Maj. Gen. Choe Gwang, an old comrade from Manchuria guerrilla days. The army's frontline commander persuaded Kim to rescind the order.[5] (After at least one more run-in with Kim, in 1968,[6] Choe nearly four decades later, in 1988, was named chief of the general staff of the KPA. In 1995, with the death of Marshal O Jin-u, the defense minister, Vice-Marshal Choe became the top-ranking North Korean military man.)

❖   ❖   ❖

When the North Koreans marched into Seoul in triumph just three days after the initial attack, Rhee's Southern forces retreated southward. The Northerners hoped the war was all but won. In Korea, all roads led to Seoul. Pyongyang expected that losing the city that had been the capital for more than five centuries would put pressure on the Rhee regime to throw in the towel.

Based on a rosy prognosis from Pak Hon-yong, the invasion plan had anticipated that Southerners would help the invaders by rising massively against their rulers. Having been the leader of South Korea's communists before fleeing to the North, Pak was eager to restore his power base through an invasion. He had assured Kim—and Stalin—that two hundred thousand hidden communists in the South were "ready to rebel at the first signal from the North."[7]

In Seoul nothing of the sort happened. To be sure, there were happy people among the Seoul populace, wearing red armbands and running about to cheer their liberators. Happiest of all may have been prisoners who shouted, as the North Koreans threw open the prison gates, "Long live the fatherland!" Soon the streets were bedecked with posters depicting Kim Il-sung and Stalin.[8] The invasion went over well with pro-communists such as an ice cream peddler who led some neighbors in chanting against the Rhee "clique" and confiscated for use as his family living quarters a mansion belonging to a former mayor.[9] But after the initially well-behaved occupiers began rounding up and killing Southern "reactionaries," even the shouts of support started to die down.[10] Yu traveled to Seoul and was surprised to see that "the people on the streets were expressionless to us. When we waved our hands to them, there were few who cheered for us."[11]

The operations plan called for North Korean troops to advance nine to twelve miles a day and take over the whole peninsula in twenty-two to twenty-seven days.[12] The Northerners made the huge mistake of halting their advance in Seoul for two days of rest and celebration—giving the South's forces time to regroup. And with further communications breakdowns, the post-Seoul plans proved unworkable in some aspects. Guerrillas did help the Northern troops in some battles. But the massive uprising Kim had counted on did not occur in the hinterland, any more than it had in Seoul and vicinity.[13] Still, the eager Northern forces rolled down the peninsula.

Meanwhile, Kim's propaganda machine swung into action to try to make believers out of the South Koreans. Schoolchildren in North Korean–occupied Seoul learned the catchy "Song of General Kim Il-sung":[14]

Tell, blizzards that rage in the wild Manchurian plains,
Tell, you nights in forests deep where the silence reigns,
Who is the partisan whose deeds are unsurpassed?
Who is the patriot whose fame shall ever last?

So dear to all our hearts is our General's glorious name,
Our own beloved Kim Il-sung of undying fame.[15]

On the home front, morale was high. Only a handful of North Koreans knew that their army had invaded the South. Most believed the North had been the target of a Southern and U.S. invasion, an invasion that the North Korean People's Army had turned back heroically. Pyongyang's phony unification appeal just before the attack had fooled Kim's own people.

In the North, once the "war of national liberation" started, youngsters heeded the volunteer-recruitment slogan: "Let's all go out and give our lives!" Kang Song-ho, an ethnic Korean from the USSR who was living in North Korea when the war broke out, appeared on South Korean television many years later and told how he and his friends had become fired up to fight the Southern forces. "At that time, there was a lot of propaganda made about North Korea appealing to South Korea, always offering peaceful unification," he said. Northern propaganda, as Kang recalled, claimed that "the U.S. had given instructions, and South Korea had already been made into their colony." Rhee was inciting his men "to go and even eat up the people of North Korea."[16]

Far more serious than the misguided assumption of quick victory was the plan's second major flaw: the assumption that the United States would stay out. Perhaps that might have turned out to be the case, if not for the Northern forces' fatal two-day stopover in Seoul. But Kim's assumption that the United States would not intervene to reverse a fait accompli more likely was mistaken — if he really believed that and was not simply handing Stalin a line to win Soviet support. Because of American policy makers' assumptions about the meaning of the invasion, response was close to automatic — and there certainly would have been sentiment in the United States in favor of retaking the South even if the North had overrun all of its territory.

Acheson and other American officials assumed that Stalin had a role in the June 25 invasion — a correct assumption, as has been amply proven with the opening of the archives of the former Soviet Union. But the Americans exaggerated the Soviet role, imagining that the Korean invasion was but the first step in an expansionist Soviet plan. They did not know that it was Kim — not Stalin — who had taken the initiative, and for his own purely Korean purposes. "This act was very obviously inspired by the Soviet Union," President Harry Truman said in a congressional briefing. Assistant Secretary of State Edward W. Barrett compared the Moscow-Pyongyang relationship to "Walt Disney and Donald Duck."[17]

Complicating matters was the universal tendency to "fight the last war," a tendency that was reinforced by the currents of domestic United States politics at the time. Strong memories remained of the negative consequences that had flowed from appeasing the expansionist Nazis at Munich. More immediately, Truman's Democrats and the Department of State had come under fire from Republicans for decisions and actions that allegedly permitted the "loss" of China: Mao Zedong's 1949 victory over Chiang Kai-shek's Nationalists.

By 1950, conspiracy theorists in a kill-the-messenger frenzy were questioning the loyalty of a host of officials who had doubted Chiang's viability. Only four and a half months before the North Korean invasion, on February 9, Senator Joseph McCarthy had begun his Red-baiting campaign by announcing in Wheeling, West Virginia, that he held in his hand a list of 205 Communist Party members working in the State Department. For Truman to let the Korean invasion stand—and thus preside over the "loss" of yet another country—would have made him instant grist for McCarthy's mill.

Although Truman certainly was aware of the compelling domestic political factors as he decided on a response in Korea, publicly he stuck to international, Cold War reasoning when he set out to rally Americans and allies to take a stand. "If we let Korea down," Truman told members of Congress, "the Soviets will keep on going and swallow up one piece of Asia after another." After Asia, they would move on to the Near East and, perhaps, Europe. The United States must draw the line. Here was an early enunciation of what came to be called the Domino Theory.[18]

It was not long before additional evidence began appearing that suggested the Truman-Acheson assumption about Stalin's expansionism was off the mark.[19] Korea bordered the Soviet Union, so Stalin naturally preferred a like-minded state there for security reasons. But Stalin's policy apparently did not call for the unlimited expansion into nonbordering states that many in the West feared—not, at least, for the time being.[20]

On the other hand, there has never been much doubt about the accuracy of another Truman assumption: Without swift American intervention, the invaders would overrun all of South Korea. The president acted quickly and decisively. A United Nations resolution, engineered by Washington just two days after the invasion, demanded that the Northern troops go back behind the 38th parallel. Wrapped in the UN mantle, Truman committed not only air and sea support but ground troops to help the beleaguered South Koreans. Lead units of the U.S. Army Twenty-fourth Division, stationed in Japan, landed on July 1, just six days after the invasion, signaling a full American commitment to the war. A UN command ultimately combined the combatant troops of sixteen nations, with thirty-seven others contributing money, supplies and medical aid.

Acheson's successor as secretary of state, Dulles, later explained the decision this way: "We did not come to fight and die in Korea in order to unite it by force, or to liberate by force the North Koreans. We do not subscribe to the principle that such injustices are to be remedied by recourse to war. If indeed that were sound principle, we should be fighting all over the world and the total of misery and destruction would be incalculable. We came to Korea to demonstrate that there would be unity to throw back armed aggression."[21]

Kim Il-sung could point his finger at underlings for misleading him regarding the Southern response, and for letting the People's Army troops stop to rest after taking Seoul. However, miscalculating American capability and intent was a higher-level responsibility. Yu Song-chol said some ranking North Korean officials had warned that the United States might intervene — but Kim had dismissed their warnings as defeatism.[22]

With the North Korean attack, and Truman's decision to defend South Korea, Americans who never had thought much about far-off Korea and were not even quite sure how to pronounce it were suddenly hearing a great deal about it. I was among them, a third-grade elementary school pupil at the time the war broke out. Comic books quickly began featuring GIs in the John Wayne mold fighting ferocious communist "gooks."[23] By the third year of the fighting Ken Pitts, a fellow pupil in my Georgia Sunday school class, had made a weekly ritual of praying: "Lord, be with our boys in Ko-rea," drawling out the first syllable for an extra beat or two.

One of "our boys," the chief supplier of war stories to the Martin family, was a brother of my mother. Edward O'Neal Logan had enlisted in the Alabama National Guard at sixteen, lying about his age, and had fought across a wide swath of the Southwest Pacific during World War II with an infantry regiment and Sixth Army staff, as a guerrilla warfare and behind-the-lines intelligence officer. Slightly Oriental in appearance himself, he looked a little like Mao Zedong; he had inherited his distinctive looks from my grandfather, who occasionally cited a family legend that one of our ancestors was a Cherokee.

Logan was all fighting man, focused on his job of killing the enemy; cultural sensitivity was not, at the time, his strong suit. In one 1944 note home, accompanied by a photo showing him as a tanned and confident young island warrior, he had passed along a survival tip he evidently was obeying: "The only good Jap is a dead Jap." Promoted to major at age twenty-two, he had signed up after the war to stay in the (much-reduced) regular army. From the Twenty-fourth Division's base in Japan, Ed Logan got to Korea a few days ahead of his unit and headed for Taejon. The bulk of the undermanned, under-equipped Nineteenth Infantry Regiment, whose commander he served as operations and training officer (S-3), disembarked at the Pusan docks July 10 and headed northwest. Its assignment: try to hold the enemy at the Kum River north of Taejon.

Kim Il-sung wanted to "put the U.S. imperialists' nose out of joint" by taking the city, according to an official biography. So Kim "mapped out a careful and meticulous operation to free Taejon, and led it in person."[24] That biography lies shamelessly about some verifiable aspects of the war, and other sources do not mention Kim's alleged role in leading the Taejon battle, which suggests it is just one more prevarication. Indeed, Yu Song-chol said Kim kept his headquarters in an underground bunker near Pyongyang—and during the entire war, as far as Yu knew, the premier visited the frontline command only once, when it was headquartered in the capitol building in Seoul.[25]

Nevertheless, if there was a time for homegrown tactics, such as those the anti-Japanese fighters, including Kim, had learned in Manchuria and elsewhere in China, one such time was mid-July of 1950. Yu said the Russian invasion planners were sent back home after their failure to match eastern front tank movements to the actual terrain.[26] And the Chinese "volunteers" had not yet entered the war, with their own ideas of strategy and tactics. Recall further that, according to Kim's memoirs, attacking the enemy's rear while keeping the pressure on at the front had been a favorite tactic of his as early as the defense of Xiaowangqing in Manchuria, back in 1933. That tactic played an important role in the Korean People's Army's assault on Taejon—regardless of whether it was Kim himself or one of his old partisan colleagues who personally came up with the battle plan.[27]

The Nineteenth Infantry Regiment had to defend forty-two miles of riverfront, a sector so large it normally would be assigned to the three regiments that comprise a full infantry division. Like the South Koreans, the Americans at first were literally and figuratively blown away by the North Koreans' Soviet T-34 tanks. The behemoths destroyed all before them, were impregnable to most weapons the Americans had on hand and created "fear and frustration that is difficult to describe," Logan would recall. "I used a 2.75-inch rocket launcher fired at less than fifty feet. Five rounds. They bounced off the wheels and the tank kept moving."[28]

Air power helped, for a time, to bolster the thin line of Americans, in which there were wide gaps. On July 15, in an attempt to ward off an enemy night crossing of the river, American mortar and artillery fire and air strikes set ablaze a North Korean–held village on the other side, illuminating the riverfront. After the loss of a three-man U.S. Air Force radio team handling ground control of the pilots, however, there was no more close air support.

On July 16 and 17, the Americans got a sample of what many of them came to describe as the North Korean forces' "disregard for human life"—or, as the Northerners themselves would have put it, their fighting spirit. "We blew the bridge but they kept coming, over dead bodies," an incredulous American machine gunner told Logan. "There must be three to four hundred bodies in the river at the major crossing and we are out of ammo."

North Korean soldiers waded across the river and passed through gaps between positions held by the overextended Americans. Then the Northerners circled around behind the Nineteenth and blocked the main highway—the Americans' supply and exit route—three miles to the rear, where the road hugged a steep mountainside on one side, a precipice on the other. His superiors wounded, Logan took command of an operation to try to break through or bypass what proved to be a mile-and-a-half-long roadblock enforced by North Korean soldiers firing down from the highlands above. A squad of North Koreans jumped the major, and four men with him were killed. He fell into the guts of one of his dead soldiers, head in the man's bloody belly, and played dead as enemy soldiers stuck bayonets in his rear to check his condition.

Rescued by some of his men, Logan got past the roadblock and found the division commander, Maj. Gen. William F. Dean. Dean sent Logan farther to the rear to establish a new position closer to Taejon, then organized an attempt to break through the blockage with two light tanks and four anti-aircraft vehicles. The attempt failed. Some five hundred American infantrymen trapped between the roadblock and the river could escape only by climbing the mountains above the road. Some able-bodied men, detailed to carry the seriously wounded in litters, could not get far with them in the punishing terrain and had to abandon them on a mountaintop. North Korean troops soon came along and killed the wounded men.

The North Koreans who had jumped Logan made off with his wallet, with pictures of my aunt Glennis and cousins Eddie and Dennis. A couple of days later, when the regiment was withdrawing south of Taejon for regrouping, war correspondent Marguerite Higgins of the New York *Herald Tribune* saw the major. "Thought you were dead," she said. Higgins told him that "Seoul City Sue," a former missionary who was broadcasting North Korean propaganda to the American troops, had announced the previous day that Glennis, Eddie and Dennis Logan would never see their husband and father again.

In late July and early August additional American ground divisions as well as air force units arrived to reinforce the beaten-up Twenty-fourth Division. The North Korean troops, having occupied most of the South, finally were halted at the Nakdong River in the southeast, paralyzed by U.S. air power. "Indiscriminate bombing created a situation in which the KPA could neither fight nor move during daylight," recalled Yu Song-chol. Support from the rear became almost impossible. "As soon as the aircraft sound was heard, one could see the serious neurotic state in which the soldiers were terrified out of their wits. This carpet-bombing strategy struck a fatal blow to the KPA. However, it also inflicted tremendous damage on innocent civilians as well."[29] Despite the turn the war was taking because of air power, Kim Il-sung pressed his troops to capture Pusan, the southeastern port and South Korea's second city. In an August 15 radio broadcast, he gave them a deadline, the end of August, explaining that "the longer this is delayed, the stronger UN defenses will become." The ensuing ferocious attacks resulted in horrendous casualties on both sides before the North Koreans' supplies ran short and they had to pull back.[30]

The Nineteenth Infantry Regiment was assigned to defend a western area of the Pusan perimeter. Casualties had reduced manpower of the regiment to only thirty or forty percent of what it should have been, as Logan recalled. Around the time Kim was goading his troops into renewed assaults, the Nineteenth got some four hundred replacement troops. American military personnel lists in Japan had been combed for anyone with any background in infantry, armored or artillery units. So urgently were replacements needed, the army had not been able to divide those soldiers into the usual racially segregated units. Receiving them in a village schoolyard that was coming under sporadic artillery and mortar attacks, "we lined them up with the words, 'This group to Company so-and-so,'" Logan told me. Guides took them to their companies, and thus occurred one of the earliest recorded cases of genuine black-white racial integration in an American combat unit.[31] Within days, many of the replacements were dead. As in World War II's Battle of the Bulge, "we had no records, just a name in the notebook."

If the Lord was answering the prayers of Ken Pitts and others by watching over the Americans, the North Koreans were still "fighting for the leader,"[32] Kim Il-sung, who by then had begun assuming deity status himself.

Mao Zedong and his Central Committee, nervously following the war from Beijing, began to fear in early August that the North Korean troops had "advanced too far in isolation, leaving their rear area vulnerable." The United States "might launch a counteroffensive." Later in August, Mao sent word to Kim through the North Korean representative in Beijing that Inchon was a likely spot for a UN amphibious landing. Kim reportedly was unimpressed.[33] Sure enough, however, with much of the North's manpower concentrated on the Pusan perimeter, U.S. forces on September 15 carried out their momentous landing at Inchon, far behind the KPA lines. They encountered little resistance. Caught between two American forces, the North Koreans retreated, the Americans chasing them.

While acknowledging that the retreat was "a sore trial," North Korean official accounts describe it as a "temporary strategic retreat." The "iron-willed, brilliant commander" Kim Il-sung, they explain, "made up his mind to lure and scatter the enemy, throwing them into the confusion of a labyrinth, not hitting them in front as before." To ensure that the trap would succeed, the KPA's main units "retreated at exhilarating speed."[34]

That is not the way Kim's operations bureau commander, Yu Song-chol, would tell it. After Inchon, the North Korean high command ordered *not* that its forces around the Pusan perimeter hightail it all the way back to the 38th parallel and beyond; rather, Kim's generals ordered a retreat only far enough to set up a new line of defense at South Korea's Kum River Basin and the Sobaek Mountain range. However, according to Yu, "the entire KPA communications network was in ruins, and we could not pass the retreat orders past the division level."[35]

Breaking out of the Pusan perimeter, the Nineteenth Infantry got the assignment as the lead unit to retake Taejon—this time supported by American tanks and air cover. As the Nineteenth's lead tanks passed them, the North Korean soldiers—far from establishing a new defense line at the Kum, scene of their earlier triumph—rapidly changed into white civilian garb and discarded their weapons. Faced with this tactic as they chased the KPA forces day and night, the Americans shot "anything that moved," according to Logan, who by then was the regimental executive officer.[36]

When the Nineteenth reached the outskirts of Taejon, a South Korean policeman flagged down Logan's jeep and said, "Hurry! Hurry! Americans being killed—buried alive at police station." Lead elements of the column, including a couple of tanks, rushed to the police station and found a ditch there with arms and legs of American prisoners of war sticking out, some moving. "We got some out alive," said Logan.

The previous day, while flying over the city in a light aircraft to reconnoiter, Logan had seen on hills north and northwest of Taejon the bodies of many other people, in multicolored clothing. He assumed that those were people the Northerners had killed as they retreated. It was impossible to get an accurate count from the air, but Logan estimated that the number of bodies exceeded two thousand. Later he heard a count of some five thousand victims of this massacre, mostly South Korean civilians.[37]

The UN forces retook Seoul on September 28. With little debate, Washington agreed to the proposal of the UN commander, Gen. Douglas MacArthur, not to stop there but to press on and take Pyongyang—a goal far beyond the original one of thwarting armed aggression. Reasons to keep going included the fear that Kim, if left to rule above the 38th parallel, would simply rebuild his army and strike again. Fatefully, the line that Beijing had decided to draw in the sand was the 38th parallel—not the Yalu River as was thought until Chinese documentary evidence clarified the matter in the 1990s. China tried to signal that it would fight if UN troops crossed the 38th. But the push north had gathered momentum and would not be stopped. MacArthur was golden after his brilliant coup at Inchon; hardly anyone was prepared to stand in his way now. Washington, in any event, would have been hard-pressed to stop Rhee from sending his South Korean troops north. Out to avenge their humiliation at the beginning of the war, the Southerners traveled night and day up the east coast in pursuit of the fleeing North Koreans. Two of their divisions took the port of Wonsan on October 10, way ahead of an invasion force that MacArthur was sending by sea.[38]

The UN forces pushed the North Koreans back above the former border on October 1. MacArthur called on the North to surrender, and Kim Il-sung answered by ordering his troops to "fight to the end."[39] The Americans crossed the parallel in full force from October 9. Logan joined the pursuit, taking command of the Nineteenth Regiment's Third Battalion a few days after his twenty-ninth birthday. With his battalion in the lead, the Twenty-fourth Division raced the First Cavalry Division northward. The first to reach a major road junction on the way to the North Korean capital, Pyongyang, would become the lead division for the push north from there. Logan "missed it by about two hours."

Kim Il-sung ordered soldiers defending Pyongyang not to retreat even "one step farther," and assigned a squad to shoot deserters. This time his effort to whip up martial spirit was insufficient. Five days later, on October 19, American and South Korean troops were in Pyongyang, where they could check out Kim's office and command bunker. Entered via four anterooms, a portrait of Stalin in each, the office contained plaster busts of Stalin and Kim. In the bunker, the former church organist had an organ.[40]

Losing their capital, the North Koreans continued retreating north. Logan's unit proceeded north on a "mopping up" mission, cleaning out pockets of resistance and sending many POWs to the rear for other units to care for. It was a messy job, and many civilians were victims. One news correspondent, appalled when Logan's battalion shelled villages and burned people's homes, said it reminded him of Sherman's march to the sea. Logan defended his actions, saying it was in those villages, in those houses, that North Korean soldiers changed from their uniforms into civilian clothes and fired on his men. If he should bypass the villages, they would then attack from the rear. There was that much truth, at least, to Kim's later talk of a "labyrinth," a "trap." (Whether or not the thought had occurred to Kim, Mao as early as October 9 cabled the North Korean leader to propose trapping the advancing UN and South Korean troops by opening another front to their rear. "It will be very helpful to the operations in the north if 40,000 to 50,000 troops of the [Korean] People's Army could remain in South Korea to undertake this assignment," Mao said.)[41]

Logan gave the critical newsman a copy of his mission statement: Attack north to rescue a surrounded unit—utmost speed—destroy anything that would jeopardize your mission. Then he asked the correspondent what he would do if he were commanding the battalion. "Before he had a chance to answer, a round landed about twenty feet from us and he bolted. The round was from a shack we had not destroyed. I didn't get an answer." Logan mused that "our wars kill more civilians, innocent or not, than battle casualties." War "is not a gentleman's game. Codes of honor and conduct are difficult to separate from the various battle situations at hand. What one would call a necessity, another, not present, would call wrong."

❊   ❊   ❊

As the counterinvasion of North Korea proceeded, it became clear that even if Kim enjoyed substantial support from his subjects, allegiance to his regime was by no means unanimous. Residents in many areas of the North— "unsound people of some social standing," as Pyongyang described them[42]— cooperated with the occupying forces. Banding together in "peace preservation corps," they helped depose local communist rulers.

In Songhwa County of South Hwanghae Province, former landowners still bore a grudge against the deputy chief of the county People's Committee for his leading role in the land reform of four years before. The man previously had been a substantial landowner himself, in local terms, farming his approximately five acres with the help of relatives. Placed in charge of redistributing the county's land, he had parceled out to those previously landless relatives more than enough to make up for the acreage he had been required to give up personally. Now his aggrieved neighbors saw their chance for revenge. Cooperating with South Korean troops who occupied the county, they threw the official's wife and six children down a 100-meter vertical mine shaft, killing them all.[43]

Kim Il-sung had already called for reinforcements, documents in the former Soviet archives show. On September 29, three months after the invasion, Kim wrote to ask Stalin to commit the Soviet Union to the war and request China to join the fighting as well. On October 1, Kim wrote directly to Mao to plead for a rescue mission.

The Chinese had anticipated being called upon. When the Americans intervened, Mao "quickly concluded that the real U.S. aim was to threaten China itself, and he began to act accordingly," say scholars Sergei Goncharov, John W. Lewis and Xue Litai. Within a week after the American intervention, the Chinese leader had begun to worry that the North Koreans could not achieve the quick victory Kim had promised. As early as July 7, when the KPA was still pressing south and demolishing all resistance, senior Chinese military officials shifted elite army units close to the Korean border in preparation for possible entry into the war. In quick succession they deployed added reserve units and put the troops through training exercises, with the Americans as their hypothetical enemy.[44]

Mao and some colleagues calculated, after a review, that they need not fear escalation beyond a conventional war because the Americans would not use nuclear weapons in either China or Korea.[45] Their troops battle-ready and in position, the Chinese leaders watched the war. Once the UN troops had landed at Inchon, Mao wrote to his top general in the Northeast: "Apparently it will not do for us not to intervene in the war." After Kim Il-sung requested help, saying North Korea could not put up sufficient resistance on its own, the Chinese Politburo met on October 2. Skeptics including

Premier Zhou Enlai continued to argue that the new communist government should concentrate on pressing domestic matters instead of sending its poorly equipped soldiers for a showdown with the U.S. Army.[46]

On top of the alarming prospect that a U.S.-backed regime soon would govern the entire Korean peninsula and knock on China's door, pressure from Stalin helped to stiffen backs. "If we do not send troops," Mao said, "the reactionaries at home and abroad would be swollen with arrogance when the enemy troops press to the Yalu River border." Secretary of State Acheson's assurances that the United States had no designs on Chinese territory inspired little trust. If a showdown with the Americans was inevitable, as Mao believed, Korea was a more advantageous place to have it out than Taiwan or Vietnam, two other possibilities. On October 8, the day after units of the U.S. First Cavalry Division crossed the 38th parallel heading north, Mao issued an official order for China's Northeast Frontier Force, under the new name of Chinese People's Volunteers, to "march speedily to Korea and join the Korean comrades in fighting the aggressors and winning a glorious victory."[47]

That still was not the last word, however. Second thoughts ensued when there was a snag over Soviet assistance.[48] Another politburo meeting was called for the evening of October 18. Yu Song-chol had gone with Pak Hon-yong to Beijing on Kim's orders. Around midnight on October 18, the two met with the Chinese Politburo to brief them on the war and repeat the request for aid. When they had finished, "Mao Zedong began by informing us that the Politburo had already decided to send volunteer forces to Korea." Mao used body language to advise on military strategy, asking his listeners to imagine that one of his legs was the U.S. forces; the other, South Korean forces. First surround and annihilate the South Koreans, and then the Americans will be helpless, he said—and he "raised one leg of his bulky body and hopped around on one foot."[49]

MacArthur countermanded a Pentagon order to use only South Korean forces near the Chinese border.[50] On October 20, he ordered maximum effort to secure all of Korea. On October 24, Mao declared that U.S. occupation of Korea would be a serious threat to Chinese security and could not be tolerated. The first Chinese participation in battle came October 25.[51] In October and November, hundreds of thousands of Chinese troops entered the fray.

According to Yu Song-chol, Kim Il-sung at that point lost overall command of the war: The Korean People's Army was reduced to a support role, in charge of the eastern front, while the Chinese ran operations independently on the central front.[52] At whatever temporary cost to his self-esteem, though, China had saved Kim's bacon. The most important military result of his "strategic retreat" up to that point had been to show so much North Korean weakness the Chinese felt compelled to help.

Khrushchev recalled in his memoir of the Korean War that the Soviet ambassador in North Korea had been writing "very tragic reports concerning

Kim Il-sung's state of mind. Kim Il-sung was already preparing to go into the mountains to pursue guerrilla struggle again"—in other words, to leave the enemy in control of most of North Korea for the time being. He would have had little choice without Mao's intervention. Stalin was adamant in his refusal to play the rescuer's role—having become resigned, as Khrushchev wrote, "to the idea that North Korea would be annihilated, and that the Americans would reach our border."[53]

United Nations forces were slow to recognize that they faced a new opponent. Early in December, while freshly promoted Lt. Col. Ed Logan's unit was halted just short of the Yalu, another regiment of the Twenty-fourth Division reported having captured Chinese soldiers. "No one believed it at higher headquarters," Logan would recall. Soon enough they had to believe, though. Logan's Third Battalion got orders to head back to the Anju-Sinanju area and hold a crossroads until the retreating First Cavalry Division could pass through to the South. "The First Cav got chopped up something awful." Logan's battalion held the crossroads for two days, helping to evacuate First Cavalry Division casualties—"a bloody job." The UN retreat continued. By December 6, Pyongyang was back in the hands of the North.

The Chinese were not using tanks as the North Koreans had in June and July. Instead, "hordes" of soldiers, hardy veterans of years of battles in the Chinese civil war, attacked at night, on foot, bypassing heavy weapons. "They could go for days with a bag of rice, an army coat, ammo and rifle," Logan marveled. Americans weren't accustomed to that sort of combat. "We are road-bound. We try to live in the field as we do at home."[54] South Korean divisions, made up of conscripts shipped to the front lines after only a few days of training, were even less prepared. They bore the brunt of the attacks and, like many of the U.S. units, completely disintegrated.

MacArthur had said it would be over by Christmas. As it happened, it was on Christmas Day that a Chinese concussion grenade blew Logan off a hilltop in the vicinity of the Imjin River, north of Seoul, where UN forces were making a stand. Both eardrums burst and his back injured, he was flown to a hospital ship for repairs. Told he would be evacuated to Japan, he refused and returned to his command, believing the Chinese would attack on New Year's Eve. Indeed, the Chinese did attack that day, sending masses of troops to attempt to cross the river. Logan's unit held until January 2, 1951. The Chinese infiltrated through the Nineteenth Regiment's flanks, which were exposed by the evacuation of units on its right. Three Chinese soldiers got to the headquarters tent area, where Logan's men fought them hand to hand. At that point he decided it was time to evacuate his unit southward, joining the general retreat.

On January 4, 1951, the Chinese and North Korean troops recaptured Seoul. The UN forces retreated to a line farther south. Logan traversed roads packed as far as he could see with South Korean civilians and dejected soldiers, once again trying to flee the communist forces, old and young carrying bundles on their heads, on their backs, on handcarts. North Korean soldiers were disguising themselves as refugees and joining the crowds to infiltrate behind the UN lines—"but how could you stop them?"

The Eighth Army commander, Gen. Matthew Ridgway, ordered the units defending the new line not to take a fight-to-the-death approach but to save their resources for another day. However, they had nearly lost contact with the enemy. "We did not know exactly where he was or in what strength—a real violation of the principles of warfare," Logan said. Against orders, the battalion commanders sent patrols northward each day—two miles, then three, then four. Not sighting the enemy, they finally reported this to the division commander "and got chewed out a little." In a couple of days, Ridgway ordered a task force of tanks, artillery and infantry to reconnoiter north toward Suwon and beyond. They succeeded, which was a great morale booster.

Logan's role in the combat was over, however. In February of 1951, Ridgway, bringing in new blood for the next phase of the war, evacuated war-weary, banged-up and sick regimental and battalion commanders who had been in Korea for the duration. Taking along two Silver Stars pinned on him for valor, Logan went to a hospital in Japan for surgery on his frostbitten toes and recuperation from a variety of other ailments.

Proclaiming a state of emergency in December of 1950, Truman had called upon "our farmers, our workers in industry and our businessmen to make a mighty production effort to meet the defense requirements of the nation." His proclamation and a drastically increased defense budget signaled that the military-industrial complex was back in business, for the duration of the Cold War and beyond.

Typical of the fruits of the Truman proclamation was the reinvigoration of my hometown, whose post–Civil War slumber had been broken early in World War II with the decision to build and operate there the world's largest aircraft plant under one roof. Government Aircraft Plant No. 6 closed after VJ Day, and by 1950 kudzu vines threatened to engulf its echoing premises. But now the plant's new contractor, Lockheed Aircraft Corporation, recalled managers, engineers and skilled machinists who had dispersed into the civilian economy.[55] True to Truman's summons, Lockheed put out the word to the chicken farmers and shade-tree mechanics of North Georgia that a huge and well-paid production workforce was needed to dust off the Marietta facility and resume sending bombers to the Air Force.

❖   ❖   ❖

Air power was the key to the evolving strategy in Korea. Two months after losing Seoul for the second time, the UN forces regained the capital. But the seesawing battles continued, with the two sides arrayed against each other in the vicinity of the former border. Carrying out a scorched-earth policy of aerial and naval bombardment in North Korea, the UN forces sought to deprive the Chinese and North Korean troops of logistical support from the rear and, ultimately, of the will to fight. Killing millions of people, in what Bruce Cumings once predicted would be recognized eventually as an "American holocaust,"[56] the bombings helped prevent reconquest of the South but fell short of defeating the communists.

As Chinese and North Korean soldiers stubbornly defended their positions, building a network of military tunnels along the front, North Korean civilians likewise dug into mountainsides to construct underground factories that could withstand bombing raids. Children, according to official accounts, kept going to school during the war "while their pencil cases rattled" from the bombing. If those official sources can be credited, the Northerners simply became more determined—and, alas, more verbose: "Hero Kang Ho-yung was seriously wounded in both arms and both legs in the Kamak Hill Battle, so he rolled into the midst of the enemy with a hand grenade in his mouth and wiped them out, shouting: 'My arms and legs were broken. But on the contrary my retaliatory spirit against you scoundrels became a thousand times stronger. I will show the unbending fighting will of a member of the Workers' Party of Korea and unflinching will firmly pledged to the Party and the Leader!' "[57]

The truth, of course, is that war takes its toll on the morale of even the most motivated people. According to defector testimony, North Koreans had become so war-weary that many had come to hope simply for an end to the fighting, regardless of which side might win.[58]

As the fighting and killing continued, MacArthur sought to resolve the bloody impasse by carrying the war to China. He wanted to unleash Chiang Kai-shek's Taiwan-based Nationalist troops for a rematch with the Chinese communists, supporting them this time with American bombing—including the atomic bomb. American generals had been considering and making preparations for the possible use of nuclear weapons since the early weeks of the war, and Truman had publicly discussed the possibility in a press conference on November 30, 1950.[59]

Truman, however, favored an essentially defensive posture, fearing that MacArthur's aggressive scheme would attract Soviet intervention (just as the Chinese, unbeknownst to him, had calculated). In the ensuing third world war, with American forces stretched too thin, Europe or Japan or both might fall to the communist forces. When MacArthur, against orders, persisted in maneuvering publicly and privately to get his way, Truman fired him for insubordination. The war would be limited to a conventional "police action."

Limited war was an unpopular concept among Americans. Right-wing forces opposed it because they wanted not mere "containment" of communist regimes at their current borders—the usual policy of Cold War–era governments in Washington—but an active "rollback" that would take on such regimes and remove them. Regime change was a minority position, however.

More important in shifting American opinion was the bloodshed that continued in Korea following MacArthur's march to the Yalu. The violence came to seem gratuitous, giving rise to cynicism in the field that later would be portrayed graphically in the movie and long-running television series *M*A*S*H*. At home, as well, more and more Americans asked a simple but compelling question: Why get our men killed capturing and relinquishing real estate by the square inch in that far-off land—especially if the United States could wipe out the enemy with a few well-placed nuclear weapons?

Ceasefire talks began in mid-1951, with American officers and one South Korean representing the UN side while the North Koreans and Chinese fielded a joint delegation. Growing American sentiment in favor of using stronger measures to halt the fighting may have been one factor influencing the other side to agree to negotiate.[60] Nevertheless, the North Koreans were ready to try to portray Washington's eagerness to talk as evidence that Pyongyang had triumphed: The United States was "frantic," "completely bewildered."[61]

The talks snagged on the treatment of prisoners of war. UN negotiators insisted that each POW be permitted to decide whether to return to his country or not. Humanitarian considerations aside, Washington's propaganda goal was to show up communism by encouraging many of the North Koreans and Chinese to reject a return to communist rule. The communist side would have none of that, and insisted on the return of all prisoners according to the terms of the Geneva Convention.

American public support for Truman waned as the talks and the fighting dragged on, and he decided not to seek reelection. Dwight Eisenhower campaigned on a promise to "go to Korea"—which voters took as a pledge to try to halt the war, even if that required more serious measures. After taking office as president in January 1953, the former general let North Korea's allies in Beijing and Moscow know he was prepared to end the stalemate by expanding the war. He withdrew orders with which Truman had neutralized Taiwan; Chiang Kai-shek was now "unleashed," and conceivably might decide to invade the Chinese mainland, opening a second front. Stalin's death in March of 1953 further complicated matters for North Korea's backers. In May, Secretary of State John Foster Dulles told Indian Prime Minister Jawaharlal Nehru that the United States was prepared to exercise the nuclear option. Nehru duly passed along the threat.

Finally, on July 27, 1953, representatives of the United Nations, China and North Korea, meeting at the neutral village of Panmunjom ("Plank-Gate Tavern"), signed a ceasefire agreement. South Korea did not sign, since Rhee wanted to keep the war going and unify the peninsula. Many military commanders on the UN side privately agreed with him. The generals feared that the ceasefire, while averting further bloodshed in the immediate conflict, postponed an inevitable final reckoning with what they still viewed as the expansionist forces of worldwide communism—a reckoning that would prove even bloodier on account of the delay.[62]

The armistice signatories fixed a border along a 155-mile-long, two-and-a-half-mile-wide "demilitarized zone." That left North and South roughly where they had been at the time of the 1950 invasion. (The North did gain the major city of Kaesong. Also the new border was even closer to Seoul than before, an advantage to the North in case hostilities should revive—and thus the cause of decades of anxiety in the South Korean capital.) In this war approximately 3.5 million Koreans had died—2.5 million of them Northerners, representing a quarter of the DPRK's prewar population. Perhaps a million Chinese had died.[63] The UN death toll including battle-related deaths of 33,629 Americans plus 3,194 others—Turks, Greeks, French, British, Canadians, Thais, Colombians and so on—pales beside the Korean and Chinese numbers. But from the point of view of the dead foreign soldiers' comrades, families and friends, there were far too many losses.

When I asked retired colonel Ed Logan what he thought the war had accomplished, his reply was positive if laconic: "Saved South Korea."[64] But as for his view of the 1950–1953 policy of "limited war" against the Chinese and North Koreans, he said bluntly: "We should've nuked 'em."

Kim Il-sung had won the respect of his foes for the military leadership he displayed in the early days of the war.[65] As Joseph C. Goulden revealed in his excellent book on the war, someone in the CIA in Washington had thought enough of Kim's importance to his country's war effort to offer a hit man a "grand prize of a considerable amount of money" to try to assassinate the North Korean premier.[66] At home, on the other hand, Kim faced a potential political problem that Truman himself could have recognized: blame for an initially successful war gone sour. North Korea lay in ruins, devastated more thoroughly than Japan had been by the time of its 1945 surrender.[67]

Kim in his Manchurian guerrilla days never had commanded more than a few hundred men in combat—and those were harassing operations, by no means comparable to the full-scale war of conquest he waged against the South. If, in the anti-Japanese struggle, he had come to be viewed as a legendary hero, now he was stuck with a bloody disaster of a war. Earlier major decisions after 1945, such as land reform, had been dictated by the Russians and had succeeded, but the invasion scheme was Kim's call—a fact that some of the other top leaders knew, even though the masses did not—and it was a failure. As Stalin told Zhou Enlai at a Black Sea meeting in October 1950, Kim had underestimated the "enemy's might."[68]

Unlike Truman, Kim was not about to step down voluntarily. If he did not act shrewdly, though, it was conceivable that he could lose the leadership, and its perquisites. Regarding those perquisites, he seems not to have denied himself. Despite his inspirational pronouncement that "when the people eat boiled foxtail millet, we must have it, too," photos from the wartime period show Kim looking very well fed indeed—a striking contrast to his rail-thin subjects.[69]

Not the least of Kim's perks was the adoring gaze of that vast majority of his people who, believing the official version of events, were totally unaware it was Kim who had planned and started the full-scale war that killed and maimed so many of them. Kim evidently could not get enough adoration. An official biography relates a telling incident: Entertaining a group of military heroes during the war, Kim asked them coyly, "There is a song you sing at the front. Please sing that song." The men obligingly sang the song—which, as Kim well knew, was "The Song of General Kim Il-sung."[70]

Part of Kim's approach to dealing with the failures of the war was to pass the buck, while harking back to the supposed golden age of his guerrilla activities. North Korean casualties in the war, he wrote, could have been cut drastically if only "flunkeyist" subordinates had taught the people the lessons of his anti-Japanese struggle, instead of directing their eyes abroad to the achievements of the socialist mother country, the Soviet Union.

"If we had educated people in our revolutionary traditions," Kim wrote in his memoirs, "they could have formed small units of five to six people or fifteen to twenty people, each carrying an axe and one or two *mal* [about half a bushel to a bushel] of rice, and moving from mountain to mountain, firing several shots now and then and posting up leaflets; in this way they could have endured one month or two in mountains."[71] There are some similarities here with the way Korean communist guerrillas in the South, as well as the Chinese "volunteers," actually did operate during the Korean War. And perhaps his remark is a regretful reference to Mao's proposal for establishing a second front in the South in October 1950.[72] However, Kim's hindsight analysis seems a bit quaint when held up against the overall military reality of that conflict—a struggle so ferociously close to total war that it can be called "limited" only thanks to its nonuse of nuclear weapons and the fact that ground fighting did not spill over into other countries.

Mainly, however, Kim dealt with the war's failure by proclaiming over and over again that North Korea had won a great victory, repelling an invasion by the South and the UN forces. "At the time when we had been able to live a worthy life, built up on our own after the liberation, the U.S. imperialists ignited the war," he told the people.[73]

As an official biographer puts it, "all the attacks of the enemy were turned, as though they dashed their heads against the cliffs. The People's Army mercilessly hit the oncoming enemy, met them and crushed their positions. The People's Army and the whole Korean people stood like a mountain towering in the sky, brandishing their sharpened arms. On top of the mountain stood Comrade Kim Il-sung, the iron-willed brilliant commander who held in his hands the general outcome of the war, looking down upon the panic-stricken U.S. imperialist aggressors with calm and shining eyes."[74]

The North's propaganda references to "the whole Korean people"—as if the people of North and South under Kim's leadership had been struggling in partnership against the South Korean rulers—would have rung hollow to many Southerners. Their own military men were bad enough, overbearing and arrogant toward civilians. But the experience with the Northern occupiers seems to have been even worse. Northern troops in the South indulged themselves in drunkenness and looting. Many Southerners saw their young relatives forbibly conscripted into the North Korean People's Army and their older relatives—civilians with backgrounds in politics or scholarship—spirited off to the North, never to return.[75] Others lost friends or relatives in mass executions of people denounced as anti-communist. Some of the executions were particularly grisly beheadings by swordsmen.[76] Christians were a key target for arrest and maltreatment. Thousands of people deemed "pro-American" were jailed and deprived of their property, as the North applied what correspondent Marguerite Higgins described as police-state techniques "far more ruthless than those I had seen in Poland."[77]

While they occupied parts of the South the Northerners tried to portray themselves positively as liberators, but with only mixed results. Communist propagandists sought to make the best of the American intervention by attacking the Rhee regime for flunkeyism, in an appeal to South Koreans' nationalist feelings. Although Moscow used its leverage as supplier of aid and skills to maintain control over much of the Pyongyang regime's basic decision making, via the Soviet embassy,[78] the Russians had gone to considerable lengths to disguise that fact. As the invasion approached, Moscow had withdrawn its military advisors in order to keep its major contributions to the Northern war effort hidden from outside view. That left Pyongyang in a position to decry the South's dependence on U.S. military backing. A talented cartoonist in the hastily established communist propaganda bureau in Seoul drew what one South Korean third grader of the time considered a very effective poster. It showed a craven South Korean President Rhee kneeling down and begging Truman for help.[79]

The Northern regime allied itself with elements in the South Korean National Assembly. Some of those had been bested in factional struggles and so might have felt they had little to lose. Others, however, were moderates who had beaten the Rhee forces in an election shortly before the invasion and had taken control of the assembly. Many such moderates decided to stay on in Seoul after the communists arrived.[80]

Having taken over the rice stocks, the occupation authorities tried to win friends by giving special rationing treatment to Southern families whose members joined communist youth orgainizations and labor unions. Offsetting the scheme's successes was the guaranteed alienation of all those who did *not* get the special rations—many of whom, having taken names, would be around after the communists' departure. In yet another bid for popular support, the occupiers set up supposedly democratic "people's committees" to govern localities—but they staffed them with mayors and other officials brought from the North, along with Southern communists.

Farmland hastily redistributed to tenant farmers came burdened with onerous quotas for delivery of crops to the government; as a result, Higgins found, the decrees "aroused little enthusiasm." After the Allies retook Seoul, the American correspondent also found a big change in the views of South Korean journalists she had known in the capital. Just before the war, they had been responsive and somewhat sympathetic to communist propaganda. But now she found that their earlier fervor to see the country unified, even if it should come under communist domination, had been transformed quickly into a panicked determination to flee the communist-occupied zone.[81]

For decades afterward, it was an article of faith among commentators in and out of South Korea that the war had left most Southerners implacably anti-communist.[82] Evidence advanced for that proposition included enormous refugee flows from north to south, the numbers not even approached by a flow in the opposite direction. Those fleeing the North had included many farmers who "abandoned their own land to become propertyless refugees in South Korea," Higgins reported. "The pitiful swarms of refugees who fled south in the wake of our retreating army were irrefutable evidence of how much the people feared the Reds."[83]

Is it possible, though, that many who moved South were not truly voluntary refugees but people who simply feared being bombed if they should remain in the North? That is the argument of scholars Jon Halliday and Bruce Cumings. "There is evidence that people in the North genuinely feared that they might be hit" with atomic weapons, they write—and "anyone who has seen pictures of the North as it was in the winter of 1950–51 and the destruction of Hungnam (or Inchon), with temperatures falling to minus forty degrees centigrade, with food stocks burned, animals slaughtered and entire villages razed to the ground, might reconsider why people moved."[84] Halliday and Cumings also say that no "important" Workers' Party officials defected to the South.[85]

    The South had already passed the legislation for a land reform of its own before the invasion. Redistribution, limiting any family to three *chongbo* or about 7.5 acres, was supposed to take place after the 1950 autumn rice harvest. Once he regained control of the South, Rhee sought to postpone the reform, but he ended up carrying it out. Halliday and Cumings believe that the Northern occupiers' brief land-reform effort, whatever its shortcomings, had been enough of a success to pressure the Rhee regime into going ahead despite the objections of the landlord class.[86]

    Still, one key to the intensity of Southern anti-communism in succeeding years no doubt is the fact that Southerners with obvious leanings toward the North had either gone north or died. Like Kim Il-sung in the North, Rhee used the war to purge his half of Korea of ideological diversity. Gregory Henderson, a U.S. diplomat in Seoul in the prewar period, wrote four decades later that people occupying an ideological middle ground had been much in evidence there as the war approached, and some of them had gone to the North during the war. But "one searches in vain for them in the North they went to. Perhaps they are hidden in northern niches where we cannot yet find them. They were stamped out also in the South."[87]

The escalation of hatred had, of course, been mutual. After the war, while the Southerners remembered Northern atrocities, there had been far more indiscriminate killing by the other side for North Koreans to remember if the victims of aerial bombings and napalm attacks are taken into account. The regime had little difficulty fanning popular hatred against both South Korea and the United States for deeds both real and imagined: "The U.S. imperialists and their bootlickers trampled underfoot and burnt everything in all quarters. They butchered innocent people en masse. They kicked children and pregnant women into the flames and buried old folks alive."[88]

    Even if many of the refugees were simply fleeing the bombing, the additional migration further reduced the numbers of malcontents in the North who might resist Kim's policies. On top of about 3.5 million North Koreans who had migrated to the South between 1945 and the outbreak of the war, another million or so refugees fled during the Korean War. Many (including such people as those villagers who had thrown a communist official's family down a mine shaft) joined the retreat of the UN forces from the North in the winter of 1950 after the Chinese joined the conflict.[89]

Although the war with which he had sought to reunite Koreans had divided them further instead, nevertheless Kim's regime remained unrelenting in repeating the lie of a great victory in a war begun by U.S. imperialists. During the brief occupation by UN and South Korean forces, some North Koreans had heard the truth about who had invaded whom. For the most part, though, people remained willing to believe the regime's version.[90]

Eventually the official version would also leave out references to Chinese help. The supposed grand victory would become a purely North Korean victory. That piece of historical falsification could not be accomplished immediately, since the Chinese "volunteer" army stayed on until 1958 to protect North Korea against any renewal of hostilities with the United States. North Koreans retained vivid memories of generous Chinese assistance—even as some of them criticized the Soviet Union and their own Korean Workers' Party for not having done enough.[91]

By the 1960s, however, Kim's official biographer would have not a single word to say about Chinese help, right up through his description of the "enthusiastic cheers of Korea and the world" on July 28, 1953. That was the day the Presidium of the Supreme People's Assembly conferred the title of Hero of the Democratic People's Republic of Korea, the National Flag First Class and the Medal of the Golden Star on Marshal Kim Il-sung, who had "organized and led the Korean people and the People's Army to a shining victory in the Fatherland Liberation War, with his outstanding strategy and tactics."[92] The account leaves out the small detail that the Hero of the DPRK title was awarded also to Gen. Peng Dehuai, commander of the Chinese force.[93]

For public consumption in North Korea, the war was pronounced a success. The North Korean people continued to be told that the South Koreans and Americans had started the war to destroy the North. To have thwarted their evil plan was a glorious victory, affirming the system and the revolutionary tradition of Kim's republic. "The spirit of the heroic soldiers who held out against the American invaders on Height 1211 [known to the UN troops as Heartbreak Ridge] was derived from the spirit of the guerrilla zones in the 1930s," Kim wrote in his memoirs. "We still maintain this spirit as we advance along the straight road of our own style of socialism within imperialist encirclement."[94]

Snatching a proclaimed "victory" from the jaws of defeat with the help of the Chinese, much as he had been able to do in 1945 thanks to the Allies, Kim could well imagine that the fates were with him. We may doubt that the Korean War failure seriously dented his confidence in himself, any more than had his ultimate failure in anti-Japanese warfare.

SIX

With the Leader Who
Unfolded Paradise

Throughout his career, starting with the skits he produced in Jilin as a student organizer, Kim Il-sung displayed a showman's sense. Thus it was that when Workers' Party officials gathered in Pyongyang for a plenary session of the Central Committee on August 5, 1953, they met in a nicely appointed meeting hall equipped to seat a thousand.

How could that be, just a few days after the armistice had been signed, in a city where the American bombing had flattened nearly every building? The story goes that Kim had ordered the building's foundation and walls constructed even before the armistice—on the theory that walls were more likely than roofs to withstand any further United Nations bombing attacks. The roofless structure had indeed survived. With the armistice, Kim had ordered an all-out effort to roof the building and finish its interior in time for the meeting.

Kim viewed the post–Korean War period not as a time to relax after the horrors of the war but as a contest, in which the two opposing systems would position themselves for further struggle. The North must build a strong and attractive economy—not just for its own people but to back up a continuing push to bring the South under communist rule. The instant meeting hall was intended as a vivid symbol of his determination. The speech he gave the party officials who assembled there was entitled, "Everything for the Postwar Rehabilitation and Development of the National Economy."[1]

In the several years following the armistice North Korea did rebuild its shattered economy, with a lot of help from its friends. The country—especially its capital, Pyongyang—became something of a socialist showcase. Meanwhile Kim consolidated power through continued purges against his rivals at home. His concern to limit the country's dependence on its larger communist neighbors inspired him to begin developing a self-reliant brand of communist economics.

Although Kim would not acknowledge the failure of the war, the country was in ruins and someone had to take some sort of responsibility. He moved to defuse the situation by blaming mid-level and low-level bureaucrats for foul-ups.[2] That was not enough, though, and he sacrificed some of the leadership.

Even as the Korean War fighting raged, Kim parceled out blame among high officials. On December 21, 1950, he addressed a meeting of the central committee of his Workers' Party, attacking named individuals for mistakes. Some of those errors were substantive snafus, but others were "defeatism" and other attitude problems. The offense of one high official who lost all his official posts was to have remarked that it would be hard to fight without more airplanes—a comment whose truth should have been evident in view of the devastation wrought when the Americans unleashed their air power.

Kim called for a purge of the party, asserting that the war had shown certain members to be disloyal.[3] His approach was to pick off potential enemies, one group at a time, before they could build enough political support to use his failure in the war to push him out. Removed from their official and party positions in the course of a long series of purges—and in many cases exiled, imprisoned at hard labor or killed—were most of the members of rival factions plus some old comrades from Manchuria belonging to his own faction. Those purged eventually included an astonishingly high proportion of the KPA generals who had been involved in the war—about nine out of ten, according to Yu Song-chol.[4]

Kim's skill at cutthroat, divide-and-conquer maneuvering can be seen in the purge of Ho Ka-i. A vice-chairman of the party Central Committee and vice-premier, Ho was also the leader of Soviet-born ethnic Koreans, including Yu Song-chol, who had come in with the Soviet occupation troops. Ho and Kim clashed over whether to make the Workers' Party an elite organization, as the communist party was in the USSR, or the mass party that Kim wanted.[5] Yu said that another Soviet-Korean, Pak Chang-ok, one day took Ho a copy of a party draft document full of flowery praise of Kim Il-sung— the sort of tribute that was to become de rigueur. Ho criticized the language as excessive, whereupon Pak invited him to edit the document. Taking the bait, the unsuspecting Ho underlined the offending passages in red ink. The other man took the marked-up document straight to Kim. Later Ho visited the premier's office. Armed now with proof of Ho's disloyalty, Kim "pulled the draft out of his drawer, his face flushed."

At a party Central Committee meeting November 1, 1951, Ho's erstwhile factional ally Pak Chang-ok led a criticism session that dredged up a number of alleged errors. Ho lost his party position and membership. He stayed on for a time as vice-premier. Kim assigned him to restore, by a certain deadline, a dam that had been destroyed during the Korean War. It was a task at which, Yu said, Ho was bound to fail. In 1953, Ho was found dead of what was described as a self-inflicted pistol wound. Yu thought it was really an assassin's bullet that killed him.[6]

In 1952, North Korean authorities secretly arrested twelve communists who had been active in the South Korean Workers' Party before fleeing to the North. According to the charges against them, "on the orders of U.S. imperialists" they had planned a coup to replace Kim with their fellow Southerner and faction leader, Pak Hon-yong. They were also accused of destroying "democratic forces" in the South and of spying on behalf of the United States. A spy gang affiliated with them, in a "vicious counterrevolutionary crime," allegedly had ignored Kim's orders to strengthen the defense of the west coast, especially the Inchon-Seoul area, in July of 1950—and thus the North Koreans had not been ready to repel the Inchon landing.[7]

In fact this group had challenged Kim's wartime leadership and sought to overthrow him, but the charges tying members to the American enemy almost certainly were trumped up.[8] The twelve went on trial in August 1953, right after proclamation of the armistice. Ten drew death sentences while the other two were sentenced to imprisonment for decades. The authorities held Pak Hon-yong himself incommunicado, from February 1953, and condemned him to death in December 1955.

Besides eliminating his most dangerous opponent, Kim used the trials to drive home the notion that U.S. and South Korean aggression had caused the war. More important, he shifted the blame for the war's failure to those rivals' alleged collusion with the United States. As an official biographer enthuses: "To have successfully fought U.S. imperialism, the strongest enemy, while such wicked spy cliques were entrenched in the Party and carrying out their intrigues! How great is Comrade Kim Il-sung!"[9] Kim had learned to fend off challenges to his rule by wrapping himself in the flag.

Yu Song-chol described the way Kim Il-sung "displayed his astute political tactics by creating dissension among the different factions. On a personal level, Kim would hand out special promotions and assignments in order to court his opponents' favor. Then, at the moment they became careless or inattentive, he would either purge or remove them like a lightning bolt out of the blue."

A core group of Kim Il-sung loyalists did his bidding in those purges. Yu counted around twenty-five guerrilla partisans who had been with Kim in

Manchuria and at the Eighty-eighth Brigade camp, then followed him to North Korea. Most of them Yu described as next to illiterate, some never having finished even the four years of elementary school. In a period when members of other groups were gritting their teeth at the ever-increasing extravagance of Kim's personality cult, the partisans were delighted to see their leader rendered such praise. "There was no ideological discord between them and Kim Il-sung," Yu said of the partisans. Because of their limited backgrounds, "they could not become a power that could challenge him, and none of them could survive on their own in case of a break-up."[10]

Kim compared the "sectarian elements" he was purging to rats that required complete extermination: "If we don't catch the rat, it will give birth to young. They will gnaw holes through the walls and finally destroy the whole house."[11]

An official biography claims that even as the Korean War raged, Kim had one eye on postwar economic development: "Can he not create vast farms on the unexplored plateaux of the north? Can he not reclaim the tidelands from the West Sea? Where is a great metallurgical base to be built and a base for light industries? How and where will the city apartments and countryside housing be built? These are the questions he thought over time and again as he looked far into the future." In the dark days of 1951, Kim supposedly came up with a vision for the rebuilt Pyongyang and called in an architect to discuss it as planes buzzed and anti-aircraft guns boomed. "Already his eyes saw the splendid, the magnificent streets extending one beyond the other, . . . the beautiful parks where children frolicked and cultural institutions of marble and granite stood."[12]

When the time came to transform the vision into reality, Kim turned the capital's reconstruction into a nationwide "battle," in the Soviet Stakhanovite pattern, with college students and office workers pressed into service to keep the building sites humming day and night.[13] Other "battles" ensued, to rebuild factories and transportation facilities as Pyongyang fully nationalized the country's industry. Clearing away the ashes and ruins of war, North Koreans laid an impressive base for economic development. Between 1954 and 1958, Pyongyang reported that combined output from mining, manufacturing and power transmission increased more than threefold.[14] Industry's role in generating national income rapidly outdistanced that of agriculture—a key indication of industrial development.[15] Between 1947 and 1967, per capita income was reported to have grown at an average rate of 13.1 percent a year.[16]

Other communist countries helped, but there is a debate whether that help came in the philanthropic form of foreign aid or in simple trade and investment. By one account, between 1946 and 1960, North Korea received foreign aid equivalent to about $125 per person (approximately the same per capita amount as South Korea received from its donors). The aid came from the Soviet Union, China, Eastern European countries and even Mongolia.[17] However, announcements of grants to North Korea are conspicuously lacking from the Soviet records of the period. That is a good reason to think that there were no grants, since Moscow in other cases was never shy about taking credit for philanthropy. Substantial Soviet shipments of raw materials, industrial equipment and fuel were extremely helpful to the developing North Korean economy—but probably came on credit, to be repaid with North Korean products.[18]

It is one thing to receive help from abroad, quite another to use it well. Many recipient countries had dismal records, but foreign analysts were impressed that North Korea used what it got to press forward with its industrialization drive. Pyongyang took effective advantage of the country's high degree of centralization, its compact economy and an unusual lack of corruption and mismanagement. Its success "makes North Korea's model unique among the world's many aid-receiving aspirants of development," said a study published by a conservative American think tank.[19]

What Kim promised North Koreans was phrased in the terms traditionally used to describe the good life. The people would "live in tile-roofed houses, clothed in silk, eating rice and meat soup."[20] Although those goals were to remain elusive, the economy chalked up so many early successes that Kim perhaps started to believe the "genius" claims his subordinates were putting forth.[21] Hearing choruses of praise for what he had done already,[22] Kim Il-sung felt a surge of confidence for the future. In 1958, he even boasted that North Korea had the ability to "catch up with Japan in the machinery industry."[23]

Underlying all his policies was Kim's unchanged determination to reunite the country. He sought more subtle ways of disengaging the Seoul government's American defenders. Still far from his mind was any notion that the capitalist South and socialist North might coexist peacefully. In the cause of ultimate reunification, the prime duty of North Korean revolutionaries was still to overthrow "the U.S. imperialist aggressive forces" and liberate the South Korean people. The DPRK must build up its economy in order to play its role as "strategic base of the Korean revolution."[24]

While moderating the recklessness that had pushed him to invade in 1950, Kim gave up none of his determination. Not even the enmity his troops had aroused during their periods of occupation of the South deterred him. There was another factor, however, that weighed heavily in Kim's calculations: Thanks to a new U.S.–South Korean mutual security treaty, it was clear now that the Southerners did not stand alone. For the decades that followed, the North lived with the danger that the United States would re-join the Korean War—perhaps with the gloves off the American nuclear ca-pability—if Kim should renew his attempt at reunification via invasion.

The regime's propaganda emphasized readiness to take on the United States again. Further, it used the Americans as bugbears to inspire passion-ate efforts to rebuild the country—as when workers at the Hwanghae steel works supposedly pledged to Kim: "We will now build open hearths and blast furnaces and surely burn up the U.S. imperialists, the enemy, in their flames!"[25]

But Kim preferred to avoid confronting the Americans directly—unless they should happen to be so busy in wars elsewhere that he could see a chance of victory. Forceful unification would be an option in case of the out-break of global war, he said in 1955. "It would be rather difficult for us to fight all alone against American imperialism," he explained. However, "un-der conditions where they must disperse their forces on a global scale it would be comparatively easy for us to defeat them."[26]

Besides preparing for such a chance to unify via war, Kim developed an-other interventionist policy aimed at bringing the South under communist rule even in peacetime. That strategy was based on subversion. It represented a return to the approach of the late 1940s, before Pyongyang had shifted to planning for the 1950 invasion. While working to get American forces out of the South and out of the picture, North Korea would break down the anti-communism of South Koreans and incite them to revolt against their leaders. For this, Pyongyang would train agents and infiltrate them into the South. The revolution would communize the South and permit unification under a single system.

Kim still saw himself as Korea's Ho Chi Minh. Girding up its military de-fenses, the North would become a launching pad—and a fortified, inviolable sanctuary—for forces waging guerrilla warfare or other military actions in support of a Southern revolution.[27] Although Kim called this process "peace-ful unification," the Pyongyang regime quickly started preparing for the vio-lence implicit in an approach that amounted to a Mao-style "people's war." And violent it was. Among the reported casualties was a South Korean woman named Park Bu-ryon, wife of Koje Island anchovy fisherman Kim Hong-jo. A pair of local South Koreans allegedly working as agitators for Pyongyang broke into her house in 1960. When she discovered them and shouted for help, they killed her and stole a boat to attempt an escape. Mourning her was the victim's eldest son: an ambitious young politician named Kim Young-sam, later to become president of South Korea.[28]

After the war the North had a vast military force—estimated at almost 600,000 men. But Kim needed to divert as much manpower and wealth as possible to economic development, and it was also in his interest to try to weaken the South's military defenses. Thus, he developed a huge "territorial militia," led by discharged soldiers working in the civilian economy and armed with automatic weapons and armored vehicles. Meanwhile he proposed to South Korea a mutual reduction so that the active-duty forces of each would number fewer than 100,000 men. Although that disarmament proposal went nowhere, Pyongyang unilaterally reduced military service periods for draftees and began gradual demobilization—sending many of the mustered-out soldiers, as well as new graduates of junior and senior high schools, to work on the farms. The military component of the state budget dropped from 15.2 percent in 1953 to 4.8 percent in 1958.[29]

Despite the many claims that the war had made anti-communists of most Southerners, it was clear that the impoverished, war-devastated South remained vulnerable to communist infiltration and subversion. A few weeks before the armistice was signed, when Washington policymakers considered whether to press for the option of a neutral, unified Korea, one official worried aloud that neutralization might provide the opening for rapid communization of the South Koreans.[30] The next day, June 17, 1953, Rhee's prime minister met Secretary of State Dulles to argue against an armistice. Prime Minister Paek Tu-chin argued that the time was right to "get the communists out of Korea, unite the country and liberate the people in North Korea." Otherwise, he warned, "the communists would rebuild their air fields, create strong military forces and soon infiltrate South Korea." The South Korean government and people "very much" feared communist infiltration and attack, Paek said.

Trying to sell an armistice, Dulles argued (prophetically, but jumping the gun by decades) that communism was a force in decline: It was possible, he said, that in the next five or ten years Russian power would have "pulled back to its historic boundaries" and the Cold War divisions of Germany and Korea ended. To help this process along, Dulles urged, "infiltration should work just the other way—that is, from the South to the North," and "the economy of South Korea should be rapidly built up so that South Korea would soon become a strong attraction" to North Koreans. Dulles also cited as protection for South Korea a proposed security treaty with the United States, plus a "Greater Sanction Statement" comprising commitments by other members of the UN Command. "The communists"—including Moscow and Beijing—would be on notice that both commitments "would mean instant retaliation if they again attack Korea, and they know that this retaliation could mean atomic attacks on Vladivostok and Port Arthur." Thus, "the communists might be reluctant to use what resources they have, which are relatively meager, to rebuild their military position in North Korea and risk continuing the expansion of South Korean and American power on the peninsula."[31]

Less than three weeks later, on July 7, 1953, the U.S. National Security Council adopted a top-secret policy statement covering the period between the signing of the armistice and the negotiation of a peace treaty—an "interim" period that even a half century later had yet to end, according to that definition. Among other measures, the United States was to "continue a program of covert operations designed to assist in the achievement of U.S. objectives vis-à-vis Communist China and Korea."[32] As for what those objectives might be, another top-secret NSC report issued that same day said that Washington could choose one of two mutually exclusive objectives in Korea. One was to continue the division of the country, with South Korea to be brought into the U.S. security system as a military ally. The other choice was to ensure that united Korea would be neutral but governed by the regime already in place in the South. The second option, of course, was available only if North and South could be unified. The policymakers decided after due debate that a reunified and neutral but noncommunist Korea was the preferred option.[33] However, a subsequent international conference at Geneva did not reach agreement on a peace treaty—much less on the reunification-with-neutralization option.

As we have seen, part of Kim Il-sung's strategy to subvert the South was to restore the prewar North Korean economy and build on it to demonstrate the superiority of the socialist system—the mirror image of what Dulles envisioned for the South. The difference was that Kim managed to show some quick successes while the Rhee regime in Seoul faltered politically and turned in a dismal economic performance.

Pyongyang made sure the word got out. Its propaganda organs portrayed the North as an egalitarian paradise. Kim's achievements permitted him to press a psychological offensive against South Korea, issuing patronizing public offers to send food aid, hire the South's unemployed and care for Southern orphans.[34]

One strong indication of the magnetic power of the society Kim was building: Overseas Koreans in substantial numbers began to immigrate to the North. Kim wrote in his memoirs of the homecoming in 1960 of surviving members of the Jo family, who had sheltered him and nursed him through his fever in 1935. The family had lived in Manchuria since the start of the century, he said, and one could imagine their feelings "at the sight of the independent homeland, a country of freedom and a state which was now rising magnificently on the debris, beneath the banner of self-reliance."[35]

More significant was to prove the case of Korean nationals who had lived and labored in Japan as an oppressed minority since the period of Japanese colonial rule over Korea. In 1955, in accordance with Kim's instruction that "the overseas citizens' movement had to contribute to the

Korean revolution," pro-Pyongyang Korean residents banded together in Chongryon, the General Association of Korean Residents in Japan.[36] Most of the members actually hailed from the southern part of the peninsula; their identification with the North over the South reflected leftist sentiment as well as the widespread perception that the North was doing better than the South economically. Starting at the end of 1959, some seventy-five thousand of those Korean residents joined in an exodus to Kim's Promised Land.[37] It was a movement similar in some respects to Zionism. The returnees embarked from the docks at the Sea of Japan port of Niigata amid great flourishes of rhetoric by Korean resident leaders and leftist Japanese students.

Chong Ki-hae[38] was seventeen years old and a recent graduate of a Korean high school run by Chongryon when he and his parents repatriated to North Korea in 1960. Chong's parents, born in what became South Korea, had gone to Japan in the 1920s and eked out a hand-to-mouth existence wandering around the country doing odd jobs. Life eventually had improved for the family—to the extent that Chong himself would have preferred to stay in Japan. But his parents' experience of harsh prewar discrimination against ethnic Koreans had made them hate Japan and long for the Korean motherland. A cousin, also living in Japan, visited South Korea and reported to them that people there lived no better than the communist North Koreans—and that the North, unlike the South, offered free health care and education. On that basis, Chong's parents decided on the North. The family boarded a ship at Niigata, taking along 500,000 Japanese yen in currency, a Toyota sedan, a truck and a motorcycle. Realizing that North Korea still was not fully developed, they also took the precaution of shipping a ten-year supply of shoes and clothing and a cache of trading goods including twenty gold Swiss watches and two hundred meters of black suiting fabric.

As a reality check on Kim Il-sung's boast that his country would catch up with Japan quickly, consider the still relatively primitive North Korea that the Chongs found. Officials classified the family members, finding that young Chong was the only able-bodied worker since his parents were of retirement age. The family rode to Chongju County in North Pyongan Province, where they were assigned to their work unit: a sewing machine factory in a community of about four thousand people. The Chongs donated their truck to the factory and young Chong signed up to drive it on delivery runs. He did that for three years until he started worrying about his future prospects. Then he began studying and training to work as a machinist, a trade he was to practice until he defected to South Korea in 1994.

North Korea was far from a paradise, the family quickly found. Living in a farmhouse with walls of sun-dried mud like everyone else's, but still owning their black Toyota, the Chongs were the center of gawking attention in the county. Not only had the concept of private property become alien, especially among the younger people who had grown up under communism. There was also the matter that private cars were almost unheard of. There were state-owned sedans, but the black ones were reserved for really high officials. Although no one applied pressure directly, the Chongs felt more and more uncomfortable about their car. Whenever a big shot came to town, local officials would ask to borrow it to convey him during his stay. Finally, after a year, the Chongs sold the car to the state for use in Pyongyang, the home of most officials who rated black cars.

The other items the Chongs had brought along from Japan turned out to spell the difference between a fair level of comfort and the poverty that characterized the lives of ordinary North Koreans despite the undeniable advances of the previous several years. Take the clothing, for example. North Koreans were wearing clothes of a fabric based on reeds and wood pulp, manufactured inside the country. Pants ripped easily and often had to be patched, especially on the seat. People seeing the twin round patches would say, "I see you're wearing glasses on your butt."[39]

Then there was food supply. Starting in 1954, North Korea had transferred the farmland from individuals to cooperatives. From 1958, China's Great Leap Forward inspired Kim Il-sung to push farm collectivization even further. He launched his own Chollima movement, named after a mythical winged horse that could leap 1,000 *ri* (about 250 kilometers or 150 miles). Using the Chollima to symbolize the "breathless speed of socialist construction and revolutionary spirit of Korea," Kim set out to remake nature, reform society and revitalize the people.[40] Perhaps forgetting that extremely rapid collectivization moves in Manchuria in the 1930s had left a bad taste in his mouth, he briefly threw caution to the winds in the late 1950s. It was a time of high excitement as North Koreans, like Mao Zedong and his subjects in China, were swept away by an almost mystical belief that the stage of true communism was at hand.

Kim grouped the original cooperatives together in even larger units, under state control, which also functioned as the lowest level of local government. Still called cooperatives, those were in fact similar to China's new communes and the Soviet Union's collective farms. Boosting production (on the theory that bigger is better) was only part of the objective. At least as important was to turn peasants, whose propertied status inclined them to bourgeois capitalist traits, into good members of the working class—and, thus, prospective communists.[41]

Remember that only a decade earlier the land had been redistributed from landlords to the tillers. The state giveth; the state taketh away. Official propaganda claimed that the peasants "found happiness in cooperative labor and beamed for joy."[42] Peasants had been "sitting alone on banks between paddy fields . . . unable to move heaps of stones." Now discovering economies of scale, they "pooled their strength and wisdom, built waterways through the hills and farmed the land with new methods, bidding good-bye to out-dated ways."[43]

The collectivization movement did bring some bigger harvests—but it failed to "resolve questions of food"—Kim's ambitious goal when he set out the five-year plan in 1956. Very quickly, in 1959, he found it advisable to back off a bit from collectivization. He restored to farm families individual kitchen garden plots and the right to use them to raise chickens, pigs, ducks and rabbits for sale. The regime urged that they use the money to build new houses.[44]

Even though harvests did increase, the increases failed to meet planners' goals. Rationing—the surest sign of scarcity—continued. Disappointing results probably explain North Korea's failure to release its agricultural results after completion of the "extended" seven-year plan that went into effect around the time of the Chongs' repatriation. The regime itself reported that wealthy farmers, along with those whose middle-income status predated land reform, tended to oppose collectivization.[45] Probably the dilution of farmers' individual incentives played a role in limiting harvests, along with frequent droughts and a persistent cold front.[46]

The food that the Chongs got every fifteen days in their official rations left them unsatisfied, even though at the beginning they always received the full ration of grain (700 grams a day for a worker, lesser amounts for children, retirees and others). Except for soybeans, which occasionally were distributed, the ration included no vegetables or meat. At that time the problem with grain was not so much the quantity but the quality. What people found objectionable was the fact that the ration usually consisted of 90 percent "mixed grains"—mostly corn (maize)—and only 10 percent rice. Like most East Asians of that time, the Chongs wanted rice at every meal. The preference for rice over corn is a matter of custom, of course—but it also reflects the body's nutritional needs since corn contains far less protein and niacin than rice does. As public health workers discovered in impoverished areas of the southern United States early in the twentieth century, subsistence on a corn-dominated diet with little fresh meat is a formula for contracting pellagra, a serious disease whose symptoms include skin changes, severe nerve dysfunction and diarrhea.[47]

Unlike Chong and other factory workers, members of agricultural cooperatives received their entire grain ration in rice. Although the state prohibited trading in grain, some farmers were willing to sell their rice on the black market for one and a quarter *won* per kilogram. At that rate young Chong, drawing a monthly wage of about 45 *won*, could not afford to supply enough rice for himself and his nonworking parents with just the contents of his pay envelope. So he bartered the family's trading stocks of watches and fabric for rice.

At farmers' markets, the farmers were permitted to sell livestock, baskets and other goods, but if they got caught selling grain they would be sent to jail.[48] Before Chong could buy grain from the farmers, he had to approach them delicately. "In the farmers' market, I'd buy some livestock and other things I didn't need, and ask that they be delivered to my home. Then when the farmer brought them we would talk about a food purchase. After that first time, I could work it out any time." Chong told me that people who remembered the economy of Japanese days understood the value of such transactions. The Workers' Party, however, "was very harsh in its treatment of the exchange of goods." The party decried the practice as a capitalist holdover. Koreans who knew Chong and his family could see that the returnees were living better than the others. "Basically people were very envious of us."

Even Kim Il-sung's official biographers acknowledge dissatisfaction with living conditions during that period—if only on the part of "people with antiquated petty-bourgeois ideas." An official inquiry revealed that such people "are without exception the people who lived well in the past. These people seize every opportunity to complain and readily waver before the slightest difficulty."[49]

Most ordinary North Koreans, however, did not have direct knowledge of Japan and other outside countries, and they knew that their own living standards had improved after the advent of communist rule. Thus, Chong told me, they were inclined to believe Kim Il-sung's boast of having unfolded a paradise.

Outside analysts' comparisons during that period bolstered Kim's claim. One study shows North and South neck and neck at the time of the 1953 armistice, with gross national product per capita of $56 and $55 respectively. By 1960, the South at $60 had barely advanced, while the North's figure had nearly quadrupled to $208—an impressive statistical advance, even if only a fraction of that increase translated into improvements in the daily lives of the masses.[50]

As Chong Ki-hae's cousin had reported before the elder Chongs decided on North Korea as their destination, the living standard was at least as high in the North as in the South. And the North was far ahead in industrial development, especially heavy machinery. That did not necessarily contribute to living standards immediately, but at least it seemed to point to a brighter future.

A student-led uprising in the South in 1960 kicked Rhee out and installed a democratically elected government. But that failed to alter the equation, as the new South Korean government of Prime Minister Chang Myon proved weak and corrupt. In April 1961—seven years after Dulles had talked about making the South attractive through an economic buildup—the

U.S. ambassador in Seoul sent a classified cable to Washington. In it he lamented that the "stark, bleak facts of economic life," along with frustrations over the peninsula's continued division, were behind Southerners' "widespread feelings of hopelessness." Add to that mix "continuing mutual recriminations among Koreans," the ambassador wrote, "and all this creates an atmosphere wide open to exploitation by enemies of a free Korea."[51]

Commentators friendly to Pyongyang seized upon the real differences and exaggerated them. "The South was literally a desolate land," wrote an East German who visited North Korea in the early 1960s and essayed a comparison. "Only helmets of the American soldiers were shining. But to the north of the demarcation line as far as the eye can reach there were fields of golden grain."[52] A Western academic's 1965 article entitled "Korean Miracle" referred not to the South Korean but to the *North* Korean economy.[53]

Kim Il-sung's personality cult was gathering momentum. The theory, earlier worked out in the Soviet Union on behalf of Stalin, was that the people, defined by communist doctrine as all-powerful, nevertheless could not function properly without becoming united under the leadership of a superior being, one without the limitations that afflict other people. Thus, an official biographer shortly would write that Kim Il-sung from the time of liberation had been the country's obvious and true leader:

> But it is not a gift that everyone has, this ability for correct insight into such a complex situation, looking far into the future to hammer out the only correct line for the Korean revolution. Ahead of the Korean revolution on this morrow of the liberation lay countless complex problems, including the people's inherent backwardness due to their history, the complex intertwined political forces and social and class relations, the occupation of South Korea by U.S. imperialism and the forced division of Korea into North and South.
>
> To correctly analyze all these issues and to chart the correct way for the revolution—this was a task to which only Comrade Kim Il-sung was equal, outstanding Leader of revolution as he is, who had gained unique and rich experience through his long-drawn revolutionary struggles, and who burned with patriotism and was armed with Marxist-Leninist convictions.
>
> This was the reason why immediately after liberation, the Korean people looked to Comrade Kim Il-sung to take the lead in the revolution as quickly as possible, in order to overcome the confusion. Political leaders of both North and South Korea, too, realizing their own limitations, earnestly wished him to lead them to the fulfillment of the long-cherished desire of the people as soon as possible."[54]

Kim Il-sung and the party "became the brain, heart, wisdom and conscience of all the Korean people."[55] While other high-level leaders had to wait until they were dead before anything would be named after them, the huge Kim Il-sung Square had been one of the first features completed in the new Pyongyang.[56]

Kim's purges continued as he moved to consolidate his rule. Soon it became the turn of the Yenan faction, made up of Korean returnees from China proper who had fought against the Japanese as members of Mao Zedong's communist forces. They showed their potential for challenging Kim in the years following Stalin's 1953 death. At a 1956 meeting in Moscow, Khrushchev criticized the Stalin personality cult and proposed collective leadership in the Soviet Union to replace the dead leader's one-man rule. Clearly, other communist countries were expected to follow that lead.

After watching Khrushchev's treatment of Stalin several North Korean officials (mostly members of the Yenan faction, although some Soviet-Koreans got involved also) were bold enough to question Kim's personality cult, management style and economic policies. They plotted to topple him. Scholar Andrei N. Lankov demonstrates their deep differences with Kim by citing memoranda of conversations between Soviet officials and the plotters, documents he found in the Soviet archives in the 1990s. "I am becoming more and more convinced that Kim Il-sung does not understand how harmful his behavior is," one plotter complained to a Soviet Embassy official. "He paralyzes the initiative of members of the Standing Committee and other executives of the Party and the State. He intimidates everyone. Nobody can voice an opinion on any question. People are subjected to repression for the slightest criticism. He has gathered around himself sycophants and mediocrities." Another man dissected Kim's economic policies: "Farmers compose 80 percent of the population. . . . After Liberation they were offered a good opportunity for a better life but they remain very poor. The government's taxation policy is incorrect. Instead of 25 to 27 percent tax they took more than 50 percent from the farmers. Such a policy continues to this day. It is not necessary to recount the methods used in 1954–1955 to gather taxes. Tax gathering was accompanied by beatings, murders and arrests. The party's activities are based on violence, not persuasion. The [agricultural] co-operative movement is based on violence." What to do? "A group of executives considers it necessary to undertake certain actions against Kim Il-sung and his closest associates at the earliest possible opportunity. The group sets itself the task of putting new persons in charge of the [Korean Workers' Party] Central Committee and government."[57]

At a Central Committee meeting where they hoped to win support for his ouster, Kim was ready for them. Those who stood to speak against Kim's idolization were "pushed back by abusive insults and shouting," according to Yu Song-chol. The atmosphere was so threatening that four of the Yenan faction members "fled to China immediately after the morning session, fearing for their lives." The vicissitudes of the Yenan faction continued until it was wiped out. Its leader, Kim Tu-bong, lost his party membership in 1958 and was sent off to a collective farm, where he died. Yenan faction members in the military were charged with plotting a revolt. The "military revolt plan" that was used in evidence against them was in reality merely a plan for suppressing anti-government uprisings, a plan they had been assigned to draw up, according to Yu.[58]

Phony as much of the evidence may have been, Kim was becoming all-powerful at home through such maneuvers. As he was to write much later, in his memoirs, "While I made many friends and comrades on the path of my struggle, there were also many people who stood in my way." Seeing potential rivals, he showed no hesitation in cutting them down in order to consolidate his own power.[59]

While Kim's praise of his role model, Stalin, had been largely sincere, Khrushchev was something else altogether. The new Soviet leader's iconoclasm and his interest in limiting the anti-imperialist struggle to peaceful competition boded ill for the North Korean premier. Kim's position depended on continuing to use real or imagined external threats to maintain his Stalinist, one-man rule.[60] His goal of reunification through any combination of violent and nonviolent means required that North Korea—preferably with allies' support—confront American power in the South directly. Fortunately for Kim, Moscow's efforts to export de-Stalinization soon proved dangerous to Soviet interests, inspiring Hungarians to rise against Soviet control in October of 1956. Khrushchev then backed off, declaring a policy of noninterference in the domestic affairs of other communist countries.

With less danger now that Moscow would retaliate against him Kim Il-sung mounted a full-fledged offensive against the Soviet faction, which had retained influence in Pyongyang even after the purge of Ho Ka-i. Part of the problem with the Soviet-Koreans, from Kim's viewpoint, was the very fact that they had been raised in the Soviet Union and had dual Soviet and North Korean citizenship—and divided loyalties, as well. There are reports that many of them mistrusted Kim and his guerrillas and looked down upon them as ignorant, backwoods types—viewing themselves as the genuine Bolshevik article.[61]

Kim was growing restive in the face of Soviet efforts to influence his policies. He had been Number One almost from the beginning in Pyongyang after the Liberation, in large part thanks to Soviet support. But he had to share some of the decision-making process, and he did not yet feel secure enough for comfort.[62] Attacks on "flunkeys" who viewed everything Russian as superior, things Korean as inferior, became a major theme in his post—Korean War utterances.[63] It is safe to say that Kim himself was tired of sucking up to the Russians.

For a time after liberation, the North Korean leaders and media acknowledged the Soviet Union's help and example. Kim himself noted in a speech shortly after his arrival in Pyongyang that the USSR (*and* the United States—this latter acknowledgment a rare one indeed) had liberated Korea.[64] In a February 1947 speech Kim praised the Soviet Union as "the most advanced democratic state," and suggested its structure was worth copying.[65] As late as 1950, when Kim was looking for help in prosecuting the war against the Americans, the party newspaper still acknowledged that North Korea had been liberated "by Soviet armed strength."[66] But it was not long before he decided that others had carried praise of the USSR so far as to amount to flunkeyism—excessive dependence on and praise of foreign countries. He wanted the praise turned around and directed to Korean benefactors of the people—mainly himself, as it turned out.

Kim later complained in his memoirs that the regime's propagandists after liberation had not sufficiently publicized the anti-Japanese guerrilla movement. "The flunkeyist fever spread by these people developed to such an extreme that immediately after liberation our people were not even aware that there had been a heavy battle fought for the defense of Xiaowangqing during the anti-Japanese war—although they knew all about the battle of Stalingrad."[67]

He had a point. Besides its all-pervasive influence in politics, military affairs and economics, the USSR had deeply penetrated the molding of popular North Korean attitudes. Organized down to the village and street levels, a "Society for Cultural Relations with the Soviet Union" promoted Soviet culture by showing films, maintaining libraries and halls and sponsoring lectures, theatrical events and exhibitions. A huge percentage of the population joined.[68] The streets of North Korean cities were festooned with Soviet propaganda posters and portraits of Lenin and Stalin, in addition to Kim Il-sung.[69] In such circumstances it would have been little wonder if, as Kim Il-sung charged, some North Korean officials got carried away with seeing the world through Russian eyes.

As noted, Kim himself had been an enthusiastic participant in the adulation of the Soviet Union. Further, his having found sanctuary in the USSR until 1945 could have opened him to the same charges of reliance on a great power that he was leveling against others. In those days, indeed, he had been a communist internationalist, taking help where he could get it, his Korean nationalism directed solely against the Japanese. The brand of nationalism he was beginning to find it in his interest to promote, however, was so exclusive of non-Korean influences as to be almost xenophobic. The regime's "historians" placed him in the Manchurian region bordering Korea—and sometimes in Korea itself—right up into 1945, continuing the fight until he led his "Korean People's Revolutionary Army" to victory over the Japanese.[70] The Russians' cooperation with this deception had definite limits.[71] Never mind such annoying facts, though, for Kim's own propagandists soon would see to it that his defeat by the Japanese at the beginning of the 1940s and his flight to the Soviet Union would disappear from history as North Koreans could read it. Hwang Jang-yop, following his 1997 defection to South Korea, reported that from 1958—the first year he served Kim as party secretary for ideology—it was the duty of himself and his colleagues to rewrite Kim's *Selected Works*, destroying any record in the ruler's reports and speeches that "gave the impression of worshiping the Soviet Union." Readers would find no "Long live Stalin" quotations in the republished volumes.[72]

Pyongyang became stingier in giving the USSR credit for its liberation role, dropping all mention of it by the late 1960s.[73] (The role of the United States and other allied countries had disappeared, of course, long before that.) Many North Koreans in 1945 had seen the Russian liberation forces with their own eyes. Nevertheless, for succeeding generations of schoolchildren reading the country's "history" Kim Il-sung would become the liberator he wished he could have been.[74] Although the Soviets (and Americans) might judge him an ingrate, he would in this fashion show that he was no flunkey or puppet.

Similarly, it would have been inconvenient to admit that Kim during his guerrilla days had taken orders from the Comintern, the Chinese Communist Party and Chinese commanders in the Northeast Anti-Japanese United Army. For his greater glory, Pyongyang downgraded or deleted the roles of not only Russians involved in the struggle but eventually Chinese as well.[75] For good measure, they slighted the efforts even of Korean communists who had opposed the Japanese in the homeland or in China-based units other than Kim's.

Eventually the purges of Soviet-Koreans got to Yu Song-chol. Yu believed there was a personal element added to the mix in his case. "Kim had an intolerant side to him that caused him to remember anyone with whom he had a negative experience and eventually seek revenge without fail," he said. While serving as Kim's interpreter back in the Soviet Union, Yu had crossed his boss. He had refused to run a private errand for Kim, citing Soviet Army regulations that forbade such use of enlisted men. As time passed, Yu had forgotten about that and likewise had forgotten another occasion on which words had passed with Kim. He lived to regret both. A decade and a half later, when Yu had risen to the rank of lieutenant general, a friend warned him that Kim still harbored ill will toward him because of those two incidents.

Yu figured that the old grudge had something to do with his being purged a bit later.[76] Yu's recollections of his personal downfall afford an inside view of the experience of being purged—at the lower end of the horror curve, since he was not killed.

Koreans generally are sticklers for formality and "face." Returning to Pyongyang in 1958 from two years of study in the Soviet Union, Yu knew something must be amiss when no one came to the airport to meet him—a three-star general, at least nominally heading the operations bureau of the Korean People's Army. Three days after his return, Yu was summoned to a meeting of the defense ministry's "Thought Examination Committee." The meeting chairman pointed to him and said: "You have committed four mistakes. Conduct self-criticism." Charges against Yu included describing the people's "loyalty" to Kim Il-sung as a personality cult; speaking as though Kim had started the Korean War; and spying for the Soviet Union. He admitted that he had said, in a chat with two other senior officers, that a drive for peaceful reunification would have been better than starting the Korean War. He denied the other charges. The most serious, the spying charge, he figured had been trumped up as Kim's way of showing that he was offended by Yu's close relations with Soviet officials: Soviet military advisors had intervened concerning Yu's assignments several times since 1945.

Removed from his job, Yu had to spend all day in an otherwise empty room writing letters of "self-reflection." At night he returned to sessions of the Thought Examination Committee, which met from 7 P.M. to midnight or 1 A.M. The committee members harassed and berated him until he conducted self-criticism to their satisfaction. Whenever he opened his mouth to speak they shouted abuse at him. "After a few days, I agreed with all their criticisms out of a feeling of hopelessness. However, they continued to torment me every night, repeating the same process over and over." It got to be too much for Yu. He begged a former subordinate, who by then was sitting on the Thought Examination Committee, to kill him—"rather than bleeding me slowly like this." Finally, though, the sessions ended with Thought Examination Committee members ripping off Yu's rank insignia. Expelled from the People's Army and the party, he became a nonperson. "As word spread that I had undergone thought examination, relatives stopped visiting and even my old friends ostracized me."

Worried about where their next meal would come from and evicted from their home, he and his family moved in the freezing January of 1959 into a former stable. Soon they were ordered to leave even that shelter. Eventually Yu was told that he was in the third category on Kim's list of purge targets— those who need not be killed or put to hard labor but might simply leave the country if they wished. Cursing Kim Il-sung, Yu left in December of 1959— one of some four hundred officials and their family members whom Kim's purges drove into exile in the Soviet Union.[77]

In reality Yu's "crimes" must have been not too terrible—considering the fact that in 1990 the Pyongyang regime, seeking to let bygones be bygones, invited him and a number of the other exiles in the USSR to visit North Korea. It was Yu's first time back since his forced departure three decades earlier. When he got to Pyongyang, he was dismayed to find in the "Fatherland Liberation War Museum" no record of the Korean War efforts of himself and other high-ranking cadre who had been purged. Even his name was missing from the list of Operations Bureau commanders. Compounding the insult, one North Korean host (as had long been customary with visitors) "asked me to write down a few words praising Kim Il-sung."[78]

As he accused his domestic rivals of flunkeyism, Kim Il-sung also glorified the opposite quality, or state of mind, which he came to term *juche*—often translated simply as national self-reliance but having the broader meaning of putting Korea first. *Juche* was to be the antidote to the tendency of Koreans, like citizens of other small communist countries, to subject themselves to the wishes of Moscow or Beijing. "What are we doing?" Kim asked in an appearance before party propagandists and agitators in 1955. "We are not engaged in the revolution of another country but in our Korean revolution."[79]

Although it was in that 1955 speech that Kim gave full voice to his arguments for *juche*, he had been talking along similar lines as early as 1948. It was better, he said, to produce finished goods at home and develop the economy independently instead of sending raw materials to be processed abroad.[80] The theme became important in a debate over what to emphasize in the reconstruction of the post–Korean War economy. Kim had chosen to go all-out with investments in building heavy industry, including armaments.[81] That meant postponing major improvements in popular living standards.

Criticism of Kim's economic policies came from Korean "factionalists and dogmatists," as Kim called them. Besides questioning the priority on heavy industrial development, they also complained that agricultural collectivization was moving too fast. And some believed he should be encouraging the country's remaining capitalists and traders through the sort of state capitalism that other socialist countries had employed at a comparably early stage.

In a sense such critics played into Kim's hands. He always needed enemies at home or abroad, or both, to make the most of his skills at negative motivation. If the "factionalists and dogmatists" had not come along he might have had to invent them (as of course he did, to the extent that he trumped up cases against them). Visiting the Kangson steel mill complex in 1956, he told its workers and managers that the country faced a situation in which "people in some country try to impose their factionalism upon us. People in another country try to get control of us in cooperation with those people. The factionalists in our country depend on their masters for support." Meanwhile, South Korea's Rhee "attempts to attack us, with help of the United States. Then, whom shall we trust? There is none other than you whom we can trust."[82]

Kim cranked up an "all-party ideological struggle" to root out his domestic critics and their subversive notions. "Wherever he went," his official biographer claims, "Comrade Kim Il-sung learned clearly that the entire party and people had strong revolutionary zeal running high, and were filled with an intense fighting spirit against both internal and external enemies. He lost no time in translating their passion and strength into action . . . to produce a big leap forward in the socialist revolution and construction and thereby completely overwhelm the factionalists."[83]

In practice, that struggle involved wholesale population relocation. Shin Myung-chul, a former member of the State Security secret police apparatus who defected to the South, told me that his family had been relocated in 1956, four years before he was born, from the major city of Hamhung to a small city, Cheongdan-eup. His parents were socialist enthusiasts, and their relocation was part of Kim Il-sung's scheme to resettle such exemplars where they could teach less ideologically advanced people. Ahn Choong-hak, a logger who defected to the South, told me that his family in 1961, the year he turned three, had been part of a mass relocation of households of "good family background" to the old capital of Kaesong.[84] Recall that Kaesong, below the 38th parallel, had been captured by the North during the Korean War and incorporated into its post-armistice territory. The ideological correctness of many remaining local people left much to be desired.

By taking "ten steps where others need only take one,"[85] Kim enthused, the country would soon move from socialism to the ultimate communist utopia. Then everyone would work voluntarily and receive goods according to need — not according to effort, as in the socialist stage. "I will take you on to communist society," he vowed in a 1959 visit to workers — formerly independent craftsmen — in the Wonsan Ironworks Producers' Cooperative. "I will take all your sons to communist society." An official biographer reports that "unity in ideology and will" grew out of the campaign. "All functionaries and working people came to take the firm *juche* position of knowing no other ideas than the revolutionary ideas of Comrade Kim. . . ."[86]

But attacks on Kim's policies had come not only at home but also from communists abroad. No less a figure than future Soviet leader Leonid Brezhnev, as a delegate to a 1956 party conference, urged his North Korean hosts to import Soviet consumer goods instead of machines. Such disagreements continued into the 1960s as Kim criticized the Soviet-backed notion that socialist countries should form an "integrated" economy, each specializing rather than trying to produce a full range of products domestically.[87] The ongoing

Soviet campaign of de-Stalinization—whose implications were so dangerous for Kim Il-sung himself—was one important factor making him hesitate to put his full trust in Moscow's guidance on other matters.

Starting in the late 1950s, a bitter competition between China and the Soviet Union became a big factor in North Korean foreign policy. Pyongyang at first sought to avoid getting caught up in the struggle between its two key foreign backers. Kim's resultant need to keep his political distance from both countries reinforced his policy of economic independence and self-reliance. *Juche* was to become a huge success in domestic propaganda, playing to Koreans' strong but battered pride and to the xenophobia that had come to characterize them over a long history often marred by foreign invasions.[88]

The United States had withdrawn most of its own troops after 1953, but had retained enough to serve as a "tripwire." In case the North should invade again, American troops would be bloodied and the United States would be at war again—automatically. The American who served as UN commander also had "operational control" of South Korean troops, which meant that in time of war those troops would serve under the joint command structure.

The North Koreans talked contemptuously of the Americans,[89] but in reality the GIs' presence was a serious obstacle. The Korean War had taught Kim Il-sung caution. After the war, furthermore, Washington had adopted the policy of what Dulles termed "massive retaliation" in case the armistice should fail to hold.[90] A formerly classified April 17, 1954, memorandum by the secretary of the U.S. Joint Chiefs of Staff spells it out: "If hordes of Chinese should attack again, U.S. air support operations, including use of atomic weapons, will be employed to inflict maximum destruction of enemy forces."[91]

Thus did Washington raise over South Korea what came to be called the "nuclear umbrella": the prospect of American nuclear retaliation for even a conventional attack.[92] From the late 1950s Kim watched as the United States introduced into South Korea tactical nuclear weapons, under the control of U.S. forces.[93]

Declassified U.S. documents show Washington's expectation that those new weapons would make Southern leaders feel secure enough to reduce the size of their own bloated, 677,000-man military by about one-tenth. Supporting South Korean troops with aid funds keyed to their numbers, Washington viewed the substitution of nukes for men as a budgetary economy measure. American officials also did not want the South to spend any more of its own

scarce funds on defense. They were concerned because defense spending accounted for 71 percent of the entire South Korean budget. They hoped that
percentage would decline in favor of spending on badly needed economic development initiatives. U.S. officials succeeded in negotiating a troop reduction—but it took months to overcome the obstinate opposition of President
Rhee, who by then was senile but continued to cling tenaciously to power.[94]

While preparations were under way early in 1958 for transferring a
nuclear-capable missile unit to South Korea, Pyongyang issued proposals
similar to those it had pushed at the failed 1954 Geneva conference. They
included simultaneous withdrawal of all foreign troops from the peninsula,
to be followed by a "free, all-Korean election . . . under neutral nation supervision with democratic rights and freedom of activity guaranteed for all
political parties and social organizations." North and South would negotiate
the terms of the election as well as "economic and cultural contacts, and
freedom of movement." The two Koreas' armed forces would be reduced "to
minimum."

The Chinese endorsed the proposals. Both Beijing and Pyongyang
pointed to the U.S. introduction of nuclear weapons to portray themselves as
the champions of peaceful reunification, the South Koreans and Americans
as its opponents. China claimed the United States had been the aggressor in
the Korean War. North Korea repeated that the U.S. military "occupation" of
South Korea was the "fundamental reason" why unification had not come.[95]
A few weeks later, on February 28, 1958, Kim Il-sung and Chinese Premier
Zhou Enlai jointly announced that the Chinese "volunteer" troops, which had
stayed on to protect North Korea against American–South Korean invasion,
would be withdrawn by the end of the year. The Soviet Union quickly endorsed the move—and added a call for de-nuclearizing the Korean peninsula,
Japan and Taiwan.

The United States treated the series of communist announcements as a
somewhat troublesome propaganda ploy, designed to exert pressure for full
American withdrawal. After all, the Chinese troops did not need to stay, in
the absence of an immediate invasion threat from South Korea. If they were
needed, they could come in quickly from across the border in northeastern
China as they had done in 1950.

Official American policy in the face of the Chinese withdrawal was that
"we must maintain our forces in Korea until a satisfactory settlement is
achieved." Such a settlement would be a unification scheme leading to a Korea-
wide government friendly to the United States—meaning noncommunist. In
case of another North Korean invasion of the South, of course, it would have
been time-consuming to get sufficient U.S. forces in from outside. More important, Washington saw the U.S. armed presence as deterring the sort of
Northern attack that had followed by one year the previous withdrawal of
U.S. troops. State Department thinking by this time apparently had reached

the conclusion that the 1949 withdrawal was the key element that had inspired the invasion.[96]

American officials had additional reasons for wanting to stay. They believed that keeping their military establishment in South Korea helped prevent communist subversion. And they thought they needed to keep operational control over the South Korean military, to make sure Rhee would not try to invade the North. Perhaps another reason for staying on was the long-term hope—challenged daily by the unpleasant realities of life under the Rhee regime—that South Korea would achieve a thriving market economy and political democracy. It may seem that keen-eyed observers from afar should have been able to note Kim's emphasis on going it alone and conclude that North Korea was growing out of its Soviet-satellite status. Nevertheless, there was no official Washington talk of pulling out the American troops—no repetition of the late 1940s finding that Korea lacked strategic importance to the United States. "Our own security interests" required the troops to stay pending a settlement, said a State Department memorandum.[97]

Washington continued to see North Korea as a Soviet satellite, also influenced by China but hardly an independent actor. The perception of communism as a monolithic force remained. The Sino-Soviet split and other conflicts among communist countries, representing fundamentally different interests, were yet to come out fully into the open.[98] Realistically, even if U.S. officials had come to perceive North Korea as acting essentially alone there would have been great reluctance to leave South Korea to the mercies of the North after all the blood and wealth Americans had expended in the Korean War.

Beyond that, probably the biggest reason for considering Korea vital to U.S. interests was the expectation that a communist Korea ruled by Kim Il-sung would be hostile to capitalist Japan—which was beginning to fulfill its promise as an engine of economic growth for the noncommunist world. It was not only American officials who felt certain that South Korea's communization would rock Japan. Belief that Korean communism posed a grave danger was and remained a powerfully felt conviction among establishment figures and others in Japan, also.[99] As late as two decades later in a Tokyo conversation with an insider in the ruling Liberal Democratic Party I heard the matter-of-fact prediction that a communist takeover of Korea would shatter Japan's fragile democracy, inspiring a quick reversion to dictatorial rule.[100]

In 1958, when the communists made their proposals, Washington saw them as representing, in part, efforts to drive a wedge between Japan and the United States. At one meeting of top Pentagon brass and State Department officials, discussion turned to Japan's reaction to Chinese troop withdrawal and the de-nuclearization proposal. Although the communist moves were calculated to appeal to the pacifism enshrined in the postwar Japanese constitution, the Tokyo government was disturbed by a belligerent tone in North Korea's references to Japan and the United States. "Since then the Japanese Foreign Office has been anxious of our assessment of the reasons for the Chinese Communist announcement and particularly whether we intend to withdraw our troops from Korea," says a memorandum of the meeting. "If so, the Foreign Office would be most distressed."[101]

Needing to respond somehow to the communist initiative, the Americans called a meeting of the sixteen countries that had contributed forces on the UN side in the Korean War. The sixteen sent the Chinese and North Koreans a note asking "whether, when the North Korean authorities speak of a 'neutral nations organization' to supervise the elections, they accept that these should be held under United Nations auspices." The Chinese responded by accusing the UN group of trying to shift the focus. With Chinese forces being withdrawn, prospects for free elections and a peaceful reunification depended on corresponding withdrawal of the UN forces.[102] Later in 1958, the Chinese dismissed the notion of holding UN-supervised elections. They charged—not without logic—that the United Nations, "under the domination of the United States, has been reduced to a belligerent in the Korean War and has lost all competence and moral authority to deal fairly and reasonably with the Korean question."[103]

The parties were getting nowhere toward the creation of the reunified, democratic Korea that both sides claimed to want. As usual, other priorities intervened. In this case the communist proposals most likely were indeed a ploy. Washington was justified in its concern that withdrawing its troops again would not advance its elections-and-reunification agenda, but merely make it easier for North Korea to carry out its own quite different version. Once the American troops were gone, an American president confronted with a crisis in Korea would find public and congressional opinion far more cautious and cynical than in 1950. The North Koreans knew that a quick, Truman-style intervention would be extremely difficult to arrange the second time around under such circumstances.

Basking in the praise he was hearing from people at home and abroad, and believing that he was gaining on his enemies across the DMZ, Kim took personal credit for the achievements of the period. There was more than a little justification for that, it appears. The 1997 defector Hwang Jang-yop, who had worked closely with Kim as party ideology secretary from 1958 to 1965, described Kim's leadership in glowing terms.

Kim Il-sung "was conscientious, wise and dignified," Hwang wrote. At the weekly party political bureau meeting, held in a meeting room next to his office, the premier "would personally brief the attendants on each item on the agenda and propose alternatives. He used easy words to give a thorough explanation so that there was no room for misunderstanding or question regarding an issue. I thought that whatever he said was reasonable. He fully presented his opinion and then asked the rest of the officials for theirs."

As an example of Kim's determination and persuasive powers once he had made up his mind, Hwang cited a scheme, begun in 1958, in which the premier tried to deal with the consumer goods shortages by having small factories built in the countryside. He assigned them to use whatever resources they could scrape together that might be left over from the big push in heavy industry. In his guidelines, Kim "strongly recommended the employment of women in these factories."

In a patriarchal society, that was revolutionary stuff. At a meeting, recalled Hwang, factory managers said that it would be better to be understaffed than to employ women. After all, women would need paid maternity leave of 90 days (later 150 days). Besides, the managers complained, women "put their children before their work, they talk too much and work too little and they tend to talk behind the supervisor's back."

Kim replied that bringing women into the workplace was not simply a response to the country's labor shortage. "If our women, who make up half our population, all stay home to work in the kitchens, they will lag behind the men in social awareness. Naturally, they will not understand their working husbands and so become a hindrance to their husbands' careers." It was necessary, Kim said, to "liberate our women from the kitchen and turn them into masters of society and the nation."

Thenceforth, Hwang noted, "child care centers, kindergartens and outpatient clinics were set up everywhere so that women need not worry about their children while at work, and this led to the flood of women entering the work force."

It was Kim himself who chose corn as the country's main imported substitute for scarce and prohibitively expensive rice—a choice he apparently made based not on nutritional analysis but on his long experience making do with rice substitutes before 1945. In 1959, according to Hwang, "the issue of importing food was discussed during a political bureau meeting." Kim listened to the discussion for a while before he said: "I've eaten a variety of grains before, and I think the best is corn. How about importing corn?" Hwang remembered being "quite impressed, because it was a judgment only someone who had gone through hard times could make."

According to Hwang, Kim "made policy decisions after taking into consideration the opinions of his subordinates." When the premier started a new project, "he always gathered the party officials to explain his idea first. The secretaries would then write down his idea with more theoretical input and send the document down to the party organizations. And when giving instructions, Kim Il-sung always summoned the official in charge or called him on

the phone. After setting the direction for a task, he left the details of execution to the independent decision of his subordinates. Kim Il-sung made frequent site inspections, from which he derived a lot of ideas. And when
putting one of his ideas into practice, he would test it at a restricted level to
gain more experience before making it the norm. He did not necessarily imi-
tate other countries but tried to make adjustments to suit our situation. Thus
he was not affected by the negative influence of other countries."

Hwang acknowledged that he had "learned a great deal from Kim Il-
sung." The premier "genuinely cared about us secretaries, and told us to accompany him whenever he made his rounds to the factories or farms." When
the aides were able to make time from the press of other duties to accept his
invitations, they found that "Kim Il-sung did a fine job when he went to visit
faraway places to personally guide the workers. He paid attention to the
opinions of the workers or farmers, and did not act in an overbearing manner."[104]

Still, for a dynamo of energy such as Kim Il-sung evidently was during
the 1950s, seemingly no detail of the country's reconstruction was too small
to deserve his "guidance." In July of 1955, visiting the newly built railway
station at Kanggye, he complained that the station signboard was too small—
and so was the greenery. Disdaining the small saplings he found planted
around the station, he said: "You've planted small trees though many good
big trees are available. . . . It'll be long before such young trees grow big
enough for old people to enjoy the view." Thereupon he instructed that the
saplings be replaced with bigger trees.[105]

In another wallow in the nitty-gritty details of running the country, in
January of 1958, Kim met with construction officials to press for increased
housing production through prefabrication. "If you reduce the per-unit rota-
tion time of cranes to seven or eight minutes, finish plastering while the units
are being made in the factories instead of doing it at the construction site,
you'll be able to build houses cheaper and faster," he is supposed to have advised them. The builders, "upholding his teachings," refined their process to
the point they could build an apartment in fourteen minutes—"Pyongyang
speed," as it was called.[106]

Visiting one of the new flats, Kim asked a resident for a critique. At first
the woman gave the formulaic praise, "We are living well with nothing to
worry about, thanks to the State." But Kim noticed that the apartment did
not have heated floors. Getting the woman to relax, he drew from her an acknowledgment that she would have preferred that traditional Korean heating system, called *ondol*. Kim told the construction officials accompanying
him to try to incorporate *ondol* in future apartment projects. Then, using a
measuring stick, the premier criticized the proportions of the rooms. "He
taught them in detail that they had better partition the flat in such an appropriate way as to provide best convenience for the dwellers, and lower the

ceilings a little. . . . He told the building functionaries that they should make the kitchen bigger so that a wife could work at ease there even with a baby on her back. 'Madame, what else do you want me to do?' asked he. 'There is nothing else,'" the woman replied.[107] That is by no means the end of the tales of Kim Il-sung as Great Builder. Telling of one new apartment complex completed in Pyongyang around 1960, for example, Kim reported that he had "personally chosen the site of this block of flats for writers and anti-Japanese revolutionary veterans and had scrutinized its design."

On August 15, 1961, the sixteenth anniversary of liberation from Japanese rule, Kim "looked around the streets of the capital sunk in deep thought," he was to write in his memoirs. "There was an animated holiday atmosphere in the streets. Sungri Street and the People's Army Street, in which the movement to build 20,000 flats was launched, and all the main streets of Pyongyang had been improved with magnificent public buildings and multi-storeyed blocks of flats. In the eight years since the war, tens of thousands of Pyongyang citizens had left their dugouts and moved into the newly-built blocks of flats which were one of the wonderful achievements of postwar construction."

To be sure, Kim added, "the work of construction was only just beginning. As yet, most of the citizens of the capital were still living in shabby dugouts and old-fashioned one-room houses. They had made painful sacrifices and suffered appalling hardships, enduring the crucible of the anti-Japanese and the anti-U.S. wars, trials which no other people in the world had ever experienced. No people in the world had shed so much blood, braved such cold winds and missed so many meals as our people did. For these people we had to build more good houses, make more nice clothes and build more fine schools, holiday homes and hospitals. And we had to bring home more of our compatriots in foreign lands, who yearned for their homeland. This was what I had to do with my life, for the sake of the people. . . . These thoughts kept me awake at night."[108]

SEVEN

When He Hugged Us Still
Damp from the Sea

Kim Il-sung might have gotten even less sleep if he had realized fully the meaning of an event in Seoul three months earlier, on May 16, 1961. Military officers led by Maj. Gen. Park Chung-hee took power in a coup d'etat. The coup snuffed out democratic rule, with which South Korea had been experimenting since Rhee's overthrow the previous year in a student-led revolution. The intensely security-conscious new leaders in Seoul not only cracked down on dissent; they also made it clear very quickly that they would raise higher barriers to inroads by Northern agents and indigenous leftists. That alone would have been bad news for Kim, who counted on subversion to spark the Southern revolution that would pave the way for unification on his terms.

Taking longer to become apparent were some even farther-reaching consequences of Park's ascension to power. Although the North had gotten the jump on the South economically in the post–Korean War period, the military takeover in the South signaled a new phase in their contest. Within a few years Park's authoritarian regime had unleashed Western-trained economists—some of them no less than brilliant—and dynamic business leaders. Their mission: build a market economy modeled on that of Japan, employing close bureaucratic guidance and taking full advantage of a low-cost, hard-working, well-trained labor force. The formula was not too different from the "state capitalism" that Kim Il-sung had rejected as inappropriate for the North. It worked for the South, producing a rapidly wealth-expanding, relatively free economy.[1]

There remained severe problems in the South, to be sure. A populace growing more prosperous, literate and sophisticated increasingly found itself in conflict with the repression that the military-backed dictatorship used to preserve its power. The North cheered Southern dissidents and lost no opportunity to attack Park Chung-hee's legitimacy: the South Korean leader had served during colonial times in the hated Japanese Imperial Army. North Korean propaganda continued to portray the South as a puppet state, where

> the U.S. imperialist aggressors have planted themselves in the top-level places of the exploiters and traitors who ride the people, and lord it over them. In shanties and dugouts the people are bemoaning their poverty and hunger, while the plunderers satiate themselves with the blood and sweat of the people, in their palace-like mansions, indulging in orgies. Brandishing their bayonets, the ruling classes, who control the power and the wealth, oppress the people struggling for liberation and unification at will, making the land one of carnage.[2]

While the South's frequent political turmoil did not derail its astonishingly rapid economic growth, the North started to bump up against the limits of what could be achieved with a command economy.[3]

Meanwhile, facing both real and imagined threats, Kim took it upon himself to militarize the economy to an unprecedented degree. "The turning point," according to Hwang Jang-yop, who was then his ideology secretary, "came in the late 1960s." Disillusioned by both the revisionists in the Soviet Union and the wild leftists then launching the Cultural Revolution in China, Kim Il-sung "decided that his party had to rely on its own strength to liberate South Korea and achieve reunification."[4] Accordingly Kim began his militarization campaign.

Although militarism would, over time, cripple the civilian economy, North Korea in the '60s still enjoyed some momentum. As late as 1965 the North's $292 per capita GNP was more than three times the South's $88, according to one set of estimates.[5] Those were the golden years of North Korean life, to hear former residents reminisce. In the 1950s and '60s, "even though it was difficult to have an easy and comfortable lifestyle, at least the rations came regularly—never delayed," Lee Ok-keum, who was born in 1949 and defected to the South with her husband and family in 1994, told me. "There were actually goods made in North Korea that you could buy in the stores— clothing, material, underwear, candy."

As South Korean economic growth accelerated, growth rates in the North gradually declined. While the multi-year state economic plans of the late 1940s and the mid- to late '50s were deemed to have achieved their goals more or less as planned, growth from then on failed to meet planners' expectations. The first "seven-year plan," begun in 1961, dragged on for three extra years. Subsequent plans likewise could not be completed without extensions of two or three years.

Those disappointing results came despite a series of campaigns and mass movements intended to wring greater output from the economy. Kim's Chollima movement had brought serious confusion around 1959, when planners misallocated resources to various sectors of the economy. Quality of production dropped, and eager-to-please economic units turned in inflated claims for their quantitative production. Kim added incentives, short of money bonuses. He combined ideological indoctrination with prizes, including free vacations, and awards of medals and honorific titles for exceeding production quotas. Those incentives proved insufficient.[6]

Kim's "Tae-an work system," named for a power plant he was visiting in 1961 when he gave the instructions, was supposed to reduce bureaucratic inefficiency. In practice, it focused all power in party secretaries who, in turn, represented the will of the Great Leader. Hwang Jang-yop, who held high posts in both the party and the administration before he defected in 1997, explained how it worked:

> Say the prime minister has given a certain factory manager some instructions. The factory manager will immediately report to the factory party committee and follow the committee's instructions. . . . The prime minister does not have the authority to give instructions to the factory party committee. The factory party committee will deliberate on whether or not the prime minister's instructions are commensurate with the will of the Great Leader, and if it decides not, then it will not carry out those instructions but report to its supervising party committee and await instructions from there before proceeding any further.

Hwang further illustrated his point by noting that as president of Kim Il-sung University he had held cabinet ministerial status. "I was also the Speaker of the Supreme People's Assembly and member of the party's central committee, and was therefore one notch above the rest of the cabinet ministers. Thus, in terms of status in the party and the state, the party secretary supervising the university was far below me. And still all power in the university was in the hands of the party secretary, and the university president was under his command." The Tae-an work system, Hwang said, "only served to paralyze the creativity and spontaneity of administrative and economic officials and legitimize the bureaucracy of party officials."[7]

Economic strength translates into political and military power. Park Chung-hee's reinvigoration of the Southern economy meant that the South now would have a shot at achieving ultimate reunification on its terms. The contest was becoming clearer. Most Koreans believed that reunification was inevitable sooner or later. One possibility now was that the South, by overtaking and overwhelming the North economically, would set the stage for a demoralized North to fall into its lap. The other possibility—that the North would win the prize by patiently pursuing its tactics of subversion, then intervening in a moment of Southern weakness to help communize the South—depended on dislodging or neutralizing the South's U.S. backers.

After using the term *juche* in 1955 to describe his self-reliant policy,[8] Kim had said little about it for a while. By the early 1960s, though, Kim was tilting toward the Beijing side in the Sino-Soviet dispute. Khrushchev in Moscow was promoting the line that communist countries should de-emphasize military preparations. Instead they should focus on peaceful competition with capitalist countries to develop their economies. Moscow assured the smaller communist countries that they need not worry; the nuclear-armed might of the Soviet superpower deterred Western attack.

To Kim such talk had one highly unwelcome meaning: He could expect no help from the Soviet Bloc in a forcible reunification of Korea. The notion of peaceful coexistence—whether the Soviet Union's coexistence with the hated imperialist Americans or North Korea's coexistence with South Korea—was anathema to him as it had been since the 1950s.[9] He still had on his agenda the big-ticket items of pushing the Americans to withdraw their troops, fomenting a Southern revolution and unifying Korea under his rule. (As an official biography put it, he was "leading to victory the revolutionary struggles of the South Korean people, to sweep away U.S. imperialism and its agents, and the struggle of the entire Korean people for national unification."[10])

In 1963, under such circumstances, Kim picked up the theme of *juche* again. Afterward he never tired of talking about it. "In a nutshell," according to Kim, *juche* means "having the attitude of master toward revolution and construction in one's own country." It means "refraining from dependence upon others." It means "using your own brains, believing your own strength and displaying the revolutionary spirit of self-reliance, and thus solving your own problems for yourself on your own responsibility under all circumstances." Kim went on to emphasize the importance for any socialist country of "applying the universal principles of Marxism-Leninism and the experience of other countries to suit the historical conditions and national peculiarities of your own country."[11] In other words: Don't let Moscow or Beijing pull your strings.

In the end, however, *juche*, Kim's homegrown twist, was to prove just as limiting for the North's economic growth as the Stalinist-style planned economy. The limitations were to become especially apparent in view of what Park Chung-hee was starting to do in the South. The Korean peninsula's own natural resources were concentrated in the North, out of the Southerners' grasp.

Even if that had not been the case, the peninsula—lacking petroleum and another industrial essential, coking coal—could not be self-sufficient and therefore could never be completely self-reliant. The Southerners turned to international trade, at the opposite pole from *juche*. They would import the basic commodities, then reprocess them using borrowed capital and cheap local labor. Finally, they would export the finished products.

In 1965, South Korea normalized relations with Japan, which provided $300 million in grants and $200 million in loans as compensation for damages inflicted during the colonial period. That money, plus enhanced business ties with Japan, gave South Korea a running start toward the "miracle" that was to make it the leader of Asia's fast-developing "tiger" economies. According to one analysis, the South's growth rate outpaced the North's from 1966—and in 1976 the South's per capita GNP surpassed that of the North for the first time.[12]

After somewhat de-emphasizing the military following the Korean War, Kim Il-sung in the 1960s resumed with a vengeance the policy of building up his armed forces.[13] While the psychic costs are hard to measure, it is clear enough that Kim's growing obsession with security was terribly expensive in economic development terms. His policy of maintaining military superiority over the far more populous South proved to be a crushing burden—and, in the long run, countercompetitive.[14]

Many South Korean and Western analysts argued that the militarization drive represented nothing but Kim's continuing dream of military conquest of the South. The North, on the other hand, always maintained that it arose from the prospect that South Korea and its American backers would start a new war and Pyongyang would have to defend itself.[15] My view is that Kim's policy combined offensive and defensive elements—although his defensive concerns to a large extent represented his fears of the consequences of his offensive policies. Despite military alliances with China and the USSR, and Khrushchev's assurances of protection, Kim feared he might not be able to count on allies to rescue him in case his contest with the South should lead to renewed war with the Americans. Without an impenetrable defense, he could not feel secure in taking offensive measures.

Kim became downright nervous from the early 1960s as he was finding it difficult to get along with his Soviet allies. An opportunity for a second southward strike came during the confusion of the South Korean student uprising against Rhee in April of 1960. Both China and Russia urged against acting, however, according to Hwang Jang-yop's reported later testimony. The Pyongyang leadership lacked the stomach to go it alone, particularly since it had just finished rebuilding the country from the ruins of the first Korean War.[16]

In 1962, U.S. President John F. Kennedy went eyeball-to-eyeball with Khrushchev in the Cuban Missile Crisis; it was the Russian who blinked, agreeing to eliminate the Soviet missile bases in Cuba that had sparked the crisis. Kim Il-sung's growing concern that he could not depend on his biggest supposed backer in the communist world inspired a major round of diplomacy to find friends among the smaller communist and Third World countries.

Just as he split with Moscow over its challenge to the doctrine of continuing revolution, so Kim eventually turned on Beijing—for failing to put aside its own disputes with Moscow in the interest of the Vietnamese revolution.[17] Before that dispute could be cooled off, Chinese Red Guards would attack Kim's very un-communist lifestyle, deriding him as "fat," a "counterrevolutionary," "a millionaire, an aristocrat and a leading bourgeois element in Korea."[18]

Meanwhile, American attempts to remove Fidel Castro in Cuba and to defeat the Viet Cong made Kim wonder if he might be next. His attitude was not mere paranoia. In addition to whatever concern he felt over the new U.S. tactical nuclear weapons, he had to worry about less direct means the United States and South Korea were using to attack his regime. While the North Koreans hoped to subvert South Korea, that was also precisely what South Korea and its American backers hoped to do to North Korea. As a control measure, the Soviet occupation regime in the 1940s had initiated what proved to be a pattern of North Korean isolation that would last for decades. Washington sought to intensify that isolation as part of its efforts to exert pressure that might cause the Northern system to break down.[19]

The installation of the new, military-backed regime across the DMZ in South Korea in 1961 certainly did not ease Kim's worries on this score. It was around that time that Kim draped over the North a shroud of secrecy and exclusivity comparable to the centuries of isolationism that had preceded the nineteenth century opening to the West and earned Korea the sobriquet "hermit kingdom."[20] A large part of his objective clearly was to make the population inaccessible to propaganda and other subversion efforts. While the South Koreans and Americans liked to imagine that isolation would threaten his rule, Kim believed that even more isolation was the way to preserve his system. In more than four decades to come, he was never proved wrong about that.

The change Kim put into effect was dramatic. During Rumanian diplomat Izidor Urian's first stay in Pyongyang, from 1954 to 1959, "the people in North Korea treated me kindly and I could meet people freely. At that time I was allowed to travel freely almost anywhere in North Korea." Urian returned to Pyongyang in 1963 and found quite a different atmosphere. Even diplomats dispatched from friendly communist countries such as his were confined to the capital and permitted only minimal contact with North Koreans. Without special permits they could visit only a few sites such as a swimming pool at Nampo, west of Pyongyang, and a Kim Il-sung museum at Mount Myohyang, some 150 kilometers north of the capital. Urian later wrote that from 1963 he "managed to meet government officials only in the Foreign Affairs Ministry and some other departments, and a few reporters." Until he ended his duties in Pyongyang in 1983, he had no further chances to meet ordinary people in Pyongyang. Even at banquets for foreigners, the North Koreans kept to themselves instead of mixing with their guests.[21]

If resident and visiting Rumanians and Cubans felt themselves isolated and restricted in Pyongyang, citizens of Western countries were barred, for the most part, from even entering North Korea in the first place. For them and for the South Koreans, the battles above the 38th parallel in the Korean War would prove to have been the last chance to glimpse North Korea for decades. Even if they should manage to get in, they would encounter a population trained to tell them nothing.

Feeling a need to know what was happening in the North, but finding human intelligence increasingly hard to come by, Washington and Seoul resorted to electronic and photographic surveillance by plane and ship.[22]

Some analysts have sought to explain what was happening in North Korea almost entirely in terms of the threat facing the country from the nuclear-armed American forces and their South Korean colleagues. Indeed, the North Koreans were being pushed extremely hard. In the end, though, the argument is not convincing. Other countries have felt themselves under siege without going to such extremes of self-isolation, of one-man rule systematically built on enormous lies and on whipping up mass hatred.[23] Whatever they were telling their people, for propaganda purposes, about diabolical American schemes, could Pyongyang's leaders really not understand that the American nuclear weapons were in Korea to deter the North from provoking or starting another war? From the other side it seemed clear that the weapons were there precisely because the United States had no desire to fight another full-fledged war—much less (for the time being, at least) initiate one. Washington just as obviously was determined to keep Seoul from sparking a Second Korean War.

Whatever threat he might have felt from American and South Korean subversion and espionage efforts, Kim Il-sung was doing his share of threatening. In September 1961, he sounded an anti-American theme, calling upon South Koreans to reject military service, to struggle against U.S. military bases and to shut down factories with strikes and sabotage. Simultaneously he ordered reconstruction of a communist party in the South. In 1964, an underground revolutionary group, the Revolutionary Party for Reunification, was founded in the South with a twelve-point program that read very much like the program of South Vietnam's National Liberation Front. The party had the mission of attracting Southerners, particularly intellectuals, to the communist movement under Kim Il-sung's leadership.

Having failed to take advantage of the South Korean student revolution in 1960, or to prevent the military coup of 1961, Kim appears to have been determined to be ready the next time opportunity might knock. In December 1962 the North Korean party leadership formally raised military preparation to equal status with economic development, citing both the international situation and South Korea's "acute crisis."[24]

As the North Korean military built its strength, its soldiers involved themselves increasingly in small-scale assaults on the enemy along the DMZ. One theory was that those clashes were intended for domestic consumption—to keep tensions high. Thus, the regime could justify the sacrifices being made to build up the military at a time when strained relations with the Soviet Union also contributed to economic hardship.[25] Border skirmishes became especially frequent starting in 1967 when the number of reported incidents exceeded 550—a tenfold increase over the 1966 figure. Between 1967 and 1969, thirty-eight Americans were killed and 144 wounded, with South Korean casualties in proportional numbers.[26]

No doubt there was a connection between North Korea's redoubled militancy and the Vietnam War. Kim Il-sung decried the massive U.S. commitment in Indochina as imperialism at its worst. From 1965, South Korean troops were dispatched to take some of the burden off the Americans—and to give the South Korean soldiers valuable combat experience. Kim followed suit, dispatching fighter planes and pilots to Vietnam. At the same time, though, the Vietnamese quagmire was a distraction of his enemies of the sort Kim had been awaiting. Weakening those enemies would be one dividend from his own support of the Vietnamese communists. Kim's identification with Ho Chi Minh and his close ties with North Vietnam suggest that Hanoi's strategy for liberating South Vietnam impressed him as valid for use against South Korea, if sufficient preparations could be made.[27]

Apparently hoping to reduce South Korea to leaderless chaos, and thus to set in motion a social revolution that would pave the way for unification under his regime, Kim unleashed a bold terrorist plot. In January of 1968, thirty-one Korean People's Army commandos crossed the DMZ disguised as South Korean soldiers. Their orders were to assassinate South Korean President Park, and they had memorized the floor plans of the Blue House, the presidential palace. On the way, they happened upon some South Korean woodcutters, who guessed their identities. Overruling others in the group who wanted to kill them, the commando leader let the woodcutters go with a warning not to report what they had seen. That bit of generosity proved fatal to the mission. The woodcutters reported the sighting to the South Korean authorities. The commandos entered Seoul and got within one kilometer of the Blue House, where police intercepted them on the night of January 21. Most of the commandos were killed, with only a few escaping back through the mountains.

Earlier that same day, off North Korea's east coast port of Wonsan, a North Korean sub-chaser had spotted the *Pueblo,* a small, only perfunctorily armed U.S. Navy spy ship on its maiden voyage. Outfitted with sophisticated electronic gear, the *Pueblo* was checking up on North Korean coastal defenses, trying to pinpoint the locations, missions and frequencies of North Korean radar installations. Such intelligence could help the Americans prepare to jam or trick those radars in the event of another war. The ship was also monitoring coded communications, to gather material for code breakers in Washington, and listening in on noncoded communications that might help in evaluating North Korean forces' order of battle, equipment and morale. Oceanographers on board were gathering information on the waters off North Korea.

Unaware of the aborted assassination attempt in Seoul and the way it had quite suddenly heightened tensions in Korea, the *Pueblo*'s skipper continued with his mission. Cdr. Lloyd M. Bucher was confident the ship was in international waters and, therefore, in no danger. However, on January 23, North Korean warships fired on the *Pueblo.* Overwhelmingly outgunned, Bucher did not return the fire but concentrated on evasive action, while his crewmen destroyed sensitive gear and data. His radioman alerted the U.S. Air Force, and help was supposed to be on the way. However, no American rescuers were actually dispatched. President Lyndon B. Johnson reportedly said to a *Time* magazine correspondent during the first day of the crisis: "If we started sending gunboats out to protect everybody gathering information we'd have a budget of $500 billion every year. That harassment is part of the job."[28]

With himself and three of his men wounded, one of them so critically that he would die soon, Bucher surrendered his ship. It was the first surrender of a U.S. Navy ship in peacetime since that of the USS *Chesapeake* in 1807— and the *Chesapeake*'s skipper had given up only after firing "one gun for the honor of the flag."[29] The attackers took the *Pueblo* into port and held its crew, charging that they had been spying inside North Korean territorial waters. The crew members, blindfolded, were marched off the ship toward a waiting bus. Along the way they were subjected to the shouts and blows of hundreds of civilians lined up on either side of the road.[30]

In a meeting at the truce village of Panmunjom, the United States protested first the Blue House raid and then the *Pueblo*'s seizure, demanding immediate return of the vessel and men. The North Korean representative, Maj. Gen. Pak Chung-kuk, replied,

Our saying goes, "A mad dog barks at the moon." . . . I cannot but pity you who are compelled to behave like a hooligan, disregarding even your age and honor to accomplish the crazy intentions of the war maniac Johnson for the sake of bread and dollars to keep your life. In order to sustain your life, you probably served Kennedy, who is already sent to hell. If you want to escape from the same fate of Kennedy, who is now a putrid corpse, don't indulge yourself desperately in invective.

Rear Adm. John Victor Smith, the senior U.S. representative in Panmunjom, at a hearing much later was to testify in kind that the North Koreans were "only one step above animals." While meeting with Pak, though, he had to content himself for the moment with blowing cigar smoke in his antagonist's face. Smith believed that the assassination attempt in Seoul, followed in such quick succession by the *Pueblo*'s seizure, showed that Kim Il-sung wanted war.[31]

Higher-ranking U.S. officials, having failed to stop the seizure of the ship while it was in progress, meanwhile were frustrated by their inability to come up with a plan to help the eighty-two imprisoned crewmen and, at the same time, punish Pyongyang for its effrontery. Hawkish politicians wanted to go to war.[32] By 1968, to a considerable extent, the nuclear option had come to dominate American thinking about Korean security. One reported reason why the U.S. Air Force did not go to the aid of the *Pueblo* during the North Korean attack was that the seven F-4s it had based in South Korea were all loaded with nuclear weapons. But some Americans were ready to use such weapons. Congressman L. Mendel Rivers, chairman of the House Armed Services Committee, called for a nuclear bombing of one North Korean city. "Bomb, bomb, bomb," he demanded.[33] Even some of the captured crewmen said later that they had hoped for American nuclear retaliation against the North Koreans.[34] In South Korea, too, newspapers and officials called upon the United States to help avenge the Blue House raid—and perhaps unify the country in the process.

Johnson called up reserve military units but in the end decided against a military response. Top officials dismissed not only nuclear warfare but also even conventional options—bombings, shellings, unleashing the angry South Koreans for a battalion-sized raid across the DMZ. Any such action would be unlikely to help get the *Pueblo*'s crew back safely, and would risk inspiring Soviet or Chinese retaliation that could lead to another world war. The South Koreans considered attacking with their own aircraft, but the problem was that their airfields were "soft"—unprotected, vulnerable to attack—while the North's airfields had been hardened. In the end Seoul agreed to exercise restraint in exchange for a U.S. promise of $100 million in aid, which was directed mainly to preventing future infiltration from the North.[35]

After thirty-six hours of imprisonment, beatings and torture, Bucher signed a "confession" that the North Koreans had written in stilted English. The captors were not satisfied with that early effort. Backing their demands with coercion, for the next eleven months they kept insisting on increasingly abject confessions and statements. The Americans sometimes submitted — but they inserted inside jokes in those documents to reassure people at home that their confessions were not sincere but coerced. Required to list partners and mentors in espionage, they kept straight faces as they named the likes of comic strip character Buzz Sawyer and television spy Maxwell Smart. One statement purporting to admit that the *Pueblo* had violated North Korean waters was, unbeknownst to the North Koreans, a direct quotation from the legal definition of rape: "Penetration, however slight, is sufficient to complete the act."

In what could pass as a metaphor for the decades-long history of Americans and North Koreans talking past one another, *Pueblo* crew members in a press conference mimicked the bombastic formulations of their captors to poke fun at the uncomprehending North Koreans. The Americans spoke longingly of "our motherland," of returning to "the bosom of the fatherland." Such stunts backfired when *Time* ran a photo of *Pueblo* captives extending their middle fingers. The magazine explained that this was "the U.S. hand signal of derisiveness and contempt." That was an unpleasant surprise for Pyongyang, since crewmen had described the gesture as a Hawaiian good-luck sign. The crew's treatment during the following week, according to its commander, was "the most concentrated form of terror that I've ever seen or dreamed is possible."[36]

The *Pueblo*'s crew members finally got their freedom on December 23, 1968, after U.S. officials hit on a formula for agreement with North Korea. It was a bizarre formula indeed. Maj. Gen. Gilbert H. Woodward, the senior U.S. representative at Panmunjom, signed a document that day admitting illegal intrusion and espionage in North Korean waters, apologizing for the *Pueblo*'s actions and assuring Pyongyang that no U.S. ships would intrude again. But before signing it, the American general announced:

> The position of the United States government with regard to the *Pueblo* . . . has been that the ship was not engaged in illegal activities and that there is no convincing evidence that the ship at any time intruded into the territorial waters claimed by North Korea, and that we could not apologize for actions which we did not believe took place. The document which I am going to sign was prepared by the North Koreans and is at variance with the above position. My signature will not and cannot alter the facts. I will sign the document to free the crew and only to free the crew.

In other words, General Woodward was telling the world that the document he was about to sign was nothing but an expedient lie. But the North Koreans did not mind that part. "It satisfied their one condition, a signature on a piece of paper," the general explained to an interviewer later. "Never mind the oral repudiation. In the Orient, you know, nothing is more important than the written word. Besides, the North Korean people would never hear about that repudiation. Their propaganda boys would take care of that. As for the rest of the world, well, they just didn't care." Or as Secretary of State Dean Rusk put it, "Apparently the North Koreans believe there is propaganda value even in a worthless document. It is a strange procedure. The North Koreans would have to explain it. I know of no precedent in my nineteen years of public service."[37]

Why did Pyongyang seize the *Pueblo*? Perhaps fear of retaliation for the Blue House raid further inflamed an already increasingly bellicose attitude in Pyongyang. Or was the seizure coolly calculated, as a diversionary maneuver and perhaps as a test of U.S. resolve? Even declassified U.S. government documents from the period have failed to clarify North Korean motivation. State Department historians can only note that some U.S. intelligence estimates and reports "suggest that Pyongyang saw the Vietnam War as an opportunity to challenge the United States, knowing that the United States was overextended in Southeast Asia and lacked the ability to respond. The North Koreans could have hoped to disrupt relations between Washington and Seoul or, perhaps, to have started a series of events that might have paved the way for the collapse of South Korea, thus succeeding where the Blue House raid failed."[38]

Perhaps it is more useful to ask what the North Koreans gained from the incident, regardless of whether they planned it that way. Besides humiliating the United States and distracting attention from their own deadly intrusion into South Korea, they were able to drive at least a small wedge between Seoul and Washington. That came about when the United States—which did not officially recognize their country's existence—negotiated with North Korean officials directly on the issue at Panmunjom, without South Korean participation.

No doubt, too, Kim Il-sung and company learned several very important lessons about American preparedness, unity and resolve. One was that Washington's trigger finger—seventeen years after Truman had intervened in the Korean War, and midway through a new and more frustrating and divisive Asian land war—was not as itchy as some might have imagined. When it came to nuclear weapons, there was much greater reluctance to push the button, even with provocation. It was possible from Pyongyang's perspective to see in the United States a muscle-bound opponent, a foe unable to use his strength effectively. Over time, with cleverness and patience, even American nuclear weapons could be made to lose their deterrent power.

Another lesson was that the U.S. government was in such bad repute with its own people, over Vietnam especially, that some Americans were ready to believe the North Korean version of events, including the *Pueblo* crew's coerced confessions. Never mind that the official U.S. denials were backed by radio intercepts, in which North Korean ships about to be involved in the attack on the *Pueblo* gave their locations as outside North Korean waters.[39] In coming years, segments of American public opinion could (and did) prove more receptive than in the past to viewpoints at least somewhat sympathetic to North Korea.

Pyongyang surely pondered with great interest the overriding American concern for the safety of the crew. No doubt an element of timing heightened that concern. The *Pueblo* incident began just as public protest over the war in Indochina was reaching a peak of intensity. Americans were in no mood to send young warriors to die in another part of far-off Asia, and especially without clear purpose. The priority that the United States put on safeguarding its military men found reflection in actions ranging from Bucher's decision to surrender the ship—without firing even one shot, and before the last of the sensitive materials aboard could be destroyed—up to Washington officials' shying away from any military action that might endanger the captives. As President Johnson heatedly vowed to an aide, the United States would "do anything to get those men back—including meeting naked in the middle of the street at high noon, if that's what it takes."[40]

A country may be more civilized when the safety of members of the armed forces starts to become more important than the policy objectives they are sent to fight for, but there is a price to pay: Even the might of a superpower loses deterrent value. That is especially true regarding an enemy who has no qualms about sending men on a virtual suicide mission, such as the Blue House raid.

No wonder navy traditionalists were dismayed with Bucher's conduct. The commander "could have been the greatest hero in the history of the U.S. Navy," said one American admiral who participated in the navy's court of inquiry into the *Pueblo* case. "For a commanding officer to do anything other than guard his ship with his life is indefensible. I'll admit it takes guts; that's what you gotta have. The thought of saving his crew is interesting, humane, but it had nothing at all to do with the job he was assigned to do." Said another: "If he had only fired one shot it would have made all the difference. Just one little bitty squirt of machine-gun fire, and that whole thing might have been over. They might not have had that boarding party in the first place."[41]

They did have that boarding party, however, and the most immediate lesson Pyongyang apparently drew from the *Pueblo* incident was that it could mount a significant but limited attack on American forces and get away with it. Fifteen months after the capture of the *Pueblo*, North Korean forces shot down an unarmed American EC-121 reconnaissance plane.[42] For decades the North Korean regime would show off the *Pueblo* as a shrine recalling its triumph over "the most vicious enemy in the world."[43]

Both the seizure of the *Pueblo* and the shooting down of the EC-121 were high-risk gambles in which Kim was prepared to deal with whatever response might issue from the United States. In both cases, according to reported later testimony by a North Korean official who defected to the South, the authorities believed war might be imminent, sent civilians to shelters and prepared the military to fight.[44]

By 1970, although he had gotten nowhere with his efforts to undermine and "liberate" the South, Kim Il-sung was determined that his people must try all the harder and must be ready to "battle staunchly at any time to force the U.S. imperialists out of South Korea and carry the revolutionary cause of national unification through to the end." Meanwhile, he was able to report that the North had been thoroughly fortified and its entire people armed. "In our country, everyone knows how to fire a gun and carries a gun with him," Kim boasted.[45]

Concern over the North's machinations helped to stimulate an authoritarian crackdown by the Park regime on the South Korean populace.[46] There was a chance that the South, under too tight a lid, would boil up. Kim Il-sung needed to ensure that American support for the South would not be automatic, in case a popular uprising against Park Chung-hee or other signs of Southern weakness should make South Korea once again a tempting target for Northern military intervention.

Kim knew that removing South Korea's U.S. protection would also remove the restraints the Americans exerted on the South's military. Yet he wanted the Americans out. Clearly he was willing to risk the chance that their absence would encourage Southern generals to choose war as the means of uniting their fractious populace. Having hardened his defenses in an effort to make them impenetrable, he would hope to repel any Southern attack, quickly shift to the offense and prevail—in a straight North-South fight, with no meddling by foreign forces that might be inclined to turn the Second Korean War into a nuclear war.

It is not that Kim actively sought another war at the time, after the years of grueling effort his subjects had put into rebuilding their shattered country. Plan A, apparently, still was to reunify via subversion of the South. But if Plan A should fail and Plan B, another war, be required, sooner was better than later for Kim. He could not afford to wait too long while an advancing Southern economy overtook the North. "The whole party and the entire people should buckle down to a further acceleration of war preparations," he said. They must strictly guard against the "trend of war phobia, to prevent it from infiltrating into our ranks."[47]

The Vietnam-inspired "war phobia" that was developing in the United States, on the other hand, seemed a favorable development for Kim, to the extent it would require Washington to rethink its global policeman role. Korea became a focal point of the U.S. debate, as the only place in Asia besides Indochina where Americans had fought a land war and one of the most likely places for another to break out. Hoping to help the Americans talk themselves out of Korea, Kim adopted—for outside consumption, especially—a less confrontational stance.[48]

Among American scholars of the period, intellectual heir's to '50s revisionist I. F. Stone advanced the argument that Truman and his aides had intentionally exaggerated the danger posed by the June 1950 North Korean invasion of the South. Some critics spied a conspiracy to win popular and congressional support for a war that was—like Vietnam—peripheral to genuine American security interests (not to mention unwinnable). Truman had "deliberately created a sense of impending disaster," one historian charged.[49]

The parallels between the wars in Korea and Vietnam, wrote another scholar-critic, "are numerous. In both cases the United States backed corrupt and unpopular governments, preferring to believe that 'international order' was more important than the legitimate nationalism of the peoples involved." In Korea, from an American standpoint, "non-intervention would have brought welcome consequences. First, the Chinese civil war would have ended with the liberation of Taiwan. And then, in all probability, Washington and Peking would have reached a working relationship. . . ." Instead, "the political price that Koreans have paid for the American intervention has been autocracy throughout the peninsula based upon the mutual fears of the two governments."[50]

One pair of Korea scholars who focused on the Vietnam comparison found it remarkable that "whereas the Vietnamese and Ho Chi Minh inspired considerable sympathy in the West, the nature and credentials of the Korean revolution were completely ignored. . . . No students charged through the streets of Berkeley shouting, 'Kim, Kim, Kim Il-sung.' "[51]

Vietnam-era critics had little but contempt for Washington's claim that its support for South Korea equated to defending freedom in a society that was evolving toward democracy. One American scholar saw the Park Chung-hee regime as "a police state with but a few trappings—the 'formal institutions' of constitutional government—to avoid foreign criticism." As for the economic gains then becoming apparent in the South, they were distributed unevenly, he wrote. "In a mixed capitalist system, without pressure from below, the chances of Korean workers and farmers getting a fair share of the increased wealth appear remote. It is more probable that they will be caught in a police state vise, working long hours for low wages, while the profits go to foreign capitalists and a small ruling elite in South Korea."[52]

In the late 1960s, several younger-generation Korea scholars of like mind helped to form the Committee of Concerned Asian Scholars, challenging more conservative academic colleagues to drop their support—active or passive—for "an Asian policy committed to ensuring American domination of much of Asia."[53] In the introduction to a book of essays, several of them contributed by fellow members of the committee, a leading spirit of that group issued a blanket dismissal of the fruits of North Korea studies in the United States as of the early 1970s. "On the one hand, career anti-communists dominate the field," he wrote. On the other hand, "the independent, objective, Korean-born researcher" would fear to tell the whole truth because of pressure from the South Korean Central Intelligence Agency, "including pressure on relatives in South Korea." For such researchers, "self-censorship prevented unbiased or sympathetic research on North Korea."[54]

A number of the concerned scholars believed that the United States must abandon South Korea. As one wrote, "The risk of being involved in another phase of the Korean civil war, the endless cost of providing weapons and military aid to South Korea and of keeping U.S. forces there, and the embarrassing dictatorial methods of the Park government all argue for an end to U.S. involvement."[55] Some Vietnam-era critics who harbored extremely negative views of South Korea adopted the logic that since the South was so horrible the North must be wonderful, or at least better than the South.[56]

The revisionists often started from a romantic, very '60s and '70s view of revolution and socialist egalitarianism. Several were scholar-activists who identified themselves with the "New Left." Not surprisingly, their arguments resonated among anti-establishment young people, in particular. The movement was by no means restricted to the radical fringes, however. Influential establishment news media organizations that came to take critical stances against the Vietnam War also eventually adopted some of the revisionists' positions on Korea.

The war allergy that developed in the United States during the late 1960s and became unmistakably apparent at the time of the *Pueblo* incident remained deeply ingrained in the American psyche. Dubbed "Vietnam syndrome," it persisted as a major constraint on Washington's policy makers at least until September 11, 2001. Only after militant Islamists in hijacked airliners killed thousands of American civilians in their suicide bombings of the World Trade Center in New York and the Pentagon in Washington did polls finally show public opinion swinging decisively in favor of sending fighting men to risk their lives in battle.

EIGHT

Flowers of His Great Love
Are Blooming

Early in the 1970s, domestic issues began to distract Kim Il-sung from his long-term mission of unifying Korea. Economic problems were becoming more and more apparent in the North. Of even more concern to Kim, as his sixtieth birthday approached, was his determination to arrange his own succession in such a way as to ensure the survival throughout his own lifetime and afterward of the system and ideology that he had instituted.

Fortuitously, in August 1971, the South Korean Red Cross proposed a meeting with its Northern counterpart to discuss the problems of divided families—locating relatives, getting information to the other side about their condition and, finally, arranging reunions. The proposal had much to do with domestic political considerations in the South, where Park Chung-hee was at a crucial stage in consolidating his regime. By showing himself ready to talk with the North, Park hoped to improve his standing with a restive South Korean populace regarding the explosive issues of unification and nationalism. Pyongyang and Seoul had been talking past each other for decades, so there was no assurance that the North would accept—or that the Southern side really expected it to accept.[1] But because Kim Il-sung needed some breathing room, the Northern side did agree to meet.

After preliminary talks had proceeded for nearly a year, Park Chung-hee sent his director of central intelligence, Lee Hu-rak, on a secret mission to Pyongyang to talk with Kim Il-sung and his younger brother, Kim Yong-ju, who then ran the Workers' Party's powerful Organization and Guidance

Department. The North in turn sent an envoy, Pak Song-chol, to talk with the South Korean president and other officials in Seoul. On July 4, 1972, North and South issued a joint communiqué that called for peaceful reunification without external interference and a reconciliation of North and South that would transcend ideological and institutional differences. Meanwhile they pledged steps to ease tension: an end to mutual slander and abuse, prevention of inadvertent military incidents and installation of a telephone hot line between Seoul and Pyongyang. A South-North Coordinating Committee would work on carrying out these agreements.

In 1971 and 1972, the United States brought home one of its two infantry divisions based in South Korea. That was in line with President Richard Nixon's Guam Doctrine, which held that Americans should shoulder a lesser burden in ground defense of their Asian allies—and that the allies should increase their own ground-defense preparations correspondingly. The new U.S. policy also may have reflected Pyongyang's apparent shift toward a less confrontational policy.[2]

The attempt to reach a North-South accommodation was short-lived. As was to become the pattern, South Korea proposed dealing first with economic and social issues. The two sides would build mutual confidence by solving some of those and then gradually work up to the ultimate, far knottier political and military issues. North Korea insisted on getting straight to the military issues. When South Korea refused to discuss the withdrawal of the rest of the U.S. troops, the North, its eyes back on the main goal, maintained that such a foreign presence interfered with the mutual pledge to unify "without outside intervention." After three plenary sessions alternating between the respective capitals, North Korea called off the dialogue in August 1973. The United States that year toughened its standing plan for responding to any new invasion of the South.[3]

Kim had not given up on diplomacy. He engaged in a contest with South Korea to secure diplomatic recognition and support from as many countries as possible, useful in rounding up UN votes. To that end Pyongyang held Kim up as a beacon to the numerous underdeveloped countries of the Third World, wooing them with aid and urging them to emulate North Korean policies and practices. In 1975, North Korea managed to gain admittance to their principal forum, the Non-Aligned Movement.

Could Pyongyang really afford an extensive foreign aid program? There are indications that the regime eventually had cause to regret its generosity. Kang Myong-do, who had been a member of the Pyongyang elite, said after his defection to the South that excessive aid to Third World countries had caused an actual worsening of North Korea's own already serious economic problems. Kim, he said, basically had given leaders of African countries such as Algeria, Tanzania and Zaire whatever they had requested—tractors and other machinery, dam construction, weapons, presidential mansions. "For

Madagascar Kim Il-sung armed the entire army," Kang said. "That's why they call Madagascar the second North Korea."[4]

Jimmy Carter won the U.S. presidency in November 1976 after campaigning on a proposal to bring all American troops home from South Korea. Park Chung-hee's military dictatorship had achieved impressive economic development but many Southerners had been left behind, for the time being. Park's government kept a very tight rein on protest and was growing increasingly unpopular both at home and among human-rights advocates in the United States.

The Carter troop withdrawal plan was music to Kim Il-sung's ears. In the new atmosphere characterized by Vietnam syndrome, the American public might very well veto any proposal to go to war to defend South Korea from a second Northern attack—unless American troops were among the first casualties. The South Korean regime all through the 1970s had been lobbying hard in the United States to keep the troops. The effort was carried on with considerable savvy, and backed with substantial resources. Eventually, though, it became so heavy-handed as to arouse widespread American resentment at what was viewed as interference in U.S. politics.[5]

North Korea was carrying out its own campaign to influence American opinion. Full-page advertisements in *The New York Times* promoted Kim and his *juche* ideology. The North Korean press reported the ads as if they were news articles or editorials written by admiring foreigners. Although *Times* readers were more bemused than favorably impressed, what really put a crimp in Kim's public relations campaign was an incident in the waning days of Gerald Ford's presidency that reinforced the North's reputation for bloodthirsty behavior. On August 18, 1976, axe-wielding North Korean soldiers killed American soldiers who were trimming a tree in the Demilitarized Zone. The killings outraged officials and the public in the United States. One North Korean soldier who was based at the time in a camp at the DMZ told me later, "Everybody on the base thought a real war would erupt. We were fully equipped and stayed in the tunnels about a month and a half."[6]

Even before the axe killings, candidate Carter's troop withdrawal plan had reminded South Koreans, ominously, of that earlier withdrawal in 1949 that had been followed by the Acheson speech and the North Korean invasion.[7] After Carter took office in 1977, critics forced him to water down his plan for unilateral withdrawal. U.S. naval and air forces would remain, as well as logistics and intelligence units, the administration decided. South Koreans by February and March of 1978 were able to relax somewhat. The influential U.S. ambassador to Japan, former Senate Majority Leader Mike Mansfield, told me and other U.S. journalists invited to his Tokyo residence that even if the troops were withdrawn from Korea it could be assumed that

U.S. ground troops would be sent in from bases elsewhere in case of another war.[8]

Then U.S. and South Korean military officials held a dress rehearsal for just such an emergency reinforcement. They beefed up and heavily publicized an annual joint military exercise code-named Team Spirit, after having played the exercise down in previous years. In Team Spirit, American units practiced moving swiftly into Korea—some in an amphibious assault surely intended to rekindle memories of Inchon—while coordinating their actions with South Korean and American units already in place. The publicity seemed partly intended to test American public backing for the commitment and prepare the way for scrapping what remained of the pullout plan. And clearly there was a message here for the Koreans, north and south alike, that the U.S. commitment to South Korean defense stood essentially unchanged.[9]

Pyongyang got the message and briefly returned to a hard-line stance. In the summer of 1978, it began making personal attacks on Carter and other U.S. officials. In October, it sent commandos to infiltrate into South Korea. That same month the U.S.–South Korean United Nations Command announced that a recent underground explosion sending water and debris up a borehole had enabled soldiers to pinpoint a Northern-dug infiltration tunnel under the DMZ. Cut through solid granite, this was the third such tunnel to have been discovered.

Meanwhile, new U.S. intelligence data indicated that North Korea over the previous four or five years had built up its military to a much greater extent than previously believed. The United States now "tentatively" estimated that the North Korean ground force totaled between 560,000 and 600,000 men, about a fourth higher than earlier estimated. "These additional units were not added in the last year; we just found them in the last year," an American general in Seoul said. "We really don't know how new it is, but it's clear you can't organize and equip a division overnight."[10] The new figures ranked the North Korean People's Army as the fifth largest army in the world, in a country whose population was only 17 million. The timing of the news, right when army generals needed ammunition to counter Carter's proposal, aroused some suspicions. But in February 1979, Carter announced he was "holding in abeyance" any further troop withdrawals pending further study.[11]

Casting about during that period for anything that could arrest the negative trend in its fortunes, Pyongyang noted the positive results of the "ping-pong diplomacy" that China had begun in 1971 by hosting an American table tennis team. Talks with Henry Kissinger and a visit by President Richard Nixon had followed, ultimately leading to diplomatic relations between Beijing and Washington.[12]

Preparing to host the world table tennis tournament in April of 1979, Pyongyang decided to try some ping-pong diplomacy of its own. It agreed to receive the first large contingent of Americans to visit the North since the Korean War. North Korean officials believed that the Americans, simply by visiting Pyongyang, would confer de facto recognition on the Kim Il-sung regime. The United States and North Korea previously had concluded only the 1953 ceasefire agreement. After more than a quarter-century, there was no peace treaty, much less diplomatic relations.

The North hoped to persuade the American visitors, and through them the American public, of the regime's peaceful intentions. It would do this partly by showing how much it had built and therefore how much it stood to lose in the case of war. It hoped also to show the bad effects of Korean division on families, and drive home the regime's argument that American troops in the South unjustly caused and maintained the division. A third objective was to portray North Korea as independent, not a satellite of either the Soviet Union or China, posing no threat to American interests if only the Americans would avoid threatening North Korean interests.

The longer-term goal was to hold talks with the U.S. government, persuading Washington to go through with the stalled troop withdrawals—and eventually, no doubt, to remove entirely the American commitment to South Korean security, including the nuclear "umbrella." If Kim Il-sung could get that far, he could then hope that Washington would react with equanimity in case the peninsula should be reunited—whether completely under his rule or, for a time at least, according to his publicly proposed formula: a confederation in which the North and South would coexist.

In April 1978, the State Department confirmed that the U.S. chapter of the International Table Tennis Federation had applied for approval to send a team to Pyongyang for the tournament. A Pyongyang operative in Tokyo then told me that Kim Il-sung himself would be on hand for the ceremonial functions of the tournament, and that the Great Leader just might chat with members of the American delegation. Pyongyang clearly hoped that, among the American players, coaches, interpreters and hangers-on, there would be someone delegated by Washington to deal with political issues.[13]

Washington remained unwilling to budge from its firm insistence that any rapprochement with North Korea must not bypass South Korea. As a demonstration of flexibility, Pyongyang in January of 1979 responded with its own twist on a South Korean proposal to reopen the North-South dialogue that had petered out in 1973. North Korea refused to talk on a government-to-government basis. Instead it insisted on its longstanding formula calling for talks between nongovernmental delegations representing the two Koreas' political parties and "social organizations." Nevertheless, its moves to appear responsive seemed to place the diplomatic ball back in the South's court (especially in the minds of non-Koreans who had yet to suspect that Kim's I-win-you-lose philosophy still had no room for a genuine live-and-let-live relationship with the South).

The South, going through a period of unusually intense domestic political strife, was aware that the Northern formula for talks would provide diverse viewpoints only on the Southern side. The monolithic Northern regime by that time allowed no dissent at home and certainly would allow no real diversity of views among its delegates, whatever their supposed organizational affiliations. Northern delegates, the Southerners believed, would merely exploit political differences among Southerners in a divide-and-conquer pattern.

Thus, despite wide grins on the North Koreans' faces and a few points for Pyongyang in its propaganda contest with Seoul, the preliminary talks at Panmunjom in the DMZ fizzled out in mutual distrust, recrimination and nitpicking. So did parallel meetings to consider forming a joint North-and-South Korean table tennis team to compete in the tournament.[14]

Working as a newspaper correspondent covering Korea, I was eager to be included in the press delegation accompanying the American team to Pyongyang. The view among Tokyo-based correspondents was that the only way one could hope to get into North Korea was through a persistent campaign of cables to Pyongyang, to a quasi-diplomatic body that specialized in dealing with the West. Those cables to the Committee for Cultural Relations with Foreign Countries, I was advised, should be supplemented by appeals to influential members of the pro-Pyongyang Korean community in Japan. I followed this program, emphasizing my open-mindedness. The North Koreans at the time were trying to persuade Washington that they had moderated their approach to South Korea, and I made note of my awareness of that effort.

The regional paper I worked for, *The Baltimore Sun*, at great expense maintained eight foreign news bureaus as well as a large Washington bureau. Circulating in Maryland and adjacent Washington, it enjoyed a fine reputation among diplomats and other internationalists. As a sales pitch, one of my predecessors as Tokyo bureau chief had taught reporter/news assistant Hideko Takayama that whenever she telephoned someone unfamiliar with the paper to ask for an appointment she should explain that *The Sun* was "read daily by the President of the United States." That claim had been more or less true at the time the former bureau chief taught Takayama her line, and she had continued to use it up to my time when she called North Korean and other prospective news sources who might lack detailed knowledge of the U.S. media. No one had thought to reexamine the procedure, even though other presidents had taken their turns in the Oval Office and it was possible the incumbent might have failed somehow to develop the same reading habit.

I myself was not above boasting to Pyongyang's representatives in Japan that the paper was to political coverage what *The Wall Street Journal* was to economics.

Anyhow, the campaign worked. Along with correspondents for the *Journal* and a few other news organizations, I received my invitation to appear at the North Korean embassy in Beijing for a visa and thence to travel to Pyongyang.

Not the first American journalist to reach North Korea, but close enough that I felt a little bit like Neil Armstrong arriving on the moon, I stepped off a Soviet-built plane at Pyongyang's airport. Peering intently at everything I saw, I was determined to miss nothing. Pyongyang rewarded me by providing much that was unfamiliar, starting with the crowds of schoolchildren who stood in ranks along the road from the airport to cheer the latest arrivals for the table tennis tournament.

Although at that time I knew very little of what I have written in this volume—and was indeed, I believe, pretty open-minded regarding what I would see—I had of course come armed with some general impressions based on background interviews and reading. And I was set to filter whatever I might hear through the skepticism that American journalists of my generation had learned to apply to official claims made by any government anywhere in the world—especially our own. The North Koreans, for their part, were intent on turning skeptics into believers.

North Korean papers and broadcasts were full of stories about the sporting events that I had theoretically come to cover, and my hosts made no secret of their opinion that I should show at least some interest in them myself. One day I did go to the matches and saw a pair of North Korean women competing against Korean-Americans who were playing for the U.S. team. Thirteen other matches were in progress at the same time, with North Korean competitors involved in some of them, but the North Korean spectators glued their eyes to this one match. Prosperous-looking Pyongyang people, mostly men in business suits and neckties, crowded the grandstand, cheering thunderously for the home team against the Korean-Americans, especially when the referee ruled for North Korea on a disputed point.

Pyongyang's heroine of the moment was Li Song-suk, who won the women's singles world championship. The Great Leader, the papers said, had given his personal attention to her training, and that had been the secret of her success. However, the buzz among the other teams in Pyongyang was that the Chinese—who had long dominated world table tennis—were not above taking a dive as a reward to their hosts. Perpetually seeking political autonomy by playing its two giant communist neighbors off against each other, North Korea since the mid-'70s had been leaning toward the Chinese.

Pyongyang had supported Chinese charges of Vietnamese aggression in Cambodia (but had conspicuously avoided comment on China's war with Vietnam) while urging nonaligned nations to keep their distance from the Soviet Union.

Reunification — to be preceded by American troop withdrawal, of course — was a constant theme wherever I went in North Korea. "Whenever the Great Leader visited us, he told us we should produce more tractors so that we could supply tractors to the southern part of the country when we reunify," said an official of a tractor plant that was on our sightseeing itinerary.

One day I accompanied some other visiting reporters to scenic Mount Kumgang in the southeastern part of North Korea, near the South Korean border. When we got there, we learned that the authorities had arranged for a group of Koreans to talk to us as we viewed the scenery. They were there to tell us of their families, divided since the Korean War, and their dream of reunifying the country. They were so poised and prosperous looking that I thought they might be actors, but I had no reason to doubt that national division was a matter of great anguish to the families actually affected, on both sides.[15]

I talked with Ko Young-il, a Korean-American who had signed on to travel to Pyongyang as interpreter for the American team in hopes of meeting his mother, five sisters and brother, whom he had not seen since the Korean War. Late in 1950, Chinese and UN troops fought over the North Korean county where they lived. In the confusion of battle Ko, then nine years old, found himself separated from his family and started to follow the UN troops south. About five miles from the county seat he met his father, and the two headed for their small town to search for the others in the family. When they got close they saw that the town was already burning, so they climbed up into some hills and looked for American troops. No one could tell them where his mother and siblings were. "Since then," Ko said, "we never met them, we never heard anything from them. That's it."

Ko lived in Seoul until 1972, when he took his family to the United States to seek "a better future for ourselves and our children." He had become the owner of an auto-body repair shop and a billiard hall in the Virginia suburbs of Washington, D.C. He still held South Korean citizenship, and had needed the approval of the Seoul government to travel to Pyongyang. Ko was preparing to reunite with his family, figuring he must have a lot of nephews and nieces he had never met. He was eager. "Since I left America I can't sleep," he said. But at the same time he was nervous. For one thing, he worried about how his family members would receive him. Perhaps they would see him and ask, "Why are you here?" With greater cause, perhaps, he worried that the Northern regime might put pressure on his family because of him—might "blackmail" them, as he put it—and use the reunion for propaganda.

I had no trouble imagining this as the sort of situation that official propagandists would play for all it was worth. Sure enough, when Ko did meet his family, the Pyongyang newspaper account quoted him as saying he would really like to stay in North Korea except that his father would not be able to join the rest of them. "Someday when we reunify the country we can live together," he was quoted as saying. As presented, the quoted remark implied that North Korea was a highly appealing place to live—the usual formula.

Two days later Pak Kyong-sik, a team leader in a hothouse on the outskirts of Pyongyang, told me that his family had seen a newspaper account of the reunion and "we sat and talked until late at night." Pak said his brother had been separated from the rest of the family in the Korean War, going to South Korea. "Many years have passed, but I still haven't had any opportunity to see my brother. I live with my parents, who worry a lot about whether my brother is alive or dead." Pak told me that although he was leading "this happy life"—the requisite note lauding Kim Il-sung's paradise—"I'm always eager to meet my brother."

On my first full day in Pyongyang, April 24, my guide told me I would be having lunch with someone. I asked with whom, and he replied, "We'll see." We went to a large private dining room in my hotel, where I was introduced to a man named Pak, a council member of the Committee for Cultural Relations with Foreign Countries. This organization, rather than the Foreign Ministry, dealt with countries that had not recognized Pyongyang diplomatically and vice versa. Over a lavish meal consisting of Chinese, Korean and Western courses, Mr. Pak and I talked for an hour and a half. We began with a lengthy chat about the weather and went on to a discussion of U.S.-Korean relations. My guide interpreted well, although he was stumped at one point by the English word "pragmatism." In this conversation a couple of things struck me. One was that Pak did not know much about the United States. He said he understood that Americans eat turkey on our independence day.

Another thing that struck me was that Pak bluntly contradicted me only once. That was when I was speaking about the pros and cons of South Korea in the eyes of Americans. I told him that, despite what was then a lack of democracy as we understood democracy, South Korea offered its citizens a certain kind of freedom that Americans could identify with: freedom to make nonpolitical choices, to be upwardly mobile economically and socially. Pak snapped: "That's not true!" And he said it with a fervid conviction that contrasted with the man-of-the-world demeanor he otherwise displayed that day. In the remainder of the conversation, while he could be ironic and a bit playful about American words and deeds, he never acknowledged anything positive about South Korea. My telling him that Americans could identify to an extent with South Korea seemed only to have reinforced his evident belief that the South was playing the flunkey role, trying to become a Western-style society—a contemptible trend, in his view of Korean cultural legitimacy.

Pak said he hoped I would learn from my visit about the Korean people's craving for independence. This got us to specifics, and it was troop withdrawal that he emphasized. I gave Pak my assessment that the Carter administration had drawn back from its troop withdrawal commitment at least partly because it would have amounted to a unilateral giveaway of bargaining chips, with nothing demanded in return. I spoke of the skepticism of U.S. allies, especially Japan. I mentioned the new intelligence estimates of North Korea's military strength—agreeing with Pak that the timing of the revelation, in the heat of the troop-withdrawal debate, did seem a bit strange. Pak made a few perfunctory attempts to arouse my outrage that Carter would go back on his campaign promise. I steered the conversation back to the real world by emphasizing that the United States had to look at such matters in the light of its role as a world power.

Pak finally rephrased what I had been saying: "So it's a bargain that the United States wants now?" I agreed that this was the assessment I would make, as a mere newspaper reporter. As the meal ended, Pak delivered a flowery farewell speech in which he said we would talk again.

I made a reply speech (at lunch in North Korea one often made speeches instead of conversation) in which I attempted to state my understanding of American opinion regarding Korea. By the 1970s, I told Pak, many Americans including myself had come to wonder if Washington had been mistaken to get the country involved in Korea's affairs in the first place. (I had never fully bought into the argument that the United States should have stayed home in the post–World War II period. But my personal views—I didn't tell Pak this part—had been influenced by the arguments of revisionist historians, starting with college exposure to William Appleman Williams's *The Tragedy of American Diplomacy*.) And maybe, I told Pak, the United States had learned in Vietnam a hard lesson about the consequences of injecting ourselves into Asian civil wars. But, wisely or unwisely, we *had* gotten involved in Korea, and a society had been building in the South for more than thirty years. We had to consider carefully how to phase out our intrusion honorably—doing violence to neither our idealism nor our loyalty.

Pak was visibly displeased by this—as displeased, apparently, as he had been when I said that South Korea's human rights record was better than Iran's. But he said we would have further talks. I assumed Pak's report to his colleagues and higher-ups would determine whether I would get more access to foreign-affairs officials.

Some fellow journalists and I had been speculating whether Washington might have empowered any member of the U.S. table tennis delegation to deal with the Northerners on political issues. Pyongyang, eager to talk, clearly hoped that was the case. Looking over the group, however, we came up with no obvious CIA types or others who seemed as if they might fill the role. I had the impression the North Koreans, likewise coming up empty-handed, might have decided to feel out the journalists accompanying the delegation to see if any of us might have pipelines to the White House more direct than mere presidential readership. I certainly was not reporting to the U.S. government or, indeed, to anyone except my editors back in Baltimore, and did not pretend otherwise. I was not sure whether the North Koreans knew of the American law that forbade intelligence agencies from recruiting journalists on the staffs of American news organizations. Whatever my hosts might imagine, however, I hoped they would decide that sending a message through me and my newspaper would be an efficient way to reach people in high places in Washington.

When I visited So Tong-bong, an editor of the Workers' Party newspaper *Nodong Shinmun* (Workers' Daily), he told me that North Koreans "want the United States not to put obstacles in the way of reunification. So we hope the U.S. will withdraw American troops from the South and give a good atmosphere to create favorable conditions for reunification." Improved U.S. relations with communist China had blunted the old justification that American troops were in the South to contain communist expansion, he observed—but still the troops remained, with the excuse of deterring North Korean aggression. "As you know, so many times we have clarified our position that we have no aggressive designs on South Korea," the editor said. "War will not break out even if U.S. troops withdraw from South Korea." (Seoul and Washington, of course, had plenty of doubts on that point. "They've got an awfully big military force for a country of peaceful intentions," as one American official observed.)

So Tong-bong told me that Americans should understand Koreans' desire for unification. After all, our own Civil War had been fought over the question of unity. Nice try. But North Korea and the capitalist South, during the thirty-four years since the division of the country, had grown into societies differing from each other far more profoundly than the Union differed from the Confederacy. North and South Korea both talked a lot about unification, but it seemed that each wanted it only if its own system would rule on the united peninsula. Pyongyang wanted to reunify quickly while it still held the stronger hand—but Seoul wanted to obtain world recognition of two Koreas for the time being, and delay reunification for long enough to build the South into a position of potential dominance.

The editor insisted that North Korea would not force South Koreans to live under the North's system, and he added that Northerners had no thought of living under the South's bourgeois system. In that case, I asked, how could the mere presence of U.S. troops in the South be blamed for preventing reunification—the sort of reunification he claimed he wanted, with the two Korean systems remaining mutually exclusive? "I think you know the answer," he replied, in what I found to be a typical North Korean rhetorical device. He added, "We are insisting that reunification should be done by the Korean people themselves. If foreign interference exists, independent reunification is impossible."

That was a reference to the longstanding North Korean position that the Seoul government was not a true representative of the South Korean people but merely a puppet of the United States, cruelly repressing the people, keeping power and maintaining national division with the backing of American troops. I had spent enough time in South Korea to know that this was a crude caricature. The South Koreans in general very much liked the wealth and opportunities their system was bringing them. Their complaints arose from uneven distribution of those gains, the dizzying pace of social and economic change and Park Chung-hee's determination to stay in power without holding democratic elections.

The sentimental appeal of the idea of reunification remained potent—and the Seoul regime was finding it difficult to reconcile that with its de facto policy of "two Koreas." Nevertheless, having experienced North Korean rule briefly in wartime 1950 and 1951, South Koreans hardly wished to replace their lot under a merely authoritarian regime with the North Koreans' fate under the totalitarian Kim Il-sung regime. Thus, I was not convinced that removal of U.S. troops from the South would aid the cause of reunification—except, perhaps, by enabling Kim Il-sung to impose his will upon the South.

As the time for my departure drew near, I got word that I was to be granted a major interview. I would meet Kim Yong-nam, secretary of the Workers' Party in charge of foreign affairs, who ranked in the top ten in the party hierarchy. I was to submit some questions in advance.

Kim Yong-nam smilingly greeted me in a Workers' Party guest house on the outskirts of Pyongyang. A slender, strong-jawed man of fifty with a mobile mouth and straight, bushy Groucho Marx eyebrows, he wore horn-rimmed glasses and a well-tailored gray plaid suit, with the requisite gold-framed portrait of the Great Leader pinned to his lapel. After some pleasantries, he proposed first to tell me about North Korea's reunification policy. What would I think of that? "I think that would be an excellent procedure," I replied, deferring to my host. Despite his superficial resemblance to Groucho, he offered no one-liners (and no cigar). Instead, he launched into a monologue, which dragged on for long enough to make me regret my politeness.

Kim Yong-nam repeated the point made by virtually every other North Korean I had met—that reunification was the ardent wish of the entire Korean people. The question of reunification, he said, "is an urgent one that cannot be delayed further." Koreans are "a homogeneous people with one language, one set of customs and one territory," he said. But because of their separation for the previous thirty-four years, "the language and customs of the people are becoming different. This is the biggest tragedy for our people. Now the North and the South are in a position of military confrontation and both keep strong military forces," he said. "To remove the danger of a new war, Korea's reunification should be realized soon."

Kim complained that it appeared "the United States does not clearly understand the sincere position of our country for independent and peaceful reunification." He said his country's proposals had gone largely unreported in the news media of capitalist countries. Take, for example, the North's proposals for economic cooperation with the South. The North had mineral and fishery resources and the South had surplus labor, so why not put them together? Stop the South Koreans from emigrating to places like the United States and send those people north, he said. Specifically, the North had offered to let low-income South Korean fishermen fish in North Korean territorial waters alongside North Korean fishermen. The North had even offered to build irrigation systems to help increase farm yields in the South. "But as the South Korean side rejected all those proposals, not a proposal could be realized," Kim Yong-nam said solemnly, looking deeply sorry for the poor Southerners thus deprived of Northern economic help.

Kim Yong-nam reprised some appeals that were standard ingredients in Pyongyang's efforts to undermine the Washington-Seoul alliance by playing to Americans critical of the Park Chung-hee regime's anti-democratic record. Such critics formed a large and growing group and included my newspaper's editorial board and myself, as North Korean officials perhaps were aware. "We think the U.S. should change its policy on Korean questions, proceeding from goodwill," Kim said. "The U.S. should not back or instigate Park Chung-hee, particularly in his maneuvers for splitting our country, his war clamor and his policy of trampling the democratic forces in South Korea. . . . The U.S. should come out to assist the realization of reunification. If it can't do that, at least it should not do things which hinder and put obstacles in the way of realizing reunification." Kim repeatedly emphasized that the improvement of U.S.–North Korean relations was "entirely up to the United States."

Making what he told me was a new offer, Kim Yong-nam said that if the United States would withdraw its troops from South Korea and help to achieve Korean reunification through a confederation, North Korea would guarantee not to "touch or harm" American interests in the South. He repeated the North Korean proposal for reunification, which envisioned separate governments coexisting in the northern and southern halves of the country for an indefinite period. Each could maintain its own social system with a guarantee of independent operation regarding domestic matters, he said. But the two would be united in dealing with foreign affairs, in which field the proposed Korean federation would pursue a "nonaligned, neutral policy."

Kim Yong-nam did not get into a detailed discussion of just what were American interests in South Korea. He did not even mention, for example, investments there by American corporations, but he did address by implication Washington's basic Cold War–era interest in seeing that Moscow would have as few allies as possible. He repeated the argument Pyongyang had been peddling for several years: that North Korea was an independent and nonaligned country, taking orders from no great power. A reunited Korea would be likewise, he promised. "What I want to emphasize is that even after reunification our country will stand independently, will not be a satellite of certain countries and will strictly follow a nonaligned and neutral policy," Kim Yong-nam told me.

Two hours and fifty minutes after our meeting had begun, Kim ended his monologue. We repaired to a lunch of several courses, lasting another couple of hours, during which he took questions. In response to a question on how the guarantees he had offered would apply, he gave no specifics but said, "That question can be discussed if the United States comes out with the intention to help the country's reunification."

Kim Yong-nam offered no new proposals to get the stalled North-South talks moving again. It seemed clear that North Korea's leaders had decided to concentrate for the time being on changing American minds in the hope the United States would resume troop withdrawal.

As for the new U.S. intelligence reports saying the North's ground forces numbered between 560,000 and 600,000 men, Kim charged that this was "baseless information. Even 400,000 would be a great burden for us when we think of our population and other conditions." North Korea was "demanding the reduction of military forces in the North and South and reduction of armaments," he said. Meanwhile it had been reducing the percentage of its budget spent on the military, from 16.5 percent in 1976 to 15 percent in 1979. "And we have many times expressed and clarified our stand that we have no intention of pursuing aggression against the South."

The account of my interview with Kim Yong-nam was the lead article on the front page of *The Baltimore Sun* the next morning,[16] and it was duly read in official Washington. The offer to guarantee "as they are" American interests in South Korea seemed intended to provide the missing quid pro quo for continued American troop withdrawal from the South. Kim Yong-nam had told me the proposed guarantees would apply not only to the United States but also to other foreign countries with interests in South Korea—specifically Japan, whose economy, as he noted, was more "organically" linked with South Korea's than was the U.S. economy.

But although Kim had insisted he was offering something new, Washington saw in what he had told me just a dressed-up version of Pyongyang's unchanging line. North Korea's military was considerably more formidable than that of South Korea alone, but the first step was for the American troops to leave—and then we would see which side could wrest control of a unified Korean foreign policy and military. If Kim Yong-nam really imagined he was offering, through *The Sun*, a deal that would appeal to Washington, either he did not understand American thinking or he underestimated the intelligence of U.S. officials.

Just a few weeks later, President Carter went to Seoul to reaffirm publicly American military support for South Korea. While there, he implicitly criticized the South Korean regime for its repression of the people. Hailing "the dramatic economic progress in this booming country," he said during a state dinner: "I believe that the achievement can be matched by similar progress through the realization of basic human aspirations in political and human rights." Carter also spoke with opposition leader Kim Young-sam, who had aroused a storm of criticism by expressing his willingness to meet with the North's Kim Il-sung. The U.S. president indicated that the time might be right for some such initiative. "We must take advantage of changes in the international environment to lower tensions between South and North and, ultimately, to bring permanent peace and reunification to the Korean peninsula," he said at the state dinner.[17] Carter and South Korean President Park on July 1 called for three-way peace talks with North Korea—not the talks with Washington alone that Pyongyang, forever seeking an end run around Seoul, insisted upon.

Sorely disappointed, rejecting the presence of the South at U.S.-North Korean talks except in the capacity of an observer, North Korea called Carter a "vicious political mountebank;" his journey, "a powder-reeking trip of a hypocrite agitating for aggression and war." But a North Korean spokesman in Tokyo said that, in the North Korean lexicon, this was a relatively moderate slur. At least the North had not called Carter an imperialist, its worst insult. North Korea would stick with its insistence on bilateral talks with Washington, the spokesman said, and "we don't think the U.S. can oppose Pyongyang's proposal indefinitely." Sooner or later, "the U.S. will be forced to go along with Pyongyang's proposal."[18]

Carter announced on July 20, 1979, that he was "freezing" troop withdrawals until 1981. While the plan had been alive, only about 10 percent of the U.S. troops in South Korea had been removed—and U.S. aircraft based there had increased in number. Gen. John W. Vessey, vice chief of staff of the army, that same month warned a congressional subcommittee that

"Kim Il-sung's only remaining course of action to achieve unification on his terms appears to be the military option of large-scale attack." Vessey's testimony echoed a remark by a North Korean foreign affairs official who had escorted me and other American journalists on a visit to the northern side of the DMZ: "I think if this tension continues, eventually it will break out into another war."[19]

In reality, Kim Il-sung had other options that Vessey did not mention. One was simply to wait, in the hope that the Southern regime would fall to a revolution and present Kim a new opportunity. As had happened in Iran—a comparison the North Koreans enjoyed making—the faster the economic growth in South Korea, the more the social fabric was rubbed raw. Southerners' discontent was flaming up, fueled by traffic jams, pollution, double-digit inflation and the widespread perception of a growing gap between rich and poor. Democratic-minded intellectuals, social-activist Christians, students and low-paid industrial workers stirred the pot, frustrated by the regime's police-state tactics for preventing organized protest.

North Koreans were jubilant when, on October 26, 1979, South Korea's intelligence chief assassinated President Park. In an atmosphere of wild excitement, the Northerners even closed their schools.[20] Months of political confusion followed in the South, as the forces for democracy clashed with a new group of would-be military rulers led by Maj. Gen. Chun Doo-hwan. Making some efforts to exploit the situation politically, the North sent Seoul a rephrased proposal for North-South talks in January 1980.

But the North did not yield to the temptation to move militarily, and some reports from Seoul to the contrary were outright lies concocted by the Chun Doo-hwan forces. *The Baltimore Sun* caught South Korean government officials red-handed in the fabrication of a report—intended to defuse student demonstrations—that Northern moves to invade the South appeared to be under way. Briefing South Korean newsmen in Seoul on May 10, 1980, Prime Minister Shin Hyon-hwack said a "close ally" had informed the government that North Korea's infiltration-trained Eighth Army Corps had been out of sight of intelligence surveillance for some time. The unit might surface in South Korea, perhaps between May 15 and May 20. South Korea had only two close allies at the time, the United States and Japan. Thus, it was a simple matter to check, and to report in the paper the next morning, that neither ally had provided this information. Instead, the Japanese said the South Koreans had been trying to peddle the "intelligence" to *them*, claiming it came from China—a country that certainly was not a close ally. "The South Korean inquiry appeared to be something of an advertising balloon," a Japanese source said dryly.[21]

North Korean restraint was sorely tested in May 1980 when South Korean special forces, enforcing martial law in the city of Kwangju, massacred some two hundred citizens. North Korean security and intelligence officials watched the news coverage on Japanese television. "At the time, we thought that everyone there was being killed," a high-ranking Public Security Ministry official recalled after his defection later to South Korea. "There were some who, watching television, felt that we could not simply sit back and watch this and instead must charge on down. If the Kwangju incident had dragged out just a little bit more, then it was possible that the problem could have become a bit more complicated."[22]

During the Kwangju incident a North Korean spokesman in Tokyo complained to me that the United States was "agitating us to do something." The spokesman, a foreign affairs official of Chongryon (General Association of Korean Residents in Japan), seemed to think Seoul and Washington wanted to lure Pyongyang into a military intervention that would unite the fractured South Korean society behind its defending army.

The South Korean government at the time was accusing North Korea of controlling from behind the scenes the student rebels who fought the military in Kwangju. Later, when I had a chance to interview people in Kwangju who had been involved at the core of the uprising, I found no evidence that this charge was any more than another fabrication by the Chun regime, as in the case of the supposedly missing North Korean army corps.[23]

For whatever purpose, though, the North Korean People's Army was on full alert during and after each major crisis. Kim Kwang-il, who rose to the rank of sergeant first class, was stationed right on the border in Cholwon, Kangwon Province, manning 105-millimeter artillery that was kept in a mountain tunnel ready to be rolled out for firing on Yeoncheon in South Korea. "When Park Chung-hee was assassinated, we all waited for war, remaining on alert in the tunnel for sixty days wearing our helmets, gas masks and boots," Kim Kwang-il told me following his 1995 defection to the South. "The high-ranking officers told us South Korea would invade, but the soldiers figured the Northern leadership would order an attack. There were six of these alerts while I was serving, following the same routine. They were prompted by the 1976 axe killings, a 1977 training exercise, the 1979 Park assassination, the Kwangju uprising in 1980, a major defection in 1981 and Kim Il-sung's seventieth birthday in 1982. At the time of Kwangju we understood there was great instability in the South, but Chun Doo-hwan emerged and stabilized the situation. In the case of Kim Il-sung's seventieth birthday, the authorities had hoped to be able to reunify the peninsula as a present to him. There were so many cases when alerts expired after nothing had happened that we grew accustomed to them, and indifferent: 'Oh, it's just another training exercise.'"

The year 1981 came and Jimmy Carter was no longer in office to consider thawing out his "frozen" troop-withdrawal plan. Worse, from Pyongyang's perspective, Ronald Reagan had replaced Carter—and Reagan quickly put

on a showy display of support for Chun Doo-hwan, South Korea's new dictator. Pyongyang was not delicate about expressing its feelings. The Voice of the
Revolutionary Party for Reunification, a North Korean radio station that
masqueraded as an underground South Korean outlet, reported a 1982 assassination attempt against Reagan as a punishment "deserved by a warmonger
and a strangler of human rights."[24]

That illustrates one of the problems a democracy such as the United
States encounters in dealing with a country ruled by a single-minded, all-
powerful individual. Although Carter and his foreign-policy team were gone
from 1980, turned out of office by the American voters, Kim Il-sung, his son
Kim Jong-il and Kim Yong-nam were still in office. More than two decades
later Kim Il-sung, although dead, remained officially the president of North
Korea. Kim Jong-il, alive, maintained the uninterrupted family rule. And
Kim Yong-nam? For all the intervening years he had continued in key foreign relations posts, eventually becoming the titular head of state.

Every four or eight years, as a new American administration started
more or less from scratch to figure out who the North Koreans were and
begin to deal with them, the ever-more experienced America-watchers in
Pyongyang waited for the newcomers to fumble.[25]

NINE

He Gave Us Water and
Sent Us Machines

When Pak Song-chol returned to Pyongyang from his secret visit to Seoul before the July 4, 1972, issuance of the North-South joint communiqué, Kim Il-sung asked him how things were in the South. One story goes that Pak gave Kim an accurate report of what he had seen, one that did not conform to North Korea's propaganda picture of a backward, poverty-ridden country. Thereupon Kim snapped: "You look at things that way because your ideology is wrong." After that, Pak dropped out of sight for three or four months, having been sent off to a camp for "reeducation."[1] Needless to say, other delegates made sure they were properly armed with skepticism when they went south. There is the famous story of their charge that the automobiles filling Seoul's streets were mere props. But in fact they saw what Pak had seen in Seoul, and some of them—while no doubt softening the story to avoid informing the emperor directly that he had no clothes—dared to be bearers of ill tidings.

Once he finally got a glimmering that the South had positioned itself to overtake the North economically, a shocked Kim Il-sung intensified his emphasis on mass mobilization. In 1973 he appointed son and heir Kim Jong-il to head Three Revolutions teams of young agitators, who would go into the factories and fields and whip up workers' zeal to fever pitch. Even though its effectiveness was dwindling, it was understandable that the elder Kim would fall back on his favorite motivational technique. It had worked reasonably well—for a limited time. Even South Korea in the 1970s experimented with mass mobilization in its successful, government-sponsored "New Village" movement for rural self-help and development.[2]

In a more substantial policy shift, the Pyongyang regime tried to change its luck by importing technology from the West. In part that was to make up for shortfalls in aid from the Soviet Union, related to troubles in the Moscow-Pyongyang political relationship. The new policy required some modification in the *juche* policy, as the North went on a spending spree. In the early 1970s, Pyongyang borrowed hundreds of millions of dollars to buy new factories from Western European countries and Japan. The plan was to repay the debts with the increased export income that the new technology would provide.[3] In the process, North Korea itself was moving to an even more authoritarian system than before. The regime stepped up surveillance to make sure Western ideas would not contaminate the citizenry as the country brought in foreign capital and technology.[4]

However, the technology-import strategy backfired, partly because of a downturn in the world economy but also because of lack of ability and experience in the most advantageous use of the new technology. Failing to repay its debts, the regime became known in international financial circles as a deadbeat. The country's reputation suffered further injury when some of its diplomats in Scandinavian countries were accused of smuggling drugs, in what seems to have been a systematic attempt to raise hard currency. Pyongyang had botched the first of many attempts to take money and technology—but not ideas and values—from the West.

In 1972 North Korea adopted a new constitution, which mandated a switch to a presidential system. Kim Il-sung gave up the premiership to take the presidency. Thenceforth, the premiership would be a useful lightning rod for the regime. The incumbent premier could be dismissed to take responsibility for any recognized policy failure—even though President Kim continued to dictate the policies. At the end of 1977 Kim reorganized the government, implicitly acknowledging the North's failure to regain the economic lead over the South. While men of military background previously had served as premier, this time he put an economist, Li Jong-ok, into the job. The question was how much leeway Li and his technocrat cohorts would have. After all, real power continued to be held by President Kim, who had established a politics-first ideology and who kept around him men who had served with him as anti-Japanese guerillas.[5]

Despite the problems, Kim stuck stubbornly to—and even intensified—his policy of Stalinist centralism.[6] Micromanagement from the top had become less and less effective with the economy's expansion, but still it seemed that no detail was too small to concern Kim Il-sung. At a meeting of financial and banking workers in December 1978, he gave an hour-long address that delved deeply into the minutiae of the country's economic administration. He complained, among other things, about the way people were misusing a synthetic textile, vinalon. "During my survey on waste of cloth, I found that vinalon strings in Yanggang Province were used for hop-vine supports, which could easily be replaced with something made from hemp or barks of lime trees," Kim said, advising that "vinalon strings should be used for webs only."[7]

Why didn't Kim do more to change his system and ideology in response to the Southern challenge, once it became apparent in the 1970s? My 1979 visit to the country gave me considerable food for subsequent thought about this question.

When I met Kim Yong-nam near the end of that visit, the party foreign affairs secretary noted that I had been touring his country. "As you have seen," he said, "we have built and constructed a lot in a peaceful atmosphere. Why should we destroy all these successes and fight with our own people?" I thought he had a point. It was not that my visit had turned me into a true believer. Indeed, I was deeply troubled to learn in my stops at North Korean schools, cultural agencies and even health-care facilities of the extent to which Kim Il-sung's attempts to remake the minds of his subjects were still going strong—and apparently succeeding. Overall, however, it would have been difficult for me, or any other newcomer, to avoid being favorably impressed by the achievements that North Koreans showed off to visitors. Even though South Korea probably had pulled ahead of the North in per capita GNP by 1979,[8] the overriding impression was of Northern success, up to a point—not failure.

Both building anew and restoring the mighty infrastructure that the Japanese had bequeathed to them, the North Koreans had achieved considerable industrialization. At the same time they had irrigated, fertilized and mechanized in their struggle to squeeze from a largely mountainous land enough food to sustain them. The parts of the country that I was permitted to see did not appear to bear out the totally negative appraisals—"economic basket case," for example—that had started to appear in Western studies and press reports. People appeared adequately housed and clothed. Although few besides the president and his son were fat, I did not notice any obvious signs of malnutrition. There was austerity, apparently rather evenly shared, but I saw no signs of destitution. All this seemed to set North Korea apart from other developing nations.

The movements of foreign visitors were minutely controlled—probably because of fear that we would learn something the authorities did not want us to know, plus fear that we would spread alien knowledge and opinions that might call into question Kim Il-sung's leadership. I was assigned to stay in the Potonggang Hotel. Disappointingly, a large surrounding park planted with willow trees isolated the hotel from the daily life of Pyongyang. I kept asking if I could not just wander around by myself, but my handlers politely forbade it.

If I wanted to go anywhere, to see anything, my guide and interpreter said, they would happily "help" by going with me. One or the other or both of them waited near the hotel's single exit. If I tried to venture out, they would join me, escort me to a waiting Volvo and tell the driver where to take us. Generally this was explained in terms of hospitality—I was a guest, new to the country, and needed guidance—but occasionally someone would allude more or less gently to the fact I came from a country that was officially an enemy of theirs. I waited for an opportunity to escape from my handlers for some unguided sightseeing. In the meantime, I preferred taking the guided tours to spending more time watching the table tennis matches.

My guide took me to sites on the approved itinerary, such as the Kumsong tractor plant near Nampo. En route, a sign at a farm village proclaimed: "All for conquering the 8.8-million-ton grain goal this year!" Mechanization was an important element in the effort to meet that goal. Another sign, closer to the tractor factory, exhorted the people to achieve the Three Revolutions— ideological, technical and cultural. But the tractor plant was a success story that predated the current Three Revolutions campaign.

Kim Il-sung's self-reliant *juche* policy on more than one occasion had meant borrowing—or, as Western patent lawyers would say, pirating—foreign designs. North Koreans were far from apologetic about this. My guide, Kim Yon-shik, told me that the country had imported tractors up until 1958. The need, however, overwhelmed North Korea's ability to pay. Fellow socialist countries were in no position to make up the difference because "they also had planned economies." The solution was to produce tractors at home, but North Korean engineers predicted problems of high cost and poor quality.

Kim Il-sung told the engineers that the problems would diminish with experience. He asked them to take a crack at it. Their first challenge was to come up with a design. Foreign suppliers, not interested in abetting an import-replacement scheme, refused to lend blueprints. "You can buy the tractors from us," they told the North Koreans. "There's no need to make them by yourself." And so, my guide related, "our workers used an old, worn-out tractor to draw up blueprints. . . . They used the rasp and the hammer to make the first tractor, and in forty days they made one."

There was just one big problem with that first North Korean tractor prototype based on a pirated Soviet design: The tractor ran fine in reverse gear but would not move forward. Nevertheless, said Kim Il-sung, "the important thing is that the tractor is moving." Indeed, the indigenous tractor industry expanded rapidly from that point. Between 1970 and 1976, output increased 8.7 times. The government claimed to have enlarged the fleet sufficiently to average seven or eight tractors for each 100 hectares of farmland. The Kumsong tractor plant had been rebuilt from the ruins of a small chemical fertilizer workshop in 1954, and had produced agricultural implements until the first Chollima ("Flying Horse") tractor rolled out in 1958. By the time I visited there, the 28-horsepower Chollima represented only 30 percent of production. A newer model, the 75-horsepower Poonnyun ("Bumper Year"), accounted for the remaining 70 percent.

Among younger workers at Kumsong I saw far more women than men, although I was told that women made up only about 30 percent of the approximately eight thousand workers of all ages.[9] When I asked my guide where all the young men were, he replied that they were "still growing up," studying in colleges and universities. I knew that the real answer was that they were in the army. The military's drain on the young male work force was helping perpetuate a countrywide labor shortage that had begun with the casualties and migrations of the Korean War era. South Korean figures said women made up nearly half the labor force.[10] Foreign intelligence agencies estimated that about seven hundred thousand men, or one in every twenty-four North Koreans, were in the various military services. Officials in Pyongyang denied that there were that many, but indirectly acknowledged that maintaining a huge and costly military force put a crimp in economic development efforts. "It's difficult to do something with one hand tied behind our backs," one told me.

In this tractor plant, as elsewhere, the authorities had compensated by introducing automation. Hong Ju-son, head of the administrative department, proudly showed off a large stone monument to "on-the-spot guidance" that Kim Il-sung had given to the factory. Thirty-one times Kim had visited to offer such advice, and 570 other times he had sent "teaching."[11] The basic thrust of Kim's messages, Hong said, had been "to free the workers from their burdens of great work." During the new seven-year plan (1978–1984), said Hong, "our main task is *juche* orientation and scientification and modernization. The main content of *juche* is thinking about man. Automating the plant means freeing the people from heavy labor, and also producing more products."

Evidently the regime found it politic to justify automation as a productivity measure and, especially, as a humanitarian gesture to improve working conditions, rather than mentioning the military-related—and therefore taboo—labor shortage that had made it so necessary. In the tractor factory, Hong said, a whole department of experts looked out for safety and "we never spare anything to provide protection of our workers." Yet, throughout the 55,000-square-meter processing and assembly building the lighting was dim, workers wore no helmets or goggles and many cutting machines had no safety shields. Nonetheless, as Hong told it, the workers had been so deeply moved by "the solicitude and warm care of our Great Leader" that they had erected the monument to his visits.

Whatever the motive for installing it, I was impressed by some of the machinery. A lone woman operated a 100-meter-long system for making the tractor's gearbox, peering down from a car riding on rails above. Another lone woman operated the console that controlled the engine block machining. "Every machine and piece of equipment in the factory was produced in our own country," Hong said proudly. With a million "intellectuals," including engineers, North Koreans "can solve our problems." Hong noted Kim Il-sung's personal approval of the gearbox-making system: "Our Great Leader said this is one of the great creations."

Despite the considerable automation already accomplished in the factory, I thought the tractor assembly line still moved slowly, compared with automotive plants I had visited in other countries. The workers had a lot of waiting-around time on their hands. Officials said the factory produced one hundred tractors a day, which seemed a low figure considering that this was mass production of just two basic models. Officials obviously agreed: They wanted greater productivity. A colorful sign exhorted workers: "All should come out to fulfill the resolutions of the Seventeenth Session of the Fifth Central Committee of the Workers' Party." One of the resolutions was predictable: "Produce more!" The sign praised model workers, showing their pictures and describing their feats. One woman "did her job 200 percent."

The factory operated six days a week, on two shifts. It wasn't clear how many hours an actual shift might be. Hong, when I asked him about it, replied: "In principle, according to the labor law, we do not allow them to work more than eight hours." The general rule of thumb, he said, is "eight hours' work, eight hours' study and eight hours' rest." Overtime work requires "approval from higher administrative organs." Considering the many reports of all-out work campaigns pushed by higher-ups in the party and government, it was easy to speculate that an eight-hour workday "in principle" could often stretch out longer in reality.

Retirement ages, Hong said, were sixty for men and fifty-five for women—typical figures for East Asian countries, including Japan, at that time. I asked if many people of retirement age stayed on in the workplace for whatever reason. I hoped the answer would hint at whether there might be pressure to postpone retirement to counter the shortage of younger workers. Hong said an occasional person of retirement age would stay on as a part-time "advisor," drawing both pension and salary. In fact I had not seen many obviously elderly people working in his tractor factory or elsewhere. If such a practice was actually rare, that might have been one measure of the extent to which Confucianism, with its deference to age, remained a cultural force in the North—or it might simply have meant the people were wearing out early by contemporary Western and Japanese standards.

Workers made an average of 90 *won,* or about $53 at the official exchange rate, per month, Hong said. But he quickly added that the wage was just frosting on the cake, since "the material and cultural life of our people is provided by the state." Thus, "if we calculate the solicitude and benevolence they are receiving from the state—such as vacation facilities, free medical treatment, free education—the workers' actual income is much more than their cash income."

Wage differentials were based on position and degree of skill. While college graduates made up the management corps, workers with ability could be promoted to team leader and workshop leader. "But the difference is not so much," Hong said. The entire range ran from about 80 *won* for beginners up to about 150 *won* for the factory manager and highly skilled technicians. I heard of similar pay ranges at other enterprises, including a hothouse.

Amazingly, Hong could not say how much the Kumsong plant's tractors cost to produce. "We don't calculate the cost of the tractors," he said. "The Agricultural Committee takes care of that." The factory supplied the tractors directly to the counties' agricultural managements. Asked about the plant's annual operating budget, Hong replied, "As I am not in charge of the plant's budget, I don't have a figure."[12] I hoped someone had some idea about the costs—if only in order to figure a rational selling price for the portion of output that was being sent abroad, mostly to Third World countries, particularly in the Middle East.

Journeys outside Pyongyang—chaperoned journeys, always—revealed towns and small cities, each a miniature Pyongyang, the men neatly dressed in Western-style suits or in Mao suits with Lenin caps, the women often garbed in the colorful Korean traditional dresses, the children marching to or from school in the uniforms of the children's corps. In the countryside I passed neat rice paddies, vegetable fields and orchards lined with irrigation canals, the trucks and tractors greatly outnumbering the bullock-pulled carts and plows, the farmers housed in substantial-looking apartment complexes or clusters of tile-roofed, masonry-walled houses. I was told that 560,000 dwelling units had been built at state expense for farmers.

One day early in the rice-planting season my handlers took me to Chonsam-ri, a cooperative farm near the east coast port of Wonsan. At dusk I came upon scenes that might have made a nice poster to promote socialist agricultural policies. The glistening water atop the knee-deep mud of the farm's paddies showed reflections of the conical, orchard-topped hills punctuating the plain. A man wearing a Lenin cap piloted a chugging rice-planting machine across one of the paddies. Two kerchiefed women, perched on the back, fed seedlings into the device, which plopped them, upright and evenly spaced, into the fertilized and smoothed ooze. Two helpers slogged along.

Beyond a stone-banked irrigation canal and a narrow road bordering it, kindergarten children sang and danced to the accompaniment of a pump organ played by a woman teacher. In the nursery next door, toddlers chanted in unison the name of the place where Kim Il-sung was born, Mangyongdae. Otherwise, there was little activity and there were few sounds. Most of the five hundred or so adults who did the farming work were nowhere to be seen. The children, it was said, had stayed late so that they could perform for me.

Perhaps the farmers had retreated into their tile-roofed houses to leave the sensitive contact with the foreigner to ideologically sound and reliable colleagues. Could it have been that enthusiasm for the collectivization of farming was not yet universal among its practitioners? But there was a more mundane, less conspiratorial possibility that could explain the adults' absence. Only a few days remained before the height of the transplanting season — the time when, as an old Korean saying goes, "even a stick of stovewood moves." Perhaps the unseen farmers were resting in preparation for those hectic days when army units, students and office workers from the cities would be mobilized to help out on farms like this one.

Recall that, before the post–World War II partition of Korea, the northern part had specialized in mining and industry while depending on the granary of the mineral-poor southern part for food. Now there was no exchange between the communist North and the capitalist South. The North must attempt to feed itself, despite its mountainous topography. The goal of self-reliance in agriculture had led to extremely labor-intensive additions to acreage through land reclamation. Irrigation channels, the result of Kim Il-sung's "grand plan to remake nature,"[13] totaled some forty thousand kilometers — long enough to girdle the world, as I was told. And Kim had taught that "fertilizer means rice; rice means socialism." Fertilizer output was reported to have increased two and half times between 1970 and 1978. Farmers were applying more than 120 kilograms of chemical fertilizer per person per year — equivalent to twice the weight of every man, woman and child in the country.

With the right timing, hard work and the water from rain-swollen reservoirs, North Koreans hoped to approach the goal of harvesting 8.8 million tons of grain for the year — although previous harvests had made clear it was difficult for the three-quarters mountainous country to produce enough food to sustain 17 million people.[14]

❖   ❖   ❖

In 1954, after the Korean War, the three hundred or so peasant families who were farming in Chonsam-ri owned two cows among them, my hosts told me. The fields were hilly and unevenly laid out. There were only a few farm implements. The peasants had suffered greatly from the fierce war sweeping back and forth across their country. In accordance with the party line dictating collectivization of all agriculture, the lands owned by the peasants of Chonsam-ri were pooled that year to make a cooperative farm. All members would own the cooperative in common. Youngsters who grew up and decided to stay on, or outsiders who might come from the cities and ask to join, would be given equal shares of the ownership automatically.

The crops would be shared among the members, not equally but according to work performed. The party leaders in Pyongyang did not think the country was yet ready to live by what communist ideology considers a loftier principle: "From each according to his ability, to each according to his needs." Along with the transition from cooperative to state-owned farms, that was to come later. (A quarter century later, those changes still had not come.)

If the farmers had yet to achieve ideal communism, nevertheless there had been plenty of other advances, as Chun To-kun was happy to point out. Chun, who looked a little like a skinny young Paul Newman, was introduced as deputy chairman of Chonsam Cooperative Farm. One of his duties was showing the occasional foreign visitor around. The government's reservoir-building program and irrigation work had allowed farming "without any worry about water supply and without receiving any influence from drought," Chun said. Farmers had smoothed out the 1,360 acres of paddy field and divided them into neat rectangles. They had terraced the hills, evenly planting 370 acres in vegetables and an equal area in persimmon orchards. The farm had the use of twenty-six tractors. "Our Great Leader provided them," Chun said.

Kim Il-sung had promised that his regime would enable everyone to live in tile-roofed houses. Indeed, the Chonsam farmers' neat white masonry houses were all roofed with ceramic tiles—the traditional Korean status symbol that only well-to-do farmers had been able to afford in the old days. The state had built the houses and turned them over to the farmers. Schools, a small hospital, a barbershop and a laundry served the 1,500 people living on the farm. About a quarter of the 270 households had television sets, Chun said, and the cooperative paid from its culture fund to bring in films to show on its three projectors.

The changes had been slow in coming at first, leaving Chonsam-ri one of the more backward of North Korea's cooperative farms. The big breakthrough, Chun said, came with 1959 and 1961 visits by Kim Il-sung. At that time there was no road into the farm and the hills were covered with pine trees. The state had begun to promote the planting of orchards only in 1958. "Our Great Leader pushed through the trees and grasses and taught

us how to develop our farm," Chun said. Monuments commemorated those
first visits by President Kim to give "on-the-spot guidance." Another monument recalled his only other visit since then, in 1976. In the fall of 1978, just
a few months before my visit, Kim had held forth on farming questions at a
party committee meeting in Wonsan, the nearby capital of the province.
There he had instructed everyone to plant persimmon trees.[15]

"Whenever our Great Leader visited and saw our farmers working in the
paddy fields with crooked backs, weeding with hands and hoes, he told us
that he couldn't eat rice with an easy mind when he saw such hard work,"
Chun said. "So he sent to our farm various kinds of insecticides, weed killers,
weeding equipment, agricultural equipment. He sent these things to all cooperative farms, but he paid special attention to this farm because of its backwardness." Still, Chonsam-ri was only an ordinary North Korean cooperative
farm, Chun insisted—not a model farm such as the famous (and, to the Western ear, confusingly similar-sounding) Chongsan-ri, where the country's agricultural policies had been incubated.[16] Indeed, three visits by the peripatetic
leader were not, relatively speaking, very many.

Model farm or not, Chonsam-ri had a prosperous look to it. The previous year, Chun said, the farm had produced 4,200 tons of crops including
3,600 tons of rice. The average share of each family was six tons of grain,
which could be sold to the state, and cash in the amount of 3,000 *won* ($1,754
at the official exchange rate). That would have made the Chonsam-ri farmers
slightly better off than average wage earners in the cities and towns. "During
the past, the young people preferred to go to the city to work," the farm official said, "but now young people from the city are coming to the countryside
because the living standards of cooperative farmers have improved."

Farmers shared in the cooperative's income according to a formula setting norms for what would be considered a day's work in a particular task.
Hand transplanting of rice seedlings is backbreaking work, and there were
not enough rice-planting machines in operation in North Korea yet to make
the old way obsolete. Bending to plant one hundred seedlings was considered
a day's work. A farmer got due credit, in the form of added fractional "days
worked," for overfulfilling the quota. On the other hand, plowing was mechanized and a day's work was considered planting one hectare (two and a half
acres). Farmers shared the grain crop, and cash earned by the cooperative
from sales of vegetables and fruit, according to each family's total days worked,
officials said. But first, the cooperative took a portion out for the common
fund to finance the next year's farming and development projects. The farm
had to buy fertilizer and tractor fuel from the state and pay the state for water supply and tractor rental.

The work on the farm remained hard and long. The farmers followed
the old East Asian custom of taking a day of rest only every ten days. In the
winter, though, there was a day off once a week, and each family could take

fifteen days' leave each year for a vacation at a state-provided beach or mountain resort. "Our farmers," Chun said, "are receiving great benevolence from the state."

Children inherited household effects from their deceased parents, Chun told me, and could stay on in the family homes if they wished. The typical family kept savings of about 10,000 *won* ($5,850 at the official exchange rate) in a state bank in the name of the head of the household. By custom another family member could use the money. Money in a savings account drew interest of about 4 percent a year. In the cooperative's early days, Chun said, farmers had borrowed money from the bank, but later they had found it unnecessary to do so. The farmers did not have much need for their savings, aside from financing weddings and the like, Chun said, because "thanks to the solicitude of our Great Leader, the state provides the goods needed for our farmers' life. Even raincoats are supplied for work at very cheap prices."

I knew that outsiders' reports of North Korea's economic shambles, even if exaggerated compared with the real situation in 1979, had their basis in genuine difficulties. Drought had affected harvests for several years. And, of course, the country had failed to repay its foreign trade debts. But officials' talk during my visit was upbeat. Rains in that spring of 1979 had filled the reservoirs, they said. They predicted a bountiful harvest. And they claimed the country would be able to pay off its foreign debts by 1984, the end of the current seven-year economic plan.

Obviously there had been a great deal of construction already—I took a trip by car on a recently completed and nearly empty multi-lane highway across a hundred miles of mountainous terrain between Pyongyang and the east coast port of Wonsan. Generally, what I saw of North Korea had a built-up and well-tended look. The seven-year plan for 1978–1984 called for nearly doubled electrical power output and steel production.

But many outsiders were skeptical about the chances of meeting the new plan's goals—especially since the capital-short regime counted on increased labor efficiency to power three-quarters of the increase.[17] Certainly there was no sign of a real boom such as capitalist South Korea had been experiencing for several years. Missing were the signs of rising affluence that could be seen in the South: streets and highways clogged with private cars and taxis, new hotels opulent enough for Dallas or Palm Springs going up in the heart of the capital, a vibrant stock market fueled with cash from a new middle class. But neither did one see in North Korea slums, prostitution, street waifs hawking chewing gum—signs easily found in the South of 1979 that some segments of society had been left behind.

North and South Korea each claimed per capita gross national product of more than $1,200. Western and South Korean estimates at the time placed the Northern figure at only about half that amount, giving the twice-as-populous South an enormous advantage in the overall weight of its economy. While it was possible that estimates from sources unfriendly to the North had overstated the difference—and while it was hard to compare the two quite different economic systems—it did seem that there was a gap in the South's favor, one that might well continue to widen.

But then again, the vagaries of the international economy and then-rampant inflation might conceivably take a heavy toll in the South.[18] North Korean officials claimed their economy was immune from such forces, and on that basis they seemed to hope that time was really on their side. A planned economy, with virtually no private sector beyond the farmers' small, household vegetable plots, meant that the state set prices. Necessities were cheap. Rice, the basic dietary staple, went for the equivalent of two cents a pound at the official exchange rate. Anything deemed a luxury, on the other hand, was very expensive. A black-and-white television cost the equivalent of $175— more than three months' wages for the average worker. The state provided housing, health care and education without levying taxes.

In Pyongyang, at the Children's Palace, a soldier packing a pistol guarded the lobby as visitors from abroad arrived for an evening performance by school-aged youngsters enrolled in afternoon performing-arts classes. One of the lavishly staged skits dramatized the youthful exploits of Kim Il-sung in guerrilla warfare against the Japanese. As children on the stage chased others who were done up as caricatures of grinning, bowing Japanese, with enormous papier-mâché heads, an English translation of the pursuers' call was projected on a screen: "Let's march forward, following our commander, to annihilate the Japs to the last man."

The day I visited the Chonsam-ri cooperative farm, a nursery school teacher was leading her four-year-old charges in one of their favorite exercises. Holding aloft a toy rifle, she called out, "How do we shoot the rifle?"

"Pull the trigger! Pull the trigger!" the little ones responded in unison, shouting at the tops of their lungs.

I quickly learned that North Korean officials took immense pride in the country's elaborate, state-financed system of nurseries, schools, "children's palaces," colleges, universities, courses for workers at their job sites and correspondence courses. Of the population of 17 million, some 8 million were enrolled, paying no fees. The society, officials said, was being "intellectualized."[19]

The basis of the system was composed of nurseries followed by compulsory education from kindergarten through tenth grade. Matriculation came when a baby, only a few weeks old, was sent to a nursery at the mother's work-place. The children would stay there from early morning until late evening. The mothers were permitted breaks from their work to feed them. After regular classes, the state kept school-aged youngsters busy with supervised activities. Youngsters might end up spending only an hour or two a day with their parents, if that much. North Korea had been one of the first Asian countries to extend free public education as far as grade ten, and that in itself was an undeniably impressive accomplishment. As a Westerner, though, I could not help finding a sinister aspect to the system's near monopoly on children's upbringing and the direction in which it guided them.

Official propaganda claimed on one level that the children themselves were the beneficiaries of the approach. "In this country," President Kim had said, "children are the kings." His disciples rhapsodically reported that the Great Leader would do anything for the children, and that the educational system was a manifestation of his boundless love for them.

I visited a Pyongyang weekly boarding nursery, whose tiny charges spent only Saturday nights and Sundays with their families. The director said enthusiastically that they "grow faster and learn more than if they were at home." Meanwhile, tots in her nursery competed in a relay race to see which of two teams could be first to complete sentences such as "We are happy" and "We have nothing to envy in the world." Two-year-olds in the showplace nursery were counting apples displayed on a visual aid: "These are four and one more makes five." In a room decorated with models of President Kim's birthplace, little ones showed the proper attitude to the Great Leader by reciting stories of his childhood and bowing before his boyhood portrait. By the time children reached kindergarten age, they would have learned to say, when they received their snacks, "Thank you, Great Fatherly Leader."

Sometimes it was the parents who were said to benefit from the country's educational system. Mothers were "liberated" for "political, economic and cultural life," the nursery director said. At the mammoth Pyongyang Children's Palace, an official explained that having the state in charge of children not only in school but after school meant that "parents do not have to worry about the children's education." The "palace" kept ten thousand middle school and high school students busy from 4 P.M. to 7 P.M. daily with classes—some rather advanced—in music, arts, crafts, vocational subjects, sports, gymnastics and communist ideology. Provincial capitals offered similar if somewhat smaller facilities.

On another level, Kim Il-sung himself had indicated that benefits flowing from the educational system to parents and children as individuals were not really what he had in mind. Rather, the education system was intended to benefit the collective mass of the people. After all, as Kim told a national meeting of teachers in a key speech in 1971, "in any society the primary aim of education lies in training people to faithfully serve the existing social system." Echoing Friedrich Engels, Kim argued that the socialist state must "prevent the old ideas of their parents from exerting influence on children's minds." Children would be taught to be militant revolutionaries. "We must educate the students to hate the landlord and capitalist classes and the exploiting system," Kim said. "If we neglect the education of the rising generation on such lines, they will lose sight of the class enemies and, lapsing into a pacifistic mood, hate to make revolution and, in the end, may degenerate and become depraved."

Any stray impulses to go in a different direction would be rooted out. Children in a socialist society, Kim said, should be guided "to reject individualism and selfishness, love the organization and the collective, and struggle devotedly for the sake of society and the people and the party and the revolution."

I saw just how seriously North Koreans took that struggle for uniformity and against individualism when I went to the Taedongmun Primary School in Pyongyang. Teachers in classrooms I visited were posing questions to classes studying, variously, birds, evaporation and the revolutionary deeds of President Kim. Upon hearing each question, the pupils, sitting perfectly erect and still at their desks, all raised their hands, barked in unison, "Me!" and then instantly fell quiet again. Whenever any pupil was called upon, he or she marched to the front of the room, stood at attention and shouted out the memorized answer in a high-pitched monotone like the one used by West Point plebes to address upperclass cadets. Among the pupils who were not called upon, no one stirred; no one whispered.

Chung Kwang-chun, the principal, bragged in an interview that this was an "all-A's school." A single teacher had charge of the same group of pupils as they passed through all four grades, she said. That teacher was responsible for making sure—through extra work, if necessary—that all members of the class progressed well. "In the final analysis, we don't believe there are people who can't learn and can't study," Mrs. Chung said. She enumerated the most important subjects taught at the school, in this order: (1) "the revolutionary activities of the Great Leader," (2) communist morality, (3) reading, (4) math. Actually, in the forty-three pages of the Great Leader's important 1971 speech, "On the Thorough Implementation of the Principles of Socialist Pedagogy in Education," he had not mentioned either reading or math.

At the time of the Korean War, Confucian filial piety had remained enough of a force that parents still had taken first place, even in Kim Il-sung's rhetoric. Speaking with the army corps commander leading the battle of Heartbreak

Ridge, Kim supposedly told him he wanted the soldiers to "realize that it is the wish of their parents and the Party's line that not even an inch of the sacred soil of the fatherland be yielded to the enemy. . . ." When his words were duly conveyed to the men, "moved by their Leader's love, all rubbed their eyes with their fists" and pledged to do as parents and party asked.[20]

More recently, however, Kim had been talking about "revolutionizing the homes,"[21] and I began to get some concrete idea of what that meant. When I asked Principal Chung about parents' role in their children's education, she said they were allowed to visit the school, and ought to help the pupils with their studies. She added, however, that parents were not called in for disciplinary problems, which were handled with teacher persuasion (no corporal punishment) and—through the school's Young Pioneers–style children's corps—peer criticism.

Actually, Mrs. Chung said, there were few behavior problems. The pupils hardly ever fought among themselves, even outside class, because "we are educating them in communist morality." She was proud of the discipline of her students. Sitting up straight in class was required for health reasons, she said. Outside class the pupils were free to slouch if they liked—"but as we teach them the healthful way, they always follow that way." Even as she spoke, I heard from the playground the unmistakable sound of schoolchildren at recess, whooping and running around. Relieved by this return to recognizable reality, I stepped to the window to photograph the scene. Mrs. Chung, however, quickly spoke to my interpreter—who strode over and grasped my arm before I could click the shutter. Those two explained, patiently and in excruciatingly friendly fashion, that such a photograph of unorganized activity might make a bad impression abroad.

Quite the contrary, I replied. Americans and many other Westerners would be favorably impressed by such evidence that at least a little freedom survived in such a rigidly controlled society.

My interpreter, though, would not buy the argument. North Koreans valued unity, he explained earnestly. As for the schoolchildren, "we are educating them in a unitary idea—thinking in the same way and acting in the same way." The playground picture, unfortunately, would not illustrate that.[22]

Even at the time of my first visit, such thinking—no matter how passionately taught by earnest ideologues—was in decline in many other communist countries. Kim Il-sung himself had warned North Korean teachers to guard against the trend in some socialist countries for the young to seek "a fast and indolent life." Such a development in North Korea could result in slowed

economic growth, he had warned. The children must be educated to "love labor." They must be "working-classized," and taught to "have faith in communism before anything else." Later, in his memoirs, he blamed the Khrushchev
brand of communists for problems with the younger generation: Such people, "who are addicted to extreme egoism and hedonism, are not taking care
of the younger generation; they are disarming them spiritually and exposing
them to all sorts of social evils."[23]

In North Korea's case, it was very difficult for a foreigner to judge how
well the regime had succeeded in achieving its goal of casting all the young in
the same mold. My interpreter, Han Yong, seemed a fairly typical representative of the earnest and zealous Kimilsungists of his generation, a star product
of the educational system that he was showing me. He was a twenty-nine-
year-old senior at the Foreign Languages University, majoring in English.
He and his entire class had been mobilized to interpret for tournament visitors. Han hoped to become an engineer, he said, and studied English because
it would help him "look at what others have done and apply the best to Korea." For his engineering training, he planned to take a correspondence
course. Han said he wanted to marry, and had a bride picked out, but thought
it "better to wait, since I returned to school at an old age." (He didn't say so,
but presumably he had served in the military before college, as was typical.)
Han said his proudest moment had been joining the Korean Workers' Party
in 1973.

Otherwise, I could see three- and four-year-olds in the accordion band[24]
at the September Fifteenth Nursery in Pyongyang who had obeyed the
Great Leader's dictum that every child should learn to play a musical instrument. The youngsters employed precisely the same technique as all of the uncounted other youthful accordionists in the country—smiling, cocking their
heads, keeping eye contact with the audience—as they pumped out a pass-
able melody. Then there were the groups of red-kerchiefed children's corps
members marching to and from school in formation, saluting passengers in
passing cars, halting to perform community cleanup projects.

A boy assembling a miniature electric motor in a class at the Pyongyang
Children's Palace might say during an interview, as twelve-year-old Jong-
hyun did, "When I grow up I want to become an electrician because electricity is very important in building our country into an independent and
powerful country, according to the teachings of the Great Leader." Still, I
could not go out freely and talk at random with young adults who had spent
most of their lives being indoctrinated, to see how much of it had taken.

Instead, I had to settle for contacts with the North Koreans whom the authorities had placed in my path—Lee Yong-ho, for example, who identified
himself as a twenty-six-year-old doctoral candidate in molecular biology at

Kim Il-sung University, one of the one million intellectuals the regime claimed to have produced in its push to develop the country.

Finding Lee on a weekday afternoon was unavoidable. For days I had been asking my handlers to let me meet some university students, and on this afternoon they finally told me it was time to visit the university. When we arrived, however, the campus was deserted. I asked them where all the students had gone. In a seminar, was the reply. "Twelve thousand students in a seminar," I marveled. "Amazing!" I contemplated the possibility that the authorities had gone to the trouble of emptying out a campus just to make sure I would not have any unscheduled conversations with the wrong people. Anyhow, when my handlers ushered me across campus and up several flights of stairs to a particular laboratory, Lee just happened to be sitting there—in a business suit, with a miniature, gold-framed, enameled portrait of President Kim pinned to his left lapel—peering intently at a textbook.

A bull-necked boxer, soccer player and veteran of army service, Lee in response to my questions professed a complete lack of interest in the two prime interests of 1970s students in the West: protest and sex. As for sex, he said that he had neither girlfriend nor wife, and never thought of such things even though the university was coeducational. "I am a student, so I am studying now, concentrating all my efforts on my subject," he said. Student dissent, Mr. Lee said, would be unthinkable at Kim Il-sung University. There were not even any campus issues, much less national issues, to arouse rebellious feelings. "Among our students you can't find a single one who believes there is some element to be criticized," he said.

(Hwang Jang-yop, a former president of the university, confirmed following his 1997 defection to the South that "student demonstrations calling for freedom on campus are unthinkable." But he contradicted student Lee on another point. "In Kim Il-sung University, the students start harboring suspicions about the Great Leader's personality cult by the time they are in their second year, but none of them dare to voice their suspicions out loud."[25])

It dawned on me during that 1979 visit that, in its zeal to create a new man, the regime had swept away most traces of the cultural achievements of Korea's past. I was astonished to learn that even the Korean classics were taught only at universities—not at either primary or secondary level in schools. Instead, an official explained, students studied the modern Korean classics of Kim Il-sung and his *juche* philosophy. The music I heard, from the choral numbers in *Song of Paradise* right down to the oom-pah-pah marches and ditties that the kindergartners pumped out on their accordions, sounded basically Western as interpreted through a Japanese filter. The architecture of the boxy buildings likewise was largely Western in style—Stalinist, I would say—as were the ubiquitous oil paintings of Kim.

I arranged an interview with Lee Sang-tae, a member of the Central Committee of the General League of Writers and Artists, and asked him what had become of the old works. After all, as Lee himself told me, Korea claims thousands of years of history and "the literature and art in our country bloomed in the tenth century"—by which time Korean pottery, art and architecture were being exported across the Korea Strait to become a formative element in what is now Japanese culture. Ironically, as Lee noted, it was the Japanese who, in the colonial period, tried to "stamp out our national literature and language."

After liberation Kim Il-sung, like the Japanese colonialists before him, sought to root out old ways of thinking—in this case "feudalistic and Confucian"—and enforce new, communist norms.[26] "While other people were traveling the world by warship and by train, our country's feudal rulers rode on donkeys and wore horse-hair hats, singing of scenic beauties," Kim later wrote in a contemptuous assessment of traditional culture.[27] "Revolution is to overthrow the old system and establish a new system," he explained in a speech. "Cultural revolution is also devoted to eradicating the old and bringing the new into being."[28]

The country's 1972 constitution called for just such a cultural revolution. Unlike the Japanese, Kim with his nationalist background knew that trying to extirpate Korean tradition completely would only alienate the people. He compromised based on Stalin's "Socialism in one country" formula, which had revised the original utopian notion of communist internationalism so as to allow for the reality of national differences. This cultural policy Kim eventually bundled into his overall *juche* philosophy of national self-reliance.[29]

Culture in North Korea would be "socialist in content, national in form."[30] In other words, old novels, plays, songs and poems unsuitable for the indoctrination of the masses might be consigned to libraries and filing cabinets accessible only to a handful of specialists—but the regime would recycle elements of the old Korean forms to support the new, approved content. In my talk with Lee Sang-tae, I observed that this content seemed limited—mainly praising socialism and Kim Il-sung. Lee did not disagree, but explained, "We think that the main function and purpose of literature and art is, firstly, describing and also depicting the sentimental, general life of the people. Secondly, they should also be means of educating the people. We educate them to love the fatherland and their socialist system and to revere the Leader and to have sound morality and sound life and to have a noble human feeling and civilized feeling and life."

Lee's organization was in charge of making sure writers and artists did their duty, assigning and enforcing production quotas on behalf of the Culture and Arts Division of the Workers' Party.[31] Having been tamed by purges of creative people in 1952, 1956, 1961, 1963 and 1964 (plus others, following Kim Jong-il's takeover of culture, as we shall see in chapter 13),

those remaining in the field presumably had a proper respect for authority
and were ready to comply.

And what were the results? In many cases, Lee told me, the regime had
produced new versions of folk songs whose original versions were no longer
sung. The traditional elements provided "interest and flavor." He hummed a
few bars of one such recent product, a song called "Moranbong." Sure
enough, it did come through with the nasal sound and the catch in the voice
that I associated with East Asian folk music. Lee said the old folk melody
might be used as the basis for a more "modern" sound—an example, in *Song
of Paradise*, being the dance and grand ensemble "Let Us Boast of Our
Bumper Harvest to the Whole World," which sounded to my ear somewhere
between Indian raga and American bluegrass.[32]

Still, I said to Lee, most of *Song of Paradise* seemed Western in feeling. Did
the use of the gigantic choirs possibly trace back to the church music brought
in by Western missionaries from the late nineteenth century? Absolutely not,
Lee replied. "We have had no such influence from the missionaries. We developed our songs based on our traditional heritage. Before liberation we had
religions—Buddhism, Christianity—but after liberation the influence of those
disappeared."

I saw or heard little in the way of overtly foreign cultural offerings, but
Lee assured me the works of the likes of Beethoven and Tchaikovsky were
studied and performed by "specialists." He added that there had been two
series of translations of foreign literary classics, one in 1955 and a second in
1977. Shakespeare, Balzac, Jack London, Mark Twain, Homer, Goethe, By-
ron, Gorky and Tolstoy were names he mentioned of authors he said were
generally available to North Korean readers. As for movies, such relatively
tame offerings as *Cleopatra* and *Spartacus* had been imported for general
distribution—but the regime drew the line at the more recent, sexier offerings of Hollywood. Nudity and sexual permissiveness, Lee said, were alien to
the "traditional way of life of our people."

I asked whether rock-'n'-roll music would be an acceptable import. That
stopped my otherwise very competent interpreter.

"What is rock-and-roll music?" he asked me. "Do you mean jazz?"

I explained, and he passed along my explanation to Lee, but Lee replied
that he likewise had never heard of rock-and-roll music.

In addition to music, Lee said, "we develop modern fine arts based on [tradi-
tional] Korean paintings." Those tended toward group efforts, however, as individualism was one of the bad old traits the regime was trying to root out.
Pictures embroidered in silk, for example, were produced by teams. Different
teams had responsibility for design and the actual embroidery, as I found on
a visit to Pyongyang's Embroidery Research Institute.

I was curious about one of the finest of traditional Korean arts, pottery making. Sadly for connoisseurs of celadon and other famous varieties of Korean pottery, ceramics as an art had become truly a thing of the past. "To meet the needs of the people we produce by industrial means, not by handicraft," Lee told me, although he assured me that "artistic features are used in the pottery and some hand touches remain, such as hand-drawn pictures on the pottery."

The health-care system offered a case study in the ways North Korea combined various threads of the country's ideology—socialism, modernization and crash development, nationalism and national self-sufficiency, the Kim Il-sung personality cult.

The official literature around the time of my 1979 visit held up health-care workers and especially physicians as examples of what the regime asked of its subjects. The doctors were expected literally to cut themselves to pieces for their patients. There was the story, told in the newspaper *Nodong Shinmun*, of a surgeon in a small hospital in a place called Ryongsong who felt sorry for a youthful polio victim. To correct a bad limp, the child needed a bone graft. The doctor cut out a chunk of his own bone and implanted it in the child's leg.

Similar stories of doctors giving their own blood and flesh to their patients had flowed regularly from the North Korean propaganda machine since the start of the Chollima movement in the late 1950s. They included cases of physicians donating skin to burn victims, and even one case of an eye surgeon who was preparing to transplant his own corneal tissue to a patient until the doctor's wife and daughter agreed to be the donors. In the latter case, when the bandages were removed and the surgery proved successful, the transplant recipient was reported to have shed tears "for the happy socialist system and the good care of the Great Leader." Whether true or not, those stories were one of the means the regime used in seeking to obliterate the last traces of pre-revolutionary thinking and acting in order to create a new type of man—unselfish, nationalistic and dedicated to the achievement of a socialist paradise on earth. Such people were "new communist human beings safely reared under the warm care of Comrade Kim Il-sung."[33]

The stories illustrated the conflict between old and new ways. Although no places of religious worship remained—officials claimed that U.S. bombs had destroyed every single Christian church during the Korean War—still old customs based on both Eastern and Western religious beliefs persisted. One of those customs was that the dead were to be dressed in new clothing, placed in coffins and buried. Removing tissue or complete organs from a cadaver was taboo. The repeated tales of doctors literally giving of themselves to their patients confronted the old religious taboo indirectly even as officials pleaded with selected bereaved families to confront it directly by permitting organ donations. This may explain why the officially spread stories were vague on the question of why the surgeons did not use whalebone or pigskin, for example.

The doctors' self-sacrifice stories came out of a propaganda campaign directed at health workers themselves, seeking to teach them by example to be more aware of their responsibility for "the welfare of the people" and to inspire them to practice "high ideology and morality in treatment."[34]

In case they might be inclined to forget their identity with the masses, doctors' salaries were kept low. The maximum, for a physician with twenty years' experience, was 180 *won* a month—$105 at the official exchange rate and only double the average pay for North Korean wage earners in general. Then there was professional review, which appeared to consist at least in part of the "criticism sessions" typical in communist countries. While interviewing Dr. Han Ung-se, the Public Health Ministry's director of treatment and preventive health care, I mentioned that workers in the tractor plant I had visited lacked safety goggles, helmets, hard-toed boots and guard plates for their metal-cutting machines. Han replied, a trifle ominously, that the doctor in charge of the plant's health and safety "will be criticized."

Saying that they were following Kim Il-sung's idea that "man is the most precious," officials took great pride in having established a system of constitutionally guaranteed, free, cradle-to-grave health care. The U.S. Navy crewmen of the *Pueblo* had reported considerable experience with North Korean medical services, and their views were far from positive.[35] But having no real opportunity to verify the state of North Korean public opinion on the quality of health care, I could not rule out the possibility that there was more than a little truth in the official assertions that the country's people were pleased with the system as it existed in 1979. The official comparison was always with what had passed for health care before establishment of the communist state—a comparison that permitted boasting of how much better a nationalistic, self-reliant, socialist system served the people. In the period preceding 1945, Dr. Han of the Public Health Ministry told me, the medical system reflected the Japanese view of Koreans as expendable cogs in the colonial economy. Consequently, there were no public hospital beds and fewer than three hundred private beds. Medical doctors (presumably excluding traditional practitioners) numbered fewer than thirty, with some records giving the figure as nine, Han said.

By the time of my visit, Han told me, North Korea had more than thirty thousand doctors—one for every four hundred people.[36] The North had ten medical colleges, a college of pharmacy and twelve other schools teaching nursing, dentistry, midwifery and so on. Hospitals ranged down to eleven-bed units serving villages. Physicians were organized to care for groups of families. Individuals' medical record cards followed them throughout their lives. During the thirty-four years following liberation from Japanese rule, health workers had eradicated cholera, plague, malaria, syphilis and gonorrhea, they said. Average life spans had increased by decades, reaching seventy for men and seventy-six for women.

I was intrigued by a nationalistic element that was prominent in North Korean thinking about health care. I heard vague, unbacked assertions that Koreans were unique in their health-care needs and that—partly because of that uniqueness, and in line with *juche* philosophy—locally developed remedies were best. Even while subscribing to some three thousand foreign medical journals, Dr. Han said, the thirty-two medical-research agencies in North Korea "develop medical science according to the physical character of our people. A few of our doctors studied abroad, but mostly we educated them in our own colleges." Han himself was one of the local products, he said, having been a "worker" prior to 1945. "Of course those who studied abroad know well about world treatment methods," he said, "but they don't know well how to treat our own people according to their own physical characteristics."

In line with this sort of thinking, North Korea was manufacturing most of its mass-consumption medicines. About 60 percent of that output represented traditional Oriental medicines, such as the ones Kim Il-sung's father had dispensed in Manchuria. "Medicine appropriate to foreigners may not suit us," Han told me. Besides, he said, the people liked the homegrown and home-brewed tonics, cold remedies and aids to digestion. The most famous of those was the human-shaped ginseng root, believed to prolong life. It grows in various parts of Asia—but the ginseng with the best medical effect grows only in Korea, around Panmunjom, I was told.

I encountered some evidence suggesting that the merger of traditional Oriental and modern Western medicine might be incomplete. At the Chonsam-ri cooperative farm I visited the little hospital. Outside the building, a farm official pointed out the herb garden. "When our Great Leader visited here, he taught us we must produce a lot of medicinal herbs," the official said. Then a woman described as an "assistant doctor" showed me around inside the clinic: surgery, internal medicine, physical therapy, lab, pharmacy, dentistry, obstetrics and gynecology.

In front of one treatment room, however, she remained silent. A gaunt, disheveled, elderly man standing in the doorway of that room stared at me. The woman guiding me appeared annoyed and tried to shut the door in the old man's face. Standing his ground, he continued to stare. The assistant doctor tried once more to shut the door, whereupon I asked her the purpose of the room. "Korean medicine," she muttered impatiently, hustling me away. Possible explanations for this odd incident that came to mind were that the old practitioner might be a crank—perhaps an extreme xenophobe—or that he might be a suspected malcontent not cleared to talk with foreigners. But

I was inclined to believe I had witnessed a minor battle in the professional turf wars. In the woman's voice I thought I detected the condescending tone some orthopedists might affect when speaking of chiropractors. As we walked past, I glimpsed inside the man's room a large, wooden medicine chest of the traditional Korean style, with scores of tiny drawers.

The official view on mental health care similarly emphasized locally developed remedies. When I asked Dr. Han whether Freudian-style therapy was employed, puzzled expressions appeared on the faces of my guide and my interpreter, both college-educated men fluent in English. The health official explained their bafflement: "Of course our doctors study this, but we don't introduce it in our country." Mental patients, he said, were hospitalized and treated with medicines and insulin shock. "We have good Oriental tranquilizers," Han said. Doctors in North Korea "don't exactly know the cause" of mental illness, he said, and so research was proceeding. Anyhow, he added, there was "not much mental illness—maybe one or two cases per one thousand"—in North Korea. "Some people ask why the rate is so low. We answer that our socialist system is good."

Rejecting vulnerability to the ups and downs of the world economy, North Korea for more than two decades had been following Kim's philosophy of *juche,* which emphasized satisfying basic needs from local industries using locally available resources. Recall that this inward focus of the economy originally sought to reduce dependence on the Soviet Union—which preferred a colonial-style arrangement of exchanging Soviet finished products for North Korean ores and other raw materials.

Juche had led the North Koreans to develop the ability to produce an impressive array of goods. At the Industrial and Agricultural Exhibition in Pyongyang, which had been built in 1956, were displayed the "achievements of socialist construction"—thousands of products, from automated, close-tolerance machine tools to locomotives and excavation and tunneling machinery to pharmaceuticals to toys, all described as having been manufactured within North Korea, a country the size of Pennsylvania. "Maybe the quality needs to be improved, by Western standards," conceded the exhibition director, a graduate of Kim Il-Sung University, "but we're proud that we made it ourselves."

Before *juche,* the country had exported its mineral ores, he said. But Kim Il-sung had taught his people to use those ores at home. Even though the country lacked coking coal, which is important in steelmaking, "the respected and beloved leader Chairman Kim Il-sung said iron can be produced with our own fuels." Kim's slogan had been: "Priority to heavy industry with simultaneous development of light industry and agriculture."

"We've developed our industry so that we can export a large amount of machinery and equipment to foreign countries," the exhibition director said. "We have plenty of natural resources and also we have laid the foundation of our economy. If our country is unified we can live a happy life." North Korean shipyards, he said, were building 20,000-ton ships, and soon would turn out 100,000-ton vessels. Output of trucks — ranging up to a colossal 100-ton dump truck for mining — was up nearly five times over 1959's figure, he said.

As for the machine-tool industry, which had interested me since my visit to the tractor factory, I learned that North Korean radial drilling machines were being exported to about fifty countries. The catalog continued: numerical controlled lathe, automatic copying multi-cut lathe, automatically programmed turret lathe, programmed milling machine, vertical lathe, universal tool milling machine, automatic thread cutting machine, gear slotting machine, air hammer, friction press, hydraulic press and so on. From 1946, the machine building industry's output had increased 1,012 times, I was told, and North Korea was 98 percent self-sufficient in machinery and instruments. Having some acquaintance with factory machinery, from summer jobs in an aircraft plant during my college years and, later, reporting trips to innumerable factories in several countries, I was impressed.

North Korea bought what it must from other countries, substituting to keep the need for imports to a minimum. The climate made cotton hard to grow and there was little land to spare for sheep to graze, so the country relied on Korean-developed processes for making fibers from locally available materials. The most notable was vinalon, made of anthracite and limestone — both of which were "inexhaustible in our country," the director explained. (He added that when it came time to build the first vinalon factory, "the Fatherly Leader selected the site personally.") Production had expanded to the point that the annual cloth allotment was 35.2 meters per person — "so the question of clothing is completely solved."

Besides coking coal, petroleum was the other big lack in otherwise mineral-rich North Korea. Oil had to be imported from China, the Soviet Union and the Middle East. To reduce demand, and thus dependence on outsiders, the government required that workers live near their workplaces and use public transit. In the cities, trolley systems used power that was generated in anthracite-fired or hydroelectric plants. The sparse traffic resulting at least in part from that transit policy helped give Pyongyang an almost deserted look, as if it were a ghost city.

The *juche* policy contrasted with the South Korean development model, based largely on pushing exports and encouraging foreign investments, a policy that in North Korean eyes made the South nothing more than a colony of Japan and the United States.[37] The difference could be seen in South Korean estimates that North Korea's total external trade in 1978 had amounted to only about $1.8 billion — approximately one-fifteenth the volume of South Korea's international trade.

❊   ❊   ❊

Whether visiting factories and farms or simply riding for mile after mile
through broad streets lined with trees and neat, multi-story apartment buildings in the park-studded capital of Pyongyang, I found the contrast between
what was being said by outsiders and what I was seeing with my own eyes
very sharp indeed. I was not the first visitor to wonder whether the authorities had arranged for visitors to see only showplaces, built—like a Potemkin
village of Czarist Russia—to disguise underlying poverty and impress the
credulous.

My chance to take an unguided tour came after I realized that my hosts
never scheduled appointments for me from roughly one o'clock in the afternoon until three or four. Instead, they kept urging me to take a rest in my
room. It dawned on me that the North Koreans observed the custom of the
siesta.[38] They were leaving that time free because the people I wanted to interview would be napping—and because the guide and interpreter themselves wanted to rest. One day after lunch I yawned conspicuously and said
I would like to have a rest. I could see the expressions of relief—the American had finally gotten with the program. We all took the elevator up together,
and I got off at my floor. My handlers continued on to the floor immediately
above me, where they had rooms. As soon as the elevator door shut, I took
the stairs back down to the lobby. There, momentarily at least, the coast was
clear. Trying to look as if I knew where I was going, I strode out into the
park. Spying a narrow footbridge, I crossed to the other side of a stream and
into what I took to be something approximating the real world of Pyongyang:
both neat apartment buildings and, mixed into the urban landscape, realistically grimy sheds and small industrial installations.

People looked at me suspiciously. I have no idea who was the first to
rush off and inform the authorities that a lone foreigner was loose in the city,
but it was only a matter of minutes before I turned around and saw a man
tailing me. He was wearing a blue blazer (with Kim Il-Sung portrait button,
of course) and gray slacks. I decided to have a little fun with him, so I turned
into an alley and then doubled back to the same street I had been walking on.
I calculated my detour to allow enough time that a man innocently walking
behind me would have passed the alley entrance and thus gotten ahead of me
by the time I emerged. As I came out of the alley, I saw the plainclothes security man. He had stopped in front of what I took to be a miniature steelmaking furnace housed in a shed, where he stood, having lit a cigarette. He
was puffing it pensively, gazing at the fire of the furnace as if it were a particularly agreeable sunset. I half expected him to start declaiming on "the
proud life of the smelters."

I stopped and waited for him to turn around, then stared at him so that
he would be sure I knew what he was up to. What came over me, to challenge

authority so blatantly? Merely the sort of irresistible rebellious impulse that a Western traveler in Pyongyang was subject to after a few days or weeks of experiencing the regime's heavy-handed control. The plainclothesman only followed me, not forcing me to turn back. So for a couple of hours I enjoyed unaccustomed freedom of movement.

I returned to the hotel after my stroll and found my handlers waiting for me outside the entrance, looking not a little panicked. One of them angrily suggested that "special spy training" had enabled me to give them the slip. I laughed and assured him that anyone who had grown up watching cops-and-robbers shows on American television was acquainted with the elementary techniques I had employed. Later, though, I thought about it and realized that with this episode I could have fueled, quite unintentionally, any speculation among North Korean officials that I might be the Washington agent they hoped to find among the American visitors. Had this been my ticket to the interview meeting with Kim Yong-nam?[39]

The parts of Pyongyang I saw that afternoon turned out to be much like the places on the official itinerary: solidly built and clean, for the most part, with real people living in more of those beige brick apartment buildings, shopping in the stores and eating in restaurants.

Still, strains and pressures were evident. Pyongyang's deserted look during most hours of the day and night was not wholly a result of mass transit and housing policy. With manpower resources stretched almost to the breaking point, people simply had little time to stroll on the streets. As I had learned at the tractor factory, the government claimed that a maximum eight-hour workday rule was enforced, with another eight hours reserved for study and the remaining eight hours for rest, according to the dictum of President Kim. Parks and housing complexes were almost empty until late in the evening. Nurseries kept children until 8 P.M. or later while their mothers, if they were not working overtime at their jobs, presumably attended group study sessions.

Among major problems facing the regime at that point, the need to provide more and better consumer goods was high on the list. When the Chonsam-ri farm deputy manager boasted to me about the people's limited need to spend money, he failed to mention there was little in the stores for them to buy.

Recall that the regime, shortly after the Korean War, had resolved policy disputes in favor of President Kim's formula of going all out to build heavy industry, putting off until later an improvement in living standards beyond the spartan level. Then came the 1960s and Kim's militaristic policy. As scholar Joseph Sang-hoon Chung noted in 1974, the average North Korean, "though his lot has improved substantially, has not benefited fully from economic development."[40] That could be seen clearly by comparing North Korea's

serviceable machine tools with its consumer goods, which were generally
scarce, crude and monotonously lacking in variety. The country made basic
appliances—refrigerators, electric rice cookers, washers, televisions—but
had yet to place them in all households. That would take "a few years," an official said. Furniture looked as if it had been banged together by pupils in a
shop class; clothing was generally poorly tailored; the radio-phonographs in
hotel rooms did not work.

For some time, North Korean officials at higher levels had acknowledged the problems.[41] Improvement had been a major goal of the six-year economic plan recently ended, but the planners had made little headway on that
score. "Improving the people's life" was a major goal of the current seven-
year plan, which emphasized upgrading the quality and variety of consumer
goods. In his New Year's speech, Kim Il-sung had said that in 1979 the country must "elevate the living standards of the people. All factories in the sector
of light industry should operate to full capacity to produce more consumer
goods."[42]

Part of the quality problem was said to result from the laziness of some
workers who lacked the communist attitude of "one for all, all for one," and
who were not behaving, in President Kim's phrase, as "masters of the nation." If a worker is not doing a good job, said a hothouse manager, "we educate him ideologically and politically so he can carry out his tasks well."
Criticism sessions might be held—"It's something like mutual assistance so
he can correct his mistakes and become a good gardener." If a worker should
work well, "we praise and honor him." But the manager said that was "not a
particularly fixed procedure."

In that stage of development of North Korean society, officials admitted,
it was necessary to employ a system of material incentives. Work teams got
extra money for exceeding not only quantitative quotas but also quality standards, and they were supposed to find their pay docked if their work fell off.[43]
"As we are applying the cost accounting system which was created by our
Great Leader, Comrade Kim Il-sung, when we produce more we can get extra money but when we produce less we get less," said the hothouse manager.

Another obvious way to improve the quality of goods would have been to reduce the reliance on locally developed technology—under which North Koreans had figuratively reinvented the wheel in a number of fields—and import
either finished products or the plant machinery to make them. Indeed, the
country's leaders wanted to import additional selected technology from the
countries most advanced in each field, which often meant from the West and
Japan. The problem here was Pyongyang's reputation for stiffing debtors.

The usual estimate by outsiders was that North Korea owed about $2 billion abroad. The Japan External Trade Organization broke that down as $300 million owed to Japanese creditors, $500 million to Westerners and between $1 billion and $1.2 billion to other communist countries. Periodic promises to pay at least the interest due on those debts had not been kept. North Korean checks written on third-country bank accounts had even been returned for lack of funds to cover them. Although officials now talked of repaying the debts by 1984, foreign creditors were pessimistic about getting their money even by then. They cited both the unreliability of past assurances from Pyongyang and doubts that the ambitious goals of the economic plan could be met.

Much of the debt was for plants and equipment imported during the crash program to raise the technological and output levels of the country earlier in the decade. Outsiders generally believed that Pyongyang had launched the effort with little planning or preparation, following the abortive Red Cross peace talks in 1972–1973 and the shocking glimpses of Southern advances that the talks afforded North Korean officials visiting Seoul. The move to import selected foreign technology represented a relaxation—but not abandonment—of the North Korean policy of *juche*.

The plan was to pay for the overseas purchases with foreign exchange to be earned from expanded exports. When export earnings lagged and the payments slowed to a trickle, the country's international credit rating plummeted. The buying spree came to a halt. For example, trade with Japan—which had been North Korea's largest noncommunist trading partner—was reduced to largely cash transactions in a few items handled through a small company the North Koreans set up in the Portuguese colony of Macao.

When I met the director of North Korea's Institute of Economic Research, Ryom Kwon-san, for an interview, Ryom emphasized external causes for the payments problem. First, he said, the worldwide economic crisis triggered by the Arab oil embargoes and oil price increases had caused "many" countries to decline to take delivery of North Korean products they had ordered. (He mentioned only one by name, Pakistan.) Cement, magnesite clinker—for making firebricks—and machine tools were left piled up in North Korean ports. Second, he said, lower international market prices for certain commodities, especially copper, had reduced foreign exchange earnings even when the goods were shipped.

Ryom did not mention it, but I heard much later of another external factor: North Korean officials may have connived in cheating their own country, in the beginnings of an atmosphere of official corruption that was to become quite pervasive later. Kang Myong-do, a North Korean trading company vice-president, told a South Korean magazine interviewer: "The country is in such a state, and officials are just taking money for themselves.

Moranbong watch factory was built in 1978 with Swiss factory components, but it's crummy stuff. The person who arranged it got a kickback from the Swiss for paying a lot of money for old machinery."[44]

When I pressed Ryom to say whether some of the fault did not lie with North Korea itself, he admitted that delays in a port-expansion program had kept shipments from going out even in cases when buyers were prepared to accept them. The country "may have" had trouble supplying goods in a timely fashion, he said, and "possibly" was a victim of its own inexperience in trade with noncommunist countries.

Ryom said the country was completing expansion projects at its ports of Nampo, Haeju, Hungnam and Chongjin. To upgrade the capacity of the North Korean merchant fleet, he said, the shipyards had moved to build 20,000-ton cargo ships in addition to the old models of only 10,000 tons. He could not give a figure for total current fleet tonnage, he said, because he was not "a specialist in this field." Ryom suggested that a visit to the Nampo port, downriver from Pyongyang near the country's west coast, would demonstrate what was happening in port development. But I never got permission despite repeated requests. Bruce Dunning of CBS Television did go to the dry-cargo port and told me he had found dredging in progress, as well as construction to add new berths to the seven or eight in place. About ten ships were in port. A Panamanian-registered container ship was being loaded, but with old-fashioned conventional cranes; farm tractors pulling wagonloads of cargo outnumbered forklift trucks.

With improvement of transportation facilities, Ryom told me, "we think that the debt will be repaid soon." Then North Korea could proceed in carrying out "the main line of our party—to make bigger efforts to develop foreign trade in the coming years." For the time being, "we are mainly exporting cement, magnesite clinker and metal products," he said. "But we are going to emphasize also exports of machine tools, manufacturing machinery. We will increase the capacity of our factories." Already foreign demand for North Korean cement was increasing rapidly, he said, and if the seven-year plan should prove successful, the country by 1984 could be earning $1 billion a year from exports of cement, steel, chemical fertilizer and zinc.

However, some outside observers did not see much indication, up to that point, of an advancing trend in exports that would help North Korea pay off its debts. An analyst with the Japan External Trade Organization in Tokyo noted that North Korea registered a decline in such principal exports as zinc and lead from 1977 to 1978 while selling more textiles and agricultural products abroad.

North Korean officials appeared not to understand why capitalists got so upset over such matters as bounced checks. For example, Ryom, introduced to me as one of the country's leading economists, said, "Our debt is not so much. I think there is no country that is not in debt." Meanwhile, the impatience of some foreign creditors was approaching open contempt, with the view often expressed that North Korea could pay its bills if it really wanted to. The leading Japanese economic daily newspaper, *Nihon Keizai Shimbun,* had reported in January 1979 that cement plants and baking furnaces, imported from Japan but never paid for, had been placed in operation in North Korea and could produce export goods to earn foreign exchange. Add that to an apparently improved domestic economy, the paper said, and Japanese businessmen—with "an increasing sense of distrust"—wondered why North Korea did not pay up.

One Western diplomat who dealt with Pyongyang was even less reservedly bitter in his comments after several years of broken promises. He suggested that North Korea could meet its economic goals and pay its debts if it got rid of the bizarre personality cult around Kim and stopped spending huge sums for festivals honoring "the Respected and Beloved Leader."

Confronted with such criticisms, Pyongyang officials tended to go on the offensive. One approach was to blame Western lenders and news media for spotlighting the debt problem. Bai Song-chul, the official who had told me his story of being an orphan, was sitting in during my interview with Ryom. In his impatient fashion Bai interjected a typically tough message for me to pass along to the country's debtors: "If you are quiet, you will be paid back soon, but if you are shouting, you will be paid back later."

I was puzzled during and after my meeting with Ryom to realize that a North Korean economist seemed to know next to nothing of what a Western economist would consider his field. I had asked that my handlers set me up with someone broad-gauged to talk about the economy. Ryom qualified, on paper. Besides directing the Institute of Economic Research, he was chairman of the economics department at People's Economic University. But he proved a far cry from the high-powered purveyors of concepts I had spoken with in South Korea and other countries. I was dissatisfied with the bits of information I had managed to squeeze out of him in our first session of three or four hours' duration, so I asked him to return another day for a second session. The second session lasted about as long but proved equally unsatisfactory. The problem may have been not so much Ryom himself but the fact that the regime intentionally kept its economic results murky.[45]

Outside analysts had suggested that the North Koreans at the time of their ill-fated venture into world markets really did not understand the up-and-down dynamics of those markets, having been accustomed only to the formal barter among communist countries. I wonder if Ryom himself was hinting at this sort of ignorance when he remarked, "Our people learned the alphabet after liberation and do not know foreign languages very well." In fact North Korea had begun to emphasize foreign language study in the schools. But how quickly could the long-isolated country produce a sophisticated corps of world trade specialists via a rigid educational system that focused narrowly on the life, times and thought of the practically deified President Kim? Kim had directed in September 1978 that "all college students should be well versed in more than one foreign language in order to learn advanced science and technology," and one list of North Koreans studying abroad as of February 1979 counted more than four hundred studying in such fields as languages, science, mathematics, medicine and foreign languages. However, not a single economics student was listed among them.[46]

Consumer goods, debt and other problems aside, Kim Il-sung's command economy did appear to have built itself an impressive foundation. I believed I could see the magnitude of the achievement as I left the country, this time riding the train from Pyongyang to Beijing. The vistas of neat, substantial farm houses, tractors and rice-planting machines and well-scrubbed, solidly built towns gave way at the Yalu River to China's squalid rural huts, urban slums, people and draft animals engaged in backbreaking labor.

The train was made up of green-painted passenger cars, most of them divided into compartments with two lower and two upper bunks each, plus a dining car. Clearly, the sociable place to be was the dining car, and there I sat for much of the trip, alternately peering out the window and talking politics with an assortment of passengers who at various times included Hungarians, Russians, Americans, Japanese, a Dutchman and a Scot. (By now I was not surprised that no North Koreans chatted me up.)

We began the trip by passing through Pyongyang's rail yards, where wooden-bodied boxcars were lined up on sidings. The urban area petered out quickly and we were in the countryside. Here as earlier I saw numbers of tractors, and some rice-planting machines. In addition, though, oxen pulled wooden-wheeled carts. Houses in some places seemed a bit shabbier than those I had seen in other parts of North Korea—but as soon as I took note of those I would usually pass by other farming villages made up of clumps of the newer rural apartment houses that the state had been building. Soil quality on the North Korean side seemed to lessen as we drew closer to the city of Sinuiju and the Yalu River, which forms the border with China. In that area the predominant, dry-looking red clay resembled the poor fields surrounding my Georgia childhood home, whose nutrients had been leached out by generations of single-crop cotton planting and which could no longer support crops much more demanding than pine trees. Still, everything was neat and in order, and I saw no scenes of destitution.

Across the Yalu, the preferred exterior treatment for buildings changed from cream-colored stucco to red brick. We had a stop in the Chinese city of

Dandong. While waiting for a different locomotive to be attached, we passed through Chinese immigration in a station building whose large, framed portraits substituted China's then-leaders for Kim Il-sung.

Then it was on through a Chinese countryside that presented a stark contrast to what I had seen in North Korea. Carts pulled by oxen and donkeys made up a great percentage of vehicular traffic outside our train windows. Even to move a huge boulder one group of workers had nothing but a donkey cart. The Chinese in 1979 had hardly any tractors. More of the houses we passed were roofed with thatch, fewer with tile, than in North Korea, and houses typically looked poorer. In villages, towns and cities the landscapes ranged from shabby to tumbledown.

Still, while what I had seen of North Korea had a settled, almost prosperous look to it, and did seem clearly ahead in such key areas of development as farm mechanization and decent housing, China had the obvious edge in one category. While one could ride for a long time on a North Korean train without seeing much in the way of human activity, China served up a constant panorama of vitality — people everywhere, on bicycles, on foot, fishing in an irrigation canal, haggling.

Of course, China was another communist country where the authorities had sought to exert totalitarian control. Partly because it was such a big country, though, Big Brother could not indoctrinate and monitor the people there as thoroughly and efficiently as in North Korea. Indeed, life in China had already started to change. Mao Zedong was dead and, with him, his catastrophic Great Proletarian Cultural Revolution. Although I did not yet know it, the vitality I saw was to power the amazing changes that were about to come to China under Deng Xiaoping's reform-minded rule.

At the time, though, if I could credit what my eyes revealed in terms of economic development, the comparison between North Korea and China seemed much more startling than any that could be made between North and South Korea.[47] That seemed a likely partial explanation, at least, of why the Pyongyang regime contemplated only minor deviations from past practice. Perhaps the North's leaders themselves were lulled by the evidence of their successes, taking reports of the South's advances less seriously than they might have if their own system had less to show for it.

TEN

Let's Spread the Pollen of Love

Kim Il-sung took the role of father of the republic literally. Easily adjusting to and expanding upon the enormous power that went with the job of top leader in a Stalinist state, Kim lived a life of increasing—eventually, almost unimaginable—luxury in mansions and villas built for him by subordinates who competed for his favor. There he sired biological children with mistresses and concubines, not to mention his two officially recognized wives. He arranged for special schools to bring up war orphans to think of themselves as his children.

The patriarch Kim ran the country as a family enterprise, filling high offices first with assorted members of his Kim and Kang clans and later with the youngsters, now grown up, who called him father or uncle. Capping this policy was his decision to name Kim Jong-il, his eldest acknowledged son, as his successor, creating the communist world's first dynastic succession.

Kim Il-sung published prolifically on almost every other subject but had remarkably little to say about his relationships with women. While still an active guerrilla, Kim "had many comrade women who were his girlfriends," a former elite official of the regime told me. The woman who became his first officially recognized wife, Kim Jong-suk, was the one who happened to be with him when he fled to the Soviet Union. "Otherwise it could have been any one of those women."[1]

Kim Jong-suk, a member of the guerrilla women's unit, gave birth to Kim Il-sung's first three acknowledged children. The eldest, Kim Jong-il, is believed by most outside analysts to have been born in the Soviet Union.[2] The regime gives his date of birth as February 16, 1942, but claims he was born in the foothills of Mount Paektu on the Korea-China border. A brother was born in 1944. Jong-il was called Yura, the nickname of a brother of a famous Soviet war heroine. His little brother was called Shura. (Among Russians, Yura is the pet name for someone named Yuri while Shura is short for Alexander.)[3] Kim Il-sung's Russian-language interpreter in those days recalled that the two boys' mother "was a good cook and a very warm-hearted individual."[4] After liberation she followed her husband to Pyongyang. There she had another child, daughter Kyong-hui. Her second son, Shura, drowned in 1948 while playing in a pond and Kim Jong-suk herself died in 1949. She is described as having been short of stature, freckled of face, "an illiterate with a dogged character."[5]

Immediately after liberation, Kim is reported to have commissioned a search for Han Song-hui, his former wife, and, after many months, to have located her in remote Kangwon Province. She had resumed communist political activity and was serving as vice-chair of the Provincial Women's League.[6] Kim established Han and her children, at least some of them his, in a mansion near Shinmiri, between Pyongyang and Sunan.[7]

Around that time, Kim spied Kim Song-ae, a "cute and especially charming" typist working in the defense ministry, and arranged for her transfer to work in his office.[8] During the period when the country's new leader was resuming relations with Han Song-hui and beginning an affair with Kim Song-ae, he was still married to Kim Jong-suk, who had been one of Han's subordinates in the partisan women's unit and like a younger sister to Han.[9] Perhaps thanks to Han's clear seniority, there are no reports of jealous strife between those two female comrades. Rather, both seem to have focused their jealousy on Kim Il-sung's new relationship with his secretary. Eventually the revived relationship between Kim Il-sung and Han Song-hui cooled on account of the new office affair.[10]

Some years following Kim Jong-suk's death, Kim Song-ae, twelve years his junior, would be recognized officially as Kim Il-sung's wife and the first lady of the country—once again, it appears, without benefit of a public wedding ceremony.[11]

Whether or not it is true that power is the ultimate aphrodisiac, certainly Kim Il-sung's newfound political power did not go just to the young ruler's head. Kim quickly began taking advantage of his position to arrange numerous liaisons with other women in addition to the three who had been or were to become his wives.

If Kim or his female conquests thought he was Heaven's gift to women, perhaps that was no wonder in view of his already extravagant but ever-intensifying personality cult. But whatever institutional help he could call upon, Kim Il-sung also brought to his pursuit of the opposite sex consider-able personal charm that only increased with age and experience. Official bi-ographer Baik Bong refers to Kim's "peculiarly moving smile,"[12] and such references seem to reflect more truth than propaganda. I think of Kim when I see and hear the dignified, deep-voiced James Earl Jones in the role of an African absolute monarch, father of Eddie Murphy's Prince Akeem, in the Hollywood movie *Coming to America*.

"Kim Il-sung is charming," a defector who knew him personally told me in an interview while the North Korean ruler was still alive. "He has been a politician for fifty years. When you dine with him, he's very generous and warm. He's a good-looking man except for that lump on his neck. His voice is very special. Most people talk from their throats. He talks from his belly like an opera singer."[13]

Armed with such an arsenal, the premier "seduced the wife of a high-ranking Korean People's Army officer and dispatched her husband to the So-viet Union for overseas study," Yu Song-chol said. At the offices of the Interim People's Committee, a typist named O Chan-bok slapped Kim's face when he tried to kiss her.[14] The 1946 reforms included a law granting equality to women. Prostitution and concubinage were outlawed, along with female infanticide. Pyongyang encouraged North Koreans to feel pride at having put such social evils behind them. They were urged to feel especially irate at the thought of American soldiers violating Korean women in the South.[15] For the premier, however, rules were to be skirted, not followed. To head off discon-tent among more straitlaced subordinates, Yu said, Kim arranged for secret love nests to be set up with code names "Number One" and "Number Two," and "summoned pretty young women there for secret rendezvous."[16]

Over the years, rumor among the Pyongyang elite had it that Kim had sired a number of children by women other than his deceased former wife and her successor as first lady. Besides unacknowledged wife Han Song-hui, "so many more had his children," one high-ranking defector told me.

Sometimes, as in the case of Han, Kim set up his children's mothers in their own households. In other cases the women married men who gave the children their names. Regardless, Kim continued to take an interest in his offspring from liaisons old and new. Because inquiring into the Fatherly Leader's personal lifestyle was an absolute taboo, "only the children of his two official wives are known," said the former official. "Even high officials don't know the head count of youngsters being brought up privately in the mansions."[17]

＊　＊　＊

It should come as no surprise that such an enthusiastic patriarch would become one of the world's premier nepotists. Kim Il-sung provided jobs for a
stupefying number of relatives in addition to his offspring. His female
cousins on his father's side did well in the regime, for example, as did their
husbands. Cousin Kim Jong-suk (same name as Kim's second wife, but a
different person) became vice-chair of the Korean General Occupational
Federations and chief editor of *Minju Choson,* organ of the administrative
council. Her husband was Ho Dam, who served as vice-premier and foreign
minister. Kim Il-sung's cousin Kim Shin-sook became deputy director of the
Academy of Social Sciences and an official of the Democratic Women's
League. Her husband, Yang Hyong-sop, rose to become a member of the party
politburo and secretariat and chairman of the Supreme People's Assembly —
the parliament.[18]

Kim Il-sung gave a vice-presidency of the country to Kang Ryang-uk,
the former Methodist minister who was a cousin of his maternal grandfather
and who had taught him at Changdok School. In the united-front facade that
Kim erected early in his rule, Kang was supposed to represent the moderate,
noncommunist forces that had allied themselves with the communists. Besides heading the token opposition Korean Democratic Party, other assignments before his death in 1983 included a vice-chairmanship of the General
League of Trade Unions. Joining Kang as a vice-president was Pak Song-
chol, who was Kang's son-in-law. Thus, of three vice-presidents serving during that period, only one was *not* a relative of Kim Il-sung's. Pak was also
made a member of the party politburo and chairman of the Central People's
Committee.[19]

Kim Il-sung's first cousins included Kim Chang-ju, who rose to become
vice-premier, and Chang-ju's brother Bong-ju, who became chairman of the
Profession League Central Committee. They were the sons of Kim Il-sung's
uncle Kim Hyong-rok — his father's younger brother, who had stayed home
to farm, taking over as head of the Mangyongdae household. Hyong-rok's
third son, Kim Won-ju, was a State Security Department officer whose assignments included rooting out disloyalty to the regime among students at
the ultra-elite Mangyongdae School. Won-ju's son Myong-su became a State
Security official; Myong-su's brother Myong-ho, a colonel in the People's
Army. Kim Byoung-il, another State Security official (in charge of inspecting the evidence brought in by investigators in loyalty cases), was married to
a niece of Kim Il-sung.[20]

It was an exaggeration but not too far from the truth to say, as did one
high-level defector, that "the topmost officials have to be relatives,"[21] Son
Sang-pil, who was ambassador to Moscow, was a relative on Kim Il-sung's
mother's side. Kim Kyong-hui, Kim Jong-il's sister, became a member of the

party Central Committee and the Supreme People's Assembly. Her husband, Chang Song-taek, also became an influential official who carried out sensitive missions for his brother-in-law.

Kim Il-sung's last wife, Kim Song-ae, became chairwoman of the Korean Democratic Women's Union. Kim Song-ae gave birth to Kim Il-sung's second set of acknowledged children. Her eldest child, daughter Kim Byong-jin, married Kim Kwang-sop, who became an ambassador to, among other countries, the Czech Republic. Kim Song-ae's first son, Kim Pyong-il, became ambassador to Bulgaria, Finland and Poland.

Hwang Jang-yop, the highest ranking North Korean defector, wrote of his great respect for Kim Il-sung during the years 1958–1965, the period when Hwang was working directly under Kim as party secretary for ideology. Kim "was cruel to his political enemies but generous to his colleagues and subordinates," Hwang said. "The only thing I felt uncomfortable with was that he put too much trust in his relatives and too much value in their opinions."[22]

Kim Il-sung's closest guerrilla comrades also were entitled to practice nepotism. Choe Yong-gon and Kim Il, before they died, were numbers two and three in the regime, and their wives were then party Central Committee alternate members. So was Choe's cousin, Choe Chong-gon, who also became director of the air force's General Political Bureau.[23]

Kim Il-sung himself, during the purge of Pak Hon-yong's followers in 1952, attacked as "petty bourgeois" the formation of factional groupings based on "kinship, friendship, connections with the same school or common regional origins."[24] But a more tolerant take on nepotism is made to issue from the mouth of no less a figure than Kim Jong-suk, Kim Il-sung's beatified second wife and the mother of Kim Jong-il. As a young, still unmarried woman in the guerrilla band, she supposedly opined that it was inevitable, at least at the village level, for relatives to work together. The important thing, she was quoted as having instructed a communist youth group, was to keep such kinship relations from influencing one's work.[25]

One need only look into Korean history, though, to find the Confucian patterns that repeated themselves in the hereditary North Korean ruling class that Kim Il-sung built. The *yangban* were the hereditary noble class of scholar-official-landlords under the Yi Dynasty, which reigned from 1392 to 1910. One Western diplomat specializing in things Korean saw "a modern-day parody" in what he called North Korea's "communist yangban class."[26]

As if not yet satisfied with the number of relatives he had to choose from for his appointments to official posts, Kim Il-sung early in his rule expanded the pool by playing father to the country's orphans. It was in December of 1950, after meeting a woman whose husband had been killed in action and who was now struggling to raise their four children alone, that Kim decided the state would rear "orphans and all the children the parents thought it difficult to bring up because of many children," he later wrote in his memoirs. Kim gave the orders to build schools for the children of "patriotic martyrs" in every province. As a result, he said, "all the orphans grew up quickly and warmly in the bosom of the country and the people. Though numerous parents were victims, the orphans were never crying nor roaming through the streets."[27]

The orphans' schools also gave Kim Il-sung a group of intense loyalists who, as Bai Song-chul told me during our train-ride conversation in 1979, looked upon Kim as their father. That was particularly true of the graduates of the Mangyongdae School for the Bereaved Children of Revolutionaries, which produced much of the country's military, intelligence and internal security elite. Kim set up the school near his ancestral home in 1947. It was to receive the children of fallen revolutionaries who had asked him "with their dying breath" to "educate their children and train them into fine revolutionaries after the independence of Korea."[28]

Whether they had really asked that or not, in Korean cultural terms Kim was no doubt correct to assume that helping to continue their lineage and make their children their elite "successors" was what those martyrs would have wanted him to do in repayment of their sacrifice. Take the case of Ryang Se-bong, an independence fighter killed in a trap set by Japanese agents. The regime sent Ryang's son through the elite school at Mangyongdae and gave him a political job with an air force unit. When the son, too, died in a plane crash, Kim "feared that Commander Ryang's lineage might be broken." Fortunately, there was a grandson, but he was crippled with polio. The party saw to his education, and he became a writer who "creates literary works in bed. He has two sons and a daughter."[29]

Kim told in his memoirs of having "dispatched many officials to various places at home and in northeast China to find the bereaved children of revolutionaries. At that time hundreds of such children came home from China. Some of those children . . . have now become members of the Political Bureau of the Central Committee of our Party."

Several of Kim's family members were eligible to attend the Mangyongdae School. Son Kim Jong-il—qualified, I suppose, by the loss of his former-guerrilla mother—enrolled there. Another pupil was a daughter of Kim Hyong-gwon, the hot-tempered uncle of Kim Il-sung who had fought the colonialists and died in a Japanese prison. "I thought I would bring her up with all care to succeed her father," Kim wrote. Alas, she was killed later in a Korean War bombing raid.[30] He expanded the school's mission to include children of Korean War dead, as well as the offspring of North Korean agents killed in the South before and after the war. From the 1960s, those target groups declined in numbers. The school widened its admissions net, while still focusing on training a future elite. As that proved more and more to be a family elite, the descendants of prominent figures in the regime had an edge in gaining admission.

Others who enrolled at orphans' school are reported to have been Kim's unacknowledged children. Indeed, it is tempting to speculate that the education of his own children as well as younger relatives was a factor in his decision to establish the school at Mangyongdae. Fortuitously or not, the North's constitution decreed an end to discrimination against illegitimate children.[31] Ultraloyal to Kim as a result of the combination of blood ties and training, some of his youngsters are said to have grown up to form a sort of bastards' honor guard. Assuming positions in important party and state organizations, they helped to run the country while functioning as the eyes and ears of their father—and, later, of their half-brother, Kim Jong-il. While "no one can be treated quite on the level of Kim Il-sung and Kim Jong-il," a former elite official told me, those offspring "get preferential treatment because they are royalty even if illegitimate."

Few names have been known for certain, even by other members of the elite, as this has been one of the ultimate taboo subjects in North Korea. As I shall relate later, however, I was told the identity of one man described as probably the most powerful, at the time, of Kim's unacknowledged children. Another, much younger man, apparently Kim's illegitimate son, was reported to have begun work in the party propaganda bureau.

Watching the de-Stalinization of the Soviet Union, starting in 1956, and later observing the abortive revolt by Mao Zedong's designated successor, Lin Biao, in China, Kim Il-sung became determined to name his own flesh and blood as his successor.[32] The idea was not only to guard against posthumous insults but also, within his lifetime, to avoid challenges to his power from nonfamily underlings impatient to take over. "Think about it," one former official of the regime said to me. "Who would let go of such a lifestyle and give up his regime?"

Even Kim Il-sung had to know that his succession plans would be seen as a betrayal of his communist ideals. (Recall his schoolboy criticism of Korea's feudal Yi Dynasty.) Indeed, Hwang Jang-yop, who became the regime's chief ideologue in 1965, believed that Kim Il-sung "probably did not have the intention of turning over power to his son from the beginning." Hwang at that stage was impressed by the senior Kim's "sense of democracy in trying to be fair to all children, regardless of whose offspring they were."

But as Kim's "personal dictatorship continued and its political foundation strengthened," Hwang recalled, "he became over-confident, believing
that he could do anything he liked. More and more he came to regard the
government as his personal property."[33] Hwang added: "In a situation where
all means of production actually belong to the Great Leader, the economy itself naturally serves the interest of the Great Leader before all else. The national economy is nothing more than the household economy of the Great
Leader. North Korea's economy exists first and foremost to serve the Great
Leader."[34]

In one post-defection article, Hwang recalled having heard Kim Il-sung
utter "relatively humble remarks" during the time when they had worked
closely together. The senior Kim, for example, said: "I wasn't a big part of the
partisan struggle against the Japanese" and "I never dreamed back then that
I would become the leader of North Korea."[35] In Hwang's view, however,
"North Korea, with the vestiges of feudalism still maintaining a stronghold
on society, was from the very beginning a hotbed for a personality cult. Personal dictatorship was established more firmly in North Korea than in any
other socialist country." In the first stage, that involved simple emulation,
"under Soviet supervision," of Stalin's cult.

After Kim consolidated power, he made his surviving younger brother a very
high official. Kim Yong-ju joined the party Central Committee in 1961, was
named party secretary for organization and guidance in 1962 and advanced
to full membership in the politburo and number six ranking in the entire
regime in 1970. At that time he was viewed abroad as likely successor to his
elder brother as top leader.[36]

In the official Kim family mythology, Yong-ju is described as having
spent his childhood in terror, fleeing search parties. Kim Il-sung wrote in his
memoirs that, while he himself battled Japanese troops, the Japanese authorities hunted for Yong-ju as part of their attempt to pressure rebels. They
distributed photographs of the youngster, Kim Il-sung said, so "my brother
had to roam aimlessly, under a false name and by concealing his identity,
about cities and villages all over the three provinces of Manchuria and even
in China proper."[37]

Yu Song-chol gave a somewhat different account, in which Yong-ju was
a guerrilla for a time but fled to China and got a job in a Japanese store
there—after Kim Il-sung told him it was his duty to survive and carry on the
family line. Yu said Yong-ju was in Hawaii during the 1940s but returned to
North Korea after liberation.[38]

In Pyongyang, high-ranking officials lived in special neighborhood enclaves. Those mimicked the exclusive communities Soviet officials had established in the city after liberation, with their own schools, shops and hospitals.[39]

Kim Yong-ju lived in the Mansu-dong neighborhood. (His next-door neighbor was Choe Yong-gon, a former anti-Japanese fighter who reached the number two position in the regime.)

Kim Yong-ju sired at least one houseful of children who grew up to take prominent posts in the regime, including son Kim Bong-ju, who became a party Central Committee member. One former high-ranking North Korean official who defected to South Korea told me in an interview that Kim Yong-ju "has lots of kids. They're in all departments of government—good jobs, of course." In a country where few people could be satisfied with the quantities of food they got to eat, "all his sons and daughters are very, very fat—real heavyweights."[40]

In the early 1970s the regime dropped a very clear official hint that a close relative would become Kim Il-sung's successor. The 1970 edition of North Korea's *Dictionary of Political Terminologies* had included this critical definition:

> Hereditary succession is a reactionary custom of exploitative societies whereby certain positions or riches may be legally inherited. Originally a product of slave societies, it was later adopted by feudal lords as a means to perpetuate dictatorial rule.

The definition failed to appear in the 1972 edition of the dictionary.[41]

Some defectors have reported that Kim Il-sung's wife, the former typist Kim Song-ae, hoped her brother-in-law would win the succession. She favored Kim Yong-ju not because she was on friendly terms with him (she was not) but, apparently, simply because he was of the older generation. That meant his tenure might be short and afterward there might still be a chance at the top job for Kim Pyong-il, her own elder son. Pyong-il, Kim Jong-il's stepbrother, was too young to be considered at that time.

It's quite possible, though, that Kim Il-sung never seriously considered his brother as his successor. Actuarial tables, after all, would have given the brother only a few years to rule beyond Kim Il-sung's own life span. For Kim Il-sung, who wanted to perpetuate his system and ideology, picking a significantly younger man probably would have seemed the sound choice. But as a consummate strategist he would not have let everyone know his decision until he had laid the groundwork.

In the meantime, palace intrigues raged in which the object was to gain Kim Il-sung's favor. A principal means of doing so was flattery. The contenders, a former high official related, "went crazy trying to idolize Kim Il-sung in order to display their loyalty to him."[42] They certainly knew the way to the Great Leader's heart. Constantly assured of his godlike attributes,

Kim became a caricature of the classic potentate. It seems there was nothing he did not consider himself entitled to. Feeding his enormous appetites and ego provided full-time and never-ending work for those around him.

Such a lofty being could not, for example, partake of the ordinary food that was rationed out to ordinary mortals. Kim Il-sung had to have special orchards and greenhouses and farms producing his food. His rice grains were polished individually to make sure he would get not a single bad grain. According to one former Pyongyang-based foreign diplomat, there was a rumor among the people that Kim's special apple trees were watered with a sugar solution—an otherwise unthinkable luxury in a country where sweets were very rarely available.

It could not have been easy finding ways to flatter Kim Il-sung further, but it seemed that every year brought something new. Kim Jong-il reportedly dreamed up the idea of having delegates to 1970's Fifth Congress of the Workers' Party wear lapel badges adorned with a likeness of the Respected and Beloved Leader.[43] By the time I visited in 1979, all citizens were wearing them. Some were simple, round pins while others showed Kim's portrait against various backgrounds. I asked a hothouse manager whether the difference in badges indicated difference in status of the wearers. Oh, no, he replied; the badges served only to "highly revere our Leader and wish him good health." Fifteen years later, a defector gave me a different version: "You can tell someone's status by looking at his Kim Il-sung portrait badge. For high officials of the party, the portrait appears against the background of a red flag. Some people want to seem important, so they buy badges that indicate higher status than they possess. Of course if you are caught . . ."[44]

Despite what foreign analysts had thought, Kim Yong-ju did not have it sewn up. Instead the nod would go to his nephew, Kim Jong-il. Testing his son's abilities before anointing him as the successor, Kim Il-sung had Jong-il handle the arrangements for the elder Kim's own sixtieth birthday. The sixtieth is a major milestone for any Korean; in the Great Leader's case, his son turned it into perhaps the most extravagant celebration in North Korean history up to that point—which helped earn him the right to try to outdo himself with the bashes honoring the Great Leader's sixty-fifth and seventieth birthdays.

Brilliantly reading his father's psychology, Kim Jong-il established (as noted in chapter 1) the Kim Il-sung Institute of Health and Longevity. In a country that advertised an average life span of seventy-three, the institute was mandated to find ways for the Fatherly Leader to live longer and enjoy himself. For medical and dietary research it used human guinea pigs whose ages and physical characteristics were similar to his.[45] A former high official of the regime explained to me that the institute focused on the aging Great

Leader's symptoms of insomnia, cardiovascular problems and advancing sexual impotence. In due course the doctors came up with a prescription: the Respected and Beloved Leader should eat dog penises at least seven centimeters (2.8 inches) long. That prescription was not, of course, the only product of the institute. One European who served as a diplomat in Pyongyang told me he treasured a box of special matches that were produced as part of the massive effort to protect the Iron-Willed, Ever-Victorious Brilliant Commander from harm. The matches would burn for a maximum of half their length, and then they went out. That way there was no risk that they would burn the Great Fingers.

Kim Il-sung and his family were accustomed to luxurious living in mansions and villas. Chinese Red Guards criticizing him for his bourgeois ways reported that his estate in Pyongyang, commanding a full view of the Taedong and Potong rivers, covered tens of thousands of square meters and was "surrounded on all sides by high walls. All sides of the estate are dotted with sentry posts. One has to pass through five or six doors before one comes to the courtyard. This really makes one think of the great palaces of the emperors in the past." Besides his main residence, Kim had "his own palaces everywhere in North Korea. . . . All of these villas are on a grand scale. Although Kim Il-sung stays in these villas for only a few days every year, such stays usually require the services of large numbers of military and security personnel."[46]

Hwang Jang-yop, who had worked in close contact with the two Kims, confirmed that account: "All around the city of Pyongyang are several special facilities, or what can be termed 'special royal villas,' equipped with all sorts of luxuries from performing arts centers to medical facilities and even exclusive hunting grounds," Hwang wrote. "There is probably no other country in the world both in the past and present that has as many royal villas as North Korea. Any place deemed to boast the slightest scenic beauty is designated as a site for one of these royal villas. An army of escorts [bodyguards] guard all these places, and hostesses are stationed there round the clock in readiness for a royal visit. . . ."[47]

But those competing for Kim Il-sung's favor believed that more was better and did not mind spending huge sums for yet more elaborate facilities to show their loyalty. As a former Public Security Ministry official observed dryly, "In the process of such competitive idolization, excessive funds were spent."[48]

In his memoirs, recalling a conflict with a wicked landlord in his guerrilla days, Kim wrote, "Long experience had bred in my bones the feeling that the richer people were, the more cold-hearted they were, the more devoid of virtue." Wealth, he lamented, is "a trap which swallows and destroys virtue." But after taking power Kim Il-sung had changed. He was no longer the outraged young revolutionary who had vowed to "wipe out the old society of immorality and corruption" and replace it with a beautiful society permitting "no gulf between the poor and the rich."[49]

A Chinese Red Guard publication that attacked him as a fat counterrevolutionary also catalogued some of the villas Kim had to choose from by the late 1960s, for weekend getaways. One was set among the pines of the Sanmien District near Pyongyang, a second in the scenic Chin Mountains, a third at Chuwol Hot Springs, a fourth in the border city of Sinuiji and a fifth along the coast in the vicinity of the port of Chongjin. The article also criticized Kim for building a cemetery to demonstrate filial piety toward his parents and ancestors. And it attacked North Korean officials for giving expensive gifts and hosting elaborate parties.[50]

For his sixtieth birthday, Kim got the most expensive mansion up to that point, costing the equivalent of tens of millions of dollars, according to a former official's estimate. The funds, this source told me, came from gold mining. "North Korea can mine up to 50 tons of gold a year, so they can afford that sort of thing."[51]

By the time of Kim Il-sung's death in 1994, he and son Kim Jong-il had some one hundred places to call home. The same source reported that out of those hundred, there were some that Kim Il-sung "has not even visited yet." He added that Kim Jong-il's younger sister, Kyong-hui, as well as his halfbrother, Pyong-il, had their own villas.[52] One former official told me while Kim Il-sung was still alive that the Great Leader "moves around, changes houses every day for his safety."

Kim Il-sung's taste in architecture was "modern Oriental style," according to an architect-engineer who worked on a project to build an elaborate, 15,000-square-meter villa for Kim Il-sung and Kim Jong-il in the mountains near the east coast port of Chongjin. The structure had "a tile roof, but straight rather than curved as is traditional. All the windows are imported from Austria. The furniture all comes from Japan." The villa was "nestled into a valley, with mountains on three sides and a tunnel coming down from one of the mountains to bring fresh air."[53]

An official who visited a lakeside villa at Songhan-Ri near Sinuiju and a seaside villa between Hongwon and Iwon in South Hamgyong Province told me that both featured underwater glass walls one foot thick, giving the interiors the feel of an aquarium. (One of those was Kim Il-sung's sixtieth birthday present; the other, a present for Kim Jong-il on his fortieth birthday in 1982.) At another villa in South Pyongan Province, at a hot spring, "all the furniture was made of ebony, very expensive," the official told me. "In the mid-'70s I visited Moranbong. It's a secret mansion of Kim Jong-il's behind the television station," in Pyongyang. Various units of the complex had been connected with underground passages.

The same official said he had visited a mansion at Tongbuk-ri at Kim Jong-il's invitation in the late 1960s. "Tongbuk-ri is beside a big lake. In several complexes there, one for Kim Jong-il, another for Kim Il-sung and a third for public banquet use, there are lots of women."

Lots of women, indeed. From mere philandering, Kim Il-sung had advanced to presiding over something not far removed from a harem. In this he may have learned from the Chinese. North Korean officials who had spent a lot of time in China picked up the traditional belief that having sex with young women prolongs a man's lifespan. After the Korean War, Choe Yong-gon, Kim's top deputy, came up with the idea of establishing a Mansions Special Volunteer Corps, which organized young women as companions for Kim.

The "volunteer" corps was a small-scale operation at first, said a former elite official, but "the extravagance built up year after year." As a birthday present for Kim Il-sung—again, supposedly to help prolong the life of the Great Leader—Kim Jong-il greatly expanded the operation. According to Kim Myong-chol, who served in the bodyguard corps of both Kim Il-sung and Kim Jong-il, bodyguards learned in the course of 1981 that female companions had been organized into three corps, called in Korean *kippeunjo, manjokjo* and *haengbokjo.* Members of the *kippeunjo,* or Happy Corps, were actresses and singers who entertained at parties and might have slept with Kim Il-sung or Kim Jong-il. The *manjokjo,* or Satisfaction Corps, was more explicitly focused on sexual services. So, too, according to Kim Myong-chol, was the *haengbokjo,* or Felicity Corps—whose members he said were recruited from the Workers' Party organization and from among the female bodyguards. (Another defector said the *haengbukjo* also performed menial work in the mansions.)

Corps members would "follow Kim Il-sung and Kim Jong-il wherever they go, and massage them," Pak Su-hyon, a Kim Il-sung bodyguard from 1982 to 1989, told me. Architect-engineer Kim Young-song, who worked on construction of villas and other projects of interest to the leaders, told me, "Whenever Kim Jong-il or Kim Il-sung were to arrive, the happy girls would come early and wait for them. They're Kim Il-sung's and Kim Jong-il's concubines."

At any given time, literally thousands of young women would be in service in positions in which they might be called upon to provide sexual favors to Kim Il-sung or his son. (Eat your heart out, Hugh Hefner.) Most were recruited systematically from among the prettiest in the land. But there was always room for one more who happened to be discovered by accident. Indeed, for any underling wishing to flatter Kim Il-sung, yet another especially beautiful girl was the perfect gift—along with health foods and elixirs thought to improve his boudoir stamina.

A special unit was established in the party's Central Committee to select girls, a former official told me.[54] Staff members would check with schools all over the country to find beautiful girls. Finding one with potential, "they tell people around her that she may become a member of the service detail, so no one can touch her." If a girl passed final scrutiny and was selected, the authorities would tell her parents something of what her assignment would be. Eager to show their loyalty, the parents were "happy to give their daughters to Kim Il-sung." Besides, after their daughters' selection, the families got preferential treatment.

Among training centers in various parts of the country, "the girls' most important training is at Tongi-ri," this former official told me. Kim Il-sung had a great mansion complex there, he explained. The training was handled with even more secrecy than the training for terrorist-saboteurs. The future Happy Corps girls "are trained as entertainers: comedy, dancing, singing—but not for public viewing. The public stars are selected differently." The girls formed classes of ten for special training. Their teachers, senior service corps women, "train them in sex education, the special characteristics and preferences of Kim Il-sung and Kim Jong-il."[55]

One such special preference was the "human bed," an arrangement in which women lie with their legs intertwined and the man lies on top of them to sleep. I had some difficulty imagining why even an aging and lecherous ruler would have wanted to lie on a "human bed," and I wondered where the North Koreans might have gotten such notions. A former official told me he understood that the companion corps trainers had gone on study tours to Poland and China. The Chinese, in particular, "have a long history of sexual culture. They bound their wives' feet and so on. Chiang Kai-shek and the Empress Dowager had similar lifestyles. The Shah of Iran was also a sex fanatic. But in modern times the three farthest out are probably Mao Zedong, Kim Il-sung and Kim Jong-il." The former official was not kidding about Mao. Soon after he spoke with me a new book by the late Chinese leader's doctor appeared, detailing a potentate's lifestyle almost as uninhibited as that of Kim Il-sung—although on a far less grand scale and without the degree of formal organization the efficient Koreans had adopted.

Quite a few scholars have assumed that defector testimony exaggerated the Kims' sexual practices, and I imagine that might be true. I have not caught any defectors lying about these sexual matters, but if I had to pick one story as being so bizarre as to set off extra-loud alarm bells I guess it might be the human bed. For the girls or young women on the bottom, the arrangement sounded gruesomely uncomfortable. My source assured me, however, that the bed was "arranged so that both top and bottom people are comfortable." The former elite official had a reputation for veracity, and I was inclined to think he had not made up the story. But in this case he was passing along a rumor, not his own eyewitness account, and rumors do have a way of becoming embellished as they pass from mouth to mouth.[56]

That source told me that the nubile human mattresses were more than happy to oblige. "North Korea, you know, claims that men and women are treated equally—after the babies are weaned, both are the same. In fact, though, it's a totally unequal system. Much more so than in South Korea, even. Women are brought up to be submissive and subservient. Being part of Kim Il-sung's human bed is an honor for them." Former bodyguard Pak Su-hyon confirmed that picture of the North Korean attitude toward selection as one of the Kims' vestal virgins: "When you hear of this group you think of them as low-class. But in North Korea it's an honor to sacrifice themselves for the Great Leader."

Once they had worked until their early twenties, the women retired. Referring to foreign newspaper articles accompanying a photo of one of Kim Il-sung's mistresses who had gone abroad with the Great Leader's five-year-old daughter, a former official explained that "women like that are ones who have already retired from Kim's personal service team." The party provided for the retirees' futures, taking responsibility for marrying off at least the childless ones when their duties in the mansions and villas were over. Promising never to talk about their experience, they were given husbands chosen from among party members, including bodyguards.

Mix with children, share their feelings, and you will feel a strong urge to live, and you will understand that they bring beauty and variety to people's lives. You will also feel inspired with a sense of the noble duty of bringing them to full bloom and safeguarding the ideals glowing in their eyes.

—KIM IL-SUNG[57]

Before Kim Il-sung's death, I interviewed a former official who told me that the North Korean president, as he aged, craved the companionship of girls in their early teens. Kim had a history of that. Recall the time he had spent while in his early twenties with pubescent and prepubescent tap dancers in the guerrilla zone. Later, after the Korean War, he took in three orphaned girls, fifteen-year-old Kim Young-ok and her thirteen- and eleven-year-old sisters, and raised them, eventually sending them to college, the former official told me.[58]

The practice developed of having one or two of the most beautiful thirteen-year-old Happy Corps recruits assigned to each mansion or villa start training immediately, instead of waiting to graduate like the rest. Kim Il-sung "wanted more than sexual satisfaction," the former official told me.

"He wanted to become younger through their *ki*—life force. The thirteen-year-olds don't sleep with him. They get training. Then at fifteen they become sexual product. Kim Il-sung likes to be with them as they mature—thinks it's good for his health. If you're in the same room with young people, their *ki* is supposed to transfer to you."

Some other very high-ranking officials also became entitled to special privileges. In the 1960s, one of Kim Il-sung's early mistresses, a well-known entertainer, became madam of a brothel established to service big-shot clients.[59] Former bodyguard Kim Myong-chol told me that in 1983 he and fellow bodyguards learned of a new division of the female companion corps established to service very high officials other than Kim Il-sung and Kim Jong-il. This was the *kwabu-jo*, made up of beautiful widows from all over the country who were recruited to participate in a sort of recycling. (In Korean tradition, widows normally could not expect to remarry.)

Mainly, though, for officials outside the inner circle, unsanctioned sexual relationships had to be furtive. A former official described to me a casual love affair. "Once I went to a rural area and was returning to Pyongyang at night in my Mercedes-Benz 230. I saw a girl in the road—roads are mostly deserted, as you know. She was waving, trying to hitch a ride. I stopped and she said she had missed her bus. She worked at a textile factory in Pyongyang. I said I'd take her there. On the way I got to know her. She was interested in me and asked for my address. I gave her my office phone number. One day she called and said, 'I have some free time this afternoon.' I took her to the Pyongyang Hotel for dinner. Somehow we grew close, and I slept with her. I went home and, the next day, went to the office as usual. My wife called and said, 'You'd better come home early today.' When I got home my underwear were on top of the bed and my wife told me to look at them. The girl had been a virgin, and there was a stain on my underwear. I got in trouble—there was a lot of hostility at home. I didn't see the girl after that, but a couple of years later when she got married I bought her some clothes. Her name was Sun-yi—same name as a famous South Korean singer. Lots of high officials have similar affairs."

On occasion the regime cracked down to show that the rules applied even to the affairs of the high and mighty. Kim Yong-sun, who later would serve as a very high-level Workers' Party secretary in charge of relations with the United States and Japan, was sent to a camp for three years of re-education early in his career, in 1979. His offense was getting caught in a compromising situation with one of the pretty young women assigned to clerical duties in the offices of the leadership.[60]

In 1965, there was a case that a defector later reported to international human rights organizations. A woman university student was tried publicly for having sex with numerous men, including influential party officials. The trial was held in front of some twenty thousand citizens, who criticized and accused her for about four hours. Finally the judge ruled that her moral depravity had violated Kim Il-sung's instructions, so she must die. The excited crowd shouted curses at her and a firing squad shot her dead.[61]

The behavior of the woman who was executed probably had been fairly tame compared with the Kims' sex lives, news of which would have shocked most North Koreans. But unlike President Bill Clinton's United States and Prince Charles's Britain, North Korea had no news media that would publicize tales of the rulers' bed-hopping and cut their images down to mere human size. And the senior Kim, for his part, although he was a sociable sort who enjoyed business-related entertaining, kept his peccadilloes private to the extent he did not, as a general rule, hold private parties even for his pals in the inner circle.[62]

Kim Il-sung, while he did not have much of a conscience, "would never flaunt his lifestyle in front of his people," a former elite official told me. "They make the girls' parents sign contracts of secrecy, tell them their lives are in danger if they talk. And people around them don't really know the nature of their work is servicing Kim Il-sung and Kim Jong-il. Most of their acquaintances think they have gone to acting school." Any unauthorized person who might happen to discover the truth would be in grave peril simply on account of the knowledge.

Some bodyguards and household servants were in on the secret, of course. In exchange for their silence they were permitted to lead "lives without normal controls—privileged lives," the former high official told me. It was through that inner circle that the word eventually leaked to other high officials outside the Kims' immediate households. Some bodyguards-turned-generals, aping the Kims' behavior, set themselves up with harems of their own. That aroused other officials' suspicion and led to some discreet conversations in which bodyguards spilled the beans. Still, the former official said, most North Koreans did not know. As for the high officials who had found out, they feared the consequences if they talked about it with anyone they did not trust implicitly.

ELEVEN

Yura

Kim Jong-il had a troubled upbringing. At age seven, already having lost a younger brother, he suffered the death of his mother. His father was often absent, preoccupied with affairs of the heart in addition to such affairs of state as his invasion of South Korea and the three-year war that followed. As the UN forces advanced across the 38th parallel, Jong-il, then called Yura, and his little sister were shipped off to the rear for the duration. Following the war, the father's paramour—the hated rival of the boy's dead mother— became first lady of the land. In classic East Asian style, it appears, the jealous new wife sought to channel her husband's affection to her own children at the expense of her stepson, on whom she spied and informed. The sadness and alienation of a boy bereft of maternal love could have been more than enough in themselves to cloud his developing personality.

To make things worse, inveterately status-fixated Koreans around him, young and old alike, deferred to the eldest son of the country's top leader as if he were a little prince, thus encouraging the bully in him. By the time he graduated from college he was well along toward developing a reputation, among both Pyongyang's Korean elite and the small foreign community, of being wild, recklessly impulsive and, by turns, cruel and warm-hearted, even extravagantly generous.

At the same time, though, Kim Jong-il had begun showing flashes of the intelligence and artistic sense that he would use later to transform the country's stodgy cinema and stage productions. More important, living with daily exposure to high statecraft and palace intrigue, he was sharpening skills of manipulation and political infighting that eventually would help carry him to the pinnacle of power as his father's successor.

The regime said nothing about the circumstances of Kim Jong-il's birth and infancy until the mid-1970s, when he had been tapped as the successor. What was said after that was crafted to lend a magical aura of inevitability to his rise. In recent years, however, witnesses have come forward who knew the boy and his parents and described their lives in the Soviet Union and in the period after they moved to Pyongyang.

The Korean-American writer Peter Hyun in an article in the Seoul monthly *Wolgan Chosun* recounted a 1999 interview with Lee Min, a comrade of Kim Il-sung and his wife during the anti-Japanese period. Kim Jong-il's mother, Kim Jong-suk, "was quite a beauty," Lee recalled. "Her face was that of a princess but her complexion was dark on account of her many years in the field. Her eyebrows were black and her eyelashes were long, making her truly attractive. Her build was even more attractive."

Lee was a member of another of the fighting units that escaped to Siberia after taking a beating from the Japanese. In 1942, she met Kim Il-sung, then a captain in the Eighty-eighth Brigade, and his wife. Lee married a Chinese who was also deeply involved in the anti-Japanese struggle in Manchuria and who eventually became governor of Heilongjiang Province. As a Korean-Chinese, she herself became a high-ranking provincial official dealing with ethnic minority issues. Sensitivities in Sino–North Korean relations may have been at the root of her reticence on one key question when she spoke with Hyun. "Kim Jong-il was born before I met Kim Jong-suk, and I don't have anything to say about his birthplace," she said.

The two women spent considerable time together between 1942 and 1945. Kim Jong-suk, according to Lee, "spent winters indoors and summers outdoors. She was quick, generous and had many talents," among them cooking, sewing, acting and singing. In the dramatic productions that Kim Il-sung produced in the Eighty-eighth Brigade's camp, Kim Jong-suk directed the dancing "and, often, danced herself."

Kim Jong-il, Lee recalled, "was a bright and agile child. He had his mother's dark eyes and dark complexion. He was a cute boy." In the afternoon, after his child care center let out, the boy enjoyed playing with a wooden rifle, marching along with fighters who were undergoing training. "When he played with Choe Hyon's daughter Gop-dan and other kids, Jong-il had to be the commander. Gop-dan was one year older than Jong-il. I would ask him if he could kill the Japanese with a wooden gun. He would reply confidently that he could. I would tell him that he needed a real gun to kill a Japanese, and then he would ask his mother for a real gun. Kim

Jong-suk told him: 'No, you cannot have Dad's gun. You must use your wooden gun to take a real gun from the enemy. That's the only way you would ever become a general like your dad.' Kim Jong-suk was quite strict with Jong-il."[1]

At a Russian nursery attended by children of Eighty-eighth Brigade members, Yura Kim and the other children received ideological indoctrination. Stalin and Mao Zedong were exalted beings, while capitalists and religious believers—especially the Germans and Japanese—were compared to wolves for their evil, cunning natures. In an interview with a South Korean newspaper, a woman who had cared for Yura at the nursery recalled him as a rough lad given to biting other children.[2]

Photographs from the period show that the home of the Kims after they moved from the Soviet Union to Pyongyang was a Western-style, multi-story house built of stone—from the look of it, probably one that had belonged to Japanese colonialists or Western missionaries. Such a house required servants. A Japanese woman was trying to return to Japan in 1946 when Pyongyang authorities dragooned her into working in the Kim residence as a maid. Not hiding her obvious feeling that she was too refined for such duty, the woman later described the mistress of the house, Kim Jong-suk, as a rustic. Lacking style or glamour, the North Korean first lady had not adapted her rough ways of dress and behavior to the unfamiliar life in a city. "She used to go out barefooted to the back yard of her house and butcher chickens whenever she was told to prepare food for guests," the Japanese woman recalled. "She was very quick in plucking out chicken feathers. It was just enough to make me imagine how she had operated during her partisan's life in the forests."[3]

Pyongyang's version of Kim Jong-il's upbringing following the family's return to Korea in 1945 begins with a visit to Mangyongdae to meet surviving relatives on his father's side. The white-bearded great-grandfather, Kim Bo-hyon, naturally made a big fuss over the three-year-old, joggling him on his knee and remarking: "On this joyous day the deceased members of our family will probably close their eyes in relief. Thank you, my dear granddaughter-in-law. You've brought our great-grandson to us and our Mangyongdae home brightens up."[4]

This typical homecoming story is charming and believable—except for one enormous, gaping hole. The account, like other official biographical works, says nothing to indicate that Kim Jong-il was not the only son whom Kim Il-sung and Kim Jong-suk had brought back with them to Korea. In fact he had a little brother, then one year old—the same brother who, three years later, drowned in a pond at home in Pyongyang. It stands to reason that the little one, even if his parents had not brought him along to take his turn being joggled on Grandpa's knee, would have rated a mention at least. In Confucian family life, after all, even though the eldest son is the be-all and end-all, it is considered important to have at least one more son—as insurance that there will be a male to carry on the line if something happens to the firstborn.

Since his official biographies were all produced after Kim Jong-il had taken charge of the country's literary and propaganda output, it would be difficult to explain the lack of any reference to his little brother other than by surmising that Kim Jong-il chose, personally, to erase the younger child's existence from history as North Koreans could read it. Why? One possible explanation is that the omission made it simpler likewise to ignore two stepbrothers born later, Pyong-il and Yong-il—Kim Jong-il's perceived rivals, whom by all accounts he hated. Also, it would not do to mention the fact that he once had a brother who, at the time of his drowning, was still called by a Russian nickname, Shura. That would not fit with the nationalism that was at the root of the *juche* ideology.

Another possible reason for the omission is guilt. One account by a North Korean official who defected to South Korea in 1960 says Kim Jong-il himself was responsible for his brother's drowning, through careless horseplay: Four-year-old Shura was trying to climb out of the pond where they had been wading but six-year-old Yura repeatedly pushed him back in, until the younger boy became exhausted and drowned. When they heard of the accident, the boys' parents ran to the pond, out of breath.

> "What's the matter?" Kim Il-sung shouted to Kim Jong-il, who was standing there like an idiot. Shura was already dead by the time his father arrived there. "I'm asking you what this is all about?" The father again spurred the child to say something. But the boy was without a word. "What have you been doing with Shura?"

The story is at best secondhand, and it dates from the pre-1988 period when a military dictatorship ruled South Korea and was widely suspected of manipulating North Korean defectors' testimony for political and propaganda purposes. Still the account should not be rejected out of hand—especially given that official biographies of Kim Jong-il published after that version came out did not counter it with any alternate, official version of little brother Shura's life and death. Such sad things do happen among young children, and it would be only natural to wish to obliterate the horrible memory.

The former official who told that story described little Kim Jong-il as "a lonely and guilty child" who enjoyed killing bugs and was known to make a pest of himself with acts of mischief. For example, he sneaked into the guard house and swiped a bayonet, which he jabbed into the calf of a guard before running away. He tormented a carpenter by vandalizing his workshop, beating on the carefully sharpened tools with a hammer and strewing things about, then hiding to watch the man try to control his anger. Once the carpenter caught the boy scraping a saw's teeth on the concrete floor, and could not resist slapping his face. Kim Il-sung happened to come out just at that moment. To the petrified carpenter the Great Leader said: "Comrade carpenter, you have done a good thing. No one can endure the mischief of a naughty boy even if he is the son of the premier." But then, according to the story, Kim told his bodyguard chief: "Get rid of that bastard carpenter right away. How can he use violence here?"[5]

Regarding Kim Jong-il's mother's death on September 22, 1949, the official biographies are vague about the cause—and, of course, say nothing about her rivalry with Kim Song-ae. But far from ignoring her death as they do the death of her son Shura, they dwell upon it at length to garner every possible ounce of public sympathy for Kim Jong-il.

Kim Jong-suk told her son she was going to the hospital, which was just opposite the house, and would be back very soon. The thirty-two-year-old woman then "left the house with a smiling face." Jong-il and his younger sister were waiting impatiently for her return, the little girl crying, when a car pulled in through the gate of the house. Kim Jong-il ran out on the porch, but it was a female relative who had arrived; she was there to get one of his mother's dresses to prepare the body for the funeral. "She could hardly tell the boy of the terrible fact, so she told him that Mother would come back when the day dawned. With this she left, concealing her tears."

The next morning, when he learned the truth, the boy was distraught, hardly able to comprehend. He grabbed his little sister's hand and tried to run with her to the hospital, but the women at the house—relatives, and some comrades of Kim Jong-suk's from the days of the anti-Japanese struggle—stopped him. "He called again and again his dear mother in a trembling voice. But Mother did not come." At the funeral in the assembly hall of the party Central Committee, Kim Jong-il "put his face to his mother's breast and wept. The women fighters picked up the boy to take him away from the side of his mother, whereupon the father leader said in a hoarse voice, 'Leave him alone. Tomorrow he will have no mother anymore in whose embrace to cry.' Taking his handkerchief from his pocket he wiped the tears calmly. At this moment the solemn strains of the dirge were intoned":

> *Bones and flesh of the martyrs lie buried in earth,*
> *But their revolutionary spirit and single-hearted fidelity remain alive.*[6]

After his mother's death, one or more women took over the job of raising him and his sister, to whom by all accounts the boy was devoted. The official biographies that were published following his selection as successor fail to name a caregiver, much less record any special bond of affection with her. Some other accounts say that Kim Ok-sun, the surviving member of the tap-dancing duo from Manchurian guerrilla days and the wife of future army chief and defense minister Choe Gwang, took on the role lovingly. This does appear to have been the case, although there are other versions that say a first cousin of their father's raised the children. In a chapter of Kim Il-sung's memoirs—a posthumous installment whose real author we can guess to be Kim Jong-il, busily polishing his own myth—the late Great Leader is made to credit Gen. Ri Ul-sol "and other comrades in arms" for having taken care of Jong-il and his sister after their mother died. (Kim Jong-il relied heavily on Ri to smooth the succession after Kim Il-sung died.)[7]

Just nine months after Kim Jong-suk's death, with the coming of the Korean War, Kim Il-sung moved out of the house and into his command bunker. His son stayed in the house only a little longer, until the war moved too close to home. He worked up an eight-year-old's strong hatred of "the U.S. imperial-ists, the sworn enemy of the Korean people for more than a hundred years, who had pounced on them again to enslave them." He vowed to grow up and make the Americans "pay a thousand times more for the blood shed by our people."[8]

In September, after the tide of war had shifted against the North, the boy and his sister were bundled off to join the retreat from Pyongyang. Trav-eling by car, the premier's family took a road that was "packed with people streaming northward. . . . The going was possible only at night, otherwise in the daytime enemy planes would raid." During the retreat Jong-il suppos-edly admonished a party official, who accompanied them, for cutting a live tree for firewood to prepare their meal instead of gathering dead twigs. "Don't touch even a single living tree," he ordered the man. The propaganda intent of relating the anecdote is to show that the eight-year-old knew the re-treat would be short-lived and wished to conserve Korean resources. To non–North Koreans, he is more likely to come across as a snot-nosed tyrant.[9]

Yura and his sister stayed for a while in the mountains near the Yalu River[10] before retreating farther to "the rear"—to a place that is not named in the official histories but was actually in China. (According to some ac-counts the place was Jilin, where his father had attended middle school.[11]) Kim Il-sung had ordered the Mangyongdae School for Bereaved Children of Revolutionaries relocated there for the duration of the war. Kim Jong-il en-rolled, living for a time in a house with his great-grandfather Kim and other refugee relatives before moving into the school dormitory. The teacher who had "the honor" of teaching him there announced to his fellow students that, since he was "a brilliant student," he was skipping a grade. Supposedly "the pupils who were going to take the first lesson with him were all filled with joy."

Another teacher "paid special attention to his education." When she was transferred to another post, she left a twelve-point memo advising her successor how to deal with Kim Jong-il. One of her points was that the boy "does not want and even detests special favors"—but the rest of the list was a formula for running the classroom precisely according to his needs, wishes and whims. For example, "the teacher should study without delay and in detail" the works of Kim Il-sung, since "these are what Kim Jong-il is most concerned about, and he inquires about them [at] any moment." The daily classroom schedule "should be laid out meticulously so that there may be no time spent idly and he should be guided to observe it strictly. His temperament is like the current of a swift river, so he does not know standstill and stagnation but always makes progress." There is more—as humorist Dave Barry would say, I am not making this up. "The teacher should always watch the eyes of Kim Jong-il. . . . When he looks away or shows aloofness from the teacher, the latter should know that his own speech or act is at fault and should correct it promptly. In other words, it will be proper to regard the eyes of Kim Jong-il as an indicator of right and wrong."[12]

The story of the list—like the anecdote about his tirade against tree cutting—was first disseminated at a time in the 1980s when the regime was trying to build a personality cult for the junior Kim, making him out to have been clever and wise (just as his father purportedly had been at the same age) and, at all times, totally devoted to perpetuating his father's ideas—in short, the ideal successor. Thus, the teacher's memo may be apocryphal in whole or in part. But the general picture that emerges, of teachers and other adults deferring to the communist prince and letting him have his way, is by all accounts accurate.

When the children were finally reunited with their father following the signing of the armistice, an official biography relates, Kim Il-sung stroked their heads and said: "Now that the war is over, let us all live together as before, papa rebuilding the country wrecked by the Yanks and you going to school. . . . What do you say? Good?"[13]

The biography does not mention that the Father-Leader during the war had found time to start a new family. The happy home life he promised fell short of materializing, as Kim Jong-il and his stepmother, Kim Song-ae, were often at odds. "I heard that Kim Jong-il himself obtained permission from his father to call his stepmother 'auntie' instead of 'mother,'" Hwang Jang-yop, who was the party secretary for ideology from 1958, wrote after his 1997 defection to the South.[14]

"Kim Jong-il always hated Kim Song-ae due to the tragic death of his mother," according to defector Kang Myong-do. And the boy felt slighted by his father's attention to stepbrother Kim Pyong-il, who was born around 1953. Pyong-il looked like his father, and in the less frenzied atmosphere of the late 1950s the father was able to spend more time with him and develop a closer, more affectionate relationship than he had managed with Jong-il a decade earlier, Kang reported. "Kim Il-sung always favored Pyong-il over Jong-il," he added.[15]

Kim Jong-il's official biographies reveal nothing of such problems, making no mention of Kim Song-ae or any of her children. Indeed, to read those accounts, it would seem the household included only Kim Jong-il, his little sister and their father—who was often away from Pyongyang for "on-the-spot guidance" trips. When Kim Il-sung was in town, he returned home late from the office, burned the lights in his study practically the whole night and only then might go for an early morning walk with Kim Jong-il, the son who had been waiting for a chance to talk with him. They strolled along the roads inside the premier's estate, which doubled as an experiment station for agriculture, fisheries and forestry. Father and son talked about "study, art, the comradeship of the anti-Japanese fighters or . . . the renowned people and famous generals in Korea."

The boy "made every effort to help his father in his work," and the regime retailed various anecdotes to show the premier's youthful aide in action. Once, for example, Kim Jong-il supposedly went to the market to price school supplies. Finding that the merchants were buying state-produced goods and marking up the prices as much as 300 percent before reselling them, he delivered to an accompanying pal a stinging critique of such vestiges of the market economy. "No matter how cheaply the state sells good for the people, merchants buy them up before they reach the people," he complained. "If we leave intact private merchants, we can neither develop the country's economy nor make the people well off. That's why the fatherly Marshal has mapped out a line of transforming all the private merchants." Walking with the fatherly Marshal the next morning, the boy turned over pen nibs he had bought as evidence. "Inspecting the nibs over and over again, the Great Leader said that those nibs proved that . . . it was necessary to remold the traders to be socialist working people." Soon the regime adopted new restrictions on the merchants and began shifting them into cooperatives. (We must forgo any disrespectful puns here about His Nibs' having been responsible.)

Another time, while walking in the garden with his father, the boy displayed the fashion sense that later would affect clothing styles in the country. Kim Il-sung, glancing at some People's Army soldiers passing by, remarked that their uniform looked out of date. Kim Jong-il instantly agreed, and suggested a new design based on the uniforms that the anti-Japanese guerrillas had worn, but with modifications "to fit in with the contemporary esthetic sense." Kim Il-sung, captivated by the idea, "stopped and looked at his son with affectionate eyes."[16]

Such stories have some basis in the truth. Hwang Jang-yop, following his 1997 defection to South Korea, portrayed the younger Kim as a teenager who—with whatever motivation—took on the role of the deeply devoted son.[17]

But there is a poor-little-rich-boy tinge to Kim Jong-il's story. With his father absent so much and his relationship with his stepmother a distant one at best, the child had to find solace in possessions, such as the automobiles he drove while still a schoolboy,[18] and in receiving expressions of admiration and deference from servants and officials, schoolmates and playmates. He "expressed an interest in power early on, acting out his role as 'premier' during childhood play," according to Hwang. The lad "appointed his friends as 'ministers' and bellowed orders while playing with them."

"We weren't allowed to play with commoners," a former playmate, who lived in a privileged suburban enclave near the premier's mansion, told me. "We sons of high officials led a very comfortable life—but compared with Kim Jong-il the differences in lifestyles were like heaven and earth. When I was little I looked up to Kim Jong-il, envied him and regretted not being the son of Kim Il-sung myself. Anything Kim Jong-il asked me, I would do, since I looked up to him so much. What I envied was the way other people admired him."

After the Korean War, Jong-il attended, in succession, Samsok Primary School, Pyongyang Primary School No. 4, Pyongyang Middle School No. 1 and Namsan Senior Middle School, according to official accounts.[19] His schoolmates were other children of top officials. Indeed, cynical North Korean "commoners" referred to Namsan, situated opposite party headquarters, as a "school for nobility"—a knockoff of Gakushuen, the exclusive Tokyo school that had educated Japan's pre-1945 nobility. (Senior middle school was the final level before work or university, roughly equivalent to American high school.)

According to the account of a North Korean education official who visited Namsan in 1956 and later defected to the South, the school youth corps uniforms were so nice and neat that Namsan students "could be distinguished at a glance" from the shabbily uniformed students of other schools. The man passed a group of final-year students who were chattering in fluent Russian among themselves, which seemed to confirm a rumor he had heard that they would be sent to the Soviet Union for their further education. "The children slipped out of the gate in a group passing by me, but no one made a bow to me. I was disappointed to see these privileged children who did not know how to behave before elders."[20]

An official biography tells of Kim Jong-il's phoning up a classmate—something that would have been impossible between two normal households in the phone-scarce Pyongyang of the 1950s. According to the same official account, at graduation from higher middle school, Jong-il held a dance party for his classmates, all of whom were going to universities instead of straight into the army as most North Korean male graduates did before they got a shot—if they were very lucky—at university education.[21]

According to people who knew him at Namsan, Kim was not enthusiastic about his studies, preferring to take fellow students home to watch movies with him. "He was a perpetual showoff. He was self-centered and his behavior was impolite. He used to boast of his high-quality watch to other classmates. Frequently, he had fun driving a car or motorbike at a fast speed in the streets of Pyongyang."[22]

The official version, on the other hand, is that during his school years the junior Kim "took honors in all subjects every school term and year, and won first prize in every study contest." Besides, he was an all-around athlete— basketball, soccer, gymnastics—and a musician "skilled at playing instruments of all types."[23]

At twelve, according to official accounts, he was elected president of the Children's Union sub-branch in his class. The "unitary idea" had not yet taken over, and many students cut classes, misbehaved, failed to study and idled away their afterschool hours. They would hang around the marketplace, buying lottery tickets from merchants who showed their wicked nature by rigging the draw. Official accounts tell of Kim Jong-il's leadership of a struggle to "remodel" his classmates. "He advanced a detailed plan for extramural activities and decided who would be in charge of studies, sports and art circles."

In honor of the seventeenth anniversary of the Great Leader's battle against the colonial authorities at Pochonbo, Kim Jong-il staged a play. Even though he is reported personally to have taken on the duties of producer, director, scriptwriter and lead actor (playing the part of "General Kim," his father), the play supposedly occupied the other pupils' attentions and helped keep them out of trouble.

So grateful were all concerned for his leadership that the next year, when he was thirteen, he was elected chairman of the Children's Union for the entire Pyongyang Middle School No. 1, although he was only a second-year student. He went on to take charge of the Democratic Youth League at Namsan. There, thanks to his efforts, "the school as a whole became a disciplined, bright and harmonious collective."[24]

Obviously it is necessary to discount the official claims, but by how much is hard to judge. As in the case of the high posts held by the wives of Kim Il-sung and other top officials, leadership status in the youth organizations may have been assured for Kim Jong-il regardless of his interest or ability. And presumably the teachers and professional youth workers involved would have found it in their interest to provide the most unstinting support for the premier's son in his supposed task of "remodeling" fellow students.

The official accounts are filled with reports of instances in which the youngster displayed utter devotion to his father, and implacable opposition to any who would contravene the instructions of the Fatherly Leader. When the two were riding along in a car together during the Korean War, for example, a guard standing at a fork in the road indicated with hand signals the direction of the main road. Kim Il-sung decided to take the other route, whereupon the guard protested, "General, the lane is very rough. And there are no guards posted along it." But Kim Il-sung insisted he wanted to take the rutted lane. The guard stood in confusion until the boy admonished him: "Why are you standing like that? Didn't the General say the car should go along the lane? Let the car go the way requested by the General."

His words, the account relates, "were full of conviction that they should do as told by the Great Leader without fail because his instructions are always correct. At his words, the guard who was standing at a loss gave a start and, repenting deeply of his wavering for a few minutes, let the car take the path pointed out by the General." As the car passed over a gorge, American planes bombed the nearby highway where the car would have been if they had not taken the road less traveled. Allegedly the Pak Hon-yong "counterrevolutionary spy group" had tipped off the Americans to Kim Il-sung's whereabouts.[25] It seems from such accounts as if every twist or turn in high policy, ranging from the attack on Kim Il-sung's personality cult to the most complicated economic debates, found reflection in Kim Jong-il's schoolboy life as he got in his licks against his father's enemies.

One incident sounds suspiciously similar to Kim Il-sung's boyhood challenge to a Korean nationalist lecturer in Jilin. Jong-il purportedly got the better of a critic who complained that Kim Il-sung's emphasis on building heavy industry was keeping living standards down. The man had made the mistake of lecturing at the school attended by the Great Leader's son, who let him have his say before responding sternly, "Denying the necessity of making our own trucks and tractors totally runs counter to the idea of the leader." The lecturer, the loyal son insisted, should give a "correct explanation on this matter."

The poor fellow "turned pale, unable to answer anything as the audience got excited. Having realized the counterrevolutionary content of the 'lecture,' the pupils glared at the lecturer with an indignant eye. The scared lecturer, a stooge of factionalists, was at his wit's end and vainly rubbed his hands. He dismounted from the rostrum and hastily took leave." Thereupon the students looked up to Kim Jong-il "with boundless admiration and adoration." The lad responded by telling them: "We should think and act only in accordance with the ideas of Marshal Kim Il-sung anytime any-where."[26]

Such stories are very hard to credit, and the question remains: Just how devoted was Kim Jong-il to Kim Il-sung? Kang Myong-do said the Kang clan's view was that the junior Kim had a love-hate relationship with his fa-ther.[27] Kim Il-sung may have slighted the boy and his late mother by shifting affection to Kim Song-ae and her brood—but on the other hand, North Ko-reans, including Jong-il and his classmates, were taught to worship the god-like Leader more and more fanatically during the years when the boy was growing up. The father's reflected glory alone gave Kim Jong-il the power that he seems to have relished using.

Stretching credulity, but perhaps not totally unbelievable, is another story, proudly related in an official biography, describing a field trip to Pochonbo by Kim Jong-il and his schoolmates. Reaching the town, Jong-il insisted on making an immediate inspection of a bronze statue of his father, which the townspeople had erected on the site of the Great Leader's com-mand post during the guerrilla assault on the town. "General Kim Il-sung, the brilliant commander of the anti-Japanese struggle, stood majestically, looking at the enemy stronghold, with a binocular in one hand, just as he had appeared when he commanded the march into the homeland." The visiting students "stood solemnly and bowed with respect to the statue. Then they sang the 'Song of General Kim Il-sung' loudly in a chorus with a feeling of infinite reverence for the Marshal."

All of them, including Kim Jong-il, were "deeply stirred"—until, that is, Kim Jong-il started looking more closely at the statue, from various angles and distances.

A stern look came gradually into his face, but no one knew why. Af-ter a while he quietly asked the officials there if the statue was not too small. Upon the unexpected inquiry, the officials could not but feel embarrassed, not knowing what to say. Then he said in a tone of anxiety that despite the fact that the leader was the peerless patriot and national hero who had defeated the Japanese imperialists on this land and regained the country, his bronze statue was too small, its representation was not made well and its location was too low in view of the surrounding area.

His words were a great shock to the officials. Until that day nu-merous people had visited Pochonbo but no one noticed the defect. And the officials themselves, living in Pochonbo, could not discover its weak points, though looking at the statue almost every day. None but Kim Jong-il, who had no parallel in loyalty and was devoted to defending and carrying forward the fatherly leader's immortal revo-lutionary cause, saw the failure to erect the statue properly the moment he visited it. Only when they listened to what he said could the officials realize that they had failed to build the statue better, with greater respect. . . . The officials dropped their heads low, feeling very sorry that there were weaknesses in their work of arranging the revolutionary battle sites and that this meant precisely a breach in their loyalty to the leader.[28]

As that field trip continued, it seems from official accounts that Kim Jong-il continued to throw his weight around. He wanted to visit Lake Samji, another site in his father's guerrilla saga, but a local middle-school student serving as a guide told him the road had not been built yet and there was only a rough path. Fine, said the fourteen-year-old visitor. His group would hike through the forest—and in the process would choose the route for the new road.

That was the time when Kim Il-sung's critics had dared to attack his personality cult. Kim and his sycophants rejected not only the criticism but the term "personality cult" itself, insisting they were simply promoting the party's "revolutionary traditions"—that is, remembrance of the feats of the Great Leader. Gazing at the forest of Mount Paektu (his "birthplace"), Kim Jong-il is reported to have uttered aloud—and, of course, "sternly"—a vow: "The anti-party, counterrevolutionary factional elements, although playing tricks to disparage the party's revolutionary traditions," would be defeated. To that end, "he said a road network should be laid out up to the ridge of Mount Paektu to link all battle sites in a chain," so that all North Koreans could visit them. Officials took his statement as an instruction and guideline for their subsequent work developing the sites for the throngs of loyal subjects who soon would be trooping there daily.[29]

If such stories seem to the non–North Korean reader to portray a spoiled-rotten brat shamelessly exploiting his father's position to get away with bossing grownups around, so be it. It is almost beyond doubt that Kim Jong-il himself approved every word before the publication of those accounts in the 1980s. Quite obviously he was appealing not to outsiders but, rather, to Korean worshippers of Kim Il-sung. Nevertheless, the subsequent publication of those biographies in numerous foreign languages—projects on which he also would have had to sign off—suggests he had no sense that the behavior attributed to him would appear outrageous to many people outside the fold.

Kim Jong-il had a narrow and sheltered upbringing, subject to relatively few influences that would challenge the world-view he was developing as the son of the North Korean god-king. Although he spent his early years in the Soviet Union, the family moved to Pyongyang when he was only three. He spent most of the Korean War years in China—but was surrounded there by relatives and fellow members of the North Korean elite, not interacting much if at all with Chinese people and not learning the language.

Before finishing high school, he did accompany his father to the Soviet Union, one of the few known instances of his traveling abroad. Indeed, the politically precocious seventeen-year-old actually involved himself in planning Kim Il-sung's itinerary for the trip, according to Hwang Jang-yop, who traveled with them as party secretary for ideology. "When Kim Il-sung left the hotel in the mornings to attend to official functions, he would help his father to the door, bring out his shoes and personally put them on his feet. Back then Kim Il-sung was only forty-seven, enjoying robust health that was the envy of much younger men. However, he was still pleased by his son's act of taking his arm and putting his shoes on for him." During that trip the younger Kim took a supervisory role over his father's doctors, nurses and assistants. In the evening he would assemble them and "ask them how they had served Kim Il-sung during the day and what they should do the next day." Jong-il "was particularly interested in me, and asked me a lot of questions," Hwang said. "I felt that he was much too politically sensitive for a seventeen-year-old."[30] Hwang "had the premonition that Kim Jong-il would one day chase his uncle out and take over or climb even higher. Anything higher would have been inheritance of Kim Il-sung's power, but back then I did not dream that things would come to that."[31]

Hwang took the opportunity of that Moscow trip to suggest that the youth enroll in the party secretary's alma mater, Moscow University, but Kim Jong-il rejected the idea. "He said that politics should be learned from his father, and that he could not assist his father while studying abroad."[32] He returned to Pyongyang to enroll at Kim Il-sung University. The official version has it that his decision was based on his "*juche*-consciousness": He realized that "his real learning and his textbooks were found in the reality of Korea and not in any other country."[33] Perhaps that's not far from the real reason. For most of his life he had been known as Yura, but shortly before his high school graduation he is reported to have told classmates to call him Jong-il.[34] It may be that he wished to present a more Korean image so his father would not look ridiculous attacking flunkeyists for aping things foreign. But Hwang came to believe that the youngster had developed ambition for his own career: "Considering his words and deeds from this time onwards, I believe that Kim Jong-il was more aggressive than his father in the process of power inheritance."

Kim Jong-il "grew up in the royal family headed by an absolute dictator, and faced no obstacles in his path," Hwang wrote. "Since his mother Kim Jong-suk's death in 1949 no one had any control over him." The lad "behaved like a prince," and was "a conceited child who flaunted his status as the son of the highest ruler among his friends. This tendency to do whatever he liked worsened as he grew and turned into the overvaulting ambition to make his father's power his own."[35]

As befits its illustrious name, Kim Il-sung University was the country's most prestigious institution of higher learning. It employed about six thousand faculty and staff members. Compare that number with a student body of ten thousand "and you'll see it's a very prominent school," one former student said. Known as the place where the country grew "pure particles for Kimil-sungism," KISU emphasized ideological studies even more than other universities did.

The official accounts describe Kim Jong-il's university career as brilliant. He took top academic honors. He led fellow students, both on campus and in the off-campus physical labor that was required of all North Korean students. And he "published some 1,200 works including treatises, talks, speeches, answers, conclusions and letters as a student"—publications that "concern matters of philosophy, political economy, history, pedagogy, literature and art, linguistics, law, military science and natural science."[36] In fact, his purported undergraduate writings, on topics such as "The Characteristics of Modern Imperialism and Its Aggressive Nature," did not draw official praise and start appearing in print until he had been picked to succeed his father in the 1970s. By then he commanded an enormous corps of writers, some of whom just might have had something to do, even retrospectively, with his prolific output.

Kim Jong-il majored in political economy. Largely as a result of his choice, economics later became the most prominent of the university's departments. "A lot of people who graduated in economics have been promoted quite well," said a former math major at KISU who took the basic political economy course. "They learn socialist economics and a touch of capitalist economics. What you learn about capitalist economics is just what Marx said in *Das Kapital.* In other words, you get a critique of capitalism."[37]

On his first day at KISU young Kim humbly greeted professors and fellow students, taking off his cap and saying, "I hope I will learn a great deal from you." Within days, however, he is said to have begun criticizing the curriculum and the textbooks—and professors and deans, of course, had begun changing them according to his instructions.

For one thing, he did not see why it was necessary to include study of computation using the slide rule and abacus in the university economics curriculum. After all, students were supposed to have learned one of those tools, the abacus, before they got there; at the university level they would do their computation on adding machines. "Surprised at the keen insight" of that complaint, the dean not only revised the curriculum but took to having a private chat with Kim Jong-il after each of his lectures to see if his words had met with the very special freshman's approval.[38] In rescuing North Korea's future economic managers from the drudgery of studying computation so they could concentrate on what he considered the really important parts of the curriculum, Kim Jong-il was following in the footsteps of his father and his father's mentor, Stalin. Both were known for their suspicion of mathematical and scientific evaluation of policies.[39]

Meanwhile Kim Jong-il saw to it that his KISU classmates were "afire with unquenchable ardor" for reading. Official accounts credit him with having started a movement in which every student was to read ten thousand pages a year—from books by and about Kim Il-sung. The younger Kim's rationale: "In order to make the Great Leader's revolutionary thought your own conviction, you must read his works ten or even twenty times until you grasp their essence, thinking deeply over the ideas conveyed by each phrase of his works." Soon—like Chinese with the little red book of Mao's quotations—they are reported to have been studying Kim Il-sung's works "no matter when and where, in libraries, while walking in parks and in their spare minutes in dining halls."[40]

Kim Jong-il joined the Workers' Party while a university student. He was not the leader of his party cell—or of the campus Democratic Youth League. Indeed, an authorized biography has it that the party cell chairman was so "greatly honored by mere registration of the distinguished name" that he told young Kim he could "do as he pleased regarding his life in the party." However, the account goes on, Kim rejected the offer, and throughout his university career he provided "a brilliant example" of the conscientious party member.

For example, he intervened to revise the cell's work plan when he saw that it had strayed from the main target into minutiae. Ashamed of their mistake, the committee members "dropped their heads." (The gesture evidently was becoming reflexive among North Koreans as the junior Kim more often deigned to offer his guidance to lesser mortals.) Kim also realized that "party-life review"—the criticism session so central to communist practice— was held too seldom. He proposed making it a weekly or even daily routine. "If we have it frequently, we will not have to keep our deficiencies for a long time before they are criticized as we do now," he explained. "We will be able to rectify them before they grow too serious." Oddly, there is no mention of any criticism of him uttered in such sessions, no listing of deficiencies he might have had.[41]

One story full of unintended ambiguity tells of news reporters who went to the campus in early 1963 to write up an award—"Double Chollima"— won by Kim's class. Already, "Kim Jong-il was widely known as a young leader," says an official biography. "Various anecdotes about this were told widely. So the people desired eagerly to see him." The reporters asked to interview him, "because they had thought that the class owed all its success to his energetic guidance." Kim Jong-il refused, however, explaining that it would be enough for them to "meet the comrades who have done good jobs." Finally he submitted to a brief interview, but was not very forthcoming. When they asked about his experience in guiding the class's work to win the award, he answered that he had "nothing to say." After thinking a bit, he broke his silence only to the point of delivering a homily of a few words on the mission of youth to carry forward the revolution.

When the journalists suggested he pose for a photograph, he refused, asking: "Why should I have my picture published in the paper?" Instead he sent them away, "asking them to write a fine article and show it to him when it had been written." They complied—this was North Korea, remember, where reporters were mere mouthpieces for the regime. After he received their draft, he returned it to them—having marked for excision all references to him.

Although they failed to photograph him alone, the journalists did get a chance to take a picture of the whole class. On that occasion they are reported to have asked Kim Jong-il to stand front and center. The story is that he refused, saying the places of honor belonged to the party cell chairman, the Democratic Youth League chairman and the class monitor, who had "done a great deal of work." The journalists insisted that having him stand in the middle was "the wish of the readers of our newspaper, the unanimous wish of all our people." Fellow students chimed in, urging him to stand in the middle. He refused, and the cameraman finally snapped the picture showing Kim Jong-il in "an obscure corner," second from the left in the central row.

The reporters were "deeply impressed with his infinite modesty," says his biographer. "On honorable occasions he always took the back seat, giving all honors to the ordinary students. In him they saw the great personality of a true leader who bears the brunt of all difficulties for the well-being of the people." That photograph, published in February of 1963, was the first one picturing Kim Jong-il to appear in the North Korean media. "This was how the dear leader whom the Korean people had craved to see so eagerly made a public appearance so unseemingly and so obscurely among fellow students. The people saw the image of their dear leader in this very humble picture."[42]

Right. Well, it sounds as if the regime, by the time the biography carrying that account was published, might have had to make a virtue of necessity. As we have seen, most of the stories officially told about him from the 1980s showed Kim Jong-il as the leader of his mates since his elementary school days. But here was his first published photograph and it showed him taking a back seat. What to do? Tell a story about his modesty, true or concocted.

Kim Jong-il may well have had ample cause for modesty that day. He was not the class leader (although presumably he could have held whatever post he wanted—if higher-ups and he himself had thought at the time that he was destined to rule the country, and had realized it would look good on his résumé for him to get his college-leadership ticket punched on the way up).

It may have been true that real credit for the achievements in question belonged to others, whether he actually said so or not. Kim Jong-il was just growing out of adolescence, while a great many of his male classmates — more than likely including the leaders who did the real organizational work — were army veterans senior to him by several years, who had shown their mettle in the military and in party work before matriculating. I do not recall having seen the photograph in question, but other photos of him with fellow KISU students show a cherub-faced boy among lantern-jawed men.[43]

In the extraordinarily faction-prone and education-worshipping Korean culture, after the family there is no group as important throughout one's working career as classmates. However shamelessly Kim Jong-il might have played the big shot among ordinary strangers, taking public credit for efforts that others in the class actually had exerted would not have endeared him to the Kim Il-sung University Class of 1964. The class was destined to be an important source of support for him. Perhaps he understood that much.

But there are other factors to consider in evaluating this story. First, the photographers were asking him to stand in the middle of the front row. Kim Jong-il was very short — perhaps five feet two inches (1.58 meters) when fully grown — and extremely self-conscious about it. In later years he would exert himself mightily to appear taller, wearing shoes with three-inch heels[44] and teasing his hair up into a bouffant pompadour to add a few more inches. (The glorious career of China's even more diminutive Deng Xiaoping evidently provided him little if any consolation.) If Kim had stood where he supposedly was asked to stand that day in 1963, he might have been seen to be the shortest male in his class. Photographers might not yet have gotten the word that they must routinely pose him standing slightly in front of others so that perspective would give an illusion of extra height.

Additionally, there are hints that young Kim had been going through a rebellious period. If his father — as seems likely — or someone else in the regime had decided it was a good idea to start publicizing him as a "young leader," perhaps he himself had not come to terms with the requirements of the public role being thrust upon him. And finally, his reluctance to be interviewed and to bask in public praise was not temporary. For decades to come he remained largely inaccessible to journalists, and repeatedly stayed out of the public eye for such long periods as to suggest an almost Howard Hughes–like aversion to the limelight.

Young Kim is described in one officially disseminated biography as having gone "deeply into the people" during his college days.[45] The phrase is an accidental but telling double entendre: Those "people" seem to have been mainly young women. Nonofficial sources describe Kim the collegian as a ladies' man leading a rambunctious life. He started out living in the premier's

mansion instead of the school dormitory, but serious family problems—
especially conflicts with his stepmother, who would report to his father on
his behavior—eventually kept him away from home for long stretches. Not
eating properly, he was expending his energies on love affairs to the extent
that one professor, Kim Shin-sook, decided the budding Don Juan needed
better nutrition to keep up his health and stamina. Whether out of sincere
concern or to earn brownie points, the professor acquired delicacies and fed
them to Kim Jong-il. The young man, on that rich diet, began to grow
chubby—eventually presenting a roly-poly contrast to the slim builds of
most of his fellow North Koreans on and off campus.

Rumors of wild partying, fast driving and sexual escapades got around
in Pyongyang. Perhaps it was partly for that reason that the regime eventually went to so much trouble to paint a contrasting picture. Jesus Christ as
Eagle Scout, doing many a good turn daily—that pretty much sums up the
official portrayals of the young Kim. China's communist propagandists once
plucked from the masses a previously anonymous do-gooder named Lei
Feng, composed songs about him and taught children to emulate Lei Feng's
selflessness. In North Korea the songs and tales of Kim Jong-il would serve
the same function.

As in stories about his father, it seems people were constantly shedding
tears at the astonishing love, benevolence and selflessness Kim Jong-il unfailingly displayed. One of countless officially peddled anecdotes relates that
a sickly youth whom he tended in the hospital and helped with studies "could
not hide hot tears welling up in his eyes." Holding in his hands the class notes
that young Kim had copied out for him during his absence, the student
"threw himself into the broad arms of Kim Jong-il and burst into sobs with
his face buried in his breast. That was something too noble to be called mere
friendship."[46]

Helping sick friends seems to have been a specialty. There is another story
telling how young Kim prescribed and delivered medicine—"a cure-all"—
for a female student suffering the aftereffects of a malnourished childhood
in South Korea. "She burst into sobs," and her mother's eyes were "wet with
tears." Needless to say, the young woman recovered.[47] Exaggerated and
over-dramatized they may be, but probably there is at least a grain of truth in
some of the stories about kind gestures to individuals. Regarding his "prescription," for example, Kim Jong-il had access to the best medicines, many
of which were unavailable to ordinary North Koreans. Considering that virtually everyone else let him have his way, the pharmacists at the hospital for
the top elite might well have let the youngster do the prescribing—perhaps
of a tonic such as Korean ginseng. In the pattern of noblesse oblige it would
become his habit to present gifts—usually elaborate and sometimes wildly
extravagant—to somewhat less fortunate people who happened to be his
friends, supporters or underlings, or who otherwise were known to him.

But against whatever signs of a warm heart the young Kim displayed must be balanced some tasteless hijinks in which he humiliated others for his own amusement. An example is a story that a former member of the Pyong-yang elite told me about Kim and his pal "Jerkoff" Choe.

Choe Hyon, a former anti-Japanese guerrilla, rose to become vice-president of North Korea and lived in the exclusive neighborhood of Changkwangdong, near the premier's mansion. His son, Choe Yong-hae, grew up hanging out after school with Kim Jong-il and Kim's other buddies.[48] After Kim Jong-il enrolled in the university and began his career of amour, he noticed that Choe Yong-hae was very shy and would not date girls. He suggested that Choe might not be a "real male." One day Kim Jong-il and his other buddies, with their girlfriends, were at Choe's house after classes. Continuing to torment Choe, Kim demanded that he take his pants off. The boy complied, but Kim Jong-il pointed out his lack of an erection despite the girls' presence and suggested that Choe must be impotent. So he had other pals tie up Choe and told one of the group to massage him. Disobedience to Kim Jong-il was unthinkable because of whose son he was, as well as fear that the disobedient one would become his next target for bullying. Those who had tied him up held the struggling victim down while the designated youngster duly complied with the instruction. When Choe became aroused, Kim Jong-il said: "Oh. You're capable. I'm satisfied."[49]

Instead of Yong-hae, from that day forward Choe was known as Yong-du, "the head is moving toward the sky," a slang term for masturbation. He eventually became chairman of the Central Committee of the League of Socialist Working Youth, the body responsible for training and guiding prospective party members following their graduation from school. He held that post until 1997, when, according to a South Korean intelligence report, he was ousted for corruption. He was known to be a trusted crony of Kim Jong-il's— and very fond of women. His childhood pals had continued to call him Yong-du.[50]

Kim Jong-il may have grown a bit more serious as he became a university upperclassman and could see looming ahead his graduation into the North Korean top elite's version of the real world. Maybe his father had a heart-to-heart talk with him about his future and the need to settle down somewhat— perhaps even mentioning Jong-il's possible eventual succession to the top post. The younger Kim did not stop partying then, it is clear, but the official accounts have him accompanying his father on frequent trips for "on-the-spot guidance." In the course of such trips the junior Kim enthusiastically picked up his father's style of micromanagement. It is a style that unfortunately had reached, if it had not already long since passed, the point of diminishing returns for the economy.

One such story unintentionally shows that Kim Il-sung's originally ad-
mirable practice of going out to the boondocks to see the real problems of the
people was becoming an empty ritual. Both officials and ordinary people
wanted only to please the overburdened Great Leader without "troubling"
such an exalted being with their problems.

Father and son, visiting a military outpost near the Demilitarized Zone
in February 1963, split up for separate inspections. The junior Kim noticed
that the only water supply was a dribble from an ice-covered spring. Mess
hall, bathhouse and laundry were all out of commission on account of the
lack of water. Kim Il-sung had already asked the soldiers if they had any
problems. Oh, no, they said. They were living "literally in plenty." Then
Jong-il approached the Great One to tell him quietly about the water shortage that the men had not mentioned, a problem that could be overcome with
just a little pipe and pumping equipment. "These comrades say that they
dared not request the material out of consideration of the nation's economic
problems," he told his father, who immediately gave orders to solve the problem. "The next day found the arrival on that hill of many technicians and a
large amount of pumping equipment, all sent by the Fatherly Leader. A fort-
night later clear water began to gush forth." The soldiers felt "boundless respect" for Kim Jong-il.[51]

During a scorching lowland heat wave the following August, the Kims
prudently chose to focus their guidance on remote Pungsan County, in
the high, cool mountains of Yanggang Province. (The accounts do not say
whether the premier's entire family, including Pyong-il and the other children, went along on that working summer vacation.) Kim Jong-il discovered
that local children's lunchboxes were packed with potato cakes instead of the
rice Koreans generally prefer. Imagining "the sorry faces of the mothers
preparing the lunches for their children every day," he "perceived the still
poor livelihood of the mountain folk, and judged the irresponsible work attitude of the officials who were not so enthusiastic for the improvement of the
people's standard of living." He passed along his findings to his father, who
called a meeting of county agricultural officials and set them right with instructions on soil building, planting suitable crops for the cold highland,
damming the river to set up an irrigation system and exchanging the potatoes grown there for lowland rice. Hearing the Fatherly Leader point out
"the bright road they should follow," the listeners cheered "at the top of their
voices."[52]

In those instances Kim Jong-il kept his role to investigating quietly, advising his father of his findings and recommendations. One wonders, then,
about the real feelings of an obsequious school official in Pungsan County
when the college boy stepped out of the staff role and decided to guide the
official directly in the work of running the Pungsan Middle School. Visiting
the school's science laboratories, young Kim noticed that they were set up

only for general teaching of the subjects, with nothing to help tailor instruction to the particular needs of the county. He advised collecting local soil samples and bringing in preserved specimens of local flora and fauna — asters, sheep, bull trout. That seems to have been sensible enough advice.

But then, "seeing that trunks of poplars around the playground had been mauled by axes and knives," Kim Jong-il said sports equipment should be provided to prevent mischievous boys from misbehaving. Additionally, he instructed that apple trees be planted on a bare hillside behind the school. Apples don't normally do well on such a cold highland, but Kim Jong-il "explained in detail" how to adapt them. That, he said, would be "very important in convincing the children that nothing will be impossible if they get down to implementing the leader's instruction to develop the highland to be as good a place as the lowland."

In a classroom he found a gap in the floor. Frowning, "he exhorted the official to fill in the chink lest a cold wind through it in winter should make the children catch a cold." The school official, astonished that the young visitor had noticed something he himself had neglected, "bowed his head, ashamed of his failure to fulfill the duty as an educationist." A little later, "reluctant to part" with Kim Jong-il, the same official "begged him to give more instructions." Kim Jong-il then produced bark he had stripped off a birch tree in the schoolyard. (Evidently that was okay, although carving on poplar trees was not.) Using the birch bark as writing paper just as his father's anti-Japanese guerrillas supposedly had done, he dashed off seven pages of "precious instruction."[53]

Back at the university that fall, Kim Jong-il is reported to have set out to use what he had learned as the starting point for a graduation thesis on the role of the county. His father was then promoting the county as the key local government level at which to "resolve all problems arising in the building of socialism and communism in the countryside." A professor suggested that the topic was too ambitious for a mere bachelor's-degree thesis, requiring so much original research and argument that it would be more like a doctoral dissertation. The professor advised young Kim to be satisfied with a typical graduation paper proving socialist economic laws. However, "Kim Jong-il said smilingly that the validity of socialist economic laws had already been confirmed and that there was no use of proving it again. He continued: 'What we need is a correct way to carry on the revolution and construction. Many lectures at the university deal with something abstract and general, and lack in clarifying such a thing.'"

Sticking with his plan, the junior Kim worked hard studying his father's pronouncements on rural economy and local industry, says an official biography. "At the same time, he himself toured different parts of the country to collect various data on politics, the economy and culture." That was, of course, a research opportunity not available to the usual North Korean undergraduate. He also had plenty of help from state agencies, normally stingy with statistics, as he "analyzed the facts consolidated by the State Planning Commission and economic guidance agencies."

After all that work, finally "he could give perfect answers to the questions raised in the revolution." In March of 1964, a few days before his graduation, he rose in a college lecture hall to deliver "an immortal work, 'The Place and Role of the County in the Building of Socialism.' " Needless to say, "the audience loudly applauded him for his firm conviction, clear-cut analysis and cogent theory and his ideo-theoretical brilliance and convincing argument by which he solved the complex rural problem in an original way from the standpoint of *juche*."[54] As in the case of his other some 1,199 college writings, though, skeptics harbor doubt that Kim himself wrote the thesis — or wrote it the way it was finally published, twenty-one years later, at a time when efforts to promote his personality cult were peaking.[55]

But even if Kim Jong-il was not quite the Big Man on Campus that such official accounts make him out to have been, it does seem he was very much a presence at his university — and not only on account of whose son he was. Partially overcoming his peculiar upbringing, he was developing some engaging qualities of his own. Perhaps he was learning something about human relations by watching his father, a past master. Relationships with classmates seem to have been relatively good.

According to a Bulgarian diplomat who was an exchange student at Kim Il-sung University, Kim Jong-il "loved to talk with friends," especially foreigners. Evidently, by that time he had acquired a proper aristocrat's set of manners. He seemed "not as arrogant as many sons of high-ranking officials in Bulgaria," Georgi Mitov recalled in a South Korean newspaper interview some three decades later. Young Kim's humility quotient was high enough, at least, to permit his becoming star-struck: Mitov was a famous volleyball player, and he thought that was part of the reason Kim Jong-il visited him in his dormitory often — so often that the Bulgarian sometimes had to pretend he was out.[56]

Another former East European diplomat has described the junior Kim in Joe College terms — soccer player, amateur pianist, at least normally intelligent student. Expanding on the latter point, a North Korean who knew him told me, "Although his mind is okay, it does not appear he studied much. There must be a strict teacher-student relationship for good education. Could there possibly be someone able to teach properly the son of Kim Il-sung?"

TWELVE

Growing Pains

Kim Jong-il, at the top of the pecking order, was by no means unique in the extent to which the experiences of childhood and youth depended on who his father was. All the way down the complicated North Korean class hierarchy youngsters typically found their treatment, from even their earliest years, to be governed by the family's socioeconomic position, or *songbun* — essentially the status of their parents, grandparents, aunts and uncles.[1]

Take Dong Young-jun, who grew up in privilege—although not even remotely near Kim Jong-il's level—in Bukchong, the big country town in North Hamgyong Province where he was born in 1965. "My family was very well off," he told me. "Whenever I met people who were undergoing hardship or hunger, I felt especially thankful for my parents."

Dong's father worked as an investigator in "internal affairs," meaning he was checking up on his fellow North Koreans. Following the turmoil of the Korean War, "many people lied about their backgrounds," Dong explained. Employed by a secret police organization that in 1973 was renamed Department of State Security, his father "was digging up their true backgrounds." On the other side of the family Dong's mother, herself a doctor, had some good connections in Pyongyang. One of her cousins was a senior colonel working at a military academy. Another was a member of the Supreme People's Assembly.

Dong grew up, he told me, as a "fanatic," idolizing Kim Il-sung and urging his schoolmates to do the same. "All through elementary school, junior middle and higher middle school, I was student body president. Even at the university I was on the student council."

At one point in our interview Dong asked if I minded if he smoked. I told him it was all right with me. He interjected then that he had grown up hating the United States. Now that he had defected to South Korea, though, "I think I actually like the United States," he told me. "Look, I have a U.S.-made lighter and I smoke Marlboros."

I asked when he had started smoking. His answer, totally unexpected, introduced me to a facet of North Korea that I had neither heard nor read about. He had started "at age eleven," Dong said. He explained: "In North Korean schools there are gangs that fight a lot. They consider the first boy to suffer a nosebleed the loser. They believe if you smoke a lot you won't get a nosebleed." So Dong the model student had led a double life, moonlighting as a member of a violent teenage gang? Naturally I wanted to know more, and Dong obliged me.

"Gangs are rated according to the social rank of the members' fathers," he told me. "These aren't formal groups, but this has been going on for years—for generations. In most cases, if your father is very high ranking you get the power. You hang out with kids from similar family backgrounds.

"You can't fight on the school grounds," Dong said. Rather, the gangs usually fought at sites where the students were doing the manual labor frequently required of them. "Or we would meet on Sunday by pre-arrangement, say near the Namdaechon River bank at such and such a time with such and such number of people. We might catch a dog around there and eat it, or hide and steal people's watches."

Dong told me he stayed in his gang until junior year in higher middle school. "But in senior year I studied very hard, so I could get into Pyongyang Engineering College."

My own very first article as a cub newspaper reporter in North Carolina, in 1969, was about a fatal fight between gangs supporting the basketball teams of two high schools. Of course, it made the front page of *The Charlotte Observer*. To hear Dong describe the fights with rocks and tools that went on in his community—an arm cut off, a skull broken in half—it was clear to me that some of them would be considered newsworthy in any country with a free press. In North Korea, however, although the official media on occasion referred vaguely to problems of young people's misbehavior, the regime did not like to shine too bright a light on such rampant juvenile delinquency as Dong was describing. "It's never in the newspapers there," Dong said.

Most interesting in Dong's account, I thought, was his description of the makeup of the gangs. "There were basically about four groupings throughout the grades," he said, and all of those were from the elite. "Ordinary people's children could hardly be part of the gangs. Say you had a fight and hurt someone. You'd go to prison. If your parents were influential, they could get you out. But the ordinary people would have no chance of getting out, so they didn't join.

"The leader of each gang was whoever had the most important father. The first group consisted of children of party or State Security men. The second group's members were children of people working in administration and technology; the third, military; the fourth, trade and commerce. I was part of the first group. Because our group was highest ranking and most powerful, the other groups would give us gifts like cigarettes. Normally the first group would fight the second and third groups. Often the second group fought the third."

And what were those fights about? Dong gave me an example. "In my district," he said, "there were a lot of special forces military men. The student who got his arm cut off was the son of a military man. The one who cut it off was the son of a technocrat. What happened was that the military man's son had just been transferred into the school and wasn't part of a gang yet. Kids can be very cruel to newcomers in school. People in the second group kicked him around and beat him up badly. The military kids took offense, even though he wasn't yet part of their gang. The whole gang got into the fight. That was in 1977, at the Namdaechon River bank. We were assigned there to collect pebbles. One guy hit a military kid with a sharp-edged spade and cut his arm off. It was completely severed. I saw it. We always sharpened the spades so they would slip easily into the ground. I was twelve years old then, and so was the kid who got hurt.

"The incident of the split skull I didn't see. It happened a year later at the same site, during the night. In that case it was a fight with kids from another school. A guy on the other side had his skull split—again, with a sharpened spade—and died."

So what happened to the young authors of mayhem and murder? "If the victim's father was of higher rank, the perpetrator would be in serious trouble," Dong said. "And if the perpetrator's father was of higher rank, things would be hushed up. The guy who cut off his opponent's arm got only three weeks of forced labor. In the case of the killing I described, the perpetrator had his head shaved and was sent to prison. He stayed only ten days, though. His father was so prominent, he was just sent to another school."

When I asked, Dong told me that from what he had heard his experience was not peculiar to his locale. "All over North Korea there are gangs like this. I don't know about the degree of brutality. Even in Pyongyang there are gangs, but they're closely watched. If there's a fight between two groups there and the authorities find out, the leader and his family are sent to a prison camp. Chongjin, Rajin and Hamhung are the worst places. Gang fighting originated with Koreans from Japan, who tended to settle in those areas. Lots of Koreans who moved from Japan are people who got in trouble in Japan and then were sent to North Korea. They were accepted because they had money."

I have no confirmation of Dong's observation that banishing trouble-makers was a significant factor when ethnic Korean families in Japan decided who among them would repatriate to North Korea. However, it is true that for decades many of the gangsters in Japan were people of Korean ancestry. (That was, at least in part, a reflection of the Korean minority's mistreatment by the Japanese majority.) So I was curious to know whether the North Korean gangs followed the rituals of the Japanese underworld *yakuza*. "No, they don't cut their fingers off or tattoo themselves," Dong told me. "But they do prick their fingers and hold them together to become blood brothers."

Dong told me that the name of his gang was a Korean word that means downpour or deluge. "Every member of my gang wore formal shoes—leather shoes with laces. Of course, the other kids had only cloth shoes. Leather shoes were rare. Just by wearing those, we showed we had prominence."

The shoe discussion led Dong to digress away from the topic of gang life into courtship customs. For a *son*, the arranged and rather formal first date between a man and woman of marriageable age, he told me, "a guy might borrow leather shoes to impress the woman."

It took me a moment to realize that Dong was relating a standard North Korean joke, whose humor derived from its essential if not literal truth about the material advantages of the elite. "The three things you need for that first date are leather shoes, a Seiko watch and a gold tooth," Dong went on, getting wound up. "Sometimes you would even borrow the gold tooth. At night the guy would take the girl to a bright spot and show those things off as he made arrangements for the next meeting. He would say, 'We have to meet tomorrow at eight,' and he would tap his Seiko watch. 'We have to meet *here*.' He would tap his leather shoe on the ground so she would look at it when he said 'here,' and then he would grin widely at her so the light would glint off his gold tooth."

As Kim Dae-ho grew up he had a life quite different from Dong's—except for the fact that he also became a juvenile gang fighter. Born across the border in China in 1959, Kim was a member of an ethnic Korean family. He formed few memories of China before his parents, motivated by patriotism, moved the family to South Hamgyong Province in North Korea when he was three. His father went to work in a food factory. His mother stayed home to keep house and care for Dae-ho and his younger brothers, of whom eventually there were three.

The parents quickly realized that the lifestyle they had left behind in China was more prosperous, and they "couldn't forget" about the differences, Kim told me. "In China we had candy stored in the kitchen for snacks"—but not in North Korea. "My mother used to cry when, as an elementary student,

I ripped my pants and she had to mend them. We were so poor. That's why she cried."

Starting his education with nursery school and kindergarten, where he began to learn about Kim Il-sung's greatness, little Dae-ho soon came to wish he had an elder brother. "When I got in a fight, a kid with his elder brother could beat me up."

Worse, Kim Dae-ho recalled being subject to "invisible discrimination from fellow pupils with more stable backgrounds. Having no relatives in North Korea I was at a disadvantage. You have to write a paper on your family. Other people could write about a father in the party, an uncle on the Central Committee. I had no relatives and my parents weren't party members, so the discrimination continued."

Not only other children but also teachers and officials meted out different treatment depending on a pupil's family background, Kim Dae-ho told me. "Even when looking over our homework the officials would praise children of high officials." (Recall the slavish praise of Kim Jong-il by his teachers.) The highlight of a youngster's life was supposed to be donning the bright kerchief of a member of the children's corps. Even there, though, "the children of the elite got in earlier. There were two inflows of eight-year-olds. The first group got in on April 15, Kim Il-sung's birthday. I was part of the second intake, on June 6. The reason given for letting the first group in early was that they were better students, brought up more uprightly."

Kim Dae-ho blamed such discrimination for having affected his personality. "I became rough and aggressive. I beat up children of high officials and disobeyed the teacher often." He grinned and added: "Since I was very rough, kids were afraid of me and the teachers didn't know what to do with me." Meanwhile some older youngsters were bullying him in turn. Junior high students, some of them repatriated from Japan, had formed gangs. "I did some dirty work for them, got on trains to steal from people, did some shoplifting. You couldn't say I was a gang member, because I was only about ten years old. They would bully me and demand that I bring money from home."

Eventually each group gave him something serious to think about. "In third grade I bullied so many kids that my classmates decided to gang up on me. I realized then that kids no longer feared me. They would throw stones at me, or spit at me." The older gang members, around the same time, "took me to the railroad, stripped me to my underwear and made me lie on the track."

After thinking things over, the boy gave up his pose of ferocious loner in hopes of becoming a leader. "I made friends and created my own gang," he told me. Indeed, from the sound of it—and despite his lack of family connections to fall back on in the event of punishment—he seems to have become a junior-grade godfather in Tanchon, the South Hamgyong Province city where he lived. "I retaliated against gang members who had used me. As I got older they came and asked for food or tickets. I got my revenge by ordering my gang members to beat them up. I had friends not only in my own school but in all the schools of the city. At a parent-teacher conference, teachers told parents to keep their kids from associating with me. But if the kids obeyed, I'd beat them up. So parents would come up to me and ask for good treatment for their kids."

Members of gangs "mostly were children of high officials and more prosperous people who came from Japan," Kim Dae-ho told me. "Even in my group, lots were kids of high officials." As for weapons, "in elementary school we used rocks. In the upper grades we learned *taekwondo* and fought with our fists and feet. I had a fight with the son of a military security officer. The kid brought a knife, so I asked my friends to bring me one. They brought me a straight razor. The kid ran away. He didn't come to school the next day; by coincidence he died of accidental gas poisoning. Otherwise, there was the occasional minor stabbing but nobody got killed in our fights."

Due to his family's unhappy circumstances, Kim Dae-ho told me, he was slow to develop feelings of worship for the country's leader. But when he reached sixteen he realized that his career choices might soon start to narrow very drastically. The dream of most North Korean males was to join the army. That was the standard route to becoming members of the party and, when they were mustered out following a decade's service, being considered for responsible civilian jobs.

Only youngsters of acceptable class background by North Korea's standards, and whose "loyalty" was unquestioned, would be accepted into the army. Kim Dae-ho's family background was merely undistinguished; it was not positively bad as it would have been if, for example, his forebears had been big landlords or prominent collaborators with the Japanese colonial regime. But his credentials were lacking in the personal loyalty department, so he proceeded to immerse himself in the organized adoration of Kim Il-sung. Still he found that ordinary expressions of loyalty wouldn't persuade the army recruiters "because I was known as a gang leader."

So what did he do? "I went to the recruitment center and wrote an oath in my blood," Kim told me. The oath read: "I will sacrifice my life for the nation and I will do my best in the army."

When I interviewed Kim Dae-ho he was slender and appeared rather studious. To look at him, he was no Bruce Lee type. It had been a little difficult for me earlier in the interview to picture him taking the lead role in a real-life North Korean version of *West Side Story*. Now I suppose my jaw must have dropped as I wondered whose idea the blood oath had been, and about Kim Dae-ho's sincerity in signing it. When I asked him, though, he didn't hesitate to reply. "I truly believed in it and it was my idea to write it in blood," he told me.

The blood-oath gesture had the desired effect. Kim entered the army in 1976 and became an artillery spotter, stationed near the front line in Kang-won Province. He was promoted to sergeant and singled out as a model sol-dier, honored with a chest full of commendation medals. When he finished his army service in 1985, his record qualified him for something that at first glance might have looked better than the farming or coal-mining jobs to which most army veterans were assigned: He went to work for an atomic en-ergy agency. We shall hear more from him in a later chapter.

A third North Korean who talked with me about juvenile rumbles was Ahn Choong-hak,[2] who said that the gang fights sometimes involved as many as fifty or sixty boys at a time. But Ahn added that there had been a crackdown starting in 1974. It "became a social issue. The authorities suggested that South Korean spies were organizing the violence. Participants were por-trayed as dissidents. So people became afraid to join in and by 1976 gang fights disappeared," as far as he knew.

Before that happened, Ahn was involved in his share of youthful hijinks. But I think his personal story mainly goes to show that one's family back-ground could be very good—yet still not good enough.

His family had quite good *songbun*, which is precisely why the Ahns were relocated to Kaesong, near the Demilitarized Zone, in 1961. As we noted briefly in chapter 6, their move was part of a mass shift of families of "good" background to replace large numbers of locals, who were shipped north to live in remote areas where there was less danger that they could be enlisted to serve the enemy. Kaesong had been under South Korean rule until the Ko-rean War, and the families that were moved out were considered suspect or worse in terms of loyalty to the North Korean regime.

Ahn found the atmosphere in Kaesong "always tense. There were always rumors of spies caught around our area. People from other provinces weren't allowed to enter freely. When I was in third grade, the teacher who had taught me in first grade suddenly disappeared. I heard other teachers say it was be-cause she was the daughter of a landlord's concubine. I had felt a special affinity for her."

Ahn's father was a university-trained civil engineer (his education alone signaling elite status) who traveled a lot in his work. Ahn's mother tailored suits at home. Alas, Kaesong did not suit her. She was constantly ill, blaming the city's "bad water." When Ahn was a fourth-grade pupil, his father man-aged—it was difficult—to get the authorities' permission to move the family back to their home city, Hamhung.

If the second move pleased his mother, it didn't help the emotional well-being of the son. "Kids in Hamhung made fun of my Kaesong dialect, which is almost like Seoul dialect," Ahn told me. He reacted, as children often do in such circumstances, by becoming a troublemaker. "My dad disciplined me a lot for misbehavior. He didn't want the whole family resettled on my account."

Ahn's boldest exploit came in the first year of senior middle school when he and two friends decided to go to the capital. North Koreans were not allowed to travel without permits. In particular, the regime was at great pains to avoid migration or casual travel from the outlying areas to Pyongyang, a city of strictly controlled population that served both as seat of the top echelons and showcase to foreigners.

"We got on a train secretly," Ahn told me. "In the restroom of a North Korean train, above the toilet, is a loose wooden plank. There's a space above it, under the ceiling. We hid there and replaced the plank. But Public Security is on to that trick. The police caught us when we reached Sunchon. They took us off the train and planned to send us to a rehabilitation center for a month. But there was such a big crowd of offenders waiting for the bus that we were able to escape. We walked to Pyongyang and stayed four days before we sneaked onto another train to go home."

"In Pyongyang," Ahn recalled, "my school uniform didn't look so good. If you see the difference between Pyongyang kids and provincial kids you get angry and want what they have. I beat up some Pyongyang kids and took a nice uniform from them."

Back home in Hamhung, Ahn said, "I got a big spanking from my dad for that exploit."

Facetiously, I asked Ahn why he had not thought to excuse himself by saying he was emulating the Great Leader's boyhood "1000-*ri* Journey for Learning." He replied: "I would have been branded a dissident for breaking the rules and presuming to compare myself to Kim Il-sung. When I was in the third grade of elementary school my friend Yong-il had a bowel movement and it froze. He said, 'It looks like Mount Paektu.' Others reported him and he had to write statements of repentance in his notebook for a couple of months. After all, Mount Paektu was where Kim Il-sung participated in the anti-Japanese struggle."

Ahn somehow managed to avoid ruining his family's good name. He was a good athlete. A newly established physical education college recruited him. (He found the coeducational classes, which were something new to him, "exciting.") After college he was supposed to go to work as a coach, the job for which he had been trained. But Ahn "wanted to join the army, because in school we were trained to want to become heroes, forerunners of national unification. Kim Il-sung was very good at instilling that kind of patriotic feeling in youngsters. Besides, it's very prestigious to become a member of the Workers' Party, and once you've enlisted and served in the army you have more chance of acceptance by the party."

He succeeded in enlisting in the army in 1974. Like Kim Dae-ho, he became a model soldier. After hauling missiles and artillery around the vicinity of the Demilitarized Zone, he drew the cushy assignment of driving the Eighth Division commander. His dream of life after the army was to enroll in Kumsong Political University, an elite school that trained spies and infiltrators. But when he spoke to an official of the State Security Department about his future, the man advised him to forget that idea and just take a normal job after mustering out.

Puzzled and disappointed, Ahn went on home leave back to South Hamgyong Province and asked his parents if there was anything in the family background that might explain why his career suddenly had run up against a brick wall. They insisted that there was nothing, but he didn't believe them. He then went to the home of his father's older brother. There, a female cousin told him the truth. Their grandfather and three of their uncles and aunts had moved to the South during the Korean War. The cousin had heard the dry rattle of that skeleton in the family closet when it tumbled out to thwart her plans to marry a Public Security lieutenant. The young policeman's seniors had pressured him to break off the engagement. The family's *songbun*, it transpired, was good enough to get Ahn's father into engineering university, good enough to get Ahn into physical education college and the army—but not good enough for the police, or the spy service.

"I was devastated," Ahn told me, his passion obviously still burning many years after the event. "My first reaction was to feel shame at having such traitors in my family. I had always sworn to destroy such people." Remaining at his cousin's house, Ahn got drunk and awaited his uncle's return home, falling into such a noisy rage that the police came to inquire what was happening. Seeing his army uniform, they checked with State Security, found he had been granted special leave from his unit and sent him back to his parents' house. There, his rage unabated, he grabbed his mother's sewing machine and threw it onto the ground in the garden before walking away from the house, vowing never to return.

"I had always pitied those who couldn't succeed due to their family background," Ahn told me. "To realize that was my situation just tore me up."

THIRTEEN

Take the Lead in World Conjuring

It is an immutable law that in the course of this historical struggle, capitalism fails and socialism and communism emerge victorious.

—KIM JONG-IL, ADDRESSING FILMMAKERS IN 1968[1]

The ink on Kim Jong-il's diploma was hardly dry before he had plunged into the political struggles that would become, under his leadership, his country's counterpart to the Chinese Cultural Revolution.

The similarities are striking. In China as in North Korea a relative of the top leader—Mao Zedong's fourth wife, former movie actress Jiang Qing, played the role in China—unceremoniously rooted out "bourgeois" literary and art forms and the officials responsible, replacing both with "revolutionary" new ones. Organizations of radical young zealots—the Mao-quoting Red Guards and the Kim Il-sung–quoting Three Revolutions teams, the latter led by Kim Jong-il—carried the attack to authority figures in non-arts fields and their old-fashioned ways of doing things.

The parallels do not go much farther, however. Mao used but did not always fully control China's Great Proletarian Cultural Revolution, part of which was a bottom-up affair, relatively spontaneous and genuinely revolutionary if horribly misguided and destructive. Kim Il-sung and his son, on the other hand, kept tight, topside control over a movement that was revolutionary mainly in the sense that it sought to change people's thinking permanently. Serving the very conservative goal of protecting and perpetuating the existing regime, North Korean mind control soon surpassed in thoroughness all other twentieth-century totalitarian political movements.

While it is generally thought that Kim Il-sung only began to push his son's selection as his successor in the 1970s, a former elite official of the regime who knew Kim Jong-il well and had frequent contact with him said systematic preparations actually began a decade earlier—even as the junior Kim was concluding his university studies.[2] It certainly does seem that someone had big plans for the youngster—in view of the high-level work he was immediately assigned in the Central Committee of the Workers' Party, the regime's nerve center.

In Pyongyang's account, "it was not by chance that Kim Jong-il began to work at the Central Committee." That seems a huge understatement, but the official version does not intend an indirect reference to his birthright. Instead, the claim is that the youngster was selected for work in the exalted "general staff of the revolution" purely on merit.[3] Indeed, Pyongyang's version has it that Kim Il-sung "refrained from doing anything that could be viewed as a bid to groom his son as future heir or to impose him on the population as such." The junior Kim was merely "trained to think and behave as a dedicated servant of the people."[4]

The first phase of his career saw him advance quickly in Central Committee staff work until he became number two in the party's propaganda department. His father during that period gave him freedom that would have been unthinkable for any other novice official. Flitting from one issue to another, often ignoring established divisions of authority and responsibility, Kim Jong-il got an overview of the regime. In the process he was able to meet many people from all classes of society.

In a subsequent stage, the younger Kim concentrated on remolding the country's cinema and opera. That was a productive period of learning and personal growth. Indeed, it was a time of triumph as he drew applause for such works as the 1969 movie and 1971 revolutionary opera *Sea of Blood*.

There are numerous reports of clashes with other officials. Throughout those early stages of his career, according to a former official who knew him, a testing process was under way to try to identify people Kim Jong-il might be unable to control when it came his turn to take power.[5]

* * *

Note that such tagging of prospective enemies of the younger Kim came as his father felt the regime's hold on power threatened, to an extent unprecedented since the Korean War. Besides any internal critics who had the temerity to raise their heads, the threat was seen as coming from enemies without. The policy adopted was to vanquish all foes by focusing the loyalty of officials and the masses, even more than before, on the elder Kim's own person rather than on the country or on some set of abstract principles.

In what may have represented a military-civilian struggle within the regime, Kim Il-sung in 1966 sacked leaders in charge of his economic policy and, the next year, turned around and dumped officials who had criticized that policy. Kim complained that some people had the temerity to suggest that, after a country achieved a certain level of economic development, it could no longer expect to maintain growth rates as high as before. Such "passivist and conservative" notions could not be permitted. A top deputy warned that North Koreans, including party leaders, must show "a revolutionary trait which accepts no other ideas but Comrade Kim Il-sung's revolutionary ideas . . . , a trait which makes thinking and action conform to our party's policy, and which accepts the policy and carries it through unconditionally, without the slightest swerving in any winds and waves."[6]

As enforcer of what the regime called its "monolithic" or "unitary" system, Kim Jong-il during the '60s and '70s presided over the shift to describing the state dogma as "Kimilsungism." The term, with its specific connotation of one-man rule, was credited to the junior Kim himself.

While the elder Kim, as we have seen in chapter 7, increased tensions with the United States, his son set out to intensify the personality cult. Kim Jong-il, starting work with the party, was convinced of the need to defend Kim Il-sung's absolute authority and his revolutionary ideas "in order to tide over this difficult situation."[7]

It was during that period that the senior Kim made the transition from mere dictator to official deity.

"North Korean leaders claimed that they opposed China's Cultural Revolution, but in reality they imitated the Cultural Revolution on a smaller scale," former party ideology chief Hwang Jang-yop observed later. "They created an even more intense personality cult for Kim Il-sung and launched an ultra-left campaign to rid society of all capitalistic elements." Since there was no "visible political force opposing Kim Il-sung," said Hwang, the campaign in Pyongyang "was a simple affair that accomplished its goal with the purging of a few intellectuals. But that simple affair was the turning point in the Kim Il-sung personality cult, which went from strength to strength."[8]

A complicating factor was a struggle between Kim Jong-il and his uncle, Kim Yong-ju, that began to develop after the younger man graduated from college and started work in the party. As we saw in chapter 10, Yong-ju seemingly was positioned to become Kim Il-sung's successor. He had backers in high places, including Kim Il-sung's wife Song-ae. Many people in leading roles in the party assumed he would be the successor.[9] But Kim Jong-il went after the job. "The two men's rivalry was based on who could put Kim Il-sung on a higher pedestal," Hwang Jang-yop recalled. "Thanks to this competition, the Kim Il-sung personality cult went beyond the Soviet-style dictatorship" and became what Hwang called "absolutism of the Great Leader."

Unofficial accounts agree with the official version that the junior Kim from very early in his working career focused his efforts on promoting loyalty toward the revolution and, especially, its leader. Koreans traditionally value "purity." Both in Pyongyang and in Seoul, the ruling regime denigrated suspected agents of the other side as "impure elements." In a typically Korean Confucian behavior pattern that Karl Marx surely never envisioned as a component of communist rule, Kim Jong-il liked to ascribe merit to himself on account of his descent from the pure revolutionary line. And he insisted that others acknowledge his superiority in that regard. After all, Kim Il-sung had demonstrated his own purity by refusing to deviate even slightly from opposition to the Japanese colonialists.

According to one account, the young man displayed open contempt toward any Korean of his father's generation who had shown any weakness toward the enemy and thus failed to meet Kim Il-sung's high standard. "Comrade, how much did you devote yourself to the revolution at the time of the Japanese colonial rule?" he would ask one of his elders. "Did you ever commit anti-revolutionary acts?" (I encountered a similar attitude in a great many *South* Korean youngsters, of his and subsequent generations, who had little direct knowledge of the pressures and complexities of life under Japanese rule. They were eager to reject and despise any authority figures—from parents right up to the late South Korean President Park Chung-hee, a former Japanese soldier—on the ground of insufficient patriotism.)

One of Kim Jong-il's early targets for contempt was his uncle, Kim Yong-ju. As director of the Central Committee's Organization and Guidance Bureau, the uncle was officially the young graduate's first boss. But according to a South Korean account, he soon learned that the little prince was not easily bossed.

Over the years various reports appeared in South Korea to the effect that Kim Yong-ju had been captured by the Japanese in the late 1930s and had turned collaborator.[10] It is not clear whether Kim Jong-il while working for his uncle got wind of such stories, true or false. Even if he did not, however, it would have been simple enough to punch holes in Kim Yong-ju's own war stories and show him up for an un-heroic sort at best whose pre-liberation experiences would not bear much scrutiny. Yong-ju made the preposterous claim, for example, that he had been a member of the political committee of the New Fourth Army of the Chinese People's Liberation Army. The actual members of that committee were such Chinese Communist luminaries as Liu Shao-qi and Chen Yi.[11]

The South Korean account says that clashes with the uncle led Kim Il-sung to transfer the young man from the party Central Committee to the party chapter in North Hamgyong Province. In the provincial party chapter, young Kim is reported to have worked under Kim Guk-tae, the boss of the local party's Organization Department. Although Kim Guk-tae was several years older and an army veteran, this was a more salubrious match-up as both men were second-generation communist nobility. Both could boast "pure revolutionary" descent. A graduate of Mangyongdae School, Kim Guk-tae was the son of Kim Chaek. An anti-Japanese guerrilla general, the equal of Kim Il-sung in Manchuria, Kim Chaek had died during the Korean War after commanding the frontline troops of the People's Army. The two young men had known each other as boys.[12]

Around 1966 Kim is believed to have returned to Pyongyang to work in his father's military bodyguard organization. One account says he took the rank of major, and clashed frequently with the chief of the Bodyguard Bureau, O Baek-ryong, a former anti-Japanese guerrilla comrade of Kim Il-sung's. There is a report that O finally became so irritated by Kim Jong-il's presumption that he asked the younger man: "Am I your adjutant?"[13]

Young Kim as a bodyguard officer continued accompanying his father on guidance tours and giving some guidance of his own. Sometimes he seems to have given advice just to hear himself talk. At the workers' dormitory of a steel mill, for example, he barged unceremoniously into a room—to the surprise of the occupant, who was just getting off his shift and looking forward to his rest. Although the rooms were already so well equipped that the visiting mothers of workers had gushed over their comforts, he demanded that flat pillows be replaced with cylindrical, embroidered, traditionally Korean pillows, and pots of cold water with hot, freshly boiled water. The story does not mention his asking workers whether that was what they wanted, but it praises him for "taking into consideration those points which even their over-anxious mothers did not notice."

Visiting a furnace at a steel mill and seeing a lot of dust, he behaved like a zealous American Occupational Safety and Health Administration (OSHA) inspector. Told that a dust extractor was being built, he insisted "in a low yet grave voice, which expressed his determination," that factory officials shut down the furnace immediately until the new anti-pollution equipment was ready for installation. They might have ignored another twenty-four-year-old bodyguard who gave such an order, but this was Kim Il-sung's son. They dutifully shut down the furnace.[14]

Officially disseminated stories go on and on telling of his tramping through woods and fields and across dangerous steel mill floors, rolling up his sleeves and getting dirty, sometimes actually joining in the work—and thereby deeply impressing his hosts. "Kim Jong-il was working in person!" an official biographer exclaims, relating an instance in which the young Kim husked some corn. An official who was on the scene "bowed in spite of himself before the noble and loyal heart of Kim Jong-il."[15] It appears that the supposedly egalitarian North Koreans believed—and were not officially discouraged in that belief—that the ordinary requirements should not apply to the son of the country's ruler. That notion is rooted not in communist doctrine but in the determinedly anti-egalitarian Confucianism represented by the Yi Dynasty's royalty and *yangban* nobility. For them physical labor was unthinkable; idly reading poetry, the most admired pursuit.

Bodyguard duty was the closest young Kim ever came to serving in the military. He had a uniform then, but photos generally show him in civilian garb. The regime had to scrounge to find a single, rather pathetic anecdote from that period indicating interest in military matters. In July of 1967, near the height of military tension with South Korea and the United States, he visited a coastal defense headquarters on the Sea of Japan. Earlier that year a North Korean coastal battery had sunk a South Korean patrol escort craft in those waters. The following January would see the capture of the *Pueblo*.

The coastal defense unit, of course, specialized in big guns. But Kim Jong-il himself was known as a crack shot with small arms—perhaps the result of many hunting trips with his father. Discussing the soldiers' training program, he complained that they had focused on artillery at the expense of rifle practice. After all, they might have to defend their positions with rifles if the big guns failed. He had the men demonstrate their shooting, but they were not very good. Then he "stepped down an emplacement and, giving an example of the right way to shoot, he taught them how to achieve first-rate marksmanship. Looking at Kim Jong-il, who was drenched in sweat, the commanders felt tremendously guilty about their neglect of small arms training." Or did one or two of them, perhaps, silently entertain dark thoughts about a privileged, twenty-five-year-old draft-dodger who had unerringly picked for discussion and demonstration the only skill in which he could show their men up?[16]

After his bodyguard duty Kim Jong-il went back to the party Central Committee, taking posts in the propaganda and agitation department.[17] There he became such a bloodhound in rooting out disloyal elements that an official version reads like a history of the Spanish Inquisition: "Kim Jong-il, who had obtained concrete information on the internal conditions of the party in a short time, found that there was a serious problem in it."

[Kim] discovered a symptom of a dangerous plot by some impure elements. He found that some party officials were leading an unwholesome life as party members. They were not sincere in their party work, ignoring party rules and concealing each other's irregularities. . . . It appeared to Kim Jong-il that there was something shady about their lives and so he made a close study of their defects and shortcomings in all fields of their activities. As a result, he discovered that an official holding a high post in the party was behind the irregularities. . . . He discovered this when he read a certain book and when he noticed in it a passage denying the purity of the revolutionary tradition of the party. Many people read the book, but there was none who pointed out this fact. Only he saw in it an attempt to slander party policy and deny the purity of its revolutionary tradition. He lost no time in examining publications related to that book. His concern proved right, as he found not a few books which advocated bourgeois ideas, revisionist and Confucian ideas and lifestyles. . . . A handful of people, centered on a high-ranking party official, were spreading unwholesome ideas systematically and in an organized way in the backstage, while pretending on the surface to support the ideas of the party.[18]

No name is given for this wicked Korean version of China's Deng Xiaoping, but the high-ranking official whom the young loyalist zealot was pursuing appears to have been Kim To-man. Chosen in 1966 as party secretary in charge of propaganda and agitation, Kim To-man was the only one of the ten people given secretary rank at that time who could not boast of either experience as a partisan general or blood ties to partisan leaders.[19] Kim Jong-il went after him and his followers, who had influence in "literary and artistic circles"—that is, party propaganda. The young inquisitor became particularly exercised over a play called *An Act of Sincerity*. He argued that the play was intended to gloss over the flaws of people he believed or suspected had not fought the good fight against the Japanese. The play, says a biographer of Kim Jong-il,

was written to enable schemers and ambitious people to utilize an "autobiography" to make themselves appear like "revolutionaries". . . . However, when the revolution faced a difficult phase, those who could not endure it raised their heads as impure and vacillating elements. Many of them had unknown careers. Nevertheless the party and President Kim Il-sung took a careful and generous attitude to them so as to allow them to hold responsible posts in the party and the state, expecting that when trusted and entrusted with heavy responsibilities, they would repay the generous treatment with sincere efforts. However, they betrayed the trust reposed in them, and as they were given leading posts and as their positions rose higher, they became arrogant, and later came to take an overbearing attitude, bent on achieving their own personal purposes in the party.

This was a case in which Kim Il-sung was rooting out perceived rivals from within the partisan group and the military—perhaps on account of their criticism of his new, extreme policies[20] rather than their views on literature—and his son enthusiastically piled on. In part the younger Kim was seeking to prove his loyalty to his father. But according to Hwang Jang-yop, Kim Jong-il also had his own axe to grind: he hoped to push aside high-level supporters of his uncle within those then-powerful groups.[21]

"Already aware of their moves," the elder Kim called a party Central Committee plenary meeting for May of 1967 "to smash the schemes of the bourgeois and revisionist elements." Before that meeting was held, the Great Leader started an "ideological struggle." However, "at first, participants in the struggle did not understand the seriousness of the situation." Kim Jong-il, coming to the rescue, "unveiled the nature of anti-party, counter-revolutionary elements who had raised their heads whenever the party faced a trial."

That started the ball rolling, and soon others joined in, spying upon and denouncing the target elements. For example,

> a certain official discovered an impure "directive" issued by an anti-party element written down in his notebook, and with an awakened eye he saw that it could serve as evidence to expose the criminal act of the anti-party element, and unhesitatingly participated in the struggle against the factionalists. Then many other party members exposed the criminal acts of anti-party elements by pointing out similar facts. The ideological struggle intensified. . . . After the plenary meeting the schemers who wanted to spread anti-party, counter-revolutionary ideas within the party were systematically liquidated.[22]

Kim To-man and several colleagues were purged at that meeting.[23] More purges were yet to come.

Hwang Jang-yop has explained in plain language what much of the literary purge entailed. Earlier Kim Il-sung had permitted, even encouraged, his old partisan comrades to publish their own memoirs. The regime's ghostwriters made sure those volumes included plenty of flattering references to Kim. "But when Kim Jong-il entered the central party in the late 1960s, he called back all the memoirs," according to Hwang. "Kim Jong-il was concerned that the memoirs detracted from the Kim Il-sung personality cult and created legends about partisans other than Kim Il-sung." By the late 1960s, North Korean textbooks were devoid of references to "many heroic figures. . . ."[24]

Taking the witch hunt on the road, in July 1967 Kim Jong-il went to South Hamgyong Province and got involved in some rough local politics. He "worked hard there to eradicate the tendencies of factionalism, parochialism and nepotism which were still found in some party organizations." In that province and South Pyongan Province, say officially sanctioned biographers, he "worked energetically to carry through the party policy of eradicating the effect of unwholesome ideas and promoting economic and defense construction simultaneously."[25] The latter was the euphemism for Kim Il-sung's policy of militarization. According to an unofficial North Korean spokesman in Tokyo, Kim Jong-il "struggled against local opponents who attempted to weaken the party leadership" and afterward "emerged as a leading theoretician."[26]

Hwang Jang-yop, who worked from 1958 to 1965 as Kim Il-sung's ideological secretary, seems to have found himself eclipsed in ideological work as the junior Kim's star ascended. While continuing to rank as one of the country's leading intellectuals, Hwang was shifted to a number of often less important jobs before he defected, in 1997, to South Korea.

Hwang was relatively fortunate in that he survived. After his defection he told of Baek Nam-woon, who, although "respected as the father of left-wing scholars, was purged by Kim Jong-il at the end of the 1960s. I heard Kim Byeong-ha, then Minister of National Security, boast that his men had taken Baek to the [concentration camp]. . . . As a scholar, Baek had not participated actively in the campaign against Kim Il-sung. He probably made a few comments that were picked up through wire-tapping and construed as complaints. Baek died in the concentration camp."[27]

More than is the case with the often fanciful-sounding accounts of his birth, childhood and youth, in my reading stories officially told about Kim Jong-il's deeds following his university graduation tend to have the feel of being based on actual incidents. It appears that his hagiographers went out in the late 1970s or early 1980s and interviewed people he had been in contact with earlier, asking them for accounts of the meetings. Perhaps the original tellers — and certainly the sycophantic retellers — made any necessary adjustments so that the accounts would conform to the formula established earlier, in which the young man invariably left his listeners scratching their heads at their own stupidity and carelessness but full of admiration for his genius and his great love for the people.

A gut reaction to such stories is that most of the people involved must have been at least normally intelligent folk. Some of them probably were smarter than he was. But it seems likely that either they felt at the time that they must play dumb in the actual meetings or, later, they allowed themselves to be portrayed as fools in order to flatter the leader's eldest son.

To someone raised on the United States' unceremonious, no-nonsense egalitarianism, it is numbing to read volume after volume of accounts such as one that describes Kim Jong-il's summoning of officials in charge of scientific and educational work. When they arrived at the meeting he let them know they were there to resolve theoretical questions, regarding which "opinions varied in the academic world at that time." He did the talking, of course. As the twenty-five-year-old rambled on, "the officials wrote down every one of Kim Jong-il's words in their notebooks." They "felt their mental horizons broadening." When he had finished, they felt confident that the academic controversies he had addressed "had come to an end." They believed that "they could open the eyes of anyone who was confused on the subject. . . . When Kim Jong-il finished his explanation, all the officials rose to their feet. 'He's truly a genius of ideas, and genius of theory!'—This is what every one of them felt. Greatly moved, they expressed their infinite respect for Kim Jong-il."[28]

Indeed, according to Hwang, Kim Jong-il "tends to dominate meetings and conferences and to lead all discussion to conclusions congruent with his own."[29] My guess is that those poor officials whom the biographers describe really did abase themselves to some such depth of fawning servility, feeling they had no other choice. Eventually the official stories had been repeated so often inside the country that many younger North Koreans—never having heard him utter more than a phrase, and having no source of information about him except the regime's teachings—truly believed that Kim Jong-il was an exalted being, quite different from ordinary people. Thus, there might be less need for conscious dissembling and acting on their part. But again the question arises of why, if he possessed any sensitivity, the junior Kim not only permitted but almost certainly gave the order that such accounts be translated from the Korean for foreign readers—to many of whom he himself was inevitably made to appear the fatuous one.

In his new role as propagandist and "theoretician," Kim Jong-il sought to promote unthinking devotion to one-man rule. He arranged for the manufacture of plaster busts of Kim Il-sung, which he placed in study halls all over the country—changing the name from Study Hall of the History of the Workers' Party of Korea to Study Hall of Comrade Kim Il-sung's Revolutionary History. That made it clear that the leader now had primacy over even the party. The young Kim also ordered a new compilation of historical photographs to place in those study halls, "knowing that the existing pictorial records were not edited so as to center on the greatness of the President."[30]

Hagiographers exaggerated and fabricated to inflate Kim Il-sung's creditable achievements into a titanic image.[31] In the 1960s, official Pyongyang biographer Baik Bong described Kim as "a legendary hero . . . who is capable of commanding heavens and earth, an unrivalled brilliant commander who, as it were, can shrink a long range of steep mountains at a stroke and smash the swarming hordes of enemies with one blow."[32]

Such a magical figure's spiritual origins naturally had to be matched with a heroic physical birth, so his hagiographers described Kim Il-sung as issuing from the bosom of a revolutionary holy family. Biographer Baik credited Kim's father, Kim Hyong-jik, with such colossal achievements as having founded, in 1917, the underground Korean National Association, largest of the anti-Japanese organizations of the time.[33]

When the propagandists ran short on exaggerations and inventions, they stole. In people's homes were placed copies of a slogan attributed to Kim: "Fish cannot live out of water. The people cannot live without the People's Army. — Kim Il-sung." The real author of the phrase was, of course, Mao Zedong.[34]

Publishing a third edition of Kim Il-sung's *Selected Works* along with volumes of commentary and biography, backing them up with audiovisual materials and developing revolutionary historical sites for mass tours, Kim Jong-il enforced systematic, daily study. The goal was to "make all party members think and act in unison according to the leader's intentions and teachings," to make people "have absolute trust in the President as their spiritual support."

Kim Jong-il was tireless in his efforts "to lead people to the way of faithfulness." One of his acquaintances, for example, had a brother who got in a spot of trouble with the authorities. Kim Jong-il was able to have the brother's case reexamined. It turned out that some "vicious elements" were responsible for the transgression and had shifted the blame. Afterward, young Kim advised the grateful acquaintance, in effect, that his whole family should go and sin no more: "If a man is deprived of his political life, or the trust of the party, he is nothing. Therefore, it is necessary to do everything in your power to keep your political life, given by the great leader, and work hard to prove worthy of his trust. Not only yourself, but all your family members and relatives must be armed with the unitary idea of the party and be educated to be faithful to the leader. You must live according to the leader's teachings anywhere, anytime, whatever you do, and judge by his teachings as a yardstick, and fight unhesitatingly against anything deviating from his teachings."[35]

When a draft document for a party congress listed several top party officials, with Kim Il-sung's name at the top, his son ordered that it be retyped to leave a space between the Great Leader's name and the rest of the list. His underlings did that, but a few days later he called an official in and asked him to print Kim Il-sung's name in larger type, as well. "Think. It's because the sun shines that the planets shed their light, isn't it?" he explained to the puzzled official. "As we could not draw the sun and the planets in the same size, so we would never write down the name of the leader and the names of his men in the same size." The official now understood what Kim Jong-il had in mind, and "bowed deeply to his noble loyalty." (The idea actually was lifted from Stalin's personality cult.)[36] It was for that same party congress, in 1970, that Kim Jong-il personally designed the first lapel badges with his father's portrait and had them passed out to delegates.[37]

Kim Jong-il had been fascinated with movies from his childhood, brought up on viewing sessions in his father's mansion that leaned heavily toward Russian movies. As that fascination converged with his interest in women, the avid film buff had begun hanging around Pyongyang's film studios, dating actresses.[38]

According to an official account, he told his father as early as 1964—the year of his university graduation—that all was not well in North Korea's tinseltown. Kim Il-sung thereupon called a party politburo meeting at the Korean Film Studio, with the studio staff in attendance. There the elder Kim gave a speech complaining that opportunists within the communist movement were kowtowing to a cultural offensive launched by the imperialists. He wanted a radical change. The industry must produce many high-quality movies, artistic yet ideologically compelling. Filmmakers must chart a straight path, repudiating two extremes: "the art-for-art's sake doctrine of the revisionists and the leftist tendency to stress only ideology while ignoring artistry." The themes of the films must fall into three categories: (1) Kim Il-sung's anti-Japanese struggle, (2) the Korean War and (3) inspiration for workers to make "great revolutionary advances in socialist construction."

After the speech, the audience "gave a standing ovation for a long time, looking up at President Kim Il-sung and Comrade Kim Jong-il. . . . It was from that time onwards that Kim Jong-il's energetic guidance of cinematic development began."[39]

While still in his twenties Kim Jong-il rose in the party Central Committee hierarchy to become deputy director of the propaganda and agitation department (under his friend Kim Guk-tae again, according to some reports) and then department director. Working as a propagandist gave the Great Leader's son an official excuse to continue his interest in the cinema—which eventually would prove a virtual obsession. On one level, he simply wanted better quality from a young and struggling backwater movie industry that was far from meeting the technical standards of Moscow, much less Hollywood. On another level, he was determined to root out of the movie industry the counterrevolutionary, bourgeois, feudalistic, revisionist, flunkeyist influences that those wicked fellows purged in 1967 had planted in earlier years to distract the people from worshipping Kim Il-sung with the proper single-hearted, single-minded unity. This would be a flip-side version of the Hollywood blacklist.

Kim Jong-il started by abolishing an annual January convention of

filmmakers from all over the country to evaluate the previous year's film output from the standpoint of artistry. Kim decried the esthetic review for its
failure to stick strictly to pushing the ideology of one-man rule. He called it a
"platform which was utilized by the babblers in order to demonstrate their
intelligence." Anti-party counterrevolutionaries in charge of cinema development for the party had dreamed up the session in a plot to "restore outdated
self-indulgence, so as to 'liberalize' cinematic creation." Instead of studying
Kim Il-sung's thoughts on art and literature, speakers at the meeting had
dwelled on theories from outside. They had even gone to the length of "suggesting the introduction of so-and-so's system of direction and so-and-so's
system of acting from Europe."

Officials hearing his complaints were "bewildered," never having seen
any harm in the get-togethers. But, now that he mentioned it, they "felt as if
their vision was opening up." Kim Jong-il then opened their vision a little
wider, decreeing that "from now on you must not use the words 'esthetic review.' Instead we must hold a meeting for the study of the great leader's artistic and literary thoughts." Now they got the picture, and "the officials and
artists left the room, bitterly reflecting on their inability to distinguish right
from wrong."

Some days later Kim Jong-il presided over the first meeting for the study
of the Great Leader's thought on *juche*-oriented art and literature, convened in
a movie studio. He humiliated the first speaker who took the floor, attacking
the man's use of foreign words such as the "moral" of a story and "suspense"
when there were perfectly good words in Korean to get the meaning across.
Bidding the "bewildered" speaker to sit down, he expressed disgust that "the
flunkeyist and dogmatic habit is even repeated in this place where we are
studying the Great Leader's *juche*-oriented art and literary thoughts. It is appalling." Without discarding that habit of "parroting" others, the filmmakers
would "never be able to make films which will genuinely do a great deal for
the Korean revolution, films which will be loved by the Korean people."

In order to make a clean sweep of past errors, "Kim Jong-il sternly ordered that all the files on the 'art review' meetings be burned. All those present at the meeting were struck by the intelligent leadership of Kim Jong-il."
After the meeting, all the papers and reports presented at previous "esthetic
reviews" were indeed burned, so that a new start could be made based on the
theories of Kim Il-sung.[40]

Although Kim Il-sung had staged skits and plays and disseminated tracts
during his anti-Japanese struggle, he had not made movies. Thus, the pick-
ings were slim for filmmakers looking for guidance from the Great Leader's
holy writ. Kim Jong-il was happy to step into the breach and propound his
own theories, always describing them as developments of his father's ideas.

At the first meeting for the study of the Great Leader's thought on *juche*-oriented art and literature, according to official accounts, and on other occasions as well, the junior Kim laid out his *chongja* or "seed" theory. He had "discovered for the first time in history the seed of the work of art, its nucleus."[41] In fact his demand that writers and directors "grasp the seed" of a work was another way of directing them to choose a theme that could be expressed in just a few words and stick to it. To that extent, of course, Kim Jong-il's idea was by no means new. But the principle of focusing tightly on a clear theme probably is the one that writers—professionals included—most often forget. (I, myself, while reading his thoughts on the "seed," realized that parts of my manuscript lacked focus and needed rewriting. Thanks, Dear Leader, for the useful reminder.) Kim's dwelling on the principle could only be a positive influence on North Korean screenwriting and film direction and editing, from the technical standpoint.

Content was a different matter. Kim Jong-il wanted artistic people to grasp seeds that would promote the regime's ideology, especially one-man rule. Talking to the makers of the film *Five Guerrilla Brothers* in 1968, he complained that they had killed off a character, making him the victim of an enemy plot to poison the guerrillas' salt supply. That went against what was or should have been the seed of the work: "that the Korean People's Revolutionary Army would be ever-victorious as long as the headquarters of the revolution existed."

Kim Jong-il also complained that the real prototype of the character the filmmakers had killed off did not in fact die in the salt incident. And he insisted that "our literature and arts must portray historical facts strictly in accordance with the principles of maintaining party loyalty and of being historically accurate." (Note that party loyalty was to take precedence over historical accuracy.) "You must not fake, in a careless manner, what is not found in life, and present scenes that vary from the truth, simply for the sake of the arts. In dealing with historical facts, you must discard, as a matter of course, what is of no substance; but you must not discard what is of essential significance, interpret it as you please or invent something."

That is good advice. I think it was taken to heart, to some extent, in the factual basis apparent in many of the stories told about Kim senior and junior in books the regime published from the 1980s on, at least until Kim Il-sung's death in 1994.

But Kim Jong-il only selectively followed his own advice. The "headquarters of the revolution" to which he referred in his critique of *Five Guerrilla Brothers* was meant to be understood as the seat of Gen. Kim Il-sung, that lofty being destined to become North Korea's Great Leader. In historical fact, Kim Il-sung's headquarters was no more the headquarters of *the* revolution than were the headquarters of any of a number of other guerrilla fighters and political leaders, based in other parts of Manchuria, in

China proper, in Korea itself or elsewhere, who were Kim's revolutionary equals or betters.

The unspoken rule seems to have been that writers should avoid lies about small, easily ascertainable facts and stick to Big Lies—such as Kim Il-sung's purported leadership of the entire "revolution" from the 1930s on and South Korea's invasion of the North to start the Korean War. Kim Jong-il did not in so many words, for publication, address the importance of the Big Lie for the regime. However, he did endorse fictionalizing historical facts: "The arts, even though based on actual situations, must not reproduce facts and instances automatically; they must identify those which are of essential significance and generalize them," he said, in the same talk in which he had emphasized fidelity to the facts. Unfortunately, he said, the unimaginative moviemakers he was addressing were "unable to make full use of this wonderful creative capacity."[42]

What his seemingly conflicting advice may have boiled down to is: Stick to the facts if fabrication would be easily detected—but if a lie would serve the maintenance of the regime, then tell the lie and overcome people's disbelief through dramatic force and constant repetition.

To get the filmmakers headed in the right direction, Kim Jong-il decided to lead them in making films based on some works—plays or skits—from the period of the anti-Japanese struggle in Manchuria. In each case those were works whose original authorship was ascribed to Kim Il-sung. The first of those was *Sea of Blood*, which is

> the story of an ordinary mother in a farm village, who is widowed in the sea of blood resulting from a slaughter carried out by Japanese imperialism. The story gives a vivid account of how the mother, realizing the truth of struggle through ordeals, rises in a revolutionary struggle. With her three children to feed, the heroine has a hard time of it under the oppressive rule of Japanese imperialism. The elder son Won-nam joins the Anti-Japanese Guerrilla Army in his early years, and the only daughter Gap-sun and the younger son Ul-nam are gradually awakened to the cause of revolution. The mother learns the truth of revolution, first under the influence of her husband and children and then educated by an anti-Japanese guerrilla political worker.
>
> One day, the younger son Ul-nam is cruelly murdered by the enemy while trying to save the political worker being pursued by a Japanese garrison troop. Firming up her will to resist in the depth of despair, the heroine indignantly rises, organizes a women's association, goes among workers and gets explosives. After remarkable

activities, she leads a popular uprising in support of an attack on the
county seat by the Guerrilla Army and joins it. On the joyful day of
liberation of the county seat, the heroine, speaking to the masses of
the truth she has learned, makes an enthusiastic appeal to them to
rise for the revolution.

Kim Jong-il's creative staff spent a year developing a screenplay based
on a novelized version of the original play.[43] Young Kim quickly demonstrated his preference for late-night work regardless of the sleeping sched-
ules of underlings, whom he expected to adjust to his hours. Staying in "a
house beside a lake"—perhaps one of his villas—he worked with the creative
staff on the screenplay. One night,

the scriptwriters, who worked until late at night, were just going to
bed when Kim Jong-il called them and handed back their manuscripts which he had been looking through. He asked them to bring
him any other manuscripts which they might have. It was already
2:30 A.M., so they hesitated. One of them suggested that he should
sleep.

"Never mind, give me manuscripts you've written, if you have
any. . . . You know, the President wrote this celebrated work, sitting
up all night for several nights, taking time off in the intervals of the
grim, bloody struggle against the Japanese. In that case, how can
we allow ourselves to write the screen version of that masterpiece,
taking as much rest and sleep as we want, satisfied with our comfortable conditions? I prefer to work in the peaceful, small hours.
Give me manuscripts you've written, please."

His eyes were glittering with eagerness. The writers were swept
by rising emotion and gave him their manuscripts. Taking the papers, Kim Jong-il again plunged into his work of revision. The night
passed and the moonlight which played on the rippling water of the
lake was fading in the grey dawn. The writers, too, sat at their desks
a little longer. Soon they were overcome by weariness and started to
doze.

How much time passed no one knew. . . . One of them was
awakened by the trickling of water somewhere. The sound undoubtedly came from the washroom. The hands of the clock were pointing
to 4 A.M. He pricked up his ears to make sure where the sound was
coming from, and there again came the sound of running water
which was now mingled with noise of splashing. The writer stood
up. He went to the washroom and was surprised to see Kim Jong-il
washing his face in cold water. A lump suddenly rose in his throat.
"He's overcoming the fatigue caused by overwork." The writer stood

spellbound for some time, staring in reverence at the dear leader who was so devoted to his work of making the screen version an enduring piece to be handed down to posterity.

Kim Jong-il also personally supervised the shooting of *Sea of Blood*. In September 1969, filming a scene depicting the burning of a hamlet, he ran hither and yon through the smoke making sure all the pieces fit together. He told off an actor playing a Japanese soldier who "ran about brandishing his sword, although he had just been slain by a peasant with an axe." At another point, "he urged the cavalry to charge towards Ul-nam's mother, who was frantically searching for her children, but they did not hear him. Immediately he rushed into the suffocating smoke and led the horsemen to where they should be."[44]

Sea of Blood premiered later in 1969, followed in the next few years by other screen versions of Kim Il-sung's "revolutionary masterpieces." In 1970 came *The Fate of a Self-defense Corps Man*, whose main character is first pressed into betraying his nation through service in the Japanese imperialists' self-defense corps. He soon finds the corps to be "a living hell of racial discrimination, insult and whipping." A friend who tries to desert is executed. Meanwhile, the Japanese drive the hero's father like a beast, as he labors to help build a gun emplacement, and then they shoot him to death. The young man, previously without class-consciousness, then changes course, taking "the path of revolution to wipe out the aggressors." The writers at first had trouble deciding on the central theme. Kim Jong-il settled it. The seed of the work, he said, was the inevitability of death, whether or not the young men joined the self-defense corps.[45]

Note that the film offers a view of life complex enough to allow for a negative character to turn positive. One who has started as a traitor can become a shining revolutionary. That sort of twist would become a hallmark of the Kim Jong-il era in cinema, as compared with simplistic "revolutionary morality plays" that the North Korean studios had churned out earlier.[46] This fact strikes a note of seeming irony: From what we are told about *An Act of Sincerity*—the play Kim Jong-il had denounced earlier as representing a treacherous maneuver by Kim To-man's henchmen—the approach appears to have been similar.

While filming *The Fate of a Self-defense Corps Man*, the cast and crew worked on location at Pochonbo in the mountainous northern part of the country. The weather was cold. Kim Jong-il "sent them a variety of foodstuffs and high-quality medicines, in addition to blankets, fur coats, fur caps and fur shoes for each member of the crew. He even sent them a letter. On receiving these gifts, the crew were choked with emotion." Pulling strings to procure special favors on such a munificent scale for people involved in his pet projects—or for people in unfortunate circumstances, whose particular needs came to his attention and moved him—was to become his pattern. The impulse to generosity seems to have been genuine enough, but in altruism and philanthropy his style was neither modest nor discreet. It appears his propagandists made sure he would get full public credit for every kindness.

At that time Kim was promoting a "speed campaign" to step up output in the film industry, paralleling similar campaigns elsewhere in the economy. He telephoned the Pochonbo location every day around midnight or in the early morning to check on progress, urging "that the shooting be done at lightning speed." The daily shooting quota was 80 meters of film, but "thanks to Kim Jong-il's solicitude and trust" the crew averaged 250 meters a day— even though the cameramen "had to work while breathing on the lenses to warm them." A film that normally would have taken a year to complete was shot in forty days. "The beacon of the speed campaign, which was raised by Kim Jong-il, spread like wildfire to all units of the film industry and astonishing feats were performed, one after another. In 1970 alone, the cinema workers produced several dozen first-rate films"—an achievement that gave the lie to the evil counterrevolutionaries' claim that "higher speed results in lower quality."[47]

Kim by all accounts was genuinely tireless in his pursuit of the revolution in filmmaking. He chose the themes of films such as *The Flourishing Village* and *A Worker's Family*, both of which won the country's People's Prize. In the latter case he looked over film already shot and determined that the creative staff had not grasped the seed. "The stress must be put on the fact that a worker must never forget his origin and that even though he knows his origin, he would degenerate if he did not unceasingly revolutionize himself," he told them. "The seed of the film should be derived from this idea." They reworked the characters and the sequences accordingly. That, says an official account, is how the film "became a work of great social impact, with people crying about the need for revolutionizing society."

Not satisfied with merely telling the staff what to do, Kim "would also work, scissors in hand, throughout the night in a narrow editing booth or in a darkroom." The story is told of an inexperienced director who himself worked late into the night before he finished inserting a scene according to Kim's instruction, then went to bed. Later the man was awakened and summoned back to the studio, where he found Kim Jong-il reediting the film with scissors. Kim had gone through nine reels and had been at it for some four hours. "The film has been developed well," he told the "utterly perplexed" director, explaining that he had "cut out some scraps of the scenes which might be dull. I am not sure you will be happy with what I have done. . . ."

"Dear Leader!" mumbled the director, who was "deeply moved."

Finally, Kim Jong-il put the scissors down and walked out, saying to the director, "Comrade director, look through it again carefully."

Then he left the studio. The car carrying Kim Jong-il glided out of the studio gate and disappeared into the darkness, which soon melted into grey light.

The director returned to the room and, as he looked through the film which had just been reedited by Kim Jong-il, he was overcome by another surge of emotion. Scenes which were similar and redundant had been cut out and the recording of boisterous orchestral music and a long chorus in the finale had been removed. Because this had been done the emotional development now had pace and force and it left one in a thoughtful mood. The director felt as if he was watching another film altogether. He blushed in spite of himself. In order to accentuate the emotion in the finale, he had intertwined similar, meaningless scenes and backed them up by prolonged orchestral music and a chorus. Now the director realized that he had simply followed the conventional canon of editing. There suddenly rang in his ears the words which Kim Jong-il had so modestly said when bidding him farewell—"Look through it again carefully."

Thus Kim, although still a very young man himself, played the big daddy role, with his filmmakers cast as children. "In keeping with the proverb, 'Spare the rod and spoil the child,' Kim Jong-il was extremely exacting while being infinitely kind to them as well. With such fatherly attention, Kim Jong-il helped them in their work."[48]

The role of the movie-going masses he envisioned as even more childish: to watch his films and, through watching, fully internalize devout reverence toward his own father as the father of them all, in accordance with the "monolithic ideology." His efforts paid off, in terms of both propaganda and art. Audiences definitely noticed an improvement. Some of the films produced under his supervision drew favorable reviews not only from the captive North Korean audience but from outsiders, as well.

Kim Jong-il's takeover of North Korean opera in the late 1960s was as blunt and, for those in the industry, as initially humiliating as his earlier move to abolish the filmmakers' "esthetic review" sessions. He attended the opening of a new opera. While he watched the performance, "his face clouded." When the curtain came down, he gathered the writers and asked them "whether they would follow the old manner they had adopted. Faced by such an abrupt question, they were unable to say a word. Turning to the bewildered artists, he explained the defects of opera one by one and said that the time had come for them to put aside operas of this kind—in which the content is shackled to the form and which do not appeal to contemporary esthetic sense."

Korea had its own classic opera form. However, due at least partly to Soviet influence, the traditional form had declined in favor of European-style opera. Viewing European opera as an aristocratic form, Kim Jong-il likewise was not interested in bringing back the traditional, decidedly un-revolutionary Korean opera. Rather, he was determined to create a new type of opera, starting with operatic versions of *Sea of Blood* and the other "revolutionary masterpieces" that he had made into movies. He would re-place the Western-style arias and recitatives with *juche* elements, including songs sung in verses or stanzas, as in Korean folk ballads. Another *juche* ele-ment would be *pangchang,* offstage solos, duets and choruses that narrate, or project an inner voice, and set the mood. *Pangchang* is described as "unique in opera."[49]

In reality there is offstage singing in European opera. Take *Il Trovatore,* for example. But it would be a mistake simply to dismiss the North Korean claim by saying that Verdi and others were ahead of Kim Jong-il there. When I had a chance to experience it in person, attending a performance of *The Flower Girl* in 1989 (I'll say more about that performance in chapter 20), I found *pangchang* peculiarly affecting—differing subtly but significantly from the usual offstage singing in Western grand opera and in stage musicals of the Broadway type.

Kim put himself into the development of *Sea of Blood* as an opera just as he had done with the earlier movie version. Says an official biography: "The unremitting application which he brought to his task can be shown by the following figures: he listened to over fifty songs on nine occasions before se-lecting the song of the village youths in Act 1; as many as ninety songs on seven occasions before selecting one for a duet in Act 2; and over one hun-dred songs on six occasions for the duet between the mothers of Bok-dol and Chil-song in Act 3."

The creative staff did not quite understand how to use *pangchang,* so young Kim "specified where *pangchang* should be used and what its content should be." For example, in a scene in which the illiterate heroine's son, Ul-nam, is teaching her how to write, the composers wrote separate songs for the two of them to sing. "But Kim Jong-il, when he saw the scene, claimed that it had no general appeal and that the deep feelings of mother and son should be brought into relief, not through their songs, but by the use of *pangchang.*" In the resulting rewritten scene, the two study silently while the offstage *pangchang* chorus "conjures up the spiritual world of the mother and son in a way which neither songs nor gestures could bring out:"[50]

The mother's voice echoes through the dark sky;
A flood of stars lights the sleepless night.
Nourishing the flower bud in her heart,
She pictures a new and joyful world.
The mother who has known such a bitter life
Learns one, then another letter this night.[51]

By all accounts, when *Sea of Blood* premiered at the Pyongyang Grand Theater July 17, 1971, in the presence of the Great Leader himself, it astonished the theatergoers with its power. "Everyone in the audience became deeply moved and stood to applaud Kim Jong-il," said a former member of the elite who defected to South Korea. The production made Kim Jong-il's name and helped to solidify his status as the most likely successor to his father.[52]

The afterglow lasted for some time. A caption attached to a photo of Kim Jong-il taken on April 6, 1973, describes him as expounding "the principles of creating the *Sea of Blood*–type revolutionary operas." It is one of the most appealing photos of him. Standing in what looks to be his office, smiling and gesturing as he addresses note-taking journalists, the thirty-one-year-old cultural czar appears confident and enthusiastic. Now he is no mere privileged kid, relying solely on his father's authority to lord it over his elders, but a mature young master of a field in which young people typically can shine, one who not only knows but loves his subject.[53]

In his work with the cinema and opera, Kim Jong-il seems to have achieved—for once in his life—the delicate combination of toughness and solicitude needed to call forth his subordinates' best work. It may be that he had been studying his father's leadership techniques closely, and learning from them.

The propaganda goal toward which Kim Jong-il directed the new type of opera and all the other arts (he also gave his attention to improving dance, orchestral music, stage drama and novels, among other forms) was, of course, quite another matter. "Works which do not cater to the Party's requirements are of no use at all," he bluntly told fellow propagandists in 1974.[54] His most outstanding achievement in art and literature, said a Pyongyang biographer, was "his brilliant solution to the question of portraying the leader." He ordered establishment of three creative centers of first-rate writers and artists: Paektusan Productions, April 15 Literary Productions and the Mansuadae Art Studio. These "were entirely devoted to the portrayal of the great leader."

When *A True Daughter of the Party* premiered, "it had little appeal. One day, after he had seen the opera, Kim Jong-il said that the reason for its failure was that loyalty to the Great Leader was not brought into bold relief and that there was no appropriate theme song." He wrote the lyrics for one himself:

> *Where is the fatherly General*
> *When the Big Dipper lights the sky!*
> *Where can Supreme Headquarters be with its light-flooded windows?*
>
> *Where he's sure to be!*
>
> *From this dark forest far behind enemy lines,*
> *We're wondering where the General is now.*
> *As the chilly autumn wind blows*
> *We yearn for his warm care.*[55]

The biggest test of his early career was managing the festivities marking the year when Kim Il-sung turned sixty. For that, Kim Jong-il gave some lyricists and composers their marching orders fifteen months in advance. They were to come up with a hymn entitled "Long Life and Good Health to the Leader," to be sung at a banquet on New Year's Day, 1972. They set to work. "Many songs were written but none of them appealed to Kim Jong-il."

With the deadline approaching, Kim Jong-il visited the composers late at night, listened to their latest offerings, but was exasperated that they still did not get it. "I trust and cherish you at heart," he told them. "Why don't you understand me? Think, the leader will be sixty years old in the new year. So I made up my mind to present him with this song on the morning of New Year's Day, but you seem to be far from understanding me." The composers, of course, dropped their eyes, feeling ashamed. Then Kim Jong-il continued:

> You do not know what great pain and burdens our leader has to bear all his life and the hardships he has overcome. Our leader has experienced all the trials, sorrows and agonies which man has ever undergone and has risked his life on countless occasions. He has shed many a tear taking in his arms his dying comrades who fell on the road of the revolution and even today he cannot sleep, thinking of them. Has our leader ever enjoyed a rest with peace of mind? He spent twenty years or more in the snow and rain of the Manchurian wilderness and worked sitting up at night to build a new country after liberation and he underwent untold trials in the three years of war. After the war he fought against the vicious sectarians and, tightening his belt along with the people, he has spent his days on the road carrying out personal inspections, missing his meals.

Kim Jong-il paused, seemingly "unable to contain himself," and the composers' "eyes grew moist." Despite all those sacrifices by the Great Leader, "they had not yet produced a single song which would pray for his long life." Kim Jong-il continued:

> He is the leader of the people who has dedicated all his life to bringing them the rich life which they enjoy today. Their happiness today has come and has flowered under the care of the fatherly leader. For this reason our people are following him until the end of the sun and the moon, holding him in high esteem and ardently praying for his long life and good health. If you express these feelings and emotions in your verses and melody, that will make the song we are so anxious to see — a song which will become highly popular. This song must not be a mere ballad; it should be a hymn of the entire people expressing their ardent hopes and wishes.

Bingo! The writers "felt inspiration taking hold of them." They rushed into their rooms and started writing. Soon they came up with these lyrics:

> *Every moment our leader's life is devoted*
> *To bringing a fuller, richer life to the people.*
> *Our happiness is great; our ardor knows no bounds.*
> *You take us to your heart with never-failing love.*
>
> *To the distant ends of the earth we'll follow you.*
> *Till the sun and the moon grow cold we'll stay with you.*
> *Your kindliness is great, we'll sing forever.*
> *We'll always remain loyal to you, great leader.*
>
> > *That you may live long in good health, our leader, our father,*
> > *Is the wish of the people in our joyous land.*

The tune was "immeasurably gentle and echoed the thoughts of the words." Kim Jong-il pronounced the hymn "flawless" and had it circulated to the public even before the big day. The New Year arrived and the singers went on stage at the banquet hall, excited that they were about to sing it for the first time in Kim Il-sung's presence.

To grasp what followed, it is important to understand that Koreans tend to be emotional people, given to public displays of grief and hysteria. In South Korea, by way of illustration, Protestant Christian evangelicals with their emotional confessions of faith have made major inroads; the fastest-growing Christian group of all in the South has been the extremely demonstrative Pentecostals, known for "speaking in tongues." In North Korea, with proselytizing for other religions forbidden, the promoters of the official faith, Kimilsungism, sought to appeal to that same emotional streak.

Now let us resume the story of the New Year's Day banquet as related by one of Kim Jong-il's official biographers.

The performers stood to sing, and followed the soft orchestral opening by singing the first few lines of the song. But then, overcome by emotion, the singers went out of tune with the orchestra and gradually stopped singing. The singers tried to start again but could not, they were sobbing so hard.

> Both the conductor and the orchestra were similarly affected and everyone at the banquet gave way to tears. Dear Comrade Kim Jong-il, who was in the audience, called in several other singers and had them resume the interrupted song. Soon the song was resumed but the voices of these singers also faltered and the audience, who were standing up, began to join them, singing between their sobs. The whole house plunged into a whirlwind of excitement. It overflowed with the hymn praying for the good health and long life of the fatherly leader—which was a song from the hearts of the whole nation, which was a paean of the loyal people. Soon afterwards the song ended but those present did not sit down; the sound of weeping could be heard everywhere. The fatherly leader put a handkerchief to his eyelids and, taking hands of veteran fighters who were standing beside him, said: "Thank you, thank you. Come, don't cry, sit down, sit down." The eyes of Kim Jong-il, as he heard his words and looked at him, also glistened.[56]

Indeed. That brilliantly outrageous display of showmanship on New Year's Day launched a year of sixtieth birthday tributes during which the junior Kim proved himself flatterer—or "loyalist," in the regime's term—beyond compare.

At one of the celebrations, Kim Jong-il unveiled the new magic acts that he had pressed the Pyongyang Circus's previously lackluster magicians to perfect. They produced a basket of flowers hung with a streamer whose inscription wished long life and good health to the Great Leader. Doves flew out of the basket and circled it. When Kim Il-sung praised the magicians, "their sight went blurred." Kim Jong-il told them to keep improving until they could "take the lead in world conjuring." After further work, they went on to win top prizes in the International Modern Magic Festival, including "Magic King of the World."

Kim Jong-il was credited with an "original theory" of the leader. In the spring of 1965, he supposedly related his theory to another Central Committee official in these words:

> The question of the leader is the core of the revolution. The desire of the masses of the people alone is not sufficient for a revolution. There should be the ideological and theoretical brain, the center of unity, to give ideas and work out strategy and tactics and unite the masses. And that is the leader. To win in the revolution without the leader is like waiting for a flower to bloom without sunlight.

The masses of the people were required, in his theory "to be firmly united with a single idea."[57]

Whether or not the twenty-three-year-old Kim Jong-il single-handedly devised that theory, there is no doubt that as the years passed he became its chief promoter and enforcer. "Kim Jong-il had a correct view of how to revere the leader," we are told. "To be loyal to the leader was the purpose of all his efforts and his life itself."[58]

Scholars debate the extent to which Western and traditional East Asian models influenced North Korea's exaltation of the leader's role. "For sustained institutionalization of personal rule," argues Australian diplomat and historian Adrian Buzo, "only Stalin's system at its height can remotely compare with the authority exercised by Kim Il-sung from 1967 to his death in 1994." The Korean political tradition offers no antecedents for the "cult of the fatherly leader, reliance on charismatic leadership and cult of personality in politics," not to mention "militarism, executive activism and pervasive government intrusion into what was previously the highly self-regulatory realm of clan and family life," Buzo writes. "They are, however, features of Stalinism."[59] In Buzo's analysis, the North Korean system melded generic Stalinism with "the tastes, prejudices and experiences of the Manchurian guerilla mind-set—militaristic, Spartan, ruthless, conspiratorial, anti-intellectual, anti-bureaucratic and insular."[60]

On the other hand, Hwang Jang-yop, who studied in Stalin's Moscow to prepare for his ideological duties in Pyongyang, argues that North Korea—with Kim Jong-il in the lead—turned Stalinism and Marxism-Leninism on their heads by reverting to Confucian notions. "Stalinism acknowledged the necessity of dictatorship of the highest leader, but maintained that the highest leader had to serve the party, working class and people," Hwang writes. Stalin's system "was an extension of Marxism, which emphasized the need for dictatorship of the working class," and thus Stalin's "orders and instructions were not considered coming from an individual but from the working class." In North Korea, "things work the other way around. The Great Leader does not live for the people. It is the people who live for the Great Leader."

In Hwang's view, the Pyongyang leadership "used the feudalistic idea of filial piety to justify absolutism of the Great Leader. Filial piety in feudalism demands that children regard their parents as their benefactors and masters because they would not have existed without their parents. Taking care of your parents, the people who gave you life—in other words, being dutiful children—is the ultimate goal in life and the highest moral code. The state is a unity of families, and the head of all these families is none other than the king." Hence the role that the leadership devised for Kim Il-sung: father of the people. In the same way that a person's physical life came from his parents, his sociopolitical life came from the Great Leader. And the regime maintained that this sociopolitical life was far more precious than mere physical existence, which even animals possessed.

Whatever future historians might end up concluding about the system's antecedents, according to Hwang there was one point in particular where the regime's propaganda agreed with the truth: The new way of looking at the Great Leader "was the work of Kim Jong-il rather than Kim Il-sung himself."[61]

Among the differences between what happened in North Korea and China starting in the mid-1960s and '70s, the most important is that in China the Cultural Revolution and related movements were a spent force after little more than a decade. Jiang Qing was arrested in 1976, shortly after Mao's death. I was in Beijing covering the proceedings at the end of 1980 and the beginning of 1981 as she and her infamous Gang of Four were tried and sentenced. Their chief target, Deng Xiaoping, triumphed. Red Guards, having spent their youth revolting instead of studying, came to their senses and faced the bleak reality of their stunted careers and wasted lives. Jiang Qing had her fun at the trial, spitting out her contempt for her accusers and judges even as they derided her as a "white-boned evil spirit." But after her death penalty was suspended, in deference to the memory of her late husband, she found life in prison not to her liking. In 1991, she hanged herself in her cell.

North Korea's version of the Cultural Revolution, on the other hand, would rage on for decades with its original leader, Kim Jong-il, in charge. In 1972, the year when the junior Kim feted his father's sixtieth birthday, a new constitution legally enshrined unlimited personal rule by the Great Leader. Gone was any chance of nagging interference by such institutions as legislatures and courts.

By the late 1970s, when China was dismantling the Mao Zedong cult, discussion of the Great Leader was in terms such as these, from the issue of *Nodong Shinmun* for his birthday, April 15, 1977:

> All through the passage of time since men came into being and history began on this earth, no one has equaled Comrade Kim Il-sung, an eminent hero revered by all people; he is the greatest genius in ideology, the genius of leadership and the driving force for revolution who distinguished himself by his exceptional intelligence, the genius

of philosophical thought and theoretical activity, scientific insight, invincible art of military campaign, infinite dedication to the task of liberating mankind, vigorous revolutionary prowess, lofty virtues, and fervent love of man. He erected a shining and immortal tower of history for assiduously promoting the Korean revolution and world revolution with unprecedentedly broad scope and depth to embody all of these assets of his.[62]

It is no exaggeration to say the Kim Il-sung personality cult operated as a religion. People were encouraged to sob, "like children," at the merciful kindness of the Leader, just as at a Protestant Christian revival meeting the penitents give tearful thanks for their salvation. The regime's stories about Kim constantly told of people shedding tears upon learning of some kindness or another.

A European who served for many years as a diplomat in Pyongyang, with postings there off and on from the 1970s into the 1990s, likened North Korea to a Catholic state in the Middle Ages. He estimated that around 90 percent really believed in the regime and its teachings—while the other 10 percent had no choice but to pretend that they believed. As opposed to other communist countries, where jokes about leaders such as the Soviet Union's Brezhnev and East Germany's Erich Honecker were a staple of conversation, there were no jokes about Kim Il-sung or Kim Jong-il, the diplomat said.[63]

Kim Il-sung was hooked on adulation, and it was Kim Jong-il's job to keep it coming. As the elder Kim would write in his memoirs: "A man who enjoys the love of the people is happy, and a man who does not is unhappy. This is the view of the nature of happiness which I have maintained throughout my life."[64] He gloried in all his tributes, seemingly never tiring of sycophancy. Unlike Hitler, who refused to allow growers to name giant strawberries for him or proud parents to name their baby daughters Hitlerine,[65] Kim happily became the namesake of a flower, developed by a foreign botanist, called "kimilsungia."

Further generations of children would undergo Kim Jong-il's indoctrination programs in the new orthodoxy. Memorizing Kim Il-sung's life story and thoughts, they would follow orders and hymn the praises of Kim the father, Kim the son and the holy spirit of *juche*—all this at dreadful cost to an economy that desperately needed new ideas and a decentralization of decision making. Every Korean suspected of being a closet Deng Xiaoping would be vanquished.

FOURTEEN

Calm and Shining Eyes

Propaganda alone, of course, was not sufficient to enable Kim senior and junior to gain and maintain unprecedented control over their subjects. The police state apparatus was modeled on the Soviet one, with similarities to that of the Imperial Japanese. But it became—thanks in part to North Korea's compact and homogeneous population—even more pervasive and thorough.

According to Hwang Jang-yop, the former party secretary who defected to South Korea in 1997, armed police at the beginning of that decade numbered about three hundred thousand. Those were divided between the regular police force, under the Ministry of Public Security, and the secret police of the Ministry of State Security. The police were considered so important to regime maintenance that they were kept outside the cabinet's administrative control. Both Public Security and State Security belonged directly to the Central Committee of the Workers' Party.

Agents from both ministries were "stationed at every level of the administrative agencies, right down to the lowest level," Hwang wrote. "They are in charge of monitoring the movements of the residents, especially those under special surveillance. Even the smallest act that is out of the ordinary is a cause for arrest," and people attracting the authorities' attention "become sacrificial lambs in the agents' overzealous urge to show off their accomplishments." Agents at the post office intercepted and inspected letters and packages. Bugging and wiretapping were used to keep tabs on even high-ranking officials. People of common sense knew "not to voice their innermost thoughts, even at home."

Hwang offered as an example the police infiltration of Kim Il-sung University, of which he had been president for a time. Each of the police organizations had established there a branch equivalent in size to a county government organization, he said. Each police unit at the university "had dozens of agents under its command, and the agents in turn were put in charge of supervising and monitoring all the university departments and administrative units." For leverage, they persuaded students to watch one another. Public Security "organized small groups among the students and controlled these groups." Meanwhile, "one out of every five students was a secret agent of the State Security branch."[1]

Chong Ki-hae, a Japanese-Korean whom we met in chapter 6, had not wanted to repatriate in 1960. He had studied Korean at school in Japan but, intent on fitting in like any other youngster, he had seldom spoken his parents' language outside. Discrimination against Koreans living in Japan had eased after the war, and "the whole idea of a motherland didn't mean much to me," he told me. Besides, the family's fortunes in Japan had changed for the better, thanks to an elder brother who owned *pachinko* — Japanese pinball — and other successful businesses. But his parents, fired with bitter nationalistic feelings, were adamant that the family would move.

Sent to a small, rural North Korean community, Chong sorely missed the bright lights of Tokyo. But "I had no choice," he recalled. "I had to go where they sent me." He had dreamed of a career as an entrepreneur like his successful brother. He laughed as he confessed to the unreality of the notion of himself at seventeen — with no skills but only aspirations — starting a business in a country whose economy was centrally controlled and highly collectivized.

When I met Chong he was wiry and tanned. I inquired about that and he told me his skin color was not the result of nutritional deficiency. He had cultivated a tan after moving to South Korea. He came to the interview wearing a sharp glen-plaid suit, white-on-white shirt and figured tie, an Yves St. Laurent buckle on his belt. He said he had not even wanted to "touch the clothes" in North Korea. "I don't want to brag, but people from Japan are more fashion-conscious and like nicer fabrics." In his decades in North Korea he never had come to believe in communism, never had grown to worship Kim Il-sung. "For someone like me, who's had a taste of capitalism, it's difficult," he said. "I could never be one of the ordinary people. They have no access to information, so they believe they're in a paradise."

Because the Chongs had brought with them knowledge of a better life abroad, "Public Security had spies planted in the neighborhood, always watching us. When I first got there, someone would come by twice a month.

At first I didn't know who they were. Neighbors said they were from Public Security. They just chatted about how our life in North Korea was turning out. After I told them about my disappointments, they would say, 'But look, Kim Il-sung has done this, this and this for the people. It would be ungrateful of you to feel disappointed.' The whole community, all the neighbors, watched each other. Even I watched the people next to me."

Chong used to travel from his rural county to Pyongyang, where he could use his Japanese money to buy delicacies such as ham or sausage in the hotels. There he met some other returnees from Japan. Seven returnees took to meeting for casual discussion of the problems they encountered living in the North. They agreed that they did not want to stay there forever but would like to return to Japan. In 1965 Chong was arrested and jailed for four months. It turned out that one member of his group had been a police spy. The spy had given the authorities a record of all of Chong's meetings and contacts. While he was in jail the authorities asked Chong to spy on his neighbors. "They figured I would be pliable, since they had me on charges," he said. Although he could not reject the request, "in fact I just decided not to talk to other people so I wouldn't be in a position to get them into trouble." From the 1965 incident, "I realized I should trust no one, talk to no one. I only concentrated on my studies."

In 1982, Kim Il-sung turned seventy and the authorities used the occasion for a crackdown. "From March 15, for one month, people who were politically incorrect were supposed to confess or be reported," Chong told me. "I was reported again by Public Security for my 1965 crime and was classified as a 'traitor to the people.' I decided to volunteer to move to a more rural area. At that time I was very sick. The place I suggested going to is very mountainous and no one who went there ever returned. So they thought there was no problem sending me where I asked to go."

Partial rehabilitation was at hand. From the mid-1980s, Chong said, North Koreans were exposed to visiting Chinese merchants and people from Japan. Seeing that visitors from abroad had money, "people began to realize that North Korea was not so great compared with the rest of the world. People got lazy. Compared with others, I was considered a diligent worker. So in 1987 they made me a party worker and in 1988 a deputy to the People's Assembly of Unhong County, Yanggang Province, where I lived."

Probably the regime "wanted to set an example," Chong said. "About half the population were families of political offenders and others with bad backgrounds, like me. The idea was to show that if we worked diligently, we could succeed despite such backgrounds. They gave some very important jobs to us to provide incentives. This was one of Kim Il-sung's methods: forgive and show off."[2]

Chong, unlike many other returnees, had no relatives left in Japan. All had repatriated to North Korea. That meant there was no one to send money after what he and his family had brought with them ran out. He started getting hungry in the 1980s. "I don't have an enormous appetite," he told me, "so it wasn't a huge problem to me, but it was very hard for my kids—two sons and three daughters. In Yanggang Province I secretly cultivated and harvested food—so probably we were better off than we would have been in the city. But real starvation started around 1990. Farmers had gotten lazy. They had no motivation. The return was always the same regardless of how hard they worked. Only between 2.5 million and 2.8 million tons of rice were produced in North Korea. The question for me was whether I would live or starve to death. In March 1993 I had no prospects for the future so decided on suicide. I had some pills that needed to be dissolved in water, and I hid those in a closet. My daughter found them. She said maybe the whole family should commit suicide. I thought about sending the whole family to China but couldn't because I was a deputy. We would be noticed and caught. So I went by myself, as if I had simply disappeared."

In North Korea, Chong said, "they won't allow you to hope for a better lifestyle. I just wanted a normal life with my family: food, the basic necessities. In socialism, they won't accept the whole idea of a person." He made his way to South Korea. "I can't forget about Japan, but there was no one waiting for me there."

The police spying had continued "the whole time, right up to the day I defected."

George Orwell's *1984* is no mere literary fantasy. If you were North Korean, Big Brother would watch you. Pyongyang's internal spies and thought police were everywhere.

Lee Woong-pyong used to be one of them, although all he wanted to do was fly airplanes. "My cousin was a pilot, and from the time I entered middle school it was my dream to become one, too," Lee told me decades later.[3] "Pilots are among the highest-status members of society. While the South Koreans might think lawyers and doctors have the best jobs, in North Korea those are no better than ordinary workers."

Born in 1954, the year following the armistice in the Korean War, Lee grew up in Pyongyang. His father taught at a police academy and served as a city assemblyman. Although those positions and the father's party membership placed the family in a social stratum that ordinary North Koreans would have envied, times were almost as hard for the Lees as for most others in the country. "I can recall from around the early '60s," Lee told me. "Pyongyang was underdeveloped, with cows wandering around, cow dung everywhere. There were no railroads. There wasn't much plastic; it was only after entering elementary school that I got a plastic school bag." Clothing tended to be hand-me-downs. Lee's father was issued a new uniform every two years.

"When he got a new one we would dye the old one a different color and someone else in the family would wear it." The grain ration came mainly in the form of flour, which went into dumplings and flat noodles. Many people ate food donated by the Soviet Army. Food "was never enough," Lee told me. "I dug into rat holes to get the rice the rats had accumulated. We led a very thrifty life." But "happiness doesn't mean the absolute value of wealth," he added. "It's comparative. Everybody was poor at that time. That was considered happiness. I was just an ordinary kid leading a very ordinary life. People's expectations weren't advanced."

The ten members of the family, including a grandmother, shared a standard two-room, sixty-square-meter unit in one of the apartment buildings built out of the ashes and rubble of wartime Pyongyang. "We all slept together. Even when I was in higher middle school I slept with my parents. The mentality was different. We didn't imagine that each person should have a separate room. It seemed normal for all of us to be in together."

Getting to know one's neighbors was assured; residents of the building bathed communally and two or three apartments shared each coal-fired furnace. ("There were many disputes about stealing coal," Lee remembered.) In one of the downstairs units lived the Workers' Party commissar of Lee's school. When Lee was sixteen and finishing higher middle school, the commissar selected him to become a pilot trainee. Donning an air force uniform, Lee went off to Chongjin on the east coast to enroll in a five-year program that started with theory and moved through flight training. He trained in YAK 18 trainers, then MIG 15, MIG 17 and finally MIG 19 fighters.

Lee had grown up idolizing Kim Il-sung from his nursery school days. Toward the end of his pilot training, around 1974, teachers started talking about Kim Jong-il, as well. Rationalizing the succession plans, they pointed out that Stalin had died without an assured successor. The Soviet Union, they complained, had then veered away from the ideals of socialist revolution. (Within a year or two Ho Chi Minh and Mao Zedong had died and their negative examples in the succession department could be used as well.) Lee, meanwhile, was becoming part of a group that was elite not only on account of its occupation but in many cases thanks to the young pilots' own family backgrounds. Among the pilots he knew were sons and nephews of some of the country's top leaders.

Payback time came at graduation in 1976. Lee found that he was expected to become an informant to State Security. The elite secret police organization, which handled the most sensitive political cases, reported directly to Kim Il-sung. It was then a department, not yet a full ministry, having split off from the Ministry of Public Security in 1973.

"Most of my family members had some relations with State Security,"

Lee told me. With such a family background, he was an obvious pick. As a practical matter he had no real choice of whether to accept or not. "To be selected to inform means State Security trusts you. To reject the job would have worked as a disadvantage to me." After listening to two or three lectures, Lee wrote out and affixed a fingerprint to an oath whose wording he recalled as something like, "As an informant for State Security I'll be loyal to the party and do my best. I'll keep the secrets." He was instructed to "report anyone saying or doing anything against party rules, anyone who exposed military secrets, national secrets, party secrets, anyone going against the authority of Kim Il-sung, any power struggles in the organization."

With that, Lee went off to an air force base to lead a double life, both flying with and spying on his colleagues. He knew he was far from alone. Although in the regular army one in perhaps a hundred soldiers was a snoop, he thought, the ratio was considerably higher among pilots—maybe one out of eighteen or twenty. Pilots, after all, were trained to fight in the skies over South Korea, learning about the terrain and other conditions in the South. If a pilot should decide to defect, he would have his transportation at hand and know exactly where to go, so he could escape more readily than a foot soldier—and at far greater cost to the northern regime. A key mission of the pilot-informants was to pick out and report any colleague who showed signs that he might contemplate defection. The predictable punishment was so harsh, Lee said, that he would have thought more than twice before making such a report. Indeed, "I didn't do any reporting on that kind of situation because, if I had, that person would have been sent somewhere. I'd have to be really sure before I'd report it."

Lee reported seldom—maybe once a month instead of weekly, which was the standard. He stuck to routine reports about pilots who received visitors (Who? What time?), played cards and committed other such minor infractions. It wasn't that he was a saint. "If I didn't like someone, I reported on that person," he admitted to me. But he said he had never gotten anyone into serious trouble with his reports—"no fatal cases and none sent to prison camps. I only did the basics, what was necessary."

Nevertheless he found his life "very stressful, because I had to do two things at once—my regular job plus working for State Security. I came to detest the mechanism of the regime," which was using informants to sustain its power. "I realized that this variety of communism could not go on. That's the first thing I said when I defected to South Korea. I defected because I thought it was unjust." On February 25, 1983, when he was a major, he flew a MIG 19 across the Demilitarized Zone and down to a South Korean air base at Suwon, tipping his wings to signal that he was defecting.

Although I was impressed by the forceful speech of the crewcut and balding, strong-featured Lee, I felt that something was missing in the story he'd told up to that point. My experience from interviewing many defectors

was that, in the usual case, systemic injustice in the abstract was not enough
to spur such a drastic act. A defector would know all too well that his family
members remaining behind quite likely would be sent off to political prison
camps, perhaps for the rest of their lives, to pay for his act. In view of that
heavy responsibility, I had found, a North Korean normally would not defect
unless he had fallen afoul of the system in some life-shattering fashion. But I
also knew that the authorities in South Korea considered Lee a sincere defector. They had shown that by letting him join their air force (in a nonflying
job, teaching about North Korea) and eventually, as he approached his fortieth birthday, by promoting him to lieutenant colonel.

I pressed Lee to tell me more of his story. And there was more, enough to
persuade me that he had experienced conflicts with the system sufficient to
motivate a self-loathing character in a Graham Greene novel. His epiphany,
it turned out, had involved the woman he loved. But I'm getting ahead of the
story.

Back at the time of his defection, Lee told me, "lots of people doubted me
because it seemed I didn't have such a decisive reason—that I just defected
for political reasons." That was his reason, though, he insisted. "At bottom
the regime just put too much pressure on people's basic rights." I asked him
for an example. "For example," he replied, "because of the concept of class
struggle you're not allowed to marry whomever you want." Now I could see
that his story was about to get more personal.

I drew him out on the rest and learned that, when he was twenty-seven,
someone had arranged for him to meet a prospective bride. "I won't mention
the full name, but Miss Chang's parents were from Seoul and came north in
1949." The couple got along well, corresponding by mail for about a year. "I
wanted to marry her, but pilots weren't supposed to marry people with Seoul
backgrounds." The mere fact that Miss Chang's parents had lived in South
Korea—before she was born—made her loyalty suspect, along with that of
her whole family. "I guess that was the turning point, the point where I
started having conflicts," Lee told me. "What right has the regime to invade
social relations?"

Lee was expected to consult with a senior State Security officer if he
wanted to marry. "They didn't specifically say, 'Don't marry.' They said, 'Do
as you wish.' But the unstated message was that there would be lots of disadvantages for my family and me. After a background check on the woman, I
knew it wasn't what we were supposed to do. I slowly distanced myself from
her, trying to persuade her that marriage to a pilot would mean a hard life."
He reminded her that North Korean military units were expected to grow
much of their own food. "I told her, 'You'd have to do farming, raise pigs.'
The last letter I got from her, she told me she was marrying another man.
She quoted a Korean saying to the effect that 'birds of a feather flock together.' She understood the real reason. She was, I guess, outraged, upset."

Meanwhile, Lee didn't have to be an Einstein to figure that there was a spy out there somewhere who was just waiting for him to say or do the wrong thing. That was the way the regime operated, after all. While Lee himself was with State Security, there was always Public Security among other spying organizations. The various agencies watched each other, even had units officially stationed inside one another's organizations to facilitate their mutual spying. Lee felt his frustration bottled up for as long as he remained in North Korea. Lacking trust in those around him, "I couldn't talk about my dissatisfaction with anyone," he told me.

Among scores of defectors and refugees I interviewed, I found Lee particularly tough-minded. North Koreans, soon after their arrival in China or South Korea, tended to accept religion, Buddhism in some cases but more often evangelical Christianity—a new set of top-down, revealed, all-encompassing beliefs to replace the faith that had failed them in the North. Lee was different in that regard. "I'm not much of an organization man, more of an individualist," he told me. "That's why I haven't taken up religion yet. It's difficult to accept it. I still have doubts. I think religion was made to maintain the social order."

Then he looked hard at me and said, "I want the North Korean regime to know that when the regime changes, they'll have to take responsibility for punishing the families of defectors. Put that in your book."

FIFTEEN

From Generation to Generation

In February 1974, Pyongyang-watchers abroad read in *Nodong Shinmun,* the North Korean party newspaper, an editorial entitled, "Let the Whole Party, Nation and People Respond to the Call of the Great Leader and the Appeal of the Party Center for Grand Construction Programs of Socialism."

It eventually turned out that the editorial had coincided with the Central Committee's unannounced endorsement of Kim Jong-il's selection as successor to his father, who was party general secretary. Shortly before, in September 1973, the Central Committee had elected the junior Kim to membership in the party's elite politburo and named him party secretary for organization and guidance—the very powerful post that his uncle, Kim Yong-ju, had held.

Thenceforth Kim Jong-il "was not merely number two in the power hierarchy," high-ranking defector Hwang Jang-yop recalled later. "This is what sets him apart from his uncle Kim Yong-ju." The junior Kim's power was far greater than his uncle had ever wielded. From 1974, said Hwang, "even the most insignificant report could not reach Kim Il-sung without going through Kim Jong-il first, and none of Kim Il-sung's instructions could reach his subordinates without going through Kim Jong-il first."[1]

Without knowing all that, foreign analysts pondered the question of who or what might be the mysterious "Party Center," so prominently singled out in the editorial. Clues began to appear. In February of 1975, Pyongyang television showed Kim Jong-il voting in local elections right behind Kim Il-sung and Kim Il, the next-ranked figure among active members of the guerrilla generation, who was not related by blood to the other two similarly named Kims. Voting order had been for decades a strong hint of rank in any communist country. In 1975, Kim Jong-il's portrait started to appear alongside that of his father in public places—but still the code term "Party Center" was used and his name was rarely heard in public. In March of 1976, the term was upgraded to "Glorious Party Center." An official announcement the same year finally made clear the junior Kim's position in the party secretariat.[2]

Although he had received the official nod, Kim Jong-il with his father's help was still in the midst of what would prove a very long process. On the one hand, the Kims had to win support for the succession plan among key officials suspected of harboring skepticism. On the other, they had to root out any exceptionally bold leading officials who might dare to oppose the scheme overtly—along with cagier officials who could be biding their time, disguising their opposition while awaiting the elder Kim's death as their cue to move against his son.

Kim Jong-il mobilized relatively young people to help him. Totally in charge of propaganda for the party starting in 1973, he commanded the newly formed Three Revolutions teams—North Korea's answer to China's Red Guards. He and his loyalists pushed aside older figures, many of whom were purged for alleged incompetence or insufficiently "revolutionary" attitudes. But age was no barrier when he sought allies for his machinations, and he also teamed up with selected members of the old guard. Rivals, including his uncle, stepbrothers and stepmother, bit the dust.

To show his fitness for the top leadership, the propaganda and cultural specialist had to present himself as more broadly qualified. That required dabbling in the larger economy. In 1972, not yet formally anointed as successor, he is reported to have told leading officials and engineers that he had resolved to take upon himself "the task of automation." Presumably his father gave advance approval; in any event, the stated reason for what might have appeared to outsiders as arrant usurpation was that a "technical revolution," begun in 1970, had not made enough progress.

The technical revolution's official goal was "finally freeing all the working people from backbreaking labor." But as we saw in chapter 9, the movement appears rather to have been a response to the fact that militarization, by enlarging the army, had created a labor shortage. Automation was the way to stretch the available labor supply. Change had proven elusive, though, because managers were mainly concerned with meeting their production quotas. Thus, they had little time to think about automation, say the regime's official historians. Besides, "some people were victims of a sort of mysticism."

They believed that "putting industry on a totally automated track was feasible only in developed countries."[3]

At the outmoded, Japanese-built Hwanghae Iron Works, Kim Jong-il demonstrated what was to become a signature element of his management style. If he decided on a project his philosophy was: Full speed ahead and the cost be damned. Steelmaking officials and technicians argued that automating Hwanghae's old, worn-out sintering plant would not be cost-effective. That was nonsense in the young Kim's view. "Money should not be spared," he ordered. "Calculation should not come first in spending money for the working class." In what seems an echo of his insistence as a university student that computation be dropped from the economics curriculum, he added: "Counting may be done later."[4] His show project of automating the old iron works was completed in short order.

In Kim Jong-il's mind, the technical revolution was an extension of the ideological and cultural work in which he had done his apprenticeship. For him, policy issues boiled down to motivation. With material rewards ideologically frowned upon, positive motivation meant propaganda and mass mobilization. His cinema and opera work merged directly into his new duties. North Koreans were encouraged to emulate the heroes and heroines of his movies and revolutionary operas. They organized "Sea-of-Blood" Guards and "Flower Girl" Guards to push for innovations. "Day after day, leading characters in the works of art became real in each factory and each workshop."[5] A magic trick he encouraged the Pyongyang Circus conjurers to develop and show off to his father highlighted the campaign to reduce women's kitchen labor.[6] To whip up support for the Hwanghae Iron Works modernization, he brought in "a high-powered economic cheering squad" composed of Central Broadcasting Commission professionals to broadcast to factories and related industries nationwide, urging them to aid the automation project.[7]

In 1973, with output of tractors and other agricultural machines failing to meet demand, Kim Jong-il and his propaganda and agitation department mounted a campaign to raise productivity at Kumsong Tractor Works and Sungri General Motor Works. "Party activists and hundreds of artists, reporters and editors rushed to the production sites, with all the means of publicity put into action, including newspapers, radio stations, TV stations and feature films." Artists sang and danced on the site, their songs "reverbrating in high pitch" as teach-ins, bulletins and wall newspapers called forth "the political consciousness and creative initiative of the working class." Thanks to the "fresh innovations" thus inspired, both factories were said to have worked wonders.[8]

Despite such successes, the country's leaders remained troubled by workplace-level resistance to the campaigns.[9] In 1973, the year of the campaigns in the two tractor plants, Kim Il-sung established a movement to remove the "shackles of outdated thinking" and promote vigor in carrying out ideological, technical and cultural revolution— "the Three Revolutions." Organized into teams of twenty to fifty members were tens of thousands of zealous ideologues—young party members, technocrats, intellectuals and college students, who had been educated completely under the communist regime. After special training, they were sent into factories, farms and offices, even schools. The elder Kim soon placed his son in command of the effort,[10] inspiring analysts abroad to suggest that one purpose of the teams was to root out opposition to Kim Jong-il's succession and install his young loyalists in positions of authority.[11]

A North Korean named Kim Ji-il, who was an elementary school pupil when the movement was launched, recalled after his defection to the South that teams "would even come to our school and inspect the kids, their lifestyles and so on. This took about ten days. They would hold a meeting each day, take one kid at a time and make him or her confess publicly to some misdeed or other. The other kids would get into the spirit of the criticism session and remind whomever they were grilling: 'You also did so and so!' I was class president so I felt a lot of conflict about this. But North Korea is an inter-critical society."

Kim Ji-il recalled that "confessions might be something like, 'I was absent,' or 'I came late to school.' 'I didn't participate well in the criticism session.' Or, 'I fought with another kid.' It wasn't the details they cared about. They wanted to intimidate you and give you stress. Each Monday we had to get up and make Kim Jong-il pledges: 'I will be faithful to the leader, blah blah blah.' Part of the pledge was, 'In case of war I will sacrifice myself as an advance-guard stormtrooper.' I had to be the first one to read it, and they always criticized my pronunciation of advance-guard stormtrooper, *keunuidaekyeolsade.*"[12]

In workplaces, the teams' official missions were to whip up fervor for over-production, combat conservative and bureacratic tendencies and "teach modern science and technology to those cadres who do not study much and who are preoccupied with their day-to-day work." Particular targets were older officials who had lost their own zeal and become mired in bureaucratic routine and sloth. Even the Central Committee of the Workers' Party was not exempted from the requirement to play host to a Three Revolutions team.[13]

Longer-lived than China's Red Guards, the Three Revolutions teams lasted for more than two decades. Former member Kim Kwang-wook, whose term in the organization ended in 1993, told me that college students had been eager to join the Three Revolutions teams because it put them on

the fast track leading to high officialdom. About 70 percent of college graduates went to work in Three Revolutions offices, said Kim, who defected right
after leaving the group—before he could put his civil engineering training to
work building underground tunnels for the army.

Despite the teams' vaunted morale-building function, in reality the members worked as snoops and spies, Kim Kwang-wook told me. Thus, in his initial assignment in Pyongyang, "I had to write down everything any of the
three hundred citizens I watched might say—anything against the regime."
The young people

> spied on ordinary citizens, but our special duty was to spy on fac-
> tory managers and government officials. We were sent to factories
> and treated like gods or kings, because they were afraid we'd rat on
> them. I was in the mines for six months, then I moved to a factory
> making excavation equipment. I took care of the transport, fueling
> and equipment departments and if anyone used them excessively I
> reported on that. If someone opposed an order Kim Jong-il had sent
> down—saying, "Why should we do that?"—we'd make a report,
> While I was in the mines an official got into that kind of trouble. He
> got fired and sent as a common laborer to an airport. It was someone
> else's report. At that time there were a lot of corruption scandals.
> We heard that Kim Jong-il said, "I'll choose more loyal and efficient
> mine officials." One official, in a department that was considered de-
> sirable, complained to his colleagues about Kim Jong-il's orders,
> and his colleagues reported him.

By the time Kim Kwang-wook joined, the teams had reached something
of an accommodation with the people they watched. Nevertheless, as we saw
in the case of pilot-spy Kim Woong-pyong in chapter 14, they could not simply stop reporting altogether so they reported selectively. "Mostly we overlooked what we heard. We got TV sets as bribes. I myself received cloth to
make a suit. We got to know those officials really well after a while. But how
could there be nothing, among three hundred people? If we called a cup a
plate, it was a plate. If officials crossed Three Revolutions team members, the
team members might simply make up stories about them."

The considerably older subjects of all that surveillance "couldn't express
animosity but I know they didn't like us," Kim Kwang-wook said. "In Oriental culture you must speak a certain way to elders. I didn't speak that
way—we used plain, not honorific, speech. Officials really hated the Three
Revolutions teams." That didn't bother the youngsters much, though. "If
you're a team member, you automatically get accepted into the party, so we
didn't feel any compunction. That was my attitude, and that's the way others
felt as well."[14]

❀ ❀ ❀

Superficially the Three-Revolutions teams were similar to the radical Maoist Red Guards who rampaged across China. In reality, though, Kim Il-sung had long opposed the "leftist deviation" of bottom-up, egalitarian democracy. His regime had made clear its opposition to the "reckless rebellion" of the Chinese Cultural Revolution.[15] Far from unleashing the masses, the Three Revolutions teams were all about control. Kim and his son kept the teams themselves under tightly centralized control and used them, in turn, to control potentially troublesome elements in the bureaucracy and the economy.

In March 1975, the third year of the Three Revolutions teams, Kim Il-sung claimed that because of the teams, the country had passed the $1,000 mark in per capita income and joined the advanced countries. Even if such claims were true, not everyone was pleased. Watching the advance of the young Kim and his likewise youthful comrades and disapproving of the aggressive behavior of the youngsters in the Three Revolutions teams, some of the old revolutionaries wondered how long it would be before they themselves were consigned to history. Kim Il-sung sought to soothe them in 1975. "The target of the Three Revolutions teams is not the old cadres themselves but their outdated thought," he said. "Elderly officials should not be simply dismissed but be remolded through the movement."[16]

As we have seen, and as we shall see again, Kim Jong-il's version of generational politics did involve selective harsh attacks on older-generation foes. He would not have been his father's son if purges had not been part of his arsenal. But he also worked hard to win the acceptance of first-generation members of the leadership, flattering and allying himself with those who supported him or who exhibited enough pliability that he believed he could deal with them.

There was no shortage of sycophants. When Kim Jong-il graduated from college and joined the Workers' Party in 1964, one former high official told me, the princeling rated his own female "mansions volunteer corps." Its organizers were Yi Yong-mu, a general in charge of the KPA Political Department, and Jun Mun-sop, bodyguard commander. Other flatterers, as well, introduced him to young women or brought him other gifts. "Kim Il-sung and Kim Jong-il both love to give and receive gifts," this former official said. "Kim Il-sung likes health food. Kim Jong-il requests presents with value overseas—gold bullion and foreign currency."[17]

Another former official, Kang Myong-do, told me that in the 1970s, Li Dong-ho, a very powerful figure in espionage in South Korea, held parties for Kim Jong-il and gave him presents. Foreign affairs specialist Ho Dam was also giving presents to flatter the junior Kim. Kang told me that Kim

Jong-il seemed to savor the attention. The gift-giving, as is traditional in East Asia, was mutual. Kim Jong-il was wont to give lavishly, whether the recipient was already close to him or was someone he had yet to bring over to his side.

Official biographies relate incidents such as his gift to a television cameraman of an apartment in 1964—the year of the junior Kim's university graduation, when his work involved him with the Central Radio and TV Broadcasting Committee. The cameraman, a Korean War orphan, was a newlywed. The intent of the story is to show the young Kim following in his father's footsteps in showing "warm affection" for orphans "as if he were their own parent." Kim summoned the cameraman and drove him downtown.

> Presently the car stopped in front of a high-rise apartment house. Leading the man up the well-polished artificial granite staircase, Kim Jong-il halted in front of Room Ten on the first floor, and produced a small piece of paper from his briefcase. "Now, take it, it is the occupation certificate. I could not allow myself to give you an old house because yours is a young family. . . . Go in and see whether you like it." With these words Kim Jong-il opened the door.[18]

"Party rules prohibit gift-giving among members," a former elite official told me. "But Kim Jong-il gave gifts to try to buy people off from forming factions against him." When he gave an imported automobile, as was often the case, the gift was marked with a special "216" license plate—the numerals representing the junior Kim's birthday, February 16. "Once Kim Jong-il gave me an Audi with one of the '216' license plates," the same former official told me.

Besides cars, Kim Jong-il's gifts included television sets, radios and watches—all foreign-made, of course. The overall scale of his gift-giving soon grew so enormous as to affect the economy seriously. Various sources confirm that a special unit in the party, dubbed Room 39 on account of its office location, was given the mission of bringing in foreign exchange to pay for Kim's purchases. To accomplish that, Room 39 had a monopoly over the export of several high-demand products.

According to defector Kang Myong-do, Room 39 was founded in 1974 and given sole authority over the export of gold and silver, steel, fish and mushrooms. "Only through Room 39 could those products be exported," said Kang. "Previously each unit handled its own imports and exports, but Kim Jong-il's order made it treason to deal in those products through any other route. Because of Room 39 activities, the government had no bank reserves and became nearly broke. So from the mid-1980s most foreign trade had to be done on credit. Anyone who could borrow $1 million from another country was considered a North Korean hero."[19]

❊ ❊ ❊

Gift-giving didn't win over all the skeptics who questioned Kim Jong-il's rise. Different approaches were needed to deal with several first-generation revolutionaries who "treated Kim Jong-il as a kid not yet weaned," in Kang Myong-do's words. Those included top civilian officials Kim Dong-kyu, Kim Il and Pak Song-chol as well as a senior general, O Jin-u, who had been a guerrilla protégé of Kim Il-sung's in Manchuria.

According to Kang's account, Kim Jong-il betrayed a bosom pal to get O on his side. The pal was Yi Yong-mu, the ambitious general and Politburo member in charge of the political department of the Korean People's Army (and, by some accounts, the husband of a cousin of Kim Il-sung's), who had oiled his way into Kim Jong-il's inner circle starting in the junior Kim's college days. "Yi was very obsequious to Kim Jong-il, and Kim Jong-il liked that very much," said Kang. "He gave lots of presents to Kim Jong-il and built him a mansion at Changwan Mountain. From the KPA orchestra he handed over nineteen-to-twenty-year-old women to Kim Jong-il as Happy Corps members—they both liked women. Yi was really friendly with Kim Jong-il. They went all over the country in a Lincoln and a Mercedes-Benz. Yi used familiar language in addressing Kim Jong-il. Kim Jong-il trusted Yi 100 percent. Yi was very confident, and O Jin-u didn't like his attitude."

Then, said Kang, "some personnel problems arose in Kangwon Province. The First Infantry commander's job was open, and Yi and O favored different people. O was a veteran of the First Infantry and he wanted a first-generation revolutionary to take over the job. Yi wanted one of his own cronies." On paper, Yi was in charge of military personnel matters, having been assigned the job by Kim Il-sung himself. According to Kang, though, Kim Jong-il realized that if he supported his buddy Yi he would "be seen as siding against the first generation of revolutionaries. Kim Jong-il, being smart, sacrificed Yi, consigning him to a secondary post in a logging area in the remote mountains of Chagang Province." Going further, Kim Jong-il suggested to Kim Il-sung that O Jin-u be given Yi's former job as head of the overall political department of the KPA. "Kim Jong-il considered O Jin-u not so smart, but he wanted somebody from the first generation on his side," said Kang.[20]

O's support apparently proved useful to Kim Jong-il in his competition with his uncle. Hwang Jang-yop is quoted as reporting that Kim Jong-il and O Jin-u "were major factors behind driving Hur Bong-hak, Kim Kwang-yop and other military men out of power between 1969 and 1970 for purposes of emasculating Kim Yong-ju politically."[21]

Kim Yong-ju was elected to the Politburo in 1970, ranked sixth in the regime. Kim Il-sung gave him the high-profile mission of negotiating with South Korean intelligence chief Lee Hu-rak in the North-South talks of 1972–1973. But in the palace politics at home Yong-ju had met his match in his cunning nephew, and the uncle's rise proved ephemeral. He lost to Kim Jong-il his post as party chief of organization and guidance in September 1973. As a consolation prize Kim Il-sung gave him a vice-premiership— negligible in the scheme of things in Pyongyang, where the party apparatus far outranked the cabinet. Kim Yong-ju was dropped from public mention entirely after his attendance was noted at an April 1975 meeting of the Supreme People's Assembly. (He was not to make another announced appearance until 1993.[22]) His follower Ryu Jang-shik likewise disappeared from public view in September of 1975.

Around that time, Kim Jong-il managed to neutralize any clout possessed by his stepmother, Kim Song-ae, who had favored Uncle Yong-ju in a bid to improve the eventual chances of her own son Pyong-il. By introducing Kim Il-sung to two women who then became favorites of the Great Leader, Kang Myong-do told me, Kim Jong-il drove a wedge into his father's marriage and reduced the first lady's influence. (Kang added that the Fatherly Leader's son by one of those women was being raised in Switzerland.) To add insult to injury, the propaganda apparatus pressed Song-ae into service in 1975 to offer public praise of her late predecessor and rival for Kim Il-sung's affections. Photographed wearing a facial expression in which some *Nodong Shinmun* readers thought they discerned distaste, she called Kim Jong-suk— Kim Jong-il's late mother, then the subject of Pyongyang's version of beatification—an "imperishable communist revolutionary fighter and outstanding woman activist."

An apparent interruption in Kim Jong-il's rise came when the regime removed his portrait from public places in October 1976 and reduced what had been practically daily references to "the Party Center," then dropped all use of the term from the early part of 1977. That curious incident remains to be fully explained, but the consensus of Pyongyang-watchers seems to be that the young Kim's disappearance from public view was a response to concern his advance had engendered among influential people.

Soviet newsmen stationed in Pyongyang told me when I visited the capital in 1979 that the key concerns leading to Kim Jong-il's public sidelining had been expressed within the military, where Kim Jong-il—as we saw in his involvement in the the contest between O and Yi—had assumed an oversight role.

The junior Kim's portaits came down just a few weeks after the 1976

Panmunjom incident in which North Korean troops, wielding axes, killed two American officers who had led a detail to trim a poplar tree that interfered with visual monitoring of the truce zone. The killings came after the Americans had refused North Korean soldiers' demand that they halt the tree-cutting. Having seen enough of the younger Kim's leadership, one of the Russians told me, irate North Korean officers had blamed Kim Jong-il for the diplomatically embarrassing axe incident and had succeeded in getting him removed, for the time being, from his military role.

An unofficial, Tokyo-based spokesman for the regime, Kim Myong-chol, insisted in a 1982 article in a Hong Kong magazine that Kim Jong-il had not been involved in the axe incident: "Kim Jong-il was preoccupied at that time with organizing the North Korean people, party and government. He was simply too busy to have had any role in that affair, Pyongyang says." Much later, however, after Pyongyang had cranked up a propaganda campaign to glorify the junior Kim as a great general, another unofficial overseas spokesman pictured Kim Jong-il as having given an order, during the axe incident, that the Americans "should be taught a lesson." When the United States responded to the killings with a display of military muscle, "Kim Jong-il was not impressed and laughed at the American moves."[23]

A Swedish diplomat who was based in Pyongyang as his country's ambassador during that period offers an intriguing aside: "The pictures of the son seemed to change." Meanwhile, Eastern European diplomats openly circulated rumors that Kim Il-sung had a son older than Kim Jong-il from an earlier marriage. "Had the elder one been required to renounce his rights as firstborn in favor of his brother?" The diplomats could only speculate, as they were unable to confirm the rumors that there was an older son.[24]

In a widely disseminated story from that period, a pro-Seoul Korean-language newspaper in Japan, *Toitsu Nippo* (Unification Daily), alleged on February 2, 1978, that young military officers led by an aide to Gen. Yi Yong-mu had attempted to kill Kim Jong-il in a hit-and-run automobile collision in September 1977, inflicting serious head injuries on him and sending him into a coma. According to the account, the young officers were immediately arrested and executed and Yi was removed from his post, while doctors specializing in treatment of "human vegetables" were invited to Pyongyang to examine the junior Kim. There is little evidence for this. Although, as we have seen, Yi Yong-mu was out of favor while Kim Jong-il drew closer to regime elder O Jin-u, Yi later made a comeback of the sort that was not uncommon in the North Korea system. He came to be ranked near the top of the regime as a key deputy to Kim Jong-il on the Central Military Commission.

280 UNDER THE LOVING CARE OF THE FATHERLY LEADER

That would have been out of the question if Yi ever had involved himself in such a seriously bad career move as a botched attempt to assassinate the Great Leader–designate.

Tales such as that assassination yarn seem to have been fed by Kim Jong-il's still-wild personal life, which was public enough to cause some in the military and the leadership to disdain him as a young reprobate. The story of his being seriously injured in an automobile wreck fits into what some others have said—one account says he was driving recklessly and caused an accident himself—even if there is nothing to the coup story. Hwang Jang-yop after his defection to the South said he had heard that Kim Jong-il "was injured when he fell during horse riding—but I don't know well."[25]

A leader more concerned than Kim Il-sung with the opinions of others might have heeded the signs of opposition or skepticism and withdrawn his son's appointment. But they did not call Kim Il-sung "iron-willed" for nothing. Kim Jong-il's retreat to the shadows was merely temporary. Meanwhile, efforts continued to remove or isolate those resisting the succession scheme.

Vice-President Kim Dong-kyu was the center of opposition to Kim Jong-il's succession within the older generation of former guerrillas in the leadership. Not only had he been an anti-Japanese resistance fighter but he also had lost an arm in the struggle. When ousted, he ranked number two in North Korea, right after Kim Il-sung. He didn't like Kim Jong-il, as Kang Myong-do related to the Seoul newspaper *JoongAng Ilbo*. When the young man was being elevated, Kim Dong-kyu said: "I think they're being too rash on this succession matter." At that point, according to Kang's account, Kim Il-sung did nothing.

Having gotten O Jin-u on his side, according to Kang's account, Kim Jong-il manipulated documents so as to be able to give Kim Il-sung a report that Kim Dong-kyu had been a traitor to the anti-Japanese movement. That got Kim Dong-kyu exiled in 1977 to a rural area in North Hamgyong Province. In 1980, Kim Il-sung happened to be in that area and caught sight of a very large mansion. He found that it was Kim Dong-kyu's and became very upset. Kim Il-sung sent Kim Dong-kyu to dissidents' camp No. 16 in Hwasong, according to Kang's version, and in 1984 Kim Dong-kyu died there "of malnutrition and despair."

First Lady Kim Song-ae's dream of seeing a child of her own succeed to her husband's position at the helm of the nation came to naught. Her elder son,

Pyong-il, had his career in the capital cut short. His younger brother Yong-il never had a place in public life in the first place.

Born in the early 1950s,[26] Pyong-il studied English in Malta in the late 1960s, attended the North Korean military academy and learned to fly light, civilian aircraft at an airport in East Germany. (Some reports say he also studied in Moscow.) He became a member of his father's military bodyguard corps, as had his stepbrother, Kim Jong-il. Kim Yong-il, for his part, studied electronics at Dresden Technical University in East Germany, becoming fluent in German. He went on to get his Ph.D. in Berlin. His plan when he finished his studies in the mid-1980s was to go back to North Korea to head an electronics factory, according to a former East German official who knew both him and Pyong-il. The German described the two brothers as "intelligent and well-educated." Both displayed the common touch, he told me. "They know life and they know regular Koreans." Both spoke Russian, he added.[27]

Kang Myong-do in his interviews with *JoongAng Ilbo* sorted out the story of Pyong-il. According to Kang's account, as North-South tension increased following the axe incident at the DMZ, Pyong-il entered the bodyguard division. A Kim Il-sung University graduate in addition to being a member of the first family, he rose quickly at first. Soon he was promoted to colonel and named vice-head of the strategic department of the bodyguards.

Pyong-il's lifestyle became extravagant, according to Kang's account. Pyong-il's cronies included Kim Chang-ha, son of Kim Byong-ha, who was head of the State Security Department, and Chon Wi, son of the head of bodyguards. They often met at the Kim Byong-ha home and held frequent parties there. Pyong-il's custom was to hand out watches engraved with Kim Il-sung's name as presents to guests. "He was very extravagant and generous and had lots of followers who flattered him by saying: 'Long live Kim Pyong-il!' You weren't supposed to say that about anyone but Kim Il-sung—it's against the one-man rule system."[28]

At that time, according to Kang's account, Kim Jong-il was spying on Kim Pyong-il and learned of his activities through Room 10 in the party headquarters, which was established in 1978 to set up spy networks to catch any deviation from one-man rule. (Kim Jong-il had no use for either Pyong-il or Yong-il, caring only for his sister Kyong-hui, one former high-ranking official recalled.[29]) "Kim Jong-il was always waiting for a chance to get his stepbrother in trouble," said Kang. "He used this information and made a report to Kim Il-sung." Kim Il-sung got angry and fired Pyong-il, according to Kang, who told me in an interview that Kim Pyong-il for a time stayed in Pyongyang. Finding that few people dared to have anything to do with him, he asked to be sent abroad. Thus were Pyong-il's political hopes dashed. In the army, where real influence resided, Kang said in his *JoongAng Ilbo* interviews, "there is no one who supports Pyong-il. No one." Kim Pyong-il was consigned to overseas embassies, far from the center of power. He drew successive post-ings as ambassador to European countries including Bulgaria and Finland.

It seems to me that Kim Jong-il must have learned from this incident a profound lesson: He must stick to the role of the modest, filial son for a *very* long time. This may help to explain his reluctance to show himself publicly and step front and center, even after his father died.

As for First Lady Kim Song-ae's other children, Kang Myong-do told me that Pyong-il's elder sister Kim Byong-jin was the wife of a diplomat, Kim Kwang-sop, who at the time of our talk was ambassador to the Czech Republic. Kim Jong-il's young stepbrother Kim Yong-il, Kang said, was liv-ing an isolated life in Pyongyang, having no job. The studious Kim Yong-il was enthusiastic about the social sciences as well as the electronics-related subjects he had studied. Unlike his elder brother Pyong-il, he had never been a political threat. But like Pyong-il he found that people avoided him. Rather than going abroad he was spending his days in his Pyongyang mansion, do-ing history. His one friend, by Kang's account, was O Il-su, O Jin-u's son. The two had studied together in East Germany.[30]

Hwang Jang-yop, who had left the Central Committee in 1965, returned in 1979 to find that the tone at the political heart of the country had changed drastically. Hwang's close, sustained involvement with both Kims makes him one of the most important witnesses to the inner workings of the regime. His testimony after he defected to South Korea in 1997 was largely favorable in its appraisal of the way Kim Il-sung had run things up through the 1960s and beyond. But from 1974, when the Great Leader designated his son as heir, Hwang's portrayal shows the country heading for disaster. The reason was partly a change in Kim Il-sung himself, who from that time "became increas-ingly conceited and turned sloppy in his work."[31]

But the main problem, as Hwang discovered, was Kim Jong-il's man-agement style and, ultimately, his personality. Hwang had worked from 1958 to 1965 as party secretary for ideology. "At that time, Kim Il-sung's younger brother Kim Yong-ju was in charge of party affairs. But when I returned to the central committee in 1979 as the party central secretary, it was Kim Jong-il who was running the show. I was shocked by the numerous changes that had taken place during my long absence. Life in the central party before had been filled with joy and pride at working at the heart of the nation's brain power, but life in the very same organization after my return was filled with unease and tension. I was constantly on my toes, fearful of getting hurt by the highly-charged wire of dictatorship so close at hand."

Highly intensified surveillance even of top-ranking officials was one big change that Hwang immediately noticed. He found that a new headquarters party committee "specifically charged with controlling the lives of workers in the party central committee" had been established under Kim Jong-il, "various departments within it controlling the organizational or ideological lives of the party officials or carrying out secret intelligence activities." Thenceforth, "the lives of workers in the party central committee were placed under two- to three-fold scrutiny and control at all times."

Another thing Hwang noticed was a change in the style and tone of Central Committee meetings. In the earlier days when Kim Il-sung presided he "gave many positive examples to encourage the participants and refrained from too much criticism. He always emphasized that strengthening the positive could overcome the negative. In contrast, Kim Jong-il focused on criticizing bad points and encouraging mutual criticism among participants. It is only when a meeting is conducted in this manner that he claims that the meeting went well amid a revolutionary mood. Those who refrain from criticizing others during meetings are denounced because of their lack of revolutionary attitude, whereas those who loudly and harshly criticize others are praised for their revolutionary zeal and loyalty to the Great Leader."

Hwang wrote that "Kim Jong-il is by nature a person who does not like living in harmony with others. He makes people fight against each other and depend only on him. Thus, when he talks about strengthening the organization, he means making strict rules to guarantee unconditional obedience to him and holding more meetings for officials to criticize each other. During mutual denunciation sessions, the yardstick used is the degree of one's loyalty to Kim Jong-il. So the more party members criticize each other and fight among themselves, the greater Kim Jong-il's authority becomes."

At the mutual denunciation sessions, said Hwang, "even the smallest defect is blown out of proportions into a serious incident," providing fodder for more elaborate "grand debates and ideological struggle rallies" to come. Then, "after making people bicker among themselves, Kim Jong-il would sit back and enjoy the fight." His pattern was to repair to his office and watch on closed circuit television as his underlings laid into each other. Hwang came to believe that Kim actually took pleasure in harassing party officials.[32]

Kim Il-sung had done business mainly through face-to-face encounters, Hwang reported. But Kim Jong-il, having turned the meetings into loyalty tests, switched to doing actual business through paperwork. "Kim Jong-il established a system of getting each department to submit policy recommendations, which he would approve before implementation. It was a strict system, especially when it came to new or basic issues, which could never see the light of day unless the recommendations were submitted for his approval. This was a system that hardly existed during Kim Il-sung's rule."

It was not exactly the lazy man's approach to governing. "No matter how busy he was, Kim Jong-il would personally read all the recommendations submitted and provide his comments or conclusions," said Hwang. "For important documents submitted personally by the party secretaries, he would put the approved documents in his special envelope, write the recipient's name on it, and seal it before passing it to the secretary in charge. All this constitutes a huge workload, but Kim Jong-il never passes this work to someone else but handles it personally."

Kim instituted a simple system of priorities regarding his rulings on the documents submitted to him, Hwang said. "Those with Kim Jong-il's signature and date of approval written on it by Kim Jong-il himself become legal documents that must be put into action at all costs. A document with only the date of approval on it is returned to the bureau that submitted it, and the bureau can see to its execution at its discretion. A document that has neither date nor signature but only two lines means that it does not matter one way or other; it is up to the bureau that submitted it to execute or cancel the plan. Besides these weekly reports, important bureaus fax papers to Kim Jong-il whenever necessary to gain his approval."

Like others who had worked in the higher levels of the regime, Hwang noted Kim Jong-il's penchant for holding drinking parties. But Hwang put them in context as "an important element in Kim Jong-il's style of politics," not merely a recreational outlet. "He throws such parties frequently, and summons artists to perform in them. These parties were probably the means through which Kim Jong-il formed his group of vassals. By inviting his trusted subordinates to a party, he can observe their personalities at close range and imbue them with pride at being close attendants of the Great Leader. But since it is a drinking party, it is often the case that those who enjoy drinking are invited more often than others. Sometimes, gossip or passing remarks at these parties can become official policies the next day. At these drinking parties, those who get drunk only need to be respectful to Kim Jong-il; they can say anything they like to anyone regardless of his title. So in a way, Kim Jong-il's system of sole leadership is strictly implemented at these parties."

Although the parties had a business function from Kim's point of view, they inevitably led to some drunken policy making. Kim at his parties would occasionally issue orders so odd that they could not be carried out, Hwang said. "Kim Jong-il is more than capable of making quick and accurate calculations guided by self-interest, but he is also fickle and impatient, resulting in spontaneous and irrational instructions. For example, he commanded everyone who went on overseas business trips to wear watches made in the watch factories of Pyongyang as a mark of North Korea's self-reliant economy. But the problem was that the watches made in Pyongyang were of very low quality, and so everyone was reluctant to wear them when traveling abroad. He also gave instructions for women to wear the traditional Korean costume in black and white, but no one follows these instructions except the women working in the party Central Committee."

The fact that Kim insisted on giving personal approval to every policy did not deter him from punishing whoever had proposed a policy that eventually caused him regret, Hwang observed. "There was once when the manager in charge of documenting the Great Leader's instructions at the Organization and Guidance Bureau got the professors of Kim Il-sung University to write a fifteen-volume [set of] Kim Jong-il literature (100 percent fake, of course) in order to publicize that Kim Jong-il was an industrious ideologist even as a student. The manager submitted every draft for Kim Jong-il's approval before publication. But later, when it was pointed out that the works could end up strengthening the authority of one individual [other than himself], Kim Jong-il punished the manager and the professors who authored the works, and ordered that the contents be completely revised."

One difference between the two Kims that Hwang noticed concerned formality. As we have seen, Kim Il-sung from his partisan days expected obedience from his subordinates. Still, the elder Kim was not one to insist on elaborate, needless formalilty, Hwang said. "But Kim Jong-il has initiated numerous formalities to guarantee the people's absolute obedience to the Great Leader. Whenever there are important functions or events, he would get people to pay their utmost respect to the Great Leader by writing and offering up grand speeches swearing allegiance to the Great Leader or congratulating him. He also ordered ceremonies for people to lay wreaths at the foot of Kim Il-sung's statue or at the martyrs' tomb. Every festive occasion, workers are made to hold 'pledge gatherings,' where they start the gatherings with songs exalting first Kim Il-sung and then Kim Jong-il and end the gatherings with songs wishing the two Kims long life and good health."

In these circumstances, North Koreans must "hold frequent meetings just to write up pledges of loyalty or letters of gratitude to the Great Leader," Hwang said. "On the night of New Year's Eve, a year-end party is held on a national scale. Kim Jong-il does not attend this official party but holds his own private one with his regular party-goers and cohorts. Then at 12 midnight or dawn of New Year's Day, he would fax out to each bureau director a brief New Year greeting along the lines of, 'Everyone worked hard last year. Let us work even harder to achieve greater victory this year.' Consequently, the bureau directors must report for work even on New Year's Day to hold ceremonies to receive Kim Jong-il's message and send a suitable reply in the form of resolutions or pledges of loyalty. That is the way Kim Jong-il prefers to do things."

Two of Kim Jong-il's least attractive qualities, Hwang found, were secretiveness and jealousy. "Whenever there is a gathering, Kim Jong-il always emphasizes two things. One is keeping the party's secrets, and the other is refraining from pinning one's hopes on any individual official. This is a reflection of Kim Jong-il's personality; he prefers secrecy to openness, and is jealous of other people's good fortune." The secretiveness might have had something to do with Kim Jong-il's well-known penchant for staying out of the public eye. "Kim Jong-il does not like to meet people on official business or

make public speeches, and prefers gathering his cohorts for parties to holding official functions. He prefers working at night to working in the day."

Kim Jong-il's "pathological" jealousy was another quality not shared
with his late father, Hwang said. "Kim Il-sung was not jealous of subordinates who were loyal to him. He disliked conceited people, but he was never
jealous of those who were faithful to him just because they had the public's
trust. But in the case of Kim Jong-il, he becomes jealous of even his loyal
subordinates if they gain popularity among the masses. He even dislikes the
good fortune of other countries, and becomes jealous of leaders in other
countries who are known to be popular with the people. This trait may well
be closely related to his thoroughly egotistic viewpoint of ideology."

Kim found a curious way of justifying his jealousy in ideological terms.
As Hwang related, Kim "says that he opposes the worship of any individual.
He is the Great Leader of the people and therefore not an individual, but the
rest of the party officials are considered individuals since they are not the
Great Leader. For example, if a party secretary in charge of a certain district
wins the confidence of the residents, he will surely get the secretary replaced.
And from time to time, he would purge officials by labeling them anti-
revolutionaries who induce illusions about individuals."

Whether it was out of jealousy or simple security concerns or both,
Hwang noted that "Kim Jong-il forbids any relationship that does not re-
volve around him. He condemns family orientation or regionalism as hotbeds
of sectarianism, and opposes all forms of socializing including class reunions.
He is even against people forming bonds based on teacher-student or senior-
junior relationships. He demands that people maintain close relationships
with those close to the Great Leader and keep those not close to the Great
Leader at arm's length. He also set up thorough measures to marginalize certain people such as his step-siblings born of Kim Il-sung's second wife from
the power circle and to keep them from relating to the masses. Not a few people were stripped of their titles and expelled for accepting gifts or letters from
Kim Jong-il's step-siblings. So even ordinary people avoid anyone blacklisted for marginalization."

The corollary was deference due to Kim's own household, Hwang reported. "Kim Jong-il becomes furious when his loved ones are not given the
hospitality due them. He loves the dancing troupe that entertains him. The
dancers are meant only for Kim Jong-il's eyes, but when in a generous mood,
he would allow Party Central Committee members to watch the performances. There was once when he ordered an ideological struggle rally because the party officials did not clap hard enough during a performance.
After that incident, party officials who attend performances by Kim Jong-il's
favorite artists make sure that they clap long and loud. They have to keep up
the applause through several curtain calls and can only leave their seats
when the performers no longer respond to their applause."

As for Kim Jong-il's secretiveness, it may have been justified by fear of the consequences in case his secrets were revealed. Kim "has cruelly killed countless people," Hwang asserted. "His worst fear is having these crimes exposed. Thus he says that 'keeping secrets is the essence of life in the party,' and forbids everyone from revealing anything more than what is reported in the papers. He has forbidden the wives of party officials holding positions any higher than vice-director from holding a job for fear that they would leak party secrets while at work."[33]

Without giving names or the date, Hwang offered a horrifying example of the intersection between secretiveness and killing: "One of Kim Jong-il's secretaries got drunk once and told his wife about Kim Jong-il's life of debauchery. The good wife, a woman of high cultural and moral standards, was genuinely shocked, and thought, 'How can a leader who leads such an immoral life safeguard the happiness of his people?' After much thought, she decided to write a letter to Kim Il-sung asking him to reprimand his son. Needless to say, the letter went to Kim Jong-il, who threw a drinking party and had the woman arrested and brought before him. In front of all the guests at the party, he pronounced the woman a counterrevolutionary and had her shot on the spot. Kim Jong-il's intention was to issue a warning to those present that leaking whatever went on at drinking parties would be punishable by death. The poor woman's husband actually begged Kim Jong-il to let him do the shooting. Kim Jong-il granted the secretary his wish, and gave him the weapon to shoot his wife."[34]

In 1979, the coast apparently clear, official pronouncements resumed their mention of the "Glorious Party Center." Still, when I visited North Korea that spring I found that questions about Kim Jong-il were discouraged. Only one official, the forthright Bai Song-chul, would confirm for me that the younger Kim was being groomed to succeed his father. While his portraits reportedly had reappeared in some public places, those did not include the usual sites visited by foreigners. Evidently the regime wished to avoid stirring up foreign criticism of the dynastic succession scheme, perhaps because the plan still needed some tidying up.[35]

So well did Pyongyang hide its cards during my visit at the time of the 1979 table tennis tournament that I had almost no idea of the enormous extent to which the country already bore the imprint of Kim Jong-il. In fact the younger Kim had exerted major influence for fifteen years already, and had served as co-ruler for five years. The economic achievements I was permitted to see were, it is true, largely those of the father, displayed shortly after they had peaked. But I realized only much later that what I had observed of North Korea's cultural life—including the extreme form that the personality cult had taken—was largely the work of the son.

It was May of 1980 before an on-the-record acknowledgment to the outside world of the plans for Kim Jong-il's future came from a spokesman for North Korea. Meeting foreign journalists, Choe U-gyun, editor of pro-Pyongyang newspapers published in Tokyo, attacked what he called the Western mass-media view that the younger Kim's accession to power would be a case of "hereditary" succession. "We understand hereditary succession normally means takeover of power by foolish, spoiled offspring," Choe said. But Kim Jong-il, he said, "is a brilliant leader. He is possessed of excellent leadership qualities in terms of policy decision-making. Not only that, he is possessed of moral integrity worthy of an excellent leader. He is endowed with unrivaled leadership capability over economic affairs, political affairs, cultural affairs and over even military affairs."

Choe extended the catalog of virtues of the junior Kim even further, piling on the sort of praise long associated with Kim Il-sung himself as he listed such a blinding array of qualities as to make dissent by ordinary mortals unthinkable. He focused especially on Kim Jong-il's artistic achievements. The Pyongyang Art Theater Troupe was then visiting Tokyo, Choe noted. Among its members, "many of those musicians and dancers, magicians and jugglers received the personal guidance of Kim Jong-il." The younger Kim even invented a system of notation for prescribing the dancers' movements, Choe said. "He's also an excellent film director — maybe something like Hitchcock but of a different genre. Lenin is credited with fostering and training and inspiring Russian novelist Gorky, but Kim Jong-il is doing a similar job."

Attending that briefing, I attempted to listen respectfully and keep a straight face during Choe's recital of Kim Jong-il's virtues. I found it a bit much, though, and finally I could not resist asking, irreverently, whether the junior Kim could juggle and dance at the same time. Choe did not answer directly, but said simply that a great composer is never the best singer, and that Alfred Hitchcock, although a great director, was never a great actor.[36]

By the time of the sixth party congress in October of 1980, Public Security Minister Li Jin-su was able to announce: "In the course of our struggle against the anti-revolutionary elements, the extremely few antagonistic elements were completely isolated." Next, he said, the regime would rally the public and "shatter" those "antagonistic elements"—presumably the opponents of the succession plan.[37] By then, according to a former high-ranking official, anyone Kim Jong-il was unable to control had been completely isolated. The elder forces knew what their role would be and were prepared not to interfere in Kim Jong-il's role.[38]

A party congress provided a rare chance for Pyongyang-watchers abroad to catch up on the relative rankings of officials. One interesting change: Kim Song-ae, Kim Il-sung's official wife and the mother of Kim Pyong-il, was demoted from number 67 on the 1970 party Central Committee membership list to number 105 in 1980.

In the competition to glorify and cater to the aging Great Leader, supreme flatterer Kim Jong-il had emerged as the winner, hands down. "Among Kim Il-sung's children he was the one who got his father's trust," a former North Korean diplomat explained to me many years later. "He supported Kim Il-sung's deification."

Reflecting his victory, at the same congress Kim Jong-il was elected to the five-person presidium of the politburo and became a member of the party military commission, chaired by his father. Celebrating this decision, *Nodong Shinmun* in a pre-Christmas editorial offered foreigners a pair of replacements for the father and son of the Christian trinity. "People of the world, if you are looking for miracles, come to Korea!" the paper urged. "Christians, do not go to Jerusalem. Come rather to Korea. Do not believe in God. Believe in the great man." At the party congress that had made the junior Kim's heirship official, "the cheers shaking heaven and earth . . . were an explosion of our people's joy, looking up at the star of guidance [Kim Jong-il] shining together with the benevolent sun [Kim Il-sung]."[39]

Cheer as they might, designating Kim Jong-il the heir was to prove "very costly," as scholar Lee Manwoo has observed, since "much of North Korea's inflexibility and isolation is due to this decision."[40] Hwang Jang-yop put it this way: "It is clear that Kim Jong-il's dictatorship is cruel and that he has a remarkable aptitude for it. It is with this remarkable aptitude that he ruined his own father, North Korean society and the naive people who follow him. I cannot help but worry that eventually, his aptitude for dictatorship will end up ruining South Koreans and foreigners and bring unprecedented tragedy to the 70 million compatriots on the Korean peninsula."[41] Hwang probably was too kind to Kim Il-sung. The elder Kim's policies were largely responsible for the disasters that were soon to befall North Koreans. But it is true that, by hewing to his father's policies, by ruthlessly cutting down anyone who suggested a new approach, Kim Jong-il ensured the ruination of the country.

SIXTEEN

Our Earthly Paradise Free
from Oppression

Woe betide any North Korean suspected of "behavior that runs counter to the will of the Great Leader." As one former party official wrote, "you are stripped of your titles or expelled from school . . . and you are chased out of your house."[1] Hundreds of thousands of North Koreans found themselves banished to the remote countryside because their devotion was deemed unsatisfactory.

Far worse would lie in store if one should be found guilty of serious disloyalty. During one of his purges of the suspected opponents of one-man rule, Kim Il-sung warned "factionalists" that their actions "will destroy three generations of a family."[2] He and his son made good on that threat. Over decades, the regime executed uncounted critics. Politically incorrect North Koreans sent to prisons and concentration camps numbered in the hundreds of thousands, perhaps in the millions.[3] In the typical case, family members including small children, spouses and elderly parents shared in the punishment given anyone identified as an enemy of the regime. For many political prisoners, the expectation—and the fact—was that they would never return from the North Korean gulag. They would die from overwork and hunger, or be shot for trying to escape.[4]

The regime set up an array of incarceration facilities, starting with detention centers for locking up citizens deemed to have broken relatively minor rules. Failure to get permission before boarding a train and being absent from work were typical of the offenses that could land a citizen in a detention center. Terms of one or two years in reformatories were reserved for heavier criminal offenses such as theft, assault and slander (as well as escaping across the Chinese border in search of food, which became common when shortages reached famine levels in the 1990s). In the reformatories, otherwise known as labor drill units, officials used harsh discipline and hard labor to attempt to "re-educate" the inmates. Regular prisons received general offenders sentenced to more than two years. The Ministry of Public Security, the general police agency, was assigned to administer the detention centers, reformatories and regular prisons.

The Ministry of State Security was put in charge of most of the facilities designed to get really tough with major political offenders. That secret police and intelligence agency was given responsibility for political prisons as well as concentration camps housing "factionalists" and other people deemed opponents of the party, the revolution or the leader. Offenders who were not executed or placed in noncamp prisons would be sent to camps. Families of offenders also would be sent to the camps, accompanied or not by the offenders depending on the fate of the latter. In one type of concentration camp, eventual release might be possible. Facilities in a second, no-hope and no-exit, category could be described as slow-death camps.[5]

Architect-engineer Kim Young-song tasted punishment at the milder end of the scale when he was sent to work in the mines in 1974. Afterward, until his 1992 defection to South Korea, he lived with the fear that he and his family would end up dying in a political prison or concentration camp. Family background was his initial problem, he told me. "We were intellectuals. Father taught at elementary school. I had five older brothers. Four attended university." While the regime encouraged education, it suspected educated people—especially pre-liberation white-collar families.

Fifty-nine years old when I interviewed him, intense and bespectacled, Kim impressed me with his obvious intelligence as well as his sardonic worldview. "I was put under surveillance for thirty years," he told me with a sort of disgusted relish. And what did the watchers find? He laughed derisively at my question and replied, "Nothing. Everybody's watching each other in North Korea."

Kim Young-song wanted to join the army when he turned seventeen in 1951, "but I wasn't tall enough yet, so I studied in Pyongyang from late 1951 to the summer of 1952. I was with my eldest brother there, so I got a food ration. In 1952, I went to Czechoslovakia to continue my studies. I couldn't go straight to university then because I didn't have a high school diploma. I attended a specialized training school, got great marks and went on to the university in Prague. It took me about two years to learn Czech. I studied architecture and engineering, and stayed from 1952 to late 1959."

During that time, in 1956, his eldest brother went to study in Leningrad—
just in time to watch Khrushchev lambaste the recently dead Stalin for his
personality cult. Picking up on that theme, the brother joined some friends in
criticizing Kim Il-sung's Stalin-style personality cult and his increasingly
one-man rule. "That got him executed," Kim told me. The brother "wasn't an
activist in the movement, just a scholar. But his friends were involved in politics. When they were executed, so was he, in 1958."[6]

In Czechoslovakia Kim Young-song was placed under special "ideological monitoring" as his brother's case progressed. In 1958 North Korea wanted
to call all foreign exchange students home to keep from exposing them further
to ideas that might be dangerous to the regime. "They told me, 'You're studying construction. You should see the work on Chollima Street.'" But a North
Korean official in need of an interpreter went to Czechoslovakia that year and
the student was kept on to help him. "The next year there was a lot of conflict.
Some questioned my ideology, but others said I was smart and my knowledge
should be put to use. They didn't want to irritate the Czech government."

When he finally returned to Pyongyang at the beginning of 1960, Kim
Young-song was "attacked on ideological grounds," he said. "First they wanted
to send me to a construction project in a rural area. That year they had a special session of ideological criticism of students who had returned from abroad.
That time, luckily, I was not kicked out. There was still a case backlog of people with ideas unpalatable to the regime—religious believers, families of people
who had defected to South Korea, the old elite class, people involved in trade
and commerce. During the late 1950s the regime started getting rid of them. I
had a couple of advantages. First, one brother had been killed in the Korean
War. Second, I was part of the new elite, educated under the Kim Il-sung
regime. Those assets helped drag my case out for fourteen years."

Kim Young-song's work in Pyongyang "involved pre-cast concrete and
the standardization of buildings. If you plan a few buildings at once, you can
standardize materials use. I was in charge of saying which materials went
where. From 1969, I was involved in planning and building the buildings on
one side of Chollima Street next to the Potong River: the Choson Arts and
Culture Center, Choson Documentary Movie Center and Pyongyang City
Stadium. Chollima Street was built for the fifth Party meeting [in 1970].
Just for that meeting they made us construct thirty buildings of ten stories
each. We built them in ten days. That epitomized construction in North Korea. But I didn't think that much about it. It was the peak of construction activity. After that, it was downhill all the way."

Kim Jong-il had not fully taken over the construction industry at that
time. "He didn't start running all construction until 1975, by which time I
had been kicked out," Kim Young-song told me. "But he was involved in the
Pyongyang Arts and Culture Center as something like the owner. He had to
OK the construction plans. I didn't meet him. Whenever Kim Jong-il was on

his way, we had to leave the place. They never said, 'Kim Jong-il is coming.'
They just said, 'We have some foreign films.' So everyone would go in and
watch them. While we were inside he would come and go." Those who didn't
get to see the Dear Leader were excluded "for security, basically, and proto-
col," Kim Young-song said. "Only the highest officials and the most beautiful
actresses would greet him."

All through his fourteen years in Pyongyang authorities watched the
architect-engineer closely because he had worked abroad and, mainly, because his family during and after the war had shown divided loyalties. "My
first and second brothers had socialist ideals, but the eldest nonetheless was
executed. The third committed suicide during the Korean War. The fourth
and fifth defected because of their capitalist ideals. So even though I was a
member of the new-era elite, they didn't really trust me. That was the period
of what I call the quiet cultural revolution in North Korea. If your background was not good enough, you would be banished to a remote area. I believe the North Korean version was more brutal than the Chinese Cultural
Revolution. It was just much less publicized. By the late 1970s, everyone
who might seem to be a threat to the Kim regime had been purged."

In all the purges, "the basic principle was survival of one-man rule," Kim
Young-song told me. "From the mid-'50s to the mid-'60s Kim Il-sung was getting rid of other factions. After that he worked on forming a base for his one-
man rule. Kim Jong-il started getting power, and a new group of his fanatic
loyalists appeared. They were not well educated, but rather people who had
gotten honors in the military and for otherwise sacrificing themselves for the
Kim regime. In this period there was little or no regard for education. The really harsh period started in 1967, the year they sought one-man, totalitarian
rule in earnest and set the foundation for Kim Jong-il's succession to power."

Kim Young-song rattled off a brief history of the later purges. "From
1967 for a decade or so, new groupings opposed to Kim Jong-il's succession
appeared. The first consisted of people who had helped Kim Il-sung establish
his own one-man rule. When Kim Jong-il appeared on the scene in 1967 or
so, they were angry: 'How dare that young boy take the second position in
power?' Then someone would report them and they would be purged. O Jin-
u was one of those who ratted. Kim Yong-ju had to be sent to a highly securi-
tized mansion—under virtual house arrest—because Kim Jong-il was chosen
over him as successor. Kim Jong-il's stepmother, too, Kim Song-ae, and her
children—relatives perceived as posing a threat were put under house arrest.
Nonrelatives were sent to their deaths along with their families. Kim Dong-
kyu of the party political bureau and Kim Chang-bong, a minister, fell into the
latter category. They and their families were sent to concentration camps,
where they were expected to die within two or three years. That was the procedure for higher-ranking people; ordinary people would be sent to the mines.
By the late 1970s, all opposition to Kim Jong-il was removed."

I asked Kim Young-song how an architect-engineer would know all those details of the palace intrigues. "It was common knowledge," he replied. "Everybody in the country knew it. That's how the Kim regime survives: everyone hears of such things and is frightened for his life. In the case of my older brother who was executed, all four of his children and his wife were sent to political prison. There has been no word from them for forty years. They probably died there. There is never an instance where families are not punished also."

The regime finally got around to punishing Kim Young-song.

"If you have experience overseas, or enough intelligence to think about the regime, or you're part of the old elite, you're put under surveillance of a very active sort," he told me. "They keep making you talk so you'll slip up and make a mistake. Many times I made little mistakes. Such minor slips of the tongue aren't too big a problem. Lots of people were watching me, but there were also a lot of people trying to help me because I was hard-working and good at my job. I was probably forgiven five or six times more than the usual person would have been. I never did anything wrong. It's just that for ten years they were purging people, and they finally got to me. When they did, it was for old reasons—my bad family background. Up until then I had taken on very important construction jobs. But they started giving me less and less important work. I figured my time was coming. One day State Security called me in and told me, 'A train leaves tomorrow for the mines. Get your things together and be on it with your family.'"

The moment Kim Young-song had dreaded came on August 26, 1974. "I went with my wife and three daughters. We were sent to a mine near the Tumen River. I worked as a janitor in the area. My wife worked in food service. State Security gave me no explanation at all. Once each spring and once each autumn they would send about 4,500 people out of Pyongyang without explanation. The place we were banished to wasn't a political prison. They didn't expect me to die from being sent there, but just to stay in that limited area and lead a very passive life. When I went to a city in the area, I met a lot of political exiles who had been sent there more than twenty years earlier from places like Pyongyang, Kaesong and Haeju."

After about five years, Kim Young-song told me, he "got very lucky." A technocrat colleague from Pyongyang was sent to North Hamgyong Province as governor. "He worked things out and got me a job in the construction engineering department of Chongjin District. There was in fact no construction going on in Chongjin. Most of the construction money was spent in Pyongyang. There was no need to build anything in Chongjin. The country had barely enough construction materials, fuel and vehicles to keep building things in Pyongyang. I was based in Chongjin until 1989 and kept my family there, but I also went around the country—mostly to Pyongyang—helping at construction sites." Villas for the leaders Great and Dear (see chapter 10) were the main exception to the Pyongyang-only pattern of construction work.

The construction industry to which Kim Young-song returned was now under Kim Jong-il's supervision. The architect-engineer found that things had changed. "Up until then, all the buildings were plain, boxy structures. Kim Jong-il asked for more intricate buildings. That led to problems not only with construction but with materials." One building that Kim Young-song worked on in Pyongyang adjoined a 105-story structure Kim Jong-il ordered built in an effort to boast of the world's tallest hostelry. "That project shows the limitation of Kim Jong-il's involvement in the construction business," he said. "Until now, whatever Kim Jong-il ordered was done. But I believe that 105-story hotel will never be completed."

I had heard that workers, piling up masonry story by story (the building had no steel frame), had not built the hotel straight enough vertically for elevators to be installed—that it was out of plumb, in builders' terminology. But Kim Young-song said that wasn't the problem. "They can put in elevators. If it's a bit off plumb we just bend the equipment a little," he said with a grin. "The problem is the shortage of funds. They don't have the foreign currency to import the air conditioners, windows, lights, fixtures, etc. North Korea has the natural resources to build the framework of such a structure, but it must import everything else."

I asked him: Do North Koreans laugh at Kim Jong-il over this failure?

"No," he replied. "They just say, 'That's the way life is here.' There are so many laughable things. If you laughed at them all, you'd be tired."

I asked architect Kim what percentage of construction work was for show as opposed to being useful for people's lives. "There is construction work only in Pyongyang, and the purpose of Pyongyang is showing off," he said. "After things are built for show, though, they often are useful." For the 1989 World Festival of Youth and Students, an extravagant North Korean attempt to outshine the 1988 Seoul Olympics, Kim Young-song "worked on a thirty-story round building on Kwangbok Avenue and a department store, also on Kwangbok Avenue, plus the table tennis gymnasium for the festival." By the time the festival opened, the new housing wasn't ready to be used as such in many cases—"only the exterior structures were in place." And even after the highrise apartment buildings were completed, "because of the electrical shortage the elevators operate two hours in the morning, two hours in the afternoon, two hours at night. At other times, you just walk up and down. A special man is in charge of elevators." (After this interview the electrical shortage worsened and elevator service reportedly ceased entirely in many buildings.)

Kim Young-song got one more chance to go abroad for the regime. "In 1989 the North Korean government was sending students to East Germany to learn computers. They needed an interpreter. I knew German very well. They made me a party member and sent me to Germany. I was there three years. I didn't have much change in my mentality. I was just leading my life as I had done in Czechoslovakia thirty years before. Nothing had changed. There were just more cars.

"But I committed a slip of the tongue and found myself fleeing for my life. In North Korea if you tell 100 percent truth you have to die. The one big slip of the tongue I committed was to say, 'East Germany is a basic example of a true communist nation, but look how poorly off they are. Probably the capitalist nations are better off than this.' I said it to trustworthy colleagues and friends while in North Korea on my annual two months' vacation leave. Trustworthy colleagues told their trustworthy colleagues, word spread and the police started investigating.

"I realized my treatment by friends was different. They started turning their backs on me. Really close friends said, 'Why vacation so long? Go back and do your work.' They didn't want me to slip up again. But on two different vacation trips I slipped up and said something wrong, and my surveillance was increased. I think when I got back to Germany the last time there was an order to return me to North Korea. The attitude of the man in charge of North Koreans in East Germany changed. He had been very lenient. But, after a while, whenever I went anywhere he went with me — even to the grocery store. In Germany when I watched TV he would be outside listening, then he would just open the door and come in. My next vacation was due in three months, but this supervisor said, 'Let's go earlier. Let's go now.' "

I asked Kim Young-song why he had been so concerned. I had heard that the punishment for saying that things might be better in capitalist countries was minor, only a month or two in prison. "Maybe sons of prominent high officials get small punishments," he replied. "But with my family background and history of trouble, a big slip would finish me. The people who were able to tell you about the lighter punishment are probably part of the family of Kim or close to State Security officials. The biggest difference between me and other defectors is that they made little mistakes, got scared and defected, while I was under surveillance for thirty years. This mistake would have been the end of me. I would have gone to prison and died there. Take the case of one of the students who studied overseas, returned to North Korea, went to a store, looked at the underwear made in North Korea and said, 'A person should wear *this* as underwear?' He was sent to political prison."

Kim's escape was made relatively easy by the fact that Germany had reunified the year following his arrival. "So I basically lived in a free country. I could defect any time, just get a cab and run away as fast as I could. I've been told by the South Korean authorities not to give details, but, briefly, I went through southern Germany. I thought of going to the South Korean consulate in Berlin, but North Korea had an embassy there so I thought it was too dangerous. The escape itself was unadventurous, though. I just got up earlier than usual one day, got my bag and left."

The unsettling part was abandoning his family back in North Korea. "I figured if I went back they would go to prison with me," Kim told me. Did that mean things were no worse for them than if he had gone back to face the music? "I can't say yes or no," he replied. "If I agree, it seems I'm rationalizing the abandonment of my family."

Kim took a pessimistic view both of his former country's future and of his new country's capacity for dealing with it. "North Korea will never change," he said. "The tragedy of South Koreans is believing that North Korea will change. There are three groups in South Korea. One group thinks, 'North Korea will change'; the second, 'North Korea is changing'; and the third, 'I will make North Korea change.' You seem to understand me," he told me, "but South Koreans don't seem to understand what I've been through. South Koreans actually believe North Korea will change."

He said he saw no way to get Kim Il-sung and Kim Jong-il out of power so that change could take place, without war. "The North Korean regime is a very brutal one. There may be internal problems, but they have the ability, the power and the brutality to suppress them." I mentioned the American plan to start Radio Free Asia, which would broadcast news of North Korea into North Korea in the Korean language. It might help a little, he thought. "It wouldn't affect ordinary people but could affect high officials. I don't see any negative aspects in influencing at least some people." The people knew that high officials under Kim Il-sung and Kim Jong-il were not the only ones responsible for all that went wrong, he said. "They just can't name Kim father and son as the reasons for their harsh lives, so they talk as if they blamed only the other high officials." In the case of the some ten thousand members of State Security, however, blame was cast sincerely. "If the regime collapses, the ten thousand are gone. People hate them so much. The radio service wouldn't affect them, but other high officials will listen. Changing a little can be positive."

Probably it is necessary to look beyond Korea to find whatever "factionalism" might have brought ruin upon three generations of Kang Te-hyu's family. Kang was one of the ethnically Korean returnees from Japan. In Kyoto, he had run a lucrative *pachinko* business. Although his wealth came from a capitalistic enterprise in Japan, Kang was a devout socialist who wore his Korean patriotism on his sleeve. Before moving his family to the communist motherland in 1963, he ran the trade and commerce unit of Japan's Pyongyang-directed Korean residents' association, Chongryon. His wife headed Chongryon's Kyoto women's group.

When the family moved to North Korea Kang gave his wealth to the state, to the tune of several million dollars. Indeed, his grandson told me, it was Kang who donated the funds to build the gigantic statue of Kim Il-sung in Pyongyang to which visitors were urged to present flowers—the statue that was golden for a while before being bronzed in reported response to Deng Xiaoping's expression of distaste.

Kang and his family rated a royal red-carpet welcome. He became vice-director of a government unit that supplied goods for department stores. His wife became a member of the Supreme People's Assembly. Kang had four sons and two daughters. The family lived well in the communist capital.

In Pyongyang at the time, Kang's grandson Kang Chul-hwan told me, "it would have been rare to find anyone with a car, but we had a Volvo. We were what you would call bourgeois even though Grandfather ideologically was very much a socialist. A Japanese reporter got a photo of our family, taken in 1966 as Kim Il-sung propaganda, and sent it to the Japanese press to show the family was living well."

That was two years before Kang Chul-hwan's birth as son of patriarch Kang's eldest son. Chul-hwan's father, in keeping with East Asian custom, remained in the elder Kang's household after going to work as a photographer, marrying another ethnic Korean from Japan and starting a family that eventually included Chul-hwan and a younger daughter. Chul-hwan recalled that the family had lived an "extravagant" life by North Korean standards— until they were imprisoned.

"We lived well," Kang Chul-hwan told me. "We lived in central Pyongyang and went to the schools attended by the children of the elite. My three uncles went to Kim Il-sung University." Not being the firstborn, the uncles as they married established separate households.

After a while, the North Korean authorities began to find it inconvenient to host the returnees from Japan and started banishing them to remote areas or sending them to camps or prisons. Fifteen years after his arrival, the elder Kang's turn came. "Grandfather was taken away at the time when the regime was getting rid of Koreans from Japan," Chul-hwan told me. "He was one of the last taken away. We didn't know what they did with him." The grandson explained that conflicts had arisen broadly because "the Korean residents of Japan who returned to North Korea were not used to a closed society. They often badmouthed what they saw—and got penalized for it. But in Grandfather's case we speculate that it was opposition to Han Duk-su, chairman of the Chongryon back in Japan, that got him in trouble."

When the grandfather was taken away, Kang Chul-hwan told me, "they sent the rest of the household including me and my youngest uncle to a concentration camp. The married aunts and uncles weren't sent to the camp, but they were expelled from Pyongyang and sent to mountainous areas in the north. They became coal miners there, at Musangun, North Hamgyong Province. My family and I were sent to the camp at Yodok. There was a separate complex there for people who had migrated from foreign countries, including Japan and Russia. We were assigned there."

Only nine at the time, Chul-hwan at first "thought I was going on something like a family camping trip. It was the first time I had seen mountains. I thought they were beautiful. But when I saw the gates with armed guards, they reminded me of a Japanese concentration camp I had seen in a movie about the evil Japanese and I thought, 'Oh! Are there such camps in Korea?' I thought only the cruel Japanese would do such a thing. I was so surprised to hear that the Beloved Fatherly Leader would build a camp so cruel. We asked why we were sent there and they said, 'Oh, you did a very wicked thing. You should be punished to death. But thanks to the benevolence of the Great Leader you are being allowed to live.' They never explained what we were accused of, but lots of Korean former residents of Japan were there and they speculated it was because Grandfather opposed Han Duk-su's chairmanship of Chongryon."

Chul-hwan attended the camp school. "The school was not for education, though," he told me. "It was for brainwashing. They weren't real teachers. They were all sent from State Security. We didn't have regular courses but they taught us courses on Kim Il-sung's revolutionary history and his thought." Even though he was a prisoner, Kang Chul-hwan believed what he was taught, for a while. "After junior high, I started to turn against Kim Il-sung. But when you're young, you believe the propaganda. Parents can't say anything, because little kids would blab and the parents would get in trouble."

Whenever the young prisoners were not being indoctrinated, Kang Chul-hwan told me, "we were used as forced labor. The principal gave us a speech: 'Your parents are political criminals, but thanks to the benevolence of the Great Leader the government is being very generous to you. It will educate you even though your parents did terrible things. To repay this generosity, you must work very hard for the country.' We had to go out and gather firewood, and also medicinal herbs that could be exported for foreign exchange. We went to the mountains to search for thick, old trees that could be cut down, and we had to help with the farming."

Brutality was the rule in the camp, Kang Chul-hwan said. "In North Korea a person has two lives, natural and political. But once you get sent to a prison camp your political life is over and you have only your natural life. You're nothing, an animal, a savage. The guards have the right to kill you without penalty because you're just an animal. If you disobey them or talk back, the guards hit you. It's human nature then to fight back, but if you do they'll shoot you. In one year's time they would stage public executions fifteen or twenty times. People who tried to escape and didn't get far were simply shot on the spot. But if you cost the guards a lot of time and trouble before they recaptured you, they would have a public execution.

"When reunification comes, people should go to the sites of the prison camps. Alongside the camps, in the mountain areas, there are so many unmarked graves. In ten years I think about twenty thousand people died at my camp. The part of the camp I was in had a population of about twenty thousand. Enough people kept dying to make room for all the newcomers. I had about eighty classmates. By the time I graduated from junior high, half were dead, mostly from malnutrition and overwork."

Kang Chul-hwan told me that the camp his family inhabited was in fact "one of the more comfortable" of some twenty camps in the North Korean gulag. I wondered how he knew that. "Most people know about those camps," he told me. "And some people in my camp came from other camps, so I heard about those."

Kang Chul-hwan described himself as one of the stronger prisoners. "I was able to survive a decade in the camp—nine years and eight months, to be precise, from August 4, 1977, to February 28, 1987." His family members came out alive, but some were not as strong as he. His grandmother and his father died soon after their release. "Grandmother had been hanging on just to get out of the camp before dying." Her motive: Dying before release makes traditional ancestral rites difficult if not impossible. Although the regime formally disapproved of such observances, "it couldn't be stopped even by Kim Il-sung," Chul-hwan said. "But the graves of people who died in the camp are there adjoining the camp, so their descendants can't go and pay homage. We were very fortunate."

Kang said the family was released only after relatives in Japan applied great pressure. "The question of restoring diplomatic ties between North Korea and Japan came up during 1986 and 1987. A lot of Chongryon members visited North Korea to see what had become of their relatives. The lucky people who had relatives in Japan filing complaints were let out of the camps. We had lots of relatives in Japan. Relatives came twice to North Korea to find us, but each time the government told them we had gone on vacation. After that, instead of coming over, they filed complaints. They finally got to meet some of the family in North Korea. Lots of relatives in Japan sent a lot of money. My uncles and aunts, who had been sent to the mountains as miners, ended up with cars and color television sets.

"After release we were sent to a farm in Yodok County. Then our relatives in Japan bribed high officials to send us to a more comfortable city in the same county. With the help of our relatives we were able to get nice clothes and other luxuries. When we met our relatives after the deaths of my father and grandmother, we weren't supposed to tell them about the camp. When the word came that they would visit us, a State Security official came and instructed us not to say anything about it. Also, State Security sent people to repair the house. They told us to say, 'We are living a very affluent life under the care of the Great Leader.' In North Korea you are supposed to get free medical care, retirement benefits when you get to be sixty and other benefits. State Security told us to show the relatives the entitlement cards. We did, but our relatives said, 'Oh, we have that in Japan, too.'"[7]

Kang Chul-hwan eventually encountered further trouble with the regime and defected from North Korea, as we shall see in chapter 34.

Kang Chul-ho and Kang Chul-hwan were not related, despite the similiarity of their names. But each could trace his troubles with the authorities back to a grandfather who was out of favor with the regime. Kang Chul-ho could not even remember the name of his grandfather. All he knew was that the old man was a respected veteran of the anti-Japanese resistance movement who was working as a party official in the east coast city of Hamhung when the authorities barged into the house at night, seized a book manuscript in which he had written critically about Kim Il-sung and took him away. The family never heard from him again. The grandmother always spoke favorably of Pak Hon-yong—the "domestic faction" leader who had been condemned to death in 1955 and presumably executed—so perhaps Kang Chul-ho's grandfather had been purged as a remnant of that faction.

What happened afterward to Kang Chul-ho is one of the more gut-wrenching of the stories I heard in my interviews with defectors. His father had been working as a management official in an electrical products factory in Hamhung. Five days after the authorities seized the grandfather, they banished the rest of the family—Chul-ho's grandmother, parents and elder brother—to Koyang in remote Hamju County. After the move, his father worked as a bricklayer and "was questioned repeatedly by Public Security," Kang Chul-ho told me. The hot-blooded father was so annoyed by the constant questions that he set fire to the local State Security building. For that he was executed, in 1976. "It was a public execution by shooting. I was there with my family when my father was executed. I witnessed it, at the public execution site near the riverside, close to Hamhung." Could it get any worse for a little boy? Oh, yes. "My mother committed suicide when my father was executed. Grandmother lived far away, and was too old to help. Local people discriminated against my family, shunned us because of what had happened," he continued. Thinking of what this poor fellow had been through at the age of eight, I already felt like hugging him.

Alas, the sudden deaths of his parents and the unkindness of his neighbors had been by no means the end of his woes. Chul-ho continued in school, and the indoctrination he received there made him blame his parents and grandfather for their misfortunes. "I believed in the party," he told me. Indeed, when the time came he applied to join the military—but was rejected. "I checked the record. There was a rule against having people of bad family background in the military. I was sent to a mine instead." Only then did he start to question the system. "I had expected to live a normal life but it was all a dream."

Whenever I heard stories like this one I could not help noting the irony:

The regime seemed to consider blood more important than ideology—while people like Kang Chul-ho were more than willing to forget blood ties and buy into the ideology if only the authorities would permit them to do so. This, even more than hewing religiously to the personality cult and refusing to adjust an imperfect Marxist vision, may prove to have been the central tragedy of the Kim regime.

At the phosphorous mine in Tanchon, Tongam County, Kang Chul-ho "suffered from the tough rules. At criticism meetings I had many arguments with group leaders, so I got a worse and worse reputation. When I was late for work, I was questioned while others weren't. We were supposed to get gloves and rabbit skins to send to the military. But since I didn't have family members I was always behind in meeting the quota.

"They pointed out my bad family background. I couldn't stand that. They used the issue of my father and grandfather as the final card. 'Because you had a bad father and grandfather you behave this way.' I argued that my father was my father; my grandfather, my grandfather. We were different people. But that didn't faze them.

"At first they didn't use the issue in the beginning of a criticism session. They would bring it up at the end. Fellow workers didn't know about my family background. But local officials did, so they brought it up at the end of the session. We had those sessions weekly. They would assemble a group of forty or so and then choose around five people who were the worst—for family background or other reasons—and put them on the stage, then question them continuously. It takes around one hour and twenty minutes. Two or three times a month I was one of those up on the stage. The party secretaries chose us. Mainly people who had no backing or support were selected, people with no influential family members to help us. They started selecting me for criticism about a month after I arrived.

"One day I had failed to obey an order to obtain gloves and rabbit skins. Others got them from their parents or other relatives who raised rabbits or knitted gloves. My monthly quota was five pair of gloves and two rabbit skins. But I couldn't steal them so I ignored it. Since I didn't have any assets, or influential family background, I argued with the secretary. After that, they said, 'Because you have a bad family background you didn't obey.'"

Following that incident, having spent only a year at the mine, Kang Chul-ho was sent to a maximum-security prison camp. I asked about the trial, and he told me there had been none. "The local party secretary and youth league leader wrote the report on me and signed it. The charge was that I didn't follow the party's orders and had a bad attitude against the party. The party worried about my influence on colleagues. They wanted to make an example of me."

He arrived at prison camp No. 19, Taeheung-dong, Tanchon, in the northeastern corner of South Hamgyong Province, on December 28, 1987.

"I remember that date because after three days in prison I realized it was New Year's Day." The prisoners were employed mining magnesite clinker, which was used to make fire bricks and was one of North Korea's main exports. Foreign exchange from its sales went to a national security fund.[8] "Once I got to prison I had no time to complain, the rules were so tough. All I could do was follow the rules." Electric fences surrounded the camp. "During working hours we were taken to the mine and guards watched us. It was both an open-pit and an underground mine."

After a 5 A.M. wake-up call, the prisoners rotated into the mess hall for breakfast. There followed a one-hour period for washing up and preparing for their thirteen-and-a-half-hour workday, after which they went to the mine at 6:30. Lunch break was from 12:00 to 1:00, supper break from 8:00 to 9:00 and the working day ended at 10 P.M. when the men returned to their cells.

"There was no mining machinery such as railroad cars. We mined with pick and shovel. We were truly confined at hard labor. Clothing was distributed every six months. The workplace was so dusty we had to wear dust coats. There was one bathroom in each cell for the forty inmates in that cell. At least the cell was relatively clean, because there were duty shifts among prisoners for the cleaning detail.

"But the most unbearable thing was hunger. The prisoners were always hungry," Kang told me. "The standard was 700 grams of staple food a day, but we were given only 300 grams a day—and that only if we mined our daily quota. If you couldn't mine enough you got a percentage accordingly. Less than 40 percent of your quota, you only got 10 to 20 percent of the ration, 50 percent got 40 percent and 70 got 70. The food was beans and corn. Only a tenth of the prisoners could make the full quota, generally. Normally we could get only 70 percent or so. This was done intentionally to keep people working hard." Although the guards didn't normally steal prisoners' food, "at the manager level there was lots of corruption."

It wasn't possible to work and survive on just 200 grams or so a day, so supplemental efforts were necessary. "I was so hungry I caught frogs in the mountains. I sometimes ate elm bark, which can be used to make noodles. I chewed the bark, dried it and ate it.

"To the guards, prisoners are animals, not human. They're beaten and mistreated all the time. But we were so hungry, if we noticed anything edible—or a cigarette butt on the ground—we tried to pick it up. Then they'd beat us. I was beaten severely many times. It's very natural to want to eat or smoke, but the guards didn't allow it. The guards were well educated and trained. They regarded prisoners as 'enemy class.'

"There were around five thousand prisoners in four divisions. Once you were in, there was no way out except escape, as a practical matter. Many were shot to death trying to escape. Theoretically you can get out for good behavior but it's very hard. I tried that approach for three years before I decided to escape. I behaved myself very well. It was so painful for me to be there that my only hope was to get out. So I was very careful not to disobey. But it takes ten years before you're eligible for parole."

What happened to those who disobeyed? "They suddenly disappeared, during the night. People assumed they were killed. There were seventy prisoners in my unit. During my stay ten disappeared—not including attempted escapees."

There were many other deaths as well. "In any one year fifteen to twenty people died of malnutrition-related causes. A total of thirty to forty people either died or went unconscious and were taken out while the authorities called family members. I guess in fact they all died. That's the other way to get out. People died of malnutrition. Some ate poisonous plants. Others had accidents with the machinery and lost arms or legs. Most died after going to the medical section.

"It's impossible to escape from there," Kang Chul-ho told me. And yet he himself managed to escape. How? "Not from the prison directly. I went to a local hospital for an appendectomy and escaped from the hospital."

After he escaped from the hospital, he told me, "I had no money until I reached China. I wasn't sure I could make it but I had no choice. I walked eight days and nights to the Chinese border, eating corn and potatoes from farms. I got to the Yalu River around 2 A.M., chose a spot where the water was up to my waist and waded across. That was on August 30, 1990. I wanted to come to South Korea but couldn't, because there were so many other North Koreans in China who wanted the same thing. I got a job at a Chinese company—the manager helped me a lot. I did an interview with *Chosun Ilbo* [a South Korean daily newspaper]. The North Korean embassy people came to my company, with Chinese police, trying to catch me, but the manager of the Chinese company helped me get a Chinese passport. Finally I arranged a job in Osaka. On the way, flying on Korean Air, I came to Seoul." That was in March 1997, after he had been in China for more than six years.

When I interviewed him in 1998, Kang had combed his hair down over his forehead, according to the Seoul fashion of the time. He was by no means a handsome man—his teeth were yellow, his chin receded and he had no eyelashes that I could see. But in a gesture typical of many defectors who began new lives in the capitalist half of Korea, he sported a gold Rolex watch.

I asked about his health after the ordeal he had been through. "I'd been trained physically when I was young, so I was OK," he said, "but spiritually . . . " Now, he said, he was studying theology, attending seminary as a follower of a new Protestant Christian denomination that had branched off from the Presbyterians.

SEVENTEEN

Two Women

Born in December 1949 in mountainous Yanggang Province, not far from the scene of Kim Il-sung's daring 1937 guerrilla attack on the town of Pochonbo, Lee Ok-keum was just one among millions of North Koreans who would be raised to revere the Fatherly Leader. But by the time she and her family fled to South Korea in 1994, their lives had come close to intersecting with Kim's in a way that would have been hard to predict. When I interviewed her that year I found her a simple woman, modest and soft-spoken—yet quite helpful to my research, thanks to a homemaker's steel-trap memory for prices and other details of living standards.

Lee's family still owned a rice farm when she was born. Like so many other youngsters of that time, she lost her father during the Korean War. That left her mother to do the farm work along with five children (three older, one younger than Ok-keum), both before and after the farm collectivization that came in 1955.

In 1959 the family gave up farming and moved to the county seat, where Lee's mother got a job doing road repairs. That work hardly paid enough to support the whole family, so an uncle suggested that the eldest son halt his education after the seventh grade and get a job. He did drop out, but it turned out there were no unskilled jobs available for him. Thus, after a time, the young man entered the army. Army enlisted men made very little. The brother didn't send money home.

Although the family budget was tight, Lee positively recalled the 1950s and 1960s as a time of optimism and of satisfaction, to a degree, with developing living standards. "After the war Kim Il-sung put all his effort into developing the economy," she told me. The main problem then was that "the people didn't have money to buy goods." Lee's mother brought home around thirty *won* a month, and much of that went to clothe the five family members who remained at home. Clothes in the stores were too expensive, so she used her wages to buy cheap, synthetic material—natural fibers were priced out of her range—and hired a tailor to make it into clothing.

A family member's wardrobe, like those of most other North Koreans both then and later, would consist of no more than one outfit at a time—basically a uniform. "Here in South Korea people change clothes every day," Lee marveled. In North Korea, she said, "you just wear one outfit until it's too tattered and filthy to wear any longer. Before I came to South Korea I had three outfits to wear outside the home: one for winter, one for summer and one for autumn and spring. At home we wore pants. I had two pair and would wear one while washing the other."

Lee's first uniform, of course, was a school uniform. "There was no kindergarten then," in the mid-1950s. "We started with elementary school from age seven. Schools were different then. Although we learned about Kim Il-sung, we also studied history and classical literature. We had much more freedom to study what we wanted. That changed from 1965, the year we really started to idolize Kim Il-sung."

That was the year when, having completed the four years of elementary school and three years of junior middle school, Lee enrolled in a two-year vocational school that was divided into agricultural and mechanical programs. "I took agriculture, but after about three months I decided to switch to mechanics. If I'd stayed in agriculture I'd have had to go to a farm. So I studied tractors and such." The mechanical training was "only theoretical," she recalled. The students had no hands-on experience with machinery parts.

At that time there was no high school for her to attend. Lee was sent off to a job not as a mechanic but as a food-processing worker. On the mechanical side of the graduating class, "everyone had a similar experience," she said. "After graduation there was no correlation between what you had studied and what your work assignment would be." At the food-processing plant she helped to make soy sauce and related products as well as candy. She lived at home then and contributed her salary to household expenses. The following year she moved to a textile plant.

After two years of factory work, Lee volunteered for the army. Her second brother was also in the army at the time, driving for an officer, and during one home leave he introduced her to his close friend and fellow driver Yeo Man-cheol, who took a fancy to her. (Although North Korean women, because of all the privation they had to endure, tended not to age well, my guess from looking at Lee during our interview was that she had been pretty as a young woman.)

"Since I didn't have any dowry I resisted him," Lee recalled. "But my mother was very sick. We had no way to treat her." High-quality medicines were in short supply, and doctors were under instruction not to prescribe, for any patient, medicine that the pharmacists were unable to supply to that person. "You had to be elite class or know someone in the hospital to get the right prescription," Lee said. "Without connections, you'd go to the hospital and they would write a prescription but what they gave you wouldn't cure you. If you had a liver problem, it was accompanied by digestive problems. They'd just give you indigestion medicine even though they knew your basic ailment was in the liver. The problem was a shortage of medicine."

(The regime not only acknowledged but boasted that some people deemed especially important got state-of-the-art medicine. Kim Il-sung, referring in his memoirs to one special case, wrote that "Kim Ryang-nam was one of the people who rendered distinguished service in the creation of the Mansudae Art Troupe and its development into one of the world's first troupes under the personal guidance of Secretary Kim Jong-il." When Kim Ryang-nam "contracted a fatal disease, Kim Jong-il organized an efficient medical team to provide him with intensive medical treatment around the clock; he also transmitted his diagnosis to our embassies in foreign countries in order to obtain adequate supplies of expensive medicines, and sent special airplanes to countries which were said to have a developed pharmaceutical industry. Kim Ryang-nam underwent operations ten times and this intensive care lengthened the span of his lifetime by almost two years.")[1]

Soldiers were considered more important than widowed road repair-women. Thus, the People's Army had "plenty of medicine," as Lee recalled. Yeo, smitten as he was with Lee, managed to obtain appropriate medicine for her mother. After that, "Mother persuaded me that he was a good man," Lee recalled. They married in 1973, despite Lee's worries about having no dowry. "The basic dowry then was a suit for your husband-to-be, underwear for him, presents for his family and basic necessities for the household. I think it's more these days. Lack of a dowry doesn't keep you from marrying, but sometimes your in-laws may be a bit harsh on you for not bringing enough. My in-laws were a little mean, but not all that harsh. I understand."

The young couple set up housekeeping in the northeastern industrial city of Hamhung. Yeo moved from the army to the Public Security force — the police. Lee (keeping her maiden name as Korean wives do) worked for ten years in a nursery and then started working from her home, as a photographer, in what was called a neighborhood cooperation scheme. "That brought in good money, so the government abolished the job," she told me with unexpected sarcasm. "Then I turned to mending clothing."

Meanwhile, like most other North Korean women, she was taking care of the housework for her husband and children. It's no wonder she learned to rattle off figures for the grain ration entitlements of various categories of people: as of 1975, 600 grams for workers; 300 for nonworkers including babies and pre-school children; 400 for elementary school pupils, 500 for older students through high school, 700 for college or university students. It was after 1975, she told me, that the youngest children's rations were reduced to 100 grams each for up to eighteen months of age, 200 grams after that. From that year, "you had to be twenty-three months old to get 300 grams." Then, starting in the early 1980s, "10 percent was cut from rations with no specific explanation, probably due to food shortages."

From 1990, the food shortage became far worse. "That year we started selling the sewing machine and other possessions and asking for help from relatives in Pyongyang," Lee said. From 1993, there was nowhere left to turn. In August that year food rations ended entirely in South Hamgyong Province, where the family lived. "I never saw rations resumed," said Lee. Seven months later the Yeo family was in South Korea, unable to ignore the fact that their son came up only to the shoulders of South Korean youngsters a year younger. "He was 148 centimeters (four feet eleven inches) tall when we arrived and he grew 6 centimeters in just two months in South Korea," she told me.

Of course Lee took minute mental note of what was available in the stores over the decades. The quality of goods improved from 1967, she told me, and the North Korean shoppers' heyday lasted until around 1975. During that time "it was possible to buy goods in stores with money you had." It was after 1975 that the authorities stopped rationing items such as shoes and clothing. While rationing normally bespeaks shortages, in that case the end of rationing did not mean plenty—it was just the opposite. "You had to go to the stores, where it was 'first come, first serve,' and the stocks of those items weren't sufficient."

From around 1977 to 1978, products were mainly displayed for show, Lee told me. And from mid-1987, "everything in North Korea is a display. You can buy maybe an eraser or a bobby pin. If we go to Pyongyang now and see goods in the stores, they won't sell to us."

I asked Lee what explanation consumers had received. The authorities "don't know the word 'explanation,'" she replied bitterly. "Sometimes in speeches they told people that although times were hard we should be loyal to the loving father Kim Il-sung."

Did the black market make up for the lack of goods in the official stores? "Take my family and socks," Lee told me. "Each family member needs about one new pair a month. When we could buy them in the stores we paid three and a half to four *won* a pair for nylon socks. In the black market, you had to pay forty-five to fifty *won*. So for the average worker one month's pay would go for one pair of socks. In fact we just had to keep wearing old, ripped socks."

If 1987 was tough on North Koreans in general, due to the increasing shortages, it was the beginning of special hardships for Yeo and Lee and their family. Yeo lost his job as a policeman that year. That happened after the family's next-door neighbor was involved in a road accident, injuring someone, Lee told me. Ordinarily the neighbor would have had to pay a fine of a month's or half a month's salary. "But my husband let him off because he was a neighbor. The neighbor was grateful and gave my husband a bottle of ginseng liquor as a show of gratitude. Public Security inspectors found out. Also, while my husband was drunk, he got into a fight with a colleague at Public Security."[2]

The Yeo-Lee couple's pretty daughter had been one of the elementary school pupils singled out by county party officials as candidates for Kim Il-sung's and Kim Jong-il's mansion service corps. The officials had not contacted the parents but had simply told the girl that if she made the final cut she would start at age sixteen or seventeen and work until her marriage, which the party would arrange. They asked her not to have a boyfriend in the meantime. Some other girls in South Hamgyong Province, where the family lived, started in the mansions corps around thirteen or fourteen. Those were usually the prettiest ones.

Lee had been delighted to think her daughter might be accepted into the corps. "I thought they worked as comedians, actresses, singers and dancers to cheer up Kim Il-sung and Kim Jong-il," she told me. She had no idea at the time that sex might be part of the job. "I only knew we would have a more comfortable life." A girl's selection was "considered a great honor, and also an economic benefit. She could send 1,000 *won* back to the family each month." That was many times an average factory worker's wage.

After Yeo Man-cheol lost his police job and took up a new career as a distributor of imported materials, "it was very hard for us to get by," his wife Lee told me. To make matters worse, people around them and "the system" began to treat not only Yeo but also his wife and children differently. His disgrace inflicted on all of them a big drop in socioeconomic status. Particularly affected was their daughter.

In 1991, when the daughter was seventeen and graduating from school, she failed to make it through the final selection process for the mansions corps. Out of seventy girls in South Hamgyong Province who were finalists to join the unit that she hoped to enter, eight were selected. Her exclusion was a major blow to the family. The country was in the midst of a prolonged food shortage. Lee's fingernails had started to grow backward from malnutrition, she told me; neighbors advised eating dog to reverse the condition. The household had counted on the girl's income to stave off hunger.

Instead, the daughter went to work as a kindergarten teacher. When she applied for what many North Koreans considered a better job, as a typist, she was turned down—because of her father's problems with Public Security, she was told. Whether or not those same problems had been the reason for her exclusion from the mansions corps, it was clear that she and other family members were expected to suffer indefinitely for their father's sins. That and the hunger that became progressively worse through the early 1990s helped persuade the family to defect, Lee told me. They had illegally listened to radio broadcasts from South Korea that suggested life there was better. Chinese traders, who had been operating in the border area of North Korea since the late 1980s, had confirmed that information.

It was only after the family had crossed over the Chinese border in March 1994 that one of them read in a South Korean book about the duties that many of the mansions corps women actually were expected to perform, including sleeping with the Great or Dear Leader. The mother told me that she had realized only then what a close call it had been for her daughter. "I was very relieved that she hadn't been accepted," she said.

Born and raised in Sinuiju on the Yalu River across from China, Shu Chung-shin was twenty-five in May 1997 when she joined her husband's family in defecting as a group of fourteen to South Korea. "I didn't know where they were going," she told me. "I just followed. Everything was arranged by my father-in-law, who had a brother in America. Uncle-in-law bought a vessel from some Chinese and in that we came to South Korea."

Shu had worked as a dancer. "I attended a college of arts for five years and learned dance," she said. "After graduation, I worked with an art troupe doing propaganda. We went around Sinuiju. We were told that Kim Jong-il had organized the dance troupe. I never met him, but I did see him at the 1989 World Festival of Youth and Students, at the stadium. There was a shortage of dancers. So the order came to Sinuiju to get more dancers. We danced in the stadium for the opening and closing ceremonies."

The family defected after having grown weary of the consequences of a bad background. "My grandfather-in-law on my father-in-law's side was a church preacher. Father-in-law's mother and younger brother had fled to South Korea during the Korean War. He wanted to follow them. The father of my mother-in-law was a landlord. So the authorities were watching us. In North Korea, if you are from a bad family background, they follow you and spy on you. Eventually somebody realized that the old woman next door was spying on us. The family had given this woman food. Grandmother-in-law was so annoyed! She said, 'How can you do this?' There was a big fuss, and we worried about the children's future. That was just the last straw. Father-in-law actually had been preparing for eight years. At first he wanted to cross the border by land so he arranged excuses in advance, staying away for a while on business. There was a spy following him. He didn't know that at first. When changing trains at Sinuiju station, he saw he was followed. So he gave up on the land route."

Shu herself came from a background that had become, as time passed, problematic: Her family were former residents of Japan. Generally returnees from Japan "are regarded as rich," she noted. "Families from Japan or from America receive money from our relatives. Officials expect bribes. If they don't get them, they find something to criticize. My mother did some business—she bought goods from China and resold them. But the police came and confiscated all the goods. She asked for them back, but they didn't return them. She had to give the police ten packs of cigarettes, or they would insist on splitting the goods. She gave them the cigarettes." Her father also had many problems, Shu told me. "He was a surgeon. He took pride in his work. But he was not allowed to be a party member, even though his assistants were members. He had to leave the room before meetings started. In school, we had a session to draw our family trees. Where you filled in the names, there was a place to check if they were party members. My schoolmates proudly checked there. When I got home I complained to my father. I think that hurt his feelings."

I asked if Shu had been a loyal believer. "The new generation in Sinuiju is different from the old," she said. "They prefer friends from overseas and they're very open-minded. For example, they like wearing jeans. The authorities forbid it, telling them that jeans came from America originally—and in the Korean War, GIs wore them while they killed North Koreans. Younger generation people reply, 'What's the problem? If you have correct ideology, what do jeans matter?' There's no organized anti-government activity. Still I heard a rumor that when Kim Jong-il visited Sinuiju he supposedly said he was worried about the young of Sinuiju in case war breaks out because they are like capitalists in their attitudes, so he must do something. Anyhow, my mother taught me to follow the party's teachings. Although I'm of the new generation, I accepted her advice. Because of our family background I knew I had to be very careful. I trusted the regime. It was only when I came to South Korea that I realized I'd been lied to. For example, Kim Jong-il had been born in Khabarovsk, not on the holy Mount Paektu."

In their vulnerable position, her parents had wanted their daughter to marry someone of good family background. They were dismayed when Shu picked a man with many strikes against him politically. "I had a lot of trouble from my parents," she told me. "But we were in love, and I insisted on going through with the marriage. I had met my husband when I was seventeen and in college. He was twenty-three then. We married when I was twenty-four, in 1995. He was a student. After our marriage, he worked as a physics teacher at a middle school. In South Korea now he studies theology. No one had followed his grandfather's example and become a minister, and his father wanted one of the children to do that."

Her husband's family, like her own, enjoyed relatively good economic circumstances, thanks to remittances from the relatives in America. "But by 1995, the whole economy had slowed down. So it was getting harder to get rice," Shu said. "Until I married, I had regarded my family as middle-class. We kept a one-year reserve of rice — 100 or 200 kilograms. After I married, in 1994 and 1995, it was different. Subsidized rice rations stopped in the Sinuiju area in 1995, for a whole year. In other areas they had stopped in 1994." Still the family did not go hungry. "I didn't have any difficulties, thanks to the dollars sent from America. Also, my father-in-law worked in foreign exchange. He moved around in North Korea and made money. He was a trader. He raised silkworms and grew seed plants, sold them to the Chinese and in exchange got wheat, as well as money that we could use to buy food." There were some things money could not readily buy. The medical system was "very poor. There is no intravenous equipment and virtually no medicine. Anesthesia is scarce, and the doctors use it only at the precise time of surgery. There are not even sleeping pills. With no medicine, the doctors have nothing to do. They collect scrap metal to sell to Chinese traders."

Here I must mention that Shu, although a bit on the gaunt side as befitted a recent arrival from North Korea, was very pretty, especially when animated by memories of love or indignation. Even the no-nonsense blue blouse and gray slacks that she wore to meet me looked good on her lithe dancer's body. Although already a mother — her three-year-old son, in Mickey Mouse shirt and sneakers, slept in her lap as we spoke — she still wore her hair attractively long. (Once East Asian women became matrons they used to exhibit a lamentable tendency to chop off their flowing tresses in favor of more practical hairdos, wishing to look the new role and no longer feeling much need to attract men. But I am told younger women have taken a different view.) Her only ornaments were a silver-colored watch and a diamond pendant on a gold neck chain. I noticed in particular her full, pouty, red lips, which reminded me of those of a former girlfriend. Shu was soft-spoken, charming — face it: she was a babe. Now, if I am beginning to sound like one of Kim Jong-il's operatives salivating over a particularly choice candidate for the mansion service corps, that is precisely the point. As soon as I caught a glimpse of Shu I felt pretty sure she would not have escaped the recruiters' notice. So after a decent interval spent talking about other matters I posed a general question, asking whether she had heard anything about girls being taken to Pyongyang for Kim Il-sung and Kim Jong-il.

Indeed she had. "There is a group called fifth division — in Korean, *okwa*. They are all women — dancers and so on. Since I lived in Sinuiju, I don't know exactly what happens in Pyongyang. But I heard that Kim Jong-il would call in some dancers from the *kippeunjo* when he was depressed at night and they would dance naked in front of him. I also heard a story that once, when some communist secretaries came from overseas, they were out driving and saw a pretty woman. North Korean officials who were with them stopped the car and had her spend the night with them. Later they sent her to a mental hospital and locked her up. One of my family members went to

Pyongyang University of Foreign Languages. He heard the story there." So far, all that she had told me about the leaders' treatment of women was hearsay, but I pressed on with my questioning: Were the girls recruited from all over the country? "Recruiting officials go to every province looking for beautiful girls," Shu replied.

And then she came out with it. "Actually, I myself was initially chosen when I was a student at the college of fine arts, when I was seventeen," Shu said. "But then I was turned down because my family was from Japan. This was for *okwa*. They didn't tell me what unit, but they did tell me I'd be with the Wangjaesan Band."

The recruiters, Shu explained further, "go to arts-related institutions. They prefer actresses and other fine arts majors, because they assume the beauties are studying in those fields." In Sinuiju, "they distributed numbers from one to ten, looked at the girls' faces and chose us by number. Then there was a second local round." Shu laughed fetchingly. "People like big eyes—that's their idea of beauty—so I did well locally and got chosen to go to Pyongyang for the third round. In the first and second rounds they just looked at our faces, judged us by our appearance. In Pyongyang they interviewed us, consulting official documents. They asked me whether my father was a party member, the ages and the dates and places of birth of my parents, their jobs and so on. Finally they said, 'You can go. We'll let you know by mail if you are chosen.' I didn't get an acceptance. They realized that my family was from Japan, so they rejected me. I know this because my mother-in-law's friend's son worked in that band, but he had to leave because his family were returnees from Japan. The government was afraid that news about *okwa* would spread to the world."

I asked Shu if she had been disappointed not to make the final cut. "I wasn't sorry at all," she said at first. "My parents had heard in the neighborhood that if I got in I wouldn't be allowed out, I would be spoiled. Most North Koreans know the purpose of *okwa*." Her rejection mainly made her think about what sort of career she could have in the performing arts. "I was worried about whether my family background would affect my chances to perform in Pyongyang." A bit later in our conversation, though, she gestured beautifully, touching the long, gracefully tapered fingers of one hand to her face and then to her heart. "Actually," she then confessed, "I wanted to go. I would have nice clothes, French makeup, imported lingerie, good food—fruit, butter, milk—that was hard to find in our local area. At the time I was young, so I didn't know the bottom line. I didn't realize sex might be part of the deal. I just thought I'd dance and live well. My parents had heard about the *kippeunjo* and didn't want me to go to Pyongyang. But I wasn't afraid because being a band dancer in *kippeunjo* was different from being in another *okwa* unit that was explicitly for sexual services. *Kippeunjo* members are supposed to give pleasure but not sexual services. Sex is not their basic job."

Shu told me she had once "met a woman from *okwa*. Her father-in-law had been sent to Sinuiju from Pyongyang because he had done something wrong. The woman was married; she had already retired from the mansions corps. But one day her husband was drinking with his friends. He had no money so he left a watch with Kim Il-sung's signature engraved on the back, as a guarantee until he could get money. The watch was a gift for high-ranking officials. The husband was so drunk, he handed the watch to the clerk, who reported the incident directly to the police. The husband was punished and had to follow his father to Sinuiju, and she came too. When I first met her I thought she might have come from overseas, because she looked totally different from ordinary people. That woman had no idea how ordinary people lived. The husband had been a foreign exchange trader and had been making big money, so his wife could spend $500 at a time. In Pyongyang, there was plenty for her to buy; it was just a matter of money. But in Sinuiju there was simply nothing to buy. It shocked her a lot." I asked if the husband had known about his wife's past. "Yes," Shu said. "It's not out of the ordinary for sons of high officials to live with former *okwa* members. Kim Jong-il orders it."

Shu told me how the women recruited for explicitly sexual duties were rounded up. "The recruiters came in a Mercedes-Benz, went to middle schools, chose seventeen-to-eighteen-year-olds and took them away. The parents didn't know what had happened, and searched for their daughters. When they gave up, officials came with gifts from Pyongyang and said, 'Your daughter is well. Don't worry.' After that the parents gave up, thinking, 'Now our daughter belongs to the state.' Some families think it's a kind of sacrifice to the country. Some families who had been hungry think it's a benefit."

I received confirmation regarding the duties of the mansions corps from several men who said they had been in contact with members. Oh Young-nam, a former captain of State Security, told me in 1996 that his "first love" had been one of the mansions corps women available for sexual services to the leaders. "I first thought they were all naive virgins. I had a sexual relationship with this woman and I realized that she wasn't a virgin. She worked at Munsu Mansion. That mansion is for the Ministry of People's Armed Forces. You can see her in North Korean films. She became a movie star with Kim Jong-il's help. She spent a couple of nights with Kim Jong-il and then had a relationship with Kim Kang-jin, vice-minister of armed forces. You enter that service at twelve and retire at twenty-two. Usually the women promise not to tell anyone, but we were thinking of marriage. My mother opposed it. The woman told me all about the training: mental training, skin treatment, light exercise to keep her figure. She had to learn massage, dance, striptease, mambo, samba and so on. She said she was noticed when she was twelve when returning home from school. Somebody took her by car; they do not ask the parents' permission.

Those who are selected for the mansions service and for anti–South Korea espionage—their parents are just told they have been given to the country. They do not try to find where their children have gone."

Kang Myong-do was a son-in-law of Kang Song-san, who was prime minister around the time of the son-in-law's defection. The defector said he also was distantly related to Kim Il-sung as a grandnephew of the late Vice-President Kang Ryang-uk, born in Chilgol, Kim Il-sung's native village, of the same clan as Kim's mother.[3] While Kang said he did meet Kim Jong-il on occasion, some of the information he was able to provide falls into the category of hearsay rather than eyewitness reports. "Kim Jong-il and I are relatives, but not too close," Kang told me in an interview. "Basically what I tell you comes from the buzz, the talk among the elite of the elite—about sixty people who run the country, and their families. I was a member of that group."[4] Having offered the reader that caveat regarding hearsay, let me say that Kang's reports generally ring true when they can be compared with the accounts of other North Koreans, including those who boasted greater seniority and more direct contact with the leadership.

Kang told me that the party Central Committee's fifth division, or *okwa*, was in charge of the palace women's corps, with staff members in each province and county to handle recruiting. The officials would check on the family backgrounds of the likeliest prospects, to make sure of their loyalty to the regime, then watch them to make sure they did not get involved with boys. The young women who made the cut at the time of graduation from senior middle school, at age fifteen or sixteen, would be given physical examinations to confirm their virginity.[5]

About two thousand girls were selected each year and given a year of training. Some five to six hundred who were expected to be available for sex would be assigned to the lodges and villas (*chodeso*) and to other mansions (*titka*) where the rulers held receptions; some also went to the bodyguard service. Others were given secretarial and other jobs where, officially, they were not expected to provide sexual services.

Kang told me that many of his friends working for the Central Committee had married mansions corps retirees, in a sort of lottery procedure.[6] Slips of paper with the women's names written on them were placed in a pile. Most of the dragooned bridegrooms he knew were aware that the women might have been available to the rulers for sexual services and thus might not have been the virgin brides much sought after by Korean males—but the men had no choice. Still, "on balance, they like it. You get rich by marrying them." Besides the women's pensions, there would be elaborate gifts. Kang said he visited two former Happy Corps dancers he knew and found "a house full of presents from Kim Jong-il." Another factor appealing to the prospective bridegrooms was: "How else would they get such good-looking women?" After all, in case nature had been in any way deficient, these were women who had access to the high-level 915 Hospital, staffed with plastic surgeons. (Doctors at 915 also operated on spies who were in need of disguise, according to an ex-spy, Ahn Myung-jin, who told me about the hospital.)[7]

Even if a prospective bridegroom wanted a virgin it would be hard to find one, according to Kang. The men figured that "it's better to marry a top leader's former woman than get a bride who's been broken in by some farm boy." To hear Kang tell it—other sources disagreed vehemently on this—hardly any virgins of marriageable age remained in North Korea. Kang was an official of an organization that supplied special foodstuffs to the elite, and sometimes he went to middle schools to recruit office workers. "One place I went, out of fifty middle-school graduates only three were virgins. This came out in the course of complete medical checkups we arranged for them at a hospital. Afterward there was a special order not to do those physicals because it upset the women."

Housewife Lee Ok-keum was one of those who disputed Kang's characterization of the younger generation. "Basically in North Korea boys and girls in junior or senior middle school wouldn't have close connections," she told me. Indeed, officially, ordinary North Korean citizens were expected to keep to very strict sexual morality. Even among university students, "there aren't supposed to be male-female relationships," a former member of Kim Il-sung's bodyguard unit, Pak Su-hyon, told me. "If women wear makeup, they will be scrutinized." Couples must keep their liaisons secret or face expulsion.

However, Kang was not alone in pointing to an increase in sexual license. "In a way North Korea may be sexually wilder than South Korea," Pak Su-hyon told me. "In South Korea when guys and girls meet, you have tea and exchange pleasantries. There's no opportunity for that sort of thing in the North. If you talk about a relationship between a man and a woman, it means they're having sex. But those relationships tend to be long running, consistent. They make love outside mostly—in parks at night, near the lake."

Kim Ji-il, who was a physics student in the Ukraine when he defected in 1990, agreed with Pak. "From outside it may seem there's a lot of rigidity in male-female relations," Kim told me, "but when you get down to it things can get quite wild. In North Korea women are very naive. If a man says, 'I'll marry you,' the woman gives everything. Many men take advantage of girls. Many North Koreans want to be party members, but that depends on party officials, who may trade a promise of party membership for sex with a woman candidate." Kim added: "Since North Korea is an organization-based society, often you're away from home with your group, even overnight. Many relationships form during the night shift. There's no sex education, so often when couples act out their curiosity it leads to pregnancy. They don't know how to deal with it, so lots of women take rat poison to kill themselves. Since so many women died from eating rat poison, in 1984 Kim Jong-il told the doctors to give abortions on demand."

EIGHTEEN

Dazzling Ray of Guidance

With the 1980 announcement of the succession, Kim Jong-il immediately established a pattern of sparking concern—at home and abroad—about his health. At the party congress where he was elevated, he looked uncharacteristically thin and pale. It was later claimed that people all over the country had written to chastise other officials for failing to look after the princeling's health.[1] Whether people really wrote such letters of their own volition, the junior Kim seems to have learned something about what in Western democracies is called a "sympathy vote."

Another pattern he established was that of *not* appearing in public. He had been reclusive before his 1980 debut as heir-designate, and he was to remain so. Pyongyang after 1980 reported that the junior Kim had been eschewing appearances at meetings, other than the party congress at which he was anointed and a series of celebratory parades. Instead he was spending his time traveling around to give "guidance" to the people.

In fact he lived much of his life in the private world of a movie fan, locked up in a room with his celluloid and videotape images of the outside. After a trip to China in 1983, it appears that he seldom went abroad. Besides absorbing movie versions of foreign places, he had his women dress up once a week in the national costume of some country, serve him the cuisine of that country and make believe.

Kim Jong-il's responsibilities increased, so much so that the contrast of his behavior with the persona he needed to project became untenable. Eventually he himself would realize the need for a conscious effort to clean up his act. But that time did not come until the mid-1980s, when—already in his forties—he was placed in day-to-day charge of the party, government and military. His youth and some signs that he harbored liberal views led to hopes that he would prove to be a reformer prince, but early evidence for that proposition was less than overwhelming.

Especially through the first half of the 1980s, although he had started a family as early as 1977, Kim Jong-il continued an active schedule of relationships with women from the world of let's pretend: actresses, dancers, members of his mansions corps. At the same time, according to Hwang Jang-yop, who was working for him in a high-ranking position in the party's central committee, Kim would go to any length to portray himself in the public eye as "above reproach when it comes to women." Hwang said Kim "forbade women to ride behind men on bicycles when out searching for food because it offended public morals. He even forbade women from riding bicycles on their own because he said it was unsightly."

If such decrees seem more ridiculous than sinister, consider the story told by Hwang, architect-engineer Kim Young-song and others about Woo In-hee, a promiscuous movie star who had received the title "people's actress." In 1980 she was making love in a garaged car—the engine and heater running—with a Korean returnee from Japan. Both were overcome by carbon monoxide and the man died. When Woo recovered, authorities interrogated her to obtain a list of men with whom she had been intimate. The story goes that Kim Jong-il then ordered her execution by shooting. Hwang wrote, "It is rumored that the main reason for deciding to kill Woo was that she had crumbled under interrogation and confessed to having slept with Kim Jong-il."[2]

While many elite North Koreans had heard about Woo, the rumors about Kim Jong-il's involvement with her awaited confirmation. The evidence was a little better in the case of another woman who talked out of school. A Happy Corps member was irate because it was time for her retirement and she had not been assigned a husband like the other retirees. She let off steam by complaining to acquaintances that Kim Jong-il "is propagandized as a holy, pure, godlike type, but he's nothing like that." Former political prisoner Ahn Hyuk told me he had met the woman in his prison camp and heard directly from her about this.

(It was Ahn, drawing on what he said that woman prisoner had told him, who said that "Kim Jong-il didn't go overseas any more, so they would have national nights. On India night, the Happy Corps would wear Indian sari and he would eat Indian food. The next time they might be gotten up as geishas." But former official Kang Myong-do told the Seoul newspaper *JoongAng Ilbo* that Kim did make some unannounced pleasure trips up until the mid-1980s. "He would take his private jet to Hong Kong, Macao, stay in the top hotels, eat Chinese delicacies including sparrow specialties.")

My point in dwelling on the Kims' sex lives at some length is to show that a great many North Koreans were affected by the rulers' systematic, even official, exploitation of girls and young women. I mentioned President Bill Clinton and Prince Charles earlier. Many people would argue that the news media and, in Clinton's case, political opponents were too keen to expose what were essentially private acts between consenting adults, the sort of affairs that many countrymen who were far less exalted likewise engaged in. I doubt that many who have read this far would offer such an argument on behalf of the Kims.

Sometimes it was men who suffered from Kim's womanizing, if that term can be used for such intricately organized hunting and gathering. One former official told me the story of Kang Yon-ok, a beautiful woman who "was able to make her acting debut because she was Kim Jong-il's mistress. Kim Jong-il kept her from age seventeen to twenty-nine. He set her up to marry an actor, Yi Sung-nam. Yi didn't know she wasn't a virgin. He was upset when he discovered she wasn't, and taunted her. She had promised not to talk about her background, but she felt she had to tell him. He was furious. He spoke to his friends, asking: 'How could Kim Jong-il do this?' Now he's in a prison camp. Lots of people in North Korea know this story."

The former official added that Pyongyang elite circles believed actress Kang and others among Kim's mistresses had become pregnant by Kim before he married them off to other men, and subsequently had given birth to his children. The official mentioned in this regard famous actresses Hong Yung-hui (who played the title role in the movie *The Flower Girl*), O Mi-ran and Ji Yung-bok. Although specific confirmation of such rumors is elusive, it is indisputable that Kim did take time out of the busy schedule of the country's co-ruler to involve himself in matchmaking—traditionally the job of parents. Consider the following story—this one from an official biography—of a hastily arranged marriage:

> One evening in January 1980, a woman anti-Japanese veteran was telephoned in her office by Kim Jong-il and was told to come to him at once. . . . Some days previously, Kim Jong-il, who had heard that she had a son who was old enough to get married, chose a fiancée for . . . her son, who was serving in the army after graduating from a military academy, and asked her opinion. She immediately agreed with Kim Jong-il's choice and was grateful for his kindness, which was as great as the warmth shown by parents to their son. Remembering his care, the veteran fighter wondered, while she was in the car, how she would thank him when she met the man who had been

worried about her family. Before she realized it, the car pulled into the grounds of a building.

But she found something else to surprise her when she entered the room. Her son and married daughter were already there. "Oh, my, what are you doing here?" Her daughter told her what had happened. Kim Jong-il had sent for her because of her son's marriage. After he had heard the opinions of both the lad and the girl as well as the parents of both sides, Kim Jong-il had thought that, because they all agreed about the marriage, it would be a good idea to have an engagement party. This was why they had been sent for. . . .

Kim Jong-il was highly delighted to see her, and shook her hand warmly. He told her that he had sent for her because he wanted to decide on her son's betrothed and hold the engagement party and then set the date of their marriage. Then he asked her for her opinion. She thanked him heartily, saying that they had no greater honor that that of having the engagement party in the presence of Kim Jong-il. They would not mind if they did not have a wedding party, she added. She said they would take the memorable engagement party as being a wedding party. Kim Jong-il thanked her and told an official to prepare the wedding party.[3]

Meanwhile, the regime's ideologists were working hard to develop a theoretical basis for the succession. As ultimately spelled out, it involved these propositions: First, it was necessary to have a successor to Kim Il-sung, because "the struggle of the working class and the masses of people is too prolonged and too complicated to be completed in one generation." Second, the heir must be someone endowed with "boundless loyalty to the Great Leader, which takes the form of a complete knowledge and understanding of the revolutionary thought of the Leader; dedication to the working-class and people's interests; and complete inheritance of the Great Leader's illustrious leadership and a full embodiment of his lofty moral virtues."[4] Of course, only one person combined all these virtues.

Kim Il-sung played Confucian ethics for all they were worth to justify the hereditary elite he established and his plans for dynastic rule of the country. It was at least partially for that purpose that the regime's propagandists—now headed by his son—glorified the elder Kim's parents, uncles, grandparents and even his great-grandfather as patriot leaders. "All of the world's people ought to learn from the record of struggle established by the Kim family," Radio Pyongyang told listeners in 1977. "The people of the world envy the Korean people who have such a family as their leaders. Therefore we must be loyal and devoted to the Kim family and their shining tradition."[5]

In fact, of course, not all the people of the world—and not even all the people of the communist world—were swept away with envy. An American

Korea specialist went to China in the early 1980s and discussed North Korea with Chinese Pyongyang-watchers. He kept trying to get their opinion on the dynasty in Pyongyang, but the Chinese were hesitant to talk about it. Finally the host said, "Let's go to lunch and stop talking about this. But before we go I will say one thing. We communist theoreticians have a difficult time categorizing this system. Is it feudal socialism or socialist feudalism?"

Lies quickly engulfed the young Kim, as they had his father. Indeed, his own official personality cult is even more ludicrous in its excess than Kim Il-sung's, because propagandists had far less to work with. In the case of the elder Kim, the regime's sycophantic biographers needed only a few steps from recounting his actual guerrilla war record during the 1930s to casting him as a magical general who could cross rivers by walking on fallen leaves. When it came to the son, though, a lack of tangible achievements made constructing a towering image more difficult. After all, Kim Jong-il fought in neither the anti-Japanese resistance nor the Korean War. Casting about for alternative legends to glorify the man who would be Great Leader but who had little apparent Great Leadership to his credit, the Pyongyang regime settled on the title of "genius."[6]

Kim Il-sung got personally involved in the new propaganda push on his designated heir's behalf. According to Hwang Jang-yop, the former party ideology secretary, with the success of the intensified efforts to glorify the senior Kim's revolutionary career "the stage was set for the birth of the first legend about Kim Jong-il—his birth in 1942 in a secret encampment in Mount Paektu. Kim Il-sung was enjoying a holiday in the resort in Samjiyeon when he summoned the people who had participated in the partisan struggle and ordered them to find the site of the secret camp in Mount Paektu where Kim Jong-il was born. Obviously they could not find something that did not exist. So Kim Il-sung said that he would have to do it himself. He looked around and picked a scenic spot and claimed that that was where the secret encampment had been. He then named the mountain peak behind it 'Jongilbong' (Jong-il Peak). The Party History Center obtained a huge granite rock and carved the word 'Jongilbong' on it. Then they accomplished the difficult task of hoisting the rock up the Jongilbong and attaching it there. Underneath the rock they built a hut called 'Home of the Mount Paektu secret encampment' and went around claiming that this hut was where Kim Il-sung had lived with Kim Jong-suk. This was where he had planted the red flag indicating the commander's headquarters and directed the partisan struggle. And this was where Kim Jong-il was born. He supposedly grew up in this hut listening to the sounds of gunshots of the partisans." One of Hwang's jobs was supervising the Party History Center, he wrote.[7]

* * *

Kim Jong-il was credited with having been the advocate of the policy of mo-
bilizing masses of workers to complete construction projects at breakneck
speed. In October 1974 "when the economy was faced with many difficulties," Kim Il-sung convened a meeting of the Party Central Committee's
politburo. "At that time Mr. Kim Jong-il set forward the policy of waging
'speed battles' to overcome the economic difficulties," a pro-Pyongyang newspaper in Tokyo reported later. Others pointed out the obstacles, but "it was
his firm conviction that there was nothing that could not be overcome if the
inexhaustible power and energy of the masses were mobilized. On October 5
of the same year, in order to fulfill the annual assignments of economic construction, Mr. Kim Jong-il proposed to start a '70-day battle' in the national
economy."[8]

Such "speed battles" became the trademark of Kim Jong-il's leadership
style, both in contruction and in the general operation of the economy.
Looking back at the end of 1980 on the accomplishments of that year, for
example, North Korea's Central News Agency credited the "dazzling ray of
guidance"—Kim Jong-il, of course—with a construction "speed campaign"
in which "grandiose monumental creations . . . have sprung up everywhere."
All those "great monuments of the era of the Workers' Party, which were
built in the land of paradise under the outstretched hand of guidance, are
gifts of great love which could be provided only by the Respected and
Beloved Leader [Kim Il-sung] and the Benevolent Party Center."

Upholding his father's "architectural esthetic," Kim Jong-il focused his
energies on massive urban-development projects in Pyongyang. "The young
secretary completely transformed the capital" by 1979, throwing up hospitals, an indoor stadium and the Mansudae Art Theater. Changgwang Street,
lined with new twenty- to thirty-story apartment blocks, normally would
have taken three or four years to build but went up in ten months in 1980,
the regime boasted.[9]

Even though he already had received his father's approval to become the
successor, Kim Jong-il continued his elaborate and expensive flattery of Kim
Il-sung. As when he was a youngster, the son was accustomed to doing as he
wished—and ordinary mortals generally were not prepared to stand in his
way. "Formally, the Supreme People's Assembly is the highest sovereign organization in North Korea," one former high-ranking official said. "In reality, even if it sets a budget, Kim Jong-il will demand unreasonable expenses
for constructing such projects as villas, the Juche Tower or the Arch of Triumph. Cases of unplanned expenses are frequent. Although there are times
when experts spin around in circles, pointing out these expenses, there is no
one who can act as a restraining force." The former official added: "Most citizens are unaware of these non-productive expenditures. However, even if
they harbor dissatisfaction, is there anyone who could express this dissatisfaction and make an issue out of it? This non-productive investment was an

important cause of the economic predicament North Korea fell into in the latter half of the 1980s. The waste was caused by the political environment leading up to the transfer of power to Kim Jong-il."[10]

In 1983 officials of Chongryon, the pro-Pyongyang association of Korean residents in Japan, which functions as a sort of de facto embassy in the absence of diplomatic relations between Japan and North Korea, invited me to a movie screening. It would be the Japan premiere of a documentary film depicting a visit to China by Kim Jong-il.

That was an irresistible invitation at a time when North Korea was very much in the news. The country had just sent commandos to Burma to bomb a South Korean delegation. Failing to harm the South's president, the North Korean agents killed four of his cabinet members and thirteen other officials. Among those who died in Rangoon was Kim Jae-ik, a brilliant, Stanford-educated economist—in my estimation the best and brightest of the technocrats involved in planning the South's economic miracle. After my 1979 visit to North Korea I had traveled to Seoul to compare notes with South Korean officials. Talking about the North was still a strong taboo, however, and every official I visited contrived to change the subject—except for Kim Jae-ik. I actually went to see him to talk about another topic, South Korea's economic plans. But when he heard I had just come from the North he was so excited that he kept me in his office for several hours, picking my brain about what I had learned there. In the fall of 1983, when I saw Kim Jae-ik's name on the Rangoon fatalities list, I felt personal loss. (It was only much later that various sources, among them former party secretary Hwang Jang-yop,[11] suggested that Kim Jong-il had ordered the attack. Some analysts say his father still retained the main supervisory role over major initiatives in inter-Korean and foreign affairs.)

I duly attended the screening and reviewed the film as follows for my employer at the time, *The Asian Wall Street Journal,* and its U.S. parent newspaper:

TOKYO—Is the virtual crown prince of communist North Korea a candidate for an early heart attack? Does he lack a skill so essential to a political leader as speechmaking? Did he harbor doubts about the intentions of North Korea's Chinese allies—doubts that Beijing sought to allay with almost two weeks of marathon banquets, talks, sightseeing and (literal) hand-holding? With President Reagan due to visit the other Korea this coming weekend, such questions may be of at least passing interest to Americans.

A North Korean documentary film, "Dear Leader Kim Jong-il's visit to China," which premiered in English here, chronicles a June visit to China by Kim Jong-il, President Kim Il-sung's 41-year-old son and designated successor. It gives tantalizing clues to the personality, abilities, attitudes and health of a leader little known outside his largely closed country. And it provides hints of North Korean and Chinese policy trends at a time when tension in Northeast Asia is heightened by the Rangoon bomb that killed 17 South Korean officials and by the earlier Soviet downing of a South Korean jetliner.

The younger Mr. Kim is secretary of the Korean Workers' (Communist) Party. He visited China June 1–12. The trip wasn't announced until after his return.

The two-hour film describes the visit as "unofficial." Yet it makes clear that the Chinese went all out to give their guest treatment befitting an officially visiting head of state. At every arrival and sendoff during a rail trip that took him to several east-coast cities, his hosts stage-managed the sort of adulation by supposedly joyous crowds of well-wishers he is accustomed to at home—where both he and his father are treated as godlike cult figures of superhuman brilliance and accomplishments.

The film covers only ceremonial and social parts of Mr. Kim's meetings with Chinese officials, who included Deng Xiaoping, Communist Party General Secretary Hu Yaobang and Premier Zhao Zhiyang. But it covers those parts interminably and in the process supports some observations and some educated guesses:

Young Mr. Kim has a heroic abdominal overhang of the sort known outside sober North Korea as a beer belly. Despite a discreet tailoring job on the gunmetal-blue Mao-style tunics he wore, he looked in the film to be perhaps 40 to 50 pounds overweight. He smokes filter-tipped cigarettes. In Beijing he slowed going up some steep steps and looked out of breath. A Chinese soldier accompanying him offered an arm, but he refused it. Most doctors would counsel dieting and exercise to reduce the chances of high blood presure, heart attack, stroke or other illness.

(On the other hand, his father carries similar bulk and also is a smoker, and he passed his 71st birthday this year. And there must be political advantages in looking like his father—which he does, except for his sylishly permed hair, right down to the boyishly round face seen in old photos of the elder Mr. Kim.)

The younger Mr. Kim may dislike public speaking. He appeared to lack talent for it. When welcoming speeches were made to him and his party during the trip, he almost always left the replies to underlings. When he did make a speech he stood reading it without expression, his head down. He made neither gestures nor eye contact with the audience. This is curious, since North Korean spokesmen in Tokyo have praised the oratorical skills of the "dear leader."

Mr. Kim seemed unsmilingly ill at ease or haughty on occasion during the first days in China. But by the time his trip ended, the film showed him positively glowing. It is possible that in the beginning he simply suffered from the usual shock experienced by a visitor unaccustomed to the mammoth banquets with which the Chinese stuff their guests. But it is more likely he took a while to decide whether to trust his hosts. Chinese leaders, only recently rid of the personality cult and nepotism of the late Chairman Mao Zedong, had been slow to recognize the junior Mr. Kim publicly as successor to his father's even more extravagant personality cult. And there had been hints of a softening in China's stance toward the North's mortal enemy, South Korea. When his stiffness turned to relaxation, and even an animated charm, around midway in the visit, it is a good bet he was responding not just to the lavish hospitality but mainly to promises of support, implied or expressed.

The film was made originally in Korean, which indicates it was intended to give the home folks the message that China was recognizing the younger Mr. Kim as heir to his father. Like the very expensive continuing propaganda campaign to portray the father as a leader revered worldwide for his sagacity, this effort testifies that in North Korea there still are doubters, if not overt opponents, of "Kimilsungism" and its provision for an hereditary succession. For several years, North Korea's officials and spokesmen have seemed extremely sensitive to foreign criticism of the Kim clan's nepotism, and this hasn't changed. One of the unofficial spokesmen for North Korea, who arranged the film premiere, pointedly struck up a conversation with me about my very young son. "So you have a successor now," the spokesman said. "Do you want him to be a journalist like you?"

The Chinese were able to swallow their very strong misgivings and embrace the scion of so un-Marxist an institution as a dynasty. That shows once again how susceptible they are to Kim Il-sung's playing off of China against the Soviet Union. The film shows how literally that term "embrace" can be taken. Hu Yaobang, the main official negotiating with Mr. Kim, had at least five sessions with him. And Mr. Hu went for the hard sell. On two occasions the film shows him trying to link arms with Mr. Kim. Both times Mr. Kim resisted. Eventually, Mr. Hu's determined overtures prevailed and they strolled along holding hands.

Finally, the film is yet another demonstration that North Korea's propaganda is the most heavy-handed in the world. The documentary

unmercifully subjects viewers to every railway station arrival demonstration, every fervent farewell, every banquet toast. Eleven sets of
talks and banquets are described as having occurred in atmospheres
characterized by combinations of qualities from this list: cordial, serious, comradely and friendly. The cameraman throughout the long
trip never failed to lean out of the train window just after a departure and film the train snaking around a curve ahead, and the editor
never failed to leave the clichéd scene in. All this belies a 1980 desrip-
tion of Mr. Kim by North Korea's spokesmen here as the country's
Alfred Hitchcock, as an artistic film director in his own right who
transformed the country's cinema even as he gave "personal guidance" to many musicians, dancers and jugglers.

The film showing was arranged and invitations sent before the
explosion in Rangoon. It is a document that hints at the state of
mind of North Korea's leadership in the months just before the
bombing: perhaps an enhanced confidence resulting from China's
overtures.[12]

I heard subsequently that the highest-level Chongryon official involved
in inviting me to the screening had been required to answer to his superiors
for my review. According to one account, he nearly lost his job over it. Our
relationship cooled decidedly after that. I was told by another official in the
Chongryon Tokyo headquarters more than five years later that the incident
still was held against me, and was remembered in connection with my continuing applications to revisit North Korea. Meanwhile, after that China
journey Kim Jong-il took few publicized trips abroad.[13] But the China visit's
diplomatic success could be seen in de facto Chinese support for his status —
and, soon, in Soviet public recognition that he would be the successor.

If that documentary had shown nothing else, at least it would have demonstrated that Kim Jong-il still had ample reason to be dissatisfied with his
filmmakers. Of course there were bright spots where they had "grasped the
seed" and produced work in which he could take pride. The film version of
The Flower Girl at one foreign film festival had been awarded a Special Prize
and Special Medal.[14] But obviously there remained much room for improvement. And indeed, as it turned out, Kim had long since made plans — bizarre
beyond anything the world had yet heard about him — to deal with his film
industry's shortcomings.

Lacking a film director of the caliber of South Korea's finest, the prize-
winning Shin Sang-ok, the Dear Leader in 1978 had arranged for the kidnapping of Shin himself. Kim's agents first lured Shin's ex-wife, South
Korean superstar Choi Eun-hi, to Hong Kong to discuss an acting role, then

bundled her off to North Korea by sea. Kim Jong-il, waiting at dockside for her arrival, said, "Welcome to the DPRK." He didn't explain why she had been kidnapped, and Choi was "afraid to ask." Kim established her in luxurious surroundings, as she related in a book Choi and Shin published after their 1986 escape.[15]

It would be five years before Choi learned that she had been taken as bait to catch Shin. The two had remained friendly—and Kim Jong-il knew this—although they had divorced due to childlessness and Shin had married another actress, with whom he had children. Six months after Choi's mysterious disappearance Shin—who had been searching for her—was in Hong Kong when Kim's agents nabbed him, too, and spirited him off to North Korea. In Pyongyang, at first, Shin likewise got VIP treatment, with no explanation of what was going on—he was not told what had become of Choi. But Shin twice attempted escape. He was sent to prison, where he learned the hard way how the regime dealt with disobedience.

Choi was assigned a tutor and put to work studying Kim Il-sung, Kim Jong-il and the North Korean revolution. On Fridays Kim Jong-il invited her to see movies, operas and musicals. Others attending those soirees were high officials Kim had invited. Kim clearly wanted Choi to get to know him and to have a favorable impression of him. If there was no party, he took her videotapes of South Korean movies and asked for her critical opinion. Eventually she realized he was intelligent and possessed artistic sensibility. He arranged for her to have reading material, including a three-volume life of Kim Il-sung's father, Kim Hong jik. Volume three alone took about three months to read, but she found it interesting. With all that watching and reading, reviewing and commenting, she wasn't permitted much free time. But on Kim Jong-il's birthday, February 16, 1978, Choi's handler-guide took her on an outing. The destination proved to be a museum, at Kim Il-sung University, that was devoted to Kim Jong-il. Never having seen such a big museum devoted to just one person, she was surprised.

Choi saw and was impressed by Kim's trademark movies, *Sea of Blood* and *The Flower Girl*. But although she knew he had overseen those productions, taking more or less the role of producer, she couldn't tell who had actually directed the films. She noticed that in North Korea the director was not identified on movie posters. Kim Il-sung and Kim Jong-il wouldn't allow it, she learned. Only industry insiders would know who had made a movie. The two Kims didn't want other people to become famous. There were exceptions, though. A few movie people Kim Jong-il liked were recognized publicly as stars. For example, Hong Yong-hui of *Flower Girl* fame was pictured on the country's one-*won* currency note.

Choi noticed another curious practice in the North Korean media world: The country televised sports matches between North and South Korea only if the North had won. The people weren't told the outcome of the losing matches. She found also that the Korean language had forked off into different directions in the North and the South. When she went shopping with her guide, he requested *bulal*. Hearing that word embarrassed her, as *bulal* in South Korea meant testicle. But she found that in North Korea it meant lightbulb.

When April 15 came, Choi noticed that Kim Il-sung's birthday parade was "more like a funeral" because the North Koreans cried at the sight of the Great Leader. They also cried as they received the gifts—clothing, mostly—that Kim Il-sung provided for the people. Of course they applauded even as they were crying. "Once I neglected to clap my hands. Someone asked me, 'Why don't you praise Kim Il-sung?' 'Uh oh. I'm sorry.' And I clapped." Then there were the formal messages of congratulation that she was expected to prepare on Kim Jong-il's and Kim Il-sung's birthdays and on the September 9 anniversary of liberation. "Someone brought very nice paper so I could write the message, and then I had to make a cover of colorful material. There were specific dimensions to be followed. I had to find a different message each year—one is not allowed to repeat oneself. It was really torture."

Choi found also that, just before one of the leaders' birthdays, all North Koreans had to gather in family or other groupings to commemmorate the occasion by listening to a 140-minute radio broadcast or recording recounting the Kim family saga. It was forbidden to talk or sleep before this Pyongyang answer to a Christmas Eve service ended. On Kim Il-sung's birthday everyone was expected to collect or otherwise acquire azaleas to present to him. Presents came from the Great Leader in return. Most prized was an Omega watch, the back inscribed with Kim Il-sung's name. Choi got one of those.

Choi, staying in a guest house, had a dog, which made her very happy. But she heard that the North Koreans exported dog fur to Russia, besides eating dog meat. The dog disappeared. The housemaid said she didn't know for sure, but it was "probably far away." As the housemaid told her, frankly, "A dog's life is only six months. A dog is an export item in North Korea." (Some South Koreans eat the meat of dogs, but in the South those normally are especially bred food animals, not pets.)

Choi met a Chinese woman who had been kidnapped to work as a language teacher and learned from her that the spies employed in such operations must be good-looking. A handsome spy, pretending to be rich, could easily pick up a targeted female victim. If a spy's natural endowments were insufficient, the plastic surgeons stood ready to perfect what nature had wrought. Choi learned that "there was a special hospital for Kim Il-sung, his family and high officials. There were always soldiers there."

* * *

Shin was kept at first in a guest house, also in Pyongyang but separate from Choi's, with a guide and a secretary. After a couple of months, however, as punishment for his two nocturnal escape attempts, he was jailed. In his cell he was required to sit cross-legged, in the lotus position, his back straight, for hours at a time, Zen-style. He was not allowed to move. No reading, no radio, nothing else was permitted. He had to look into the eyes of his instructor, not shifting his gaze. A guard remained with him all day long. Meals were corn or rice, with salty soup.

"I awoke around five each day, then as soon as I got up I had to raise my arms straight up until the 7 A.M. breakfast, as punishment," Shin recalled. "After breakfast I could wash my face with the remains of my drinking water. Then I had to sit in the lotus position for three hours. After that punishment, I had three minutes to relax. Following lunch, it was the lotus position again from 12:30 to 6:30. Electrical brownouts occurred on average three times a day. Someone would bring a candle to each cell then, because the guards needed to see that we were in the lotus position. Once a week I had to strip and face the wall for a 'physical exam.' It was not a real physical, and I hated to show them my nudity."

In jail, after a couple of years of that routine, Shin felt his sanity starting to unravel. On Christmas morning in 1980, he was struck by an urge to send a greeting to his family back in South Korea. It was a white Christmas. Sent out with a shovel to clear the grounds, Shin used his urine to write "Merry Xmas" on the snow. "Anyone who saw me would have thought I was out of my mind, but I had to do it," he wrote. (That passage reminded me of my own nutty 1979 fantasy of escape across the Demilitarized Zone, described in chapter 1.)

Eventually Shin requested a consultation with someone in authority. The request was refused. He was told he must write a letter of apology to Kim Jong-il for his escape attempts and his other disobedience. "I decided to write a letter of apology. It took three days to get it right. I wrote: 'I will obey your rules. I want to become a DPRK citizen and follow and praise Kim Il-sung and Kim Jong-il. Please free me.'"

After he wrote his apology letter, Shin found that his status changed. Under the tutelage of a State Security agent, he began studying the lives and thoughts of the Kims. Wake-up time was still 5 A.M. And he had to obey rules that were posted on his wall: "Obedience is essential. Do not try to learn of the private lives of other prisoners. Don't listen to other prisoners' conversations. Don't converse with other prisoners. Accuse any prisoner who is at fault. Patients, obey the doctor. Don't waste the blanket, which is the property of the nation." Each prisoner had only one blanket, one set of clothing, one pair of socks. Before Kim Il-sung's birthday the prisoners had to clean the premises furiously. Some called that "the torture of April."

Shin found the rules ridiculous, especially one that limited each prisoner's shower to five minutes. He obeyed for a while but eventually got so fed up with prison that he resumed attempting to escape and even tried to fast to death. At first, his guards simply told him to go ahead and die of starvation if he wished. But then some "guidance" officials came to his cell and force-fed him with a funnel, pushing the food down his throat. After that horrible experience a guard told him, "I've never seen that before. They never cared about a fasting prisoner. You're the first." The guard said his treatment indicated Shin must be very important for North Korea.

Shin continued his studies and eventually was awarded his own outing to the Kim Jong-il Museum. There he was shown a mineral well whose water was highly praised. He should drink from it, he was told. He declined but his hosts insisted he "drink in remembrance of Kim Jong-il." It isn't clear whether this touch had been borrowed from Christian observance or from the ritual purification rite performed at the shrines of Japanese Shinto, the religion that had been used to support emperor worship.

In 1982, when Kim Il-sung's seventieth birthday drew near, Shin worked on composing a congratulatory letter as his political tutors had urged. They told him ordinary paper would not do, and gave him the proper stationery, magnificent and colorful. Opening the cover, he could see the faint outlines of the magnolia flower, Kim's favorite. He wrote his note on that paper. When Kim's birthday came, Shin received as a present from the Great Leader his own inscribed Omega wristwatch. He was also awarded a national medal.

The following year, on February 23, Shin's letters of apology and flattery finally paid off when Kim Jong-il sent a letter releasing him from jail. A guard ordered him to stand at attention while the guard read it and watched Shin's eyes. "I forgive you even though you are a sinner and your guilt was very large," Kim Jong-il had written. "I just want you to devote yourself to achieving revolution in my country." Shin's handler took him to a restaurant. There, Shin bowed automatically, at the requisite forty-five-degree angle, before a portrait of Kim Il-sung. Then, still standing before the portrait, he vowed aloud to "do as you order, Great Leader." The guide was pleased. "You are doing very well," he told Shin. "Let's have a seat."

Earlier that month, Kim Jong-il had told Choi for the first time that her ex-husband was in Pyongyang, promising her that she would meet Shin soon. On March 6, Shin's handler told him: "You will have good news today. You should get dressed." He was taken to meet Kim Jong-il and Choi. Kim suggested to Choi: "Why don't you hug him?" Then Kim announced, to the security people and others present, "Mr. Shin will be my film advisor from now on." Kim had a suggestion for the divorced couple: "Why don't you get married on my father's birthday?" He assured Shin that he was returning the still-glamorous Choi to him "without having touched her. I am a real, purified communist."

Kim held a party for the couple and there he astonished them by apologizing for having kept each of them in the dark about the reasons for the kidnapping and the whereabouts of the other. The date was March 7, 1983, and presumably Kim knew that it was the twenty-ninth anniversary of their original marriage. "Please forgive me," Kim said to them. "I was just playing a role." Kim got drunk during the party and sang South Korean songs (which were forbidden to his subjects). He showed some documentary films in which citizens displayed adulation toward him. When Shin complimented him on the people's evident devotion, Kim replied: "It's all a lie. They're just pretending to praise me."

Before meeting him, Shin had thought Kim must be crazy. Now, however, upon hearing Kim's apologetic and humble remarks, Shin concluded that the young leader had real humanity and was very generous. "I was amazed that he was a communist."

Shin and Choi were happy to be reunited. After the party, they were taken to see the Dear Leader's personal film library, which they found to be a three-story building where some 250 employees cared for an astonishingly full collection of more than 15,000 films from around the world. Around 300 of those were from South Korea, and one of them came as a major shock to Shin and Choi. Years earlier, without taking the precaution of making copies of his new film *Tale of Shimcheong*, Shin had sent it to a representative in Hong Kong who had asked to have it shipped there so that subtitles could be made. The film thereafter had gone missing. Now Shin saw that Kim Jong-il had it in his library, which meant that the Dear Leader was the only person in the world who could screen it. The couple figured Shin's Hong Kong employee had been Kim Jong-il's secret agent, involved first in stealing the film and then in kidnapping them.

Kim asked Shin and Choi to watch and critique films, four per day, mostly from the communist bloc but also including the occasional Hollywood production such as *Dr. Zhivago*. All that viewing would not have seemed to Kim an onerous chore. He himself was watching movies every night. Shin and Choi concluded that he was using foreign films to make up for his lack of foreign travel, gathering from them information about foreign countries. Wherever he went, a video setup was expected to be provided. Shin learned that Kim personally vetted in advance each film proposed for showing in the country. Kim phoned the couple every day, dialing directly rather than having his secretary make the calls. "How are you? Is your health OK? If there's anything you need, just tell me." Shin developed considerable respect for

Kim's film knowledge and sensibility, deciding that the young ruler was "smarter than his directors and writers."

One day, Kim phoned Shin, thanked him for his help and said he had a favor to ask. Kim had done the preliminary planning for a film and wanted Shin to direct it and enter it in an international contest. At the same time he said he was preparing an office for Shin at Pyongyang's Choson Film Studios. When Shin saw it he was astonished. "It was a wonderful office, three stories, of semi-European architecture, lined in marble." Shin was doubly happy: Not only would he be able to resume movie-making, he would also be given a passport, which meant there might be a chance for escape eventually.

At the time of his kidnapping Shin had been on the outs politically with the military-backed government of South Korea. He and Choi knew that if they should ever escape and try to return to the South they would need proof to persuade the tough and suspicious anti-communist officials of the Korean Central Intelligence Agency that they had not defected willingly. So they adopted an extremely risky gambit. When they visited Kim Jong-il in his office at party headquarters for an audience on Shin's fifty-first birthday, Choi secreted a tape recorder in her handbag and managed to record forty-five minutes of the three-hour conversation. The date was October 19, 1983 — ten days after the Rangoon bombing (and just a few days before I saw and panned the China trip documentary that had been assembled by far lesser talents than Shin). Choi noted with interest that Kim had monitors mounted on his office wall showing three South Korean television networks.

More than a decade later the South Korean monthly magazine *Wolgan Choson* combined the tapes of this conversation and some subsequent tapings onto a cassette and distributed it in connection with a magazine special report. As one South Korean listener commented to me, the Kim on the tapes talked "volubly" and "straightforwardly." He "doesn't embellish but just comes out and says what he wants to." His voice was "normally pitched, resonant and pleasant. But he speaks with a slight stutter and the words don't always fit together. He jumps around." Kim seemed to like to talk — on the tape he left little time for others to talk. Although the accented Korean spoken by people from the North and the South can be quite different, Kim "speaks with only a slight accent. He could communicate easily in the South."[16]

In this first secretly taped conversation Kim offered an explanation, remarkably frank, of the thinking behind the kidnap plot. He had heard of Shin's political troubles with the Seoul regime, which had resulted in revocation of the Shin Studio's South Korean film license, he told the couple. Thus he figured that Shin, then spending time in Hong Kong and the United States, might be preparing to move his operation overseas. Shin had been born before liberation in the northern part of Korea, which also helped make him a plausible convert to the North Korean side. He doubted he could get Shin to come on his own, though, so Kim had ordered Choi brought to

Pyongyang "to lure director Shin." Kim explained that "at the time, the thing I was advocating was: How can the people from the Southern part come to us, to our republic's bosom, and with genuine freedom, genuine, uh, in producing films, do so without worries?"

Kim then launched into a soliloquy on why South Korea had achieved a higher standard of moviemaking than the North. The difference, he suggested, was that North Korean film industry people knew that the state would feed them even if they performed only minimally, so they didn't try hard. Their Southern counterparts, meanwhile, especially in earlier years when the economy was struggling, knew that they must work to eat. "Because they have to earn money," Kim said, Southern movie industry people expended blood, sweat and tears to get results. South Korean actors, he said, obviously had been aware that instant stardom wouldn't last; they must work to improve their acting because the public soon would tire of just a pretty face. Newcomers to the North Korean screen lacked that understanding and motivation, and thus failed to make the effort to grow in their craft after making their film debuts, Kim said.

Besides recognizing the motivation problems in a socialist system, Kim in that conversation also acknowledged that the North's insistence on national self-reliance made it difficult for others in the country to speak, as he was doing privately to Shin and Choi, about the superiority of outside ways. "If someone else says this, the others will criticize him for being a malcontent," the Dear Leader said. "He might be termed a toady." As a result, he said, filmmakers in the North worked dogmatically. "There are many repetitive scenes and the stories are already schematized. . . . There are so many crying scenes, like a funeral. Why aren't there any movies without crying scenes?"

Kim told his forced guests, apologetically, that he could not have it known that he had kidnapped Shin and Choi to the country to upgrade the local film industry. "It is not propitious to talk about it truthfully," he said. Then he taught them the cover story they should use when meeting people from outside North Korea. They should say that "South Koreans do not have democracy. No freedom, no democracy. Next, say there is too much meddling when it comes to creative invention. The intervention is what you [in the South] call the anti-communist law. Uh, [in the South] they only tell you to do anti-communism, so there is anti-communism here and there and thus no freedom." Shin tried to interject a remark at that point but Kim ignored him and continued laying down his script for the couple to follow: "That is why, because there is no freedom, in seeking genuine freedom, pursuing genuine freedom, to be ensured freedom of creativity, you have come here. And as for the plot of a movie, we can start following the developed countries and even exceed what they have done. With this slogan, 'exceeding,' we will march forward. This way, everything will be natural. It's better than saying you came here by force."

Kim later explained his remark about movie plots, acknowledging that films made for internal propaganda purposes might not be suited for entry into international contests. Thus Shin would be permitted to select themes more likely to be accepted abroad. Kim told the couple a story of one contest in Cambodia, a country then ruled by Kim Il-sung's close friend Prince Norodom Sihanouk, in which North Korea had tried to enter a guerrilla-themed film. Sihanouk was not amused. After all, Cambodia had rid itself only recently of the Khmer Rouge, the genocidal former guerrillas whose dead victims included some of Sihanouk's children. Sihanouk complained that the pro-revolutionary North Korean entry was "a film opposing myself." Kim recalled that Sihanouk was "fuming with rage." North Korean representatives spent the rest of their time in Phnom Penh aplogizing. "It is evident," concluded Kim, "that we don't have a properly made film to enter in a film festival."

Resuming his comparison, Kim said North Korea's filmmakers were "like kindergarten students who just learned how to walk, but in the South they all possess mid- to high-level technologies. [The Southerners are] university-level, and we are kindergarten level, but still when new ideas are introduced they [North Korean film people] reject them and are firm about it." He worried that "in ten years, if we don't catch up, frankly speaking, in an international perspective, because our movies are so backwards, we might rank number one among the most backward films. Ah, I'm saying that we might be the last among the lagging films."

Shin started work October 20, 1983, at his new office. Kim provided Shin with millions of dollars, practically a blank check, for the quest to win international film awards. Once the couple went abroad together, under close guard, and gave a press conference in which they denied having been kidnapped, claiming that they had gone voluntarily to Pyongyang. They had no choice at the time, they were to write later. But lying at that press conference helped them prepare for their eventual escape (which came in 1986), by persuading Kim that they were loyal and need not be guarded so closely when they traveled.

The Choi-Shin episode revealed much about Kim Jong-il's personality and work style. When it came to his favorite subject, movies, Kim proved to be not so rigid an ideologue as might have been expected based on his attacks on others who fell short of ideological purity. His published movie writings focus tightly on promoting the unitary system, yet he told Shin not to worry about political statements but just to make prize-winning films that would show off North Korea.

The liberal attitudes that Kim showed to Shin and Choi could have been role-playing, to an extent. The couple reported that Kim described Shin's

Kim Il-sung in 1965. (AP)

Women in their finest outfits line up to view Kim Il-sung's childhood home at Mangyongdae. (COURTESY OF THE AUTHOR)

Mural shows Kim Il-sung surveying well-tended farmland.
(COURTESY OF THE AUTHOR)

Suffer the little children to come unto Kim Il-sung. (COURTESY OF THE AUTHOR)

The Pyongyang subways are full of murals like this one, which shows Kim Il-
sung in another rural scene. Note the ornate columns.
(COURTESY OF THE AUTHOR)

The holy family goes riding on Mount Packtu, but without little brother Shura.
(COURTESY OF THE AUTHOR)

First Lady Kim Jong-suk accompanies a children's musicale. Can you spot her son, Kim Jong-il? (COURTESY OF THE AUTHOR)

Inspecting the West Sea Barrage, Kim Jong-il's gigantic public works project near Nampo, Kim Il-sung seems about to exclaim: "This is my beloved son, in whom I am well pleased." (COURTESY OF THE AUTHOR)

As he eased into semi-retirement, Kim Il-sung switched from "people's clothing" to Western-style suits. Here he is shown relaxing before the "secret cabin"
on Mount Paektu. (COURTESY OF THE AUTHOR)

Father and son give on-the-spot guidance to peasants.
(COURTESY OF THE AUTHOR)

Now doing the guidance tours on his own, the fashion-conscious Dear Leader shows off one of his trademark outfits. (COURTESY OF THE AUTHOR)

In Pyongyang, a bronze statue that used to be gold makes clear how insignificant ordinary mortals are in comparison with Kim Il-sung. (COURTESY OF THE AUTHOR)

The holy of holies in the lobby of the Potonggang Hotel in Pyongyang features Kim Il-sung atop Mount Paektu. (COURTESY OF THE AUTHOR)

In 1979 and for decades after, the lack of bustle on the streets of Pyongyang was notable. (COURTESY OF THE AUTHOR)

Kim Il-sung Square looks better when it's filled with people.
(COURTESY OF THE AUTHOR)

The regime paid serious attention to improving the Pyongyang skyline, erecting many of these buildings in the run-up to the 1989 World Festival of Youth and Students.
(COURTESY OF THE AUTHOR)

The sets for *Song of Paradise* in 1979 included this example of idealized housing. (COURTESY OF THE AUTHOR)

Child entertainers at a school in Pyongyang show their practised smiles in 1979. Did their parents realize that some of the youngsters might be recruited all too soon to serve in the Mansions Special Volunteer Corps? (COURTESY OF THE AUTHOR)

Schoolchildren learn about Kim Il-sung and his family.
(COURTESY OF THE AUTHOR)

The teacher is never alone at the head of the class. (COURTESY OF THE AUTHOR)

A salesclerk exhibits a North Korean wristwatch made with machinery imported in the 1970s from Switzerland. Pyongyang stiffed the machinery exporters when they sent their bill. (COURTESY OF THE AUTHOR)

A statue of Kim Il-sung surveys an exhibition of industrial machinery made in North Korea. (COURTESY OF THE AUTHOR)

Factory workers make men's suits for export to Japan. (COURTESY OF THE AUTHOR)

Chun To-kun, deputy chairman of Chonsam Cooperative Farm, shows a visitor around in 1979. (COURTESY OF THE AUTHOR)

North Korea goes all out in "mass games" in which the masses hold up colored cards to depict the greatness of their leaders. (COURTESY OF THE AUTHOR)

The country went wild when South Korean dissident student Im Su-gyong visited in 1989 and Kim Il-sung himself received her. She returned to serve a jail sentence in South Korea. Meanwhile, North Korean artists competed to portray her as a leader of street demonstrations, struggling against riot policemen and as the defendant in her court case. (COURTESY OF THE AUTHOR)

The author gets a friendly welcome at a Pyongyang nursery. (MIKE THARP)

American journalists Edith Lederer (Associated Press), John Wallach (Hearst) and Mike "Buck" Tharp *(The Wall Street Journal)* look past North Korean soldiers standing guard at the demarcation line in Panmunjom to the soldiers representing the United Nations forces. (COURTESY OF THE AUTHOR)

Kim Yong-nam, then foreign policy chief for the Workers Party, sits for an interview in 1979. He later became titular head of state.
(COURTESY OF THE AUTHOR)

High-ranking intelligence official Bai Song-chul, alias Kim Jong-su, demonstrates his characteristic feisty posture and sardonic expression. Standing behind him are interpreters and other handlers of the American journalists who visited in 1979.
(COURTESY OF THE AUTHOR)

Kim Jong-il salutes during the celebration to mark North Korea's fifty-fifth birthday on September 9, 2003. (AP/KOREA NEWS SERVICE)

The Seaview Casino Hotel was built to accommodate visiting gamblers from across the Chinese border. (HIDEKO TAKAYAMA)

Kim Jong-nam, the eldest son of Kim Jong-il. (AP/SHIZUO KAMBAYASHI)

harsh treatment in jail as a dreadful mistake, the result of poorly performing security personnel who provoked Shin's rebellion. In that case the Dear Leader seems to have sought to present his "good cop" face. Following in the footsteps of his father, he would make frequent use of the device of publicly blaming subordinates for failed policies—and punishing them—even though the policies were his.

Note the tendency unashamedly to play god, planning the lives of people under his control, as when Kim suggested that Choi and Shin remarry even though Shin still had a legal second wife in the South. (The second wife subsequently died in a motor accident.)

And there is the fact that, even with a whole country to look out for as the co-ruler, Kim Jong-il still spent a great deal of his time and effort on movies. Subordinates seeking to justify his fascination with foreign movies might explain it as a means to learn English and thus learn about Western economic methods. But that hardly accounts for his having received four critiques a day from Shin, for example. One may question how much time and effort he had left over to spend on improving the people's livelihood—aside from exhorting them to work ever harder and faster.[17]

Shortly after Kim Jong-il's formal elevation to the heirship in 1980, Pyongyang's Central News Agency praised the "Party Center" for an "economic agitation campaign" through which "a leaping advance has been made in economic development."[18] The people of North Korea would have had to be instructed where to look for evidence of such an "advance." Agitation was the old, top-down motivation method used in the Chollima campaign, Kim Il-sung's knockoff of China's Great Leap Forward. By the 1980s the method had lost much of its usefulness, but the elder Kim had been loath to adopt the un-socialist Western approaches that were being introduced into other communist economies.

As the poorly traveled Kim Jong-il gained power over his country's affairs, the top-down, closed-to-the-outside-world approach was all that he had been taught, all that he knew. It was during this period that his committee of sympathetic biographers troubled to tell us, in *Great Leader Kim Jong-il*, that as a primary school pupil in the period immediately after the 1953 armistice the junior Kim often visited private rice shops in the market and "made a close study of rice prices and citizens' purchasing power. At night, he showed to his father his pocketbook in which the prices of goods were written down." By the time he was a political economy major at Kim Il-sung University, private shops were a thing of the past and Kim Jong-il was lending his talents to the regime's micromanagement of the economy. He would, his biographers say, drop into a mountain food shop, check the soybean paste, find it sour and deliver a speech urging shop employees to protect consumers by cracking down on suppliers "when there are shortages of goods or the goods supplied are inferior in quality."

It was the Chinese who now tried to teach Kim Jong-il some different ideas about economic development. And he listened, at least to an extent. But much of what he heard seems to have worried him, or baffled him, as much as it inspired him. He began talking of plans to open North Korea soon after returning from his 1983 trip to China. In the recorded portion of his October 19 conversation that year with film couple Shin and Choi, Kim noted that China like Yugoslavia had "opened itself up. . . . Hu Yaobang said: 'Now here, uh, Chairman Mao, Chairman Mao, when Mao Zedong was still around, the doors were tightly locked and thus [the Chinese] people saw nothing. When they see other people's things they say without consideration that the other people's goods are good while theirs are bad. In reality, their goods aren't so bad. They have to make efforts to improve theirs to do better than others, but instead of making efforts they continually claim that the other person's goods are good, which is a major problem. After opening up a little, what do they learn first, instead of Western technology? They learn to grow beards and [long] hair. Ah, tell them to acquire technology but all they do is take in external things, thus they have nothing in them yet. The education system should generally be reformed.' That's what Hu Yaobang said to me."

Kim talked then about how the lesson applied to North Korea: "It's the same in our case," he told the couple. "If we continually show Western films on television, show them without restraint, then only nihilistic thoughts can come about. Eh, then, in a situation where we are divided, how can our national pride and next patriotic struggle—all those things, patriotism, patriotism—we have to increase this, but we only make them idolize Western things, Western things. So we must advance the technology before opening, but this is one of the problems that cause us to fall into internal contradictions." His conclusion was a cautious compromise: "Eh, thus, because of this, I want to give rights to a limited degree. That is my intention."

Kim then returned to his concern about the failure of the regime's incentives to make North Korean movie industry people work hard. He had more than an inkling that the North Korean system was at fault. "What I'm saying is that this—ever since the end of the Korean War, speaking in materialistic terms, what you call, eh—unless we make them have desires, uh—I think it is related with the system. What I'm saying is that even if only one piece is written in a year, living expenses are still given. When a piece is written, only the cost of the paper can be earned. It should be their main job but it is only a side job. Eh—what one has to really, really do [for a living], that is a side job while even if one does not do this, living expenses are still given by the government. Thus the people have no desire or need. So if we say, 'Write three pieces a year,' thus they've already become too full in the stomach. Then they say that they can't write it at their home and thus request that they be sent to a resort. That's how people have become." Once, Kim said, "I called on my propaganda department workers and said to them that the socialist system is said to be good, but that there are a lot of internal discrepancies that must be resolved. Yes. So what I'm trying to say is that they have no motivation to work."

Months later, after one of their new films won an award at a festival in Czechoslovakia, Kim invited Choi and Shin to his office—and again the couple managed to tape the conversation. This time, Kim broadened his economic analysis a bit to touch upon aspects beyond his beloved movie studios: "Ten years ago, twenty years ago, what did we say? 'People should tighten their belts. In a situation where the North and the South are separated, we must ourselves prepare a revolutionary capacity. Thus we must tighten our belts and work to build our defense.'"

From this historical note Kim abruptly shifted his thoughts to the competition from South Korea, which was then getting favorable worldwide publicity for its success in launching an indigenous automobile industry. Kim felt the praise was undeserved because the Southern automakers relied heavily on overseas suppliers of components. "Localization, localization is what they claim, but in engine development the South Koreans, the South Korean people, in producing a motorcycle they import the engine, bring in this and that. . . . It is basically an assembled good. The automobiles, what do they call it [perhaps he was attempting to recall the name of the Hyundai Pony, which was the Model-T Ford of South Korean industrialization], even those are completely assembled. What they claim as localization is only 40 percent. How can they call what they assemble localization? They themselves—we shouldn't do it that way. We must show the machines in the planning stages. Show this, show them from the first stages, then the reporters will go to the South and will compare our factory to the South Korean one."

Kim then returned to his earlier theme: "So now, in what direction are we heading? Yes, the defense industry or heavy industries are our priority. While encouraging this, what else should we do? It's time to raise the living standards of the people. This is because tightening the belts of socialist people is—I have said already. Look at our comrades."

Kim continued his monologue, harking back to popular support for the socialist system at the time of the Korean War—and in the process acknowledging to Shin that the North had attacked the South, something that the South Korean would have known very well but that most North Koreans were not permitted to know. "How were the sentiments of our people when the war broke out in 1950?" he asked rhetorically. At the time, he asserted, people in both North and South had favored the Northern system and opposed what he asserted was the system below the 38th parallel: "a society for a minority of capitalists and mid-level people. Thus because they said the [socialist] system at the time was favorable at the time, what did we have? There were only a few weapons given by the Soviets. Because we knew that the system was good, we went out to secure it. Thus in South Korea there were capitalists, landlords and comprador capitalists. Thus we said, 'Let's go and liberate.'"

Things had changed, though, in the intervening period, Kim acknowledged. "After doing socialism for thirty years, feeding the people cannot be done without reaching out to the Western world. We are definitely behind the Western world. So the people, this livelihood problem—this ideological problem—is very important. To overcome this, Eastern European countries are having a hard time."

It seems Kim still did not fully understand how the South had done so well, and would in coming years do so well, economically. He wanted to improve living standards for North Koreans, sensed that socialist methods were failing in his country and elsewhere in the communist bloc—but at the same time he rejected integration into the market economy that South Korea had joined. He still thought it possible to stick with his father's *juche* approach, producing everything at home from scratch.

The Chinese continued to work on him, though. Hu Yaobang had made a return visit to North Korea since Kim's earlier recorded conversation with Shin and Choi. During that return visit, Kim told Shin, Hu had asked him: "Why aren't you doing the tourism industry? The tourism industry brings in a lot of money." Kim acknowledged the rationality of the argument, although in the same breath he expressed ambivalence about the issue: "I understand, so we will do the tourism industry now. We will start now. But it wasn't because we didn't want to do it—of course we didn't want to do it—but now I've decided to do it."

Kim agonized over the opening of his country that would be necessary if he should go after tourist dollars. Speaking to Hu Yaobang, he said, he had worried aloud that North Korea was so small, with so much of its territory fortified, that it would be difficult to show off tourist sites without giving enemies a clear view of its defenses. "In your case," he said he had told Hu, "since you have a vast continent you can do whatever you want. In our case the border and the shoreline aren't very long, and are tightly fortified. If this is opened up to tourism, how would it be different from withdrawal of troops? If everyone comes and looks over everything, if everything is opened up—ha ha! And if Pyongyang is opened up in the end it will be the same as calling back the forces from along the border. Next it will, must be in Pyongyang. It's the same as being disarmed. Being the same as disarmed—I propose this after we reunite. But with your [China's] experience, like your case, we will do it. We will do it, and there is a way. We will do tourism."

Kim had figured out, he said, that at most he could open certain east coast areas to tourism: the port city of Chongjin and parts of Kangwon province. "I said to this Hu Yaobang: 'Now we will pursue the open door policy. We will initiate the open door policy"—but only in those limited areas. "Yes, we will do tourism." He quoted Hu as having replied: "Let's see you do it." And, said Kim, "I promised him."

In December 1984, Kim called the couple to his office and told them that "he"—Kim Il-sung—was "very satisfied" with their work. Having received Choi's letters every year, the Great Leader now would greet them on New Year's Day, 1985. They took along their tape recorder when they went to the palace for the reception. The conversation they recorded there reveals much about the attitudes of the man who remained North Korea's ultimate ruler, for the time being, even as he was ceding more and more authority to his son.

Kim Il-sung and first lady Kim Song-ae engaged Shin and Choi in small talk about their movies, and then the president quickly changed the subject. He wanted to talk about a recent international proposal that North Korea and South Korea enter the United Nations at the same time. That would divide Korea "forever," Kim Il-sung complained. "Instead, what we are proposing is to retain the systems and autonomy of North and South while uniting [in a confederation], and enter the UN as one country. That way would not perpetuate the division."

Then the Great Leader got in a dig at South Korea, in the process proving that he understood South Korea's economic success and prospects no better than his son did—perhaps not even as well as his son did. "It's impractical to ask the South Korean government to get rid of the rotten system there overnight," Kim Il-sung told Shin and Choi. "They have a $50 billion debt. Fifty billion: think about it! Fifty billion is not a simple problem. Our debt is $1 billion. We are going to earn foreign currency and thus within a couple of years we are going to fully pay it back. Do you know what [Japanese lawmaker] Tokuma Usunomiya said to me? The Japanese give a lot of money to South Korea, but that amount is equivalent of what the South Korean government has to pay each year as interest on its loans!"

The receiving-line conversation with Shin and Choi ended there, as a North Korean functionary offered his New Year's greeting: "Long live the Great Leader!"

"Thank you," replied Kim Il-sung.

It was around that time that the balance tilted in the relationship between the president and his heir-designate. Mainly involved with matters of ideology and propaganda previously, Kim Jong-il from the mid-1980s is reported to have taken day-to-day charge of the party, the military, the administration— even international affairs. "By 1985, Kim Jong-il had in reality taken complete control of most of the areas in politics," according to Hwang Jang-yop, "and he got his men to spread the word that he was top leader in North Korea."[19]

The extent of his new responsibilities and the amount of work involved seem to have required him to face up to the need that he change his behavior. "From 1985, Kim Jong-il's lifestyle changed totally," elite defector Kang Myong-do told *JoongAng Ilbo* in Seoul. "His life of no constraints ended and the number of Happy Corps members declined. There was a lot of work to do from 1985. Each day he had thousands of reports to take care of and had to work until 1 or 2 A.M. sometimes. He adopted a routine. On Monday he would take care of the party propaganda department's work; Tuesday, the Korean People's Army; Wednesday, the president's office and party finances; Thursday, government officials; Friday, the Central People's Committee. Weekends, he would rest."[20]

If there was any hope for the country short of a major regime change, then, it was that Kim Jong-il would turn out to be a reformer. Pyongyang offered tantalizing clues that he might. Here is what an unofficial spokesman for the regime wrote about Kim's modernizing ways in the Hong Kong–based magazine *Far Eastern Economic Review*: "An enemy of regimentation, Kim Jong-il views it as contradictory to the concept of man as a free, independent and creative being. He advocates modern lifestyles while preserving traditional values. He even encourages people to date more openly, in a traditional manner. Since he first appeared with a modern hairdo, such things have been in vogue among North Korea's young people. City and rural barbers and beauty parlors cater to customers with dozens of different hairstyles. People are encouraged to wear a variety of fashionable and colorful costumes, both traditional and modern."[21]

Beyond such superficial matters, there were some changes in economic policies, including a 1984 law intended to encourage foreign investment in joint ventures in North Korea. But positive change in substantive matters came slowly through the 1980s and into the 1990s. Part of the reason has to be that, as we have seen in this chapter, Kim Jong-il was not completely clear in his own mind about the direction in which he should take the country.

In fairness, we should note that he still did not have full power. While Kim Jong-il was running things on a day-to-day basis from 1985, one former elite official told me nearly a decade later, the younger Kim inevitably encountered some conflicts with his father, who was still the president and the Great Leader. "Kim Jong-il will be the successor, but Kim Il-sung is not handing over power all at once. Kim Jong-il may want it faster. Since Kim Jong-il is younger he's more open-minded regarding foreign affairs than Kim Il-sung. Even if he wants to change the policy, though, he has to go through Kim Il-sung."[22] The former official's point is well taken. Still, even if Kim Il-sung had died in 1985 and left the whole family business to Kim Jong-il, we may doubt based on what we know of him that the younger man would have moved immediately to change the system in a major way.

NINETEEN

A Story to Tell to the Nations

In 1989, during a brief thaw in the otherwise mostly unremitting enmity between Pyongyang and Washington, the first delegation of North Korean "scholars" visited the East Coast of the United States. At a dinner party in their honor in a friend's New York apartment, I was introduced to the North Korean delegates including their leader, Professor Kim Jong-su. Something about him, perhaps the oval yet strong-jawed face, or the sardonic look of his downward-turned mouth, looked familiar. Kim and I looked at each other for a while, and it was he who spoke first to ask: "Haven't we met before?" Indeed we had, I replied—but I had been with *The Baltimore Sun* at that time, in 1979. Now, ten years later, I was working for *Newsweek*. I decided not to mention that I had known him the first time not as Professor Kim, deputy director of a scholarly think tank called the Institute for International Studies, but as Bai Song-chul, the orphan who had been brought up by Kim Il-sung to become a diplomat working for the Society for Cultural Relations with Foreign Countries.

It was an extraordinarily pleasant evening. The North Korean guests and a group of Korean-American scholars joined together to sing Korean songs around the piano after supper and talked of their hopes for reunification. Everyone was in shirtsleeves and relaxed. At one point Kim Jong-su asked sociably if I had been back to North Korea.

That was just the question I had been waiting for. Kim Yong-nam, the foreign affairs secretary, had told me during our interview in 1979 that

I ought to revisit North Korea in the future, as I had "made many friends" in his country. "Later on we'll have much opportunity to meet again," he had assured me. But then the North had rolled up the welcome mat. Over the following decade I had written and cabled Kim Yong-nam and others in Pyongyang asking permission to revisit the country, but each request had been ignored. The World Festival of Youth and Students was scheduled to open in Pyongyang just a few days after this New York dinner party and I had applied to cover it, but the prospects did not look good.

When I explained all that to Kim Jong-su, he unhesitatingly offered to intercede on my behalf, assuring me that I would be admitted. He was as good as his word and soon I was back in Pyongyang, ensconced once again in the Potonggang Hotel.

In the decade since my previous visit to North Korea, rival South Korea's gross national product had expanded to nearly $5,000 per capita while economic performance in the North had continued to lag. Persistent reports reaching the outside world had told of serious food shortages in the North, although the regime did not acknowledge them. Indeed, it had not talked much about such occurrences since the hard times of 1946, the year after liberation, when Kim Il-sung had told his countrymen: "Everything is short with us—foodstuff, personnel, materials and so on. But this is no reason for us to be idle." In 1989 it was not yet clear to outsiders that what had been intended as a propaganda gesture to South Korea had instead confirmed the North on a collision course with famine. Kang Myong-do reported in 1995 that North Korean organizations responsible for destabilizing and spying on the South had come up with the idea of publicly offering massive rice aid in 1984 when the Southerners were hit with floods. The assumption was that Seoul as usual would reject the offer. To the Pyongyang leadership's horror, the Southerners accepted. In Pyongyang, "Kim Jung-lin, the person in charge, was exiled," Kang reported. "He dug privies for six months."[1]

Now Kim Il-sung and Kim Jong-il seemed determined to banish any problems by intensifying the same old approaches. Communist leaders in China, Hungary and elsewhere were experimenting with individual incentives and free markets. The Pyongyang leadership meanwhile dreamed up ever more costly and elaborate schemes to burnish prestige with grandiose monuments and extravagant festivities, hoping to persuade its subjects that their sacrifices were worthwhile. But the evident confusion and panic within the Northern leadership increased as old allies in Eastern Europe and the Soviet Union cast off communism—and with it, their special relationships with Pyongyang.

One by one, countries that had favored North Korea or tried to maintain equal relationships with the two Koreas were wooing the South and all but ignoring the North. For those countries, North Korea no longer had much to offer. South Korea on the other hand was a model of capitalist development, a potential source of trade, investment, technology, advice and aid. The trend could be glimpsed from the time Hungary and South Korea set up trade offices in each other's capitals starting in late 1987. Other East European countries followed Budapest's lead, and diplomatic recognition followed trade.

From early in the decade the Northern leaders had responded to the signs Pyongyang was losing the contest with Seoul by resorting to terror. There was the 1983 Rangoon bombing, in which North Korean agents assassinated South Korean cabinet members. In 1987, Pyongyang agents bombed a Korean Airlines civilian passenger jet, killing all 115 people aboard. The attack was an effort to spoil Seoul's plans to host the Olympics. The two agents swallowed poison when they were caught, but one survived. Under South Korean questioning she said she had been told by her superior in Pyongyang that her orders came directly from Kim Jong-il. (Former party secretary Hwang Jang-yop has blamed Kim Jong-il for the incident, without giving details.)[2] Maddeningly for Pyongyang, the South went on to increase its lead over the North not only economically but also politically. In 1987, student-led demonstrations forced President Chun Doo-hwan to agree to free elections. Permitting the South's people to choose their leaders tended to neutralize Pyongyang's chief remaining talking point.

Among South Korea's successes, none galled the North's leaders more than the 1988 Seoul Olympics, which celebrated and spotlighted the South's newfound international status. Pyongyang first tried to muscle in on Seoul's act, demanding that it be allowed to co-host the Olympics. The South agreed to discuss the matter, but negotiations collapsed. Then came the bombing of the Korean Airlines plane. Finally, North Korea's leaders decided to use their turn to host the World Festival of Youth and Students—a sports-and-ideology bash well known in the socialist world but virtually unheard of in the United States—as a showcase of their own. (The psychology of that decision was typically Korean. In the South, for example, a recurring problem for economic planners was that if one top *chaebol*—big business combine—went into, say, the automobile business, then the others felt they must do exactly the same. Their prestige depended on it, in the Korean way of thinking.) Having kept Western journalists at a distance in response to the largely unfavorable coverage at the time of the 1979 table tennis tournament, Pyongyang officials decided once more to admit a press contingent.

Like so much else that the leadership had tried, the scheme to stage the festival as a means of enhancing North Korea's international prestige backfired badly. Through an accident of timing, the Pyongyang festival opened right after the Tienanmen Square massacre in China. Not only journalists but also delegates from European countries with relatively moderate socialist movements focused on obvious similarities between the human rights situations in China and North Korea. Those of us who attended the festival's opening ceremony, in a brand-new stadium, witnessed an astonishing demonstration that may have been the first in decades to oppose the regime. As Scandinavian and Italian delegates marched around the stadium, they briefly held up signs questioning human rights policies in North Korea and in China. Danes in the audience who brandished a sign just as Kim Il-sung began speaking found themselves in a scuffle with male North Koreans—students who acted spontaneously, not police, Kim Jong-su assured me later. ("We are a hot people," he explained, using the incident as an illustration that the people were not automatons as some foreigners thought.)

Alerted in advance, North Korean officials clearly were concerned about the foreign criticism. A day or two before the opening ceremony a group of foreign correspondents asked a taxi driver to drive to the Italian delegation's headquarters, where a party was scheduled. We expected to get news there of the coming protest. The driver indeed took us for a ride—out into the countryside. For an hour, he pretended to be lost. Eventually he returned us to our hotel. It may be that he had exceeded his brief; one of our handlers apologized and said it had been a mistake. Before the evening was completely gone, we were duly ferried to the Italians' party.

The demonstration in the stadium was, to be sure, a foreigners' protest. The assumption must be that the North Koreans witnessing it were members of the privileged class of loyalists permitted to reside in the capital, and therefore were unlikely to be inspired to action by the protesters' signs. Not only did the Pyongyang residents fail to join in the foreigners' demonstration; foreign residents I talked with said they had seen no evidence of indigenous protests, either. "Oh, they might complain about a policeman who stops their car," one foreigner said, "but I've never heard anyone criticize the policy or the system." North Koreans insisted, as in 1979, that they enjoyed complete freedom. What about the reports by human rights groups that tens of thousands of citizens were imprisoned for political offenses? "There is no one against the government in our country," a festival guide replied. "It's a lie."

North Koreans also insisted that their country was virtually crime-free. During the festival, uniformed guards carrying automatic weapons continued to patrol both in the cities and at bridges, airstrips, railways and other sensitive sites in the countryside. But checkpoints between the city and its airport were left unmanned, perhaps to give less of an impression of Big Brother–style interference.

In any case, just as other communist-ruled societies had faced enormous challenges that forced them to deviate from the teachings of Marx, Lenin and Mao, North Korea was experiencing frustrations that in time might turn even avid revolutionaries against their government. Economic problems had continued, and there were some signs that the regime's handling of the economy had begun to cause popular disaffection. Defectors to South Korea and other countries had complained, for example, that people were exhausted from the almost constant demands for "voluntary" labor and "speed campaigns."[3] At Kim Chaek University of Technology, officials in an interview denied a report from a human rights group that forty students at Kim Chaek and another college campus had been arrested a year before the festival, after posters appeared questioning the regime's economic policies.

Electrical power was in permanent shortage, so stores were not switching on their lights except during weekends and on special occasions. The entire period of the youth festival was a special occasion, though, with huge amounts of power used to light up Pyongyang and cool the visitors. The practical effects of the shortage could be seen when trolley buses stopped one morning as the result of an apparent electrical blackout.

Consumer durables clearly were a problem, although here again the regime sought to counter the impression. During the youth festival the authorities stepped up shipments to the stores. I doubted that the stores shown to foreigners were representative of those where ordinary North Koreans routinely shopped. In any case, the department store displays in 1989 were an improvement over the dreary selection seen a decade earlier. Designs of some goods such as women's handbags had clearly improved. Clothing, especially women's garments, showed more color and variety. The improvements, however—whether real or contrived—had done no more than to bring those stores up to the fairly low standard of department stores in Beijing when I had lived there from 1980 to 1982, before the Chinese economy's new direction had started to show major tangible results.

Despite the shipments for the festival, some items were notable for either their unavailability or their poor quality. One currently popular item among North Koreans was a stereophonic portable cassette-tape player, but the shortage was severe. Not a single one could be found in any of three downtown Pyongyang department stores. Instead shoppers were offered tinny-sounding, primitive phonographs. Predictably, those elicited little enthusiasm.

Department stores emphasized what they had. Piles of buckets, basins, bowls and other plastic housewares in bright colors occupied the most prominent ground-floor displays. A buyer could select from some twenty-five styles of women's shoes, all made of vinyl; a shopper insisting on leather shoes would need to come up with some foreign exchange to buy them in a special hard-currency outlet for foreign goods. At the Changkwan Department Store a bicycle was 175 *won*—a good month's pay. A small North Korean-made refrigerator cost twice that, 350 *won*. A Daedong River-brand black-and-white television cost 620 *won*. A Japanese-made National-brand color set was priced at 1,400 *won*, more than the annual salary of a starting North Korean worker (90 *won* a month).

Although North Korea on my previous visit had seemed to be ahead of China economically, the Chinese since then had benefited from ten more years of economic reform. With no major reform program of their own, the North Koreans had far less to show for the intervening decade than the Chinese had. On paper, still, North Korea remained far ahead on a per capita basis, by comparison with Beijing's own official economic statistics. The visual evidence suggested, however, that the Chinese had overtaken the North Koreans decisively. (The suspicion that the statistics failed to tell the real story got support at the end of 1992 when an Australian government report challenged the Chinese figures.)[4]

Meanwhile, traffic remained very light by the standards of other developing countries. Highways might have five or even seven lanes (the center one reserved for Kim Il-sung, I had heard), but very few vehicles used them. The lack of traffic allowed sweepers to keep both city streets and highways spanking clean. City streets lacked the bustle of even a Beijing, with its swarms of people and bicycles and carts; the automotive traffic jams of a capitalist metropolis would have been unimaginable. Aside from a few Soviet and Japanese models, most of the cars in use were Mercedes-Benz and Volvo sedans imported for the elite.

North Korea did not produce the ultimate consumer durable, civilian passenger cars—but clearly wished it did. I had grasped the symbolism of the automobile during my 1979 visit. When I had asked the Chonsam-ri cooperative farm's deputy chairman about the lack of private cars on his farm and in North Korea generally, he had minimized their importance. The Chonsam-ri farmers did not need them, because there were plenty of farm trucks and buses. Maybe so, but the eyes of one group of Pyongyang officials who ranked high enough to rate chauffeured imported sedans had lit up during a discussion of the relative merits of various foreign makes. Those officials had listened with evident fascination to my description of South Korea's fast-developing automotive industry, then assured me that the North one day would have mass-produced private cars.

A handmade prototype of a sedan had been displayed at Pyongyang's Exhibition of the Achievements of Socialist Construction during my 1979 visit. A guide there had said the country hoped to go into mass production. By 1989, the earlier model was gone, replaced by two new handmade prototypes of a car to be called the "Pyongyang"—out-and-out copies of the Mercedes-Benz 190, of which the country had recently imported a fleet. Production would start soon at a factory then producing military Jeep-type vehicles, said an exhibition guide. I decided not to hold my breath.[5]

Enough sophisticated foreign goods were getting into the country to let North Koreans glimpse what they were missing. Pyongyang residents were excited about special shops opened during the festival that sold foreign goods. Even during nonfestival times there was a steady flow of such goods to some North Koreans—particularly to former residents of Japan who had repatriated and whose remaining relatives in Japan kept them supplied. Officials were sensitive about the broadening gap in living standards and tried to persuade foreign journalists to ignore it. "Don't compare us with the advanced countries," said one official. "Remember, we had to build everything from the destruction of the war. And we had to do it so that everyone could share the same level. That's not easy." But the regime seemed to know it could not sell its economic philosophy forever on the basis of equality only. It would have to offer more of the good life, especially consumer goods.[6]

Catching up would require upgrading technology in such fields as electronics. North Korea did have some people capable of working in high-tech fields. Kim Chaek University of Technology boasted computer rooms equipped with personal and mainframe computers imported from Europe (especially Poland), Japan and Singapore, as well as people who knew how to use them and how they were made. The university exhibited robots constructed in campus labs. But factory production of such high-tech machines would be another matter, and there was little evidence the country was making much progress there. As with automobiles, the North Koreans seemed more successful at taking apart foreign-made machines and building hand-made prototypes than at starting mass production.

At the Exhibition of the Achievements of Socialist Construction, plenty of North Korean–made high-tech machinery was on display—but on inquiry it turned out in many cases to be prototype equipment from the labs at Kim Chaek or other universities, not production goods.

Trying to develop at home all the elements of modern technology clearly was out of the question, even for an intelligent, educated population. Obviously it would be hard to meet North Koreans' rising expectations without importing huge quantities of goods—or, more practically, the foreign technology to produce them. Importing technology would mean a need for joint ventures and other dealings with the capitalist world. A halfhearted and sketchy stab at that, enactment of a joint-ventures law in 1984, had failed to attract much investor interest.

Business dealings with the noncommunist world remained difficult. North Korea had little or no foreign exchange and could not get credit because it still had not repaid its loans from the 1970s.[7] Creditors were particularly exasperated that, before even making much of a gesture toward paying its debts, Pyongyang had spent what some Westerners estimated at the equivalent of four to eight billion U.S. dollars importing materials and machinery for the construction campaign to prepare for the youth festival. That history disposed many foreign companies against any dealings with the North, unless they could see cash up front. The one reliable group of overseas business partners comprised pro-Pyongyang Korean businessmen resident in Japan, who had invested in dozens of joint ventures.

Despite Pyongyang's determination to stick with the Stalinist status quo, it was possible to detect a few striking, if relatively modest, changes in attitudes and behavior. The authorities wanted to banish North Korea's image as an Orwellian horror of brainwashed people. Kim Jong-su complained to me that foreigners kept saying North Koreans were "like machines, answering mechanically and smiling mechanically." That, he insisted, was "not true. Everybody is different."[8]

I reflected that the regime's promoters of the "monolithic" philosophy had worked hard to earn for their country the automaton label. But I did notice that people who were cleared for dealings with foreigners appeared to have been permitted to lighten up just a bit. Overall, North Koreans seemed somewhat easier and more relaxed—among themselves and with Westerners, including Americans—than their counterparts a decade before. Indeed, normal human reactions described the biggest change I found. Although North Koreans still sang the praises of *juche*, for example, they seemed less obsessed than before with giving the impression that everything was Korean-made. At the Taean Heavy Machinery complex near Nampo, when officials conducted a tour of a factory making electrical generators, they identified as foreign-made (Italian, in some cases) many of the machine tools. They offered no excuses.

Spontaneity, which in some quarters had seemed almost to be considered a sin back in 1979, was much more in evidence. North Koreans I saw smiled and laughed more in the presence of foreigners. In some cases they exuded so much warmth and hospitality as to make almost plausible the government's goal of increasing tourism several-fold in the next few years—to fill up thousands of hotel rooms that were either newly built or still under construction by attracting groups from the West and elsewhere. It was clear, however, that the officials concerned had their work cut out for them projecting an image of their country that would appeal to masses of foreign tourists.

One new tourism facility was the Pyongyang Golf Club, the first and only one in the country, built in 1987 to serve mainly foreigners and overseas Koreans from Japan. Caddies, young Korean women, chirped the Japanese-English compliment "Nice *shotto*" as the golfers teed off. Kang Kyong-chul, thirty-seven, wiry and tanned, had been a tennis coach before going to Japan for two months in 1986 to learn golf in preparation for becoming the course's pro. He told me his handicap was 10. Golfing had not really caught on—an average of only seven foreigners and overseas Koreans and three North Koreans played each day, according to Kang's figures, and he said those did not include any high-ranking Korean officials. "Our country is divided, as you know," Kang explained. "There are many things to do for our people if our country is unified. At that time we will expand golf and other sports to larger scale."

After rummaging through Pyongyang's arts-and-crafts and souvenir shops, I had to conclude that Western tourists would find little to inspire shopping sprees. Typical of the offerings was a landscape painting in traditional East Asian style, on sale in a downtown Pyongyang gallery. It depicted the breathtaking gorge, the autumn leaves, the waterfall—but also the highway bridge supporting a gleaming tour bus conveying happy masses of sightseers smack through the middle of the scene. As jarringly, an embroidery picture of a girl in flowing traditional garb swinging on the traditional high swing also showed, in one corner, a modern concrete park bench. I suppose such touches made sense in the North Korean context. After all, Kim Il-sung's *juche* philosophy celebrated man as the "master" of the earth, so why hide the evidence of man and his creations? (Pictures were done without shading, and I guess that also fit with the ideology.)

A visible change of questionable significance was construction of the first Protestant and Catholic churches permitted to operate in Pyongyang in decades. In the early days of the North Korean communist regime, all the churches had been closed. (The authorities claimed that American bombs destroyed every last one of them during the Korean War.) According to human rights groups, religious people had been persecuted as members of the "disloyal" class. Churches were regarded as symbols of imperialist oppression.[9] At the Korea Feature Film Studio lot during that same visit I saw a large gothic church structure, built—obviously for use in propaganda films—in 1980, when the country had no real church buildings. The regime accorded special treatment to Chondoism, an indigenous, patriotic religion founded by a former independence fighter who was said to have "prayed to the mystical wonders of Nature on Mount Paektu to deal out divine punishment to the Japanese and bless the Korean nation."

At the Protestant Pongsu Church on a Sunday during the youth festival, Korean and foreign cameramen snapped away as worshipers sang "Jesus Loves Me," in Korean. Many of them appeared to know it by heart. Then a pastor, The Rev. Li Song-bong, prayed "in the name of Jesus Christ" for the success of the festival, under its "banner of anti-imperialist solidarity." Later, Li preached on the need for removal of nuclear weapons from the peninsula and prayed for Korean reunification—all in all, a heavier political than spiritual agenda.

Although people involved with the church thus hewed to the official North Korean political line, perhaps the more striking fact in such a tightly controlled society was that they showed less than full participation in the Kim Il-sung personality cult. The church was in Mangyongdae District, birthplace of the Great Leader himself, but there were no portraits of Kim or his son on the church walls and congregation members during services did not wear the miniature Kim portraits on their breasts. Perhaps this was for the benefit of us foreign visitors. I watched one man walk up the hill toward the church, wearing his Kim badge. Near the gate, he turned his back and made a motion as if he were reaching for a pack of cigarettes. When he turned again, the badge was gone, discreetly pocketed.

No church members or clergy were members of the Kims' ruling Korean Workers' (communist) Party, a clergyman explained, because "we Christians believe in God." People attending church denied human-rights groups' reports that they suffered discriminatory treatment in economic benefits and legal treatment, but I thought most of those people had a haggard look that suggested their lives had been less than easy. There may have been unconscious irony on that festival Sunday as the congregation opened blue-bound hymnals and sang, in Korean, "We've a story to tell to the nations that shall turn their hearts to the right."

Previously only home church services had been possible for the still-faithful remnants of the old church memberships, I was told; Protestants who did not attend the Pongsu Church services still practiced home worship. Among both the Pongsu Church worshippers and a home-worship group I visited on a different Sunday, participants under forty were rare. Worshippers told me they found it difficult to attract their own children to the faith of their fathers. They did not have to explain the reason. The young ones, after all, had been indoctrinated from shortly after birth, in state nurseries, kindergartens and schools, to worship the Kims. They revered Kim Il-sung as "more than a god," as a non-Christian student interpreter for one of the foreign visitors to Pongsu Church described the president to me.

In an atmosphere so overwhelmingly hostile to competing religions or other different ideas, it was but a small change to have church buildings — not so much a real shift in domestic policy as a cosmetic ploy to influence public opinion abroad. Several years later, in a similar effort, Kim Il-sung was to receive American evangelist Billy Graham in Pyongyang, after conceding in his memoirs that many Korean Christians of times past "were respectable patriots," like Kim's benefactor, Sohn Jong-do.[10]

This attempt to show a tolerant attitude toward Christianity was intended to improve Pyongyang's standing in the West. North Korea at the time it built the churches was involved once again in a campaign to drive a wedge between Seoul and Washington, in hopes of triggering the withdrawal of the some 40,000 U.S. troops that were still in South Korea.

American Christians remained concerned about the persecution of North Korean Christians. Recall that Protestant missionaries from the United

States, especially Presbyterians and Methodists, had led the missionary effort in Korea from the opening of the country in the late nineteenth century. Staying on through the decades until the 1930s, when the Japanese occupation made their work impossible, they had passed the faith to millions of Koreans—ironically, with even more success in the northern half of the country than in the South. Certainly the Pyongyang regime hoped to influence such groups with the highly publicized church openings.

Over time, of course, even such externally targeted measures could inject a note of unaccustomed pluralism into domestic society. For the time being, though, the average North Korean probably felt little effect. Indeed, one American Protestant who visited Pyongyang in the fall of that same year, 1989, found evidence that religious belief still cut very much against the grain of the Kim regime. Virgil Cooper, a Seoul-based Southern Baptist missionary, attended services at Pongsu Church. He told me he had found the associate pastor's sermon to be suitably "Bible based," but considered it odd that the congregation did not belt out the hymns with the Korean gusto he was familiar with in Seoul. Later, in his hotel, a Christian woman who had seen him at the church approached him. Pointing to the ceiling, she urged him not to talk loudly. Christians remained subject to considerable discrimination and repression, she told him.

The woman Cooper met, assuming she was a sincere believer, may have been an exception even among the churchgoers. According to a high-level defector, former chief ideologist Hwang Jang-yop, "all the churches in Pyongyang are fake churches built for show. The monks living in the Buddhist temples are of course fake monks. Genuine believers in North Korea cannot profess their faith; only fake believers are allowed to do so."[11]

The more immediate question was whether Kim Il-sung and Kim Jong-il were flexible enough to make far more drastic changes, especially in the economy. The obvious economic policy changes would conflict with the regime's need to maintain control internally. Stepping up contacts with foreigners via trade and technology transfer would give the people more opportunities to test what they had been taught against other versions of the truth. Solving economic problems would require admitting past mistakes at least implicitly—but Kim Il-sung and Kim Jong-il were, of course, infallible; any hint of contradicting their past "precious teachings" would weaken their claim to absolute loyalty and obedience. What I saw in 1989 did not give me confidence that major changes would come in timely fashion. In the end, adding up every change that could be detected on that visit produced a list that seemed unimpressive at best and, when compared with the exciting things happening elsewhere in the communist world at the time, downright pitiful.

It was the heyday of Mikhail Gorbachev's *glasnost* and *perestroika* in the Soviet Union, but North Koreans knew little or nothing about Soviet liberalization and restructuring. They did not even know about the popular protests that had been raging next door in China. My guide, a twenty-nine-year-old college English teacher, mentioned that he hoped to go the following September to Beijing to study English and Chinese. I asked him if he knew what had happened at Tiananmen Square. "A little bit" about it was in *Nodong Shinmun*, the party newspaper, he said. When I told him that China's army had killed thousands of its own young people, he seemed to try to mask a reaction of surprise. "Students?" he asked. Getting his information from the only source available to him, the party-lining North Korean media, he had not even heard the terms *glasnost* and *perestroika* before I taught them to him. Once he understood the meanings, though, he dismissed any need for reform in North Korea. "Our country has no *glasnost* or *perestroika*," he boasted. "Our policy is unchanged for forty years. No one wants to change."

My guide and every other North Korean I met, just as in 1979, constantly praised Kim Il-sung for having built a socialist paradise guaranteeing jobs and food, decent housing, free medical care and education. The difference in 1989 was that they also added references to Kim Jong-il, by then no longer spoken of only in code terms but long since officially proclaimed his father's successor, the "Dear Leader." A mammoth effort was under way simultaneously to continue building the Kim Il-sung personality cult and to stretch it enough to envelop the junior Kim, who represented the regime's hope of continuing on *without* major change or reform. Not only Kim Jong-il's name but also his picture and his words were everywhere, and his abilities were described in close to superhuman terms.

This effort was evident during my visit to the Grand People's Study House, a grandiose pile of masonry billed as the country's central library and "center of intellectual activity." Predictably, a gigantic chalk-white statue of Kim Il-sung, seated in an easy chair and reading the *Workers' Daily*, dominated the vast lobby. Several rooms of the library were devoted to an exhibit of books published in North Korea. A librarian there, Li Hyung-ran, boasted that more than 1,300 volumes of Kim Il-sung's works and more than 700 volumes of works by Kim Jong-il had been published. The latter included a fifteen-volume set of Kim Jong-il's achievements in guiding the country's literature and art.

The shelf for Korean literature in general—novels, poetry, criticism—was considerably smaller than the shelf for the works of Kim Il-sung, and even there it was impossible to escape the main theme. Here, said the librarian, was a historical novel, also in fifteen volumes—a fictionalized account of the deeds of Kim Jong-il. And over here, "these are the illustrated fairy tales told by the Great Leader and the Dear Leader," she said. "And this picture album illustrates the immortal flower Kimjongilia. It was newly cultivated by a Japanese gardener"—and named, of course, for the Dear Leader. Over there, finally! A book bearing a different name in the title. "This book introduces the noble life and revolutionary history of Comrade Kim Jong-suk," said Miss Li. "She was the most loyal to the Great Leader, an anti-Japanese heroine and a communist revolutionary fighter." Um, wasn't she Kim Il-sung's wife? "Yes, you guessed well. And she also was the mother of Dear Leader Comrade Kim Jong-il."

As on my earlier visit, adoration of the elder Kim appeared genuine, even when foreigners would consider that it had gone to bizarre extremes. When the Great Leader appeared for an ice-skating show, the entire audience of Koreans leapt to its feet as one person and bellowed "Hooray! Hooray! Hooray!" over and over and over for close to three minutes. When performers or marchers passed before Kim's seat in the May Day Stadium during the festival opening ceremony, they jumped up and down on their toes, their arms raised, palms open toward the leader, in very much the posture of a tiny child asking her father for candy, or a dog begging for a bone.

When I asked my guide about the Kim Il-sung portrait badges that he and every other North Korean "voluntarily" wore on their breasts, he replied, "We want always to have the Great Leader near us. I want to have his portrait on my heart. As you know, the Great Leader liberated the country. He dedicated all his life for the people." The badges, he added, were gifts from "the Dear Leader Kim Jong-il."

My hosts' idea of a museum to show off to visitors was the International Friendship Exhibition, a massive, windowless stone structure at Mount Myohyang, a resort three hours' ride by train north of Pyongyang. The exhibits consisted solely of gifts from foreigners to the Great and Dear Leaders. "The presents are precious to our country, the pride of our people," an exhibition guide, twenty-five-year-old Chong Sun-hyang, told me. They showed "how much respect the rest of the world has for the Great Leader," she said. Four-ton copper doors embossed with the hybrid flower named Kimilsungia (developed by that same Japanese botanist who gave the world the Kimjongilia) swung open noiselessly to admit visitors to a tomblike interior. Inside, the practice was to cover one's shoes with cloth booties to keep from tracking dirt, then to pad pristinely into the holy-of-holies, where another enormous, eerie, chalk-white limestone statue of the Great Leader seated in an easy chair loomed over a selection of presents from world leaders.

Once a visitor had made his way around that first room, there were only forty-four more rooms to go to complete the tour of gifts to Kim Il-sung—a vase fashioned from a lump of coal, from Poland's Jaruzelski, for example, and a woven saddle from Libya's Khadaffi. Then there were eight more rooms full of similar gifts to Kim Jong-il, who was represented by another limestone statue. It seemed African leaders had sent the two Kims enough elephant tusks, carved and un-carved, to justify an all-points bulletin by the World Wildlife Fund. The full tour took four hours, and I was assured that only a quarter of the gifts on hand were being displayed at the moment.

I could only speculate that, after decades of indoctrination and purges, those North Koreans who remained alive and not in prison had by and large bought into the entire program. "But what if someone wants to say: 'I don't believe in the Great Leader?'" I asked my guide. "You don't understand," he replied. "All our people believe in the Great Leader. . . . There is no one in the country who doesn't believe."

No doubt one big reason people could still muster loyalty for the elder Kim despite the economic and other failings of his regime was that in his public and television appearances he came across as an engaging figure. On television during my 1989 visit he was shown striding along with the some-what shambling gait of an elderly but still reasonably healthy man (perhaps the longevity research had helped—although the camera never showed the grapefruit-sized tumor on the back of his neck). He smiled confidently, taking the inevitable tributes graciously. In his public appearances he spoke in a gravelly, avuncular voice. He seemed very much the politician.

The campaign to transfer to Kim Jong-il his father's deity status was in full cry at Pyongyang's Revolutionary Museum of the Dear Leader Comrade Kim Jong-il. The museum, which kidnapped movie director Shin and actress Choi had visited during their stay in Pyongyang, consisted of twelve rooms set aside at the younger Kim's alma mater, Kim Il-sung University. A student guide told me that at age eight the prodigy read Lenin's "State and Revolution" and wrote a commentary on it. When he was eleven during the Korean War, Kim Jong-il wrote these immortal song lyrics: "Father General, you will build a paradise in this land of heroes who crush the Yankees." When he entered college a few years later, the guide said, practically the first thing the precocious teenager did was to climb a campus hill and there compose and recite a poem that included this line: "Learning the leader's great idea, I will be the master of the revolution."

The guide sang the 1953 song and requested special care with cameras to make any photos showing the Dear Leader "beautiful." Then she proceeded to point out paintings that showed the cherubic Kim Jong-il of a quarter century before, always at the center of things, striking sagacious and leader-like poses as fellow members of the class of 1964 beamed up at him in evident adoration. Studying alongside Kim Jong-il, said a fellow student's diary entry that was on exhibit in the museum, was "my pride and honor."

A mural at the West Sea Barrage, a gigantic, recently completed public works project to regulate the water level of a river mouth near the port of Nampo, showed Kim Jong-il in his role as the executor of his father's will. The Great and Dear Leaders stood together, the younger man's overcoat flapping heroically in the breeze, his left boot lifted up on a high piece of the machinery. He gestured with his left hand to show his smiling father what he had built. The Dear Leader, in that picture very much the energetic young man of action, wore his trademark jumpsuit with zipper front, while the Great Leader appeared in Western suit with tie, the costume he had adopted as elder statesman.

Without having been either a guerrilla hero or the father of the country, Kim Jong-il needed some basis for legitimacy as the country's leader-designate. He hoped he had found it in his role as chief commentator and expositor of his father's *juche* philosophy. "As you know, the Great Leader created the *juche* idea during the struggle against the Japanese imperialists," Kim Ho-sok, director of Haksan Cooperative Farm, told me. "Then the Dear Leader Comrade Kim Jong-il developed and enriched the *juche* idea."

The succession had been as carefully prepared as could be imagined, and there were no discernible signs of opposition. Still there was reason to suspect the junior Kim might prove unequal to portrayal of the living-god role he was to inherit. Kim Jong-il's credentials as a god-king were sketchy. Among the few foreigners who had met him, some had described him as testy—totally lacking in charm or grace, not to mention the sort of charisma or presence that bespeaks a world-class statesman. Indications were that he was well entrenched as the successor, so much propaganda having flowed about his magnificent qualifications that youngsters and perhaps some of the more credulous among their elders might have begun believing it. But it seemed he was no Kim Il-sung. Foreign and South Korean analysts wondered whether, if a major crisis arose after his father's death and his own accession to the top job, he could weather it.

Although still largely a figure of mystery, Kim Jong-il (as noted in chapter 18) was well known for having brought North Korea a surface modernity in fashion and popular culture. He had encouraged girls and young women to fix themselves up, wear makeup and look nicer. North Korean women—among the most beautiful in the world to begin with—obviously were taking far more care with their appearance than a decade earlier.

Our hosts invited the foreign news media contingent and some others attending the festival to a banquet held in the Mongnankwan, an immense marble hall decorated with crystal chandeliers and fitted with the latest audio equipment. Young female members of the Pochonbo Electric Band, named for the site of Kim Il-sung's successful 1937 raid on the Japanese, entertained us. The band's musicians played peppy music, influenced perhaps to some extent by Western rock but more by the Japanese and South Korean versions. (I was amused to recall the uncomprehending stares of ten years earlier in response to my mention of rock 'n' roll.) Dancers, stunning young women, came out in costumes so skimpy as to suggest we were being treated to a striptease. Then the guests were invited to dance with women from the stage, who had more or less clothed themselves for that duty. I danced with one. (It was only several years later, after I learned of the existence of the Happy Corps, that I was told my dance partner and her entertainer comrades had been corps members.)[12]

While the rock played by Kim Jong-il's band members was for us foreigners, I found that the genre was being introduced to Pyongyang's young people just then by festival visitors from abroad who had brought cassette tapes of their favorite music with them. I saw youngsters who did not disguise their appreciation of rock music that foreigners were playing in and out of their high-rise lodgings. One young woman shook her booty to the beat as a parade passed by. I thought the loss of musical innocence probably foreshadowed bigger changes in attitude.

Visiting the Korea Feature Film Studio I had a chance to check out the results of the junior Kim's vaunted efforts to inspire filmmakers to create more appealing works. The outdoor sets maintained at the studio represented a rural village, with thatched huts surrounding the landlord's grand house; a Japanese street in the 1930s; and a Chinese street in the same period—all used in epics about the Great Leader's struggle against Japanese colonialism and landlord greed. A back alley filled with girlie bars depicted what the North called the decadent, exploitive lifestyle of contemporary capitalist South Korea—a staple of the studio's films promoting reunification on the North's terms. Studio officials boasted of twenty visits by Kim Il-sung since the studio's founding in 1947—and 320 by Kim Jong-il. "The Dear Leader, Comrade Kim Jong-il, leads our art and literature to a brilliant future," explained studio spokesman Li Sok-kyu. "He gives precious teachings for good films."

The studio was filming a swashbuckler, set in olden times, featuring a hero who employed swordplay and the Korean martial art of taekwondo to wipe out dozens of enemies at a time in the style of Hong Kong kung fu epics. Apparently the film was aimed more at light entertainment value and box-office appeal than heavy political ideology. It was not difficult to imagine that Kim Jong-il would need all the box-office appeal he could muster to deal with what lay ahead.

TWENTY

Wherever You Go in
My Homeland

One day during the 1989 World Festival of Youth and Students, my guide excitedly said I would be meeting a high official. "The Dear Leader?" I asked. No. The VIP turned out to be Professor Kim Jong-su, who soon arrived and invited me to a folk festival. In a lovely woodland setting, the site of the ancient tomb of a dynastic founder, we watched performances of traditional skills such as spear-throwing and then tucked into a copious picnic feast.

Once again I decided not to bring up the matter of my host's dual identity. In any event, he did not repeat his orphan story this time. Indeed, in the course of our chat, it turned out that Kim Jong-su had a mother, then still living. I mentally noted that interesting fact but said nothing, making allowance for the likelihood that one who had lost only his father might be considered orphaned, particularly in that patriarchal, still Confucian-oriented society.

Kim Jong-su quoted his mother on the extent of improvement in living conditions since the old days, when inferior grains had to be substituted for scarce rice. He recalled that, in his own youth in the 1940s and 1950s, times were so hard that a kind of grass or hay had to be mixed in to make pounded-rice cakes. Recently, he said, his children had been complaining about how bland everything tasted. He had given them some old-fashioned rice cakes with just a little hay in them, he said, and the youngsters had pronounced the taste wonderful.

Throughout my visit, North Korean officials had been denying persistent reports of food shortages. Officials acknowledged that rice was rationed, but the figures they gave for rations (700 grams a day for an adult, 500 for a child) seemed adequate assuming they were accurate. The question was what the diet might include beyond the staples (grain and beans, mainly) and kimchee, the national dish of spicy pickled cabbage, cucumbers or other vegetables. Foreigners living in Pyongyang said that eggs were available but that meat was a rarity on most North Korean tables. Visitors to the youth festival did not confront any shortage personally—far from it. Our hosts fed us great quantities of meat, fulfilling the dictates of traditional Korean hospitality even as they sought to persuade us that meat was plentiful in the diet of ordinary Koreans.

At the picnic, country air and an endless supply of the local beer sharpened my appetite, which even normally was large—but as soon as I finished off one plate of roasted meat, another appeared. I was skeptical of Kim Jong-su's assurances that food had become plentiful, but I did not know at the time just how bad the situation had become. Later, when I learned more, I felt ashamed of having pigged out at Kim's picnic. The truth was that the food supply was miserably (although not yet disastrously) bad. The regime had come up with special supplies for the festival, but soon North Koreans once again would be eating grasses out of necessity, not nostalgia, and not mixed in with their rice but instead of rice.[1]

Even while I was there, a look at North Korea's agriculture suggested that the country was stuck, dabbling in slight changes to the formula but unwilling or unable to commit wholeheartedly to reforms that would deviate seriously from the original line of Stalin and Kim Il-sung—now, in its basics, the line of Kim Jong-il as well.

That official line contradicted the clear evidence of what worked best. In small private plots, to take the most readily gauged example, the corn was taller than corn growing in nearby fields that were farmed collectively. Despite such visual proof the authorities publicly continued to denigrate those private plots, and the markets at which their produce was sold, as shameful relics of the bad old pre-socialist days. While other communist countries were experimenting with private enterprise, North Koreans still were allowed to cultivate privately only their patches of dooryard. The proclaimed long-term policy was not to expand that tiny private sector but to phase it out, to collectivize farming even further—in other words, to redouble approaches that long since had passed the point of diminishing returns.

Travel outside Pyongyang during my 1989 visit revealed that North Korean farmers were cultivating practically every available square inch of arable soil. Soil appeared generally not particularly good, and in places very poor—red clay or sand, with little or no topsoil cover.[2] The land available was used not for pasture or fiber production but overwhelmingly for growing grains and other foods for direct human consumption. I saw few animals. Those I did see, in almost all cases, were not meat or dairy animals but oxen for plowing and pulling carts.

At Haksan Cooperative Farm north of Pyongyang, rice paddies, green and glistening in early July, filled the lowlands while corn was planted on steeper land. Houses and apartment buildings clustered tightly together on high ground to conserve land. I met farm director Kim Ho-sok, who said he was in charge of 2,600 farmers cultivating 15 million square meters and living in 1,100 households. Kim boasted that harvests had continued to increase in the previous decade,[3] but the farm director's claims conflicted with the picture of North Korean agricultural stagnation that foreign and South Korean analysts were painting.

Haksan's dooryard private plots were limited to 66 square meters each. Farm officials said free markets were held every ten days where farmers could sell or barter some of the produce of their private plots—but the officials insisted those markets were a dwindling, unwelcome holdover from the bad old days and would not be needed any longer once the country achieved full, pure communism. "Gradually the free market is declining now," said farm director Kim. After all, he explained, "the state supplies the people with the necessities of life."

Reminded that the Soviet Union was emphasizing *glasnost* and *perestroika*, and along with China had been increasing the use of free markets, Kim replied: "We don't know much about that, but we don't want to follow their lead. 'Openness' and 'reform' are for the Russians and Chinese. It's their style." In theory, at least, farmers collectively owned the so-called cooperative farms such as Haksan, which sold their produce to the state. But cooperative farms were supposed to be converted soon into "state farms." Their land would be owned by the state and the farmers would become salaried employees of the state, director Kim said with evident pride.

A visit to a farm family's home illustrated both the old-style incentives that were still considered ideologically correct and some financial incentives that the regime scorned but had to tolerate during the "transitional" period. Kim Myong-pok showed off an apartment of three rooms plus kitchen that she said her farming family had occupied since the previous year. Haksan's farmers were gradually moving out of old fashioned, single-story houses into such newly built, modern apartments, similar to those of city-dwellers. Mrs. Kim explained that her husband had been high on the list to get the new housing because he was a "labor hero." She was watching a Japanese Toshiba television set that she said had been donated by the Great Leader to the husband for his labor heroism. Heroes got their special awards based on effort, for going all out.

On the other hand, cash payments to Haksan's farmers were based on time worked, skill level and unit-wide production. The previous year,

Mrs. Kim had made 3,400 *won* and her husband 5,200 *won*, she said. The to-tal, 8,600 *won* for a year, was two or three times as much as a typical urban-dwelling, two-income couple might bring home for factory or white-collar work. Since there was no need for farmers to spend money on housing or on food, Mrs. Kim said, theirs went for home furnishings, or into savings to pay for their children's weddings, parents' wedding anniversary parties and other foreseeable social obligations.

North Koreans insisted that financial incentives were passé, but their actions suggested the opposite. By 1989, reports had reached the outside world of self-seeking behavior among the country's supposedly puritanical communists. For example, high-ranking officials demanded that underlings bribe them with scarce goods such as color television sets in exchange for promotions.

One diplomat who was stationed in Pyongyang intermittently for years illustrated the change that was taking place by citing two identical incidents when his family visited a beach resort and an adventurous child swam out too far, so that the concerned diplomat had to ask a lifeguard to row out and bring the youngster back. The first time that happened, in the mid-1970s, the lifeguard had to be pressed to accept some lollipops as a gesture of thanks. When it happened again more than a decade later (an amazing coincidence, but that's the diplomat's story), the lifeguard refused the proffered candies, asking to be rewarded instead in U.S. dollars.

I had a similar experience in 1989 when one of the North Koreans as-signed to help foreign newsmen asked me to give him some American cur-rency. He said he wanted dollars to spend for foreign goods that were for sale in the special hard-currency shops established for the youth festival. Some Adidas sports shoes, in particular, seemed to have caught his eye. I re-flected at the time that he might have been instructed to ask for money as part of the regime's efforts to accumulate foreign exchange. But the amount involved was insignificant, so I leaned toward the explanation that he had made the request on his own initiative and for his personal benefit. This in-stance of seemingly individualistic behavior reinforced a sense that the regime had given up some of its rigid control, perhaps to a greater degree than planned. And I thought that the authorities had better brace themselves for a sharp rise in consumer expectations, now that Pyongyang residents at-tending the festival had seen what they were missing.

On the level of official incentives, the regime had paid a bonus of one month's salary to the country's workers before the festival opened in recog-nition of their hard work in a "200-day speed campaign" to meet production and construction goals. In practice, then, the gradual shift was continuing from the old-style "moral" incentives, such as medals for labor heroes, to financial incentives. The latter were officially keyed, to be sure, to group rather than individual performance. Even such relatively mild heresy, however, was not something the regime's ideology permitted it to take pride in.

Chinese followers of Deng Xiaoping by then had become communist in name only as they pursued economic reforms nakedly intended to unleash the individual's profit motive, but North Koreans were still required to praise the communist ideal of selfless behavior. "All for one and one for all" was the rule.

The propaganda machine promulgating such beliefs, heavy-handed though it was, still succeeded well enough that even in 1989 North Koreans were reciting their collectivist catechism smilingly and with evident sincerity. Whatever bourgeois sins they might be tempted to commit, they gave every appearance of believing in—or believing that they ought to believe in—old-fashioned communism, tied closely to the leader cult. Call it brainwashing or education, or credit the art of a host of well-trained actors; no matter how the authorities had managed to pull it off, a visitor was left with the feeling he had traveled to the center of a great and still-burning faith. Instead of Pyongyang it could have been Teheran.

Again, as in 1979, national beliefs were nowhere more accessible to visitors than in Pyongyang's theaters, and it was on this trip that I saw one of Kim Jong-il's "new type" revolutionary operas, *The Flower Girl*. In New York a few days earlier I had seen and been moved by the Broadway version of *Les Misérables*. Almost certainly the creators of that hit musical had not seen the North Korean production, and vice versa. Yet the similarities between the two were remarkable. Both were beautifully staged melodramas, evoking with consummate skill that hatred of privilege that was the ideological starting point of both the French Revolution and Kim Il-sung's regime. The stage version of *The Flower Girl* struck me as world class—much better than the 1972 movie version, which itself had been singled out for considerable praise at home and abroad. If what I saw was fairly representative of the genre, Kim Jong-il had much cause for pride.

The plot of *The Flower Girl* is simple: In the 1920s, cruel landlord-usurers take advantage of a small loan of rice to enslave the family of heroine Ggot-bun. Reduced to going to town to sell flowers in the street in order to buy medicine for her sick mother, she is insulted and molested by Japanese colonialists and their Korean henchmen. One moonlit night she is falsely charged with theft. The police whip her as punishment, and she happens to learn that the landlords are about to sell her into bondage. Returning home, she sings about her sad fate:

> *On the petals dewdrops glisten.*
> *Is it there that my tears flow?*

The moon is bright but in this dim,
Dark world I know not where to go.

One moon shines up in the sky.
But different people gaze upon it.
Some are happy to see the moon,
While others grow most melancholy.

(Kim Jong-il, chain-smoking until he got his thoughts in order, is reported to have taken a personal hand in sharpening the lyrics' focus on the different moods in which people would react to the moon, depending on their social station in a pre-revolutionary society full of contradictions.)[4]

The heroine's troubles only get worse. After the landlords sell her to a textile mill, they beat her mother to death and blind her sister. In the second act, a show-stopping *pangchang* sung by an offstage ensemble of women—the lyrics again reportedly showing Kim Jong-il's personal revision[5]—expresses Ggot-bun's feelings and those of other women of her class:

Moon, bright moon, you shine sadly.
Do you know how hard our fate is?
We're assaulted by woe and woe,
Ill-treated and humiliated.

At the climax, guerrillas swoop down from the hills to execute the wicked landords and reunite Ggot-bun with her siblings.

At that point in the evening when I saw *The Flower Girl,* if there was a dry eye in the house it certainly did not belong to me. But then came the finale, apparently an even more exciting moment for other theatergoers. The image of a red sun appeared on a backdrop, symbolizing Kim Il-sung (who claimed to have come up with the story line as a teenaged revolutionary)[6] and the good life that liberation and his communist regime would bring. Koreans in the audience, all wearing their miniature enameled portraits of Kim on their breasts, stood and cheered for the leader. Finally the curtain fell and the evening's performance ended. As we turned to leave, my guide explained that the revolution symbolized by that red sun was far from over. "We are continuing until we establish in this land communism, an ideal society," he asserted earnestly.

Pyongyang continued to rely on propaganda campaigns to whip its people into a revolutionary frenzy of overproduction. Even given the potency of its propaganda, it was remarkable after so many decades how much the regime had to show (and "show" is the operative word here) for its seemingly anachronistic, circuses-before-bread approach. Carried on at breakneck speed

and referred to in borrowed military terminology as "speed battles," its or-
gies of construction were the sort of exercise of which even the most dedicated ideologues must soon have tired. Yet North Koreans had battled on,
out of whatever combination of fear and fervor, so that those visiting for the
youth festival found new wonders to behold. In downtown Pyongyang we
could see that the basic concrete work had been done on the 105-story hotel
structure that was intended to be Asia's highest building.[7]

Soldiers had helped build the West Sea Barrage, consisting of a five-
mile-wide dam, with ship locks, across the Taedong River where it meets the
Yellow Sea. Guides boasted that the construction project had produced 103
"labor heroes." At Sunchon, an hour and a half's drive north of Pyongyang, a
largely military workforce was putting up an enormous complex to produce
the indigenous synthetic fiber vinalon.

A major construction goal in 1989 clearly was to try to outdo Seoul's
Olympics, and no effort or expense was spared. Besides stadiums and other
venues for the festival's sports events, North Koreans had built streets lined
with high-rise apartment buildings. Those housed festival participants. After
their departure the apartments were to be turned over to citizens. Pyongyang's
skyline soared, and the opening and closing ceremonies for the youth festival
proved more elaborate even than the extraordinary shows Seoul had put on
for the Olympics.

"We're in a hurry," Kim Jong-su explained to me. "Everyone's in a hurry
here. Our leader said we are a backward country. If the others take one step
forward, we must take ten. If they walk, we must run."

Glorification of the leaders was the focus of much of the frenzy of construction. It was impossible to miss Pyongyang's version of the Arc de Tri-
omph, larger than the Paris original. It had been built in 1982, the year of
Kim Il-sung's seventieth birthday, to commemorate his triumphal return
from exile in 1945 to take command of a country he supposedly had liberated
from the Japanese. Kim Jong-il had overseen the recent monument building, which foreign economists were calling a major drain on the economy.

If in retrospect the gargantuan effort of the 1980s is seen to have been a
last hurrah before Pyongyang's world fell apart in the 1990s, in the process it
may have provided history the definitive last word on just how very far a
people can be led with propaganda.

Whatever cosmetic touches the regime had employed to inflate its claims of
having created a "paradise," and however far behind South Korea—and even
China—the country had fallen in reality, North Korea in 1989 still managed
an appearance of dynamism that appealed to some people outside its borders.

Third World leaders were impressed with Kim Il-sung's credentials as an
anti-imperialist freedom fighter. Some of them also admired the North's

economic development—or at least appreciated Pyongyang's foreign aid programs and arms supplies. (Some had adopted personality cults similar to Kim's. At the youth festival, Iraqi, Afghan, Syrian and Cote d'Ivoire delegates all carried—or, in the last case, wore stamped on their clothing—portraits of their own national leaders.) Naturally, any hint of foreign approval the regime could muster was translated instantly into domestic propaganda. "I recommend to you *The Pyongyang Times*," my straight-faced guide said to me when I asked him about reading matter. He referred to a weekly tabloid devoted mainly to chronicling Kim Il-sung's meetings with and tributes from foreign dignitaries.

The ideology was even proving exportable to South Korea. A virulent Pyongyang fever on campuses had become a severe complicating factor in the South's quest for stability. Radically inclined South Korean students were attracted to Kim's teachings of revolutionary egalitarianism, economic self-sufficiency, unification zeal and anti-Americanism. His pre-liberation guerrilla opposition to the Japanese made him a patriot hero in their eyes. Based on that interest, the Kims appeared still to hope that a resurgence of unrest in the South would lead to a leftist insurrection, reversing the otherwise clear course of history, and pave the way to reunification on Pyongyang's terms.

Until not long before, after all, the major influences on Koreans in the South as well as the North had been authoritarian. They had lived under the dynastic system of royalty and hereditary nobles backed up with Chinese Confucian thought, and then under the emperor-worshipping Japanese colonial regime. The only major difference was that from 1945 South Korea received American influence while North Korea received Soviet and then Chinese communist influence. American-style democracy was far from transforming South Korean politics completely. The authoritarian tradition held sway among political leaders of all stripes even after a relatively free election in 1987. Thus, it was not unreasonable to imagine, as did many in the North and some in the South, that American influence was just a thin veneer that could be replaced with socialist and communist ideas.

By 1989, the campus atmosphere in the South had become reminiscent of Americans' 1960s slogan, "Don't trust anyone over thirty." The substantial number of South Korean scholars who had learned enough overseas about communist thinking to reject it were, by the time of their return to teaching posts back home, too old and established to be considered trustworthy advisers by the student radicals. Outright pro-communist propaganda had some enthusiastic fans. So did some left-leaning foreign scholars' theories that condemned the roles of the American and South Korean governments while going easy on criticism of the Northern regime.

Earlier, the South had banned books on such topics; South Koreans attracted to Marxist ideas while studying abroad were in no position to propagate them publicly after their return home. But a belated grant of democratic freedoms after 1987 had suddenly allowed Southerners to flirt with Marxism and North Korean ideology. After decades without contact with such ideas, perhaps it should not have been surprising that substantial numbers in the South were not inoculated with the skepticism needed to counter the simple if often deceptive appeal of Northern propaganda. The inherent attraction of the new and previously forbidden enhanced the attraction.

With North Koreans themselves practicing pretty much the Stalinism that briefly appealed to leftist Americans in the Depression years of the 1930s, it was almost as if Koreans on both sides of the Demilitarized Zone had traveled back five decades in an intellectual time machine. South Korean officials were at wit's end trying to cope. American military and diplomatic policymakers, too, were concerned. Some U.S. officials saw the most prolific and influential of the American scholars as a pied piper and went so far as to implore him to go to Seoul and help disabuse student radicals of their distorted notions. He declined.[8]

A big part of the problem was that South Korean students did *not* know the North—still were not permitted to go there without special permission. When their government insisted that the North was a bleak place, they considered what the government had told them previously and, perhaps understandably, decided not to believe it.

The evening I went to see *The Flower Girl* the guest of honor swept into the theater just before the curtain rose for the first act, receiving a standing ovation. Im Su-gyong, a beautiful South Korean university student, had defied her government by visiting Pyongyang via a third country to attend the youth festival. She was promoting a pro-unification scheme for a student march from the northern end of the peninsula, across the normally unpassable Demilitarized Zone and down to the southern tip. Her arrival in Pyongyang created pandemonium. Northerners, evidently genuinely delighted and moved by her visit, mobbed her. In the televised arrival scene, the jostled cameraman was unable to keep his camera still, resulting in a rare bit of spontaneous television.

Im Su-gyong soon returned to the South, where she was jailed until Christmas Eve of 1992 for violating the National Security Act. That only made her a martyr to the Southern radicals' cause—to the delight of the propaganda authorities in the North. During another visit to Pyongyang three years later, I was taken to an art studio where the main non-Kim subject of the artists turned out to be Im. There were sculptures of her and paintings galore, in a variety of poses, the most dramatic a courtroom scene from her trial in Seoul.

Hwang Jang-yop, following his 1997 defection, told of another way the

North sought to appeal to the South. Recall Baek Nam-woon, "the father of left-wing scholars," whom Kim Jong-il purged at the end of the 1960s. Although he died in a concentration camp, Hwang reported, Baek's remains were later moved to the Shinmiri Patriotic Martyrs' Cemetery. Hwang said the same procedure was followed with others who were popular among South Korean nationalists. "Anyone with some value in maintaining the sympathy of outsiders is buried here, even if he had died at the hands of the North Korean rulers."[9]

The image of ideological purity that Pyongyang projected appealed to the South Korean radicals' tendency to see issues in black and white. The propaganda mills of Pyongyang never failed to point out that the South still suffered the ignominy of having foreign troops on its soil, "controlling" its armed forces, buying its women, golfing on its prime real estate and disseminating crass American culture over one of the most desirable of the scarce television channels. (The fact that those troops were there to deter another invasion by the North like the one in 1950 was never mentioned—Northern propaganda still claimed it was the South that had invaded.)[10]

Pyongyang's call for immediate reunification—its means for completing the revolution—had a simple appeal compared with the more complex and cautious South Korean policy. Pyongyang presented early reunification as a spiritual as well as a practical imperative for achieving Korea's destiny as a major nation, free of contaminating foreign influence and able to stand alone, whole, atop the North's considerable mineral resources—including coal, iron ore, gold and uranium—combined with the South's arable land and its technological and business prowess. "If our country is reunified it will be rich in food," Haksan Cooperative Farm's director told me.

In one sequence in the mammoth opening ceremony of the youth festival scores of doves or pigeons representing peace were released inside the stadium. Immediately, there was a multiple-gun salute—twenty-one guns, I suppose, but I did not count—during which the booming noise and the smoke of the explosions drove the already frightened birds into panic so that they veered all over the stadium in apparent efforts to escape. (Shu Chungshin, the dancer once rejected as a candidate for the *okwa* on account of her family background, told me when I met her in South Korea several years later that she had been on the field performing during the dove scene.) That incident could have symbolized the ambiguity of North Korea's reunification policy: On the one hand, Pyongyang continued to insist publicly that it had no interest in unifying the peninsula by force. On the other hand, its enormous military was poised to attack southward on short notice.

Besides its reunification policy, North Korea's emphasis on economic equality exerted enough pull on some South Korean radicals to overcome the clear fact that South Korea had advanced much farther and faster economically through capitalism. Internally, the North Korean regime's ideological

WHEREVER YOU GO IN MY HOMELAND   367

and economic needs conflicted badly, in the long run tending to box it in. Still, Pyongyang's leaders could hope to use the appeal of Kim's ideas to young South Koreans to revolutionize the South and win the race despite Seoul's advantages.[11]

Of course, North Korean propaganda concerning the South was pitched not only to South Koreans but also at least equally to Northerners, and it was intriguing to see how the Northerners reacted. "I am young, so I want to know about the South Korean students' struggle against the U.S. imperialists and the South Korean puppet clique," my guide Pak said to me one night when I took him and our driver to supper. I explained that the demonstrations had tapered off to some extent following the movement's success in forcing a free presidential election in 1987. A bit later, Pak said: "As you know, the United States provoked the Korean War in 1950." No, I said, it was well established that the North had planned the invasion of the South. Pak laughed and told me that what I had said was just too ridiculous to credit. He did apologize a few minutes later for using the term *imperialist*— obviously not the thing to call one's guest. But it was clear that he and his fellow Northerners had been given a hugely distorted view of South Korea as a uniformly horrible place in need of salvation by the Great Leader, a land where the fruits of capitalist economic development had accrued to the wealthy few. Among North Koreans who were permitted to speak with foreign visitors, even those sophisticated enough to know that the South had the higher average living standard insisted that the North's system was better because the wealth was shared more evenly.[12]

(Equality in the North was not quite what the regime and faithful subjects portrayed it as being. It had little to do with the lives of top officials and their families. One illustration could be found on any street or road. Scarce passenger cars were used mainly to carry big shots, while the masses walked, or rode in the backs of trucks or on buses. The passenger car drivers almost without fail propelled their vehicles at high speed. They clearly operated on the presumption that they were entitled to the right of way against pedestrians. Drivers approached intersections without slowing down, scattering pedestrians, who would fall back to avoid being run over. Drivers apparently felt that the importance of their high-ranking passengers justified their arrogant behavior. At the entrance to the tomb of the founder of the Koguryo Dynasty, Kim Jong-su pointed out to me an ancient inscription: "Men great or small must dismount before entering here." I asked whether that applied to the Great Leader. Kim Jong-su's face assumed a pained look and he replied, "Don't make such comparisons.")

South Korea did have a few thousand radical disciples of Kim Il-sung, problem enough for the authorities in Seoul. But to hear it from North Korean propaganda one would have thought almost the entire Southern population was ready to worship Kim. Since there was virtually no information available to the contrary, people in the North seemed to believe all this. As was often reported abroad, radios available to ordinary citizens really were fixed so that they could receive only government broadcasts. The newspapers purveyed strictly the party line. "According to the newspaper almost all South Koreans respect the Great Leader and want reunification," said my guide, who added that he believed everything he read in the North Korean press.

Of course, the real elite had sources of information much better than the regular North Korean media. Very high-ranking cadre who needed to keep up with the outside world could listen to foreign broadcasts, including South Korean programming and the U.S. government's Voice of America. A slight but studied relaxation of U.S. antagonism toward the Pyongyang regime had permitted the delegation of North Koreans led by Kim Jong-su to visit Washington shortly before the youth festival. Much as sightseers in Hollywood want to see the studios and the homes of the stars, the North Koreans were keen to visit the offices of the Voice of America—where they expressed puzzlement when told of a U.S. law that prohibited broadcasting VOA programming within U.S. borders.[13]

High officials' superior sources of information about how North Korea compared with other countries did not produce any hint of humility in their conversation and pronouncements. Rather, one of Pyongyang's chief objects in permitting some Western journalists to visit for the youth festival was to issue a warning to the United States against continuing what amounted to a policy of letting North Korea stew in its own juices.

Strategists in the United States and South Korea had developed a theory, over the preceding few years, that the balance of power in the Korean peninsula was about to shift. According to that theory, South Korea's economic growth rate was so much higher than the North's that it would be a matter of only a few years before the South's military expenditures—while representing a much smaller percentage of gross national product—would match and exceed those of Pyongyang. When that happened, the theory went, South Korea would be able to field enough of a defensive force of its own to provide a credible deterrent against North Korean attack, without the help of U.S. troops. (Unspoken was the obvious corollary that if the South should develop aggressive intentions toward the North, Seoul would have the force advantage to contemplate carrying them out.) According to the theory, North Korea was desperate to do something to keep the balance from shifting decisively against it. Adding to North Korean frustration were the flight from communist orthodoxy of Pyongyang's allies, their flirtations with South Korea and pressures on Pyongyang from within to reform its own lagging economy.

Seeing all that, American and South Korean policymakers figured they could deal effectively with the North Korean threat simply by leaving the U.S. troops in place as a deterrent, taking modest steps to ease tensions and allowing time to pass. Thus, neither Washington nor Seoul seemed to feel any great urgency to push vigorously for negotiated solutions to the stand-off in the peninsula. That disturbed North Korean officials. Although they showed no real interest in genuinely negotiating with Seoul, nonetheless they still obviously hoped to play up to the United States sufficiently to get the U.S. troops removed from the South. True, American and North Korean mid-ranking diplomats had begun to meet periodically in Beijing. But this was really little more than another aspect of Washington's measured, very slight approach to relaxing tensions. Pyongyang—in search of diplomatic, military and economic concessions—wanted higher-level, more frequent contacts to get the talks off dead center. Kim Jong-su complained to me that the Beijing talks were proceeding like a very slow-moving bicycle—in danger of falling down for lack of momentum.

Kim Jong-su let me know that his government had not issued its invitations to American journalists lightly. "You have to understand that it's difficult to invite Americans here," he said. "Our people are very sensitive about the United States. In America you are maybe not so sensitive about Korea." What seemed to have overcome Pyongyang's reservations about inviting us was an urgent need to convey a message to Americans and others in the Western alliance. The message: North Korea was a powerful country, a country to be reckoned with, not only militarily but as a revolutionary society of impressive economic and social achievements, a beacon to the poor and to those oppressed by inequity in South Korea and the Third World.

Although it was tempting to imagine that North Korean leaders had started to believe their own propaganda, there was much more than that to their demand for respect. They meant to leave us with the impression of a country we should take seriously, if for no other reason than the enormous amount of trouble it could cause. Washington must not assume that the continued presence of U.S. troops in the South, coupled with an American policy of benign neglect of other issues, would solve the Korean problem. Americans should not make the mistake of assuming it was only a matter of time before North Korea would collapse or otherwise decisively lose the race with South Korea. More to the point, we had better realize that Pyongyang simply would not permit itself to lose without doing something drastic.

There did seem to be some basis for questioning the U.S. policy of deterrence-plus-malign neglect. North Korea still had gold and other mineral resources to barter abroad. Militarily, reports had started to appear that Pyongyang might be trying to develop nuclear weapons. Already it was known that the North had the capability to launch another surprise attack with conventional weapons. Add the factors of Pyongyang's ideological penetration of the South and uncertainty about what would happen after Kim Jong-il's succession, and the picture of what was yet to come looked a bit less reassuring. Those troubling facts were reason enough to intensify the search for new policy approaches. Arms-control experts, including John W. Lewis of the Center for International Security and Arms Control at Stanford, were indeed talking with North and South Korean counterparts about confidence-building measures that could lead to a reduction of the danger of war on the peninsula.

On balance, though, it would have been hard to justify an immediate and drastic shift from the basic watch-and-wait policy—especially a shift to any of the alternatives Pyongyang was pitching. Kim Il-sung had proposed a "confederation" in which the Northern and Southern systems supposedly could thrive separately, with no need for American troops to guard the peace. The catch was that there would be a common army and a common foreign policy—under whose control? The South Koreans understandably were not interested in taking a chance that the North would gain control of the army and impose its system on the South, completing Kim's revolution. North Korea's proposal for a nuclear-free zone in the peninsula seemed more worthy of discussion, but an agreement clearly would be worthless unless the North opened itself to permit verification.

New ideas would have been welcome, but no one seemed to have any. The regime was loath to open the country in any way that could admit outside influences, which might challenge its control of the people. So for Pyongyang's adversaries there remained a good argument in favor of waiting for internal strains to intensify further—meanwhile ensuring that the North's rulers would always have a way out, would not feel cornered.

Still, I left pondering the thought that North Koreans, after all, were Koreans—possessed of the toughness and determination that had made their fellow Koreans extraordinarily successful, not only in the South but as immigrants in the United States and other countries. Waiting for them to fall on their faces could be a long wait.

North Korean officials were unhappy with my coverage of that visit for *Newsweek*. As a Chongryon official told me later, the main complaint was that the articles had dwelled on Kim Il-sung's personality cult. Pyongyang vehemently insisted that the popular worship of Kim Il-sung was purely voluntary and from the heart and should not be described in the same terms as a state-imposed Stalinist personality cult. During my visit, an official had told me pointedly that the bottom-line minimum was that Westerners who wanted any sort of relationship with Pyongyang at all must stop making fun of its leaders. "Some parts of the body are more sensitive than others," the official told me, advising me not to hit him "in the eyes." In the monolithic society that North Korea boasted of having become, as I knew well enough, talk of the regime's "eyes"—or "brains"—was intended as a direct reference to Kim Il-sung and Kim Jong-il.

Presumably as a result of the official unhappiness with my articles, Kim Jong-su after that visit treated me distantly, ignoring my letters. Eventually I heard that he had gone to Peru as a diplomat. Some time later he reappeared in New York with ambassadorial rank as deputy chief of the North Korean mission to the United Nations. Still, despite calls and letters from me, he showed no interest in resuming our acquaintanceship.

Toward the end of my 1989 visit I had learned of his meeting with some foreign televison journalists—but under his earlier name, which this time seemed to be spelled Bae instead of Bai. He had explained, when I mentioned it, that his two names involved his having been orphaned and then later having acquired a stepfather; only "old friends" knew him as Bae. That didn't make much sense; the TV people now calling him Bae were strangers while I had known him earlier and was now calling him Kim. I could only continue to wonder about who and what—with his changes of name and occupation, and the orphan story he had told me—he really was. I guessed that he must be some sort of intelligence official and that Bai/Bae was his name when dealing with foreign visitors to North Korea while Kim was his traveling name. Other foreigners dealing with North Koreans had encountered such name changes.

Still, the mystery continued to intrigue me. Eventually I heard a vague report—no names were attached—about Kim Il-sung's unacknowledged children who had filled important posts in the regime. I wondered if Kim Jong-su might be one of them. Comparing photos, I thought I detected a physical resemblance to the young Kim Il-sung, particularly in facial bone structure. Kim Jong-su shared part of his given name with Kim Jong-il—the way Korean siblings often do. He had been virtually the only North Korean willing to talk forthrightly with me during my visits. Then there was the obvious and, as things turned out, justified confidence in his own influence that he showed when he guaranteed that he could get me—a reporter out of favor with the regime, at least since publication of my negative film review—admitted to cover the youth festival. All those factors suggested a status above that of ordinary mortals. I did once see him carelessly garbed in a suit of which the grays of the trousers and jacket did not match, more rumpled than royal, a costume appropriate to his current role as an academic intellectual. However, other North Koreans treated him with deference, close to awe, that the average think-tank scholar would not expect or receive.

Eventually, I started asking former elite North Korean officials about the country's backdoor royalty. Only one admitted to having heard details, and he told me, "If anyone in North Korea talks about it, it's immediate death." He was reluctant to say more at first. But finally he said that among high officials in the know, Kim Jong-su—for that was the man's real name—was considered to be the most powerful of Kim Il-sung's unacknowledged sons. His mother's home was in Sosong, an elite Pyongyang neighborhood. His influence derived not so much from his ancestry as from his real job, which was at a considerably higher level than his formal titles would suggest. "In North Korea we have a dual system, official and unofficial rank," my source told me. "Kim Jong-su is part of the party's intelligence organization, so his rank should never be known. People who don't know the inner workings of the system might think his rank is not so high. But in fact he's much, much higher than most people. He has the authority to contact Kim Jong-il by phone—so you can assume he's more powerful than a minister. Kim Jong-il knows their biological relationship."

If the age that Bai/Kim gave me—thirty-nine in the spring of 1979—was correct in Western terms, he was actually Kim Jong-il's elder. Even if he was giving me his age the way Koreans traditionally figured it—you are already one year old the day you are born—he was around the same age as Jong-il. That suggested his mother might have been one of Kim Il-sung's companions in the guerrilla days or early in his exile in the Soviet Union, between his first two marriages, or overlapping one or both of them. The source who told me Bai/Kim's identity said the mother was one of Kim Il-sung's favorite mistresses, a woman who became famous as a dancer after liberation. She eventually married another man, who was considered Kim Jong-su's official father, he said. The orphan story that Bai had told me was "the story that everyone gives to foreigners to explain his faithfulness," this source explained.[14]

I wished that I could find other people who could tell me they had heard it in Pyongyang, to confirm that this version of Kim Jong-su's paternity was indeed a rumor that spread among some members of the elite. Although my source's information on other matters generally checked out, I could not absolutely rule out the possibility he had made up this story. And even assuming that the rumor about Kim Jong-su did circulate, it might have been baseless in fact.

All I could conclude with reasonable certainty was that Kim Jong-su was not the person(s) he pretended to be. His diplomatic appointments and his brief incarnation as a scholar, two former officials told me, were cover for intelligence work. Former career diplomat Ko Young-hwan, who defected to South Korea in 1991 after postings in Africa, told me he did not know about the ancestry question. Ko said, however, that "Kim Jong-su is not a true diplomat like Ho Jong"—who was number three in the UN mission in the late 1980s and early 1990s, also with ambassadorial rank. Rather, Kim Jong-su "was sent to the United Nations as a spy. He's in that department. I assume he went to Mangyongdae School. He never went to the foreign language schools that most diplomats have attended."

In his diplomatic postings (prior to the one at the United Nations, at least) Kim Jong-su "was there to make sure false reports were not made and to watch the ambassador, in case he should work as a channel for right-wing members of the host-country government to be in touch with anti–Kim Jong-il forces," another former official told me. "When other North Koreans came from Pyongyang, people in that position reported on anything the ambassador might try to hide."

I tried to contact Kim Jong-su at the United Nations in the summer of 1994 when I wrote a note of condolence on the death of Kim Il-sung, the man whom, as I noted he had told me, he had grown up considering his father. As I was writing this book I mailed, to the address I had for Kim Jong-su, draft versions of chapters 2 and 3, about the young Kim Il-sung, and requested his help in arranging for me to do further research in Pyongyang on the Great Leader's life. He did not reply to my overtures.[15]

TWENTY-ONE

If Your Brain Is Properly Oiled

After each of my visits a major question remained in my mind: How effective, really, had all the indoctrination been? Had it produced a population filled with individual examples of the ideal communist "new man," an altruistic citizen devoted to the welfare of his countrymen? Were people truly fanatical in their loyalty to—or worship of—the leaders? Were they ready to follow orders, no matter what? Even as early as 1979, I was to learn, people had been hungry—but they had lied with alacrity to foreigners like me, boasting of full stomachs. "My country was very poor before, but thanks to the wise leadership of our Great Leader the country became a powerful state," a hothouse manager had told me. "Now we are leading a happy life."

Fear of the consequences if they should fail to play their roles was part of the reason they showed the face they did. But I don't believe that was the only reason. I think the people for the most part genuinely revered Kim Il-sung. They wanted to praise him and his works. They had expected their lives to improve based on his policies and decisions. If North Korea was not yet the paradise that they tried to convince me it was, many still believed or wanted to believe in the ultimate vision. I came to that conclusion after interviewing a number of defectors who told me they *still* revered Kim even after having fled to South Korea. Appearances, I realized then, were by no means totally deceiving. Many defectors' statements confirmed that the feeling of religious awe was real.

Take Kim Jong-min, who defected in 1988 after reaching a high rank in

the Ministry of Public Security. Before I met him, he told a South Korean interviewer that, even after arriving in Seoul, he had found himself "unable to
denounce Kim Il-sung for the first year." True, that was partly because "the
thought that someone might be listening was too deeply rooted in my consciousness," he acknowledged. But "even if I had thought of hating a person
whom I had only worshipped for forty years, there was no way to really express it." He explained that "there is no one in North Korea who would say
Kim Il-sung is bad." North Koreans were taught to believe that "through his
anti-Japanese activities, the nation was saved, and through land reform a
state centered around the people was established. He established a party
which directs the state, and led the country to victory in a war with the
United States. He remodeled socialism. The taxation system and social welfare system were completely realized under him. All of this was said to be
done by Kim Il-sung, so who would dare to call him bad?"[1]

Kim Jong-min had found reason, where his personal life intersected
with public life, to abandon the regime and throw in his lot with the enemy.
That made his confession of loyalty to Kim Il-sung all the more believable.
After all, the South Korean authorities of the period were not urging him and
other defectors to go easy on Pyongyang in their comments for publication.
(That form of manipulation would be left for the Kim Dae-jung administration, 1998–2003, and its successor, which did try to mute or silence some defector testimony that might challenge the government's "sunshine policy" of
North-South detente.) Consider also that the defectors were among the tiny
minority of citizens who had found the situation back home so intolerable
they were moved to risk their lives to escape. The vast majority had stayed
behind. Those who stayed behind would have tended to be, if anything, even
more devoted.

Andrew Holloway, a British social worker and socialist who lived in the
country in 1987–88 while working to revise English translations of the
regime's propaganda, paints in *A Year in Pyongyang* an affecting picture of an
apparently sincerely felt socialist spirit that he found displayed then in the
lives and deeds of Pyongyang residents with whom he came in contact. It can
easily be argued that those capital dwellers were an elite group by official decree, people who got to live in Pyongyang partly thanks to their ability to act
as exemplars. One could also note that they had little freedom of thought
(virtually none on the larger issues) and had been misguided regarding the
long-term efficacy of the Kims' policies. Nevertheless, I think, readers of
Holloway's book who were not consumed with knee-jerk loathing for socialism might be hard-pressed to adjudge as evil beyond redemption a society so
apparently successful in inculcating values such as kindness and modesty.[2]

Still, altruism and loyalty do not exist in a vacuum. The fervor of North
Koreans who bought into the system totally could not but be tested severely
once food problems became endemic. For the regime it had been an article of

faith that without near-complete isolation, *juche* could not go unchallenged. As eye-opening contacts with the outside world became more frequent, results proved the correctness of that calculation.

One North Korean who changed from zealot to critic was Dong Young-jun, who studied transport economics in Poland at Gdansk University until he defected from there in May 1989. When I met him I found a pleasant-looking fellow with a long-jawed—I would say horsey—face topped with springy hair. Married, with one son, he was studying economics at Seoul's Korea University. He was an English-speaker, and had made a Western fashion statement by wearing to our meeting a Lacoste sweater with embroidered crocodile logo. He carried a gold-plated lighter with leather inlays to light his Marlboros. In chapter 12 we heard Dong's account of the gang fights of his youth—fights he participated in, even though this son of a State Security official as a junior and senior middle school student was by his own description a "fanatic" regime loyalist. By the time of his graduation, he had settled down and become a good enough student to go straight to college, with six months of military training replacing the usual decade of service.

Dong told me about the ideology courses he had taken during his student days at Pyongyang Engineering College. The classes required students to memorize Kim Il-sung's main ideas and then "think of the best way to put them into effect." Were those classes interesting? I asked him. "I cried often," he replied. "I was so touched by the consideration Kim Il-sung showed for his people." Dong related an example of the Great Leader's concern. "Kim Il-sung passed by a workplace one cold day and saw women removing the roe from fish, blowing cold vapor from their mouths. He took a knife and started gutting fish himself, and he asked, 'How can I improve your lives?' Kim Il-sung then sent an order to our university, saying, 'Make a machine that can do this work.' Even to this day, it really touches me when I think of it and I feel like crying. When I thought of my mother making *kimchee* during the cold winter, it didn't affect me. But when I thought of the Great Leader touching the smelly fish with the dangerous knife, that got me very emotional."

Dong was assigned as a member of a group of students who were ordered to dream up the fish-cleaning machine. "In one and a half years we succeeded. The machine we made was very good, had hardly any flaws and didn't make any mistakes. We made it with fanatic devotion. I heard a saying then, 'If your mind is at the highest state, your product is at the highest state also.'"

Kim Il-sung made a stop on campus to commend the students who had produced the machine. Dong was not one of those who were notified in advance they would be permitted to talk with the Great Leader, but he was thrilled nonetheless. "When Kim Il-sung visited us at the university, I real-ized for the first time that he traveled in an American Ford limousine," Dong said. "I was very proud. There's an amusing story about Kim Il-sung and for-eign cars. In the mid-1970s he met with foreign reporters. Someone asked him, 'You hate the United States so much, how can you ride in an American car?' He replied, 'I'm not riding in it. I'm *driving* it.' Just seeing him in it made me proud. I was three or four meters away." However, Dong con-fessed, "Now that I have come to South Korea, I'm used to free thinking. I feel a discrepancy between *juche* and his riding in a foreign car."

I asked whether he believed the story about Kim's gutting the fish and deciding on the spot to do something for the workers. "He may have done it for show, for effect, but I still believe it actually happened," Dong replied. "There were people who saw Kim Il-sung do this and wrote books about it."

Dong's loyalty to the regime and its leaders was a complex feeling, not all positive, he acknowledged. "Once when I was a junior at the University, I went to a friend's birthday party. At the party my friend, the host, said, 'There is something wrong with the Kim Il-sung regime.' I replied, 'How could you say that?' When I think about it now, I was reacting not only out of fanaticism but also out of fear and apprehension. A big reason why I tried to shut him up was that I was afraid he would say it somewhere else, be put under surveillance, get caught and confess that he had made the same re-mark at his birthday party. Then they would ask, 'Who else was at the birth-day party?' State Security would ask me why I hadn't reported it. I was afraid of being punished. I was also concerned because once every three months they would have a big meeting of all the students. There they would make a show of expelling at least one or two students on the basis of State Security's findings."

Dong explained that "when you're small, all you think of is gratitude to Kim Il-sung. When you're older, you think, 'He has done so much for me, I should not do anything against him.' And I also feared punishment if I should do anything against him. There was no way for me to get access to informa-tion that went against Kim Il-sung or showed discrepancies."

I mentioned to Dong how, on an afternoon in 1979, I had gone to Kim Il-sung University but had found the parts of the campus I was shown utterly deserted and had not believed my guides' explanation that everyone was in a meeting, all 12,000 students. Dong surprised me by saying there really were such meetings. "*Everyone* goes. Otherwise, at the next meeting you'll be the one expelled. We would meet on the grounds of the campus. The university president attends plus one agent from State Security, one from Public Secu-rity, the regular dean and the party-affiliated dean. Professors attend only the very serious annual session. They also go to separate faculty meetings every three months."

Dong told me a bit about how the universities taught. "There's one advantage to a North Korean university," he said. "Even the professors study along with the students. There's no difference between a professor and a student. If the student excels to the point he's better than the professor, the student will be acknowledged." But that student would have to excel within the context of what Kim Il-sung had said and written. "In North Korea there's only discussion, no debate. Most ideology courses require memorization of principles, but to excel in class you need to come up with an improvement. Of course you can't change Kim Il-sung's principles, but you can think of the best way to put them into effect."

I asked Dong's view of the regime succession. "I thought very highly of Kim Il-sung," he replied. "I was proud and honored to work for such a high being. As for Kim Jong-il, I thought of him as a human. I liked Kim Jong-il because he was young and understood the younger generation. I thought he could bring a lot of change to North Korea. Understanding the younger generation, Kim Jong-il allowed men to grow their hair longer and let women have permanent waves. He even permitted access to famous foreign literary works. When you see festivities in North Korea, sometimes you can find Koreans dancing. This was allowed thanks to a decision by Kim Jong-il. I participated in that dancing, too, and was very grateful to Kim Jong-il. In 1983 on the thirty-fifth anniversary of the North Korean People's Army I joined in the dancing, too."

Dong's remarks reminded me that I had danced around a maypole on May Day, 1979, in Pyongyang's Kim Il-sung Square, wearing a Lenin cap newly purchased in a department store. I had not realized at the time that even that sort of dancing, based on folk dancing and to my eye totally devoid of sexual suggestiveness, was a newly granted privilege for which I should thank the Dear Leader.

Dong told me that he had kept his ideological purity until he left North Korea to study abroad. "Our political and economic system was based on dictatorship by Kim Il-sung—one-man rule," he said. "When I was in North Korea, I thought Kim Il-sung was God. I did everything by his command. I had no doubts about the regime until I went to Poland in 1985. Then, for five years, I heard a lot of news of the West—the United States, Germany, England. I thought, 'Which system or country is better politically or economically?' And I saw the life of the Polish people. In my mind, I saw that life in the West and in East European socialist countries, as well, was better than life in North Korea.

"I watched the Seoul Olympics on television—all the games. On the television monitor I saw Seoul and other cities. Before seeing the 1988 Olympics, I had been taught that South Korea was very poor. Many, many people were dying there, fighting against dictatorship, I was told. But I saw something different during the '88 Olympics. Of course I was interested in the games, but I was mostly interested in the street scenes that were televised, how the people were dressed. I realized I had been thinking wrong. I'd always been taught that South Korea was a poverty-stricken colony of the United States with no freedom, but when I watched boxing and saw that the South Korean beat the American, I thought, 'Maybe it's not the way I've been told.' Up until then I had thought that the colony could not go against the imperialists. Seeing that the South Koreans upheld their flag and competed in the games as South Korea, I was astonished that they could beat the United States."

After the Seoul Olympics, "people in many Eastern European countries including Poland were eager to find out about South Korea," Dong said. "There were a lot of special reports in the news—magazines, television, and so on—about how South Korea could develop into such an industrialized nation, and about how much power South Korea had to have to be able to host the Olympics. This was the channel I used to get knowledge of South Korea. I think it's a tragedy we had to get information that way. When I was in Pyongyang we could not learn such things."

Dong noted that radio, for example, "is a product of capitalism." In North Korea, "people can't have access to normal radios, because that would allow them to hear broadcasts from all over the world. It's hard to buy radios except the one-channel radios. The central government sends people to inspect radios every three or four months, so just having a radio can put people under fear and apprehension."

I asked Dong what he thought of the plans then being discussed for U.S. radio broadcasts to North Korea of news about North Korea in the Korean language, via Radio Free Asia. "It's a very good idea but not very practical," was his opinion. "Not enough North Koreans have access to radios to receive the transmissions—maybe just one percent, the high officials, a few people with power like those in State Security. The broadcasts won't be known nationwide. But the people with power to change things could listen and think. I myself got a lot of help from Radio Free Europe and BBC broadcasts."

It was not only what he heard on the radio and the televised revelations about South Korea that rocked Dong's worldview. "The changes in Poland—especially Solidarity—influenced me a lot," he said. "I had lots of Polish friends in Solidarity. They kept telling me, 'If your brain is properly oiled, you won't go back to North Korea.' I was shocked when a South Korean embassy was set up in Hungary, but I felt encouraged, because with a North Korean passport I couldn't go to a Western or neutral country but I could go to Hungary."

Soon, another factor arose that made Dong feel he had only a narrow window of opportunity if he wished to escape. When the embassy was established in Hungary, all the North Korean students there were sent to Poland to keep them from having contact with the Southerners. "When I heard of a plan for a South Korean embassy in Poland, I figured the North Korean students in Poland would be removed, too." With nowhere else to go in Europe, "I would be sent back to North Korea. That's what triggered my defection. I went by plane to Hungary and found the South Korean embassy in Budapest. They sent me to the South Korean embassy in Vienna." That was in May of 1989, six months before the South Korean embassy in Poland opened. "When I defected," Dong told me, "the main thing that troubled me was that my family would be punished. But I feel I'm a very egocentric man, to be able to defect. I guesss I was egotistical enough to overcome that concern."

I asked Dong how North Korean youngsters managed to learn anything substantive in school, what with all the gang fighting, labor, ideology instruction and so on. Had he felt he was far behind his Polish fellow students? "I thought I was way up there, because I entered in Poland as a university freshman," he replied. "All my classmates had only graduated from high school, but I already had three years of university education. So I was ahead of them. In general, though, I think North Korea lags in all fields with the possible exceptions of math, basic science—physics and chemistry—and English and Russian."

Before entering the prestigious Korea University in Seoul, Dong told me, he had taken an entrance examination and failed Korean. (That is not as surprising as it may sound. After all the decades of separation, the versions of Korean used in the North and South had many differences in vocabulary. As for the writing systems, although North Korea had long before halted the use of Chinese characters, South Koreans continued to use them in tandem with what had become the sole Northern writing system, the indigenous Korean *hangul* alphabet.) Nevertheless, Dong said, "I had very high scores in physics, chemistry and math. I'm a senior now. When I graduate, I'll enter Daewoo Corporation and specialize in East European trade. I speak Polish."

I asked Dong if he still worshipped Kim Il-sung, years after his defection. He hesitated. "It's hard to answer," he said. "When I think of Kim Il-sung, he did very cruel and wrong things. Still, when you contemplate it, the degree of his wrongdoing lessens. Since coming to South Korea I've come to realize that much of his history is fabricated, but still I'm moved by Kim Il-sung's leadership." Kim Il-sung, Dong noted, formerly had worn "people's clothes"—*inmin-pok* (what Americans call Mao suits although the Chinese actually call them Sun Yat-sen suits, for the 1911 founder of the Chinese republic, who wore the garb before either Mao or the North Koreans did)—with a Lenin cap. "Now he wears Western-style suits. That symbolizes that his health is good and he has the intent of cooperating with the West. The former, the health symbolism, is for his people; the latter is for the outside world."

By the time I spoke with Dong, the United States and North Korea were embroiled in the first dispute over Pyongyang's nuclear weapons program. Dong read into that an interesting observation about the regime's staying power. "I don't believe North Korea is going to collapse suddenly," he said. "To be able to have this conflict with the United States means Kim Il-sung has something to rely on: the support of the people." I asked if this was real rather than feigned or imaginary support. "I believe he *has* the people's support," Dong said. "Here's proof. Now they're having two meals a day, they're overworked, but still there's no uprising. That proves he has the people's support. People now understand that North Korea is not the most powerful nation. But they still believe it is among the most developed nations in the world. For me, when I left for Poland, I thought, 'North Korea is the best nation.' When I visited North Korea before the 1988 Olympics I met people who realized North Korea was not the best nation, but they thought it was certainly among the higher-ranking ones."

Dong noted that "Kim Il-sung is old" and said that "people realize he'll die soon. Until Kim Il-sung's death the regime will stay put. After his death, Kim Jong-il will succeed him. People don't trust Kim Jong-il as much as Kim Il-sung, so they will be a bit troubled. But there's still backing, and the regime won't collapse all that suddenly. From then on there will be a lot of change in North Korea—change like in China, maintaining the socialist system but adapting the free-market system. But the problem is, there will be turmoil caused by people who want revenge for all the hardship they've gone through. I believe Kim Jong-il doesn't have the kind of leadership ability Kim Il-sung has. So the people who have been oppressed will rise up and take revenge."

I asked Dong what he thought South Korea and the United States should be doing. "I would like to see the U.S. put more pressure on North Korea," he said. "Sanctions, demanding to inspect the human rights situation. Meanwhile South Korea should play the good cop and say to the U.S., 'Don't press them so hard.' Thus there could be a good channel for North-South talks. But the U.S. still would have to maintain the pressure. Even if there are North-South talks, the International Atomic Energy Agency, the United Nations and the United States should be able to step up the pressure if the talks don't go well. But I do believe that to achieve normal ties between North and South will be very difficult. It would be easier to normalize relations between the U.S. and North Korea or between Japan and North Korea."

Chung Seong-san, a soldier until his January 1995 defection, gave me a "yes, but . . ." answer to the question of whether the communist "new man" (or woman) really existed in North Korea. Chung told me he had contracted polio as a child and suffered from "stiff" legs. A man of very casual demeanor and dress, wearing a white-on-white windbreaker, light plaid slacks and loafers, Chung exhibited no obvious physical symptoms other than swollen knuckles. (Those were not uncommon among North Korean army veterans, trained in knuckle-smashing martial arts.) Evidently Chung's had been a mild case of polio or the diagnosis was faulty.

At one point in our conversation Chung said to me: "I've met a lot of North Korea specialists. Theoretically they know more about North Korea than I do, but they don't know the North Korean heart." Chung's heart story was a complicated one, sometimes self-contradictory, it turned out. "I was bald until I was eleven or twelve," he told me. "I got special treatment because of my illness, due to the benevolence of the party."

Hearing Chung say that, I remembered that neither I nor other visitors had seen handicapped people in Pyongyang. Lee Woong-pyong, the MIG19 pilot who escaped with his plane to the South, had told me that, in Pyongyang, "before the 1970s you could find many beggars and people disabled by the war. After that they were exiled to rural areas in the provinces. The reason the authorities gave was that Pyongyang is a cultured city, with lots of foreign visitors and there should be no distractions from the scenery." Ahn Choong-hak, a former soldier and logging camp worker who became a Kia automobile salesman when he reached the South, told me, "In the early 1980s they rounded up all the midgets in North Korea and placed them in Maemu-ri. Relatives started complaining, so around 1989 or 1990 they released them."

I told Chung I was surprised by his remarks; I had understood that the regime treated handicapped people shabbily. "There's different treatment for each group, but basically North Korean society is for the handicapped," he replied. "They have a specific policy regarding handicapped people. The best treated are those who become disabled while in the army—amputees and people who lose their sight, for example. Kim Shi-kwon, who became paralyzed in the Korean War, is the symbol of the disabled. He gets the most from the regime. There's always a car waiting to take him anywhere; doctors come to check him."

When I spoke with Chung he had been in South Korea for under half a year since his defection—he was still in the custody of the intelligence service pending his qualification for citizenship—but already he felt prepared to make a comparison. "The South Koreans don't have the kind of compassion the North Koreans have," he asserted. "In North Korea a friend lost a leg when a grenade exploded. He was helpless for the time being, but a very attractive woman factory worker volunteered to live with him. This is the result of training in selflessness."

In each North Korean province, Chung said, "there are two special schools for the disabled. They call them 'schools for the blind'—even if the problem is cerebral palsy. They have all the basics for dealing with problems such as sight and hearing impairment: braille, sign language and so on. There are special factories for the handicapped to work in. The North Korean regime says that, as long as you have that revolutionary spirit burning inside you, you get this special treatment."

Recent history, however, had been unkind to the disabled along with everyone else. "It's true that discrepancies are developing in the socialist countries," Chung said. "They don't have the resources for the normal people, so how can they provide properly for the disabled?" North Korea's special schools, he said, "don't have the resources for improvement." Still, "even though North Koreans may not have the doctors and the medicine, they're trying."

Up to this point, Chung had been positive in his recollections. But he abruptly changed his tone when I asked him to estimate what percentage of the people had internalized the officially encouraged attitude of loving and helping the other person—had become examples of North Korea's "new man," similar to the ideal Christian. "Although the system provides special privileges for the disabled, you can't fool human nature," he replied. "People are not all that kind to the disabled. In the 1960s, Pang Hwa-su, an elementary pupil, got third degree burns all over his body. Doctors really did peel off their own skin to graft onto him. Now he's a well-grown man. But the doctors today are like vampires. They're not for the people. The case where the woman volunteered to live with the amputee—that hardly ever happens. In North Korea there are about twenty-five severely paralyzed people a year. For each of them, the regime selects a woman and forces a marriage. Basically the women go through that kind of ordeal because they get rewarded by the government and because the summons is like the word of God. They get color televisions, money, and so on, if they agree, but if they refuse they'll be sent to prison camp."

I asked if there had been some turning point when popular altruism started to decline. "It's hard to say," Chung repled. "Maybe it was after 1985, possibly because of the food shortages. The second major cause may be repression, but they probably don't even realize that. I realized it while I was working there, visiting the schools for the blind to do research."

Chung was born in 1969 in Pyongyang, the capital. His father was a warehouse clerk. His mother stayed home to keep house. He told me he had gone to Chanhyun Elementary School and Songbuk Junior and Senior Middle School. That set me off on a line of questioning about the top schools in Pyongyang. The real elite, he told me, attended Mangyongdae Revolutionary School and Namsan Junior-Senior Middle School. "Namsan Junior was called, in 1948, Pyongyang First Elementary Junior School. After the Korean War they called it Namsan Junior and it was specifically for offspring of Korean War heroes and very high party officials." Over the decades, Chung said, the regime—unhappy with the qualifications of the class of 1958 at Kim Il-sung University—had tried various strategems for expanding the pool of Namsan applicants in order to bring in brighter youngsters. The children of somewhat less exalted officials were admitted if they were relatively gifted intellectually. "In 1984, they changed the selection system. Before 1984, 100 percent of those accepted were high officials' kids, but after 1985 two out of five were not from that background but were geniuses—although they still had to have proper class backgrounds. After 1985, the competition was about 300 to one, and you could enter from any part of the country."

I asked about the difference between Namsan Junior-Senior and Mangyongdae Revolutionary School. "Mangyongdae was an orphanage for children of Korean War martyrs, and it also accepted children of especially loyal members of the regime—spies working in South Korea for example," Chung said. "There are special cases where high army officers send their kids or grandchildren to get them trained for the army. You couldn't term this a normal, average school. More members are sent to the army and become the central members of the army."

After his own graduation in 1986 from the lesser Songbuk Senior, Chung himself went into army. "I was a writer in the army, writing propaganda for the regime," he told me. "North Korea has ten army corps. I was in the Second Corps, Ninth Division. At the same time I was taking a correspondence course in film production from Pyongyang Research Movie College and was a member of the national Writers' Coalition. In the Ninth Division I was in the mobile propaganda unit. I did my studying while I was with my military unit and occasionally visited the college for an exam. My work was to go around boosting the morale of my fellow soldiers. We put on stage shows, comedies, song and dance performances. I was both producing and writing. From 1988 until I defected I worked as a producer. At the beginning I had a goal in mind, which motivated me. The goal was to work diligently, enter the party and attend university."

So, I asked, had he been opportunistically trying to get ahead without particularly believing in the propaganda? "Yes," he replied. I asked when he had stopped believing. "I can't give you a turning point," he said. "It was gradual change while I was growing up. Since I know a lot about the regime, I started to know the discrepancies. That's when my heart changed. In Jilin Province, China, in 1938, Kim Il-sung formed a 'soviet' and made a speech: 'My ultimate goal is for the people to to eat rice with meat soup, live under a tile roof and wear silk clothes.' Over the decades he has done none of it. One incident comes to mind: My elder brother's marriage ceremony in 1990. It's a tradition that you put rice cakes and chestnuts on the table. The 'rice cakes' at his wedding were made of radish and the 'chestnuts' of dirt."

A more specific turning point for him, Chung said, came in 1991 — "after

I heard South Korean radio programs. South Korea sent propaganda balloons. I got a radio from a balloon and started listening to South Korean
broadcasts — MBC, CBS [the Christian Broadcasting System], KBS. When
I acquired the radio I was suffering from self-contradictions. I had to write
North Korean propaganda saying that all the people were living well and
had plenty to eat. I felt the discrepancies. I listened to KBS programs specifically targeted to North Koreans. At first I didn't believe them but later I acknowledged some of what they said. Even to this moment I don't believe all
of it."

I asked what he thought of the U.S. plan for Radio Free Asia broadcasts
to North Korea. "It will fail," was his first reaction. "People don't have the radios. The frequencies would be blocked. For that to be possible, to try to
move North Korean society through mass media, you'd have to make radios
available first. Loyal people are selected to pick up the South Korean balloon
drops. I was part of that. It's government policy to pick them up. It's hard because they usually fell on residential areas. I think the balloon-drop strategy
is very effective. They mostly come in July or August. North Koreans always look up to the sky then: 'Maybe today I'll be lucky.' When the balloons
drop, dogs run toward them to get food. If this is so successful, you may ask,
why isn't it changing North Korean society? The answer is there are usually
only one or two radios per balloon — not enough."

Radio was involved in Chung's own decision to defect. "I had entered
the party last year and had a chance to enter university, but I got caught with
a radio," he told me. "I could have gotten out of it and gone to the university,
since I knew people, but it would have been a black mark against me all
through my career. But my main reason for defecting was artistic. In North
Korea I could only produce what the government told me to make. I wanted
to express myself creatively. I want to study to become a producer in South
Korea."

I asked him whether North Korean soldiers wanted war. "Any ordinary
soldier wants to fight," Chung said. "He's never experienced defeat. Ignorance makes him want to fight."

Although Chung argued that the "new man" attitude had decayed, especially
among doctors, I heard a somewhat different view from Stephen Linton.
Linton, an American, grew up in South Korea as the son of missionaries and
organized a North Korea–focused philanthropic foundation that he named
for a missionary forebear, the Reverend Eugene Bell. I had first met Linton
when he served as interpreter for the U.S. table tennis team in Pyongyang in
1979. I trusted him and his organization to use effectively my own periodic,
modest contributions. His brother John was a medical doctor working in
Seoul, and one of the Eugene Bell Foundation's specialties was providing

equipment and medicine to help North Korean hospitals cope with an alarming jump in cases of tuberculosis. "I don't know about doctors giving flesh," Steve Linton told me, "but take fluoroscopes—you can look through somebody and use a screen instead of film. There's a crude kind of fluoro-scope that requires the radiation source on one side, the patient in the middle and the doctor on the other side, to diagnose TB. They know it's hard on the doctor. Cataracts are the first effect. If you're lucky, that's all. Otherwise brain damage. I can't help respecting somebody who will look into an X-ray machine."

Even as my hosts in Pyongyang in 1989 were assuring me that all was well in paradise, North Korea was in trouble. A visitor, tightly restricted in what he could see while inside the country, could only sense that something was amiss. But evidence was building up outside to show that the regime was failing in its elementary duty of feeding the people.[3] That failure threatened Pyongyang's single-minded efforts to maintain loyalty to Kim Il-sung and Kim Jong-il at a fever pitch. More and more of the Kims' subjects started to make the connection, as Chung Seong-san did, between economic backwardness and the policies of their top leaders.

The connection came most readily to the minds of North Koreans who, like Dong Young-jun, were stationed abroad, and who thus were exposed to information and viewpoints unavailable to their stay-at-home countrymen. Food shortages worsened to the point where even some elite expatriates feared for their livelihoods if they should return home. Kang Myong-do, son-in-law of a prime minister, Kang Song-san, told the Seoul newspaper *Joong-Ang Ilbo* that North Korean spies in China, to avoid being sent home, had fabricated and submitted reports setting out a need for them to remain in China. Their specific scam was to tell their Pyongyang masters that South Korean special forces had been sent to kidnap North Koreans in China and take them south. "Kim Jong-il and Kang Song-san still believe that," Kang Myong-do told the newspaper.[4]

The story illustrates the fact that China had become more prosperous than North Korea. People living just across the border in China's Yanbian region were in perhaps the best position to notice that shift. "North Koreans were better off than people in China, including Yanbian, until the early 1970s," one such person, an ethnic Korean professor at the Yanbian Academy of Social Sciences, told me.[5] "During the 1960s lots of Koreans from China went over to North Korea because life there was much better than in China. There was a lot of internal strife in China during the 1960s. From the 1970s, the situation in North Korea started deteriorating because the government spent too much on the military after the 1962 Cuban missile crisis and the Vietnam War. Gradually China, including Yanbian, pulled ahead.

The difference was that people in China not only had money; they also had something to spend it on. The North Koreans got their salaries but there was nothing to buy with their money."

The professor, speaking in 1992, said that people in North Korea had been "hungry, although not actually starving, since the mid-1970s. The exception is Pyongyang. I have an aunt in Pyongyang who is the widow of a 1930s martyr in the anti-Japanese struggle. I visited her and found she had plenty. She was well taken care of. She had lots of sacks of rice. For the others, the government has been trying to improve the situation but there's been no real improvement since the 1970s. Laborers get eighteen kilograms of grain per month; office workers, fifteen kilos. Both China and North Korea distribute food directly to the people as a means of coping with scarcity. The basic principle is: If there's a scarcity, the state must ration. If there's a surplus, let people buy it in the stores. There are a lot more side dishes in China, and meat is now very common in China. Chinese can buy meat in stores. In North Korea, the stores' stocks are very limited. Meat and dairy products there are still rationed by the state, because of their scarcity."

Still, the professor told me, it would be a mistake to imagine that people's natural complaints translated into significant active dissent. "I can't judge the amount of complaining, since it's suppressed," he said, "but people do complain everywhere. The government won't tolerate dissent. People get executed. So an uprising would be next to impossible. It's important to note that, whatever happens, people do conform to the rules and regulations. They believe in the ideology."

Not everyone believed, though. There were cynics like Ko Chung-song, who had been an employee of a district office for preservation of revolutionary historical sites before he defected in June 1993.[6] The office was all about ideology, but Ko's job was about food, fuel and other essentials of life. The day I met him in 1994 Ko wore rimless, rectangular glasses, a nice suit and tie, a gold watch. All in all, he looked like a typical young South Korean bureaucrat or corporate official.

Ko told me that as a young student in North Hwanghae Province, he had "basically believed Kim Il-sung was a god, a savior. In high school I thought my uniform had been given to me by Kim Il-sung. 'He's educating me for a good life,' I believed. So I thought very highly of him. All the education is centered around Kim Il-sung. The first thing you say when you wake up is, 'Oh, Great Leader Kim Il-sung.' The first thing you learn to say as a baby is 'Kim Il-sung.' So how can you *not* worship him? At the nursery they have a portrait of Kim Il-sung. Before you eat you say 'Thank thee, thou great Kim Il-sung.'"

In school, "if you don't get 100 percent on your ideological test you're a failure." All the ideological instruction, combined with "volunteer" labor, left little time to study other subjects or have fun. "I did more labor in my school days than after I entered into society," Ko told me. "Out of a year, four months would be spent laboring. All I can remember is toiling away my days. If I had been paid I would have gotten a lot of money. We would study in the morning and work in the afternoon."

It was a specific incident after he had finished high school, though, that really sparked Ko's cynicism. "Once the district party told me: 'We'd like you to volunteer for a very special, high-level mission.' I thought it was some kind of reward, but after I agreed to volunteer I was told to go to the coal mines. I was a diligent, hard worker, so they took advantage of me. I had believed them, and I felt really betrayed." It sounded, I told him, very much like the classic ploy of the U.S. Army recruiters whose posters urged young men to see the world and learn a wonderful new profession—which turned out to involve cleaning latrines and peeling potatoes.

"High blood pressure kept me out of the army," Ko said. "I asked my brother to get me exempted at the time of the August 8 [1976] axe-killing incident at the Demilitarized Zone." After falling for the "special mission" bait-and-switch maneuver, Ko said, "I protested for a year, refusing to work in the mines, and then was sent to do forced labor on a farm near Pyongyang."

I was surprised to hear he had managed to hold out for so long before being punished. "Luckily I had good family connections," Ko explained. "I got out of the forced farm labor quickly thanks to my uncle. When you're sent for a job you need a *munkwan*—party permission document. Once you're sent to forced labor, without strong backup you can't leave. But my uncle got my *munkwan* changed. I went to work in the Hwangju irrigation office, and then from 1984 to 1987 I worked in Kanggye Military Factory No. 26, which made missiles for anti-submarine warfare, and rockets. It had a false name, 'Kanggye Tractor Co.'"

But Ko told me he had "still felt rebellious. Lots of my relatives were high officials, and I had attended a specialized school. So until I was betrayed by the government with that 'special mission' trick, I'd held high hopes for my career. Now there was forced labor on my record, and that goes against you. I never trusted the authorities again. I was sick of the brainwashing and started listening to South Korean broadcasts.

"In 1987 I went to work for the Kanggye Food Supply Department. The food shortage then was worse than usual. When I arrived things were already in a pitiful state, but in 1989 the situation started getting far worse still. It gets worse and worse each year. To meet North Koreans' food requirements, about six million tons of rice are needed. But only about four million tons are produced. That means two million tons should be imported. In Kanggye there are 400,000 people. Kanggye is a mountainous area that can't grow its own rice. We got it all from North Pyongan Province, or it was imported—say from China. We were always behind in distributions by two months or so. The average worker supposedly is entitled to 700 grams a day. For unemployed people, it's 300 grams. But the authorities said they needed to store up rice for use in case of war, so we had to take some out of the ration. So the actual supply was about 530 grams. Around 1989 and 1990, while I was there, we were providing about 530 grams."

That food-supply job, Ko told me, put him where the power was at a time when ordinary people had begun to turn to theft and scavenging to fill their stomachs. "In North Korea right now, food is equivalent to money. In rural areas, if you want to buy things like appliances you have to pay in food instead of money. I never stole, but generally to sustain life in North Korea you have to steal. If you work in a pencil factory you have to steal pencils, which you then trade in the black market for food. I didn't have to steal because I could fix up the documents to supply me enough food. In North Korea any job having to do with food was a high position. Sons and daughters of high officials liked to work there."

I told Ko about the youth festival helper who had asked me for $100 to buy goods at the special store selling foreign goods. "To earn $100 a North Korean would have to work 10 years. That guide is probably quite a rich man. One month's salary is about 60 *won*, while $100 equals 7,500 *won* or so. You made a wealthy man there." I asked Ko whether the man might have been instructed by the regime to ask for foreign exchange. "Of course he did it on his own," Ko replied. "The North Korean government is too proud to make those workers ask Americans for money." (I pointed out to Ko that the regime was not too proud to make its diplomats smuggle drugs and pass counterfeit bills for hard currency.)

When Ko left the Kanggye Food Supply Department he continued to be involved with food. His new job was supplying food, coal and so on for the forty-five people or so—workers and management—in the Chagang Province Preservation Office for Historical Monuments, in Kanggye city. Chagang province is close to Manchuria—Northeast China—and includes much of the route of Kim Il-sung's storied boyhood journey for learning. There is, for example, the inn whose keeper back in 1923 gave Kim Il-sung an extra blanket at no charge. The high command during the Korean War was in what later became Chagang Province, and Kim Jong-il spent part of his childhood in Kanggye.

The preservation office was in charge of historical monuments including "slogan trees." "In the mountains during the struggle against Japanese rule some people peeled back the bark of trees and scratched praise of the 'great general Kim Il-sung' in the wood. A couple of those *kuho* (inscribed trees) are authentic, but others later popped up all over North Korea—put there by the authorities. I haven't personally seen it done, but I've seen the evidence of their work. A committee established by the party proclaimed, 'We're totally faithful to Kim Il-sung, so we'll go to the mountains to find the inscriptions.' They reported the ones they had 'found' and I went to look at them. I could tell they had just cut into the trees a few days before—not decades before. They're propaganda to make people worship Kim Il-sung."[7]

It was a similar story with other "historical" monuments, Ko said. "Kim Jong-il was born in the Soviet Union, but they made a monument on Mount Paektu saying he was born there. In Mangyongdae, Kim Il-sung's birthplace, you can find markers for the place where Kim studied, the place he played and so on. Well, the authorities have put up the same sort of monuments for Kim Jong-il, in Kanggye. 'Here's where he thought about the revolution. This shows why he must be the leader.' 'Here's where he played.' Actually, Kim Jong-il stayed only three months or so in Kanggye, then went to China with his sister, Kim Kyong-hui. But they still made the monuments. The whole district of Hankye-ri in Kanggye city is one big 'historical' monument."

Ko worked for the historical office from mid-1991 until he defected in June 1993. "From the moment I started working there I felt it was all fake," he told me. "No one talked about it. You could have your own feelings about it, but you couldn't openly talk about it. I'm pretty sure a lot of people felt that way, but they didn't dare express it clearly." As for the reaction of the general public, "In the past, all those historical monuments had great effect," Ko said. "People went to those places and studied the inscriptions. But now they don't pay any attention. People started changing two or three years ago [1991 or 1992], expecially in the elite classes. University students got stirred up. With the downfall of communism in Eastern Europe and the Soviet Union, people were starting to think, 'Maybe there's something wrong with communism.' Also, there was no more aid coming from the Russians. So the economy declined terribly. People today no longer care about ideology—they only care about their survival. People think something is bound to happen in North Korea. That's what I meant by saying the students got stirred up. Members of the elite believe that North Korea will be influenced by international changes."

Ko told me he had "felt some of this before starting to work in the monuments office. I began listening to radio—KBS from South Korea, radio from Yanbian, the Radio Moscow Korean-language service. From around 11 P.M. to early morning, you can tune in the KBS social education station well. I started listening in 1985 and began doubting the regime in 1989. The state doesn't know, but people listen to secretly imported radios." He had bought his radio, a Sony shortwave model, from a man he met on a business trip. Maybe 5 to 6 percent of the population had radios capable of receiving at least AM—medium wave—transmissions at the time he left, he estimated. He guessed that a third of those with the equipment—perhaps 2 percent of the population—listened to foreign stations.

"My friends and I would even get together to listen to the South Korean broadcasts and debate what we had heard," Ko said. "Kim Il-sung was saying in his speeches that in order for us to have a lavish life and prosper we must reunify. I wanted to learn the prospects for reunification. On the radio I heard about the downfall of foreign socialism and about the virtual capitalism rampant in China. I wanted to find out the prospects for Korea. I ultimately defected because I came to believe the regime could not survive for long. It's bound to fall. Everybody believes something is going to happen in a couple of years. When friends get together, they debate how North Korea will change. Someone might say, 'What do you think about the collapse of the USSR? Do you think capitalism or socialism is better? What about Chinese-style, free-market socialism?' The regime's propaganda backfires. On North Korean news they show footage of students demonstrating in South Korea. Ordinary people say, 'Oh, society must be very harsh there.' Educated people think, 'To have such demonstrations, they must have a very democratic society.' Other issues people talk about in these private discussions include oil. The oil supply that the Soviet Union used to provide is now cut and oil from China drastically reduced. So what is the future of North Korea?"

I asked him what people thought was the answer to that question. "Everybody believes a war will break out sooner or later," he said. "A hundred percent want war to occur. The food shortage is terrible. Distribution is halted, so people figure they will die of hunger or die in war. They're even prepared to die in a nuclear war. A hundred percent believe that North Korea would win, so they support war. They were brought up to worship Kim Il-sung. No matter what changes occur, they always worship Kim Il-sung. They've been so brainwashed since birth that they're willing to die for the country."

So was it the case that the people did not connect Kim's rule to their problems? "They don't blame Kim Il-sung, but they do blame Kim Jong-il," Ko said. "The moment Kim Jong-il came into power the problems started, they think. All North Koreans believe Kim Il-sung is a war hero who brought about the independence of Korea. They worship him. Even though I betrayed North Korea, I still revere Kim Il-sung, think very highly of him. Probably all the defectors here think that way. It's such a closed society."

Ko had found, he said, that "people in South Korea are not alert enough. I know that Kim Jong-il is brutal enough to start a war. Most people in North Korea believe the reason North and South cannot reunify is that the U.S. military is stationed here. And if the U.S. moves out, they think, reunification is only a matter of time. But removing U.S. troops won't bring about reunification. Kim Il-sung knows that if free markets and other foreign influences come in, his regime will collapse. I support economic sanctions. But for economic sanctions to work China would have to give up its socialist ideal.

Without that change we can't have change in North Korea, because the regime has the support of the Chinese."

I told Ko about Washington's plans for Radio Free Asia broadcasts in Korean and asked if he thought those could help open the society. "That's an exciting idea!" he said. "A lot of people listen to the radio so it has a high chance of disrupting the regime. It would be effective. Most North Koreans don't know what's happening in North Korea. When I was living there I was waiting for someone to tell me what I should do. No one ever did. On those broadcasts, defectors should talk and persuade their friends in North Korea—let them know we're alive. Maybe that would inspire them. Put it in terms they can understand. Instead of having someone say that South Korea is experiencing an economic boom, get defectors on the radio to give examples of what can be bought down here." As a percentage of the respective average incomes, "the price of a Hyundai Sonata II here, for example, is equivalent to the price of a suit in North Korea."

I asked him about the leaflets the South Koreans dropped by balloon. "I've read them myself," he replied, "although you're forbidden to read them. If word gets out they have been dropped, State Security sends lots of people out to watch. If anyone is seen picking up one of the leaflets to read it, someone will tattle and the person reading it will go to prison."

Another North Korean who told me about the growing criticism of Kim Jong-il in the 1980s was Kim Nam-joon, who defected to the South in August 1989 while serving as a People's Army second lieutenant. "The food shortage got worse in the early 1980s," Kim Nam-joon told me.[8] "Most people tied that to the appearance of Kim Jong-il on the political stage. Kim Jong-il is a very unlucky man. He graduated from Kim Il-sung University in 1964. Until the late 1970s he worked quietly in the party. In the 1980s he started appearing in public. People connected all the failures to him. In 1984, when there was flooding in South Korea, North Korea offered aid to the South. Each month at a military hospital in my area a two-and-a-half-ton truck had come, filled with supplies. After we started aiding South Korea, the truck would show up with only two kilograms or so of supplies per month. For workers, the grain ration had been 700 grams a day. The authorities would subtract 20 grams to store in case of war. Then they started taking another 20 grams out for aid to South Korea." Military men got a larger ration—800 grams was the standard—but still, when that was cut, "I could feel it," Kim said.

Kim Nam-joon told me that in 1989, "fifteen more grams were cut from the grain ration to pay for the youth festival, so we were down to 645 grams a day." I asked about what Asians refer to as "side dishes," a catchall term for the rest of their diet besides grain. He laughed bitterly. "If it was the season for Chinese cabbage, that's what we'd have. Maybe just salted. Or if it was radishes—salted. To try to make us think we were getting a variety of dishes, they would cut the vegetable in different shapes: a bowl in which it was cut into cubes, another in which it was sliced—the same vegetable. Soup was just the water that had been used for washing rice, with a little salt added."

Actually, Kim Nam-joon told me, blaming Kim Jong-il in that case was unfair since the shortages of the 1980s could be traced directly back to the early 1970s "when Kim Il-sung made his declaration about national farming. It was nonsense. He did it because there wasn't enough coal, so people had to go to the mountains and cut trees for firewood. So the mountains are bare. Kim Il-sung said since there are no trees on the mountains we'll use them for farmland. OK, you guys, cut the trees—we'll farm there. 'Reclaim more land' was the motto, but you can't fight nature. After a couple of years the mountains started eroding from the rain, and the runoff clogged the rivers. The water supply couldn't get to other farm areas."[9]

That struck me as a rather sophisticated analysis of agricultural policy for an army junior officer to have recited, so I asked Kim Nam-joon if people really had talked in such terms about the Great Leader's policy failures. "They're so simple-minded they don't complain," he replied. "They only see what's in front of them." What he had told me was "something I figured out after coming to Seoul. I only speculated about it while I was in North Korea. But I had a calculator in 1987 or '88. I once calculated something. All the people were hungry, but the media said that each year North Korea was harvesting 8.8 million tons of grain. I calculated, even assuming there were around 30 million people in North Korea"—the actual population was only something over half that—"and applied the standard grain rations to see how much grain that would be. I came up with a figure of 4.5 million tons. So I wondered where the other 4.3 million tons had gone. I realized it was another lie."

The thought of the regime having lied to him set Kim Nam-joon off on a bitter tirade. "Kim Il-sung is such a liar, such a hypocrite, such an imitator," he raged. It was Kim Nam-joon who told me of the slogan theft mentioned in chapter 13. "At people's homes there's a slogan, 'Fish cannot live out of water. The people cannot live without the People's Army.—Kim Il-sung.' When I came to South Korea I learned that Mao Zedong was actually the one who said that. Kim is such a copycat. He's so stupid. In the early '70s he said, 'Find land.' In the '80s he said, 'Find water,' after all the rivers had been clogged from mountain erosion. He said that for farming we would have to find underground water supplies. Of course, there's not enough water underground. All this brought about the decline of North Korean agriculture."

Kim Nam-joon recalled that he had been a typically faithful believer through high school. His parents were ethnic Koreans who had lived in the Russian Far East, near Khabarovsk, where his father served in the Soviet

Navy. In 1959, three years before Nam-joon's birth, the father retired and the family moved to Chongjin, a major port on the east coast of North Korea.

"The family moved because my father had been a member of the Communist Party in Korea before moving to the Soviet Union in 1945, after liberation," Kim Nam-joon told me. "Father was sixty, had his pension and wanted to come home. He figured he would get special privileges thanks to his political history. Chongjin was a place where a lot of returnees were sent to resettle—especially those from Japan. The government told them to go there. Mother opposed returning. In the event, their life in North Korea was so deprived they wished they could go back to the Soviet Union. Growing up, I heard them complaining all the time. When they lived in the Soviet Union, they had radios, bicycles—all the luxuries. Many people who came to Chongjin from the Soviet Union were married to Russian women. They were allowed to return to the Soviet Union if they wished. But my parents were both Koreans so they weren't allowed to leave once they had returned to Korea."

Despite his parents' complaints, Kim said, he had not felt any contradiction between reality and what he was taught in the North Korean schools. That was "because my father was a totally committed communist. Of course my mother was not used to the lifestyle in North Korea, but I didn't really feel a conflict until I graduated from high school. I thought everyone in the world lived the way I did. The general mentality in North Korea is, if they tell you it's red, you say it's red even if it's really blue.

"In 1983, though, I entered the Kankon Military Academy and became more internationalized. The academy is a two-year military college in Pyongyang where they train officers. I entered after three years in the military. When you enter the military academy you are supposed to start to get a feel for the foreign world. To be able to teach our subordinates to deal with reality, future officers had to be in contact with reality. We needed to see foreign newspapers. It wasn't that open, really—we could only have a taste. But they did let us have a glimpse of the real world. North Korea teaches that capitalism is on the brink of collapse, but from all my reading at the academy, I realized capitalism has a better future than socialism. Take the case of Hungary, which was starting to prosper in those days. At first I thought the Hungarians were rich because of socialist ideas and the communist system. Then I realized that they had grown prosperous thanks to capitalist ideas. The most important thing that influenced me was the knowledge I got of South Korea. I had thought of South Korea as corrupt and poorly governed. But at the military academy they had a catalog of South Korean weaponry. I realized they had high-tech weapons, and far more military vehicles than North Korea. Before entering the academy, I thought all South Koreans were poor. I believed that their housing was like refugee camps. But at the academy they taught a course on the Republic of Korea, telling us about lifestyles and so on. I started to think maybe the people in South Korea were not as miserable as I had thought.

"At the academy, although I was beginning to get a little suspicious of the regime I still didn't have so many real doubts. And I didn't talk with people at the academy about my suspicions. It was after I graduated, got my commission and was stationed at the Demilitarized Zone that I began to really face facts. We had binoculars and could compare the reality across the DMZ with what we had been told. Near the DMZ there's a South Korean town. I realized it had beautiful houses. I saw lots of helicopters and other vehicles. I figured it would take a prosperous country to maintain it.

"A big impetus to my defection came in July 1987 when I saw South Korean television broadcasts. I was head of the border guard unit, which gave me a lot of authority despite my low rank. I had access to the camp commander's room. There was a Japanese television in there with the channels blocked. Accidentally one day I saw that the back was open and I moved a switch. I got to see the U.S. Armed Forces Korea Network (AFKN), which was totally surprising. I got up my courage further and changed channels to KBS, where the *Midnight Debate* was on. Sometimes I watched it after that. Even the highest-quality television sold in North Korea is the dial-type. They move the dial to channel nine and solder it in place. But from the back you can still turn the channels. I liked to watch the *Midnight Debate*. A weekly 40-kilometer [25-mile] hike was from 10 P.M. Friday to 6 A.M. Saturday, so everyone was out of the camp at the time when I turned that program on each week. I didn't really know what they were talking about. I was just looking at the people. South Korea was supposed to be poor and ugly, but they were lavishly dressed and had some fat on them. All the students in the studio audience were wearing watches—that would be almost a miracle if it were North Korea.

"I just watched once a week for four weeks before I got caught. I was afraid I would be sent to prison then. But in order to be part of this border guard brigade you had to have a good family background. Even Premier Yon Hyon-muk's son was in the border guards. I had *paek* [connections] so I was only demoted and sent to a front-line infantry brigade. That was in August of 1987. For two years I had so much conflict in my mind. Should I commit suicide? Defect? There was no prospect of promotion for someone who had been demoted and sent to the infantry. If I had children later on, they would be deemed to have a bad family background because of me."

In 1988, Kim Nam-joon felt the impact of a momentous announcement by South Korean President Roh Tae-woo. On July 7 of that year, emulating West Germany's *Ostpolitik,* or outreach to East Germany, Roh issued his own six-point *Nordpolitik* proposal for an improved North-South relationship, including economic and personnel exchanges. "A balloon dropped a copy of *Saenal* [New Day]," Kim told me. "One of the articles dealt with the July declaration of Roh Tae-woo. After reading that, I decided I had to go to South Korea. For twenty-five years I had been hearing Kim Il-sung's New Year's proclamations. Every time I heard them, I thought, 'That's a pack of lies, but I guess that's what leaders have to say.' But when I saw Roh's July 7 proclamation I analyzed it for forty minutes, underlined parts of it and decided, 'This is true.' Even regarding the North-South issue, Roh showed real intent. Kim Il-sung would always say, 'We have to reunify peacefully.' You didn't really see much eagerness in it. But in Roh's proclamation I saw the yearning.

"Two other guys read it, too. Kim Kwang-choon defected with me and the other man was supposed to, but he couldn't get out. I suppose he must have been caught. Most other people who have defected did so on the spur of the moment, but I deliberated for a whole year. After I had planned it for eight months, the other two came into the picture four months before the actual defection. I hear the brigade I was in was dispersed. Maybe the people close to me are in big trouble."

Ko Young-hwan was one of the North Koreans who had to go abroad before starting to realize what was really happening at home. Born in 1953, the year the Korean War ended, Ko studied for seven years in a foreign languages institute before enrolling in Pyongyang's Foreign Languages University. After graduation, he joined the Foreign Ministry. He was stationed as a diplomat in Geneva for one year, in Zaire twice for a total of five years, then in the Congo. He was first secretary in the North Korean embassy in the Congo when he defected in 1991. After that, South Korea put him to work as a researcher at the Institute for North Korean Studies in Seoul. Skinny with gold-rimmed glasses, when I interviewed him in 1993 he presented the sort of studious appearance that made me feel certain he would adjust well to life in the South Korean capital.[10]

"Most North Korean citizens believe that when Kim Il-sung was in full power the economy was better," Ko told me. "They believe the economy has gone down since the late 1970s when Kim Jong-il started appearing on the political scene." But Ko, like Kim Nam-joon, felt that the declines of that period resulted from the policies of the father, rather than those of the son. "This is the buzz in North Korea: 'When Kim Il-sung was in power, everything was perfect, but now that Kim Jong-il is taking over it can be very bad.' The truth is, in the 1950s and '60s the economy thrived because support from communist countries—the Soviet Union, China and Eastern European countries—made possible a stable economy. But in the late 1960s the country started using half its gross national product for the military. That's why the life of the people worsened. The change almost coincided with the time Kim Jong-il came into power. Thus Kim Il-sung's faults are blamed on Kim Jong-il."

I asked Ko about the origins of his decision to defect. "Three events really shook me up regarding communist ideology," he told me. "First, I heard Gorbachev's speech on *perestroika* in 1987. I wanted to know more. Second was the reunification of East and West Germany. Third was the political turmoil in Albania. The Gorbachev speech was the first time I doubted the socialist ideal, but earlier, while I was in Zaire from 1981 to 1983, I experienced my first concerns and doubts about the education I had received in North Korea. I heard about South Korea from other people and learned that what I had been taught was not true. That's when my ideas began to be shaken. After 1987 I believed socialism could not succeed in North Korea."

We talked about my observations regarding fanaticism as a quality that had seemed to be at its peak when I first visited Pyongyang in 1979. Ko agreed, saying things were changing. "The younger generations of the late 1970s and today are totally different," he said. "I was one of the fanatics until 1987. Up until about 1985, most people were that way. But toward the end of the '80s people started having doubts about the socialist ideal, and about whether we could really beat South Korea in war. The difference is that the new younger generation are doubters, not fanatics. That earlier younger generation of the late '70s—those people have now become family men, mainly interested in stability." Ko said people tended to develop doubts between the ages of twenty-two and twenty-nine.

The challenge for people who harbored doubts was to keep their lips zipped. Regarding Kim Jong-il, "the only thing they can talk about is the fact he is the son of Kim Il-sung," Ko said. "They don't dare discuss whom he married, who his half-brother is, the fact that he's short—any of these could send them to prison. There is twice as much repression as when Kim Il-sung was in power. After the late '70s it got so bad that if you went to a store, asked for toothpaste, were told there wasn't any and complained, asking, 'What kind of a store is this?' you could be sent to prison as a political dissident. While I was in university there were about 1,000 students. Each year about ten students disappeared for such transgressions—even for saying there was bad blood between Kim Jong-il and Kim Pyong-il," his younger stepbrother.

I asked Ko how, if people could not talk freely, he had learned how people viewed Kim Jong-il. "Inside North Korea you can't hear that kind of complaint," the ex-diplomat told me. "But when people visit an overseas embassy and have a drink, they say things like 'Kim Jong-il should maybe spend more time on the scientific and technical side'—something very indirect, so that if there were any repercussions they could hope to get away with it. Another indirect conversation you could hear among high officials relates to China's reforms. They would say, 'China is doing very well nowadays.' They don't directly say that North Korea should be like China."

*   *   *

Another North Korean who experienced a moment of truth while abroad was Kim Ji-il, who studied physics in Kharkov, Ukraine (then part of the Soviet Union), from 1984. (In chapter 15, we met Kim as an elementary school class president who in criticism sessions stumbled on the pronunciation of that mouthful of a Korean word for "advance-guard stormtrooper," *keunuidaekyeolsade.*) He defected to Seoul in 1990.[11] A handsome fellow with heavy eyebrows, Kim—like only one other male defector to South Korea among the dozens I spoke with—did not wear a gold watch. His timepiece was a black, plastic, digital sports model. "My wife tells me I should wear a formal watch, like other businessmen, but I like casual," he explained when I commented on that nonconformist fashion touch. As for being a businessman, he was working at Sunkyong Corporation in the foreign trade department, developing exchange projects with other countries. He told me he hoped to get involved in trade with North Korea eventually, but wasn't yet pursuing any deals with Pyongyang.

Born in 1964, Kim Ji-il grew up in Pyongyang, where his father was a construction engineer building factories and energy projects. His mother was a professor of Russian at the Foreign Languages University. Maternity leave was seventy-seven days, so Kim was sent to a nursery at around two months of age. Later, "in kindergarten, when they gave us our snacks, they would say, 'Our Great Leader gave us these.' The kids would have to say, 'Thank you, Great Fatherly Leader.'" I had been wondering how family relationships had fared in a country where the Great Leader was everyone's father. I asked Kim Ji-il whether, despite exposure to the constant propaganda focus on Kim Il-sung, he had been close to his parents. "Very close," he replied. "When my father returned from a business trip, he would bring me snacks. He helped me with my homework. I remember walking around with my parents, being with them quite a lot."

Kim Ji-il seemed to have had an unusually happy childhood. Even an involuntary family move away from Pyongyang when the boy was twelve was a positive experience for him. "Because of the 1976 axe-murder incident there was a fear of war, so everyone at my father's workplace moved to Kujan County in North Pyongan Province. That was my first real encounter with nature. I could see down into the river, could jump from a cliff into the river. I took hiking trips into the mountains, hunting for rabbits and game."

I asked if he had loved the Great Leader. "I wouldn't say I loved Kim Il-sung," he replied. "I didn't know him personally. But we were brought up to *idolize* Kim Il-sung. There was an element of habit in it. Everybody idolized Kim Il-sung. It was the thing to do." I told him that reminded me of the situation in a small Southern town in the United States where pretty much everyone is an evangelical Christian and one either believes in that faith or at least gives it lip service. He had been away from North Korea long enough to grasp the comparison. "The mechanics of Kim Il-sung's ideology and religion are the same," he said. "In Christian society if you say, 'I'm an atheist,' they'll point their fingers at you. It's the same in North Korea. If you say, 'I don't believe in Kim Il-sung,' you'll get in trouble. In religion, though, God is invisible. In North Korea, Kim Il-sung is alive and you can see him."

Kim Ji-il had been a rather cool customer, though, in the ideology department. And his impression was that his approach had been pretty much universal among his countrymen. "The extent of idolization of Kim Il-sung is about the same for everyone," he asserted. "In religion there may be fanatics, but no one in North Korea is a fanatic." I pressed the point: How about hysterical young people crying because they are so touched by the benevolence of the Great Leader? "At official gatherings I've seen it, but normally you would never see it," he said. "I think it's acting." (Tell that to Dong Young-jun, who assured me his tears had been very real.)

I told Kim Ji-il the story of how, on my first trip to North Korea, in 1979, my interpreter grabbed my camera to keep me from photographing children running around on a schoolyard. The photographer's argument was that such photos would not convey the unity, the single-mindedness, of the North Korean people. "That's what the people at the top want foreigners to see: unity," Kim commented. "But as I say, all that idolatry you saw in the schools is habitual behavior. When no one was watching, we would just go wild like any kids around the world."

Kim did his undergraduate studies at Kim Il-sung University, from 1980 to 1984. It was then that he began to harbor real doubts about the regime. "When I was little and they said our uniforms had been given by Kim Il-sung, I though, 'Wow, for free? What a kind and generous man!' But after I went to university, my mentality began developing. When they gave us presents, I said, 'Where does Kim Il-sung get the money to supply all these presents?' I knew there was a Kim Il-sung fund, but where did he get the money? That was the start of my doubts. Twice a year they would give 'gifts' to all the students around the nation, so I began to wonder how fat that fund was." Expressing such doubts could be dangerous. "Two or three spies were assigned per thirty people at the university—one from the party, one from State Security, one from Public Security. Most people can speculate who the spies are. You just have to watch your back."

I wondered whether it was because he came from an elite background that Kim Ji-il thought the fanaticism of other North Koreans that he had encountered was feigned. Were the common people more likely to be genuinely fanatical? "I didn't think of myself as elite," he told me. "At the university there were so many people of higher rank than I." He did recognize that he was different, in terms of privilege, from the great mass of North Koreans, but he said he did not believe there was a great difference in ideological fervor. "The common people are overworked and hungry," Kim said. "Maybe outwardly they would profess faith in the regime, but behind the officials' backs they would complain more than the elite, I think."

He himself, while living in North Korea, was "never full, but I didn't have such a problem that I was reduced to eating weeds. Harking back to the 1970s, I don't remember thinking, 'We don't have enough food.' You never had a feeling there was plenty, but it wasn't as bad as in the '80s." After he began his studies abroad, he had a two-month home leave in 1987 and noticed that things had started getting worse.

I asked how he had managed to go abroad to study. "From the early 1950s to the late '60s, many students were sent to Eastern Europe to study," he said. "My dad went to East Germany. From the late '60s until the early '80s no more students were sent. But then, in 1984 or so, Kim Il-sung went to Eastern Europe. He realized North Korea was far behind, so he said we'd better send some students. That's how the opportunity came to me. Those sent overseas were all science and engineering students. They selected students still in the university who they believed had intact ideology that wouldn't be swayed by encounters with capitalism. The ones who made the judgment were officials sent by the party to work in a special university department where they inspected students' lives. The procedure was first to select the 'ideologically intact' students and then test those in their fields to find the ones to send abroad."

With the doubts about the regime that he had told me he harbored even as an undergraduate, I wondered how Kim Ji-il had passed the scrutiny of the screening committee for overseas study. Was it acting? "I did have some doubts at the time but I didn't oppose the regime so I didn't really have to pretend or act," he replied. "In North Korea even if you had doubts, you couldn't satisfy your curiosity because you had no way of hearing the truth."

However, Kim continued, "the moment I set foot in the Soviet Union I changed. I saw a wave of individualism. People all dressed differently. Party members weren't forced to attend every single meeting but could skip some. I liked the way the stores worked: If you had money, you could buy, unlike the ration system in North Korea. This was a totally different world. I got to know the real details by making friends with Russians and talking with them. In essence, I think the mentality of Russians and Americans was essentially the same. I got there during the time when Konstantin Chernenko held the top job, but he was quickly followed by Gorbachev. I watched the unfolding of *perestroika* and *glasnost*. I became anti-regime after about a year in the Soviet Union. I went back to North Korea in the summer of 1987 for two months of home leave. My intent was not to say anything but to wait until I came back for a longer time before trying to change people's minds."

In 1988, Kim Ji-il began thinking he really did not want to return to

North Korea. "But I didn't think of defecting to South Korea until the moment of my defection," he told me. "If it were only a matter of ideological changes, everyone in North Korea should defect." For anyone who might actually go so far as to defect, "there's always a plus alpha. My plus alpha was my wife and my daughter. I had met my wife, a Soviet citizen, on campus. She was willing to go with me anywhere in the world. North Korea would have been no problem for her. But North Korean society would not have accepted her. An international marriage would be unthinkable there. It was a secret marriage. My daughter was born in 1989 and I didn't tell my government." I wondered: How could he have kept his marriage secret? "That shows how much freer we were in the USSR than in North Korea," Kim replied.

At first Kim's wife advised him, "Go back to North Korea. Defecting would affect your parents." Kim was "in a dilemma," he told me. "It was time to return to North Korea and I had to choose between my family in North Korea and my wife and daughter, whom I couldn't take back with me. I chose the wife and child. I didn't want my daughter to be brought up without a father." Having made his decision, he defected by traveling to Eastern Europe and presenting himself at a South Korean embassy.

At the time of Kim's defection, his father was in Germany making a deal with a German company. His mother back in Pyongyang worked in broadcasting as an editorial writer. A younger sister worked at Yongseong Nutrition Institute, which had a factory that packaged high-quality food for consumption by the elite. A younger brother was studying at Kim Chaek University of Technology. He told me, hopefully: "Coming to South Korea doesn't mean I'm losing my parents. I believe they're alive. They may have suffered, but I believe they're alive. The trend is such that for North Korea to survive it must adapt to the free-market system as the Chinese have done. I believe North Korea will do it. That will bring openness and a lot of foreign cultural influences."

I mentioned the plans that were brewing at the time in Washington to broadcast North Korean news to North Koreans in their own language via Radio Free Asia. "It's a good idea," Kim said. "I listened to Radio Free Europe and the Voice of America in Russian. They were a success in the Soviet Union. They reported stories that weren't in the Soviet press. My wife's family also listened." Among the radios owned by North Koreans, "some of the Japanese imports are shortwave. At customs they are stuck on one channel. But civilian and military high officials have shortwave radios that are not fixed to one channel."

TWENTY-TWO

Logging In and Logging Out

North Korean defectors to the South up until the 1990s were so rare that the Pyongyang regime and its sympathizers in the West could dismiss those few citizens who did make the break as malcontents—often criminals—whose testimony about conditions back home amounted to little more than artful propaganda, manipulated on behalf of the military-backed South Korean dictators by the sinister spooks of the Korean Central Intelligence Agency. But as conditions in the North worsened, the numbers of defectors increased dramatically. Meanwhile Kim Young-sam, a longtime democratic opposition figure, won the South Korean presidency in the election of December 1992 and set out to reform the intelligence agency. Soon there were in the South enough defectors, evidently free to speak their minds, that an interviewer willing to spend time unburdening them of their life stories could start to discern a combination of large patterns—recall, for example, the custom of gang-fighting among youths, covered in chapter 12—and small variations. Considered together, these suggested an essential truthfulness in what they had to say.

Take, for example, the men who had worked in the Russian Far East at logging camps and in a few cases at mining camps. I found that this group was largely misunderstood by Western reporters and commentators. Quite a few of my colleagues in the media suggested that armies of North Korean men had been forced to travel to Siberia to work in slave labor camps.[1] In fact, as interviews with a number of them demonstrated to me, the men had gone of their own volition. Indeed, they had competed fiercely, using bribes and any other means available, to exert enough influence on North Korean officials to get themselves on the list. They saw going to Russia as their tickets to wealth otherwise almost unimaginable by North Korean standards. The work was approximately as arduous as what they would have experienced back home. The big difference besides huge salary increases was that it was possible to leave the camps occasionally and interact with Russians and ethnic Koreans and Chinese in nearby communities. Many loggers were transformed by experiencing Russia's relatively liberalized atmosphere. Here are some of their stories.

Chang Ki-hong defected in November 1991, while working at a North Korean timber camp in eastern Russia not far from Khabarovsk. When I met him Chang was enrolled as a Russian language student at Seoul's Yonsei University, one of South Korea's top-rated institutions, and had married a fellow student. With his round face, strong jaw, reddish complexion and wiry hair, he had something of the appearance of a soldier—classic Korean looks.

Chang was born in Yomju, North Pyongan Province, in 1963. Not only had his father fought in the Korean war, Chang told me, but "before the Kim regime came to power, our family were neither landlords nor capitalists. So we were considered to have a good family background. Mother worked in a salt factory. Father couldn't work because he was disabled and couldn't walk well. He stayed at home and did some wood-cutting." The household's living standard was in the middle-to-high range.

Chang told me he had begun his education with nursery school and kindergarten. "They didn't give us much training in nursery school. It really started in kindergarten. When we played soldier with toy soldiers, we would always say, 'The general is Kim Il-sung.' We would learn about his family, his upbringing, where he was born, how brave he was in fighting Japanese imperial rule. They had a room where they put up pictures of Kim Il-sung's life. We would have to memorize the pictures and the stories that went with them. The pupils who did best at that got red stars for exemplary work. And if you excelled in studies of Kim Il-sung, you got more snacks than other pupils. I got a lot of red stars."

After kindergarten, "basic education is eleven years," Chang said. "But when I was in school it was nine years—four years of elementary school followed by five years of junior and senior middle school. You would finish around eighteen. I remember I was always hungry. Another thing: Even in elementary school I was so accustomed to being part of a highly organized system. When I went into second grade I had to become part of the children's corps. In junior high I switched to the socialist youth league. You stay in that until you're about thirty years old. Then you either get into the party, which is good, or become part of some other organization for adults. You're always part of some organization. You're never on your own. All these are basically subsystems within the system called the party. They make people more manageable." (Since North Koreans while remaining in the country were trained to avoid asking why things were the way they were, as Chang himself said a little later in our talk, I suspected that last observation about making people more "manageable" to have been something of an afterthought, the product of fairly recent reflection.)

"The basic thing you learn in youth organizations is that you can't be an individual," Chang continued. "You're part of a system. You learn more about the Kim regime, about Kim Il-sung and Kim Jong-il—that they are gods on their own terms. They told us that the family is another organization. Parents can feed you, they brought you into the world. But as for the party and government, even after your death they can allow your political life to continue eternally. Because of the existence of the party and government, the family can exist. Kim Il-sung comes first. He is the father of all."

I asked him whether parents would ever have objected to putting Kim Il-sung, party and state ahead of the family. "They figure everyone in the world must be living like this, so there is nothing to object to," Chang replied. "Of course, they have small complaints about the Kim regime, food shortages and so on, but nothing they would speak out about. To make sure we wouldn't complain, in each New Year's speech Kim Il-sung reminded us that 'we all have to suffer and sacrifice as long as imperialism exists in this world and the United States and South Korea are preparing to make war on us.' He made that speech every New Year's until 1991.

"Basically the mental processes of North Koreans aren't so complex," Chang continued. "They do acknowledge they are poor. Even those who don't have exchanges of information with relatives in Japan and China recognize they lead poor lives. Maybe 80 percent imagine that South Koreans live better. But their mentality is separated between lifestyle and politics. They don't connect the two and blame the government for their poverty." Again, I figured this was something Chang had sorted out for himself fairly late in life, after his arrival and debriefing by government officials in the South—although that did not keep his words from ringing true.

When Chang was growing up, "most of the people in my town worked in factories or on collective farms," he said. "Besides such regular jobs, there was a law passed in 1985 permitting 'household cooperation communities.' Those without work could stay home or stay in the neighborhood, engage in cottage industries and go to the markets to sell things they had made, such as cigarettes. Before 1985, there was a market every ten days where people could sell their own produce or industrial products. After 1985, small consumer goods like cigarettes could be sold there also, and you could go to the seashore to get clams to sell. If you wanted to be part of the household cooperative community you needed to get government permission."

I asked Chang about the regular distribution system for food grains. "The distribution systems were different for workers and farmers," he said. "Farmers got their year's supply of rice after the harvest. Workers got their supplies every fifteen days, between 700 grams and one kilogram per person depending on their work. Unemployed people got about 300 grams; children, 400 to 600 depending on age. Even if you ate very sparingly, you could only live on the ration for twelve days. So for three days you would starve or hunt for roots to eat."

Like all the other North Koreans I interviewed, Chang could remember with some precision the fluctuations of food supply for people where he lived. "It was always hard and seemed to be getting worse," he said. "Until the 1970s maybe it was all right. In the early '70s, when I was in elementary school, we could still find jams in the stores and eat them. Later, from around 1975, they were unavailable. From the mid-eighties things started getting really much worse. In 1988, I was still getting all my regular grain distribution. I left North Korea in 1989, for Russia and started getting letters from relatives saying the distribution center didn't have rice, or other grain. The center gave people tickets instead of grain. Later on, if the food arrived, they could exchange the tickets for food."

Although residents of Pyongyang got special privileges, Chang told me, people like his family who lived outside Pyongyang were "not as envious as you would think. The general run of people don't even think of living in the capital. If you reach a certain rank you may get a call from Pyongyang City Hall. The population is always controlled at two million. Once in a while if they get too populous they send people elsewhere."

I asked Chang what he had done for fun and excitement as a child. "Of course childhood activities are different for children in Pyongyang and the provinces," he said. "I didn't have much time to play. I had to do my social labor—work in the fields after class—even in elementary school. In winter, the schools usually didn't get coal supplies so we had to go get corn husks and dry them to use for fuel. In the summers, I do remember playing. We went to an apple orchard, ate some apples and ran around."

Chang managed to get accepted into a university right out of school, which was unusual, and thus he was not required to put in the usual decade-long stint in the military. "You're exempt if you enter university, as long as you spend six months in a military training course," he told me. "I went to Sinuiju University and studied to become a teacher. In North Korea teaching is not considered a very good profession. It's hard to sustain a normal life as a teacher. And the basic image of a teacher is not very positive. It may seem a bit sissy. Lots of women are teachers. So after I graduated I went to work for the railroad, where I was in charge of controlling the tracks, coupling and uncoupling the trains. It was very dangerous work. I worked on the railroad until 1987. From then until 1988 I was applying and preparing for my Russia assignment."

The competition to get to Russia was severe, Chang explained. "For North Koreans, to be able to go to Russia is the chance of a lifetime. You can earn lots of money. The average income in North Korea is about 60 *won* a month. In Russia I got 900 *won* a month. Actually I would have gotten 3,000 *won* a month, but the North Korean government kept 2,100 *won.* A special committee selected me. You have to have a good family background. My elder brothers were high officials in the party and my third brother was an actor in Pyongyang. Eighty percent of those selected are party members. I wasn't a party member, but they checked to make sure I was ideologically stable—not susceptible to subversive influences. In each workplace there's a party secretary. My party secretary at the railroad recommended me."

When he arrived in 1988 Chang found that "the lifestyle of the camp was basically the same, a miniature North Korea with 15,000 to 20,000 North Koreans working there. My work was analyzing statistics of the operation. I had an eight-hour day, but had to study ideology during my off hours. I was in Russia but I was controlled by North Koreans. To get out of the restricted area I needed a pass."

I asked Chang how his outlook had changed while he was working at the camp. "Until I got to the Soviet Union I believed in the regime," he said. "But when I got to the Soviet Union and started meeting people there, I realized there must be something wrong back home. It was after I had been there about six months that my mentality started to change. We are taught that the whole world worships Kim Il-sung. I met Russians who made fun of this Kim worship, and then I realized that he was not in fact worshipped by the whole world. Cultural differences played a big role in the changes I went through. In North Korea there are no entertainment facilities. All you can do is drink a lot. In Russia I saw cinemas, discos. I didn't go to discos often, because there would be big trouble if I got caught; I would be sent back to North Korea. The North Korean authorities wouldn't allow us to go because they thought it would make us lazy." But Chang did manage to get out on the town occasionally. "I was affected. I realized this was the kind of life people should lead—not suppressed and controlled."

Although he liked the lifestyle in Russia, Chang didn't think of defecting on that account. Rather, it was radio that set him off. "I'm the curious type, and my friend and I started listening to South Korean and other foreign broadcasts. He was caught and sent back. I was put under surveillance because we were such close friends. It was one month before I was due to go back to North Korea myself, but I was afraid if I went back I would be executed or sent to a prison camp." Chang had listened to South Korea's state-owned KBS, which broadcast special programming to Korean-speaking people in communist countries. He had also heard Korean-language programming from the Soviet Union and from China's ethnically Korean Yanbian region. As for KBS, "I could listen in the afternoon but the reception was bad. At night from eleven o'clock I could listen. At first I had a hard time understanding the South Korean dialect. They had people criticizing the government on various issues. And at that time they were running a series on the rise of the Kim Il-sung regime in North Korea. It was very interesting to get a different perspective. So I experienced some ideological change. My friend and I kidded each other, 'Let's go to South Korea.' Ultimately it was that ideological change coupled with fear of execution that prodded me to defect."

I told Chang that the U.S. Congress was preparing to fund Radio Free Asia, which would likely have a Korean-language service directed to North Koreans. "Of course it would be good! What bad could come of it?" he said. "But there's a saying in Korea: 'Listening 100 times is not as good as seeing it once.' Actual interchange is needed, too."

When he decided to defect, Chang realized it would not be easy. "The problem was that the North Korean and Russian police worked together. If anyone tried to escape, the Russian authorities would capture him and turn him over to the North Koreans. Many tried, but most were caught and sent back, to death in most cases. One day I read an ad from a Moscow department store saying that South Korean–made goods would be sold there to people with dollars to buy them. I decided to go to Moscow in the hope of meeting some of the South Koreans there. A Russian friend got me a ticket to Moscow. Most escapees don't have good plans for getting away. They just run for the mountains—it seems to be a Korean instinct. The authorities know that, so they just go to the mountains and recapture the escapees. But the Russian cops didn't think of looking for me en route to Moscow. Unfortunately, by the time I got to Moscow the August Revolution had broken out there and the South Koreans had all gone back home. So I figured I had to cross the Russian border. My job experience on the railroad helped. I realized that all Eastern European countries except Hungary required a visa. I bribed a railroad worker to let me climb a ladder in the restroom to the roof of the car, where I stayed until the train crossed the border into Hungary. I went to the South Korean embassy."

Kim Kil-song, when I interviewed him in 1994, appeared to be something of a dandy. He was fussily gotten up in long-oval, gold-framed spectacles, a rectangular gold watch with gold band, starched white shirt, a floral print tie with tie bar, double-breasted brown-checked sports jacket and dark trousers. But on his left hand, in the web between thumb and forefinger, was a tattoo, and after I had heard his story I knew he had not always been a fashion plate.

Kim was born in 1962 in Pyongyang. His father, injured in 1952 while fighting in the Korean War as an officer, had been mustered out in Pyongyang. After recovering from his wounds, the father held management jobs in a porcelain factory, which made household crockery. There he met Kim's mother. The couple married, first living at the factory and later being assigned an apartment. Eventually his mother stopped working at the factory and took a job as a salesperson at a textiles store near their home. His father at that time commuted to work by trolley bus.

In 1964, there was a reassignment in which less "loyal" North Koreans were moved out of the good jobs and out of Pyongyang to menial positions in the provinces. Kim's father had been a landowner—he had owned an orchard in Northern Hamgyong Province. That was enough to bar the family from the loyal class. They were sent to Sinuiju, on the Yalu River across from China, where the father worked loading shipments on trucks at a synthetic textile factory. The mother worked in a sporting goods factory, making balls. From then on the family remained in Sinuiju.

Such treatment for a wounded Korean War veteran shocked me a little, and I asked Kim whether it had made his parents bitter. "They blamed their ancestors," he replied. "Possibly they felt the regime was at fault for their treatment, but they would have had very little chance to express it. Once or twice when times got very hard Mother would express some dissatisfaction with the regime: 'How could they question our past background?'" By hard times, Kim meant that "housing was terrible," at least for his family. "We lived in a house that had been damaged in a Korean War bombing raid. Up through 1968, there was no food problem, but then food conditions worsened. We didn't have enough food. There were few goods in the store. Before that, I remember taking pocket money and going to stores to buy candy. I could see the products on the shelves. But shortages began in 1969. Just in one or two years they ran out of supplies. It happened all over the country. We heard from neighbors who had visited relatives in other provinces. There, too, there were no goods in the stores."

In his youth, Kim told me, he had been "very faithful to Kim Il-sung. Even though life was hard, I was thankful. Without Kim Il-sung we would be in an even worse situation, I thought. I learned that way of thinking from kindergarten and elementary school. Once in a while, my parents, too, would say, 'You have to be faithful to Kim Il-sung.'" I asked how he expressed his faithfulness. "In each household there was a portrait of Kim Il-sung," he said. "If my father brought home some clothes or snacks or a toy for me, instead of thanking Father I would go to the portrait of Kim Il-sung, bow before it and say, 'Thank you for the wonderful gift.'"

I wanted to know more about the family's housing. "We lived in the same house until I was in high school," Kim told me. "Because of the bombing it was leaning, about to fall down, but we couldn't get any help from the authorities to fix it because my father was an ordinary worker. He worked at a big factory. Finally, though, the factory built a housing complex and we moved to an apartment. That apartment was about eighteen square meters, with two small rooms to house my parents, two brothers, two sisters and myself—altogether seven people. Lots of families of seven people lived in one-room apartments. We considered ourselves very fortunate to have two." The apartment was unfinished when the family moved in. "There was a little room meant to be a bathroom, but it didn't have plumbing except for a water faucet. The equipment had been unavailable when the apartments were built. We made a cement tank to store water for bathing. We had to go downstairs to use a communal toilet. Anyhow, in North Korea, except in Pyongyang, when they say, 'We have housing for you,' you can't expect to find it ready to move in. The interior is just the rough concrete structure. You have to finish it yourself, with floor covering, doors, and so on. Usually in Pyongyang you do get a finished apartment, but in the provinces, no."

Kim told me he had remained loyal to Kim Il-sung throughout a ten-year army enlistment that started in 1979 when he was seventeen. He was stationed in Kaesong, near the border with South Korea, as an artilleryman. "I worked on launchers with thirty separate warheads. I became a sergeant, commanding one launcher and a squad of twelve men attached to it." I asked what he had been taught about his mission. "While I was in the army, conditions in North Korea worsened," he replied. "We had about three hours of ideological studies each day, and they taught us to believe that all our difficulties were due to the U.S. Army and the South Korean government. I believed I had to fight. I even wanted to sacrifice my life for the country. They constantly taught us about the superiority of socialism and the greatness of Kim Il-sung and Kim Jong-il. I believed socialism was the best. They continually told us stories about South Korea that highlighted the negative aspects of capitalism—the gap between rich and poor, beggars and homeless people living in the streets and under bridges, people getting no education because the South Korean government could not provide equal opportunities to the people. I believed it totally."

Kim explained that North Koreans believed because they had no alternative sources of information. I asked him about broadcasts from abroad, but he said he had never heard one while he was in North Korea. Well, then, wasn't there a grapevine, as other defectors had told me? "I'm skeptical about the powers of the grapevine," Kim replied. "All right, an ethnic Korean living in Yanbian [in China] might have visited South Korea. He might pass the word that South Koreans are wealthy. But even if I had heard it, I was so brainwashed I wouldn't have believed it. And even if I had believed it, I wouldn't have dared to spread it. But there may be some difference between civilians and soldiers in this regard. I would be pretty sure such rumors don't spread in the army even now. But among civilians, rumors of South Korean wealth are spreading and there are some people who are envious of South Koreans' lives."

His remark about the military's resistance to outside information intrigued me and I asked Kim to explain. "During your ten-year hitch in the army you get no leave," he explained. "There's no contact with the outside world. No outside information can penetrate. There's much more ideological study than civilians undergo." I pressed him on whether there was some way that the United States and South Korea could get through to soldiers despite those circumstances. "It's very difficult to penetrate the army," he said. But he added that the situation was not entirely hopeless. "Just continue the drops of propaganda leaflets and the propaganda broadcasts through DMZ loudspeakers. Even though they try not to listen, how can they not hear some of those?"

I went back to Kim's remark that he had been ready to fight and asked him to talk about that. "The North Korean government tells the civilian population that unification will come through peaceful means," he said. "In the military, though, they taught us that reunification would be possible only through forcible measures, so we had to be prepared for war. Then, after reunification, we would restructure South Korea with socialism. They taught us that food shortages are the result of isolation caused by the capitalist societies' sanctions. Through a war, we believed, we could come out of that isolation. We believed that through reunification on North Korean terms, if we had South Korea, we would then have enough farmland to cultivate enough food to sustain life."

That sounded to me a little like Hitler's concept of *Lebensraum*. I asked Kim to try to recreate for me the lectures he had heard in ideological training, in the words of the instructors to the extent he could remember. Here are some of the spiels he remembered: "We have to reunify the peninsula by 1995, even if we must use force to achieve it. Everyone serving in the army now must be prepared for this war. You must be prepared to sacrifice your life for the country. Capitalism is an evil, a vice. Socialism is the system that works for the people. We military must fight together to enforce a socialist regime. South Korea is a very anti-humanitarian regime. For the sake of Koreans north and south, for the betterment of the whole race, we must ensure the triumph of socialism. Even though South Korea has the U.S. Army to help it, North Korea is prepared. We're better than the U.S. Army. We've been preparing since the Korean War. We have enough men and matériel to fight the war and win. There's a basic difference between us and the other side. The South Korean and American armies are structured according to the capitalist ideal. Their soldiers fight for money. They aren't prepared to sacrifice their lives to win the war. North Korean soldiers are prepared to sacrifice our lives. We are not fighting for money but to create an ideal society for the people. During the Korean War, eighteen countries helped South Korea but we still won. We didn't have enough matériel then, but now we have what we need. We definitely can win this war."

Kim interrupted his memories to tell me that North Korean soldiers had no actual knowledge regarding the weaponry facing them, which could help explain their strong confidence of victory. Then he continued recalling the teachings that had been drilled into him in the army: "As soon as we have won the war, we will root out capitalist ideas in the South. We army men, stationed there, will teach the people about socialism, teach them to follow the leadership of the Great Leader Comrade Kim Il-sung. Whoever resists will be killed. Right now the United States is basing nuclear weapons in Okinawa and other places. But there is no need to fear them. We have better arms than the U.S., and we can win. So feel confident, soldiers, and do not fear the nuclear arms of the U.S. If a war is staged in South Korea, that will not be an invasion but a war for justice. Once we are unified, we no longer have to use our money to build up our military might. We can use all our resources for the betterment of the people's lives. Having the South Korean farmland, with the country united under the leadership of Kim Il-sung, we can produce enough staple food not to be threatened by the Western world's economic sanctions. As soon as we are reunified, we will all be able to 'eat rice with beef soup, wear silk clothing and live in houses with tile roofs.' Right now we don't have enough food supplies and we must train strenuously. This is because our army is an army for war. As soon as the war is won we will have a better society."

I asked Kim whether the indoctrinations had changed in any way during his ten years in the army. "The basic objectives remained the same, although there may have been some change in structure," he replied. "According to political events the structure might change. Right now [October 1994] I'd speculate they're teaching with reference to the North Korea–U.S. talks — maybe something to the effect that the United States won't give up what we want so we'll still have to advance reunification through force. Each year the New Year's teachings by Kim Il-sung and Kim Jong-il were emphasized. From 1986, there was more emphasis on getting South Korea's farmland and eating better: 'This ordeal is continuing because of South Korea and the United States. We have to defeat their armies and unite the North and South.'"

Kim said he had been subjected to the lectures "right up to July 14, 1988, the day before I was mustered out. In North Korea, we have 'Strategic Sundays,' for study, plus three hours of ideological study daily." He acknowledged that those sessions could become tedious. "Of course, if you hear the same thing over and over, you'll get bored. But the punishment for drowsing during the lectures is so severe you can't even think of allowing yourself to doze off. Punishments include from ten hours of continuous ideological studies to a whole week of them, around the clock, with no sleep. They may hit you, or make you run around the mountains." But Kim didn't study just out of fear, he said. "I was enthusiastic because diligence would pay off later. If you want to climb the career ladder, knowing ideology is essential. I wanted to enter a university after my enlistment, and the very first exam to screen applicants is on ideology. At the same time, I was very loyal."

In the end, he said, "I was not selected to take the exam. Only two out of a hundred were selected. It turned out they had to be the sons of high-ranking officials or of workers very loyal to the regime. I had some hopes but was disappointed in the end." Although he was disappointed, he was not disillusioned. "Even if I had been dissatisfied, there was nothing I could do. My fate would not have changed. So I just accepted the outcome. If I felt some disappointment, I blamed my parents: Why wasn't my father a high-ranking official?"

I knew that the usual procedure for anyone ending his military hitch was to be sent to work in the mines, unless he managed to get into a university. I asked Kim how he had avoided that fate. "In principle, everybody ending his enlistment is sent to the mines," he said. "But the regime makes sure parents have at least one child at home to look after them. My two elder brothers had already been sent to the mines, so I was allowed to go home to Sinuiju. I worked there in a company making textile-dyeing equipment. Afterward I went to Pyongyang on temporary assignment as a construction worker under the central party's management department. I worked on the Koryo Hotel, Kim Jong-il's gift apartments—those he awarded to people—and the 105-story hotel, until April 1992. I went back to Sinuiju then, and in August went to Siberia."

He explained the lure of Russia. "When I got back from the army, my father was seventy-two and my mother was in her sixties. Neither could work any longer. I had to work hard to support them. The problem was, you couldn't get extra pay for diligence. That's why I decided to go to Siberia. It paid twenty times what you could make in North Korea." Getting there was "very difficult," Kim said. "There are about 10,000 North Koreans working in Siberia. Each year a third of them rotate home, so there are some 3,000 openings. Around 9,000 sign up, which means a three-to-one competition. To be selected you have to give side gifts to officials. The family had no money. I borrowed 1,000 *won*—a couple of years' wages. With that I managed to get a three-year contract."

There was more indoctrination before his departure, but this time he quickly had an opportunity to see that what he was being taught wasn't true. "I had to undergo an intense ideological training session. They taught us that Russians were having a hard time since they'd given up socialism, so we shouldn't associate with Russians in Siberia. When I got there, I secretly visited stores and discovered that the situation was not at all as I had been told.

Russians worked very diligently and got paid accordingly for their work. I also came into contact with some Chinese merchants who had visited South Korea. I learned from them about the real situation in the South. I also associated with some immigrants from Korea, and listened to South Korean radio. So I started to become affected. What really made me decide I'd been lied to was when I visited department stores in the larger cities, which had lots of South Korean goods on sale."

I had understood Kim's job to have been logging, but he corrected me on that. "Among the Koreans sent to Siberia," he said, "a few are sent to mines instead of doing logging, to earn Russian currency that can be used to pay for trucking the timber and so on. I was one of those, and I realized I was getting only 10 percent of what my Russian co-workers got. The other 90 percent was going to the [Korean Workers'] party. I got upset at that and argued about it, getting into trouble. At dawn on the day I would have been arrested for insubordination, I escaped to Vladivostok. Two Chinese-Korean immigrants there helped me, and when I heard of a ship in port that was bound for Pusan, I stowed away aboard it. I got to South Korea December 30, 1993. Now I work for a pharmaceutical company, in the personnel department."

I asked Kim to permit me a personal question about his tattoo. "Some friends and I got tattooed when we went into the army," he replied. "This says, 'Martial Spirit.'" I wondered if he had talked to any former soldiers, mustered out more recently than he, and learned whether their indoctrination had been like his own. "Yes, I knew some in Siberia. They were told: 'No one here is going to end his hitch before a war comes.' They call the soldiers 'reunification soldiers.'" Would they fight? "They don't have any fear. They'll just run down to South Korea once war erupts." Could the North win? "With what I know now, they don't have a chance of winning. I don't believe they could take Seoul—although Seoul certainly would be affected by a war."

I met Chae Myung-hak the same day I spoke with Kim Kil-song in October 1994. Chae had arrived in Seoul the previous February. He sported an early Beatles sort of bowl haircut with heavy bangs down to his eyebrows. From there down his face featured high cheekbones and a strong jaw.

Chae was born in 1960, in Kuson, a city in North Pyongan Province, he told me. His father had been a policeman. Leaving the force in 1963 after eleven years, the father had then become a communal farmer. Chae's mother was also a farmer. Chae heard from them that "before my father became a farmer, we lived a comparatively wealthy life." His own memories of material conditions dated to the late 1960s, "when we didn't have basic necessities like shoes and clothing, and couldn't find them in stores. But from the time I was seventeen I have no perception of how the society worked because I was in the army. We were allowed to write letters, but officers would read them first, and when we received letters they only gave us the parts that were cleared. Besides, we had our hands completely full with strenuous mountain training for war. There was no time to think of the rest of society."

Chae did not know at the time he enlisted that he would be assigned to the special forces—an elite posting. "For special forces, they pick about 10 percent of recruits, choosing on the basis of good family background and healthy bodies," he told me. "They trained us to attack certain sites in South Korea, including Kimpo Airport and certain Honest John, Hawk and Patriot missile sites. We specialized in nuclear missile sites. We had spies in South Korea who took pictures of the sites and mapped them. We had exact mockups of the installations we were to attack. We were trained so thoroughly we could even attack blindfolded." Pending war, only higher-ups knew the actual locations of the targeted sites in South Korea, he said. Meanwhile the men prepared to deal with the first obstacle, the heavily mined Demilitarized Zone. "We were trained to cross the DMZ. For training we had the same set-up, fences, mines and all, and we had to practice getting through."

I wondered if his trainers had predicted how a new war would begin. "Since my childhood I had been taught that the Korean War erupted because the United States pushed the South Korean army into it," Chae said. "We were taught that the Americans at some time would start another war, so we must be prepared. It would bring a lot of casualties on both sides. But we had to beat the United States. They told us that a war, which the U.S. would start, was necessary to bring reunification. We would have to win it. They told us the war would start with a U.S. attack, but in looking back on it since my defection I have to assume the plan was for North Korea to invade South Korea."

Reunification would bring material benefits, the trainers told their military charges: "They said, 'We are deprived now because of the United States. But once reunification comes, North and South will prosper together and Korea will become the head of the Asian world.' We were taught that North Korea was poor because the U.S., with its forces in South Korea, prevents reunification of the peninsula. They said North Korea is very mountainous compared with the South. We don't have much farmland and can't grow enough rice. But South Korea has great farming potential while North Korea has mineral resources and advanced heavy industry. They told us that even though South Korea has lots of farmland, they don't use it to the fullest but instead build army and air bases on it. Therefore, South Korea is poor. So once we reunite, Korea will emerge as the leader of Asia."

When I pressed him on the connection in the indoctrination sessions between making war and getting more to eat, Chae replied: "I should clarify that we were not taught that we would invade South Korea to gain its land so we could increase our agricultural production. We were taught that the U.S. and South Korea would invade North Korea, and we then would have to bring about reunification. The benefit of increased food is just an incentive given to soldiers."

Chae said he had been taught that Kim Il-sung would be in charge of the reunified Korea—"but then I couldn't have imagined anything else. He had been our sole leader for decades. I had no doubts. I just presumed that would be the natural outcome." Soldiers like Chae had "no specific orders" regarding their post-reunification role, "but basically all the political instruction taught me that once reunification came the South Korean army and others, being enemies, would have to change their ideology to socialism. We would have to keep a watch on them." That didn't seem a terribly difficult task, in light of what the North Korean soldiers were taught about the South. "I thought South Koreans would be delighted to be reunified by the North Koreans," Chae said. "In North Korea they broadcast news of South Korean student demonstrations, anti-government and pro-unification. After seeing those broadcasts we assumed that South Koreans were anti-government and would favor the North Korean regime after reunification. When I was in North Korea I believed people were basically the same. The only differences were due to their leaders. The South Korean and U.S. governments, not the people, were the villains, I thought. I even thought I understood U.S. soldiers. I was a sergeant, with a squad of eleven men under me. Being a low-ranking soldier myself, I knew the American soldiers just followed orders."

Starting in 1984 when the North sent food aid to the South following flooding there, Chae told me, even for the military "the food problem was an important issue." Civilians who were supposed to get 600 grams of grain a day got 520. The military suffered a lesser reduction in rations. "We went from 800 grams to 760." Reasons given were that "the harvest was not so good that year. And we were told we had to help our brothers in South Korea in their desperate straits. Each year the situation worsened, and they explained that the harvests had not been satisfactory. From 1985 through 1988 things got worse, but not so drastically. When I left the military in April of 1987, I was sent to North Hamgyong Province. When I got there I realized the grain ration had been delayed. January, February, March and April rations were not provided. Finally, in June, they gave us the delayed ration. North Hamgyong was an exception, though. Other places were only a couple of months late. People blamed the provincial governor, saying he lacked the ability to overcome the problem by bartering with another province." The central government did not, however, punish the governor. After all, Chae noted, "the government had sent him there."

Chae said that, in civilian life, "my first job was as an engine repairman, but I couldn't earn much so I took a job as a diver in Rajin. It would pay better and I could buy food on the black market. I dived for marine products on the sea floor—crabs, octopus, clams and so on—which were exported for foreign exchange. That meant I could make more money." Chae told me he had harbored no doubts about the system at that point. "I just thought the food shortages were due to poor harvests."

Chae went to Russia in October 1989. "According to what I heard from people at home, the youth festival earlier that year caused things to get drastically worse. I heard from some officials that if a country wins the right to host the Olympics, there are lots of economic benefits. The youth festival, on the other hand, drains a country's treasury so badly it takes five years to recover. To hold the festival the government spends a lot, and the people have to pay."

Chae wanted very badly to go to the Soviet Union as a logger. But he found that "it's very difficult to be sent to Siberia if you're single. Only 1 or 2 percent of those who go don't have families." The authorities reasoned that a family's presence back home would serve as a guarantee of a logger's return after his contract was up. Chae devised an ingenious strategem. "I made a contract marriage with a woman who had a child. She was the wife of a coworker who was sent to a prison camp, which meant they were automatically divorced. I knew him. He was a senior official, head of the production line. He stole a lot of products that were supposed to be exported, and got caught for embezzlement."

That was an economic crime, but Chae said that even in the case of political crimes it was no longer automatic that the offender's family would be sent away with him. There had been a change of policy. "In 1991 a woman defected with two men and went on television to talk about North Korea. The broadcasts could be seen near the DMZ. This brought about a lot of problems, so the government wanted to get rid of all her relatives. But there were too many, including a number of high-ranking officials. From 1992 the regulations changed. Whoever betrayed the regime, that person was the only traitor. That's the reason there have been more defections since 1992. People don't have to worry so much about families they leave behind. Family members now just lose social privileges—no promotions, no central party membership, etc. There's the report that Marshal O Jin-u's son escaped to China. This won't affect O Jin-u."

Chae said one big reason he was so eager to go to Russia was that, although he had not picked his bride, he did hope eventually to have a real marriage. Meanwhile, "the diving job was too dangerous. I almost died three times, twice because of a blocked oxygen hose and another time because of a compression problem. I knew this dangerous job would kill me, but I couldn't earn enough in normal jobs to get married. So I decided to use my pay from the diving job to give gifts to officials so I could go to Siberia and

make more money. I used about 3,000 *won* to pay off officials: the party secretary at my work unit, the city director in charge of sending people overseas, the vice-head of the State Security office." I asked him if having to
make payoffs to those officials had caused him to doubt the system. "No," he
replied. "It just seemed the natural route to get to Siberia. I wanted very
badly to go."

It was his arrival in Russia that started to change his attitude. "I realized
Siberia and Russia were decades ahead of North Korea. This brought out a
discrepancy, because I'd been taught that the Soviet Union was the poorest
country among European nations. I realized the government was lying to us.
From Koreans I met in Russia, I learned it was North Korea that had invaded South Korea, and that Kim Jong-il hadn't been born in Korea on
Mount Paektu but near Khabarovsk. That was shocking. While I was in
Siberia I saw a documentary on [then South Korean President] Roh Tae-
woo's meeting with Gorbachev. The documentary showed South Korean automobile assembly lines. I realized that to sell all those products that I saw in
the markets of Khabarovsk, South Korea had to have become industrialized.
Over the course of about a year I realized all the facts through conversations
with Russians, reading newspapers, watching movies from France, Italy and
the United States, watching TV. My ideology shifted and became unstable.
There was no time to listen to the radio, but occasionally I heard South Korean popular music."

Still, it took a series of additional shocks before Chae started contemplating defection, he told me. "Even though my ideology had changed, my
basic sentiment was that I planned to go back to North Korea. After three
years in Siberia I wanted to return. But due to some agreement with the
Russians, everybody had to stay another year. My father passed away then.
They wouldn't let me go home for the funeral. That enraged me, and I came
up with the idea that I should escape, go to the Russian authorities, obtain a
Russian passport and then fly back to North Korea." Hearing Chae relate his
desperate plan, and feeling certain he would have been caught and either executed or sent off to a camp if he had attempted it, I was reminded yet again
of my equally screwy 1979 thoughts of fleeing across the DMZ.

"Even though I hatched that scheme," Chae continued, "the occasion
didn't arise. And while I was still thinking about it, my roommate got drunk
and stabbed a fellow worker. He was going to be sent back to a prison camp,
so he escaped. The authorities started questioning me to find out where he
was so they could capture him. They threatened that if I didn't help them they
wouldn't let me return to North Korea. There were three opportunities to return that year. Although I had been on the list for the first group, they took
my name off. So I decided to escape. I still had that plan of going back to
North Korea, but people demanded too much money for a passport. I decided to go to Moscow with a friend. There I met some South Koreans who

were managing a restaurant. I worked as a security guard at night and carved jewelry in the daytime. With the money, we asked the Russian mafia in Siberia to make Russian passports. But we realized we would just be sent to prison camps if we did go back to North Korea, so finally we decided to go to South Korea. We thought of going to the United States, but South Korea is, after all, Korean. Arriving at Kimpo Airport as tourists with Russian passports, we turned ourselves in. We had return tickets to Russia in case we should be rejected. We went through immigration and then asked people how to find the intelligence officials. We caused some confusion because North Korean spies might come in the way we did."

Chae said he was working at Sempyo Company, a South Korean maker of soy sauce, in the factory. "It's temporary work," he said. "Then the government will send us somewhere else."

Chae had teamed up with a friend, Kim Tae-pom, for the escape from their logging camp and defection to South Korea. When I went to interview Kim, I met a slender man wearing a light green suit, a floral necktie with a big knot, metal-rimmed glasses and a black plastic watch—unusual, as noted earlier, among defectors, who typically sported expensive timepieces.

Kim was born in Pyongyang, in 1962. In 1976, when he was in high school, the family was sent to South Pyongan Province because of his sister's polio. "Kim Il-sung and Kim Jong-il didn't want disabled people in Pyongyang," he told me, echoing what I had heard from other sources about a policy of removing handicapped people, midgets, beggars and anyone else considered unsightly from the showcase capital. The forced move came despite a "good" family background. Kim Tae-pom's mother was a Korean War orphan. There were siblings in the army and at the Mansudae Art Theater. "My parents were upset," Kim told me, "but this was a government order. What could they do? My father took a demotion from a high party official's job in the Department of Administration to become a much lower-ranking member of the local economic committee in Songchon. The clothing we could get there was not as nice, and our house was smaller. But we still had relatives in Pyongyang. With their influence we eventually moved to a bigger house. Because of my father's demotion, our food rations were smaller. In Pyongyang our grain ration had come in rice, every week, and we had received two kilograms of meat weekly. After the move we got mixed grain, which was lower in quality. It was distributed only every ten days, along with one kilogram of meat."

I asked Kim to recall for me a time when he had been really happy. He replied: "Do you have a religion? In North Korea the *juche* ideology is another form of religion. I was very faithful to that. I felt ecstatic when we got presents from Kim Il-sung—clothing, food." I asked him then about negative feelings. "I never felt any dissatisfaction toward Kim Il-sung himself," he said. "Maybe I had some criticism of the regime, especially regarding the food situation. But unless you're a true dissident, there's no crticism of Kim Il-sung—only of the government." He added, however, "Before we moved we were part of the elite, but after we moved I felt some discrepancies in the social structure, the gap between the elite and others."

After graduating from high school, Kim Tae-pom had gone to a trade school but dropped out on account of eye problems. He went to work in a car factory, then became a member of an elite paramilitary "shock unit" of the Central Committee of the League of Socialist Working Youth. Everyone joined the youth league (around age fourteen), and there were chapters even in the army, but those shock unit members were special. They came from "good" family backgrounds. To be accepted, applicants had to demonstrate ideological stability. They got paid well and were in line to become cadre. Kim Jong-il had founded the shock units and they were somewhat similar to Three Revolutions teams, which were run by the party itself.

Kim Tae-pom and his colleagues wore military uniforms and had military ranks. From 1982 to 1984 his unit was responsible for security at an arsenal. The members spent from 8 to 9 A.M. studying the life and works of Kim Il-sung, then worked from 9 A.M. until evening constructing facilities. After supper, from 9 to 10 P.M., they attended indoctrination sessions. Following a full hitch, a member was entitled to party membership and a factory job back home without having to go to work in the mines. Kim's post-shock unit job, which he held from 1984 to 1989, was as an equipment repairman in a thread factory near his South Pyongan province home. At the factory, 90 percent of the employees were women.

Eventually Kim Tae-pom wanted to leave the thread factory, and his salary of 80 *won* per month, for better pay and a better life. He applied to go to Russia. "Pay in Siberia would be 70 times what I'd made before, even after the government had taken its big cut. The men who go there expect to make enough to live on for the rest of their lives. Usually they buy household appliances in Russia that are not available in North Korea. Sometimes they sell those back home; in other cases they use them."

Basic requirements for getting sent to Russia included party membership, no criminal record and a good family background with no capitalist forebears. But Kim said that, when he applied, the ratio of largely qualified applicants to those who actually would be employed was fifteen or twenty to one. "To get on the list, you had to give or promise a television set or refrigerator to a higher official involved in the selection process. Some applicants actually wrote contracts promising to send the appliances to their official patrons after a year's work in Siberia." I wondered how such an obviously corrupt contract could be enforced. "The worker is bound to come back," Kim replied, "so they get him one way or another. This official would have enough power over your later career to ensure misery if he so chose."

I probed in vain for any sense of revulsion on Kim's part concerning such arrangements. "I feel it's justified," he said. "The official works hard to send the worker to Siberia, so there should be a payoff for him. Above that official there may be higher officials. This lower official has to work hard to get his own candidate to Siberia, has to pay off higher-ups. I just thought that was the way things were. I thought it was understandable. This system is prevalent throughout society. For example, if I couldn't make it to the factory one day, I'd see the manager and give him some gifts and ask him to look the other way. In North Korea most bribery involves goods, not money. When my father worked as an official at a county economic committee he received so many 'presents' from farmers—potatoes, green onions and so on. In North Korean law, if a person receives a present in the form of goods, that's a 'friendly present.' Money is a bribe."

In 1989, Kim Tae-pom went to Russia as a truck driver, hauling food from local markets to a logging camp. For his third year the assignment changed to loading the food onto trains. His story was, I realized, a typical one: He arrived as a young man devoted to the regime of Kim Il-sung and Kim Jong-il, but soon started to have his assumptions challenged. "Factors that influenced me included conversations with Russians and being able to find and read South Korean newspapers. Other parts of the world became accessible. I learned that the rest of the world was different from what I'd been taught. There was more freedom to criticize the regime because we were in Siberia. Among friends, people often let out their dissatisfaction. The situation in North Korea had drastically worsened in 1986. And by 1989, when I left, it was far worse still. Letters from our families back home openly described problems with food. But the North Korean official broadcasts always insisted that things were getting better. I was aware of the discrepancies. I listened to Radio Moscow, Yanbian [China] radio and KBS."

In 1992, Kim said, "I bribed officials to alter my papers so I could get home leave for five months, see my family and give them some money. In December 1992, I returned to Siberia, realizing that nothing had changed in North Korea and feeling that I could no longer endure North Korean society. Coincidentally, I learned I was going to be sent home on account of the bribery. That's why I escaped." On February 1, 1993, Kim Taepom fled to Khabarovsk, where he hid until he met some Americans and a Russian reporter who were able to help him get to Moscow and then to South Korea.

The reader has met Ahn Choong-hak already. In chapter 6 Ahn told us about his childhood pal who had been punished for comparing his frozen pile of feces to the sacred Mount Paektu. In chapter 12, we saw Ahn, enraged at learning that his family background was too flawed to get him into an elite college for spies and infiltrators, flinging his mother's sewing machine to the ground. After that outburst he returned to his military unit, where he was a model soldier and the driver for the Eighth Division commander, and remained there for four more years until his ten-year hitch ended in 1984.

Ahn did not leave the military entirely then, but took up a post as an inspector at the army's Hamhung Military Equipment Plant, which made parts. Later he transferred to the South Hamgyong Mining Rear Equipment Supply Center at Kwangop as a staff member. "It was a good job," he told me. "This was a distribution center so we had enough to eat. It was one of the hardest organizations to enter. You needed a lot of bribery to get in. Liquor, cigarettes—I got it on the black market using money my mother made tailoring suits. I also knew the younger brother of a high-ranking administrator of South Hamgyong Province." Ahn stayed in that second post until September 1991, when he went to Russia. Getting there required "even more bribery than before, a lot of goods: a sewing machine, two boxs of liquor, women's shoes, cigarettes."

Since the rejection of his application to attend Kumsong Political University, Ahn told me, "I had been disappointed but still hadn't blamed Kim Il-sung and Kim Jong-il. Until I went to Siberia, I didn't blame them for my problem. I knew that I was limited in what I could achieve politically because of my family background, so I wanted to become wealthy and, through that route, be somebody. I decided to go to Siberia and make a lot of money. My father's sixtieth birthday was coming in 1993, and I wanted to do something lavish to celebrate it."

Once he got to Siberia, though, Ahn "realized that the Russians made fun of us for our Kim Il-sung badges. They said we were ignorant, stupid people who still worshipped Kim Il-sung even though he did nothing for us. At first I fought with them. I still believed in the system and had aspirations for my children's future. But the Russian stores were so well stocked that I felt what I guess you could call material shock. I was also frustrated because our lives were restricted. We weren't allowed to walk around freely. From December 1991, they prohibited us from watching Russian television. South Korea had come into the news. I had thought of South Korea as a poor country but that image started to change. I started asking, 'Why? Why?' Once the foreign media, including South Korean reporters, got interested in the logging camps and requested a visit. One morning the authorities took all the loggers by truck to a cucumber field and replaced them with a model platoon of soldiers who pretended to be loggers. Although I was a party member, because of my family background I was sent to the cucumber field. I wasn't considered fit to meet the reporters. Those who were put there were not allowed to speak with reporters individually but only in twos and threes, and they had answers to eleven questions memorized in advance.

"I had turned thirty," Ahn continued, "and I realized that the principles of Kim Il-sung that I had been learning were all lies. I felt a sense of loss, but at the same time I became very curious about the world. I bought a radio and started listening to South Korean broadcasts, which came at certain times only. In the other room they heard something and figured out I must be listening to the broadcasts. An accountant was on the point of deciding to report me to State Security, but a friend warned me and told me not to listen to the broadcasts. I stopped, but after three or four days I couldn't resist and listened again. I realized South Korean broadcasts were very different from North Korean ones. North Korea only criticized South Korea. South Korean radio gave very clear accounts of real news. It was more humanistic. The next day my friend came over and said, 'You listened, didn't you? I think the other guy is going to report you.' At that point I had no further hope, so I ran away. I took the money I'd saved and a knife and walked 35 kilometers [22 miles] in freezing weather to a train station and went to Moscow. I waited in Russia for a year and eight months before stowing away on a Russian ship at Nakhodka and coming to South Korea."

When I met Ahn in August of 1996, he had been in South Korea only a year or so. He had made a truly impressive transition from logging camp worker to salesman. Cars were his product—he had been named in advance to become the post-reunification manager of a Kia Motors dealership in his home city back in North Korea, Hamhung. But I felt that his propensity to sales talk included an obvious urge to expound on the differences between South and North Korea. I had to keep telling him to forego the lectures and just give me his personal story. Round-faced, with the usual metal-rimmed glasses and what looked like a gold and platinum watch, Ahn wore on the lapel of his business suit—in place of his old Kim Il-sung button—a pin bearing the Kia Motors logo. He had already sold an automobile to fellow defector Yeo Man-cheol, husband of Lee Ok-keum (chapter 17).

Ahn had married in the South and was considered well enough adjusted that he was no longer the subject of full-time attention by the South Korean authorities. I inquired whether the Agency for National Security Planning (as the KCIA had been renamed in an attempt at sanitizing it under the democratically elected government) made any efforts to censor his accounts of North Korea. No, he replied. "Now South Korea is stronger and won't collapse if people know about North Korea." As we talked I realized that what I took to be Ahn's sales pitches could represent something more complicated. "I consciously make efforts to forget about North Korea because if I think about it I can't do my work," he told me. "When I first had to speak out in a press conference, I couldn't speak. All images of my childhood, parents, friends were all mixed up. But now I feel at ease in this interview." A bit ashamed of my earlier feelings of impatience with his preachy pronouncements, I realized that for Ahn our conversation represented a catharsis of sorts.

✶   ✶   ✶

Shin Myung-chul had been described to me as a logger, but when I met him in August of 1996 he turned out to have been a policeman. Shin, very young looking, came to the interview in jeans and a T-shirt on which were printed a cartoon picture of a shark and the English phrase "Hot Summer." Wiry of build, he had combed his short hair forward in front, in the style popular in Seoul, and wore the gold-rimmed spectacles that were de rigeur. Shin had joined the air force straight out of high school and served in the Ninety-seventh Radar Battallion, stationed at Chongjin, at the time one of the most militarily sensitive port cities. "When I was growing up, socialism seemed superior to capitalist society. Someone like me who learned Russian in high school got preference. From each of the nine provinces, ten like me were chosen to be tested and of those ninety tested, nineteen were finally selected to go to the radar division of the air force. The radar equipment came from Russia. You had to know the language to read the manuals."

When his ten-year military hitch ended in 1988, Shin went to work in a county outpost of State Security, in the communications office. "I was selected," he told me. "They look at family background, how long you've been in the party and so on before deciding who goes to State Security and who goes to the mines." When I asked if he had been a true believer, he flashed an odd smirk. "I was very devoted to the ideology," he said. "I entered the party at twenty."

Shin told me how one's military assignment affected later job prospects:

- Bodyguards had the best assignment and could go back home after completing their service.
- The air force was the most prestigious of the main services. Radar was a key skill. One could go from there either to State Security or back home. Anyhow, "radar guys like me aren't robust enough for the coal mines," Shin said.
- Others, who had recommendations from universities or had been named most outstanding in their units, could go home.
- The rest were relocated en masse.

Shin quit his job in State Security to go to Russia because he wanted more money. "Usually in North Korea you have to save for thirty years to buy a television set," he explained. In Russia he had worked for the party in a police role, limiting reception on loggers' radios and connecting them to propaganda feeds from home. "Of course, I was still loyal then. The loggers have shortwave radios. I opened them up and set the gearing that controls band selection, made a connection with aluminum. Those don't last forever, so sometimes the loggers could listen to forbidden broadcasts in Korean from KBS, Radio Moscow, China, America. So I had to do it continuously. I was like a cop, restricting loggers' lives, but not in such a big way. And I didn't create the propaganda broadcasts. I just connected the loggers' radios by cable to programming that I got over radio frequencies. I worked there about two and a half years."

Like others who went, "I started realizing there were vast differences between Russia and North Korea. I started facing a dilemma. What really changed me was the fact that I had a radio room that no one could enter. There I listened to Korean-language broadcasts every day, usually KBS and broadcasts from Moscow. There was so much difference between their accounts of events and the North Korean version.

"I had a wife and a one-year-old daughter in North Korea when I left there. While in Russia I sometimes went to Khabarovsk to buy things to take back to North Korea. It was a seven-day round trip. One day, while I waited in a park to return to the camp, by chance I met a South Korean preacher and we struck up a conversation. Nothing serious, but we planned to meet again. The next time I was in Khabarovsk, the preacher had returned to South Korea and another preacher, Yu Jae-hee, came and we talked a while. I was always concerned that State Security would find out.

"A close friend and schoolmate was at the camp as a logger. I let him listen to all the overseas radio broadcasts, and I was concerned they'd find out about that. On August 20, 1994, he was caught by the manager of the logging camp and arrested. As soon as I heard that, I knew I had to escape. I didn't intend to come to South Korea. I went to Khabarovsk, and had to work for my living expenses. After two months I went to the South Korean consulate in Vladivostok to apply to defect. Permission didn't come easily. While I waited I worked as a merchant. That made me known to some Korean residents of China, who reported me to North Korean State Security because there was an $8,000 reward for catching me.

"On August 30, 1995, State Security officers in cooperation with armed Russian police came after me. I was cornered on top of a three-story building. I ended up on the ground with both legs broken and was sent to the Russian police hospital for casts. The State Security officers thought I couldn't escape with two casts, but I got away that night. I stayed in seclusion for a while and then applied to the International Red Cross in Moscow to become a refugee. The Red Cross and the South Korean consulate helped me."

Shin had no job at the time I spoke with him but said he hoped to put his radio and cable experience to work in the telecommunications field.

For me, on the basis of those interviews, the verdict on the Russian logging and mining camps was obvious: from the standpoint of human rights the camps were far more an opportunity than they were a problem. Even that great majority of workers and officials who did not defect would have returned to North Korea with some changes in their outlook as a result of their liberating experiences in Russia. Their knowledge of the real world would, to some extent, have percolated into the common understanding. While some foreign editorial writers and activists for human rights campaigned against the camps and urged the Russian leadership to shut them down, I only wished there were more of them.

Instead, the number of North Korean workers in Siberia peaked at around 15,000 and then approximately 90 percent were sent home when Russia experienced a financial crisis in 1998. In April 2002, during a period when Pyongyang was focused on reinvigorating its economy, its national airline instituted twice-weekly service between Pyongyang and Khabarovsk. North Korean Prime Minister Jo Chang-dok, on a trip that month to promote economic exchange, asked the Russians to accept at least ten thousand laborers. The request was denied.[2]

TWENTY-THREE

Do You Remember That Time?

If any North Korean's story ought to be made into a sequel to Joseph Heller's novel *Catch-22*, that might be Pak Su-hyon's. Pak was born on October 28, 1966, in Kyongsong, North Hamgyong Province, the son of a disabled father who was on welfare and a factory-worker mother. Considered to have a relatively "good" family background in the North Korean context, he grew up getting his ticket punched in all the right places for a young man eager to rise in station. He was a member of the leaders' bodyguard service—a super-loyal military unit, so large that Pak never personally encountered Kim Il-sung. Studying at a medical college in the east coast port city of Chongjin, Pak by the early 1990s was hungry like most other people but at least could look forward to a good career. But then his brother was caught stealing food. On the North Korean principle that the misdeeds of an individual call into question the loyalty of his whole family, Pak was forced out of college and reduced to working in the electrical factory that employed his mother.

Disillusioned, he defected to South Korea in 1993. When I met him on February 7, 1994, I encountered a passionate and humorous man who was preparing to resume studies of traditional herbal medicine, which he had begun in the North. His stature was small; his face, pointed. The word "elfin" came to my mind. Wearing a generously cut new suit with wide lapels, grinning a survivor's wry grin as he related some of the worst of his misfortunes, Pak listened intently to my questions and took his own notes on them before he replied to each. Here is his story, pieced together from his answers:

The biggest problem now is the food shortage. There isn't enough food for the people. How can they have food for cattle and other livestock? That's why you didn't see any during your 1992 visit.

Until the 1970s it was all right. From 1976 to 1979 the food shortages started. Those shortages were even worse than the ones of the early 1990s. They cut the rice ration in half. We speculated it was due to lack of supplies donated by the Russians. Or it was used for something else instead of being distributed to the people. But in the 1976 to 1979 period, people still had hope. North Koreans believed very strongly in the ideology of Kim Il-sung. And from 1979 the government did resume supplying all the rations. Also from that year some people plowed their own land. That was the "privatization" movement.

Things did improve around the end of 1979. But in 1984 the government sent rice to South Korean flood victims. That caused a great shortage at home. Certain amounts of grain had been provided regularly to each household, but from that point supplies became irregular. When the 1989 youth festival came we worked up some hope because there were lots of food supplies for that one week of festivities—although, of course, the rural areas were not as favored as Pyongyang.

Kim Il-sung and Kim Jong-il said we would concentrate on improving agriculture and put factory workers into the fields. People believed in those intentions, but by 1992 we felt it was only words and had given up hope. Now people realize it's not going to get better. It's going to get worse year by year.

In the distribution of food grains to each household, they started substituting all kinds of grain and even flour for rice. Sometimes the supplies didn't get through. From January to March you would get the food supply. Then for a long time they wouldn't give you any. Then later, in July, they would give you imported grain. Again, with the harvest, they would resume the supply. From March to July people would borrow food. In July they'd have to pay it back with the rations they got then, so they would have little left to eat. After coming to Seoul I saw a South Korean documentary of the Korean War period. It was called, "Do you remember that time?" But in North Korea conditions were that same way, again, forty years after the war.

Even when food was distributed, sometimes there wasn't enough for everyone in the village or neighborhood, so you would have to be on your guard to make sure your family would get its rations. They wouldn't give advance notice of when the distribution would be held, so little kids were assigned to watch. If those children saw someone getting food supplies they would run home and shout, "It's time!" Previously, people had thought it was shameful for a man to line up for rice—that was women's work. That changed. It had become like a war. Lots of people would sleep in front of the distribution center waiting for the time.

In our family there are four brothers. I'm the second. The brother who got caught stealing food is the third brother. All of us were in the military. No family has sacrificed more. My third brother entered the service in 1989. He was maltreated in the military and caught pneumonia, so he was mustered out in the spring of 1991 and sent home. When he got home there was nothing to eat in the house.

Earlier, this had been a problem that everyone shared, which made it somehow more tolerable. But some people had become wealthy—they might have relatives in Yanbian, China, or in Japan, who would help them out. My brother couldn't stand it, so in May of 1992 he went to the storeroom of a wealthy family who had relatives in Yanbian, and he stole grain. South Koreans are horrified by the thought of a thief. But in North Korea, two out of three people have stolen. The fields are collectivized. At harvest time people sneak in and poach food. It's the government's property, so they figure whoever gets there first gets the food. There are military guards, and lots of people are shot dead when they try that. If you're not shot, for stealing one handful of grain you can go to prison for maybe two or three years. Or you might go to a camp for unpaid labor in the fields for six months or so. North Koreans used to think field work was the lowest. A factory worker caught stealing food and sent to the fields thought he'd gotten the worst punishment. In 1991, Kim Jong-il decreed that anyone stealing food would be sent to do farming. But the thing is, now people *want* to go.

I've stolen food many times. It would be hard to find a university student or soldier who had not stolen. Both men and women steal food. In the collective fields the managers would display posters saying, "This field is my field." The poster was supposed to encourage the farmers to work harder. But I took it to mean that this collective field was *my* field. Even after four months in South Korea I have to be careful about what I eat because I've got stomach ulcers, like 80 to 90 percent of the North Korean population. The digestive juices flow, and there's no food in your stomach, so the juices eat through the wall of your stomach. Ulcers aren't even considered an illness, since everybody has them.

Even though I had to steal food, I didn't question the ideology. The education system makes you think of politics and real life as two separate matters. So I thought that, even though life was hard, our ideology was sound.

I was in Chongjin Medical School studying traditional herbal medicine. I had studied almost four years when, in July of 1992, my brother was caught and sent to prison. The family whose grain was stolen asked me to replace the stolen grain. I replied: "My brother is in prison. How can you ask me for the grain?" We had a brawl and they said, "How can such a person as this be a university student?" They tattled to the authorities and I was expelled from med school. That was the time when communism in the Soviet Union and Eastern Europe was collapsing. Universities were enforcing strict discipline. Kim Jong-il said, "Now's the time for action. Punish the ones who should be punished." When I was expelled in 1993, about twelve others were expelled at the same time.

In your later career, Kim Il-sung and Kim Jong-il would judge you according to three qualifications: Had you been a party member? A university graduate? In bodyguard service? I was a party member. After bodyguard service I was on the way to earning my university degree. So I had figured my life would be great. But getting expelled from the university ended my dreams. That's why I defected. At the time when I was joining the bodyguard service, Kim Il-sung had warned, "Trust is everything. Don't betray us and we won't betray you—but if you ever become a traitor then we want you out of our sight."

I had kept my part of the bargain. I didn't have big doubts while I was in the bodyguard service. And in university all they talk about is the continuance of socialism. I agreed that socialism was the only ideology for our country. My major doubts came only when I was expelled.

The authorities said I could come back and try to be readmitted the following year. But they knew I had no way of leading my life after my expulsion. Generally if you are expelled from university they send you to the mines. I didn't do anything for two months, then went to a factory. A high official helped me avoid being sent to the mines. During those two months' rest before going to the factory, I thought a lot and realized that ideology is irrelevant to the lives of ordinary people. What's important is the people's lives. As long as life is good, any regime is all right. I turned my back on the regime in an instant.

Most people's opinions of Kim Il-sung and Kim Jong-il haven't changed. Most ordinary people don't know about the extravagant lives of those two, or about their faults. They blame high officials under the Kims for their problems. They believe Kim Il-sung and Kim

Jong-il are well-intentioned but that high officials working under them don't carry out their policies properly. But those high officials do know all the faults of Kim Il-sung and Kim Jong-il. I've talked to some officials. While ordinary people blame them, high officials blame Kim Il-sung and Kim Jong-il.

But you have to be very careful about saying anything critical, even to someone you consider your close friend. No one can say anything about the Kim family dynasty, for example. One word equals prison. Oh, people who knew each other well might remark that Kim Il-sung's regime was more totalitarian than Hitler's—but being more totalitarian than Hitler wouldn't be considered necessarily a bad thing. People like one-party rule. Kim Il-sung explained that European socialist countries fell because of the multi-party system.

I had one friend with whom I was especially close. We had known each other for a very long time, and our families also knew each other well. Our fathers worked together. My friend was also expelled, from Pyongyang University in 1993 because of family background. He had come home in hopes of defecting to South Korea. We were able to open up to each other after getting drunk. In bantering fashion one of us said, "Let's go to South Korea." We realized we meant it. We didn't tell our families or even our girlfriends.

At first we planned very secretly to go via China on September 15, 1993, but we didn't have the money so we decided to wait. I sold some things—antique porcelains—to a Chinese trader who came to North Korea, and then we had the money. We crossed the border into China October 1. There are lots of military guards at the border, so it's very difficult to get across. We bribed a guard, saying we would just go across and return the same day. For that we spent 4,000 *won*, enough for one TV set on the black market. It's about four years' salary for a university graduate.

Even after we crossed the border to Yanbian in China it still wasn't easy. We visited friends and relatives but couldn't tell them our real plan. We told them we would be going back to North Korea. A relative gave us some money and we went to Tianjin port in China, where we stowed away on a ship that people said was going to Inchon in South Korea. A crewman found us but sympathized and hid us again. We showed ourselves when the ship was in sight of Inchon.

There was a lot to surprise me about South Korea. In North Korea I had read about South Korea's world-record accident rate and had felt critical of the South Koreans, considering them disorderly and violent. At the time I couldn't imagine a place with so many cars, or I would have understood. I was shocked to see such huge numbers of South Korean–made cars on the streets. And I was actually impressed with the traffic order compared with the chaos of China, where cars drive wherever the drivers want.

I like Seoul. I had not imagined it would have all these high-rise buildings. I'm surprised there is a place like this in the world. I'm very fortunate to realize before I die that there is a place like this. I'm sorry for North Koreans who will die without learning about such a life.

I first looked at people's shoes, because in North Korea shoes are often stolen. South Koreans are much taller than North Koreans. And I noticed that compared with North Koreans, South Koreans are heavy. They have more meat on them, look like they have drunk a lot of milk. If there's a war between North and South, the North Koreans don't have a chance, physically. South Koreans have nice complexions. In North Korea it's very hard to find a beer belly, but here everybody's stomach is bulging out.

I was shocked, also, at the reaction of South Koreans to foreigners. In North Korea everybody looks up to foreigners. In Seoul they don't pay that much attention.

I saw a sign after I arrived in South Korea that said, "Love Your Neighbor as Yourself." I was astonished to think that South Koreans had the concept of love.

When foreigners visit, North Koreans have to pretend that their stomachs are full and that they lead wonderful lives. Pamphlets instruct people how to behave in front of foreigners. In fact, even during 1976–79, despite the food shortages, I believed that North Korea was better off than the South. But as the years went by, South Korea became a very prominent country while North Korea declined. Now, except for really uneducated people, most people know that South Korea is a much more powerful country in world politics. They're very distressed by the knowledge.

I was in Kim Il-sung's bodyguard service from May 1982 to August 1989. To be a bodyguard, you don't volunteer. You have to be selected. Fortunately my family background was very stable. At the time, I felt delighted. It was a great honor.

One forbidden thing I was able to get away with as a bodyguard was listening to radio stations other than the official one. Starting in the 1990s lots of radios got into North Korea from China. You could buy them in the dollar stores. Kim Jong-il and Kim Il-sung also give radios as presents. When you bought one, the government person would fix it so that only one frequency could be listened to. But high officials, national security and military people, can get radios without such blockage, both shortwave and regular AM-FM radios. As for a radio stuck on one frequency, of course you can reverse that. However, they check it periodically. If they find you've altered it, they'll take it away. A lot of people alter their radios, listen, then change them back before the next inspection.

Listening to KBS from Seoul, it struck me that while North Korea's broadcasts would often criticize South Korean President Kim Young-sam, the South Korean broadcasts didn't say much at all about Kim Il-sung and Kim Jong-il. Nothing bad was said. Once, though, I did hear some criticism. A broadcast quoted a French reporter as saying Kim Il-sung had put a lot of political offenders into prison. I was very surprised. Of course, I knew about that. But how did people in France know so much about North Korea?

Real change started with the 1989 youth festival. During 1989 a lot of foreigners came into North Korea. We heard about that. And lots of music cassette tapes were brought in [from the ethnic Korean region of] Yanbian in China. Foreigners brought their culture. That aroused curiosity. The regime loosened up a little. When Kim Il-sung realized that people were getting a bit free, he put the lid back on. That aroused more curiosity: Why were we being suppressed?

I'll tell you about an incident at Kim Il-sung University. Some sons of high officials were having parties, playing *jupae,* a Korean card game. They also danced the disco style they had learned from watching the foreigners during the youth festival. Besides dancing and drinking, they got naked with women and played *jupae* on their naked stomachs. When Kim Il-sung and Kim Jong-il heard of it, they kicked them out of the university.

In the old days people used to shout "Long live Kim Il-sung!" But after hearing this disco music, people would shake their hips. Not only in Pyongyang but in other places as well, people were getting wild. In the late 1980s, a song called "Huiparam," meaning "Whistle," came out. It was the kind of song that made people want to move their bodies. But the government suppressed the original song and changed the rhythm before re-releasing it.

You wonder how news and pop culture got all the way out to North Hamgyong Province? Most North Koreans don't rely on broadcasts. Instead, news spreads very quickly via the grapevine. Whenever officials weren't around, everyone danced, and even sang South Korean songs. I did, too.

The slogan about university life was the same as in the 1960s: If you're cold and hungry, you study more because your mind is clear. Meals were rice and soy sauce or beancurd. The soup was saltless, tasteless. There was no heating. Actually there wasn't enough time for study. We had to do our labor, in the fields and elsewhere. Most students study their major subject plus Kim Il-sung ideology. You would be expelled if you didn't do well in ideology. I used to give speeches in the university about how great the Great Leader was. I was a member of the Propaganda Club. But I used to read novels and study English surreptitiously during the Kim Il-sung ideology class. If I got caught, they would accuse me, saying: "Your ideology is wrong." There are special spies—I don't know how many. Party secretaries act as their controllers. We don't know which people are spies, so we can't really trust each other.

I think North Korean university graduates would cope all right with reunification. Students in North Korea don't really have aspirations while they're in the university because, even if they study very hard, the government decides where to assign them. When students return from abroad, I hear they get two months of re-indoctrination. And wherever they go, someone is with them, so they can't talk. And they've signed contracts saying they will not talk about what they saw overseas. Still, it gets around.

Things will be worse for my family now, but even if I had stayed in North Korea I couldn't have been much help to the family. I have a new vision now. I'm waiting for reunification and then I think I'll be of more help to my family. But I believe the regime will not collapse without outside influence, such as the flow of foreign culture. Otherwise, unless high officials turn their backs on Kim Il-sung and Kim Jong-il and stage a coup, there won't be any collapse. Now, looking from South Korea, I can see so many reasons to believe the Northern regime has to collapse—but when I was in North Korea I never thought such a thing. So why should others there think so? The authorities have this special magic: If there's a war even the criminals in North Korea would unite and fight for the country. I like the American plan to start Radio Free Asia and broadcast in Korean to North Korea. I hope it would help North Koreans open their eyes to the faults of the regime. If the regime does collapse, it won't happen peacefully as in Russia. If people turn against the regime there will be bloodshed. They'll kill the high officials.

In my home area only about 30 to 40 percent of factory capacity is in use. People still go to the factory sites each day, though. They may cut the grass and do maintenance work. I don't know how the living standard could decline much more. People figure there has to be a war or something. The government told us all the resources had to be devoted to military needs to prepare for a war. I think about six months' worth of food is stored up for war. I heard that from people in the military. I don't know about fuel. People believe that if there is a war, and if reunification comes, the sacrifice will have been worth-while. The problem is, people want war. They believe they are living this hard life because there's going to be a war. If there's going to be a war, why not just get it over with? They believe they'll die either way, from hunger or war. So the only solution is war. What Kim Il-sung and Kim Jong-il are saying now is that even if foreign nations force economic sanctions on the nuclear issue, we can survive. The ordinary people say, "OK, let's have a great harvest."

Foreigners and South Koreans believe it's the North Koreans who will bring war. But ordinary North Koreans believe the Ameri-cans will invade them. I used to believe the Americans were ruthless, scary people. If anything went wrong in North Korea, it was "be-cause of the Americans." Still, North Koreans underestimate the United States. Despite the Americans' global policeman role, the North Korean mentality holds that Americans are no threat if a war breaks out. The real threat is Japan, they think. They have experi-ence with the Americans in the Korean War and say, "We can beat them again, any time." Most people, civilian and military alike, think that way. But university students know that the U.S. has great power. In university we study international institutions like the United Nations. And a lot of high officials when they talk say that war is out of the question.

TWENTY-FOUR

Pickled Plum in a Lunch Box

Why would a nuclear reactor for peaceful use be built with no electrical power transmission grid; a heavy-water reactor without an adjoining commercial reactor? Why would the plant complex include a nuclear fuel reprocessing facility of the sort used to produce bomb-grade plutonium? Those were key questions Western and South Korean analysts raised about the mysterious North Korean reactor complex that had risen beside a winding river at Yongbyon, about 55 miles north of Pyongyang. Logical explanations that sprang to mind were that: (A) North Korean leaders were trying to make atomic bombs, or (B) they wanted their antagonists to think they might be doing so. Concern in Washington and Seoul grew as American and French satellite photos showed the complex taking shape. But without sending in inspectors there was no way to prove that the reactor was for weapons production.

Pyongyang had signed the Nuclear Nonproliferation Treaty in 1985 — but then had not carried out its treaty obligation to permit full International Atomic Energy Agency inspection of its nuclear facilities. North Korean spokesmen trotted out increasingly elaborate defenses of the refusal to accept IAEA inspection. But "the more they dig their heels in, the more you think they really have something to hide," a Western diplomat in Seoul said. It seems that, when North Korea signed the NPT, parts of the Yongbyon facility were already in place. There were reports that Moscow had demanded that Pyongyang sign the treaty as a condition for the export of Soviet power reactors similar to the one at Chernobyl, for use not at Yongbyon but elsewhere in the country. North Korea under the terms it had agreed to was then expected to sign an IAEA safeguards agreement by June 1987. That turned out, coincidentally, to be a month when South Korea was consumed in rioting that offered Pyongyang its best hope in years of seeing an indigenous southern uprising or revolution, a situation that the North might then exploit. Instead the chaos of that month led to the collapse of the South's military dictatorship and the introduction of democratic elections. The IAEA safeguards signing deadline kept slipping, and it was April 9, 1992, before North Korea's rubber-stamp Supreme People's Assembly ratified an agreement. Even then Pyongyang refused to accept "overall" inspection of any and all facilities, including some of the newer construction at Yongbyon. Only years later would a high-ranking defector, Hwang Jang-yop, report that North Korea in 1991, before accepting the IAEA safeguards agreement, had carried out underground nuclear weapons testing.[1]

Meanwhile, in the West and South Korea the reports that the North might be developing the bomb at Yongbyon came with greater frequency. Few details were made public. Washington did not care to show the precise capabilities of its satellite and other intelligence. "I gather they can identify a pickled plum in a lunch box," said a Japanese researcher.[2] Still the reports were persistent enough that North Korea in February 1990 felt compelled to respond. A comment distributed by its Korean Central News Agency strongly denied that Pyongyang was producing nuclear weapons. It said the focus should be not on the North but on the South, where it alleged the United States kept some one thousand nuclear weapons. The publicity was "helping the bad and attacking the good," the KCNA complained.

For a while, the people paying attention were mainly officials and specialists. From shortly after the reactor complex was started, global media focused on the dramatic end of the Cold War—not on the continuing danger from a lone, unreconstructed Stalinist holdout. From August 1990, media and public interest shifted to the first Persian Gulf crisis. The North Korean nuclear issue simmered along, drawing only sporadic outside attention. But then Japan turned up the heat near the end of 1990 by moving abruptly toward diplomatic recognition of Pyongyang—recognition that Tokyo planned to couple with financial aid worth billions of dollars to the cash-strapped regime. Alarmed American and South Korean officials warned that such aid could help the Kims strengthen a military already ranked the world's fifth largest, its forces forward-deployed along the South Korean border in what the U.S. military claimed was an offensive posture. Washington quietly sent a delegation of intelligence people to Tokyo with stacks of satellite photos of the suspicious reactor complex. Chastened Tokyo officials backtracked and handed Pyongyang a list of tough preconditions for normalization—including acceptance of the IAEA safeguards. Even that flap didn't get very big headlines outside Asia. But once Saddam Hussein was beaten, for the time being, in April 1991, anyone asking where other potential Saddams might be lurking was pointed in Kim Il-sung's direction.

Kang Myong-do, son-in-law of North Korean Prime Minister Kang Song-san, gave a Seoul newspaper, *JoongAng Ilbo*, his take on the situation in 1995, after he defected to the South. "If you really want to know the North Korea problem," Kang said, "you have to know the apprehension the ruling class feels. Their fears started with the August 1976 tree-cutting incident at the Demilitarized Zone. At that moment they were on the verge of war. North Koreans believed they would lose because South Korea had one thousand U.S. nuclear weapons and the North Koreans had none. I think that was when Kim Il-sung and Kim Jong-il decided they needed to develop nuclear weapons." Yuri Andropov, the KGB boss who became the top Soviet leader in 1982, "wanted conflict with the United States so he sent a secret message saying, 'The Soviet Union will help you, so attack.' From that moment, the Russians suggested a North Korean nuclear development project. They sent about seventy nuclear specialists to North Korea. The specialists stayed until August 1993. I heard of Andropov's urging when I was at the People's Armed Forces. In 1992, North Korea acquired two nuclear submarines from the Soviet Union, saying they would be used for scrap. But they weren't scrapped."

North Korea, Kang said, set up its nuclear system with Kim Pong-yeul, a graduate of a Soviet military academy, as the "key person in the Moscow-Pyongyang nuclear pipeline. Because he leans toward Russia, he's not very close to Kim Jong-il. But his ties to the Soviets made him valuable. The people in charge of nuclear policy are officials of vice-ministerial rank in the Central Committee Information Department. Mr. Chang and Mr. Choe of the Research Department are in charge of nuclear policy. They are in their 50s. The nuclear strategy procedure is for Kim Jong-il to give an order to Kim Yong-sun, who instructs the Research Department to collect data and formulate policy proposals. The proposals go to the Research Department head, Kwon Hi-kyong, and to Kim Yong-sun, who is in charge of spy activities in South Korea. They discuss it, send it to Kim Jong-il, revise it and do final drafts. In 1992, they absorbed the Workers' Party International Department into the Research Department's North American Division. They wanted to use the nuclear issue as a way of bettering relations between North Korea and the United States. Kim Yong-sun had been in charge of the International Division."[3]

Kim Dae-ho, one of the teenaged gang fighters featured in chapter 12, matured enough to become a model soldier and was able to land a job with many special benefits including extra food rations. However, it was a job that turned out to have some serious disadvantages. Starting in 1985, he treated waste water at the Atomic Energy April Industry, so named because it had been founded in the month of Kim Il-sung's birthday. Situated in Tongsam-ri, North Pyongan Province, April Industry was a uranium processing facility. The waste water that Kim Dae-ho treated had been used in uranium processing. He put limestone into the water, causing the solids to sink to the bottom, and then sluiced the somewhat cleaner water into the river system.

"The authorities claim they're concerned about the environment but it's not the case," Kim Dae-ho told me. "The trees next to the river died and so did all the fish. Workers' white blood cell counts were down. They had liver problems and their hair fell out. In 1990, I had to work in vanadium processing, using sulfuric acid. I worked in that for about a week. For a long time blood seeped out of my mouth. Even now if I put something in my mouth and suck on it I can see blood."

Eighty percent pure by the time the plant finished with it, the uranium then was taken to Yongbyon for further purification. "At Yongbyon they made it 100 percent pure and used it for power generation," Kim Dae-ho said. "They used it in the experimental reactors. In October 1986 and February 1987, I visited Yongbyon. In 1986, I heard from workers that someone working there got exposed to plutonium rays in the reactor. His whole body deteriorated. In 1988 Kim Il-sung and Kim Jong-il inspected Yongbyon. I heard they gave the workers presents such as Japanese TVs as a reward for achieving the extraction of plutonium, but I have no idea if it was weapons grade. It was also in 1988 that I heard about a special military unit for nuclear development that had been assigned to make a storage place and store plutonium."

In 1988, Kim Dae-ho transferred to Namchon in North Hwanghae Province, which he described as "the other place besides April Industry where they processed uranium. That year while I was there I got a Toshiba color TV from Kim Jong-il. Color sets were a big deal. The government didn't sell them. In the black market one cost 4,500 or 5,000 *won*—five or six years' pay. I got mine for being a good, steady worker—nothing to do with plutonium."

As Kang Myong-do suggested, the nuclear weapons issue needed to be seen against a background of a generally perceived lessening of the North Korean military threat. It was not that Pyongyang's military was shrinking. Rather, Seoul increasingly had the resources to counter it. By the time the project to build A-bombs at Yongbyon began in earnest in the 1980s, it was becoming clear that South Korea's economy was growing so fast that the North's military superiority soon would be a thing of the past. The Kims evidently thought they needed nuclear weapons for a variety of purposes: to keep alive the possibility of reuniting the peninsula by force, on their terms; to deter South Korea and its American ally from trying to reunify on *their* terms; and to force concessions from the United States and other countries. Even with a nuclear equalizer, the Kims were confronted with more and more compelling evidence that they could not win a second Korean war. Everybody would lose grievously, not least the North. Perhaps the most daunting evidence was Operation Desert Storm, in which American equipment like what the Americans and South Koreans were deploying south of the Demilitarized Zone was credited with having chewed up Soviet-supplied Iraqi equipment similar to what North Korea had bought.

Some observers still worried that Saddam Hussein's invasion of Kuwait proved that irrational or foolhardy dictators do start wars, even when it should be obvious they will lose. The question often asked was whether Kim Il-sung was rational. Certainly there was plenty of evidence suggesting megalomania in the giant statues and portraits of the Great Leader everywhere in Pyongyang. Like Saddam, Kim wanted to hear nothing but good news from his minions and consequently was given a distorted version of events. But, reassuringly, in the four decades since he had started the immensely destructive Korean War, Kim had not started another one—although there could be little doubt he had been tempted several times.

At the beginning of the crisis North Korea's suspected bomb-building capability was less a military threat than a threat to the concept and practice of nuclear non-proliferation. "North Korean nuclear weapons are for deterrence, not offense," Kang Myong-do told me. "They don't have enough strength to strike." But the lessons of China, India and Pakistan strongly suggested that if North Korea were allowed to get away with refusing to allow inspection of Yongbyon, then both South Korea and Japan would feel strong pressure to acquire their own nukes. Neither would have much trouble with the technical aspects if they went ahead, and the chain reaction might not end with them.

Kim's challenge to the non-proliferation regime was not merely an implied one. His regime launched an uncharacteristically sophisticated public relations campaign against the NPT, blasting the treaty as partial to nuclear powers such as the United States and unfair to have-not, non-nuclear nations. Indeed, even if the NPT was all that stood between the world and Armageddon, it never could stand close scrutiny in terms of equity. If Pyongyang should persist in its refusal to admit inspectors and halt any bomb development, the whole non-proliferation structure might start to unravel.

The preferred means to move Pyongyang were diplomatic. But in case diplomacy should fail, a slip of the tongue by South Korea's defense minister in April of 1991 offered one clue that at least some thought had been given to a preemptive strike to take out the Yongbyon facility, as Israel had done to Iraq's Osirak facility in 1981.

The nuclear issue remained obscure until a bungled diplomatic foray by a Japanese politician forced Washington to turn up the heat.[4] In September

1990, Shin Kanemaru visited Pyongyang as co-leader of a political parties' delegation that also included a Japanese socialist leader. A master of domestic politics, a powerful behind-the-scenes elder in Japan's ruling Liberal Democratic Party, Kanemaru was a diplomatic tyro. Kim Il-sung by all accounts charmed his pants off, inviting him for repeated tête-à-têtes and pushing a sudden campaign for normalization of diplomatic relations. Kim hoped to counter the forays of South Korean President Roh Tae-woo into the communist bloc, where Roh was establishing diplomatic relations with Moscow and trade relations with Beijing. Western policy basically favored "cross-recognition" in which the respective allies of each of the two Koreas would recognize the other Korea as a means of increasing contact and reducing tensions. But Kanemaru was too eager and just about gave away the store. He agreed to normalize quickly and, in the process, to "compensate" the North for the effects of Japan's 1910–1945 colonization of the Korean peninsula. In fact he spoke in favor of generous "reparations" for the damage Japan had inflicted on North Korea not only during but also *after* its time as colonial overlord there.

In the West, Kim Il-sung was seen as a fearsome dictator, but in person by all accounts he was charismatic. Kanemaru was so moved by all of Kim's attentions and, presumably, by lingering Japanese national guilt over the treatment of the Koreans that at one point during a press conference in Pyongyang he wept.[5] It was in that atmosphere that Kanemaru, at the behest of his accompanying Foreign Ministry advisors and only perfunctorily, raised the issue of North Korean nuclear weapons development. Kim denied everything, insisting that all he had at Yongbyon was a research facility. He said he would accept inspection if U.S. nuclear weapons in the South would also be inspected. He literally asked Kanemaru to "trust me." That pretty much disposed of the nuclear issue for the time being. It wasn't even mentioned in the joint communiqué issued at the close of the meetings.

Kanemaru's diplomatic foray enraged South Korea, which he had not consulted ahead of time. In Seoul it quickly aroused suspicions of an ulterior motive: Tokyo, fearing a united Korea next door, was trying to prop up Kim's regime with cash so that Japan could play a divide-and-conquer role on the Korean peninsula and reap the commercial advantages of being seen as a North Korean friend. One South Korean official, speaking privately to me after several glasses of Scotch whiskey in the Oak Room of Seoul's Hilton Hotel, raged, "North Korea was almost on the brink of going down the drain! And these Japanese coming into the picture, they are willing to provide more than five billion dollars—goddammit!—thereby making it difficult for the country to be unified!"[6]

Embarrassed over Kanemaru's commitment to a sudden policy shift that did not accord with their plans, Japanese foreign policy professionals sought to restore bureaucratic control over foreign policy. They emphasized that this had been only a political party delegation, not an official one, and therefore Kanemaru's promise was not binding. To provide them the needed ammunition, Washington, according to an account that first appeared from Japan's Jiji Press wire service, sent in an intelligence delegation led by a high-ranking military officer to brief officials of the Japanese Foreign Ministry, Defense Agency and Cabinet Research Agency—the main civilian intelligence organization—for three days from October 31.[7]

The Jiji account was the first detailed report made public on what the North Koreans had at Yongbyon as shown in the U.S. KH11 satellite photos and the American intelligence people's briefing. Jiji cataloged: (1) a research reactor built by the Soviet Union in the early 1960s, and given to North Korea, mainly used for basic research; (2) a small reactor, of 1950s Soviet technology, in use at Yongbyon since 1987, capable of producing seven kilograms of plutonium per year—enough for one bomb—although it was not known if it had been used to do that; (3) a larger reactor in the 50–200 megawatt range, of French 1950s technology, under construction in Yongbyon since 1984 and expected to be completed in 1994, which would be capable of producing 18 to 50 kilograms of plutonium a year or enough for two to five Nagasaki-sized bombs; (4) a factory to produce enriched uranium (North Korea mined natural uranium); (5) a nuclear fuel reprocessing plant with high chimneys and meter-thick walls to keep radioactivity from escaping, almost completed and expected to be in full use in 1995; (6) remains of a pre-1988 low-level explosion experiment; (7) Kim Il-sung's mountain resort villa nearby. The bottom line: Jiji quoted the U.S. briefer as telling his Japanese listeners that North Korea would be able to develop nuclear weapons by 1995.

Although the world still had both eyes on the Persian Gulf, specialists involved were in earnest by then about doing something to stop North Korea's nuclear weapons development. Various approaches began to get considerable attention. One of the more promising was to use Pyongyang-Tokyo normalization and the money North Korea would get from Tokyo as the carrot. After Kanemaru flew to Seoul to apologize to an angry President Roh Tae-woo for his hasty approach, the professional diplomats again took the driver's seat in Tokyo and parked Japan on that firm, quid-pro-quo approach. The first rounds of government-to-government normalization talks, in Pyongyang in February 1991 and in Tokyo a little later, made clear that signing the IAEA safeguards agreement was a precondition Tokyo had set for normalization.

The carrot was thought potentially effective because the North Korean economy was in serious trouble. Kim Chang-soon, an early defector from the North who presided over Seoul's Institute of North Korean Studies, told me that during 1991's opening months there had been some 150 reports of crowds—perhaps 200 people at a time—gathering to protest food shortages in various parts of North Korea. He cited reports from Korean residents of

Japan whose relatives had moved back to North Korea some years previously. The country had not had a bumper harvest since the 1970s, Kim noted, and grain rations often had been arriving late or not at all. This also affected what on the surface appeared to be good military morale, he said: "Naturally some of the soldiers sneak into farm villages and steal food." Kim Chang-soon told me it would be very difficult for the low-level protests he cited to grow larger and coordinated. North Koreans were kept to their work groups and locales; they lacked the freedom of movement and communication it would take to develop a mass movement. But although the North Korean leadership was not in imminent danger of overthrow by the masses, he said, "they are in a very difficult position and they have to compromise with the Japanese. . . . They really are badly in need of Japanese money."

A deal with North Korea would involve Tokyo's payment of the equivalent of billions of dollars. Tokyo knew how much clout it had acquired. I spoke with Katsumi Sato, editor of *Gendai Korea* and a leading Japanese Pyongyang-watcher. Because of fuel shortages that resulted from a Soviet decision to move away from bartering oil on favorable terms to Pyongyang, Sato noted, factories were closed and ships could not sail. With its zero credit rating, when Pyongyang looked around for a quick financial fix the only possibility in sight was Japan and the aid and, perhaps, trade that normalization would bring. "Japan is actually the casting vote," said Sato. "Whether they live or die is up to Japan."

Pyongyang wanted more than just Tokyo's diplomatic recognition and aid, though. It wanted development of higher-level relations with the United States—to counter Seoul's approach to Moscow and Beijing and bypass Seoul. If it should succeed in getting all of those in exchange for giving up its nuclear weapons card, its ploy would have to be counted as successful.

One diplomatic approach that was mainly stick, favored by Seoul, was to line up international support for demands that Pyongyang cease and desist. The nuclear powers were on board for that. Moscow had abandoned its agreement to export reactors, by most accounts in order to back its demand that Pyongyang sign the safeguards agreement and admit inspectors. (Some said the export halt was merely a sort of factory recall: Moscow wanted to fix the flaws in the Chernobyl-type reactor before proceeding with exports.) In reality, if Pyongyang was already past the point of needing help to continue its weapons program, Moscow's embargo would have little more than political effect. Even that could be important, though, as Moscow was such an old ally of Pyongyang's and the growing estrangement between them was painful.

Several things occurred to heat up the North Korean nuclear issue further. In February 1991, a bilateral committee set up by the East-West Center in

Honolulu and the Seoul Forum for International Affairs issued a recommendation that U.S. nuclear weapons could be removed from South Korea without endangering that country's security. Members of the group included former high officials from both countries: a former chairman of the U.S. Joint Chiefs of Staff, a former South Korean defense minister, a former U.S. assistant secretary of state for Asia and the Pacific and a former South Korean ambassador to the United States. Their argument was that South Korea could remain under the American nuclear umbrella without having the weapons physically in South Korea, thanks to the development of longer-range, precision weapons. They also argued that there would be political advantages for the South in being able to say the weapons were not present. The United States, for its part, could continue its not always followed "NCND" (neither confirm nor deny) policy regarding the presence of nuclear weapons in South Korea. North Korea had been seeking to link the demands for IAEA inspection of its facilities to its own demand that U.S. nukes be withdrawn or inspected. The committee rejected that as an apples-and-oranges linkage, but at the same time appeared to recognize the public relations reality: it would be just as well not to have to try to explain to non-specialists why Kim's proposal was off the mark if indeed there was no compelling military reason to keep the U.S. nukes on Korean soil.

To learn that public relations reality, one had only to visit a South Korean campus and talk with just about any student. The presence of U.S. troops, and their nuclear weapons, was a hot-button issue with them, but most knew or cared little about North Korean nukes. South Korea's government had cried wolf so often about North Korean schemes for imminent conquest that young South Koreans simply ignored reports of North Korean nuclear weapons production. North Korea, long known for its heavy-handed propaganda, had learned to play skillfully on the nationalistic sentiments of South Korea's young.

The North also had gotten its act together in propaganda directed outside Korea. An English-language booklet, "U.S. Nuclear Threat to North Korea," was published in March 1991 in the name of a magazine called *Korea Report,* an organ of Pyongyang's unofficial "embassy" in Tokyo, the International Affairs Bureau of the Central Standing Committee of the Chongryon. It was a thoroughly professional piece of research that read as if it might have been prepared by a Western scholar or peace activist. No author was listed, but I suspected that the Korean residents' group or someone in Pyongyang acting through the group had commissioned just such a person to do it. There was one place where a reference to American "impudence" seemed to have been inserted by one of the old guard propagandists, but otherwise the document stuck to an unemotional approach that worked very well.

The booklet made the linkage argument about as persuasively as it could have been made. It skillfully turned Pyongyang's refusal to allow inspection into a valiant defense of the rights of the less powerful countries against the superpowers. The booklet recited a history of U.S. planning for the use of nuclear weapons in Korea in the Korean War and listed in startling detail the various nuclear weapons the United States was alleged to keep in the South. "South Korea is the only place in the world where nuclear weapons face a non-nuclear 'foe,' namely North Korea," it said. The booklet called for denuclearization of the Korean peninsula, to be accomplished through talks among North and South Korea and the United States. (The other side pointed out that American nuclear weapons faced Russian weapons just a few miles from North Korean territory in the Vladivostok area. Washington was suspicious of local nuclear-free zones generally, and argued that in order to work they must include all the nuclear-power neighbors.)

The booklet attacked the "unfairness" of the Nuclear Nonproliferation Treaty. The United States had issued a blanket guarantee that any non-nuclear nation that signed the NPT would not be attacked first with American nuclear weapons unless it allied itself with N-powers attacking the United States or its allies. Pyongyang demanded that this "Negative Security Assurance" be made specific and legally binding toward North Korea in particular, another of the demands the booklet set out. There was also a UN Security Council resolution of 1968 promising immediate action by the permanent members of the council to aid any non-nuclear power attacked by a nuclear power. But "the non-nuclear powers, while welcoming these guarantees, do not regard them as providing a complete guarantee," the booklet said. Non-nuclear powers wanted more "effective" international guarantees.

Even more controversial was a long and comprehensive article published in Seoul in the March 1991 issue of the monthly magazine *Wolgan Choson*, written by a leading South Korean investigative reporter, Cho Gap-jae. Cho argued forcefully that South Korea's military should not simply watch quietly to see whether diplomacy succeeded in persuading Pyongyang to abandon its nuclear weapons program. It should be adding to the pressure, planning a last-resort preemptive strike. He said both South Korean and American military people were at least considering such a strike. Cho recalled that Washington had made life miserable for the late South Korean President Park Chung-hee until Park gave up his own nuclear weapons program in the 1970s in exchange for a U.S. promise to protect the South and keep the North from developing nukes. That sort of pressure in the long run could be hard for Kim Il-sung, too, to resist—but if he timed it right Kim had much to gain by hitting up Japan and the United States for payment once he agreed to accept inspection. Even then the North would retain superiority over the South in terms of being able to crank up a nuclear program again if the situation demanded it, Cho wrote. Still, "a compromise involving a with-

drawal of U.S. nuclear weapons from South Korea together with a termina-
tion of nuclear development by North Korea is the most possible and most
peaceful solution under the current conditions."

Lest anyone think South Korea was fully resigned to permanent non-
nuclear status, Cho wrote that "an extremely small circle" of South Koreans
was thinking ahead to Korean unification and a world in which a unified Korea would face "hypothetical enemies" such as Japan, China and the Soviet
Union. Those Southerners were wondering whether Pyongyang shouldn't
be allowed to continue with its nuclear weapons development. Such thinking, of course, was a nightmare to the anti-proliferation mavens in Washington and elsewhere.

The Cho article was on many people's minds in April of 1991 when Defense Minister Lee Jong-koo told a group of journalists that the country
ought to work out "punitive measures" in case North Korea persisted in its
nuclear-weapons development. Mixing up his Israeli raids, he spoke of an
"Entebbe" solution. Entebbe is in Uganda, and that wasn't the nuclear
weapons case. But Lee got in plenty of hot water anyhow. Pyongyang
called his remarks a "declaration of war" and opposition parties demanded
he be sacked because he had hurt the chances for North-South rapprochement. The government tried to hush the whole thing up, asking newspapers not to write about it, and Lee himself withdrew his remarks. The
incident illustrated, among other things, the fact that nuclear weapons
were not that much talked about in South Korea. There was a kind of
taboo, it was said.

Besides nukes there were North Korea's chemical and biological weapons.
"They have one of the five biggest stocks of chemical and biological
weapons," Kim Chang-soon of Seoul's Institute of North Korean Studies
told me. "I can't go into details, but from the Mount Kumgang area on the
Eastern front they can use such weapons, taking advantage of seasonal
winds, and destroy a corps of enemy forces [three divisions] in an hour.
That's part of the North's aim for supremacy. They aim at quick attack and
quick resolution. Their idea is to resolve everything before the U.S. side
makes preparations to help us out."

North Korea also had Scud missiles, which were of particular interest in
1991 after Saddam Hussein had used them. Cha Young-koo, an arms control
expert at the Korea Institute for Defense Analysis, noted that Saddam's use of
Scuds was mainly intended to try to draw Israel into the Gulf War. A renewed
Korean War would not offer a similar temptation to provoke a neighbor, Cha
told me. But if North Korea should fire Scuds at South Korea in peacetime,
"it means they want war," he said. "And in wartime if they use Scud missiles,
we'll use *our* missiles, with the assistance of the United States."

The *Wolgan Choson* article said that the North Korean newer-model Scuds had been made broad enough in diameter to carry low-tech nuclear warheads of the type that could be achieved by countries just joining the club and unable yet to miniaturize. So the presence of the Scuds presumably pointed to a viable nuclear delivery system.

The many good reasons for removing U.S. nuclear weapons from South Korea finally persuaded President George H. W. Bush. Pyongyang meanwhile had a number of apparent reasons to use the occasion to open up its relations with South Korea, as Seoul's business interests hoped. The controversy over suspected nuclear weapons development had turned Kim Il-sung into the international bogeyman to replace Saddam Hussein for the time being. Even as Pyongyang desperately wished to normalize relations with Japan, Tokyo had made clear that normalization must await Pyongyang's submission to international inspection of its nuclear facilities.

North Korea evidently intended to announce it would comply, but no sooner than necessary. It may have seemed to Pyongyang that its interest lay in distracting attention from the nuclear issue to buy time—perhaps for further development and concealment of what already had been done—before permitting international inspections. Perhaps the leadership thought that taking a constructive approach to issues regarding the North-South relationship would provide just such a distraction. It was also a way to produce an accomplishment that could be cited in the upcoming April 15 celebration of Kim Il-sung's eightieth birthday.

For whatever combination of such reasons, members of the Northern delegation to a December premier-level meeting in Seoul said they had orders from no less than the Great Leader himself not to come back empty-handed.[8] They even held out the possibility of a summit meeting between Kim Il-sung and South Korean President Roh Tae-woo. They went home bearing an agreement of "reconciliation, nonaggression, exchanges and cooperation" between North and South. Within a few days South Korea had traded cancellation of the 1992 Team Spirit exercise for North Korea's agreement to permit IAEA inspection. On December 18, South Korean President Roh was able to announce that no nuclear weapons were in South Korea. The two Koreas then concluded an agreement pledging that neither side would have anything to do with nuclear weapons or the facilities for manufacturing them; each would permit inspections by the other to verify that. The North's Supreme People's Assembly finally ratified the IAEA safeguards agreement on April 9, 1992, and the international body the following month was able to send inspectors to start to find out just how sincere Pyongyang was about its no-nukes promise.[9]

TWENTY-FIVE

I Die, You Die

Kim Jong-min was one of the higher-level defectors from North Korea. After rising to a rank equivalent to brigadier general during a career in the Ministry of Public Security, he had become a businessman as president of the Daeyang Trading Company. The company's purpose—like that of some 150 other trading companies that had been set up in various units of the regime including the military since 1971—was to raise foreign currency. Daeyang was assigned to acquire millions of dollars to help finance the 1989 youth festival. Kim went abroad on that mission in 1988. His efforts failed and, he told me, he believed he would be punished upon his return to North Korea. Thus he defected, via the Netherlands, to South Korea. In Seoul following his debriefing he was given a post at Kyungnam University's Institute for Far Eastern Studies, researching and writing on North Korean political, economic and military matters.

Kim showed up for our first talk in November 1993 looking the part of a businessman in a crisp, starched white shirt, a nice silk tie and a well-tailored blue suit. He wore a gold wristwatch. He showed a facial resemblance to members of the Kim Il-sung family and, tantalizingly, he called attention to that resemblance. "Don't you think I look like Kim Jong-il?" he asked me, noting that the Jong of his own middle name was the same character as the Jong in Kim Jong-il's name. He quickly denied any blood relationship, though, saying the resemblance was mere coincidence. He told me he had known Kim Jong-il while growing up, especially between 1957 and 1961;

they had hung out together, along with other children of elite officials, although Kim Jong-il was several years older. Kim Jong-min's father had been an editor of *Nodong Shinmun*, the party daily, he told me.

Kim's testimony was useful in helping me to understand the mindset of North Korean high officials at the time of the first nuclear weapons crisis. Ways of thinking in North Korea changed slowly, and his remarks remained illuminating after the country's nuclear weapons became, once again, the center of attention. Thus I offer much of our exchange in the following pages.

Q. You keep joking about how your middle name is the same as Kim Jong-il's and you look like him, but you say you're not one of his brothers. I'm trying to figure out how a less-than-top official like your father, who wasn't the top editor of *Nodong Shinmun*, could live in the neighborhood with Kim Il-sung and the rest of the top leadership, the people you mentioned earlier as your neighbors.

KIM JONG-MIN: "My father was unofficially the most powerful guy on *Nodong Shinmun* despite his title. He was one of the most educated of the North Korean elite. In the end he had to go back to his home district because he had been part of the Korean elite under the Japanese occupation. He was a very prominent figure in the media, but he died in his home province. My father wrote editorials and critical essays. My middle name is just a coincidence. [He grinned.] I laughed because of the meaningful look you gave me. If I were the illegitimate son of Kim Il-sung I would have had no reason to defect. Under those circumstances I wouldn't have feared punishment."

Q. How do you assess economic trends in North Korea?

A. "South Korean and foreign analysts see the North Korean economy as being in bad shape. It is, *but* for thirty years the North Korean economy was based on *juche*. The end of the Cold War era has reduced trade among communist countries. But the economy can't just collapse overnight, because North Koreans have existed this way for thirty years. In Western society the goal is to maintain the highest quality of life. But we could say that the goal of the North Korean economy is simply to survive despite the lowest possible living standards.

"You can see how this way of thinking works out in practice by imagining a wartime crisis. Even if Western countries have better weapons technology, the North Korean military men were trained to overcome any hardships and disadvantages to win. Take the case of shooting a missile by pressing a button. Maybe in Western countries the order would come over a TV monitor. In North Korea they may relay the order with an ordinary phone call, but the result would be the same.

The North Korean economy is not set up to help people lead extravagant lives but to put maximum resources into the military while merely sustaining life.

"There are problems with the stores, more demand than supply. Department stores are not for show. You can buy things there. But to buy most of the products you need not just money but government coupons. Only shoes and a few other products can be bought freely with currency alone. Televisions and refrigerators are not for anyone to buy. You have to do something for the government. Then as a reward you get a coupon allowing you to buy one. Those coupons are only for merit, because they can't satisfy the demand of everyone. But even if you have a coupon you may not be able to get the goods. Store employees tell relatives when things arrive. They get them first. Then, when everything is sold, even people with coupons can't buy."

Q. What's the shopping situation in the provinces?

A. "Only certain places have department stores: Hamhung, Chongjin, Sinuiju, Wonsan—big cities and the larger towns. The government sets all the prices. They try to distribute the same products to all the department stores around the country, but of course Pyongyang is the capital and largest city so it gets more. The diversity is the same in the provinces, but the quality of goods and the quantities delivered differ. The better products are for Pyongyang, the older styles for the provinces."

Q. I didn't see any livestock in 1992. Is there no meat?

A. "You probably couldn't see the livestock because they are concentrated in specified areas. There *are* livestock, but not as many as in South Korea."

* * *

Q. When serious demonstrations break out in South Korea, do those in North Korea feel that the South Korean government will collapse?

A. "There is probably no one in North Korea who thinks like that now. No matter how chaotic the situation may have been at Kwangju, that was a different time and place. There is no one today who believes that the South Korean government is on the verge of collapsing. Even as late as the mid-1970s, there were expectations that, with a good effort, the South Korean regime could be toppled. Now, however, because of the difference in economic power, no one feels like that."

Q. But is another war possible?

A. "Considering the international political environment and North Korean internal problems, war in the near future seems almost impossible. But with one-man rule, strong feelings of nationalism are brought up. If there's an irritation to that ideal, a war is possible."

Q. Is it the case that people may be questioning the system, or Kim Jong-il,

but they still have total faith that the enemies are the United States and
South Korea?

A.   "They believe the South Korean government maintains its system thanks
to dependence on the Western systems. So they're enemies because the
ultimate goal is the unification of Korea."

＊   ＊   ＊

Q.   What are your thoughts on the nuclear weapons issue?

A.   "I don't really know very well about South Korean and American policy,
but people may be pushing it a little early. People are underestimating
North Korea too much. The South Korean people are not very interested in the nuclear issue or shocked about it, and are not quick to analyze its impact. They think it's just a political move. But there's more to
it. I agree the United States is a strong country, but it believes in its
power too much. In my opinion, in a word, the big question is not
whether North Korea develops nuclear facilities or not. There are other
more important things. Even if they did develop some nuclear weapons,
they could hide them and they wouldn't admit to it. I assume North Korea specialists in the United States already can speculate regarding the
limitations of North Korean nuclear weapons. But finding out about
North Korean nuclear weapons is less important than trying to prevent
mass production of nuclear weapons.

"Isolating North Korea is not a very wise thing to do. I'm almost
sure North Korea has developed one or two nuclear weapons. North
Koreans don't believe the United States is here for defensive reasons.
They think the U.S. is here for aggression, especially an attack on the
North. They say they are defending their country. I've learned from my
experience—I was in the military about twenty years—that the number
of people isn't what's most important. Most important in winning a war
are high-tech weapons. They will pursue that principle forever. All this is
in a way a defensive move. They believe to win a war you have to have
the right equipment and facilities to fight off a nuclear attack. Without
nuclear capability, no nation could win a war. With this intention they've
been developing nuclear weapons for a very long time. To stick with socialist ideology they must have something to back them up—to be this
stubborn despite the economic downfall.

"I'm not a specialist who can tell you there is a nuclear weapon in
North Korea. I'm just telling you this is the mentality in the North. So
it's very likely they have it. From all my experience serving in the military, I feel there are nuclear weapons in the North. Even if they did develop nuclear weapons, though, the size and quantity would be small.
They're developing these nuclear weapons not with the intention of going against the South but as a card to preserve their ideology versus

South Korea. Post–Cold War they want the U.S. to take heed of their ideology and their existence. I believe the U.S. should be the one to help bring North Korea out of isolation."

Q. What is Kim Il-sung's bottom line? What can Washington offer him?

A. "We're in a very tough situation right now. If the agreements with IAEA backfire, there will be a lot of conflict here in South Korea. Even if the UN Security Council forces sanctions, that won't stop North Korea from developing nuclear weapons. If they force military sanctions upon North Korea, I'm sure there will be a second Korean War. Leaks regarding placement of Patriot missiles here, changing the South Korean helicopter model, visits by the CIA chief and so on—those won't deter the North Koreans. That's the wrong idea. All the talk regarding economic sanctions is useless because they already are planning for such sanctions.

"North Korea can mine up to 50 tons of gold a year. Each ton is $15 million. Even if the United Nations forced economic sanctions on the nuclear issue, while it would be a problem for the North Korean economy, it wouldn't be as big a problem as people think because they have so much gold.

"The most important thing Kim Il-sung wishes for is improved U.S.–North Korean relations. He wants normalized relations with the U.S. The U.S. supported South Korea after the Korean War for ideological reasons, but there are other principles. To expect the North to submit to U.S. power is senseless. The basic principle behind North Korean ideology is nationalism. If the United States does not take heed of these nationalistic aspects, normalization will never occur. First Kim Il-sung and Kim Jong-il want their ideology to remain unaltered. Then they can talk about relations with the U.S. and South Korea. They want to have the same standing as the South Koreans. They're raising these issues. I think they have other intentions. First, in this post–Cold War era they want their ideology to be known. They want it known that they still have a stronghold, unlike the other nations that faced downfall. Second, they want the U.S. to admit the existence of North Korean ideology and the stability of relations among the people in North Korea. They want to be acknowledged. I hope the U.S. understands these intentions."

Q. How can agreement be reached?

A. "First, North Korea is a totalitarian country. They have other, very peculiar characteristics. There are a lot of characteristics I could talk about. But let me say that only the real specialists in North Korean issues should deal with the North Koreans, because it's very delicate. Their political center is the party. They are going to stick to this, and the members of the party have a lot of influence. The most important thing is for the U.S. to stop showing favoritism to South Korea. The high South Korean officials when they go into a news conference say that the U.S.

supports the policies of South Korea. But that is like setting a bomb. That is not advisable. Of course, they believe South Korea is a democratic society, so they can say whatever is true or they believe to be true. The North Koreans also know the U.S. is the most democratic nation in the whole world. If they did not acknowledge American democratic policies, the North Koreans would never have agreed to talks.

"Hypothetically, if Kim Il-sung and Kim Jong-il's power declines, the U.S. should show that they could defect to the United States. Look at the case with South Korea. One former high official [Kim Chongwhi] wants to defect to the United States. It shows that the U.S. presents such an image of democracy that anyone in a difficult spot would want to defect to the U.S."

Q. If they were being forced out domestically, would they rather go into exile or bomb everyone?

A. "At the moment they'd rather bomb everyone. I die, you die. Kim Il-sung feels he's immortal. Even if everybody dies, he won't die. This development of nuclear weapons started about thirty years ago with the intention to survive in case of a nuclear war. I believe Kim Il-sung is ready. Even if there is a nuclear attack he has a shelter ready. Even if he pushes the button he'll survive."

Q. Is his bottom line to save his family, to make sure they can remain in powerful positions despite any external or internal threat?

A. "I don't believe in an internal threat. I don't think Kim Il-sung feels a threat internally. Kim Il-sung considers his family very important, just as you think. But to Kim Il-sung the more important thing is to be able to live the high-class life. That is more important than the family. In the U.S. you have the Bill Clinton scandals, but there is no comparison. In fact I don't understand how the president of such a strong country as the United States should be scrutinized. Kim Il-sung has formed a regime in which he can do anything and no one can ever say anything about it. He can lead the expensive, extravagant life. For example, the food in Kim Il-sung's mansions is planned two years ahead. He has the power to demand such high treatment. Each grain of rice that Kim Il-sung and Kim Jong-il eat is individually selected from a whole heap of rice."

Q. Do you think the country has changed substantially since your defection in 1988?

A. "Maybe, but the essence of the system could not wholly change."

Q. Is it possible for the regime of Kim Il-sung and Kim Jong-il to reform North Korea?

A. "It depends on what we mean by reform. But because of the essence of the social system, it is very hard for any *real* change to occur. For true political reform to occur there needs to be democracy. But democracy would threaten one-man rule in North Korea."

Q. Were you a totally loyal believer in Kim Il-sung and Kim Jong-il? If so, when and why did you change?

A. "For someone to survive in a country, it's necessary to follow the norms of the system. For forty years I followed the norms. But due to my occupation I traveled abroad often and saw discrepancies between reality and what I had been told—that foreign countries were corrupt, rotten. Altogether, the reasons for my defection in the end were: (1) North Korea was too undemocratic. (2) Economically it was not very rational. (3) I could see from neighboring countries that the system lowered the standard of living. In that society I was considered one of the higher officials. For higher officials it's easy to adjust to the norm, be satisfied with the standard of living. But moving around brought about the change in my thinking."

Q. Are the interests of other elite officials the same as those of the two Kims?

A. "For a single leader to have so much power, there had to be the force of the elite ranks. Along with Kim Il-sung and Kim Jong-il, they should get the blame. At the moment the elite claim to have the same interests as the Kim Il-sung and Kim Jong-il regime. But in the long run that's less certain. No one can say whether those interests will diverge. But I think the elite ranks and the regime of Kim Il-sung and Kim Jong-il are striving for the same goals. Looking at the United States and Western nations, they see people who would take away their power and perquisites. For the moment, based on ideology, they believe they have to follow the leadership of Kim Il-sung and Kim Jong-il to keep power."

Q. Would it be useful for the United States to offer fellowships for study, on the theory that the Pyongyang regime would choose relatives of the Kims or of other top leaders?

A. "It might be all right, but what's really needed is normalization of relations through political means."

Q. What good would come of normalizing relations?

A. "You can talk forever regarding the advantages and disadvantages. But having a formal embassy in the closed society of North Korea and having a North Korean embassy in the United States would bring a natural channel for cultural exchange. Cultural exchange would be bound to set the stage for more opening of North Korean society. There's definitely a great deal of opening coming once the U.S. and North Korea establish relations. People in their forties and fifties tend to be anti-American, but younger people have fantasies about the United States. Seeing the reality of the U.S. will accelerate the trend to openness. Maybe capitalism can flow in naturally. Through this cultural exchange there's bound to be economic exchange. That will give the U.S. leverage in North Korea. Once North Korea gets into an economic position that's subordinate to the U.S., it will not be able to go against the U.S. What North Korea is today is a direct result of the country's terrible human rights situation. They've been able to exploit their people without regard to human rights, and that has made this sort of regime possible. Later the U.S. will want to talk about human rights. Once the issue is focused on, then the regime is bound to collapse."

Q. What do you think of the idea for Radio Free Asia broadcasts in Korean to North Korea?

A. "You should do Radio Free Asia at the same time. To destroy the Kim Il-sung regime, the radio broadcasts are very important. You have to let North Koreans understand U.S. society and see the decency in the U.S."

Q. Are there enough receiver sets in North Korea?

A. "Of course, ordinary citizens won't have the equipment, but the people specializing in relations with the U.S. and South Korea are very curious and lack the real information. Satisfying their curiosity will help to spread that influence to others.

"There are most definitely people inside North Korea who are against the regime. They don't feel they have any backing. Finding that the U.S. backs them would help. In view of my position if I had been in a Western European country and gotten in contact with the CIA there, for me to have returned to North Korea could have been better for re-unification."

Q. You mean if you had returned to North Korea as a spy?

A. "Not exactly as a spy. But I could have acted as a guide for the press coming to North Korea, given them good access, helping to open up North Korea society."

Q. Are others trying to do that sort of thing?

A. "I believe there are quite a few, but it's hard to distinguish just who."

Q. What's the highest level of people assuming such roles?

A. "I believe they're spread around—two or three may even be among those closest to Kim Il-sung and Kim Jong-il. But Western forces can't accomplish internal collapse of the regime because they have no way of contacting those anti-regime people inside. The most important thing is getting in contact with those people."

Q. Can you identify those open to such direction?

A. "Only by common sense."

Q. Did you hear complaints?

A. "A lot. But no one would say socialism is bad. Some would say one-man rule is corrupting society.

"Among the first generation of the revolutionaries—around the age of Kim Il-sung—no one has any doubts. The second generation is mostly Kim-worshippers, excepting only a few who have had contact with the outside world and are highly educated. I guess I'm between second and third generation. But don't get me wrong. The third generation could be as fanatical as the first generation if there's been no outside contact. But in each generation there are some highly educated people who can analyze reality. Those people realize the discrepancies. Those people need some guidelines from foreign nations."

Q. Who can provide those guidelines?

A. "Foreign specialists in North Korea should have the most contact with people coming from North Korea, or go into North Korea and have some influence there."

Q. Should the U.S. broadcast, say, lessons in how to pull off a coup d'état?

A. "Do it through unofficial channels. There must be unofficial channels as well—so it's special contact, personal contact. Even that is going to be very difficult. Take the case of the two North Korean soldiers the South Koreans recently saved at sea. They wanted to go back. That's how rigid and blockheaded they are. Those two military men were part of the State Security marine division. Before they were sent back to North Korea, I told the KCIA to ask them if Im Eung-seong was still three-star. They said yes, he's still a hotshot at State Security. We were colleagues for fifteen years. Im is very conservative."

Q. I'm still not quite clear on what you think about holding out to the Kims the possibilty of exile in the United States, since you said they wouldn't actually be interested and would rather bomb than leave.

A. "In the current situation of course they'd bomb us first. But after normalization, with diplomatic ties, then when the time came they would consider exile to the United States."

Q. Can a policy of guaranteeing North Korea's external security be combined with starting a radio service that would attack the ideology of its leaders?

A. "It would be possible only if you put some buffer between the U.S. government and this new station. You should give the feeling the U.S. government does not dominate it. I do like the idea of the U.S. taking a neutral stance, guaranteeing the security of both North and South Korea against attack by the other Korea."

Q. What do you think of a policy like this: The United States says, "We'll guarantee the external security of both Koreas but we don't agree with the system. We'll hope for the ultimate collapse and will propagandize, just as North Korea propagandizes." Would they buy it?

A. "They would like that proposal. Ensuring that the U.S. would pose no threat to the regime is very important. They'd like it. But of course, they'd have doubts. They'd go along with it—catch the bait. It would go deeper down their throats. When it got down far enough, they wouldn't be able to spit it out."

Q. Suppose the Americans said, "OK, you say your system is great. We don't agree, but we'll give you a chance to prove it. Chop your military spending, as Seoul will, and concentrate on your economy. See what you can achieve under socialism, without the excessive military burden. We know you'll still proselytize the Southerners. We'll propagandize in favor of capitalism and democracy. But you'll have time to see what you can do."

A. "They wouldn't go directly to spending all that military money on the civilian economy. But the U.S. could guide them to shift their spending. If a relationship develops between the U.S. and North Korea, U.S. influence should spread. The economic infrastructure should be influenced by the U.S. economy, so that it couldn't stand alone. They don't have much trade with the old East Bloc any more."

Q. But how can the United States trust them if they don't drastically cut military spending at the beginning? History makes Americans doubt them.

A. "Basically you should not think that way. First, normalization of diplomatic ties should come. This shows the United States acknowledges both North Korea and South Korea. If the United States hesitates, another century will go by. This is the post–Cold War era!"

Q. So Washington just *gives* them diplomatic recognition?

A. "From the North Korean standpoint, this is the way the United States should be in both North Korea and South Korea. The way things are now, if it got cold, the U.S. would give the South Koreans clothing and tell the North Koreans to take off their clothes."

Q. How can the nuclear weapons issue be resolved? It's a matter of face for the United States, and it's a worldwide concern regarding the future of the Nonproliferation Treaty. How do we get past that to diplomatic recognition?

A. "As far as this nuclear issue is concerned, if the United States insists on saving face it will be impossible to resolve. The only way to resolve it with U.S. face saved is to have a war. No one wants that. The United States should stop now and acknowledge the situation as it is, then *afterward* move to control the situation."

Q. Recognize a fait accompli? But things have gone so far with IAEA demands.

A. "The North Koreans think the IAEA is not an international organization but a sub-department of the United States. North Koreans—all the people—have been going hungry so they could develop nuclear weapons. All those thirty years of work would go up in smoke if they submitted to the IAEA or followed its principles. To North Korea, just having these weapons in case of a war with South Korea is enough. Of course, Pyongyang knows that if North Korea bombs South Korea the United States is not going to just stand by and let it happen."

Q. But how can the United States be neutral if North Korea has the bomb

but South Korea does not? Don't the Americans have to let South Korea
build one, or at least continue to be ready to bomb North Korea?

A. "It's not important whether nuclear weapons are based in South Korea.
They have Team Spirit [joint annual U.S.–South Korean military exer-
cises]. Pyongyang sees that as training for nuclear war against North
Korea. In a few hours all the U.S. weapons could be shipped to South
Korea and missiles could be shot from the U.S. to North Korea. That's
why the United States has to be neutral. If the U.S. shot a missile from
Okinawa, how long would it take to get to North Korea? How long from
North Korea to South Korea?"

Q. To recognize a country that has cheated on the NPT and to guarantee its
defense would pose a very difficult political problem in U.S. terms.

A. "Acknowledge all the nuclear weapons already made. Before signing
diplomatic relations, go and inspect."

Q. So North Korea would give up its nuclear card in the process of getting
recognition?

A. "After diplomatic ties are established, they'll want to safeguard their
credibility, especially if the IAEA comes up with a more internationally
equal system. My recommendation of diplomatic ties is not based on the
nuclear war issue. Rather, the reason is to increase contact with North
Korea, so that foreign culture can infiltrate. People then will eventually
figure out what they want, and that will bring about the downfall of the
regime. Trying to find out if they made nuclear weapons or not—that's
not the important issue right now. They've been made already. Other
than that, the only solution is a war. If you keep forcing them into a corner, it's 90 percent sure there will be a war."

Q. Making IAEA more equitable is a contradiction in terms. The organization is inherently inequitable, based on raw power. But what is to replace it?

A. "What difference does it make? India and Pakistan are already making
nuclear weapons regardless of the NPT."

Q. They're not members.

A. "Still, they're part of the world."

Q. So North Korea withdraws from the NPT; China refuses to approve
sanctions; the United States says, "OK, Kim, you win this one. Now let's
talk." Is that the scenario?

A. "No. You should not allow North Korea to leave the NPT."

Q. How could it be kept in?

A. "If there's a third round of U.S.–North Korean talks, maybe the United
States should give in on some of North Korea's demands so North Korea
has no choice but to stay in the NPT."

Q. Like what demands?

A. "For example, acknowledging the regime, ending Team Spirit. Now

North Korea has proposed a certain number of sites for inspection. The U.S. wants two more included. Maybe you shouldn't force the issue on those extra sites, but have periodic *regular* inspections."

Q. Americans should just close their eyes and pretend they're enforcing NPT?

A. "Yes. The North Koreans have a strong standpoint now. They have weapons to retaliate against attack, and they're ready to fight."

❊   ❊   ❊

Q. What economic training did you have for your role as a businessman?

A. "I graduated from political officers' school and took engineering. I never had any real economic experience but learned on the job. Most of my subordinates, though, graduated from the People's College of Economics in the international relations unit, and were well-trained."

Q. I had the impression that the society changed in the 1980s to become more corrupt and cynical.

A. "On your next trip I can show you women who ask for money. [He laughed.] Even in Pyongyang that kind of girl emerged. With North Korean currency they can't buy foreign goods. Girls who would do anything for foreign currency emerged, behind officials' backs, eager to buy clothing and other foreign goods.

"Before, when people had foreign currency they would ask people going abroad to buy things for them. Kim Jong-il heard of this and allowed people to buy foreign goods *inside* North Korea. That started around October of 1977, but people were wary at first. They feared it was a trick to get their foreign exchange. It was more effective starting in the 1980s. Starting in the 1980s you could buy food with foreign currency in shops. People had always been able to go to shops, just in Pyongyang, where they could buy food according to the numbers of their family members, but buying with foreign currency started in the '80s."

Q. In your day, how much meat was available to a member of the elite such as you?

A. "I was satisfied with the amount provided. I don't have hunger for meat. I can't be compared to other officials, though. I was dealing in foreign currency, so I could always go and buy meat. I can't say the other officials were the same as I. But most officials in North Korea are very satisfied with their lives. The basic necessity is just three meals a day. They were guaranteed that. If they just worked hard for the government and stayed in their places, they could be sure of those three meals.

"As for the quality of housing, South Korean apartments are much larger. But in North Korea the question is how many rooms you have. I had $100,000 to $150,000 worth of furniture in my home. I had command of foreign currency. When I traded with other countries, I got gifts. So

I had access to expensive foreign things. The dollar currency is so powerful in North Korea. With $100 you can buy ten of the best-quality suits.
The KCIA was very surprised when I defected. I had over $100,000
worth of currency with me when I defected. None of the other defectors
had access to the lifestyle I experienced."

Q. Why did you defect, really? You had a comfortable life within the
system.

A. "Even though I had a very comfortable life, I felt uncertainty and apprehension. During the Cold War, my cousin came to South Korea. Then,
under orders of the South Korean government or the U.S., he returned to
North Korea. He was prosecuted and executed. When I was young
I didn't have problems on that account, but it became a problem as I became a prominent member of society. In North Korea circumstances like
that are considered very important for the other members of a family.
Having a defector or traitor in the family can be a big minus. This is the
main reason why I defected to the South. I feared that because of that
background if there arose a situation where I could not fulfill one of Kim
Jong-il's orders he might bring it up. I had trouble with Kim Jong-il's orders. He wanted to do something like the Olympics in North Korea—the
World Festival of Youth and Students. The company I was with was supposed to take care of the money problem for the festival. I had to be the
money resource. I was president of the company, Daeyang Trading Co.
I was supposed to come up with about $10 million—first $3 million, then
another $3 million, and finally $4 million. I was going to import cobalt
from Africa and re-export it for $15 million. But the buyer insisted on pay-
ing *after* delivery. The problem was that Kim Jong-il wanted the money
quickly. A government official called me in Moscow and we had a big
argument. There wasn't time to get the money. That's when I defected.

"At first I regretted defecting, very much. Everything was so alien to
me. So I considered defecting again to a third country. I'm still here because if I go back to North Korea it will only mean death. Life has gotten
better, but still there's a lot of psychological stress in being a defector.
South Koreans say they want reunification but they are distant toward
me. I wonder how it would really work out.

"South Korean officials have hardly made any use of my information. I met U.S. military intelligence people three times, but they just
asked general questions. [On the other hand] I was writing a book and I
discovered that my typist was taking pages of the manuscript back to the
KCIA. I got rid of her and have refused to publish the book. I can't publish it because some of my high government-official friends might be
hurt, people who are outwardly loyal but who have some doubts. Exposing them to reprisal could damage prospects for reunification. Kim
Jong-il is very upset. I imagine my family was sent to a harsh place. If

Kim Jong-il had cause for even greater anger, I'm afraid he would get to my family in a worse way and even get to me. I thought Bill Clinton could bring reunification, since I believe the U.S. has power to influence the situation. But I have some fear that reunification would allow family members of defectors, and others in North Korea who have suffered on account of defectors, to come and kill the defectors."

I met Kim Jong-min several times in informal circumstances. As I got to know him I realized he was truly unhappy with the way his life had turned out. He spoke more than once of how much he missed his family. One daughter—like his mother—was very beautiful; if she came to the South she could enter the pageant and become Miss Korea, he boasted. Once, he failed to show up for a morning appointment with me in a coffee shop. Later he explained that he had stayed up drinking with a friend and slept too late. I learned that he had married in the South, but then had divorced and was left with alimony problems. I worried that he was not making and never would make the adjustment to living in Seoul. And, as he had done, I extrapolated from his situation, worrying how North and South Koreans would fare living together in any eventual reunification.

In July 2001, Kim left Seoul on a trip to China and promptly disappeared. By that time, it was not uncommon for defectors to travel to the China–North Korea border and mount rescue operations to try to bring out family members. Sometimes they employed Chinese who could travel freely in North Korea, but some of the defectors actually went in themselves—sometimes succeeding, sometimes not. At least one defector who went in himself was captured and publicly executed. The Seoul newspaper *JoongAng Ilbo* in reporting Kim Jong-min's disappearance the following February quoted colleagues as recalling his often expressed wish to bring his daughters to South Korea.[1]

TWENTY-SIX

Yen for the Motherland

Hong Song-il, also known by his Japanese name, Seichi Tokuyama, might have seemed an anomaly. Forty years old when I interviewed him,[1] the third-generation Korean resident of Japan owned a chain of eight *pachinko*—Japanese pinball—parlors in and near Tokyo, drove a Mercedes-Benz and was both objectively and in his own mind a rich capitalist. Nevertheless, he contributed substantial funds both directly and indirectly to communist North Korea. In our talk he explained why he and many other capitalistic Koreans looked north to Pyongyang rather than south to Seoul for their Korean homeland.

Q: How do you and your family happen to be among the 700,000 Korean residents of Japan?

A: "My grandfather came first. Around 1929 my father at age seven came over to join him, and ended up working as a day laborer in Osaka. After Japan surrendered in 1945, my family could go back and forth often to our home town on Cheju Island. But my grandfather supported the 1948 mutiny by Cheju people opposed to Rhee's rule in South Korea. After Rhee's government put down that uprising, the whole family—all my father's brothers and sisters—came to Japan."

Q. Could they still go back and forth to South Korea?

A. "No. The South Korean government prohibited entry by anyone affiliated with Chongryon, the pro–North Korean residents' association in Japan.

I think my father had joined that shortly after the single Korean group here split into pro-North and pro-South groups in 1945."

Q. Why did he take the pro-North side?

A. "Before 1945, he opposed Japanese imperialism, which dominated and colonized Koreans. He came to Japan for economic reasons, to earn bread for his family. He believed socialism or communism would provide a better life for Koreans. He also realized the bitterness of statelessness under Japanese domination."

Q. It's been many years since that time. Why do you and other second- and third-generation Korean residents support North Korea and Chongryon?

A. "Upbringing has something to do with it, at least in my case. Not only did my father support the North, but I attended a North Korean school in Japan and so did my wife. In fact the cultural role of Chongryon is one of the reasons many in the younger generations continue to support it. It functions as a rallying or unifying agent in maintaining the Korean community and keeping up traditional culture. It even conducts weddings and funerals."

Q. Is that enough to persuade even a businessman such as yourself to support a pro-communist organization?

A. "To survive in capitalist Japan you need some political support. The economic policy of the Japanese government is very hostile to Koreans. My business, pinballs, requires a license. The more successful my business becomes, the worse the police and political harassment becomes. Chongryon champions our rights. That's the reason we support it. Kim Il-sung is something like a father figure for us."

Q. In Juzo Itami's movie *A Taxing Woman* the female tax inspector goes after a *pachinko*-parlor operator. When you talk of official harassment, is tax one of the things you're talking about?

A. "There is overt and covert harassment."

Q. After all these years in Japan, have you thought of becoming naturalized?

A. "After graduating from the North Korean school here, I did waver and think of becoming naturalized. But one day two young drunks kicked my car, and when I spoke to them about it we got into an argument. At first witnesses and the policeman who came to the scene were very cordial to me, blaming the two drunks and sympathizing with me as the victim. But after the policeman asked for my driver's license and saw that I was Korean, his attitude changed abruptly and he blamed me for the incident and incited the witnesses to blame me as well, telling them I was Korean. He threatened not to let me go home until I confessed I had started the whole thing. When my wife and newborn baby came to get me out, I looked at my baby's sleeping face and realized I must remain Korean. Although Koreans speak Japanese and live Japanese-style, we remain Koreans."

Q. Do you believe in the North's communist system?

A. "Frankly, I don't have much faith in communism. I think there needs to be a sort of Korean-style *perestroika* to reform it."

Q. Have you been to North Korea?

A. "Yes, in 1982 and again in 1987, to visit an uncle and an aunt who had moved there from Japan. The uncle and his family live in the mountains of North Pyongan Province. The aunt lives in Wonsan."

Q. What did you think of what you saw?

A. "I felt some contradiction between what I saw in North Korea and what I had been told. They have a party-first system. The Workers' Party is everything. The basic requirements of living are met, yes, but there is little luxury in food, housing or amenities. Pyongyang has developed impressively but once you get outside the capital there is much to be desired. However, on the plane back to Japan I reflected that contradictions couldn't be helped. In view of the military situation facing North Korea, its confrontation with the United States and the fact that it's almost surrounded by major countries, its survival is at stake."

Q. What about the question of personal freedom?

A. "What you call 'freedoms' in the capitalist countries cannot be found in North Korea, but they do enjoy sovereignty and independence. Just look: There are no foreign troops in North Korea."

Q. How were living conditions at your uncle's place?

A. "Pretty bad by Japanese standards, although if you went there from certain Asian countries you would find better conditions than you had left at home."

Q. If your uncle moved there voluntarily, why was he put in such a remote corner of the country instead of being allowed to live somewhere with some urban comforts?

A. "That kind of economic condition is just the same everywhere in the country."

Q. What sort of work do your relatives do?

A. "My uncle is a mining engineer. His son drives a truck and his daughter is a clerk. Another of my uncle's sons graduated from medical school in Pyongyang."

Q. One recent report by Asia Watch and another human rights group describes a North Korean class system in which people are ranked according to how well they can be trusted to support Kim Il-sung, with those opposed to the regime given the hardest living conditions. Does that jibe with what you saw?

A. "I detected nothing that would suggest the presence of any opposition to the government. Wherever I went I saw no sign of opposition to or disaffection with Kim Il-sung or Kim Jong-il. I did see differences in political treatment. Of course the best treated are Kim Il-sung's family, then the anti-Japanese guerrilla fighters in World War II. Then come those who fought against the Americans in the Korean War."

Q. How were you received at your uncle's place?

A. "I got the most fervent welcome and warm hospitality—for the reason that I was a pro-Pyongyang Korean businessman who had donated money to the town. I've given hundreds of millions of yen to the pro-Pyongyang organization in Japan, mostly for Korean schools here as a sort of repayment of my obligation for what those schools did for me. The North Korean government started sending money to Korean schools in Japan right after the Korean War. I've given tens of millions of yen directly to the North Korean government in cash, trucks and heavy equipment. But still my donations are a joke compared with those some businessmen have made."

Q. Will your family stay in Japan, or maybe try to go back to South Korea?

A. "If Korea is reunified I'll go back to South Korea. For the moment it's politically impossible to go back. I'm telling my children, 'Never think Japan is the only place where Koreans can live. You may go to Canada or the United States but still remain Korean.' Japan is racially and politically intolerant. We think Canada or the United States is more tolerant and comfortable for Koreans. People of my parents' generation are always talking of returning to the homeland. My generation's main concern is how to live as Koreans wherever we live. Maybe in the fourth generation the attitude may change, I don't know."

TWENTY-SEVEN

Winds of Temptation May Blow

It was clear that something was going on in the spring of 1992, when North Korea's Ministry of External Economic Relations sponsored a weeklong tour by more than one hundred business executives, scholars and officials. Most were from Japan and South Korea but small delegations came from China, Russia and the United States. The visitors would travel though remote areas that few Westerners had seen for decades. The unusual arrangements signaled unprecentedly serious efforts to attract foreign investment—and for good reason. Despite Kim Il-sung's trumpeting of *juche*, national self-reliance, his country for four decades had gotten more than a little help from its socialist friends abroad. Now, the rest of the communist bloc had shrunk to China, Cuba and not much else, and that flow of aid and subsidized trade was squeezed off. A clear sign that Pyongyang's external partnerships were falling apart had come in the summer of 1990, when South Korean President Roh Tae-woo's "northern policy" of wooing the Soviet Union and Pyongyang's other communist allies paid off spectacularly: Roh flew to San Francisco (I was the lone foreign reporter on his plane) for an epochal meeting with Soviet leader Mikhail Gorbachev. Diplomatic relations followed—and by late 1992, China, the last major communist holdout, would exchange ambassadors with Seoul.

With 21 million people to keep reasonably satisfied, the regime had little alternative but to look to the global free-market economy. Belatedly following China's example, Pyongyang had decided to set up its first free economic zones. The North Koreans welcomed the visitors from capitalist countries in the hope they would funnel investment into infrastructure and manufacturing. The goals were simple, explained Kim Song-sik, vice-chairman of the Committee for Promotion of External Economic Relations: "Introduce more modern factories of international standard, and generate more foreign exchange." (I noticed that Kim Song-sik was wearing proletarian garb: Lenin cap, Mao jacket. But he set those off with a modern accessory of more or less international standard, for which someone had expended foreign exchange: his belt buckle, which bore a *Playboy* bunny motif.)

Besides the knowledge that they were being blamed for their countrymen's plight, another factor had been helping to coax Pyongyang officials out of their shell. That was an international scheme for developing manufacturing, trade and shipping among countries facing the Sea of Japan, with help from the United Nations Development Program. Meetings in various cities in the region had explored multinational development of a triangular area of Russia, China and North Korea surrounding the mouth of the Tumen River, which formed the border among the three countries. Pyongyang's turn to host a conference on the proposal was the occasion for our tour in North Korea.

The tour provided a chance for North Korea to stage what one American called "a rolling party through the countryside" and play up its ambitious plans to expand tourism. Kim Do-jun, director of the Bureau of Tour Promotion, said around 100,000 foreign visitors were arriving annually, bringing in a total of about $100 million. Hong Kong, Thailand and Australia were being considered as the origins of new tourist flights. Pyongyang wanted to increase the visitor total to 500,000 foreigners, in addition to South Koreans and overseas Koreans. And Kim Do-jun spoke of long-range plans for such developments as "a Disney World" in Kangwon province, near the South Korean border in the mountainous eastern region. Clearly, though, there was a long way to go before the infrastructure would be up to handling such an influx. Counting those of us in the press, the delegation's numbers were so great that hotels outside the capital couldn't or wouldn't house the group—so we had to bunk together for nights on end in the sweaty compartments of a slow-moving passenger train.

The only delegates from the United States who had been invited for the 1992 affair were a pair of researchers at the East-West Center in Honolulu. I happened to be working at the center as journalist in residence (starting on a project that eventually turned into this book) and I applied to make the tour with them. I hoped that in the years since 1989 the Pyongyang authorities somehow would have removed my name from their list of unwelcome scribes—or, otherwise, that I would manage to go unrecognized as a blacklisted reporter thanks to my new scholarly affiliation. Perhaps,

I hoped, there were separate bureaucracies involved in screening scholars and journalists. After all, commentators on the top-down North Korean political system had noted that there was remarkably little in the way of lateral communication among parallel governmental units—apparently they needed to save their breath and paperwork for dealing vertically with their bosses and subordinates.

Whatever the cause for my good fortune, I not only was accepted for the trip but received V.I.P. treatment including a first class seat on the Air Koryo plane that took our delegation and others from Beijing to Pyongyang. When we arrived at the airport it turned out that a pair of young foreign affairs officials, assigned as handlers of the foreign reporters who were expected, did know who I was. "Have you really left *Newsweek*, Mr. Martin?" one of them asked. "Oh, yes," I replied, truthfully. (I was happy that they did not ask whether I had left journalism. Would they have branded me an imposter and put me on the next plane back to Beijing if I had revealed, there at the airport, that I would return to full-time journalism after my fellowships ran out—and that I planned to pay for that trip by writing an article for a magazine?[1])

In the past, normally, it had been North Korean officials who restricted foreigners, while the foreigners demanded more freedom of movement—but early in this visit the tables were turned somewhat. Our *Japanese* tour organizers insisted that the accompanying foreign newsmen stay in the hall to cover the two-day Tumen conference. Then the two North Korean press handlers, officials in their twenties who were both named Kim, struck an unaccustomed blow for a free press. They heatedly argued the journalists' case for skipping conference sessions to leave time for seeing more of Pyongyang. By that time the press corps had developed considerable affection for the two, to the point of giving them nicknames. A relatively tall and handsome Kim worked for the Ministry of Foreign Affairs. He was dubbed Slick Kim because he always wore a well-tailored pinstriped suit. (It was the same suit day after day, I noticed eventually; probably he couldn't afford a spare.) His shorter, slightly chubby colleague—who resembled Kim Jong-il and other ruling-family Kims—was called Fat Kim. Fat Kim, who worked for the Society for Cultural Relations with Foreign Countries, told us that Slick Kim was on the fast track to eventual cabinet position.

Successful as it had proven up to that point, my Clark Kent–style change of identity had begun to threaten my mission. When we arrived at the conference hall where the official delegates were to convene I found that the scholar Martin had been classified as an official delegate. Not only that, I had been assigned a front-row seat facing the dais, my name in very large letters affixed to a placard on the table in front of me. I couldn't bug out without being noticed. Fearing that I would end up wasting precious days vegetating in that conference room, I approached Fat Kim and Slick Kim and won their kind permission to give up my V.I.P. status and join the rest of the crew of foreign reporters to look around in Pyongyang and environs.

With the notable exception of Kim Jong-su, whom I did not meet on this visit, North Korean officials had been notorious for bland, filibustering, prevaricating replies to interviewers; they would talk for hours but give little useful information. Speaking with the foreign reporters who were covering this tour, however, our chief host, Deputy Prime Minister Kim Dal-hyon, was a refreshing departure from the rule. Kim Dal-hyon frankly acknowledged that the collapse of Soviet and East European communism had hit his country hard. "Because of the rapid destruction of the world socialist market," he lamented, "we can't export our goods to socialist countries and import oil in exchange."

In particular, longtime barter partner Moscow had begun demanding payment in hard currency, which was in very short supply in North Korea. Trade with the former Soviet republics had accounted for 38 percent of Pyongyang's global trade in 1990, but dropped to less than 14 percent in 1991, according to South Korean figures.[2] Not only was North Korea importing less from its old ally; its exports were down even more, since its products generally were not competitive with rival free-market products. Analysts were saying the North's economy actually had shrunken each year since 1990 (including, by one estimate, a sickening drop of as much as 30 percent in 1992 alone).[3] China reportedly had joined Russia in demanding hard-currency settlement, further fueling the alarming trend. Not surprisingly, Pyongyang appeared determined to squeeze every possible dollar or yen out of foreign visitors: A European businessman living in Pyongyang's thirty-five-story Koryo Hotel said his daily room rate had doubled to $200 not long before our arrival.

Nickel-and-diming, however, would not solve the problem. Evidence of poverty and economic stagnation was too abundant for the authorities to hide as we rode by train and bus from Pyongyang across the central mountains to the east coast and northward to the Russian and Chinese borders. In previous years I had seen progress in farm mechanization in other parts of the country, but it seemed not to have occurred in this area—or, if it had occurred, to have been reversed, perhaps because of the oil shortage. Farmers plowed far less often with tractors than with oxen, which were among the few farm animals visible. Beanpoles lining the dooryard of almost every house along the route were the only visible source of protein—helping to explain a propaganda campaign that recently had pushed the slogan: "Let's eat two meals a day instead of three."[4]

Little nonfarming work could be seen. At the port of Rajin, for example, we were told that the dockworkers were taking a "holiday." In Pyongyang, large numbers of people were out and about in mid-afternoon, a marked change from the semi-deserted streets noted during most daylight hours on earlier visits. My guide explained that new working hours permitted people to start early and finish early—but reflection suggested that there were reasons other than humanitarian that kept them from the workplace. All this tended to confirm reports that up to half the factories and working population had been idled by energy and other material shortages resulting from the collapse of the international socialist barter economy.

Whether operating or not, factories looked old and inefficient—and their products showed it. Of course, there were occasional bright spots. In a downtown Pyongyang department store, a new display featured stylish jogging suits. But who in North Korea could afford 148 *won*, about $67 at the official rate and more than a typical worker's monthly pay, for a jogging suit? As for the choices provincial residents were offered, there was no chance to find out. The train we were living on did not stop in cities and towns overnight but instead poked around in the countryside and sat on rural sidings. Our suspicion that this was intended to keep us from exploring the provincial towns and cities became a certainty when we visited the port of Chongjin. Some journalists attempted to walk out of the port's gate to a nearby department store, but a port guard stopped them at gunpoint.

The most jarring scene that confronted me as I sat peering out of the train window was a trainload of North Koreans passing us in the opposite direction. They were a ghastly sight. Their clothing was ragged and filthy, their faces darkened with what I presumed to be either mud or skin discolorations resulting from pellagra. There was no glass in the windows of their train. At that moment I figured I must have glimpsed accidentally what it was the authorities with their elaborate scheduling and preparations tried so hard to prevent visitors from seeing. Another surreal experience of lavish hospitality in a starving land, such as I had experienced at Kim Jong-su's picnic in 1989, drove the image home later in the trip when we were served a magnificent feast of giant crabs on a beach in the Rajin-Sonbong area.

With almost nothing positive happening in the domestic economy, a hint of change could be seen in North Korea's approach to the outside world. The Tumen River proposals clearly had sparked major interest in Pyongyang. China had initiated the discussions, seeking access to the Sea of Japan from landlocked Jilin Province. China's Hunchun, about ten miles up the Tumen from its mouth, had been a bustling small port with navigation rights guaranteed by a regional treaty before Japanese troops in 1938 drove pilings into the mouth of the Tumen to cut off shipping. Conference participants traveled to Friendship Bridge, the railway crossing between North Korea and Russia just south of Chinese territory. One look was enough to convince most of them of the impracticality of China's proposal to dredge the Tumen for ocean-going ships. The river was so silted up that dredging obviously would be constant and very expensive.

A compromise proposal aired in Pyongyang by officials of the United Nations Development Program suggested focusing development efforts on North Korea's coastal Rajin and Sonbong ports. China could tie in by rail and road and use those as its own ports, free of customs-clearance or visa formalities. China was studying that proposal. But I heard from my East-West Center colleague Mark Valencia, a specialist in maritime matters, that "China wants the rights of navigation on the Tumen, even if it's a rowboat. They're thinking generations down the line."

Besides the river port versus coastal port controversy, countries involved disagreed on whether management of specific zones should be multinational or national. China sought multinational management, and its delegates mentioned Hong Kong and Macao, neither of which it had yet taken over, as models for placing territory under the management of an entity other than the sovereign. Sovereignty was not at stake, the Chinese insisted, but only management. Those questions were to be taken up at further international meetings later that year in Beijing and Vladivostok. But North Korean officials were skeptical already about the part of the proposal that called for multinational management of the zone—which would mean sharing power in their own territory.

Thus Pyongyang was proceeding with a parallel go-it-alone approach. On paper, North Korea had already established its first special economic zone at Rajin and Sonbong, inside the territory that would be part of a Tumen Delta multinational zone if the Chinese and others should have their way. Trying to lure investors there—regardless of how the multinational negotiations might turn out—clearly was a big part of what the government had in mind when it admitted our group of visitors. Rajin and Sonbong port officials planned to expand cargo capacity from six million to 50 million tons a year in two stages—and also planned to build a brand new port in the area with annual capacity of another 50 million tons. Unlike some nearby Russian ports, they boasted, the North Korean ports didn't freeze up in winter. A slick brochure complete with four-color maps projected that the population of 131,000 North Koreans living in the vicinity of the two ports would grow into a modern industrial city of a million people.

Conceivably a purely North Korean economic zone could work, if South Korean, Japanese or other foreign interests invested in factories there. But Yasuhiro Kawashima, deputy director-general of the Bureau of Port and Airport Development of Japan's Niigata Prefecture, cautioned that proposals to expand port facilities in Rajin, Sonbong and nearby Chongjin might go nowhere unless Pyongyang persuaded neighbors to trans-ship cargoes through the North Korean ports. Lately, the trend had been the other way.

China had tried large-scale exports through North Korea's Chongjin port several years before, but had backed off when its freight cars weren't always returned after they were unloaded. Chongjin port manager Chong Chi-ryong said the total of transit cargo handled on behalf of China and other countries was only 100,000 to 150,000 tons a year. Restoring China as a major user of the North Korean ports might require concessions to Beijing on the questions of multinationalism and access to the Sea of Japan. Future conferences would try to sort out the issue. But regardless of the outcome, said Lee-Jay Cho, East-West Center vice-president and senior researcher, it was significant that North Korea at least was talking about the various proposals.

The country, at least partly thanks to China's prodding of Kim Jong-il, had sounded the general theme of welcoming outside investment since 1984. But only some one hundred businesses had resulted from the joint-venture law enacted that year. Those businesses had brought in foreign funds estimated by South Korea's Unification Board at only about $150 million[5]—most of the money coming from pro-Pyongyang Korean residents of Japan. In those ventures the government permitted—but only unofficially—some capitalist-style incentives, such as "gifts" of merchandise to more productive factory workers.[6] From an investor's viewpoint, key points remained unclarified in the joint-venture and foreign exchange regulations. Outsiders' distrust combined with internal inertia to keep real change to a minimum.

If there were reasons in 1992 to imagine that more investors might respond to the new initiatives, a most intriguing factor headed the list: North Korea had managed something of a generation shift. In a typically Korean pattern also found in South Korea, Kim Jong-il had formed his support network partly from alumni of the schools he had attended: Namsan Junior and Senior Middle School, Mangyongdae Revolutionary School and Kim Il-sung University. By 1987, the Mangyongdae school's graduates accounted for 20 percent of the party central committee, 30 percent of the party politburo and 32 percent of the military commission of the central committee.[7] The school "produces revolutionary warriors to carry on, generation after generation," according to a 1982 speech by O Guk-ryol, then-chief of the armed forces general staff and by one account a classmate of Kim Jong-il's who had been with him as a child at the Eighty-eighth Brigade camp.[8]

Mangyongdae provided military training along with the regular junior-high and high-school curriculum. Graduates entered the army for three years and could become party members during that time. After their hitches, they could enroll in Kim Il-sung University or the military academy. The graduates—about 120 students per year—formed an elite. "They're very loyal," one high-level defector told me. "Most of the people around Kim

Jong-il have graduated from Mangyongdae." According to Kang Myong-do, son-in-law of a prime minister, applicants whose parents were still living were eligible to enroll in Mangyongdae if they were the children of officials at least at the level of party department head—higher than vice-premier. "It's a great privilege to be admitted," he said. Children of the elite who in the past would have gone to Namsan now went to Mangyongdaae, he said.

Not only alumni of schools he had attended but also some other people who had worked for Kim Jong-il in the Three Revolutions teams became prominent among his militant followers.[9] Youth coming to the fore was a positive omen in the eyes of many outside analysts. "There is an ascendance of the younger, more pragmatic elite . . . who are of Kim Jong-il's genera-tion," South Korean scholar-diplomat Han Sung-joo told reporters in Tokyo in 1992. "They are saying their country has to open up a little bit . . . or they will lag hopelessly behind South Korea and the polity will collapse."[10]

Kim Jong-il, who turned fifty on February 16, 1992, remained a mysterious figure who almost never met foreigners—but as day-to-day chief of the gov-ernment and party he had placed protégés in a great many key economics and foreign-relations posts. Some, such as Kim Dal-hyon, the deputy prime minister who was our host, were relatives. Still they represented "a changing of the guard," as Kim Duk-choong, former chief executive officer of South Korea's Daewoo Corporation, said during the trip. "All are young genera-tion— fifties and forties," he noted. "They're much more forthcoming than in the past."

True, Kim Dal-hyon's acknowledgment of serious economic difficulties had not yet become the party line; subordinates such as Kim Song-sik con-tinued to assert that all was well and the country was experiencing little ill ef-fect from the changes in other communist nations. And even Kim Dal-hyon insisted that his countrymen "do not have any worries about food, clothing and housing." Significantly, though, he acknowledged bluntly that "the world is changing" and that creation of special economic zones "is for our survival," in a world where "there are only a few countries following the so-cialist model."

Another small example of the new, more enlightened approach: North Korean officials seemed to have realized that outsiders had little stomach for hearing worshipful encomia to the wondrous leadership of President Kim Il-sung and his son Kim Jong-il. During our 1992 visit, unless they were asked specifically, they mercifully refrained from spouting the interminable old lines about how the Great or Dear Leader provided this or that factory of school out of love for the people, blah blah blah.

Some of the younger officials also embodied a fascinating answer to a very real question: In a country that neither taught nor understood free-market economics, where could one find competent managers for a push to join the global economy? It turned out that some of the rising economic stars had been trained in the sciences—one of the few areas in which a North Korean could get an education with a relatively small component of ideological cant. Kim Jong-u, vice-minister of external economic affairs and chairman of the Committee for the Promotion of External Economic Cooperation, had been a nuclear scientist. Deputy Premier Kim Dal-hyon himself had been a chemist and head of North Korea's Academy of Sciences.[11]

I had a glimpse of the quality of Kim Dal-hyon's mind during a press conference. He announced at the outset that he would take all questions first, and then answer them at once. Reporters groaned, fearing that this was his trick to avoid answering any questions he considered challenging. He insisted, though, so the reporters one after another stood to ask questions, giving Kim their toughest shots. Kim acknowledged the questions as they came, but did not note them down—which intensified our concern that we were about to be spun big time. But when all the questions were in, he gave a lengthy overall reply that actually answered all but a couple of the questions. When reporters reminded him that he had missed those, he answered them, too. The impression he gave with that performance was one of electrifying brilliance. Just listening to him raised my level of optimism about the North Korean economy by several notches.[12]

Alas, even the scientists-turned-economists offered no cure for North Korea's perennial allergy to dealing in hard statistics. "The main shortcoming of socialism is that we are not accustomed to figures," Kim Dal-hyon explained wryly, as he begged off giving cost figures for April 15 celebrations so extravagant that Kim Il-sung's eightieth birthday would do for a run-up to the Second Coming of Jesus. But at least the deputy premier showed some understanding of prospective investors' need to know just where they stood. "Detailed laws and regulations on preferential treatment for investors, free flow of people, visa and tax exemptions will be promulgated within this year," Kim promised. In the future the country could open additional free-trade zones in such cities as Wonsan and Nampo, "and also create free tourism areas." North Korea had joined the United Nations, simultaneously with South Korea in 1991, and Kim Dal-hyon hoped for help from international organizations in financing the infrastructure projects. "The major cost will be undertaken by our country, the Asian Development Bank and banks and businesses of other countries," he said. "We'll soon be admitted to the ADB."

The regime knew that it still had work to do before very many outsiders would be ready to plunk down their money. "We want to revise laws, and make special new laws for the zones alone, to satisfy your demands," Kim Dal-hyon said. "Our intention is to make a better zone than China's Shen-zhen." (Indeed, it turned out that new regulations were enacted on October 5,

1992. They offered foreign investors tax breaks, guaranteed them property rights and allowed remittance of some profits back home. Not only joint ventures, as before, but also wholly foreign-owned ventures were now permitted. South Koreans, barred by the 1984 law, could invest in the North under the law's new version.[13] Tax rates, published February 6, 1993, were more favorable to foreign investors than China's rates.[14])

While hardly anyone in North Korea had much experience with market economics, Yoo Jang-hee, president of the Korea Institute for International Economic Policy (KIEP), a Seoul think tank, and leader of the South Korean delegation, was encouraged that such new-generation officials at least understood "*their* kind of economics." Intriguing as the new approaches were, however, they did not represent a decision in favor of fundamental change. North Korean authorities remained impaled on the horns of an old dilemma: Although failure to open to investment by capitalists could doom the Pyongyang regime, so could the attitudes, knowledge and ideas that would enter the country along with such change. After all, how could a separate North Korean regime be justified once its subjects could see it had become merely an inferior imitation of the wildly successful capitalist Korea to the South?[15]

The solution that Kim Dal-hyon and his technocrats proposed sounded like the ultimate test of totalitarianism: establish free economic zones, but segregate them so tightly they would have no effect on people and institutions elsewhere in the country. Kim insisted that there should be little problem of other North Koreans envying the wages and living conditions of workers inside the zones, since "we believe in our people." But Kim Duk-choong and other visitors speculated that the regime had picked Rajin and Sonbong as the first free-trade zone precisely because the area was remote from main population centers. (Years later it was reported that the state was clearing out the zone's population, replacing it with new residents whose ideological commitment was considered beyond reproach.)

The experience of other countries such as China suggested that the economic apartheid envisioned would not work for long, and that real economic takeoff would both require and contribute to real market reform and opening. Pyongyang officials, however, had their marching orders. While capitalistic methods would be allowed in the trade zones, Kim Song-sik said, "we think we can keep those methods from affecting enterprises elsewhere in the country, where the government's economic policy is unchanged."

In addition to more rather than less control over the people, the strategy to accomplish such a containment of capitalist ideas envisioned even more intense propaganda efforts to whip up mass enthusiasm for the status quo. In April 1992, the regime unveiled a new stage extravaganza, *Song of Best*

Wishes, featuring a cast of thousands who wished Kim Il-sung a happy eight-ieth birthday and praised the system he had installed. "Winds of temptation may blow," the gigantic chorus sang, but "we'll go our way forever. Hey, hey, let's defend socialism!"

"There are quite a number of people on earth who are anxious to see our style of socialism corrupted by the filthy germ of revisionism," Kim Il-sung explained in a volume of his memoirs published around that time. "We do not want our Party to be reduced to a club or a market-place by the tendency of ultra-democracy. The suffering inflicted upon us by the evils of ultra-democracy in military affairs during the anti-Japanese war and the lessons of Eastern Europe cry out to us that we must not allow this."[16]

To prospective foreign investors, officials audaciously pointed out the discreet charms of totalitarianism—social stability not least among them. At his press conference, Kim Dal-hyon was asked whether workers for foreign firms would be subjected to the time-consuming ideological cheerleading sessions that workers in other enterprises were required to attend. Perhaps not, he indicated, but "I think our ideology will help the creation of the free economic zones. There won't be any thieves, punks or pimps in our zones. We are constantly educating our younger generation and our older population to work as hard as possible. In fact, the mission of the Three Revolutions teams—not that they will be in the zones—is to stimulate overproduction."

Indeed, a South Korean lawyer who was one of my companions on the trip marveled at the "naive, pure, unsophisticated" personalities of North Koreans he met. "These people know how to cooperate," he said. He noted the attentive hospitality and prompt service in hotels and restaurants, contrasting with the lackadaisical and even sullen behavior he had experienced in a communist neighbor, China. Irreverent Westerners might be tempted to credit lobotomies, or at least lifelong brainwashing, for the discipline displayed by North Koreans. But I reflected that true-believer cults everywhere do tend to produce devotees who exhibit sweet personalities—just think of the starry-eyed young cultists who, around that time, were accosting passersby for contributions in Western cities. The Kim Il-sung cult was no exception.

Still, most outsiders reacted warily. They were put off not only by the unlikely strategy of development without real change but also by Pyong-yang's general profile—from its record of debt default to its reputation for aggression to doubts about political stability once Kim Il-sung should pass from the scene. Particularly unexcited were Japanese, who had the resources, the proximity and the history of interest in the Korean peninsula to become a major factor if they should wish to do so. North Korea still had not paid its debts despite repeated reschedulings. Japan had heard offers to repay its portion in fish and in gold, but nothing ever had come of those, either. The Japanese government in the 1980s made export insurance payments to companies left in the lurch. In the process, Tokyo refused to offer any more export insurance. Some Japanese suggested it would be hard to take Pyongyang seriously until it began paying off the old debts with some of the money that had been going for monuments and birthday bashes. (Japanese general contractors were an obvious exception to the usual caution. Contractors eyed the Rajin-Sonbong and Chongjin port-expansion projects hungrily. They figured that normalization of Tokyo-Pyongyang diplomatic ties would come before too much longer, and with it Japanese aid. Such funding would pay for expensive construction contracts, of which Japanese contractors could hope to win the larger share.)

To those focused on the debt, Kim Dal-hyon asked for patience. "There is no reason we should pay these debts right at this moment," he said. "Creditor countries should understand the economic situation faced by socialist countries." Blood ties could go a long way toward producing the sort of understanding for which Kim Dal-hyon was pleading. In some periods there had been considerable talk of economic cooperation between North and South Korea. There were even reports of South Korean proposals to buy up some of the North Koreans' overseas debt, as a fraternal gesture.

South Koreans and their counterparts in the North had talked of cooperation in the past without much coming of it. In a July 7, 1988, special declaration, South Korean President Roh Tae-woo said it was time to improve North-South relations. As part of the process, he proposed introducing tariff-free North-South trade as if the two were a single country. Analysts at the time doubted that immediate results would amount to much. Actually, Roh's economic olive branch to the North had been motivated in part by a wish to give China and the Soviet Union an excuse to betray their Pyongyang ally by stepping up economic and political ties with Seoul.

Predictably, North Korea—still smarting over the 1988 Olympics and loath to get involved in an exchange that would expose its economic inferiority to its own people—had immediately dismissed Roh's offer as "nothing new." But Pyongyang's long-term need remained. North Korea with the collapse of communism elsewhere was thrown back on a form of *juche* that was too truly self-reliant for comfort. Now forced to do without the vital resources it had been accustomed to receiving from its communist brethren, the North badly needed reunification from an economic standpoint. To Seoul business leaders, meanwhile, the economies of North and South offered a complementary fit that was equally tempting, in a pure pocketbook sense. Transportation was one factor. Gaining rights to use North Korean railways and to overfly the North could save substantial sums for the South as it expanded its continental markets, particularly in China and Russia.

For the South, labor was another key factor, more important than natural resources. After all, South Korea had done without Northern natural resources, going abroad to buy replacements. Resource-poor South Korea now had enormous experience and know-how in producing world-class manufactured goods. But its very success had become a problem. By the 1990s, the South had encountered the typical rich-country problems of overpaid and complacent labor. Southern industrialists paid their workers ten times North Korean wages, while the picky Southern workers increasingly turned up their noses at jobs that combined the "three D's": dirty, dangerous and difficult. "Here we're trying to trade in our Hyundai Stellars," a Seoul resident said to me in 1991. Meanwhile in North Korea, he noted, the latest catchy public campaign slogan was, "Let's watch the stars while we work." The South's need for a cheap, hardworking labor force to continue its "economic miracle" sparked a revival of economic interest in unification.

Industrialists from the South could see considerable attraction in a polite, well-behaved population and a labor force that was low-paid for the moment and, apparently, highly disciplined. When we visited Pyongyang's Eguk Moran Garment Factory, the general manager, Jon Song-won, said of his employees: "They don't even know the word 'strike.'" His factory made suits for ethnic Korean buyers in Japan in exchange for materials and management costs plus a flat labor charge of $10 a suit. Someone asked Jon if he would be surprised to learn that the Japanese merchants buying the suits marked them up ten-fold or more before sale. Jon, almost as naive as his workers, replied: "I don't think they would do such a tricky thing."

For South Koreans, argued Kim Duk-choong, investing in the North was "less risky than investing in Southeast Asia. You're investing in your own country, in the long run." He was pleased that Kim Dal-hyon at his press conference remarked that he hoped South Koreans would be the first to invest in Rajin-Sonbong development, "because they are our own compatriots." Kim Duk-choong marveled: "It's the first time they expressed that: 'We welcome our brothers.'"

The fact that North Korea was playing up to prospective Japanese investors had helped—despite the unenthusiastic Japanese response—to trigger a competitive urge in the South to beat the former colonial master to the punch. The largest Southern corporate groups—Hyundai, Samsung, Daewoo, Lucky-Goldstar—had been excited enough by the long-term prospects to race each other in establishing task forces that would try to increase indirect trade with the North via third countries, and prepare for the day when direct trade would become a reality. Finally, on October 17, 1988, the government in Seoul had authorized private companies to trade with the North and permitted businessmen's exchanges.

Hyundai founder Chung Ju-yung had been the first to take advantage of the new dispensation, traveling to the North in January 1989 and returning with a tentative agreement on a $700 million joint project: development of a resort on both sides of the border around North Korea's scenic Mount Kumgang near the east coast. It was time to test Kim Jong-il's promise to China's Hu Yaobang that he would promote tourism. The Kumgang idea didn't sound totally preposterous. As Seoul architect-planner Kwaak Young-hoon told me, first-time visitors from the South tended to react to aspects of North Korea the way surveys showed first-time visitors reacting to Disneyland: Both were seen as "clean and friendly."

Political considerations had intervened, however. The collapse of East Germany in 1990 had triggered a major reassessment on both sides of the Korean Demilitarized Zone. The euphoria in Seoul had been palpable as some people predicted Korean reunification within five years. Southerners had licked their lips at what seemed the near-certainty that communism would self-destruct in North Korea without the South's having to lift a finger. As in Germany, reunification would come through absorption of the former communist state by the victorious capitalist state. Only then would the South invest in the North.

As a bonus, meanwhile, news of the demise of European communism had nipped in the bud the leftist radical movement in the South, in which Pyongyang had placed some hopes for the eventual peninsula-wide victory of Kim Il-sung's revolution. The idea of doing anything that could feed money into North Korea and help prolong its separate existence had become anathema in Seoul, especially to government officials. For two years after Chung Ju-yung's 1989 visit to Pyongyang, no other top-ranked South Korean businessman had followed in his footsteps.

Members of the North Korean elite had gone into shock upon hearing the fate of their East German counterparts. In the new, unified Germany, Easterners initially seemed to have no claim to leadership and its perquisites—or even, in some cases, to decent jobs. That precedent had been as horrifying to Pyongyang as German unification had been inspirational to Seoul. Indeed, avoiding "absorption" had become an obsession in Pyongyang.[17]

By early 1992, Pyongyang's panic over the prospect of absorption seemed to have abated slightly. The regime might have felt that a campaign to frighten any wavering members of its elite class and unify them around the Kim Il-sung and Kim Jong-il leadership was succeeding. As part of the campaign, North Korean television broadcast a documentary showing former East German officials looking for jobs and peddling hot dogs on the street.[18]

No doubt another cause for at least momentary relaxation in Pyongyang was a shift of opinion in South Korea so drastic that it appeared, for the moment, that the interests of the Northern and Southern regimes might actually overlap. German unification had proven so expensive that many South Koreans who had looked forward to a quick, German-style reunification of

Korea now came to hope for a more gradual process, one that would allow time for the North to build up its economy so it would represent less of a burden to a prospective merger partner.

"German reunification is a good example of the worst case," said Park Young-kyu, a scholar at Seoul's Research Institute for National Reunification and one of the South Koreans on the trip. South Korea's Finance Ministry estimated that the price tag, if the South should have to absorb the Northern economy before the year 2000, would be $980 billion—more than three times the South's then-current gross national product of $280 billion.[19] Such estimates took into account the needs for worker retraining, improvements in infrastructure such as roads and ports, social welfare benefits for Northerners and costs for environmental cleanup and administrative integration. One South Korean government-sponsored think tank reported that some 70 percent of East German firms would fail to survive reunification, and 20 percent of East Germans would lose their jobs in the process. As the North Korean economy stood then, the post-reunification job loss there would be far greater, on the order of 50 percent, said the Korea Institute of Economy and Technology.[20]

Many economists feared that the gap in incomes and living standards had grown too wide to permit splicing the two Korean economies together. The South was approaching a $7,000 per capita income, while the North was declining from a high that might have approached the $1,000 level.[21] A consensus was building in South Korea that Seoul must help Pyongyang close that gap—and in the process help prop up the North Korean economy. As a theoretical bonus, prosperity presumably would make Pyongyang easier to deal with.

Meanwhile, soaring labor costs had punched the export-based South Korean economy in the solar plexus—driving home the humbling lesson that a relatively scrawny Seoul would be much harder pressed than heavyweight Bonn to avoid the consequences of a sudden reunification. In their nightmares, Seoul residents saw their capital overrun by destitute Northern cousins fleeing south to pursue dreams of the good life. The Finance Ministry proposed severe limits on cross-border travel in the initial post-reunification period—with an exception for the divided families whom the South sought to reunite.[22] One Western diplomat with long experience studying Korean society painted for me an even more forbidding picture. "Abrupt unification along the lines of East and West Germany would be a disaster," he told me in August 1991. "If they were to reunify today, the South Koreans would take over everything. North Koreans would be the underlings—the guys sweeping, or wiping the babies' asses." Unlike the people from South Korea's Cholla provinces, who previously had taken such menial roles in Seoul, North Koreans "are not stoic," the diplomat said. "They wouldn't take it. They'd get real violent real quick."

Seoul's Korea Institute of Economy and Technology, among others, argued that the South should help develop new, more competitive industry in the North *before* reunification to minimize such disruptions. The message went over expecially well with one particular group of South Koreans. Shin Woong-shik, a Seoul lawyer specializing in legal dealings with Pyongyang, went on the trip and told me that much of the Southern interest came from among the millions of South Koreans who hailed from the North. Before and during the Korean War people from the North, many of them from the upper socioeconomic groups purged by the communists, had migrated to the South. Himself the grandson of the operator of a gold mine in what became North Korea, Shin said many rich, Northern-born South Koreans had sentimental reasons for helping to develop their home region. Topping the list were Daewoo Group Chairman Kim Woo-choong and Hyundai founder Chung Ju-yung—the latter an unsuccessful candidate for president of South Korea, in the December 18, 1992, election.[23]

In May of 1991, Daewoo's Kim Woo-choong had gone to Pyongyang and discussed both commodity trade and joint manufacturing ventures in such fields as textiles and electronics. The South had traded rice for North Korean coal and cement later that summer—directly, without routing the ship through a third country as in past trade arrangements. That was a third-flag ship, to be sure, but the South had begun to study the possibility of opening a regular shipping service between the two Koreas. Also under study were a proposed settlement account between Seoul's Export-Import Bank and Pyongyang's Foreign Trade Bank, to clear payments once direct trade should become active, and eventual issuance of soft loans to North Korea. In August of 1991, the South's President Roh himself had registered his government's support for joint ventures, not just the trade that had been encouraged in the past. Negotiations resumed on joint tourist development around Mount Kumgang. Besides such projects and joint development of North Korean natural resources, there had been some talk of joint fisheries zones and of joint ventures in third countries—specifically, using North Korean labor in construction and development projects overseen by South Korean contractors in places like Pakistan and the Middle East and in logging schemes in Russia.

Up to the time of our visit, Daewoo Group had made the closest thing to an actual investment deal. Chairman Kim Woo-choong (whose brother, Kim Duk-choong, was on our trip) had gone to Pyongyang at Deputy Premier Kim Dal-hyon's invitation in January 1992. While there, he had signed a contract for a joint venture in which the Northern regime would provide the land and the labor for a big industrial complex at the west coast port of Nampo—which Pyongyang would designate as another free trade zone. Daewoo would provide capital and technology and help operate nine factories, making textiles, garments, shoes, luggage, stuffed toys and household utensils. The Daewoo chairman was on record as expressing confidence that the factories could export $10 billion worth of goods a year.

In view of such developments, it was tempting during much of 1992 to foresee that investment in North Korea might proceed according to what might be called the China pattern. When China a decade before had set out to reform its economy and attract outside investment, Japanese and Western business people and financiers had watched with interest—but put down relatively little money, particularly at the beginning. The largest part of the outside investment came from co-ethnics: Chinese in Hong Kong and abroad. Seoul lawyer Shin argued that North Korea, like China, was more fortunate in its built-in overseas network than the likes of Vietnam, Cambodia and Cuba—which "don't have brother countries." Indeed, it seemed a good bet that, for a while at least, the bulk of any significant investment in North Korea would come from ethnic Koreans abroad—not only in Japan and the United States[24] but, especially, in South Korea.

Although some South Koreans still argued that the South should not lift a finger to prevent a collapse of the North's system, Southerners who were on the tour generally took a contrary view. To many of the visitors the odds at long last seemed to have shifted decisively in favor of economic reform in the North; although the process would take years, they wanted to encourage reform because it would bode well for North-South detente and, down the road, a relatively smooth reunification. "If you get wealthier you'll get more flexible," observed economic researcher Kim Ick-soo.

Such optimistic thinking, however, soon fell victim to more politics. Shortly after Daewoo's Chairman Kim signed letters of intent with Pyongyang—and before a contract could win the required approval by the South Korean authorities—the Seoul government suspended all economic cooperation talks and banned all economic exchanges. To get the ban lifted, the government said, Pyongyang must go through with its agreement to permit inspections by North and South Korea of each other's suspected nuclear-weapons facilities.

TWENTY-EIGHT

Sea of Fire

One is pleased to see the bugs die in a fire even though one's house is burned down.

—KIM IL-SUNG[1]

Was Kim Il-sung an East Asian Saddam Hussein? There certainly were some similarities. With a ruthlessness that would have won Saddam's approval, Kim consolidated his power after being installed by Soviet troops in 1945, purging members of rival factions. Afterward he displayed what we might now describe as a Saddamesque love of sycophancy and aversion to hearing straight factual reports that might conflict with his views. And when Kim started the Korean War in 1950 by invading the South, he guessed wrong—as Saddam was to do in 1990 and again in 2003—about American resolve and found his own military capabilities quickly overrun. If the Chinese "volunteers" had not come to the rescue and taken over the war effort from Kim and his Korean People's Army, the struggle would have ended in regime change.

That was not to say, however, that he would make the same mistake twice. Kim had presided over an enormous amount of construction. Although his people suffered, and were about to suffer even worse, up until the 1990s the citizens of truly destitute Third World countries would have welcomed a North Korean standard of development. Miscalculating and waging a war—without Soviet or Chinese help—would have brought the certain destruction of all the North's economic achievements and of Kim's and his son's dreams of dynastic rule. Kim's caution in not attacking since that first mistake in 1950—he didn't move even when Seoul was engulfed several times in anti-government riots—suggested, as did his age, that he would not do so now that South Korea's superiority had become so evident.

Seoul-based analyst Kim Chang-soon said as the first North Korean nuclear crisis raged that in the wake of Desert Storm, the U.S.-led assault that cancelled Iraq's conquest of Kuwait, "I don't think any North Korean leaders believe they can win a war with their present weapons systems. They are developing nuclear weapons not to win a war but to deter and to avoid losing a war." Japanese Korea-watcher Katsumi Sato offered a similar assessment: "They don't have enough oil to make war." Still, it was believed that Kim could not help but dream that the South's people would prepare the way for him or his son one day. "They are thinking of keeping a military balance, and also they hope that the South may some day experience a crisis of domestic chaos so that a Vietnam-type war could be waged," said Kim Chang-soon.

Kim Il-sung had pretty much transferred day-to-day power to his son except in three fields, experts believed. Those three were foreign diplomacy, North-South relations and the military. Kim senior remained chairman of the military commission while Kim Jong-il was number two. The military had always been the older man's base, and there was little evidence of disloyalty. But many in the South and elsewhere theorized that once Kim Il-sung died, a movement would arise within the military to kick out Kim Jong-il and install a military government similar to the one under which South Korea had modernized. That was only speculation, of course. The point is that Kim Il-sung himself—not his son—was believed to be in charge of the military and of any decision to attack or not. The assumption was reassuring to many analysts. The elder Kim had been around for long enough and seen enough world leaders that they could at least make a stab at figuring him out. The younger Kim had been unwilling to have much to do with foreigners and was a largely unknown quantity. Only a few odd traits such as his movies fetish were known.

The consensus of those abroad who had thought about it—and it was faint praise, indeed—was that they would much rather try to deal with Daddy while he remained alive than take their chances with Junior.

Not only in title, however, but also in fact—as defector testimony since then makes clear—Kim Jong-il's power was increasing, so much so that his father became almost a figurehead. People's Army First Lieutenant Lim Yong-son, who defected in 1993, recalled that in 1988 Kim Il-sung had instructed the army, "As you have been following me in participating in a revolution, from now on follow the orders of the Central Committee's secretary for organization, Kim Jong-il." At that point, "inside the military, people thought Kim Jong-il didn't have the ability to rule," Lim said. Some officers pointed out, "He didn't even enlist in the army. He went to university and spent only one month or so in military camp. He doesn't know how to lead the army. If we make war with Kim Jong-il as our leader, we will all die."

The Kims brushed aside soldiers' private reservations. In December 1991, Kim Jong-il took over as supreme commander of the People's Army. In April 1992, he was named to the top military rank of marshal alongside only one other soldier of that exalted status, O Jin-u. (His father was promoted that year from marshal to a newly created super rank translated as generalissimo or grand marshal.) That day, said Lim, Kim Jong-il "was supposed to wear a marshal's uniform, but he declined. O Jin-u told him, 'You should wear it!' But Kim Jong-il said, 'It's not suitable for me to wear a clean marshal's uniform. That uniform should be torn with shrapnel.'" Lim related this bit of army lore (which I also heard from another former military man) explicitly to illustrate the new marshal's bellicosity. But the anecdote also suggests that Kim Jong-il felt—or wanted to be perceived as feeling—something akin to modesty.[2]

On April 25, 1993, the sixtieth anniversary of the People's Army, Kim Jong-il became chairman of the party's military commission. Reviewing a military parade that day, he had to give a short speech before an assembled multitude. Although he uttered just a single sentence invoking glory upon the armed forces, delivering a message in person to such a vast audience was an unaccustomed task. One former high official who watched the event on a videotape in Seoul told me, "I saw Kim Il-sung turned toward Kim Jong-il with an expression of concern—could he make it through his phrase?"

The younger Kim did make it through, smoothly enough. But rumors spread that he had a speech problem, a former army sergeant, Lee Chong-guk, told me. Even if that was the case, however, public speaking may have been the least of Kim Jong-il's problems. "Kim Il-sung was idolized," Lee said, "but for Kim Jong-il, there are only bad rumors, like the *kippeunjo*. Although there were rumors that Kim Il-sung had a five-year-old son, he was idolized anyhow because of his role in the anti-Japanese struggle and the Korean War. As for Kim Jong-il, it's rumored that he sleeps in the afternoon, parties at night and has affairs with actresses. Nothing good is said about Kim Jong-il."

"At first, Kim Il-sung made a conscious effort to hand over power to his son," said former party secretary Hwang Jang-yop. "But as Kim Jong-il began to take control of every area of the government, there was nothing Kim Il-sung could do to control his son anymore. By the 1990s, Kim Il-sung was merely an advisor to his son. But they were father and son, with father having an

interest in passing his power down to his son and son having an interest in
using the authority of his father. So any conflict between the two did not surface." Kim Jong-il's promotion to commander in chief of the People's Army
in 1991 signaled "the end of the transition of power from father to son," according to Hwang. "The entire party and nation of North Korea must swear
unconditional obedience to the commands of the People's Army commander
in chief. Eventually things came to the point where Kim Il-sung actually had
to suck up to his son. On Kim Jong-il's fiftieth birthday in 1992, Kim Il-sung
wrote a ridiculous ode of praise about a king honoring his royal heir, proving
once again the cold-hearted political theory that power defines everything."
The poem:

> Heaven and earth shake
> With the resounding cheers
> Of all the people
> United in praising him.[3]

Kim Jong-il proceeded to use his chairmanship of the military commission to change the North Korean system from a party dictatorship to a military dictatorship. "In the army," said Hwang Jang-yop, "there is the Defense
Headquarters, which is under the direct supervision of Kim Jong-il. Agents
of this Defense Headquarters are stationed at every level of the military right
down to the platoon, and are in charge of monitoring the movements of the
soldiers. The Defense Headquarters has enormous power, authorized to arrest even civilians if necessary. In this regard, even the Ministry of State Security and Defense is under the surveillance of the Defense Headquarters.
In recent years, as the North Korean economy faced bankruptcy and food
rations got cut off, the regime could no longer maintain its tight control over
the people through the old methods alone. So the North Korean rulers are
committing armed forces to the effort to maintain the dictatorship of the
Great Leader." Calling the results a "blatant military dictatorship," Hwang
said the army began "keeping law and order in all the agricultural cooperatives, factories and markets in North Korea."[4]

Starting in May 1992, Pyongyang permitted some international inspections at
Yongbyon. In view of its economic straits there was reason to hope it might
soon decide the price was right to accept a complete inspection program or
otherwise relinquish its nuclear card. South Korean companies hoping for a
breakthrough on the nuclear issue continued to prepare to act quickly once
the ban on dealing with the North should be lifted. Executives of the Daewoo,
Samsung and Lucky Goldstar conglomerates had meetings with North Korean Deputy Premier Kim Dal-hyon in Beijing as late as December of 1992.[5]

On March 8, 1993, though, Kim Jong-il announced that he was placing the nation on a "semi-war" footing during the U.S.–South Korean Team Spirit exercise. At rallies, North Koreans pledged loyalty to Kim Jong-il. "If the enemies trample upon an inch of land or a blade of grass of our country, we will become bullets and bombs to annihilate them," one participant said.[6]

In the capital, where soldiers from elite families tended to be posted, Sgt. Lee Chong-guk joined 5,000 comrades rallying in a gymnasium. "All heads were shaved in the army; I thought war was coming soon," Lee said after his defection to South Korea the following year. A small man, looking younger than his twenty-five years, Lee when I met him was no longer shaven-headed; he had let his hair grow long according to Southern fashion. He described the atmosphere of hysteria among those rallying in the gym and elsewhere in North Korea: a widespread feeling that North Koreans had nothing more to lose and might as well embrace their fate, fight to the end and be done with it. "I felt isolation," Lee recalled. "I believed North Korea was on its own, without allies. In the case of East Germany, the high-ranking people hadn't done well after reunification. I thought change was not good for us in the elite class. We were singing and waving red flags." By that time, Kim Jong-il's name had replaced Kim Il-sung's in military slogans and songs; soldiers were studying the "revolutionary history" of the younger Kim. Lee recalled the verses of the song the soldiers had sung that day, "Without You There Is No Country":

Pushing away the fierce cyclone,
Marshal Kim Jong-il gave us faith.

(Chorus) Without You there is no us,
Without You there is no country.

Takes care of our future and our hopes,
Our nation's fate: Marshal Kim Jong-il.

Even though the world is overturned a hundred times,
Still the people believe in Marshal Kim Jong-il.

"We were crying together at our fate," Lee told me. "Kim Jong-Il attended, without saying anything—but then Kim Jong-il never says anything in public. As we sang about the world being 'overturned a hundred times,' we were thinking that *our* world would be overturned and it would be bad for *us*. We were crying for ourselves." Soldiers in Pyongyang normally were not supplied live ammunition, presumably for fear they would mount a coup, Lee said, but on that occasion bullets were issued even to troops in the capital.

They were told to don helmets. The government announced a curfew, and residents who did not already have bomb shelters began digging them.

Lee had been assigned as a noncommissioned officer to the Bureau of Nuclear and Chemical Defense since 1990. "Since the enemy is the United States and the United States possesses nukes, North Koreans feel they should also possess them," Lee told me. "I believe they'd use them if war broke out."

Lee believed that war was imminent and that it would be cataclysmic for all Koreans, North and South. In that regard, he had more to say about chemical than nuclear weapons. One of the privileged young men permitted formal study beyond high school, he had majored in biochemistry at Pyongsong University before enlisting. His military job was translating foreign journals. Following his arrival in Seoul in 1994, he warned publicly that his military superiors had claimed that North Korea had the capability to wipe out the South Korean population with chemical weapons as well as wreaking havoc on Japan.

I asked Lee how his superiors justified their talk of killing 40 million South Koreans. "They're saying every South Korean is full of anti-communist ideology," he explained. "When we reunite the country we can't make them communists, so we should get rid of them." One officer in Lee's unit, Lieutenant Colonel Hwang Chang-pyong, had made clear that genocide was on his mind when, in August 1993, he taught in an ideology course that "not only the U.S. army, or the South Korean army—everybody should die."

Lee was less than a true believer by the time he heard those chilling words. "I had started having doubts about the regime when I was in the university," he said. "I wondered if capitalism was better." He failed to buy Hwang's argument, believing that fighting American and South Korean soldiers was one thing; massacring civilians, quite another. He kept silent, though—"It's hard to voice your opinion," he said—and had no idea how many of his comrades agreed with the officer.

Lt. Col. Hwang, who from Lee's description sounded to me like Pyongyang's version of Dr. Strangelove, was "one of the North Koreans most intensely loyal to Kim Il-sung," Lee said. "He graduated from three universities and is a very important person in the development of nuclear and chemical weapons in North Korea. The development wouldn't take place without him. Kim Jong-il during his birthday celebration personally thanked Hwang and gave him a commendation."

Lee explained the structure of chemical weapons development. "The Thirty-second Division is involved in making chemical weapons in Sakju, North Pyongan province, and Kanggye in Chagang province," he said. "The products are sent for storage in Yongsong Maram in Pyongyang, also to Ji-hari Sansa in Anbyon County and to Anbyon County in Kangwon Province. Then they are distributed to each army section. There is a training and experiment site in Sokan-ri, Pyongwon County, South Pyongan Province. The nuclear and chemical Eighteenth Division is there."

Next to the Eighteenth Division, Lee added, "there is a cemetery for victims of experiments gone awry, and of accidents. Soldiers are trained for chemical war, but even though they wear gas masks some of them die accidentally. Often they die inside the tanks, even with their masks on. They basically think that inside the tanks they are safe."

Quoting North Korea's warning that it could turn Seoul into a "sea of fire," Lee said he believed it was possible and believed that the North had delivery systems sufficient to ensure that chemical weapons could figure in a major way in such an assault. While he was in North Korea, he said, he had expected "a nuclear war, spreading chemical weapons, in which the South Koreans would all be killed." But death would be the lot of the Northerners as well. "It wasn't a matter of winning or losing. If war broke out, everyone would die, North and South. Everybody else in the North also believes it."

When I asked him to reconcile that assertion with his earlier statement that North Koreans actively wanted the war to start, he explained, "Even though they knew the outcome, they were so starved. It's either die of starvation or die in war." Lee, who as a member of an elite unit was not starving, did not want war and, he told me, believed it was up to him to do something about it. Because his parents were dead and thus out of the regime's reach, "it was easier for me than for others to decide to defect and tell South Koreans about the current situation with chemical and nuclear weapons."

Contributing to Lee's sense of urgency, Kim Jong-il had told the military to plan on achieving reunification by 1995, which the Dear Leader believed—mistakenly, as it turned out—would be in time for his father to see the promised land before his death. "I believed that I had to warn South Koreans about these weapons," Lee said. "I didn't want either North or South to be destroyed." He rode by train to the North Korean side of the Yalu River, managed to cross the river and, in China, met some South Koreans who helped him get to Seoul via a third country. When I met him he had not yet made plans for a new career.[7]

On March 13, 1993, Pyongyang stunned the world with an announcement that it was withdrawing from the Nuclear Nonproliferation Treaty (NPT.) The statement complained that proposed International Atomic Energy Agency inspections of two secret North Korean sites—which it called non-nuclear military installations—would be an unjustified intrusion on sovereignty. It also cited the U.S.–South Korean military exercise Team Spirit, then in

progress, calling it a rehearsal for a nuclear attack on the North. If not reversed, Pyongyang's withdrawal could seriously undermine the global NPT
system and set off a nuclear arms race among the two Koreas and Japan.
Thus it triggered a flurry of consultations in world capitals.[8]

Pyongyang went out of its way to let it be known that the decision to
withdraw from the NPT had been made by Kim Jong-il. The implication
was that he had so fully taken over the reins of state from his father that he
could make such an important decision on his own. Advertising his take-
charge role seems to have been part of the decades-long process of making
his succession a fait accompli.

Assuming that he did make the withdrawal decision himself,[9] what was
Kim Jong-il thinking? Consider some of the background to the presumed
decisions to begin and then to continue work on nuclear weapons. For many
years the obvious trend had been toward a reversal in the military balance,
from Northern to Southern superiority. Then, the Gulf War had shown Kim
Il-sung and Kim Jong-il two important facts. First, the U.S. military had
conventional forces so potent, thanks in part to new weapons systems, that
they could all but wipe out the Iraqi military in a matter of a few days—and
probably would have a similar conventional-war advantage over North Korea. For Pyongyang that emphasized the need to develop an equalizer. The
second thing Pyongyang learned reinforced the lesson: Despite all that the
United States and its allies threw at him in 1991, Saddam Hussein nonetheless hung on to power, thumbing his nose at Washington and at international
nuclear inspectors.

There is another factor that must have figured in Pyongyang's ferocious
reaction to Team Spirit. Kim Jong-il would have recognized that elements in
the North Korean military might use a future exercise and their own responsive maneuvers as, respectively, pretext and cover for a coup d'etat.

By March of 1993, in South Korea, a new president with a totally civilian background, Kim Young-sam, had taken office and begun immediately to
dismantle the remaining police-state apparatus instituted by his army general predecessors—making Pyongyang look even worse than before by comparison.

Talks with Japan finally had been suspended in November of 1992, after
North Korea had objected that Tokyo was making nuclear inspections a condition for establishing diplomatic ties.[10] Pyongyang's main ally in wringing
money out of Japan, Kanemaru, had lost his post as ruling party boss and
fallen so low as to be indicted, in March of 1993, for massive tax evasion.
With Japan, the United States and South Korea united in insisting that the
North prove itself atomically clean before receiving any aid, it was hard to
find the leverage to work out a favorable deal.

Subsequent events suggest that Pyongyang never had really reconciled
itself to the idea of giving up whatever nuclear capability it had developed,

but reasoned that the bomb was useful insurance and hoped to hang onto it through subterfuge while pretending to submit to NPT restrictions that had been less than effective in deterring other countries from bomb programs.

Under such circumstances, when the International Atomic Energy Agency set a deadline for the stringent new inspections and forced his hand, Kim Jong-il may have figured he had little to lose by raising the stakes for Washington, Tokyo and Seoul. Possible gains could include the direct high-level negotiations with Washington that Pyongyang had sought for years, focusing on both economic incentives and security inducements for Pyongyang to drop out of the nuclear club. As a bonus, the move would shock Kim Young-sam's fledgling administration, perhaps contributing to the political instability that Pyongyang liked to see in Seoul. And the decision gave Kim Jong-il the chance to swagger on the world stage and impress his own people.

Citing Team Spirit as justification for the North Korean move might have seemed at first glance largely a rhetorical flourish. The exercise was an otherwise annual one that Washington and Seoul had suspended the previous year as an inducement to the North to settle the nuclear and other issues. Even after resuming it they invited Pyongyang to send observers so they could see for themselves that it was a "purely defensive" exercise.

Former North Korean diplomat Ko Young-hwan told me the leadership whipped up the "threat" for popular consumption. "Up to now," Ko said, "Kim Jong-il and Kim Il-sung know that Team Spirit will not be an invasion. But they used that kind of mentality to manipulate North Koreans' feelings. They're still using that mentality. Most people believe that it is true. You might speculate as to how the citizens of North Korea actually believe in the Team Spirit threat. You can't understand it unless you've lived in North Korea. They have regular civil-defense exercises, black sheets over the windows. Such frequent practice makes people believe in the threat. From all ranks, up to higher officials, people still blame Americans and South Koreans for their problems. If some have a different view, they are probably diplomats or others who have traveled abroad."

On the other hand, Pyongyang's own war plans for achieving surprise in the invasion of South Korea in 1950 had emphasized the use of mock military exercises as a cover for hostile troop movements. "We had put a particular amount of effort into concealing this large-scale troop movement as training," Yu Song-chol, one of Pyongyang's Korean War planners, told a South Korean interviewer in 1990. "To do this, we passed bogus mobility training plans not via encoded communications, as is normally done, but rather through plain-text wire communications. Even training evaluation reports were passed in plain text via wire. . . . Of course, the South had monitored such exchange of messages."[11] Thus Pyongyang's perennial complaints that Washington and Seoul could use Team Spirit in just that way did represent the voice of experience.

But Pyongyang's shrillness on the Team Spirit question if anything had increased. Besides apprehension of a threat of an invasion from the South, that may have involved new factors that had surfaced domestically. One such factor, often noted, was the severe fuel shortage: Cranking up tanks and trucks and planes to shadow the other side's troop movements during Team Spirit—just in case they might turn into actual aggression—must be paid for with further reduction of economic activity. Also, Kim Jong-il had personally taken credit for the suspension of Team Spirit in 1991. Thus, as South Korean Foreign Minister Han Sung-joo told foreign correspondents,[12] Kim would have felt when the exercise was resumed that he needed to regain face that he had lost.

Lt. Lim Yong-son offered another bit of army scuttlebutt describing a meeting among Kim Il-sung, Kim Jong-il, Marshal O Jin-u and Prime Minister Kang Song-san in which the Great Leader asked what would happen if war broke out and North Korea lost. O and Kang agreed: "We would never lose." Kim Il-sung then asked Kim Jong-il; "*But*, what would happen if we *did* lose?" Kim Jong-il's reply: "If we lose, I will destroy the world." According to the story, Kim Il-sung thereupon said, "You're very brave and it's good thinking. You're definitely talking the way a marshal should talk."

How dire was the situation of North Koreans as the first nuclear crisis played out? Kim Dae-ho, the former teenage gang fighter whose job was treating water that had been used for uranium processing, received good material benefits by North Korean standards, he told me—but only until 1993. "To be able to work in an industry like this means you're better off than other North Koreans," he said. Beginning in 1993, however, "my ration was delayed just like others. In that atomic industry facility at Namchon there had been a great commissary. We had received rations like cooking oil and 80 to 100 grams of candy a day. Starting in 1993 those rations were cancelled and we didn't get any. In May of 1993, the grain ration was delayed. In September of 1993, the commissary was closed. Since 1986 the government had been giving reasons for delayed rations. Every year they had given the same reasons. Now they just said, 'We don't have it so we can't give it to you.'" Kim Dae-ho defected in February 1994, in his thirty-fifth year.

Outsiders knowledgeable about the North could not help speculating darkly about some act of back-to-the-wall desperation, something that might feel good to the Pyongyang leadership at the time and distract the people from their very real and increasing problems. Pyongyang was likely, some thought, to lash out externally; the NPT withdrawal and the "war footing" could be seen as precursors. One Japanese Korea-watcher speculated that the fallback position was for Pyongyang, following imposition of international sanctions, to announce it had the bomb—and then actually threaten to use it, on South Korea or on Japan. A British defense expert, Paul Beaver of Jane's Sentinel intelligence database, said Pyongyang still lacked the delivery system but had a bomb—so "the only thing they could do at the moment is blow themselves up." Beaver added that he couldn't rule out a suicidal gesture.[13]

North Korea, thanks to the Kims' reluctance to change, seemed to offer the perfect example of what Yale University historian Paul Kennedy had begun referring to as a "failed state."[14] That only accentuated the questions of sanity and judgment asked about the Kims for decades. Thankfully, however, ever since 1953, Kim Il-sung's military behavior had been more or less in his regime's rational self-interest. And while Kim Jong-il was much less of a known quantity, his NPT withdrawal was not irrational. In the end it would have to be counted a shrewd ploy that increased his negotiating leverage and his regime's short-to-medium-term security.

But the pressure was on Kim Il-sung and Kim Jong-il in a way it had not been on European communist leaders who failed to foresee their fate. The Kims knew the Europeans and had already seen the fate of, for example, Nicolae and Elena Ceausescu, the Romanian dictator and his wife who were executed by a firing squad during the December 1989 anticommunist revolt.[15] Their own symptoms of megalomania aside, the Kims were busily inducing paranoia in people loyal to them. During the "semi-war" footing in March of 1993 Pyongyang reported that some 1.5 million people volunteered to join the army, and many signed oaths in blood declaring their readiness to fight with their lives for Kim Il-sung and Kim Jong-il in a "sacred war of reunification."[16]

The thought of millions of Kim-worshipping youngsters willing to make themselves cannon fodder troubled outsiders who were aware of what was happening. The timing was eerie. Even granting a Russian expert's contention that the rate of fanaticism among adult members of the elite was as low as 10 percent,[17] there were grounds to worry that North Korea in the worst case might come to resemble what authorities in Waco, Texas, were facing at precisely the same time in dealing with the Branch Davidians. That was a cult not so very different, except in scale, from the North Korean cult of Kim and Kim. But waiting out Pyongyang would be many, many times more harrowing. After all, David Koresh was not thought to have stocked an A-bomb in his compound.

Speculation centered on how long the junior Kim could last in power before being challenged by elements in the elite party bureaucracy or the military, and on what sort of regime would emerge and how it would approach the South. In the Gang of Four scenario, which appealed to some foreign analysts, the younger Kim and others who had been close to his father could be blamed for the excesses of the elder's regime—recall how Mao Zedong's reformist successors had jailed his widow and top ideologues for having orchestrated the disastrous Cultural Revolution. Some Pyongyang watchers, on the other hand, still hoped the junior Kim could turn out to be a credible reformer in his own right, a Korean Gorbachev. Others suggested that elements in the North Korean military might inaugurate a new development-oriented regime modeled on the highly successful, albeit authoritarian, government that General Park Chung-hee had established in the South in 1961.[18]

"If the teenagers wail and lament at the chaos of reality, and bear a grudge against their parents, people in power and the world in general," Kim Il-sung wrote in a volume of his memoirs published in the early 1990s, "then the revolution of that country has no future or its prospects are at best gloomy."[19]

Former diplomat Ko Young-hwan had told me that the Team Spirit invasion threat was hyped for popular consumption. I asked Ko whether Kim Il-sung saw the real threat as an internal one. "Based on his actions I think he knows the threat is internal," Ko said. "The formation of the secret police could reveal his fear of internal foes. When I say secret police I mean State Security, formed in the 1960s, whose power has been ever increasing. This shows Kim Il-sung's concern."

Although the education system up through high school and the military still produced fanatics, Ko added, "the 22–29 group is a threat to Kim Jong-il because they know only his [poor] rule. The 30s-to-50s group still has nostalgia for the Kim Il-sung days, which they can remember. There's so much reform all over the world. The young ones hear the news and look for a change in North Korea, too. In the meantime the regime is emphasizing reeducation of the youngsters regarding ideals. It fears they are caught up in bourgeois ideas and think that poses a great threat."

There was considerable evidence during the period of that first nuclear crisis that the Kims, father and son, were afflicted with a serious case of the jitters. According to Lt. Lim Yong-son, Kim Jong-il early in 1991 ordered State Security political officials to be "owl-eyed" and to step up regulation, in order to preserve the regime. "When selecting party members, diligence and loyalty had been the most important criteria but that changed to family background," Lim said. "In the past about 80 percent of KPA members had been able to enter the party, but now only around 10 percent get in."

In 1992, Lim said, "Kim Jong-il issued another order, number 0027, to all soldiers in the People's Army, saying we must increase our struggle against the nonsocialist forces and build a revolutionist and belligerent state.

In the Ministry of the People's Armed Forces they increased the State Security presence and changed the structure some. All leaders in the army, especially those known to be political dissidents and those who had taken bribes, were subjected to intensified telephone bugging. It was the same on our base. I heard this from the person in charge of the communication department. General officers were bugged. Starting in October 1992, any army officer against whom there was evidence of opposition to the regime, bribery or improper use of government property was expelled. I guess that was because of what had happened in the eastern European countries. Kim Jong-il feared outside influences and wanted to strengthen the regime."[20]

Kang Myong-do, son-in-law of Prime Minister Kang Song-san, recalled that the fearful atmosphere affected members of the elite in general. "People would always get together and ask, 'Can North Korea survive this year? Should we defect to Europe or the United States?' In 1992 and 1993, the leaders' apprehension was more severe than South Koreans thought. They became more distressed when East Germany, Hungary and the Soviet Union collapsed. The biggest shock was the collapse of the Soviet Union. The worst year was 1993. The harvest was bad and there wasn't enough food. As people became distressed, lots of them secretly prepared to defect. They hoped to get their children out first, in foreign study programs. Also, they accumulated lots of dollars secretly. Even Kim Jong-il was sort of scared. He has special armed teams around him, a Swiss bank account with maybe a couple of billion dollars. He appointed an honor guard in case of coup d'état and kept them armed even as he prepared for exile in that contingency. Near Pyongyang he has a special airstrip with planes kept in case he needs to make a getaway."

Former ideology chief Hwang Jang-yop elaborated on the facilities for a top-level escape: "To guarantee secrecy of the Great Leader's daily activities as well as his personal safety in times of war, there is a whole network of underground tunnels in Pyongyang that run deeper than the subway," which is 80 to 100 meters deep. "Those underground tunnels are connected all the way to Mount Jamo in Sunchon, South Pyongan province," about 25 miles from downtown Pyongyang. On that mountain, Hwang said, "there is not only a royal villa but also an airport. The North Korean leaders claim that they built the royal villa there because the air at 600 meters above sea level was ideal for the Great Leader's health, but considering that the place is accessible through the underground tunnels, it was probably built with an emergency escape route in mind."[21]

According to Kang Myong-do, North Korean members of the elite "felt a lot of tension and fear in May 1993 when Secretary of Defense William Perry talked about bombing Yongbyon. Kim Jong-il could not even go out. He stayed in his office. All Central Committee members were wearing military uniforms and carrying guns. From outside, North Korea seemed very confident, talking of full-scale war. But the ruling class in Pyongyang was really apprehensive of a U.S. attack, even though I believe North Korea possesses nuclear weapons—five nuclear missiles. This I heard from the State Security person in charge of political affairs at the Yongbyong nuclear facility. I see no reason why he would have lied to me." Kang said a number of Russian specialists, freelancing for lack of remunerative work at home, "were working with the People's Army on nuclear weapons. In August of 1993, Moscow asked that they be sent back. We had to send fifteen back. The person in charge of Russian scientists was a friend of mine. They had come of their own free will, but Russia requested their repatriation."

As an indirect result of all the tension, Kim Jong-il seriously injured himself in a fall from a horse, Kang said. "In 1993, Kim Jong-il was really edgy due to the NPT crisis. He had no time to relax. He liked untamed horses. Finally in September he went riding but he fell, injuring his head and arms and breaking all his teeth. All his teeth now are false. He brought a famous dentist from France to make them."[22]

Colonel Ed Logan was worried early in 1994 as he pondered, from retirement in Alabama, the prospect that the United States would refight the Korean War. "Thank God we are militarily a little better positioned than in June 1950," he told me. "However, it is difficult to predict what happens to casualty count when a million ground troops engage in face-to-face combat with one side not accountable to anyone for the number of casualties. You can fly over and drop bombs. You can sail and control the seas. But actual control of real estate is just forward of the bayonet carried by the infantry soldier."[23]

By the spring of 1994, as a Fulbright fellow in Seoul, I had interviewed enough recent defectors to apprehend the widespread readiness of North Koreans to fight and get it over with. The Kims, requiring tension for their survival, were keeping their people on a dangerous edge, primed for war but not yet actually fighting. The North Korean military was a gigantic, cocked weapon. Who could know how and when it might go off? The tendency of many in Washington to try to isolate North Korea even further seemed to me dangerous under the circumstances.

I also had learned from defectors that, despite the regime's Big Brother surveillance and control, some people had gotten hold of forbidden short-wave receivers and begun listening to foreign broadcasts. Ordinary North Korean radio listeners had long been limited by available equipment to a single government medium-band frequency. The U.S. government's Voice of America was accessible to the small group of North Koreans allowed to hear short-wave broadcasts—that is, trusted members of the leadership class whose work absolutely required familiarity with events abroad. But reports said that in January 1993 the regime had begun jamming the transmissions of VOA.[24] Recall that, ironically, some members of the country's elite had become regular VOA listeners—even fans. [25] In Pyongyang during our 1992 visit one official astonished the veteran VOA Asia correspondent Ed Conley[26] by giving an imitation, near-perfect in intonation, cadences and pauses, of Conley's trademark signoff: "Edward Conley . . . Voice of America . . . Tokyo." The North Korean said he had been a Conley fan for years. It was not clear whether the government specifically wished to deprive such elite officials of the VOA news source.[27]

In any case, instead of isolating North Korea further, I thought that what was needed was a way to break through the regime's lock on information and help North Koreans become aware of reality outside their country. I saw in then-current efforts in Washington to start Radio Free Asia an excellent vehicle for doing just that—if those in charge of RFA would make sure its broadcasts went out not merely on short-wave frequencies but also on medium wave, also known as AM, which my research showed far more North Koreans equipped to receive.

I wrote up my findings in a policy paper and with the help of some friends put it into the hands of the top Washington officials making policy on Korean and RFA matters, including the secretary of state and the national security advisor. They sent thank-you notes. One high-level U.S. official concerned with Korean issues told me my paper contained new and important information. He was struck by my use of defector testimony, he said, since U.S. officials had long assumed defectors were of little value. It was time to reassess that notion in view of what I had learned, he said.

More than eight years later I met that official again. He was still deeply involved with issues involving North Korea. If, as promised, he had reassessed his view of defector testimony, however, the reassessment had not changed his mind. He obviously did not recall our earlier conversation and told me he had little use for what defectors said. Radio Free Asia by that time had been broadcasting in the Korean language for years, but only over short wave frequencies. In 2003 the organization finally managed to acquire facilities in a neighboring country to broadcast over AM frequencies but it soon stopped doing so, for "budgetary reasons."

It was former President Jimmy Carter who managed to cut through the mutual suspicions and fears, finding a temporary compromise resolution of the standoff over nuclear weapons. As both sides contemplated going to war momentarily, Carter accepted an invitation to visit Kim Il-sung in Pyongyang. There he won from Kim an agreement to freeze North Korea's nuclear program in exchange for resumption of dialogue with Washington.

At a June 18, 1994, press conference in Seoul, which I attended, Carter said that Kim had conveyed through him two requests to Washington. First, he wanted the United States to help Pyongyang replace its current nuclear power technology with a more modern technology—one that would not produce large quantities of plutonium as a byproduct. Second, he wanted official assurances that neither the United States nor any other outside forces would attack North Korea.

Although Carter had informed the Clinton Administration about his talks with Kim, he was seen in the White House as something of a freelancer. There were some ruffled feathers. However, Washington signaled that it was prepared to talk. The threat of immediate war receded.[28]

One measure of how serious a possibility war had become in the minds of the leaders: Hwang Jang-yop reported that "because Kim Il-sung's statue must not be damaged even in times of war, the recently-made statues are mostly knockdown style, so that the statues can be easily and safely moved underground in times of emergency. All Kim Il-sung statues are guarded round the clock by armed soldiers."[29]

TWENTY-NINE

Without You There Is
No Country

In a ruined country neither the land nor the people can remain at peace. Under the roofs of houses in a ruined country even the traitors who live in luxury as a reward for betraying their country will not be able to sleep in peace. Even though they are alive, the people are worse than gutter dogs, and even if the mountains and rivers remain the same, they will not retain their beauty.

—KIM IL-SUNG

Writing those words in the memoirs that he began publishing in 1992,[1] Kim Il-sung meant to contrast the horrors of Japanese colonial rule with the wonders achieved during his rule of nearly half a century. The main ruination brought by colonialism, in his view, was to national dignity. But by the time of his death in 1994 it would have been clear to almost any reader of his words that the harsh description applied, in material even if not in nationalistic terms, to the North Korea that he had created.

Indeed Kim Il-sung himself seems to have begun in the final three years of his life to contemplate some new approaches to dealing with his country's immense problems.

*   *   *

Yoshimi Tanaka was one of nine Japanese Red Army terrorists who hijacked a Japan Airlines jumbo jet in March 1970 and flew to North Korea. Tanaka ran afoul of the law again in 1996. He was arrested on the Cambodia-Vietnam border and whisked to Thailand to face charges that he had been part of a plot there to cash counterfeit $100 bills, hard-to-detect "Super-K" forgeries produced by North Korea's ruling party as part of its drive to obtain foreign currency. He spent almost three and a half years in a Thai jail, and then, in 1999, he was about to be extradited to Japan, where he could expect further prison time. At that point he spoke with an interviewer for the Japanese weekly *Gendai*, saying: "I now recollect my life in Pyongyang with a warm heart." Tanaka related that he had lived amid greenery in a quiet section of Pyongyang, along the Taedong River. About twenty North Koreans had been assigned by the state to work at the residences of the Japanese Red Army members and some Ecuadorian guerrillas who lived next door. The helpers "were there to manage the waterworks and boilers, transport coal and propane gas, secure foods and daily necessities and repair our Mercedes Benz cars."

The interviewer took that as his cue to observe: "You seem to have enjoyed a higher living standard than those of ordinary citizens." Tanaka acknowledged that some people had disparaged the ex-terrorists' circumstances as "life within a palace." But he himself had no complaint on that score. "I think the president"—Kim Il-sung—"simply wanted to treat us as foreigners." At that point Tanaka acknowledged that, living in an affluent residential area that was something of a cocoon, isolated from most North Koreans, he "did not know what the ordinary life in the republic was. So I cannot tell whether I lived a luxurious life or not." He added, "As to the issue of hunger, as well, I really do not know about it."

Tanaka's comments ring a bell. There is evidence that Kim Il-sung's vastly more splendid isolation in real palaces—combined with the efforts of underlings to report only good news and expose him to Potemkin villages that oozed fake prosperity—kept the Great Leader from realizing the full extent of his people's plight.

There is other evidence, however, that even on some occasions when Kim did know what was really happening he was having such a good time as Great Leader that he didn't want to inconvenience himself in order to deal with such mundane matters. Former ideology chief Hwang Jang-yop told of "an incident that occurred during the time when electricity supply was so poor that there were frequent blackouts even in Pyongyang." Hwang gave no date for the incident, but power outages in Pyongyang were reported from the 1980s. "During a meeting of the party Central Committee chaired by Kim Il-sung, he called the minister of electric power to account for the inconvenience he had been experiencing recently while watching movies due to voltage drops.

The ever-conscientious minister stood up to reply: 'Currently there is not enough electric power to meet the requirements of the factories. Because of the heavy load in transmission to the factories, the voltage of electricity supplied to Pyongyang tends to drop.' Kim Il-sung responded with, 'Then why can't you adjust the power supply transmitted to factories and allocate more to Pyongyang?' When the Minister explained, 'That would stop operations in a lot of factories,' Kim Il-sung cut him off and ordered, 'I don't care if all the factories in the country stop production. Just send enough electricity to Pyongyang.' "[2]

Probably it is unnecessary to choose between the image of an unknowing Kim and Hwang's harsh portrait of a knowing but uncaring Kim. It should not be surprising that he behaved on occasion like the despot that he was. Absolute power does, after all, corrupt absolutely. But it appears that his knowledge was in fact imperfect for quite a long time up until the early 1990s.

Statesmen approaching death—even the most vicious tyrants among them—look to their reputations, their places in history. Kim Il-sung was no exception. "Just as in the past, I still feel nowadays the greatest pride and joy in enjoying the love of the people," he wrote in his memoirs. "I consider this the true meaning of life. Only those who understand this true meaning can be the genuine sons and faithful servants of the people."[3]

Kim wrote—as if writing it could make it true—that he would be leaving behind a "revolution progressing triumphantly and our country prospering, with all the people singing its praises."[4] The people indeed had no choice but to sing the revolution's praises, and Kim's. But conditions had reached the point where no one could ignore the stark evidence that the country was descending deeper and deeper into poverty and hunger.

Economic conditions only grew worse in the early 1990s. Food distribution became increasingly irregular, with much smaller quantities of inferior grains such as millet substituted for the usual rice rations. People survived by using their cash savings to buy grain in the private sector—especially in a black market dealing in grain that had been held back illegally from collective-farm harvests. (This form of corruption had taken hold by the mid-1980s.) Beef, the Korean meat of choice, had become a once-a-year delicacy for most North Koreans. More than 50 percent of manufacturing had been idled due to shortages, and the workers who showed up had nothing to occupy them but cleaning the facilities. Even new factories built in the late 1980s were not operating. A largely military work force built an immense factory complex at Sunchon to make the synthetic fabric vinalon; it had its opening ceremony in 1991, but could not go into production. Supplying the clothing needs of the populace had been one of the prides of the Kim Il-sung regime, but now people's clothing was growing shabby.[5]

Word certainly was getting back to substantial numbers of North Koreans from relatives and others who had traveled or lived abroad that life in

South Korea and the West—and even in China—was richer. Getting caught saying so brought a one-month sentence in a reeducation camp.[6] The economy could hardly improve if the regime's nuclear gamble scared off anyone considering significant investment from outside. No doubt it was significant that the government had been at pains to patch even tiny holes in the tight lid it kept on information from outside. Reports told of a crackdown on contact even with Chinese.[7]

What was the need for all the frantic unity campaigns and rallies pledging loyalty to Kim Jong-il if there was not a growing recognition of a split in interests between the ruling pair and other groups of North Koreans? In particular, we now know, some people in the elite—civilian and military alike—wished that they were permitted to reform the system enough to preserve their status. That is not to say there were fully developed factions in high places in North Korea. Factions could not flourish for want of strong leaders who had not yet been purged. Nevertheless, some influential members of the elite possessed survival skills and were more amenable to change than some of their colleagues and they did engage in power struggles.

The record of "change" under the Kims could only dismay such people: In the 1970s, the North had begun to lag behind South Korea, but had rejected major change. In the 1980s, the economy had remained stagnant and the ideology of egalitarianism and altruism had started to ring hollow to North Koreans. Reform had been the watchword in other communist countries, but Pyongyang had redoubled its commitment to its hard-line ideology. Now it was the 1990s and European communism was dead, while in North Korea the stench of failure had become almost overpowering.

Experience had shown how difficult it was for North Korea to change while the Kims remained in power. Kim Il-sung, his longevity, his identification with the system and the lies on which he built his personality cult seemed to stand in the way of even Chinese-style reforms. The regime feared that reform of the system would imply criticism of Kim Il-sung. Opening the country to foreign ideas and information would admit views critical of Kim Il-sung. But clearly the Great Leader could not be seen to have told or condoned lies, behaved brutally toward his subjects or made mistakes. Therefore, the regime had viewed opening and fundamental reform as out of the question. Limited to halfway measures, the ruling class had been helpless to take the serious steps many believed were needed to prolong their rule—as, for example, Chinese economic reformers under Deng Xiaoping had been able to extend Communist Party rule. With Kim Il-sung and son occupying the status of permanent royalty, their more expendable subordinates in the bureaucracy felt the pressure from above and below to perform—or, barring that, to find someone else to blame for the system's failures.

If there ever had been a possible way out of this historical bind for Kim Il-sung since the time it became apparent his system was losing the race, that may have been somehow to recreate himself. Could he remake his image through positive tactics such as replacing lies with truth or through destructive tactics such as blaming subordinates and evil advisers for the excesses of his system? If he could do that, then maybe, just maybe, he could permit his technocrats to go for something resembling a Chinese-style economic reform — while leaving the political system and leadership relatively unchanged for the time being. Like Mao Zedong, then, he could retain his place in history as a towering patriotic figure and the father of the republic. Evidence suggests that something like that actually occurred to Kim and that he made a beginning in that direction.

Kim's memoirs were one indication that an image makeover was under way. The first two volumes, covering the period from his birth in 1912 until early 1933, nearly twenty-one years, went on sale in Pyongyang during his birthday celebration in 1992. Those turned out to be a partially revisionist work containing a number of attempts to distance Kim from earlier fabrications and embellishments and lies by commission and omission, as well as from some of the most widely condemned aspects of his system.[8]

An example of distancing himself from old lies: Kim had been a legitimate hero of the anti-Japanese struggle of the 1930s — but only one of a number of heroes.[9] To justify a personality cult, however, he had to outshine the others vastly. For his greater glory Pyongyang over the decades had downgraded or deleted the roles of others involved in the struggle — not only fellow Koreans but Chinese and the agents of the Soviet Union as well. In the memoirs, however, Kim acknowledged that he had worked as a cadre of a Chinese Communist Party organization and fought in a "joint struggle" with Chinese forces. He recalled by name many previously ignored comrades, including Korean and Chinese guerrilla leaders. And he revealed that he had accepted appointment by representatives of Moscow's Communist International as a youth organizer in Manchuria's Eastern Jilin Province in 1930.

Besides those modest efforts to respond to outside challenges regarding his historical record, Kim also tried to distort that record further. In his new incarnation as revealed in the memoirs he miraculously appeared, for example, as a lifelong, staunch opponent of discrimination against people on account of their class or ideological background. It would be hard to banish the suspicion that Kim's self-portrayal as the soul of tolerance was designed to shift the blame for his police state. Some of his claims to having uttered pro-tolerance views can be interpreted as almost a plea for Koreans of subsequent generations to honor him and his anti-Japanese guerrillas, and treat their descendents well, even if the communist system should be tossed on the rubbish heap of history. Thus, he complained that, after liberation, some communists had rejected people with other ideologies, including the non-communist nationalist independence fighters. Kim said he admonished such "narrow-minded" people: "Even if we are in power, we communists must not fail to appreciate our patriotic seniors. The trend of thought differs from age to age; then why do you ostracize them, guard against them and avoid them? Are they guilty for fighting for Korea's independence at the risk of their lives when others were living with their families in warm houses, eating hot rice?"[10]

Beyond the pure public relations effort that his memoirs represented, there is evidence that Kim also concluded he could risk—and his legacy might gain from—some significant substantive changes of policy. After all, the regime's grip was so tight that hardly anyone thought it would collapse while Kim Il-sung was alive. Most foreign and South Korean scholars ruled out a Ceaucescu scenario for Kim. Partly due to brainwashing but also because he was seen as a genuine nationalist hero, his subjects' personal loyalty to their Respected and Beloved Great Leader remained "too great for them to butcher him like a pig," one American professor remarked. Indeed, since they loved Kim Il-sung so much, it seemed he might be able to tell them he had decided the world was not yet ready for North Korea's exalted version of socialism. (Recall that it took anti-communist zealot and longtime China-basher Richard Nixon to establish U.S. relations with Mainland China.) Wouldn't North Koreans gratefully accept whatever Kim Il-sung proposed as an imperfect interim system?

In the end, while he did not propose a new system, he did seek a shift in emphasis within the old system. According to defector Kang Myong-do, the event triggering Kim's belated efforts to change policy occurred in April of 1992—coincidentally, the month I was in the country for the Tumen River conference. "Every morning when Kim Il-sung awoke, he liked to look at the Pyongyang skyline to see the chimneys of the power plants," Kang told reporters for Seoul's *JoongAng Ilbo*. "In April 1992, Kim Il-sung was really angry because smoke was coming from only two of the smokestacks. The reason, he found after investigation, was that the Anju mines were not supplying coal. So Kim Il-sung became really curious. The reports claimed 120 percent overproduction compared with the planned goal. Kim secretly sent to the mines someone who found that the miners had nothing to eat. 'How can we work?' they asked. They were supposed to get 1,100 grams of rice, 200 grams of meat, 100 grams of corn oil per day. But for a week they had eaten only salt soup. It shows how little Kim Il-sung knew. It was the first time he realized the people were not getting their rations. He was surprised."[11]

Kim pursued the matter and received an accurate report on horribly grim conditions in mountainous North Hamgyong province, which adjoins the Chinese and Russian borders in the northeastern part of the country.

North Hamgyong, throughout North Korea's economic decline, suffered more than most other provinces. (I suspect a census of refugees who were desperate enough to flee to China would show that a majority of them hailed from North Hamgyong.) Kang Myong-do told one interviewer that his father-in-law, Kang Song-san, then the governor of that province, had leveled with the president. Shocked into action, the semi-retired Kim re-involved himself in domestic issues, author Don Oberdorfer relates. Kang Song-san, who had held the prime ministerial portfolio earlier, was brought back in the same capacity that year. Meetings on economic policy the following year led to a dramatic admission at the end of 1993 that the country was in trouble economically. The regime would move to new policies de-emphasizing heavy industry in favor of activities that would more directly improve the people's livelihood.[12]

In the meantime, the standoff with the United States continued. Kim Jong-il was busy consolidating his position with the military—often at the expense of the civilian economy. Eventually Kim Dal-hyon, perhaps the government's most promising reformer, fell afoul of powerful military interests. In the atmosphere of the time, that meant he had to go. "Even in the party there was conflict," Kang Myong-do said. "They didn't have a specific guideline for opening up and reforming." That set the stage for the clash, a personal one between Kim Guk-tae and Kim Dal-hyun. Kim Guk-tae, a second-generation revolutionary, eldest son of partisan and fallen Korean War general Kim Chaek and a graduate of Mangyongdae Revolutionary School, reportedly had been Kim Jong-il's supervisor when the younger man was starting his career. (See chapter 13.) Kang described him as "not very bright—he doesn't know what 'opening' means." Kim Dal-hyon was also a second-generation revolutionary, said Kang, who described him as Kim Il-sung's nephew-in-law. "He's very smart," Kang said. "He's a very powerful, gutsy figure."

The conflict between the two, according to Kang's account, began in 1992 when the regime was selecting the chairman of the external economic committee. "Kim Dal-hyon had been the chairman. With his promotion he wanted Yi Song-dae to be his successor. Yi was vice-head of the governments' trade department. Kim Guk-tae wanted Choe Jong-keun. Kim Guk-tae was secretary of the party Central Committee department in charge of personnel." In December 1992, there was a meeting of the Supreme People's Assembly, Kang said. "During a break, Kim Jong-il called out Kim Dal-hyon for a chat and told him, 'We decided on Choe.' Kim Dal-hyon's face became contorted and he said if Choe became the next chairman he would quit as vice-premier. Kim Jong-il asked whom he wanted. 'Yi Song-dae,' Kim Dal-hyon replied. Kim Jong-il didn't know him, but since Kim Dal-hyon was so adamant he agreed to appoint Yi. When they returned to the assembly, Choe was very surprised to learn he had lost it."

At that point, "Kim Guk-tae started maneuvering to oust Kim Dal-hyon." His strategy was to show his adversary as an opponent of the military-first policy. Kim Dal-hyon, while serving as acting prime minister, "wanted to salvage the North Korean economy, so he diverted to the mines 30 percent of the energy that was to be supplied to the military equipment factories," Kang said. "He is on bad terms with Kim Chol-man and Chon Byon-ho, high officials in charge of armaments. They were involved in a power struggle complicated by personal dislike. Kim Jong-il in a meeting asked why there had been no innovations in armaments. They answered, 'Because Kim Dal-hyon took over our energy supply.' Kim Jong-il is very smart. He knows how things work, knows what happens in the world. But he's very rash. If someone under him makes a mistake he makes a hasty decision to get rid of that person. He also doesn't like anyone else having too much power. He will get rid of such a person." Kim Dal-hyon was demoted, becoming manager of a synthetic fabric factory complex. His absence from Pyongyang probably slowed the impetus for change. "Kim Dal-hyon is for opening," Kang said. "There are bright people among the elite, but nobody else as gutsy as Kim Dal-hyon. When he's abroad he's even bold enough to say things opposed to Kim Jong-il's views."[13]

To the extent that Kim Jong-il during that period had an interest in economic reform, it seems to have been fleeting, not very profound and offset to a considerable extent by conservative impulses and his determination to seal the military's support for his succession. In March 1993, probably to back his claims to being the chief priest of his father's ideology, he warned in a twenty-two-page thesis against private ownership and other "abuses of socialism." Those he blamed for the collapse of socialist systems abroad.[14] Even at that late date, then, he was demonstrably unprepared to make major changes in the system.

There is little reason to believe that even the senior Kim's newfound enthusiasm for change went much beyond emphasizing food and consumer goods more, heavy industry less. But rumors had it that a disagreement between father and son contributed to the father's death.

I spoke with Oh Young-nam, a former captain in State Security who defected to the South. His family home in Pyongyang was across the street from the elite's social hub, the Koryo Hotel, a location that signified to me the family's considerable prominence. He mentioned, without naming, a powerful relative who had died. (I had heard that a relative of Marshal O Jin-u had defected, but Oh Young-nam refused to answer when I asked if that might be the connection.) Oh Young-nam gave me an account of Kim's last days that he said was pieced together from what he had heard from other members of the elite—especially sons and daughters of very high officials, whom he named for me.

"The more Kim Jong-il took power, the more Kim Il-sung regretted it," Oh said. "Kim Jong-il is very dogmatic. Kim Jong-il divided the bodyguard service into two separate forces. Force One was for Kim Il-sung and Force Two was for Kim Jong-il. That was a threat; Kim Il-sung was regretting it. But when he met Jimmy Carter, he was jubilant. He believed Korea would reunify under [a confederation plan allowing for] two systems. He told Lee Yong-u, the head of transport and former head of the surveillance department, that they should relink the North-South railroad in Pyonggun so he could go for negotiations.

"Kim Il-sung was at Mount Myohyang and Kim Jong-il was at Samjiyon pond at a resort for high ranking people such as Lee Jong-ok, Pak Song-chol and Choe Gwang. Kim Il-sung was so jubilant regarding reunification. He said in meetings of heads of ministries that he would de-emphasize defense and emphasize improving the lives of average civilians. He ordered that more electricity be delivered to people. But [during a meeting] he had a phone conversation with Kim Jong-il, who said, 'Relax, enjoy your old age. We'll take care of it.' Kim Il-sung was really angry. He couldn't continue the meeting. He went back to his office and told Chong Il-shim, a woman who was helping him with his memoirs, 'I am very angry at this moment. I want to emphasize civilian life. With the negotiations with the United States, I hope aid will be given to North Hamgyong.' He was too angry. He asked his chief secretary to leave him for one hour.

"The chief secretary after two hours entered the office. Kim Il-sung had dropped off the bed, face first on the floor. The chief secretary raised him up, got the phlegm out of his mouth and asked for the main doctor. But Kim Jong-il had fired that doctor, saying he was too old. Only a young doctor was there. They arranged for two helicopters to come, but the one carrying emergency equipment crashed. The medical team couldn't help Kim Il-sung and he died. When Kim Jong-il heard it, he said, 'Do not announce it to anyone else. Restrict the movements of State Security, Public Security and the People's Army.' [Here Oh named his sources for this detail, but I choose to omit those names.] Because Kim Il-sung died in such a way, his chief secretary, whose name I don't recall, shot himself in the head.

"The media showed North Koreans weeping in front of the statue of Kim Il-sung. That only lasted three days. Kim Jong-il was astonished that people wept only three days. Kim Il-sung had been in power so long. Kim Jong-il realized he would be the leader and the people would worship him. But what would happen when he got weak? So he made every organization send a certain number of people to weep each day in front of the Kim Il-sung statue. They were not allowed to drink alcohol during mourning. Everyone who was in the mansion at Mount Myohyang when Kim Il-sung died was under great scrutiny. Those who were there included Kang Jong-hyon, a great grandchild of Kim Il-sung's mother; Kang Jong-ho, from the Kang clan; a son of Choe Jung-nam, who heads the North Korea trade office in Guangzhou. All high-ranking sons and daughters considered Kim Jong-il to have been at fault. The day that Kim Il-sung's body was transported from Mount Myohyang, all soldiers were confined to barracks or recalled. They didn't want any movement. The next day, O Jin-u went to the presidential palace in Pyongyang and was disappointed to find that the doorknob was rusty and the chandeliers' light bulbs were out. Maintenance was poor. How could Kim Jong-il treat his father that way?

"Most of this account was from sons and daughters of high officials. It's well known in Pyongyang right now."

On July 8, 1994, Radio Pyongyang issued a grave announcement: "The Great Heart stopped beating." Kim Il-sung had been "a great national hero who regained the sovereignty and dignity of the country," *Nodong Shinmun* said in an editorial. Kim had "triumphantly led the twenty-year-long rigorous anti-Japanese revolutionary struggle and put an end to the distress-torn history of the nation and brought a new spring of liberation to our people. This was an undying feat that marked a new turning point in the history of our nation spanning 5,000 years."[15]

Japanese analyst Katsumi Sato watched the changing lists of the funeral committee for clues that might bear on the rumors—already rife—that Kim Il-sung had been arguing with his son when he died. Name order in North Korea traditionally indicated status. First lady Kim Song-ae started off as number 104 on the committee. Eventually she became number seven. Kim Song-ae had spoken with Carter during his visit. Also, Sato said, Kim Il-sung had told the visiting widow of a former Japanese prime minister, when she stopped over in Pyongyang, that his good health was thanks to Song-ae's son Pyong-il: "He's been helping me lately." Sato thought a real power struggle had been afoot at the end. He watched the televised funeral rally as Kim Jong-il whispered in O Jin-u's ear. O ignored him "as if he were a child," said Sato, who suspected the old marshal was angry because Kim Jong-il had "caused" his father's death.

As at the party congress fourteen years earlier at which his succession had been made formal, Kim Jong-il appeared pale and sick when he attended the televised funeral event. Slack-jawed and dazed-looking, he could have been mistaken for the corpse. He was reported to have fasted for four days. His appearance also gave rise to intense speculation about the state of his health, although some analysts suspected he was just trying to look as bad as possible to project deep grief. (We now know about his fall from horseback the previous autumn. He may have been showing still the effects of that accident.) In a book published in 2003, a Japanese who claimed to have worked as Kim Jong-il's chef said the Dear Leader after his father's death confined himself to his room for long periods. One of Kim's wives, Ko Yong-hui, found him keeping a pistol next to him once, and asked him what he was thinking about, the chef wrote.[16]

A New Year's 1995 editorial that ran in the newspapers of the party, army and League of Socialist Working Youth referred to Kim Jong-il as "Great Leader of our party and people," "our Fatherly Leader" and "Supreme Commander of our revolutionary armed forces." If Kim Jong-il was ever going to do anything radical on his own, it might have seemed that now was his time. In the event, however, he had his father made president in perpetuity and kept the country in official mourning for three years.

As Hwang Jang-yop recalled, "The entire country was swept up in a flood of tears. Most of the mourners were crying because they had been brainwashed by Kim Il-sung's personality cult, but there was also the fact that anything other than mourning was not allowed. The party conducted surveys to see who displayed the most grief, and made this an important criterion in assessing party members' loyalty. Patients who remained in hospitals and people who drank and made merry even after hearing news of their leader's death were all singled out for punishment. In the Juche Science Institute, which I was supervising, Professor Hong Seung-hoon, the director of economic research, was demoted for remaining dry-eyed and busy repairing his bicycle. This incident eventually took its toll on Dr. Hong's health and led to his death."[17]

After Kim's death, Hwang said, "there was a debate on whether the party should continue publishing his memoirs. I firmly stated my opinion that the party should stop publishing the memoirs. I pointed out that quite a few people already questioned the integrity of the memoirs published so far because they were too intriguing to be true. So if the memoirs continued to be published even after Kim Il-sung's death, people would lose their faith in even the volumes that had been published while he was alive. I also had another reason in mind. It was all right to stretch the truth about the partisan struggle before liberation, since no one would take issue with that. But exaggerating about the post-liberation period, which is public knowledge, was a different matter. I was afraid it might cause problems in diplomatic relations.

"Kim Il-sung's partisan warfare was carried out under the guidance of the Chinese Communist Party, but the struggle in Northeast China [Manchuria] was not a significant part of the communist struggle in China as a whole. Furthermore, Kim Il-sung's partisan struggle was but a small part of the struggle in Northeast China. So the Chinese could turn a blind eye to the North Korean leaders' exaggeration of Kim Il-sung's feats, since his struggle was a drop in the bucket compared with the struggles of the Chinese Communist Party led by Mao. However, the Chinese people would react differently if the historical facts that were being distorted occurred after the liberation. That was what I was afraid of. Overzealous officials ignored my advice and submitted the sequel to Kim Il-sung's memoirs for Kim Jong-il's approval. The memoirs are still being published, long after the death of Kim Il-sung."[18]

"By handing over the reins to his son, Kim Il-sung committed a total and irrevocable mistake," Hwang Jang-yop wrote. "And his final mistake was sucking up to the power acquired by his son, thereby losing everything he once had. If Kim Il-sung had ruled only until the end of the 1960s and died then, he would have gone down in history as a hero of the armed struggle against Japanese colonialism and a capable leader of North Korea. But by handing over the government to his son, he walked down the same dishonorable path as Kim Jong-il, smearing the honorable first half of his political career. The mess in Kim Il-sung's life was made not so much by himself but by Kim Jong-il. The most serious defect in the lives of the two Kims is the hereditary passing down of power. Who is the one more at fault in this matter? Most people say that it is Kim Il-sung, but I believe that more than half the blame lies with Kim Jong-il."[19]

Former North Korean diplomat Ko Young-hwan said he had been very surprised when he went to South Korea because "many professionals thought there would be political turmoil and Kim Jong-il couldn't succeed. I didn't think that way. There's a big problem with his credibility, but I still think he'll rule for a period of time. His supporters are filling the highest official ranks, military and ciivilian, including economic officials. But he's going to collapse anyway because government officials believe he's only half the man his father is. That will bring him down. People around him think Kim Jong-il has a bad character and leads an extravagant life. He seems to put too much emphasis on unimportant issues. He doesn't have much interest in what's happening inside North Korea. He's not very interested in the economic crisis, the people's welfare or educational change. He's only interested in issues that can be seen, or that he can be acclaimed for. He's not interested in the big picture. He's interested in movie-making, operas, little gestures like sending a bus to a school or putting up buildings for a school."

So, I asked Ko, is Kim Jong-il basically a fool? He agreed with that characterization but I wanted a more nuanced estimate from him so I asked whether Kim wasn't bright in a way. "As far as I can see, I don't agree," Ko replied. "He has some talent in culture and arts. He can tell when the violinist hits the wrong note. But regarding the economy and statecraft he's a fool. The technocrats don't expect much from him in those areas, but at least they wish he'd show in the field of technology some of the zeal he displays toward art and culture. If he did that, maybe he could be seen as a better leader, but there's no chance of it now."

Former President Carter had arranged for then South Korean President Kim Young-sam to meet Kim Il-sung, and plans for the summit were being made when Kim Il-sung died. Pyongyang hoped that Kim Young-sam would attend the funeral. But communism was a personal issue for Kim Young-sam. North Korean agents, as we saw in chapter 6, had killed his mother in the family home on Koje Island in 1960. After his election in 1992, he had gone to the island and reported to his dead mother on his achievement, offering the election certificate before her grave.[20] As North Korea retreated into mourning Kim Young-sam buckled to domestic pressures, insulting the dead leader's successor son by refusing to send a delegation to mourn the "war criminal." In a taped April 25, 1998, conversation in Pyongyang with visiting Japanese-Korean officials of Chongryon, Kim Jong-il cited the incident and called Kim Young-sam "a filthy dirt-bag."

"One thing I feel sorry for him," the North Korean leader told his visitors, "is that he surrounded himself with bad advisors. When Leader Kim Il-sung passed away, Kim Young-sam could not attend the funeral because of his advisors. I hear Kim himself regrets having bad helpers. When Leader Kim Il-sung died, I discussed with Secretary Kim Yong-sun what to do if Kim Young-sam wanted to attend the funeral, and made a detailed plan to receive him. But he did not come, and we were very upset with him. If he had any wisdom, he would have come to the funeral. If he had come, he might have taken over North Korea and become president of a united Korea. What an idiot!"[21]

The nuclear negotiations that Carter had arranged went forward despite Kim Il-sung's death. In agreements reached in October 1994 and June 1995, Pyongyang promised it would neither restart its suspect reactor nor reprocess the spent fuel. A consortium of countries with interests in the region agreed to provide light-water reactors to replace the existing graphite-moderated technology.

Nevertheless, in the regime's propaganda an ominous theme became increasingly evident: a negative fate awaited North Koreans and they must embrace it. "We must be prepared to die for the leader." "Life is not valuable without valuable deaths." "Your life is meaningless except in the context of the party." "We must be prepared to share the fate of the leader, good or bad." A diplomat in Seoul saw parallels to the atmosphere in Nazi Germany during its final days. The Allies tried to starve the country into submission but Germans instead showed resilience and—when all hope was gone—readiness for catastrophe, the diplomat noted.

THIRTY

We Will Become Bullets and Bombs

In that part of the world there were neither shops nor markets nor merchants, nor any money in circulation. Here the law of value had no effect. Shoes and clothing for the population were obtained by capturing the enemy's supplies.

—KIM IL-SUNG, DESCRIBING CONDITIONS IN THE
MANCHURIAN GUERRILLA ZONES IN THE 1930s[1]

Consider a typical war scenario widely circulated in the waning years of the twentieth century and the early years of the twenty-first: Like Japan in 1941, the Pyongyang regime decides its survival is at stake and war is its last realistic—albeit desperate—chance. Responding to a real or manufactured provocation, and counting on problems elsewhere in the world to distract Washington and slow any American response, North Korea unleashes artillery barrages that destroy Seoul. Meanwhile fanatical troops sneak into South Korea, disguised as locals. Some infiltrate via larger-scale versions of a September 19, 1996, coastal landing by a band of armed northern commandos aboard a submarine. Others ride tanks and armored personnel carriers through secret tunnels beneath the Demilitarized Zone. Soon swollen by troops victorious in conventional battles along the DMZ, the Northern force sweeps south and bowls over its rich—and therefore soft—foe to reunite the peninsula in a matter of days.

Other scenarios could be imagined as well, of course. But regardless of the specifics, the message that defecting North Korean soldiers repeatedly took south was this: If war should come, South Koreans and Americans would have their work cut out for them fighting an enemy more formidable than they might realize. Lulled by the passage of time since the last Korean war ended in 1953, civilians in South Korea and the United States at times were tempted to brush off such warnings. Drawing confidence from their state-of-the-art armaments, many expected that their combined forces would turn back an offensive by the merely medium-tech North Koreans, with more or less ease.

Military and intelligence professionals based in South Korea, on the other hand, were more inclined to cast a respectful eye at their prospective foe. Whatever the technological gap, North Korea had a significant advantage in the location of the border—just to the north of the suburbs of Seoul, which put the Southern capital easily within range of the North's massive artillery. Besides, the Pyongyang leadership had spent decades of effort and vast sums honeycombing the North's hills to turn the country into an underground fortress, which it boasted would prove impregnable to attack or counterattack.

Despite such factors, the Gulf, Kosovo and Iraq wars inspired confidence that the American arsenal of "smart bombs" and other conventional weapons could tip the balance in Korea—without the need to use nuclear weapons. But an intangible remained for knowledgable South Koreans and Americans, even those possessed of unbounded faith in the latest gizmos. That intangible was morale.

For a long while, Northerners' fighting spirit withstood—indeed, thrived upon—food shortages. Shortages became a regular fact of life in the 1970s and by the start of the 1990s had seriously afflicted much of the North's population. The regime fanned popular hatred of outside enemies, blaming all internal trouble—notably citizens' reduced and intermittent grain rations—on South Korea, the United States and Japan. Ordinary people bought into that theory massively, defectors and refugees reported. Most North Koreans did not find the cause of the food shortages in the top leadership or in the country's political-economic-social system, both of which they had been taught to revere. Rather, they blamed their troubles on the military threat from their enemies. It was on account of that threat, they were told—and they believed—that they had to sacrifice in order to keep up a credible military capability.

For many years grain rations had been reduced across the board with the explanation that the difference was going into the nation's war reserves as a patriotic contribution. But when would the sacrifice and consequent misery stop? Defectors in the 1990s began saying that an overwhelming percentage of the people believed only war could end the North-South impasse, which they saw as the cause of hard times. "The North Korean people have been suffering a long time," Bae In-soo, a truck driver who defected to South Korea in 1996, told me. "They've been investing everything" in preparations for war. And so, for them, "war is the only answer."

Ominously, those who felt that way included the younger soldiers who would have to do most of the fighting and dying if war should break out. Youngsters serving their hitches in the army were—the overwhelming majority of them—not only ready but eager to fight. Combined with the war reserves of grain and fuel made possible by popular sacrifice and foreign aid, such focused hatred among the troops could be a formidable advantage in wartime—especially against a generation of South Korean and American soldiers raised on abundance and more focused on consumption, leisure-time activities and post-military careers than on fighting.

How would the South Koreans and Americans perform once the bullets started flying and their buddies started dying? Ahn Young-kil, a former North Korean army captain, saw enough following his defection to the South to warn that "in case of a long, drawn-out war—anything over two months— the South Korean army doesn't have the potential to continue and the Americans would lose interest." The South Koreans' "mentality is not as strong as North Koreans'," said Ahn. "South Koreans don't have a strong sense of war and the sacrifice needed when war erupts." North Koreans, on the other hand, because of what they had been taught, "believe that they have to root out the main problem." That main problem was that "the food shortage and other difficulties in livelihood result from U.S.-led economic sanctions, and from the fact the United States and South Korea have been preparing for war and forcing North Korea to prepare for war." Get rid of that problem, they believed, and "they won't have this economic difficulty. So they are determined to have this war."

Choi Myung-nam, who served in the 124th Special Forces (the unit whose members had infiltrated to try to attack the Blue House in Seoul), offered a similar view: "The mentality and morale are very different. In South Korea, discipline is very loose. Soldiers only have to stay in the army for three years. During that time they can take leave to go meet their girlfriends." North Korean soldiers, in contrast, Choi said, were in uniform typically for ten-year hitches filled with tough, intensive training. In their Spartan lives, the Northern soldiers had "no chance to meet girlfriends," Choi said. They constantly shouted Kim Il-sung's slogan: "We don't want war but we are not afraid of war." In fact, Choi said, "all my comrades wanted war to break out—partly because they wanted to flaunt their potential, but also partly because the economic situation was so harsh they just wanted some change." While he was in the North, Choi "thought we would win. I knew that in a single day we would go all the way to the Naktong River" in the southern part of South Korea. His experiences in South Korea did not change his mind materially on that point. "Coming to South Korea, I realized that in a one-on-one war with South Korea the North would always win, assuming the Americans and others didn't get involved," he said.

True, North Koreans looking at the South might "miss the fact that pluralism in a democratic society has potential strength," as Kim Kyung-woong, an official in the South's Ministry of National Unification, noted. "In troubled times, society becomes cohesive." But in terms of the prospects for the outbreak of a second, probably bloodier Korean war, the more significant fact was that fighting spirit reached such a height in the North that the leader—Kim Il-sung or his son, Kim Jong-il, after him—had only to say the word and the masses would march off enthusiastically into battle.

A big question after the mid-1990s was whether all that Northern mental readiness for war had peaked and started to decline. Some in Washington saw reasons to think so. A congressman, Tony Hall, said at a September 12, 1996, hearing that during a trip to North Korea in August that year he had seen soldiers looking as undernourished as civilians, thin and hollow-cheeked. "That may be the best evidence that most of North Korea's military isn't getting much more to eat than the rest of the people," Hall said.

Rear Admiral William Wright, director of Asian affairs in the Pentagon's Bureau of International Security Affairs, said at the same hearing that hunger could lead to a breakdown in discipline among the North's soldiers. "They will begin to see indiscipline, perhaps, and infractions . . . as they continue to struggle to look after their own families and their own survival," Wright said. Such slippage did indeed occur. Several defectors told me that hunger and associated health problems were starting to become more of a hindrance than a spur to military performance.

Historians a generation hence may well point to August 1995 as the high point on a chart of North Korean fighting spirit. August 15, 1945, was the day when the Korean peninsula was liberated from Japanese colonial rule— only to be divided into the American-ruled and Soviet-ruled zones that subsequently became South Korea and North Korea. In the early 1990s, the Pyongyang regime made much of the necessity of ending Korean division in time for the approaching fiftieth anniversary of the liberation, August 15, 1995. North Koreans believed that "if division still prevailed on the fiftieth anniversary, it would continue forever," said Choi Kwang-hyeok, a twenty-five-year-old former KPA sergeant who escaped across the DMZ to the South. He said Northerners were also determined to achieve reunification as a gift to Great Leader Kim Il-sung during his lifetime, as Kim Jong-il repeatedly promised.

By 1992, the widespread belief was that all able-bodied young men should join the army so that they could take part in the war for reunification expected before that fiftieth anniversary, said Choi, who was a university student but made the patriotic decision in the war fever of that year to enlist as a soldier. Already the food situation was severe enough, even for the military, that the usual strenuous training had to be deemphasized, Choi said. Ideological readiness sessions that emphasized hatred of the enemy filled much of the soldiers' time. But then Kim Il-sung died, in July 1994, having ruled for almost a half century. Like many others, Choi Kwang-hyeok was "devastated" by the Great Leader's death. He "started doubting that reunification would occur, doubting the whole regime" and its future. When August 15, 1995, came and went, reunification still only a dream, "people started thinking, 'Maybe war will happen—but maybe it won't,'" said Choi.

Like an apocalyptic sect confronted with the world's failure to end on the scheduled day, the regime did its figures again and pushed the date forward, telling the people, "We'll have reunification by the end of the 1990s." People still bought in, but not as thoroughly as before. "They still think war may break out, but motivation and morale are not as high," Choi said. "Even the [military] trainers complain, 'With that kind of morale, how are we supposed to win the war?'"

Ahn Young-kil cited "two factors needed to keep morale up: Feed the soldiers well, and give them hope." In fact, that formula was Kim Jong-il's highest priority. In a speech near the end of 1996,[2] Kim gave himself and the armed forces' political commissars high marks on the second part. "I am satisfied that our soldiers have the ideological thinking to become guns and bombs to protect the revolutionary leadership in a fight to the death," he said. The problem he saw was too much contrast between the levels of military and civilian morale. The speech marked the 50th anniversary of Kim Il-sung University, and that day Kim had watched a performance by the university's arts performance team. He was disappointed that the performers "were lacking in spirit." By comparison, "the performance I saw a few days ago by the mobile propaganda unit of the People's Army was full of stamina and vitality."

For the morale problems in civilian life and for the economy's failure to provide enough food, especially to soldiers, Kim blamed slothful, bureaucratic party officials. "I assisted the Great Leader's work from 1960, but there are no party workers who can assist me correctly," he complained. "I am working alone." Although the military was his top priority, he also took notice of civilian suffering. "When I was visiting Chollima Steel Mill, I saw many people on the road looking for food, and in other areas the road, trains and train stations were full of such people, I was told. In many regions these heartbreaking events are happening, but all the party worker does is stay at home and study for meetings and lectures. How can we overcome our problems with such behavior?"

Kim blamed subordinates for the fact that "the people are forced to wander aimlessly looking for rice" during what he called a "march of hardship." Party officials, "who do not use their brains to solve problems, who just sit at their desks complaining and studying words," were at fault, he asserted. "I cannot solve all the problems . . . as I have to control important sectors such as the military and the party as well. If I concentrated only on the economy there would be irrecoverable damage to the revolution. The Great Leader told me when he was alive never to be involved in economic projects, just concentrate on the military and the party and leave economics to party functionaries. If I do delve into economics, then I cannot run the party and the military effectively."

Exhorting party officials to take "measures to guarantee rice for the military," Kim told them that socialism had collapsed in many countries because "the party changed and could no longer control the military." (He might have been recalling how elements of the Romanian military had executed the Ceaucescus.) Enemies, "seeing our temporary troubles, are crying out that our socialism has collapsed and are seeking the chance to invade. If the U.S. imperialists know that we do not have rice for the military, then they will immediately invade us."

The solution, Kim said, was to politically educate the people, especially farmers, to spare more food for the soldiers. But the officials were going about that in the wrong way. Instead of leaving their desks to make direct appeals to the people, they were relying on print and broadcast media—which people could hardly receive due to energy shortages. "Currently the farmers and miners are hiding food at every opportunity," for the black market, Kim said. Party workers must preach to them: "'Who is going to supply food to your sons and grandsons in the army? If we cannot give them rice, then when the yankees invade us we cannot defeat them and your sons and daughters will become imperialist slaves once more.' It is this logic that must be used to persuade those who hide and smuggle food, to regain their consciences."

In fact, food became so scarce that many soldiers took to stealing it from civilians, even deserting from the army. "Physically they're very frail now, very weak," the former army captain Ahn Young-kil told me. "So their mental state has weakened, too." Meanwhile, the soldiers were losing the hope that they might enjoy good lives following their army hitches, Ahn said. "They are very depressed because they go home on leave and see their parents improperly fed. They see no hope." In case of war, Ahn predicted, "the majority wouldn't run away. But their fighting power and spirit would not be the same as in the past when they were well fed."

Choi Myung-nam, the special forces veteran, said theft and embezzlement had increased drastically in the military, starting in the 1990s, as soldiers began to leave socialist ideals behind and adopt the attitude that
"without money, you can't survive in society." More and more, they focused
on the means—almost all illicit—of accumulating the money and material
goods they believed they would need if they hoped to marry and live reasonably well after finishing their army hitches, Choi said. Their talk turned to
dreams of the goods—radios, fashionable clothes—that they hoped to buy
once they returned to the civilian world. That did not mean they had begun
to fear war, he cautioned. They continued to think "it would be an honor to
die as a martyr in war."

Ex-sergeant Choi Kwang-hyeok said the changed situation had taken
such a toll that "man for man I don't think North Korea is a match for South
Korea." That would not mean the North could not call upon its other advantages if it made the fateful decision for war. Its military remained far larger
than the South's, for example, so the man-for-man comparison need not apply. And its ability to inflict enormous punishment on the South with its artillery remained. The North's "main weapon is artillery," said an intelligence
professional in the South. "It doesn't take that much practice and physical
conditioning to shoot that stuff."

In terms of supplies, if outsiders had let North Korea suffer alone the aftermath of disastrous flooding in 1995, said Ahn, the year 1996 "would have
been the most critical point." Regarding their ability to make war, the North's
leaders would have had to conclude that it was a case of use it or lose it. In
the absence of aid, by 1997 "North Korea would not have been able to retain
the support system for waging war," Ahn judged. But China, the United
States, Japan, South Korea and other countries did come to the North's aid
with food shipments. Ahn criticized that aid as appeasement and complained it
was "only making North Korea more confident."

It was questionable how much comfort South Koreans, Americans and
Japanese should take from evidence of declining North Korean military
morale. Even if the North's war capablility declined past the point where an
attack could represent a rational last-ditch decision, the top leadership might
not realize that because of North Korean underlings' notorious reluctance to
convey bad news to the boss. Kim Jong-il in his December 1996 speech insisted that military commanders knew they could not fool him because he
had made it a habit to "visit them unexpectedly. Therefore in the People's
Army the commanders are always prepared to meet the supreme commander, so they are always on alert with clean barracks and they attempt to
improve their soldiers' living conditions while always being ready to fight."
But he acknowledged that civilian party officials had tried to pull the wool

over his late father's eyes. Once when the Great Leader visited Hamhung, "some party workers brought goods by train to fill the stores in the city. This is typical pointism that deceives the leader, so I ordered them punished. However there are still many party workers doing this."

Besides the possibility of delusion there was that irrational loser's choice, reportedly articulated by Kim Jong-il in a meeting with his father and top military leaders: to "break the world." In sum: Fireworks on the Korean Peninsula could not be ruled out, as the following interviews with former military men (presented in order of the times of their defections, from earlier to later) helped to persuade me.

When I interviewed Kim Nam-joon five years after his 1989 defection, the former army second lieutenant was a university student in Seoul but he still looked like a soldier—with his prominent jaw and what Americans call a "whitewall" haircut, almost down to the scalp near his ears but longer on top. Kim told me that besides food problems (which he has described in chapter 21), military men also suffered from a shortage of clothing and shoes. "I got one new summer uniform a year, and a new winter uniform every two years—not enough, considering all the training. Once a week we had to walk 40 kilometers [25 miles] in a day. I had one pair of boots to wear during the winter. That wasn't enough. You sweated, and you had to wash and dry your boots. The problem was, there was no way of buying them. The more cunning soldiers would steal others' boots. The training was so burdensome I even thought of killing myself. By the time soldiers finish their ten-year hitches and are mustered out to civilian society, their minds are dead. All they can think of is shooting."

Kim, a commissioned officer, had befriended, and later defected in company with, a noncommissioned officer. In some other countries' armies that would violate fraternization regulations. "In communist society we don't put much stock in rank," he explained when I asked him about it. "We believe in equality. We don't address each other with honorific or humble speech based on rank or age. We don't call higher-ranking or older soldiers *songsaeng-nim* [honorable elder, teacher]. I commanded a platoon of thirty men. Kim Kwang-choon was my deputy. We had to be close. We became very close as people, rank aside. That was the basis of the relationship. Kim often came to my home."[3]

Q. Tell me about the morale of the military. If orders were given to go to war, how would the soldiers feel?

A. "In the first stages, 90 percent of the soldiers would do as they were told—invade South Korea, say. They are ignorant, they don't yet know right from wrong. Kim Il-sung and Kim Jong-il may know an invasion would be evil, but the soldiers don't. They just do their jobs. Officers who graduated from the military academy like me might have some doubts, but they lack the courage to do anything about them. Even if they had access to a television set they wouldn't take advantage of the opportunity to watch South Korean television. Soldiers truly believe that invading South Korea would be for the purpose of expelling the U.S. imperialists.

"In the second stage, though, if soldiers get down to South Korea they'll see cities full of well-dressed, well-fed people. They'll comprehend the reality of North Korea. If I went to North Korea dressed like this [nice suit of a charcoal hue, gold watch, starched white shirt with French cuffs, tie], everybody would faint. When I see South Koreans walking around, I still feel they're so fortunate. Even the dogs I see wouldn't be pets if they were in North Korea—they'd all be eaten. The North Korean soldiers when they see all this will become aware, but their officers will be ready for that. They train North Korean officers to be prepared for just this situation: 'When all the people are dead with their watches on, North Korean soldiers will run to scavenge the corpses. You have to teach them not to. They already give that training to officers back in North Korea. I had it myself.

"But all this ideological turmoil in the end would lead to a South Korean victory. Those North Korean scavengers would be beyond control. North Korean soldiers are soldiers first, human beings second. But when they come to South Korea and see all the advantages of the free-market system, they'll be humans first and soldiers second. There's a Korean saying, 'Even a king if starved for three days will go out and steal.' Even if they are brainwashed, people are still human."

Q. What about relations among the soldiers?

A. "Each 120-man company has a commander, who is a captain, plus a party commissar. These days they're like cats and dogs. If war broke out, they'd have the right to fire their weapons and they would shoot each other. They hate each other.[4] There's a great possibility of North Korea invading South Korea, but the South Koreans would win for all these reasons.

"By the way, I heard there's a tunnel that comes all the way down to Seoul, near Kimpo Airport. I told the South Korean authorities about it and they're trying to find it. That tunnel is intended to take advantage of the fact that most of South Korea's military is posted near the DMZ and there's virtually nothing south of Seoul. So they can just come through the tunnel, going under the South Korean defenders, and head south. Bypassing the defenders, they could take over much of South Korea. Three days ago they started digging for the tunnel. It could be a couple of hundred meters deep."

Q. What sort of food and petroleum reserves does North Korea maintain for wartime use?

A. "We're taught that we have a three-year supply of food and petroleum. But I speculate there isn't much left. It's just a pitiful situation. Even when I was there they would take rice from the wartime reserves. Now things are much worse, so it's very probable they're using the petroleum reserve now. There are colonels who inspect the DMZ lines in their trucks. When they don't have enough fuel, they have to walk, maybe twenty miles, back to camp."

Q. What happens following Kim Il-sung's death?

A. "I don't believe in a military coup. The military wouldn't have that much power. But inside the central party apparatus they're not all Kim Il-sung's family. There are also members of [Marshal] O Jin-u's family and other first-generation revolutionaries' families. They'll be the leaders in any coup attempt."

Q. What did your superiors think about Kim Jong-il and his orders?

A. "They follow the orders because they have to. But they hate following him. He's a very authoritarian personality. Take the West Sea Barrage. A Soviet engineer came and said it would take twenty years to build. Kim Jong-il said to do it in five years. They did it in six years. Probably all twenty million citizens were involved. Kim Il-sung went through lots of hardship to get where he is. But most people feel just being Kim Il-sung's son hasn't earned Kim Jong-il his position."

Q. Soldiers serve for ten years or so. Do they go without sex all that time?

A. "Although it's not allowed, guys fantasize and masturbate. Others go to nearby villages and rape women, or seduce them with promises of marriage. Officers who have graduated from the military academy are allowed to marry and bring their wives to the camp. I was married. I never heard the word 'homosexual' until I came to South Korea, but I saw a lot of that in the military. The veterans would latch onto new, seventeen-year-old recruits. It's not like homosexuality in the West. It's just that there are no women. In their sleep, the men are lined up in their bunks. A young guy with soft skin may seem like a woman. Around half of the soldiers were involved in that sort of thing."

Q. Did you notice any changes in the military from the cultural inroads made by foreigners at the 1989 youth festival?

A. "No. In the military you can't satisfy your cultural wishes. There wan't that big a change. From a foreigner's viewpoint it may have seemed bigger. The government made people wear colorful clothing, and brought in discos and disco music. A foreigner may have imagined North Korean society had opened up, but the government's policy actually has become more rigid by the year in terms of restraints on behavior. Kim Jong-il has a slogan about openness. 'If you want openness, you open a window.

But flies and mosquitoes can come in then. So we'll have mosquito nets.'
We actually had to become more tightly knit than before, rather than
opening up."

Q. What do you think about Radio Free Asia?

A. "It's a very good idea. I have a lot of expectations for the U.S. role in
opening up North Korea. South Korea has limitations in dealing with
that. The U.S. should do its utmost to knock at the door and make the
North Koreans open up."

Q. What about radio availability?

A. "Most people don't have radios. If people could listen to this kind of
broadcast the regime would have collapsed years ago. The people who
can listen are those who already have power—those in the central committee of the party."

Kim Kwang-choon, the master sergeant on the front line who defected in
1989 with Kim Nam-joon by swimming the Imjin River, was a handsome,
clear-eyed man of twenty-nine when I met him in 1994. He was quite short.
If I had not known he was Korean I would have assumed from his appearance that he was Southeast Asian, perhaps Thai.

A native of Pyongsong in South Pyongan province, Kim had been assigned for eight years to security details of the city of Kaesong, just north of
the border. "While I was working near Panmunjom I got to know about
Seoul and South Korea," he told me. "When you first enter the military you
don't know, but if you work four or five years around the DMZ you get to
realize what's happening. There's an atmosphere of war. Both sides spread
leaflets and broadcast propaganda. South Korea gives away watches and
stockings, and the South Korean literature includes articles from newspapers like *Dong-A Ilbo* and *Chosun Ilbo*. The watches are electronic. Now that
I'm in the South I see them everywhere. They're pretty cheap, too. The
South Koreans would send up balloons filled with those materials during the
night. They were supposed to explode after two hours—usually around
Kaesong. So I would pick them up. I had to give them to State Security, but
while picking them up I got to see the materials."

Q. I notice that just about every defector I've interviewed so far, including
you, has worn a fancy gold watch.

A. "When I came South I bought a gold-plated Seiko. In North Korea gold
is very rare, so every defector wants a gold watch. A government person
takes us to a watch store and says, 'Pick the one you want.' Then the
government pays for it."

Q. You were able to read *Dong-A Ilbo* and *Chosun Ilbo* even though the North
Korean school system doesn't teach Chinese characters?

A. "This is part of psychological warfare. The Ministry of National Defense in Seoul replaces the *hanja* [Chinese characters, which are used by most South Korean publishers for many loan words] and reprints the articles all in *hangul* [the indigenous Korean alphabet, which is used in combination with *hanja* in the South but whose use Kim Il-sung made exclusive in the North as an affirmation of linguistic nationalism]. Sometimes they leave the *hanja* in, but we can try to guess the meanings.

"When I was low-ranked I couldn't look at those. I had to turn them in. Actually I didn't even want to read them. But later, starting around 1986 as I got promoted in rank, I was able to read them secretly in the woods. I didn't really grasp the South Korean political scene, but I read articles on foreign affairs and the outside world. I got interested in articles about demonstrations and crime. I was fascinated because in North Korea you couldn't possibly dream of having a demonstration or riot. I was amazed that people could have their voices, could even criticize the head of state. I read a lot of articles on that. I was very surprised and thought, 'There must be a lot of freedom in South Korea for them to have these demonstrations.'"

Q. Why were you interested in crime stories?

A. "In North Korea they don't put that bad stuff in the papers. At first I thought South Korea must be in turmoil. Everybody must be a criminal. Ultimately, I started thinking that South Koreans must have a lot of time for theft and such. It must be an individualistic society."

Q. How could you think such thoughts, having been raised in North Korea?

A. [Evidently he didn't quite get the question.] "Even to this day I don't know how I defected. But to tell you the truth, it was the lack of material goods in North Korea that made me defect. The biggest difference between South and North is that the North Korean economy is based on rationing. I realized that South Korea was a free-market society where people could go to the market and get what they liked."

Q. Were you hungry?

A. "To be in the military in North Korea is far better than being an ordinary citizen. I got 800 grams of rice a day. But with all the heavy training even 800 grams was not enough. From reading the South Korean materials I gathered that South Korean military men got their rations but then also could have their snacks. This was totally unthinkable in North Korea. We got snacks only on holidays, when the military got more than civilians. Once in a while when I had to work night shifts, from 6 P.M. to 6 A.M., I would get about 500 grams of candy. Outsiders never really quite grasp North Korean society. I'm appalled because when I meet youngsters in South Korea I tell them I was hungry and they reply, 'Why should you go hungry?' I reply, 'Without living there you couldn't understand.'"

Q. Why did you stay in the military?

A. "Of course when you're young you are determined to enter the military because after your hitch you become a party member. It's usually a seven-to-ten-year hitch. You stay in until you're twenty-seven. Most enter at seventeen, so spend ten years at it, but some have worked in factories after high school so may have only seven years or so before they hit twenty-seven. In South Korea to become a commissioned officer you would go to the Korea Military Academy right out of high school. In North Korea, though, new cadets entering Kankon Military Academy are chosen from among soldiers with three or four years' service. I didn't go to the military academy. Instead, after three years I went to a training program for noncommissioned officers.

Q. Did soldiers discuss complaints such as you have mentioned?

A. "Yes. We would sit around and talk about our complaints. Of course, you would be hesitant to talk to just anyone. I would only talk to a couple of very close friends."

Q. Did they want to defect?

A. "They had to consider their families. In my case, my parents died while I was in the military. I'm the youngest of six siblings. I thought, 'Why would the government bother my brothers and sisters?'"

Q. Could you see South Korean soldiers across the border, and did you note any difference between them and North Koreans?

A. "I had no way of knowing their lifestyle. I only knew we had the same bloodlines."

Q. Were they taller, fatter?

A. "I didn't think much about that because the North Korean soldiers sent to Panmunjom are the taller ones of good family background. So I thought maybe the South Koreans had the same policy."

Q. Tell me about your family background and childhood.

A. "My family lived in Harbin [in Northeast China]. We left there when I was two—it was the time of the Chinese Cultural Revolution and we couldn't live there any more.

"When I was two and three years old, I went to nursery school every day while my parents worked. From age four to six I went to kindergarten at seven in the morning and returned home at 6 P.M. Since my parents were out working, there were times when I would come home early and find no one there. I would just play by myself. I didn't get much love from my parents and didn't have much time to spend with them. My father was a chauffeur. Mother did sewing in a neighborhood cooperation group. Because of my education, I felt more gratitude to Kim Il-sung than to my parents. I believed that Kim Il-sung was a savior, providing my education and my food. I did my utmost to be faithful to Kim Il-sung."

Q. When you were planning your defection, did you feel any guilt toward Kim Il-sung?

A. "I think Kim Il-sung is basically a nice guy. He's not to blame. All the brainwashing is done by the high officials just for their vested rights. They make this ideology so their privileges will stand. Kim Il-sung did a lot of painful things to his people. But he shouldn't be blamed. His followers did it with him. High officials made Kim Il-sung into an idol so they could lead lavish lives and hold on to their privileges. I do understand he wants permanent one-man rule, but it's the will of his followers, too. Kim Il-sung as one individual can't be solely blamed. It's those under him who have brought the people to this situation — people like former Premier Yon Hyon-muk and current Premier Kang Song-san."

Q. How about Kim Jong-il?

A. "I don't like him at all. I have lots of complaints about Kim Jong-il. He never experienced war, never knew hardship. He's conceited, showing off his activity and power. But he has the power because of his father. Kim Jong-il wants to head the military. This brings up a complaint about Kim Il-sung. Kim Il-sung is making Kim Jong-il the head of the army when there are so many more able men, just to extend one-man rule. Kim Jong-il never served in the military.

"Kim Jong-il has curly hair. They call him 'Curly'. They say he's so brutal, when he sits on the ground somewhere and then gets up, grass won't grow there anymore. Nights and days are reversed for Kim Jong-il. He sleeps days, works nights. He phones people at odd hours — that brings about complaints. I acknowledge that he's an artistic genius, but he's leading a sinful and dirty life. He likes women too much. Who doesn't like women? But he's notorious. Lots of ordinary people know about his flings with women. We heard about Kim Jong-il's Happy Group, Kim Il-sung's Satisfaction Group. There's an institute of studies for Kim Il-sung's longevity."

Q. Did you hear about some of this after you came to the South?

A. "I'm telling you only what I knew when I was in North Korea."

Q. Why blame only Kim Il-sung's followers? He set out to have himself idolized.

A. "I know he's the boss behind idolization but the followers should get together and have a coup d'etat."

Q. It seems that North Koreans who are dissatisfied enough to do anything end up defecting instead of rebelling. What must happen before people will stay and struggle rather than defect?

A. "When I was in North Korea, after having all those complaints I wanted to form some kind of anti–Kim Il-sung movement. But I alone could do nothing, so I defected. But middle-level officials know about the outside world and they do nothing. There should be a lot of pressure from the outside world. Ordinary people need a *lot* of pressure from the outside."

Q. What do you think of the idea for Radio Free Asia?

A. "It would be very effective. I'd be very glad. I've heard them talking about it at the [South Korean] Defense Ministry."

Q. What sort of programming should it offer?

A. "Instead of looking at the big picture, take a more micro approach. Start reporting on North Korea's lifestyles, crime and so on. Then, later, tune it up a bit and talk about the state of economics and politics. You would have to interpret this for people, in a way, or they wouldn't be able to understand. Make it simple."

Q. Do people have radios to listen?

A. "Only about one in fifteen homes has the right equipment. It would be difficult."

Q. What did you learn about the ability or willingness of soldiers to fight if Kim Jong-il should give the order?

A. "I sort of doubt they would really fight. In the brigade there's a line commander plus a party commissar. The military person should have the power, but the party commissar is struggling for power. There's a split. Some are for the commander, others for the commissar. If war should come, the initial problem would be whose command to follow."

Q. Can you envision ordinary soldiers and officers throwing down their arms or shooting their commanders?

A. "Since there are two factions in each unit, I thought in case war should break out I would shoot the commander. I was thinking of that when I got promoted, and it gave me an incentive to treat my subordinates very warmly. I figured if war broke out and they had the same mentality as I had, maybe they would shoot me. I can't really say how many, but there certainly are others who think the way I did."

Q. Some young civilian defectors told me the people of North Korea think it would be better to die in war than die of hunger, so they want war.

A. "That's a widespread attitude. I myself thought war would have to break out. I was suffering too much from hunger. When I first entered the army, I was 100 percent certain North Korea would win a war. But after four or five years of studying the South Korean enemy, I realized North Korea doesn't have the economy to support a war. So I thought a war would destroy both South Korea and North Korea. Officially the government warns that war between South and North would be the third world war. But in military training we are taught we have to fight the South and win."

Q. Tell me about your senior officers.

A. "I think they have the same sort of complaints against the regime.

I talked with them and they would complain indirectly: 'Look at the rations my family is getting. Can they live on that?'"

Q. Other defectors I've interviewed had moments of crisis when they were faced with jail or loss of their positions, so they felt they had little to lose in defecting. How about you?

A. "After ten years of military service they assign you to a district other than your home district. Since you're still young, they make you go to the mines for a couple of years. I was scared of that. I didn't know about it at the time I entered the military, but after I got in it started to worry me. [Unless chosen for something more important] you have no way of avoiding mine duty, although if you work diligently you may get to cut it short earlier than otherwise. From 1987, I started thinking of coming to South Korea through China, once I got mustered out. I was thinking of just a visit en route to my new posting. It wouldn't have been too difficult because my home town is Harbin and all my relatives except my siblings are in China. So I could set out to visit relatives in China. A high officer in my brigade promised to send me to Kim Il-sung University. But in 1988 he sent another officer instead. I got angry. With the combination of anger over that incident and fear of life in the mines, I decided to defect."

Q. One high-ranking civilian defector suggested a scenario in which mine workers aided by military-trained people rise up against the regime and overthrow it.

A. "I don't really know for sure the mentality of the people at the mines, but it certainly sounds plausible. Among my fellow soldiers, others besides myself were worried and angry at the prospect of being sent to the mines."

Q. Why did you swim the Imjin River when you had a relatively painless escape route through China?

A. "I used to discuss these things with Kim Nam-joon, my friend who ultimately defected with me. At first we did plan to go via China. But then we said, 'We're so near the border, why not take the risk now instead of waiting a couple of years to be mustered out?'"

Q. What did you expect after defection?

A. "I didn't have specific expectations except that South Korea was a more affluent society. I just wanted to get away from the miserable life of North Korea."

Q. Tell me exactly how you escaped.

A. "We got all our preparations ready. There are four lines of fences, electrified from 6 P.M. to 6 A.M. The first two are 220 volts; the third, 3,300 volts; and the fourth, 10,000 volts. We got some wire cutters for the first two and planned to crawl under the third and fourth. To do that we needed a mine detector. We had guns. The Imjin River was the place where I worked. After cutting the first two fences we came to the 3,300-volt third fence. We

had an iron rod and a three-meter rubber hose. The plan was to swing this
and throw it at the fence, putting the fuse out. It didn't work, although
there was an enormous electrical flash, like lightning. We defected on September 10. The previous day had been a holiday, so people on the night
watch were sleeping on the early morning of the tenth to rest up from the
festivities. We accidentally fired a gun once, but they were too sleepy to
hear it.

"Since we couldn't get past the third fence, we crawled back to the
night-watch camp and found the soldiers on watch asleep. Luckily we
found a sewer. It was low tide, so there was no water in it. We went
through that to the Imjin River. We had life jackets and swam the 4 kilometers across the river, taking three hours. We went to a South Korean
marines camp."

Q. What are you doing now?
A. "I'm still dealing with the National Security Planning Agency. South
   Korean people can figure from seeing me whether I'm a North Korean
   spy or not. I'm attending Kyongwon University, studying administration. I'm also studying *hanja*. I'm not married yet, but will marry soon."

Choi Seung-chan, an army sergeant turned factory supply official, defected
in July 1996. When I interviewed him in 1998 he was thirty-one years old.
There was no smile on his immobile face. His eyes were wide, his hair
combed forward. He had clothed his small frame in a beige suit.

Q. Why did you defect?
A. "I had been in the military for ten years and afterward worked to supply
   a factory. I came via Kangwha Island, near Inchon. The main reason is,
   I was watching people starve. While people starve in North Korea, Kim
   Jong-il only prepares for war. He visits military camps, not the ordi-
   nary people. I thought, 'This country is not for the people, only for the
   military.' I also heard that South Korea was richer than North Korea."
Q. Were you in trouble?
A. "The main trouble I had was starvation. I thought it was better to come
   to South Korea than to get shot while stealing."
Q. People in charge of supply are usually better off than the others.
A. "The only advantage I had was more free time than ordinary people had.
   The problem with working in the supply department was a total lack of
   supplies for the factory. I had to sell my personal assets to supply the fac-
   tory. It was a brick factory in Kaesong. That's my home city."
Q. Tell me about your family.
A. "I'm the third son of five siblings. Father was retired when I was born.
   He was a trucker, delivering supplies. He worked for a marble quarry.

Both my parents were Kaesong natives. My father was seventeen when the war broke out. He was a farmer. Seven family members all died from American bombing and my father was severely burned. The family was pro-North so they could remain in Kaesong after the war when others were moved out."

Q. What was your military assignment?

A. "Sergeant in the Parachute Corps, stationed in Pyongyang."

Q. Is it true that military units made up of people from one region are always stationed elsewhere so they won't mind opening fire on the locals in case of demonstrations?

A. "I'm not sure. It's true that they station people away from their homes, and units can be dispatched to other provinces but not where they're from, but I don't know if the reason has to do with demonstrations."

Q. So in your unit, for example, you met no Pyongyang natives?

A. "Right, basically, although there were some sons of high officials who had been brought up in Pyongyang."

Q. Why were paratroopers stationed in Pyongyang?

A. "Two missions: One is war reserve. The other is to fight South Korean paratroopers when they come to Pyongyang. I joned in 1983 at sixteen and had my whole tour in Pyongyang."

Q. Was it a good assignment?

A. (He finally smiles a little.) "I was very proud to be in Pyongyang. I had some free time and was able to relax."

Q. Rations?

A. "I started in the military in 1983. Rations came at first. But in the end it was terrible. There was no oily food more than once a week. We had meat only on special holidays. Rice couldn't be cooked properly because of the fuel shortage, so we had to eat it partly cooked."

Q. Quantity?

A. "We could have only one-third to two-thirds of the standard due to corruption. Higher-ranking soldiers took the food. So when the military came to a village, the local people were afraid because they knew lower-ranking soldiers were hungry and would steal their food."

Q. You, too?

A. "I had to survive. There was no exception. Villagers understood our problem but asked us not to steal the farmers' individual crops from their own plots but just take from the collectively grown food."

Q. When did military theft of food start?

A. "Before I joined. When I was a private I was ordered to go out and get food. Although I told you the situation was good when I first enlisted, I was speaking in relative terms."

Q. What was the proportion of stolen to rationed food by 1983?

A. "I was in a seven-man squad. When we went out to steal, we stole

20 kilograms. We did that two or three times a month. The total I stole was maybe one ton. Some bad guys would steal a ton at one time, sell it and keep the proceeds for their marriage."

Q. You knew someone who did that?

A. "Yes. You cannot live in the military without stealing."

Q. Did military men find any contradictions in the fact they were supposed to be defending the socialist revolution and at the same time had to steal from the civilian population?

A. "Officially the military banned stealing. Those who were caught were supposed to be punished with demotion. But you cannot live the official way."

Q. Did the men talk about contradictions?

A. "I could only think about them. I couldn't speak about them or I'd be reported."

Q. How did that relate to morale, fighting spirit?

A. "There's an indoctrination effect. The men thought their hardship was caused by South Korea and the United States. The worse their difficulties, the angrier they became at the U.S. and South Korea. More and more people wanted war, to escape reality."

Q. Yourself?

A. "Everyone including myself."

Q. What can you tell me about the ability of the North Korean military?

A. "While I was in North Korea my colleagues and I thought South Korea wasn't any match for North Korea. The South Korean army was so weak. Even in the Korean War our side had gone all the way to Pusan. Without American intervention we could have conquered the peninsula then. After I moved to South Korea and saw the technology and the status of the military I thought the South Koreans could fight with North Korea. I think North Korean army morale is still high. They're in a life-or-death situation. If there were a war they would fight to the death. They're so starved."

Q. Who would win?

A. "You never know."

Q. How did you avoid getting sent to the coal mines after the army?

A. "Normally infantrymen go to the mines. Paratroopers—they valued my military contributions and sent me home. At first I worked at the stone quarry where my father worked, in the grinding and cutting department. The work was not too heavy—we used machinery. But the noise was a problem."

Q. Did you leave because of the noise?

A. (Becomes relatively heated.) "The work itself was OK. But the rules were too tight. It was a military quarry. There was a meeting every week at which I was subjected to criticism. That was a total pain. So I wanted to move to a civilian job. I moved to a brick factory."

Q. What can you tell me about the food situation over the years?

A. "From 1987 there were problems with the government-provided rice. They would skip one or two months' rations. By 1993, it stopped for over six months. I spent seven months of 1996 in North Korea and received no rice ration. In between, in 1994 and '95, they skipped seven or eight months a year."

Q. What precisely was your job at the brick factory?

A. "Collecting coal from a state agency in Kaesong. To do that I had to bribe them. We needed the coal to fire the clay into bricks."

Q. Was a lot of production stopped by that time?

A. "In Kaesong, 20 to 30 percent of factories were still working. In my factory, 20 to 30 percent of the departments were working."

Q. Why didn't you report the coal agency's demands for bribes?

A. "There's much more demand than supply. So everybody bribed the officials. You had to use special gifts, liquor or meat, to make them happy."

Q. What did you have to sell to get those presents for them?

A. "I had some private assets: eight goats, one pig and two dogs for eating, plus my bicycle, which I sold. Every year I sold 50 percent of my remaining assets and from those sales used 40 percent as bribe money. I was getting low and I couldn't see any hope for the future."

Q. Why didn't you use all your assets to live on and forget about the factory, saving the bribery costs?

A. "The factory gave me free time, which I needed to raise the animals and build my assets. If I couldn't get the coal I'd be dismissed from the factory and would have no place to go. Public Security would get me. Every day the police check the attendance and if someone's not there they go to his home and catch him. If I had no job for six months the police would catch me and charge me with theft. The theory is: If you have no income for six months, how else, except by stealing, could you get by?"

Q. Were you raising your animals on brickyard property?

A. "No, on a mountain near my house. I moved my house so I could raise them. If you sell one goat you can get 20 kilos (44 pounds) of rice—just a month's worth."

Q. Your animals weren't breeding fast enough to keep you ahead?

A. "It takes one year for goats."

Q. Did you think of switching to rabbits?

A. "One out of every three households raises rabbits. The value is too low. They only weigh a kilo or so. It was a relatively good job I had in the brick factory. But I'd sold all my goats by the time I decided to come here. So I thought maybe that was my last chance: 'Die here or be shot crossing the border.'"

Q. Did you have surviving family?

A. "Brothers and sisters but no wife or children. I came alone."

Q. How did you cross?

A. "I used the tides. Because I'd been trained as a paratrooper I could have come by land, but I thought the sea route was easier. I first tried in June, one month before my successful attempt, but the water was too cold so I postponed it to July 8, 1996, the second anniversary of Kim Il-sung's death. At midnight, like in *Papillon,* I got in at low tide. I swam three days and nights using a small bicycle tube for flotation. It would be only a one-day swim, but I had to hide during daylight beneath fences. I followed the coastline for three days, still in North Korea, before I crossed the border. That's my military training: I was sure I could make it."

Q. Tell me about your military life. Ten year hitch, no home leave, no girls?

A. "I had no choice. Just life or death. No visits. No dates. All I could do was follow orders."

Q. Even in Pyongyang?

A. "It's just a slight difference. In some ways soldiers in rural areas have a better situation—they can steal more rice. My base was on the outskirts of Pyongyang. We could go to the rice mill or the dog farm."

Q. Did you have any rough confrontations?

A. "Although the guards were armed they couldn't keep the military out. We were trained. Normally guards are beaten by military robbers. When theft occurs, 70 percent of the stock goes. Once the manager of a farm told the miliitary commander, 'Please just hit one section of the farm. I'll calculate the number of dogs stolen, report it to the commander and get compensation.' Many guards were knifed to death."

Q. Did you fight people?

A. "I used stones to frighten the guards. Normally they'd get frightened and back off. I didn't kill anybody. One out of ten times there'd be a fight, but nobody ever fights with the military and wins."

Q. Did you ever see donated food?

A. "Not international aid, but in 1995 South Korea donated food. I saw it. I got three or four kilograms. We were told the rice was from the Chongryon—that they had bought it from the South Koreans and sent it. That was the official North Korean story. After several months I found a leaflet from a South Korean balloon and heard South Korean radio reports so I realized the truth."

Q. How long did you listen to radio and read leaflets?

A. "Leaflets I could see even when I was a kid. Radio I could receive when I was in the military. I could even watch KBS2 when I was in the military, but I had to be very careful."

Q. Were you an early doubter?

A. When I was young I didn't believe what the South Koreans said. And there was government-subsidized food in North Korea then. When I grew up, the economy was in worse shape and there was no more subsidized food. Kim Jong-il only visited military camps. He didn't show interest in ordinary people. So I came to believe what the leaflets said. I decided in 1993, one year after I quit the army, that I would defect eventually. My first idea was to escape to China, but I didn't know the Chinese border area well so I decided to go to South Korea."

Q. What are you doing now?

A. "I work with the farmers' cooperative."

Yoo Song-il, a supply colonel until he retired to civilian life in 1992, noted when I met him in 1998 that military service was not mandatory in North Korea. "But we're taught all our lives that joining the military is the greatest honor. You can't be a party member or hold a high position without military experience. So every young man's dream is to join the military. I reached the rank of colonel in logistics and supply. I was based in the same place in Kangwon province, right across from the DMZ, for twenty-four years, supplying eastern DMZ posts."

Q. What was the military supplies situation as of 1992?

A. "Until 1992 we did have the basic rations needed, and supplies for war. In the military everybody had enough food for three days in reserve, plus two days' worth of other necessities. Also, in a warehouse, we had some more. In total, we had nine days of food in reserve. There are set amounts of daily food and other necessities for soldiers: 560 grams of rice, 240 grams of other grain, 100 grams of meat, 1 kilogram of vegetables, 20 grams of soy sauce and 10 grams of cigarettes. They're supposed to get that even if they're not fighting. But while we got rice, cigarettes and salt, Kim Jong-il said to produce our own meat and vegetables. As a practical matter, soldiers didn't get what they were supposed to get."

Q. Had the soldiers missed rations by 1992?

A. "No. One reason they didn't get all they were supposed to get was that whenever such and such quantity of meat was supposed to come to my base officials on the way down would take some. By the time it arrived, there wasn't enough. In reality, some soldiers were malnourished. We put malnourished people together and fed them separately. If they improved, they were sent back to their units. Otherwise they were hospitalized or discharged."

Q. What proportion were malnourished?

A. "About 2 percent."

Q. Did the army reduce war reserve stores?

A. "Yes, there were times when that happened, because of the economic crisis. The nine-day supply included food, fuel, ammunition, explosives and uniforms, kept in a war-staging area on each base."

Q. Did you examine those stores?

A. "Yes, once a week we checked and replaced old rice with new."

Q. How would you compare the army with your civilian life in Chongjin, regarding food supply?

A. "It's like the difference between heaven and earth. When I was in the military I never had to worry about food or clothing. When I got out, rations were scarce. We were supposed to get them every fifteen days but it didn't always happen, so we had to worry about food. Officials always took what they needed, but most people relied on their rations."

Q. What if war comes?

A. "There's always a possibility of war. The soldiers have been raised all their lives to think if Kim Jong-il is in charge they'll win. The civilians are starving. They've been taught that the only way to live well is through reunification. Now they're starving. What can they lose? They all think once there's a war they'll win."

Q. What do you think?

A. "War is possible if Kim Jong-il is threatened enough. North Korea is a place where people can't protest. The country for fifty years has been preparing for war. But the people are starving. If the situation gets worse and Kim Jong-il's power structure is threatened, he might start a war as a last resort. Although I don't think it would happen easily, it's definitely a possibility.

    "After the July 14, 1973, statement for unification, in the military we had hope, we started thinking about unification. But the party used that to reinforce the military and put everything into defense. The party used this propaganda to say, 'When unification comes, we'll have to liberate the South. We must reinforce and invest in the military.'"

Q. I calculate that you would have joined the army around the time of the *Pueblo*'s capture, 1968.

A. "Yes. Lots of people joined the military then, because we thought there'd be a war."

Q. How did you become an officer?

A. "Through effort. Kim Jong-il was backing the military. It was the most popular occupation. I didn't go to the academy. Rather I was picked for three months of officer candidate school and promoted."

Q. What did your fellow field grade and senior officers think of the chances of victory?

A. "When they think of war they think of fighting the United States and Japan, rather than South Korea. They used to say, 'China and the Soviet

Union shouldn't be involved. This is our own war, against the U.S. and Japan.' They think we'll win. They're brainwashed to think so."

Q. You thought so?

A. "Yes."

Q. Now what do you think?

A. "In terms of will, indoctrination, the South is at a disadvantage. North Koreans are single-minded. In the South they're talking of peaceful unification. That's not how the North thinks. In the North, everyone is ready mentally for war. But in the South most citizens don't think of it, and they don't have that resolve to win. Technically, North Korea lags behind. But they say a fight goes to the single-minded. That's what North Korea has. Unless South Koreans prepare themselves mentally for the possiblity, who knows what will happen?"

Q. Some say North Korean soldiers' morale will crumble when they see the riches of the South—they'll just start looting instead of fighting.

A. "I don't think so. Yes, they'll be shocked, but they're disciplined."

Q. What are you doing now?

A. "It hasn't been a year since I got here. I was in an education camp, started living as a civilian last July. Now I'm checking job possibilities, lecturing on the North Korean situation. I want to get my South Korean driver's license, so I'll be taking classes for that."

Q. Are you helping the South Korean army?

A. "Yes, a little. After all, I was in for twenty-four years."

Ahn Myung-jin had served in a special spy force with military ranks whose mission was to infiltrate into South Korea. With his thick forearms, Ahn looked strong. And after I had heard his story late in June of 1994, just a few days before Kim Il-sung's death, I reflected that he could represent both the wildest dreams and the deepest fears harbored by Kim Jong-il.

From 1979 to 1987, Ahn told me, he had studied at Wonsan Foreign Language Institution. When I noted that I had visited Wonsan, an east coast port, during my 1979 visit, he replied curtly, "That was in better times." At the school, he said, "I specialized in English but the course wasn't very good. There is one of those foreign language institutions in each province. You go to language school right after four years of elementary school and spend eight years of middle and high school there. Future spies are selected from among the graduates.

"From 1987 to May 1993 I attended the university-level Kim Jong-il Political-Military Academy in Pyongyang. The term of study there is five years and six months. They basically teach espionage, terror and other undercover tactics there, including how to kidnap important government officials and lure potential defectors from South Korea and, in the event of war, how to get into South Korea ahead of the People's Army and destroy the important institutions."

The junior member of the team that bombed the South Korean airliner in 1987, Kim Hyon-hui, who had posed as a Japanese traveler, had survived a suicide attempt with a poison capsule after capture (her senior colleague died). She ultimately told her South Korean captors the details of the mission. "Kim Hyon-hui had gone earlier to the same school, when it was called Kumsong Political-Military University," Ahn said. "There are two tracks. She went through the one-year espionage course. The six-year program is for people who will be involved in the war effort." Ahn boasted that Kim "didn't do a tenth of what I did. Compared with what we had to do, her work was very light."

He was passionate as he elaborated on the superiority of his training: "Because Kim Hyon-hui had only one year of training, she would not have been the one in charge of an order given by Kim Jong-il. She wouldn't pull the trigger, or kidnap someone. Kim Hyon-hui was in the Department of External Information, concerned with Japan. She wasn't being trained to infiltrate but just to *become* Japanese. I was in the Strategic Division of the Party Central Committee's Espionage Department, of which the academy was a part and where we needed military training. She only got input and didn't learn how to output information. I would inspect important sites that might be ordered blown up and study the interiors to see where the explosives could be placed. As for swimming, I had to swim 10 kilometers; she only had to make four kilometers. I practiced scuba diving and all kinds of shooting—long distance, short-range, moving objects.

"We studied the geography of South Korea. I knew it by heart. And I knew how to act like a normal South Korean. [My interpreter, Rhee Soo-mi, noted that Ahn indeed did not speak with so obvious a Northern accent as other Northerners she had helped me interview.] I could use the local currency and so on. I wasn't surprised by South Korea when I came here."

Q. Had you studied the "Orange Tribe" (as a species of trendy young Seoulites was dubbed in the mid-'90s)?

A. "We learned all about the people who live here, from the Orange Tribe to beggars. [In spy training] people are classified demographically, by occupation and age group. We used audiovisual aids and studied dialects."

Q. Were you trusted to know anything whatsoever about South Korea?

A. "I read all the dailies published in South Korea. We also knew that South Korea was a much freer country with much higher living standards."

Q. If they let you know that, how did they keep you loyal?

A. "Actually they changed the system after the Kim Hyon-hui case. She hadn't been taught what I was taught about South Korea. She was taught

WE WILL BECOME BULLETS AND BOMBS

about Western capabilities but she thought South Koreans didn't live as well as North Koreans. When she was taken to Seoul and saw the South Korean living standards, she betrayed the regime. So they decided it was better to teach the reality, to avoid such surprises."

Q. But how did they keep you loyal?

A. "First you should not imagine that we were ordinary North Koreans. Our living standards were up to those of the higher class in South Korea. We would do our best to conduct espionage in South Korea. In the past, though, if spies failed they would commit suicide. What the regime doesn't know is that the current crop would not commit suicide in case of failure but surrender, since we had learned that defectors live pretty well here."

Q. Tell me about your family background and your attitudes toward the regime as you grew up.

A. "My family was part of the elite. All who attended the academy were selected for good family background, meaning no history of association with South Korea.

"I was a fanatical believer in the ideology. Every true rejection of ideology has a practical reason. In my case, I had wanted since my childhood to be a diplomat, and I was supposed to go to the External Information Department, the one that Kim Hyon-hui was in. But in my senior year at the foreign language school, I got into a fight with a soldier and that ruined my chances to go to the External Information Department and become a diplomat. Diplomats from my background are in fact spies who spy on other countries, not on other North Korean diplomats. Instead I had to go to the Central Party Espionage Department's Strategic Division.

"At the Kim Jong-il Political-Military Academy my ideology began to change. Ideological change combined with the damage to my career made me turn against the regime. I always knew about the discrepancies in the North Korean regime and felt dissatisfaction, but the main point that made me defect was this: If you're in the Strategic Department you can no longer meet your parents or other family members. You live like the upper class but you're isolated all your life."

Q. Why isolated?

A. "Three reasons. First, we had been exposed to the realities of capitalist countries and the regime was afraid we might influence others who had not. Second, they also feared that ordinary people would see our much more opulent lifestyle and resent it. Finally, many trainees were killed in training, which could cause problems with parents—it was thought best they not know what we were doing."

Q. But wouldn't the first reason have applied also to ordinary diplomats, who weren't isolated?

A. "Diplomats know, but they don't have the detailed knowledge of South Korean society that I was taught. Anyhow, diplomats who graduate from the academy are also isolated."

Q. So you had expected isolation anyhow?

A. "Yes. But if I had become a diplomat the isolation wouldn't have been so extreme—I would have had occasional chances to meeet my family. Also, the work wouldn't have been so strenuous."

Q. You were isolated from women?

A. "When I was at the language school I had friends who were girls, but the instant I entered the academy I was isolated from them. Once I reached twenty-eight or twenty-nine I would be given ten to fifteen days to get a woman. I would write to request my parents to propose a bride for me, then I'd go marry her and bring her back. In the agency there are a couple of women, but they are in great demand."

Q. Any other reasons for your disappointment besides the isolated life?

A. "In the Strategic Division, there was lots of strenuous training. And I would have to kill people even though I didn't want to."

Q. You disliked your assignment in Strategic? (I waited for him to mention any moral repugnance or sense of injustice.)

A. "Yes. While I was growing up my parents always taught me to be good. In the Strategic Department they teach you to hurt or kill others to protect yourself. It bothered me."

Q. Did you have a moral objection or was it more a matter of convenience?

A. "It cannot be only a matter of convenience. I just couldn't stand doing over and over all my life things I didn't want to do."

Q. What was your opinion of your unit's basic mission of destroying South Korea?

A. "That it was possible and necessary in order for there to be reunification on Kim Il-sung's and Kim Jong-il's terms."

Q. The end justifies the means?

A. "Yes."

Q. (I told him about the chemical warfare colonel who wanted to wipe out the whole South Korean population.) Is there a lot of such thinking in North Korea, that the end justifies the means?

A. "No one ought to say we should kill all the 40 million civilians in South Korea. I was taught we should not kill all the South Koreans, but if they opposed our regime then we would kill them."

Q. Have you met Lee Chong-guk (the man who had issued the chemical warfare warning), the only defector I've met who didn't describe any personal problem as part of his motivation for defecting?

A. "Most of those who escaped from North Korea are people who couldn't stand their low living standards. I also am surprised by Lee Chong-guk. Could it be possible to defect with no reason?"

"In my case, if you asked for the one big reason I defected I would answer: Being exposed to unlimiited outside information I realized that if reunification came it would be by North Korean collapse or absorption into South Korea. I would become unemployed and because of my status as a spy my parents would be in danger."

Q. Do you think any of the defectors is an agent provocateur?

A. "I don't think so. That's not the way they infiltrate spies into South Korea."

Q. Tell me more about the spy trainee lifestyle.

A. "Rations for us were different. I got high-quality rice, 900 grams a day, eggs, chocolate, butter, drinks. At the academy I lived in a dorm, four people to a room equipped with air conditioning, television, video, refrigerator. After graduation and before I defected I was in an accommodation of that same standard.

"I graduated May 20, 1993, then defected on September 4. In the interim I spent one month practicing infiltration by water—swimming, scuba practice. The second month I studied *taekwondo;* the third month, wireless telecommunications plus reality training in a facility resembling South Korea.

"A big tunnel, 12 meters high, 30 meters wide and 8 kilometers long, in the same area as the KJIPMA contains a 100 by 50 meter scale model of Seoul and, separately, approximately one-fourth-scale mockups of some of the more important institutions. I remember seeing the Blue House, the police department, the Agency for National Security Planning, the Kyobo Building, the Shilla Hotel, Lotte and Shinsegye department stores, as well as small cafes. When you walked through the streets you felt you were there: discos, South Korean—made cars, South Korean products inside the buildings. The scale model of all of Seoul has all the important buildings in Seoul, and the subway entrances. Next to each building is a brochure showing its whole interior.

"In the tunnel they broadcast all the programs from South Korean television and radio. It was my work to watch and listen. Even during practice sessions we had transistor radios attached to our belts and continually listened. In the tunnel you get 700,000 to 800,000 South Korean *won* in fifteen days and you have to use it up. The tunnel has its own economy. You live there fifteen days or one month a year for training and during that time you buy products."

(I nearly gasped in wonderment as Ahn described that elaborate facility set up to train spies in conspicuous consumption while much of the rest of the population went hungry. To me it remains an unforgettable image.)

"I've been in there three times. It's like a holiday. But there aren't any girls in the discos. Men demonstrate how the hostesses pour drinks.

If women were inside the tunnel it would be too much like South Korean society and there would be trouble. But we were instructed in how to interact with South Korean women.

"Training in the tunnel was to enable us to meet other spies, kidnap important officials and so on. Fifty South Koreans have been kidnapped. The people who teach you South Korean customs and dialect in the tunnels were kidnapped from South Korea. The authorities wanted to bring important figures for that, but it's hard, so those were ordinary citizens. One was a university student who was kidnapped while camping in a tent with friends during vacation in a coastal area. Basically the whole practice drill is so that we can adapt ourselves to South Korean ways during peacetime missions to the South.

"We got other training for wartime. We practiced wartime kidnapping of generals from a moving vehicle, and from a building whose security force we had to penetrate. We learned to destroy South Korean telecommunications, get on a warship secretly and destroy it, bomb an institution. We had highly developed lightweight explosives and learned the basic structure of a ship, the layout of the bridge, where to plant the explosives."

Q. Does the regime plan reunification by force?
A. "They always have that dream of reunifying through force, but there aren't enough resources now—they're very weak. So they're trying to find other ways. Thus, they're holding the nuclear card and trying to negotiate. Whenever they get their strength back they'll start dreaming their dreams again. Peaceful reunification can only occur through capitalist South Korean society overtaking North Korea. [If a federation or confederation is arranged] people in North Korea will be influenced by the lifestyle of the South and will oppose the northern regime. So to maintain their regime they believe they have to take over South Korea and get rid of capitalist ideas. They teach you that."

Q. The elite must save their positions?
A. "They don't put it that way. They would say 'for the people.' They say that basically socialism is for the people while capitalism is for an elite few. They propagandize by saying if North Korea is absorbed into South Korea it will be a world for the small elite instead of a society for the people."

Q. How could anyone believe that in a country where the elite live well and the people live like dogs?
A. "Ordinary North Koreans didn't know the real circumstances in South Korea. They're brainwashed. Now, most North Koreans do know that South Korea is wealthier. There's been a lot of change in the way people think since the 1989 youth festival brought lots of capitalistic lifestyle into the country. But even if they acknowledge that South Korea is

wealthy, people believe that if reunification takes place they have to take its wealth and distribute it among themselves."

Q. How firmly are reunification and food supplies linked together in North Koreans' minds?

A. "Reunification is not the only prospect for eating well, but food is one factor in their hope for reunification."

Q. What's the level of fanaticism among student spies?

A. "At the academy there are between three hundred and four hundred students, sixty to eighty per class year. I have no way of knowing how many are fanatics. But not all are. And even those who are fanatic adopt that posture because it's the way to get ahead. They aren't fanatics on general principle. If the North Korean regime were to collapse, the people who would be the leaders in helping to bring it down would be the people in the South Korea infiltration unit."

Q. Did people say that?

A. "I never heard such talk, it's just an opinion. There's a saying in North Korea: 'The dog you trust the most will bite you.' I did hear that saying. The people in the division hate Kim Jong-il more than anyone else does. Everyone used to be willing to sacrifice for the mission, for Kim Jong-il. But some things happened to change that. In 1989, he visited the South Korea infiltration division. He likes speed. He got on one of the speedboats there. And he did lots of promiscuous stuff with women he had brought there. People talked against him— 'How come we sacrifice for him?' Eight people disappeared suddenly after Kim Jong-il's bodyguards ratted on them.

"There was the Kim Hyon-hui case, too. She did her best, but when she was caught her parents were sent to a camp. The old man who died on that mission—Kim Sung-il—his family was sent to prison. After seeing that, we thought, 'No matter what we do, if our missions become known to the world we'll be in trouble.' So we were very unsure about our futures. Even if we did our missions well, if the fact we had done espionage became known our families would be sent to political prisons."

Q. Did you meet Kim Jong-il?

A. "I never personally met him but saw him during training."

Q. Does he have a speaking problem?

A. "I hear he speaks well one-on-one, but doesn't talk in a very courteous way. He's not deferential." (Ahn interjected that he admired my "objectivity." The regime hated that, he said. It wanted people to be either positive or negative. If they were negative, it could change them.)

"High officials in North Korea are getting prepared just in case the regime collapses. All ordinary people hate the elite and everyone hates Kim Jong-il. Ordinary people still worship Kim Il-sung."

Q. How did you escape?

A. "I made a run across the DMZ into Kyonggi Province, carrying two bombs to blow myself up if necessary, an AK47 assault rifle and a small pistol [assembled on the pretense of a training session]. The South Koreans saw me cross. I headed for a South Korean camp. No North Koreans noticed me leave."

THIRTY-ONE

Neither Land nor People
at Peace

"The Supreme Committee for the Struggle of National Salvation has reviewed Kim Il-sung's and Kim Jong-il's crimes, and sentences them to seizure of their wealth and execution."

Lim Young-sun claimed to have printed that sentence on slips of paper, then distributed them in the northeastern part of North Korea in September 1991. On the reverse side of the fliers, which were about one-fifth the size of a standard sheet of typing paper, was this further message: "All you soldiers and working citizens, form combat units and fight. Hurray for a triumphant, free people!" The former People's Army first lieutenant said that he and some anti-regime colleagues had carved a rubber stamp from a tire to print the fliers. He picked up a young woman passenger and bribed the conductor to give them both seats on the crowded train, then used his chatting with her as a cover while he tossed handfuls of fliers from the window as the train moved through the desolate region. Lim's motive? As usual with defectors, it had begun with personal disappointment. Lim said he was outraged that his father had been mistreated by the regime and that his own career was limited on account of questionable family background. In his twenties, he "decided to get revenge on the regime for what it had done to my family name."

A slender, rather good-looking man, Lim was thirty when I met him in 1994. (Yes, he wore a gold watch.) "When I started learning to write," he told me, "the first thing I learned to write—even before my own name—was 'Kim Il-sung'. Even though I didn't know my parents' birthdays, I knew the birthdays of Kim Il-sung and his ancestors. I was a very ideal student. I participated in a parade with Kim Il-sung and went on stage wearing a red kerchief as a children's corps member. I don't know if you could call it love, but I did revere Kim Il-sung and I would have done anything at all to show my loyalty. The whole process of daily life is a testing of loyalty toward Kim Il-sung. I just thought everybody lived that way. It seemed normal to me at the time. I was in my twenties before I started thinking it was strange.

"Father came from South Korea to the North during the Korean War. He was a volunteer in the *Uiyonggun*, the army of South Koreans fighting on the North Korean side. All those were volunteers. But there are always conflicts between Koreans from different regions. North Koreans don't like South Koreans, because they're more intelligent and better educated, and they have the potential to take over the regime. Father was one of the five best architects in North Korea, but his work was not properly acknowledged as the others' work was. He resented that. Superiors or subordinates were given credit for his work. People from South Korea always confront a limit. It's hard to break through that, regardless of your abilities."

When Lim was born in 1963, the family lived in the captial, Pyongyang, where his father was designing buildings. The father was a party member. Lim's mother worked in retail. Lim was the third son in a family of three boys and two girls. "We were comparatively well off, living in a three-room masonry house with television, radio and phonograph—but no refrigerator at that time. Then my father's South Korean background got in the way of his career." In 1976, the year of the Panmunjom axe-killing incident, "we had to move to North Hamgyong Province, to a cooperative farm where my parents both became farmers. Father was reduced from high party official to ordinary party member. The reason they gave was, in preparation for the war to come, they had to decrease the Pyongyang population. Of course, my parents understood the real reason: family background.

"I heard my father complain a lot. But I was too young to think of much. I just thought the family was moving. In the country, we lived in one room of a farmer's mud-walled house. There was no kitchen. We had to build our own outside, with planks. We took our TV with us but there was no reception in that remote area then, so we sold it eventually. As life got harder, we also sold the radio and the phonograph. We had a Japanese-made loom and sold that, too. As for clothing, it wasn't that bad. We took a lot with us, and some of my dad's schoolmates in Pyongyang sent us clothing. But the food I ate was mainly potatoes and corn. There were some Chinese cabbages and radishes, but we couldn't make kimchee without the other ingredients— pepper powder and so on. We just soaked the vegetables in salt water. The place is near Mount Paektu, very mountainous. I had to walk six kilometers to school, each way. Actually you could hardly call it a school. It was a storage room. The teachers had licenses but their standard was low. In some aspects, I knew more than the teachers. It was very undeveloped, like a feudal society.

"I took the university entrance exam. Since childhood I had dreamed of studying economics at a university. But because my father had been expelled from Pyongyang, and despite lots of bribes by my mother to school officials, they assigned me to an agricultural college. I didn't want to attend it, so I didn't go. To ameliorate my family background I decided to enter the army in 1980, when I was seventeen. I was an ordinary soldier for eight years, then took one-year officer training and got a commission. I served at a missile base and underground airbase in South Pyongyan province. When I was in the army, I was second to none in study and practice. I was so diligent I won seven medals. But always there were limitations on account of my family background. I couldn't go to the academy.

"From 1986, I acted as a screenwriter for the army movie studio. The studio is in Pyongyang, but I remained in my army unit and wrote scenarios based on observing other soldiers. Through this I started meeting high officials, people from the central party. I got to know about the high life they were living. I don't care that much about Kim Il-sung's lifestyle, but to keep his power he's destroying the people. In most aspects my own situation was improving, but I doubted the regime: Why were my opportunities always limited because of my family background?

"The head of the Department of Movie Creation under the Ministry of the People's Armed Forces was Li Jin-u. I got close to him. He talked about the problems of the regime. I became associated with the anti-regime movement within the ministry. In 1989, Kim Jong-il issued an instruction that as a present to Kim Il-sung we had to reunite North and South by 1995. But when Kim Jong-il gave that instruction, some people in the ministry did not want forceful reunification. They wanted it done peacefully, no matter how long it might take. Their goal was to get rid of Kim Jong-il in a coup d'état. They wanted to attempt a coup d'état either when Kim Il-sung got physically feeble or when Kim Jong-il really wanted to start a war." I asked why the plotters opposed starting a war. "Do *you* want war?" Lim replied. "These are the normal people. It's the abnormal people who would want war."

Lim said he had not been directly a part of the plotters' organization, which numbered in the hundreds of members. But he and some young colleagues were moved to form their own, much smaller organization. "First, I wanted to oppose war. Second, I didn't like the succession of Kim Jong-il. I wanted minimal freedom for the 20 million North Koreans. But basically, we did not want to be the people to initiate change. Because I was young, I didn't want what I was doing to have any political color. But since I knew all the guys in other organizations I wanted to prepare to help if some organization started a coup d'etat. We pondered for about a year on how to make the biggest impact." In September 1991, he boarded the train from Mount Komu in North Hamgyong Province to Chongjin and, during his ride, distributed about 400 of the printed fliers. Colleagues on different routes distributed about 600 more.

"The authorities investigated for about a year to find out who did it," Lim said. "I was always stressed, fearing capture. Probably the reason I wasn't caught is that my people were among the searchers." But meanwhile the larger anti-regime organization in the military was discovered and crushed. "State Security agents in the ministry found out about their attempt. They got rid of them by late 1992, arrested them all. At the New Year in 1993 Kim Il-sung made a speech. The State Security man who caught the plotters was promoted from major general to full general. The group arrested included a vice-marshal and nine or ten other general officers, one of them four-star. They were going to have an armed coup, get rid of Kim Jong-il and resume talks with South Korea. Yi Bong-yol was rumored to be the four-star general involved. I'm not sure of the others. I didn't dig up details for fear I'd be arrested myself. Word on this came via the State Security people in the military units. I never saw the documents, but in each department they had official discussions of what had happened inside the ministry. When State Security felt something was fishy, they bugged the houses of some officers, got evidence and secretly arrested them. People thought they'd just gone on long trips, and only later heard they had been arrested. Along with the generals, about 200 to 300 were said to have been arrested, with half of those executed and half sent to political prison. I don't know the method of execution, but at that time they had started using the electric chair in North Korea.

"A year after we distributed the fliers it seemed the coast was clear for me, but in February 1993 they resumed investigating the incident. In North Hamgyong, my home province, a special State Security force was formed to find the criminal. They investigated anyone who had ridden a train there in September 1991. It was discovered I had visited the province September 24, 1991, and stayed about ten hours, so State Security suspected me. In March of 1993 they found some evidence at my home." While the authorities worked to nail down further evidence, Lim made his preparations and fled to South Korea via a third country.

There is much drama in Lim's account. Perhaps that owes something to his skills as a screenwriter. In South Korea he published two books about his experiences. "When I first defected, South Korean intelligence people knew of the flier incident very well," he wrote in the second volume, *River That Runs South.* "One of them said, 'Did you know that Kim Jong-il promised to bestow the title of "hero" on whoever could find the truth of this incident?'"

While Lim's accounts were gripping, some readers were skeptical. Defector Oh Young-nam said he had been a captain in State Security in Pyong-yang from June 1991 until April of 1993, covering the entire period when Lim supposedly was the object of intensive investigation. Oh told me he had not heard of the flier incident even though he was in charge of an inspection department combatting spies and anti-government movements. He added that the regime was "very fast to act in such a case. If someone puts out a leaflet with anti-government information, there's no possibility of getting away. The intelligence network is very well kept. Sometimes sons would report on fathers. I never really trusted my wife, because I've seen too many cases where wives reported on husbands. Thus there is no open opposition." Due to extreme shortages, Oh added, "you can't find clean A-4 paper anywhere, even in an office. You can use a kid's notebook, but I can't imagine someone tossing full packs of leaflets."

That is not to say there were no opponents of the regime. Oh told me that his father, a bodyguard, had died in a 1960s shootout with special forces soldiers at a mansion where Kim Il-sung and first lady Kim Song-ae were staying in Changson county, North Pyongan province. "It was Kim Song-ae who shut my father's eyelids," Oh said. "This is widely known in North Korea." The coup plotters, he said, turned out to be under the control of Minister of National Defense Kim Chang-bong, who was not present for the gun battle.

Other sources indicated that anti-regime activities had not been infrequent. Kim Myong-chol guarded both Kim Il-sung and Kim Jong-il during his stint in the bodyguard service from 1976 to 1985. When I met him in 1994 he was suntanned, with coarse hair and a toothy smile. Oh yes, and he wore a gold watch. "When I entered there were only about 3,000 to 4,000 bodyguards," he told me, "but after the killing of Ceaucescu and his wife in Romania in 1989, they increased the number and now it's about 70,000." Kim Myong-chol had left by then but he learned of the increase from old colleagues when he visited headquarters.

"Externally we were guarding against enemy countries; internally, counterrevolutionaries," he said. "There was a 300-page book published by the Bodyguard Service detailing past incidents involving people who opposed the government. I remember a lot, but I can't remember dates and names. Around 1977, in Anak County, Hwanghae Province, a person stole an AK assault weapon from a soldier, cut it down—sawed it off—and hid it inside his jacket. He was headed for Pyongyang to terrorize a high party official when a plainclothes bodyguard caught him. His chest was bulging. There were similar incidents involving different weapons. Some people decided they wanted to give a letter of complaint to Kim Il-sung personally and tried to get through the bodyguards to him, but they got caught." He mentioned also a large student anti-regime movement, led by the son of a vice director of State Security, that he said was uncovered in 1991 at Wonsan University.

"I didn't realize any of the contradictions while I was a bodyguard," Kim Myong-chol said. "I was prepared to give up my life for Kim Il-sung and Kim Jong-il. Bodyguards are more loyal than the army. Bodyguards are people with a sturdy background of loyalty. Even a dog wouldn't go against an owner who had raised him."

Aspects of Lim's story did check out. For example, army movie creative boss Li Jin-u was a real person who got into real trouble. Lee Chong-guk, former sergeant in the Bureau of Nuclear and Chemical Defense, related to me a rumor that Li Jin-u had been killed for spreading secret information about nuclear weapons. "In 1989, Li Jin-u was making a movie, *Red Maple Leaf*," Lee said. "Researching for the scenario, he had to use data processing and look up information. He found some information about nuclear weapons and told Western reporters about it. That upset Kim Jong-il, who had Li killed. That's a rumor, but for sure Li was never seen again."

And the 1992 purge of dissident or at least disgruntled officers in the Ministry of People's Armed Forces did happen, by the accounts of many sources. According to Kang Myong-do the leader was Vice Marshal Ahn Jong-ho, and forty other elite officers were involved. Ahn Jong-ho, Kang said, had graduated from Mangyongdae Revolutionary School. As an officer he had studied at a Soviet military academy before returning to the KPA for assignments in the strategy and battle training departments, heading the latter. He had been a rising star, Kang said. Others involved were the deputy commander of the battle training department and the vice head of the strategy department, Kang said.

Kang said the officers harbored doubts about the regime and personally disliked Kim Jong-il. All had studied for three to four years at the Russian academy and had experienced considerable freedom, comparatively speaking. It was natural, he said, that they had some doubts after that experience. They also abhorred Kim Jong-il's distortion of history. Quite a few had been his classmates at Namsan Senior Middle School, so they knew his "promiscuous lifestyle. They disliked his changing his birthplace to Mount Paektu." The forty, Kang said, were executed, and the authorities "got rid of " fifty others who had studied in Russia. Kang listed previous coup attempts from as far back as the 1960s led respectively by Ho Bong-ha, Yi Hyo-seun, Kim Chang-bong and Kim Byong-ha. "Even in this tightly controlled regime there is always a possibility of coup d'etat," he said.[1]

Former party secretary Hwang Jang-yop added that in addition to the leaders who were executed, "almost all the people who had studied in the

Soviet Union were deemed to have been influenced by the anti–Kim Jong-il organization even if they were not soldiers. These people were not allowed to travel overseas, and anyone found to have the slightest connection to the anti–Kim Jong-il organization was executed, resulting in the death of almost all the students who had studied in the Soviet Union in the 1980s. I used to supervise the Juche Science Institute, where I met a Russian literature graduate of Kazan University in the USSR. The professor who had supervised his graduation thesis was the dean in charge of foreigners, and such professors usually had connections with the Security Bureau of the Soviet Union. Based on this flimsy reasoning, the People's Army arrested the graduate and had him shot."[2]

Choe Joo-whal, a former People's Army lieutenant colonel who defected, said the purged officers' offenses included giving military information to Russian intelligence. The internal spy who discovered the plot was Won Eung-hui, said Choe, who put the number purged by Won on Kim Jong-il's orders at around three hundred. Kim Jong-il, he added, was going all out to build support among other military officers. In 1992, Kim had a "very fancy" apartment building constructed on the Taedong River in Pyongyang so that he could give the apartments to influential generals. In 1995, he gave twenty generals new Mercedes Benz automobiles as presents, Choe said.[3]

In his December 7, 1996, speech, Kim stated that "currently, there are no anti-revolutionaries within the party," although there was "huge chaos due to the poor performance of the party in constructing socialism," and those party workers who had "stood by with folded arms during this hard time will have to account for their actions in the future." In the event, after the three-year period of mourning for his father ended and he made good his threat, he seems to have found some officials to accuse of being outright oppositionists.

From 1997, according to reports that filtered out of the country, North Korea publicly executed over fifty high officials. According to South Korean intelligence chief Lee Jong-chan, one of them was Ri Bong-won, a four-star general who supervised KPA personnel decisions and was accused of spying for South Korea.[4]

There were rumors, reported abroad, of a coup attempt by elements of the Sixth Army Corps in North Hamgyong Province. Kim Jong-il told some ethnic Koreans from Japan in April 1998 that the rumors were "a baseless lie. There was no such attempt. What really happened was that we found some defects in the political indoctrination program of the corps and had to remove some officers after self-criticism meetings. Contrary to the published reports, neither the corps commander nor the political commissar was executed. The joint chief of staff, who was the corps commander in question, is here today. After the so-called coup attempt, he was promoted to the chief of the joint staff. Now the enemy propagandists claim that the political commissar was behind the coup and that it was he who was executed. The truth of the matter is that the commissar was relieved because of his stomach cancer."[5]

Back to the account by Lim Young-sun of his adventure on the train, I see three items of circumstantial evidence in favor of crediting Lim's story. First, there were afterward quite a number of new and credible reports of anti-regime leafletting and graffiti writing. Second, the single provocation Lim claimed to commit was so modest (except by North Korean standards) that I would expect a movie scenarist exercising literary creativity to come up with something more heroic—car chases, shootouts, that sort of thing.

Finally, I found Lim to be perfectly plausible in the role in which he cast himself: leader of an ambitious movement. He seemed to me the sort of man who in traditional Korean cultural terms would be accepted as a leader and thus would be capable not only of dreaming up but also of carrying out an important movement. That is to say, he came across as an impatient authoritarian—the same bossy type as Kim Il-sung, Kim Jong-il and the South Korean military coup leaders-turned-dictators who had opposed them. Lim showed that side of himself in his behavior toward my interpreter, Rhee Soo-mi, pounding home his points to her. (An ambassador's daughter, accustomed to big shots, she refused to let him rattle her; following her work with me, she went on to become a New York lawyer.) I was not sure whether Lim intended irony in one peculiar exchange. "You should go to live in North Korea," he told me. I asked what I would learn there. "To obey," he replied with no sign of mirth.

Lim said he wanted to study for a while and then work in a corporation. I figured that in no time he would be CEO.

THIRTY-TWO

In a Ruined Country

[N]o man might buy or sell, save he that had the mark, or the name
of the beast, or the number of his name. Here is wisdom. Let him
that hath understanding count the number of the beast: for it is the
number of a man; and his number is six hundred threescore and six.

—THE REVELATION OF ST. JOHN THE DIVINE

Kim Jong-il's election on July 26, 1998, to the Supreme People's Assembly,
North Korea's parliament, was unanimous, according to the official Korean
Central News Agency. The current Great Leader won election from Pyongyang's District 666. Whoever picked the military-dominated district for him
may not have been aware that the number has satanic associations. (Perhaps
someone realized it later. In 2003, Kim was elected instead from District
649.)[1]

The KCNA reported that the voters in District 666 sang, danced and
shouted wishes for Kim's longevity after they had voted. Exulted one: "Experiencing the same glee that our people felt when they held Great Leader
Kim Il-sung in high esteem as head of state fifty years ago, I cast my ballot
for the Supreme Commander, Kim Jong-il." Many outside analysts believed—
mistakenly, as it turned out—that the hoopla was preparation for the junior

Kim's formal takeover of the country's presidency. That title had been vacant since his father's death in 1994, even though the son as head of the military and the Workers' Party had exercised effective control over the machinery of power. In the end, the expertly embalmed father was kept on as the country's president in perpetuity.

All the folderol about unanimous elections and titled glory aside, how were the fifty-six-year-old Supreme Commander's subjects really feeling about their leader? On his watch a famine, brought on by flooding and drought—and, to a large extent, by refusal to change failed economic and agricultural policies—had killed countless countrymen in the three years since 1995. Whether estimates of up to two or three million dead from famine-related causes during that period were correct or not,[2] there was no disputing that hunger was extremely widespread. It afflicted even the best-fed large segment of the populace, which was the Korean People's Army. The soldiers "get more than other North Koreans but they're not getting enough," an official with close ties to the Republic of Korea (ROK, South Korea) and U.S. militaries told me in June 1998.

The man told me a story that harked back to H. G. Wells's frail, flushed, four-feet-tall Eloi. In the first year of the most devastating period of the famine, he said, "two North Korean soldiers from a frontline unit in the southwestern islands got washed away in a boat while checking their nets, seeking protein. They stayed approximately two days in the boat, and were almost dead when rescued. The ROKs picked them up, and let the North Koreans know we'd return them. While they had them in the ROK Navy hospital they examined those boys from asshole to appetite. They found both had liver dysfunction due to chronic malnutrition. Both had kidney dysfunction and skin discoloration. Both had severe dental problems. The big one was five feet five and a half inches tall. The other one was four-foot-eleven. The big one, nineteen years old, weighed 98 pounds. The little one, twenty-one, was eighty-nine pounds. We don't get a lot of North Korean soldiers to do in-depth medical analysis. We didn't know whether we had the runts of the litter. We repatriated them through Panmunjom. About ten days later we saw on Pyongyang television these guys returned to their unit for a heroes' welcome. Everybody in the unit was the same size.

"We can't extrapolate but we can draw a very firm conclusion that in that unit on the frontline islands the men were all little, all chronically undernourished and not in very good health. And when I look at other North Koreans, other than in Panmunjom, I see little scrawny guys. North Korean defectors arriving in Seoul plump up after three to six months in the South. You can conclude all are undernourished—perhaps not malnourished, but not up to their genetic potential. In South Korea there are lots of six-foot-two, 180-pound guys. Even North Korea's big guards at Panmunjom are not nearly as big as South Korean JSA [Joint Security Area] guards. Anecdotally, I'd say it's clear about the KPA: their gas tank is running pretty close to empty."

This jibed with what World Food Program Assistant Executive Director Jean-Jacques Graisse told me and other journalists in Tokyo that same month. In North Korean kindergartens, Graisse said, "the children look far better than they did two years ago when the food assistance started. The food *was* delivered and *has* produced positive results among children." But still, along the Pyongyang-Wonsan-Chongjin route, said his colleague, Eri Kudo, "we really saw in nurseries and kindergartens significantly undersized children with very, very thin limbs." Said Graisse, "I was shocked to see in most classes that the children on the average looked two years younger than they were"—a judgment that he said medical doctors working for aid organizations confirmed.[3]

On family visits the WFP officials asked to see kitchens so they could learn what people were eating. One old woman had only a large rice bowl containing a watery porridge of rice and grated corn—mainly water. The woman explained it was for her entire family—three bowls of that porridge for the day for five family members. Walking around, Kudo found an old man lying down—her husband. He could not stand up. His digestive system was too weak to take even the porridge. Kudo saw swollen faces. One aspect of East Asian culture, she noted, is the high value placed on forebearance: "'Try to put up with the situation, don't complain too much.' So we imagine there are many more like that."

Was the regime's collapse, or at least its leader's overthrow, at hand? That might have seemed a likely outcome in almost any other country similarly afflicted—and especially in an East Asian country traditionally imbued not only with the desire to show forebearance but also with the notion that a ruling dynasty keeps power only until the "mandate of heaven" is withdrawn. In that old way of thinking, natural disaster itself is blamed on the ruler, seen as a sign of heaven's disapproval of a lack of righteousness in his administration and a signal that it is time for a change. It seemed clear to me and some other outsiders that the Kim dynasty really was responsible for long-term policy failures that exacerbated the disasters befalling the land.[4] And in truth, North Koreans were not so far away from the traditional ways of viewing their rulers otherwise. Did some of the more simple-minded among the populace also see their woes in the mid- and late-1990s as the revenge of heaven upon the system the Kims had built?

Leaving aside heavenly portents and omens, a study entitled "Pattern of Collapse in North Korea," written by an American expert and circulated among Pyongyang-watchers in the latter half of the 1990s, hypothesized a seven-phase process. Much of North Korea seemed already to have passed through the first three phases listed in the paper by Robert Collins, who based his theorizing on accounts of communism's collapse in the Soviet Union and Eastern Europe and on his decades of experience as a U.S. government employee observing North Korea.[5]

The Democratic People's Republic of Korea long since had encountered resource depletion, which was Collins's Phase One. The country then had moved into Phase Two, prioritization, in which someone had to decide either that everyone would suffer equally or—the decision actually made—that certain groups such as the party elite and the military would be given priority in distribution of scarce food and other resources. (American food aid specialist Andrew S. Natsios argues in *The Great North Korean Famine* that this setting of priorities in favor of Pyongyang and nearby west coast areas meant cutting off the east coast of the country from food subsidies. Natsios calls such a policy "triage," a term normally applied to decisions by frazzled military medics, following bloody engagements, that certain wounded soldiers will be treated—because their chances of recovery seem high—while others, whose prospects are considered relatively hopeless, must be left to die.)

Robert Collins's Phase Three, local independence, also seemed well established in much of the country by mid-1998. In that phase, working-and-living units—even whole localities—that got little or nothing from the center because they were left off the priority list had to adopt their own means of coping. That often involved circumventing regime policies, as we shall see in chapter 33.

Thus, as the end of the millennium approached, North Koreans should have been moving into Phase Four—suppression—if the regime was heading toward imminent collapse according to the pattern Collins posited. In what he called a "most pivotal phase," the core group of the regime would feel its ultimate political control threatened by the new disdain for the rules shown by groups pursuing survival-at-any-cost schemes. So Kim Jong-il and company would crack down, handing to their formidable internal security apparatus "maximum, even indiscriminate, powers" to suppress actions that contradicted state policies.

In case suppression should fail to put a cap on local independence, it would instead push the country into Phase Five: resistance by organized groups and leaders. If the drama should play out fully, there would then ensue Phase Six, the fracture of the core group, a splintering that would occur because of opposing views about how to handle increasingly violent resistance; and, finally, Phase Seven, realignment of the national leadership without necessarily eliminating all of the core group.

Were things happening the way Collins, writing in 1996, had postulated? No outsider could know for sure about much of anything that happened in North Korea, of course. But there were always the Pyongyang-watcher's fall-back techniques of analysis based on scraps of information from all kinds of sources including defector testimony and the regime's news media and propaganda—the sort of "tea leaf reading" that also characterized the work of kremlinologists and sinologists.

Thus, my attempt to solve another, seemingly unrelated mystery—why the DPRK had barred United Nations World Food Program aid monitors from thirty-nine of the North's counties—turned out to be instructive. My findings suggested that Kim Jong-il and company so far might have avoided falling into the trap of Phase Four, as Collins defined it. In that case, the Kim family regime (let us eschew obvious comparisons to Satan and his beastly manifestations) still might have some staying power.

The Democratic People's Republic of Korea deserved its title as the most secretive country in the world. In the atmosphere of constant preparation for a new war that had prevailed in North Korea since the end of the first Korean War in 1953, secretiveness had always been about regime survival, first and foremost. Besides the obvious wish to prevent hostile, spying eyes from seeing the country's strengths and weaknesses, the authorities were determined to keep ordinary North Koreans from contact with foreigners who might inform them that much of the information their rulers drummed into their heads about their own country and the outside world was bla-tantly false.

So it was news when the regime's need for international aid to respond to a full-blown food crisis forced it to ease the restrictions on foreigners' presence and movements. More than one hundred international aid workers based themselves in North Korea. Their organizations demanded freedom of movement sufficient to assure themselves that the food reached hungry peo-ple. World Food Program monitors from abroad numbered thirty-six by 1998. They had visited 171 counties. They worked out of six offices spread around the country and drove about in their own Toyota Land Cruisers to avoid the interminable delays of the creaking public transportation system. "The DPRK two years ago barely had an international presence," said the WFP's Graisse. "This has been a breakthrough." Indeed, an optimist could see in those developments a positive omen presaging a wider opening by the regime.

Why, then, did I focus on the negative—on the thirty-nine counties that were *not* open to WFP monitors and whose inaccessibility had led the Rome-based organization to announce on May 18, 1998, that it was withholding

55,000 metric tons of food worth some $33 million? (That was 7 percent of the aid it had planned to deliver that year, the proportion based on the fact that those counties accounted for about seven percent of the total population.) My lack of optimism stemmed from having watched North Korea for more than two decades. Always eager to credit signs of opening in the isolated and rigidly controlled country, I had become increasingly skeptical as I saw how little actually changed—and as I came to realize how very strong was the interest of the Kim family and other members of the top elite in resisting change, regardless of the citizenry's needs.

The regime continued to display a remarkable ability to thwart both external and internal forces for change. Take, for one example, the very concept of monitoring aid deliveries. In the mid-1990s, in the immediate wake of flooding that had devastated much of North Korea and precipitated the food crisis, one Westerner who was raising funds for aid insisted that he must deliver it personally. Renting trucks, he traveled through country seldom seen by Western visitors and handed over the goods directly to people identified as the end-recipients. That relief organizer prepared a lecture that he illustrated with slides showing one of his deliveries. I attended his presentation in Tokyo and saw that the supposedly needy North Koreans who were pictured lining up to receive his gifts were not gaunt and haggard, shabbily dressed people. Their faces did not appear discolored by the malnutrition-caused disease pellagra. Rather, in those slides they looked well dressed, robust and well fed—in some cases exceptionally handsome or beautiful. I guessed that they were either local party officials or actors. Did the fund raiser who was showing those slides realize that the recipients of his handout did not look like ordinary North Koreans? If so, he did not tell his listeners on the night when I sat in on his presentation.

Insisting on accompanying aid to the end-users was not the only technique used by visiting foreigners. Journalists no less than aid monitors and visiting U.S. congressmen asked or demanded, in the midst of their travels within the country, to see places not on their previously arranged itineraries. Visitors hoped, thus, to find the real, unvarnished truth instead of prepared scenes. Were the famine's effects on the condition of the population worse than the authorities wanted the world to know? Was the food aid getting to the people—or, rather, was it being diverted to high officials or the military? Sudden requests for schedule changes were one of the few means for trying to check. Any visitor who did not relish being fooled was duty-bound to try that tactic, but often the effort was futile. One international aid worker told me he had learned while in North Korea that the authorities typically dispatched sound trucks to alert residents of districts that were about to be subjected to "surprise" visits by foreigners. The trucks' loudspeakers warned that only party members were authorized to speak with the guests.

Sometimes, a last-minute request elicited more or less full disclosure, but usually not without a struggle. "Of course we have to indicate in advance we wish to visit this or that," Graisse of the World Food Program said in Tokyo, "but there can be small deviations from the plans." He had just returned from a visit to the city of Sinuiju, across the Yalu River from China. His original itinerary there had emphasized kindergartens and nurseries, since the WFP's aid program focused primarily on feeding children. But his organization was planning a new program of assistance to hospitals, so Graisse after his arrival in the city asked to see a pediatric hospital. He got his wish, but after he arrived at the hospital he ran into trouble when he asked to see the kitchen. That request caused "visible pain on the face of the hospital administrator." A long discussion ensued before the administrator permitted his visitor to open pots and see what was inside, which was not much: a bit of rice brought by the family of one patient and some "very clear" soup made of weeds, spinach and seaweed.

But let's return to the part of the WFP's batting average that especially intrigued me: those thirty-nine counties to which it had failed to gain access. Aside from the Hitchcockian spy-chase associations of the number (*The 39 Steps*), what was so special about those counties? How were they different from the 171 counties to which the monitors did have access? With foreigners permitted to go to the other counties, why were thirty-nine still closed tight? Here was a mystery. And anyone who disliked trying to solve mysteries would have no business spending his or her days watching so secretive a country as the DPRK.

Pyongyang itself vaguely cited reasons of security for barring foreigners from those areas. But in a country where the regime's security was the be-all and end-all, that explanation hardly narrowed down the practical possibilities. The authorities did mention sensitive military installations, and I phoned a Western diplomat in Seoul to ask him if those might explain the exclusion. "I can't comment on that at all," he said. "You're asking me to discuss USFK [United States Forces Korea] targeting information on an open line for publication."

North Korea did have plenty of military installations, all of them more or less sensitive. The fact that food monitors were permitted to travel to certain food-distribution centers certainly did not mean they were welcome on military bases within the same county jurisdictions. Presumably the authorities could, if they wished, give access to food-distribution centers in some or all of the thirty-nine still-closed counties while forbidding the monitors to travel near military installations.

Pondering the whys of keeping thirty-nine counties closed to outsiders, I noted that some of them were in areas where—as former political prisoners and prison guards had told me—the regime had maintained concentration camps for political offenders. And in the same harsh and remote northern

mountains were communities largely comprising families that had been banished from Pyongyang and other desirable parts of the country on account of
"bad family background." In the 1990s additional families had been tarred
with the designation because relatives had defected to South Korea.

I wondered: Were some of the thirty-nine counties off limits precisely because the regime did not want outsiders to see what was happening to the
members of the "hostile" and "wavering" classes who lived there? A worst-
case scenario occurred to me. I knew that prisoners already had been half-
starved as a matter of policy. Their official daily grain ration even in times of
relative plenty had been as little as 300 grams per person, versus the 700
grams rationed to a normal working adult.[6] Now the food shortage had become so severe that grain rations failed to appear for months on end. Even
citizens classified as loyal were reduced to receiving as little as an average of
100 grams a day or less. So what was happening to those North Koreans
who were politically out of favor? Were the prisoners in their camps and the
banished families in their mountain communities being treated even worse
than before? Specifically, had the regime systematically abandoned them to
starvation?

There were some ghastly communist precedents. Stalin used famine "to
achieve mastery" over the Ukraine, as the North Korea demographic expert
Nicholas Eberstadt has written. "Soviet troops were actually emplaced at
border points to prevent travelers from smuggling food into the desperate region." Pol Pot's Khmer Rouge, once it had taken power country-wide, says
Eberstadt, "selectively inflicted" hunger on a group that the communists
called "the new people"—Cambodians who had not been with the movement
from its guerrilla days.[7]

Could the Pyongyang regime be so brutally cynical as to have devised a
genocidal policy of ensuring that all or most of the people classified as disloyal would die quickly from hunger—while the survivors of the famine
would include the people whose loyalty was considered essential for regime
survival, especially the military and the police? Had Pyongyang calculated
that the regime would thus emerge from the period of famine stronger than
before, because almost all the survivors would be loyalists? It was a horrifying thought. Knowing something of the ruthlessness of the regime, and with
the example of Hitler and the Holocaust so fresh in the West's collective
memory, I could not dismiss the theory out of hand. I arranged a round of intensive interviews, in Seoul, of Koreans and non-Koreans who had knowledge of the North. I showed all the people I interviewed a map of North
Korea, downloaded from the Internet. The counties that had been visited by
WFP monitors were shaded in green. I asked them to venture explanations
of why the areas in white were still closed.

✻ ✻ ✻

Officials who were familiar with Pyongyang's military deployment shared my doubt that military installations were the sole sticking point regarding the closed counties, most of which are in the mountainous northern part of the country. "I don't think they're hiding another nuclear site up there," said one official.

"Obviously they have the bulk of their forces echeloned right at the Demilitarized Zone," another official offered. But only eight of the thirty-nine counties bordered the DMZ. And in the far north "they don't have very much stuff." Sensitive military installations in the excluded mountain counties "would surprise me." As for missile launching sites, "It's my personal understanding that even the Nodong is on a missile launcher, and the Scuds are on mobile launchers. They don't want a fixed site because they know we can go after it." The North Koreans would not have excluded a county "just because there's a launcher," he continued. "A county is, like, really big. It's not like a launcher is so dominating that, like bam! you run into it."

A third official looked at the map and wondered if missile manufacturing might account for some—but not all—of the excluded territory. He noted that North Korea's "two invasion corridors, Chorwon and Munsan, are both in the middle area on the Z"—slang for the Demilitarized Zone. "The Ongjin Peninsula is on the west. Presumably they have significant defenses there, too. Where they build the Nodong missiles may be somewhere in the west—I heard that. They wouldn't put that too close to the Z."

"Kanggye is a defense industry center," said another official. "But that doesn't justify making the whole province off-limits." He was not certain about his assertion, though. Later in our conversation he remarked that he did think it possible that county officials might block access to their entire territory just to protect a single sensitive installation. "County administration can't be broken up," he said. "It makes sense to keep the whole county off limits if there's something you don't want people to see. Everywhere within that county there's one political boss—the party boss, who also sits on the economic committee and controls the whole jurisdiction. North Koreans never break up jurisdictions [in such a way that in] this part of the county you can, that part you can't. It would lead to conflict between policy and lifelong training, [which] starts with ideology training in kindergarten."

That same official mentioned the presence of coal mines, full of disappointed former soldiers who had hoped for better assignments when their hitches expired, as an explanation that might apply to some of the counties. Due to the shortage of electrical power, water could not be pumped from the bottoms of the mines. Fuel shortages and other transportation problems made it difficult to move coal from the mines. Thus many miners (who in many cases remained reserve soldiers, with some access to arms) were effectively out of work. "I don't see a military reason in the middle area" of the map, that official said, noting that mountainous Kangwon Province had seen very little combat during the Korean War. However, the North Koreans "consider the coal-mining areas highly sensitive," he said. "There are lots of coal mines in the top right of the middle white area." (In 1999 a Beijing correspondent of Seoul's *Chosun Ilbo* quoted "people who frequently visit North Korea" as reporting a riot in North Hamgyong's Onsong mining district.)[8]

Several officials mentioned concentration camps as a possible explanation of why those counties were closed. "There's been some speculation that they might also include prison camps," one said. "I do think that part of the reason they do it is not just for military installations but for various criminal camps they have up there," said another.[9]

But one official sought to shoot down that theory, arguing that the public distribution centers for rationed foodstuffs in a given county would not likely be situated very near any prison camp.

One promising category of answers could be summed up by an official's pithy remark: "I suspect that what's really stopping the WFP from going there is probably that conditions really suck there." He began tapping on his computer keyboard and soon had called up from the Internet a map from the U.S. Agency for International Development, showing distribution of supplies.[10] The distances between ration distribution centers were great in the white regions of the WFP map, he noted. He suspected the roads were bad, as well.

Another official, looking at the map, said similarly: "They don't have the resources to assist the [aid workers] to get to these areas. Almost all are incredibly high mountains. Their infrastructure in these areas is no better than Rwanda or the Central African Republic—miserable." He thought this factor might combine with the presence of prison camps. Yanggang Province "is so isolated, so hard to get to, and there are many camps up there. And the camps are very large."

One official spoke of the map's white regions this way: "We've heard the government has just written them off as far as getting food to people. They're completely on their own. No doubt in large part these are mountain areas with bad infrastructure."

I heard several variations of the write-off theory. One of them imputed thorough cynicism to North Korean leaders. In that case an official said: "I suspect these are places that the North Koreans have written off and decided to let them starve." He added that he found the estimate of up to three million dead to be credible. He noted a certain Korean cultural trait: officials tend to be fiercely protective of their home regions, sharply antagonistic to rival regions. I had seen that trait at its most deadly in South Korea's 1980 massacre of more than two hundred citizens of the southwestern city of Kwangju by paratroopers, sent from a rival region in the southeast to put down pro-democracy demonstrations. In the Korean political culture, "regions without important native sons get nothing," the official observed. (In this case, though, as we saw in chapter 29, Kim Il-sung himself reportedly had taken pity on North Hamgyong Province although it was not his home province.) The official had heard that the North Korean People's Army, just as the South's army had done, "raises regional units but assigns them to other regions so they won't hesitate to shoot."

The North Korean economy, that same official asserted, "never worked. It was subsidized. When big neighbors bugged out, the North Koreans were on the margin. They were unable to respond to natural disaster. They had to prioritize. The military is always first. Whenever you prioritize something, you have to deprioritize something else. The concept that they've written people off is right. It's inevitable they're going to write people off. They can't afford to feed those who are not critical to the survival of the regime, such as coal miners. If you're in a factory or cooperative that's [even less] necessary to support the regime—a doll factory, an ice cream or widget factory—you were deprioritized long ago. You close down a factory, it becomes a ghost town. The ration center moves. If you're not part of the group, you get screwed and have to go down the road. There is definitely a fringe population that is being intentionally sacrificed. They don't really have much choice."

There was one other notion that imputed bad faith to the North Korean officials. That was the theory that those thirty-nine counties were off limits because authorities didn't want food monitors to know that the populace was secretly growing enough food to produce a surplus that could have alleviated the shortage elsewhere in the country. I heard no support for that idea during my interviews, although I did hear that North Koreans farming leased land in the Russian Far East were producing more than their compatriot workers there needed and were shipping the extra supplies back to North Korea.

But I felt I was getting especially warm in my quest when one official told me: "My gut instinct is that because the region is so blighted they just don't want people to see it." The strong points of that theory include its acknowledgement of the importance of face in Korean culture.

* * *

Besides officials, I interviewed recent defectors. One was Lee Soon-ok, a distribution center chief who had been imprisoned on what she said were trumped-up criminal charges related to her work. I asked her what was in those thirty-nine counties. "Special military factories," she replied. "North Pyongan, Chagang and Yanggang Provinces are special military production areas. Hamhung has a huge chemical research center. It does research both for the military and for the civilian economy. There's a military research center in Chagang Province."

Q. Anything else?
A. "That's where all the regular prisons and political prison camps are. There's a huge prison in Kyowaso, Yongdam, Kangwon Province. There's a big political prison at Mount Chol, Tong-nim, North Pyongan Province. In fact [that white part of] North Pyongan is all prison camp area. The white part near Pyongyang is Kaechon. That's where I was. In the far northeast, at Hoeryong and Kyongsong are two political prison camps. Hoeryong is No. 13 or 14 and Kyongsong is No. 11. I know that because my son was a prison guard. Looking at the map, probably the places are where they have camps. That's the likely reason for keeping the monitors out."
Q. Would the authorities fear simply that foreigners would see that there are prison camps? Or is the fear that they would see that people are starving in the camps?
A. "There's no way they'll let foreigners in those areas. It's not just the food—people do starve—but when they see the conditions that are created, it's worse than any starvation that can be imagined. If the outside world sees that, North Korea can't survive. Prisoners get beaten with belts while working. When you enter prison you get a uniform. You're supposed to use it for ten years. You don't wash it. People's skin has turned dark gray due to malnutrition. The natural oils from their skin build up in the uniforms and they become like synthetic leather, like part of your skin."
Q. Do you think it's possible the authorities now have decided to cut or eliminate the rations for prisoners, in effect kill them off?
A. "It's possible. But each of these prison camps is given an annual quota to produce so many truckloads of clothing and so on. It takes about six months to adjust to the environment, but lots of prisoners die off first. Because of those quotas there are also certain regulations. You have to have a certain number of prisoners. If you lose some you have to get more prisoners. If those die you have to get more."

Q. So it's in the interest of the prison authorities to keep them alive?
A. "Right."

Choe Dong-chul, Lee's son, had been a prison guard until 1986 when his mother's troubles with the authorities ruined his career and got him sent away. "I don't think the prison camps are the reason" for aid workers' exclusion from the thirty-nine counties, he said. "The camps are already remote, isolated, not so easy to see. The white areas on the map in Chagang and North Pyongan Provinces are where there are military factories. The Yongbyon nuclear complex is in North Pyongan. In Hwadae, North Hamgyong, there are Nodong missile launchers, not mobile but from tunnels.

"There are prison camps in Dongshin County, Chagang Province, and in Chonma County, North Pyongan Province. Chongjin has another camp, and it also seems to be in the white area. Dongshin is a coal mine; Chonma, a gold mine; Chongjin, a factory making bikes and military equipment. The Yodok prison camp is in the white area of South Hamgyong Province. The Hoeryong, Hwasong and Kaechon camps are in the green area. Kaechon is where my mother was sent. [It makes garments, artificial flowers, doilies and furniture covers for export.] Yodok, Hwasong and Hoeryong mainly farm and raise livestock. Anyway the monitors can't visit every corner of a county. A prison camp is very remote. They wouldn't necessarily see it. Generally, a prison camp is forty to sixty kilometers from any ordinary village. Ordinary people can't go in. But camps could be part of the reason why some areas are off-limits."

Q. Are the prison camps still producing goods? Do they receive food?
A. "I haven't heard [from more recent defectors] about any change. There's a quota. You have to meet the quota. You can die, but you have to produce. The farms at the camps are not for the inmates. If they steal anything, even a grain of rice, they'll be shot. So the situation is all the same."
Q. Why should we think these prison factories and mines are operating when so much of the rest of the manufacturing sector has closed down?
A. "We don't know for sure. But the reason to operate these camps is that it's the easiest way to produce. Prisoners can be controlled."

I digressed, asking Choe Dong-cheol whether he thought outsiders should continue to provide food aid to North Korea. "Continue it, but monitor it and insist on better protection of human rights in North Korea," he said. "We need more control of distribution. And it's not necessary to send high-quality grain. Send corn instead of polished rice, and there will be more possibility that ordinary North Koreans will get it. Officials want polished white rice."

Choe Seung-chan, an army paratroop sergeant turned factory supply official in Kaesong, told me: "I don't think there are military bases up north. It's a tough area for farming. It's the fertile areas the monitors have been to—the white area is the bad land for growing. I guess for propaganda they wanted to show better places. The roads in general up there are not paved."

Q. Are there underground military facilities up there?
A. "Yes. Missile factories. But they're underground so foreigners wouldn't be able to see them anyhow. I doubt that's the reason."

Nam Chung and his family had been exiled to Tongpo mining camp in Onsong County, North Hamgyong Province, in 1992. "From around April 1994 we got no rations at all," he told me. "People sold everything they could, to buy food. We did get 500 grams a person on the three holidays. The situation varied from area to area from April 1994, as I knew because I worked for the railroad. Farming areas of the country got a little."

Q. Did that situation apply to people in your area who were not being punished as well?
A. "They didn't get rations either, although the people who watched us got paid every time they gave information to the authorities. It's not that everybody was without rations. Officials, State Security and party people, the military and bureaucrats always got rations. Sometimes they got more than they needed and would sell the leftovers. The officials' theme song is 'These Days Are So Good; Don't Let Them End.' They make incredible profits. They buy things from the ration centers. If they pay eight cents, they sell for 150 *won* for a 2,000 percent profit."
Q. How do you analyze the map?
A. "In Chagang Province there are lots of military factories. Workers there were given rations. The two areas in the northwestern part of the map are well known for military factories. There are lots of political prison camps in the middle of the map. In the far northeast are marine and navy bases. There are lots of military bases in Kangwon Province. Near Pyongyang, that's a political prison camp. As for the northeastern mountains that aren't on the coast, I don't know why they are shown in white. The southwestern areas are military. Most camps are in the middle of the map in South Pyongan and South Hamgyong Provinces. As for Yanggang Province, I don't know. Chagang and North Pyongan Provinces have lots of military factories, mostly in tunnels carved underground. There

are few people living above ground. People living in the villages eat more than other people. They usually don't show outsiders those areas. Also, I heard that in South Hamgyong near Tanchon they mine uranium; I heard it's for nuclear weapons. My friend's father worked for a nuclear reactor plant. He used to go on a lot of trips to South Hamgyong." (Nam was a recent enough defector to retain a South Korean police minder. The minder was present in the room during the interview, but had shown no interest in other parts of the interview. He paid close attention to this map talk.)

Q. Were any areas of the country written off, treated unfairly during the food crisis?

A. "I don't think so. Each area has its quotas, how much it has to give Pyongyang. A certain portion of the leftovers goes to Pyongyang, a certain portion to the military. They decide in the province how to distribute the rest."

Q. Yanggang Province?

A. "Their basic staple is potatoes. They produce a lot of them. Farming areas are in most of the green shaded area. They carve out the mountains and make farmland."

Nam Chung's mother, Chang In-sook, had been a prominent architect-engineer in Pyongyang before the family's exile. "Chagang Province is military factories," she told me, "the 'second economy,' as that sector is called. Yanggang Province is forest area with a very low population. That could be a reason—it may be the poorest area. Maybe Kangwon is white on the map because it's mountainous and faces the DMZ.

"UN agencies came thorugh Sinuiju and Onsong. I saw people from the UN several times while I was in Onsong. I'm not sure about South Hamgyong Province. In North Pyongan there are the Yongbyon and Pakchon nuclear power plants."

Q. What do you know about actual prison camps as opposed to areas of exile such as yours?

A. "Susong camp is just next to Chongjin. Yodok is in North Hamgyong, Tokson in South Hamgyong, Kaechon in South Pyongan. I've only heard of them. I'm not exactly sure where they are. They're supposed to be in remote areas to prevent escape."

Q. I heard Kim Jong-il issued a decree, "Don't make internal enemies."

A. "There are some policy changes, but still there are people sent to political prisons. I think Li Kwan-gu, who was in that stranded submarine in 1996 that directly affected North Korea's worldwide reputation, could be sent to political prison camp because he talked too much before returning. And still there are public executions, to warn people."

Q. So what are the actual changes?

A. "There are six major changes. First, from the 1990s, political prisoners' camps received people more selectively. Second, there are more joint ventures with Russians and Chinese. Third, border control between China and North Korea was loosened. People used to need a passport, but now just a permit document is sufficient. Fourth, there are public relations changes, especially toward the media. In the past when people were interviewed they said, 'We're the best, we want for nothing.' Now when the United Nations comes people say, 'Thanks, please give us food again.' This caused a controversy between State Security and the local party of Ongson. State Security wanted people to beg for further food aid but the local party in Ongson didn't want them to. They produced a children's show before the UN team came, so that when the team arrived they could see kids eating the donated food.

"Fifth, there are changes in the attitude of local people. People were compliant and always obeyed. They believed in the party and nation and talked of the Great Leader. Now they complain while watching TV and say, 'I'll believe it when I see it. What I can get is what I'll believe.' Sixth, government attitudes have changed. Smugglers who got caught used to be sent to prison camp but now get just ten days in a police station."

Q. Did these all come about in the 1990s?

A. "Especially since 1994."

Q. What happens to donated food?

A. "It's a trickle-down situation. I can't say none gets to ordinary people. Maybe 10 percent does. The rest goes to the military and to local officials."

Q. The monitors are foreigners?

A. "The UN monitors go to the local yard and see workers get rice. But they take it to subdistribution centers, not directly to the people. The rakeoffs come at the sub-level distribution centers. [She smiled sardonically as she described the scam.] On the way to the people, the truck goes to a military camp, to officials, finally gets to the people. Now local people don't trust announcements that rice has arrived. I had neighbors who worked for the local storage yard. I heard, 'Rice is stored in the local yard.' But there was no rice. Other people told me where it went."

Although the responses varied, I was relieved to find that the interviews in Seoul did not bear out my worst-case theory. In particular, in the interviews with defectors, not a single person agreed with the notion that there was a conscious policy to starve political prisoners and the members of banished families more systematically than had been the case in pre-famine times. For example, Kang Chul-ho, a former inmate in prison camp No. 19, which had been situated in the map's white area (see his story in chapter 16), figured that inmate deaths from malnutrition would have increased as the famine worsened. But "in a state-operated prison camp, I guess the authorities try to keep the prisoners eating barely enough to sustain life," said Kang, who had defected in 1997.

"I heard the political prison camp I had been in was moved in 1993 and that site was made into a regular prison camp. The camp I was in, No. 19 Public Security prison camp, maximum security, used to mine magnesite clinker. The result wasn't good enough so they sent inmates elsewhere and now use the site as a general prison."

Q. Why do you think the thirty-nine counties have been kept off limits?
A. "Basically military reasons. In the north there's a concentration of air force bases, military matériel factories, special forces. One reason it took me eight days to escape is that I had to be so careful. There were so many guards, I had to move only at night.
"Also maybe this area has only very poor people. It's a mountainous area."

The response of defectors I interviewed on this question was strong if anecdotal, speculative and thus inconclusive evidence against my worst-case theory of the regime. (At the same time it was evidence that defectors and refugees during much of the decade of the 1990s did not, generally speaking, devote themselves to badmouthing the North one-sidedly, as propaganda proxies for the South Korean intelligence service, which quite a few of their predecessors had been accused of doing.[11])

Even the official in Seoul who suspected that the Northern regime was intentionally starving some groups to death acknowledged that prison camp inmates probably were not among the targeted groups—if only because of the prisoners' value in continuing productive work. "At a camp, the guy in charge is in charge of everything including self-sufficiency," that official told me. "He must support the prisoners and the guards. They've got to keep most of them alive to do the farming."

My effort to solve the mystery of the thirty-nine counties ended up providing additional evidence for a view of the North Korean government as being at least marginally less diabolical than might have been suggested by Kim Jong-il's election district number and my worst imaginings. It fit into a picture that I had been developing since conducting some of my earlier defector interviews in the early and mid-1990s. In that picture, the DPRK not only proclaimed that its citizens had rights and entitlements; furthermore, the apparatus attempted some of the time to act as if that were definitely the case. And the citizens tended to believe, until something untoward happened to make them doubt it, that they possessed some or most of the rights they were guaranteed and that officials were at least somewhat sympathetic to their needs.

To put it another way, in this view North Korea was a country that functioned to some extent under the rule of law or regulations, and written procedures. The wheels of justice normally ground exceedingly slowly, and that afforded time for people to anticipate what was coming. They also had some opportunity for petition and appeal, and where that was the case it was not always a totally empty formality. What made the DPRK a highly repressive country, a nightmare by human-rights standards, was not so much aspects of the formal system itself as the number and severity of the lapses from the officially prescribed standards.

Consider, by way of illustration, the story of Yoo Song-il, an army supply colonel turned university administrator who fell afoul of the authorities over a chance remark. The elfin Yoo when I met him looked—with his big ears, big nose, high cheekbones and sleepy eyes—exactly like a cartoon hero of my teenage years, Alfred E. Neuman, the "What, me worry?" mascot of *Mad* magazine. His hair combed forward over his forehead in the style so many men were displaying in Seoul in the late 1990s, Neuman—I mean Yoo—wore a brown, chalk-striped suit; brown, blue and white figured tie; white, starched shirt; gold, rectangular watch. His military career (which figures in chapter 30) had taken place entirely along the DMZ in Kangwon Province's Kimhwa County, one of the closed counties I was inquiring about.

"I was in the military for twenty-four years, until April 1992," Yoo told me. "It was only after I became a civilian that I realized how unequal everything was and starting thinking about Kim Jong-il's politics, which I decided were self-centered—not for the people.

"In June of 1992 I started work for O Joong-hup University as chief of general affairs, in North Hamgyong Province. It's a teacher-training university. One day in January 1995, when I went to work, there was a *Nodong Shinmun* on my desk. One article told of students demonstrating in South Korea against imports of rice and beef from abroad. There were about thirty other employees in the office. People come to work at 7:30 A.M. and spend the first thirty minutes hearing lectures on the greatness of Kim Il-sung and Kim Jong-il. After I saw the article I said, 'Those sons of bitches are too well fed and they're protesting about imported beef!? I wish they'd bring it up here and let us eat it!' After that, my colleagues started thinking South Korea must be doing much better than we were. I was jailed for ten days, accused of inciting pro-South Korean thinking. Besides my remark, there were other, personal transgressions. I used to wager with friends, with cigarettes and alcohol. That's prohibited.

"I was released, after those ten days, because I'd been a military career man and they said I didn't really know civilian society well. Others would have gotten much longer sentences. I returned to my job, but in December 1995 the North Hamgyong provincial office ordered me to move to the Kilju Ilshin coal-mining area as a 'revolutionary laborer.' They told me that this is what they do—they send people to work with coal miners. 'They spend two to three years repenting, reforming their thoughts, and then return to their old jobs.' But in reality no one ever returns to his job."

Q. What actual work did you do at the mines?
A. "I never went. I was only dispatched there. Once that happens, politically and otherwise you are finished in society. When I was given the assignment I went and argued at the provincial office: 'I've dedicated my life to Kim Jong-il, spent twenty-four years in the military, didn't do anything wrong. I refuse to go.' I knew I'd be watched all the time. I didn't want to live like a dog. Suddenly I wasn't part of the society any more. I had always thought Kim Jong-il's policies were for the people. I was extremely disappointed. I wanted to live like a human being so I decided to leave. It took three months or so of back and forth but finally they told me I had to go to the mines. I refused, but they said, 'If you refuse, we'll give you a worse assignment.' I said, 'Go ahead and do it, then. I didn't do anything wrong.' This all went on for about three months."
Q. Is North Korea in any way a society of laws?
A. "People in North Korea do have certain rights. You can buy time because of the layers of bureaucracy. Sometimes you have time to write to Kim Jong-il and argue with the authorities."
Q. Did you write to Kim Jong-il?
A. "To the Central Party, twice: once in August 1995, the second time in January 1996. I said that citizens' rights were part of the constitution. 'This is not what I was taught. How could they be doing this?' Writing made me seem more of a troublemaker."
Q. The top-down structure of the regime, with very little horizontal communication—is that a weakness of the system?
A. "I see it that way. Once the command comes down from the top, that's it."
Q. Your order came all the way from the top?
A. "Every province and other subdivision has a top authority who usually belongs to the central party. My decision came down from the provincial party. I got no answer to my letters to the central party. If the central party wrote to the provincial party, I never saw it."

I told Yoo the story of the woman who said she had been framed, Lee Soon-ok. She quoted central party people as telling her they had determined that her accusations against influential people in her office and community who had gotten her punished were true—but nevertheless she mustn't rock the boat.

"Yes, that happens a lot," Yoo said. "Everybody knows of a case like that: Many people are involved, and if the authorities wield the axe it will bring them all down. So they ignore cases like that. North Korea does have an organized system and they do check things out."

Q. Did they tell you, too, that you shouldn't rock the boat?
A. "Because I was in my hometown, Chongjin, I knew the provincial officials. Throughout the argument process they were saying, 'Let's see if we can try to give you a post in Chongjin as a laborer.' That gave me a little more time to plan my escape. I finally crossed the border on March 4, 1996."
Q. Was your whole family supposed to go to the coal district?
A. "Of course."
Q. Did you bring them out?
A. "Yes. My mother, my six-year-old son, two daughters and my wife all went to China with me. Mother died while we were in hiding there. We lived around the Beijing train station about a month. I thought once we got to Beijing we could go to South Korea through the embassy. But I found that was impossible. My wife and I argued a lot during that time. She was resentful that my prediction hadn't worked out. It was pretty bad. I think the North Korean embassy people found out we were there and started following us. My wife said she was going to keep trying to come to South Korea through the embassy. But I took the children and left. I don't know if she's still there or back in North Korea.

"When we were in China I started listening to KBS. That's when I learned that the route to South Korea was to go to Guangzhou, then Hong Kong, and thence to South Korea. I didn't have money and needed to earn some to do that. Some Chinese-Korean people helped me. With their help I got on a ship January 22, 1997, with the children. We landed on a deserted island and got help from the South Korean Marine Police. From there we took a helicopter to Inchon."
Q. Tell me about hunger and starvation in Chongjin.
A. "People were dying of starvation. I saw them. I heard my friend's father was sick. I visited him and the doctors told me he was just malnourished. He was skin and bones. They said if he ate he'd get better. But there wasn't any way to feed him. He died three days later. I didn't see people dying on the streets, though."
Q. What about conditions in the coal mines?

A. "I don't know much about it. I don't think their rations were better than others."
Q. What about the estimates of two to three million dead?
A. "That's probably very true. By the time I left in 1996 we were getting only two days' worth of food per month. People who didn't have money or anything to sell could only starve."
Q. Who were they?
A. "Laborers, people without power. Usually the officials and party members have food."
Q. How about prisoners?
A. "Usually prisoners are treated like dogs. When I was jailed for ten days I got a corn ball with three beans in it, this big [shows six finger joints] three times a day with a small bowl of salt soup, just enough to sustain life. I lost eight kilograms during the ten days. I didn't eat the first four days, the food was so disgusting."

Stories like Yoo's made more plausible the claim of First Lieutenant Lim Young-sun (chapter 31) that the regime's increasingly careful and deliberate system of investigation and punishment had enabled him to have months of warning that he was likely to be arrested for distributing anti-regime leaflets and must make plans to defect. In April 1993, Lim wrote in his second book, "I went to check the Onchon underground runway construction site, and the political committee member instructed me to stay overnight. The next day some officers arriving from my corps informed me that the security guard had gone through my things. I realized that I was in for it. But, fortunately for me, they couldn't find definitive evidence of my guilt, so they just increased surveillance of me.

"Why did State Security waste all that time trying to find incriminating evidence, when past practice had been to arrest and execute anyone considered even slightly suspect? In the past, many innocent people had been killed that way—because once a person was taken to a secret place it didn't matter whether he or she was guilty or not; even an innocent person would have seen the inner workings of State Security by then and would have to be executed to preserve security. But from the mid-1980s, to end such abuses, concrete evidence was required for an arrest.

"Why did the investigation take so long? This was because of structural problems among security organizations. The head of North Korea's authority system is State Security. Under it there are provincial and city security authorities. The People's Armed Forces security is [formally] under the direction of State Security but the PAF maintains its own security department and trains its workers at its own security school. For State Security to investigate or arrest an army member it needs the cooperation of the military security authorities. They usually don't work well together. In my case, State Security requested cooperation from the PAF Security Department but the PAF authorities didn't cooperate. That left it to civilians in State Security to investigate me with no help. Military security authorities hoped State Security would give up due to lack of evidence so they could then solve the case, arrest and charge me and keep all the credit for themselves."

One American involved with private relief efforts took note of the somewhat less harsh face the justice system had begun to present. "North Koreans break the rules on internal passports for the starving," he said. The authorities had been permitting unprecedented freedom of movement so that desperate people could search for food. "They're not shooting people for cutting trees on the hills or farming on slopes even though it causes erosion and means deforestation that will deprive the military of hiding places." Meanwhile, he said, "enlisted men are almost starving."[12]

There had been a policy since Kim Il-sung's day to "root out three generations" of the families of disloyal subjects, and the prisons continued to be used for that purpose. (See the testimony of Ahn Myong-chol in chapter 34.) However, as other researchers also have found,[13] apparently that did not translate into a special starvation regime for prisoners once the famine began in earnest. While more and more inmates died as a result of malnutrition, the political prison camps continued to be run more as slave-labor and slow-death camps than as instant-death camps. It may seem a small distinction, but it shows that in this regard at least Kim Jong-il was no Hitler.

Choi Myung-nam defected in 1995. I asked him what he thought had happened to the family he left behind. "I believe they would have been resettled to a rural area in the mountains, maybe in South Pyongan Province," Choi said. "From 1993, families of defectors are not sent to prison camps but just resettled in the mountains. From 1993, unless a person actually commits a crime he's not sent to prison camp. It's just a policy of Kim Jong-il's."

That sort of leniency, as opposed to the crackdown that Robert Collins would have predicted if the regime were entering his fourth phase, suppression, in the process of collapse, suggested to me that the regime might be around for a while.

In fact, although of course he had not used those terms, reversing the local independence of Phase Three and avoiding Phase Four had been main thrusts of Kim Jong-il's December 1996 speech. As for local independence, his argument was: "If the party lets the people solve the food problem themselves, then only the farmers and merchants will prosper, giving rise to egotism and collapsing the social order of a classless society. The party will then lose its popular base and will experience meltdown as in Poland and Czechoslovakia." Kim clearly feared that party officials were opting for suppression. Instead, he insisted, they must persuade the people that "this is the time of the march of hardship" and thus permit the regime to "control the situation without resorting to using law enforcement bodies."[14] One can see in his handling of the situation hints that in the aftermath of his father's death he had become an effective national leader in his own right, correctly analyzing the reasons for communism's collapse elsewhere and taking steps to avoid that outcome in North Korea.

It turned out that Kim Jong-il in 1998, only shortly before I started inquiring into the mystery of the thirty-nine counties, met with Japanese-Korean representatives of Chongryon and spoke to them enthusiastically about what he saw as the need for more attention to legality in North Korea. "Our people have incorrect understanding of how our laws should work," Kim complained. "In a socialist country, party organs, government officials and social groups are keen on political indoctrination but little attention is paid to the laws of the land." It appears that although some of the examples of leniency during the famine would prove to have been merely temporary expedients, Kim contemplated changes of a more permanent nature that could make the system less arbitrary.[15]

The immediate impetus for Kim's new stance apparently had been an incident at Hwanghae Steel Mill that forced him to confront the extent to which corruption had taken hold since the 1980s. "I will tell you what really happened at the Hwanghae Steel Mill," he said to his visitors from Japan. "We spent three years mourning the death of our Leader Kim Il-sung and coincidentally were hit with natural disasters. We found ourselves in a dire situation and could not provide enough electric power to the Hwanghae Steel Mill. The mill had to stop operation. Some bad elements of our society in cahoots with the mill management began to dismantle the mill and sell its machines as scrap metal to Chinese merchants.

"By the time we got wind of what was going on, more than half of the mill had been stripped away. For nearly a year, the thieves took over the mill and stole the people's property at will. They bought off party leaders and security officers and, consequently, no one had informed us about their thievery. Everybody was on the take at the mill and we had to send in an army to retake the mill. The army surrounded the mill and arrested the thieves. The army recovered the people's property from the thieves. Some of our trading people were involved in this massive fleecing of the mill."

Was Kim extolling the rule of law because he wanted to crack down on the leniency that rank-and-file officials had exercised in the face of the population's difficulties? Perhaps the facts of the mill incident as he recited them could permit the interpretation that local officials had been trying heroically to raise cash with which to feed the population of unemployed mill employees. Suggesting a different interpretation, however, is the fact that people connected with the mill incident were by no means the only ones made to answer for corruption around that time. There were high-level targets, some very close to Kim himself. South Korean intelligence chief Lee Jong-chan told his country's National Assembly in July 1998 that seven members of the Kim Il-sung League of Socialist Working Youth had been executed in the fall of 1997 while the league's chief, Choe Yong-hae, had been dismissed for corruption. That's the same "Jerkoff" Choe who, as we saw in chapter 11, hung out with Kim when they were youngsters. Chang Song-taek, Kim Jong-il's brother-in-law and the man rumored to be his closest friend and advisor, had been sent off to atone for corruption by going through a "revolutionary education" course and had already returned to Kim's good graces, the Southern spy boss reported.[16]

In his talk with Chongryon representatives Kim spoke with evident respect about the legal systems of capitalist countries. In North Korea, he complained, "party cadres and security officers operate outside the law without exception." In capitalist nations, on the other hand, "people abide by the law from cradle to grave," he said. "All persons must obey the law and the law is enforced universally." That praise was in contrast to his father's dismissal of legal impartiality as nonsense.[17] To be sure, Kim Jong-il's interest was thoroughly mixed with caution, as he then emphasized. "Revisionists," he said, using the term applied to anti-Stalinist communist reformers such as Khrushchev, "weaken socialist systems by overemphasizing laws and ignoring political indoctrination. Gorbachev brought down the Soviet Union using this tactic. Today, the Chinese leaders are on the same path."

But he quickly resumed praising Western systems: "As you comrades know so well, having lived in a capitalist nation for so long, people in a capitalist society must obey the law no matter where they live. Chongryon, too, must obey the Japanese laws, otherwise the Japanese police will crack down." A North Korean ship calling frequently at the Japanese port of Niigata was under official Japanese scrutiny at the time, in view of evidence it was being used for smuggling prohibited items, among other infractions. "I hear that our cruiseship *Mangyong 92* has to cater to Japanese businessmen and bribe the police with large sums of money in order to get anything loaded," Kim told his visitors. "In our country, a few hundred dollars are enough to bribe some security officers. This shows in a way how bad our judicial system is in comparison to that of a capitalist nation."

Kim observed, "In a capitalist nation even the prime minister and the president are prosecuted if they break the law. We must study how to strengthen our legal system. Japanese police fear the prosecutors. Whom do the prosecutors fear? Do they fear the police? You said that the police will go after any prosecutor who breaks the law. Few prosecutors have been arrested in Japan. The main reason is the strict process of selecting prosecutors. Law graduates take tough exams to become lawyers, judges or prosecutors. Only the best get to become prosecutors or judges."

Thus, Kim said, "cops and prosecutors are miles apart in qualifications. [But] in our nation, any college graduate can become a prosecutor, if the college so wishes. Because of this, prosecutors in our nation carry no special authority. In a capitalist nation, prosecutors are sworn to uphold the law and defend the nation. Kakuei Tanaka, a former Japanese prime minister, was arrested by a prosecutor."

Kim wanted a system in North Korea in which "law graduates must pass a special exam in order to become prosecutors, and only the best qualified people should become prosecutors. Currently, prosecutors are appointed just like other jobs and they stay chummy with their former classmates. It is tough for prosecutors to wield any authority in this kind of system."

In the same conversation, Kim talked about food and agriculture policy. North Korea's agriculture minister, So Kwan-hui, had been executed in September 1997, accused of intentionally ruining the country's agriculture as a spy in the service of the United States. At the same time the regime had dug up the remains of Kim Man-kum, So's predecessor and mentor, from the Patriots' Cemetery and subjected them to ritual execution by a firing squad—a modern update of the feudal custom of exhuming and decapitating the corpse of a posthumously disgraced official. The two officials' fate had then been held out to officials, the military and the public as examples of what would befall any other "traitors."[18]

Kim alleged to his visitors that So as agriculture minister had "failed to introduce higher-yield seeds and distributed non-existent fertilizers to our farms. This traitor ensured that our farms failed to produce enough food for our people." The minister "was a long-time party member and did everything he could to ruin our agriculture," Kim said. "For a long time, So refused to send a farm delegation to Japan using one excuse after another because he feared that they might receive better seeds from Chongryon. Better seeds would have worked counter to his plan to starve us slowly. So became a traitor in 1950. He would hardly do anything at the party meetings for discussing farm problems. Even when he was the party secretary for agriculture, he had precious little to say about farming. He was a filthy traitor loyal to his masters to the very end.

"We continue to ask the International Red Cross for food assistance, because we are in fact short of food; but the main reason is that our seeds have degraded thanks to So Kwan-hui's treachery. Our production has declined steadily because of the bad seeds. We are replacing them with better seeds but it will take about three years to fully recover. We need food aid to tide us over during this transition period.

"You may have received letters from your relatives living here about the food shortage. The situation is not as bad as it may appear. We make sure that the army has enough to eat, and the farmers and government workers get less food. The residents of Pyongyang receive many benefits from the government and they live better than the people in the rest of the country. For this reason, we cut back rations to the Pyongyang residents and at the same time, increased rations for the rest of the people. Ignorant of this, some people panicked and wrote you that our nation had only a week's supply of food left, and so on.

"Last year, the whole army was mobilized to grow food. The main finding of the army is that the seeds must be replaced, and we have began to bring in better seeds. But it will take two to three years at the least to replace the old seeds with the new. Until then, our food shortage will persist.

"We have been on a forced march for several years now and we are finding a number of structural problems. Had we held a Party Congress or the Supreme People's Assembly plenum before the end of the three-year mourning period after Leader Kim Il-sung's death, we would be facing food shortages for ten years or more. The lesson learned is that you need to know who is who. Today, all of the senior leaders are old revolutionaries who had worked with Leader Kim Il-sung. We have to ensure that they stay on for a long time to come."

The previous year, high-ranking defector Hwang Jang-yop had reported that even an arms factory in Chagang Province had received no food rations for nine or ten months straight. Despite the emphasis placed on military security, the state had permitted some two thousand weapons engineers to starve to death, according to Hwang.[19] Kim Jong-il tried to knock down such reports in his conversation with Chongryon representatives. "Our enemies report almost daily so many millions have starved to death and so forth, and do all they can to defame and demonize us," he said. "You comrades are here to witness the truth and report what you have seen here when you are back in Japan. That is why I took you along on my on-the-spot guidance trip to an armament factory in a remote village. I wanted you to see how the factory workers lived and how they differed from the residents of Pyongyang. I wanted you to see if there were people dying on the roadsides from hunger. As you have seen from your auto trip, there were no starving people on the roadsides and the factory workers are healthier than the people in Pyongyang. I hope that you saw the might of our nation and the optimism of our workers."

Nevertheless, Kim explained, it had been necessary that pride before foreigners give way to begging for food. "Previously, only our foreign service people cried for help but now all people do so," he said. "Thus, all of us tell foreigners about this shortage or that shortage, and take them to the worst place for them to see. In the past, foreign visitors were taken to the best show places and people were taught to say that they were living well. But now, faced with the economic isolation forced on us by our enemy, we need foreign aid and so we present sad pictures to foreign visitors."

There were, of course, no sad pictures of Kim's own table to be presented. Throughout the period of the famine, Kim had been dining like the king he was, according to a Japanese who claimed to have been his personal sushi chef since 1988. Kim kept a 10,000-bottle wine cellar and liked shark's fin soup several times a week, Kenji Fujimoto (that's a pseudonym) told the Japanese weekly magazine *Shukan Post*. "His banquets often started at midnight and lasted until morning. The longest lasted for four days."

All this still leaves us without a final solution to the mystery of the thirty-nine counties—most of which, according to the World Food Program's Web site, remained closed to the agency. I suspect that most of the theories related above—with the exception of my worst-case scenario involving a genocidal plot to starve to death immediately the people suspected of lack of loyalty to the regime—are partially correct.[20] But a full answer probably would have to emphasize national pride and the East Asian concept of face. "The nature of North Korean society is not to admit that things do not function properly," the World Food Program's Jean-Jacques Graisse said. His Foreign Ministry contact, a vice-minister, had told him that national pride was behind much of the denial of access. The official "admitted I had seen only 50 percent of the problem," he said.

Another aid worker, who requested anonymity, told me she had spoken with an anguished North Korean official who told her: "Our country's not Africa! We used to assist some African countries!" The aid worker added: "They believe it's just a natural disaster, not a structural problem, and therefore it is not fair to compare them with Africa. Extending the argument, they're probably afraid that if we take note of these places [in the off-limits thirty-nine counties], the only medium of communication is the oxcart."

After all, even where that aid worker had been permitted to visit, soldiers walking around "don't even carry a stick, much less a gun. They're in the fields, or repairing the truck. The cities look like car repair shops." Even in the fancy Pyongyang guest house where she and some other visiting aid workers had stayed, there was no running water. Relatively privileged women had to manage to stay presentable despite lack of water. They used a lot of foundation makeup, she told me. Female aid workers were experiencing gynecological problems due to lack of water. Just imagine, she said, what conditions must be in the thirty-nine counties.

Then again, Kim Jong-il's boast to his Chongryon visitors about well-fed armaments workers in a remote village suggested one last, if fanciful, theory. Maybe counties populated by invisible people, living and working underground with their machinery[21] like H. G. Wells's Morlocks, were so well off at the expense of citizens above ground that they had no need of foreign aid—much less of monitors to see to its proper delivery.

THIRTY-THREE

Even the Traitors Who Live
in Luxury

Interviewing North Korean defectors, it did not take me long to realize that quite a few of them had practiced an occupation that would have been rare earlier. They had been traders, in some cases entrepreneurs. They had often earned very large incomes from buying, selling, bartering, deal-making. Trading companies had been set up in response to Kim Jong-il's demand for foreign currency. The companies had multiplied. Not only high-level government and party organizations but military, agricultural and industrial units at lower levels, as well, had their own trading subsidiaries.

Trading is a challenging occupation even for those who are trained for it. North Korea's new traders had no training in business. Most had only military or police experience. Some traders who ended up defecting did so because, ultimately, they had failed at their new jobs. But many had succeeded.

The new occupation attracted people from the highest to the lowest levels of society. Kang Myong-do grew up as a member of the Pyongyang elite. His father headed the capital's construction department and his mother taught party history at the Potonggang district party headquarters. Kang majored in French at Pyongyang Foreign Languages University, graduating in 1979, and joined the staff of the League of Socialist Working Youth, guiding foreign V.I.P. visitors. I asked him if he knew the crude nickname of the league's top boss, Choe Yong-hae. He did not—the age gap was considerable and the two men were not on intimate terms—but he did tell me that Choe was reputed to like women.

In 1982, Kang went to work in party headquarters' Room 39, which was in charge of foreign exchange schemes. He became a party member the following year. In 1984, Kang—described by other defectors who knew him in Pyongyang as the playboy type—married a mansion "volunteer," a waitress at the Majolli palace in Hamhung, against his parents' opposition. They soon split up. He got in some sort of scrape around that time. "I was on the losing side in a power struggle in the KPA between the military and political officers, siding with the military officers," was the way he described it to South Korean reporters. He was sent off to the No. 18 Revolutionary Work Class to have his thinking corrected. Most elite officials eventually got sent to such camps, Kang said. The drill was mainly study of the leaders' history. The usual term was two to three years but a friendly member of the bodyguard service recommended Kang's release after one and a half years. Although he had a fairly soft life in that revolutionary work camp for the elite, next door was a camp for ordinary detainees and they did hard labor. Kang said he began to dislike Kim Jong-il during his stay. After his release he moved to a rural area as vice director of the local party management department.

Kang married a daughter of the former and future prime minister Kang Song-san in 1992. She also had been married once, during her father's first term as premier, to another graduate of the Foreign Languages University, someone Kang knew. When her father was demoted and sent off to be governor of North Hamgyong Province, her husband started treating her cruelly, Kang Myong-do said, and her father urged her to divorce that man. Kang and his bride-to-be met on a blind date, a *son*. Kang Myong-do's uncle had been a schoolmate of Governor Kang's at Mangyongdae Revolutionary School, so there was no opposition from either family—although someone did mention as a drawback his having gone to revolutionary work class.

His father-in-law arranged for Kang to become a cadre in the Presidential Palace Accounting Department, "but outside the North I was known as the vice-president of Neng-Ra 888 Trading Company," he said. He seemed well cast in the role, pleasant and charming while displaying an authoritative manner.

"This Neng-Ra 888 Trading Company is a nominal company, an alias for the department," Kang said. "It took care of everything for Kim Jong-il and Kim Il-sung, including their clothing and food. It would import televisions, refrigerators, suit fabrics, spices, soy sauce, beer and whiskey, all from Japan. Kim Jong-il likes Kikkoman and other Japanese brands. The department also owned a factory and a farm exclusively producing snacks and cookies and pastries for Kim Jong-il and Kim Il-sung, as well as meat—mutton, beef, pork—for their bodyguards. Inside the department was a special

EVEN THE TRAITORS WHO LIVE IN LUXURY   581

division called 'Presents.' Anyone who attended a political event involving Kim Il-sung or Kim Jong-il always received a present—usually a bag, some sort of luggage."

Using startup capital of $600,000 provided by the state, Kang imported Japanese cars through the Chongjin and Rajin ports and then exported them across the Tumen River to China, which lacked a seaport convenient to the more remote parts of its northeastern region, the former Manchuria. He specialized in high-end Toyota Crowns, three to four years old, which he could buy by the hundreds for around $3,000 each and then sell in China for $8,000 to $12,000. He gave port officials cigarettes to ensure smooth passage. When Beijing asked Pyongyang to halt the imports in 1993 due to oversupply, Kang simply switched from legal exports to smuggling. He made $600,000 profit dealing in cars, he said, and used those proceeds to import petroleum, earning him an achievement award from Kim Il-sung.

Taking home about $2,000 a month, Kang was rich by North Korean standards. (A Kim Il-sung University professor's salary was only the equivalent of around $10 a month.) He was living well, in a six-room home on Pyongyang's Changkwang Avenue, and frequented the Koryo Hotel. When groups of officials got together for drinking and carousing, he said, they always made it a point to include one trading company official like him because they needed his dollars. In the company of his impecunious pals, Kang—despite his newlywed status—was dating actresses, buying them clothing and lingerie.

"Personally, this was the greatest time of my life," he said. "Many times people came to me to ask favors. Their family members were sick or something. I gave them $100 or $200—it was nothing to me. In North Korea there's always a big shortage of beer, liquor and cigarettes. The presents I gave were a big deal to the recipients. Even a high official in North Korea couldn't have the kind of lifestyle I led—if they did, government officials would always report on them. A couple of times I gave money to my father-in-law, who went to the foreign goods store to buy a rice cooker, a massage machine and snacks for his grandson." Kang Song-san, who by then was prime minister again, was able to boast: "I've been to a foreign goods store for the first time, thanks to my son-in-law."

In May 1994, Kang went to Beijing, and got into trouble. "There were two reasons for my business trip to China," he said. "One was to come to an agreement about a fertilizer plant joint venture with China. With China we usually traded bags, pollack, automobiles and steel. But as trade increased, the Chinese proposed a joint venture with North Korea. They proposed building a composite fertilizer plant in Hoeryong. The second reason I went was to collect overdue payments from the Chinese automobile merchants."

Kang had not received permission from the North Korean authorities to go as far beyond the border area as Beijing, and once he got there he stayed for such a long time that they feared he was preparing to defect. "I didn't intend to defect at all," he said. "It was accidental. While I was trading with the Japanese, one guy said he was going to Beijing. I wanted to meet that Japanese. He was old, so it was hard for him to go to the North Korean border to meet me. I stayed in Beijing twenty-five days, waiting for the guy. I was heading back to the border, when I called a friend and he said to be careful because there were forty people out to catch me." The search party had been sent from Pyongyang to make sure the prime minister's son-in-law would not defect. "I knew if I got sent back to Pyongyang I wouldn't be able to leave again and would have a hard life," he said. "If I could have gone back voluntarily it would have been no problem. But if I had gone back after they sent men to capture me, it would have been like they caught me and forced me to return." So he boarded a plane and escaped.[1]

Kim Myong-chol, former bodyguard for Kim Il-sung and Kim Jong-il, ended his hitch in the bodyguard service in 1985 and went to work for a laser arms factory at Kim Il-sung's home village, Mangyongdae. There his job was to trade, to accumulate foreign currency. He exported seafood to Japan in exchange for yen. The proceeds were to go to the party for use by the top leaders. I told him I was surprised to find that around 15 percent of the defectors I had met had done similar work. "We got more access to outside information," he said, explaining why traders might be more likely than others to defect.

"Because of my job I had lots of foreign currency and foreign products," Kim Myong-chol said. "Lots of higher-ups pressed me to bribe them. In 1992, I had a success and accumulated a lot of foreign exchange. There were around 1,900 people working for me, exporting clams, fish, sea cucumbers and red fish roe. To boost morale in view of the food situation, I inported three tons of sugar from China and distributed it to those workers. That caused a problem. The party said that whatever I got from business must be given to the party. I couldn't put up with it.

"I decided that with my ability I could make a good living in China. So I went to China. I went over the Tumen first, walked across the ice in winter. I wanted to get into business in China. I wasn't in great danger. I just didn't like where the system was heading. I believed that I'd done something good for my workers but the party was criticizing me. I ran away before I could be punished. I would have had to go to a reeducation camp for a year. Then my career would be ruined. I wouldn't be able to get a good job. I left for China January 29, 1993, but I found I couldn't be a legal resident and couldn't go into business there. Now I work for Donghwa Bank in South Korea."

*   *   *

Like Kang Myong-do, Choe Shin-il seemed well cast as a wheeler-dealer in imports and exports. A handsome, slender man of middle age with a nice haircut, Choe the day I met him wore a gray suit and a necktie, gold watch, gold-rimmed spectacles and a gold ring with a big stone. He was tanned, and he spoke with a deep voice that could have had something to do with the Dunhill cigarettes he smoked. Cementing the impression that he was some-one who got around, he told me he had seen me at the Koryo Hotel in 1992. He had worked for the trading arm of a major government agency. Choe Shin-il is not his real name; he was the only defector I interviewed who asked to be identified by a pseudonym. This, he said, was to protect his family from reprisals.

"When I look back I have to say that from the moment I graduated from the university I had a very good lifestyle compared with others," Choe told me. "I changed cars four times in eleven years. My last car was a Toyota with a 2,400-cubic-centimeter engine, which I got as a commission from some Japanese." That commission was a kickback. If Choe's employers asked him to sell a certain product for 1,000 yen, he might tell the Japanese buyers the price was 1,200. After haggling, he would let them have it for 1,000 plus his "commission." Such a procedure is illegal in North Korea, "but it happens anyhow," Choe said. "And if I got a commission of, say, $50,000, I couldn't keep it all for myself. I had to bribe high officials to keep their mouths shut. The biggest commission I ever got was $120,000. That was in 1986 when I was trading mushrooms.

"All departments have their own trading companies. Every government and party organization has at least one. From the 1970s the central party had its secret Room 39. In the 1980s Kim Il-sung said to gain foreign exchange, so this expanded from the central party through the ministries. In 1985 and '86 there were only about fifty of us doing that sort of work. But entering the 1990s, Kim Il-sung said that everybody must go and gain foreign currency, so there are lots more traders nowadays.

"Starting in 1986 I traveled a lot on business to China, Japan, Hong Kong, Russia. I stayed home only three months out of the year. When I went on a business trip inside North Korea I always stayed at a hotel. Women knew we were from trading companies and had dollars, so we could have any woman we wanted: hotel employees, movie actresses, dancers. North Korea is basically run on dollars. The higher up you are in the hierarchy, the more important dollars are. My salary was 137 *won* a month. The company president got 148 *won* a month. We just laughed at it. To me, the North Korean currency is just valueless paper. It would take 10,000 *won* to equal $100. Since production has virtually stopped, there's almost nothing you can buy in the store with North Korean currency. Only dollars—you can use those at the dollar store.

"There is a feeling of animosity and jealousy toward the returnees from Japan. People call them call them *han-joppari*—half-Japanese dwarves. You say you saw a wedding in the Koryo Hotel. Not even high officials could have a wedding there. Either they couldn't afford it or there would be too much gossip. Only people whose relatives in Chongryon would come and arrange the wedding and pay for it could do that. Most of the Korean-Japanese are very stingy. If the line to Japan is cut they have no recourse, so they're very frugal. They're called unpatriotic, perceived as having run away to Japan during the colonial period. But now the attitude has turned from jealousy to envy: 'How come *my* grandfather wasn't in Japan?'

"Ordinary people don't even have soap to wash their clothes, coal for the public baths. So people aren't clean anymore. The people who are well off are concerned, on the one hand, because they have relatives in the rural areas. But to a greater extent they're proud of themselves for having this lifestyle, very condescending to the rest of the population.

"The first factor that led to my defection was discrepancies between what I was taught and what I later learned in China and the Soviet Union. When I was little I was taught Kim Jong-il was born on Mount Paektu, but Russians told me 'No, he was born here.' Also life in North Korea is very stressful with its emphasis on group teamwork. I couldn't adjust after trips abroad where I had felt such freedom.

"Before I defected to South Korea I had many business trips to rural areas. I was astonished to see Kim Chaek Steel Works. It was totally shut down. I thought, 'If this factory isn't working, what's the situation in the rest of North Korea?' After the fall of the Soviet Union, North Korea totally disintegrated. Just before I left I estimated about 70 percent of the economy was dead.

"I started having positive, optimistic thoughts about capitalism and freedom. Starting in 1990, I listened to KBS-AM radio. I could listen on my car radio to the social-educational broadcasts.

"I can't say there's no one who truly believes in the regime, but belief is mostly based on self-interest. There are people who still believe in the regime because they want to maintain their status. From 1993, the authorities taught people, 'Look at Eastern Europe. Former high officials are beggars in the streets. If our regime collapses, you are also doomed.' This is strictly taught to high officials only, in high officials' conferences.

"During New Year's Kim Il-sung always made his annual speech. People stopped believing in those speeches. The content never changed. People are so desperate they want war. They're sick of their life and they want things to spill over. They want a new something to come.

"I was in China when Kim Il-sung died. When I heard the news,

I couldn't believe it at first. I never expected Kim Il-sung to die. I thought it was the end of North Korea. It could last at most four or five years—that would be the end. I have no faith in Kim Jong-il's rule. He doesn't have the capability to rule. Kim Il-sung had charisma. People thought of him as a god. Nobody reveres Kim Jong-il. High officials don't revere him, but only fear him, because his character is very bad. He's very mean, cruel. He doesn't show respect to elders. He acts impulsively. If he's in a good mood he can be very generous. He *is* very smart. In history, many people who came to power were the sons of later wives. Kim Jong-il is the son of the first wife, so he must have some intellect to maintain his power.

"From the 1980s Kim Jong-il told people, 'We should help the old father in economic, political and cultural life.' Every report had to go through Kim Jong-il before reaching Kim Il-sung. In the summers Kim Jong-il didn't work—he'd go to Mount Paektu or other resorts. In 1988, South Korea had the Seoul Olympics. Kim Jong-il wanted to top that, so he put on the youth festival. That's an example of poor economic decision making. They invested in buildings, hotels, Kwangbok Road. The deficits were so immense, North Korea never got out of the slump.

"I knew Kang Myong-do very well when he was there, although he was younger than I. Now that we're here I look for a lot of emotional support from him. I defected when I was in China for the trading company. Things weren't working well. At that time I heard the news that Kang had defected to South Korea. I thought I should do the same. The government had set a price for the commodity I was trying to sell, but I couldn't get it. There was a gap of a couple of million dollars. So I thought if I returned to North Korea I'd be in trouble."

In chapter 21, we met Ko Chung-song, an employee of a district office for preservation of revolutionary historical sites. Ko's work there was supplying coal, food and other necessities for the office's forty-five or so workers and managers. To do so, in the circumstances of the 1990s, he had to become a small-time trader.

"I had to find the materials that the people in my office needed," he told me. "It was difficult to buy those directly. By the 1990s there were shortages and the government couldn't supply what we needed. At my workplace they had extra money. On my business trips, besides dealing with the government, I did my own trading. I played around with the money and bribed people. I went to another company, bought materials from it and brought them to our unit.

"For example, to get coal once I started by trading tires for silkworms. Tires were scarce, but I had access to some, so I was able to trade them for two tons of silkworms. I took the silkworms to another company, which accepted them in exchange for 220 meters of fabric and 150 pairs of shoes. One pair of shoes was worth three months' salary for the average North Korean. With those I was able to continue trading until I got the coal that the unit needed. I had a pass to travel around the country on business, and I traveled about two hundred days a year doing that sort of trading.

"I decided to defect when I was put under surveillance because they suspected me of being 'anti-socialist.' The head of one company I had bought from was caught [for accepting a bribe] and reduced in rank. I was sure they would come after me next. Sure enough, lots of phone calls came to the office, asking that I go to State Security. But my colleagues told them I was away on a business trip. The office was very appreciative of my work. They also knew that if I got nailed everyone there would be demoted or fired along with me.

"Anti-socialist is the term they used for a competent businessman like myself. Lots of North Koreans operated as I did. It started in the '90s with the shortages. It's impossible to manage an organization in North Korea without doing that. They say the society is communist, but internally there are many capitalist aspects. I believe they'll open their markets slowly. Pyongyang fears it, so it formed an Anti-Socialist Surveillance Committee.

"Since I had a pass for business travel, no one would have been too surprised that I didn't show up for several days. Taking advantage of that, I went to the Tumen River. I first tried to cross to China at Sosong, but couldn't make it so went to Hoeryong and failed there, too. I thought of returning home. I went back to Musan and tried to bribe a guard but couldn't. I stayed close to the border then, and for two days watched the way the guards walked their rounds until I knew their pattern. When I saw my chance, I ran for it across the river, which was frozen then, about 50 meters across. I could run 100 meters in thirteen seconds, so probably it took me only six and a half seconds to get across. It was 7:30 P.M." Ko grinned as he recounted his adventure.

"I didn't have money. I starved for about five days in China. In Beijing, at a diner in front of the train station, I met a South Korean who gave me some money. Then I went to Dairen and stowed away on a ship. When we got far out of port I revealed and identified myself. In South Korea I want to become a businessman, but as yet I lack the capital. Now I'm just sightseeing and making speeches." I asked if he had thought of going to business school. "In North Korea I couldn't apply for university because of the forced labor on my record," he replied. "Now I'm too old." I told him Americans would not consider thirty-two too old for business school.

Some who took up this new occupation did so because other avenues of advancement were blocked. Kim Dae-ho, whom we first met as a China-born member of a youth gang, ended up as a trader after having become a model soldier and a worker in the atomic energy industry. "Basically I had no prospects due to my family background," Kim told me. "I decided to participate in the raising of foreign currency for North Korea. I was working on the western coast. Officially I was supposed to be selling clams, sea cucumbers and oysters to buy equipment for the atomic energy industry. But I was also trading on my own account, selling Korean antiques to Japanese businessmen."

Kim ended up a failure at that unfamiliar game, he said, when some people he dealt with tricked him out of $25,000—money belonging to the state. "First, I was conned by the brother of someone who was working for me. He said he knew of a gold antique that he wanted to buy so he could resell it to a Japanese trader, but he didn't have enough money. He asked to borrow it. I went to the trading company and borrrowed $25,000, saying I would use it to make foreign currency profits for the state. The guy took the $15,000 I advanced him and never came back."

The second time, Kim said, "I was swindled by the head of the Taekwondo Department along with Chang Song-taek, Kim Jong-il's sister's husband. I wanted to pay back the $25,000 I had borrowed from my employers, but I needed to have my own import department to make enough money for that. Those two said, 'Give us money to bribe officials. We can help you set up a trading company.' I gave them the remaining $10,000. Chang's elder brother was in State Security then, the head of the political department. So I had no way of getting my money back from them. Then I decided I was really in trouble and had to defect." Kim defected via China, in 1994.

Kim Kwang-wook as a university junior became a black market dealer in antiques. He did not look the part. With his crudely cut hair, big black-framed glasses and acne he looked more like, say, a computer nerd.

"I applied for a fellowship to study in China," Kim told me. "Although I believed I was qualified, I was rejected. I checked it out and found the reason was my relatives in China. My parents had lived in China and had come to North Korea before I was born. I realized this family background would keep me from becoming a high official like a policeman or journalist. I could only go so far as an administrator. So I figured the only way to succeed in the society was to earn money so I could bribe officials, and then I could be somebody.

"I sold North Korean antiques to Chinese and Japanese merchants in Pyongyang. These were the antiques rich people had owned before the Korean War. After the war they had hard lives. They sold them for money—or one could excavate rich people's tombs to find antiques. I didn't excavate them myself, but I bought, cheap, from those who did. Then I resold them to Japanese porcelain merchants.

"I continued to work in antique trading even while I was a Three Revolutions team member. [His experiences as a team member are related in chapter 15.] Then a lot of the people who worked with me in the antique business got caught in the act and sent to prison camps. During interrogation they told about me. Since I was an antique dealer I had a lot of money. Money buys friends. I had friends all over, including police. One policeman warned me I had been reported. My friends got caught in July, and in September I learned that I had been fingered. I defected the next month, October.

"I crossed the Yalu River secretly at night. Just before crossing I was apprehensive, but looking back on it now I think it was pretty easy. Even if I'd been caught, I wouldn't have gotten in trouble. I had a certificate saying I was from a Three Revolutions team, signed by Kim Jong-il's secretary's office, and I also had a counterfeit travel permit. To get by in China I had plenty of foreign exchange left over from my antique business. In fact I never had a hard life after I started dealing in antiques. I never intended to come to South Korea. I just wanted to live in China. When I first defected I really believed the North Korean propaganda that said South Korea was full of economic strife, and I didn't want to come here. While I was in China I realized South Korea is a democratic, wealthy country.

"I'm certain North Korea can't last long. Kim Il-sung and O Jin-u are dead. Kim Jong-il's reputation is bad. Hunger is so prevalent. I give it three to five years. When you look at South Korea there were lots of demonstrations during the 1980s. That was possible because South Korean students could compare their situation with those of other countries. North Koreans couldn't, but by the time I left in October 1993 people had more perception of the outside world. So I think these complaints will swell and explode. They learn about reality mainly from Siberian loggers and from Chinese and Japanese merchants visiting North Korea. At the moment the economic situation won't permit the regime to kick those merchants out. It can't do without the foreign exchange they bring."

Bae In-Soo's father studied tractor design at a Chinese university and became the chairman of the metal and steel industry inspection department in the government division of the Workers' Party Central Committee. His mother ran the accounting department at the Kumsong tractor factory—the factory that had produced the famous tractor prototype that only moved in reverse. In 1968, the father was one of many members of the Yenan (Chinese) faction who were purged. He was sent to political prison camp—Bae did not know which camp—and was never heard from again, Bae said, even though many political prisoners were released between 1984 and 1986. Eventually Bae, his mother and his elder brother were exiled from the port city of Nampo, where they had lived, to a rural area in South Pyongan province.

"Most of our belongings were confiscated," Bae, a handsome, thoughtful-seeming man, told me. "We still had our color TV. We were the only family in the area who had one. After four months someone set fire to our house. Everything was lost except the underwear we had on. Probably it was a vil-lager, one of those people who were calling us anti-communists. After our property was set on fire, Mother kept demanding an investigation. The Cen-tral Party said she was crazy and put her in a mental hospital when I was seven, in 1976. For three years she stayed there while my brother and I dined only on small rations. I had eyesight problems. I couldn't see. I couldn't at-tend the elementary school because schoolmates would call me anti-communist and teachers would hit me. My brother taught me a little. But if anyone had offered us help, that person would have gotten in trouble. No one helped.

"My uncle on my mother's side was vice-commander of the Second Army Corps. He met the governor of the province and asked him for clemency. The governor arranged for us to be resettled. In 1980, we moved to Maengsan County, 120 kilometers east of Pyongyang, where Mother worked as a farm-hand. People who were deemed anti-communists, capitalists or landlords, or who had helped South Korea during the war, were resettled in Maengsan County. Seventy percent of the people there are like us. It was a difficult place to survive. The soil was poor. Transportation was poor. It was in remote mountain terrain. The nearest train station was 30 kilometers and the way to get there was on foot.

"Every time I start talking about the past I just start crying," Bae said. "I don't recall any good experiences. When I was in senior middle school, my only hope was that some day I could enter the army. I had no hope of going to a university. But by the time of graduation, I realized that I could not even enter the army because of my father's status. So I had lost all hope in life. North Korea should be called the Feudal State of Korea. It's like during the Yi Dynasty, when it was the *yangban* [nobles] against the ordinary people. We started bribing authorities and I was allowed to go to Maengsan County automotive school, where I learned to drive. I went to work driving a truck for a truck-and-driver-hire organization. I did that from 1988 to May 1993.

"On the side I was making money by trading. Normally, on Kim Il-sung's birthday, each family got a fish. They sold them instead of eating them. I bought those fish for 10 *won* each on the black market and dried them at home. My workplace sent me to get fish for employees. I would barter 50 liters of liquor, 140 kilograms of oil and 100 of coal for a truckload of fish. The barter was unofficial. We would steal some of the load on the way back.

Eventually, I would drive to the border with a full truckload of dried fish and trade. The company head and the rest often participated. I was not fooling anyone in the company.

"For three years I made strenuous efforts to show my loyalty and enter the party. But when I tried to sign up, the official in charge said: 'Look at your background. How dare you apply to join the party?' After that I lost all faith in the regime. In 1993, the announcement came that war was about to erupt, so anyone under thirty should volunteer and prepare to fight. I didn't want to go to war. At graduation time, the army had represented my hope to erase my bad background and have a decent career. But I had come to realize that no matter how hard I worked, my background never would be erased. I would always be mistreated and discriminated against.

"I had problems with State Security people, but bribed them to send me to Sunchon City to work as a driver hauling export goods, a better job than the one I had. Bribery started in big way in the early 1980s and became very prevalent in 1988, especially in 1989 with the youth festival. In 1988, because of the coming festival many foreign countries donated goods. People started realizing the value of foreign goods and realized that you have to have money to buy them in the black market. So officials and others developed a greed for foreign exchange.

"In the past, if girls prostituted themselves and used the proceeds to buy fancy clothes, the authorities might inquire into where the money had come from. These days no one even asks any more. So many girls sell themselves to foreigners. Even in the Sunchon area, in the train stations, women approach and ask 'Do you want to buy a squid?' People in the know understand this to be the code. In the past the code would be 'flower basket.' Even in Pyongyang, if they find a foreigner with a North Korean woman, State Security will follow them, then approach her and demand the money. The women usually turn over the money. The customers are not only foreigners. A North Korean man with five *won* can get that service. Some of the women have approached me. In the past people scorned them, but now people are understanding, as long as they earn money. Usually in North Korea, all villagers know where the prostitutes are.

"I worked in Sunchon from May to October, 1993, then crossed the Tumen River to China on October 1, 1993. On January 28, 1996, I came to South Korea. All I want to do is get a South Korean driver's license and drive a big container truck. At first, I thought of becoming a tractor designer, but they've got enough of those."

North Korea with its one-man rule and brainwashed society always had appeared to scholars as a country in which the real story was that of the leader. But the basis of that assumption started to shift during the 1990s. A nanny state that had provided everything was unable now to provide much of anything. North Koreans found they had nothing left but ideology, which they could neither eat nor wear. Required for their survival to become traders and individual strivers, many had found a certain freedom. Although under the circumstances it would have been surprising if many of Kim Jong-il's subjects welcomed that development, it seemed to me likely to have some profound — perhaps ultimately positive — consequences for North Koreans' future.

THIRTY-FOUR

Though Alive, Worse Than Gutter Dogs

In March 1999, North Korean diplomats and other agents kidnapped twenty-year-old Hong Won-myong, along with his diplomat father and his mother, who were attempting to defect, from a Bangkok apartment. The parents escaped in the confusion of an automobile wreck, but young Hong was in another car that was not involved in the wreck. His captors held him as a hostage while, with a degree of chutzpah that none but North Koreans could muster, they used him as a bargaining chip as they demanded that the Thai government turn the parents over to them and absolve Pyongyang and its gang of thugs of blame for the kidnap. Not buying that audacious pitch, the Thais threatened to break off diplomatic relations if the North Koreans refused to give up hostage Hong. Pyongyang considered Bangkok its most useful Southeast Asian diplomatic and trading outpost, so young Hong was released.

Amazingly, after his release, Hong held a press conference at which he announced he wanted to go home to North Korea, with or without his parents. "I love and respect my father very much," he said—adding, with emotion in his voice: "But if my father refuses to return I will ask to cut parental ties and return home alone."

No doubt rewards awaited him. His countrymen would make a big fuss over him upon his arrival back in Pyongyang. They would parade him around as an example of the type of selfless patriot that the country's educational system for decades had sought—with remarkable success up to a point—to produce. I could visualize thousands of chanting, flower-waving schoolchildren lining the route of young Hong's motorcade from Pyongyang's airport into the capital, where he would be hustled onto state television (the only television there was in North Korea) to repeat in Korean his performance in Thai at the press conference.

There were various versions of why the parents were unwilling to go home to Pyongyang. North Korea alleged that the father, as number three in the embassy, had embezzled $83 million that the country was preparing to pay for Thai rice imports. There was no way the regime would have entrusted him with that much money, I thought. But financial irregularities of some degree had become a way of life for North Korean officials, in the environment of extreme uncertainty and rapid moral decline in which their country found itself. It would not have surprised me to learn that a defecting diplomat had dipped his hand into the cookie jar.

What the father told the son, the latter said, was that he wanted to live in a country that would offer the younger Hong more comfort than North Korea. "But for what should I go to live in a foreign country?" the son asked at the press conference. "Should I live comfortably like a selfish person, or should I return to join more than 20 million people in my homeland to bring prosperity and development to it?" And there was more: "I don't think my country is poor, but it is very rich, because everybody works for the single aim of bringing progress to the country."

Here is another switch: The young man claimed that it was he who, for a time, had not wanted his embassy captors to turn him over to the Thai authorities. He finally agreed when he saw that it would be an opportunity to be with his parents for long enough to persuade them to go home, reunite with his elder brother and other relatives and friends, admit their mistakes and be accepted back into the bosom of the country. He did not think his father had been the traitor he was accused of being, young Hong said—but the elder Hong might have made some mistakes. "I believe that if anyone admits a mistake and asks for forgiveness, my country will give him another chance," he said. And he himself would "work wholeheartedly" to make up for any mistakes his father might have made.

It was obvious that, during his two weeks in an undisclosed place of captivity, the youngster had received some great coaching from the A-team Pyongyang sent in to help him see the light. Even though he had been living outside North Korea for years, he managed to get the party line down pat in his press conference performance. No doubt he would do just as well in public appearances back in Pyongyang.

He probably would not be arrested immediately. Kim Jong-il had issued in 1993 a new policy—"Do not make internal enemies"—encouraging leniency toward defectors' family members who were willing as Hong put it to "cut family ties." But after he had served the regime's propaganda machine sufficiently, he would be of no further use. The people in charge would not make him a diplomat, like his dad, and take advantage of his qualifications as a foreign-educated linguist, because they could never banish the suspicion he might some day try to defect and join his parents. That cosmopolitan background of his would count against him, not for him. After all, the North Koreans most inclined to complain about the regime were the cosmopolitan elements. Think in particular of the ethnic Koreans born in Japan or China who immigrated with high patriotic spirit to help "build the homeland" but, having in their minds those inevitable points of comparison, found they did not much like what they found.

Judging from what I had learned about the North Korean system by talking with many of his former countrymen who had managed to escape abroad, I thought young Hong after the inevitable waning of his propaganda value most likely would be found wanting in the loyalty department. He might be exiled to one of the poorest, most barren and mountainous parts of his country. If he were lucky, his lot there might be to try to eke out a living, as a farmer or miner, in one of the communities of people cast out of normal communities because their loyalty to the ruler was suspect—not on account of any crimes they had committed but due to problems of "family background." Some were people whose families had been abroad and who had been overheard comparing North Korea unfavorably with other countries.

If he were really unlucky, despite the new policy young Hong might— like an estimated two hundred thousand of his countrymen[1]—be sent to a prison camp. If his parents returned with him he might accompany them or not depending on whether the regime decided to just get it over with and gag the parents with stones—or bring the son forward in an arena, before a crowd screaming for justice, to accuse them of crimes—and then shoot them as he looked on.[2] The alternative would be to let the Hongs rot in one of the camps housing political criminals who had seriously offended the regime and the accompanying families of some of those criminals. Forget about the quaint notion that high-ranking would-be defectors could simply admit their mistakes and be forgiven.

Shin Myung-chul, a former State Security telecommunications staff member whose story features in chapter 22, told me the sad tale of a fellow defector named Yoo he met after arriving in South Korea. That man had defected to South Korea in 1987 while he was an officer on the DMZ, Shin said. "In March 1988, I witnessed the family of Mr. Yoo being sent to Aoji in North Hamgyong province. It's one of the three main prisons where they send families of defectors. The procedure for sending them off takes three days. The first day a wire comes from district State Security to village State Security to watch the family. There are various communications back and forth. On the day for sending them away, the State Security officials arrive in a truck around 2 A.M., with no warning, and take the whole family quietly. It's all over in forty minutes.

"After I came to South Korea, Mr. Yoo kept visiting me. Finally, after the tenth visit, I told him what had happened to his family. He had expected it, but he was devastated all the same. They usually take the wife, children, parents and siblings of the defector—all the direct relations, except in the case of a sister who's married off; her husband can be reprimanded or have his job taken away. I believe it's to help the regime retain power. It shows people the consequences of defection so people will feel responsibility. It takes forty minutes because the law says people who are resettled are entitled to take about 500 *won* worth of property with them. Anything over that the government takes.

"There are two categories of people. One group would be sent to a provincial State Security evaluation department when they're removed from their homes. They get evaluated for about a year: Are they spies for South Korea? Do they oppose Kim? But in cases like Yoo's relatives they have no hope of ever returning from the camps."

Did young Hong know the bleak reality that most likely would await him if he should go back home? Maybe not. Maybe all he remembered of North Korea, from the time before his family had last moved abroad, was life among the elite of Pyongyang: enough to eat, in those days at least; schools where you grew up learning to worship the Kims, father and son, and to believe more or less wholeheartedly in the sort of sentiments the just-released hostage gave voice to so stirringly at his press conference. It would not be unusual for such a privileged young man to know little of the darkest side of his country—until his turn came to experience it.

More likely, I thought, he did have some idea—but was really the nice, sincere kid his Bangkok college friends said he was. In which case it should not have been too hard for the team that worked on him for the two weeks of his captivity to use, as leverage, reminders of his remaining relatives and friends in North Korea—and hints of what would happen to them in case he should defect.

That kind of pressure could make it a tough call for anyone, but if he had asked me (I was in Bangkok at the time) I would have sat him down to go over the interviews that follow, several of them with members of families that had suffered together. Then I would have given him some unambiguous advice: "Don't go back to Pyongyang. Stick with your parents. If the three of you get to the United States or Canada or South Korea, especially if your dad has even a few grand, not to speak of the $83 million he is accused of having ripped off from the regime, you will find that for a price a rescue expedition can be dispatched into North Korea via the China border to bribe authorities and bring out a whole family of internal exiles, even prisoners. Don't go back, kid."

Hong, at twenty, was young but that would not win him special treatment. Ahn Hyuk was even younger, eighteen, when the junior table tennis champion was imprisoned. At age eleven, in 1979, Ahn entered and won a tournament for elementary school pupils. Thenceforth, he was groomed at a training center in Nampo to become national champion. (A woman star named Pak Yong-sun had won two world championships—although she didn't make it into the finals for the 1979 tournament that I attended. It was Pak's winnings that had been used to build the Nampo training center.)

Q. How did a table tennis champion end up in a concentration camp?
Ahn Hyuk. "I went to a ski resort used by sons and daughters of high officials. Skiing down Mount Paektu one day in February of 1986, a group of us came close to the Yalu River. Some ethnic Koreans living on the Chinese side started talking to us. They said, 'You talk about Kim Il-sung's paradise. You ought to come to China and see how we live.' Six of us walked across the frozen river, just out of curiosity, and stayed in China for three months. Then we returned to North Korea. I was sent to the camp as the youngest political prisoner there."
Q. Why did you return?
A. "Because of our families. They would be worried. I had $200 when I went skiiing. I used that to go around China for a month or so. We returned to the Yalu River to find the ice melting. It was still too cold to swim across, so we waited until May. That's when my destiny was overturned.
    "I had no idea what would happen. I was the only son, pampered, the son of a high official who had access to a lot of foreign currency for his work. I thought my father had enough power to fix it. The other guys when they got back went to their parents, who told them, 'Don't ever mention that you've crossed the Yalu.' But I first went to see my relatives, not my parents, and my relatives said, 'You're dead meat.' I realized I'd done something wrong, and I was scared. So without seeing my parents I went on my own to State Security. I thought if I went and confessed it would be all right. I told the authorities I was the only one who crossed, so the others didn't get caught. North Korean society works on criticism. I thought if I went to State Security they would criticize me and forgive me. But after my confession State Security sent me to its secret prison at Malamdong in the Yongsong area of Pyongyang. My Kim Il-sung portrait-badge was taken away, and I felt like the lowest thing on earth.

"At the prison I was kept in a dungeon for about twenty months. The cell was 2 meters by 180 centimeters. From 6 A.M. to 11 P.M. I had to sit very straight, with my fists extended in front of me. I wasn't allowed to utter a word without permission. I was supposed to raise my right fist when I needed to pee, raise my open right hand for a bowel movement. Raising the left fist meant, 'I have something to ask you,' and raising the open left hand meant 'I'm very sick.' We only got to leave the dungeon to see the sun once a month.

"I was the youngest, so I ended up doing a lot of the cleaning. My fellow prisoners included Yang Sung-hyon, former ambassador to Libya, and Kwon Song-chol, former vice foreign minister, along with a student returned from Guangzhou in China and one of the chauffeurs who drove the Volvos and Mercedes Benzes around. Yang hadn't done his job right, somehow. Kwon had been with Kim Jong-min when Kim defected from Russia, but hadn't defected himself. He was being punished for not stopping Kim Jong-min's defection. The chauffeur had merely noticed that Western passengers carried a lot of foreign currency and remarked, 'Wow, the West must be really developed.' That's all he said.

"The only food in the dungeon was cooked corn in a bowl. No side dishes. You can hardly get rice outside, so how could we get it in prison? They cut the handle off the spoon to help prevent suicide. They give you the bowl but you can't eat right away. You have to say, 'I'm ready to eat now.' All six in your row of cells have to say that before the warder says, 'OK, you may eat.'

"When I went out to get my monthly sunshine I had to strip first. I thought, 'I can't go on living this way. I must commit suicide.' On my way out I would look for a nail, or even a toothpaste cap to put under my tongue. But there was no way. I did swallow a nail, trying to kill myself with internal bleeding. I cut the inside of my mouth with the nail, then swallowed it. I sat for about ten minutes and fainted. I was sent to the hospital. They treated me there and I lived."

Q. Did they ever explain why you were being punished?
A. "They said I had acted against the people. Kim Il-sung and Kim Jong-il are the most dignified leaders of the world, and by going to China I had injured their dignity."
Q. How did you get out?
A. "After twenty months I was sent to a camp at Yotokun in South Hamgyong Province, a place surrounded by 1,800-meter mountains. I was lucky that I had connections, so I was able to get out of the dungeon. Others would never get out."
Q. Who else was at the camp?
A. "There was a son of the ambassador to China who had said the Soviet Union was a good nation. State Security inferred that he meant

Gorbachev's rule was better than Kim Il-sung's, so he was sent to the camp.

"The camp was divided into two parts. Prisoners in one part never get out. Kim Hyon-hui's family is there. In the other part are people who may get out some day. In the center of that part are individual political prisoners, and around them are the prisoners who have their families with them. The rations are the same in both parts of the camp."

Q. Tell me about conditions at the camp.

A. "I got 120 grams of corn three times a day, the same as in prison, plus salt and a weed called *shiregi.* That's all. They worked us tremendously hard in the mines or timbering. I talked with some other defectors and even they don't believe all I went through. Nowadays when I go to give speeches, I tell my audiences there is nothing on earth you can't eat. You can eat any grass that grows, mice, snakes, anything crawling on the floor. Many people die from lack of vitamins. I'm 175 centimeters tall· [5 feet 7 inches] and weighed 38 kilograms [84 pounds] when I came out of the camp in 1989. My parents had prepared two boxes of ginseng to help me recover. Now I weigh 68 kilograms [150 pounds].

"It still hurts me to this day to talk about my life there. I was very lucky. Grandfather wrote letters and I got out after one year and four months.

"I buried so many people there who died of malnutrition. The pitiful thing is that when someone died, everyone rushed to get the dead person's clothes to wear them.

"They hit you with an iron pole for talking without permission. My front teeth are all fake—the originals were smashed in prison. My lower teeth were broken, too, in camp. One day we were working and I was too hungry to go on. I looked on the ground and found the bone of a pig—someone had left it. So I crushed it and put it in a pot to make some soup. The guards saw it and said, 'You aren't supposed to eat food thrown away by regular people.' I was tied to a stake and beaten. That's when my lower jaw was smashed. I've invested so much in my teeth since I came to South Korea.

"Once we were so hungry that about twenty of us went to the pigsty and started eating the pigs' feed. When I think of it it's so disgusting. The pig keeper reported us. He complained that the pigs would get thinner because we were eating their feed. They sent us to the river and made us put our heads in the water. The first to put his head up would be beaten brutally. We had to do this until we drank enough water to urinate in our pants.

"The prison guards used to shoot birds that came into the camp. There were so many gunshots, the birds got to the point they weren't frightened and wouldn't move. So the guards sent prisoners to climb to the tops of the trees and shake them so the birds would fly out and the guards could shoot them.

"One of my campmates died after a falling tree cracked his ribs. He got no medical treatment. When you bury someone in Korea, you make a mound of dirt over the grave. I did that for him, but the prison guards said, 'Why make a mound for someone as low as a dog?' They beat me.

"When Billy Graham visited North Korea, he returned and said Christianity is reviving. I'll tell you the real story of religious life in North Korea. There's absolutely no religion in North Korea. I saw so many people in camp who came in because of religious belief. Even secretly praying is enough to get you sent to camp. Probably everyone in North Korea who is a religious believer is sent to a camp. I want to write a letter to Billy Graham: 'If you really want to know religion in North Korea, go to a prison camp.' When Billy Graham went to a church service, he should have asked people in the congregation to recite Bible verses."

Q. You eventually got out of the camp, and later defected.

A. "I left the camp on Kim Jong-il's birthday [February 16], 1989. After I got out, I tried to lead an exemplary life since I had caused so much trouble for my relatives. But I was put under surveillance. To live in a society that closed, one that wouldn't allow me freedoms—I had to defect.

"I could have led an affluent life if I had wanted. Many who defect to South Korea do so out of greed and materialism. For me, since I had money in North Korea, I wouldn't have thought of defecting if there had been a slight chance of individual freedom.

"Before I was accused of political crimes, I didn't even know the word politics. But after I got out of the prison camp I was really a political offender. I talked with my friends. I almost got caught again for listening to KBS Radio. My whole family would have gone to a camp. That would have been the end of everything. There were about ninety party members in my family. My parents were forced to divorce on account of me. Someone in State Security said I might be sent back, and then all ninety would have gone, too. So the head of State Security advised them to make me an orphan by divorcing."

Q. What was your father's job?

A. "He headed a department of external management. Its role was to get investment and money to maintain the hotels around Pyongyang. He was working as a foreign trader, exporting mushrooms and so on, both bartering for goods and selling for money. He gave some of the money to Kim Jong-il and the rest went to the hotels."

Q. Were you still playing table tennis when you were arrested? And how did the regime feel about ruining the career of a future champion?

A. "I was still at the table tennis institute when I was arrested. Even the vice-president's son is sent to political prison. Why would they spare a mere Ping-Pong star?"

Q. When Li Song-suk won the 1979 women's singles world championship, the Pyongyang papers said she had been able to win thanks to the guidance of the Respected and Beloved Great Leader Kim Il-sung. Is he indeed such a renaissance man that, besides his other accomplishments, he was a top table tennis trainer as well?

A. "Kim Il-sung didn't know how to play. That's just the usual North Korean formula."

Ahn Hyuk escaped from North Korea in January 1992 in company with Kang Chul-hwan, and they made it to South Korea the following August. As we saw in chapter 16, Kang Chul-hwan and his parents and grandmother, who had been Korean residents of Japan, spent ten years in a prison camp before relatives in Japan pressured and bribed officials to treat them better. Kang had been only nine when he was imprisoned. After his release he got in further trouble.

When I met him Kang was in his mid-thirties but still boyish looking. With his hair in bangs over a thin face, he looked perhaps sixteen—an impression accentuated by his student garb: a jacket, like American high-school athletes wear to display their letters, over a turtleneck sweater. He was studying business at Hanyang University.

"It's such a shame a place like that [prison camp] still exists in this world and is not known to the outside world," Kang told me. "Because of the nuclear issue, people are not focusing on human rights. That should come first. Along with inspections of nuclear sites, they should have inspections of the prison camps. Isn't human life the most important value? Just for opposing the Kim Il-sung regime people are sent to such places. Does that make sense at all?"

Q. What sort of work did you do after you got out of the camp?

A. "At first when we were sent to a farming district I was assigned to a farm group, but I didn't farm. A little later when we moved to town I got a job in a factory for recycling shoes. I worked as a supplier of raw materials. It helped that I had access to foreign exchange from my relatives. I went to other factories and traded to get the raw materials my factory needed. I wanted to go to Kim Chaek University, so I tried to bribe and study my way in, but I wasn't admitted. I applied then to Hamhung University, but it was such a poor university that I decided not to enroll.

"While working for the shoe recycling factory I was feeling negative about things, so I started participating in anti-regime activities. I was listening to South Korean broadcasts and telling friends what I heard. I would sing South Korean popular songs to them. Because of my work as manager of supply, I had a pass to travel all around North Korea. And because I was young I wanted to travel. My friends were all members of the elite. I would propagandize to them against the Kim Il-sung regime. Most university students have anti-regime feelings.

"At 1 A.M. we would put a blanket over our heads and listen to South Korean broadcasts. A department store in Pyongyang deals in foreign goods, including radios that are not fixed to a single channel. You need foreign exchange to buy them, and they're intended for foreigners. I had a shortwave radio."

Q. What do you think of Radio Free Asia?

A. "Very good idea."

Q. What percentage of people would have access to it?

A. "I guess about 6 to 7 percent, usually high officials — the ones with the power."

Q. Does it make sense to try to reach those people?

A. "Of course. They already know a lot about the Western world and about discrepancies involving the Kim Il-sung regime. I knew some people working at Nodong Publishing Company [publisher of the party newspaper, *Nodong Shinmun*, and the party journal, *Kulloja*]. In front of other officials they would hail Kim Il-sung, but in private they would criticize him. They don't know as much as they need to know, though. Giving them more access to the facts would change them more. The trend today is to listen secretly to foreign broadcasts. Since there are so many fabrications in North Korea, they're interested in getting information from the outside world. All they get now is KBS, and it can only be tuned in from 11 P.M. to 2 A.M., so it's not very convenient. Usually KBS broadcasts talk just about South Korea. North Koreans sometimes can't even imagine what they're talking about. What's needed is to report on what happens in North Korea."

Q. What kind of equipment do the potential listeners have available? Do many have shortwave radios as you had?

A. "Most of them have AM/FM radios with cassette decks."

Q. You were in the camp at the same time as Ahn Hyuk, and you two defected together. Did you know him in the camp?

A. "We were in different parts of the camp, so we didn't know each other there. He was in the central part, and I was in the family complex. Anyway, he went in about the same time I got out. But one of my friends in the camp got out at the same time as Ahn, and he introduced us in 1989. Ahn and I talked a lot. Both of us were dissidents, so we had similar ideals and we grew close. We were listening together to KBS, singing popular songs and dancing disco. That caused problems, because rumors spread. One day we wanted to have fun. We went to the mountains with some other friends, taking our stereo and some drinks. We started listening to South Korean popular music and dancing. A passerby reported us. We had some talks with State Security but used bribery to get out of it. That's when the intensive surveillance started, though.

"After some more bribery, we were able to move to Pyongsong city, a 'science city' very near Pyongyang, late in 1990. Before going to the camp, my youngest uncle had graduated in science with a grade average of 4.0. North Korean law says if you get a perfect score, you can have a job at any university in your field. So he worked at the Institute of Science and Technology at Pyongsong. That took a lot of bribery, too, but this time we handled it ourselves with money from our relatives. North Korean society is very corrupt. From top to bottom in the society, all ranks are linked with bribery. Without bribes you can't get anywhere.

"At Pyongsong I tried to get a job at the Institute of Science and Technology as a lab assistant, but the job didn't come through so I didn't work there. I got caught by State Security again after I moved there because one of my supposedly close friends there was a spy sent by State Security. He reported all my criticisms of Kim Il-sung. I was taken in for questioning and was under surveillance. I knew I would be sent to a camp again. Ahn was in trouble, too, since we had been to the mountains together and hung out together.

"We were close to one Public Security guy we had bribed a lot. From him we got travel passes. In January 1992, we took a train from Pyongyang to Haesan on the Chinese border near the Yalu River. We bribed some border guards, telling them we were traders and wanted to buy some goods in China to resell in North Korea. The river was frozen then, and we were able to walk across it. We had thought of going to South Korea, but our first priority was just to get out. We went to China and hung around there. We heard that it was better to go to South Korea."

Q. You said most university students have anti-regime feelings.
A. "Just by watching as China has changed to a free-market system they can see that people are living better. And look how well the Japanese live. University students believe that if the regime stays in power, it will be the downfall of North Korea."
Q. How would the regime lose power?
A. "The only way to get rid of them is a united uprising. If it were a scattered uprising, they could suppress it and send the people involved to camps. The problem is, it's impossible to get a united movement together. Even your closest friend may be a spy from State Security. To

have a united force you need to talk with each other, and that can't happen. There's no one in North Korea who has hope for the future. North Korea is as good as ruined.

"Most North Koreans don't even care about the nuclear issue. All this attention to the nuclear issue is not important. What people should focus on is human rights, saving people from the camps. As a citizen, I knew there were nuclear weapons. So why all the fuss about whether North Korea has them or not? Why all this fuss about inspection?"

Q. How should we deal with the human rights question?

A. "I don't have any specifics. I was shocked when [South Korean] Unification Minister Han said, 'We should not talk about human rights at this point.' The essential reason reunification doesn't come is a matter of human rights. Everything in North Korea is done for just two people, Kim Il-sung and Kim Jong-il. They have no consideration for the people. We can only reunify the country if North Korean society opens, so that people can stand up and talk freely about their complaints. The whole world should focus on human rights in North Korea."

Q. Would the people fight if a war came?

A. "People want war to break out. It's the only way to bring about the fall of the regime, or to end their misery. Young kids conscripted into the army at age seventeen are all brainwashed to believe that South Korea and the United States are the enemy. Of course they would fight. But once they got to Seoul and saw the reality of South Korea, there would be chaos and they would change. And while the new recruits don't know the real world, I imagine the veteran soldiers have more understanding of reality."

Q. Tell me about the food situation.

A. "While I was there, people were having two meals a day, sometimes rations of animal feed. That's what I got in the industrial city where I worked in the factory, a city with a big population and not enough food. In the camp, people like Ahn got around 300 grams a day. [Ahn himself said 360.] People like us, in the family complex, got around 500 grams a day. Corn and salt. The corn was uncooked. You had to cook it yourself."

Q. What is your goal now that you're out?

A. "I want to be part of the exchange between South and North. My dream is, when reunification comes, I want to make a monument in front of the camp to all those who were sacrificed there."

In the meantime Kang became a journalist, watching North Korea for the influential Seoul daily *Chosun Ilbo* and publishing a book about his experiences.[3]

✳   ✳   ✳

Powerfully built, suntanned, his hair cut short, his belt buckle big and gold like the buckle on a cowbow belt, Ahn Myong-chol very much looked the part of a former prison guard. He thought he recognized me when we met: "I think in 1989 or so I saw a picture of you in *Nodong Shinmun,* getting a bouquet from a little girl," he told me.

"I dropped out of agricultural college to join the army," he said. "If I'd graduated from that school I wouldn't have been able to apply for the military. I wanted to join because they usually treat those who haven't done military service as fools; unless they're technocrats they can't join the party. When I first joined the army I worked as a prison guard for three years, then for five years as a driver delivering food for an army base.

"I know about ten prison camps total and worked at four of them. Friends and colleagues worked at the other six. Usually the offenders were separated from their families. All four of my camp jobs were where the families were kept. Ahn Hyuk and Kang Chul-hwan's camp was totally different from mine. Prisoners were divided according to whether they had any prospects of leaving or not. The ones where I worked were all hopeless prisoners. No one would get out. All would die there. The guards kept urging them to work harder—'You can get out, get married.' So they believed there was some reason to hope."

Q. How did you convince them if they couldn't see anybody leaving?
A. "People did leave—but for other camps. At night some prisoners were taken from the camps by truck. Guards told those left behind that these were going out to society, to a new life. But basically they were sending them to another camp, another 'country.' I was in the Seventh Department of State Security. Country and department in Korean are both *guk. Samguk,* the Third Department, is just like Hitler. They do biological experiments on their prisoners. The Third Department facilities are right next to the prison camps. In North Korea when a person dies we usually bury his body. Cremation is rare. But in *Samguk* I could see the smoke coming out from burning bodies. I worked as a driver delivering prisoners to *Samguk.* Once I entered the basement and found it full of blood. But basically I heard about *Samguk* from guard friends, who told me. One rumor was that they squeezed fat from people to make soap for Kim Jong-il and Kim Il-sung and mixed wombs with other substances to make an injection that would stimulate Kim Jong-il's sexual activity. Friends told me these stories."
Q. Did guards inflict violence on prisoners?
A. "That's just a part of daily life. Not to be very aggressive would be seen as condoning the offenders."
Q. How many times a day did you hit someone?

A.   "I can't say I did it once or a hundred times. But when a prisoner sees a guard he has to bow at a ninety-degree angle. Any less is reason to hit him with a stick or rock or whatever. If they don't respond loudly, 'Here!', you hit them.

"Inmates' housing from the sky would look like an ordinary village, but the border is a 3,300-volt electrical fence. Guards usually call the dwellings pigpens. They look like traditional rural houses. There's one very small room per family plus kitchen, regardless of the number in the family.

"As for food, they're supposed to get 500 grams of corn. But the guards take a lot of it, so they can barely sustain life. They get corn alone only on holidays. Other times they mostly mix it with grass and pine bark. Before 1989, guards didn't feel hunger. But as Kim Jong-il took over, we got hungry and had to steal rations from prisoners. The military people are the best fed in North Korea, but from August 1994, guards got pears instead of corn. For a month guards lived on pears, usually boiled, but then started having heavy diarrhea and couldn't train. Afterward they started providing rations from the war reserves. I was a driver hauling foodstuffs by then, not a guard.

"Prison personnel are better nourished than other soldiers because the prisons grow food. As a driver I was able to steal more food. There's a law Kim Jong-il passed. Anyone caught stealing food would be sent to prison camps. A military man caught stealing food would be demoted or prevented from entering the party. But it's human nature. How can they not steal when they have the opportunity?

"I had a 700-gram ration. Anyone who was able to eat the full 700 grams would be considered well off. But they took out 'patriotic rice' and 'war-reserve rice' and there were only 500 grams left. All together, including stolen food, I ate almost 800 grams a day. Yes, prison camp is the place to be to keep in good health—if you're a guard. Prison camp guards are treated second only to fighter pilots. After finishing their terms they go to State Security, like the KCIA in South Korea. They are trusted by the regime. Three categories of people get the prison guard jobs: (1) kids of high officials; (2) kids of State Security members; (3) kids of camp workers. When I entered the army my mother paid a bribe to get me a good job. She worked in a dry goods store, so when they decided to make me a prison guard she gave officials some textiles, foreign liquor and so on. She just asked for a good job. She didn't specifically ask for a prison guard assignment—in fact, she didn't know prison camps existed. Now through the grapevine lots of people know, but when I entered in 1987 hardly anyone knew."

Q.   [I mention the demonstration at the 1989 youth festival.]

A.   "During the youth festival we were on alert. Kim Jong-il feared the in-
      mates would escape and tell the world about the camps. I hardly got any
      sleep because we had to be constantly alert and heavily armed.

           "The four camps I worked at were: No. 11, Kyongsong city in North
      Hamgyong province, where I trained; No. 13, in Jongsong district, On-
      song county, North Hamgyong; No. 22, Hoeryong City, North Ham-
      gyong; and No. 26 in Hwachon, Pyongyang City. The numbers go up to
      27, to my knowledge.

Q.   What offenses landed people there?

A.   "Calling the name of Kim Il-sung or Kim Jong-il without using the hon-
      orific prefixes, for example. One man went to the food ration depart-
      ment and they told him to come back again since there was no food that
      day. He said, 'In a socialist country like ours, how can this happen?' He
      was sent to a camp. Factionalists, people who opposed Kim Jong-il's
      succeeding Kim Il-sung in power of course were sent to camp. It's not
      just political attitudes that will get you there. Religious fanatics are im-
      prisoned, too. The prisons where I worked were for dissidents and fac-
      tionalists."

Q.   Did you agree they were bad people?

A.   "In army training they taught us that those were serious offenders who
      should be punished; if they tried to escape we had the right to kill them.
      But after three years as a guard, when I switched to driving, I had more
      personal contact with prisoners and realized they were not what I had
      thought. Sometimes I had to deliver produce grown by prisoners, and I
      chatted with them when I picked it up. I had to distribute rations from
      the central distribution point in the center of the camp to the outlying
      areas.

           "The first incident: I was still a guard but learning to drive a truck. I
      took the truck to prisoners and told them to repair it and clean it up. I
      was nineteen. One prisoner was about forty-five. He bowed to me ninety
      degrees and said, 'I'm all finished, thank you, sir.' I thought, considering
      his age, he could be my father. I felt sudden pity and decided to give him
      a cigarette. He cried. We talked and I realized he had been sent to prison
      because of his father's offenses. Kim Chang-bong, who was head of the
      KPA in the 1970s, was ousted by Kim Jong-il and sent with his family to
      camp. Others under him were also sent to prison camps with their fami-
      lies. This man's father probably worked under Kim Chang-bong."

Q.   After that incident did you start treating prisoners nicely?

A.   "At that time I was just learning what sort of people had come to the
      camps. I didn't really change my behavior. It was 1992 when I started
      being kinder toward them. Even from the moment I entered the army I
      felt some pity for them. But 1992 was when I totally changed my mind
      and decided to do something active. I gave them my meat. Once in two

weeks I got about this much [shows the final two joints of three fingers—maybe 50–100 grams or two to four ounces]. I had more access to meat, so I was able to give them some and still eat meat myself. Some other guards did the same and had to quit when they were discovered. I didn't discuss this matter with any other guards. I did talk with my most intimate friend about how the dissidents were not so bad. He agreed."

Q. Did you dislike Kim Jong-il then?

A. "I can honestly say I lean toward liking Kim Il-sung. As for Kim Jong-il, when I was in North Korea I was indifferent to him. That's not to say I hated him. I sensed some discrepancies in the regime's policies. They propagandize that North Korea is a very peaceful society, but they say in all the orders to prison guards to be very aggressive, make sure you get rid of three generations of prisoners, root them out of society."

Q. Why did you defect?

A. "I went to my hometown. My father had committed suicide but I hadn't been told that. My father worked in a granary. One day a friend said, 'My son is starving. Please get me some food for him.' Father stole a bit for that man's son. He didn't get caught then. But the granary boss stole two tons of rice. He framed my father as the culprit. My father was to be sent to prison camp, but he committed suicide, in January 1994. They didn't tell me. I knew my father had died, but the letter said it was a heart attack. I learned the truth in May when I visited my hometown. When I arrived, I found my house gone, totally demolished. In April, my mother had been sent to prison as a traitor. If any family member commits suicide, other family members including the spouse, are 'traitors.' Someone who worked under her wanted her job and said she had poisoned my father. So there were two charges against her—spouse of a traitor and murderess. He did die of poison—alkali. I found that my younger sister was by herself. My younger brother was working as a border guard and didn't know about father's death. [They were sent to prison after Ahn defected.] In Oriental society there's a family head. If the head commits suicide the spouse is a traitor. If the children commit suicide the parents are criticized and banished from the village, not sent to prison camp. I stayed in my hometown for a week, then went back to Hoeryong. When I went back, they termed me the son of a traitor and had someone watch me. It meant they didn't trust me any more. During my time at home I had already realized that if I stayed, in the end, I probably would be sent to a prison camp myself. So I had to defect to South Korea."

Q. Why South Korea?

A. "I wanted to tell the world about the reality of prison camps. The only country that came to mind as an enemy of North Korea was South Korea."

Q. Did you know anything about South Korea?

A. "Only that it was better off economically than North Korea."

Q. How did you know that?

A. "I heard rumors. When I watched televised demonstrations in South Korea I could see the buildings in the background—the South Koreans looked pretty well off. I heard rumors of vast numbers of cars. The big year was 1989. After Im Su-gyong's visit, people's thought changed. They figured North Korea couldn't feed them, but South Korea was better off. It was seeing her appearance—she seemed well off, acted free and confident."

Q. How did you defect with someone watching?

A. "I thought I had to make the watchers believe in me. I worked really diligently to instill trust. Kim Il-sung's death brought the perfect opportunity. After his death there was a mourning ceremony at Hoeryong. We didn't tell the prisoners—this was for the guards and their families. Only women cried, not the guards. So that night they had rigorous training to make the guards cry at the next mourning ceremony. Still none of them cried. I cut my finger and wrote in blood: 'Loyalty to Kim Jong-il.' From that moment they really trusted me and didn't watch me anymore.

"Initially I wanted to bring my brother and sister along but timing didn't allow it. I did take a pair of prisoners from camp—a brother and a sister—in a truck. These were the people I'd given meat to. I was close to them. They got scared in mid-escape and decided not to defect. They got on the truck inside the camp. I said, 'Let's go to South Korea.' They initially agreed, but then got scared before we got out of the camp. They weren't confident we could get across the border. She was twenty-six. Her brother was twenty-four. She wasn't my sweetheart. We were just friends. I took the truck to the border and swam across the Tumen River."

Choe Dong-chul had been miscast as a North Korean prison guard, I thought. His build was too skinny, his facial features too sensitive for someone doing such brutal work. He neither walked the walk nor talked the talk. When I asked him what he thought of post-defection life in South Korea he replied with a nuanced critique: "I don't like the consumerism of Seoul. It's not good to spend so much on these fashions. I always tell people, 'Our generation will experience reunification. You should save the money you're spending now so you can use it after reunification to build some factories in North Korea.'"

Suitability aside, Choe entered the army after high school and was stationed for three years at political prisoners' camp Number 11 in Kyongsong, North Hamgyong Province—the same camp where Ahn Myong-chol trained later. "The prerequisites were good family background, a university entrance-level exam and an interview — so they could see your appearance," he told me. "I was lucky to get in. The benefits are good. In 1982, Kim Jong-il issued a new regulation: To be a member of State Security you had to have spent at least three years in the army and have a university education. So from 1983, they started selecting elite young men as future State Security officers. We would do our army hitch, get recommended to universities and, after university graduation, would become members of State Security.

"After I got into the army I found there were political prisons numbered from 11 to 22. At Number 11 there were about twenty thousand prisoners," he said.

Q. What did you see and hear at the camp?
A. "Very gruesome stories."
Q. We can handle them.
A. "The summer of 1985 a family of five tried to escape. They were caught after three days. After a week the grandmother and father were hanged in public and the three kids — none of them even ten years old — were executed by gunfire.

"The camp was in a typhoon region. On April 5, 1986, heavy winds spread a forest fire. The prisoners were forced to fight the fire. Afterward we counted forty prisoners dead — no State Security or guards. State Security officers didn't pity them. 'It's a good thing.' 'Serves them right.'

"Some families were sent there during the land reform period — mainly capitalists and moneyed people. Some others might have been families of people who were pro–South Korea in the Korean War or 'factionalists' or families of defectors to South Korea. The prison camps were established when Kim Il-sung was vowing that factionalism would destroy three generations of a family. The factionalists themselves were sent into coal mines, separated from their wives and children, who went to prison camps. The separated people were not to know if the others were alive or dead.

"The houses at the camp were made of clay; the roofs, straw; the floors, clay or rocks, or straw on clay. Most prisoners were short — 140 to 150 centimeters [4 feet 6 inches to 4 feet 9 inches] — probably because their jobs were burdensome. They always carried loads on their backs.

"Soldiers in a guard unit usually wear a uniform almost a year. The previous year's uniforms are dyed another color and given to prisoners. It's the same with shoes, which the soldiers had worn every day.

"Prison guards weren't permitted to go in and see the inmates' food situation but from appearances I could speculate they usually had potatoes or corn. They were too skinny when you looked at them. If someone lives on a diet of mainly potatoes, the face puffs up grotesquely.

"The guards treated them like slaves. We could beat them at will. Some guards or State Security officers would kill prisoners for fun."

Q. Did you see it happen?

A. "No. I just heard a story that a guard asked a prisoner to pick up a very sharp farming tool. As the prisoner held it, the guard shot him. He explained: 'I thought he'd kill me with that.'"

Q. You?

A. "As you can see from my face I'm not that cruel."

Q. What was in your mind?

A. "I stayed three years, a short time. We were taught: 'These were the people who exploited your parents. They are enemies.' I heard that some who worked there for seven or eight years got to thinking this was too cruel even for a political prisoner. But I didn't get to that stage. I have to admit that when I was in a favorable situation I was very devoted to the regime. Only my mother's troubles later made me question the regime."

After three years as a guard Choe entered Kim Il-sung University, majoring in computer science. From June 1986 to April 1988 he lived in a dorm.

Q. How advanced is the computer science program?

A. "While I was at KISU the computer center had about fifty computers, half of them Bulgarian. We had Sharp N2-1200 and N2-800 models. The center was open to all in the university, and it wasn't adequate. You had to wait a couple of hours to use a computer once. You needed to hurry to make it available to others who were waiting. The software was in English: BASIC."

Q. When I visited the campus they told me all twelve thousand students were in a meeting.

A. "It's really true they have meetings of all twelve thousand on campus, but they don't have a big enough room for them all to be physically present. The auditorium seats seven hundred. The rest sit in classrooms and listen via loudspeaker to the teachings of Kim Il-sung, lectures on new books, ideology and so on. Unfaithful students have to stand and confess their wrongdoings. Everyone is either in the auditorium or in a classroom. You can't find anyone walking around the campus. It usually happens on Saturday. And even at other times students don't stroll around on campus or have outdoor classes as South Koreans sometimes do. They're outside only for coming and going. The rest of the time they stay in class. All students have lectures from 8:00 to 9:30 A.M., from 9:40 to 11:10 A.M. and from 11:30 A.M. to 1:00 P.M.

"Usually when foreigners come, they're invited when all students are in class. I saw some foreigners myself while at KISU, but the North

Korean government is very cautious about American reporters like you. First, the police and military men don't wear their uniforms while you're visiting and all universities and schools keep their students on campus for the duration of the reporters' stay.

"I never heard of any demonstrations. Those rumors are unfounded, especially regarding People's Economic University. All students there are current officials getting on-the-job education. Why would they demonstrate?"

(Choe's elite status as a student at the country's top university and a future State Security officer ended when his mother got in trouble.)

"My mother was in charge of a distribution center back home. The police chief and other authorities framed her and forced her to sign a confession to an alleged crime. In court, in November 1987, she got a thirteen-year prison sentence. After that, the authorities told me, 'Your mother is in prison so you can't stay in the university.' My father and I were sent as farmhands to a tobacco field about 25 or 30 kilometers from our hometown. It was the 4/25 Tobacco Farm in Onsong, North Hamgyong Province."

It was two years after I first met Choe that I was able to interview his mother, Lee Soon-ok. She was grandmotherly-looking, with graying hair, wearing gold-rimmed glasses. I asked her how she had arranged travel permits for her trips to China. "Even if they can't eat, people can find a way to get a bottle of liquor or some cigarettes to use as bribes for permits," she said. "Often the food that's supposed to go to ordinary citizens goes to officials instead."

Q. What was the police chief's scam?
A. "He used to come to the distribution center and demand things that were supposed to go to others. I had to comply at first. But he would take ten sets of underwear when some people got none. I started resisting toward the end. After I returned from China the last time, he wanted cloth as a bribe. I refused to give it to him. I thought that was what got me imprisoned. The real reason, I found out, was that since the early 1980s there had been economic difficulties due to Kim Jong-il's policies.

"They tortured me because I refused to confess to sabotaging Kim Jong-il's economic policies. I held out for one year and two months. I said, 'How could I be responsible for something as big as that—Kim Jong-il's policies?' Finally they promised me that my husband and son would be permitted to keep status. I was just holding on to life then. I gave in and signed the confession.

"My son went to the judge and asked what I had done. The judge said, 'I don't know what she did. I was told by the party to give this sentence.' I went to a prison at Kaechon in South Pyongan Province. I came to realize I'd been part of a national purge of all the people who had run distribution centers. They wanted to blame us for the failures of the policies. For the first seven months I thought I was the only one. But in the winter they would send us out for an hour in our underwear to freeze. I went out and there were twelve people there. There were twelve distribution centers in North Hamgyong Province, where I lived, and the chiefs of all of those were imprisoned there. Six men out of that group died of torture; one got twenty years; one, fifteen. Being a woman, I got only thirteen years.

"While I was in prison I saw some people starve to death. By that time I had abscesses in my body that were full of fluid, because of torture. The organs on my left side were filled with water. After I left I couldn't work for a year. I was puffy, swollen. My leg didn't work."

Q. What was the food situation in your prison?

A. "We got 300 grams of corn and would make it into a cookie-sized cake. That plus a small cup of salt soup three times a day."

Q. Prisoners had to work?

A. "They had thirty-three factories in the prison where they made military goods, from helmets to shoes. There was a coal mine, too. I didn't have to do physical labor but the men worked eighteen hours a day. There was a rubber factory, a gun holster factory, a uniform factory. The men who worked got the same 300 grams. There were more people dying than staying alive. We were all living together. Hundreds died during the seven years I was there. Six months is the turning point. After that, people's bodies start adjusting to less food and hard labor. If you survive the first six months, you should be OK. Lots of people don't. They think of how the food compares with what they got back home. Lots die of dehydration and hunger the first six months. We were working in an enclosed place, with nothing to pick from trees or fields. No food. Sometimes we'd use such things as wallpaper glue as food. Lots of people died that way. People who were dying of dehydration cried out for water, but the guards wouldn't give it to them. They got none. Just the salt soup, three times a day. So, with the last breath of their lives they'd crawl across the room and suck on the mops—shit water—and they'd die drinking that. I worked in the office in charge of accounting for the factories. After work we'd be lined up to go back to the cells. I saw hungry, dehydrated people who became delirious. The path from factory to cells wasn't paved. Sometimes a small pebble or piece of dirt looked like food. I saw people pick such things up, swallow them and die on the spot.

"There was an export factory. They'd get commissons from abroad to make goods to export for foreign exchange. For Russia, work uniforms, shirts, brassieres. For Japan they knitted sweaters. Prisoner labor. The Japanese sent the yarn and the patterns. My friends used to make roses for France, small roses, twelve to a box. For Poland they made doilies and embroidered chair covers."

Q. So this was a regular prison, not a political prison? What was the difference?

A. "Right. Even political prisoners like me are sent to prisons, not camps, if their crimes are severe enough. In a regular prison we were worked more, and the treatment was harsher, than in a political prisoners' camp. My son knew the camp situation and I compared notes with him. The treatment is so much worse once you're put into such a prison. Your rights are taken away. They can work you eighteen to twenty hours a day. There are quotas. If you don't meet them your food gets reduced to 240 grams a day. If you fail to meet the quota for five days, you get 60 grams per meal—180 grams a day. If you're in isolation you get 30 grams per meal, 90 grams a day. Prisoners can go to the toilet only three times a day. You get up at 5:30 A.M., go to the toilet once in the morning, once in the afternoon, once in the evening and stop work at 12:30 A.M., with no rest period except the three toilet times and three meals that take one hour total.

"I was a political prisoner because I supposedly messed up Kim Jong-il's plan by unfairly distributing goods, not doing a good job. I wrote a letter to Kim Jong-il after I was paroled. I couldn't write it while in jail or I'd get a double sentence for refusing to repent. I sent four letters to the central party. I wasn't supposed to. I was being watched. But there was an official I'd been close to when I was at the distribution center. I asked him to post them when he went to Pyongyang. I think two of them got through. I know one arrived because one central party official came to talk to me. My husband, a school principal, had been sent to a farm, along with my son when I went to jail. The central party official acknowledged that things had been done unfairly. But what to do? Lift the punishments off my son and husband, let my son return to university, that's what I wanted. The official's initial response was, 'I understand.' He left. Then he came back from the party center and said, 'If you ever petition like this again, you'll be sent back to prison.' I asked, 'Why, if you know that I was punished unlawfully?' His answer was, 'If your son and husband were reinstated, many layers of the officials who sent them off would have to be fired. We can't do that. Please make a sacrifice for the revolution. What's done is done.' He also said, 'You should be thankful you got out of prison alive.'"

Q. What was his name?

A. "I never knew it. He was a high official. They don't usually give you their names. He was chief of the central party Petitions Department.

"The local authorities had taken all our material goods away, I didn't know where, when they took my husband and son away. I went to the judge who had sentenced me. I found out from my friends that the people who had put me in prison—judge, policemen—divided my goods. The judge got my color TV; the prosecutor, my refrigerator; somebody else, my sewing machine and so on. The police chief got the bicycle. I took my son, with the help of a friend who still worked at the distribution center, to each of those houses and saw my things there. When I petitioned Kim Jong-il, I wrote all those points down as well. When the central party man came, he went to the houses and saw that it was true. 'But if we take those things back and exonerate you, then all those involved will have to be punished,' he said. He pointed out that I was already on the bottom while they were holding official posts. Therefore, he said, the central party was on their side. Although he acknowledged completely the wrongdoings, including my wrongful punishment, these were party members. For all those several members to be punished as thieves would undermine the party's image and credibility. I just requested that they reinstate my son in school. But, no, we would have to live the rest of our lives in the place of banishment. We decided to leave, my son and I.

"Our place of banishment was a large tract in Sansong-ri, Onsong County, North Hamgyong Province, where they formerly had a political prison. It's in the far northwest of the county. We had lived in the county seat. I heard when I got out of prison and joined my husband and son that the political prison had been closed and the prisoners moved. It had been a huge prison holding about thirty thousand inmates. Some were sent to Hoeryong, some to Kaechon, some to Kyongbuk in North Pyongan. North Korea claims it has no political prisons. The reason they moved the prisoners is that the place is right on the Chinese border. They feared other people from outside would see it because border residents have contact with foreigners. I heard that from officials who used to work at the prison.

"The place had been turned into a tobacco farm although it was on very difficult mountain terrain with not enough water. They called it 4/25 Tobacco Farm, after the founding date of the People's Army, because it supplied all the military's tobacco. The prison had used that land to grow corn before.

"When I got up there from prison my son had no shoes. They'd never given him any. His one pair of pants weighed five kilos, he had patched it so often. The pants were all patches. Those were the pants he'd been wearing when he was kicked out of university. He wore them for five years. On his feet he had only soles, with rope wrapped around them and around his feet to keep them on."

THOUGH ALIVE, WORSE THAN GUTTER DOGS

Q. What was the food situation at the tobacco farm?

A. "The rations didn't come regularly. I couldn't work and wasn't given food. I had to share my son's rations. On his way home from the farm each day he'd bring grasses and so on. We'd grind the corn we got into meal, add greens to make porridge or steam it to make corn cakes."

Q. Another woman who had been banished told me that there was less starvation in the banishment areas and maybe in prison camps than in cities, because prisoners and banishees grow their own food.

A. "I only lived in the banishment area about a year but, yes, it's a little better on the farms than in the cities regarding starvation. In the villages, if you plant, you have to do it secretly. People usually go into the mountains and make small plots there. I got there in December. I was only able to get food from my garden patch for a few months. We escaped before it yielded much produce. We lived on grasses and weeds from January to September. The grain harvest is October, November, December, so we lived on weeds until then."

Q. Do the prison camps and prisons have farmland?

A. "The prison camps usually do a lot of outdoor work: farming, raising animals or mining. Just plain prisons are enclosed with electric wire fences and are mostly factories making things."

After meeting Lee I looked up her son, Choe, to talk with him again. His face had filled out and he had matured since our first meeting two years earlier, in 1996. I felt that he had turned into quite a fine young man. He was studying hard at Hangyang University, determined to finish although he told me it was sometimes tough. He had joined RENK (Rescue the North Korean People), a human rights lobbying organization that I knew well from having talked with one of its leading figures in Japan, Professor Lee Young-hwa. "It's getting bigger," Choe said. "It has a newsletter and publishes a monthly paper, *Life and Human Rights*. The organization helps defectors overseas and we help those in South Korea who get into difficult situations."

From talking with more recent defectors, Choe said he had learned that seven political prison camps still existed. Some had been closed. "Two in the northwest were too close to the border," he said. "Many escaped, and people could find them easily from China. The authorities wanted to hide them. The camp that had been at Kyongsong in North Hamgyong Province moved because Kim Jong-il's summer palace was built in that area. Sungho closed around 1990 because it was too near the capital. Prisoners were sent to other camps. The authorities expanded existing camps."

✵ ✵ ✵

Joo Young-hee, a handsome woman of fifty with thin lips and slightly hooded eyes, her short hair permanently waved, her mature figure clothed in a black dress with white stripes, looked the typical middle-class Seoul matron except for her thick fingers and wrists. I thought those might reflect training in the martial arts, but learned she had been a basketball player in high school and a knitter afterward, had been imprisoned once at hard labor, farming, and eventually had been banished to a rural area.

Her first husband, a Korean-Japanese, had died in 1982, she told me. "After that I worked in a housewives' cooperative as a knitter, but only nominally from 1984. That year I started my own business, trading with Chinese on the border—TVs, squid. Also, Chinese traders came to my town to trade with me. I was still getting money from my husband's relatives in Japan so I could buy televisions in the stores in Pyongyang and Hamhung. A TV cost about 15,000 *won*, but we could sell it for 40,000 or 50,000 *won* to Chinese. I had been to China, with a proper passport. I had an invitation from a Chinese trading friend who I claimed was a sister-in-law. If you can afford it, it's not hard to get a proper passport and go to China. To get the passport I bribed officials with Chinese medicine. In 1989, I was imprisoned for two years for violations related to my trading. I went to Prison Number 11, Chungsam County, South Pyongan Province."

Q. How was it?
A. "I was in the country's only women's prison. You don't lose your citizenship rights there. It's more of a training camp than a prison. Inmates there were fortune-tellers, traders, thieves, people convicted of attempted murder. They didn't give us enough food. The labor was hard. Young people learned how to be criminals. I farmed there for two years until 1992. My children stayed with my mother-in-law at home.

"In 1993 my son defected to China. In January 1994, my other two children and I were banished to a village called Sangnam-ri in Hochon County, South Hamgyong Province.

"My son worked for a trading company. When it closed he went to China alone sometimes, to try to do trading on his own account. He got caught during a state of emergency around March 1993. Four border guards who suspected him of spying stripped him down to his underwear and beat him from 9 A.M. to 4 A.M. Around 5 A.M. he asked if he could go to the toilet. They let him go alone and he escaped. He went to China. That was at Kanpyong-ri in Hoeryong County, right on the Tumen River. He figured he would be punished, either banished or sent to a political prison camp. Calculating the pros and cons he decided to cross the river and escape.

"In January 1994, not a year after his escape, they came after the family. Before our banishment I was taken to State Security and was a prisoner for about a month. They questioned me because they thought I must know something about my son's escape. State Security people went to the house and packed up. The kids were at home. We were allowed to take one trunk and two sacks. I was released in time to catch the train."

Q. What was the charge?

A. "There was no charge."

Q. I heard Kim Jong-il had come up with a new directive: "Make no internal enemies."

A. "Yes, in the early 1990s there was a new law—no reprisals against the families of defectors. In reality it didn't help anyone."

Q. But you were banished, not sent to a political prison camp.

A. "That's true.

"When the three of us went to Sangnam-ri we were sent to a cooperative farm but weren't allowed to work for fifteen days. So they didn't give us food or a house. We did have twenty kilograms of rice with us and one set of clothing. We had to carry in the trunk our portraits of Kim Il-sung and Kim Jong-il. We moved in for one month with a family of four in a single room. Then we moved to the storage space of the same house. The roof leaked—we could see the sky. There were mice everywhere, even under the blankets when we slept. In August that year, we moved to a better storage room.

"We were there two years and five months, constantly being watched secretly. They'd come at night and flash a light to see if we were sleeping. We had to be careful what we said. The only freedom we had was walking within the village. We couldn't go even one step outside. Sangnam-ri traditionally has been a place of banishment. This is where families of political criminals were sent. There were a few normal people but not that many.

"We didn't see any rice. We only had corn, potatoes and beans. People living there originally, those not banished, had their own plots providing such things as vegetables, but people like us didn't have land to grow them so we had to buy them. [Gets emotional.] When we lived there, because it's a farm, we only got rations once a year at harvest share-out time in October or November. We had only brought 20 kilos of rice. Because we were watched, we couldn't use money to buy food or the seller would get in trouble. There were times we had no food even though I'd brought money. Sometimes people would secretly throw corn cakes into our house because they knew we were starving.

"Sometimes late at night I'd take the train to the county seat or to my mother's home in Hamhung. When they realized I was missing they thought I would escape to China. They would call my mother's house while I was on the train. She said no, I wasn't there. I'd get found and taken back.

"When I was banished I was told I wasn't being watched. But I knew I was. Sometimes I'd stay ten or fifteen days at Mother's before they'd come and take me back. I'd say, 'You say you're not guarding me. Why did you come to get me?' They'd say, 'No, we're not guarding you.' After every trip I'd be put on the stand. Once I was taken to State Security because of so many trips. They said I could go—but I needed seven people to approve a trip. I used to fight with them. 'I don't need all this. All I need is food. The reason I go is I'm not being rationed food and can't buy it here, so I go to buy it.' They didn't have much to say. I had to be put on the stand each time, but nobody would find anything criminal.

"Everybody called me a madwoman because I wouldn't submit. Toward the end I thought I needed to remarry. With a husband as a protector maybe life would be better. I married a train conductor. Everybody was opposed, including the party. The neighborhood people tried to discourage him because I was 'anti-party.' They put a lot of pressure on him, but we married in June 1996. Because of his unyielding personality he died of a stroke after our marriage. He went through with the marriage because his daughters told him he needed someone to care for him in his old age."

Q. How about the food situation for other banishees who don't have money?

A. "Most of the people had been there a long time. Over the years they had carved out plots in the mountains to grow things. They also stole enough food by winter to last a year. Of course, you can get caught."

Q. Did you see people starving?

A. Yes, by March or April they had run out of the harvest share-out rations. In two years and five months there I saw one child and an adult die of hunger, plus one of disease, and one by drowning. I left in 1997."

Q. Not an epidemic of starvation?

A. "No, because it was a farming community. But in one family the mother and child died of hunger and the father was so weak that he drowned while crossing a shallow river. The one who died of disease was relatively well off but had acute dysentery.

"One couple were not all there in the head. They boiled their child and ate it, took the buttocks meat to sell it in the village. The man got caught. He was imprisoned but she was released."

Q. What do you think of the reported estimate of two to three million dead of starvation?

A. "It's probably true. Before I left, near Hamhung Station, I saw lots of people dead on the streets. On the train I would see dead bodies beside the tracks. Mostly those were city people, I think. Starving people would hang around the station because it's warmer, but the guards didn't want to deal with their bodies so they kicked them out of the station."

Q. So it's better to be banished to a rural village than to stay in the city?

A. "It was a little better in the farm village. But for families like ours, with money, it would have been better to live in the city. Now all the material goods from the cities are going to the farm villages, traded for food. People from the city come to the farm villages to trade for food. In the past, after sundown the village people would let them spend the night in their houses, but the city people started stealing during the night and running away so the farmers stopped letting them in. People had to go into sheds or barns to sleep. I heard of one young man who had a bag of rice and slept in a barn. He froze to death, holding tightly to the rice.

"On the farm, if you're hungry you don't have the strength to work. So people recently started grinding corn cobs and mixing them with other stuff to make noodles. It comes out the color of cow dung and tastes horrible. It's not really edible. People in my community started eating tree bark."

Q. Did you ever see donated food?

A. "I never saw it in the village. But in Hamhung once I got a bit of South Korean rice rationed to me. Donated goods including rice are being sold in stores. You have to use foreign exchange to buy it. The government rations it to foreign currency stores, which sell it. Only people with foreign exchange could buy it. I didn't buy that but I've been to those stores in Hamhung and heard the goods there were donated."

Q. What sort of person is starving to death?

A. "In Hamhung, usually it's people with no money, no goods to sell, no gumption or trading skill. So a lot of elderly people and children die first."

Q. How do the authorities react to the hunger?

A. "What the central government tells each province is, 'Take care of the food shortages locally.' But if the officials locally can maintain their posts they're happy. They're not sacrificing, or running around finding food for citizens."

Q. How did you get out?

A. "The son who had defected got me out. He was responsible for getting relatives in China to put together our escape. The authorities in South Korea told me not to give details. I left North Korea February 16, 1997, and got to South Korea May 29."

Q. Now?

A. "I didn't know anything about South Korea. I had just heard rumors. I found that it's free. But it's not easy to live with all the freedom. I got a bounty from the government and opened a small shop selling North Korean–style sausage."

❊   ❊   ❊

The day after I had met Joo I interviewed her younger son, Hon Jin-myung. His freckled face resembled hers but at twenty-one he lacked her savvy. He was still a youth, speaking in a husky high-pitched voice. His haircut looked as if it had been done with a bowl, bangs combed forward in front as seemed to be the fashion. He wore a T-shirt with a collar, jeans and sneakers.

Q. Tell me about the place of banishment.
A. "Sangnam-ri is a well-known place where people with anti-regime thoughts including anti-communists were banished as early as the 1960s. Ex-landlords and their children were there when I got there. There were no cars. It was a mountainous rural area. We had no house at first, lived with a family that used to work for the local party. They reported every move we made. After a month we asked for a house and got to move into the shed full of mice at the same family's house. We weren't given work for three months. But then my mother went to work in a cornfield. I was in my last year of school. My sister was married but still she was forced to come with us. After a while she left to go back to her in-laws. Just my mother and I were left. The place had terraced plots but no flat land.

"After two months I wanted to join the military. But when they held the physical exam my name wasn't on the list. That's how I found out I couldn't enlist. The local party people had been telling me, 'We won't look at your past. Everything depends on your behavior.' I had believed them until then. I went to work in the cornfields like my mother. After giving up the idea of joining the military, I got to know the local people and found that nobody was allowed to leave, so we might as well come to terms with it. I talked with people in their forties and fifties who had been there since they were children. They couldn't join the party or hold important posts.

"Mother felt sorry for me when I started working in the cornfield. That's when she thought of marrying, as a way out. But they told us that even if she married, her husband would have to come live in that village. That's when she started thinking of escaping. Trading in Hamhung, she knew lots of security people. She kept asking around whether there wasn't some way out of the village. She was told there were certain people who could help get her out, people who used to be involved in the independence movement, pilots, train conductors, coal miners. She was advised to marry one of those and maybe she could get out. She wasn't supposed to leave, but she left for Tanchong City for two months and found a suitable groom. They registered the marriage and she brought back the certificate, but the authorities told her she couldn't leave even with that. The man she married had been a conductor since he was nineteen years old, back in colonial times. He had lost all his family during the Korean War. They investigated him but couldn't touch him so they stamped the certificate and we left the village."

Q. Why do conductors have so much juice?

A. "I don't know. But even when others didn't get rations, they did. Pilots are the same, maybe because they could escape in a plane. It's difficult to become a pilot. The train conductors deal with lives. Mostly they're party members. I think a conductor can join the party automatically after one year.

"We went to the town. Before we left the village we prepared documents saying I was a train conductor. But once we got to town the town refused to register us at our home address. So I couldn't work for four months. I never actually worked for the railroad.

"Mother had asked her husband-to-be for help, told him her story. He agreed to marry her for humane purposes. But he died in October 1996, after we had been there for four months. During those four months he argued with town officials about registering us to that address. After he died there was no one to take up the argument. We stayed for four months after her husband's death and did the rituals for him."

Q. Did you see people starve?

A. "Yes. It was pretty severe by the time I left. I saw three or four a day dying in Hamhung, where we stayed after the four months following the conductor's death."

Q. What sort of people died?

A. "Probably they were all laborers and farmers. Officials of a certain rank wouldn't starve. Old people and children, dressed very badly, were dying. The authorities weren't checking for passes because the food situation was so bad. People could travel to look for food."

Q. In 1992, I saw some really bad-looking people, filthy, unwashed, in bad clothing, riding a train in the northeast. The windows were glassless.

A. "That's what happens when you ride a train. From Seoul to Pusan takes only three or four hours. But from Hamhung to Chongjin, because of lack of fuel and electricity what's supposed to be a seven-hour ride takes up to a week. There's no food on the trains. At the stations you can buy food, but most people don't have money. So they travel for a week without much food, without washing facilities. At home they look a little better. It's probably just as bad in Pyongyang, but when I watched television they looked fed and relaxed. It's better than any other city—they still get rations."

Nam Chung was banished from Pyongyang along with his mother and two of his brothers after the eldest brother, a student in Russia, defected. In 1992, the family was sent to Tongpo mining camp in Onsong County, North Hamgyong

Province. "My mother's an architect," Nam told me. "My father died twenty years ago. My second brother studied in an East German military academy. My third brother graduated from Mangyongdae Revolutionary School and was a pilot for four years and six months. After we were sent off my mother was put to work at the mining camp as an architect. My second brother worked as a laborer; my third brother, in a paper factory. I was put to work laying railroad track. I had graduated from Pyongyang No. 1 Senior Middle School and enrolled in the Railroad College. I was expelled from college when my brother defected.

"We didn't have any choice although we wanted to go somewhere better. The camp used to be a full prison camp with wire fence, but the wire was taken down in 1990 due to the furor abroad over human rights. Worse offenders were sent to other prisons while lesser offenders were kept there. We were watched by six families who had been assigned by State Security. Even if we worked two or three times harder than others we weren't recognized. But I managed to graduate from the Railroad College via correspondence course. My father had graduated there, and his friends helped me. Usually it's impossible. Anyhow, my degree wasn't recognized in the camp.

"Due to the food shortage, other people didn't work for ten days or so a month. But if we missed even one day we'd be fingerprinted and reported. They collect those reports. If we do something worse they tack it on and punish us. The reason we weren't treated even worse was that Mother was a very well-known and accomplished architect in Pyongyang."

Q. Food situation?
A. "It's difficult to describe in words. We used to eat one spoon of rice per day per three adults, which we bought. So we had to go out to the hills and mountains and fields and pick any greens that weren't poisonous. We'd mix 'green porridge': assemble anything we could find, grind the greens, take the juice from them, add it to a single spoon of rice and make porridge. If you made porridge with pine bark and acorns, that was considered high-quality food. We also used to go to the farm fields and take the roots left after the rice harvest, or corn roots and corn cobs—we dried them and ground them to make porridge. Until 1993, the rations were pretty regular. From 1994, we got no rations at all in that area. By the time we left, it was on record officially that they owed us 1,800 kilograms—one ton and 800 kilograms—of grain. The fifteen-day ration was supposed to be 11.8 kilograms of grain per person. My second brother had married, so our household had three people and was supposed to get rations for three. We were supposed to get 700 or 800 grams per day per person, but because of the shortage we didn't. We bought food but by July 1996 our resources were so low we could only

buy 100 grams to divide among three people—33 grams a day per person."

Q. Which areas were best and which worst for food, based on what you learned working for the railroad?

A. "The best places were Hwanghae Province's Yonbaek Plain. In South Hamgyong it was generally OK south of Hamhung. I heard that the worst areas were in North Hamgyong, Chongjin City and Musan County."

Q. What was your railroad job?

A. "Railroad guard."

Q. They trusted you?

A. "I could never work alone. Three to five people were always together. When I was talking about rations, I wasn't referring to rice but to corn. But we wanted to have a little rice to make the soup starchy. We didn't receive anything as rations. We had to buy food. To pay for it, starting in 1994, we sold the TV, refrigerator, camera and tape recorders. Toward the end we had nothing to sell, and from July 1996 we were reduced to buying ony one spoon of rice a day, from having eaten a little better before that. We were starting to sell our blankets, blanket covers, anything we could. Some people sell everything. A family finally sells its house and becomes homeless. They go to try to find food any way they can. When it comes to the point when they can't get food, they die."

Q. Sell their homes?

A. "You do it illegally, secretly. And women sell their bodies. If you go to any big city train station like Chongjin, you see a lot of starving people, thieves, homeless people.

"My family's worst time was the latter part of 1996, before my eldest brother sent money starting in December of that year. We heard about my brother from some Chinese people. He had met a lot of Chinese while studying in the Soviet Union, and he paid about twenty people to find out about the family. Eventually, one of them succeeded, and my brother sent us money. We couldn't leave, but we weren't in cells. Other people could get in to give messages and so on. The camp wasn't completely closed to visitors. Chinese came in and gave us money directly. We were a little better off once we got money from my brother. But rations hadn't resumed."

Q. But I never heard of any place with no rations for three years.

A. "That's it. We felt it. It wasn't uniform nationwide. Pyongyang was better. Hwanghae Province was better. Some areas were better."

Q. Did you hear of or see donated food?

A. "Because I worked on the railroad I saw some, but it never got to the people where I was. I didn't care because it wasn't going to us."

Q. To whom, then?

A. "To the military. In that area there's one military ration center. All the food went there. Soldiers came and got about 50 percent, officials got some, restaurateurs got the rest."[4]

Q. You went to the distribution center?

A. "Yes."

Q. When?

A. "That was in the area where I was working, the railroad area. Fifty percent or more of the rations went to the military. There were a couple of bases in the area. It was the county distribution center. You are supposed to ration to the rest of the distribution centers, but there wasn't any left. It was mainly rationed to the military."

Q. Did people feel bitter about that?

A. "There was nothing we could do. The military has the highest priority. Especially since Kim Jong-il became head of it, you can't fight it. If a soldier comes up and hits you, you can't do anything. They have all the authority.

    "In 1997 the agriculture minister, So Kwan-hui, was executed for the agricultural failure. Poeple don't dare talk badly of Kim Jong-il. If something like that happens, Kim Jong-il orders someone executed, putting all the blame on that person. People are taught to worship Kim Jong-Il so they don't think of criticizing him."

Q. Do people die of starvation?

A. "Yes. Most people when they die of starvation, contrary to what you might think, get swollen up. They drink a lot of water because they're hungry and dehydrated, skin and bones. People who can afford to travel on trains usually eat one meal a day. At stations, beggars get on and beg for even a spoonful. Some get it, some don't. A lot die on the trains. Railroad workers have to dispose of the bodies. I didn't have to do that, but I've seen so many. The people who care for the dead bodies are delinquents. That's a punishment—to take care of the dead. After they collect the bodies, if no one claims them, they dig a hole and bury several in a mass grave.

    "When you talk about people who die of starvation, mostly the direct cause is a related disease. So many are dying they can't handle them. There aren't enough coffins. They make a metal coffin, put the body in temporarily. It costs 500 *won* to rent the coffin for the final trip to the grave, but still it's so hard to arrange that people often wait a day or two to rent one."

Q. How did you defect?

A. "We got help from my eldest brother Nam Hyun, the one who defected from Russia. I first heard in 1994 that my brother was in South Korea. I started wondering why he would go there, after all the bad things I had learned about South Korea. I saw Im Su-gyong and Moon Ik-hwan on television, then reports of their jailing after they came to North Korea. But when they came we could see they were well fed. Then she got out of jail, after only three years, and had a child. I thought they must have a lot of freedom in South Korea—only three years, then marriage and a child. Then there are the film clips of students demonstrating. It's unthinkable in North Korea—we couldn't even dream of such a thing. The North Korean media played it as a problem, but I thought, 'If they have that kind of freedom to fight the police, what's the rest of the society like?' And they weren't starving. That's when I started criticizing the cronies under the Kims. I wouldn't dare criticize the Kims themselves."

Q. When did you escape?

A. "In August 1997 we left. My second brother is in an isolated cell under State Security. He told his wife about the plans and asked her to leave, too, so he was taken away."

Q. Is she in jail?

A. "No, of course not. She has a strong revolutionary mind. She probably was rewarded."

Q. His children?

A. "They have one child who was with the mother. If she requests a divorce it will be granted."

Q. Do you resent her?

A. "Death would be too good for her. No, not her. It's her family who went to the police. She couldn't decide. [Fearing all would be punished], the family took hold of her and wouldn't let her come."

Q. What are you doing now?

A. "Working as an assistant manager at a trading company founded by my eldest brother, Nam Hyun."

Q. School?

A. "Next year I want to go. I'm thinking of working for the Railroad Authority."

Q. Maybe you'll put track across the DMZ.

Nam Chung's mother, Chang In-sook, was fifty-seven when I interviewed her in 1998, and with her weathered face and short hair she looked her age. Her face, like that of her son Nam Chung, was wide and she resembled him. Her previous occupation as an architect-engineer showed in her tastefully chosen clothing and accessories: navy jacket, deep blue patterned blouse with white collar, big brooch on the jacket, gold ring, gold watch with black leather strap.

Chang had a brilliant résumé by North Korean standards. Having earned multiple degrees in civil engineering, specializing in tunnel and bridge construction, she had worked for twenty-six years as an architect in

the Pyongyang city planning department. Considered one of the top three female architects in the country, she had participated in construction of about
thirty bridges and the Juche Tower, a monument lighting the night sky with a
huge flame representing the *juche* ideal. She had received nine awards, several
of them directly from Kim Il-sung or Kim Jong-il. She had been photographed
three times with Kim Il-sung, and on the last of those occasions Kim Jong-il
also had been in the picture. She was Workers' Party secretary for her unit.

Q. What did you do on the Juche Tower?
A. "I was in charge of the structure of the tower. As party secretary, I led
   weekly meetings and designed the structure."
Q. Tell me about the national construction policy.
A. "The policy can be summarized as showing the world North Korea's
   pride. Construction is to give pleasure to Kim Il-sung and Kim Jong-il.
   This is to show the *juche* spirit to the world. The Juche Tower and the
   memorial tower commemorating the founding of the party are examples—
   and also the West Sea Barrage. Lots of money and manpower went into
   that. It was big propaganda. But in fact its practical effect was very
   small. They just wanted it to show the power of socialism and the party.
   Even in Pyongyang there are so many buildings but you can't operate
   them so they remain empty: the new tall hotel, for example, the world's
   widest road and so on. They shouldn't have built the hotel. The Koryo
   isn't even full yet. Also, they're now building a dining hall for 10,000
   people. Nonsense!"
Q. Tell me about the problems you had after your eldest son defected.
A. "My son had been studying in Russia for five years. He came to South
   Korea in December 1990. All of a sudden the family changed from a revolutionary family to a family of traitors. I lost my job. When they kicked
   us out of Pyongyang they gave us forty-eight hours' notice to evacuate.
   Our household goods were to be packed in twenty-four hours and we
   would leave ourselves in forty-eight hours.
       "If it had been 1989, we'd have been sent to a political prison camp.
   But after the 1990s there were so many like us that there were no vacan-
   cies. So people started getting sent to coal mines, and to cut timber in the
   forests. My son who defected knew we wouldn't be sent to a prison
   camp. And he thought North Korea would collapse in a year. He was
   wrong."
Q. But I'll bet you were angry with him.
A. "Yes, at first I felt a great bitterness. He had betrayed the nation and the
   Great Leader."
Q. I've heard that the Pyongyang population is shifted every two years.
A. "Not every two years but it's shifted frequently. After the Korean War
   the landlord class was kicked out, and people who had gone to South

Korea during the war. A big transplantation came in 1976 when the Panmunjom incident occurred. Also, at times of international festivals and conferences the government wants firm control so it moves questionable people out. In addition, whole groups belonging to laboratories and factories are moved because of environmental questions, to clean up the city.

"They want people in Pyongyang who can be trusted. Whenever American reporters come, the government tells citizens to wear the best clothing they have. The authorities distribute sample questions and answers to prepare people. If someone is questioned by a reporter, he or she will be debriefed afterward on the exchange.

"When we were banished from Pyongyang we were sent to Onsong Mine. There used to be two prison camps, Changpyong and Tongpo, in Onsong County. They moved Chanpyong camp to Tokson in South Hamgyong Province in 1988. Tongpo camp moved there in 1990 to get it farther away from the border. I was in Tongpo. Both of those are tough areas developed by political prisoners. After the camps moved, at Champyon the government sent free settlers, but those people ruined the soil. So in the case of Tongpo the government sent organized people — factory workers and union people—to control the cultivation and mining. I was sent there as a settler after they moved the camp from Tongpo. They moved the camp because they were worried about human rights organizations' condemnations. And during high-level North-South meetings South Korean officials expressly named those camps. The other reason was that they were near the border and the authorities worried about what the prisoners might do. Those were the only two camps in border areas.

"When I arrived at Tongpo it was in the final stage of evacuation. I met some of the remaining prisoners and heard the story from them. I didn't start at Tongpo but at Onsong because I met someone I knew who was in charge of the mine. I could move there instead. Onsong is relatively better because it has farmland in addition to mines. Tongpo has coal mines only. I stayed at Onsong for six years and seven months, working as an architect-engineer. I was the most experienced person in the area, so I was designing bridges and railways and a big storage tower for coal. I also participated in financing of railway construction. I didn't participate in prison-camp architecture. Bridges were my field. But when I went to the camp in Onsong and saw the harsh reality—people lived in dugouts, no heating . . .

"Our relationship with the Onsong people was good. We weren't prisoners; we were just people expelled from Pyongyang. Our social class was unchanged. We stayed in a normal people's area. People thought it should be the party that would take responsibility for my son's actions, not the family. Before that my family had a very good social station. When people visited my house they could see three pictures of me with Kim Il-sung or Kim Jong-il and a watch signed by Kim Il-sung. We were the only family with a color TV. I worked hard. My sons behaved very well. State Security came once a year only and checked on us.

"Meanwhile, my son was trying to get us back and he finally got in touch with us. For eight months I rejected his offer to bring us to South Korea. In September 1997, though, I crossed the border with two of my sons. After I got here I realized why he wanted us to come.

"The first I knew that he was alive was in 1993. A leaflet about my son's marriage came from the Chinese border. It was a leaflet from South Korea that said he was studying at a university. I thought it was propaganda and figured the South Koreans would kill him after taking his photo. But when I heard he was on TV I realized it wasn't so. We heard that my son interpreted a meeting between Gorbachev and Kim Young-sam in 1994—it was on NHK [Japan Broadcasting System]. My second son's friend watched it, and told him about his elder brother. Then I realized if someone has ability he can be treated well in South Korea. So I calmed down.

"Our first direct news from him came November 1, 1996. From then he wanted the family to come to South Korea. I was afraid, but considered it for eight months and finally made the decision. Blood is thicker than water. Hatred became forgiveness. Then I missed my son a lot. Finally, we had a reunion. We all live in the same house here, with his Russian wife. My daughter-in-law is my son's professor's only daughter. When he consulted with his professor the professor said, 'Do what you think is right.' Now his daughter lives in South Korea, having left her family behind."

The end of the second millennium saw increased foreign interest in North Korea's human rights situation, a positive if belated development. Clearly there was more concern in Japan, Europe and North America, as well as South Korea, for oppressed North Koreans. This had much to do with news that thousands of refugees who had crossed the border into China, principally in search of food, had to hide there for fear of being captured and returned to North Korea.

Pyongyang-watchers who were not blinded by ideological sympathy had known all along, of course, that Pyongyang gave full expression to the theory and practice of totalitarianism. As late as 1972, when Scalapino and Lee published their landmark two-volume *Communism in Korea*, this was said freely, in strong terms. But pointed criticisms largely went out of fashion later in the 1970s after the revisionist movement took hold among those young Korea specialists in the United States who were influenced by leftist thinking. Well into the 1990s quite a few of them refused to credit the accounts of North Koreans who defected to the South.

Take away the defectors' accounts and there was almost no firsthand information available on which to base assessment of human rights abuses. Unfortunately, leftist scholars were not alone in dismissing the defectors as propaganda tools of Seoul's Korean Central Intelligence Agency. Many in foreign governments agreed.

Around 1999, though, the credibility of the defectors in Seoul started to receive a major boost from the availability of a new crop of first-hand stories about the realities of North Korea—this time told by refugees who had crossed into China. What they were telling interviewers corroborated, in spades, the main points of what the all-but-ignored Seoul-based defectors had been saying for years.[5]

The former trickle of defectors, refugees, escapees—call them what you wish—turned into a flood due to food shortages and the collapse of the North's economy. That meant there were thousands of North Koreans testifying or ready to testify—a large proportion of them not in South Korea or under South Korean government supervision. Thus, even the most skeptical researcher might be hard-pressed to keep a straight face while citing "lack of reliable information" in dismissing wholesale the many accounts of how North Koreans had been systematically oppressed.[6]

Starting in 1999 and 2000, long-isolated Pyongyang tried to improve relations with old enemies and old friends alike, an effort that seemed to offer some carryover to its human rights situation. North Korea's quest for new relationships in Europe, in particular, aroused hopes of an accompanying increase in sensitivity to international concerns over the regime's treatment of its subjects. Encouraging in that regard was a report, during a "dialogue" in November 1999 with the European Union, that Pyongyang had issued a large-scale amnesty to mark the September 9 founding anniversary of the Northern government.

The South's Yonhap news agency in a dispatch from Seoul a few days later quoted an unnamed diplomatic source as having reported the claim. But the source said the North Korean delegates, speaking with EU counterparts in Brussels, had given no details on the contents of the amnesty. Rather, they had followed up with the assertion that the regime always worked to enhance its people's rights. To bolster that claim, they had added that the country intended to join an international covenant banning gender discrimination; that United Nations human rights standards had been translated for domestic publication; and that a national judicial committee on juvenile rights had been established.

Sketchy as those remarks were, "It's a big change for the North to have elaborated on its human rights situation," said Yonhap's diplomatic source, attributing the change to Pyongyang's mounting concern over international criticism of its human rights record. To understand part of the reason for such concern, one had only to recall North Korea's dismay at NATO's Kosovo intervention, which was justified on the basis of human rights.

In the quest for better foreign relationships, establishment of diplomatic relations with Italy was viewed as a milestone. Previously no members of the Group of Seven industrialized countries had relations with Pyongyang. Australia, the Philippines, France, Taiwan, Japan, even Britain were on the list of countries that contemplated joining in the diplomatic dance. But with all the additional diplomatic activity there were few reports of positive results in human rights terms.

Some analysts worried that, on the contrary, having more polite government-to-government relationships might be giving the regime added leverage to do as it pleased with—and to—its own people. After all, outright enemies and long-time critics or detractors of a country don't hesitate to condemn its human rights violations—but countries that are in the process of improving diplomatic relations think at least twice before speaking their minds in such cases.

John Pomfret of *The Washington Post* in a February 19, 2000, article reported that the situation of North Korean refugees in China had worsened precisely because of Pyongyang's improved relations with other countries. The article quoted a United Nations official who lamented the "total silence" with which the international community greeted the forced repatriation of seven North Koreans who had fled to China and thence to Russia. "In most parts of the world the Americans would be outraged," the UN official continued. But the article quoted aid officials as saying foreign (read American?) officials' gratitude for progress on weapons issues had made them less eager to put pressure on North Korea regarding refugee issues.

Pyongyang had further plans to use diplomacy in ways that could bode ill for starving or otherwise unsatisfied, or dissatisfied, citizens of North Korea who might wish to vote with their feet. Those plans involved the country most interested in improved relations, South Korea, whose President Kim Dae-jung was pursuing a "sunshine policy" to try to lure the North into a peaceful relationship. South Korean press reports quoted a unification policy official in Seoul as saying on February 17, 2000, that North Korea had offered Seoul some secret reunions of families divided by the Demilitarized Zone—a hot-button issue in South Korea. In exchange, though, Seoul would have to agree to help Pyongyang deter the defection of North Koreans with relatives in the South. That category had accounted for a large percentage of successful defections, since the Southern family members were often willing to pay for agents to undertake rescue efforts.

Face the fact that dealing with human rights issues in the North would be a slow process, the South's President Kim advised early in 2000. "Interest by the international community in North Korea's human rights conditions may have effect to some extent," he told an international conference on engagement policy toward the North. "But it would be difficult to produce great results under any circumstances." Kim added that "solving poverty is most important in terms of North Korean human rights. Dialogue with the West and wider investment must take place before one can expect improvement." While perhaps a pragmatic and realistic assessment, that would have been a bitter pill for anyone in or out of North Korea who was hoping for a flowering of human rights as a result of all the current diplomatic activity.

But there was some encouraging evidence that Pyongyang's change of policy amounted to more than just such cosmetic touches as moving political prison camps from border areas to more remote, less easily observed sites. In October 2002, former political prison camp inmate Kang Chul-hwan, in his capacity as a *Chosun Ilbo* reporter, was able to report:

"It has recently been learned that the notorious public executions carried out across North Korea in the latter half of the 1990s are all but gone since 2000, and that the family life of political prisoners has eased significantly. 'Under Kim Jong-il's order issued to the State Security Agency and border guards early in 2000, "Don't fire shots in the Republic," no public executions have been carried out in the North, particularly in the border area,' said a North Korean who has fled to China and who had served with the border guard. . . . The reported suspension of open [as opposed to secret] executions is reportedly ascribed to censure by the world community. Pyongyang is also said to have suspended punishing the families of political criminals, unless involved in grave offenses."[7]

Such changes, if real, might have been too late to help Hong Won-myung, the twenty-year-old ex-hostage in Thailand, if he had returned to North Korea in accordance with his shock announcement to the press. But a Thai newspaper reported after his press conference appearance that the real reason Hong had expressed the wish to return home was that he wanted to protect his remaining family members there from retaliation by the Pyongyang regime; in fact he had decided to defect with his parents to the United States.

His captors each day had made him telephone his brother in North Korea, who had told him he should follow the North Korean officials' instructions or the brother and the brother's wife would come to serious harm, perhaps be killed, according to the account in the vernacular daily *Naew Na*. The paper attributed to unnamed Thai intelligence sources its version of what young Hong recounted privately after having been reunited with his parents. His captors fed him his lines for the press conference, telling him they wanted to make sure North Korea's image would not be hurt further, the article said.

Naew Na's sources quoted Hong as saying his captors had tranquilized him and kept him in his underwear after the kidnapping. Using a carrot-and-stick approach, besides arranging the daily calls to his frightened brother they had promised him an elite career if he would do as he was told and return to Pyongyang. Hong would be made a diplomat and dispatched to Bangkok in two years as a third secretary in the North Korean embassy there, they assured him. The captors also offered to return cash amounting to some $100,000 plus 200,000 Thai baht that they had seized when they broke into the family's apartment, according to the *Naew Na* account.

THIRTY-FIVE

Sun of the Twenty-First Century

Stern-faced soldiers stood every few hundred meters along a road that skirted freshly plowed and flooded rice paddies, the dark brown ooze ready for planting. A few goats grazed. Oxen pulled plows; one pulled a "honey wagon" full of night soil—human excrement, traditionally used as fertilizer. People carried loads of firewood or straw on their backs, going to and from the single-family houses and small apartment buildings that dotted the countryside. Long winter underwear hung out to dry.

This was the North Korea that a tourist like me could see from one of the tour buses that pulled up every day at the base of Mount Kumgang, home of the 100-meter Nine Dragons waterfall. The buses parked in a vast lot surrounded by souvenir stands and snack shops. After hiking up a steep, river-hugging trail, the drill was to admire ancient Buddhist inscriptions and contemporary communist slogans that had been chiseled into the rock faces. When we had taken in enough of the scenery, we could spend our hard currency bathing in therapeutic hot spring water or watching circus performers from Pyongyang perform in a covered stadium.

North Korea always put its best foot forward in areas frequented by visitors. Mount Kumgang, when I went there in the spring of 2000, proved to be no exception. As the well-fed locals who maintained it could have attested (were they permitted to speak about such matters), the site bore little resemblance to most of their country. The Dear, now Great, Leader Kim Jong-il had remained adamant in his refusal to endorse capitalism. He continued to isolate citizens from outside influences. Like Cuba, North Korea remained an economic outcast in a world mostly folded into the market economy. Next-door China, while still politically a one-party communist state, was growing rapidly and was on course to become an export powerhouse—the next Japan. Pyongyang's ideological intransigence had left it far behind China, farther still behind South Korea. Yet this mountain resort thirty miles from the border, developed by South Korean conglomerate Hyundai, offered a tantalizing clue that the rulers in Pyongyang might be ready, at long last, for major economic change.

Some people, both Korean and foreign, were hoping that a summit meeting between Kim Jong-il and South Korea's president Kim Dae-jung would prove to be a turning point. And when those leaders did meet in June 2000, the initial signs were promising. In an atmosphere akin to a love-in, the two Koreas agreed to live in peace while pursuing eventual reunification. Seoul was to promote South Korean investment in the North. Pyongyang, in turn, agreed to permit meetings of family members separated a half-century earlier. A few days after the meeting, President Bill Clinton agreed to relax most U.S. economic sanctions against North Korea, a move heralded (prematurely, as it turned out) as clearing the way for trade in all goods and services except for the most politically sensitive.

Up to that point, interest in North Korea as a business destination had been confined largely to South Koreans who had been born in the northern part of the peninsula—including Hyundai Group founder Chung Ju-yung. But the American Chamber of Commerce in South Korea was attempting to schedule a trip north by Seoul-based representatives of such major U.S. companies as Goldman Sachs, General Electric, Coca-Cola and Procter & Gamble, all of which had big investments and operations in the South. Optimists pointed to evidence that North Korea's decade-long economic decline had bottomed out in 1998. According to a report by the South Korean central bank, the North's economy had grown by 6.2 percent in 1999. Grain production was up by 8.5 percent, to 4.22 million tons—still at famine level, but an improvement. By the end of 1999, production had resumed at the giant Kim Chaek steel complex and thousands of other factories that had been idled earlier as a result of energy shortages and a general logistical breakdown.[1]

The south's Unification Ministry, which supervised North-South relations, predicted that North Korea would try to join multilateral organizations such as the International Monetary Fund by 2001. The country already had resumed diplomatic relations with Italy and Australia and was about to do the same with the Philippines. It had arranged a low-interest loan from the Organization of Petroleum Exporting Countries. The help was badly needed. Foreign lenders, like foreign investors, had shunned North Korea since the 1980s, when it defaulted on its debts to the West and Japan. With the interest compounding, Pyongyang's hard-currency debt had mush-roomed to around $14 billion. The general unwillingness of Westerners and Japanese to extend credit, coupled with the collapse of communism in the So-viet Union and Eastern Europe, blocked major improvement in Pyongyang's trade figures. Those had been factors, along with mismanagement and natu-ral disasters, in causing the drastic economic decline—the near-collapse—of the 1990s.

In 1994 North Korea had been growing weaker by the day. My own re-search like that of others had suggested a real danger that it might choose the last-ditch means of war to avert the extinction of its regime and system. It had made sense then for the United States, South Korea and Japan to agree to a deal in which Pyongyang would receive $4.5 billion worth of light-water reactors to boost its energy output, in exchange for freezing its nuclear weapons development program. The unspoken assumption in Washington had been that any war threat eventually would peter out as the regime con-tinued to decline—indeed, that the regime would collapse before the donors had to make good on all their promises.

As the 1990s ended, North Korea was publicly wielding long-range mis-siles, in place of 1994's nuclear weapons, as it attempted extortion against old enemies. And while the gap with South Korea continued to grow, the North again was growing stronger in absolute terms. The food crisis had abated somewhat—in large part thanks to aid from its enemies. Kim Jong-il clearly had consolidated his domestic position. He had kept the allegiance of the mil-itary, partly by extracting lucrative concessions from old enemy countries and doling out large shares of the proceeds to those in uniform. At a time when the country could think about starting to rebuild its economy, it had al-ready begun beefing up its conventional warfare capability. Donor countries had to ponder whether aiding a strengthening adversary could ever be a wise policy.

There seemed little problem with the process Clinton had started of eas-ing some economic sanctions against North Korea, pending further negotia-tion of a possible freeze of Pyongyang's missile development program. Most analysts agreed that following through on the gesture would not result in a major immediate windfall to Pyongyang. While Americans would become legally free to invest in the country, other reasons besides sanctions re-strained them from looking upon North Korea as a high-priority investment target. Poor infrastructure was one. Another was that trust of a country that had repeatedly failed to pay its foreign debts was close to non-existent. The bigger, political-military question was where former U.S. defense secretary William Perry's "comprehensive" approach might lead—with regard, for ex-ample, to Japan.

Kim Jong-il naturally saw the missiles program as his other card, besides nuclear weapons. He would not relinquish it cheaply. North Korean representatives would demand large sums of cold cash. In talks with Washington they were reported to have said the price for suspending missile exports would be $1 billion a year. Pyongyang had little production of any sort left to export, other than missiles. Thus the regime schemed to find new ways of earning foreign exchange. It needed hard currency, at the most basic level, to buy weapons that it could not make at home and to maintain the standard of living of the ruling class and military. Restoring the devastated manufacturing and agricultural sectors to the levels of the 1980s—not to mention achieving a real takeoff into third-generation Asian tigerdom—was no more than a dream, barring a huge influx of foreign exchange.

Pyongyang knew that it would be all but impossible both politically and legally for the Clinton administration to pay cash to a blackmailing country. In the North's calculations, this was where Tokyo came in. In the wake of the Clinton commitment on sanctions, Prime Minister Keizo Obuchi said Japan would consider lifting its own sanctions—including its freeze on diplomatic normalization talks—"in the event the North clearly shows a positive attitude" by suspending a planned missile launch. Any renewed Tokyo-Pyongyang normalization talks would, of course, quickly focus on money. Pyongyang had resumed demands for Japan to compensate the North for the colonization of Korea in the first half of the twentieth century, among other offenses. Japan had sent South Korea more than $500 million in grants and loans following their 1965 normalization of relations. Factor in generous amounts for inflation and interest on that sum and such compensation to Pyongyang could mount up to as much as $5 billion, by some South Korean and Japanese estimates. Pyongyang was demanding $10 billion, with the extra amount to represent compensation for damage caused by Japan's backing of the United Nations side in the Korean War.

Compensation or aid in the billions of dollars could serve in part as a payoff for an end to North Korea's missile threat to Japan. But Japan would not be an easy sell. When North Korea lobbed a rocket over the Japanese archipelago on August 31, 1998, the effect was not—as Pyongyang almost certainly expected—to soften up the Japanese people and frighten them into a submissive mood. Rather, the launch electrified many Japanese and got their backs up. With public opinion finally amenable, the government in Tokyo was able to push ahead with a defense buildup intended to make constitutionally pacifist Japan a more "normal" country. Among other things, Japan planned to launch its own spy satellites and it formally agreed to do joint research with the United States on a missile defense system. A law passed in May 1999 authorized the Japanese Self-Defense Forces, during a regional crisis, to give stronger support to the U.S. military than had been permitted formerly.

But there was considerable Japanese interest in resolving longstanding problems with North Korea. And to make it easier for Tokyo to agree to a payoff, Pyongyang—in a show of newfound flexibility—embarked on a program to smooth off some of the rough edges of the image it presented to the Japanese. To a visiting group of Japanese parliamentarians in August 1999 North Korean authorities suggested that a joint Red Cross effort could be mounted to search for missing Japanese. Searchers would seek not only those who had been abandoned in northern Korea in the confusion following 1945's surrender. They would look also for at least ten other Japanese who were suspected of having been abducted by North Korean agents in more recent years. Pyongyang's refusal during earlier bilateral talks to discuss the abduction charges—which so far it was denying—had led to the failure of those talks.

Should Tokyo take the bait and reach for its wallet? A clue to what Pyongyang might do with a windfall came in reports that the country had imported parts for assembly into MiG 29 and MiG 21 fighter planes. MiG 29s, ten of which reportedly were imported in knockdown form, were selling for $50 million each, used—suggesting a possible outlay of $500 million. The question facing Tokyo was similar to one that faced the South Korean government: Should Seoul permit the Hyundai group to continue sending tens of millions of dollars a year to Pyongyang as "fees" for Hyundai's tours to Mount Kumgang? For weeks the South Korean press tried to pin down whether it was Hyundai's money that paid for MiG imports. The question was a naive one. Foreign exchange income from any source—from Hyundai, from Japan, from wherever—would increase the total amount of foreign exchange available to the regime. If there were not strictly verified external controls, such income would facilitate big military purchases. And that was true regardless of precisely which account the money might go into initially. But the case against what some Washington hardliners were calling "appeasement" was by no means open and shut. The theory behind Perry's comprehensive report and behind South Korean President Kim Dae-jung's sunshine policy was that, yes, North Korea would strengthen as a result of aid. However, it would strengthen not just militarily but also economically. In the process it would begin to join the global market economy. With its security guaranteed by no less a power than the United States, its interests would grow intertwined with those of its old enemies. It seemed at least conceivable that the attempt to engage Pyongyang could work that way, although North Korea had an impressive history of refusing to change itself in any fundamental way. As Perry himself emphasized, it would be necessary to maintain strong military deterrents; any aid given to Pyongyang should be tied to particular projects in the non-threatening civilian sector and supervised closely to thwart diversion to the military.

* * *

Desperation had driven North Korea to tone down its boast of having created a communist paradise. During a January 2000 cabinet meeting, Kim Jong-il and industry leaders had pledged that this would be the year for mending the economy.

Hyundai had given Pyongyang a sample of just how much the North stood to gain. The Mount Kumgang project was bringing North Korea nearly $200 million a year in hard-currency tourist revenues. The giant conglomerate, by far North Korea's largest outside investor, promised to pay the country $950 million spread out over the five-year period from 1998 through 2002 in exchange for a thirty-year monopoly on tours to the resort. In addition, Hyundai planned to invest as much as $1 billion more at Mount Kumgang for an airport, shopping malls, restaurants, duty-free shops, golf links, condominiums, ski facilities and an amusement park. Hyundai officials were vague about when they expected to make money on the venture. For the time being they treated the project as a loss leader while they negotiated other deals, such as the development of an industrial complex on the west coast of North Korea. Expecting eventually profitable North-South relations, Hyundai officials were eager to get a head start on competitors.

Worker salaries of about $1,500 a month had priced South Korea out of the markets for many labor-intensive goods, such as shoes and apparel. Now South Korean companies wanted to get back into those markets by teaming their capital with the cheap labor of the North, where workers for foreign-invested joint ventures earned $100 to $400 a month. With cost savings like those, "we can even overcome the Chinese," predicted Hong Yeon-dal, a Hyundai executive.

Before many non-Koreans could consider the North a viable investment, there would have to be improvements in energy services, railroads, highways and ports. North Korea's infrastructure had deteriorated badly during the 1990s. Power shortages remained a constant problem, and logistical complications still outweighed the labor cost advantage. North Korea looked to Japan for one solution to the infrastructure mess. After months of talks, many observers believed Tokyo and Pyongyang would agree to establish diplomatic relations by the end of 2000. At that point, Japan was thought likely to pledge billions of dollars for infrastructure projects. Big money from Japan and South Korea was "really the only thing that's going to save them," a diplomat in Seoul said of the North Koreans.

Many Japanese and Western lenders continued to believe that Pyongyang could meet its obligations if it would stop pouring money into its military. Now, in particular, outsiders were demanding that North Korea stop developing weapons of mass destruction. "What we all want them to cough up," said a diplomat in Seoul, "is to reduce their threat." Indeed, declaring a moratorium on long-range missile tests had been the quid pro quo for Washington's easing of sanctions.[2]

Historical guilt was not the motive for what the South was offering: a combination of public and private investment plus assurances that Seoul would not interfere in Pyongyang's domestic affairs. Other South Korean companies were starting to follow Hyundai's lead. Samsung Electronics Company and LG Company had begun assembling television sets in North Korean plants. A joint venture 30 percent owned by the Unification Church's Tong-il Heavy Industries Company and 30 percent by North Korea was gearing up to assemble Fiat automobiles in the western port city of Nampo, using components shipped from Tong-il's joint venture with Fiat in Vietnam. And a pharmaceuticals plant sponsored by the South's Korea Welfare Foundation was under construction in the Rajin-Sonbong Free Economic and Trade Zone in northeastern North Korea. Still, Hyundai was by far the most visible corporate agent of the South's policy up to that point.

Before the North-South border cut it off, the Mount Kumgang region had been a popular getaway destination for residents of Seoul. But the old infrastructure was long gone. It had been necessary for Hyundai to start from scratch to build what was needed to handle its tours. Company officials admitted to having spent about $30 million on roads, port facilities, the spa, the stadium, food and souvenir stands and a customs and immigration building equipped with computers and metal detection devices. Outsiders guessed that the cost was several times higher.

Despite its investment, the company—and its customers—had to put up with inconveniences that could not be fixed. Because the resort had only a Spartan, 150-room hotel, Hyundai had decided to turn its tours into three-day cruises between the South Korean port of Tonghae and North Korea's Kosong. Tourists, most of them South Koreans, slept on their ships and disembarked twice for all-day excursions. Thus each person had to pass four times through North Korea's rigid immigration and customs. (The North Korean officials checked them with state-of-the-art security devices that Hyundai had donated.)

Pyongyang was so insistent on controlling North Koreans' exposure to outsiders that Hyundai's buses traveled on an exclusive road bordered on both sides by chain-link and barbed-wire fences. The North Koreans who were cleared to work as park rangers, tourists and Hyundai staff had been instructed to discuss nothing beyond innocuous subjects such as the weather—although the rule did not prevent one senior female guide from asking me earnestly to urge American investors to bring their dollars. (I had entered on a tourist visa arranged by Hyundai—thus perhaps avoiding once again any lingering consequences of my 1989 blacklisting as a journalist. But I made no secret of the fact I was on assignment to write an article for a financial magazine.[3])

The low-wage manufacturing model for developing an economy definitely had drawbacks. Why pack your people into sweatshops to inhale fumes from the benzene used for gluing together athletic shoes? After all, the greedy foreigners who financed and oversaw such enterprises and sold the products abroad would grab the lion's share of the profit. And as soon as your people started demanding higher wages and better treatment, those foreigners would close up shop and head off to Somalia or some other godforsaken place where they could hire workers even cheaper.

A top North Korean official considering the matter would have added another argument: Those foreigners, if you let them into your country to oversee their manufacturing businesses, would corrupt your hitherto carefully isolated and indoctrinated people with alien notions sure to highlight the enormous gap between the regime's teachings and reality as known to the rest of the world. The process eventually would threaten the continued existence of the regime. And if the businesspeople coming in happened to be South Korean—as were a large percentage of outsiders entering the North to do business—the problems would boil up sooner rather than later. South Koreans, sharing a language with the North Koreans, would be harder than other outsiders to isolate.

Pyongyang officials appeared to have pursued some such line of reasoning. Oh Seung-ryul, a research fellow at Seoul's Korea Institute for National Unification, reported in 1999 that the North was consciously deemphasizing manufacturing as its key legal means of earning foreign exchange. (The turnaround was by no means complete, and apparently it had no effect on the illegal means of bringing in hard currency, such as manufacturing and smuggling heroin or printing and passing hard-to-detect counterfeit U.S. dollars, the "Super-Ks.") More prized than manufacturing was tourism. The shift was particularly evident in the Rajin-Sonbong free economic zone. There a new casino opened, mainly targeted at people coming across the border from China. "North Korea is modifying the function of the Rajin-Sonbong area from a manufacturing base to a tourist attraction and center for transit trade," Oh said. He added that the Pyongyang regime had banned South Koreans from visiting the zone and had begun taking down advertisements for Western businesses there.

In the Rajin-Sonbong case, the danger of ideological contamination probably was not the only factor militating for a change. (There was some question as to why it should have been a factor at all, if one credited the earlier reports that the regime had moved all the original residents out and replaced them with people considered super-loyal to Pyongyang and relatively immune to foreigners' blandishments.) Another big factor was that outside investors had not been enthralled with the zone's remote location. Their investments from 1991 to 1997 had totaled only a disappointing $62 million, according to South Korean government statistics.

Corruption by the previous team of officials also seemed to play a role. A 1998 report quoting Chinese sources in Beijing said North Korean authorities had arrested seven officials including the head of the Rajin-Sonbong Special Development Project, who had been investigated by central party officials on corruption charges. Allegedly they had extorted money from foreigners who hoped to do business there. The report said the project office in Yanji, just across the border in China, had been closed.[4] While it was too early to predict whether tourism and gambling would do the trick for Rajin-Sonbong, advantages to the regime of relying on tourism could be seen clearly in the Mount Kumgang case. Try to earn *that* kind of money manufacturing textiles or assembling television sets.

But didn't South Korean tourists pose the same sort of "contamination" threat as businessmen? Not since June 1999. That was when North Korean authorities arrested and questioned for several days a touring Seoul housewife and mother. They accused the woman—who said she innocently chatted to a North Korean park ranger about the lives of North Korean defectors in the South—of being a spy. Reported to have begun psychiatric treatment for the trauma she endured, she told interviewers for *The Korea Herald* that she believed she had been set up. Indeed there were indications that Pyongyang had been looking for a tourist who could be made an example, in order to scare future tourists into reticence. If that was the intention, it certainly worked. The tour was suspended for forty-five days. When it resumed, a columnist for *Chosun Ilbo* went along and later reported: "On the cruise ship, on the bus and whenever there were a small number of people gathered together, Hyundai personnel continuously asked the Kumgang mountains tourists not to say anything to the North Korean tour guides other than 'hello' and 'thank you.'" The tourists complied.

As we have seen, steps toward rationalizing economic management and luring outside investment in the early 1990s had clashed with the aims of the military men whom Kim Jong-il was cultivating. Those steps had essentially come to a halt when South Korea turned its back on the North during the first nuclear crisis. The years of mourning and extreme famine that followed the death of Kim Il-sung in 1994 saw few indications of a renewed push to reform the economy. But on September 5, 1998, the Supreme People's Assembly adopted a new constitution for the Democratic People's Republic of Korea. Its third chapter covered the economy. Article 33, radical by past standards, read: "The State shall introduce a cost accounting system in the economic management . . . and utilize such economic levers as prime costs, prices and profits." Article 37 added that the state should encourage "joint venture enterprises with corporations or individuals of foreign countries within a special economic zone."[5] The following year the country enacted an elaborate External Economic Arbitration Law.

For a time after that, change once more slowed. Pyongyang-watchers warned that signs of relaxation in the North must be read carefully. Jean-Jacques Grauhar, secretary general of the Seoul-based European Union Chamber of Commerce, previously had worked and lived in Pyongyang for several years. He told me in 2000 that North Korean leaders apparently had no objective beyond repairs to their economic system. Their goal was "not to change the system—and that shouldn't be the objective of foreign investors," he said. Grauhar and other experts advised non-Korean companies to team up with South Koreans and emulate their style, doing business in ways that were minimally threatening to a regime leery of change. "I've been pushing Club Med to do something there for years," he said. The French company's resorts were often built in pristine environments secluded from the surrounding reality—much like Mount Kumgang. In addition, Club Med got its profits from outsiders, not from hard-pressed locals of the host countries. The notion of Club Med's bikinied guests playing bar games in North Korea seemed far-fetched—but then, until not long before, so had the idea of Hyundai tours of the Nine Dragons waterfall.

In his taped conversation with Chongryon's Japanese-Korean delegates on April 25, 1998, Kim Jong-il addressed economic issues. "We are not isolationists, but we want to keep the status quo," he said. "We don't want hordes of tourists to come here and spread AIDS and pollute our land."[6]

Kim in that conversation showed a lively interest in the details of other economies, particularly those of Japan, South Korea and the United States—all of whose nationals he referred to as "devils." He saved his most favorable words for the United States, specifically then-President Bill Clinton. "Clinton is doing well in the White House," he said. "Jack Kennedy tried to make a name for himself but he was rubbed out before he had the chance. This Clinton fellow is only fifty-two, but he got elected to the White House twice. He is quite a guy." Kim praised American-made computers. "Today," he said, "South Korea brags about its computers on TV commercials, but the South Korean computers don't even come close to American computers. We have to butter up the Americans and get the best they have. Our People's Army regards the United States as its sworn enemy, but our people engaged in trade address the Americans with much respect. This is called the principle of 'hard inside, soft outside.'"

Kim showed himself to be a news junkie, ever ready to call forth odd facts from his memory. However, his failure to travel widely could be seen in misconceptions and examples of naiveté. He asserted that Japan could do much more with damming rivers to produce hydroelectric power than it had done, taking advantage of its "many tall mountains with high volumes of water." In fact, Japanese rivers are short and not especially mighty—a big reason why the country had chosen to emphasize nuclear power. By looking through Japanese product catalogs, Kim had discovered the installment plan. "How long have they been using this method of payments?" he asked his visitors from Japan. "Even shoddy products are being sold on the installment plan. It appears that the installment plan is due to slow sales."

His characterizations of South Korea, which at the time was suffering from a severe Asian financial crisis that had begun in 1997, were full of exaggeration and misrepresentation—perhaps simply his wishful thinking: "The real ruler of South Korea is the United States. Today South Korea is in turmoil politically and economically. Seoul officials are trying to restore economic stability but I doubt they will make it." Of course, following that economic rough patch, they did make it. Revealing his faulty perception, Kim observed that, after having prospered "for about ten years starting in 1988," the South Korean devils were "broke and dirt poor."

In an illustration of Kim Jong-il's peculiar sense of proportion, he related at some length his wish that Chongryon officials search in Japan and South Korea for two species of native Korean dogs that were approaching extinction in the North. We can speculate that the beasts' scarcity had to do with the famine and the unavailability of other sources of protein. (East Asian joke: What do you call a Korean with seven dogs? Answer: A caterer.) But Kim ascribed their absence to a lamentable lack of popular devotion to the maintenance of the breeds. "We don't want our own native dogs to die out," he said earnestly. "We must make sure that *pungsan* and *jindo* dogs prosper and propagate. Our people are quite indifferent to the future of our dogs. That is wrong. These dogs belong to Korea and we must preserve them."

Kim first explained North Korea's power shortage in terms that blamed nature and let the regime and its policies off the hook. "We had ample electricity when Leader Kim Il-sung was alive," he said. "You may wonder why it is that we are short of electric power now. The reason is simple. We had natural floods several years in a row, which was unprecedented in our history, and our coal mines got flooded. We could not dig enough coal to keep our thermal plants going. That is why we are short of electricity and our people are suffering. Our economy is suffering for lack of electric power because our coal mines are flooded."

❖ ❖ ❖

To outsiders hoping for major changes in North Korea, though, Kim's some-what mixed-up view of the capitalist world might seem less significant than his reiteration of the failings of socialism as he saw them. As his talk with the Chongryon representatives progressed, for example, he took a different tack on the causes of at least part of the power shortage. He criticized colleagues who insisted on taking *juche*'s self-reliant principle to extremes. "During my 1983 visit to China, Hua Guofeng and I visited the Baosan thermal power station," he said. "It was imported from another country. China was techno-logically advanced enough to build its own power plants but it decided to buy the plant abroad. I asked Hua why." The Chinese leader "said that China could have built the station but the foreign plant was better." In con-trast, Kim observed, "Our people reason differently. Their idea is to buy only those parts that we cannot make and the rest we build here. This kind of attitude has led to many costly failures. . . . We are paying dearly for our mis-takes. . . .

"Our socialist system is people-centered and we say that we serve the people, but the truth of the matter is that our economic system is not quite like that," Kim told his visitors. "In a capitalist society, customers are catered to and their pockets are picked clean in every possible way." He elaborated: "The socialist system is ice-cold and indifferent to the customers. In our country, our store workers take the attitude that they don't care if the cus-tomers buy anything or not. Instead of servicing the customers and trying to sell something, they would rather that patrons did not show up so that they won't have to do anything. In a capitalist nation, service is everything. When our people visit Japan, they are courted everywhere with 'Welcome, wel-come, please come in.' Japanese eateries have managers who supervise the servers, and any service boy in trouble with a patron is severely reprimanded or punished. In our country, our servers are never fired for poor service. On the contrary, the patrons are expected to pay and bow to the servers for the privilege. It should be that those who receive money should thank the givers, but alas, here in this country, it is just the opposite. Capitalism has been around over one hundred years now and it tries all sorts of things to stay alive."

Kim spoke of some management changes that could help his system stay alive. One was to hold qualifying examinations instead of assigning people more or less at random to such demanding jobs as handling foreign trade. "In organs like Foreign Economic Cooperation, anyone who knows Kim Guk-tae can join his outfit," he remarked (mentioning the official who had gotten reformer Kim Dal-hyon demoted and sent off to the provinces). "We need to change this and require specific knowledge of foreign trade." He spoke favorably of sending students abroad for training. "In China, one of Deng Xiaoping's great feats was to send two thousand or so students abroad annu-ally to study, and upon their return they were given important jobs," Kim said. North Korea should emulate Deng on this point. "We have people at the top who don't have even the vaguest idea of how to get our economy moving. All they are able to think about is how much pay they are getting. Such is our sad situation and we must change it fast. Many of our workers have poor or no concepts of money. They are completely in the dark on making profits. They know about meeting production quotas, but they have no idea how to sell the products and make profits."

Those were strong criticisms indeed. But it was not that Kim Jong-il was ready to praise the capitalist system, after having struggled against the alien Western system throughout his career. "To be honest, we like the current financial meltdown in Asia," he told his visitors. "Some of our people in charge of our economy had harbored some illusions about emulating the capitalist economy of Asia, but now the current crisis made them realize how wise Leader Kim Il-sung's policy of *juche* is. It was a rude awakening to these people." He added, "Currently we are poor and our life is hard, but you won't see any people on earth that is as united as we are."

Casting about for reasons to be optimistic, Kim imagined that North Korea could reverse its fortunes by turning into what, in his vision, sounded like a new Kuwait or Brunei. "We have untapped oil fields, and once we develop our oil fields our economy will change dramatically. Once we get the oil flowing, we won't need to work our farms. We will sell our oil to the Japanese devils and buy their rice. Our oil will be like a nuclear weapon."

On a more mundane level he showed a willingness to buy from successful countries their used equipment, such as tile factories and steel-rolling mills, to facilitate the manufacturing that North Korea still would need to do in addition to encouraging tourism. The problem was to avoid loss of face, a fate almost worse than death for a traditional-minded East Asian. So he asked his visitors to have Chongryon serve as intermediary in such deals. "Of course we can obtain these things through normal trades," he said. "But how can we save our face and ask the Japanese devils for cheap used merchandise? Our trading people are reluctant to negotiate such deals, and Chongryon should step in and help us here."

Economic backwardness had become so apparent as to tarnish the North's image among impressionable young South Koreans. Many of them idealized Kim Il-sung as a great patriot and studied his *juche* philosophy, even after the successful end to South Koreans' struggle against military-backed dictatorships at home. By the time Kim Il-sung died in 1994, though, the economic failure of the North Korean system had become too obvious for any but the most devout Southern leftist to ignore. The South Korean news media, overcoming the taboo I had encountered in the 1970s, were throwing major resources into reporting on North Korean affairs. Of course there was far more negative than positive to report. If there was a defining moment in the decline of the North's image among idealistic South Korean leftists, perhaps it came in 1997 when no less a figure than Hwang Jang-yop defected to the South. Hwang was the North Korean senior official widely credited with having developed the *juche* ideology.

A 1999 scandal in Seoul illustrated the disillusionment that resulted among some South Koreans who had been beating the drums for Pyongyang. Kim Young-hwan, one of the most prominent leaders of pro-Pyongyang 1980s student radicals who called themselves Jusapa, the *juche* ideology faction, was reported to have confessed that he was a spy for Pyongyang. According to the National Intelligence Service (the former KCIA, in its latest renaming), Kim Young-hwan, by then a practically middle-aged thirty-six, confessed that he had joined Pyongyang's spy service in 1989 at the behest of a North Korean agent. Kim said he was then taken to the North on a semi-submersible spy vessel and there joined the Workers' Party, received a medal and met Kim Il-sung—who directed him to undertake development of a pro-Pyongyang underground and start a legal political party in the South. That he did, bringing in other veterans of the student anti-government movement.

Kim Young-hwan grew disillusioned with the North Korean system. In a 1995 magazine interview, he denounced the *juche* ideology. He asserted that Pyongyang had been seriously on his case from then on, scheming to assassinate him for his betrayal. He did not go to the South Korean authorities right away but, in fear for his life, fled to China. When he returned home and spilled the beans, the prosecution recommended leniency.

Such incidents did not by any means cause the South Korean left to disappear. Sympathy for the Northern brethren would remain strong. The anti-Americanism that had become pronounced in the 1980s would continue to thrive and even grow in the South. But Kim Jong-il, unlike his late father, could hardly be seen realistically as leader of or role model for a future South Korean revolution. To the extent he recognized that, it was all the more reason why he needed to do something about the economy.

Being able to point to South Korea as an implacable enemy had been, from the beginning, an essential element in the North Korean regime's control of its people. Thus it seemed significant that in April 2000, practically on the eve of South Korea's National Assembly elections, Pyongyang appeared to endorse blatantly the soft-line "sunshine" policy on North-South relations of South Korean President Kim Dae-jung. The endorsement came in the form of a mutual announcement of plans for a June summit in Pyongyang. The agreement for the South Korean president to meet Kim Jong-il was reached in a Beijing session, five days before an election that observers deemed too close to call. It seemed clear that both sides hoped the announcement would give Kim Dae-jung's party the push it needed to achieve a majority in the national legislature, so that its policies could be continued.

That move came despite the fact that Southern hard-liners, if they took power in Seoul, would provide more convincing bogeymen for the benefit of Northern propagandists. The South's chief opposition party was highly critical of Kim Dae-jung's use of aid to lure North Korea into shifting its emphasis from military preparations to economic reconstruction. "Keep it at home," opposition representatives repeatedly urged. "South Koreans need the help more."

The fact that North Korea at the moment had decided to endorse soft-line South Korean candidates did not prove it had said a permanent farewell to enmity and militarism. Long-time Pyongyang-watchers believed that the Northern leadership kept various strategies for interim survival and some form of ultimate victory going at once and would shift back and forth among them as it saw advantage in doing so. In that regard, it was noteworthy that the North's version of the announcement differed from the South's in saying Kim Dae-jung's visit to Pyongyang would be at his request, instead of at the invitation of Kim Jong-il. The first conclusion to be drawn was that Pyongyang did not think enemies should be made to look like sought-after guests. (Only later would it become clear just how accurate Pyongyang had been in saying this was Kim Dae-jung's show.)

News of the summit announcement suggested that Kim Jong-il had looked over the possibilities for fixing his busted economy and realized that it could hardly be done without the participation of the estranged but filthy-rich Koreans living south of the Demilitarized Zone—who by that time had shown their staying power by weathering the Asian financial crisis. Hyundai, with its tour cruises to Mount Kumgang, had given Pyongyang a tantalizing sample of just how much help the South could provide if relations improved. And the basic strategy embodied in both Kim Dae-jung's sunshine policy and the South Korean–American-Japanese "Perry process," named after the former defense secretary, was to combine aid with credible assurances of domestic non-interference and hook Pyongyang on peaceful coexistence. The eventual goal was to end the military threat that Pyongyang posed to the South and, with its development of weapons of mass destruction, to other parts of the world.

The cynicism of South Korean opposition politicians was understandable enough. After all, the two sides had gotten that far in 1994 only to see a planned summit fall through. Many, many, many lesser initiatives also had come to naught over the decades. Was there anything different this time? There was, and the differences provided some grounds for hope that something might eventually come of the new initiative.

One difference was that the North's economy, despite some visible recovery from the worst years of the mid-1990s, was in far worse shape both absolutely and relative to South Korea's than it had been when earlier initiatives failed. Kim Jong-il, although confused or naive on occasion, was not stupid. Neither he nor anyone else in Pyongyang could be unaware that the economy needed to be fixed. Kim Jong-il had blamed fall guys at home: ministers and other high-level officials who had tried to use the inherited Stalinist policies but (predictably enough, from a capitalist perspective) always failed. Some foreign intelligence people believed that the executions and banishments of thus-failed officials had begun to backfire, causing other officials who feared they might be next on the list to reflect privately upon where the blame really lay.

Kim, as we have seen, harbored many private reservations about his own regime's policies. He had told South Korea's Hyundai Group founder Chung Ju-yung he wanted to learn about the New Communities movement that military dictator Park Chung-hee had employed in laying the foundations for South Korea's largely successful market economy. Perhaps, commented a writer for South Korea's Yonhap news agency, "2000 will be the year to test whether [Kim Jong-il] will transform himself into the North Korean version of Park Chung-hee."[7] That did not happen, although in May 2002 Park's fifty-year-old daughter, Park Geun-hye, received a VIP reception when she visited Pyongyang.[8]

Why had Kim not moved faster to change things? Like some foreigners,[9] reform-minded North Korean officials might blame hard-line communist traditionalist holdovers, including military men, for tying his hands. Still, some officials had to find it hard to escape the thought that Kim's power was enormous; if only he had sufficient will to take risks in pursuit of a clear vision of meaningful change, he should have a good chance of succeeding. Regardless of his status as dictator, Kim must have realized that some in the elite circles just beneath him would not accept his policy failures forever. Such reasoning could help explain why he saw detente with South Korea as a major opportunity to make some changes that might help ensure his longer-term survival.

The televised reception given Kim Dae-jung in Pyongyang on June 13, 2000, was a revelation to many non–North Korean viewers. It showed a relaxed, confident and witty Kim Jong-il, the perfect host. Seventeen years after his first, initially sour foray into diplomacy in China, he appeared at last to have developed charisma worthy of the heir to Kim Il-sung. He personally went to the airport to receive Kim Dae-jung, clasping his hand and showing the deference due to an elder. "I am sure the people in South Korea were surprised to see you come to greet me," Kim Dae-jung told him as they began their first substantive meeting the next day.

Kim Jong-il displayed a previously underappreciated talent for making sly jokes. "Some Europeans have wondered why I am so reclusive," he remarked to his Southern counterpart. "I am not such a great figure worthy to be called a recluse. The fact is I have made many secret trips to countries like China and Indonesia. How is it that people say I made a rare appearance to welcome you? Whatever the case, I have been here and there without people knowing."

In one remark he revealed both his addiction to news and something that could pass for compassion. He had watched South Korean television broadcasts to see how Kim Dae-jung's reception had been covered, he said. "I saw how excited the South Koreans were—especially those who have hometowns in the North, and North Korean defectors. I saw how many of them had tears in their eyes, anxiously waiting for news about their hometowns." Turning to a high official who accompanied him, he added, "There were scenes of people actually crying."

An article by a Seoul correspondent of Taiwan's *Taipei Times* reported Southerners' altered perceptions. Along with the historic handshake, "his casual and jocular manner yesterday is transforming his rogue image in Seoul," the article said. It quoted one Seoul resident as saying, "I always thought of him as a loser with a complex, but seeing him on TV has really changed my image of him. He behaved like the guy next door and appeared normal." The writer reported that on television "Kim Jong-il appeared comfortable and spoke in a booming voice in contrast with the seemingly fatigued South Korean president." The North Korean leader's "confident behavior during the summit is changing his image from one of a weak, second-class heir to that of a statesman."[10]

Speaking the same language, the two leaders were able to pack some serious and sometimes frank discussion into their main session. As related in a Seoul speech soon afterward by General Hwang Won-duk, the South Korean president's foreign affairs and security advisor, one exchange went as follows: "Kim Jong-il said, 'The Korean problems must be resolved by the Koreans themselves. Don't you agree?' Kim Dae-jung replied, 'Yes, indeed. That is what we have been asking for and we agree with you completely.' Kim Jong-il shot back, 'Then why do you promote your alliance with the United States and Japan to stifle us?'"

Kim Dae-jung replied, "That is a misunderstanding on your part. The three-nation alliance is not for the three nations to conspire to destroy you. On the contrary, it is to help you. . . . My North Korea policy is 'sunshine' for peace, reconciliation and cooperation. It is because of my sunshine policy that we are here today. Our policy of reconciliation is to help you—not to destroy you. The three-nation alliance is to support my sunshine policy. . . . We may come up with some self-determining agreements, but if our neighbors ignore our agreements and hinder their realization, what good would they be? They would be meaningless. Therefore you must establish friendly relations with other nations. You must be friendly to the United States and also you ought to kiss and make up with Japan. In this way we'll be supported by the four big nations around us" — including China and Russia.

Kim Jong-il, Hwang continued, "intently listened to Kim Dae-jung's sermon and said, 'I understand,' and bought Kim Dae-jung's theme." The two leaders discussed whether U.S. troops should be withdrawn from the South. "Kim Dae-jung stated, 'The U.S. troops in South Korea help to prevent war in Korea. In addition they are needed to maintain military equilibrium in the Far East. They will be needed even after unification.'" Hwang said he believed that Kim Jong-il accepted the argument. In any case, Kim Jong-il did not return to "his theme of going alone against the foreign powers."

"In this way," Hwang said, the two Korean leaders "argued and agreed upon one issue after another. Some issues took less than twenty minutes and others took more than thirty minutes to resolve." One thorny issue was the South Korean request that Kim Jong-il promise to make a return visit to Seoul, Hwang said. "When Kim Dae-jung stated that Kim Jong-il must come to Seoul, Kim Jong-il said, 'Oh, no! I cannot go to Seoul in my present capacity.' Kim Dae-jung: 'Why not?' Kim Jong-il: 'I cannot go there in my present official capacity. If I were to go there my people would get upset.' Kim Dae-jung: 'Nonsense! You must come. You and I have been discussing reconciliation and if you don't come to Seoul who else will push our agreements. You have to come.' Kim Jong-il: 'No, I cannot go. . . . [A]s an official it will be impossible for me to visit Seoul.' Kim Dae-jung tried various approaches to no avail. As the last-ditch try Kim Dae-jung said, 'You have mentioned several times that you practice the Oriental ethics. I am much older than you are, right? An older man came to see you and you, the younger man, refuse to pay the older man a return visit. Is that ethical?'" Kim Jong-il finally accepted wording in the joint declaration that said he "agreed to visit Seoul at an appropriate time in the future."

The final argument was over who would sign the declaration. Kim Jong-il insisted that Kim Yong-nam, who as chief of the Supreme People's Assembly was officially head of state, should sign for North Korea. "Kim Dae-jung said, 'No, that will not do. You are the real leader of North Korea. The real leader must sign it. I am the president of South Korea and it is only proper that I should sign it. You must sign it, too.' They argued over this issue for some twenty-five minutes. Things were going nowhere. Finally [Kim Dae-jung's aides] broke in and said, 'You two have met and have been ironing out the agreements and it is not right for any other person to sign it.' At last, Kim Jong-il agreed to sign it himself." The Southerners, Hwang said, wanted it signed that very night so that it would make the news in Seoul the following morning, before their return. "Kim Jong-il chuckled and said, 'You want to return as a triumphant hero, right?' Kim Dae-jung said, 'Well, what is wrong with you making me a hero?' Kim Jong-il said, 'OK, OK, let's sign it today.'" They signed it that night, the fourteenth. However, they postdated it to the fifteenth so that the date would not include the unlucky number four, which, when pronounced in Korean, sounds like the word for death.[11]

The completed declaration was a short and simple document starting with an agreement that North and South would "solve the question of the country's reunification independently by the concerted efforts of the Korean nation responsible for it." In one item the leaders pledged to seek common ground between the North's proposal for a federation and the South's for a looser confederation. They also promised to work on humanitarian issues involving separated families and some North Korean soldiers and agents who were still imprisoned in the South for refusal to recant their loyalty to Pyongyang. They pledged cooperation and exchanges in various fields and promised to "promote the balanced development of the national economy through economic cooperation."[12] The remaining items on Seoul's wish list were saved for later negotiation by lower-ranking officials.

The South Koreans believed that Kim Jong-il was seriously interested in a new approach. For the last meal of the Pyongyang summit, the North Korean leader invited all of his top subordinates in the party and the military and called upon them to toast Kim Dae-jung as a show of support for the agreements in the declaration. At one point Kim Jong-il turned to the chief of the People's Army's political commissars and asked if he had halted anti-South propaganda broadcasts along the Demilitarized Zone. "We will stop it today," the commissar said. Kim Jong-il did not like that reply and said so: "Why haven't you stopped sooner? Stop it now!" It was done. The South followed suit the next day, ceasing its own propaganda broadcasts.[13]

Hwang's speech in Seoul detailing the summit talks was delivered to a military veterans' group. One of the veterans asked him, "Prior to the summit, North Korea was our enemy. How shall we view the North now?" The general replied, "Both you and I have served in the military. We have to view the North using the best of our judgment and our job function. For example, it should be clearly stated that the North is the enemy as far as our front line troops are concerned. If our soldiers treat Northern soldiers as their friends, they will be unable to defend our country. Another example: if our business people dealing with North Korea considered Northerners as enemies, there would not be any economic cooperation." Note that his formulation was virtually identical to what Kim Jong-il had said to his Chongryon visitors in 1998 regarding North Korea and the American devils.

"When we talk about changes in the North, we are in fact talking about changes in Kim Jong-il's mind-set," Hwang told the South Korean veterans. "Kim Jong-il was quite different from what we anticipated." The North's leader "speaks well and is jovial, well informed and intelligent." Reflecting that view of Kim Jong-il, Hwang said, "the North's politics, economy, society and culture have changed. They are not what they used to be in the past. If we add momentum to the changes, no one will be able to stop them now. We must make sure that the changes continue on."

The South's "sunshine" policy of engagement, with the summit symbolizing its supposed success, won Kim Dae-jung the Nobel Peace Prize for 2000. Kim Jong-il, gracious as he had been in his role of host, had to settle for being named *Time*'s "Asian of the Year." Worldwide, the magazine named as its "Person of the Year" George W. Bush, winner of that year's close and disputed U.S. presidential election.[14]

Kim Jong-il gave a further signal of big things to come when an article in large type bearing his name appeared in the January 4, 2001, issue of *Nodong Shinmun*. Entitled "The Twenty-first Century is a Century of Gigantic Change and Creation," it put North Koreans on notice that "things are not what they used to be in the 1960s, so no one should follow the way people used to do things in the past." As in the case of the 1998 constitution's stress on costs, prices and profits, it could be argued that Kim's exhortation represented not mere rhetoric but genuine ideological change. In the view of one German scholar, "In 2001 a far-reaching reform policy finally entered into its implementation stage in North Korea after some years of preparation, discussion and formulation."[15]

Kim Jong-il had told visiting Chinese officials that he would like to visit their country again.[16] He made the visit in January 2001 with a retinue that included military leaders as well as civilian economic officials. He did much of his sightseeing in Shanghai, the showcase city of the new China, where he saw high-tech installations and toured a joint venture Chinese-General Motors automobile plant.[17] He even visited the Shanghai Stock Exchange—twice. Chinese reform had been in full swing since Kim's visit in 1983, when he had gleaned a few ideas but—evidently not terribly impressed overall—had criticized his hosts for "revisionism." This time, he appeared to take the bait, reportedly exclaiming that "Shanghai has had unbelievable change and attracted worldwide attention."[18] He was quoted as having told Chinese officials he would build in North Korea a high-tech city modeled on Shanghai. To his accompanying subordinates he said, "Let's build skyscrapers. China has succeeded in economic reforms. Why have we failed?"[19]

Kim returned to Pyongyang and, later in 2001, ordered his economic advisors to pursue "practical benefits" while maintaining socialist principles. In

March 2002 Prime Minister Hong Song-nam announced that "dramatic" measures had been taken. The changes indeed appeared dramatic. Low, government-set prices would give way to prices that bore realistic relationships to the market. This involved enormous inflation from the old prices. Pyongyang bus and subway fares rose ten times. Rice sold through state agencies went up a stupendous 550 times, to reflect what people had been paying for the grain on the private market. "Resident fees," house and apartment rents paid to the state, went from token to very substantial figures. A country that had boasted of being free of taxes now instituted taxes on household electronic devices—still considered luxuries.

Wage increases on the order of twenty-fold were announced to help citizens cope with the new system. Jettisoning a relatively uniform wage structure, the state would now take account of the nature of the work. Miners, stuck with the nastiest job of all, were to receive pay three times higher than factory wages—and twice what was paid to trading company managers. The new compensation structure also took into account regional factors and—reflecting Kim Jong-il's decades-old, privately expressed gripe about lazy workers—job performance. Foreign currency exchange rates were brought closer to the black market rates, so that the official exchange rate for the U.S. dollar became 200 *won* instead of 2.2 *won*.

Impressive as those measures were, questions remained. In particular: Did Kim Jong-il envision a market economy in a communist party-ruled country—a structure similar to the hybrid structure that China had created? Or was he trying, yet again, to shore up a basically socialist, non-market—in large part unchanged—economy? Analysts differed on that question.[20] Skeptics noted that the new prices, while reflecting market realities, still were not market-set prices but state-set prices.

Would the changes, regardless of intent, lead to more fundamental changes? A reporter for Seoul's *Dong-A Ilbo* first visited North Korea at the time of the July announcement of the new measures. He returned three months later and found intriguing anecdotal evidence. During the summer Pyongyang had hosted a festival called Arirang, to celebrate the country's return to economic growth after the horrible period of famine—now dubbed the "arduous march." The festival represented a huge drain of funds with few discernible gains, and to that extent suggested that the regime might have failed to learn the lesson of the 1989 youth festival. Just as in 1989 a prime motive was rivalry with the South—which, with Japan, co-hosted soccer's 2002 World Cup matches. On the other hand, though, the Arirang festival had been the occasion for officials to issue operating permits for Pyongyang street stalls selling beverages, snacks and takeout food. The permits were temporary. However, as the *Dong-A Ilbo* reporter observed, after the festival concluded in August the bustling stands continued to line busy streets near subway stations and bus stops. Their operation now had been legitimized by the July measures. Such stands were not confined to Pyongyang but could be found in other places such as the parking lot for tourists visiting Mount Myohyang. The reporter quoted a guide as saying the mania for street vending had affected bricks-and-mortar enterprises. "During the summer, street vendors sell more soft drinks than regular stores. Many enterprises want to branch out into the street vendor business, which has triggered a fierce competition for good spots."

A new spirit had affected farmers, as well. "It was the normal practice for civil servants and soldiers to go out to help with the weeding," the reporter wrote. "This year, however, the farm workers informed them that no one needed to come because they would do it on their own." The farmers, he explained, "have realized that each person can make more money by increasing production and reducing costs. They have also come to understand that accepting nonessential helping hands in exchange for daily wages chips away at their profits." Income of goat-and-corn farmers whom the reporter visited had soared thanks to the July price increases. Introduction earlier of an "individual competitive system" had transformed many of the farmers' attitudes and work habits. "Based on last year's output, the difference in income between those who worked cleverly and the lazybones is five-fold," the farm manager said. The former "herded goats up the hill at eight in the morning with a lunch box and returned at eight in the evening." The slackers "slept late. Then they came down the hill with the goats to have lunch and take a nap before climbing back after two in the afternoon, only to come back early." As the reporter asked rhetorically, "Is it not natural that there is a difference between the goats that grazed the whole day and those that came and went with the shepherd?"

Buzz words appearing often in the North Korean media included "innovation" and "good at calculation," the reporter found. "In the past, 'good at calculation' meant 'selfish,' an utterly insulting expression in North Korean society. At present, however, being good at calculation for both companies and individuals is turning into a virtue."[21]

One could look for further clues in subsequent events. It would be difficult for North Korea to join the world economy if the U.S. market remained essentially closed to its products. On that point, the outlook did not seem promising. Both the Clinton and George W. Bush administrations, citing security, had restricted the scope of the relaxation of U.S. sanctions that Clinton had promised. The Bush administration had rather contemptuously rained on Kim Dae-jung's sunshine policy, starting with a reception of the South Korean president in Washington in which Bush presented a studied and insulting contrast to the deference and hospitality that Kim Jong-il had provided.

In April 2002 South Korea hoped to invite Pyongyang delegates to the annual assembly of the Asian Development Bank, to which North Korea had applied for membership. But politics, once again, thwarted business deals. Washington, the bank's leading shareholder, vetoed the invitation.[22] Even more ominously, the *Dong-A Ilbo* reporter noted during his October visit that "our delegation caught sight of six Mercedes-Benz sedans taking U.S. delegates to Pyongyang, including James Kelly, U.S. assistant secretary of state for East Asian and Pacific affairs." As we shall see in chapter 36, Kelly's visit would slam the door on hopes for U.S. cooperation in the near term.

And there was still more bad political news to come. In 2003 allegations surfaced in Seoul that Kim Dae-jung's aides, through Hyundai, had bought Kim Jong-il's participation in the 2000 summit by transferring $500 million or more to the North Korean leader's account. Chung Mong-hun, fifth son of Hyundai founder Chung Ju-yung and chairman of the Hyundai group company that had developed the North Korea projects, was to be tried for violating foreign currency regulations with the secret transfers. On August 4, 2003, Chung Mong-hun leapt to his death from the twelfth floor of the Hyundai Building, leaving a note saying: "This foolish person has committed a foolish thing." The following month six Hyundai and government officials were convicted in the case but given suspended sentences. The scandal called into question both Kim Dae-jung's Nobel Prize and Kim Jong-il's sincerity about reconciliation. Pyongyang bitterly blamed the right-wing main opposition party in the South for pushing the investigation, saying instigators would be unable "to escape the crimes that they committed in the face of their people and history itself."[23]

THIRTY-SIX

Fear and Loathing

While events around the turn of the millennium suggested that Kim Jong-il had become willing to yield some points on economic and legal policies, he had other, less peaceable things on his mind as well. His continuing policy of placing heavy emphasis on military readiness led to a high-stakes war of nerves with Washington, Tokyo and Seoul. That struggle put at risk any gains the North Korean people might hope to derive from his other initiatives.

The official position, expressed at the beginning of 2000 by an economics professor at Kim Il-sung University, was that Kim Jong-il's emphasis on "military-first" politics meant guns *and* butter. Yes, it was intended to "defend the nation from the invasion of hostile forces." But it was "a comprehensive plan which includes an effective means for an economic buildup." The policy had "nothing to do with military rule or a military regime." And the "powerful state" that the Dear Leader wanted to create did not mean a country pursuing hegemony. Rather, the policy had "two goals: defending the system and restoring the economy."[1]

Following September 11, 2001, and the Al Qaeda terrorist attacks on the World Trade Center and the Pentagon, speechwriters working on President Bush's State of the Union address for 2002 liked the catchy phrase "axis of evil." Partly to avoid making it appear the United States focused only on Muslims in the new War on Terror, they added North Korea to the original "axis" members Iraq and Iran. Many people felt that the stance was justified when Washington acquired evidence suggesting that North Korea might be continuing secretly—despite the 1994–95 agreements—to develop nuclear weapons. A second nuclear weapons crisis erupted.

Even as international attention focused again on North Korean weaponry, however, Kim Jong-il's regime continued to experiment at home with potentially far-reaching adjustments to the Stalinist-Kimilsungist system. By 2004 foreign visitors and other outside analysts were hopping aboard what seemed to be a developing consensus: Pyongyang was more serious than before about accepting—and even encouraging—economic change.

Early in 2000 South Korea's Ministry of National Defense reported that North Korea had stocked enough food for a yearlong war and enough oil for at least three months, in addition to ammunition. Interpretations varied. A substantial body of foreign opinion held that North Korea, far from being an aggressive state that might attack the South at any moment, was a weak country that simply sought to defend itself against a feared attack by the United States and South Korea. Of course that school of thought had long included sympathizers with North Korea and its socialist ideal. But quite a few others coming from elsewhere on the ideological spectrum had concluded in the 1990s that the North—with the collapse of communism in the Soviet Union and especially with the economic disaster that afflicted the country through much of the decade—had irreversibly fallen into weakness. Pyongyang must know that the days were past when it could have mounted a successful southward invasion. Looking at the matter from that point of view, the North could be squirreling away war rations, fuel and ammunition purely for the sake of deterring its enemies from attacking. After all, the South Korean ministry claimed to know where the North's storage facilities were—presumably thanks to satellite photos and other intelligence. Knowing it was being watched and hoping to discourage attack, Pyongyang would have to make sure it put up a credible front of being ready, indeed eager, to fight effectively.

There were plenty of reasons for being skeptical about that argument, and I was skeptical. One could suspect that the Pyongyang regime's adamant refusal for so many decades to change in any basic way applied fully to its more than fifty-year-old objective of ruling the whole peninsula. For the regime to relinquish that goal and settle permanently for taking its chances in peaceful competition with its Southern brethren, wouldn't there have to be an enormous change? There might be temporary policy shifts, such as emphasizing deterrence more than preparations for aggression whenever the regime felt itself temporarily weakened. But if such a huge change of long-term policy as the renunciation of conquest were to occur, wouldn't we know about it? How could it be accomplished without internal turmoil sufficient to register on Pyongyang-watchers' seismographs? Remove one element of the "unitary idea," Kim Jong-il himself had warned for decades, and the whole system would start to unravel. Along with such a major policy change, wouldn't we see, at the minimum, some new faces at the top, rather than continuing to watch a country being ruled for better or for worse—usually for worse—by the same people who had been in charge for decades?

But people who met Kim face to face continued to get the impression he was prepared to make deals that would permit him to abandon old policies so that the country could move on. One of those people was then-U.S. Secretary of State Madeleine Albright, whose memoir includes a chapter describing a visit to Pyongyang in the waning days of the Clinton administration.[2] She found Kim "an intelligent man who knew what he wanted." Exuding confidence, he made clear he wanted normal relations with the United States that would "shield his country from the threat he saw posed by American power and help him to be taken seriously in the eyes of the world."

Albright was in Pyongyang for preliminary talks looking toward a possible summit meeting between President Clinton and Kim—and what both sides hoped would be a comprehensive agreement on missiles and the other issues that kept the two countries at odds. In her first meeting with Kim ("I was wearing heels, but so was he") she told him she could not recommend a summit meeting without having an agreement on missiles. Kim told her his country was selling missiles to Iran and Syria because it needed foreign currency. "So it's clear, since we export to get money, if you guarantee compensation it will be suspended." Indeed, he offered to halt not only exports but also production for deployment within the country. "If there's no confrontation, there's no significance to weapons," he explained.

Describing a meeting the following day, Albright wrote, "I said we had given his delegation a list of questions and that it would be helpful if his experts could provide at least some answers before the end of the day. To my surprise Kim asked for the list and began answering the questions himself, not even consulting the expert by his side."

Kim told Albright that he could see a post–Cold War role for U.S. troops in South Korea: maintaining stability. But he said his military was split down the middle on whether to improve North Korea–U.S. relations and that some in his foreign ministry had argued against his speaking with the Americans. "As in the U.S.," he said, "there are people here with views differing from mine, although they don't amount to the level of opposition you have."

Kim confirmed that his country was in severe economic difficulty, and Albright asked if he would consider opening the economy. Not if it would "harm our traditions," he replied. He said he was not interested in the Chinese mix of free markets with socialism, preferring the model of Sweden, which he saw as more socialist than China.

"On a personal level," Albright wrote, "I had to assume that Kim sincerely believed in the blarney he had been taught and saw himself as the protector and benefactor of his nation. . . . One could not preside over a system as cruel as the DPRK's without being cruel oneself, but I did not think we had the luxury of simply ignoring him. He was not going to go away and his country, though weak, was not about to fall apart."

Albright concluded that Kim was serious about negotiating a deal on missiles, and that the costs to the United States "would be minimal compared to the expense of defending against the threats its missile program posed." But efforts to arrange for Clinton to meet with Kim and seal such a deal ran into obstacles. First, Albright wrote, there was considerable opposition in Washington from people who "feared a deal with North Korea would weaken the case for national missile defense," or who "argued that a summit would 'legitimize' North Korea's evil leaders." But what really scuttled the proposed trip was a competing demand for Clinton to deal with the latest Mideast crisis during his fast-dwindling time in office.

The George W. Bush administration took over in Washington early in 2001. Republican officials in charge of foreign policy, suspicious of the Clinton administration's efforts to find accommodation with Pyongyang, set out to review U.S. policy. After President Bush's Axis of Evil speech, there was more to come. In October 2002 U.S. Assistant Secretary of State James Kelly and other officials visiting Pyongyang surprised their hosts with evidence that North Korea was continuing nuclear weapons development using uranium enrichment, a different and separate process from the plutonium process the country had frozen earlier. The delegation returned to Washington to report that its counterparts had come clean on the uranium project, defiantly insisting there was no reason why the country should not have its own nukes.

Washington sought to keep the issue on the back burner while it took on Iraq first. North Korea used various provocations to try to force the United States into making concessions while the Pentagon was occupied in the Middle East. In December 2002 the country expelled International Atomic Energy Agency inspectors and started reactivating a reactor that had produced plutonium before the 1994 freeze. In January 2003 North Korea withdrew from the Nuclear Nonproliferation Treaty.

The quick initial success of the Iraq war most likely was blood-curdling news to Kim Jong-il, whose whereabouts were not known for a number of days. He was presumed to be in hiding for fear one of those smart U.S. weapons, launched in the preemptive attack that the Bush administration openly contemplated, would find him. After all, Bush had told author and *Washington Post* reporter Bob Woodward that he "loathed" Kim Jong-il, whom he referred to as a "pygmy."

In October 2003, Pyongyang said it had reprocessed some eight thousand spent fuel rods that had been in storage during the period of the freeze. "If that is indeed the case, it could have produced enough fissile material for an additional five or six nuclear weapons," Kelly said.[3] When Pyongyang hinted broadly that it might simply declare itself a nuclear power, China, for one, did not like that idea and cut off North Korea's oil supplies for several days to enforce a demand for negotiations. By early 2004 Pyongyang had offered to re-freeze its plutonium-based program (evidently realizing its admission had been a tactical error, it now denied it had acknowledged having a uranium enrichment program) while negotiating with the United States, South Korea, China, Japan and Russia to see what sort of deal it could get. What it wanted from Washington included a non-aggression pact and diplomatic relations.

While the first nuclear crisis had appeared pretty much to halt movement toward economic change, Pyongyang the second time around kept moving on a parallel track—to the extent that quite a few foreign skeptics started to become believers that something major could be happening this time.

One implication of Kelly's confrontation with North Korean officials on the bombs-from-uranium issue was, of course, that there would be no progress for the time being on resolving economic issues between Washington and Pyongyang. The month after the Kelly visit, however, Kim Jong-il's brother-in-law, Chang Song-taek, led a high-powered delegation to South Korea to learn from the Southern economy. Ignoring super-high-tech, capital-intensive operations that were way out of their league, the Northern visitors focused on what seemed within their reach: standard industrial commodities such as steel and fertilizer, which they had been producing and could hope to produce more efficiently, and smaller businesses including golf and tourism. "So while their South Korean guides expected they would like to see Samsung Electronics' cutting-edge technology," reported a Seoul newspaper, "they were more interested in how an LG subsidiary makes toothbrushes." Pak Nam-ki, the North's chief economic planner, looked intently at what he was shown and asked many detailed questions. South Koreans speculated that the travelers, upon their return to Pyongyang, would first disabuse Kim Jong-il of his misconceptions about the South Korean economy and then draft a new blueprint for restoring and reforming the North's economy.[4]

What about that old assumption that reform would unravel the ideology that kept the populace in thrall to the leader? For mass consumption, continuity was the byword. By February 2003 the regime had cranked up its propaganda machine to insist that the new initiatives fit right in with received scripture. *Nodong Shinmun* published an article on Kim Jong-il's "wise leadership for improving socialist economic management"—an article that mentioned the term "profits" several times. Explaining the timing of the publicity, the paper said it marked the thirtieth anniversary of a work by his father, "On Several Issues for Improving Socialist Economic Management." Kim Jong-il had accomplished a "great feat," the paper said, by maintaining "the socialist economic management principle amid the imperialists' encirclement and mounting difficulties." Meanwhile, he "leads us to thoroughly guarantee real profits in the socialist economic management." Perhaps the one-time political economy major had thought better of his student-princely disdain for instruction in computation. "Economic management requires scientific calculations," said that article on his management approach.[5]

Addressing the Supreme People's Assembly—the parliament—on the state budget for 2003, Finance Minister Mun Il-bong went farther. "In all institutions and enterprises a system of calculation based on money will have to be correctly installed, production and financial accounting systems be strengthened, production and management activities be carried out thoroughly by calculating the actual profits," Mun said. German scholar Ruediger Frank found in another passage of Mun's speech an effort to graft onto the old socialist ideology a new recognition of the role of entrepreneurs. "Our people, holding high the Great Leader's ideology of nation-building after liberation, have built a new democratic Korea upon the rubble," Mun said, "those with strength using strength, those with knowledge using knowledge and those with money using money." Frank noted that strength stood for the workers and peasants and knowledge for the intellectuals—the three groups represented in the hammer-sickle-writing brush emblem on Pyongyang's Juche Tower. "But 'money' is a new component," he wrote. "It stands for those who excel in economic activities." Frank found it "remarkable that the leveling of the ideological battlefield has begun so early. Kim Jong-il may be no Mikhail Gorbachev, nor a Deng Xiaoping, but the evidence makes it hard to believe he is a stubborn opponent of reform."

At the 2003 parliamentary budget session came an announcement of another initiative, issuance of People's Life Bonds. "Why would a state like North Korea care about collecting large quantities of its own currency?" asked Frank. He speculated that "the one-time extra revenue created by issuing the bonds will be used to pay wages until the new price system functions." Frank discerned in the issuance of the bonds "not only a sign of a desperate effort to prevent a failure of the reforms, but also another indicator of the strong determination of the North Korean leadership to stabilize . . . with the goal of creating a domestically functioning and internationally compatible national economy in the future." He worried that circumstances—especially unavailability of loans and grants from outside—would block the achievement of that goal. The scholar concluded that "something has started which can hardly be stopped anymore, unless it either becomes a brilliant success or a miserable failure."[6]

I remained skeptical, for the time being, that the changes were truly momentous, and I was by no means alone. The head of one foundation dedicated to medical and food aid for North Koreans traveled through the country a couple of months after Finance Minister Mun's speech. Compared with what he had seen on earlier trips, the aid organizer found that the lives of ordinary people remained "difficult almost beyond description." Starting with the years of most acute famine, "North Koreans have had to turn to informal coping mechanisms," he told a U.S. congressional committee. But an illustration he offered could just as well have been taken as an omen of change for the better. "Even individuals who work in government ministries rely on outside sources of income to acquire the goods and services they need for their families," he said, reporting that "the North Korean economy has slowly improved over the past few years," thanks mainly to "the informal economy." He told how informal coping mechanisms, including produce from private plots and farmers' markets, had "halted North Korea's precipitous economic slide toward oblivion."

But the foundation chief still found the country unable "to move beyond an 'informal economy' on the macro level." Missing, he said, was "the structural reform needed to promote legitimate international trade. . . . While some would argue that attempts to set up special economic zones and adjustments in currency represent a genuine willingness to embrace economic reform, these policies aimed at promoting economic growth have yet to make a meaningful impact on everyday life."[7]

Nevertheless, anecdotal evidence continued to pile up, suggesting a breakthrough that had ended the regime's stubborn resistance to major change. At the very least, North Korea was displaying that sense of bustle that I had found so lacking by comparison with China in earlier decades. A Russian scholar visited North Korea in July 2003 and found brighter lights in Pyongyang, where the electrical system had been repaired and was being modernized with Swedish assistance. Cellular phones were in wide use in the capital, which had begun to experience the predictable safety problems caused by people chattering away while driving or cycling. Bicycles in large numbers were a relatively new feature of the urban landscape; I had seen few on my visits starting in 1979. Strikingly, "people were using the word 'reform' without any reluctance," the Russian said. Because of the older generation's suspicion of a buzzword connected closely to the collapse of Soviet and Eastern European communism, North Koreans until the previous year had stuck to the euphemism "national measures." Touring outside Pyongyang, the Russian saw evidence that "the overall economic situation has been gradually improving and the economic reform is being continuously carried out despite the 'nuclear crisis,' while the internal situation has stabilized."[8]

Whether the regime was serious about reform was quite a different question from whether reforms would succeed. Regarding the latter, the evidence was mixed. An official of the Catholic aid organization Caritas who visited North Korea in August and September 2003 found smoke rising from factory chimneys and housing construction under way. She encountered fewer electrical brownouts than before. "Small, family-size businesses or small cooperatives are providing services or producing goods (repairing bicycles, transporting wood, selling and bartering of agricultural products and consumer goods). A 'bottom-up' process seems to have started; there is more drive as people are left to fend for themselves. Under- or unemployed workers are engaged in the search for different coping strategies."

She found that flourishing kitchen gardens of farming families were providing a "support network for relatives without access to land." The gardens meant extra income for farmers, whose regular farming work paid them mainly in food. Corn and rice were still the main crops, but "since the start of the economic reform process cooperative farm managers tend to have more freedom to plant. By now cash crops, such as tobacco, sesame, mulberry, fruits and vegetables, have been widely introduced." Those crops "provide farms not only with a higher income but also with access to diesel fuel and other farm inputs for which foreign currency is needed. Farmers' markets have evolved into general markets selling a variety of consumer goods and marketplaces are to be developed all over the country." Prices, while kept within set limits, were fluctuating according to supply and demand.

That aid worker saw both positives and negatives in what she had observed in her travels. "The cradle-to-grave security has disappeared," she said. "Individuals are given, for the first time, more responsibility and thus feel more in charge of their own destiny. This has set capacity free, but at the same time there is a growing need to support people who have difficulties in coping with these changes. Haves and have-nots are developing; families tend to spend from 50 percent to 80 percent of the family income on food." She warned that the economy was "balanced on a knife edge" and that international help was required if the reforms were to succeed: "The attention of the international community is focused on the nuclear crisis, ignoring—after years of calling for reforms and change—the fact that the DPRK leadership is now working hard to develop policies for economic reforms and opening-up." Her organization did not expect quick results, "because real change has to come from within," she said. But she emphasized that "Opening up the economy can only work if the international community is willing to help."[9]

In September 2003, Pak Pong-ju, who as chemical industry minister had been part of the high-level study delegation visiting Seoul the previous year, took over as North Korea's prime minister, the top post running the domestic economy. Meanwhile fine-tuning of the new economic measures proceeded. The original 2002 devaluation of the *won* had not sufficed to attract people to the official moneychangers. In the summer of 2003 the rate reportedly was adjusted to match the black market rate.[10]

At the end of September 2003, Pyongyang issued what were seen as re-alistic tax and labor regulations for a new industrial park planned for Kaesong, the old royal capital near the South Korean border. The minimum wage there was set at fifty dollars a month plus a social insurance package computed at 15 percent of the wage. Businesses created in the park by out-side investors would pay 14 percent of their profits in corporate income tax.[11] (Still, some of the surviving members of the founding family of Hyundai, which had invested in both the Mount Kumgang development and the Kaesong industrial park, were becoming discouraged by the lack of return on the investments.[12]) Other rules announced later in the year included a ban on entry into the territory by "international terrorists, drug addicts, lu-natics."[13] As the Kaesong regulations were being issued the South's unifica-tion minister called the North's reform efforts "meaningful." He added that Pyongyang officials had explained to their Southern counterparts that they were obeying a previously ignored instruction by Kim Il-sung that they study the capitalist economic system.[14]

The regime put out the word that it would license one foreign accounting firm and one foreign law firm to set up shop in Pyongyang,[15] and moved to merge some insolvent banks.[16] Some European investors said they would es-tablish a capital company in Pyongyang, advise in restructuring the financial system—perhaps starting a credit card settlement system and opening a bond market—and encourage foreign investment.[17] In January 2004 the Eu-ropean Union Chamber of Commerce in Seoul opened a two-person satellite office in Pyongyang.[18]

Pyongyang envisioned a major thrust in the information technology in-dustry to power its economic takeoff. In 2003 the country shifted its focus from software development to telephony, the Internet and hardware. It was able to announce that in the course of the year the number of mobile phone subscribers increased nearly seven-fold to 20,000. Its hardware production capacity had risen to 135,000 computers and 100,000 monitors a year. Plans included providing fixed telephone lines to every North Korean home within five years. But the country faced a severe cash shortage that threatened all its ambitious projects. A North Korean official noted at the end of 2003 that expanded international cooperation—read "technology transfer"—would help things along. South Korean officials cautioned, though, that the level of progress would depend on whether the nuclear weapons issue could be resolved.[19]

The South Korean government's theory was that a sense of vulnerability had spurred Pyongyang to build nuclear weapons. Certainly it was not some inexplicable case of paranoia that led Kim Jong-il and his colleagues to worry that they might be attacked. North Koreans had been "staring down the barrel of American nuclear weapons for decades," said arms control expert Peter Hayes. "Indeed, it is a large part of the explanation of why they have built a subterranean society."[20]

In 1998 journalist Richard Halloran reported that United States and South Korean forces had replaced their Korean peninsula war plan. The old plan had called for simply repelling any North Korean invasion of the South, pushing North Korean forces back behind the Demilitarized Zone. The new plan was far more ambitious, and included the possibility of preemptive strikes if the U.S. and South Korean presidents should agree that war was imminent. Americans and South Koreans would invade the North to capture Pyongyang, wipe out the regime and its military and place the country under South Korean control. Halloran quoted a senior American official as saying, "When we're done, they will not be able to mount any military activity of any kind. We will kill them all." One officer told Halloran that the plan responded to concerns that the North Koreans, contemplating the evidence that their force was deteriorating, might decide they had to "use it or lose it."[21]

The new plan and the tough talk accompanying it obviously could be sobering to Kim Jong-il and perhaps could deter him from any such adventure. No doubt that was part of the intention. In 2003 Halloran reported further details of what was officially called Operation Plan 5027. "The North Koreans are believed to know the general outline of plan 5027," he wrote, suggesting that the plan was "a factor in North Korea's latest threats and its desire for a nonaggression pact with the United States."[22]

While South Korea's military worked with the Pentagon on the new plan, civilian officials in Seoul were taking a separate tack. They believed that a successful shift to economic interdependence with the outside world would lessen Pyongyang's feelings of insecurity (as well as its shortage of hard currency) and facilitate a solution to the problem of weapons of mass destruction. Indeed, the Southern unification minister in October 2003 agreed with Pyongyang's claim that Kim Jong-il's "military-first" policy could actually be seen in part as a bid to make the economy more efficient.[23] How in the world could that be? German scholar Ruediger Frank explained how, in a provocative essay.[24] Frank said that the military-first policy was methodically removing the socialist elements of the country's ideology, leaving the nationalist elements intact. He quoted the party newspaper *Nodong Shinmun* as saying on March 21, 2003, that the policy—now called the "military-first ideology"—raised the military above the working class. That quite explicitly meant jettisoning Karl Marx's mid-nineteenth-century *Communist Manifesto*, as the newspaper signaled in an April 3 article: "In the past, it was recognized as an unbreakable formula in socialist politics to put forth the working class. However, the theory and formula . . . generated one and a half centuries ago cannot be applicable to today's reality."

Determining people's status according to their relationships with the military instead of their economic class would permit granting legitimacy to North Korea's new moneyed class, Frank argued. The argument was interesting. After all, as chapter 33 of this book makes clear, many of the new traders had emerged from the military and quite a few of their companies were tied to the army or other military organizations such as bodyguards and police. It could be a relatively small matter to decree that the rest of the enterprises belonged to the military-industrial complex. In any case Kim Jong-il, as Frank wrote, would not have to "force the group of entrepreneurs, who will very likely emerge as one of the results of successful economic reforms, into an obviously anachronistic ideological and propagandistic corset."

Kim had displayed "exceptional foresight to deal with this issue now, in this early stage of economic reforms," the scholar wrote. "The working class loses its position as the leading group in the North Korean society. Without the working class, what happens to socialism and its final stage, communism? Very simple: they are gone, although this is not openly admitted in North Korea yet." The replacement? "There is a simple answer to that, too, and we call it nationalism, also known as *juche,*" Frank wrote. "The transition will be smooth, because already since its introduction in 1955 *juche* began to gradually replace Soviet-style socialism in North Korea anyway."

Frank was right to say that nationalism should be seen as the core of *juche.* Korean self-reliance was only one component and, as we have seen from Kim Jong-il's conversation with Chongryon officials in 1998, the Dear Leader had come to believe that the self-reliant component had been overemphasized to the detriment of the economy.

There was more to Frank's analysis of how "military-first" fit with economic reform. The military wanted modern weapons, but the country could not afford them. "Where does the money come from? Economic reforms."

By early 2004 the accumulation of ideological and practical measures had reached something of a critical mass, persuading quite a few longtime skeptics that Kim Jong-il probably was serious about change. Although I had not managed to receive permission to visit the country since 2000, a tally of what others were finding tentatively persuaded me. Journalist Hideko Takayama heard from a Japanese investor who recently had renewed a repeated entreaty to his North Korean joint-venture partner to please turn off the propaganda announcements that blared incessantly in their processed seafood plant. Instead of huffily refusing, as before, the partner silenced the loudspeakers. He explained by saying, "Politics is now separate from economics." Meanwhile, *Newsweek International* reported, videotapes of South Korean soap operas were for sale in North Korean markets and Pyeonghwa Motors had rented billboard space in the capital to advertise its locally made Fiat sedan, the Huiparam (whistle).[25]

Stanford scholar John W. Lewis (whose lectures on arms control I had attended in 1983) found "dramatic" changes on his ninth visit to the country since 1987. "The real shocker was the massive semi-private market in Pyong-yang where potential buyers can find quantities of meat, vegetables and fruits as well as hardware, furniture and clothes," Lewis reported. "A market economy, however limited, has arrived in the North."[26]

For years the regime had vociferously refused to commit to the model of China or any of the other communist countries that had changed course. Fi-nally, though, *Newsweek International* reported, some officials acknowledged to South Korean counterparts that their model was Hungary's 1970s experi-ment in grafting market measures onto the basic state planning structure.[27] Indeed, many of the measures adopted in North Korea between 1998 and 2004 were similar to the Hungarian "goulash communism," as it had been called back then because of its stew-like mixture of market and central plan-ning measures.

To the extent that naming the model provided an affirmative answer to the question of whether Pyongyang was contemplating some sort of market economy, the news was encouraging. And yet the Hungary of the 1970s seemed a curious model for Pyongyang to have chosen. There had been many problems with Hungary's reforms in that period. The long-entrenched bureaucracy had dragged its feet, forcing reversal of many of the new mea-sures until a second wave of reforms began in 1978. Perhaps an attempt to avoid that trap was behind a reported order by Kim Jong-il to downsize the North Korean party and state bureaucracy—by as much as an astonishing 30 percent.[28] (Of course the Hungarian economy required further drastic changes, starting in 1989–90 with the full retreat from communism.)

China and Vietnam had been the models often proposed by outsiders. But economist Marcus Noland observed that neither of those Asian coun-tries would be a good fit—because both started the process as predominantly rural economies, able to use the rationalization of inefficient agriculture to drive industrial development.[29] North Korea, like Hungary, started its re-forms as an already industrialized country. To free up enough surplus labor to staff all the new non-state enterprises that Pyongyang wanted to see built would require downsizing not only the bureaucracy but also the bloated mil-itary. That peace dividend would be available if the North could end its mili-tary standoff with the United States and South Korea—or, as Kim Jong-il evidently had calculated alternatively, if it built its nuclear arsenal into a credible enough deterrent to compensate for slashing its conventional forces.

Further probing into the reasons for choosing the Hungarian model, we could guess that at least one top North Korean planner was an alumnus of a Hungarian university. We might also speculate that the supposed Hungarian model was to some extent a proxy for a real model much closer to home, a model that could not be publicly identified without thereby branding as lies the propaganda that had gushed forth from Pyongyang for decades. South Korea, while under military dictatorship in the 1970s and 1980s, had very successfully combined broad central planning with market decisions.

While recognizing that Kim Jong-il had spent much of his career pounding down every would-be Deng Xiaoping who popped up, South Korean officials evidently believed that no one was beyond salvation. An ideologically born-again Kim himself could be seen as the prospective Deng for his country if he got the right encouragement.[30] And so the South tried to help, although still cautiously. South Korea was moving ahead of Japan and China in the value of total imports from North Korea. The South's imports from the North in the first ten months of 2003 were up almost 30 percent over the same period a year earlier.[31] Plans were afoot to rebuild roads and railways across the border.

If Kim Jong-il really was serious about changing course, what would explain why it was happening at this particular time and why it had taken him so long? Many of the factors have been discussed above. Others are summarized in the table below. My then-and-now comparisons suggested that even if Kim Jong-il had been eager to reform the country much earlier, the country might not have been ready and other conditions also would have been unfavorable.

How would that inference fit with what we thought we knew about Kim Jong-il? Had he lain in wait for decades, intending to play the reformer as soon as conditions might permit? The available evidence indicated that from his student days in the 1950s through the 1980s and early 1990s Kim had been—if not always a sincere opponent of significantly changing the system his father had built—at best a cautious opportunist. If he was ready for far-reaching change now, I thought, it was because of overwhelming circumstances—many of them the same circumstances that had changed the minds of other people similarly raised in North Korea to be true believers.

CHANGED CONDITIONS POSSIBLY AFFECTING PROSPECTS FOR SYSTEM REFORM

Early- to mid-1990s	1998 to early 2004
South Korea still was governed by hard-liners who halted economic cooperation over the first nuclear crisis.	South Korea, under the "sunshine" policy, continued talking about economic cooperation as second nuclear crisis raged.

Early- to mid-1990s	1998 to early 2004
Many in the North still thought armed victory over the South a possibility; youths joined a mass movement to volunteer for the military in time for 1995 reunification.	The relative decline of military strength, known to high officials, had continued; hungry soldiers' morale had suffered as 1995 came and went without reunification.
Kim Jong-il, still considered weak, was buttressing his rule by focusing on winning over the military while leaving oversight of the economy to subordinates.	Firmly ensconced as military dictator, Kim had proven his staying power and turned his attention to the economy; three military leaders joined him on his 2001 China trip.
Country was racked by Kim Il-sung's death (just as he may have become interested in major change), and then by floods, famine.	The worst of the famine (and the traditional three-year mourning period) over, the economy was recovering.
Shin Kanemaru, point man favoring reparations for North Korea, lost his clout in Japanese politics in 1993.	North Korea's 1998 rocket firing over Japan gave Tokyo a new long-term reason to consider buying a better relationship.
Saddam Hussein provided a model: have it your way and thumb your nose at the U.S.	Saddam Hussein was captured in December 2003 in a "spider hole."
Isolated, xenophobic North Koreans were not ready to interact with foreigners.	Contact with foreign aid givers was changing some attitudes.
Most North Koreans had bought into socialism, expected an "iron rice bowl" and submitted meekly to the regime's extreme control over their lives. Many had tried hard to emulate the selfless communist "new man" personality, viewing calculation as wickedness.	Lacking sufficient food to ration, the government had relaxed many restrictions on individual mobility and people had learned to fend for themselves. The fierce struggle for survival required them to replace collectivist morality with the naked self-interest that fuels market economies.
Personnel lacked the training, experience to run a market-oriented economy.	Traders and entrepreneurs had emerged; young people studied business in the West.

Another hypothesis could be drawn from the facts summarized in the table. If the limited change in 1970s Hungary really was the model, those same circumstances would tend to force North Korea's economic managers to move farther—just as had been the situation of Hungarian planners. But there was the danger that even if Kim finally had decided to reform in a major way, the decision would not necessarily translate into successful reform and the new policies could be reversed. Marcus Noland warned that the reform efforts could "ultimately generate unmanageable social changes."[32]

Scarcity did not begin to describe the situation regarding the resources that would be needed to proceed with the reforms already approved. The regime had its work cut out for it just to feed the people. The UN World Food Program announced that it would have to halt food aid in February and March 2004, except to some 80,000 pregnant and nursing women and youngsters in day care.[33]

Improved revenues to North Korean enterprises would come only *after* a period during which they spent far more than before due to the officially mandated inflation. Ruediger Frank noted that this created a serious gap, "which must be bridged by loans. If loans are not available, the enterprises will be technically bankrupt and not able to pay bills and wages." But because bankruptcy and unemployment "are not acceptable for a state like the DPRK, these enterprises will be brought back under the umbrella of the state-run distribution system, which will effectively mean a failure of the economic reforms and most likely their end."[34]

Where would the money come from? Like the United States, South Korea was going through its own jobless recovery,[35] a reason to spend available funds at home. And even as Seoul continued to consult with Pyongyang at the ministerial level, many of its actual and planned cooperation measures were on hold pending a resolution of the nuclear dispute. Frustrated that Seoul was teaming up with Washington to apply pressure, Pyongyang officials talked rather wildly of perhaps shutting down the Hyundai tours of Mount Kumgang.[36]

Japanese public opinion meanwhile was inflamed even more by the abductions issue than by the nuclear weapons threat. Kim's confession to Prime Minister Junichiro Koizumi in 2002 that the North had indeed abducted thirteen people and that eight of them had died seemed intended to put the issue to rest—but had the opposite effect. Although the five survivors returned to Japan, Tokyo demanded that all their family members be released, as well, to return home to Japan. And it wanted much more information on those who were said to have died. Given the Pyongyang regime's human rights record, it seemed possible that its failure to be completely forthcoming might arise out of reluctance to avoid confessing to some atrocities even worse than the original abductions—imprisonment leading to starvation and death in the gulag, for example. Far from sending reparations money, the Japanese parliament early in 2004 passed a bill that would permit the government to impose economic sanctions if the abductions issue should fail to be resolved. Sanctions could block remittances (mainly from Chongryon members) to the North, and could stop trade. Pyongyang's Korean Central News Agency raged that history had never known "such an untrustworthy country as Japan."[37]

The moves to reform the economy seemed to point to the sort of policy that might lead to resolution of the nuclear issue. It seemed by early 2004 that North Korea had little interest in remaining a "rogue" state. Kim Jong-il wanted to join the international system and was willing to give up his country's role in proliferation of weapons of mass destruction in exchange for sufficient help in reaching that goal. If he and his military colleagues could be persuaded that they would never be attacked by the United States or South Korea, they might even give up the longer-range missiles and the atomic bombs in their stockpile.

Trust and verification were the big issues, however, regarding proliferation and—especially—the matter of existing stockpiled weapons. On the latter point, it seemed to me that it would be extremely difficult to persuade Pyongyang to trust Washington sufficiently to relinquish the nuclear "deterrent." The non-aggression pact that Kim sought could help in that regard. Pyongyang clearly hoped the Democrats would win control of the U.S. government. However, Kim had sufficient experience dealing with Washington that in dealing with a Democrat he would naturally worry about some future partisan reversal of policy that could place him once more in the Pentagon's crosshairs.

Who could persuade him he had nothing to worry about from the Americans? Perhaps President Bush could. There was the obvious comparison to Red-baiter and China-basher Richard Nixon's 1972 visit to China. Perhaps only a Republican president already on record as loathing Kim Jong-il could lead Republican hardliners to accept an accommodation with him. But there were major differences between the two cases. Nixon had not demanded that China relinquish its power to deter attack. And no doubt China had been very glad, every time its name rose for a season to the top of Washington's list of prospective enemies, that it had its own nuclear and other weapons.

Besides inability to trust American promises Kim perhaps had an additional motive for hanging onto his nukes.[38] Whenever Korean reunification might come, the weapons that would make a united Korea of 70 million people automatically a member of the nuclear club could help to equalize the assets North and South would bring to the table—and entitle Pyongyang to a say in the arrangements. The match would be wildly unequal, otherwise, unless North Korea in the interim managed to pull off its own economic miracle.

Rather than promoting a leap in the North's prosperity, Washington was enforcing sanctions and pursuing other policies whose effect would be to slow economic advances in North Korea. Some major prospective foreign investors found the risk too great, under those circumstances, to proceed with giant infrastructure projects they had been considering.[39]

Some observers believed that powerful people around the American president expected the problem to resolve itself if serious negotiations were delayed long enough. "Reluctant in an election year to request a congressional appropriation to compensate North Korea for bad behavior, the Bush administration appears content to bide its time, hoping North Korea will simply collapse," Marcus Noland of the Institute for International Economics wrote in January 2004. Noland attacked such calculations. In view of a short-term economic boost that was resulting from the reforms, "the odds today on regime change are not particularly high, about 5 percent in any given year," he argued. "If the White House seeks regime change in North Korea, it will have to give history a shove. The country is unlikely to collapse under current conditions."[40]

Some in Washington dearly wished they could give history that shove and take Kim out. There had been various proposals for removing (surgically or otherwise) Kim himself, perhaps along with his family and closest advisors, à la Saddam Hussein and the other Iraqis pictured on that famous deck of cards. South Korea was not up for such a scheme, fearing that even if it resulted in a relatively easy defeat of the North the burden of absorbing such a poor economy and strange society would overwhelm Southern resources. But what if North Koreans did the dirty work by ousting Kim and his family in a coup and setting up an authoritarian military dictatorship in Pyongyang, similar to the Park Chung-hee government that had developed South Korea so rapidly in the 1960s and 1970s?

Defense Secretary Donald Rumsfeld and Deputy Defense Secretary Paul Wolfowitz reportedly favored regime change—on the basis of an intelligence assessment that Pyongyang under no circumstances would negotiate away its nukes. One leaked idea of how to proceed was to "get the Chinese military to lead the way by telling North Korean military leaders that their future is dark as long as Mr. Kim rules." Northern generals then would mount a coup against the Dear Leader.[41]

There were serious problems with such a scheme. For starters, even if some KPA men were disgruntled enough to mount a coup, success would be particularly unlikely in view of the near-impossibility of penetrating Kim's ironclad security. Rumors of a coup attempt in 1995 by elements of the army's Sixth Corps (rumors denied by Kim in his 1998 meeting with Chongryon visitors) had it that the upstarts were put down, although with some difficulty.[42]

Beyond that, who might replace Kim? A fresh, competent military re-former from a younger generation, such as Park Chung-hee had been when he took over in Seoul in 1961? Good luck. Defector Hwang Jang-hyop had said that there was someone in North Korea—he declined to name the per-son—who could do a good job of ruling the country after Kim. But the best prospective rulers are not always the people who win military struggles for power. A hard line is the stock in trade of men in uniform the world over, and North Koreans had taken especially enthusiastically to the tough-guy role. Even if a coup were successful, the risk would have been high that whoever came out on top would become an even worse—more dangerous—leader than Kim Jong-il. Nastiness tends to trump benevolence. Recall the discour-aging precedent in South Korea in 1979–80. Park Chung-hee's intelligence chief assassinated him—and then the bloodthirsty, corrupt and profoundly anti-democratic Major General Chun Doo-hwan took over in his own coup.

Possibly the Washington officials launching their trial balloon for a coup in Pyongyang did not know what readers of chapter 31 know: Relatively cosmopolitan elements of the North Korean military—officers trained at an academy in Russia, who had returned home and sought changes in the North Korean system—were purged in 1992. Evidence that visionary reformists not only survived that purge but held sway in the senior officer corps was sparse, to put it mildly. For years, insider accounts cast military men as the heavies in policy disputes with civilian reformers. In 1995, for example, one elite defector published a chart dividing the top thirty civilian leaders almost equally among three categories: reformers, conservatives and "opportunists" (the swing-voting middle category, where the defector placed Kim Jong-il). Another segment of the chart, in which the defector categorized eleven mili-tary chiefs as either hawks or doves, was lopsided, however; he listed nine hawks and only two doves among the top brass.[43]

One Korean-American who visited Pyongyang on multiple occasions as a Clinton administration official warned that if the Bush administration was serious about regime change "it should be careful what it wishes for." North Korea's "leaders in waiting—now in their late forties and fifties—are more isolated than their elders ever were, and there is a distinct possibility that this cadre promises to be all the more hostile to the West," Philip W. Yun wrote in 2003. Yun had been senior advisor to William Perry when Perry was special advisor to the president for North Korea policy. He told of a 1999 visit when the host was a senior colonel, equivalent to a U.S. brigadier-general. "An in-tense man in his mid-fifties, the officer made it quite clear his presence was not of his choosing" and showed "palpable disdain for our entire group," Yun recalled. "The senior colonel's contemptuous manner substantiated stories I had heard of North Korean military officers and party officials—just below the top tier—being much more aggressive than their superiors. For this group, fifty years of communist ranting arguably have evolved into a form of fundamentalism, North Korean style—the idea of a unified Korea turned to sacred aspiration and armed conflict."[44]

Sad to contemplate, there was the possibility that Kim Jong-il himself was the North Korean with the most realistic chance of pulling off a Park Chung-hee–style act, as a dictator whose encouragement of economic reform might promise better times for his people. Perhaps it was as fortunate as it was predictable that the Chinese showed no apparent interest in the Pentagon's imaginative scheme to initiate a military coup against Kim.

Instead of a coup, for the time being at least a consensus built in Washington in favor of an in-between policy that essentially meant simultaneously containing and engaging Pyongyang, giving Kim Jong-il a chance to show that negotiations could work to resolve the problem. Or as pessimists saw it, Kim would be given enough rope to hang himself by demonstrating incontrovertibly to other countries that negotiations would *not* suffice. Then Washington could do a better job of lining up international support for a get-tough approach than it had managed regarding Iraq in 2002–03. Korea specialists Victor D. Cha and David C. Kang called that sort of policy "hawk engagement."[45]

The State Department's Kelly described a U.S. policy in which "North Korea has an opportunity to change its path. As some Americans might put it there is a chance for redemption. . . . With continued international solidarity, there is good reason to believe that North Korea will eventually rethink its assumptions and reverse course."[46]

If the policy worked smoothly, perhaps it was possible to imagine a result similar to Libya's 2004 agreement to give up its nuclear weapons program. Sensing the determination of the United States, Kim Jong-il might realize that refusal to deal with all issues fully would mean further isolation, economic sanctions and other measures to destabilize his regime or destroy it outright. At that point he might decide to submit, relinquish even his existing nukes (if he actually had any; their existence was mainly a matter of rumor and surmise) and take his chances on the American guarantees given in return. But imagining such an outcome required considerable optimism.

Here is how the deputy chief of the North's delegation to the six-party talks laid out his country's position: "If the U.S. fundamentally changes its hostile policy toward North Korea, we would also give up our nuclear deterrent. That is, only when a legal and systematic security mechanism guaranteeing that the U.S. will not threaten us is in place, and a certain level of trust is built and we no longer feel threatened by the U.S., will we be able to discuss with the U.S. issues relating to nuclear weapons we have already built. The criteria for judging that the U.S. has given up its hostile policy toward North Korea are as follows: First, provide in a manner believable to us a non-aggression guarantee stating that the U.S. will not attack us. Second, diplomatic relations between North Korea and the U.S. must be established. Third, the U.S. must not interfere with North Korea's economic transactions with South Korea and other nations."[47]

Six-party negotiations in Beijing in February 2004 made few discernible advances toward resolving the issues. John Kerry, the presumptive Democratic presidential nominee, complained that progress was "so slow, and it's begrudging" because the Bush administration refused to build on Clinton administration initiatives and talk one-on-one with Pyongyang. Some analysts thought Pyongyang was dragging its feet just as much as Washington was — but in the hope that Kerry would defeat Bush and change the tone of the confrontation.[48]

Pyongyang reacted with alarm in March 2004 when the South Korean National Assembly impeached President Roh Moo-hyun on charges of election law violations, incompetence and corruption. The South raised its level of military vigilance while the North said it was taking steps to strengthen its "nuclear deterrent." During a little more than a year in office, Roh had followed predecessor Kim Dae-jung's sunshine policy. Officials in the North worried that hard-line conservatives incited by the United States were about to take over in Seoul and reverse the policy.[49] South Korean voters weighed in on Roh's side, giving his supporters a big victory in National Assembly elections in April.

Whatever transpired in the South, it seemed unlikely that the North Koreans would become convinced, in the course of negotiating sessions over a period of only weeks or months, that the United States had abandoned all its hostility to the regime. (That would represent the flip side of Washington's own inability to trust Pyongyang enough to drop its hostility.) Kelly addressed that by saying Washington did not necessarily expect to "resolve the nuclear problem in a matter of a few weeks or even a few months,"[50] but patience inside the Beltway certainly was not unlimited.

What would happen if the engagement phase of "hawk engagement" failed to produce a resolution? Next would come the hawkish part, efforts to remove the regime — but how? It would be foolish for Americans to presume that they knew the will of the North Korean people, beyond the certainty that refusing to kowtow to the American devils remained a top priority. Still indoctrinated, still proud, North Korean citizens would welcome any would-be American military liberators with more bullets and bombs than flowers. Their society was not one that anyone outside the country would choose, but a great many North Koreans still endorsed much of its ideological foundation.[51]

There was the danger that if an unconvinced Kim refused to budge on the matter of his existing weapons of mass destruction, at least some in Washington would be tempted to seize on his obduracy as justification for war in one form or another. President Bush, in a February 2004 television interview, had provided a minimalist justification for the invasion of Iraq when he described Saddam Hussein as "a dangerous man" who "had the ability to make weapons, at the very minimum."[52] Obviously a similar argument could be put forward to justify military action against Kim Jong-il. Kim had the ability to make weapons and, to at least that extent, was dangerous.

For the United States and any allied forces that might launch even a limited preventive attack—say, a "surgical" strike against identified nuclear facilities—initial success might not come anywhere near as cheaply in terms of casualties as in Iraq. North Korea's "response would be prompt," a Russian specialist in East Asian studies wrote in a Seoul newspaper following a visit to Pyongyang in July 2003. "After studying this matter for a long time, the North Korean leadership reached the conclusion that since a limited attack could lead to an even more lethal attack, they must respond immediately with all their strength before their military strength becomes ineffective." The target of their retaliatory attack could be Seoul, he wrote.[53] Recall the vow Kim Jong-il was rumored to have made when he was promoted to marshal (see chapter 28), that he would "destroy the world" rather than accept military defeat. General Gary Luck, former commander in chief of U.S. forces in Korea, calculated that a second Korean war would cost a million lives and $1 trillion in damages and lost business.[54]

A prudent U.S. administration obviously would stop to think very hard about whether it really needed to go to such extremes to remove all of Kim's weapons of mass destruction right away. In an imperfect world, would Washington eventually hold its nose and strike an interim deal guaranteeing a halt to North Korea's weapons' manufacture and export, demolishing the plants and establishing a thorough inspection regime—but leaving any already deployed nukes and missiles in place for the time being, pending development of the sort of trust neither side yet felt? While an improved tone at the June 2004 talks in Beijing might have pointed vaguely in that direction, little overt support for such a compromise could be heard in Washington.[55] Then again, Washington was trying to speak with one voice about the proposition that Pyongyang had better forswear its nuclear ambitions now, or else.

The most desirable "or else," some in Washington seemed to feel, would be imposition by a united global community of sanctions far more stifling than the ones already in effect.[56]

The United States had accepted the entry into the unofficial nuclear club of India, Pakistan and Israel. Catching Pakistan red-handed in a global scheme of wildly extravagant proliferation to various U.S. enemy countries, including North Korea, the George W. Bush administration accepted a solution in which a single scientist took the rap and Islamabad promised it wouldn't happen again. Washington's rationale was to avoid doing anything that would destabilize Pakistan, whose own stockpiled bombs—even if the country ceased to proliferate—posed a grave long-term danger to the United States. An Islamic militant takeover of Pakistan and its atomic arsenal seemed a horrifying but real possibility down the road. Helping a friendly government stay in power there seemed almost a no-brainer.

But there was little sign of a substantial constituency in Washington for forming an alliance with North Korea—something that might be possible, in my view, since the two countries' fundamental needs could with some patience be reconciled—as a means of ensuring that Pyongyang's arsenal would not be used against U.S. interests.

If the United States should feel compelled to fight with North Korea, I had been saying and writing for a decade, the war should be fought with information rather than bullets. Defector Ko Jun, a former truck driver, told me in a 1998 interview, "If North Korea's citizens knew the outside world, how students demonstrate on campuses, 100 percent of the citizens would rise. They wouldn't care if they got shot. But they don't know how. They have no idea of the outside world." Bills introduced in Congress in 2003 and 2004 called for such means of breaking the information barrier as dropping radios into North Korea and broadcasting longer each day in the Korean language over AM and FM frequencies.[57] Fortunately there was the precedent of some pretty nasty states, the former Soviet Union and its Eastern European satellites, that had changed their ways on their own—without foreign occupation or the direct application of outside force—at least in part thanks to outside broadcasting.

Expanding broadcasts was a good idea regardless of the overall policy that might be chosen, I felt, if the broadcasters kept to straight news and did not resort to shrill and one-sided propaganda. Even if the United States chose to avoid suddenly destabilizing the North Korean regime, it still would make sense to try to improve the people's understanding of the outside world. In any case, successes in changing hearts and minds via broadcasting would be relatively gradual, cumulative.

As drafted by a private organization concerned with religious freedom, the Senate bill in particular had many flaws. It would inject congressional micromanagement into policy decisions beyond the competence of the U.S. legislative branch. The draft went so far as to settle upon an economic model—the Vietnamese model—for North Korea to follow. And it called for active U.S. efforts to reunify Korea—at a time when South Korea wanted only to postpone unification. It sought, in short, to legislate regime change.

The bills would authorize handing tens of millions of dollars to nongovernment organizations, which would be entrusted with performing aid work or public diplomacy (that's a euphemism for propaganda) on behalf of the U.S. government. Prominent among the organizations apparently in line to receive such grants were certain religious groups, commendably in the vanguard of a growing movement to expose North Korea's human rights violations and help the victims. Such groups also had a separate agenda. Their other and deeper interest beyond promoting human rights was in preaching religion, typically evangelical Christianity, to North Koreans. When they prepared balloon drops of small transistor radios, the packets also included Bible literature. The Senate bill's drafter, especially, apparently sought to encourage groups to tap into President Bush's proposed spending of tax funds on "faith-based initiatives. The House bill became law.[58]

Recall how missionary zeal was mixed up in the final voyage of the *General Sherman*, which got the U.S.-Korean relationship off to such a tragic start in 1866 (see chapter 2). I much preferred that religious groups continue to rely on free-will private contributions to finance their good works. Tax funds allocated for aid and public diplomacy directed to North Koreans could best be administered by dedicated, professional experts. The sort of communication expertise called for had resided in the U.S. Information Agency—until the end of the Cold War prematurely signaled that the agency was no longer needed, and it was disbanded. In view of America's enormous problems with foreign opinion—not only in North Korea but in the Muslim world and pretty much everywhere else, as well—I felt the time had come when the government should revive the agency, recall some of its retirees and put their experience to work. As for U.S. government food aid to North Koreans, it could continue to be funneled through the UN's World Food Program.

Whatever the ultimate decision might be, Americans could not afford to decide another war-and-peace question on the basis of misunderstanding and false information. A clearheaded, factual approach was needed. Thus I was concerned as I watched many people fail to let the facts get in the way of stories that cast Kim Jong-il as an offender in every category—as evil incarnate.

An example seemed to be a lobbying campaign that persuaded President Bush to impose sanctions against North Korea in September 2003 for what some human rights groups alleged was "human trafficking."[59] Their case looked weak. First there was that old canard about "forced" labor by North Koreans in Siberia. (See chapter 22 for my view that sending guest workers to Russia had far more positive than negative implications, from the standpoint of freedom and human rights.) Second, North Korean refugee women were being sold as wives and concubines to Chinese men. The evidence presented by human rights groups actually pointed mainly to Chinese nationals, acting on Chinese soil, as the guilty parties in such trafficking.[60] Pyongyang had not authorized the women's flight to China and authorities had shown disapproval of such liaisons by forcibly terminating the pregnancies of women who returned to North Korea—a human rights abuse documented far more thoroughly than was any official North Korean involvement in the trafficking of the women.[61]

A Washington psychiatrist who had done profiling work for the CIA decided that Kim suffered from "a serious mental illness." In a draft report circulated in Washington and widely quoted in news media accounts, the psychiatrist backed his long-distance psychoanalysis with a lengthy recital from the public record of negative information about Kim Jong-il.[62] We have seen that Kim grew up as a pampered prince, permitted to have his way on whatever his little heart might desire. That, the doctor said, inclined him toward a narcissistic personality. I had no argument there. But then, surmising that even the mature Kim Jong-il (by then in his sixties) must have felt inadequate compared with his father, the profiler followed that train of thought to suggest that Kim's narcissism qualified as what he described as the most dangerous form, the malignant version. Justifying that extreme call, he sweepingly characterized the North Korean ruler as so self-absorbed and grandiose that he completely lacked capacity to empathize—not only with enemies including Americans, South Koreans and Japanese but also with his own people. *No* capacity to empathize? The doctor had overlooked plenty of evidence that this was an exaggeration.[63]

I hoped that Americans, whenever they might start to hear a loud chorus of political and opinion leaders calling for the invasion of one more country led by one more dangerous "madman," would subject the diagnosis to elementary scrutiny. I'm no doctor, but I thought Kim Jong-il *was* crazy—like a fox. To scare off invaders and extort aid, he and his publicists had encouraged enemies to believe that the Dear Leader—who was in fact genuinely peculiar—might be seriously nuts and on that account should not be provoked. I thought it would be helpful if Western analysts, rather than breathlessly buying into the seriously nuts part, looked more closely before making up their minds. As Seoul-based Pyongyang-watcher Michael Breen put it, "while being neutral in the face of bad leadership is unacceptable, being objective is essential in assessing it."[64]

Missing in the accounts by those who demonized Kim was any hint that there might be two sides to the story.[65] Surely there are unrelievedly evil people. Saddam Hussein's sadistic sons Uday and Qusay perhaps qualified. But I could not fit the real Kim Jong-il comfortably into the role of total monster. Having studied Kim rather intensively for years, I would describe him as an often insensitive and brutal despot who had another side that was generous and—increasingly, as he matured—charming. He was an incompetent economic manager during the decades when stubbornness or insecurity kept him from risking needed changes in the system. But then, having found somewhere a new decisiveness, he had become the apparent sponsor of reform efforts. Sale of his regime's weapons of mass destruction to other enemy nations could cause the United States, both at home and in its role as global policeman, immense problems—but for a price he appeared willing to relinquish at least his capacity to make and sell them.

North Korea's human rights situation truly piled atrocity upon atrocity, as readers of chapters 14, 16 and 34 know. The system in which secret police fed political prisoners to the gulag was his father's creation, but Kim Jong-il had either actively or passively retained it. There was precious little on the positive side of the ledger page to balance the horrors of the camps. After complaints by human rights groups, the regime had closed some of those. But the prisoners had been transferred to locations that were more remote, where the eyes of the outside world could not penetrate. The most favorable inference from that incident was that Kim could be moved by outside opinion. Then there were his moderating instructions to "avoid creating internal enemies" and his encouragement of more attention to legality. In the end, still, there was no sign that he had come close to phasing out the camps and the oppressive system of surveillance.

I wondered what Kim might be persuaded to do now that he was changing his country's ideology. In my most optimistic daydream I imagined a very high-level envoy from a U.S. president or presidential nominee meeting Kim, perhaps in the early autumn of an election year, and saying, "Mr. Chairman, I know that you would like to meet with the man I represent. With your permission I will speak frankly on that point. In view of what we have learned about treatment of North Korean citizens who are deemed to have deviated politically from the official line, it would be hard for him to agree to meet with you. There is growing public concern in the United States regarding that situation.

"You and I have discussed measures that might begin to resolve our other mutual problems. But you are asking that we not insist upon your country's immediate nuclear disarmament. You ask that we accept simply a freeze of your capacity to make such weapons during a period of watching and waiting, while the two sides develop mutual trust. Without a breakthrough on human rights, I have to tell you, it would be politically difficult to justify a deal that offered no more than the Agreed Framework of 1994 had provided—a deal, moreover, that would hinge on trust. Let me also suggest that it would be difficult for *you* to trust our professions of non-hostility in such circumstances. After all, you might think, whenever American public opinion became seriously aroused by news of the human rights situation here, a policy reversal in Washington could lead to renewed hostility. So let's talk about how we might fast-forward the development of trust."

In my daydream Kim Jong-il would listen intently as the interpreter turned those words into Korean, before the American envoy continued: "The man who sent me understands that many of the prisoners were incarcerated originally because their attitudes and class backgrounds, or those of their parents or grandparents, were considered unsuitable in the sort of economy and social system your country was building from the 1940s. He knows of your reported instruction to 'avoid making internal enemies.' He knows about the adjustments you have begun to make to modernize the economic system. He wonders whether you might have contemplated going farther to create a role for the surviving political prisoners—and their jailers—as free people working in the new economic enterprises that you expect to see formed. If you were to free the prisoners, he would meet with you gladly."

We have seen how decisively (or, if you prefer, impetuously) Kim Jong-il had reacted to frank but polite talk in his meetings in 2000 with Kim Dae-jung and Madeleine Albright. His responses in person had been a far cry from the usual bloody-minded stonewalling his subordinates resorted to when they negotiated on his behalf.[66] At the conclusion of our hypothetical envoy's human-rights pitch, I imagined the Dear Leader grinning conspiratorially and asking, "So he wants me to make him the Great Emancipator here in the DPRK, in time for what your political writers call an 'October surprise'?" The envoy at this point would smile and reply, a bit playfully, "What's wrong with your letting him take some of the credit? But seriously, he wants *you* to be the Great Emancipator."

And then, who knows? Kim might turn to one of his functionaries and say, "Get the State Security and Public Security chiefs into my office immediately. Call the governors in from all the provinces for a meeting tonight to plan for turning those camps into ordinary communities. I'll probably regret this, but I'm taking down the fences—within the month."

Such an approach would be a long shot indeed, but something of the sort seemed to me worth a try. The polite talk would be essential. A former U.S. president would have the appropriate stature to serve as envoy. "In dealing with a nation that is attempting to reform, the form matters as much as the content," writes political scientist David C. Kang. "You can't *tell* a Korean anything, but suggestions of a solution might be met by receptive ears."[67]

One could dislike or even loathe Kim Jong-il. In my personal opinion, North Korea and the rest of the world would have been far better off if the boy called Yura had drowned in that wading pool with his little brother Shura back in 1948. Under the circumstances existing as of early 2004, however, it was no more relevant to ponder what might have been than to decide whether one liked or disliked the Dear Leader. What was essential, I thought, was to avoid overlooking anything about Kim that might point the way to a satisfactory, non-military resolution.

I felt that in my years of studying Kim I had succeeded to some extent in my goal of getting into the mind of that traditional Oriental despot, who happened to be my own age. A key, perhaps *the* key, I concluded, was the importance of maintaining face. For years I had believed that Kim Jong-il remained determined to win—to rule all of Korea. Lately, though, I had come to think that his real bottom line was to avoid humiliation. I remembered and pondered anew his odd 1998 remark (see chapter 29) about South Korean President Kim Young-sam's refusal to attend the funeral of Kim Il-sung: "If he had come, he might have taken over North Korea and become president of a united Korea. What an idiot!" Perhaps Kim Jong-il wished he could have carried out his father's dying wishes and brought into being the long-discussed federation or confederation, in which the two separate states could coexist, trade and gradually merge into one. In any case, the remark did not sound to me like the words of a ruler determined that he would either win or destroy the world. Kim did not, after all, speak of victory. It sounded more like the words of a ruler who could not accept the loss of his own and his country's face. As one of his negotiators put it in December 2003: to the North Koreans, capitulation meant "death itself."[68]

If that part was right, it followed that negotiated solutions to the United States' and other countries' problems with Kim should be possible. He could compromise if they also compromised—and if they showed respect rather than hostile contempt. Verification could be negotiated. Defector Hwang Jang-yop, who had almost nothing good to say about Kim, was skeptical when a *Washington Times* reporter asked whether the Dear Leader could be trusted to keep an agreement on nuclear weapons. But Hwang conceded, "People can change, and conditions can force a person to follow a certain path."[69]

THIRTY-SEVEN

Sing of Our Leader's Favors
for Thousands of Years

How much longer could North Korea survive as a separate country? Although no one knew, as of 2004 it seemed that the answer might turn out to be: a while yet.

After all, it was by no means clear that forces favoring speedy Korean reunification were strong enough to prevail any time soon. Each of the major players, on and off the peninsula, had interests in seeing division continue. For Beijing, continued existence of a separate North Korea would leave a communist party-ruled buffer state between the Yalu River and the U.S. troops in South Korea. In Washington the Pentagon liked the idea of keeping U.S. troops in Asia, but countries willing to play host to them had dwindled in number. A separate South Korea might well be more willing than a unified Korea to tolerate a contingent of GIs. Moscow could derive some satisfaction from seeing a former Soviet client state remain outside the American sphere of influence. Even in Tokyo people might sleep better knowing that the Koreans, whose resentment of Japan formed a common bond between North and South, had yet to manage the creation of a politically and militarily united country. For South Korea, continued division would postpone the dreaded time of reckoning when Seoul would have to attempt to develop the northern part of the peninsula quickly enough to keep a horde of hungry and homeless job-seekers from rushing south.

Would a separate North Korea continue to change internally, as rapidly as in the period since 1998 or even faster? To the extent that Pyongyang could find ways to proceed with its planned experiments in special zones, it did not seem unreasonable to guess that the country would change economically. Especially once long-forbidden information from outside became widely available, it could change politically as well. Still, political changes might come more slowly than economic ones—in that regard following the Chinese pattern rather than the Russian one. Meanwhile, for the reasons discussed in chapter 36, coup-dreaming outsiders might think better of the notion that a new, military leadership should be installed.

Under such circumstances, the Kim dynasty might last long enough to crown a successor to Kim Jong-il. At dinner with U.S. Secretary of State Madeleine Albright in 2000, Kim signaled that this was his plan. When Albright asked if there were other models he had considered emulating besides Sweden (itself a constitutional monarchy), Kim replied: "Thailand maintains a strong royal system and has preserved its independence through a long, turbulent history, yet has a market economy. I am also interested in the Thai model."[1]

Pyongyang began soon after to prepare the world for the next succession. A long essay in the party newspaper *Nodong Shinmun* for October 2, 2002, spun out an elaborate claim that Kim Jong-il had been the right choice to succeed his father precisely because he was "a partisan's son," specifically the son of Kim Il-sung. (The emphasis on the blood tie was far greater than had been the case when Kim Jong-il was put forth initially. Then, the propagandists' argument was that he just happened to be the most capable man for the job, regardless of his lineage.)

The *Nodong Shinmun* article then quoted an article, printed in an unnamed Japanese newspaper (perhaps one published by Chongryon), entitled, "The Korean Revolution Carried Out From the Son's Generation to the Grandson's Generation." It said, "Already a long time ago President Kim Il-sung expressed his determination to win the final victory of the Korean revolution by his son, if not by himself, or by his grandson, if not by his son. President Kim Il-sung reportedly expressed this determination at the secret camp on Mount Paektu in the spring of 1943."[2]

The appearance of the *Nodong Shinmun* article indicated that Kim Jong-il had decided it was time for people to start thinking about his ultimate successor. Recall that it was shortly after Kim Il-sung turned sixty that he made his choice of Kim Jong-il known to high-level intimates. Kim Jong-il himself turned sixty on February 16, 2002.

In the normal scheme of things in a Confucian society, the eldest son would be expected to carry on the family enterprise. Younger sons are, essentially, spares. But having multiple wives traditionally has complicated matters. The ruler's favorite wife is in a good position to push the case of her own son.

❊   ❊   ❊

In April 2001, Japanese public security authorities got word from a friendly foreign intelligence service that a person believed to be Kim Jong-nam, the eldest son of Kim Jong-il, would travel to Tokyo from Singapore on May 1. The passenger manifest of a Japan Airlines flight from Singapore that day listed a man who was going by a Chinese-sounding name, Pang Xiong. With him were three traveling companions: two women and a four-year-old boy. Security officials at Tokyo's Narita Airport approached the four at the immigration desk and took the man into an Immigration Bureau room to question him. He refused to answer at first, but after an hour or so he told them, "I'm Kim Jong-il's son." He explained that the group just wanted to visit Tokyo Disneyland. The date of birth given on his forged Dominican Republic passport, May 10, 1971, was Kim Jong-nam's birth date. The man said he had paid $2,000 each for the passports. His had been stamped to record entries into Japan the previous year. Questioning went on for several hours. At one point the man announced that he was hungry, peeled off a 10,000-yen note (worth around eighty dollars) from a wad of large U.S. and Japanese bills and asked that someone be sent out for food.

After spending the night at the airport, the travelers were transferred to a detention center for illegal immigrants. (The aliens who normally were confined in the center tended to be poor job-seekers from Southeast and South Asia.) Meanwhile Japanese officials wrangled over whether to (a) arrest the man and question him at length while trying to confirm the identities of all the group members, as the police and the Justice Ministry preferred, or (b) simply deport the group, which was the preference of the Foreign Ministry. Radio Moscow had quoted a denial by the North Korean embassy in Moscow that Kim Jong-il's son had traveled to Japan with a forged passport. Thus it was clear that prolonging the inquiry would irritate Pyongyang. Along with the boy, who was thought to be his son, the man stayed in the facility for male detainees and uncomplainingly ate the regular meals provided. Officials noted the detainee's "gentlemanly manner."

Foreign Minister Makiko Tanaka, who wanted to avoid troubles with Pyongyang, won the argument on May 4 and the government decided to deport the group without charges. "Now that we have saved face for North Korea, there may be some positive reaction from the North," a government official told the newspaper *Yomiuri*. The travelers then left the detention center for the airport and a flight to Beijing. The man who said he was Kim Jong-nam thanked immigration officials "for taking care of us." At various times during his detention he had spoken to his captors in Japanese and in English.[3]

Thanks to journalists' cameras at the airport, the world then got a good look at this possible heir to the North Korean throne. Not as unusual in his appearance as Kim Jong-il, he nevertheless showed in his round face and paunchy body a clear enough family resemblance. (A South Korean newspaper columnist observed that the man walked like Kim Jong-il and Kim Il-sung.[4]) There were several skin discolorations—perhaps moles or birthmarks—on his face. On his chin was a light stubble of beard, seen on enough other occasions to suggest that this was intended as a fashion statement. He wore his hair in a crew cut. His spectacles were the oblong metal-framed granny glasses favored by hip young Asians. He was dressed as a tourist, in a black knit shirt under a brown, quilted vest. He wore a gold neck chain and a gold wristwatch.

As for the man's retinue, the child wore jeans; new, white sneakers; and a red, white and blue jacket. (Those were the colors of the North Korean flag.) One of the women, a bit chubby and with a slight double chin, was holding the boy's hand and seemed to be in charge of him. Her beige leather bag and high-heeled shoes matched and they looked expensive. The other woman was sleeker and wore sunglasses. Her shiny black bag was large enough to hold business papers.

An immigration official testifying later before a Japanese parliamentary committee identified the matronly looking woman as Kim Jong-nam's wife, Shin Jong-hui, reportedly a daughter of the president of the North Korean airline, Air Koryo. The official identified the slimmer woman as Yi Kyong-hui, one of Shin's relatives. News reports said the bags both women carried were of the Louis Vuitton brand while the man's watch was a diamond-studded Rolex.[5]

Kim Jong-nam's mother was Song Hye-rim, an actress who had made her screen debut in *Border Village*.[6] Kim Jong-il met her in the 1960s, after he started hanging around at the studios, and began living with her. Besides being several years older than Kim Jong-il, Song was already married to another man and had a young daughter. After a divorce, Kim had the husband sent abroad to work. "From what I heard, my aunt was disappointed in her marriage and was quite taken by Kim Jong-il," her nephew, Li Il-nam, wrote decades later.

Kim Il-sung had hidden his own extramarital affairs while publicly espousing conventional family values. Kim Jong-il, according to Song's nephew's account, worried about the Great Leader's reaction to the potentially scandalous situation he had gotten himself into. But the young father seems to have welcomed paternity. One story has it that he was so excited to learn that the new baby was a son that he honked his car horn to awaken everyone in the hospital.[7] Li told of several instances that suggested Kim Jong-il was a doting father. Once when the child was two or three and dining with his father, he asked, "Papa, is it good?" "Of course," Kim Jong-il replied. "Everything tastes good when you are around."

Kim kept Song Hye-rim and little Jong-nam with him in a palatial mansion, the No. 15 Residence, which was staffed by around 100 servants and 500 bodyguards. (Eight cooks worked there. One had been trained in Japan and specialized in sukiyaki, a favorite of Kim's.) Song Hye-rim's mother; her widowed sister, Song Hye-rang; and the sister's two children, the boy Li Il-nam and a girl, Li Nam-ok, came and went in the household for varying periods. Song Hye-rang and her children all later left North Korea and gave public accounts of their lives in the palace.[8]

At home, Kim referred to Song Hye-rim as *yobo*, wife, according to her sister, while to others he introduced her in the Korean way as "my son's mother." But around 1973, while living with Song Hye-rim and their son Jong-nam, Kim Jong-il got involved with Kim Yong-suk, who would become his recognized wife. (Sister Song Hye-rang has argued that it is a mistake to refer to Hye-rim as a mistress: "Outsiders say Kim Yong-suk is the lawful wife, but it has no other meaning than that she was acknowledged by President Kim Il-sung.")

Kim Jong-il deputized his sister to break the news to Song that she would never be able to become his recognized wife and must leave the No. 15 Residence, according to Li Il-nam's account. The sister, Kim Kyong-hui, would take care of Jong-nam, she told the boy's mother, while Song herself would be provided for throughout her life. Song was terrified that she was about to have her son taken from her, so she ran away with the boy. But the two were soon found and brought back to No. 15.

Having grown up motherless, Kim Jong-il was moved by Song's determination not to leave the child, the nephew related. Kim, whom Li described as "a cultured person and a thinker," also retained an intellectual bond with the former actress. He reserved mansion number 15 as the home of that family. (Kim had other mansions, of course, and around 1982 he built one designated No. 55 as his new official residence.) But during the decades that remained to her Song was to be hospitalized in Moscow for long periods, treated for ailments that reportedly included depression, nervous exhaustion, diabetes and hypertension.[9] Whatever health problems were involved in her move, high-ranking defector Hwang Jang-yop alleged that there was another factor: Kim Jong-il exiled her in an effort to stifle gossip within North Korea about their relationship. "Naturally, rumors started spreading among the North Korean students studying in the USSR," Hwang wrote. "Kim Jong-il ordered the security commander of the People's Army to punish the gossipers. The commander interrogated the North Korean students living in Moscow, and executed all the students who simply replied that they knew that Song Hye-rim was living in Moscow."[10]

Likewise because of concern about gossip, Kim Jong-nam as a boy was isolated in the No. 15 Residence, lacking the relationships with playmates his own age that even his father had known. In partial compensation Kim Jong-il appeared at No. 15 for supper three times a week, emerging as if by magic from a tunnel that connected the residence to his office. When he slept in the mansion, after working late, he liked to creep into his little son's bed. Kim Jong-il pampered the boy as Kim Il-sung had pampered him. Even after Li had become a student in Moscow, he had to return to Pyongyang each May to join in the annual grand celebration of the new little prince's birthday. At No. 15 Residence Jong-nam had a playroom full of electronic game machines. On his birthday, aides packed the playroom with clothes, shoes, diamond-studded wristwatches, model guns and other foreign-made goods. "They had a special team to purchase birthday goods for Jong-nam," Li wrote. Li had a toothache once. The dentist had run out of the gold needed for a top-quality filling. When Jong-nam learned of that he opened his safe and handed his older cousin a 10-kilogram gold bar, telling him to use some of it for his dental work. The safe also contained wads of U.S. bills, Li said.[11]

Apparently the boy was denied nothing. Once when he suffered a toothache of his own, he defiantly said that his price for going to the dentist would be a car as big as his father's. Soon "a dark blue Cadillac was delivered to No. 15," according to Li. "I used to spend a lot of time with Jong-nam on my summer vacations. We would ride in the Cadillac when we went along on inspection tours." Jong-nam was permitted to read South Korean books and watch both South Korean and Japanese television. When he was eight, the boy took a liking to one South Korean comedian and ordered the mansion retainers to bring the entertainer to him. Fortunately they did not kidnap the comedian. Instead they searched until they found a North Korean farmer who looked just like him and had the farmer trained in comic routines before presenting him to Jong-nam. The impersonation worked briefly but Jong-nam soon saw through it. "I know this is fake," he said, leaving for his room.[12]

In 1979, the year Jong-nam turned eight, his thirteen-year-old female cousin Li Nam-ok moved into No. 15 Residence to become the boy's full-time playmate and Kim Jong-il's "adopted daughter." In a 1998 interview with the prestigious Japanese monthly *Bungei Shunju* she offered further details on life in the household, beyond those provided by her older brother Il-nam. (The brother had been only a visitor in the palace. He was usually away — first at a North Korean boarding school and eventually in Moscow, where he continued his studies while living with his ailing aunt Song Hye-rim.) "We did not use dollar bills for wallpaper, but we did have a very comfortable life," Li Nam-ok said. "Kim Jong-il was a man who loved a comfortable life."

Nam-ok's mother and grandmother, who were Jong-nam's aunt and grandmother, also moved in. The boy's aunt became his teacher. The grandmother looked after him for a while, but as he grew older and livelier it was hard for her to keep up. "After that I was by him all the time," Nam-ok said.

Otherwise, Jong-nam's isolation continued. "We sometimes went around the city in a chauffeur-driven Benz, but we were not allowed to get out of the car," she said. "Attendants always came with us when we went outside." Still, she thought her cousin had some idea of the reality of the common people's lives. "We could make guesses by looking at people from a moving car. Besides, there were employees at the official residence and we could hear stories from them. Jong-nam was a very curious person. My view is that he knows a lot."

Kim Jong-nam "has a good mind and sense of humor," Nam-ok said. "He is very energetic. He is a permanent optimist and a pleasant young man who can laugh all day long from morning to evening. He also has an artistic sense like his father's." Jong-nam, she added, "was a very early riser and led a well-regulated life. He always found something to do. He liked to draw pictures when young. He watched movies and read many books." Like his father, Jong-nam loved watching movies and videos for days on end. He "was very much interested in taking videos, too."

When her interviewers asked how the boy had reacted to being isolated in the palace, Nam-ok said he had accepted the situation "because that was what his father had decided for him. He was totally submissive to his father and never criticized what Kim Jong-il decided for him." Jong-nam's mother, her aunt, "was prone to sickness and was often away from home in Moscow for medical treatments. But Kim Jong-il poured his very deep love into his son in childhood, so I don't think the child felt lonely. His mother's absence was covered up by his father's presence. Besides, he did get to see his mother on a regular basis." Kim Jong-il occasionally shouted at the children when they disobeyed but he always had a reason for raising his voice and he never used violence at home.

Kim Jong-il encouraged his son's play with toy battleships and guns — all North Korean boys were expected to be militaristic in their play. He even gave the boy a real pistol at one point, instructing him to keep it locked up in his safe when he was not training with it. Jong-nam became "a sharpshooter," according to his cousin. Kim Jong-il encouraged the children to exercise so that they could grow taller. "He was very proud of his son, who is tall," Nam-ok said.[13]

Kim Jong-il did have other family responsibilities elsewhere, even beyond the official family he had established with Kim Yong-suk, with whom he had a daughter. He got involved with a woman named Ko Yong-hui and in 1981 she gave birth to a son, Kim Jong-chol. The Dear Leader and Ko set up yet another mansion household. Jealous members of the Song family took to calling Papa's new favorite "Hammer Nose."[14]

Coincidentally or not, it was around then that Kim Jong-nam was sent abroad for schooling. In 1980 he briefly tried one Soviet school but complained that the toilets were too dirty. Thereafter, he alternately attended

Swiss and Soviet schools. For a while the boy posed as the son of the North Korean ambassador to Switzerland. Already good at mathematics, he eventually became fluent in French, English and Russian. Accompanying him were his cousin Nam-ok and her mother. His mother generally was with them when they lived in Moscow and Geneva. They lived comfortably in villas in those cities and Song Hye-rim was able to save substantial sums out of what Kim Jong-il gave her. The youngsters habitually returned to Pyongyang during school vacations.[15]

The children were exposed to non-North Korean news media—in Geneva, to Western media—and what they saw by no means always agreed with Pyongyang's official version of events. However, Nam-ok said, "when there were contradictions between what he had been told in Pyongyang and what he learned in Geneva, Jong-nam wanted to believe in what he had been told in his country because he was loyal to his father and to the Motherland. When something happened and North Korea was blamed for it, North Korea always denied the accusation, and he believed what North Korea said."[16]

Kim Jong-nam saw little of his grandfather in person as he was growing up. According to some analysts, this was because of the Great Leader's disapproval—or feeling that he should disapprove—of the illicit relationship in which the boy had been conceived. Li Nam-ok said she did not know Kim Il-sung's thinking, having met him only once as a little girl when she was chosen to present flowers to him. For whatever reason, she said, the youngster saw his grandfather "not at all." She suggested that the decision was more Kim Jong-il's than Kim Il-sung's: "Probably Kim Jong-il did not want to show his private life to his father."[17]

According to Nam-ok's older brother, Il-nam, Kim Jong-il found an opportunity to clear up the question of his first son's pedigree. Kim Il-sung had fathered a boy with his young nurse and turned to Jong-il to advise on how to handle the potentially messy situation. Kim Jong-il arranged for his newborn half-brother, who was named Hyon, to be registered as the son of one of the siblings of Chang Song-taek, Jong-il's brother-in-law and confidant. That instance of male bonding between first and second generations boded well for the status of the third. When told of Kim Jong-nam's existence the Great Leader, according to Li Il-nam, "was angry at first, but he could not be harsh" in view of his own situation. Kim Il-sung, meeting Kim Jong-nam for the first time when the boy was a chubby and jolly four-year-old, "immediately liked him and gave him the name Jong-nam." He recognized the child as his first grandson, although he never acknowledged the boy's mother as his daughter-in-law.[18]

* * *

After he left school in Switzerland and returned to Pyongyang, Kim Jong-nam—a young man by then—still found himself isolated in his home, tightly restricted as to when he could leave the house and where he could go.

Cousin Li Nam-ok defected to Europe in 1992 "to live my own life." In her interview with *Bungei Shunju,* the Japanese magazine, she told of an incident that occurred shortly before her defection in which Kim Jong-il cut off the food supplies to their mansion, because she and Jong-nam had gone out without permission. Kim Jong-il was so strict because, she explained, he "wanted to keep his private life hidden from the eyes of the public." The Dear Leader "did not like other people to talk about him and make him a target of gossip or rumor," she said. "He did not want people to know that he lived with my aunt or that he had a child from her. He did not like to draw attention."

She seemed to hint that there might be some truth in reports that the young man at that stage in his life was undisciplined, and that Kim Jong-il was trying to rein in his son's hell-raising. "No doubt there was a change in his attitude toward his son," she said. But she put it in the context of East Asian child-rearing practices, in which children typically find their parents catering to their every whim or tantrum—and then reach an age at which suddenly they are expected to learn to live by society's rules. "Jong-nam being no longer a six-year-old kid, Kim Jong-il decided he should deal more strictly with, and demand more of, his son. In that sense his attitude did change, but I do not think that meant he did not love his son anymore." If her analysis was correct, note that Jong-nam by the time Kim Jong-il cracked down on him was already around twenty. The more usual age for undergoing such a forced transformation would be five or six.[19]

Defector Kang Myong-do, son-in-law of a prime minister, said that Kim Jong-nam during his early manhood, like his father before him, had become known for showing too much of a liking for cars, nightlife and women. Kang told the South Korean newspaper *JoongAng Ilbo* that in 1993 a rumor went around among the Pyongyang elite that Jong-nam had grabbed his bodyguard's gun and pointed it at another man with whom he was quarreling publicly over a woman.[20]

I heard from Oh Young-nam, a former captain in State Security, what Oh described as his own eyewitness account of not only one but two gunplay incidents. Oh's family home was across the street from Pyongyang's Koryo Hotel, he said. Lesser beings outside the young prince's circle who used the Koryo Hotel coffee shop "had to bow to Kim Jong-nam and leave the shop" whenever he entered. "We did not like the extravagant way that Kim Jong-nam lived," Oh told me. "I know Kim Jong-nam. He is younger than I am. Kim Jong-nam wears a military-style uniform even though he was not in any part of the service. He just dresses like that. On his shoulder flaps he wears four stars, suggesting he's head of the joint chiefs. He goes around flaunting his power, saying he'll be the next after Kim Jong-il. I didn't like the way Kim Jong-il ran the country, but I couldn't imagine Kim Jong-nam taking over.

"He's violent. On April 26, 1993, the day after the anniversary of the establishment of the Korean People's Army, Kim Jong-nam drank heavily, went to the Koryo Hotel and shot the place up. A cabbie had parked in Kim Jong-nam's special parking place. King Jong-nam drove up in his car — license number 216822 — and parked just behind the taxi." (Having been a traffic policeman, Oh had no difficulty remembering and spotting cars.) "Then he went in and shot up the ceiling of the lobby. After that he found the driver and kicked him in the shin." Oh witnessed the incident because, he said, "I walked across from my house to take a taxi, and that was when Kim Jong-nam roared up and started shooting."

On the second occasion, "around June of 1994 Kim Jong-nam went to the disco and started shooting. That night, I was there at the nightclub. Actually I was with Kang Myong-do's nephew. The manager of the nightclub was formerly part of the bodyguard service. I believe Kim Jong-nam and the manager had a relationship. Kim Jong-nam came in and shouted for everyone to leave. People like me did not leave so fast — I was irritated at this younger guy making such a demand. Kim Jong-nam is very rash, very impudent. Out of frustration, he started shooting.

"Kim Jong-nam continued to visit the coffee shop at the Koryo every day. Then he would go to the forty-fourth-floor restaurant of the hotel. Choe Yong-lim, who fought with Kim Jong-nam in the nightclub incident, is in prison now."

Oh's wife worked at the cashier's counter in the Koryo coffee shop, he told me. "One tower of the Koryo is for guests, the other for bodyguards. Kim Jong-il comes through the back door, the bodyguards' private entrance. The sixteenth floor in the right tower is exclusively for Kim Jong-il. Among Kim Jong-il's other children, his daughter also came often to the Koryo. She drove herself and didn't make a fuss."

Li Nam-ok said she never saw any explicit sign that Kim Jong-il planned for Kim Jong-nam to inherit his power. "Of course Jong-nam is Jong-il's eldest son, and it is always the oldest son who succeeds to the house," she told *Bungei Shunju*. Thus Jong-nam was educated "to have self-awareness and sense of responsibility as the oldest son. But I cannot think preparations were being made for a transfer of power. Even if Kim Jong-il was warming up that thinking in his heart, he never would have revealed that to anyone else. I personally have great doubts he had that thinking."

Indeed, it seemed logical from what we knew of Kim Jong-il that he would not have made any overt moves to position his son or anyone else as his successor as long as Kim Il-sung remained alive. After all, a period of testing as his own father's successor remained before he could consider his consolidation of power totally successful. The image of the selfless, absolutely filial son that he projected before and after Kim Il-sung's death was subject to being tarnished if too many secrets of his private life became widely known. Such considerations might help to explain why he was determined to keep Jong-nam under wraps, at least for the time being.

And then there was the fact that Kim Jong-nam's family background left something to be desired. Aside from the scandalous aspects of his parents' original liaison, relatives on the maternal side had developed the intensely disloyal habit of defecting. The first to jump was male cousin Li Il-nam, who disappeared in 1982 while in Switzerland. Although the fact escaped public notice, he defected through the South Korean embassy there and moved to South Korea. There he underwent plastic surgery and changed his name. Over the succeeding years he told the authorities much of what he knew about Kim Jong-il and his household.

In 1992 Li Nam-ok, tired of being locked up in the fenced mansion compound with her cousin, made her own break, to Europe. "I'd wanted to study," she explained later. "But there was no way to learn or to work in North Korea. I'd just wanted to choose my own life."[21] For several years before then, Kim Jong-nam had not even visited his mother in Moscow. There was suspicion among his relatives that Kim Jong-il had intensified his son's confinement out of fear the young man also would defect.[22]

The Seoul authorities found Li Il-nam a good job with a broadcasting organization but he gave it up to go into business. The business failed. Adjudged a bankrupt, he served ten months in prison.[23] In his effort to start again, Li Il-nam needed money. Having spoken not a word to his mother in ten years, he phoned her in Moscow and encouraged her to defect and publish a tell-all memoir. For her the notion was by no means out of the question. She had grown tired of the surveillance to which her family was subjected, even in Moscow. Il-nam taped his phone conversations with her, perhaps hoping to use what she told him in his own attempt to make money by showing himself once again as someone who possessed fresh and valuable information about North Korea.[24]

Li's mother, Kim Jong-nam's aunt Song Hye-rang, did defect to an undisclosed country in the West. Out of the surviving members of the Song family only Kim Jong-nam and his mother, Song Hye-rim, did *not* defect. (The grandmother had died and been buried in North Korea.) Although a flurry of press dispatches at the time her sister defected claimed that Hye-rim had gone with Hye-rang, in fact she continued to live in Moscow until she died in May 2002. Her niece explained that the former movie star had stayed put out of consideration for the future of her son, Kim Jong-nam.[25]

According to one report it was on Kim Jong-nam's twenty-fourth birthday in 1995 that Kim Jong-il gave him a People's Army uniform with general's badges. Thenceforth Jong-nam was addressed as "Comrade General." According to Lee Kyo-kwan, Pyongyang watcher for the Seoul newspaper *Chosun Ilbo*, the gesture had to do with a supposed incident in the early 1990s when Kim Il-sung, Kim Jong-il and Kim Jong-nam visited Mount Paektu together. Jong-nam's horsemanship impressed the old man, who supposedly remarked, "Another general has been born in our family." In North Korea, a successor would need a personality cult, and this story has the ring of propaganda devised for that purpose.

Kim Jong-nam as he grew up was by all accounts an enthusiastic computer geek, especially fond of electronic games. In his late twenties, some say in 1998, in recognition of his skills and interests in information technology he was named chairman of the country's Computer Committee. And around 1997 he reportedly took up the study of economics; his aunt Kim Kyong-hui, Kim Jong-il's younger sister, tutored him, passing along some of what she had learned as director of the Workers' Party Light Industry Department. Before his death, Kim Il-sung was concerned that the ruling family find a way to compensate for Kim Jong-il's lack of economic expertise, and was said to have suggested that Jong-nam "study economics to lead the nation."

Note that the four-year-old boy who traveled with Kim Jong-nam in May of 2001 would have been born in 1996 or 1997. As fixated as Kim Jong-il appeared to be on the subject of male heirs, it seems possible he might have taken the birth of his first grandson as a signal to draw closer to the child's father and start preparing him for an eventual succession. Kim Jong-nam perhaps had started to settle down a bit by then, in keeping with his new paternal role; his wife and son often traveled with him when he went abroad.

In 1998 someone bearing the name Kim Jong-nam but otherwise unidentified was elected Supreme People's Assembly delegate for constituency number 685. Jong-nam was occasionally sighted in filmed documentaries, accompanying his father on visits to local areas to provide guidance. So was his younger half-sister, Kim Sol-song, born in 1974 to Kim Jong-il's recognized wife Kim Yong-suk. Sol-song reportedly was trained in economics.[26]

Kim Jong-il gave his son sensitive posts in the army, the secret police and the party. Jong-nam became an instructor in the central party's Propaganda and Agitation Bureau, then got an additional job with the Organization and Guidance Bureau. The Young General got to pull rank in a high-level job in the Security Bureau of the Ministry of People's Armed Forces. He also began climbing the ladder at the State Security Ministry. His mentor there was a three-star general who had been one of his father's Kim Il-sung University classmates. His special assignment at State Security starting around 1999 was to deal with the increase in defectors and refugees, according to reported testimony by Lee Young-guk, who had been one of Kim Jong-il's bodyguards before he defected.[27]

The South Korean monthly *Wolgan Choson* suggested that Kim Jong-nam himself, upset at seeing his family's dirty laundry aired abroad, ordered the assassination of his defector cousin Li Il-nam. Li was ambushed and fatally shot on February 15, 1997, in a suburb of Seoul. South Korean authorities later said they had learned that hit men sent by Pyongyang had done the job. The magazine's claim of Kim Jong-nam's involvement did not refer to those who had actually done the shooting but to a team that Jong-nam allegedly had ordered to kill his cousin earlier; the earlier team was said to have failed, whereupon its leader—a major general named Jang Pong-rim—had been executed as punishment for that failure.[28]

In 1996, as his mother was making her break as a defector, Li had emerged from seclusion and published his book on Kim Jong-il's family life.[29] His killing seemed intended in part to retaliate against South Korea and to demonstrate Pyongyang's long reach immediately following the high-level defection of Hwang Jang-yop, an enormous loss of face for Kim Jong-il. But it was also a reminder to Song Hye-rang and her surviving child, daughter Li Nam-ok, wherever in the world they might be hiding, to be careful about what they might say regarding Kim Jong-il's private life.

There was no smoking gun with Kim Jong-nam's fingerprints on it. The evidence the magazine offered for his involvement in the alleged earlier, aborted attempt on his cousin's life was contained in a memorandum from an unnamed North Korean defector in China.[30] One might wonder whether, by early 1997, the Young General really was in a position to send minions off on such a deadly and sensitive mission abroad. There were reports that Kim Jong-nam began working in State Security as early as 1996, although according to Lee Young-guk's account it would be two or three years before Jong-nam would take charge of defector and refugee issues. And according to a high South Korean government official quoted by *JoongAng Ilbo*, "Kim Jong-nam traveled in Europe with five young women, without any particular task," until early 1999. A State Security job that he took at that point was "the first step related to the succession," that official was quoted as saying.[31]

Starting around 2000, the regime began publicly mentioning Kim Jong-nam in ways that suggested big things were expected of him. In August of that year the first group of South Koreans who had been separated from their family members in the North arrived in Pyongyang for a visit. A guide showing them the Juche Tower said Kim Jong-nam had designed it.[32] In April 2001, when pro-Pyongyang Koreans from Japan traveled to North Korea to celebrate Kim Il-sung's birthday, a party official surprised them by delivering a lecture on Kim Jong-nam's "outstanding qualities," *Newsweek International* reported.[33]

A human rights activist, reporting on a trend toward moderating the punishments inflicted on North Koreans caught trying to escape to China, told *Chosun Ilbo* that authorities had explained released prisoners' good fortune by telling them: "You owe all this to Kim Jong-nam."[34] Easing the policy against defectors might well have seemed a no-brainer to someone who had as many defectors in his family as Kim Jong-nam still had, even after the murder of Li Il-nam. Still, it appears that the relaxation—which probably encouraged more escapes—was short-lived. In January 2003 Chinese police caught seventy-eight North Korean refugees who were planning to travel by ship to South Korea and Japan. A Los Angeles–based Christian minister involved in the aborted scheme asserted in Tokyo that Kim Jong-nam at the time was "in Beijing, taking care of the refugee roundup."[35]

When Kim Jong-nam got caught at Narita Airport, some analysts suggested it would be the end of his chances to become the next Great Leader. The argument was that he had embarrassed his father, who at the time was playing host to a large group of European Union officials. Kim Jong-il reportedly canceled a trip that he had planned to China's booming Shenzhen special economic zone—a journey on which Jong-nam had been scheduled to accompany him. They had planned to leave May 7, just three days after the Japanese deported their illegal visitor.[36]

Indeed, Kim Jong-nam seems subsequently to have spent quite a lot of his time traveling and living abroad. Seoul's *Chosun Ilbo*, quoting an intelligence source in Seoul, reported in September 2002 that he had never set foot in North Korea in the more than a year following his expulsion from Japan, "probably because he has lost the confidence of the North Korean leader."[37] A Japanese daily, *Sankei Shimbun*, reported in 2002 that he had been making frequent trips to Moscow, where he dressed casually as a tourist, spent time with a young Russian woman and in general seemed to be on vacation rather than working.[38] When he was not in Russia, it appeared he was living in a villa on the outskirts of Beijing.

We might well wonder how much leadership, budding or otherwise, Kim Jong-nam could exert back home while spending so much of his time globetrotting and shopping. Any one of the high-level jobs he had been said to hold in his father's regime could require a full-time commitment.

On the other hand, some of Kim Jong-nam's travels might have been an expression of the Confucian filial piety that Kim Jong-il often went out of his way to promote. Song Hye-rim was dying in Moscow, and apparently her son spent much of his time in that city. Using a Russian first name and the surname Oh, Song had been in and out of a downtown hospital before she was taken there the final time on May 17, 2001. After her funeral in a Moscow cemetery, ethnic Koreans reported watching Kim Jong-nam send off his wife and son on a flight to Beijing.[39]

In any case, traveling incognito was something that Kim Jong-il himself had done, as he had hinted to Kim Dae-jung in 2000,[40] so he should have been aware it was risky behavior. Besides the mere fact that Kim Jong-nam got caught, and thereby focused media attention on the secretive Kim Jong-il's private affairs, it would seem the son while in Japan did nothing extraordinarily embarrassing to his father. Indeed, Kim Jong-nam showed himself very much his father's son in some of his interests at home and abroad.

"Chairman Kim and his son are similar not only in appearance but also in personality," Jong-nam's defector aunt, Song Hye-rang, told a South Korean magazine in 2000. "Their similarities include being hot-tempered, sensitive and gifted in arts. Kim Jong-nam is an excellent writer. Since he was young, he has written movie scripts and made movies." Kim Jong-il even had a small movie set built for Jong-nam to practice with, she said.[41]

Japanese news articles reported speculation that Kim Jong-nam's visits to Tokyo were not only for sightseeing but also for his education—either as heir to the leadership or as head of North Korea's push to develop information technology and build high-tech weaponry. Other news reports said he had begun traveling to Japan incognito as early as 1995, when members of Chongryon met him at the airport and escorted him on sightseeing excursions that took him to Tokyo Disneyland, among other places.[42]

Shukan Shincho, one of Japan's popular weeklies, eventually reported that the young North Korean had become a familiar figure at a Korean nightclub in the Akasaka entertainment district and at a bathhouse in Yoshiwara, a red light district in the Japanese capital. A bathhouse attendant, described as "curvaceous," was quoted as saying he had visited her before his ill-fated May 2001 trip. When his picture appeared in the news media, she said, she recognized him as an enthusiastic customer. "He visited the shop and asked for me three days in a row," the woman said.

The customer, a big tipper who paid with a credit card, told her that he did business in Hong Kong. "He showed me photos of his children and invited me to accompany him to Chinatown in Yokohama, but I begged off," she said. "Who knows? There's all that talk about Japanese being abducted to North Korea; it might have happened to me, too." The masseuse said the man she called "Wong" had a tattoo of a dragon on his back. The magazine quoted a Tokyo-based Pyongyang-watcher as saying Kim Jong-nam had such a tattoo.[43]

An article in a sister publication, *Shincho 45,* told of another Tokyo nightlife worker, a Korean who said she had spent a night with Kim Jong-nam in 1998. The woman painted a picture of a classic East Asian big spender at table. Kim, she said, sang Japanese songs until he was covered with sweat. He ate three plates of flounder sashimi, washing it down with many glasses of Hennessey Extra cognac. She said he reminded her of a yakuza godfather in the movies, speaking softly and slowly and treating her politely and with respect. She was impressed with his Japanese language ability and his knowledge of Japanese culture.[44]

What were we to make of the Young General? He might be considered just a tad undisciplined, by the standards normally applied to rising world leaders. But let's play optimist one more time and consider the half-full glass analogy. At least the youthful jet setter had somewhat more experience than his father with the realities of the outside world—indeed, it appeared he was a linguist. And he had that affinity for high technology. A dispatch by South Korea's wire service when he was detained at Narita airport put it this way: "Diplomatic sources say that although he is not thorough in personality, he has a certain degree of knowledge in international affairs and state-of-the-art industry."[45]

Still, it seemed worth noting that Jong-nam's aunt in an interview with a South Korean magazine in 2000 said flatly that her nephew "does not wish to succeed his father." Kim Jong-il, she said, "seized power not because he is the son" of Kim Il-sung. "It is because he was the most capable person and he could carry on President Kim's task better than anyone else. However, hereditary governance is against the true nature of socialism and his mother does not want it, either."[46]

We might well doubt that Kim Jong-il would wish at such a late stage to alter the North Korean tradition of father-to-son inheritance, which he had helped to establish. But it also seemed important to recall that Jong-il's raw desire for power and his strength at behind-the-scenes maneuvering had been important factors in his ultimately being named Kim Il-sung's heir. He might be looking over his own youngsters to see which if any of them displayed that fire in the belly that American political commentators look for as a sign that a U.S. presidential candidate is prepared to do whatever it takes to get elected.

Thus various analysts suggested that the succession would go not to Kim Jong-nam but to another of Kim Jong-il's children. Daughters were never mentioned in those scenarios. Confucian tradition would militate against naming a woman, and the propaganda about the third generation specifically mentioned grandsons.

One supposed candidate who was put forward was a newly discovered "son" of Kim Jong-il's named Kim Hyon or Kim Hyon-nam, whose mother was unidentified. The Japanese wire service Jiji Press in September 2002, citing unnamed sources in Beijing, reported that Kim Hyon, thirty years old, had been appointed head of the Propaganda and Agitation Department of the Workers' Party. Actually it seems likely that Jiji got the story at least partly wrong and that Kim Hyon was not Kim Jong-il's son at all but Kim Il-sung's secret, late-life progeny. Recall the elder Kim's child by his nurse, a boy named Hyon, whose future Kim Jong-il undertook to arrange in tacit exchange for his father's recognition of his own son, Jong-nam.

Was there any propaganda that might be intended to prepare for the rule of another son of Kim Il-sung? An article in *Nodong Shinmun* whose focus was praise of Kim Jong-il said he "accomplished the heavy task given by history that can be shouldered and discharged only by a partisan's son." Of course a half-brother of Kim Jong-il's also would be "a partisan's son," whether acknowledged by his father or not. But that article was the same one that pointed to succession by a grandson.[47]

In any case, it might seem a long shot that Kim Jong-il, having fought his uncle Kim Yong-ju and half-brother Kim Pyong-il for the top job, would pass over his own offspring and name a younger and illegitimate half-brother as his heir. If Kim Hyon was indeed Kim Il-sung's love child, his career in service of the regime—like that of my old acquaintance Kim Jong-su—seemed unlikely to place him at center stage.

Seemingly closer to the mark were the analysts who suggested the succession would go to one of the sons of Kim Jong-il's third wife, Ko Yong-hui.[48] Those theories were based in part on the reported fact that Ko was Kim Jong-il's favorite among his live-in women. Envious relatives of Jong-nam's in Moscow and Seoul noted in one 1990s telephone conversation that "Hammer Nose" was living well, apparently getting better treatment than Papa accorded Jong-nam's mother.[49] In Confucian societies, it had often happened that a favored junior wife or concubine maneuvered to have her son chosen over the first-born as heir. (Recall that Kim Il-sung's last wife was reported to have initiated such an effort on behalf of her son Kim Pyong-il. Perhaps she might have succeeded if her stepson Kim Jong-il had not, as former official Kang Myong-do told me, attacked her power base directly by introducing his father to two new women.[50])

Ko Yong-hui by most accounts was born in Osaka of a Korean family that had migrated to Japan from Cheju island, off the southern tip of the Korean peninsula. Her parents reportedly took her with them to North Korea around 1961, during the great homecoming of Koreans from Japan. There she became a folk dancer, working in the Mansudae Art Troupe, the country's most prestigious. According to the Japanese magazine *Aera*, she met Kim Jong-il in the mid-1970s when she performed at a party he hosted. She gave birth to their first son, Kim Jong-chol, in 1981, a second son, Kim Jong-un, two years later and a daughter after another four years.

One argument against taking either of Ko's sons seriously as a possible heir was that Kim Jong-chol and Kim Jong-un were not long out of college. But Kim Jong-il himself had started his career at a rather high level, straight from university. His father might already have had him in mind as heir at that time.

An intelligence source cited by Seoul's *Chosun Ilbo* described Kim Jong-chol as an intelligent young man who had studied in France. He was reported to have begun work in the central Workers' Party apparatus.[51] Other sources said he had studied in Switzerland at an international school, watched over by the North Korean ambassador—and there had developed a passion for American NBA basketball. Oh Young-nam thought he had studied in Singapore.

Even less was known of Kim Jong-un, said to be two years younger than Jong-chol. In early 2003 a Japanese chef, who said he had traveled to Pyongyang frequently to cook for Kim Jong-il at home, talked about the two sons on television. He told Japanese viewers that, in contrast to his polite elder brother, the younger lad when very small exhibited to strangers a suspicious mien. Jong-un's glaring ferocity, the chef said, pleased Kim Jong-il.[52] The chef said Papa had indicated he would not choose Jong-un's elder brother because he considered Jong-chol too girlish. Being mean, after all, could help round out the résumé of a dictator in waiting.

Ko Yong-hui's own family background might have seemed a negative influence on her children's prospects, in view of the dismal fate of other returned Japanese-Korean families. In the end, though, if Kim Jong-il said someone had a good family background, then the definition of "good" simply changed. As we have seen in chapter 36, the old doctrine of placing the working class first was on its way out and the moneyed class—which included many Japanese-Korean families—was becoming recognized as valuable to the country.

From Kim's point of view as a leader obsessed with propaganda and hard currency, Ko's family background might seem ideal. First, as a migrant from Japan she might be presumed to have some influence with the remaining Korean residents of Japan, whose money Kim Jong-il continued to covet. Additionally, her father's reported birthplace near Mount Halla on Cheju island would fit nicely with a pro-reunification slogan Pyongyang had spouted for several years: "From Mount Paektu to Mount Halla." The vision was of a single, united Korea stretching from the northern tip of the Korean peninsula, where Kim Jong-il allegedly was born, to the southern tip. The slogan was thus seen in some quarters as a device either originally intended or later adapted to further the development of a personality cult centering on Ko and, through her, one of her sons.

❊ ❊ ❊

With that background, consider an August 2002 article published by North Korea's People's Army Publishing Company entitled, "The Respected Mother is the Most Faithful and Loyal Subject to the Dear Leader Comrade Supreme Commander." The South Korean monthly *Wolgan Choson*, which told the rest of the world about the article in its March 2003 issue, reported that several experts believed it referred to Ko Yong-hui.

It could not refer to Kim Jong-nam's mother, Song Hye-rim, because she was dead; the language indicated a live person, the magazine's experts said. The unnamed *omonim*, or "Respected Mother," according to the People's Army article, was "the most faithful of the faithful." She "devotes herself to the personal safety of the Comrade Supreme Commander," Kim Jong-il. "Accompanying the Comrade Supreme Commander, she has climbed front-line hills for over eight years." Kim Jong-il himself was quoted as saying of her, "She understands me deeper than anyone else, devotes herself to me. It is utter happiness to have someone like her right beside me."

Respected Mother was boundlessly considerate of the troops of the People's Army. Knowing that the country was in a "difficult" situation, she showed her concern by asking if soldiers had enough soap and other essentials. Like Kim Jong-il as a young marksman accompanying his father, and like Kim Jong-il's own, deified mother, *omonim* was portrayed as a fine shot, free with advice to soldiers on how to shoot better with small arms. "You should hit a moving object," she was said to exhort the soldiers she visited.

Why could all that not apply to Kim Yong-suk, who had been recognized as Kim Jong-il's wife by his father? The analysts' thinking seemed to be that Kim Yong-suk had been dumped, more or less, and wasn't getting as much quality time as Ko Yong-hui with the Dear Comrade Supreme Commander. The magazine quoted high-level defector Hwang Jang-yop as saying, "An heir must be the child of a woman a king loves, and it is true that Kim Jong-il loves Ko Yong-hui most."[53]

Note that the eight years during which *omonim* was said to have been accompanying Kim Jong-il on visits to front-line military units would have begun almost precisely at the moment in July 1994 when Kim Il-sung died. Possibly Kim Jong-il had hesitated to show Ko Yong-hui off publicly before then, for fear of sparking an uncomfortable discussion of family values with his dad. Now that he himself was the Dear Comrade Supreme Commander, however, he could arrange for public opinion to shift to recognize as his consort whomever he might choose.

The South Korean magazine's expert consultants focused particularly on a phrase in the People's Army article that said the unnamed Respected Mother "assists the Comrade Supreme Commander closest to his body." That seemed to be a reference to a wife or concubine, they argued. And if legal wife Kim Yong-suk was intended, they wondered, why wouldn't the propagandists come right out and name her?

A further argument for assuming that Respected Mother was not Kim Jong-il's recognized wife Kim Yong-suk was that there would be no need to deify a woman whose child could not expect to be named heir. Kim Yong-suk had only a daughter. The propaganda about a third-generation succession specifically mentioned a grandson of Kim Il-sung.

Respected Mother, then—like the Glorious Party Center of the 1970s— was supposed to be recognized and deferred to first, identified only later after people got used to the idea that there was a new deity in town.

Ko Yong-hui fell ill of cancer and died in August 2004. Since she would no longer be around to press the succession case of a son, foreign analysts had to refigure the odds. I considered a long shot: What if Kim Jong-il looked over his offspring and judged daughter Sol-song—who, as we saw earlier, had been accompanying him and advising him on his guidance trips—the most competent and "loyal" of the lot? An article in the leading South Korean daily *Chosun Ilbo* had quoted an unnamed source who described Sol-song not only as her father's frequent companion on his trips to offer on-the-spot guidance but as the apple of Papa's eye. Beautiful (resembling her mother, official wife Kim Yong-suk), Sol-song was also beloved of her father "because of her good and kind nature," the paper's source said. She was modest. As a political economy student at Kim Il-sung University, she had insisted on alighting from her car a hundred meters before reaching the campus, then walking the rest of the way so that she would not appear to put on airs as the Leader's daughter.

Add that Sol-song, born in 1974, was considered an economic specialist. The article didn't mention the likelihood that her college training in that field might be no better than her father's, since she graduated in his department at KISU. But maybe she had a private tutor. Maybe under an assumed name she had joined one of the groups of North Koreans who went to study Western-style business administration in Australia.

In any case, *Chosun Ilbo*'s source said that Kim Jong-il on his guidance trips "is often seen asking Sol-song, who is standing behind him, what her opinion is, after receiving a briefing from the supervisor. The scenes of father and daughter exchanging questions and answers on economy occasionally appear in North Korean documentary films." The paper's account concluded: "Some view the fact that both Sol-song and Jong-nam accompany Kim Jong-il on his on-the-spot inspections as grooming them for their separate roles as the regime's successors." Like her aunt, Kim Jong-il's sister Kim Kyong-hui, the light-industries boss for the party, "Sol-song could take charge of the economic sector."[54]

Indeed, thinking from Kim Jong-il's point of view, why not anoint her as Respected Mother (maybe she was such a good daughter she trimmed his toenails, thus assisting him "closest to his body")? Then Sol-song could eventually reign—alone or in combination with the Young General or another half-sibling. It would be a simple matter to order the propagandists to adjust the late Great Leader's alleged remark about a grandson to make the word read, thenceforth, "grandchild" or "grandchildren." Designating a daughter as heir would be in line with efforts Kim Jong-il had made early in his career to reduce discrimination against women. And—no small matter to him—he would have the satisfaction of having outsmarted, once again, most of the people who presumed to figure him out.

The Asian royal model that Kim Jong-il told Madeleine Albright he was interested in emulating, Thailand, had been a limited rather than absolute monarchy since a 1932 revolution. Still, while living there as a Peace Corps volunteer in the 1960s and then decades later as a journalist, I encountered a deep-seated, old-fashioned popular reverence for the royal family. The king from time to time would call in feuding politicians and lecture them, insisting that they straighten out messes they had created and look to the welfare of the people. Agonizing over the monumental traffic jams caused whenever a royal entourage took to the streets of Bangkok during rush hour, he might suggest construction of a new expressway or river bridge. But for the most part he left the management of the country to a prime minister chosen by a more or less democratically elected parliament.

I was not confident Kim Jong-il personally could make an easy transition from absolute monarch to Thai-style limited monarch—although the limited role might have been what he thought he was playing in 1996 when he bemoaned the poor work of subordinates he had entrusted to take care of the economy. It seemed more likely that a younger representative of the dynasty—perhaps one of those who had been educated, like Thailand's King Bhumibol Adulyadej, in Switzerland—could make a go of it.

On the off chance that Kim Jong-il might summon me to Pyongyang as a consultant advising him how to apply the Thai model, I drafted a memo for him:

> Permit me to summarize the points I made in yesterday's discussion, Mr. Chairman. I advised that if your son Jong-un is as ferocious as we have heard he is, you should pass him over as your successor. Pardon me for the odious comparison, but Saddam Hussein chose Uday and Qusay—and look where they are now. Since your intention is to choose a modern, limited monarch instead of a dictator, you should pick not the toughest[55] but the most humane candidate. The chosen successor should then work ceaselessly and devotedly to improve the people's welfare.

In Thailand, as I told you, the people are especially fond of one of His Majesty King Bhumipol's daughters. But while the rather saintly Princess Sirinthorn is hugely admired for her charitable good works, her older brother is first in line to succeed to the throne at the conclusion of the reign of the deeply beloved present king.

In the case of the DPKK (Democratic People's Kingdom of Korea—I hope I'm not getting ahead of myself here) you have not publicized a formal choice and therefore you are still in a position to consider elevating your own reputedly modest daughter, Sol-song. With her knowledge of the economic issues that are so important to your subjects, she might become a monarch who could win hearts and minds.

Assuming that your daughter is of the caliber of the Thai princess, you could even avoid the expense of cranking up a brand-new propaganda campaign to create reverence for her. How? When instructing young writers I often pass along (in addition, of course, to your own trenchant observations on the importance of grasping the "seed" of a work) the advice that they "show us; don't tell us." By applying that same principle to statecraft, showing her greatness rather than telling about it, your daughter could inspire the people to recycle the old propaganda slogans on their own initiative. That way they would continue to believe in the slogans despite intrusion of the sort of foreign influences that otherwise might incline them to disbelief. "Under the Loving Care of the Motherly Leader" has a nice ring to it, don't you think?[56]

I do not know much about the other candidates. Perhaps one of them is better cast as Respected and Beloved Leader than your daughter. I simply suggest, strongly, that in judging all of them you use this criterion of humanity.

As we discussed, the second point is that crowning your designated heir sooner rather than later could improve the prospects that the economic transformation would succeed and the Kim dynasty survive—perhaps even for thousands of years, as those immortal lyrics from *Song of Paradise* envision. Once out from under the worst of the present economic and diplomatic crisis, having delegated to competent and trusted officials the task of running the country, you could abdicate and retire to Cannes—or even to Hollywood, assuming a breakthrough in relations with the United States.

So there you have it, Mr. Chairman. On a personal note, I am full of gratitude for your very kind hospitality. The guesthouse was wonderfully appointed, and my lack of appetite at dinner last night certainly was no reflection on the quality of the cuisine, which was magnificent. (I imagine I simply had not adjusted to the time difference.) The karaoke party was great fun, all the ladies truly lovely. Please convey my parting regards especially to Miss Choe, along with my regrets that I was not in a position to accept your very generous offer of her hand in marriage. About my consulting fee: I took your sage advice and confided to your bursar my plan to donate the amount to an aid foundation. When he realized it would be coming back to your country in that fashion he agreed to pay me in real dollars this time, instead of Super-Ks.

Well, I see that my vehicle is waiting in the tunnel to take me back. Goodbye, Mr. Chairman. May the future bring great things for you and your people.

EPILOGUE

Pyongyang, October 2005

Just as the paperback edition was about to go to press, I received permission to visit Pyongyang, for the first time since 1992. I went as a member of a Western journalists' tour group. We saw the same old tourist sites plus a few new ones that had been added. Under those circumstances especially, North Korea seemed in many ways to be a land that had stood still. On the Air Koryo plane from Beijing, many of the North Korean passengers avidly perused the Pyongyang newspapers and magazines that the cabin staff passed out. It seemed the old propaganda remained potent, at least with the "loyal" class. In the capital itself, tens of thousands of apparently devoted subjects in the May Day Stadium performed "mass games" in a hugely expensive, elaborately synchronized celebration of the wonders wrought by the Kims. It was much like what I had seen at the 1989 youth festival.

One of our group's three young interpreters was Pang Yu-gyong, a twenty-year-old university English student and granddaughter of a former chief of internal security, who was planning to work as a military interpreter after graduation and already called us all—male and female alike— "sir." One day I mentioned to her that I would be writing a magazine article for prospective investors. I asked why the tour did not highlight economic changes in the capital. Weren't our hosts missing an opportunity by restricting us to the usual cultural-political sites? "Sir," she replied with apparently sincere puzzlement, "how do you want Pyongyang to change?"

On the third day of the visit we rode south to Kaesong. Farmers along the way had continued contour plowing of steep hillsides, without taking the precaution of terracing, just as they had done for decades on the instruction of the late Kim Il-sung. It was as if the floods that had washed those rocky, deforested hillsides into the plains below had not helped cause the deadly famine of the 1990s and left the farmers with the mammoth task of clearing rocks and poor hillside soil from paddies, fields, and waterways. I could not help wondering: Do these people never learn? Meanwhile, I saw far less farm mechanization than I had observed in 1979. The paucity of fuel seemed to have left most tractors and other farm machines rusting in storage sheds while humans and oxen did the heavy work. All three of Kim Il-sung's vaunted agricultural achievements—mechanization, electrification and irrigation—seemed to have suffered serious setbacks, at best.

Eventually, closer examination and talks with resident foreigners did turn up evidence of some of the real changes I had heard about from others since my previous visits. Big public markets had sprung up in cities and towns, down to the county seat level, offering foodstuffs and predominantly Chinese consumer goods. We were not permitted to see those because, our hosts said, the markets were closed so that urbanites could help bring in the harvest and celebrate the Workers' Party's sixtieth anniversary—the occasion for the Arirang festival to which we had been invited. Still, we could see that increased trade had brought more disposable income to some urban dwellers, putting more cars, motorbikes and bicycles on the newly repaved main streets of Pyongyang and packing new restaurants with diners. The government had, as reported in Chapter 36, adjusted official foreign exchange rates to price the local currency closer to black market rates, although there remained a huge gap.

Citizens had started businesses—restaurants, street kiosks—on state-owned real estate. Richard Ragan, resident chief for the UN's World Food Program, told of an entrepreneur to whom Kim Jong-il had assigned an empty building next to Pyongyang's Juche Tower, a prime tourist location. The budding businessman then had gone to Singapore, met a sympathetic trader through other North Koreans doing business there and borrowed—with no collateral—forty thousand U.S. dollars' worth of goods needed to start a restaurant and karaoke bar. Ragan had visited the packed and thriving shop in the company of the Singaporean businessman, who had similar tales to tell about other North Korean clients.

Ragan had first visited Pyongyang in 1996 as a Clinton administration National Security Council staffer and "found it completely abysmal," he said. "I traveled all over the country and there were no signs whatsoever of a market economy. You would travel down the road and you'd see somebody dash out with cigarettes or whatever." Because "it was a crime to be involved in commercial activities," he recalled, "they'd disappear when they saw you. Now at all the rest stops there are people selling." Estimates of how many traders were involved countrywide as of late 2005, he said, ranged from 150,000 to 500,000.

Nevertheless, it was obvious that many in the North Korean establishment had not reached the point of being sufficiently pleased with the new economic system to call attention to it. Indeed, our interpreter and guide Miss Pang insisted that there was "no private business." She said the street stalls selling ice cream, soft drinks, and sweets were all units of state-owned enterprises. Ragan, on the other hand, said he understood that shops, street stalls and market stalls could be run by individuals but had to be licensed. They apparently paid taxes or tariffs back to the state in return for permission to operate and become productive, he said, because "the state owns everything."

With the new wage system in state-connected organizations, the authorities had sought to pay more to hard workers and achievers, less to slackers and incompetents. Employees of two organizations, a film studio and a local government office, replied vaguely when we asked how the new system worked. At an embroidery-arts studio, however, we were told that, while employees were never fired, the ones who were not performing up to expectations did not get raises. Finding themselves unable to live on their minuscule salaries—equivalent at black market rates to less than a dollar a month—they eventually quit and went elsewhere to try to make more money.

A project was under way to build a special economic zone at Kaesong, the ancient capital that had changed hands in the Korean War and ended up on the northern side of the Demilitarized Zone. Our group was not permitted to inspect the dozen factories operating or nearing completion there, but viewed the zone's vague skyline from a bridge a mile or so away. The Kaesong city official who escorted us, Choe Kyong-jin, either was not aware or was reluctant to say that a primary motivation of South Korean companies investing in the zone was to take advantage of low-priced North Korean labor. Rather than labor cost savings, he pointed to expected savings in transport costs—because finished goods from factories in the zone could be sent by railway across North Korea, China, and Russia to Europe. "Of course we have different systems, but North Korea and South Korea are one nation," Choe said. Asked which system he preferred, socialism or capitalism, he replied: "Socialism, of course."

Few of the North Koreans I was permitted to meet talked with real enthusiasm about free markets. What outsiders called reforms our Miss Pang described as simply adjustments to a basically sound socialist system. More significantly, the regime appeared to have slammed the brakes on change for the time being—or even to have shifted into reverse. In one major signal, the authorities had told most foreign organizations providing food aid to stop doing so, asking that they shift their contributions instead to economic development aid. Pyongyang cited a bumper harvest—the best in many years and roughly estimated at ten percent bigger than the previous year's harvest—as the main justification. Pointing out that North Korea had once been a donor country itself, officials had explained that the government was concerned lest a "culture of dependency" develop. But they also had acknowledged the regime was tired of having foreigners roaming the countryside in intrusive attempts at monitoring to assure that food aid went to those for whom it was intended. The agencies scrambled to redefine some of their handouts as "transitional" development aid so that some of their people could stay on.

Perhaps a stronger signal was that the much-diminished official grain rationing system was being restored, and private grain sales, which had constituted much of the business of the public markets, had just been banned. Restored grain rationing was an idea that foreigners would not necessarily oppose, as an expedient for dealing with out-of-control inflation, Ragan said, "if it works, and people are able to get a fair ration." The price of rice had risen so high—between three hundred and seven hundred won per kilogram, out of a typical salary of perhaps two thousand won a month—that only the best-connected and most resourceful North Koreans could readily make ends meet. On the other hand, a Western diplomat said he had been told by a North Korean foreign ministry official that the move was an attempt to squeeze out traders and speculators. The diplomat's analysis was that the North Koreans were trying a halfway version of market economics, and realized that the incentives the state gave farmers were far less than the speculators and traders had provided. "Maybe they think prices are too high. Maybe they think these guys are getting too big for their boots." The pattern seemed to be that the state tolerated grassroots experiments until they threatened to get out of hand, then pulled back to socialist fundamentals.

Still, rather than a complete abandonment of economic reform policies, the shift signaled "that they're grappling with how to deal with an emerging economy," Ragan said. He pointed to the somewhat reassuring precedent of China's experience. "I lived in China in the nineties, really the period when reform started kicking in," he said. "That was a thirty-year process, basically. You've got a lot of the same dynamics here." Far from enjoying a smooth trajectory of reform, he noted, the Chinese "have gone through all kinds of fits and starts."

On balance, the visit made me somewhat less optimistic about the prospects that Pyongyang would soon agree to relinquish its nuclear weapons program in order to become a more or less normal member of the world economy. While it seemed true that the leadership wanted a better relationship with the United States, to me an overriding perception was of the North Korean elite's stubborn determination to maintain the basics of the system that the

Kims had built. I had to wonder whether the United States, in particular, would have the patience to keep trying to chip away at Pyongyang's hard façade for as long as it might take to reach an agreement.

An obvious example of the regime's reluctance, or inability, to change was its maintenance of Pyongyang as a showcase city whose function was to impress foreigners and reward the North Korean loyalists who were entitled to live there. The city was lit up with so many neon signs during our stay that a visitor could have imagined himself in Las Vegas, and we experienced only one momentary power cut during our four-day stay. But even at the World Food Program headquarters in Pyongyang, said Ragan, "we still have brownouts. We run generators." And he said the interior of the country remained extremely short of power. The disparity between Pyongyang and the rest of the country was "huge," he said, "like night and day." He added, "Get out of the southern rice basket and you're in the mountains. Only eighteen percent of the country is arable." North of Pyongyang in the blighted Hamgyong provinces, the climate was inhospitable, there were few paved roads, energy was scarce, and the economy was generally poor.

There seemed to have been another construction boom in Pyongyang— but again it had thrown up showy structures that had little to do with economic development. We saw some grandiose monuments—the Workers' Party monument, the Unification Arch, the Tower of Immortality ("Kim Il-sung is always with us")—that had been built since my 1992 visit, with scarce funds that could instead have put food on many a table. On television one evening I saw Kim Jong-il, in dark glasses, making the rounds of a number of projects to offer on-the-spot guidance, mostly talking and gesturing, seldom listening. At least one factory was included on his rounds, but what really appeared to animate the Dear Leader was his visit to a new concert hall featuring a lot of marble and a pipe organ. Remaining totally in character, he lingered there, enthusiastically offering comments on the architectural details and the finish. If Kim was planning to become North Korea's Deng Xiaoping or Park Chung-hee and preside over an economic takeoff, he was taking his own sweet time about it.

The North Korean leadership clearly remained determined not to follow the examples of countries, such as Russia, where political change had preceded or accompanied economic policy shifts and thrown up new elites, which ultimately had challenged the entrenched communist party apparatus. The message our hosts most wanted to convey, I felt, was: "We're back. We're strong. We're not going to cave pathetically, like Libya." The Arirang festival performances were heavily loaded with militaristic imagery, including a scene depicting "female warriors, blooming like azaleas" and celebrations of Kim Jong-il's *songun*—military first—policy. Unable to point to great achievements by Kim in bringing prosperity to the people, the show's producers had fallen back on praising his vaunted ability to keep at bay a far more powerful enemy. "Thanks to the leader, we are enjoying a free and independent life," spectators were told.

Like the Chinese Communist Party, North Korea's leaders intended to keep their power indefinitely—apparently, at any cost to the economy. For example: North Korea had established mobile telephone service—and then confiscated phones purchased by its citizens, for fear their increased communication with one another and outsiders was undermining the regime's control. By the time of my visit, only foreigners were permitted to carry cell phones, and the landline phone system had been segmented so that citizens could call only fellow North Koreans and foreigners could call only foreigners. As a Western diplomat said: "This is a country which has survived, thrived on its own isolation. They're determined to keep that."

The regime's extreme caution suggested that it could be a long time before the country moved into the ranks of Asia's economic tigers. Success in ongoing six-country negotiations to end its nuclear weapons program might well speed up the process, but failure in those talks probably would lead the United States to press for additional sanctions that could nip the changes in the bud. As I visited, Washington was offering a taste of what it might have in store if the talks failed. The U.S. Treasury Department had accused a bank in the former Portuguese colony, now Chinese special region, of Macau, Banco Delta Asia, of laundering money on behalf of North Korean smuggling and counterfeiting interests. The Treasury action had effectively tied up millions of dollars of deposits by both North Korean entities and foreign companies doing business in Pyongyang. This was one economic matter that resonated with Miss Pang. "Sir, your country stopped assets in the bank," she complained to me.

I would have preferred to end this epilogue on a more positive note, but clearly there were difficult times ahead for both the North Koreans and the outsiders who sought to deal with and make sense of them. I could only hope that the North Koreans would manage enough flexibility, and the Americans, Japanese, and others enough patience, to put pessimism to flight.

ACKNOWLEDGMENTS

This book has been thirteen years in the making. I received major help and encouragement over those years from Hideko Takayama. She spotted and translated pertinent materials, conducted some interviews for me, shared her own articles done for *Newsweek* and other publications—even sent a telegram to my mountain hideout, which was unequipped with phone or TV, to alert me when Kim Il-sung died. I am deeply grateful for all her many contributions.

I began with the notion of writing about Koreans in the South as well as the North. Richard Halloran, who invited me to the East-West Center in Honolulu as journalist in residence for the 1991–1992 academic year, fortuitously suggested as an interim project a comparison of my findings during visits to North Korea in 1979, 1989 and 1992. In the process of sorting out what had changed in the country over that span of years (which was precious little, as I reported in a 1993 EWC publication, *Intruding on the Hermit: Glimpses of North Korea*) I concluded that simply getting North Korea right would be a sufficient challenge. Others who were helpful in Honolulu included Muthiah Alagappa, Lee-Jay Cho, Admiral Ronald Hays, Robert Hewett, Meheroo Jussawalla, James Kelly, Charles Morrison, Michel Oksenberg, Professor Glenn Page, John Schidlovsky, Professor Dae-sook Suh, William Wise, Mark Valencia and Caroline Yang. For terrific staff support I am grateful to June Sakaba, Laura Miho and Lear Budinger.

In 1992 I received a Fulbright grant for research in Seoul. Professors Auh Taik-sup at Korea University and Lee Manwoo at Kyungnam University's Institute for Far Eastern Studies generously provided affiliation and facilities. Korea Fulbright staff members, especially then–Executive Director Frederick Carriere and Deputy Executive Director Shim Jai-ok, were enormously helpful.

Although I studied Korean intensively under the excellent teachers at Seoul's Language Training Research Center, a working level of fluency was but a distant dream. Rhee Soo-mi (whom my old friend Professor Kim Young-seok of Yonsei University recommended for the assignment) served brilliantly for several years as my principal Korean interpreter and translator. Others who ably undertook such work for me included Meehee Park Burton, Jungeun Kim and my former *Newsweek* colleague Lee Young-ho. Sydney A. Seiler generously shared with me his translations of Korean-language materials and a manuscript version of his book.

Kim Il-sung in his memoirs recalled a bit of family lore from his father's childhood. A village schoolteacher, often in his cups, repeatedly sent pupils to buy wine for him. The boy who was to become the future Great Leader's father obeyed meekly for a while, but lost his respect for the teacher one day when he saw him fall facedown in a ditch on his way home. The next time the teacher sent him off with a bottle to get a refill, the boy intentionally smashed the bottle on a rock outside the school. Then he told the teacher he had tripped while being chased by a tiger. The pupil's father, Kim's paternal grandfather, heard of the incident and observed: "If pupils peep into their teacher's private life frequently, they lose their awe of him. The teacher must give his pupils the firm belief that their teacher neither eats nor urinates; only then can he maintain his authority at school." A teacher, Kim's grandfather added, "should set up a screen and live behind it."

The rule is all the more important for a dictator. After his rise to power, Kim adopted with a vengeance the notion that an authority figure must live behind a screen. His son, Kim Jong-il, did the same. Indeed, the two men placed the entire country behind a screen. My task has been to try to see through, or around, those screens. Since the use of such standard reporting methods as on-scene observation was severely restricted, I turned to propaganda analysis—which often meant reading between the lines of officially disseminated stories like the one just quoted. But I needed more, and I found the third leg of a methodological tripod in defector interviews. I spoke at length with fifty former Northerners, mainly during the mid- to late 1990s.

The use of defector testimony is controversial. This is particularly the case among American scholars of a certain group. The fact literally came home to me one summer evening in 1994 when some Dinner Guests from Hell ganged up to mount a vicious verbal assault on my bona fides (even as they ate my barbecue). Evidently I had set them off when I innocently started to hold forth on what interesting and important things I was learning in defector interviews. The evening fell apart completely when I spoke approvingly of another American scholar, not present, who had used defector testimony extensively in his work. "That puts you completely beyond the pale," snapped the man who had assembled the war party on my veranda. Perhaps I should thank those people. That experience of being blindsided sent me reeling to the library. I read for years to catch up and keep up on the scholarly and ideological disputes that swirl around the Korea question. The book probably is better for it, although at the time I would have preferred friendly, constructive criticism.

Anyhow, I offer here full disclosure of the circumstances of my defector interviews and leave it to the reader to judge the information thus obtained and the ways I have used it. First, I acknowledge with thanks the help of the South Korean Ministry of Information and its Korean Overseas Information Service in arranging many of those meetings. I needed the help of KOIS staff members because, until defectors completed their official debriefings, South Korean security authorities had charge of them and required that they be accompanied on any outings by government minders. (I was told that this was partly for the benefit of the defectors, who were new to the country—but then, that was how my Pyongyang minders had justified accompanying me everywhere during my visits to North Korea.) Some of those police personnel waited in anterooms; others sat in on the interviews while displaying varying degrees of interest or boredom. I remember only one case when a handler's presence became intrusive and I had to ask him to let the defector speak for himself.

It would seem natural if some defectors tried to please South Korean officials by emphasizing aspects of their knowledge that most interested their hosts. Thus I wondered what to make of it when, in several of my interviews, defectors volunteered negative information about Kim Jong-il before I asked. I inquired of another, elite defector, Oh Young-nam (whose minder was off getting a haircut at the time), whether intelligence authorities were encouraging such remarks. "No," he replied. "They don't urge you to say anything. I heard they did it in the past to some extent, but I didn't get that kind of impression." (When a defector exaggerated, it was on that defector's own initiative, in the hope of becoming "a star in South Korea," Oh also told me—insisting that he himself did not do such a thing.) There were a few other cases when interviewees wondered aloud whether they should give straight answers to my questions (answers that, as it turned out, would tend to show aspects of North Korea or its leaders in a positive light). I can report that their minders in all such cases promptly assured them that they should.

I make no claim that the former Northerners I spoke with constituted a scientific sample. For a while, though, I probably was speaking with the majority of the recent arrivals. My KOIS contacts knew that I was interested in meeting former political prisoners, officials, military people and broadgauged people in general—but also anyone who could shed light on the lives of ordinary people. They knew, as well, that I was engaged in a book project that would take some time, and that I did not place top priority on angling for news scoops concerning, say, the status of North Korean programs for developing weapons of mass destruction.

KOIS staff members did some culling. They advised me on occasion, for example, that so-and-so, who had just defected, reportedly had proven in official debriefings to be not very talkative or interesting—and thus I might be wasting my time if I met that person. In no case did I discover later that a defector whom KOIS officials had flagged as probably less worthwhile as an interviewee had gone on to say important things to other interviewers, whether Korean or foreign.

Of course, I was cognizant at all times that spin of one sort or another could be involved in the help I was receiving. Without dictating to a defector what he should say, for example, the South Korean authorities could try to determine the most opportune time to present him to the public. After all, while finding the truth was my goal (and again, it's up to the reader to judge the extent to which I found it or failed to find it), polishing the image of South Korea and promoting the policies of its government constituted the main work of KOIS. What I can point out, though, is that it was a time when democratically elected governments sought especially to show that the bad old days, when many official fabrications and manipulations of information had been justified on grounds of anti-communism, were past. Any spin that furthered that goal of theirs, I calculated, might also further mine.

Eventually, I heard that the pendulum had swung so far that the Kim Dae-jung administration had taken to discouraging defectors from giving interviews for fear they would antagonize Pyongyang and cloud the "sunshine" policy. The Roh Moo-hyun administration reportedly continued such a policy. I had pretty much completed the defector-interviewing phase of my research by then, fortunately.

There were, in fact, a couple of high-level defectors whom I was not able to interview because they were under wraps for whatever reasons at the times I tried to meet them. One was Hwang Jang-yop. (I had met and spoken with Hwang briefly at a Tokyo reception just days *before* his 1997 defection. He had not, alas, revealed his defection plans to me and the other two foreign correspondents questioning him that evening. But in hindsight I thought he had seemed to be under some strain—perhaps on account of the swarm of minders surrounding him, who quickly spirited him away before he could say much of anything to us. That line of thinking occurred to me after it came out that Hwang had hoped to defect while in Japan, but had not been able to shake the people watching him—and so had waited and made his escape after arriving in Beijing, en route home to Pyongyang.) Following his defection, fortunately, Hwang wrote prolifically for publication.

One further note: I learned that the practice of KOIS, when arranging for foreign reporters to meet defectors, was to provide each interviewee a per diem "transportation fee" of 100,000 *won*, the equivalent of something under $100. Although such modest compensation of interviewees for their trouble was accepted as normal in the East Asian context, to put money and interviewing together always raises a caution flag in American journalistic ethics. I was not in a position to change the system, but I did undertake payment of the fees out of my pocket (in envelopes that I personally handed to the defectors when the interviews were over) in order to avoid having the South Korean government subsidize my research.

Speaking of subsidies, the financing of my project hit a dry spell after my Fulbright grant expired in 1993. I hereby offer thanks to my lucky stars, and to the gods of Wall Street, for the fact that timely bets—first on Southeast Asian and later on Russian stock funds—produced returns sufficient to permit continued work on the book until I returned to full-time newspaper work for *Asia Times* in 1995, and to resume work on it after the newspaper ceased print publication in 1997.

I am grateful for the opportunity to work on the book at Dartmouth College in 2002 as "distinguished journalist in residence" at the John Sloan Dickey Center for International Understanding. Thanks to Prof. Michael Mastanduno of Dartmouth, Prof. Joseph Massey of the Tuck School of Business and Margot E. de l'Etoile, who keeps the center humming, for making possible a very productive period. Special thanks go to Dartmouth professor David C. Kang, an old colleague from my Seoul Fulbright days, who put me forward for the Dickey fellowship. Dave also read and commented on huge chunks of the manuscript and was otherwise endlessly helpful and encouraging.

At Ohio University's E. W. Scripps School of Journalism in 2002–2003, and since then at Louisiana State University's Manship School of Mass Communication, I have spent practically every waking, non-teaching moment working on the book. I acknowledge with thanks the financial support of the Scripps-Howard Foundation and (through the LSU Foundation) of the Manship family and the State of Louisiana's Board of Regents. I am grateful also for the help and patience of my colleagues and students at both universities.

Among friends offering valuable encouragement when I decided to try my hand at producing a book, William Chapman, former *Washington Post* Tokyo bureau chief, was the author of a volume about Japan that I greatly admired. Daunted by the prospect of undertaking such a huge effort, I asked Bill how I might come up with an overall theme. (I had not yet learned Kim Jong-il's term, "seed.") "Just report," he told me, "and then go back and try to figure out what it all adds up to." In our journalistic trade, as Bill did not need to remind me, the worst thing we could say about another reporter was that he or she never let the facts get in the way of a good story.

I followed Bill Chapman's advice, gratefully, and he helped again when he introduced me to the New York literary agency Scovil Chichak Galen.

Jack Scovil made Herculean efforts to interest publishers in my partial manuscript. When one after another told him that Americans weren't very interested in reading about Korea, he refused to give up. He told me later that he had lost sleep worrying that *Under the Loving Care of the Fatherly Leader* might go unpublished. Jack finally found the perfect publisher, and a highly perceptive editor, in Tom Dunne. I am deeply grateful to both men for making it all happen. My appreciation goes also to Sean Desmond, my editor at Thomas Dunne Books, who has done a bang-up job of shepherding the book into print, and to the impressively meticulous production editor, Mark Steven Long.

Thanks to Ray Downs, Richard Read and Mike Tharp for providing helpful comments on the manuscript.

At the Seoul home of Jack and Meehee Burton, the sofa bed always awaited me. I am deeply grateful for their friendship and warm hospitality. In Seoul I also received valuable help from, among others, Prof. Ahn Byung-joon, Prof. Ahn Chung-si, Michael Breen, Dr. Cha Yong-koo, Prof. Chay Pyung-gil, Chi Jung-nam, Cho Gab-je, R. S. C. Gimenez, Jean-Jacques Grauhar, Kenneth Kaliher, Dr. Kil Jeong-woo, Kim Chang-soon, Dr. Kim Choong-nam, Kim Key-man, Dr. Kim Kyung-won, Kim Yong-min, Amb. Juergen Kleiner, Catherine Lee, Lee Dong-bok, Dr. Lee Hong-koo, Shim Jae-hoon, Christopher Torchia, Kate Webb, Won Yong-chol, Dr. Yang Sung-chul, Yoo Kun-il and Alexander Z. Zhebin.

United States officials and former officials who helped out included Desaix Anderson, Amb. Stephen Bosworth, Steve Bradner, David E. Brown, Hugh Burleson, Richard Christenson, Jim Coles III, Bruce Donahue, Edward Dong, Rust Deming, Amb. Donald Gregg, Morton Holbrook, Amb. Thomas Hubbard, Amb. Charles Kartman, Jim Keith, William H. Maurer Jr., Aloysius M. O'Neill III, David Pierce, James Pierce, Larry Robinson, Danny Russel, Steve Rounds, Jack Sears and David Straub.

Old friend Park Shin-il called upon members of his vast network of colleagues to lend assistance. South Korean officials and former officials who were particularly helpful included Byun Chang-yull, Hwang Hyon-tak, Kim Myong-sik, Kim Ryu, Park Jung-ho, Park Sung-soo, Shin On, Sohn Woo-hyun, Suh Sang-myun, Yang Yun-kil, Yi Chan-yong and Yoo Il-han.

In Japan I had help from, among others, Takao Goto, Richard C. Hanson, Lee Hyon-suk, Prof. Lee Young-hwa, Yoshiko Matsushita, Katsuko Saito, Katsumi Sato, Kim Myong-chol, Larry Kelly, Mark Schreiber, Geoffrey Tudor and the staff of The Foreign Correspondents' Club of Japan.

Elsewhere I had valuable help from Greyson Bryan, former congressman George "Buddy" Darden, Dr. Young S. Kim, Stephen W. Linton, Leonid Petrov and John Einer Sandvand. Thanks to all of those.

Going way back, I remember with gratitude William Carter, especially, and the other gifted public school teachers in Marietta, Georgia, who taught me to write, including Iris Collins, Imogene Keck, Christine Hutcheson and Clara Nolen. A passion for history came over me after I arrived at Princeton, where I studied under such great professors as David Herbert Donald, Eric F. Goldman, James M. McPherson and—my initial guide to Asia—Frederick W. Mote. (Two decades later, thanks to the Professional Journalism Fellowships—now John S. Knight Fellowships—program, I had the opportunity to study with outstanding Asia experts on the Stanford faculty including Masahiko Aoki, Peter Duus, Harry Harding, John W. Lewis, Melinda Takeuchi and Robert Ward.)

Finally, Angsana Saengsawang rates special mention for her unflagging support and for putting up with my many absences from our home in Bangkok. And to my son Alexander K. T. Martin go my congratulations that he has turned out to be such a fine young man, even though the book soaked up too much of the parenting that should have gone to him during his boyhood.

I'm sure I have overlooked someone I should be singling out for public thanks. I apologize for that. Of course neither the people named nor the many other benefactors who go unnamed—the latter group including North Korean and Chongryon officials to whom I am grateful for help with information or arrangements—are to blame for shortcomings in the book. For those I am totally responsible.

Bangkok, July 8, 2004

Two foundation grants following publication of the first edition enabled me to do additional research, first on American opinions of North Korea and later on getting information into North Korea. For those I am grateful to University of Hawaii Professor Dae-Sook Suh and his Research Institute for Korean Affairs, and to Dr. Choong-nam Kim and Dr. Lee-jay Cho of the East-West Center in Honolulu and the POSCO Foundation. I also thank my EWC colleagues and, especially, Susan S. Campbell for help and friendship during a very rewarding Hawaiian summer.

Tokyo, October 21, 2005

NOTES

Prologue.

1. Quotations are from H. G. Wells, *The Time Machine: An Invention,* edited by Nicholas Ruddick (Peterborough, Ontario: Broadview Literary Texts, 2001).

1. To the City of the God-King.

1. While many visitors to Pyongyang have suspected as I did that actors and actresses were performing as ordinary citizens, it would have been hard to prove. But a diligent search undertaken by a Seoul-based newsletter may have unearthed the smoking gun. *Korea Countdown* (published by Breen & Gustaveson Consulting, Ltd.) stated in its August 1994 issue that its editors had found two places in Kim Il-sung's own writings where Kim complained, in so many words, that the "actresses" who lined Pyongyang streets to greet foreign VIPs were not giving a good enough impression. Alas, the newsletter did not cite the specific passages.

   Evidently the North Koreans learned from the Soviet Union the idea of using a subway to impress visitors. American Gen. Mark Clark in 1954 related "the old tale of the American engineers who visited Moscow" and were shown the Moscow Metro: "The Americans were astounded. They had never seen such a clean subway, so well appointed and so beautified with murals. Finally an American said: 'This is wonderful, beautiful, much better than anything we have at home. But we have been here thirty minutes now and haven't seen a single train, or a customer. Tell me, when do the trains run?' 'Ah, ah, ah,' admonished the Russian host, 'how about your lynchings in the South?'" (Clark, *From the Danube to the Yalu* [New York: Harper & Brothers, 1954], p. 34).

2. Byoung-Lo Philo Kim, *Two Koreas in Development: A Comparative Study of Principles and Strategies of Capitalist and Communist Third World Development* (New Brunswick, N.J.: Transaction Publishers, 1992), pp. 169–170.

3. Being put on night trains turned out to be the rule rather than the exception. I found on my later trips to North Korea that the authorities booked foreign visitors on night trains most of the time—perhaps because there were sights they did not want us to see.

4. He spelled his surname "Bai" in the Roman alphabet, and pronounced it "Bye." That name (also transcribed as "Pai") is fairly common among Chinese, but the more usual Korean surname is pronounced something like "bag" without the *g* and is usually Romanized as "Bae" or "Pae."

5. Author's interview with a student at Kim Il-sung University.

6. Officials mentioned the president's busy schedule of on-the-spot guidance as the reason he would not be able to meet me during my stay.

7. Kim Il-sung, "Educate Students to Be Genuine Successors of Socialist and Communist Construction," speech to a meeting of educational workers on March 14, 1968, cited in Park Yon-hon, "Cultural Policy of North Korea," *Vantage Point* (August 1979), p. 10.

8. *Theory of Public Education* (Pyongyang: Social Science Publishing House, 1975), pp. 115–121, cited in Park, "Cultural Policy," p. 8. While the North Korean state under Kim took the leading role in education and tried to eliminate clan groupings that had underlain the old order, it did leave the nuclear family more or less intact. See Charles K. Armstrong, *The North Korean Revolution, 1945–1950* (Ithaca, N.Y.: Cornell University Press, 2003), pp. 97–98.

9. Chango Machyo, deputy national political commissioner of the secretariat of the National Resistance Movement of Uganda, quoted in "DPRK President's Reminiscences Disseminated Worldwide," *People's Korea* (pro–North Korean newspaper published in Tokyo), December 25, 1993. High-ranking cadres in North Korea get their own, more accurate news from a daily compilation that is circulated internally, not for the eyes of ordinary people. This seems to resemble the printed daily news briefing from his aides that U.S. President George W. Bush was reported to rely on in lieu of a personal reading of the newspapers.

10. I attended some of those sessions in Tokyo. They were small gatherings made up primarily of people associated with the Old or New Left. By the end of 1992, according to a South Korean government count, North Korea had established 1,687 propaganda organizations in 132 countries (*Korea Herald*, June 19, 1993).

11. Quoted in an abstract of an article by Prof. Song Min-ho of Korea University in Seoul, "Characteristics of North Korean Literature," *Vantage Point* (June 1978): p. 14.

12. Almost as North Koreans came to do in the case of Kim Il-sung, the Japanese reverently ascribed unlimited benevolence to their emperor, as shown, for example, by a government document issued after the Great Kanto Earthquake of 1923: "September 4th, 1923. H.M. the Emperor, sympathizing with the hard lot of the subjects in the afflicted districts, graciously bestowed a substantial sum of money from the privy purse in aid of the sufferers' relief funds, through the Prince Regent. Premier Count Yamamoto, deeply impressed by the gracious Imperial donation, issued a proclamation addressed to the nation (Cabinet Proclamation dated Sept. 4), in which he called the attention of the nation to the benevolence and profound concern of the Imperial House for the interests of the

nation" (*The Great Earthquake of 1923 in Japan* [Tokyo: Bureau of Social Affairs, Home Office, 1926], p. 16). I am grateful to Geoffrey Tudor for sending me a copy.

Asia shows other examples of worship of the ruler. In Thailand, for example, lese majesty is among the most serious of crimes. The cult of Mao Zedong in China was an obvious prototype for Kim's cult, although most observers believe it was a case in which the student, Kim, outdid his teacher, Mao, in carrying things to an extreme. The most direct inspiration for both the Chinese and the North Korean leader cults was the cult of Stalin. For an excellent discussion highlighting Stalinism's contributions to the system that Kim Il-sung built, see Adrian Buzo, *The Guerilla Dynasty: Politics and Leadership in North Korea* (St. Leonards, Australia: Allen & Unwin, 1999), pp. 28–56.

2. Fighters and Psalmists.

1. Hwang Jang-yop, *The Problems of Human Rights in North Korea (I)*, trans. Network for North Korean Democracy and Human Rights (Seoul: NKnet, 2000), http://nknet.org/enknet/data/hwang1-1.htm.

2. Kim Il Sung's *With the Century* was published serially by Pyongyang's Foreign Languages Publishing House. The first two volumes were released in limited numbers in 1992, in Korean as well as in English and Japanese translations. Volumes 3 and 4 were published in 1993, volume 5 in 1994 and volume 6 in 1995. Those six volumes (which apparently had only small printings in the English version and are difficult to find outside North Korea) take Kim's story from his birth in 1912 up to the late 1930s, when he was a guerrilla commander in Manchuria. Page references here to those volumes are to the English version.

Thanks to Kim's newfound concern for accuracy, *With the Century* is a very important and welcome new resource. Nonetheless, in an attempt to produce a truthful account for presentation in the present work, I have found it necessary even with these relatively forthright memoirs to hack through embellishments, anecdotes that do not ring true and out-and-out prevarications that range from minor fibs to Big Lies in which Kim claims that he defeated the Japanese to liberate Korea, and that the Americans and South Koreans started and then lost the Korean War. Part of the winnowing process involved comparing Kim's latest claims with his earlier ones and with the findings of outside scholars, whose works are cited at appropriate points.

In the preface (vol. 1), Kim described the genesis of the work as follows: "Now that a large part of my work is done by Secretary for Organizational Affairs Kim Jong-il, I have been able to find some time. With the change of generations, veteran revolutionaries have departed from this life and the new generation has become the pillar of our revolution. I came to think that it was my duty to tell of the experiences I have gained in the common cause of the nation and of how our revolutionary forerunners gave their lives in their youth for this day. So I came to put down in writing what has happened in my life, a few lines each time I found a spare moment."

Be that as it may, he clearly had considerable help with the memoirs, as Hwang suggested. An Omaha, Nebraska, pathologist, Won Tai Sohn, Kim's friend from Jilin days, told a U.S. newspaper interviewer that during one of his

1990s visits to Pyongyang a professor from North Korea's History Research Institute had tagged along for every meeting, taking notes on the Great Leader's recollections as the conversations progressed. See Geraldine Brooks, "Two Old Friends: One Became a Doctor, the Other a Dictator," *Asian Wall Street Journal,* September 19, 1994.

Whether his helpers merely researched and edited the work or, as seems more likely, actually ghostwrote it, their contributions are evident in the provision of considerably detailed historical background for periods and episodes touched upon by Kim—background that even the all-powerful North Korean leader would not likely have had at his fingertips, even if he had enjoyed the leisure to pore over his records. For example, when Kim describes his transfer to Yuwen Middle School in Jilin in January 1927 (vol. 1, p. 208), he refers to the files of a Chinese newspaper, *Jizhang Ribao,* for accounts of the school that had appeared in its pages years before his enrollment.

One helper allegedly was South Korean dissident novelist Hwang Suk-young, who visited North Korea numerous times without his government's permission while living abroad in the 1980s and '90s. When he returned to South Korea in 1993, professing satisfaction that President Kim Young-sam had inaugurated a "civilian" regime after the years of military-backed government, Hwang was arrested, tried and sentenced to seven years' imprisonment for violating the national security law. One of the charges was that during his final stay of six months in the North he had "participated in the writing" of *With the Century,* which the prosecution deemed "a pro-enemy publication praising Kim Il-sung and North Korea" ([South] Korean Overseas Information Service, *Backgrounder,* October 12, 1994).

Perhaps thanks to the involvement of such professionals as novelist Hwang, much of *With the Century* is a cracking good read, laced with adventure sequences, humorous anecdotes and vignettes of people Kim encountered.

For more on the significance of the early volumes of the memoirs see Bradley Martin, "Remaking Kim's Image," *Far Eastern Economic Review,* April 15, 1993, or the author's similar Korean-language article, "Revisionism in Pyongyang," *Newsweek Hankuk-pan,* April 1, 1993.

As for later volumes of the memoir, which were published in Korean posthumously, there is additional reason for skepticism about accuracy. Those go to great lengths to present claims designed to build up the personality cult of Kim Jong-il, who after his father's death was in complete charge and thus in position to shape the account as he wished.

3. There is precedent among his communist forebears. Stalin had been a Russian Orthodox seminarian. I am grateful to George L. Olson, a retired Lutheran missionary who spent his career working in East Asia, for pointing this out to me. "Some people say communism is a heresy of Christianity," Olson noted, because the two share "a lot of the social emphasis."

4. Kim, *With the Century* (see chap. 2, n. 2), vol. 1, p. 6.

5. Kim offered a different version of what had happened. "When the U.S. imperialist aggressors' ship *General Sherman* sailed up the River Taedong and anchored at Turu Islet," he wrote, "my great-grandfather, together with some other villagers, collected ropes from all the houses and stretched them across the river between Konyu Islet and Mangyong Hill; then they rolled some stones into the water to block the way of the pirate ship. When he heard that the *General Sherman*

had sailed up to Yanggak Islet and was killing the people there with its cannons and guns, and that its crew were stealing the people's possessions and raping the women, he rushed to the walled city of Pyongyang at the head of the villagers. The people of the city, with the government army, loaded a lot of small boats with firewood, tied them together, set them on fire and floated them down towards the aggressor ship, so that the American ship was set on fire and sank with all hands. I was told that my grandfather played a major role in this attack" (*With the Century,* vol. 1, p. 10).

6. See Fred Harvey Harrington, "An American View of Korean-American Relations," in Yur-Bok Lee and Wayne Patterson, eds., *One Hundred Years of Korean-American Relations, 1882–1982* (Tuscaloosa, Ala.: University of Alabama Press, 1986), pp. 46–54. "Martyred on the bank of the Taedong River" is the description of the missionary, Rev. Robert J. Thomas, in the dedication to Thomas J. Belke, *Juche: A Christian Study of North Korea's State Religion* (Bartlesville, Okla.: Living Sacrifice Book Company, 1999). For a Korean scholar's version, marshaling evidence that the expedition's main goal was to rob tombs of their valuables, see Yongkoo Kim, *The Five Years' Crisis, 1866–1871: Korea in the Maelstrom of Western Imperialism* (Inchon, Korea: Circle, 2001).

7. From Kang Myong-do's testimony, compiled by Tae Won-ki in a twelve-part series in the Seoul daily *JoongAng Ilbo,* starting April 12, 1995.

8. "The monthly tuition fee at Sungsil Middle School at the time was two *won.* To earn two *won* my mother went to the River Sunhwa and collected shellfish to sell. My grandfather grew melons, my grandmother young radishes, and even my uncle who was only 15 years old made straw sandals to earn money to help his elder brother with his school fees. My father worked after school until dusk in a workshop run by the school to earn money. Then he would read books for hours in the school library before returning home late at night" (Kim, *With the Century,* vol. 1, p. 9).

9. Ibid., pp. 7–8. (Korean women keep their birth names after marriage.)

10. Ibid., vol. 1, p. 7.

11. Ibid., vol. 2, pp. 83–84.

12. Only later, in the 1920s and '30s, did the Japanese manage to co-opt large numbers of Koreans.

13. Kim, *With the Century,* vol. 2, p. 401.

14. Ibid., vol. 1, p. 47. Imagining that the Versailles conference of great powers settling the peace after World War I would be Korea's salvation, in view of Wilson's ringing promises of self-determination for the nations, the demonstrators "were not aware that the American President Wilson was not the good guy he claimed to be," writes Young S. Kim in "Anti-Japan Movement: 1911–1920" *(Korea Web Weekly),* http://kimsoft.com/korea/eyewit02.htm.

15. "After 1898 the P'yongyang station became the center of all Christian activities in northern Korea. . . . The common people in northern Korea are comparatively free from stubborn conservatism. They have been hard workers, fighting against the mountainous environment in which they till the ground. Not many of the Northerners held high offices in the government, but were rather subject to the oppression and extortion of the officials sent from Seoul. Their social customs were also somewhat different from those of the capital. There were no strict class distinctions, as in Seoul and the southern provinces, neither was there rigid separation of the sexes—a custom resulting from literal interpretation of one of

the five relations of the Confucian teachings. Religiously, the people largely professed Confucianism, but it had no such hold on them as it had in southern Korea. Shamanism was the prevailing belief. When the country was opened to the West, the energetic people of the North soon caught the spirit of the times. Thus the character of the people, the political vicissitudes, the social background, and the religious conditions made possible the success of Christianity in the North" (Lak-Geoon George Paik, *The History of Protestant Missions in Korea 1832–1910* [Pyongyang: Union Christian College Press, 1929; reprint, Seoul: Yonsei University Press, 1987], pp. 272–273).

16. See Yur-Bok Lee, "Korean-American Diplomatic Relations, 1882–1905," in Patterson and Lee, *One Hundred Years*, pp. 12–45. It was in the Taft-Katsura Memorandum of 1905 that the Theodore Roosevelt administration traded recognition of Japanese interests in Korea for Japanese recognition of U.S. interests in the Philippines.

17. See Wi Jo Kang, "Relations Between the Japanese Colonial Government and the American Missionary Community in Korea, 1905–1945," in Patterson and Lee, *One Hundred Years*, pp. 68–85.

18. Chay Pyung-gil, "Following the Conclusion of the Serialization 'Yu Song-ch'ol's Testimony,'" *Hankuk Ilbo* (Seoul), December 1, 1990 (translated in the appendix to Sydney A. Seiler, *Kim Il-song 1941–1948: The Creation of a Legend, the Building of a Regime* [Lanham, Md.: University Press of America, 1994], p. 196).

19. Kim, *With the Century*, vol. 1, p. 107.

20. Ibid., vol. 1, p. 20. A missionary report said that the curriculum at Sungsil "presupposed considerable knowledge of the Chinese characters, so as to enable the pupils to begin the use of all available text-books in that language. It contemplates the study of the whole bible, and special histories of the nineteenth century. In mathematics, it contemplates arithmetic, algebra, and geometry. In science, it covers the elements of physiology and hygiene, botany, zoology, physics, astronomy and chemistry, geography, physical geography, Korean grammar, map-drawing, composition and calisthenics." Students in the school's "self-help" program worked half of each day to earn their board (W. M. Baird, "History of the Educational Work," *Quarto Centennial Papers* read before the Korea Mission of the Presbyterian Church in the U.S.A., 1909, pp. 67–68, 259, cited in Paik, *History of Protestant Missions*, p. 320).

21. Kim, *With the Century*, vol. 1, p. 21. Is it too easy to note that his son seems to have taken this notion to heart? As far as Kim Il-sung's subjects are concerned, he might as well have engraved in stone the commandment "Thou shalt have no other god before me."

22. Ibid., vol. 1, p. 69.

23. Ibid., vol. 1, p. 106.

24. Ibid., vol. 1, pp. 106–107.

25. By 1944, 11.6 percent of Koreans resided outside Korea (Bruce Cumings, *The Origins of the Korean War, vol. I: Liberation and the Emergence of Separate Regimes 1945–1947* [Princeton, N.J.: Princeton University Press, 1981, cited hereinafter as *Origins* I], p. 54).

26. Kim, *With the Century*, vol. 1, p. 62.

27. Author's 1982 interview with Ju Yuanjung, official of the Committee on Minority Nationality Affairs of China's Jilin Province. See Jilin-datelined article: Bradley K. Martin, "China's Koreans ignore Pyongyang's praise of Kim," *The*

Baltimore Sun, April 6, 1982. For reminiscences of a third-generation Soviet-Korean whose grandfather moved to the Soviet Maritime Province in 1870 seeking a decent living, see Yu Song-chol's testimony in *Hankuk Ilbo,* November 2, 1990 (translated in Seiler, *Kim Il-song 1941–1948,* pp. 101–104).

28. Robert A. Scalapino and Chong-sik Lee, *Communism in Korea. Part I: The Movement* (Berkeley: University of California Press, 1972), pp. 138–140.
29. Kim, *With the Century,* vol. 1, p. 62.
30. Ibid., vol. 1, p. 64.
31. Ibid., vol. 1, p. 70.
32. Ibid., vol. 1, pp. 78–79.
33. The fact that most of his education was in non-Korean schools is something Kim had been loath to dwell upon until publication of his memoirs, presumably for fear it might detract from his Korean nationalist credentials.
34. Kim, *With the Century,* vol. 1, p. 84.
35. "None of the assertions about revolutionary activities can be verified in any Korean or other records," writes Kim's biographer, Dae-Sook Suh, of the University of Hawaii. Kim's father "may have joined an anti-Japanese nationalist group, but his activities were of little importance." Efforts to depict the parents as major revolutionary figures "seem to be directed more toward upgrading the attributes of Kim as a pious son who reveres his parents. . . . [H]is parents were ordinary people who suffered the poverty and oppression of the time and died early without giving much education or assistance to their children" (Suh, *Kim Il Sung: The North Korean Leader* [New York: Columbia University Press, 1988], p. 5). Kim himself at one point in his memoirs describes his father as attending a meeting of "veterans or the leaders of medium standing of the independence movement" (*With the Century,* vol. 1, p. 120). And elsewhere he notes that his father's deeds had not been known as "widely to the people as they are now"—i.e., now that Kim's publicists have emphasized them (vol. 1, p. 114). Such references may represent modest attempts to tone down previous accounts of his father in response to attacks on their veracity by Suh and other scholars, including Scalapino and Lee (*Communism in Korea,* pt. I, p. 204 n.).

    Dr. Won Tai Sohn of Omaha, Nebraska, son of Rev. Sohn Dong-jo, a well-known figure in the Korean independence movement and a friend of Kim Hyong-jik, wrote to the author in January 1995, "As far as I remember, my father regarded Mr. Kim Hyong-jik as a fighter for independence playing a key role."
36. Kim, *With the Century,* vol. 1, p. 31.
37. Ibid., vol. 1, pp. 80–85.
38. Scalapino and Lee, *Communism in Korea,* pt. I, p. 205.
39. Kim, *With the Century,* vol. 3, p. 44.
40. Ibid., vol. 1, pp. 92–93.
41. Ibid., vol. 1, p. 89.
42. Ibid., vol. 1, p. 86.
43. Ibid., vol. 1, p. 94.
44. Ibid., vol. 1, p. 95.
45. Ibid., vol. 1, p. 148.
46. Ibid., vol. 1, p. 143.
47. Ibid., vol. 1, p. 163.
48. Ibid., vol. 1, pp. 156–157.
49. Ibid., vol. 1, p. 159.

50. Ibid., vol. 1, p. 158.
51. Ibid., vol. 1, p. 159.
52. Ibid., vol. 1, pp. 174–178.
53. Ibid., vol. 1, p. 211.
54. Ibid., vol. 1, pp. 207–208.
55. Ibid., vol. 1, p. 248.
56. See Suh, *The Korean Communist Movement 1918–1948* (Princeton, N.J.: Princeton University Press, 1967), p. 263. Kim in his memoirs seems to suggest that his Chinese-language abilities contributed to his career in the anti-Japanese movement in Manchuria. That does indeed seem to have been the case, as we shall see in the next chapter.
57. Kim, *With the Century*, vol. 1, pp. 208–210.
58. Letter from Dr. Won Tai Sohn comprising written answers to the author's questions, January 1995. Kim himself in *With the Century* wrote simply that he lived with friends in Jilin, not mentioning the Methodist dormitory.
59. Kim, *With the Century*, vol. 1, pp. 213–226. Previous North Korean biographical works claimed Kim read *Das Kapital* in 1927. Outside biographers, however, had noted that this was highly unlikely, since neither the Korean nor the Chinese translation was published until after World War II. See Lim Un, *The Founding of a Dynasty in North Korea—An Authentic Biography of Kim Il-song* (Tokyo: Jiyu-sha, 1982). Like many points in Kim's memoirs (and whether true or not), the explanation that a friend read Marx's magnum opus in Japanese and told him about it seems to be an adjustment that responds directly to the outside biographers' challenge.
60. Kim, *With the Century*, vol. 1, pp. 240–245.
61. Ibid., vol. 1, pp. 227–239. "Literary works play a great role in the formation of the world view of people, so every time I meet writers, I tell them to produce many revolutionary stories and novels," Kim wrote (vol. 1, p. 215).
62. Mark O'Neill, "N. Korea's Dead Dictator Remembered as Star Pupil According to Chinese Teacher's Daughter" (Reuters dispatch from Beijing), *Korea Times*, September 10, 1994.
63. Kim, *With the Century*, vol. 1, p. 236.
64. Ibid., vol. 1, pp. 222–224.
65. See Scalapino and Lee, *Communism in Korea*, pt. I, p. 19.
66. Kim, *With the Century*, vol. 2, p. 12.
67. Ibid., vol. 1, p. 267.
68. Ibid., vol. 1, pp. 281–292.
69. Ibid., vol. 1, pp. 293–306. Dr. Won Tai Sohn told me in a letter (January 1995) that he had been present, seated in the front row, at An Chang-ho's lecture. He vouched for Kim's account: "Still vivid in my memory is the scene of Kim Song-ju [Kim Il-sung's name at the time] asking the speaker questions as well as the scene of Ri Kwan-Rin, a heroine of the Independence Army, rushing toward the policemen on the stage to stop them when they were arresting An Chang-Ho," Sohn told me. "Actually I was arrested too because I was trying to climb on the stage to release An Chang-ho."
70. Kim, *With the Century*, vol. 1, pp. 309–315.
71. Ibid., vol. 1, pp. 315–317.
72. Letter to the author from Dr. Won Tai Sohn, January 1995. Also see Kim, *With the Century*, vol. 1, p. 21.

73. Kim, *With the Century*, vol. 2, p. 8.
74. Letter to the author from Dr. Won Tai Sohn, January 1995. Also see Geraldine Brooks, "Two Old Friends: One Became A Doctor, the Other a Dictator," *Asian Wall Street Journal*, September 19, 1994.

    Dr. Sohn, who knew Kim in his middle-school days in the Chinese city of Jilin, told me, "Had I written about my days in Jilin, I would have written just the same as he did." But Dr. Sohn also told me he had not replied to my letter of inquiry immediately but first had taken it along on a trip to Pyongyang. Although I do not doubt his basic story, I can't help wondering whether he perhaps received help in the preparation of his literary-sounding accounts from some of the people involved with researching, ghostwriting or polishing Kim's memoirs. The physician eventually published a book of his own. It is glowing, indeed almost worshipful, in its account of Kim, as the University of Pennsylvania's G. Cameron Hurst III and Bradley University's In Kwan Hwang noted in forewords they contributed. See Won Tai Sohn, *Kim Il Sung and Korea's Struggle: An Unconventional Firsthand History* (Jefferson, N.C.: McFarland & Company, 2003).

75. Kim, *With the Century*, vol. 2, p. 8.
76. Letter from Dr. Sohn to author, January 1995.

    Kim also played the guitar, according to a reference in his memoirs: "Once I went to Ryang Song Ryang's house and played the guitar there. I did not do it because I was merry or free from anxiety. Frankly speaking, I felt gloomy at that time" (*With the Century*, vol. 3, p. 314).

77. Kim, *With the Century*, vol. 2, p. 10.
78. Letter to the author, January 1995.
79. Kim, *With the Century*, vol. 1, pp. 245–246.
80. Ibid., vol. 2, p. 11.
81. Ibid., vol. 1, pp. 254–257. Kim gave the founding date as August 28, 1927. In a typical boast, he wrote that this organization "played the vanguard role in the Korean revolution."
82. Ibid., vol. 1, pp. 354–357.
83. Letter to the author from Dr. Won Tai Sohn, January 1995; Geraldine Brooks, *Asian Wall Street Journal*, September 19, 1994. Kim, *With the Century*, vol. 1, pp. 359–367; vol. 2, pp. 4–8.

3. On Long Marches Through Blizzards.

1. "Some time near the beginning of the century there seems to have existed in Korea a legendary patriotic national hero named Kim Il-song who fought courageously against the Japanese and so won the admiration and respect of the Korean people. The true identity of this *legendary* Kim Il-song is not known. . . . [T]he lack of uniformity in the tales of the legendary Kim suggests strongly that this Kim *is* only a legend. These tales, without concrete evidence, have led some to discredit the legend as a fiction designed to belittle the North Korean premier. The *legend*, however, does exist, and while the originator of the legend cannot be identified, there are many Korean revolutionaries, Nationalist and Communist, who, by deliberate adoption of the name, contributed to the legend" (Suh, *Korean Communist Movement* [see chap. 2, n. 56], pp. 256–257).

    Note that in scholarly literature the last syllable of Kim's name is often transcribed as "song," with a diacritical mark over the vowel, in accordance with the

McCune-Reischauer system of Romanization. In the Seoul dialect, at least, to my ear the syllable as pronounced by native Koreans does sound more like the English "song" than "sung." Confusing Westerners further, in a transcription system recently adopted by South Korea the syllable would be spelled "seong." Fortunately for people who can read Korean, the marvelously rational and compact *hangul* writing system gives a phonetically precise rendering of any syllable at a single glance.

2. Kim, *With the Century* (see chap. 2, n. 2), vol. 2, pp. 23–24.

3. Ibid., vol. 2, pp. 136–137. In his memoirs he overcomes his earlier reluctance to reveal any affinity for things foreign when he acknowledges that learning Chinese stood him in good stead in later life. "If my father had not made me learn Chinese at an early age I might have had to face a great language barrier at every step of my life for the quarter of a century I spent in China," he writes. Because he was able to dress in Chinese clothing and speak fluent Chinese, "the Japanese detectives, who were said to have a hound's sense of smelling, and the Manchukuo police did not suspect me to be a Korean when I was walking in the street" (vol. 1, pp. 63–64).

4. Ibid., vol. 2, pp. 159–160.

5. Suh reports in *The Korean Communist Movement* (see chap. 2, n. 56), p. 259, that *Chokki* (Red Flag), organ of a communist group in Manchuria, carried an article in its March 1930 issue mourning the death of a Kim Il-sung.

6. Kim, *With the Century,* vol. 2, pp. 107–108.

7. The Kim Il-sung who became North Korea's leader "undoubtedly received or inherited some of the credit due to other revolutionaries, but the rumors around his name are the consequence of his own success. Prior to his accession and consolidation of power in the North, Kim Il-song, with his own record, was well known to the Koreans as well as to the Chinese and, of course, was well known to the Japanese police. . . . He is certainly not a nonentity who inherited everything from the legendary patriot or from the revolutionaries named Kim Il-song" (Suh, *Korean Communist Movement,* pp. 260–261).

8. As recently as January 2000, the South's Unification Ministry aroused controversy in Seoul by describing Kim as an "independence fighter." Some critics questioned this "policy change" (Kim Ji-ho, "New Unification Ministry Publication Calls Kim Il-sung Independence Fighter," *Korea Herald,* January 13, 2000). In fact, however, South Korea's government-funded Naewoe Press, affiliated with the organization then known as the Korean Central Intelligence Agency, had published an essentially accurate account of Kim's life as early as 1978, including the information that he "became a leading member of the [Chinese Communist] Party's anti-Japanese guerrilla forces in the latter part of the 1930s." See "Kim Il-sung," *Vantage Point* (May 1978): p. 19. It might surprise some foreigners interested in Korea to realize that such accurate information had issued from the KCIA, whose reputation was so universally sinister that the government thought it wise to change its name (to Agency for National Security Planning, or NSP) after the 1987 revival of democratic elections. The reputation of the KCIA's professional analysts of North Korean affairs was tarnished by association with the organization's dominant group, secret police who carried out internal political repression of dissidents on behalf of South Korea's military-backed rulers. The analysts' reputations also were not helped by the work of government propagandists who were less than eager to let the facts get in the

way of anti–North Korea broadsides. Further, the South Korean military rulers from time to time concocted imminent threats of Northern invasion, claiming to base their warnings on "intelligence reports." The situation in some ways parallels that of the American CIA, whose conscientious professional analysts also suffered in reputation during much of the same period due to the unlawful exploits of some of the true "spooks" in their agency.

The author has reviewed much of the output of Naewoe Press's monthly *Vantage Point* from its first volume in 1978. I find much of the information presented even decades ago to be consistent with the best information available today. True, some contributors reveal very strong unscholarly biases against the North, strong enough to affect the credibility of their conclusions and in some cases their information. But more often than not the South Korean and Korean-American contributors to *Vantage Point* appear to have struggled against great difficulties to get the basic information right. This stands to reason. For South Korea, after all, accurate information about the North was a matter of life or death.

Nonetheless, despite such long-ago efforts by South Korean government-affiliated professional analysts to set the record straight, the scenario that casts Kim Il-sung as an impostor still has credibility among some anti-communist zealots and just plain sloppy researchers, not only in South Korea but abroad. Thus it was considered news in 1994 when Naewoe Press published *A Bird's Eye View of North Korea*, which implicitly repudiated the theory. See "NK's Kim Acknowledged as Independence Fighter," *Korea Times*, May 1, 1994.

9. Scalapino and Lee (see chap. 2, n. 28), pt. 1, pp. 66–136.
10. For a provocative analysis of this political culture focusing on South Korea, see Gregory Henderson's classic *Korea: The Politics of the Vortex* (Cambridge, Mass.: Harvard University Press, 1968).
11. See Scalapino and Lee (see chap. 2, n. 28), pt. I, p. 190.
    A high Comintern official explained, "Over the years . . . factional disputes have taken place in many Parties. There are Parties which have achieved a certain amount of notoriety in this respect such as the American and Polish Parties, but the Korean factions hold the record" (Otto Kuusinen, "O koreiskom kommunisticheskom dvizhenii," *Revolyusionyyi vostok*, nos. 11–12 [1931]: p. 108, translated in Glenn Paige and Dong Jun Lee, "The Post-War Politics of Communist Korea," in Robert A. Scalapino, ed., *North Korea Today* [New York: Praeger, 1963], p. 20).
12. Kim, *With the Century*, vol. 2, p. 69. Outside scholars have long written of Kim's membership in the CCP, but prior to publication of his memoirs he and his propagandists for decades seem to have tried to disguise the fact by simply ignoring it—presumably for fear that Koreans' knowledge that the Great Leader had taken orders from a foreign party would detract from his all-important nationalist credentials.
13. Ibid., vol. 2, p. 128. Kim is careful to emphasize that he retained his independence despite having gone on the Soviet payroll. Later he turned down an offer of a Soviet scholarship, he says, because to "eat Russian bread" might make him "pro-Russian" (vol. 2, p. 175).
14. Some biographers suggest that it was his mother's remarriage or other relationship with a man that caused her to move to Antu instead of going back to Korea, where her relatives and those of her late husband lived. See Lim Un, *Founding of*

a Dynasty (see chap. 2, n. 59), p. 257, where Lim discusses the claims of biographer Yi Myong-yong. Yi is quoted as reporting that Kim himself, around the time of his father's death, had become the foster son of a Chinese named Moo.

15. Kim, *With the Century*, vol. 2, p. 252.

16. Kim offers a complicated explanation of why he fought under a Chinese nationalist commander: Chinese units were terrorizing and killing Koreans, having branded them as Japan's agents in Manchuria. Korean communist guerrilla groups "were small in size; there were only a few dozen guerrillas in each county," says Kim. "They were in danger of being annihilated if captured by the Chinese nationalist units, so they could not expand their ranks." To ensure that his own tiny guerrilla band could survive and grow, Kim offered to subordinate it to a Chinese commander as a "special Korean detachment." The commander accepted—and promptly appointed Kim propaganda chief of the larger, nationalist unit. The irony of a communist running propaganda for anti-communists is not lost on Kim. "This was a ridiculous development, and not something we had desired, but it was a step up the ladder we had to climb," he writes (*With the Century*, vol. 2, p. 294).

17. "Here again Kim [in the official hagiography] emerges as a ready-made leader. . . . There are reports that after the Manchurian Incident, students from various schools in Kirin [Jilin], including Yuwen Middle School, did form a small guerrilla band of twenty or thirty students, led by a Kirin college student named Chong Su-yong, but no Kim Song-ju (Kim Il-song) was reported. The earliest record of Kim's military activities is not until early 1935" (Suh, *Korean Communist Movement*, p. 268).

 Suh adds (p. 281), "The earliest record thus far available of Kim Il-song's military activities in Manchuria . . . shows that in December 1935 Kim was commander of a small guerrilla company in Weiho, a town midway between Harbin and Chiamussu. Thus it is perhaps safe to assume that he did begin his activities one or two years earlier than 1935. The earliest Japanese police report of the military activities of a person named Kim Il-song (unmistakably the North Korean premier) is in May 1935; the report states that Kim was leader of the Third Detachment, the First Company, the Second Army of the NEPRA [Northeast People's Revolutionary Army], operating primarily in the Chientao [Jiandao] region. Ch'oe Hyon related that he first met Kim Il-song in September 1933, which coincides with the general rise of the Chinese Communist guerrillas in Manchuria. Im Ch'un-ch'u related that Kim began his guerrilla activities with Yi Yong-pae, Kim Ch'ol-he and others but fought in a company commanded by Yang Song-yong as early as the spring of 1932. Yang Song-yong was a Korean who commanded a small detachment of the Second Company of the Second Division of the Second Army. This generally coincides with the fact that Kim fought under the Second Army, but it also confirms that he was a relatively minor figure if he fought under or with Yang Song-yong."

18. Kim, *With the Century*, vol. 2, pp. 324–326.

19. Ibid., vol. 2, p. 358.

20. Ibid., vol. 2, pp. 419–424.

21. Ibid., vol. 2, pp. 206–212.

22. Ibid., vol. 2, pp. 332–334.

23. Ibid., vol. 2, pp. 431–435.

24. Ibid., vol. 2, pp. 435–436.
25. Ibid., vol. 2, pp. 83–92.
26. Ibid., vol. 1, p. 12.
27. Ibid., vol. 1, p. 13.
28. Chung Dong-joo, "Two of Kim Il-sung Unit's Members Talk After 50 Years," *Wolgan JoongAng* (Seoul) (October 1993): pp. 650–667, this portion translated as "Testimony on Kim Il Sung's Unit (2)," *People's Korea* (Tokyo), January 29, 1994.
29. Kim, *With the Century*, vol. 2, pp. 436–453.
30. See Scalapino and Lee, *Communism in Korea*, pp. 160–161.
31. Kim, *With the Century*, vol. 3, pp. 3–8.
32. Ibid., vol. 3, pp. 10–13.
33. Ibid., vol. 3, pp. 30–31.
34. Ibid., vol. 3, pp. 29–57.
35. Ibid., vol. 3, pp. 65–66.
36. Ibid., vol. 3, pp. 29–57.
37. Ibid., vol. 3, pp. 58–83.
38. Ibid., vol. 3, chap. 8, sec. 4, pp. 202–221.
39. Scalapino and Lee, in *Communism in Korea*, p. 35, quoting a 1928 Japanese report, describe the different styles of the Korean communists in Manchuria and the Soviet Union's Irkutsk around 1921: "Manchurian forces adhered to strict military discipline, in the fashion of the Japanese army, but the Irkutsk forces called each other *tovarich* [comrade] and made 'no distinction between superior and subordinate.'" This was long before Kim became involved, but the reference at least suggests the tradition in which he would be trained.
40. Kim, *With the Century*, vol. 3, pp. 84–108.
41. Ibid., vol. 3, pp. 231–232.
42. Ibid., vol. 3, pp. 233–255.
43. Bruce Cumings reports that the fame of Kim's unit had spread even to the Soviet Union. An adulatory article in the journal *Tikhii Okean* (Pacific Ocean) in 1937 said, "The men in this detachment are very brave. All the most dangerous operations are carried out by this detachment. Its actions are usually well planned, quick and precise. Two heavy machine guns in the possession of the detachment make it possible to withstand serious encounters with the Japanese troops" (*The Origins of the Korean War: Liberation and the Emergence of Separate Regimes, 1945–1947*, cited hereinafter as *Origins* II [Princeton, N.J.: Princeton University Press, 1981], p. 37).
44. Haruki Wada, *Kin Nissei to Manshu konichi senso* (Kim Il-sung and the Manchurian resistance war against Japan) (Tokyo: Heibonsha, 1992), p. 140, cited in Gavan McCormack, "Kim Country: Hard Times in North Korea," *New Left Review* (March–April 1993).

Seiler (*Kim Il-song 1941–1948*, p. 25 [see chap. 2, n. 18]) writes that Kim's Chinese Communist mentor, Wei Zhengmin, "attended the 7th Congress of the Communist International in 1935 and reported on the situation in the region, going into detail on armed activities by Koreans in the region, particularly those of Kim. This is believed by some to have been Moscow's first knowledge of Kim as an anti-Japanese partisan." Seiler here cites testimony by So Yong-gyu, former high-level cadre of the Workers' Party of Korea, in the Seoul daily *JoongAng Ilbo*, August 19, 1991.

45. Chung Dong-joo, "Unit's Members Talk," in *Wolgan JoongAng;* this portion translated as "Testimony on General Kim's Unit (3)," *People's Korea* (Tokyo), 5 February 1994.

46. "Item 52: Declaration of the Establishment of the Northeast Anti-Japanese United Army," translated in Dae-Sook Suh, *Documents of Korean Communism 1918–1948* (Princeton, N.J.: Princeton University Press, 1970), pp. 441–443.

47. Suh, *Kim Il Sung: The North Korean Leader* (see chap. 2, n. 35), pp. 46, 52.
    McCormack, "Kim Country," relates, based on Wada, *Kin Nissei,* p. 306, that Kim was known to the Japanese "on their October 1940 'wanted' list as 'the tiger' (*'tora'*), while other guerrilla leaders were known as 'bear,' 'lion,' bull,' 'roe deer,' 'cat,' 'horse.'"

48. "Item 55: Threatening Notes," translated in Suh, *Documents of Korean Communism,* pp. 449–451.

49. Suh (in *Kim Il Sung,* pp. 38–39) cites such press reports in stating that Kim often provisioned his unit by taking hostages, sometimes by offering to protect opium and ginseng farmers in exchange for portions of their crops.

50. Kim, *With the Century,* vol. 3, p. 386.

51. Chung Dong-joo, "Testimony on General Kim's Unit (3)."

52. Kim, *With the Century,* vol. 2, p. 99.

53. Ibid., vol. 2, pp. 125–132. Elsewhere Kim describes Han as a hard-working member of the propaganda squad of the communist youth organization he helped to found. "She, as a member of the Ryugil Association of Korean Students, had fallen under our influence during art performances and at the gatherings where impressions on books were swapped. . . . A pupil of Jilin Girls' Middle School, she was good-natured but reticent and usually passed unnoticed. However, she carried out every task given her, be it difficult or irksome, for the sake of the revolution. . . . She was known as a girl orator for the fiery speeches she made in Korean and Chinese to hundreds of people in the streets" (vol. 1, p. 288).

54. Ibid., vol. 3, pp. 120–121.

55. "Declaration of the Establishment of the United Army," pp. 441–443.

56. The guerrillas also used weapons captured from the Japanese, so "it was very hard to distinguish a Korean unit from a Japanese one," Choi Jin-sok said. Chung Dong-joo, "Testimony on Gen. Kim Il Sung's Unit (2)."

57. Kim, *With the Century,* vol. 3, pp. 170–171.

58. Ibid., vol. 1, pp. 188–202.

59. Choi Jin-sok, quoted in "Testimony on Gen. Kim Il Sung's Unit (2)."

60. Kim Ik Hyon, *The Immortal Woman Revolutionary* (Pyongyang: Foreign Languages Publishing House, 1987). An editor's note says that Kim Jong-suk was "born into a patriotic and revolutionary peasant family on December 24, 1917, in Hoeryong township, Hoeryong County, North Hamgyong Province. . . . Early in her life she lost her parents and her brothers beneath the bayonets of the Japanese imperialist aggressors. In the early 1930s, as a teenage girl, she embarked upon the road of revolution against the aggressors. She grew up as a member of the Young Communist League. . . . In the spring of 1935 she met the great General Kim Il Sung, the peerless patriot and national hero, and this marked a milestone of decisive significance in her struggle and her life. Under the leadership of the great General Kim Il Sung she developed into an indomitable revolutionary and joined the Korean People's Revolutionary Army in

September 1935. From that time she fought alongside the Comrade Commander and defended the headquarters of the revolution at the risk of her life."

61. *The True Story of Kim Jong Il* (Seoul: The Institute for South-North Korean Studies, 1993), pp. 27–28.

62. An official biography of Kim Jong-il tells of his first visit, with his parents, to Kim Il-sung's ancestral home at Mangyongdae, in the fall of 1945, after liberation: "'You two had no wedding ceremony, so today's banquet is for your honour,' Kim Bo Hyon said as he held his great-grandson on his lap" (Choe In Su, *Kim Jong Il The People's Leader* [Pyongyang: Foreign Languages Publishing House, 1983], vol. I, p. 8).

63. Kim, *With the Century,* vol. 3, p. 280.

64. Ibid., vol. 3, p. 107.

65. Suh, *Kim Il Sung,* p. 51. Suh adds that he found "no record of such a woman partisan in any of the Chinese or Korean sources."

66. See Lim Un, *Founding of a Dynasty,* pp. 47–50. See also Yu Song-chol, "Transferred to the Position of Korean People's Army Operations Bureau Commander in 1948," *Hanguk Ilbo,* November 12, 1990 (translated in Seiler, *Kim Il-song 1941–1948*). Yu, a comrade of Kim's in the 1940s, places the arrest in 1939.

67. Kim, *With the Century,* vol. 3, p. 297.

68. Ibid., vol. 3, p. 282.

69. Ibid., vol. 3, pp. 279–305.

70. Ibid., vol. 3, pp. 369–370.

71. Ibid., vol. 3, p. 394.

72. Chung Dong-joo, "Testimony on Gen. Kim Il Sung's Unit (3)."

73. Kim, *With the Century,* vol. 3, pp. 402–403.

74. Ibid., vol. 3, pp. 406–411.

75. Ibid., vol. 2, p. 53.

76. A resolution adopted by Korean partisans of the First Route Army of the Northeast Anti-Japanese United Army in March 1940, at one of their last meetings, describes the situation as it was developing in the months before Kim's flight to the USSR: "The concentration and movement of a big company, as in the past, now provides an easy target for the Japanese punitive force; therefore, as a policy of the army, in the future the army should be divided into small units and should be scattered. Because of the Japanese punitive force's operation among the masses, the people in the guerrilla districts have since winter become distrustful of our army." See "Item 62: Resolution," translated in Suh, *Documents of Korean Communism,* p. 471.

77. Kim, *With the Century,* vol. 1, preface.

78. Suh, *Kim Il Sung,* p. 54.

79. Kim, *With the Century,* vol. 3, p. 394.

80. Ibid., vol. 2, p. 451.

81. Ibid., vol. 3, p. 356.

82. Ibid., vol. 3, pp. 412–415.

4. Heaven and Earth the Wise Leader Tamed.

1. Since 1970 the 1941–1953 period has been examined in whole or in part by many authors, including: Robert A. Scalapino and Chong-sik Lee (*Communism in Korea* [see chap. 2, n. 28], and other works) and Dae-Sook Suh (*Kim Il Sung*

[see chap. 2, n. 35], and other works), who are often categorized as taking an orthodox or traditional approach (or, in some critics' terms, an anti-communist,
Cold War approach; historians' debates for decades have been fraught with ideology); Bruce Cumings (especially *Origins* I [see chap. 2, n. 25], and *Origins* II
[see chap. 3, n. 43]) and several contributors to a volume edited by Frank Baldwin, *Without Parallel: The American-Korean Relationship Since 1945* (New York:
Pantheon, 1973), scholars who have been labeled "left-revisionist" by some of
their fellow historians; and Erik van Ree (*Socialism in One Zone: Stalin's Policy in
Korea, 1945–1947* [Oxford: Berg Publishers Ltd., 1989]), Sergei N. Goncharov,
John W. Lewis and Xue Litai (*Uncertain Partners: Stalin, Mao, and the Korean War*
[Stanford: Stanford University Press, 1993]) and Kathryn Weathersby (various
papers published by the Woodrow Wilson Center's Cold War International History Project), who have presented evidence made available from sources in the
Soviet Union and China, and have taken stances that might be characterized
variously as neo-orthodox or post-revisionist. The version presented in this
chapter offers a brief, critical synthesis. For a fuller listing of contending historians and a useful effort to sort out their views, see James I. Matray's 1998 review
essay "Korea's Partition: Soviet-American Pursuit of Reunification, 1945–1948,"
http://www.mtholyoke.edu/acad/intre/korpart.htm. Matray applies the label
"right revisionism" to the neo-orthodox works, even as he argues that Korean
War scholars should "abandon the outdated analytical dichotomy of traditional-
ism versus revisionism and use new communist archival materials to provide a
better understanding of the reasons for Korea's division and why two Koreas
still exist today."

2. This and other details of Kim's stay in the Soviet Union are taken from a remarkable nineteen-part series in the Seoul daily *Hanguk Ilbo* beginning November 1,
1990. The series presents the reminiscences of Yu Song-chol, a former colleague
of Kim Il-sung's who had been purged in 1959 and since then had lived in the Soviet Union, as told to Prof. Chay Pyung-gil of Yonsei University in Seoul.

    Installments of the series were translated by Sydney A. Seiler. They form
an appendix to his book, *Kim Il-song 1941–1948* (see chap. 2, n. 18). Besides citing Yu's testimony, the valuable Seiler book marshals an array of additional primary sources to establish beyond question that Kim Il-sung did indeed live in
the Soviet Union from 1941 to 1945 and served there as a Soviet Army officer —
a point that had been questioned by some Western historians and obfuscated by
Kim Il-sung and other North Korean sources. I am greatly indebted to Mr.
Seiler for having provided, before publication, a copy of his Yonsei University
thesis of the same title, on which the book is based.

    In addition to Yu's recollections of the 1941–1948 period covered by the
Seiler study, I make considerable use of the translated Yu testimony from
the Seiler book's appendix for my treatment, in the following two chapters, of
the Korean War and the purges that followed.

3. See McCormack, "Kim Country" (see chap. 3, n. 44). Kim Il-sung's unit history
was eventually published as "Kanglian diyi lujun lueshi" (Brief History of the
First Anti-Japanese United Army), in Zhongguo gongchandang lishi ziliao
cungshu, ed., *Dongbei kangri lianjun zilao* (Materials on the History of the North-
Eastern Anti-Japanese Army), vol. 2 (Beijing, 1987), pp. 665–679. McCormack
reports that "the revelation of the authorship of these materials was made in various Japanese sources in 1991."

Sydney A. Seiler (*Kim Il-song 1941–1948*, p. 31) relates that Zhou had sought to keep the old Northeast Anti-Japanese United Army units intact under Chinese Communist Party command, even though operating from Soviet soil to launch actions against the Japanese across the border: "Yet the NEAJUA remnants were essentially unable to survive, let alone operate, without Soviet assistance, and the Soviets were reluctant to support such actions especially after entering a non-aggression treaty with Japan in April 1941. An eventual compromise in which former units of the NEAJUA were allowed to operate under CCP directives but had to receive approval from the Soviets for all operations placed those units veritably under the 'domination and guidance of the Soviets.'" Seiler here cites Kim Chan-jong's interviews for the South Korean magazine *Shindonga* (July 1992, p. 368) with Korean-Chinese who had been members of the Eighty-eighth Brigade.

4. See Kim's memoirs, *With the Century* (see chap. 2, n. 2), vol. 2, pp. 42–43, where Kim recalls criticizing, at a 1930 meeting, an anti-Japanese colleague's argument that "if the great powers help us, we will win our independence." Based on the historical record, Kim had a point. When Japan had moved to dominate and take over Korea, no other great power—most disappointingly at the time, not even the United States—had stood in the way, even though Korea's King Kojong sent a secret emissary to appeal to the nations assembled at the Second International Peace Conference at The Hague in 1907.

In a later volume of memoirs, published posthumously, Kim did discuss having spent time at a "training base" in the Soviet Union, but in such a way as to suggest he had been back and forth between there and a secret guerrilla base on Mount Paektu in northern Korea. The Paektu "secret base" is where the official North Korean literature, since the 1980s, has claimed that Kim Jong-il was born. See Kim Il-sung, *With the Century*, vol. 23, "Alliance with International Anti-Imperialism Camps, January 1941–July 1942," sec. 9, "Nurturing the Root of the Revolution" (translated by Lee Wha Rang for *Korea Web Weekly*, http://kimsoft.com/war/r-23-9.htm).

5. *Hankuk Ilbo*, November 1, 1990, translated in Seiler, *Kim Il-song 1941–1948*.

6. See Seiler, *Kim Il-song 1941–1948*, p. 40.

7. *Hankuk Ilbo*, November 1–3, 1990. Chay Pyung-gil, who compiled Yu's testimony, adds, "From the aspects of both character and physical strength, Kim Il-sung was a political soldier more than a professional career soldier. He had more of an interest in organizational matters than in guerrilla or conventional warfare training" ("Following the Conclusion of the Serialization 'Yu Song-ch'ol's Testimony,'" *Hankuk Ilbo*, December 1, 1990).

8. *Hankuk Ilbo*, November 3, 1990.

9. *Hankuk Ilbo*, November 4, 1990.

10. The quotation is from a War Department cable paraphrasing the views of Gen. Douglas MacArthur, commander of U.S. forces in the Pacific theater, cited in Joseph C. Goulden, *Korea: The Untold Story of the War* (New York: McGraw-Hill, 1982), p. 18.

11. Van Ree, *Socialism in One Zone*, p. 65. The author asserts that a Korean report of heavy fighting at the port of Unggi is not borne out in the Soviet literature. He adds, "I did not come across information on how many of those [4,717] casualties were wounded or died in Korea (as opposed to Manchuria). Perhaps the Red Army lost only very few men in Korea, so few that the 'heroics' of its Korean

war are lost if the numbers become known. . . . It was truly a micro-war, barely scratching Korea."

12. Historian Kathryn Weathersby, based on analysis of recently declassified Russian documents, says Stalin mainly wished to ensure that the Korean peninsula would not be used as a staging ground for future aggression against the USSR and that a "friendly" government would be established there. See Weathersby, "Soviet Aims in Korea and the Origins of the Korean War, 1945–1950: New Evidence from Russian Archives," Working Paper No. 8, Cold War International History Project, Woodrow Wilson International Center for Scholars, Washington, D.C., November 1993.

13. Van Ree acknowledges (*Socialism in One Zone*, pp. 125–128) that there were various reasons why it might have been difficult for the Soviet authorities to arrange deliveries, but asserts that it was their refusal even to discuss the matter that showed, as early as October of 1945, a conscious Soviet policy of "closing off the northern zone." The Russians, he says, "wanted to put their zone into order and they did not want American lookers-on, or American interference in the economic process within their zone. In order to achieve that, they were willing to give up . . . the delivery of rice from the South."

14. O Yong-jin, a defector cited by Suh (*Kim Il Sung*, p. 50), quoted Kim as having told him ruefully that the speedy Japanese surrender had spoiled a plan for his band of former guerrillas to parachute dramatically into Pyongyang. On the other hand, Seiler (*Kim Il-song 1941–1948*, p. 46) says Stalin himself apparently refused to permit the Eighty-eighth to join in the fighting—perhaps thinking that having fought would entitle the Koreans to more say in the occupation government north of the 38th parallel than Soviet policy envisioned granting them. Seiler here cites Kim Chan-jong, "Bbalch'isan manga, kim il-song kwa 88 tongnip yodan" [Funeral march of the partisans, Kim Il-song and the 88th Independent Brigade], *Shindonga* (Seoul, July 1992): p. 381. Van Ree (*Socialism in One Zone*, p. 66) conjectures that Moscow wanted to use Kim's group to help administer the occupation zone, and on that account did not wish to risk their lives in battle. See footnote 83 on that page for van Ree's summary of sources that assert, vaguely, that Kim's men did participate in the fighting.

15. "Other, better-known or older Korean guerrillas such as Kim Chaek and Choe Yong-Gun trusted him and chose him as their leader. Chinese, Soviet and Korean anti-Japanese forces at the Khabarovsk camp in the Soviet Union reached a common view in appointing Kim leader of the 'Korean Task-force' (*Chaoxian gongzuotuan*) detachment sent in September 1945 to spearhead the process of takeover from Japan" (McCormack, "Kim Country," citing Wada, pp. 330 ff.).

Seiler reports (*Kim Il-song 1941–1948*, pp. 46–47), based on testimony in *JoongAng Ilbo*, August 19, 1991, "The Soviet Far East Command did dispatch one officer to the 88th Brigade to interview a handful of potential leaders from among the Koreans there. Toward the end of August 1945, Lt. Col. Grigori Konovich Mekrail, then a political officer with the Soviet Far East Command who would later serve with the 25th Army that occupied North Korea, was suddenly ordered by his headquarters to go to Pyongyang. On the way, he stopped in Khabarovsk to visit the members of the 88th Brigade. There, Mekrail claims to have met Kim Il-song and three or four other leaders among the Korean partisans. He had received orders from his headquarters to evaluate the partisans and attempt to select one among them to be a leader. Mekrail, playing down the significance of the meeting, emphasized, 'Prior to the meeting in Khabarovsk, I had not received any special mention of Kim Il-song by name.'"

16. *Hanguk Ilbo,* November 6, 1990. Seiler notes (*Kim Il-song 1941–1948,* p. 58, n. 21) testimony by the Soviet-Korean interpreter for the Soviet officials who greeted the ship, Chong Sang-jin (*JoongAng Ilbo,* August 26, 1991), that Kim introduced himself by his birth name, Kim Song-ju, when he disembarked.

17. *Hankuk Ilbo,* November 7, 1990.

   Lim Un says Kim's preliminary appointment was not police or garrison chief, but a position equally high or one step higher: deputy commander of the Pyongyang *komendatura,* the chief political operative for the city (Lim Un, *Founding of a Dynasty* [see chap. 2, n. 59], pp. 124–128). *Komendatura,* or bureaus of local commanders, as van Ree explains (*Socialism in One Zone,* p. 85), were organized throughout northern Korea right after the Soviet troops arrived: "They safeguarded local order and took possession of Japanese military property and armaments. . . . They were headed by a commander. His deputy was the chief of the Political Department. Another important official was the garrison chief."

18. Kim, *With the Century,* vol. 3, p. 22.

19. Ibid., vol. 1, pp. 293–302.

20. Yu Song-chol's testimony, *Hankuk Ilbo,* November 7, 1990. (See Seiler, *Kim Il-song 1941–1948,* p. 55, for an account of the meeting based on additional testimony.)

21. *Hankuk Ilbo,* November 7, 1990.

22. O Yong-jin, "An Eyewitness Report," Pusan, 1952, p. 143, cited in Scalapino and Lee, *Communism in Korea* (see chap. 2, n. 28), p. 324. O is identified as personal secretary to Cho Man-shik.

23. Scalapino and Lee, *Communism in Korea,* p. 338.

24. Baik Bong, *Kim Il Sung Biography (II): From Building Democratic Korea to Chullima Flight* (Tokyo: Miraisha, 1970; hereinafter cited as Baik II), p. 53.

   Once he had taken office as premier, the regime arranged photo opportunities, including one in which the youthful leader, in shirtsleeves, wielded a shovel alongside a work team. "Let us work hard and complete the work as early as possible, so that someday we may have a good time together," he said to the workers. In another photo op, Kim, wearing traditional Korean garb, bent to join peasants transplanting rice plants. See Baik II, pp. 162, 203.

   It was made known that Kim lived fairly simply and rejected elaborate special treatment: "Ryu Woon-hyung, invited to Kim Il Sung's private residence, looked at the furnishings and furniture with a look of disbelief. It was far removed from what he had imagined. It was clean but the furniture was too simple for the leader of a country. Presently, dinner was served. There were no special dishes on table, an ordinary table without mother-of-pearl inlay" (Baik II, pp. 150–151).

   "[A]s he was about to enter [a coal-mining] village he suddenly stopped and his eyes followed the road ahead where there lay a long piece of white cloth, about 300 meters long. . . . He was supposed to walk on the cloth, of course, but having declined all honours offered while going through hardships, he could not do it. He said to the Chairman of the Kangdong County Committee of the North Korean Workers' Party, who was on hand to greet him: 'Why do you do such a thing? This is no good. The cloth is to be worn by the people. It is not a thing on which I should walk. Please remove it quickly.' Moved deeply by his words, the villagers hung their heads. As the cotton cloth was removed, he started walking. The people, still feeling somewhat abashed, praised his lofty moral virtue and then gave him even more enthusiastic cheers" (Baik II, pp. 178–179).

25. *Seoul Shinmun,* January 10, 1946, p. 2, as cited and translated in Baik Bong, *Kim Il Sung Biography (I): From Birth to Triumphant Return to Homeland* (Tokyo: Miraisha, 1969; hereinafter cited as Baik I), pp. 543–544. Besides that on-the-scene reporter's guess of five-feet-six, the only other estimate of Kim Il-sung's height that I recall having seen is a description of him (Bruce Cumings, *North Korea: Another Country* [New York: New Press, 2003], p. 155) as "standing over six feet." I would have to call that quite a stretch unless perhaps the Caucasians with whom Kim often stood to pose for photographs after liberation were not Russian officials, after all, but NBA basketball players.

26. Van Ree, *Socialism in One Zone,* p. 117.

27. Ibid., pp. 117–121.

28. Ibid., pp. 129–130.

29. See Suh, *Korean Communist Movement* (see chap. 2, n. 56), p. 306.

30. Van Ree, *Socialism in One Zone,* pp. 130–140. In the conclusion to his book the author adds (p. 276), "In terms of responsibility for the continuation of Korea's division in the two years after the Second World War, the Russians carry undoubtedly most of the blame, though the logical counterpart of this is that they were much less a threat to the other's zone than the Americans."

Kathryn Weathersby argues that, in the short run, publicly supporting trusteeship "was a perfect solution to Moscow's dilemma regarding Korea. It allowed the Soviet Union to meet its security needs by maintaining control over the northern half of the peninsula and at the same time protect its position politically by posing as the true defender of the agreement on Korean unification. In the long run, however, this crude solution to the Korean question, which completely disregarded the strong desire of the Korean people for unity and independence, created such a volatile situation on the peninsula that Moscow was eventually persuaded to risk supporting an attempt at reunification by military means—an outcome that had profoundly negative consequences for Soviet security interests" (Kathryn Weathersby, "Limits to Revisionist Interpretations: New Russian Archival Materials and Old American Debates"; for permission to cite her paper I am grateful to Dr. Weathersby, who, at the time she presented the paper, was with the Kennan Institute for Advanced Russian Studies of Washington's Woodrow Wilson International Center for Scholars, where she was involved in the Cold War History Project).

31. Weathersby, ibid., argues that Korean division was "the product of American and Soviet strategies toward Korea that were unworkable and that ignored the fundamental aspirations of the Korean people. President Roosevelt's proposal for a joint trusteeship ignored Korean national sovereignty, the American occupation command's focus on thwarting leftists in Korea ignored the political desires of Koreans, and the Soviet Union's decision to protect its borders by maintaining the division of Korea ignored the most basic desire of the Korean people for national unity."

32. Scalapino and Lee, *Communism in Korea,* p. 340; Cumings, *Origins* II (see chap. 3, n. 16), p. 488. A North Korean account says vaguely but chillingly that Cho and other "alien and accidental elements in the people's committees . . . were completely eliminated" (Baik II, p. 102).

33. The Soviet authorities had helped Kim by disarming this pro-China group upon its return to Korea, observes Suh (*Kim Il Sung*, p. 101). "Furthermore, any reference to their military hero Mu Chong as a leader in the North was immediately denounced as promotion of individual heroism by the Soviet-Koreans and the occupation forces."

34. See van Ree, *Socialism in One Zone*, pp. 76–81. "A Seoul-based People's Republic promised to make Syngman Rhee president over 'Russian' North Korea, from a comfortable position in 'American' South Korea," van Ree says on p. 81. "This plan from Pak Hon-yong was something which Stalin could never accept. Moscow was not, in any circumstances, prepared to sacrifice its northern zone, not even in favour of a united front initiative which might provide the southern communists with a more secure position in the political life of the capital." Van Ree adds (p. 131) that Moscow "gave priority to northern consolidation over penetration of the South."

35. Speech at the November 15, 1945, second meeting of the North Korean Bureau of the Korean Communist Party, quoted in van Ree, *Socialism in One Zone*, p. 132.

36. From a speech published in the 1963 edition of Kim's selected works and cited in Scalapino and Lee, *Communism in Korea*, p. 339.

37. Wayne Patterson and Hilary Conroy observe that "Wilsonian idealism, missionary support and American public opinion [favoring Korea against Japanese imperialism] stood in sharp contrast to government policy, which did not 'come around' until Pearl Harbor. The fact that it was not until World War II that the United States supported Korea lends credence to the view that this support came only because it coincided with the interests of the United States. While the United States was a Johnny-come-lately to the cause of Korean nationalism, the Soviets and the Chinese supported the Koreans and Korean nationalists to a greater extent than the United States had. This led, at least in part, to divided loyalties among Koreans when liberation came, after thirty-five years of colonial rule. The United States, which had not opposed Japan in Korea, began by relying on the Japanese in Korea during the early months of the occupation. By contrast, the Soviet Union (in the north) did not. It is hardly surprising, then, that many Koreans, perhaps still hoping to depend on a stronger foreign power, began to look to the Soviet Union and the Communist bloc for support after the war" ("Duality and Dominance: A Century of Korean-American Relations," in Lee and Patterson, *One Hundred Years of Korean-American Relations, 1882–1982* [see chap. 2, n. 6], pp. 7–8).

38. Yu Song-chol's testimony, *Hankuk Ilbo*, November 7, 1990.

While scholars generally agree that Soviet help played a major role in Kim's rise, they disagree on just how great that role was. Suh says Col. Alexandre Mateevich Ignatiev "was the key person who maneuvered Kim Il Sung into power, sustained him there and supported him in the North" (*Kim Il Sung*, p. 62).

A similar view more forcefully stated is that of Scalapino and Lee (*Communism in Korea*, p. 381), who argue, "This obscure young man [Kim Il-sung] could not possibly have come to power without consistent Soviet support and backing. From this point of view, Kim was a puppet of a foreign power to an extent unmatched by any other individual's relationship to a foreign power during this period."

Cumings (*Origins* I [see chap. 2, n. 25], p. 426) credits the Soviets with "creating" the regime. But he observes (p. 401) that "Kim's public emergence in the north . . . may have been his own doing as much as that of the Soviets. He was in a position to confront and face down Korean opponents on the following bases: (1) his anti-Japanese record was known to all the parties concerned with Korean liberation . . . ; (2) he had never been captured by the Japanese police and subjected to their methods of interrogation, and therefore, unlike most other Korean communists, there was no possibility of his apostasy or of his having turned in or named his comrades; (3) he had an armed force under his own control; and (4) more than most Korean leaders, he was vigorous and even charismatic and melded communism and nationalism in an appealing combination."

Sydney A. Seiler splits the difference, arguing that it was Kim Il-sung's "political adeptness and his usefulness to the Soviet Union, not his popularity as an anti-Japanese hero, his ability as a military strategist, or his charisma, that allowed him to consolidate and maintain power" (Seiler, *Kim Il-song 1941–1948*, p. 3).

Van Ree (*Socialism in One Zone*, p. 270) observes that "precisely those North Korean communists who were closest to the Russian authorities obtained predominant power in the party. This points at the essentially satellite status of North Korea from 1945 to 1948. The comparison of North Korea with Yugoslavia that some authors [Jon Halliday and Bruce Cumings] have made seems inappropriate because the partisan group around Tito had liberated Yugoslavia on its own, while Kim Il Sung had changed his partisan status for a Red Army uniform and it was the Red Army which liberated North Korea as it had liberated other Eastern European countries. Soviet policy in the early postwar period (1945–1947) was, incidentally, more dictatorial in North Korea than it generally was in Eastern Europe." (Cumings's verdict on van Ree's work based on a reading of the 1988 dissertation version: "a well-researched study that I believe overestimates Soviet influence in North Korea" [*Origins* II, p. 832, n. 1]).

Goncharov, Lewis and Xue (*Uncertain Partners*, p. 131) say simply, "Throughout the early postwar years, Kim was wholly dependent on Moscow, and North Korea can be justly called a Soviet satellite."

In one example of the Russian evidence that has come to the surface, former Soviet occupation leaders interviewed by the South Korean newspaper *Joong-Ang Ilbo* in 1992 reported that Kim Il-sung and Pak Hon-yong made a secret visit to Moscow in August 1946, during which Stalin reviewed the Soviet generals' elevation of Kim instead of Pak and gave Kim his personal stamp of approval. McCormack, "Kim Country," cites the Japanese translation of the interview text, "Stalin ga Kim Il Sung o mensetsu tesuto" (Stalin's interview test for Kim Il Sung), *This Is Yomiuri* (February 1992): pp. 84–87.

39. Suh, *Kim Il Sung*, p. xii.
40. Charles K. Armstrong on p. 77 of *The North Korean Revolution* (see chap. 1, n. 8) says that "a careful reading of *both* North Korean and Soviet sources reveals a dynamic interaction among the Soviet government, the Soviet occupation authorities, the North Korean leadership, and grass-roots demands for reform."
41. Baik II, p. 123.
42. See Van Ree, *Socialism in One Zone*, pp. 152–154; and Lee Wha Rang, "The March 1, 1946 Plot to Assassinate Kim Il Sung," *Korea Web Weekly*, http://kimsoft.com/2002/kis-4631.htm. The latter account (based on articles in the Seoul daily *JoongAng Ilbo*) says that a key figure in plotting both attacks, Kim Yong-ji,

had fought in China for Korean independence and considered Kim Il-sung a Soviet puppet who stood in the way of independence.

Baik II, p. 121, says Kim around that time sent propagandists to "crush the false rumors and counter-propaganda spread by landlords and other reactionaries. . . . He also took steps to remove vicious landlords from their villages in order to put an end to resistance on the part of landlords, and prevent their reactionary influence from spreading to the still unawakened peasants."

43. Byoung-Lo Philo Kim, *Two Koreas in Development* (see chap. 1, n. 2), p. 168. Scalapino and Lee say a conservative estimate would be eight hundred thousand. They observe that South Korea's population "increased by a phenomenal 22 percent between 1945 and 1947, and certainly a major factor in that increase was migration from North to South" (*Communism in Korea*, pt. I, p. 349 n.).

Cumings (*Origins* I, pp. 425, 437) cites U.S. government figures indicating that dissatisfied peasants originally from the southern part of Korea who had been farming in Manchuria or working in factories in North Korea formed the largest part of the migration, returning home in the winter of 1945–1946. A little later came the dispossessed landlords. Both groups together he likens to a "Trojan horse." He suggests they were loosed by the North "to polarize and radicalize southern politics."

44. "Qualitative information on individual poor peasants demonstrates the extraordinary change in personal fortunes that came with Kim's open-door [to party membership] policy, a kind of instant upward mobility that made most of them grateful for his 'benevolence.' . . . These cases delineate the microcosmic evidence of a thorough social revolution, a class structure stood on its head. At any time before 1945 it was virtually inconceivable for uneducated poor peasants to become county-level officials or officers in the army. . . . Even something as fundamental as Korean marriage patterns began to change quickly. It became important to marry a woman with the proper class background, meaning poor peasant or worker, because this was a ticket to better life chances" (Cumings, *Origins* II, pp. 302–303).

Because "the majority of Korean experts and intellectuals" were among those who fled south, Cumings adds (p. 336), "[t]he regime was one of worker-peasants, most of them illiterate before 1945. The absence of expertise required an open-door policy toward intellectuals, who have never been denigrated in the DPRK the way they were in Mao's China."

Cumings asserts that from this point class struggle was the dominant element in North-South struggle: "After these reforms, unification of the peninsula could only occur in two ways: through a similar revolution in the south, or through a war that would be fought both for unification and the domination of classes—that is, unification would occur through revolution or counterrevolution" (*Origins* I, p. 414).

45. North Korea was "dependent on the Soviet Union for technical and administrative expertise. Japanese colonial policy had limited the number of Koreans who were allowed to gain a higher education or management experience, and the politics of the occupation from 1945–48 prompted most northerners who possessed such skills to flee to the South. Consequently, the DPRK in its early years desperately needed persons who could run factories, railroads, telegraph stations, hospitals, schools, etc. Because of autarkic Soviet policies, Pyongyang could

only turn to the USSR for such personnel" (Weathersby, "Limits to Revisionist Interpretations").

Seiler (*Kim Il-song 1941–1948*, p. 63) observes that for the Soviet occupiers "[a] blatantly obtrusive posture in the occupation of North Korea was not necessary. Soviet-Koreans, many of whom retained their Soviet citizenship and [Communist Party of the Soviet Union] membership, were able to execute Soviet policy objectives with the legitimacy and respect indigenous officials would have been afforded." The term "Soviet-Koreans" here refers to ethnically Korean Soviet citizens who went (in most cases were sent) to North Korea. For an excellent account of their experience and contributions see Andrei Lankov, *From Stalin to Kim Il Sung: The Formation of North Korea 1945–1960* (New Brunswick, N.J.: Rutgers University Press, 2002), pp. 110–135.

Balazs Szalontai of Central European University reports that Hungarian diplomats in Pyongyang found the North Korean judicial system quite similar to the one that had been established in Hungary after it became a Soviet satellite. But he argues: "Paradoxically, this dependence on Soviet expertise partly resulted from the nationalist stance of the Kim Il-sung regime. Although Pyongyang initially retained certain Japanese laws and many Japanese-trained judges, the purge of 'pro-Japanese elements' proved thorough enough. . . . Thus it was quite understandable that the regime turned to the Soviets for legal expertise, though Korean traditions also influenced North Korea's constitution, criminal code, and legal system." Balazs outlines a number of other compromises between the Soviet model and conflicting local needs in his paper, "The Dynamic of Repression: The Global Impact of the Stalinist Model, 1944–1953," originally published in *Russian History/Histoire Russe*, Nos. 2–4 (Summer-Fall-Winter 2002), pp. 415–442. A copy is posted on *Korea Web Weekly* at http://www.kimsoft.com/2003/balaz.htm.

46. Baik II, pp. 167–168.
47. Baik II, pp. 204–205; 198–199.
48. In 1945, "the North had heavy industrial complexes and energy sources that were quite formidable. Furthermore this complex was barely touched by American bombing in World War II; in the last stages of the war the North Korean economy was stronger than Japan's, with [so] much more energy output (double that in Japan), that Japan's atomic bomb project was moved to Korea to make use of these facilities" (Cumings, *Origins* II, p. 335).
49. See Philip Deane, *I Was a Captive in Korea* (New York: W. W. Norton & Co., 1953), p. 71.
50. Van Ree, *Socialism in One Zone*, p. 153.
51. Scalapino and Lee, *Communism in Korea*, p. 384.
52. According to Baik II, p. 127, the regime eschewed nationalization of the land in 1946 because Kim "clearly saw that the enthusiasm of the peasantry would reach a peak if their desire for land was met, so the thorough land reform was carried through on the principle that the land be distributed to the peasants." Cumings (*Origins* II, p. 299) emphasizes that, while the regime followed the Soviet advisors' views on the surface and "never spoke publicly of socialism as a goal in the 1940s . . . nonetheless the land could not be bought and sold, and village-level mutual aid and cooperation began quickly."
53. Against *hangul*'s very real advantages—relatively easy literacy campaigns, nationalistic appeal—must be weighed one severe disadvantage. Chinese characters

remain the linguistic glue that binds other countries of East Asia — China, Japan and South Korea — together. Not knowing them has the effect of isolating North Koreans even further from what is happening around them — a plus in terms of the Kim regime's control over its subjects, but surely a minus in terms of efforts, for example, to expand foreign trade and attract investment.

54. Baik II, pp. 216–219. Universal compulsory elementary education was fully in place by 1956. Ibid., p. 615.
55. Deane, *I Was a Captive*, pp. 68–69.
56. Baik II, p. 223.
57. Ibid., p. 128. On p. 118 Baik claims that the land reform bill was "drawn up by Comrade Kim Il Sung himself," and on p. 134 that Kim "formulated" the labor law. Any role by Soviet occupation officials goes unmentioned.
58. Ibid., pp. 124–125.
59. Kim for his first couple of years in power was still "an affectionate and attractive person with normal thought," says Lim Un in his critical biography. "It was later that he was infected with megalomania, transmogrification into a cruel dictator and an incurable person" (*Founding of a Dynasty*, p. 50). The pseudonymous Lim, whose controversial manuscript in Korean was published in a Japanese translation and a rather poor English translation, is identified as a former longtime colleague of Kim's who had been "active at the core" of the Kim regime, but who had gone into exile in the Soviet Union. Since publication it has been reported that Lim Un is a pseudonym for Ho Jin, identified as vice-chairman of Moscow's Association of Soviet Koreans. A "Soviet Korean" was an ethnic Korean who had been living in the Soviet Union at the time of Korean liberation and had been sent by the Soviet government to help its military occupation administration develop the new regime in North Korea. Kim eventually purged many such "Soviet Koreans," and those purged generally returned to the Soviet Union.

Hoki Ishihara, president of the Tokyo publisher Jiyusha, explained in an interview with my associate Hideko Takayama (November 1994) that Ho Jin approached him in Moscow after Ishihara had served for some years as chairman of a Japan-Soviet roundtable conference. "It seemed that Ho Jin had been watching us for some time," Ishihara said. Ho Jin told Ishihara about his manuscript, invited the publisher to his Moscow home and asked him to take the manuscript out of the country. Ishihara accepted and enlisted the Moscow bureau of *Mainichi Shimbun* to get the sensitive document out via pouch. It went first to Denmark and then to Ishihara's home in Tokyo, the publisher recalled. When he left Moscow, Ishihara carried out with him the photographs that illustrate the text in the published version. Once back in Tokyo, Ishihara said, he asked a friend at the South Korean embassy in Tokyo to introduce him to a translator.

The South Korean government took a hand in distributing the book after translation and publication, as is shown by the bookplate in the copy belonging to the library of the Foreign Correspondents' Club of Japan, which says the copy was donated by the [South] Korean Embassy.

Prof. Haruhisa Ogawa of Tokyo University visited Moscow in 1990 and saw Ho Jin, who was living there. Professor Ogawa said in an interview with Hideko Takayama (November 1994) that beyond Ho's own direct knowledge, the book reflects experiences related to him by his seniors, such as Yu Song-chol and Yi Sang-jo. (Perhaps that was one reason for using a pseudonym and making the narrator and purported author a composite character.) He began writing it in 1973, in Korean, and spent nearly ten years on the project. Professor Ogawa said he also learned, in an interview with Ho's brother in Tashkent, that the publication had embarrassed the Moscow government, which in 1982 was competing with Beijing for influence in North Korea while not yet recognizing South Korea. The KGB questioned Ho, the brother told Professor Ogawa. As for the origin of Ho's pen name, Lim Un is the site of the Ho family's ancestral home in southern Korea, Professor Ogawa was told.

Goncharov, Lewis and Xue, in *Uncertain Partners*, say (p. 327, fn. 29) that "Lim Un" obtained most of the materials for the book from Yu Song-chol and Yi Sang-jo. They base that conclusion on an interview with Yu.

In June of 1995 Russian scholars told me that Ho Jin was still living in Moscow, where he was operating a theater.

Lankov *(From Stalin to Kim Il Sung)* gives a different name for the author: Ho Un-bae. When I queried him by e-mail, Lankov was kind enough to reply: "The person in question normally called himself Ho Un-bae, but the name of Ho Jin was used frequently as well. I do not know how he came to have two names, but they were used interchangeably."

Scholars have reacted to the "Lim Un" book in various ways. Seiler (*Kim Il-song 1941–1948*, p. 14) writes, "This book, a compilation of interviews conducted with exiled Soviet-Koreans who played pivotal roles in the establishment of the Kim Il-song regime, corroborates much of what other Soviet-Koreans and former Soviet officials are revealing now on the background of Kim and the founding of his regime." He notes, however, that in some academic quarters the work "has been dismissed as yet another personal vendetta against Kim."

One scholar who has dismissed the work is Bruce Cumings, who refers to Lim as a "mysterious high-level defector" and observes that "Lim takes it upon himself to refute every anomaly in the record. . . . This is the surest evidence of any that the book was ghost-written in Seoul" (*Origins* II, p. 591; p. 884 n.).

As for being a "defector," perhaps the term can be used. However, it was not to South Korea but to the USSR, his home country, that Lim/Ho fled. And while *The Founding of a Dynasty* is a bitter book, I do not find it informed by Seoul-style anti-communism. To the contrary, the author's voice consistently comes through as that of a dedicated Soviet communist of Korean extraction, horrified by what he views as Kim Il-sung's perversion of sacred Soviet-communist doctrine. He contrasts Kim's personality cult and lavish lifestyle with the behavior of Lenin, who once stopped a comrade's speech to scold the speaker for praising him—and who refused special rations during a food shortage, fainting from hunger in his office one day (p. 318).

As Cumings's remark about refuting every anomaly suggests, the book does show evidence of considerable access to research materials, especially in the portions concerning periods after Lim/Ho would have left North Korea. However, I see no reason to assume on that basis that the book was ghostwritten in South Korea. Presumably, considerable materials on North Korea were available in the Soviet Union, particularly to former high-level officials such as Yu and Yi and to an official of the Association of Soviet Koreans, such as Ho Jin. And the USSR had definite ideological and other disagreements with Pyongyang during the period before and after Ho left North Korea, disputes regarding which Lim/Ho consistently argues the Soviet case.

Dutch scholar Erik van Ree relies to a great extent on Russian sources for his 1989 study, *Socialism in One Zone*. He describes Lim Un (p. 30) as "very favorably disposed towards the USSR" and adds that Lim's "factual information on the Soviet military establishment is, according to my assessment, generally correct. . . . Lim's account is, moreover, the most detailed and lively version available to my knowledge."

While the English version reveals many lapses, especially in clarity, I, too, find that much of the work rings true, both in its account of the facts and in its assessment of Kim Il-sung. (Kim "was mediocre, but there is no doubt that he was real," Lim says on page 148, summing up his lengthy and persuasive rebuttal of the many theories advanced by others calling Kim a "fake.")

60. The South Korean ruling group, according to a 1948 CIA analysis, "has been forced to support imported expatriate politicians such as Syngman Rhee and Kim Ku. These, while they have no pro-Japanese taint, are essentially demagogues bent on autocratic rule" (cited in Jon Halliday and Bruce Cumings, *Korea: The Unknown War* [London: Viking, 1988], p. 23). Cumings (*Origins* II, pp. 190–192) also observes, "The object of every Korean ruler is to inculcate proper ideas in everyone in the realm, to push a uniform pattern of thought to the point that it becomes a state of mind, and therefore impervious to logic and argument. This is taken to be the essence and ideal of stable rule."

61. Halliday and Cumings (*Korea*, p. 57) note that the intent of eliminating non-leftist political opposition "was the same as that of the right wing in the South, to squash alternative centers of power." The Northerners, however, "did it much more effectively because of their superior organization and the general weakness of the opposition."

62. Pak Pyong-so, quoted in Suh, *Kim Il Sung*, p. 78.

63. Quoted in Scalapino and Lee, *Communism in Korea*, p. 360.

64. Ibid., p. 382.

65. Ibid., p. 348.

66. Speech at the meeting ratifying the united-front policy and creating the North Korean Workers' Party, quoted in Cumings, *Origins* I, p. 420. Although his regime enacted a women's rights law outlawing sale of women into concubinage and prostitution, Kim himself was no stranger to *kisaeng* houses.

67. Van Ree, *Socialism in One Zone*, pp. 157 and 197, cites two such speeches, in April and August of 1946.

68. See Scalapino and Lee, *Communism in Korea*, pp. 298–311.

69. David Halberstam observes that "the postwar drawing of lines between the communists and the Western powers probably had a historical inevitability to it. Two great and uncertain powers were coming to terms with each other . . . like two blind dinosaurs wrestling in a very small pit" (*The Best and the Brightest* [New York: Random House, 1972], p. 106).

More specifically, Van Ree's analysis (*Socialism in One Zone*, p. 275) is that the Russians "showed remarkably little interest in moves toward Korean reunification via the Soviet-American negotiations." Reunification would have meant shared influence throughout Korea and "Moscow found American influence in the northern zone more threatening than it found its own in the southern zone attractive."

Kathryn Weathersby put it more succinctly in the 1995 conference paper cited earlier: "Once Korea was divided at the 38th parallel into Soviet and American occupation zones, the chances for unification of the peninsula became very slim. . . . The Americans would only accept a government hostile to communists and the Soviets would only accept a government thoroughly sympathetic to Moscow. The goals of the two great powers were thus mutually exclusive."

For a contrasting view, that "Soviet documents seriously undermine the argument that Moscow was responsible for the deadlock perpetuating Korea's division," see Matray, "Korea's Partition."

70. Suh, *Kim Il Sung*, p. 97.
71. According to the North's account, Kim charmed Southern delegates into becoming born-again believers in him as Korea's rightful leader. Rightist South Korean leader Kim Ku, for example, was "converted," was "captured by his character and personality," was "reborn as an enlightened human being in the rays of the shining sun of the nation, Comrade Kim Il Sung" (Baik II, pp. 243–251). Suh dismisses such claims, saying, "Nothing could be further from the truth" (*Kim Il Sung*, p. 366).
72. "Since two years of direct negotiations with the Soviet Union in Korea had failed to bring agreement on peninsulawide elections, the American move was actually intended to obtain a UN sanction for U.S.-sponsored elections in the South—the political division of Korea" (Frank Baldwin, in his introduction to *Without Parallel*, p. 11).
73. Baik II, p. 225.
74. Yu Song-chol's testimony, *Hankuk Ilbo*, November 9, 1990.
75. *New York Times*, March 2, 1950, quoted in Robert R. Simmons, "The Korean Civil War," in Baldwin, *Without Parallel*, p. 143.
76. "[T]he moral condemnation and one-sided portrayal of North Korea as 'aggressive' and 'bellicose' was a cold war contrivance. Assuming that North Korea started the Korean War, one man's 'aggression' is another's patriotic duty to restore national unity" (Baldwin, *Without Parallel*, p. 32).
77. Goncharov, Lewis and Xue say (*Uncertain Partners*, p. 152) that in buying into Kim's invasion plan "the Soviet dictator would be pursuing his goals on several levels—to expand the buffer zone along his border, to create a springboard against Japan that could be used during a future global conflict, to test the American resolve, to intensify the hostility between Beijing and Washington, and, finally and foremost, to draw U.S. power away from Europe."
78. Scalapino and Lee, *Communism in Korea*, p. 393.
79. In early 1950 Yu Song-chol's KPA operations bureau received intelligence reports suggesting that Rhee would attack the North in August, after the summer rainy season (*Hankuk Ilbo*, November 9, 1990). That does not necessarily refer to a full-scale invasion but could refer to yet another of the series of lesser attacks that each side had launched against the other.

Cumings notes the border clashes along with other fighting in his argument that the question of who started the shooting on June 25, 1950, is secondary, since it was merely a phase in a revolution that had been in process on the Korean peninsula since 1945. "The basic issues over which the war in 1950 was fought were apparent immediately after liberation, within a three-month period, and led to open fighting that eventually claimed more than one hundred thousand lives in peasant rebellion, labor strife, guerrilla warfare, and open fighting along the thirty-eighth parallel—all this before the ostensible Korean War began. In other words, the conflict was civil and revolutionary in character, beginning just after 1945 and proceeding through a dialectic of revolution and reaction. The opening of conventional battles in June 1950 only continued this war by other means" (Cumings, *Origins* I, pp. xx–xxi). In an interview after the Soviet archives had started to yield their information pointing to Stalin's role, Cumings told Prof. Paik Nak-chung of Seoul National University that "by 1949 if not earlier, both Korean states thought that war was the way—perhaps the only way—to settle the national division. . . . Even if new information should disclose a North Korean invasion apart from any southern provocation June 25, that would still not mean the North 'started' the conflict, only that it took the existing armed conflict to a new and more destructive phase" (*Korea Herald*, January 20, 1993, excerpting from an unspecified recent issue of *Korea Journal*).

While Cumings advances understanding by focusing on civil origins of the conflict, his "only" seems a curiously mild way to talk about an invasion that led to the deaths of millions of people. Somewhat in contrast to the way he minimizes the importance of the question of who invaded whom, Cumings emphasizes that it was the South that had made the first moves toward the creation of separate regimes, in the final three months of 1945. "We could argue, of course that a separate northern regime was inevitable. But the sequence remains undeniable: the south moved first" (*Origins* I, p. 403).

80. This part of Khrushchev's recollection is translated from tapes studied by John Merrill. See Merrill, *Korea: The Peninsular Origins of the War* (Newark, Del.: University of Delaware Press, 1989), p. 25. (A nearly identical translation is in Nikita Khrushchev, *Khrushchev Remembers*, translated and edited by Strobe Talbott [New York: Bantam Books, 1970], p. 401.) Goncharov, Lewis and Xue, quoting it (*Uncertain Partners*, p. 138), say it appears to relate to Kim's first visit to Moscow, in 1949, not his 1950 visit.

81. These documents were translated by Kathryn Weathersby and published in articles in *Bulletin of the Cold War History Project*, nos. 4 and 5 (1995), Woodrow Wilson International Center for Scholars, Washington, D.C.

As for Kim's political worries about the mood of his subjects, recall that the wing of the Workers' Party whose members hailed from the South still had strength in North Korea.

82. Goncharov, Lewis and Xue, *Uncertain Partners*, p. 137, citing a 1966 Soviet Foreign Ministry top-secret account of the Korean War. On page 143 they say the visit lasted from March 30 to April 25.

83. Khruschev, *Khrushchev Remembers*, pp. 401–402.

Regarding the North's economic reasons for planning a war, Suh says (*Kim Il Sung*, pp. 114 ff.), "One cause of the war that has often been neglected is the economic situation in the North. Kim had completed two one-year economic plans for 1947 and 1948, which he claimed were resounding successes. By the time of the Korean War, he had instituted a two-year economic plan for 1949–1950 which was in considerable difficulty. . . . Kim may have been advised by his comrades of the futility of trying to develop an independent North Korean economy with only half the labor force of the South while military conquest of the South and economic plans for all Korea seemed so close at hand."

84. See Weathersby's 1995 conference paper, "Limits to Revisionist Interpretations."

85. One Korea specialist wrote, "If the United States should have to fight Russia, the rugged mountains of Korea, some 5,000 miles from Moscow, would be the last possible place chosen for battle with the Soviets. The military argument for the withdrawal of every American soldier from Korea is unanswerable. In war with Russia, Korea would not be a Bataan but a Guam, with every soldier lost to the enemy in a few days. That is the military picture—if we should have to fight Russia. If we don't, then this is not the military picture. Today there seem to be no signs that war is coming in the immediate future. If that is so, then it seems that political rather than military considerations should govern the withdrawal of the last few United States troops still remaining in Korea. Many observers believe that the North Korean communist army will not attack the south so long as American soldiers are there to get in the way" (Harold J. Noble, "Korea Must Stay Half Free," *New Leader*, June 18, 1949).

86. David Halberstam, *The Fifties* (New York: Ballantine Books, 1994), pp. 65–67. "As Acheson once noted," Halberstam adds, "the foreign policy of the United States in those years immediately after the war could be summed up in three sentences: '1. Bring the boys home; 2. Don't be Santa Claus; 3. Don't be pushed around.'"

87. Goncharov spoke of the document on June 13, 1995, in the author's presence, at the Seoul conference "Rethinking the Half Century of Liberation," sponsored by Korea Press Center and the Graduate School of Journalism and Mass Communication of Korea University.

88. See Cumings, *Origins* II, for a lengthy and rather compelling recital of the evidence. On pp. 64–66 Cumings argues that the American policy of seeking containment in Korea through the United Nations instead of unilaterally—a policy he dates to several years before the June 25, 1950, outbreak of full-scale war— "was essentially the product of the State [Department]-military stalemate over how to defend southern Korea. Instead of an internationalism that abjured containment—the standard interpretation—American policy garbed containment in internationalist clothes. . . . Acheson could bring the prestige of the UN to bear on his desire to maintain American credibility in Korea, in the face of military and congressional unwillingness to back the $600 million [aid] program for Korea. He later noted that the problem was turned over to the UN because the military was pressing to get its troops out of Korea, something that 'we delayed until June 29, 1949.'"

89. See Cumings, *Origins* II, pp. 42–61. On the question of Korea's military-strategic importance, Cumings notes that not everyone in the Pentagon agreed that it was negligible. The War Department's director of intelligence said Korea "had 'high strategic value to the USSR,' completing 'a perfect outer perimeter protecting the Siberian Maritime Province' and especially the base of Vladivostok; it put Soviet ground and air forces 'within easy striking distance of the heart of the Japanese islands'" (p. 59).

90. Ibid., p. 161.

91. Arguing Acheson's case for him, Cumings says (*Origins* II, p. 428) that "telegraphing" to the Soviets that Washington intended defense of particular places aside from the big ones, Japan and Germany, "would be the height of stupidity." Why? Cumings does not elaborate here. Did Acheson envision a predatory Moscow using the information to bring about, by remote control, a war

in a place—such as Korea—that would tie U.S. forces down so that they could not defend against a later blow planned in Europe? Later (p. 430), Cumings suggests the possibility that the speech was purposely ambiguous to keep Moscow and Pyongyang guessing.

92. Cumings (*Origins* II, pp. 615–619) says it is legitimate to speculate that "a small group of officials in Tokyo and Washington saw the attack coming, prepared to meet it, and then let it happen—while keeping Congress in the dark, then and thereafter." He approvingly quotes Stone: "The hypothesis that invasion was encouraged politically by silence, invited militarily by defensive formations, and finally set off by some minor lunges across the border when all was ready would explain a great deal" (I.F. Stone, *The Hidden History of the Korean War* [New York: Monthly Review Press, 1952]; paperback, 1970, p. 44). Cumings states outright (*Origins* II, p. 602) that Acheson "wanted the communists to strike first along the containment periphery."

Cumings makes the comparison of the Korea and Pearl Harbor theories, observing that "even a lifetime of research would not prove definitively that Roosevelt was either guilty or innocent of 'maneuvering the Japanese,' and the same is true of Acheson and Korea. We do not have signals intelligence that would suggest American advance knowledge of North Korean action, a major lacuna that we do have for Pearl Harbor" (*Origins* II, p. 435).

Maneuvering by Acheson was not Cumings's preferred scenario for how the invasion came about. Rather, in *Origins* II, he favored the theory that South Korean troops striking north provoked a counterattack by North Korean troops who had been hoping and planning for just such a provocation so that they could unleash a full-fledged invasion in response. Evidence since publication of that book has shown that awaiting a Southern provocation "with the riveted mix of alarm and relish of a cobra lying in wait" (*Origins* II, p. 574) had indeed been Kim Il-sung's posture earlier—because Stalin had told him not to attack first—but that Kim, tired of waiting for Rhee to hand him a provocation, had persuaded Stalin to back his unprovoked invasion.

By the way, in this chapter and others that follow I use the term "revisionist" as a neutral descriptive term, not as a value judgment. I would estimate that I agree about as often as I disagree with positions taken by many of the Korea scholars to whom the term has been applied. As one of my best teachers at Princeton, the eminent historian James M. McPherson, writes, historians "know that revision is the lifeblood of historical scholarship. History is a continuing dialogue between the present and the past. Interpretations of the past are subject to change in response to new evidence, new questions asked of the evidence, new perspectives gained by the passage of time. There is no single, eternal and immutable 'truth' about past events and their meaning. The unending quest of historians for understanding the past—that is, 'revisionism'—is what makes history vital and meaningful" ("Revisionist Historians," from the President's column of the September 2003 *Perspectives, The Newsmagazine of the American Historical Association,* http://www.theaha.org/perspectives/issues/2003/0309/0309pre1.cfm).

93. Goncharov, Lewis and Xue, *Uncertain Partners,* p. 142, cite Lim Un (*Founding of a Dynasty,* p. 181) as saying that Kim, after the Acheson speech, "was convinced that 'the U.S. would not enter the Korean War,' or 'even if they did enter the war, they would not hold sway over the destiny of the war.'" The authors add, "Although considerable controversy surrounds Pyongyang's reaction to Acheson's

speech, we believe that Kim used the speech to bolster his case with Stalin irrespective of what his 'true' attitude to the speech may have been."

For a contrary view see Cumings, *Origins* II, pp. 410. Cumings argued—before the Russian archives yielded their evidence—that "[e]ven the premise has always been stupefyingly improbable: that Stalin, of all people, or for that matter Kim Il Sung, would be misled by a public speech into thinking the United States would not defend South Korea. Stalin's usual modus operandi was probably to put negatives in front of Acheson's public statements, as a first cut at discerning enemy intentions. A dialectical logic of interacting opposites would immediately course through his mind on reading the speech: Acheson says he won't defend them, so probably he will; maybe he means it; in any case he's trying to mislead us; maybe by pretending to believe him we can suck the Americans into a stupid war, so on and so forth."

94. Nikita Khrushchev, "The Korean War," *Ogonëk*, p. 28, cited in Goncharov, Lewis and Xue, *Uncertain Partners*, p. 143; also translated in *Khrushchev Remembers*, p. 401.

Russian scholars Aleksandr Orlov and Viktor Gavrilov, in an article whose title translates as "The Long Echo of the Korean War" (*Nezavisimoye Voyennoye Obozreniye*, Moscow, October 12–18, 2001 [summary at http://www.nautilus.org/napsnet/dr/0110/oct17.html]) say that the U.S. military response was a complete surprise to Moscow, Beijing and Pyongyang.

95. During talks in Moscow in January 1950, Stalin "told Mao that a 'confrontation with the United States is inevitable, but for us it would be favorable to delay its beginning. At present, war is not feasible, because we have just tested the atomic bomb, the country is exhausted, and the people of the USSR would not understand and support such a war'" (Goncharov, Lewis and Xue, *Uncertain Partners*, p. 108). Noting that the hydrogen bomb was not yet a part of the American arsenal, the authors cite political scientist David Holloway's conclusion "that Stalin had decided that the maximum danger of an American strike would come around 1954, and that the Soviet Union might be wise to back, though not to wage, a preemptive war before then." Stalin's remark to Mao, they write, "suggests that Stalin was leaning toward what might be called a limited preemptive conflict" (ibid., pp. 108–109).

Goncharov, Lewis and Xue say (pp. 130 ff.) that Mao, although he approved in principle Kim Il-sung's plan for forcible reunification, was a reluctant partner at first. He wanted to focus his resources on reconstructing his civil war–ravaged country and, by invading Taiwan, fully uniting it. Stalin, however, insisted that he needed China to back up North Korea so that the USSR could remain in the background—since a more visible Soviet role might bring on World War III prematurely.

96. Ibid., p. 146. The authors say Mao, evidently more worried than when he had messaged Stalin earlier, raised to Kim the possibility of U.S. intervention, "and this time in a way that did not exclude the possibility. Mao asked him whether he would like China to send troops to the Sino-Korean border if the Americans did become involved." Kim replied that he could win the war within a month, before the United States could intervene, and thus he "rejected the need for sending Chinese troops to the border and appeared confident that the Soviet assistance in hand or in the pipeline was all that would be needed."

Also see Son Key-young, "Kim Il-sung Masterminded Korean War," *Korea Times*, July 21, 1994, and Yonhap News Agency dispatches from Moscow published in the *Korea Times*: "Russian Nat'l TV Airs Documentary Proving NK Provoked Korean War," May 24, 1994, and "Stalin, Mao Gave Their Blessings to Kim Il-sung's Korean War Plan," August 8, 1993.

On Mao's need for Soviet aid as the decisive factor in his acceptance of Stalin's request, see George Wehrfritz, "History Lessons, Take Two," *Newsweek International*, July 14, 1997, pp. 28–30. The article cites articles by a Chinese revisionist historian, writing under the pen name Qingshi, in the Chinese Communist Party magazine *Hundred Year Tide*.

97. Goncharov, Lewis and Xue, *Uncertain Partners*, pp. 132–133, citing reports from Kim to Stalin, and p. 140, citing interviews to the effect that "Stalin appears to have been taken in." As the authors note, John Merrill has argued that Kim intensified guerrilla activities in the South and exaggerated the successes of those operations as part of his campaign to persuade Stalin that the success of a southward invasion was assured. Merrill, *Korea*, pp. 187–188.

Goncharov, Lewis and Xue also marvel (p. 146) at "how skillfully Kim had achieved his ends by playing on the complicated relations between Stalin and Mao. We would predict that if any transcripts of conversations turn up, they will reveal a pattern of Kim exaggerating Stalin's support to Mao, and vice versa. In the process, Kim was restricting his own future options and his ability to hedge against failure."

98. Interview in *U.S. News and World Report*, May 5, 1950.

99. Cumings, *Origins* II, p. 431.

100. Both comments quoted by Cumings (*Origins* II, pp. 420 and 503), who adds on the latter page that "Koreans viewed Dulles's speech as, in Chong Il-gwon's words, evidence of 'an absolute guarantee' to defend the ROK."

101. Yu, who was present at the meeting in Moscow, told the Goncharov-Lewis-Xue team in an interview that Kim argued, "(1) it would be a decisive surprise attack and the war would be won in three days; (2) there would be an uprising of 200,000 Party members in South Korea; (3) there were guerrillas in the southern provinces of South Korea; and (4) the United States would not have time to participate" (*Uncertain Partners*, p. 144). On p. 146, the authors describe Kim as likewise telling Mao during their meeting in May 1950 that North Korea "would achieve victory within a month, and that the United States could not deploy its forces before then."

102. "Stalin had no incentive to question Kim's arguments, but he gave the go-ahead on the basis of Soviet interests and on the condition that Mao agree. . . . Stalin was willing to support Kim only if the possibility of a Soviet-American clash in Korea would be excluded. He determined that the way to do this was to implicate Mao in the decision and thereby make him bear the full burden for ensuring Kim's survival if the Americans intervened. A Sino-American war, should it erupt in Korea, would have the added benefit of widening the break between Beijing and the West" (Goncharov, Lewis and Xue, p. 214).

103. Kim and Stalin, if they were both mistaken on U.S. capability, were not necessarily mistaken on the same grounds since their interests were different. However, they may well have held some common assumptions. For speculation on the grounds for Stalin's judgment, see Goncharov, Lewis and Xue, *Uncertain Partners*, pp. 151–152: "Stalin would have concluded from press reports and

intelligence that, though the Americans might want to aid Taiwan or even South Korea, it would take them many months to amass and get that aid to the western Pacific. The timing was on Kim's side if he moved quickly and decisively. In the worst case, U.S. intervention would lead to a clash between Beijing and Washington and a denial of Taiwan to the Chinese Communists. The resulting rise in Sino-American hostilities would only increase Mao's reliance on Stalin.

"Furthermore, Stalin was well aware that the United States would be most reluctant to go to war with the Soviet Union over Korea. With an army that had been sharply reduced after World War Two, it could not run the risk of Soviet retaliation against Western Europe or Japan. Moreover, the Soviet leader reportedly minimized the danger of any such escalation because he had bought Kim Il Sung's argument that a North Korean attack would touch off a revolution in the South, making for a quick and easy consolidation of control.

"Thus, we would argue, it was a mixture of short- and long-term estimates of the U.S. posture in Asia, as of April 1950, that finally led Stalin to become directly involved in Kim's military designs."

On p. 214 the authors add, "In our view, the decision to go to war cannot be laid alone to Stalin's pressure [on Mao], or to Kim's adventurism, or to a Soviet–North Korean (let alone Sino–North Korean) conspiracy. In fact the decision came in bits and pieces and was never coordinated or even thoroughly scrutinized by the three states. It was reckless war-making of the worst kind. Each of three Communist leaders was operating on premises that were largely concealed and facts that were fabricated or at best half true."

5. Iron-Willed Brilliant Commander.

1. *Hankuk Ilbo*, November 9, 1990, in Seiler, *Kim Il-song 1941–1948* (see chap. 2, n. 18).

Goncharov, Lewis and Xue say (*Uncertain Partners* [see chap. 4, n. 1], p. 149) that Kim and Mao at this point were in a race to finish war preparations first and fire the first shot in their reunification campaigns, since China could not fight a war on two fronts as it would have to do if it joined North Korea in fighting the United States while invading Taiwan. If China failed to act first it would have to wait. China did fail to build up its invasion troops opposite Taiwan by the summer of 1950 as planned (p. 152)—and thus had to wait for decades without getting another chance at Taiwan. The authors add (p. 153) that while Mao knew Kim was preparing for war, "there are good reasons to accept the conclusion of Korean and Chinese authors that Mao was not informed about the details of the Korean plans or the timing of the assault. . . . Keeping Mao out of the picture was Kim's intention. A striking fact about the two months before the war is that the North Koreans—and the Soviets—took steps to keep the Chinese in the dark about their military preparations."

Newsweek's George Wehrfritz ("History Lessons, Take Two" [see chap. 4, n. 96], p. 30), reports that a revised history by a Chinese scholar writing under the pen name Qingshi and using both Chinese and Soviet sources begins "with Stalin playing China against North Korea to serve his own interests. In 1949 Mao asked for 200 Russian warplanes and pilots to support an invasion of Taiwan. . . . Stalin was supportive but noncommittal. What Mao didn't know, says Qingshi, was that the Soviets had trained and supplied North Korea's military in preparation for an attack on South Korea. Indeed, Stalin urged Kim to seek Mao's approval only because he assumed, correctly, that Mao needed Soviet aid too much to say no. Stalin got his way. The invasion came five weeks after Kim's Beijing visit. Within hours the Americans vowed to turn back communist aggression in South Korea. To thwart Chinese adventurism, the U.S. Seventh Fleet sailed into the Taiwan Strait to shield Chiang Kai-shek's Nationalists in Taipei. Mao's planned invasion of Taiwan was thwarted. He quickly grew dismayed by events in Korea, particularly when Kim's assault crumbled after U.S. Gen. Douglas MacArthur's landing at Inchon on Sept. 15."

2. Baik II (see chap. 4, n. 24), pp. 267–268.

3. Harold Joyce Noble, *Embassy at War*, edited with an introduction by Frank Baldwin (Seattle: University of Washington Press, 1975), p. 221.

4. Cumings (*Origins* II [see chap. 3, n. 43], pp. 582–583) tells of one American military intelligence officer whose warnings of enemy activity led to cancellation of passes for the South Korean Army's Sixth Division. On that basis he writes, "So much for the North Koreans mounting an unexpected surprise attack against an Army on leave for the weekend. It is highly implausible that this advance information, and the 6th Division alert, would not have been communicated to other elements in the ROKA." Nevertheless, according to Yu Song-chol, it was for the very reason that many soldiers would be on leave that the Russians and North Koreans planned the invasion for June 25 (*Hankuk Ilbo*, November 11, 1990).

5. *Hankuk Ilbo*, November 9, 1990. A former KPA lieutenant colonel, Chu Yong-bok, quoted the chief of the operations directorate, Maj. Gen. Kim Kuang-hyob, as telling assembled officers on June 11, 1950, that the "maneuvers" they were about to engage in were so important that weaknesses and mistakes of the sorts that had been tolerated in previous exercises would be the subject of courts-martial this time (Chu Yong-bok, "I Translated Attack Orders Composed in Russian," in Kim Chullbaum, ed., *The Truth About the Korean War: Testimony 40 Years Later* [Seoul: Eulyoo Publishing Co., 1991], p. 117). It is not clear whether this policy was an original North Korean touch. Chu notes that the Russian-language "engineer operation orders" that he translated said: "If orders come down to begin an attack, the various engineer units will guarantee the technical preparedness of their divisions or regiments for the attack." This suggests that formal punishment for failures may have been Soviet Army operating procedure.

6. He and two other veteran military men were purged "amid rumors of a fiery denunciation of these men by Kim Il-song himself.... Behind the spoken charges . . . there was probably an unspoken one: the failure of the southern 'liberation campaign'" (Scalapino and Lee, *Communism in Korea* [see chap. 2, n. 28], pp. 614–615).

7. Suh, *Kim Il Sung* (see chap. 2, n. 35), p. 121; Goncharov, Lewis and Xue, *Uncertain Partners* (see chap. 4, n. 1), pp. 143–144.

8. See Max Hastings, *The Korean War* (London: Michael Joseph, Ltd., 1987), pp. 79, 105–106.

9. Choe Hun-sik, "Lesson of the Korean War," *Korea Herald*, June 24, 1994.

10. Hastings, *Korean War*, pp. 79, 105–106.

11. *Hankuk Ilbo*, November 13, 1990.

12. Goncharov, Lewis and Xue, *Uncertain Partners*, p. 137, citing a top-secret 1966 Soviet Foreign Ministry report on the Korean War.

This is one point on which Yu's memory may have failed him, as he insisted that the planners, assuming a quick Southern collapse after the capture of Seoul, had made no further plans. "Any war outside of three days was one that was not in the playbook of the KPA," he recalled. When it turned out that the Northern forces would have to keep fighting, they lacked operational plans, lacked linkage of artillery and infantry—lacked "even a basic strategy. Each division simply pushed southward on its own" (*Hankuk Ilbo*, November 14, 1990). Contradicting Yu on this point, Sergei Goncharov said during a conference in Seoul in June of 1995 that he had personally seen the operations plan in the Russian archives, and it did set out plans for the invasion after the taking of Seoul.

13. Yu related (*Hankuk Ilbo*, November 13, 1990), "It is said that Kim Il-song gave a speech to some military officers in 1963 along the following lines: 'Pak Hon-yong, the spy employed by the American scoundrels, exaggerated that there were some 200,000 underground party members in South Korea, with 60,000 in Seoul alone. Far from 200,000, by the time we had advanced to the Nakdong River Line, not even one uprising had occurred. If only a few thousand workers had risen in Pusan, then we certainly could have liberated [South Korea] all the way down to Pusan, and the American scoundrels could not have landed.'" Yu concludes, "In this manner, our war scenario was flawed from its basic conception."

Yu's account of the Kim speech is secondhand at best, since Yu himself went into exile in the Soviet Union in 1959. Note, however, the finding of Scalapino and Lee (*Communism in Korea*, p. 312) that official hostility in the South from 1945 had long since pushed the communist movement there "to poorly timed extremist measures that progressively estranged it from the people. By the time of the Korean War, it was largely the true believers who remained."

Cumings has a different view: "Kim Sam-gyu, Robert Simmons, the State Department, and the North Koreans are . . . wrong in alleging that no southern 'uprising' occurred. In the early days of the war there was no need for an uprising, since the southern regime collapsed quickly; no one with any brains 'rises up' in the face of army and police violence when armed help is on the way. But when the KPA arrived its efforts were greatly aided by activities of the southern people in the Cholla and Kyongsang Provinces. . . . It may be that Kim Il Sung and his allies found it convenient to let Pak Hon-yong and the southerners dangle out front in promoting an assault that everyone wanted, which would be politically shrewd. But more likely the thesis about Pak's role became useful only in 1953, when he and the other southerners could be scapegoated for the debacle of the war, which brought a holocaust on North Korea" (*Origins* II [see chap. 4, n. 1], p. 457).

Cumings cites an impressive array of guerrilla activities in the countryside as evidence for his proposition (see *Origins* II, pp. 686 ff.). However, he points to no uprising of 200,000, or even 20,000 or 10,000, at the North's signal. Nor does he offer evidence that would challenge the specific Northern complaint about the Pusan workers. It seems implausible that Pusan communists "with brains" would have failed to see (a) that Northern help was *not* on the way since it had been blocked at the Pusan perimeter; and (b) that their own efforts from inside the perimeter might make the difference between victory and defeat for their cause. Their failure to rise up does indeed call Pak's boasts into serious question.

More basically, piling on after the conquering troops have arrived requires far less courage and determination than rising up in a rebellion ahead of the arrival of the troops, and therefore seems quite a different matter.

As Goncharov, Lewis and Xue observe (*Uncertain Partners*, p. 214), experience before the invasion had already found the guerrilla struggle in the South lacking, and had given Kim ample reason not to pin too many hopes on a popular uprising. "Kim Il Sung had decided on the need for an invasion by conventional forces because his guerrilla tactics, approved by Stalin in March 1949, had miscarried. Kim presented his case for the invasion on the grounds that these tactics would somehow succeed in the wake of a full-scale attack, but he never fully apprised Stalin of the reasons behind the earlier failures."

Also see p. 155, where the authors suggest that Kim himself prevented any uprising by maintaining such secrecy before the invasion that Pak could not organize the Southern communists. A cynic (or, as Cumings puts it on p. 601 of *Origins* II, someone not "prey to what might be called the fallacy of insufficient cynicism," which he believes afflicts Americans), if aware of Kim's power struggle with Pak, might harbor a suspicion that this was deliberate, because a successful uprising might give Pak too much of a boost in stature and entitle him to share power. Such a calculation would have been more or less along the lines of Stalin's own supposed reasoning in denying Kim and the other partisans a role in the military liberation of Korea in 1945. In any event, Goncharov and his co-authors quote Yu as saying in an interview that Kim had counted on Pak to take care of the uprising, "but he failed."

14. Choi Yearn-hong, in a Washington-datelined column of reminiscences entitled "The Korean War," *Korea Herald*, June 21, 1994.
15. Those lyrics comprise the second verse plus the chorus. The first verse (according to Tak Jin, Kim Gang Il, and Pak Hong Je, *Great Leader Kim Jong Il*, vol. 1 [Tokyo: Sorinsha, 1985], p. 114) goes:

Bright traces of blood on the crags of Changbaek still gleam,
Still the Amnok carries along signs of blood in its stream.
Still do those hallowed traces shine resplendently
Over Korea ever flourishing and free.

16. From the transcript of "Testimony from the North," a telecast on South Korea's MBC-TV program *Current Debate*, June 22, 1990. The transcript is excerpted in Kim, *Truth About the Korean War*, pp. 92–93.
17. Glenn D. Paige, *The Korean Decision: June 24–30, 1950* (Glencoe, Ill.: The Free Press, 1968), pp. 117–118.
18. Cumings describes Acheson's mindset: "If in 1950 the problem was the Korean civil war, Acheson would judge it a war about Europe, or the world, that happened to occur in Korea" (Cumings, *Origins* II, p. 44).

In disagreeing with the Pentagon's view, Acheson argued that American prestige "would greatly suffer if we should withdraw." Cumings observes, "The distinction was between what we might call Korea's *military-strategic* significance and its *political-strategic* significance. Regardless of whether Korea was a good place to fight or not, the United States was there and committed, and thus had to emerge as a good doctor or cause a perceived weakening of its stand elsewhere. Such logic could survive every military argument that Korea was not important strategically . . . because the premise was psychological and political, not material or martial" (*Origins* II, p. 48).

19. See Gardner's introduction to *The Korean War,* which he edited. Gardner observes (p. 6), "The State Department's initial soundings of Moscow's intentions brought responses which satisfied the experts that Korea was in fact *not* the prelude to a general Soviet offensive. But no one in the U.S. government corrected or amended the President's assertion that the Russians had passed beyond subversion to armed invasion and war."

20. For a discussion of this point, quoting Isaac Deutscher and Daniel Yergin, see van Ree, *Socialism in One Zone* (see chap. 4, n. 1), pp. 8 ff.

   As an example of the conventional Western view at the time, consider a New York *Herald Tribune* correspondent's comment: "If we cede the Asian mainland to the Communists without a fight, we will greatly strengthen our enemy. We will give the Chinese military dictatorship time to build an even stronger and better army. We will give them the opportunity to 'liberate' the rich prizes of Indo-China and Thailand. But we will not be giving them only man power and raw materials. We will be giving them something of great strategic importance. If we pull out of Asia we say to the Soviet world, 'Your eastern flank is now comparatively secure. Go ahead and concentrate on Europe.' If we do the Soviet world this favor, Europe will eventually go under" (Marguerite Higgins, *War in Korea: The Report of a Woman Combat Correspondent* [New York: Doubleday, 1951], p. 215).

21. Confidential letter from Dulles to South Korean President Syngman Rhee, June 22, 1953, declassified and published in U.S. Department of State, *Foreign Relations of the United States 1952–1954,* vol. XV, Korea (Washington, D.C.: Government Printing Office, 1984), pp. 1238–1240. This was a rationale that Washington officials might have done well to recall and ponder carefully in September of 1950, before sending their troops across the 38th parallel to "liberate" North Korea.

   The swift UN Security Council decision figures in a 2001 argument by Russian scholars that the United States secretly hoped for an invasion and had plans to meet it. Aleksandr Orlov and Viktor Gavrilov (see chap. 4, n. 94) are reported to contend that the resolution must have been drafted beforehand by the U.S. State Department as part of its preparations. However, the remarkable haste was not in the drafting of the resolution. That is the sort of work, after all, that the department's diplomats and lawyers were trained to do expeditiously. Rather, what was remarkable was that the UN Security Council acted almost immediately. For that, there is a plausible explanation that does not involve a high-level U.S. conspiracy to invite an attack. Korean War correspondent Denis Warner reports that the United Nations at the time of the invasion already had dispatched a pair of Australians to observe, from the southern side, the outbreaks of violence that had been occurring along the 38th parallel. The day before the Northern invasion Maj. Stuart Peach and Squadron Leader Ron Rankin reported to the UN Commission in Seoul, saying they had found the South Korean military defensively oriented, not in condition to wage a major attack on the North. When the invasion occurred, the commission urgently cabled the report to the UN secretary-general in New York. "No report could have been more timely," Warner observes (*International Herald Tribune,* June 14, 2000, p. 7). "The UN Security Council did not have to rely on information from the U.S. Embassy in Seoul, the South Korean government or other observers whose impartiality might have been open to question. It had its own report from its own specialists in its own commission in Korea, of which neither the United States nor South Korea was a member." Warner adds that "if the Peach and Rankin report had not been immediately available, days might have passed before the Security Council could have mustered enough evidence to persuade its members to act. By that time, the Soviet Union [then boycotting the council] would have resumed its seat and used its veto." Without the Peach and Rankin report, North Korea "probably would have won the war," taking over the whole of the South before the UN forces could intervene.

22. *Hankuk Ilbo*, November 14, 1990.

Yu cited Choe Yong-gon as one who "was said to have opposed all-out war, pointing to the possibility that the United States would intervene." He added that because Choe and Kim Il-sung "were not getting along at the time," Kim Chaek was made frontline commander, a position to which Choe would have been entitled by rank order (*Hankuk Ilbo*, November 11, 1990).

23. "Gook" is a racial and ideological slur applied, in recent decades, mainly to Asians. A retired U.S. Navy admiral in a 1970 book used the word fifty-four times, by the count of one reviewer. The admiral defended his language in this way: "Throughout this book I use the word 'gooks' in referring to the North Koreans. Some people object to this word. By 'gook' I mean precisely an uncivilized Asiatic Communist. I see no reason for anyone who doesn't fit this definition to object to the way I use it" (Daniel V. Gallery, *The Pueblo Incident* [New York: Doubleday, 1970], p. xi., quoted in Frank Baldwin, "Patrolling the Empire: Reflections on the USS Pueblo," *Bulletin of Concerned Asian Scholars*, [Summer 1972]: p. 60).

William Safire has reported ("On Language," *Asahi Evening News*, May 14, 1995) that "gook" began as a term to describe a Spanish-speaker, particularly a Filipino, "and was later used in South Korea and Vietnam to denigrate all non-whites."

Reading Safire's account soon after I had devoted much of a year in Seoul to studying Korean, I wondered about continuity. Could the term, after a period of disuse, have been re-minted independently after 1945 based on the Korean word variously Romanized as *gook*, *guk*, *kook* or *kuk*? The word means "country" or "nationality," as in *Hanguk* for South Korea and *Miguk* for the United States of America. Each of us, regardless of race, creed or color, is from one *kuk* or another. But I found evidence against my theory in a John D. MacDonald novel published in the middle of the Korean War, *The Damned* (Greenwich, Conn.: Fawcett Gold Medal Books, 1952), which applies the term to Mexicans. MacDonald on page 31 describes killer Del Bennicke as follows: "He had an ungrammatical flair for languages, came from New Jersey, and thought of all other races as gooks."

24. Baik II, p. 299.

25. *Hankuk Ilbo*, November 14 and 16, 1990. Yu says the frontline command moved south from Seoul to a mountain temple for the Taejon offensive, with Chief of Staff Kang Kon in charge until Kang was killed when his jeep hit a mine. Kang's temporary replacement, Yu, had to report Kang's death to Kim Il-sung, sending the message off to "higher headquarters." From Yu's account, then, it seems Kim would not have been with Kang and Yu in the frontline command headquarters at the time of the Taejon offensive.

If, as Yu implies, Kim as commander in chief stayed away from actual combat situations, that seems a wise enough move for the country's leader—even if Kim's propagandists preferred to picture him recklessly throwing himself into the thick of the fighting. Baik Bong claims that Kim personally led the three most successful battles—the capture of Seoul, the capture of Taejon and the defense of Height 1211, or Heartbreak Ridge. He "visited wretched villages, falling down and burning under the enemy's bombs and fire bombs, comforting the peasants and encouraging them to join the struggle to rout the enemy; called at the smoking front at night when enemy aircraft showered bullets like hail, with star shells. It appeared that he took no care of his own personal safety, so there was no inducement for adjutants to take things easy" (Baik II, pp. 293–294, 613).

Dae-Sook Suh cites a Russian's epic wartime poem recording that Kim was wounded in a battle near Hamhung (*Kim Il Sung*, p. 155). There is, however, no mention of such a wound in Baik Bong's biography, and it is hard to imagine Kim passing up a chance to enhance his image with a genuine battlefield wound.

26. Yu Song-chol's testimony in *Hankuk Ilbo*, November 11, 1990.

27. As an official U.S. history put it, "this North Korean method of attack had characterized most earlier actions and it seldom varied in later ones" (Roy E. Appleman, *South to the Naktong, North to the Yalu* [Washington, D.C.: U.S. Government Printing Office, 1961]). (Lacy C. Barnett, in a manuscript chapter, "19th Infantry at the Kum River," quotes this passage. I am grateful to Colonel Logan for passing along his copy of the Barnett chapter, which I have found useful.)

Cumings writes (*Origins* II, p. 687) that "Americans first felt the combination of frontal assault and guerrilla warfare in the battle for Taejon. Local peasants, including women and children, would come running along the hillsides near the battle lines, as if they were refugees." On signal they would reach into their packs, pull out weapons and attack the Americans. "The retreat from Taejon ran into well organized roadblocks and ambushes, often placed by local citizens. From this point onward, American forces began burning villages suspected of harboring partisans."

28. It is not the purpose of this book to break new ground on the military conduct of the Korean War, which itself has been the subject of a great many books including several very good ones. But evoking the sheer ferocity of that war is important to the story as it will develop in later chapters. My uncle saw about as much fighting as anyone there at the time. His role figures in some military histories of the war, but they seldom quote him at any length on what he saw. Perhaps the reader will indulge me as I relate a few episodes as seen through Ed Logan's eyes.

29. *Hankuk Ilbo*, November 14, 1990.

30. Goulden, *Korea: The Untold Story of the War* (see chap. 4, n. 10), p. 183.

31. Cumings observes (*Origins* II, p. 691) that the average GI "came from an American society where people of color were subjugated and segregated, and where the highest law officer in the land, Attorney General McGrath, had called communists 'rodents.' It thus did not take long for soldiers to believe that Koreans were subhuman, and act accordingly."

32. Baik II, p. 289.

33. See Goncharov, Lewis and Xue, *Uncertain Partners*, pp. 163, 171–172.

34. Baik II, pp. 311–313.

35. *Hankuk Ilbo,* November 14, 1990. Yu adds, "On 28 September Seoul fell, and the new defense lines became meaningless. Each individual was engrossed in flee-ing . . . , with the KPA command structure in total collapse. Contact between the Front Line Command and the Auxiliary Command Posts was cut off. Mass confusion set in to the point where we did not even know the whereabouts of commanders. Kim Il-song had no choice but to have us establish a defense line north of the 38th parallel. . . . We desperately tried to halt the northern-advancing . . . forces who had broken through the 38th parallel. However, there was nothing we could do with our strength alone. Just as the South Korean regime was rescued at the last minute from a burial at sea by the United States, it was the Chinese forces' entry into the war which saved Kim Il-Song's regime at the last moment."

The first on the communist side to bring up the possible benefits of a "strategic retreat" may have been not Kim but Mao Zedong, who told Yu Song-chol in August or early September, *before* Inchon, that the South Korean and American enemy, pushed into a corner in Pusan, naturally would "unite tightly like clenched fists. . . . On such an occasion, it is not so bad for you to retreat to some extent and untie the enemy. Then they will dissolve their union as they stretch bended fingers. . . . By doing this, you can dissipate their strength by cutting off their fingers one by one" (Lim Un, *Founding of a Dynasty* [see chap. 2, n. 59], pp. 187–188).

36. The Americans' fear of North Korean soldiers disguised as civilians apparently led to one incident grave enough to have been compared to Vietnam's notorious My Lai massacre. A team of Associated Press reporters won the Pulitzer Prize for investigative reporting with a 1999 account of the shooting by the Seventh Cavalry's Second Battalion of scores, perhaps hundreds, of South Korean refugees under a bridge at No Gun Ri between July 26 and July 29, 1950. The same reporters investigated further and revealed in a book that they had found nineteen examples of orders by American commanders to fire on civilian refugees in 1950 and 1951. See Charles Hanley, Sang-hun Choe and Martha Mendoza, with Randy Herschaft, *The Bridge at No Gun Ri: A Hidden Nightmare from the Korean War* (New York: Henry Holt & Co., 2001). The Pentagon de-clined to comment when asked whether the orders showed there had been a pat-tern of decisions at high levels to fire on civilians, according to Richard Pyle, "Book Details More US Killings of Civilians During Korean War" (Associated Press dispatch from New York, *Bangkok Post*, Dec. 1, 2001).

37. "Since we were the lead unit we did not stop in Taejon proper but continued our attack through the town to [the] north and west," Logan told me. "I did not pur-sue who did it, how many [victims], whether civilian, military, etc.—more im-portant things to do at the time."

Military historian Clay Blair gives the following account of the atrocity: "North Korean security police had murdered an estimated 5,000 to 7,000 South Korean civilians and 40 American GIs and 17 ROK soldiers. The bodies were found wired together in shallow trenches. Six men—two American GIs, one ROK soldier, and three civilians—had survived the massacre by feigning death. They were buried alive in shallow graves, still wired to the dead" (*The Forgotten War: America in Korea 1950–1953* [New York: Times Books, 1987], p. 312).

It cannot be ruled out that this massacre might have been preceded by a South Korean police massacre of some 1,700 imprisoned North Korean guerrillas just before the North Koreans captured Taejon. Deane (*I Was a Captive* [see chap. 4, n. 49], p. 91) describes what he considers reliable reports of such an earlier massacre. Halliday and Cumings (*Korea* [see chap. 4, n. 60], pp. 90–92) offer their own version of the evidence for such a massacre between July 2 and 6, 1950, with the victims numbering 4,000 to 7,000.

Logan, who first arrived at Taejon with the Nineteenth's commander, Col. Guy Stanley Meloy Jr., around July 6 and stayed in the area until around July 17, told me he had never heard of these allegations before I called them to his attention in a letter of January 15, 1995. While in the Taejon area he neither heard nor saw anything that would back them up, he said, noting that in all likelihood such a huge massacre "would not go unnoticed in a fluid operation underway."

"But who knows?" he added, acknowledging that the limits of an infantry-man's knowledge are "about the range of rifle and machine-gun fire. . . . Ground plodders do little investigation—accept what we just passed and move on to the next objective. Those behind might know more, but we just keep up the pressure."

38. See Clay Blair, *The Forgotten War*, pp. 325–327; Halberstam, *The Fifties* (see chap. 4, n. 86), p. 84; and Goulden, *Korea*, p. 249.
39. Goulden, *Korea*, p. 248.
40. Dwight Martin, *Time* article, cited in Goulden, *Korea*, p. 251.
41. Cable to Kim Il-sung and the commander of the Chinese Volunteer Forces, Peng Dehuai, quoted in Goncharov, Lewis and Xue, *Uncertain Partners*, p. 185. Mao at this point was about to send his troops to Korea in response to Kim's pleas, so his advice would have carried greater weight than earlier when he had warned, futilely, about an Inchon landing.
42. Baik II, p. 334.
43. The official later remarried and had another family. His family's grisly history was related to me by a son from that second marriage, Kim Myong-chol, who was born in 1960 and defected to South Korea in 1993 after what he described as an argument with his superiors regarding the disposition of foreign currency earned on his job.

His grandparents were also killed during the war, in an explosion, Kim told me when I interviewed him in June 1994. He said he believed his father had been an honest person who distributed the county's land fairly without any attempt at self-aggrandizement. "As far as I know, people at that time weren't that greedy." But his father's formerly well-to-do neighbors nonetheless considered him a traitor.

Cumings reports (*Origins* II, p. 717), "On the day American forces moved into [Pyongyang], Rhee announnced the abrogation of the northern land reform, prompting the CIA to comment that this 'reflects political pressure by the landlord class to nullify . . . land reform in order to maintain their traditional controlling position in Korean political and economic life.' Pyongyang's new mayor chose United Nations Day to announce that land would be returned to its 'rightful owners.'"
44. Goncharov, Lewis and Xue, *Uncertain Partners*, pp. 159–163.
45. Goncharov, Lewis and Xue say (ibid., pp. 165–166) that in a "high-level meeting, the Politburo studied the argument that U.S. planes might drop atomic bombs on advancing troops in order to defeat human-wave assaults, a tactic

then under consideration if China entered the war. The majority of Party leaders reasoned that this would be most unlikely, but even if the bomb were employed on the front lines, Chinese troops would not face a catastrophe. They could devise tactics to minimize the danger to themselves and bring the U.S. defenders within their range of damage.

"These conclusions on both the strategic and the battlefield use of nuclear weapons were based on several different arguments. At the most general level, the advocates for action held to the precepts of People's War and its line that only men, not a weapon of mass destruction, could determine the outcome of any war. Moreover, what the Americans would later call a nuclear umbrella had been extended to China by the terms of the Sino-Soviet alliance. The Americans would be deterred, a word never used but clearly implied.

"The advocates further argued that the nation's industry and cities could not be effectively targeted by the small number of nuclear weapons then assumed to be in the U.S. arsenal. The industrial base was underdeveloped, mostly small-scale, and scattered, and the urban population was less than 10 percent of the country. A nuclear strike against China would be highly destructive but not decisively so. All these views found official expression throughout the next decade.

"The Politburo deduced that Washington might want to select the PLA's bases and troop concentrations in the Northeast as the priority targets for a U.S. nuclear strike. The Soviet Union had vital interests in the Northeast, thanks to the secret agreements reached in February, and Moscow would have to retaliate in order to protect its own bases in Lushun and other places. The high command restated its conviction that the Americans would have to weigh possible Soviet retaliation when they pondered the pros and cons of a nuclear strike against China.

"The foregoing arguments mostly concerned an attack on China proper, but the advocates of action [i.e., intervention] also argued that the United States would not resort to nuclear weapons in Korea either. The Chinese forces were experienced in mobile and guerrilla warfare; they could scatter and hide, as indeed they did prior to their massive intervention in October. After entering Korea, they could take cover in strong, concealed fortifications, and the Chinese believed that the role of tactical nuclear weapons in the mountainous battlefields of Korea would be limited. Finally, the Chinese and UN forces would be confronting each other in what was called 'jigsaw pattern warfare.' . . . In this confusing and ever changing battlefield, the Americans could not avoid hitting themselves."

46. Ibid., pp. 174–180.
47. Wehrfritz, "History Lesson," p. 30; Goncharov, Lewis and Xue, *Uncertain Partners*, pp. 180–185.

China understood that the war in Korea—like the later Vietnam War—was a "proxy war," Cumings observes (*Origins* II, p. 763)—"with the Chinese revolution being the real issue."

48. Goncharov, Lewis and Xue, *Uncertain Partners*, tells the astonishing tale of this turn of events on pp. 187–199.
49. *Hankuk Ilbo*, November 16, 1990.
50. Goncharov, Lewis and Xue, *Uncertain Partners*, p. 199.

David Halberstam observes that American China experts "predicted accurately what China would do, not based on Communist intentions"—i.e., the policies of a supposedly Moscow-dominated bloc—"but on *Chinese* history." However, because they had been discredited by McCarthy and others, "the State Department did not heed their warnings on what American moves would bring the Chinese into the war. The warnings unheeded, the Chinese entered, and the anti-Communist passions against the China experts mounted. It was a Greek thing" (*Best and the Brightest* [see chap. 4, n. 69], pp. 108, 118).

51. Newly released Russian documents quoted in "Kim Il-sung Masterminded Korean War," *Korea Times*, July 21, 1994.

Mao's longtime personal physician quotes his patient as having confided that he had asked Stalin to intervene as well, arguing that American conquest of Korea would threaten both China and the USSR. But Stalin, arguing that it would be the beginning of the Third World War, refused, Mao complained. Thereupon the Chinese leader asked Stalin to give or—if Stalin feared such aid would provoke the West—at least sell China weapons it could use to intervene. Stalin agreed only to a sale, and some 90 percent of munitions China used in the war came from Moscow—financed by loans totaling $1.3 billion (Dr. Li Zhizui, *The Private Life of Chairman Mao* [New York: Random House, 1994], pp. 117–118, 643).

52. *Hankuk Ilbo*, November 17, 1990.

53. Goncharov, Lewis and Xue, *Uncertain Partners*, on page 191 translate this passage, which they describe as having been left out of Khrushchev's "Korean War" as published in English.

54. As Yu Song-chol and Pak Hon-yong returned from their Beijing trip, they watched advance units of the Chinese forces crossing into North Korea. Yu recalled, "The Chinese were crossing the border with all of the military equipment loaded on handcarts, with three people pulling in front and two people pushing from the rear. This scene showed us the fighting potential of the Chinese forces" (*Hankuk Ilbo*, November 16, 1990).

55. Among those who were delighted to be recalled was my father. After spending 1942 to 1945 as a flight-test engineer on the plant's newly built B-29s, he had found himself grounded in peacetime as a Dodge truck salesman.

56. *Origins* II, p. 774.

57. Baik II, pp. 341–349.

58. "The Armistice was greeted with relief and approval by the people of North Korea. The strains and privations of the war—incessant bombing, prolonged fear, extended working hours, food shortages, and loss of relatives—had resulted in widespread 'war-weariness' (*yomjonjuui*, literally "hate war–ism"). During the conflict, however, there had developed a striking ambivalence in attitudes toward military violence: on the one hand, it was abhorred; on the other, it was welcomed since it might bring quick victory to one of the antagonists and the end of mass killing" (Glenn D. Paige and Dong Jun Lee, "The Post-War Politics of Communist Korea," in Robert A. Scalapino, ed., *North Korea Today* [see chap. 3, n. 11], pp. 18–19). Lee, a defector to South Korea, evidently of Soviet-Korean background, is described as having been "a writer for *Pravda* in Pyongyang for four years until February 1959."

59. Halliday and Cumings, *Korea*, pp. 88, 121. "Contrary to what is generally suggested, Truman's remarks were not a *faux pas*; they were a carefully weighed threat based on contingency planning to use the bomb. The crisis in Korea led to intense high-level discussions about the possible use of, or a threat to use, what

Washington liked to call 'weapons of mass destruction': atomic and chemical weapons." In December, right after British Prime Minister Clement Atlee visited him and won the President's oral assurances that he would not use the A-bomb in Korea, "Truman secretly moved non-assembled bombs to an aircraft-carrier off Korea and later, equally secretly, carried out dummy nuclear runs over North Korea" (pp. 123–124). "US policy-making was treading a razor's edge over atomic weapons. It would seem that the USA came closest to using them in early spring 1951. On 10 March MacArthur asked for something he called a 'D Day atomic capability.' At the end of March atomic-bomb-loading pits on Okinawa were operational; the bombs were ostensibly carried there unassembled and put together at the base. It is not clear whether the bombs were assembled and ready for use. But on 5 April the Joint Chiefs ordered immediate atomic retaliation against Manchurian bases if large numbers of new troops came into the fighting, or, it appears, if bombers were launched from there against American forces; and on 6 April Truman issued an order approving the Joint Chiefs' request and the transfer of a limited number of complete atomic weapons 'to military custody'" (p. 155).

60. Halliday and Cumings (ibid., p. 160) say that in early June of 1951 U.S. Defense Secretary George Marshall "is reported to have said that he would recommend to Truman that they tell the Chinese leaders . . . that unless the fighting stopped 'we are going to give them a taste of the atom.'" The suggestion seems to be that such a message might have been passed to the Chinese, disposing them toward negotiations—which began the following month. The authors add (pp. 163–164): "The first tests of tactical nuclear weapons had been held in January 1951. In June that year the Joint Chiefs again considered using the bomb, this time in tactical battle circumstances. Robert Oppenheimer was involved in 'Project Vista,' designed to gauge the feasibility of the tactical use of atomic weapons. On 5 July 1951, in the interval between the agreement to start peace talks and their actual opening, the Army Operations Division produced a memorandum recommending the use of the bomb if there was a deadlock in the talks. In the meantime it recommended field tests. Korea was the obvious place for these. In September and October 1951, while the peace talks were suspended over violations of the neutral zone and during the fiercest land battle of the war between US and North Korean troops, on Height 1211/Heartbreak Ridge, the USA carried out 'Operation Hudson Harbor' in conditions of utmost secrecy. Lone B-29 bombers flew over North Korea on simulated atomic-bombing runs, dropping dummy atomic bombs or heavy TNT bombs. . . . [T]he project indicated that the bombs were probably not useful (for purely tactical reasons)."

61. See Baik II, pp. 252, 266.

    Halliday and Cumings argue that "these negotiations were an immense breakthrough for North Korea and China. . . . This was a double psychological victory: over the USA because Americans were negotiating with people they did not 'recognize' and over the South Koreans, who were subordinate to the USA" (*Korea*, p. 160).

62. Clark, *From the Danube to the Yalu* (see chap. 1, n. 1), p. 82.

63. Halliday and Cumings, *Korea*, p. 200. The Chinese figures are particularly murky. Halliday and Cumings say that one source estimates the Chinese dead at 3 million. Other sources say that even the 1 million figure refers to total casualties, not deaths. See, e.g., Kim, *Truth About the Korean War*, p. 42.

64. That is an achievement whose value became clearer to him and many others after the South had progressed, providing its people prosperity and substantial
personal and political freedom, than it had been at the time. From the early
1950s to 1987, Western policy makers repeatedly had to make excuses for not-
very-nice South Korean governments while seeking to portray the Demilitarized Zone as "Freedom's Frontier."

65. See, e.g., Mark Clark, *From the Danube*, p. 85.

66. Goulden, *Korea*, pp. 471–472.

67. Robert F. Futrell, *The United States Air Force in Korea, 1950–53* (New York: Duell,
Sloan and Pearce, 1961), p. 648, cited in Rosemary Foot, *A Substitute for Victory:
The Politics of Peacemaking at the Korean Armistice Talks* (Ithaca, N.Y.: Cornell Uni-
versity Press, 1990), p. 207.

68. See Goncharov, Lewis and Xue, *Uncertain Partners*, p. 188.

69. See Baik II, pp. 342, 399.

70. Ibid., p. 339.

71. Kim, *With the Century* (see chap. 1, n. 1), vol. 3, pp. 333–334.

72. Halliday and Cumings write: "Most Western sources suggest that the guerrillas
were a short-lived phenomenon that soon dwindled away. This is not true."
They consider guerrilla warfare to have been "the most important factor charac-
terizing the nature of the conflict" (*Korea*, p. 146).

73. Baik II, pp. 381–382.

74. Ibid., pp. 399, 403.

75. See Deane, *I Was a Captive*, p. 17, regarding South Korean soldiers' arrogance; p.
79, regarding drunkenness and looting on the part of North Korean soldiers; pp.
96 ff. regarding capture and imprisonment of South Korean politicians; p. 223
regarding conscriptions of young South Koreans.

76. Hastings, *Korean War*, p. 132.
    The U.S. diplomat Harold Noble (*Embassy at War*, p. 205) wrote that Kore-
ans and Americans returning to Seoul in 1950 after the Northern occupiers withdrew for the first time found the bodies of South Koreans "trussed up and shot
through the head. . . . Bodies were so numerous, especially lying in alleys just off
the main streets, that their removal and burial was a major problem."

77. Higgins, *War in Korea*, pp. 209–211.

78. Weathersby, "Limits to Revisionist Interpretations" (see chap. 4, n. 30).

79. Choi Yearn-hong, "Korean War."

80. Cumings writes (*Origins* II, p. 671), "About sixty members of the National Assembly remained in Seoul, and toward the end of July, forty-eight of them held
a meeting expressing their allegiance to the DPRK." The decision of moderates
to remain in Seoul, Cumings says (p. 495), "has a retrospective eloquence" regarding Northern efforts to woo them.
    The American diplomat Harold Noble made a study of the North Korean
occupation, interviewing some Seoul residents who escaped south after the occupation was under way and many more of them after the South Korean and
American forces had returned to Seoul. Regarding the 210-member National
Assembly, Noble calculated that those members who stayed behind numbered
about thirty-eight. He concluded that, although "a few of them appear to have
been somewhat sympathetic to the communist cause, I'm convinced that most of
them were not but simply became confused that last day, remembered their resolution never to desert the people, and stayed behind until it was too late. The

communists picked up a few of the most leftist among them very quickly, and took them to Pyongyang, but left the rest alone for about ten days." Then the authorities brought those more than thirty remaining members in for a speech (telling one that his situation was like that of "a rat in a jar"), placed them under surveillance and later brought them back for interrogation. "None of them appears to have been heroic in refusing to sign confessions of crimes against the people, although in fairness I must add that those I've talked with assured me they had no doubt of an early UN and ROK victory and reoccupation of Seoul, and believed that if they could keep alive in the interim it wouldn't matter what they signed. . . . On three occasions, when the communist captors presented documents for their signature, these assemblymen signed. Two were petitions to the Security Council of the United Nations protesting against UN and US action in Korea. One of these men has told me he knew he had to sign, so he did, but he didn't bother to read the document." Some members were asked to broadcast propaganda speeches. "One little man who doesn't possess a great deal of physical courage cleverly agreed to their invitation knowing he would be turned down. He removed and hid his false teeth, and when the radio technicians heard him mumbling his prepared speech they said he wouldn't do." Among others, "some of the ablest promptly agreed to broadcast after being shown the blunt end of a pistol or the open blade of a knife." The occupation study is summarized in two manuscript chapters, "Seoul Under the Communists" and "Communist Last Days in Seoul," which were not included when Noble's *Embassy at War* was published posthumously. I am grateful to Mrs. Noble for kindly providing copies and permitting me to quote from the manuscript chapters.

81. Higgins, *War in Korea,* pp. 209–211.

   Noble ("Seoul Under the Communists") wrote that the first occupation was "so bitter a lesson that although nearly the whole population stayed behind in June, 1950, the next winter when it appeared that Seoul would be captured again by the communists, despite the snow and ice and bitter cold, well over a million people left the city and scarcely a hundred thousand remained a second time. . . ."

82. Scalapino and Lee write that, as the war came to an end, South Korea was "one of the most staunchly anti-Communist societies in the world. On the other hand, every speech and action of the North Korean officials reflected their deep anxiety regarding the loyalty of their own people and the deplorable conditions prevailing throughout their country" (*Communism in Korea,* p. 462).

   Cumings (*Origins* II, p. 669) acknowledges that South Koreans retained horrible memories of the Northern occupation, but he questions whether their memories were true ones: "In the early days of the new regime, the released prisoners settled scores with their antagonists who had abused and jailed them, mainly members of the Korean National Police and the rightist youth groups. People's courts arraigned and denounced them, after which summary executions took place. This experience has led to a general judgment, reinforced by American propaganda, that the occupation of the south was a living hell for those who experienced it. I myself seem always to be running into Koreans who say the experience was terrible, while also saying they successfully hid out during the entire three months. Evidence from the time, including interviews with ROK officials who fled Seoul, does not suggest that the occupation was politically onerous for the majority of Seoul's citizens, although generalized fear, food shortages and the American bombing made it an often hellish experience."

83. Higgins, *War in Korea*, pp. 209–211.
84. Halliday and Cumings, *Korea*, p. 143.
85. Ibid., p. 132.
86. The communists' redistribution was carried out "in every province outside the Pusan perimeter; although it was hasty and done in wartime conditions, it cleared away class structures and power that later made possible Rhee's land-redistribution programme—because the Americans would not fight merely to restore land to this class that had ruled Korea for centuries" (Halliday and Cumings, *Korea*, p. 87). Also see Cumings, *Origins* II, pp. 471–472 and, especially, p. 760, where the author observes that the war "transformed South Korea; it was the partial equivalent of the revolution its social structure demanded but did not get in the previous five years. The revolution was capitalist and the war foreshortened and hastened it, above all by ending landlordism."
87. Gregory Henderson, "Korea, 1950," in James Cotton and Ian Neary, eds., *The Korean War in History* (Manchester: Manchester University Press, 1989), pp. 175–176. In the Seoul of 1948, in contrast, Henderson wrote, "those leaning northward and those serving the south had then a kind of intimacy they no longer have. One was not quite so abruptly communist or anti-communist then. There was middle ground. All of the [South Korean security forces'] officers personally knew those who had either chosen the other side or leaned in some way toward it. Nor had they always disliked them. The fact that the—as we say in the United States—'Southern way of life' was a little more on the collaboratory side while the North was steelier, more Spartan, more hard-bitten, more ideological and less yielding and opportunistic, all this was known and recognized although not usually thus baldly articulated."
88. Baik II, p. 315.
    One film, according to an official description, told of Jo Ok-hi, a woman party member who joined a partisan force opposing the occupying UN troops in her county. American troops supposedly captured her and "subjected her to every kind of torture in an attempt to wring out of her secrets about the partisan detachment. They pulled out all her fingernails. But the enemy always got the same answers: 'You fools! No one gets secrets from a Workers' Party member!' The bloodthirsty U.S. cannibals . . . gouged out her eyeballs, burned her with a red hot iron and cut off her breasts" (*History of the Just War for the Liberation of the Fatherland of the Korean People* [Pyongyang: Foreign Languages Publishing House, 1961], pp. 133–134, cited by Kiwon Chung, "The North Korean People's Army and the Party," in Scalapino, *Korea Today*, p. 117).
89. Hong Soon-il, "Refugee Village," *Korea Times*, April 20, 1994.
90. "Despite the war-time destructiveness and psychological strains there were few signs of social malaise in North Korea at the end of the war. There appeared to be little murder, theft and personal violence, although there were growing signs of sexual license, especially among the young. Thus, while there were points of popular dissatisfaction, basic [Korean Workers' Party] control over the people of North Korea was not in jeopardy. The Communist version of how the war began was still widely believed" (Paige and Lee, "Post-War Politics," p. 19).
91. "The war-time experience was accompanied by the development of certain unfavourable attitudes toward the KWP and the Soviet Union as well as by the

growth of certain favorable attitudes toward Communist China. The principal discontent with the KWP was that it had not been vigorous enough in its relief and reconstruction work. It was popularly regarded in this respect as the 'do-nothing' party. The Soviet Union suffered in popular esteem because it had not given greater assistance to the North Korean war effort. The North Koreans were aware that South Korea was free from Communist air attack and there-fore hoped for direct retaliation by Soviet airpower against American attacks upon the North. The knowledge that Russian fighter pilots were flying defen-sively over North Korean territory and that the Russians were providing mili-tary and relief supplies did not satisfy the demand for deeper Soviet military commitment, including the participation of Soviet infantry divisions. By con-trast, the North Koreans were favorably impressed by Chinese military assis-tance. Mao Tse-tung's injunction to the Chinese soldiers in Korea to 'love the Korean Democratic People's Republic, the Korean Workers' Party, and the Ko-rean people as your own government, party, and people—and treasure every mountain, every stream, every tree, and every blade of grass the same,' was widely respected and appreciated. This did not mean, however, that Korean-Chinese relations were without points of friction. There was some evidence of professional jealousy, for example, among North Korean army officers who had to take orders from Chinese commanders" (Paige and Lee, "Post-War Politics," pp. 18–19).
92. Baik II, pp. 400, 405. To portray North Korea as the victor, Baik uses American military leaders' public expressions of regret over their side's failures. See pp. 404–405.
93. Kiwon Chung, "North Korean People's Army," p. 112.
94. Kim, *With the Century,* vol. 3, p. 255.

6. With the Leader Who Unfolded Paradise.
1. Baik II (see chap. 4, n. 24), pp. 428–430, provides the meeting-hall anecdote. Baik says (pp. 421–422) that Kim "considered that golden opportunities offered by the armistice should be fully used to promote the socialist revolution and so-cialist construction at full speed, in order to provide a firm guarantee for consol-idating peace and completing the historic cause of the unification of the nation."
2. Scalapino and Lee, *Communism in Korea* (see chap. 2, n. 28), p. 425.
3. *Hankuk Ilbo,* November 16, 1990, in Seiler, *Kim Il-song 1941–1948* (see chap. 2, n. 18).
4. *Hankuk Ilbo,* November 18, 1990.
5. Baik II, p. 369.
6. *Hankuk Ilbo,* November 18, 1990.
7. See Baik II, pp. 308, 388.
8. Suh, *Kim Il Sung* (see chap. 2, n. 25) , pp. 105–108, 127–136.
9. "The trials provided the supreme rationalization for defeat," as Scalapino and Lee say. The North's tribulations could be portrayed as "due not to the mistakes of the Kim group, but because traitors from within had given overt assistance to the enemy" (*Communism in Korea,* p. 451).
10. Chay Pyung-gil, "Following the Conclusion of the Serialization 'Yu Song-ch'ol's Testimony,'" *Hankuk Ilbo,* December 1, 1990, translated in Seiler, *Kim Il-song 1941–1948.*

Bruce Cumings (*Origins* II [see chap. 3, n. 43], p. 830, n. 26) discusses the importance of this group:

"To my knowledge only one source in all the published and unpublished literature on North Korea grasps the central importance of Kim's peculiar style of leadership, and that is thé formerly classified study done in the early 1960s by Evelyn McCune for the U.S. State Department Bureau of Intelligence and Research ('Leadership in North Korea: Groupings and Motivations,' 1963). She correctly terms the relationship between Kim and his close allies 'a semi-chivalrous, irrevocable and unconditional bond . . . under iron discipline.' It is a 'deeply personal' system, 'fundamentally hostile to complex bureaucracy.' Kim and his allies were generalists, jacks-of-all-trades who could run the government or command the army, show a peasant how to use new seeds or cuddle children in a school; Kim would dispatch them as loyal observers of officials and experts or specialists outside the inner core, that is, in the realm of impersonal bureaucracy. McCune thought correctly that the powerful glue holding the Kim group together made it much more formidable than typical Korean political factions, based on weaker patron-client relations and given to splintering in power struggles and personal competition; thus it was able to assert dominance over rival groups rather easily. She also understood the concentric circle metaphor, providing a chart of the leadership radiating outward from Kim."

11. Kim Il-sung, *Selected Works*, vol. 1 (Pyongyang: Foreign Languages Publishing House, 1976), cited in Lim Un, *Founding of a Dynasty* (see chap. 2, n. 59), pp. 221–222. Kim's philosophy of life was, "Don't trust strangers," Lim observes. Thus, Kim not only purged his opposition "but precluded the entire potential of any possible formation of new opposition. For instance, once he pinpointed an object of elimination, he hunted its fellow travelers and collaborators and purged all of them. He further eradicated their relatives, business contacts, and even acquaintances. When an army general was purged so were his relatives, relatives on his wife's side, his leaders, staff, adjutants, drivers, and all relatives of these people, persons from the same home town and schoolmates, and so forth. The extent of the victimization spread like a creeping potato vine."

12. Baik II, pp. 378–380.

13. Ibid., p. 456.

14. Yoon T. Kuark, "North Korea's Industrial Development During the Post-War Period," in Robert A. Scalapino, ed., *North Korea Today* (New York: Frederick A. Praeger, 1963), p. 54.

15. "[B]etween 1946 and 1965 the share of industry and agriculture as components of national income was almost exactly reversed: from 16.8 percent and 63.5 percent to 64.2 percent and 18.3 percent" (Aidan Foster-Carter, "North Korea. Development and Self Reliance: A Critical Appraisal," in Gavan McCormack and John Gittings, eds., *Crisis in Korea* [London, Spokesman Books, 1977], p. 81).

16. Joseph Sang-hoon Chung, *The North Korean Economy: Structure and Development* (Stanford, Calif.: Hoover Institution Press, 1974), p. 145.

17. Kuark, "Industrial Development," p. 61.

18. Van Ree, *Socialism in One Zone* (see chap. 4, n. 1), p. 182.

Suh (*Kim Il Sung*, p. 140) mentions a Soviet loan of 1 billion rubles in 1953, along with an extension of repayment time for previous Soviet loans. The same year the Chinese provided a loan of 8 trillion yuan. "The Chinese were more generous than the Soviet Union and canceled all North Korean debts to China, including materials supplied by the Chinese during the Korean War from 1950 to 1953."

19. "North Korea has been generally free from the kind of factionalism, frequent revolutions, corruption, ineptitude, inflation, unemployment, and so on that demoralized and undermined many an emerging economy" (Chung, *The North Korean Economy,* p. 158). Chung says Kim's tight dictatorial control brought a stability that probably contributed to economic development even as it dampened private incentives.

20. Baik II, p. 448.

21. Although in 1945 Kim was reported to have asked to be called by the plain title *dongmoo* (comrade), Paige and Lee report that in the 1950s "[a]t least one high official has been fired from his post" for referring to Kim as *dongmoo* instead of *t'ongji,* the honorific version ("Post-War Politics" [see chap. 5, n. 58], p. 28).

22. "In the nine years since the fighting stopped, North Korea has become something of a showcase, with plenty of window-dressing and propaganda for Communism in Asia" (Kuark, "Industrial Development," p. 51).

23. Kim Il-sung, "On Communist Education," November 28, 1958, quoted in Kim Chang-soon, "North Korea Today," *Vantage Point* (March 1979): p. 12.

24. Baik II, p. 423.

    Proponents of North–South Korean coexistence, Kim Il-sung said on November 3, 1954, "seem to think that the responsibility for the revolution in South Korea rests entirely upon the South Korean people and that we, the people in North Korea, are not responsible for liberating the South. This is nothing but an attempt to justify the division of the country and perpetuate it. Such a tendency must be thoroughly done away with." See "On Our Party's Policy for the Further Development of Agriculture," in Kim Il Sung, *Selected Works,* cited in Scalapino and Lee, *Communism in Korea,* vol. 1, p. 545.

25. Baik II, p. 438.

26. Kim Il-sung, "Sasang saopeso kyojojuuiwa hyongsikchuuirul t'oejihago chuch'erul hwangnip hal te taehayo" ("On Exterminating Dogmatism and Formalism and Establishing Independence in Ideological Work"), in *Kim Il-song Sonjip (Kim Il-sung Selected Works) IV* (Pyongyang: Korean Workers' Party Press, 1960), p. 343, translated in Glenn D. Paige and Dong Jun Lee, "The Post-War Politics of Communist Korea," in Scalapino, *North Korea Today* (see chap. 3, n. 11), pp. 26–27. Paige and Lee note, "Such thinking as this may [underlie] apparent Korean sympathy for the Chinese emphasis on widespread wars of 'national liberation.'"

27. See Scalapino and Lee, *Communism in Korea,* pp. 461–462; 543–548. As for the policy in the immediate post-liberation period, the authors report (pp. 300–301) that within a year after liberation, American and South Korean officials had begun to hear from informers about a "communist master plan" for South Korea. Under this plan, it was alleged, communists in the South would spin off front groups that would publicly take issue with the communists and assume a pose of neutrality. The Southern communists, pretending to be weakened by such maneuvers, would then offer to compromise, joining the rightists and "neutrals" in a united-front government. Believing that the communists' share of power was small, the Americans would accept this united-front government and withdraw their troops from the South. Then disguised communists planted in the security forces would take advantage of made-to-order controversies and disorders to come forth, restore order and seize power.

28. *Korea Times*, May 12 1995, and my June 1995 conversation with Park Jin, presidential spokesman.
29. See Baik II, p. 510, and Kiwon Chung, "The North Korean People's Army and the Party," in Scalapino, *North Korea Today*, pp. 118–119.

    Note that in the five-year plan promulgated in 1956, "[s]pecial steps were taken to deal with new war preparations and subversive plots being intensified by U.S. imperialism and its stooges, for which [Kim Il-sung] stressed the need to enhance the roles of home, police and judicial organs, and bring to light and destroy every kind of enemy subversive scheme as quickly as possible" (Baik II, p. 491).
30. "Personally I think if we could get a neutralized Korea that I would buy it. I do worry though as to whether we would be able to help a neutralized Korea sufficiently so the ROKs [South Koreans] wouldn't go Communist in a fairly short time" (Frank C. Nash, assistant secretary of defense for international security affairs, quoted in a declassified, formerly top-secret "Memorandum of the Substance of Discussion at a Department of State–Joint Chiefs of Staff Meeting," June 16, 1953, in *Foreign Relations of the United States 1952–1954*, vol. XV: *Korea*, pt. 2 [Washington, D.C.: Government Printing Office, 1984], p. 1187).
31. Ibid., pp. 1193–1194.
32. NSC 154/1, ibid., pp. 1341–1344.
33. NSC 157/1, "U.S. Objective with Respect to Korea Following an Armistice," ibid., pp. 1344–1346.
34. Paige and Lee, "Post-War Politics," p. 27.
35. Kim, *With the Century* (see chap. 2, n. 2), vol. 3, p. 429.
36. "Victorious History of Chongryun," *People's Korea*, 20 May 1995. In Japanese the group is called "Chosen Soren."
37. "[B]etween 1959 and 1974," says Foster-Carter, "92,000 Koreans left Japan to settle permanently in the DPRK . . . . Of these, 75,000 or over 80 per cent went in the short period 1959–1962." ("Development and Self Reliance," p. 104). He cites a Chongryon source quoted in *Sekai*, no. 3 (1975), p. 190, for the overall figures. For the 1959–1962 figures he cites G. A. De Vos and W. O. Wetherall, *Japan's Minorities*, rev. ed. (London: Minority Rights Group Report no. 3, September 1974). Foster-Carter also cites De Vos and Wetherall (p. 15) for this observation: "North Korea most effectively courted . . . Japan's Koreans in ethnic education and national identification, in contrast with the South Korean Government, which provided practically no assistance and seemed at times, in alliance with the Japanese Ministry of Education, even opposed to such concerns." And he cites Jonathan Unger ("Foreign Minorities in Japan," *Journal of Contemporary Asia*, vol. 3, no. 3, p. 307) for these further indications of the comparative appeal of North Korea over South Korea during this period: "In 1960, 445,000 of Japan's Koreans designated North Korea as their mother-country, while only 163,000 opted for South Korea—despite the fact that almost all of Japan's Koreans originated from Korea's South."
38. Interviewed June 1994 in Seoul, Chong was among several Japanese-Koreans who defected from North Korea to South Korea. Available evidence strongly suggests that a very high percentage of repatriates from Japan had found their experiences in North Korea to be highly unsatisfactory.
39. This detail comes from an interview (Seoul, June 1994) with another defector, Kim Myong-chol, who was born in the North the year Chong emigrated from Japan.

40. Baik II, p. 547.
41. See Baik II, pp. 497–516. Also see Chong-sik Lee, "Land Reform, Collectivisation and the Peasants in North Korea," in Scalapino, ed., *North Korea Today*, pp. 65–81. In another article in the same volume, "North Korea's Agricultural Development During the Post-War Period," Yoon T. Kuark observes (p. 91) that the Chollima movement was less radical than China's Great Leap, and that Pyongyang quickly drew back from some of the more extreme measures it did impose—although the radical land collectivization remained in force.
42. Baik II, p. 515.
43. Ibid., pp. 505–506.
44. Kuark, "Agricultural Development," p. 91, citing North Korean official sources.
45. Baik II, p. 503.
46. "Since entering the 1960s, coinciding with the Seven Year Plan, the pace of over-all economic progress as measured by national income began to drop sharply. Average annual rate of growth in national income declined to 8.9 percent during 1961–67 [as opposed to an average growth rate of 16.6 percent for the entire 1954–67 period]. The fact that no mention was made of the status of national income (as well as agricultural output) for 1970 in Kim Il-song's speech to the Fifth Congress suggests that the Seven Year Plan target of raising national income to 2.7 times the 1960 level by 1970 (originally by 1967) was not fulfilled" (Chung, *North Korean Economy* [see chap. 6, n. 16], p. 155).
47. I am grateful to Prof. Youngok Seo-Kim for pointing out this information.
48. Grain dealers had been eliminated in 1954. See Lee, "Land Reform," p. 78.
49. Baik II, pp. 555–556. Baik adds (p. 556), "On the contrary, the workers and peasants who could not live well are now satisfied and never complain, because their livelihood has been improved."
50. Byoung-Lo Philo Kim, *Two Koreas* (see chap. 1, n. 2), p. 66.
51. Ambassador Walter P. McConaughy, "Telegram from the Embassy in Korea to the Department of State," April 11, 1961, Document No. 210 in *Foreign Relations of the United States 1961–1963, vol. XXII* (Washington, D.C.: Department of State, 1996), http://www.state.gov/www/about_state/history/frusXXII/201to240.html.
52. Karl Mener, "Seeing Is Believing," in *Impressions of Korea* (Pyongyang: Foreign Languages Publishing House, 1961), p. 23.
53. Joan Robinson, "Korean Miracle," *Monthly Review* (January 1965): pp. 545–548, quoted in Chung, *North Korean Economy*, p. 151. Chung comments, "Calling the North Korean feat a miracle perhaps overstates the case but nevertheless dramatizes her achievements as evidenced by various indicators: rapid growth and the absolute level (total and per capita) of national income and of strategic industrial products (per capita output of 1,184 kilowatt hours of electricity, 1,975 kilograms of coal, and 158 kilograms of steel in 1970); a long-term change in the composition of national income in favor of industry; change in the structure within the industrial sector in favor of heavy industry, especially the machinery sector; change in the commodity composition of foreign trade and evidence of significant import substitution as well as impressive growth in exports; shifts in the occupational distribution of population in favor of secondary industry at the expense of the primary; increasing urbanization of population; and so on."
   Another scholar's summary: "[E]ven if one makes allowances for Communist propaganda and window-dressing . . . it appears indisputable to this author

that North Korea has made greater economic strides during the post-war period as a whole than has South Korea. In the industrial sector there is good reason to take at face value the Communist claim that 'in 1959 the North produced ten times as much steel as South Korea and five times more cement.' . . . It remains to be seen, however, whether the Communists can surpass Japan's *per capita* industrial production in ten years as the ambitious premier, Kim Il-song, prophesied in 1959. . . . In a nutshell, the recent economic offensive of the Communist North, with the usual dazzle of unconfirmable statistics, may have a grave impact upon the people of South Korea in their current plight. For there is no better bait to poverty-stricken people than economic advance" (Kuark, "Industrial Development," pp. 63, 64).

54. Baik II, pp. 28, 29. This book was published in the 1960s but the characterization of Kim and his destiny is not unlike what could be heard in the '50s.

55. Ibid., p. 138.

Dae-Sook Suh observes, "The fundamental reason for the North Korean endeavor to build up the image of Kim Il-song as the father of the Korean revolution is, primarily, his non-Korean revolutionary past. He fought under a Communist army and became a Communist, but it was with the Chinese, and possibly the Russians, not with the Korean Communists. In the Korean Communist movement and among Korean Communist leaders, Kim Il-song is an alien who advanced through the ranks of the Chinese Communist revolutionaries in Manchuria and was educated and trained by the Chinese Communists as one of their own, not as a delegate or a representative of Korean Communists among the Chinese. Kim's revolutionary past is a remarkable one, considering that he was only thirty-three in 1945—even if it was in the Chinese army. He was a Korean, a Communist, and he fought against the Japanese, scoring some important victories in Manchuria against them. It is his effort to build the image of a towering mountain from a molehill past that brings the perplexities, denunciations and doubts of his Communist revolutionary past" (Suh, *Korean Communist Movement* [see chap. 2, n. 56], p. 293).

56. Kim Il-sung Square opened in 1954 (Baik II, p. 457). Kim Chaek, who had died during the Korean War, was one of the few leaders besides Kim Il-sung whose names were carried on institutionally. Kim Chaek had a steel works and the city in which it was situated named after him, as well as the leading technical college, in Pyongyang.

57. Lankov, *From Stalin to Kim Il Sung* (see chap. 4, note 45), pp. 154–193. (Some extended quotations are from an earlier, manuscript version of that chapter.) Evaluating the outcome of this open challenge to Kim Il-sung's power, Lankov says (p. 193) that it "determined the direction of North Korean development over the following decades. Before 1956 the country had been a typical 'people's democracy,' in many respects not unlike the regimes of Soviet-dominated Eastern Europe, but after 1956 it began to transform itself into a much more idiosyncratic Communist state: thoroughly controlled, extremely militarized, devoted to a fanatical personality cult and a particular type of ideology, and far removed from 'orthodox' Marxism-Leninism. The very term for this ideology, 'chuch'e' [juche], was coined on the eve of the 1956 crisis, in December 1955."

58. *Hankuk Ilbo*, November 18 and November 20, 1990.

59. Kim, *With the Century*, vol. 1, preface.

Bruce Cumings (*Origins* II [see chap. 3, n. 43], p. 292) criticizes use of the terms "Stalinist" and "oriental despot" to describe Kim Il-sung when "there is no evidence in the North Korean experience of the mass violence against whole classes of people or the classic, wholesale 'purge' that characterized Stalinism, and that has been particularly noteworthy in the land reform campaigns in China and North Vietnam and the purges of the Cultural Revolution."

Hungarian scholar Balazs Szalontai ("The Dynamic of Repression: The Global Impact of the Stalinist Model, 1944–1953" [see chap. 4, n. 45]) says that Kim's purges during this period were "comparable to the attack Stalin had launched on the intra-party opposition in 1926–1928, and even to the Great Terror of 1937, 1938, but its methods proved rather different. First of all, the number of party members expelled between July 1957 and July 1958 did not exceed 4,000, i.e., less than one per cent of the total membership. By contrast, the Soviet *proverka* of 1935 had resulted in the expulsion of 9.1 per cent of party members. On the other hand, the enforced participation of the whole membership in the screening process certainly filled each KWP member with fear and a sense of insecurity. . . . [P]arty members, assembled in groups, had to practise criticism and self-criticism. If a person proved unable to name two witnesses testifying that he had not been involved in any anti-regime activity since the outbreak of the Korean War, his self-criticism would not be accepted. Since one was prohibited from naming relatives, friends, or acquaintances as his witnesses, the psychological pressure thus created became extremely intense. In the second half of 1958 the regime purged the provincial party committees and People's Committees, replacing most of their chairmen, and at the end of the year it organized a public trial in each province. The courts usually meted out death sentences (executions were also public), and in some cases the incited audience beat the accused unconscious. The methods . . . had more in common with Maoist practices than with Soviet Stalinism. Nevertheless, the events that happened in North Korea between 1957 and 1969 had a logic somewhat similar to that of the Soviet purges of 1926–1938."

60. Kim's official biographer obviously had Khrushchev and company in mind when he wrote scathingly of those communists who "baulked at the struggle against imperialism, and putting principles aside, entered into compromises with it. Spreading illusions about the nature of imperialism, in particular U.S. imperialism, they did everything within their power to dampen the revolutionary struggles of the peoples seeking social and national liberation" (Baik II, p. 485).

61. See van Ree, *Socialism in One Zone*, pp. 121–122. This sort of attitude can be seen throughout Lim Un's book, *The Founding of a Dynasty in North Korea—An Authentic Biography of Kim Il-song*, which is one of the reasons for doubting Bruce Cumings's suggestion that it is actually a South Korean–produced work.

Suh observes (*Kim Il Sung*, p. 108) that "Soviet-Koreans lost much when the Soviet Union withdrew and did not return to fight for [North] Korea during the Korean War."

62. Cumings (*Origins* I [see chap. 2, n. 25], p. xxv) says that Soviet policy in North Korea "failed to create a docile satellite state . . . because the Soviets sponsored a group of radical nationalists who had cut their teeth in anti-Japanese conflict and who chafed under Soviet controls."

63. Kim complained in his memoirs that misguided North Koreans even referred to Ri Su-bok, a communist hero of the Korean War battle to retake Heartbreak Ridge, as "the Korean Matrosov," a reference to a Soviet war hero (Kim, *With the Century*, vol. 3, p. 333).

    In China, Mao Zedong had reached a similar stage of dissatisfaction with the tendency of many of his colleagues to imitate Soviet practice. As his personal physician writes, "[i]nstitutional and organizational arrangements were being copied without regard to the special circumstances of China. . . . It was this dis-affection with his own party that would fester for years and grow, leading finally to the catastrophe of the Cultural Revolution" (Dr. Li Zhisui, *The Private Life of Chairman Mao: The Memoirs of Mao's Personal Physician* [New York: Random House, 1994], pp. 118–119).

64. October 13, 1945, speech to Five Province Conference, cited by Scalapino and Lee, *Communism in Korea*, p. 330. Judging from pp. 253–254, there may be some question whether the "Comrade Kim" who was speaking was Kim Il-sung, but on p. 330 Scalapino and Lee say this speech is found in a different version in Kim's selected works, published in 1963. In any case, this was not an isolated ex-ample. Scalapino and Lee refer on p. 347 to Kim's "lengthy and obsequious eu-logies of the Russians."

65. Van Ree, *Socialism in One Zone*, p. 159.

66. *Nodong Shinmun*, July 2, 1950, as cited by Cumings, *Origins* II, p. 633.

67. Kim, *With the Century*, vol. 3, p. 333.

68. Van Ree, *Socialism in One Zone*, p. 165. The author adds, "In the 1945–50 period Soviet radio broadcasts were relayed at least three times a day to North Korea. Soviet news was distributed through the North Korean news agency. In 1947 English was discontinued in all senior middle schools; Russian became a com-pulsory subject. There was a large influx of Soviet literature and films. From 1946–8 a total of ten million books were published in North Korea. In one of his 1948 speeches Kim Il Sung revealed that after the merger of the parties the Cen-tral Committee of the North Korean Workers' Party published nearly three mil-lion books of propaganda and on Marxism-Leninism, including the translation of Stalin's notorious history of the Soviet communist party. We can safely as-sume that of these three million political books a substantial portion were trans-lations from Russian." Besides, "Moscow had a strong—an unfriendly observer would say strangling—economic leverage in the form of its quasi-monopoly on P'yongyang's foreign trade."

69. Van Ree, *Socialism in One Zone*, p. 168.

70. A typical account in a 1976 *Nodong Shinmun* (Workers' Daily) article by Yi Chan-gol says, "The great leader Comrade Kim Il-sung issued orders to all com-manders and soldiers of the Korean People's Revolutionary Army to defeat the Japanese imperialists." This force then "delivered the decisive blow to the Japanese Kwantung Army" in Manchuria before moving to Korea, where it "fi-nally defeated the Japanese completely and liberated the whole country" (quoted in Lim Un, *Founding of a Dynasty*, p. 109).

    An official biography is slightly more generous to the Russians: "On August 8, 1945, the Soviet Union finally declared war on Japan. General Kim Il-sung, who had already completed his operational plan for the final decisive offensives against Japan, immediately ordered the mobilization of all units under the Ko-rean People's Revolutionary Army. . . . In the face of the strong attack by the

Korean People's Revolutionary Army and the Soviet Army, Japan's 'impregnable defense line' guarding the border collapsed like a wall of clay, and the main forces of the Kwantung Army, so proud of its might, were completely crushed" (Baik I [see chap. 4, n. 25], pp. 529–530).

71. Seiler (p. 46) cites an August 26, 1991, interview article in *JoongAng Ilbo*, a leading Seoul daily, in which the Soviet occupation chief, Maj. Gen. Nikolai Lebedev, recalled that Kim had asked him directly, "Commander, sir, please make it so that it appears as though the anti-Japanese partisans participated in the war of liberation." Lebedev declined.

72. Hwang Jang-yop, *Problems of Human Rights (1)* (see chap. 2, n. 1).

73. Suh, *Kim Il Sung*, p. 104. He adds, "They claim that it was Kim who returned triumphantly and founded the Communist republic of the North. These assertions deserve no refutation."

74. "If, in North Korea, one were to say that 'Korea was liberated from the yoke of Japanese imperialism by the Soviet Russian army,' the reaction would be most curious to observe," Lim Un wrote in his 1982 book. "Those between their teens and 30's in age will give a confident answer that it is propaganda of imperialists and the domineering class. It is a malicious lie . . . . Korea was liberated by the People's Revolutionary Army led by comrade Kim Il-song. Those Koreans in their 40's and 50's will say that from the memory of our childhood, we think the Soviet army liberated Korea. But in looking back upon those days, they will say meekly that they thought the Korean People's Revolutionary Army liberated the fatherland. Those above the age of 50 would not give any answer. For them silence is the only answer, as if to agree with the statement that Korea was liberated by the Soviet army" (Lim Un, *Founding of a Dynasty*, p. 265).

75. Suh reports that Pyongyang museum curators literally cropped the likeness of Kim's Chinese superior from a photograph showing Kim with guerrillas (*Kim Il Sung*, pp. 8–10).

76. *Hankuk Ilbo*, November 4, 1990.

77. *Hankuk Ilbo*, November 20 and 26, 1990.

78. *Hankuk Ilbo*, November 29, 1990.

79. Kim Il-sung, "On Eliminating Dogmatism and Formalism and Establishing *Juche* in Ideological Work," December 28, 1955, quoted in Baik II, p. 479. According to the scholar who served as Kim's ideology secretary from 1958 to 1965, before the Korean War the word *juche* "did not even exist. The North Korean leaders started using that word during the purging of pro-Soviet and pro-Chinese people from the party, and 'Juche ideology' became an established phrase only in the 1960s" (Hwang Jang-yop, *The Problems of Human Rights [1]*).

80. Kim Il Sung. *Selected Works*, vol. 1, p. 36, quoted in Bruce G. Cumings, "Kim's Korean Communism," *Problems of Communism* (March-April 1974), p. 36, cited in Foster-Carter, "Development and Self Reliance," p. 75.

81. "In postwar economic construction we must follow the line of giving priority to the rehabilitation and development of heavy industry, while simultaneously developing light industry and agriculture," as Kim put it (Baik II, p. 431). Baik says (pp. 432–433) that it was possible to carry out this "bold and original basic line" because of "the revolutionary ideas and seasoned guidance of Comrade Kim Il Sung, the great Leader of the 40 million Korean people, peerless patriot, national hero, ever-victorious, iron-willed brilliant commander."

82. Quoted in Baik II, p. 558.

83. Ibid., pp. 554–555.
84. I interviewed Shin and Ahn, separately, in Seoul in August 1996.
85. Baik II, p. 560.
86. Ibid., pp. 477–481, 517–523.
87. Some foreign analysts believed for a time that Kim had made the right choice. For example, Aidan Foster-Carter ("Development and Self Reliance," pp. 77–78) praised Kim for "a difficult decision to chart a course not previously mapped out by any other country. In that sense his far-sightedness can be said to be a major cause of the DPRK's subsequent remarkable development." As evidence piled up that Pyongyang's economic policies had become counterproductive, Foster-Carter revised his opinion drastically to become a leading critic of those policies. He acknowledged the error of his former ways far more forthrightly than was the case with some other analysts who had started out in the same camp. A blurb introducing his contributions to the Web site *Asia Times Online* (www.atimes.com/atimes/about.html) noted with a touch of self-deprecating humor that Foster-Carter had "followed Korean affairs for over 30 years, starting (embarrassingly) as a young fan of Kim Il-sung."
      (Full disclosure: Although I would not by any means have described myself as a fan of Kim's, I acknowledge having been pretty impressed [see chap. 9] by what the Great Leader, to a 1979 first-time North Korea visitor, appeared to have wrought with the economy.)
88. Kim Jong-min, a former high-ranking official of North Korea's Ministry of Public Security, said when interviewed by a South Korean magazine in 1991 that he still considered it "quite an impressive accomplishment that Kim Il-sung has been able to silence the mouths of the North Korean people, people who ordinarily would have much to say." Emphasizing *juche* was the key to this, since "even among Orientals the pride of the Korean people is extraordinary," he said. "Kim used this psychology in his politics in creating juche. Kim Il-sung skillfully uses the nationalistic self-reliant consciousness of the Korean people" (Cho Gap-jae, "Interview of Former High-level Official of DPRK Ministry of Public Security Who Defected to South Korea," *Wolgan Choson* [July 1991]: pp. 290–303; translation courtesy of Sydney A. Seiler). The article referred to the former official using a pseudonym, Choe Sang-kyu. In a later interview with me, Kim Jong-min confirmed that he was "Choe" and said that he had been quoted correctly in the *Wolgan Choson* interview. He gave me permission to attribute that material to him using his real name. I also have permission from *Wolgan Choson* interviewer Cho to identify his interview subject as Kim Jong-min.
89. "The defeated U.S. imperialists continue to squat in South Korea, sharpening their tusks. But the heroic Korean people under the leadership of Comrade Kim Il Sung, the ever-victorious iron-willed brilliant commander, will not let them live on. It is complete defeat that is waiting for U.S. imperialism in Korea" (Baik II, p. 417).
90. It is open to question how much the atomic threat frightened China, in particular. As we have seen, Mao Zedong had already decided it was unlikely the United States would dare to use nuclear weapons against either China or North Korea. Mao's personal physician writes that it was apparent "as early as October 1954, from a meeting with India's Prime Minister Jawaharlal Nehru, that Mao considered the atom bomb a 'paper tiger' and that he was willing that

China lose millions of people in order to emerge victorious against the so-called imperialists. 'The atom bomb is nothing to be afraid of,' Mao told Nehru. 'China has many people. They cannot be bombed out of existence'" (Dr. Li Zhisui, *Private Life of Chairman Mao*, p. 125).

91. "WASHINGTON (AP)—The United States had explicit plans for dropping the atomic bomb on mainland China in 1954 if the Chinese violated the tenuous truce that had brought the Korean War to an inconclusive end, according to a newly declassified Pentagon document. The April 17, 1954 memo, signed by Brig. Gen. Edwin H. J. Carns, who was secretary to the Joint Chiefs of Staff, showed the extent to which the Eisenhower administration was ready to use nuclear weapons in enforcing Secretary of State John Foster Dulles' Cold War policy of 'massive retaliation.'

"'In light of the enemy capability to launch a massive ground offensive, U.S. air support operations, including use of atomic weapons, will be employed to inflict maximum destruction of enemy forces,' the memo said, detailing the U.S. response for the war's resumption with Chinese forces again massively involved. The document also showed that the United States planned to blockade China's coasts, seize offshore islands and use Chinese Nationalist forces to stage raids on the mainland in the event of renewed hostilities. The memo—of which only 30 copies were made, each numbered—was among 44 million documents from World War II and the postwar years and from the Korean and Vietnam wars that were declassified in a blanket order signed by President Clinton last month" (from an Associated Press dispatch, *Korea Times*, December 14, 1994).

92. See James R. Lilley, "U.S. Security Policy and the Korean Peninsula," in Christopher J. Sigur, ed., *Korea's New Challenges and Kim Young Sam* (New York: Carnegie Council on Ethics and International Affairs, 1993), pp. 129–130.

93. Halliday and Cumings (*Korea*, p. 215) note, "In 1957 the USA announced that it would no longer recognize the authority of the Neutral Nations Supervisory Commission, which had been set up to supervise compliance with the armistice, and that it regarded itself as at liberty to bring in new armaments, including nuclear weapons." As of 1987–1988, they add, there were "approximately 41,000 US military personnel in South Korea, with nuclear weapons. South Korea is the only place in the world where nuclear weapons are used to deter a non-nuclear force.... There are no ... nuclear weapons in the North."

94. See, e.g., items 204–209 in U.S. Department of State, *Foreign Relations of the United States, 1958–1960*, vol. XVIII: *Japan and Korea* (Washington, D.C.: Government Printing Office, 1994), pp. 424–432. Also see "Telegram from the Commander in Chief, United Nations Command (Decker) to the Department of State, Seoul, April 4, 1958," item 220, for a U.S.–South Korean agreement that yields insight into the extent of American attempts to exert budgetary controls over the South Korean military. "Republic of Korea forces construction projects will be limited to essential requirements approved by CINCUNC [commander in chief United Nations Command, an American general]," it states. "The Republic of Korea military budget will be jointly reviewed and analyzed by the Republic of Korea and CINCUNC in order to assure that the military program will produce the most effective forces at minimum cost.... No Republic of Korea Force asset shall be expended for any project which is not clearly and directly a military requirement unless specific concurrence for such diversion shall have been granted by CINCUNC."

A formerly top secret memorandum of a meeting of the U.S. National Security Council paraphrases the remark of President Eisenhower that "some of those at the meeting apparently did not know Rhee. Difficulties had been experienced for many years with Rhee, who was so emotional he had once proposed sending ROK forces up to the Yalu River. The situation became worse as Rhee became senile. But we must persuade him or lose prestige" ("Memorandum of Discussion at the 375th Meeting of the National Security Council, Washington, August 7, 1958," item 236, *Foreign Relations of the United States, 1958–1960,* vol. XVIII, p. 482).

It was November of 1958 before the American negotiators finally persuaded Rhee to agree to maintain a maximum eighteen-division army, with total armed forces numbering no more than 630,000 men. See footnote 3, *Foreign Relations of the United States, 1958–1960,* vol. XVIII, p. 507.

95. See "Memorandum from the Director of the Office of Northeast Asian Affairs (Parsons) to the Deputy Assistant Secretary of State for Far Eastern Affairs (Jones), Washington, February 8, 1958," item 213 in *Foreign Relations of the United States, 1958–1960,* vol. XVIII, p. 436.

96. "Memorandum from the Assistant Secretary of State for Far Eastern Affairs (Robertson) to Secretary of State Dulles, Washington, February 28, 1958," item 215 in *Foreign Relations of the United States, 1958–1960,* vol. XVIII, pp. 440–441.

Another U.S. State Department memorandum of 1958, formerly secret, refers to "the withdrawal of U.S. troops in 1949 and the *resultant* Communist invasion" (italics are mine). See "Memorandum from the Deputy Assistant Secretary of State for Far Eastern Affairs (Parsons) to the Assistant Secretary of State for Policy Planning (Smith), Washington, July 11, 1958," item 231 in *Foreign Relations of the United States, 1958–1960,* vol. XVIII, p. 472.

97. Judging partly on the basis of a rosy evaluation of the May 2, 1958, National Assembly elections, a State Department "Progress Report on Korea" claimed, "Gradual but tangible progress has been made in the development of democratic institutions and political stability in the ROK." But the report listed a slew of economic problems yet to be solved—and its optimistic prognosis on the political side was to prove premature by decades. See "Memorandum from the Director of the Office of Northeast Asian Affairs (Parsons) to the Assistant Secretary of State for Far Eastern Affairs (Robertson), Washington, June 4, 1958," item 225 in *Foreign Relations of the United States, 1958–1960,* vol. XVIII, p. 460. Also see item 215 (n. 96)

98. In a conversation with the South Korean vice-president on June 19, 1958, the American ambassador expressed his personal opinion that "the Communist Chinese would have to follow the Soviet Union's policy" regarding Korean unification. "Memorandum for the Record, Seoul, June 27, 1958," item 228, *Foreign Relations of the United States, 1958–1960,* vol. XVIII, p. 464.

The image of monolithic communism was to prove, for a time, impervious even to the contortions that some communist countries such as North Korea went through once the Sino-Soviet split became apparent. America's leaders during that period were simply unable to understand nationalism's offsetting power against direction of other communist countries from Moscow or Beijing—as the escalation of involvement in Vietnam showed clearly. Robert S. McNamara, secretary of defense in the Kennedy and Johnson administrations, in a regretful memoir of his involvement in the Vietnam War writes that "the top East Asian and China experts in the State Department—John Paton Davies Jr., John Stewart Service and John Carter Vincent—had been purged during the McCarthy hysteria of the 1950s. Without men like these to provide sophisticated, nuanced insights, we—certainly I—badly misread China's objectives and mistook its bellicose rhetoric to imply a drive for regional hegemony. We also totally underestimated the nationalist aspect of Ho Chi Minh's movement. We saw him first as a Communist and only second as a Vietnamese nationalist." President Lyndon Johnson was "convinced that the Soviet Union and China were bent on achieving hegemony. He saw the takeover of South Vietnam as a step toward that objective" (Robert S. McNamara, "We Were Wrong, Terribly WRONG," *Newsweek*, April 17, 1995, pp. 46, 48). (The article is a pre-publication excerpt from McNamara's book, *In Retrospect* [New York: Times Books, 1995].)

99. A once top-secret 1958 U.S. policy statement says, in part, that "U.S. interests are deeply involved in Korea. Unless the United States continues to provide strong political, military and economic support to the Republic of Korea, the Communist bloc probably will ultimately succeed in extending its control over the whole of Korea. Such a development would undermine Free World security in the Northeast Asia area" ("National Security Council Report NSC 5817, Washington, August 11, 1958," *Foreign Relations of the United States, 1958–1960,* vol. XVIII, p. 486).

100. Pyongyang fueled such fears with apocalyptic propaganda. In 1965 North Korea "called upon the Koreans in the South to 'throw their bodies in front of the frenzied drive of the American imperialists, the Pak Chong-hi puppets and the Japanese reactionaries.' The treaty between Japan and South Korea was ratified. Japanese investment began to flow into Korea, and this development, along with others, stimulated the first sustained high-level growth in the south. From this point on, North Korean spokesmen were to regard 'the menace of Japanese militarism' as second only to 'the threat of American imperialism.' " In an October 1966 major address Kim Il-sung charged that "Japan's Sato government, with the active support of U.S. imperialism, has not only mapped out the plans of war to invade Korea and other Asian nations but has already started stretching its tentacles of aggression into Korea" (Scalapino and Lee, *Communism in Korea,* p. 536).

101. A senior State Department official characterized the Japanese unwillingness to take Beijing's and Pyongyang's bait as "a most encouraging development." See "Memorandum on the Substance of Discussion at a Department of State–Joint Chiefs of Staff Meeting, Washington, February 28, 1958," item 216 in *Foreign Relations of the United States, 1958–1960,* vol. XVIII, pp. 443–444. The memorandum also quotes Adm. Arleigh Burke, chief of naval operations, as mentioning "that the Chinese Communist troops were apparently having difficulties with the local population (marriages, food) which may have been one reason why it was decided to effect the withdrawal."

102. Editorial Note, item 221, *Foreign Relations of the United States, 1958–1960,* vol. XVIII, pp. 455–456.

103. See "Memorandum from the Assistant Secretary of State for Far Eastern Affairs (Robertson) to Secretary of State Dulles, Washington, November 18, 1958," item 247 in *Foreign Relations of the United States, 1958–1960,* vol. XVIII, p. 504.

104. Hwang Jang-yop, *The Problems of Human Rights in North Korea (2)*, trans. Network for North Korean Democracy and Human Rights (Seoul: NKnet, 2002), http://nknet.org/en/keys/lastkeys/2002/8/04.php.
105. Baik II, p. 449.
106. Ibid., pp. 457–459.
107. Ibid., pp. 460–461.
108. Kim, *With the Century,* vol. 3, pp. 431–433.

7. When He Hugged Us Still Damp from the Sea.

1. "The same Confucian value system held by the two Koreas has produced two fundamentally different outlooks toward development. Korea, generally speaking, has traditionally emphasized the importance of the Confucian belief in scholarship over commerce and material things. The Korean *yangban* [nobles, gentry], for example, were clearly not commercially minded. Confucian ideology disdains commercial activities, resulting in the economic stagnation of the Yi dynasty. This tradition was easily carried on in North Korea where communism disdained commercial and service activities. People were mobilized not by material incentives but by moral exhortation. In a way, Korean Confucianism was strengthened by communism in North Korea. This particularly explains the lack of development of the service sector and consumer goods in North Korea. . . . Pluralistic values help explain the extraordinary commercial bustle, the materialism, and conspicuous consumption of the people in South Korea. Christians are somewhat overrepresented in the entrepreneurial population in South Korea . . . . This is particularly helped by a Weberian 'spirit of capitalism' abetted by aspects of Protestant dogma thought to encourage commercial activities as a means of achieving personal salvation" (Byoung-Lo Philo Kim, *Two Koreas in Development* [see chap. 1, n. 2], pp. 179–180).
2. Baik II, p. 528 (see chap. 4, n. 24).
3. "Central planning was highly effective and capable of developing the North Korean economy at the beginning stage—the first seven or fifteen years—relying on mobilization measures. As the size of the economy grew, the complexity of planning and choice-making multiplied, making the central decision-making process more inefficient and wasteful than in the formative and reconstruction period" (Kim, *Two Koreas in Development,* p. 123).

   Andrei Lankov (*From Stalin to Kim Il Sung* [see chap. 4, note 45], p. 135) points additionally to unintended aftereffects of the purge of Soviet-Koreans, who had comprised a large percentage of North Korea's best-trained officials: "The mass exodus of Soviet Koreans in the late 1950s and early 1960s became one of the factors contributing to the deceleration of the country's economic development."
4. Hwang Jang-yop, *Problems of Human Rights (1)* (see chap. 2, n. 1).
5. Byoung-Lo Philo Kim, citing a U.S. Central Intelligence Agency report among other sources, observes (*Two Koreas in Development,* p. 66), "Although a GNP comparison is hard to draw because of the lack of reliable data and differences in measurement, several estimates agree on the suggestion that the North had a higher per capita output than the South at least until the mid-1970s."
6. "Mass movements, exhortations, political campaigns, 'socialistic competition,' and the like have been widely and consistently relied upon as substitutes for

pecuniary incentives. . . . [T]hese movements tend to create sectoral imbalances, secondary disruptions, overambitious targets, and planning errors. Defaulting of product quality is another consequence. Moreover, mobilization of the general populace, even if successful, would have economic limitations. Except in the areas of such highly labor-intensive projects as food processing, irrigation facilities, and construction of unpaved roads, continued substitution of labor for capital will produce, after a point, very small or near zero marginal output. Eventually, expansion in labor must be accompanied by an increased supply of capital or other inputs" (Chung, *North Korean Economy* [see chap. 6, n. 16], p. 155).

As for the use of titles and medals, "an authoritarian character has been inherent in the national character of the Korean people," observes Prof. Koh Young-bok of Seoul National University. "The socialist version of authoritarianism is combined with the traditional base to reinforce and intensify their common authoritarianism. The titles of 'hero' and many other medals and honors so freely lavished upon the people contribute to breeding and furthering the authoritarian trend in north Korea" (Koh, "The Structure and Nature of North Korean Society," *Vantage Point* [December 1979]: p. 10).

Kim's "Chongsan-ri method" in agriculture sought to get the bureaucrats from the local level to stop shuffling papers in their offices and go out to guide the farm leaders directly. See Scalapino and Lee, *Communism in Korea* (see chap. 2, n. 28), pp. 562, 575.

7. Hwang Jang-yop, *Problems of Human Rights (2)* (see chap. 6, n. 104).
8. He first used the term in a report whose main purpose was to "slander" several returnees from the Soviet Union, Lim Un alleges. "In this report, there were a few points which emphasized national pride, but the basic purpose was to inspire an anti-Soviet and an exclusionism spirit" (*Founding of a Dynasty* [see chap. 2, n. 59], p. 301).
9. Suh, *Kim Il Sung* (see chap. 2, n. 35), p. 144, and Scalapino and Lee, *Communism in Korea*, pp. 624–635.
10. Baik II, p. 3.
11. Translated in Scalapino and Lee, *Communism in Korea,* p. 660.
12. Kim, *Two Koreas in Development,* p. 66.
13. "As far as is known, the military spending of North Korea jumped from around 19 percent in the early 1960s to over 30 percent in 1967–71. (In 1968 it hit a high of 32.4 percent.) With the beginning of the south-north dialogue it dropped to below 20 percent" (Cha Byong-gwon, "The Financial Structure of North Korea—Its Characteristics," *Vantage Point* [January 1979]: p. 5).
14. Here is a South Korean explanation of how the South prospered while the North stagnated: "The wide discrepancy in the economies of south and north Korea today resulted from the phenomenal growth of the south Korean economy through successive development plans in the 1960s and 1970s, which have reached the stage of heavy and chemical industries. On the contrary, north Korea failed in its economic planning in the 1960s, lost much of its overseas market in the 1970s, brought in increased foreign capital and equipment in excess of its debt-servicing and managerial capacity and spent too much for military purposes to realize its Four Major Military Policies. These factors combined to delay the growth of production" (Kim Chang Soon, "North Korea Today," *Vantage Point* [March 1979]: p. 11).

15. In an interview conducted by the author in 1992, Prof. Zhao Fengbin, a North Korea specialist at Jilin University in China, implicitly backed Pyongyang's version. Zhao said North Korea had overemphasized its heavy industry—and as a result had fallen behind the South economically by the early 1970s—because of concern aroused by American policies in the 1960s in Cuba and Vietnam.

   Hwang Jang-yop, a former Workers' Party secretary who defected to South Korea in 1997, is quoted as having said that the Cuban Missile Crisis sparked Kim's policy of simultaneous development of the economy and the military. "Money in your own pocket is better than money in your brother's, and it is always best to keep one's wallet full," Kim said after he heard of the crisis, Hwang is said to have recalled ("Preparations for War in North Korea" in *Testimonies of North Korean Defectors: True Picture of North Korea According to a Former Workers Party Secretary* [Seoul: National Intelligence Service], an undated summary that was posted on the NIS's Web site as of May 17, 2002, but is no longer available there).

16. Hwang Jang-yop, quoted in "Preparations for War."

17. See Scalapino and Lee, *Communism in Korea,* pp. 638–641. By the time he made a key October 1966 speech, "The Present Situation and the Task Confronting Our Party," the authors relate, Kim Il-sung "was dispensing criticism against *both* major Communist states in almost equal amounts, and in neither case was the criticism trivial. The attitude that one took toward 'US imperialist aggression in Vietnam,' proclaimed Kim, showed whether or not one was resolutely opposed to imperialism, and whether or not one actively supported the people's liberation struggle. . . . The importance Kim attached to the Vietnamese issue is manifest in the prominence given that issue in his speech, the urgent tone used in discussing it, and such passages as this: 'If all the socialist countries assist the Vietnamese people in shattering U.S. aggression, U.S. imperialism will be doomed like the sun setting in the west and the revolutionary movements of all countries in Asia and the rest of the world will surge forward greatly.'"

18. *Wen-ko T'ung-hsün* (Gwangjou), February 15, 1968, translated and cited in Scalapino and Lee, *Communism in Korea,* p. 641.

19. A formerly top-secret 1958 update of the U.S. statement of policy on Korea includes the following three items regarding North Korea:

   • "Make clear that the United States does not regard the North Korean regime as a legitimate regime.
   • "Encourage the non-Communist states and the UN to continue to refuse to recognize the North Korean regime, and to treat it as a non-legitimate regime condemned for aggression and discourage any non-Communist political or economic intercourse with North Korea.
   • "Encourage the people of North Korea to oppose the Communist North Korean regime and to sympathize with the Republic of Korea" (NSC 5817 [see chap. 6, n. 99], p. 491).

   Halliday and Cumings note that the United States "maintains its toughest embargo *vis-à-vis* any state in the world on North Korea." They argue, "This long-term attempt at isolation reflects powerful and unresolved psychological and political issues left over from the Korean war" (*Korea* [see chap. 4, n. 60], p. 216).

20. One Yi Dynasty ruler in the seventeenth century outlawed the mining of silver and gold to reduce foreigners' interest in intruding into the country.

21. Izidor Urian, "The 10 Years I Spent in Pyongyang," *Chosun Ilbo* (Seoul), January 1, 1991, translated in *Vantage Point* (January 1991): pp. 15–18. Urian's diplomatic duties kept him in Pyongyang intermittently from 1963 until 1983. During that time he rose to the position of chargé d'affairs.

22. "The highly publicized 1968 *Pueblo* and 1969 EC-121 incidents were preceded by thousands of clandestine operations and electronic surveillance missions launched from U.S. bases in Japan" (from Frank Baldwin's introduction to *Without Parallel* [see chap. 4, n. 1], p. 24).

23. An enlightening discussion of this and related issues may be found in McCormack, "Kim Country" (see chap. 3, n. 44).

24. See Scalapino and Lee, *Communism in Korea*, pp. 564, 590–595, 647–653.

25. Ibid., pp. 596–597, 601, 609.

26. Baldwin, "Patrolling the Empire" (see chap. 5, n. 23), p. 73, n. 66, citing hearings held by a Senate subcommittee. Baldwin (pp. 63 ff.) asserts that the North Koreans adopted a harder-line policy in response to American and South Korean initiatives. North Korea "*did* increase pressure along the Demilitarized Zone from October 1966, and encouraged subversive and guerrilla activity in the South. . . . Nevertheless, an objective examination of the Korean situation and the Pueblo incident indicates that North Korea was *reacting* to . . . U.S./South Korean provocations" (italics in original). Besides espionage gathering, those included covert North-South warfare. Baldwin gives few details on the subject of "a private, covert war between North and South Korea," but he cites an exchange in a hearing in which Senator J. William Fulbright asked, "Have there been no raids from the South to the North? No action?" In reply, William J. Porter, ambassador to South Korea, said, "Nothing on the scale that could be called as provocative as that which, for example, the North launched in 1968 against the residence of the President of South Korea." Later the ambassador denied that there had been any South Korean raids on the North.

27. Baldwin (ibid.) suggests that the American use of South Korean troops in Vietnam from 1965, with the seasoning it gave those troops, brought about "a dangerous shift in the military balance in Korea" and thus was seen by Kim Il-sung as another provocation.

A Hanoi-datelined March 29, 2000, dispatch by South Korea's Yonhap news agency said that Yonhap reporters, "in a joint search with the South Korean embassy here for evidence of North Korea's participation in the Vietnamese war, found Wednesday a graveyard of North Korean soldiers killed in the war near here. . . . The graveyard, with a memorial monument erected in honor of 14 North Korean air force soldiers killed in the war, is located in Bac Giang, 60 kilometers north of the capital city. . . . The 14 North Korean soldiers killed in the war included 11 fighter pilots and three mechanics and included in the pilots were Ri Chang-il and Pak Tong-jun. People in Bac Giang said the North Korean soldiers fought against U.S. fighter-bombers during U.S. air raids on Hai Phong in 1967."

Scalapino and Lee (*Communism in Korea*, p. 595) say that, for Pyongyang, using the Vietnam strategy "would require substantial preparations. A southern branch of the Party and a substantial guerrilla force would have to be built, and the north would have to be guarded against retaliation when the military pressures upon the south mounted. In short, South Korea was not South Vietnam at this point. Kim and his generation were determined to 'liberate' the south on their terms, and a full decade might be required."

The same authors add (p. 647) that "there is some reason to believe that the major shift in priorities undertaken in December 1962, and the new emphasis upon large-scale militarization, were directly connected with a decision that South Korea had to be 'liberated' in the early 1970s at the latest. The frustration of being unable either to take advantage of Rhee's overthrow or to prevent the subsequent military takeover undoubtedly contributed to this decision. But there was also rising concern over Japan's potential role in Northeast Asia. Later, the increasing signs of economic growth in South Korea were to have the same effect. With respect to their public, political formula for unification, the Communists stood by their proposals at the Fourth [Workers' Party] Congress [in 1961]. However, it was also in that Congress that Kim had called openly for the establishment of 'a true Marxist-Leninist Party' in the south, and asserted emphatically that Korea would be 'peacefully unified' only when the Americans had been driven out of South Korea and the [Park Chung-hee] government overthrown. This, Kim certainly implied, would require a revolution, and a violent one. Thus the renewed 'liberation' drive was to be conducted on the pattern of Vietnam, not the Korean War. The north would serve as a training and infiltration base while a revolutionary movement was constructed in the south. Only when that movement had become strong would further steps be taken, combinations of legal and illegal action, as well as guerrilla warfare. At this later stage, North Korea could determine its role in accordance with the circumstances, supposedly secure in the knowledge that its internal defenses were impregnable."

28. Biographer Robert A. Caro quotes Johnson as having made the comment to an unnamed *Time* correspondent on January 22, 1968 (Caro, "The Compassion of Lyndon Johnson," *The New Yorker*, April 1, 2002). (The rest of the quotation, which Caro used to illustrate Johnson's ambivalence on racial issues: "It is just like you driving home at night and you come up to a stoplight, and there's some nigger there bumping you and scraping you.")

29. See Trevor Armbrister, *A Matter of Accountability: The True Story of the Pueblo Affair* (London: Barrie & Jenkins, 1970). For the basic account of events of January 21–23, including the Blue House raid and the capture of the *Pueblo*, see pt. 1, pp. 3–78. Reference to the *Chesapeake* is on p. 350. Armbrister covered the case as a journalist and interviewed a great many of the participants. Commander Bucher and his second in command also published, separately, their own memoirs.

30. Ibid., pp. 232–233.

31. Ibid., pp. 245–246, 381.

32. Ibid., p. 249.

33. *New York Times*, January 25, 1968, cited in Baldwin, "Patrolling the Empire," p. 55.

34. Armbrister, *Matter of Accountability*, pp. 212–214, 264, 273, 288.

35. Ibid., pp. 259, 262, 275–277.

36. Ibid., pp. 319–330.

37. Ibid., pp. 335–343. Washington had warned Pyongyang after the U.S. presidential election in November 1968 that only one more effort would be made to

resolve the issue before the inauguration of Richard Nixon, who was expected to take a harder line against the North. See Document 324, *Foreign Relations of the United States 1964–1968*, vol. XXIX *Korea*.

Scalapino and Lee observe (*Communism in Korea*, p. 644) that getting the American letter "was the equivalent of having 'American imperialism' kowtow before the leaders of P'yongyang, and they were subsequently to boast repeatedly that, because of the impregnable defenses that had been created in the north, the enemy did not dare to take military action and was forced to admit his crimes before the world."

38. "Without recourse to North Korean or other revealing documentation from Moscow or Beijing, it is impossible to know the other side's motivation" (*Foreign Relations of the United States 1964–1968*, vol. XXIX: *Korea*, Pt. 1 [Washington, D.C.: Department of State, 1999], http://www.state.gov/www/about_state/ history/ vol_xxix/summary.html).

Cdr. Richard Mobley in "*Pueblo*: A Retrospective" (*NWC Review*, Spring 2001, http://www.nwc.navy.mil/press/Review/2001/Spring/art8-sp1.htm), p. 3, quotes a February 5, 1968, Central Intelligence Agency briefing package as having given the CIA's view that the *Pueblo* "was almost certainly taken as a result of a decision at the highest levels of the North Korean government. . . . It seems likely . . . that the North Koreans had identified the ship and her mission at least a day in advance. It is possible that the original intent was only to harass and drive off the *Pueblo;* the final decision to take the ship into Wonsan may have only been taken when it eventually appeared that U.S. forces were not coming to assist the *Pueblo*."

Frank Baldwin argues that "North Korea kept heavy pressure along the DMZ and increased subversive and espionage activities elsewhere in South Korea from 1966 to 1969 as a contribution to the Vietnamese war effort. The U.S. was forced to keep about 50,000 troops in South Korea and public uneasiness in South Korea inhibited the R.O.K. government from further troop dispatch to Vietnam. The sequence of these events is crucial to an assessment of North Korean motives in January 1968. The increase in North Korean guerrilla and subversive operations came *after* South Korea became deeply involved in Vietnam, in fact only shortly after the second South Korean infantry division was dispatched [in 1966]. The fragile, tentative detente, which had kept violence at a relatively low level in Korea since 1953, was upset by the American–South Korean escalation in Vietnam. To North Korea, the massive South Korean intervention in Vietnam was a moral challenge; sympathy for North Vietnam's cause ensured a North Korean response." Baldwin makes clear such considerations were not "the sole operating factors in North Korean decision making. Obviously, other policy objectives were intermingled; for example, North Korea's oft-expressed intention to create a socialist revolution in South Korea" (Baldwin, "Patrolling the Empire," p. 67 and n. 46 on p. 72).

A more recent author argues that the key motivation for carrying out the capture could be found in Kim Il-sung's wish to show himself domestically as a fierce nationalist, to offset popular disappointment over the regime's failure to make adequate improvement in the people's livelihood. See Mitchell B. Lerner, *The Pueblo Incident: A Spy Ship and the Failure of American Foreign Policy* (Lawrence, Kans.: University Press of Kansas, 2002), pp. 99–122. It may be a mistake to emphasize "suffering" (p. 110) by North Koreans as an overriding political concern of Kim Il-sung's early in 1968. It is true that some of Kim's struggles with rivals had involved their calls for devoting more resources to providing consumer goods, less to heavy industry. Kim had resisted those demands successfully, however, and had purged all overt rivals. That is not to say that spotlighting his nationalism and independence was not important for Kim. As we have noted, it had been an important factor in a great many decisions since his elevation to power courtesy of the Soviet Union. But I am not persuaded that international and inter-Korean considerations played only a minimal role in motivating the *Pueblo*'s capture. (Judging from the lack of a citation, it appears Lerner may not have been cognizant of Baldwin's important arguments for an international view of the incident in "Patrolling the Empire.")

39. Armbrister, *Matter of Accountability*, pp. 263, 284. Washington claimed that the *Pueblo* was legally situated in international waters when captured and cited the 1958 convention on the law of the sea, which guaranteed ships on the high seas immunity from the jurisdiction of other nationalities. Pyongyang, however, had never signed the convention. Pyongyang went to great lengths to claim that the ship was inside North Korean territorial waters, and to that extent bolstered Washington's argument that the territorial waters issue was relevant. However, in the state of war still obtaining between North Korea and the United States, peacetime rules such as the 1958 convention would hardly seem applicable to an enemy spy ship. For a discussion of these issues see Baldwin, "Patrolling the Empire," pp. 61–67.

40. Armbrister, *Matter of Accountability*, p. 285, quoting Arthur J. McCafferty. In naval regulations, destroying classified materials takes priority over saving lives (p. 371).

41. Quotes from Vice Adm. Harold G. Bowen Jr. and Rear Adm. Marshall W. White, respectively, in Armbrister, *Matter of Accountability*, p. 385.

42. "In 1969, within a few months of Nixon's taking office as President, the North Koreans shot down a US plane, killing all thirty-one people on board. Nixon and Kissinger at first recommended dropping a nuclear bomb on the North but later backed off" (Halliday and Cumings, *Korea*, p. 216).

43. Reuters dispatch in *Korea Times*, April 29, 1995, reporting a visit to the ship by Mike Chinoy of CNN, the first American reporter allowed to see it.

44. Hwang Jang-yop, cited in *Testimonies of North Korean Defectors*.

45. Kim Il-sung's report to the Fifth Korean Workers' Party Conference, Pyongyang, November 2, 1970, cited in Scalapino and Lee, *Communism in Korea*, p. 660. It is interesting to consider the idea of arming all citizens of a totalitarian state in the light of the libertarian argument often heard in the United States that citizens' right to bear arms prevents government tyranny.

46. Byoung-Lo Philo Kim notes that in South Korea in 1972 "a popular referendum approved the Yushin (revitalizing) constitution that greatly strengthened presidential power. Key provisions included indirect election of the president through a new body, the National Conference for Unification (NCU); presidential appointment of one-third of the National Assembly; and presidential authority to issue decrees to restrict civil liberties in times of national emergency. President Park was reelected by the NCU and [his Democratic Republican Party] obtained a decisive majority in elections for the new National Assembly. . . . In South Korea, economic development was on the rise and it needed social security to attract more and more international capital when it entered a deeper level

of expansive development; this necessitated a more authoritarian state. . . . [T]he *Saemaul* (New Community) Movement, a mass mobilization measure in 1972 that took aim at rural development encouraging self-help by villages with small government grants . . . was probably stimulated by the nature of the early success of North Korea. . . . North Korea publicly called for the revolution in South Korea toward the end of the 1960s. [Such] threats stimulated South Korea to introduce a tightly controlled authoritarian state" (*Two Koreas in Development*, pp. 123–124).

47. Report to the Fifth KWP Conference.
48. James B. Palais writes that the aggressive policy had "failed to stimulate a revolutionary reaction among the generally conservative rural populace in South Korea. Moreover, because Chinese and Russian support became less dependable in the late 1960s, the North Koreans decided to abandon their aggressive tactics in the south after 1968" ("'Democracy' in South Korea, 1948–72," in Baldwin, *Without Parallel*, p. 340).

   Scalapino and Lee cite examples showing that that "infiltration did not cease, although it was considerably reduced from the high-tide of 1968" (*Communism in Korea*, p. 680).
49. Lloyd C. Gardner, *Korean War* (see chap. 5, n. 17), p. 7.
50. Robert R. Simmons, "The Korean Civil War," in Baldwin, *Without Parallel*, pp. 168, 170. Simmons's suggestion that Beijing's "liberation" of Taiwan coupled with the absorption of South Korea into North Korea would have been positive outcomes was put forth before their speedy economic development made South Korea and Taiwan the biggest and second biggest, respectively, of Asia's "Four Tigers." With the benefit of hindsight we now know that the four have, in turn, become the inspiration for China's shift to the market economy, bringing rapid wealth expansion in place of the poverty and widespread starvation that had accompanied Maoist rule.

   One might ask why the term "legitimate" should apply to a nationalism that insists on placing fellow nationals under a system that is alien to them, as was the case on both sides in Korea. It was understandable, perhaps, even inevitable. But legitimate? Australian scholar Gavan McCormack wrote much later (in "Kim Country") that "[t]he interpretation in terms of beleaguered nationalism does not distinguish (legitimate) nationalist substance from the use of nationalist symbols for other ends (maintenance of entrenched power) . . ."

   Simmons seemed to suggest that Kim Il-sung would not have been an autocratic ruler if only he had been permitted to absorb South Korea. The sum of available information about Kim indicates that this was wishful thinking. Modeling his rule on Stalin's, Kim had shown, even before the invasion, many signs of developing into the complete autocrat he was to become.

   In another Vietnam-era analysis, Frank Baldwin asked (*Without Parallel*, pp. 15–16), "What would have happened in Korea if the United States had not intervened?" His answer: "The war would have been over in two or three weeks with total casualties of perhaps less than 50,000. Several million people opposed to communism would have come under communist rule and probably, but not certainly, there would have been reprisals. A single communist Korean state would have been established, the unity of a millennium restored, and national energies immediately directed to urgent economic and social reconstruction." Baldwin listed negative consequences of the Korean War, including: "a very costly commitment to South Korea's security, reversal of the tentative policy of accommodation with the People's Republic of China and the subsequent twenty years of hostility to China, domestic mobilization and the creation of a garrison economy (Pentagon capitalism). . . . The United States intervention prolonged the war by more than three years, bringing an estimated 4.5 million Korean, Chinese and American casualties. The United States achieved its objective of keeping the Southern half of the peninsula non-communist, but the Koreans remain divided almost three decades later."

51. Halliday and Cumings, *Korea*, p. 204. A photo caption (p. 209) reads, "Kim Il Sung and Vietnamese leader Ho Chi Minh, Hanoi, November 1958. The manifest contrast in personalities does not explain the different responses that the two leaders and the two revolutions evoked in the West. Yet the two wars had much in common, including the same enemy."

   Compare McCormack's argument quite a few years later that the character of the Communist Party of Vietnam "has long been completely different from that of North Korea. Leninist and authoritarian, to be sure, but even during the life of Ho Chi Minh the cult of the personality was abjured, and after his death in 1969, a collective leadership brought the nation to victory in the war against the United States without resort to the dismal monolithicity of opinion so vaunted in North Korea" ("Kim Country").

   One might argue, further, that the contrast between the personalities of the two leaders alone was sufficiently stark to explain the different responses of many Americans. While Kim Il-sung might have sought since the 1930s to emulate the Indochinese leader, in the end he was no Ho Chi Minh. Ho Chi Minh did not purge his colleagues; he won wars—instead of losing them and then concocting elaborate lies to pretend he had won them; he was a man of "goodness and simplicity" (see David Halberstam, *Ho* [New York: Random House, 1971], especially pp. 14–17; 42).

52. Baldwin, *Without Parallel*, pp. 23–24.

53. From the "Statement of Purpose" of the Committee of Concerned Asian Scholars, adopted March 28–30, 1969, in Boston. The group sought "to develop a humane and knowledgeable understanding of Asian societies and their efforts to maintain cultural integrity and to confront such problems as poverty, oppression and imperialism." The committee reportedly argued in 1970 (this according to op-ed contributor Stephen B. Young, "Vietnam War: Washington Was Right" [*The Wall Street Journal*, November 13, 1995, p. 6]; I have not found the original source document) that "communism has generally proved itself dynamic and viable in developing nations." Regarding North Korea, that was a defensible argument in 1970.

54. Baldwin, *Without Parallel*, pp. 31–32.

55. Ibid., p. 35.

56. Journalists and other writers who visited the North got encouragement for such logic from North Korean officials. The officials made it very clear that if they should judge one's work unfair, one would not be welcome back in the country. Quite a few reporters failed the test and never were permitted to return. On the other hand, the officials were understandably pleased that several reporters and researchers who visited North Korea returned home to write almost unremittingly glowing accounts of the brave new world they had witnessed there. I think, for example, of a pair of Tokyo-based researcher-activists who were

campaigning for U.S. troop withdrawal from South Korea and reconciliation with the North. I have lost my copy of their report for an American church group of a 1980 North Korea visit (they likewise misplaced their only copy, as I learned when I contacted them in 2003); but I clearly recall reading it at the time with a feeling of amazement that so little about the country seemed to have troubled them.

However, sympathy with the North Koreans' revolutionary society did not always or necessarily translate into unstinting praise of the regime. As Frank Baldwin noted, "the apparently totalitarian controls and the personality cult of Kim Il-sung left even empathetic foreign observers puzzled and ambivalent about North Korea" (*Without Parallel*, p. 31).

8. Flowers of His Great Love Are Blooming.

1. Scalapino and Lee, *Communism in Korea* (see chap. 2, n. 28), p. 677.
2. "Very recently, some reduction of military expenditures appears to have been undertaken" in the North, Scalapino and Lee wrote just after the joint communiqué appeared (p. 684). They argued however (pp. 678–679) that "current North Korean policy does not represent an abandonment of past pledges to 'liberate' the South. In intent, at least, the shift is a tactical one, with greater emphasis to be placed in the immediate future upon a political-diplomatic offensive designed to put the [Park Chung-hee] government on the defensive with its own people by making a strenuous bid for the 'peace, unification and national independence' vote in the South. Thus, the Communists advance a liberal exchange program, advocate substantial military reductions, emphasize peaceful unification, and focus attention upon getting rid of the American presence in South Korea. All available evidence suggests that Kim Il-song hopes to utilize the new era to penetrate the South more deeply politically, setting aside military efforts at this point. If this accords with the present international environment, it also accords . . . with the current needs of the North—where intensive militarization and extreme tension had reached a point of greatly diminished returns. Secure in the control of their own society, with a complete monopoly of organization and media in the North, the Communists hope to cultivate 'people to people' relations so as to exploit the looser, more open political system of the South. Already they have caused a considerable tightening of the latter system in response."
3. Selig S. Harrison argues on pp. 118–119 of *Korean Endgame: A Strategy for Reunification and U.S. Disengagement* (Princeton, N.J.: Princeton University Press, 2002) that the "danger of a war triggered by 'misunderstanding and inadvertence' has been magnified by a basic transformation that has taken place in Operations Plan 5027, the Pentagon's official scenario for the conduct of any new conflict in Korea. During the first decades after the 1953 armistice, Op Plan 5027 envisaged a replay of the Korean War. The United States and South Korea had a limited objective: repelling a North Korean invasion and reestablishing the DMZ at the thirty-eighth parallel. In this defensive strategy, Seoul was to be evacuated. American and South Korean forces would pull back in phases to the Han River, which bisects the capital. In 1973, however, the United States proclaimed a new "Forward Defense" concept in which U.S. forces would seize Kaesong, a key North Korean city close to the DMZ, while round-the-clock B-52

strikes would stop a North Korean advance north of Seoul, ending the war in nine days. In response to this new strategy and the accompanying forward deployment of U.S. and South Korean artillery along the southern edge of the DMZ, North Korea moved its own artillery forward, where it has remained ever since." (A further, "more dramatic" shift in the U.S. strategy was to come in 1992, as Harrison notes.)

4. Kang Myong-do's testimony in *JoongAng Ilbo* (see chap. 2, n. 7).

5. See Nathan N. White, *U.S. Policy Toward Korea: Analysis, Alternatives and Recommendations* (Boulder, Co.: Westview Press, 1979), pp. 58 ff.

6. Author's August 1996 interview with Ahn Choong-hak. For a U.S. Army Korea specialist's description of the response to the axe-killings, see James V. Young, *Eye on Korea: An Insider Account of Korean-American Relations*, edited and with introduction by William Stueck (College Station, Texas: Texas A & M University Press, 2003), pp. 21–26.

7. "Such shifting policies as those of President Carter's zigzag on maintaining American ground forces in South Korea have reminded [South Koreans] of Truman-Acheson's lukewarm commitment to the defense of South Korea, which was at least partly responsible for the Korean War of 1950 to 1953. Many Koreans think it terribly ironic and inconsistent for the United States to divide the Korean peninsula along the 38th parallel in 1945, then fail to unify the country, refuse to train and equip South Korean troops (unlike the Soviets in North Korea), and withdraw its troops and phase out its commitment in South Korea — then get reinvolved when the North attacked the South and modernize the South Korean forces (under Eisenhower, Kennedy, Johnson, and Nixon), then cause anxiety about the reliability of the American commitment (under Carter) and, finally, reassert a firm pledge for the security of their country (under Reagan)" (Wayne Patterson and Hilary Conroy, "Duality and Dominance," in Patterson and Lee, *One Hundred Years* [see chap. 2, n. 6] pp. 10–11).

8. Bradley K. Martin, "Mansfield Says Troops Would Go to Korean War," *Baltimore Sun*, March 2, 1978.

9. Bradley K. Martin, "Korea Maneuvers Test U.S. Mood," *Baltimore Sun*, March 19, 1978. The United States always insisted that Team Spirit was not provocative but essentially a defensive type of exercise.

10. Bradley K. Martin, "U.S., South Korea 'Kind of Outflanked' by North's Willingness," *Baltimore Sun*, March 1, 1979.

11. "Suddenly the estimate of North Korean capabilities was almost doubled," Carter told Harrison in an interview in 2000 (see *Korean Endgame*, p. 179). "I have always felt that the intelligence community played fast and loose with the facts, but I couldn't prove it." Carter earlier had said much the same to Don Oberdorfer (*The Two Koreas* [Reading, Mass.: Addison-Wesley, 1997], p. 103).

Young (*Eye on Korea*, pp. 39–56) provides a detailed account of officials' ultimately successful effort to derail the troop-withdrawal plan. He offers no support for the proposition that the intelligence was doctored: "The findings were initially challenged by the U.S. Defense Intelligence Agency and the CIA, but in every case our army analysts were able to conclusively defend their findings, methodology, and conclusions" (p. 42). Young proudly acknowledges, nevertheless, that the effort to persuade Carter to change his mind was an all-out one. Among the civilians involved, notably Assistant Secretary of State Richard Holbrooke, a bureaucratic strategy emerged: "declare support for Carter's plan officially and publicly while delaying its actual implementation" to buy time for Congress to put its foot down (p. 48).

12. The Chinese example already may have inspired Kim to seek accommodation with Seoul in the early 1970s. See Scalapino and Lee, *Communism in Korea*, p. 678.

13. Bradley K. Martin, "North Korea Eyes Ping-Pong Diplomacy," *Baltimore Sun*, April 22, 1978. Nearly a year later, as the tournament opening approached, the same operative told me, "Whether some important persons are included in your delegation, we don't know." Clearly he hoped that there would be. And he volunteered a suggestion that U.S. congressmen visiting China that month might drop into Pyongyang. Bradley K. Martin, "Side Visit to North Korea Suggested for Congressmen Who Will Be in China," *Baltimore Sun*, April 20, 1979.

14. Bradley K. Martin, "North Korea Asks South to Talk Unity" (February 6); "Korean Reunification-Talk Furor May Produce at Least New Meetings" (February 13); "North, South Korea Agree on Time for Talks" (February 14); "North and South Korea Agree on Meeting Site" (February 16); "Friendly Approach Taken by North Koreans at Talks" (February 18); "2 Koreas Talk Detente" (February 23); "Big Question: Is North Korea's 'Smile Offensive' More than Skin Deep?" (March 3); "The Two Koreas Play Diplomatic Ping-Pong" (April 15), *Baltimore Sun*, 1979.

15. Editor-in-chief Andre Fontaine of *Le Monde*, visiting Pyongyang in 1974 along with a French television crew, had heard similar stories of divided families. Some North Koreans told Fontaine their parents were on the other side of the DMZ—whether dead or alive, they did not know. Fontaine's party, planning to go on from there to Seoul, asked if the North Koreans had messages they would like to have passed on to relatives in the South. "Don't do that!" they responded. Fontaine assumed their alarm at the notion showed their fear of "the consequences of any attempt to establish contact with family in South Korea" (Andre Fontaine, "A Postcard from Pyongyang," *Japan Times*, July 24, 1994).

16. Bradley K. Martin, "Pyongyang Offers U.S. Guarantees," *Baltimore Sun*, May 8, 1979.

17. Bradley K. Martin, "U.S. Joins Appeal to North on Korea Unification Talks" and "South Korean Leader Park, like Carter, Finds Support Eroding," *Baltimore Sun*, July 1, 1979.

18. Bradley K. Martin, "Seoul Could Attend Talks, North Says" (July 11) and "North Korean Voices U.S.-talk Confidence" (July 25), *Baltimore Sun*, 1979.

19. Bradley K. Martin, "Quick Resolution of Korean Standoff Unlikely," *Baltimore Sun*, August 12, 1979.

20. The recollection is from a North Korean defector to the South, who is quoted in *The Korea Times*, July 12, 1994.

21. Bradley K. Martin, "Where Is the Large North Korean Army Unit?" *Baltimore Sun*, May 11, 1980. For this report I contacted U.S. officials in Seoul and Hideko Takayama in Tokyo contacted Japanese officials. On May 13, the U.S. Department of State issued a statement to the press dismissing the South Korean claims: "From our information we see no movement of troops in North Korea out of the usual and we see no movement which would lead us to believe that some sort of attack upon the South is imminent" (Young, *Eye on Korea*, p. 98).

22. The former official was Kim Jong-min, quoted in Cho, "Interview of Former High-level Official of DPRK Ministry of Public Security Who Defected to South Korea" (see chap. 6, n. 88).

One aspect of U.S. policy after the incident began was to "[c]ontinue signals that the U.S. will defend South Korea from North Korean attack." U.S. forces in Korea were beefed up with AWACs early warning aircraft and naval units. (Young, *Eye on Korea*, p. 103).

23. Bradley K. Martin, "Kwangju Revisited," *Far Eastern Economic Review*, May 26, 1994, and Bradley K. Martin, "Yun Sang Won: The Knowledge in Those Eyes," in Henry Scott-Stokes and Lee Jai Eui, eds., *The Kwangju Uprising* (Armonk, N.Y.: M.E. Sharpe, 2000), pp. 87–105.

24. Bradley K. Martin, "N. Korea Halts U.S. Courtship with Anti-Reagan Blast," *Baltimore Sun*, April 15, 1982.

25. If it is any consolation for Washington, outgoing U.S. officials have had the opportunity to use an impending change of administration as an opportunity to try to wring concessions from Pyongyang by playing "good cop/bad cop," warning that the next administration would be tougher so it would be wise to make a deal immediately. Democrats have tended to take advantage of such opportunities. This is precisely what the Johnson Administration did to win the release of the *Pueblo* crew after the 1968 election. And it is what the Clinton Administration attempted late in 2000 as the inauguration of George W. Bush loomed—but without great result.

Part of the problem for the United States has been that very few of its officials have focused entirely on North Korea, even for the length of their time in office. And officials with responsibilities covering the larger Asian region often have had other things on their minds. I met then–Assistant Secretary of State Richard Holbrooke at a Tokyo reception shortly after my 1979 North Korea trip and immediately mentioned the trip, naively thinking he might be interested in hearing about it since very few Americans then could claim such an experience. Holbrooke didn't miss a beat. He gazed past me, spied someone more important across the room, turned and strode rapidly away.

9. He Gave Us Water and Sent Us Machines.

1. Katsumi Sato, editor of *Gendai Korea* and a leading Japanese Korea-watcher, told me the Pak story in a 1991 interview. Sato said he had heard from several North Korean sources that the vice-premier was sent to a Workers' Party school for ideological reeducation; if he had not been a relative of President Kim's, his punishment would have included loss of his job and authority. Sato suggested, "The point is, everybody has seen this sort of thing happen, and therefore nobody working for Kim and his son will tell them the truth."

2. "One of the important factors in South Korean success is the introduction of the mass mobilization movement in the 1970s, which South Korea probably borrowed from the successful experience of the North Korean mass movement during the 1950s. This moral incentive worked quite well because it was practiced for a relatively short period of time. Through the measure, the gap between urban and rural income narrowed. Both Korean experiences suggest that a mass mobilization technique based on moral incentive can be a successful measure, as long as it is only implemented for about seven to ten years. The idea is that in human nature any firm determination cannot last too long a time. . . . Mobilization of the general populace, even if successful for a short period, has economic limitations in the long run. It proves to be more advantageous at the early stage of

development where development can be achieved by expansion of the utilization of natural resources and unemployed labor. Except in the areas of such highly labor-intensive projects as food processing, irrigation facilities, and construction of unpaved roads, continued substitution of labor for capital will produce, after a point, very small or near-zero marginal output, so that it seems to fall behind in productivity and efficiency at the later stage of intensive development where productivity must be raised through more advanced technology" (Kim, *Two Koreas in Development* [see chap. 1, n. 2], pp. 147–149).

3. "[T]he critical factor for the failure in the first seven-year plan in the 1960s was troubled relations with the Soviet Union, the major capital and technology supplier to Pyongyang. Under the six-year plan in the 1970s, North Korea brought in capital from Western countries, including West Germany, France and Japan." See "Pyongyang Continues to Rely on Juche Economic Policy," *Vantage Point* (August 1994): p. 3.

Sweden was a major supplier, receiving orders for hundreds of millions of kroners' worth of goods. Besides factory equipment, the North Koreans ordered 1,000 Volvo sedans (including the one I rode in for most of my 1979 visit, after rejecting as too expensive to rent a higher-status black Mercedes that my hosts first provided). Swedish companies pressed successfully for the establishment of an embassy in Pyongyang. For a delightful and informative account of the first ambassador's two tours of duty, see Eric Cornell, *North Korea Under Communism: Report of an Envoy to Paradise,* translated by Rodney Bradbury (London: RoutledgeCurzon, 2002).

4. South Korean scholar Byoung-Lo Philo Kim observes, "Both South and North Korea experienced an authoritarian transformation of the constitutions and states in 1972. . . . In North Korea, a new 'socialist' constitution was promulgated. The new constitution declared Kim's political thought, *juche,* to be the ideology of the state. The formal authoritarian adaptation of both Korean states in 1972 was the result not only of the economic situation per se of each side in the late 1960s, but of the 'comparison effect' formed by the awareness of each other through the Red Cross Conference in 1972. . . . North Korea contrasts with South Korea in that economic growth slowed down in the late 1960s. Economic activity, which depended on only mass mobilization, needed to be revitalized by introducing Western capital, which led to a more authoritarian transformation of and surveillance within North Korea so as not to be exposed to the external world" (*Two Koreas in Development* [see chap. 1, n. 2], pp. 123–124).

5. "The economists are considered to be fulfilling only secondary and administrative functions," said a former North Korean newspaper editor, who had defected to the South and become a prominent analyst of Pyongyang affairs (Kim Chang Soon, "Korea Today," *Vantage Point* [March 1979]: p. 12).

6. "Except for minor and scattered cases of innovations which tend to be stop-gap devices, the North Korean system has not diverged fundamentally from the Stalinistic command system. . . ." (Chung, *North Korean Economy* [see chap. 6, n. 16], p. 155). "Unlike the Soviet Union and other East European countries which tended to decentralize business management gradually, North Korea adopted in 1961 a policy of further centralizing and tightening up entrepreneurial control and management" (Cha, "Financial Structure of North Korea" [see chap. 7, n. 13], p. 3).

7. Speech quoted in "Bankers Given 5-Point Guideline," *Vantage Point* (January 1979): pp. 23, 24.

8. Byoung-Lo Philo Kim estimates South Korean per capita GNP of $518 versus $605 in North Korea in 1975, the last time he thinks the South was behind (*Two Koreas in Development*, p. 66).

9. At a hothouse growing vegetables for the residents of Pyongyang, most of the workers likewise were women. "Our principle is, if it's easy work we give preference to women because they are not so physically strong," an official told me. Hothouse gardening was considered light work.

10. Forty-five percent in 1981, according to the South's National Unification Board. By 1989 (as demographers Nicholas Eberstadt and Judith Banister reported in *North Korea: Population Trends and Prospects* [Washington, D.C.: U.S. Bureau of the Census, 1990]), the far greater participation of women in the North's workforce was reflected in a total participation rate for both men and women of 78.5 percent. That compares with an official South Korean workforce participation rate for the same year of 58.3 percent (Byoung-Lo Philo Kim, *Two Koreas in Development*, p. 92).

11. This factory evidently was one of the installations most frequently visited by the Great Leader. A guide at the industrial and agricultural exhibition in Pyongyang told me, "The respected and beloved leader Chairman Kim Il-sung visited 199 units 699 times in the fields of heavy industrial factories," which averages out to about three and a half visits per factory.

   The pride shown by hosts at factories, farms, and schools in the president's historic visits to give "on-the-spot guidance" seemed unaffected, although close questioning of recipients of those visits usually revealed that the leader had offered little more than compliments, words of encouragement and general suggestions.

12. I got a similar answer at a suburban hothouse, officially a state farm, which produced off-season vegetables and fruits for Pyongyang residents. "I'm not a specialist in financial matters," said a management official whom I asked to tell me the annual budget.

13. Baik II (see chap. 4, n. 24), p. 161.

14. "Although lagging far behind industry and ridden with seemingly insurmountable obstacles, growth in agriculture has not been unimpressive. However, self-sufficiency in food has not yet been achieved; North Korea is a substantial net importer of food" (Chung, *North Korean Economy*, pp. 151–152).

   Cornell reports (*North Korea Under Communism*, p. 44) having heard during the mid-1970s from East European diplomats that "food production in the country was only sufficient for twenty-five daily rations a month."

15. "At an expanded plenary session of the Party's Kangwon Provincial Committee held on October 5–6 in Wonsan, the capital of the province, Kim put emphasis on farming, fishing and industry. 'For effective transportation of farming tools in the countryside,' Kim said at the meeting, 'more trucks and tractors are needed in the province.' He also said that every household should plant at least two persimmon trees in its yard to increase the production of fruits.' He praised the 'great achievements' of East Coast farmers despite various adversities and personally set the next year's production goal for grains" ("Kim Makes On-the-Spot Guidance Tours," *Vantage Point* [November 1978]: p. 26).

16. Kim supposedly spent fifteen days at the more famous Chongsan-ri in 1960, thinking through what was later named the "Chongsan-ri Method." A foreign journalist visiting that farm eighteen years later heard a guide explain that the

method, "still used today," involved "the cadres coming to the workplace to stim-
ulate the ardor and the creativity of the peasants." See "'Market Economy
Doesn't Apply to Our Country': Visit to NK Model Farm," AFP dispatch in
Korea Times, May 4, 1995.

17. "Summing Up of the 1970s," *Vantage Point* (December 1979), quoting North Korean Premier Li Jong-ok. The plan's goal was to increase electrical power generation to 56–60 billion kilowatt hours, coal production to 70–80 million tons,
steel production to 74–80 million tons and the grain harvest to 10 million tons.

18. At the time, examined in historical context, that seemed to some foreign analysts
a strong possibility. For example, "South Korea . . . for all its belated 'miracle
growth,' is a house built on sand, utterly vulnerable to the storms of the world
economy, a classic example of extreme dependency. The crucial point is that,
contrary to the advocates of so-called 'export-led growth,' there is no evidence
of any Third World country having attained self-sustaining growth on the basis
of an open export economy" (Foster-Carter, "Development and Self Reliance"
[see chap. 6, n. 15], pp. 85–86). Foster-Carter added (p. 98), "Far from signify-
ing an economy in deep trouble, they [North Korea's debts] may paradoxically
testify to its long-run advance and strength despite short-term problems of cash
flow."

19. "A rapid expansion in investment in human capital, especially in technical education, . . . must have substantially contributed toward productivity gains. North
Korea was reportedly successful in eradicating illiteracy within a few years after
the division of Korea. . . . Since 1967 North Korea went even farther by adopting a free nine-year compulsory system of education with greater emphasis on
technical education, the first such program in the Far East. (Both China and
Japan have six-year compulsory systems with tuition partially free.) Beyond the
level of primary education, North Korea has exerted all-out efforts to increase
the supply of technical-scientific personnel by expanding the enrollment at and
resources of technological colleges, vocational schools, and 'factory colleges,'
and by sending selected groups of students abroad (primarily to the Soviet
Union) for scientific and technical education. The whole educational system
seems to be geared to the goals of industrialization" (Chung, *North Korean Economy*, pp. 158–159). Chung cites statistics showing the numbers of engineers,
technicians and specialists increasing from 21,872 in 1953 to 293,506 in 1964.
Source: *Choson chungang yongam, 1965* (Korean Central Yearbook) (Pyongyang,
Korean Central News Agency, 1965), p. 482.

20. Baik II, pp. 359–360.

21. Viewing the home as "the hotbed of outdated institutions, outdated ideology and
outdated customs," the state undermined the family's role through a variety of
policies. The virtual abolition of private land ownership—and its inheritance—
was the most obvious. That chipped away at the authority of the family patriarch in a country where Confucian patriarchal teachings had reigned supreme
for centuries. Korean custom required city-dwelling families to return regularly
to their hometowns and villages for ancestral memorial services—which were
also reunions promoting close family ties. But the regime's system of restrictions
on freedom of movement, perhaps the most stringent in the world, took a heavy
toll on such observances. The old custom in which parents arranged their children's marriages gave way to a new system in which the party's intervention su-
perseded that of the parents ("Building a Socialist Culture," *The Principles of Kim*

Il-sungism [Propaganda Bureau of the Unification Revolutionary Party Central Committee, 1974], p. 182, cited in Park Yong-hon, "Cultural Policy of North Korea," *Vantage Point* [August 1979]: pp. 10–11).

22. One defector in a 1994 interview assured me that what I had seen out the school window was typical. See chap. 21 for his remarks.

23. Kim, *With the Century* (see chap. 2, n. 2), vol. 3, pp. 302–303.

24. Kim Il-sung's youthful organ playing may help to explain the curious taste in music that, since liberation, has channeled the talents of countless North Korean youngsters into playing the accordion—a portable version of the instrument that would have been found in a small Korean church in those days, the pump organ. The Kim Il-sung regime's ties to Eastern European communist countries where the accordion was in favor, and the frequent cultural exchanges accompanying those ties, may also have been a factor.

25. Hwang Jang-yop, *The Problems of Human Rights in North Korea (3)*, trans. Network for North Korean Democracy and Human Rights (Seoul: NKnet, 2002), http://www.nknet.org/en/keys/lastkeys/2002/9/04.php.

26. "His teachings covered the whole realm of literature and the arts. They became the programmatic guide for each branch in upholding its Party spirit, class spirit and popular spirit and raising its artistic quality. The 'golden arts' which peoples of the world admire today had their new beginning immediately after liberation under his wise guidance, and by his boundless effort and proper guidance, the northern half has now come to full bloom in its national culture, built and consolidated on the democratic base, rock-firm" (Baik II, p. 223).

27. Kim, *With the Century*, vol. 1, p. 5.

28. Kim, "Building a Socialist Culture," in Park Yong-hon, "Cultural Policy," p. 2.

29. "Stalinist ideology did have one thing to teach the Koreans that fit like a glove with their own preconceptions. This was the Platonism of Stalin, the architectonic, engineering-from-on-high quality that marked his thought and his praxis. Stalin was a hegemon in the era of 'late' heavy industrialization, and his discourse, like his name, clanked with an abased, mechanical imagery that valued pig iron over people, machines over bread, bridges over ideas, the leader's will over the democratic instincts of Marx. When he had Zhdanov impose his suffocating doctrine of socialist realism on the cultural realm in 1932, the metaphor of choice was that artists and writers should be 'engineers of the soul,' and that may serve as a general metaphor for Stalin's rule.

"Koreans think a maximum leader should be an engineer of the soul, too, but through exemplary behavior instead of by ramming it down your throat. They think a leader should be benevolent instead of brutish. And they think good ideas come from right thought—rectification of the mind—proceeding from the leader down through the masses, who learn the teaching by rote mastery of received wisdom. These Confucian residues melded with Soviet doctrines to make Kim a kind of benevolent Stalin, the fount of ideas, leading to a profound idealism and voluntarism at opposites with the materialism of Marx. The Koreans still refer to artists as engineers of the soul. They still surround Kim with a cult of personality. They still depict him as the source of all good ideas. This aspect of Stalinism stuck like glue in Korea, and if it had not existed in Moscow, it would have had to be invented in P'yongyang" (Cumings, *Origins* II [see chap. 3, n. 43], pp. 296–297).

30. Kim, "Building a Socialist Culture."

31. Thirty percent of all artistic creations were supposed to deal with revolutionary tradition — meaning "Kim Il-sung's exploits in his struggle against the Japanese and the idolization of Kim and his clan," according to a South Korean scholar's analysis. Another 30 percent should deal with war, including the North Korean People's Army's heroic struggle in the Korean War. That left 40 percent divided between socialist development of the country and unification of the peninsula (Lee Han-gu, "The State of Literature and Arts in North Korea," *Vantage Point* [December 1983]: pp. 4–5).

32. The regime's "folklorists" employed a similar procedure to appropriate surface elements of the Korean folklore tradition. But when South Korean folklorists met their Northern counterparts to compare notes at a time of tentative detente in the 1970s the Southerners were "confused and dismayed," one of them wrote later (Kim Yol-gyoo, "A Survey of the Character of North Korean Folklore," *Vantage Point* [March 1988]: pp. 5–10). "A glance through the papers and other materials prepared and published by north Korean students of folklore disappointed us in the south beyond measure. It was not so much a feeling of despair as a sense of betrayal that gripped us. The folklore as presented by the north Korean publications was anything but folklore." Even the nursery rhymes glorified Kim Il-sung. For example, "in the course of an instruction trip, Kim Il-sung happened to see a group of children who were learning their lessons, while singing songs. Kim made some comments on the spot, and the contents of the comments were instantly woven into the lyrics of the song. It became an 'instruction song.' A north Korean folklorist proudly mentioned the episode in his published paper."

The sense of betrayal reflected a feeling that something binding the two halves of the peninsula together had been tossed out in the North. "Koreans used to sing the time-honored song 'Oh, the moon, oh the moon, the bright moon,' perform the traditional mask dance, and play *yut*. As long as they enjoy these activities together, the division of the country into the south and north might come to an end. We felt as if Koreans in both parts of the land would share the same feelings of family ties when they kneel before the altar of ancestor worship at the tomb of their forefathers. Such feelings must turn out to be true. When a glance at the materials from north Korea made it known to us that such an expectation was a mere illusion we were confused and dismayed. As far as I felt, the north Korean folklore was a folklore alien to me. Part of it had a veneer redolent of its sameness of our folklore heritage, but the substance was totally different from that of ours." The South Korean folklorist was horrified to find poems and tales preoccupied with "labor efficiency, animosity aimed at struggle and blind devotion to the cult of personality of Kim Il-sung."

This tendency, he added, "is not limited to the study of folklore in north Korea. Such pretended and deliberate reliance on the authority of the Leader is prevalent in all papers and publications in all disciplines and artistic pursuits. For instance, the so-called *Outline History of Korean Literature* devotes two chapters to commentaries on some poems attributed to the mother and father of Kim Il-sung." The folklorist said he had watched a documentary film on the life of ethnic Koreans living around Tashkent in what was then Soviet Central Asia (Tashkent now is the capital of independent Uzbekistan). "The cultural distance between them and us is far smaller than that between north Koreans and south Koreans as far as current folklore is concerned," he concluded sadly.

33. Baik II, p. 582.

34. The health worker as prototype of the "new man" continued as a main theme. In a September 22, 1994, broadcast that I heard, a Radio Pyongyang narrator told of a hospital patient in a Pyongyang neurological ward who, at visiting time, received no visitors. One day at visiting hour, however, an old woman appeared with chicken and soup, which she urged him to eat to ensure a quick recovery. He asked who she was, but she refused to identify herself, saying that the whole country was one family with Kim Jong-il as the father. After further inquiries she revealed that she was the wife of the doctor who was treating the lonely patient. As is typical of such propaganda stories, her name was not mentioned— but Kim Jong-il's name was repeatedly brought into the narrative.

35. "Almost everyone had diarrhea. Some suffered from scurvy, others from pneumonia and hepatitis. Scratches became infected, and the infections spread. . . . Dale Rigby developed a rash over 90 percent of his body. The skin above his waist peeled off; ugly sores formed on his legs. The North Korean doctor wouldn't let him disrobe; the sight might 'embarrass' the nurse. He prescribed a mud-pack. Rigby's condition worsened. The doctor gave him a liquid ointment. That didn't help, either. Bill Scarborough's feet began to swell. The doctor tried acupuncture. He stuck four needles in one foot and three in the other.

"'Doc' Baldridge asked for permission to treat his ailing shipmates. The North Koreans produced a medical dictionary and told him to prove that he was a corpsman. They interrogated him at length about his personal life: Why had he married a Japanese? Then they told him he couldn't help; he couldn't even offer advice" (Armbrister, *Matter of Accountability* [see chap. 7, n. 29], p. 291).

36. This is one area in which official figures, at least, show North Korean superiority over South Korea—which boasted only a quarter that ratio of physicians to population (.6 doctors per 1,000 people in the South in 1982 versus 2.4 in North Korea). In hospital beds per 1,000 people, North Korea similarly showed a huge lead over the South: 12 to 1.6 (Kim, *Two Koreas in Development,* p. 90).

37. "Kim Il-sung believes that South Korea is a colony of both the United States and Japan. Even if South Korea does possess technology, that is only dependent technology, not technology obtained through nationalist development. When it comes to foreign debts, Kim insists that North Korea, if it desired to, would borrow as much money as it likes, as well. However, when I finally arrived in South Korea and saw for myself, I felt that Kim's claims were erroneous" (Kim Jong-min quoted in Cho, "Interview of Former High-Level Official of DPRK Ministry of Public Security Who Defected to South Korea" [see chap. 6, n. 88]).

38. As did the Chinese.

39. I was pleased with my escapade that afternoon, but later found that my friend Mike "Buck" Tharp, then Tokyo bureau chief of *The Wall Street Journal,* had one-upped me. Tharp had brought jogging shorts and shoes to Pyongyang, and he told his handlers that it was his custom to run every morning for his health. They were welcome to come along, he told them blandly. The first day, a hardy handler tried to keep up with the fleet-footed Tharp. After that, they let him have his run unescorted.

Besides breaking free from our handlers for an unfettered look around, the other major fantasy of every correspondent visiting Pyongyang was to land an interview with the Great Leader himself. The late John Wallach, then foreign editor of Hearst Newspapers, trumped the rest of us with his ingenuity in pursuing that goal. Wallach while at the theater paid attention to the large baskets of flowers that symbolized respect for Kim Il-sung. He cleverly went to the hotel florist and ordered one to be delivered to Kim. He definitely pushed the right button, as this proved to be a gesture that Kim would not ignore. Wallach was taken to a guest house and permitted to greet Kim briefly. The president thanked the reporter for the flowers and immediately turned him over to foreign policy chief Kim Yong-nam for an interview similar to the one I had. Wallach had exchanged only a few words with Kim Il-sung, but being able to write that he had been in the presence of the big guy certainly dressed up his story. (My consolation was being first in print with the story of Kim Yong-nam's proposal.)

40. Chung explains, "Per capita income by itself provides no direct measure of how well off the North Korean populace is economically, as it conceals the distribution of income and the portions of national output expended in capital formation and defense" (*North Korean Economy*, p. 150).

41. In 1970, for example, vice-premier Kim Il complained of poor quality and variety of consumer goods (ibid., p. 150).

"[A Japanese study by Fujio Goto calculated that] personal consumption accounted for an extraordinarily low share of North Korean [gross domestic product] in the late 1950s: less than 35 percent of GDP on what economists call an 'adjusted factor cost basis.' Just to put that figure in perspective: it would have been over twenty points lower than corresponding estimates for the Soviet Union for the same period" (Nicholas Eberstadt, in Edwin J. Feulner Jr., ed., "Orwell's Nightmare: Human Rights in North Korea," The Heritage Lectures No. 394 [Washington, D.C.: The Heritage Foundation, 1992]). A South Korean scholar calculated that the state budget of North Korea accounted for 70 percent of gross national product, high even for a communist country. He attributed much of this to the emphasis on investment in arms buildup (Cha Byong-gwon, "Financial Structure of North Korea," *Vantage Point* [January 1979]: p. 2).

42. "Kim Il Sung's New Year Message," *Vantage Point* (January 1979): p. 20.

43. "Each work-team operates on its own independent accounting system whose balance sheet indicates the team's performance and supplies the yardstick for material reward and preferential treatment by the Communist Party. Incentives for over-fulfillment of state production plans in farm, livestock and sericulture output are given up to 40 per cent of excess production in the form of products or cash or grain; penalties for failure to fulfill the plans are imposed in terms of products or cash or grain between 10 and 20 per cent of the deficit production. The head of an agricultural work-team receives an additional reward of 10–20 per cent of the reward given to him as a team member if his team has over-fulfilled its production plan.

"In the case of agricultural products, the incentives and penalties are applied to the individual work-teams. If a work-team grows more than one crop, it will receive rewards for those crops whose output has surpassed the assigned production plan; but the work-team must pay a penalty on the other crops whose output falls short of the production target. The penalties for deficit output of products of all types are added to the cooperatives' collective income.

"A work-team must fulfill not only monthly production plans but also daily and ten-day production plans. Specific measures concerning production plan implementation are taken by the Party as a result of analysis of so-called 'production rhythm assurance.' Thus, a work-team must always maintain its 'rhythm' of production performance or pace of work, under the slogan, 'Let us produce more with existing labour and facilities'" (Kuark, "North Korea's Agricultural Development" [see chap. 6, n. 41], pp. 86–87).

Another writer observes, "The Communist regime has set 'the egoism and individualism' harbored by the people as the target of attack—a scheme designed to reform the character of the north Koreans. . . . There is a limit to the efficiency of symbolic compensation such as medals. Therefore, the Pyongyang regime now gives material rewards as well. North Korea, however, is very scrupulous in presenting awards in kind as 'material awards are likely to have a bad influence on the people. Therefore, material impetus and political and moral impetus should be mixed properly'" (Choe Hong-gi, "Mobilization System and Labor Efficiency," *Vantage Point* [January 1979]: p. 13).

44. Kang Myong-do's interview testimony in *JoongAng Ilbo* (see chap. 2, n. 7).

45. As one analyst said, "Insofar as the rates of growth are concerned the so-called 'law of equal cheating' may be applied with caution. Theoretically, to the extent that the proportion of falsification, omission, grossness, errors, and the like remains stable, *rates* of growth would not be affected. . . . Omission, rather than falsification, tends to be the communist means of concealing any unfavorable development" (Chung, *North Korean Economy*, p. 174). Chung adds that "North Korean economic data must be scrutinized carefully for their reliability. Although they seem more or less internally consistent, North Korea presents them in an ambiguous manner or withholds them in times of poor economic performance. Physical data tend to be more reliable than those made available only in index numbers. . . . By and large, North Korean data are usable if handled with extreme care and investigated carefully" (pp. 176–177).

Another analyst notes that "official statistical information on the economy has become scarcer since the mid-60s and almost non-existent in the 70s (apart from relative indices, which are hard to interpret)" (Foster-Carter, "Development and Self Reliance," pp. 71–72).

46. "N. Korea Puts Emphasis on English Teaching," *Vantage Point* (March 1979), p. 26.

47. Leaving aside the question whether North Korean officials had given the Pyongyang-style showcase treatment to the towns and villages along routes traveled by foreigners—something I had no doubt they were capable of—I worried at the time that the comparison might be unfair for another reason: My route took me through China's Tangshan region, site of a devastating earthquake shortly before. Indeed, around Tangshan was where I saw the worst living conditions—many houses made of nothing but woven straw mats, a devastated village of brick houses that looked as if bombs had hit it. But Tangshan was not the only area I passed on that trip. And the year after the trip I moved to China as Beijing bureau chief for *The Baltimore Sun*. Two years of traveling widely in China seemed to confirm that what I had been permitted to see of North Korean development was in important respects more impressive than the general run of what China had to show at that very early stage of Deng Xiaoping's reforms.

10. Let's Spread the Pollen of Love.

1. Author interview with the former official, who insisted on anonymity.

2. He was born in the camp of the Eighty-eighth Brigade, according to testimony by two Korean women and a Russian interpreter cited in an article by Kim Chan-jong in Seoul's *Dong-A Ilbo* in September 1992 and cited in *The True Story of Kim Jong Il* (see chap. 3, n. 61). The birth is described as an extremely difficult one, the labor continuing through a night and Kim Jong-suk's life endangered until an unlicensed Russian veterinarian was brought in to assist. That account fits other information that Kim Jong-suk had suffered one miscarriage already and eventually died delivering a stillborn child. There is a timing question about the *Dong-A Ilbo* account, however. Although Kim Il-sung had been in the USSR since 1940 or 1941, the Eighty-eighth Special Independent Sniper Brigade was only established in the latter part of 1942, according to Yu Song-chol's testimony carried in *Hankuk Ilbo*. In that case, if Kim Jong-il indeed was born on February 16, 1942, his birthplace would not necessarily have been the site of the Eighty-eighth's camp but could have been some other part of the Soviet Union where his parents were temporarily living. There are reports that Kim Il-sung, after being stopped at the border upon his entry into the USSR, was sent to work as a farmer for a time before the activation of the Eighty-eighth in August 1942. Seiler (*Kim Il-song 1941–1948* [see chap. 2, n. 18], pp. 31–32) cites a *Korea Herald* interview with a Soviet Korean in suggesting that Kim may have "spent some time farming in the small Soviet village of Vyatka, some seventy kilometers northeast of Khabarovsk before moving on" to a camp at Okeanskaya, near Vladivostok, and then, from around May of 1942, to the camp where the Eighty-eighth was established. According to a Reuters dispatch from Beijing in *Korea Times*, July 30, 1994, a book by an official Chinese publishing house (book title translates as *The Situation in Each Country and Covering Asia*, the publishing company's name as World Knowledge Press) said in 1994 that Kim Jong-il's birthplace was faraway Samarkand, in what was then Soviet Central Asia. The spotty evidence uncovered so far undoubtedly makes it easier for Pyongyang to press its claim that the junior Kim was born in a log cabin in a secret guerrilla camp on Mount Paektu. For an argument in favor of the regime's version see Lee Wha Rang, note to "Nurturing the Root of the Revolution: How Kim Jong Il Became the Heir," a chapter in Lee's translation of Kim Il-sung's memoirs, *With the Century*, on *Korea Web Weekly*, http://www.kimsoft.com/war/r-23-9.htm. Further complicating the question of where he was born are persistent claims that Kim Jong-il actually was born February 16, 1941, and that his year of birth was changed when he was chosen as heir so that his major birthdays would be celebrated in the same years as those of his father. See Sohn Kwang Ju, "Focus Analysis Kim Jong Il" (Seoul: Network for North Korean Democracy and Human Rights, 2003, http://www.nknet.org/en/keys/lastkeys/2003/12/04.php). Sohn says Kim Jong-il was born in Khabarovsk in the USSR. Sohn says the birth date was changed in 1982 so that father and son could celebrate their seventieth and fortieth birthdays in the same year. Celebration of Kim Jong-il's fortieth birthday had already been announced in February 1941, Sohn says, but it was not yet the huge holiday it was to become from 1982 and it was possible to announce a second fortieth birthday in 1982 without totally confounding the citizenry. As for why Kim Il-sung and Kim Jong-sook would have been in Khabarovsk then, he says in his memoirs that he participated in

a Comintern-organized conference that was held there from December 1940 to mid-March 1941 (Kim, *With the Century,* Lee Wha Rang translation, chap. 23.1, http://www.kimsoft.com/war/r-23-1.htm).

3. Testimony of Li Jae-dok, Kim Jong-il's former nurse, in *JoongAng Ilbo,* October 4, 1991, cited in *True Story of Kim Jong-il,* p. 11.
4. Choe Pyong-gil, "Yu Song-chol's Testimony," *Hankuk Ilbo,* November 4, 1990, translated in Seiler, *Kim Il-Song 1941–1948.*
5. *True Story of Kim Jong-il,* p. 28.
6. Yu Song-chol's testimony, *Hankuk Ilbo,* November 8, 1990. According to one account, Han by then had become estranged from her non-communist second husband. She explained to Kim that she had not come forward earlier to reveal to him her whereabouts and new identity because of her shame at having submitted disgracefully to the Japanese authorities' demands. Kim thereupon pulled from his pocket a foot cover that she had woven of strands of her own hair to protect him from frostbite. He said he carried it always and had never forgotten her for a moment (Lim Un, *Founding of a Dynasty* [see chap. 2, n. 59], pp. 48–50). Han Song-hui is not recognized in North Korea as Kim Il-sung's wife. Although Lim asserts that Han was indeed his "wedded wife," one defector (who asked for anonymity when discussing the Kims' personal lives) told me his understanding was that the two had been engaged but never formally married.

Intriguing to note are strong similarities between her story and the story of Han Yong-ae, the female Harbin comrade of the early 1930s whose picture Kim said he still gazed upon. Possibly the Han Yong-ae story, whether or not important details are fictionalized, is told partly in an attempt to suggest that the story of Han Song-hui is wrong in important details—got the wrong Miss Han, perhaps—and particularly to refute widespread gossip in Pyongyang's elite circles to the effect that Kim resumed relations with his first wife and set her up in a mansion despite her remarriage to another man.

Consider: Kim Il-sung says that Han Yong-ae, while carrying out his assignments, "was arrested by the police in the autumn of 1930"—a decade before the reported arrest of Kim Hye-suk/Han Song-hui. In prison, Han Yong-ae (unlike Han Song-hui) bravely refused to submit, Kim writes. She declined a chance to better her lot by cooperating with a Japanese scheme to persuade Kim Il-sung to submit to the authorities. (In evaluating this claim, it is useful to recall that Kim Il-sung in 1930 was only eighteen years old and a small fish, years away from making such an impression on the Japanese that they would mount "submission" campaigns against him personally.) After her prison term, she eventually went to Seoul, married "belatedly" and "buried herself in her family life," Kim says.

"I inquired after Han Yong-ae's whereabouts in the homeland after liberation," Kim writes, "but she was not in the northern half of the country." During the Korean War, when North Korea briefly controlled much of South Korea, she took charge of a women's organization in the Seoul area, where her husband had been active in the underground work of the Korean Workers' (communist) Party, he says. The husband was "murdered by the enemy during the retreat in the Korean war." After that, Han Yong-ae "came to Pyongyang with her children to see me. But she could not meet me and, on the night of the 14th of August 1951, she and her two children were tragically killed in an enemy bombing raid."

True or false, this story of a woman so devoted to Kim and the revolution that she would *never* submit fits the pattern of North Korean propaganda heroes and heroines far better than would the story of Han Song-hui and the human weakness reported to have led her to abandon both her husband — Kim Il-sung — and the revolution. "Revolutionaries, even on a solitary island, should, like Han Yong-ae, not lose faith or abandon their conscience," Kim Il-sung writes.

The account in his memoirs, implicitly denying the reports that Kim had been married to another before Kim Jong-suk, may have been seen in Pyongyang as helping to clear up any doubts about the pedigree of Kim Jong-suk's son, Kim Jong-il, as Kim Il-sung's eldest legitimate child. Besides, for public consumption it simply would not do to tell of a woman who had been married to the incomparable Sun of the Nation but then went off to take up with some ordinary farmer.

7. My source for the location of Han's secret mansion is a former member of the elite who also confirmed other aspects of her story: "It's true that Kim Il-sung located her in Kangwon-do after Liberation and took her to Pyongyang as head of the Democratic Women's Party, then put her into a secret mansion to hide her away. . . . She had children by Kim Il-sung, but I can't remember the names."

8. Yu Song-chol's testimony, *Hankuk Ilbo*, November 8, 1990.

9. Lim Un, *Founding of a Dynasty,* p. 49.

10. See Yu Song-chol's testimony, *Hankuk Ilbo*, November 8, 1990; and Lim Un, *Founding of a Dynasty*. The story is told that Kim Jong-suk died literally on account of her jealousy of the secretary, Kim Song-ae. Suffering a stillbirth, Jong-suk began bleeding profusely. But she refused medical attention while waiting to see whether her husband would come to show his concern for her. A doctor could have saved her, but she refused to open her door. Kim Il-sung did not arrive, and she died in the room of excessive bleeding on September 22, 1949, only thirty-two years old. This is from the testimony of Kang Myong-do, compiled in a series of articles by Tae Won-ki in *JoongAng Ilbo* (Central Daily News, Seoul), April 1995. According to a 1993 South Korean report, rumors at the time of Kim Jong-suk's death were that that she had shot herself to death, or had been poisoned, "but the official announcement was that she died of a heart attack" (see *The True Story of Kim Jong-il,* p. 31). The information that the child was stillborn comes from the Japanese communist newspaper *Akahata*, September 28, 1949, as cited in Suh, *Kim Il Sung* (see chap. 2, n. 35), p. 51.

11. Yu Song-chol's testimony, *Hankuk Ilbo*, November 8, 1990.

12. Baik II (see chap. 4, n. 24), p. 447.

13. The defector is Kim Jong-min, who told me his characterization was based on his having met Kim Il-sung many times for both official and non-official occasions. "As for personally drinking and talking with him, I've done that about fifteen times." He told me he had "a watch given by Kim Il-sung with my name inscribed on it."

14. *Hankuk Ilbo*, November 7, 1990.

15. See, e.g., Deane, *I Was a Captive* (see chap. 4, n. 49), p. 229.

16. *Hankuk Ilbo*, November 7, 1990.

17. This source insisted on remaining anonymous. He said he feared that those at the top of the regime, either before or after reunification, might find a way to avenge the ultimate betrayal: exposing the Kims' private lives.

18. Yoo Sok-ryol, "The Rise of Kim Jong-il and the Heir-succession Problem," pt. I, *Vantage Point* (November 1987): p. 7.

19. Ibid., pp. 6, 7.
20. These identifications come from high-level defectors and also from Yoo, "Rise of Kim Jong-il," p. 7. There are some discrepancies among the various sources regarding the precise positions of several of these relatives, but the sources agree that all have been well placed in the regime.
21. University of Hawaii scholar Dae-Sook Suh, who visited Pyongyang in 1989 and spoke with several high-ranking officials, observed afterward that Kim's old partisan buddies had formerly exercised influence, but they had died off. "In North Korean politics today, it's mostly Kim Il-sung's relatives who are in charge," Suh said.
22. Hwang Jang-yop, *Problems of Human Rights (2)* (see chap. 6, n. 104).
23. Scalapino and Lee, *Communism in Korea* (see chap. 2, n. 28), p. 663.
24. Cited in Scalapino and Lee, *Communism in Korea*, p. 439.
25. Kim Ik-hyon, *The Immortal Woman Revolutionary* (Pyongyang: Foreign Languages Publishing House, 1987), p. 15.
26. The diplomat does not wish to be identified further.
    Consider Byoung-Lo Philo Kim's discussion of Confucianist influence:
    "The values of Marxism and Leninism in North Korea have brought about radical changes in the nature of society. Loyalty to one's family or lineage has been largely extended to loyalty to the nation as a whole, a shift from an extreme particularism to a limited universalism. Nationalism is expressed through the ideas of *juche*, which stresses national and cultural self-reliance and independence. Yet the Five Relations of Confucian culture are well retained in communist North Korea. There is no concept of privacy, self-determination, or the rights of the individual. According to Confucianism, what makes people human is not their freedom or individuality, but their acceptance of social roles that integrate them into a preestablished, collective whole, a notion coincident with the collective spirit of communism emphasized in North Korea. Family-based politics, the succession to rule of the leader's son, and the extraordinary veneration of Kim Il Sung are the Confucian legacies" (Kim, *Two Koreas in Development* [see chap. 1, n. 2], pp. 179–180).
27. Kim, *With the Century*, vol. 2, p. 183.
28. Ibid.
29. Ibid., pp. 381–382.
30. Ibid., pp. 184, 193.
31. Since the late Yi Dynasty period, writes Charles K. Armstrong (*The North Korean Revolution* [see chap. 1, n. 8], p. 95), "discrimination against 'secondary sons' (*soja*), or the sons of upper-class men and their mistresses, had been a social issue in Korea. The 1949 explanation of North Korean law pointed out that in the past, 'children born out of wedlock to concubines or *kisaeng* had suffered great discrimination as "secondary sons" (*soja*) or "bastards" (*sasaenga*).' They were not even allowed to call their fathers '*aboji*' ('father') and were denied entrance to school. This discrimination had continued unabated during the Japanese colonial period. The DPRK constitution eliminated such 'feudal' practices and guaranteed that henceforth such offspring would be treated no differently than 'legitimate sons' (*chokcha*)."
32. "In 1956, at the Twentieth Congress of the Communist Party of the Soviet Union, Khrushchev launched a formal denunciation of Stalin, challenging the supremacy and infallibility of Stalin as a leader. The de-Stalinization campaign

was undoubtedly a rude shock to Kim Il-sung. A second trauma occurred in the 1960s, when Mao signaled his wish to groom a political heir after his demise, thus putting the nation in a state of heightened anxiety and uncertainty. In September 1971, Mao's handpicked successor, Marshal Lin Biao, revolted against him and allegedly was killed in a plane crash while seeking to defect to the Soviet Union. These incidents convinced Kim Il-sung that he should carefully prepare a smooth political transition" (Kong Dan Oh, *Leadership Change in North Korean Politics: The Succession to Kim Il Sung* [Santa Monica, Calif.: RAND Corporation, 1988]).

33. Hwang Jang-yop, *Problems of Human Rights (2)*.
34. Ibid.
35. Hwang Jang-yop, *Problems of Human Rights (1)* (see chap. 2, n. 1). Hwang does not address the question of whether Kim's modesty in those remarks had been merely feigned, as so often seems to be the case with some other self-deprecating portions of Kim's memoirs—an invitation to others to pile on more praise.
36. "Kim YJ Makes 1st Appearance in 18 Yrs.," Yonhap News Agency dispatch in *Korea Times*, July 28, 1994; Kong Dan Oh, *Leadership Change*, p. 8.
37. Kim, *With the Century*, vol. 2, p. 435.
38. Choe Pyong-gil, "Following the Conclusion of the Serialization 'Yu Song-chol's Testimony,'" *Hankuk Ilbo*, December 1, 1990 (Sydney A. Seiler translation).
39. "The Soviet communities were a replica of how the Stalinist high officials lived in the USSR, as a privileged elite, separated from the rest of society" (van Ree, *Socialism in One Zone* [see chap. 4, n. 1], p. 165).
40. "I never saw anyone in North Korea as fat as his eldest daughter," he added. "One of her legs is fatter than my whole body. She's well proportioned [but] unfortunately she insisted on wearing a miniskirt. In North Korea, miniskirts were prohibited to the general population. Only members of Kim Il-sung's family could wear them. It's like a privilege for family members to wear them. That heavy daughter of Kim Yong-ju insisted on wearing a miniskirt."
41. As cited in *Leadership Change* by Oh (who maintained the dictionary change indicated not just hereditary succession but the choice of Kim Jong-il). South Korean scholar O Tae-chin also noted the dictionary change in "Three Personalities Rising as North Korea's Next Generation of Leaders," *Chugan Choson*, January 3, 1990, p. 66.
42. Cho, "Interview of Former High-level Official" (see chap. 6, n. 88).
43. Choe In Su, *Kim Jong Il: The People's Leader*, vol. 2 (Pyongyang: Foreign Languages Publishing House, 1985), p. 52.
44. This information comes from Chang Ki-hong, who had been working in a timber camp in Russia when he defected in 1991.
45. "Centered around the Ponghwa Medical Clinic, the entirety of the Red Cross Hospital is a research center. Actual practice is done entirely at the Red Cross Hospital under the guidance of the Ponghwa Medical Clinic. Those who are the same age or older than Kim Il-sung, or have the same blood type or physical condition, regardless of whether they are healthy or sick, are subjects of practice. However, no physiological damage is inflicted upon them. Instead, long-term observation of how these patients react to dietary conditions or medication is conducted" (Kim Jong-min quoted in Cho, "Interview of Former High-level Official"). "In Pyongyang there is a large Longevity Institute dedicated to researching ways to prolong the Great Leader's life, and any foods discovered to

ensure longevity are procured from the world over. All living conditions necessary to guarantee Kim Il Sung and Kim Jong Il's longevity are meticulously
taken care of, right down to the tiniest detail, and maintained at the highest standards possible" (Hwang Jang-yop, *Problems of Human Rights [2]*).

46. *Wen-ko T'ung-hsün* (Gwangjou), February 15, 1968, translated and cited in
Scalapino and Lee, *Communism in Korea*, p. 641.
47. Hwang Jang-yop, *Problems of Human Rights (2)*.
48. *Wolgan Choson* (July 1991).

Here is a description of the main presidential mansion in Pyongyang: "The
elder Kim lives opulently just minutes by car from the center of Pyongyang in a
palace circled by a moat and reached by a sweeping driveway decorated with
playing fountains. Pheasants and red-crested cranes wander freely over ex-
panses of manicured lawns. Last month the elder Kim threw a party for delegates to an Inter-Parliamentary Union conference, a party for 1,200 people held
in a hall the size of two full-sized soccer pitches in a marble-lined rotunda next
to his own elegant, square residence. At least 20 waiters served each table. The
glasses were crystal, the cutlery silver and the napkins linen. From a table at the
back of the vast dining hall, Kim appeared as a black speck on the edge of a
small white disc of table cloth" (Andrew Browne, Reuters dispatch from
Pyongyang: "The Great Leader Is an Enigma Even to His Own People," *Daily
Yomiuri* [Tokyo], June 3, 1991).

49. Kim, *With the Century*, vol. 3, p. 350.
50. *Wen-ko T'ung-hsün* (Gwangjou), February 15, 1968, translated and cited in
Scalapino and Lee, *Communism in Korea*, p. 641.
51. Interview with Kim Jong-min, former president of Daeyong Trading Company
and earlier a brigadier general–level officer in the Ministry of Public Security
(police).
52. *Wolgan Choson* (July 1991).
53. Interview with Kim Young-song. He said this mansion is near Kyongsong.
54. Kim Il-sung and Kim Jong-il "like to receive beautiful women as gifts," he said.
"Those who give women are party special department people in charge of that
aspect, or bodyguards. They scout the girls and give them as presents." I asked
how the women could be considered gifts if finding them was part of the giver's
job. My source replied: "The girls who are discovered accidentally can be considered gifts."
55. Kim in his later years, my source told me, was "still capable of performing in
bed, but the methods of arousal are such that I don't want to talk about them in
front of your interpreter. They melt 200-year-old beehives to get a wax supposed
to enhance his prowess."
56. For Mao's physician see Dr. Li Zhisui, *Private Life of Chairman Mao* (see chap. 6,
n. 64). Regarding embellishment, Bruce Cumings writes of "a bevy of female
servants on the old [Korean] royal model; chosen from among 'the pretty and
healthy virgins' from elite families, they were recruited to serve the king. The
ways in which they served him remain in dispute; they were not a harem or even
his concubines, although liaisons certainly happened. The main idea, though,
was to make the king's life comfortable. Defectors often say Kim and his son
continued this tradition, but they of course embellish this practice with endless
allegations of frolicking and womanizing." Unlike some other, similarly dismis-
sive scholars, Cumings at least attempts to marshal evidence that the defector

accounts are wrong. Citing a book by the niece of Kim's de facto first wife, Cumings says that Kim Jong-il "is not the playboy, womanizer . . . of our press. . . . He is so discreet about his private life that Nam Ok can only relate rumors about the foreign women imported to sate his sexual appetites; she never saw any of them, and after reading her account one doubts that Jong Il has much of a libido" (*North Korea: Another Country* [see chap. 4, n. 25], p. 165–166).

I must say I don't see the testimony by Li Nam-ok—herself a defector who ran away to Europe—as particularly useful on the subject of Kim Jong-il's libido. For a time living as a relative in one of Kim's households, Li would not have had anything comparable to the window on his life outside that particular household that was available to bodyguards and male cronies, not to mention the female recruits themselves. And it must be noted that Li's brother, also a defector, was murdered in South Korea by men identified as North Korean assassins after he had gone public with his account of palace life (see chap. 32). In her cautious account, Li clearly attempted to avoid inviting a similar fate.

57. Kim, *With the Century*, vol. 3, p. 282. Kim also wrote, "Today an epidemic of hedonism is cutting a wide swath across the rest of the globe. The extreme egoism of caring only for oneself and not thinking about the younger generation has encroached very far upon the minds of many people. Some of them do not have children, alleging that they are a nuisance, and others give up the thought of marrying. Needless to say, it is a matter of personal choice whether one gets married or has children. But what pleasure is there in living without the younger generation?"

58. Referring to Kim's practice during his guerrilla days of sleeping with children, Bruce Cumings offers an innocent explanation, calling it "an ancient Korean custom, still practiced" (*North Korea: Another Country*, p. 106).

59. From an interview with a former official of the regime.

60. I heard this from Kang Myong-do, who was sent to the same revolutionary work camp five years later.

61. Oh Sang-ik, "Public Executions in the DPRK," *Wolgan Choson* (January 1992): pp. 472–491 (Sydney A. Seiler translation). Oh, a lawyer, writes that Asia Watch and the International Human Rights Commission revealed this case based on testimony by a defector who had been a State Security official in North Korea.

62. Hwang Jang-yop, *Problems of Human Rights (2)*.

11. Yura.

1. Peter Hyun, "My Comrade Kim Il-sung Has Erred in Personality Cult and Power Succession," *Wolgan Choson* (February 2002), trans. Lee Wha Rang as "Lee Min—the Unsung Heroine of the Korean Independence War, Part II: Prolog," *Korea Web Weekly*, http://www.kimsoft.com/war/leemin2.htm.

2. Testimony of Park Jae-dok in *JoongAng Ilbo*, October 4, 1991, cited in *The True Story of Kim Jong Il* (see chap. 3, n. 61), p. 12.

3. Kazuko Kobayashi, "I Was a House Maid of Kim Il-sung," in *Records of Returnees from Abroad* (Tokyo: Mainichi Shimbunsha, no publication date given), pp. 119–122, cited in *The True Story of Kim Jong Il*.

4. Choe In Su, *Kim Jong Il*, vol. I (see chap. 10, n. 43), pp. 8–9.

5. Testimony of one Mo, former assistant to Agriculture Minister Kim Il, who defected to South Korea in 1960, in *Jayu Kongron* (April 1983): pp. 164–166, cited

in *The True Story of Kim Jong Il,* pp. 36–38. The author says that, once the facts of the drowning had been investigated and ascertained, Kim Il-sung "kept it a secret" and ordered gate guards, who had seen the boys playing in the pond but were not watching them carefully enough to prevent the drowning, not to talk about it.

Bruce Cumings (*North Korea* [see chap. 4, n. 25], p. 138) says Kim Il-sung "was so deeply distressed at the drowning of his younger son in 1947 that he had a *mudang* [shaman] carry out rituals on the very spot a decade later; the 'captured documents' in the U.S. archives contain long scrolls written by Buddhist monks, trying to assuage his loss and pain."

6. Choe In Su, *Kim Jong Il,* vol. I, pp. 49–51.
7. Lee Young-hwa, *Rescue the North Korean People,* leaflet, Osaka 1995, quotes scuttlebutt in Pyongyang as saying Ms. Kim raised the boy "as if he were her own child." Kang Myong-do, a defector to the South who claimed to be a Kim Il-sung relative on the maternal side, named Kang Bo-bi as the first cousin. See Kang Myong-do's testimony, compiled by Tae Won-ki, in a twelve-part series in the Seoul daily *JoongAng Ilbo,* starting April 12, 1995. For the Ri Ul-sol story see Kim Il-sung, "Nurturing the Root of the Revolution: How Kim Jong-il Became the Heir," chapter of *With the Century,* trans. Lee Wha Rang, *Korea Web Weekly,* http://www.kimsoft.com/war/r-23-9.htm. Lee Wha Rang in notes to this translation supports the view that it was Kim Ok-sun who raised Kim Jong-il.
8. Choe In Su, *Kim Jong Il,* vol. I, pp. 62–65.
9. Ibid., pp. 67–68.
10. Ibid., pp. 69–70.
11. *The True Story of Kim Jong Il,* p. 49.
12. Choe In Su, *Kim Jong Il,* vol. I, pp. 77–117. The memo is quoted on pp. 85–86.
13. Ibid., p. 118.
14. Hwang Jang-yop, *Problems of Human Rights (2)* (see chap. 6, n. 104).
15. Kang Myong-do testimony in *JoongAng Ilbo,* April 12, 1995. Choe In Su, *Kim Jong Il,* vol. I, pp. 16–17, observes, "Busy with state affairs, the father leader could find no special time for the education of his son [Kim Jong-il]; his daily life was in itself the process of bringing up and guiding his son in a revolutionary way."
16. Choe In Su, *Kim Jong Il,* vol. I, pp. 168–177.
17. Hwang Jang-yop, *Testimonies of North Korean Defectors: True Picture of North Korea According to a Former Workers' Party Secretary* (see chap. 7, n. 15).
18. See, e.g., Choe In Su, *Kim Jong Il,* vol. I, p. 203.
19. Tak Jin, Kim Gang Il and Pak Hong Je, *Great Leader Kim Jong Il,* vol. I (see chap. 5, n. 15), p. 22. A former high official who knew him told me that according to his recollection Kim Jong-il also enrolled for a second time at Mangyongdae School after leaving Namsan.
20. Yun Ki-bon, *The Land of North Korea in My Memory* (Seoul: Kapja Munhwasa, 1973), cited in *The True Story of Kim Jong Il,* pp. 49–58.
21. Choe In Su, *Kim Jong Il,* vol. I, pp. 249–250.
22. *JoongAng Ilbo,* January 14 and 28, 1993, quoting Kang Yong-gu, former superintendent of Namsan Junior High School, and Kim Dan, a classmate of Kim Jong-il's among others who had known him at Namsan and later moved to Russia, cited in *The True Story of Kim Jong Il,* pp. 59–60.

23. Choe In Su, *Kim Jong Il*, vol. I, pp. 129, 134–135.
24. Ibid., pp. 141–147; Tak, Kim and Pak, *Great Leader Kim Jong Il*, pp. 38–39.
25. Choe In Su, *Kim Jong Il*, vol. I, pp. 74–76.
26. Ibid., pp. 178–181.
27. Kang Myong-do testimony in *JoongAng Ilbo*, April 12, 1995.
28. Choe In Su, *Kim Jong Il*, vol. I, pp. 184–187.
29. Ibid., pp. 190–195.
30. Hwang Jang-yop, *Problems of Human Rights (2)*.
31. Ibid.
32. Ibid.
33. Tak, Kim and Pak, *Great Leader Kim Jong Il*, vol. I, pp. 50–51.
34. *The True Story of Kim Jong Il*, p. 59.
35. Hwang Jang-yop, *Problems of Human Rights (2)*.
36. *People's Korea* (a Chongryon newspaper in Tokyo), September 16, 1995, quoting a September 1, 1995, dispatch by Pyongyang's Korean Central News Agency.
37. Interview with Kim Ji-il, who defected to South Korea in 1990 while pursuing graduate studies in physics in Kharkov, Ukraine.
38. Choe In Su, *Kim Jong Il*, vol. I, pp. 298–301.
39. Adrian Buzo makes the comparison regarding the two older men in *The Guerilla Dynasty: Politics and Leadership in North Korea* (St. Leonards, Australia: Allen & Unwin, 1999), p. 43 and fn. 34.
40. See Choe In Su, *Kim Jong Il*, vol. I, pp. 261–267.
41. Ibid., pp. 311–316.
42. Ibid., pp. 323–326.
43. See, e.g., the photo facing p. 80 in Tak, Kim and Pak, *Great Leader Kim Jong Il*, vol. I.
44. Kang Myong-do testimony in *JoongAng Ilbo*, April 12, 1995.
45. Tak, Kim, and Pak, *Great Leader Kim Jong Il*, vol. I, p. 90.
46. Choe In Su, *Kim Jong Il*, vol. I, pp. 218–223.
47. Ibid., pp. 317–319.
48. Among the other officials who lived in the neighborhood were Choe Yong-gon, Kim Il, Kim Dong-kyu, Im Chun-chu, Pak Song-chol, Li Jong-ok, Kim Chang-bong, Chon Mun-sop and Ji Kyong-soo.
49. Among the young people at Choe Yong-hae's home that day, I was told, were Choe Young-sook, daughter of Choe Yong-gon; Pak Choon-sik and Pak Choon-hoon, sons of Pak Song-chol; Ji Kwang-jae and Ji Kwang-hwa, children of Ji Kyong-soo; plus the young men's girlfriends.
50. "S. Korean Agent Reports North Has Executed at Least 50 Officials in Purge," Seoul-datelined dispatch from Agence France-Presse.
51. Choe In Su, *Kim Jong Il*, vol. I, pp. 331–333.
52. Ibid., pp. 333–336.
53. Ibid., pp. 337–340.
54. Ibid., pp. 341–346.
55. According to *The True Story of Kim Jong Il*, p. 65, the thesis was published in full in the party theoretical journal, *Kulloja* (Worker), March 1985 issue.
56. Kim Kyeh-won, "Bulgarian Envoy Recalls Memories of Kim Jong-il," *Korea Herald*, January 16, 1991.

12. Growing Pains.

1. *Songbun* is discussed in Armstrong, *The North Korean Revolution* (see chap. 1, n. 8), pp. 71–74; and in Helen Louise Hunter, *Kim Il-song's North Korea* (Westport, Conn.: Praeger, 1999), chap. 1 ff. The latter book is a declassified Central Intelligence Agency study originally done in the early 1980s.
2. I interviewed Ahn in August 1996.

13. Take the Lead in World Conjuring.

1. Kim Jong Il, *Some Problems Arising in the Creation of Masterpieces* (Pyongyang: Foreign Languages Publishing House, 1989), p. 4.
2. Kim Jong-min, quoted by Cho Gap-jae in "Interview of Former High-level Official of DPRK Ministry of Public Security Who Defected to South Korea" (see chap. 6, n. 88).
3. Tak, Kim and Pak, *Great Leader Kim Jong Il* (see chap. 5, n. 15), vol. 1, p. 108.
4. Kim Myong Chol, "Biography of an Infant Prodigy," *Far Eastern Economic Review*, March 5, 1982. An informal spokesman for North Korea in Japan, Kim Myong Chol at the time he wrote this article was editor of the pro-Pyongyang Tokyo weekly *People's Korea*. He had translated Baik Bong's Kim Il-sung biography into English. He is not to be confused with the ex-bodyguard defector of the same name.
5. Cho Gap-jae, "Interview of Former High-level Official" (Interviewer paraphrases Kim Jong-min's remarks:) "Since the 1970s, Kim Jong-il began to prepare all-out to become his father's successor. As such, his relationships with those surrounding him became rigid. Meetings between him and [Kim Jong-min] also became infrequent."
6. See Scalapino and Lee, *Communism in Korea* (see chap. 2, n. 28), pp. 608–612.
7. Tak, Kim and Pak, *Great Leader Kim Jong Il*, pp. 109–110. The authors continue that Kim Jong-il "thought that establishing a revolutionary view of the leader among Party members was the key to closing the ranks of struggle for the revolution." Thus, he "developed an original theory on the Juche-oriented view of the leader."
8. Hwang Jang-yop, *Problems of Human Rights (1)* (see chap 2, n. 1).
9. Kang Myong-do testimony in *JoongAng Ilbo*, April 12, 1995.
10. A memoir credited to a purged North Korean official and published posthumously in Seoul in 1989 said the author in the course of his work in Pyongyang had access to a file of newspaper clippings from the pre-1945 period. In them, the author said, was an account in the leading newspaper *Dong-A Ilbo* of Kim Yong-ju's capture in 1938. Broken by the authorities, he supposedly signed a pledge of loyalty to the Japanese and went to work for them as an interpreter. Other accounts say Yong-ju worked for U.S. intelligence. For a discussion of all of those accounts see *The True Story of Kim Jong-il*, pp. 67–78. The account cites Ko Bong-ki, *Posthumous Manuscripts* (Seoul: Chunma Printing House, 1989); Lee Yong-sang, "My Friend Kim Yong-ju," *JoongAng Ilbo* (May 1991); and a book by Lee Myong-yong, *Kim Il-sung Stories*.
11. Lim Un (*Founding of a Dynasty* [see chap. 2, n. 59], p. 258) cites the claim from Kim Yong-ju's autobiography. "This is obviously dreamy talk," says Lim.
12. *True Story of Kim Jong Il*, pp. 78–79. The official biographies do not mention Kim Jong-il's having worked under Kim Guk-tae—or under anyone else except his father, for that matter.

13. *True Story of Kim Jong-il,* pp. 78–80.
14. Choe In Su, *Kim Jong Il,* vol. 2 (see chap. 10, n. 43), pp. 22–26.
15. Ibid., vol. 2, p. 12.
16. Ibid., vol. 2, pp. 40–42. I use the term "draft-dodger" loosely, to evoke a comparable American situation for Americans of that generation. North Korea did not have the military draft per se, since there was no shortage of willing recruits. Enlistment was considered an honor, and career-enhancing, so most young men who were not members of the very top elite wanted to serve.
17. *True Story of Kim Jong-il,* pp. 78–80; Kong Dan Oh, *Leadership Change* (see chap. 10, n. 32), p. 7.
18. Tak, Kim and Pak, *Great Leader Kim Jong Il,* vol. 1, pp. 119–120.
19. Suh, *Kim Il Sung* (see chap. 2, n. 35), p. 223.
20. See ibid., pp. 128–129. Also note the claim of an unofficial North Korean spokesman in Tokyo that the junior Kim "played a leading role in the watershed ideological and theoretical campaign to *defend the present leadership*" (emphasis added). See Kim Myong Chol, "Biography of an Infant Prodigy."
21. "True Picture of North Korea According to a Former Workers' Party Secretary," in *Testimonies of North Korean Defectors.*
22. Tak, Kim and Pak, *Great Leader Kim Jong Il,* vol. 1, pp. 121–125.
23. Suh, *Kim Il Sung,* pp. 228–229. Suh reports, "In his lecture to party cadres on October 11, 1969, Kim Il Sung said that a number of 'bad fellows' who had been in charge of ideological work had failed to propagate the party's great achievements and had not taught young cadres the great successes the people had achieved."
24. Hwang Jang-yop, *Problems of Human Rights (1).*
25. Tak, Kim and Pak, *Great Leader Kim Jong Il,* vol. 1, pp. 125–126.
26. Kim Myong Chol, "Biography of an Infant Prodigy."
27. Hwang Jang-yop, *Problems of Human Rights (3)* (see chap. 9, n. 25).
28. Choe In Su, *Kim Jong Il,* vol. 2, pp. 16–21.
29. "True Picture of North Korea."
30. Choe In Su, *Kim Jong Il,* vol. 2, pp. 31–35.
31. In *With the Century,* Kim Il-sung gives an example of his personal involvement in the rewriting of history. The incident involved assessment of an 1884 coup attempted by reformist Kim Ok-gyun against the decrepit Yi Dynasty. Kim Il-sung says that in his own boyhood, "most of my teachers in Korean history regarded Kim Ok-gyun as pro-Japanese . . . because he had received help from the Japanese in his preparations for the coup." After assuming power, Kim Il-sung relates, "I told our historians that . . . assessing him as pro-Japanese simply because he had drawn on the strength of Japan would lead to nihilism . . ." (vol. 1, pp. 26–27). I cannot help smiling at the image of a platoon of obedient scribes, earnestly jotting down their instructions from the Great Historian.
32. Baik I (see chap. 4, n. 25), preface.
33. Ibid., p. 23. Kim backed off a bit from such claims in his later memoirs. Likewise he steered clear of such extravagant tales as Baik Bong's David-and-Goliath account (vol. 1, p. 145) of a sturdy Kim knocking down with "a single blow" a Chinese policeman's son named Beanstalk who displayed contempt for Koreans and possessed "Herculean strength." Yet another story that bit the dust in later versions was Baik's claim that Kim at the age of sixteen—while still a middle-school pupil himself—established an elementary school in a Manchurian village that he

was trying to organize. "The General"—even as an elementary school pupil Kim rates this rank in Baik's reverential account—"provided education free of charge for peasant children who had been unable to study because of poverty, and conducted classes at night to educate youth and the middle-aged and women. On the basis of such activities, the General then rallied the residents around organizations formed according to each stratum of society, and trained them politically. He gathered them into the Juvenile Corps or the Juvenile Expeditionary Party, and youth into the Youth Association (Anti-Imperialist Youth League), women into the Women's Association and peasants into the Peasants' Union." Kim organized the people into a military unit to defend their village, taught Marxism-Leninism, published a political magazine called *Bolshevik*; in short, Baik related, the adolescent General was "tireless." And when he was older, was it not Kim Il-sung who had returned to Korea in 1945 as "the greatest hero Korea has ever produced, the Leader of the nation, who had promised a resurrection and a shining victory to the Mother Earth of Korea"? (Baik II, p. 53).

34. February 15, 1994, interview with Kim Nam-joon, a former Korean People's Army second lieutenant who said it was only after he defected to South Korea in 1989 that he learned who the real author was.

35. Tak, Kim and Pak, *Great Leader Kim Jong Il*, vol. 1, pp. 140–159.

36. Buzo, *Guerilla Dynasty* (see chap. 11, n. 39), p. 43.

37. Choe In Su, *Kim Jong Il*, vol. 2, pp. 49–54. The Chinese had lapel badges with portraits of Mao earlier.

38. Kang Myong-do testimony in *JoongAng Ilbo*.

39. Choe In Su, *Kim Jong Il*, vol. 2, pp. 55–57.

40. Ibid., pp. 59–64.

41. Ibid., vol. 2, p. 74.

42. Kim Jong Il, *Some Problems Arising*, pp. 10–13. He is described as having given the talk April 6, 1968.

43. Tak, Kim and Pak, *Great Leader Kim Jong Il*, vol. 1, pp. 172, 191–192.

44. Choe In Su, *Kim Jong Il*, vol. 2, pp. 64–70.

45. Tak, Kim and Pak, *Great Leader Kim Jong Il*, vol. 1, pp. 172–175.

46. See Koh Chik-mann, "'Theory of Cinema—' Offers Clues to Kim Jong-il's View on Arts, Politics," *Korea Times*, July 13, 1994.

47. Choe In Su, *Kim Jong Il*, vol. 2, pp. 70–74.

48. Ibid., pp. 78–83.

49. Ibid., pp. 84–87.

50. Ibid., pp. 89–90.

51. Tak, Kim and Pak, *Great Leader Kim Jong Il*, vol. 1, p. 197.

52. Kang Myong-do, *Pyeongyangeun mangmyeoneul kumgungda* (Pyongyang Dreams of Exile) (Seoul: Joongang Daily News, 1995).

53. See Choe In Su, *Kim Jong Il*, vol. 2, photo facing p. 88.

54. Kim Jong Il, *Let Us Create More Revolutionary Works Which Meet the Requirements of Our Socialist Life* (Pyongyang: Foreign Languages Publishing House, 1988).

55. Choe In Su, *Kim Jong Il*, vol. 2, pp. 92–94.

56. Ibid., pp. 115–120.

57. Tak, Kim and Pak, *Great Leader Kim Jong Il*, pp. 110–111.

58. Ibid., p. 116.

59. Buzo, *Guerilla Dynasty*, pp. 40, 48.

60. Ibid., p. 26.

61. Hwang Jang-yop, *Problems of Human Rights (3)*.
62. Quoted in Lee Sang-min, "The Personality Cult in the North Korean Political Process (II)," *Vantage Point* (September 1989): pp. 1–2.
63. I interviewed the diplomat, who asked not to be further identified. Another foreign resident, an Englishman who was employed by the Foreign Languages Publishing House as a reviser in 1987–1988, noted that comedy programs were not among the entertainment offerings on North Korean television. See chap. 8, p. 7, of Andrew Holloway, *A Year in Pyongyang* (published in 2002 on the Internet Web site of Aidan Foster-Carter, http://www.aidanfc.net/a_year_in_pyongyang.html).
64. Kim *With the Century*, vol. 3, pp. 421–422.
65. "New Book Adds Insights into Hitler's Personality," Bonn-datelined article by UPI-Kyodo, *Japan Times*, December 2, 1983.

14. Eyes and Ears.

1. Hwang Jang-yop, *Problems of Human Rights (2 and 3)* (see chap. 6, n. 104, and chap. 9, n. 25, respectively). Further details of the security organizations' interlocking operations from Kim Jong-min, who rose to the brigadier-general level in Public Security, appear in Cho Gap-jae, "Interview of Former High-level Official" (see chap. 6, n. 88).
2. An official biographer quoted Kim Il-sung as saying, "The consistent principle our Party adheres to in its work with people who have complicated social and political backgrounds, is that we should appraise them case by case, always attaching utmost importance to their present behavior, isolate hostile elements to the maximum and win even one by one over to the side of the revolution." The biographer continued, "Introducing such a principle, he was able to educate and remold all the people except a handful of purposefully hostile elements of exploiting class origin, and brought all into the bosom of socialism. He . . . went deep among the people, embraced all warmly, trusted them and actively helped them to give full scope to their talents and exercise a passion for socialist construction, himself setting a practical example, and teaching this to Party organizations."

    For example, Kim supposedly forgave the chief engineer of a steelworks who had come up under the Japanese and who, during the Korean War, had started to move south but thought better of it. "Noting that he had returned again to follow the Party after realizing that the U.S. scoundrels were bad, even though he had hesitated for a while during the war, the Leader held that it was possible to educate and remold him."

    Visiting the wives left behind by some men who had fled south during the war, Kim noted that the men were from backgrounds of poverty. Thus, they must have been deceived by enemy propaganda. "Some of your husbands who have gone to South Korea are probably begging for some food with a tin [can] in hand," he told the abandoned wives, who were described as repenting of their "inadvertent" failure to dissuade their husbands from fleeing. "Some are likely to be fighting against the Syngman Rhee clique. Achieving something in their fight, they may come back. Generally speaking, those who went there from the northern half are mostly saying frequently that the politics of the Republic is better. We know this well. Therefore, we cannot say that all the families are bad

simply because their members went to the South." He told the women, "When your infant children ask questions about their fathers, you must clearly answer. If their fathers went there after doing something wrong, tell them that their fathers are a class enemy. Educate them, telling them that they must become revolutionaries, taking the right road though their fathers took the wrong road. If their fathers went there unwittingly, please tell them that their fathers are guiltless and went there unwittingly. Inform them that it is because of U.S. imperialism and the Syngman Rhee clique that they cannot see their fathers. Teach them that U.S. imperialism and the Syngman Rhee clique are our sworn enemies. Educate them that 'You receive equal treatment as citizens of the Republic. There is no discrimination against you simply because your family members went to the South. Don't worry! You must study well, work well and become labor innovators.'" The women "shed copious tears" at his words, and after he had gone "they all gave more energy to the country's service and came to enjoy a lively life. It was because of such personal education by Comrade Kim Il-sung that the people with complicated backgrounds took the road to hope, in countless cases. People who had a shameful past drew boundless inspiration from the wise policy and warm love of Comrade Kim Il-sung and learned to give all their energies to proud socialist construction, embraced to his broad bosom" (Baik II [see chap. 4, n. 24], pp. 530–543).
3. June 1994 interview in Seoul.

15. From Generation to Generation.
1. Hwang Jang-yop, *Problems of Human Rights (2)* (see chap. 6, n. 104).
2. "Can Kim Jong-il Maintain His Father's 'Inviolable' Authority?" *Vantage Point* (July 1981): pp. 11–15.
3. Tak, Kim and Park, *Great Leader Kim Jong Il*, vol. 1 (see chap. 5, n. 15), pp. 222–223. Another report, by a North Korean spokesman in Tokyo, says it was in 1974 that Kim Jong-il formed a crisis-management task force to try to salvage the foundering six-year plan (1971–1976), which sought to complete the country's "socialist industrialization" and—the "technical revolution" again—to mechanize or automate difficult, dangerous and dirty tasks in the factory, on the farm and in the home. At an extraordinary Politburo meeting called to discuss economic problems, "no one responded to the exhortations of Kim Il-sung. Then Kim Jong-il volunteered to take over the job. He organized young volunteers into shock brigades and led the six-year plan to fulfillment of its goals ahead of schedule. For this work he was awarded the title Hero of the Nation in 1975" (Kim Myong Chol, "Biography of an Infant Prodigy" [see chap. 13, n. 4]). Here we have either two different events or, perhaps, two conflicting dates for the same event.
4. Tak, Kim and Pak, *Great Leader Kim Jong Il*, vol. 1, p. 226.
5. Ibid., pp. 204–205.
6. Choe In Su, *Kim Jong Il*, vol. 2 (see chap. 10, n. 43), p. 129.
7. Tak, Kim and Pak, *Great Leader Kim Jong Il*, vol. 1, pp. 228–229.
8. Ibid., pp. 248–250.
9. "The north Korean government is well aware of the negative feeling of the people against the mobilization system and it, therefore, keeps the people always

under strain. . . . . North Korea has admitted that small-scale resistance activities
of the people occur in a wide sphere of life. . . . According to a speech by Kim Il-
sung, there are 'workers and clerks who do not work hard and observe labor
regulations' as well as those 'who waste the valuable social and national proper-
ties' [including] those who lavishly use chemical fertilizer, leave foodgrains piled
up on moist ground and those who do not keep their farm tools in good shape
or plan to harvest chestnuts. In the case of factory workers, there are those
who think only of the quantity, not the quality, of industrial products and who
pack commodities without care. Kim Il-sung believes that these phenomena are
related to individualism. In other words, he thinks such phenomena occur as
workers do not believe in the coincidence between the national interest and personal interest" (Choe Hong-gi, "Mobilization System and Labor Efficiency,"
Vantage Point [January 1979]: pp. 12, 13; no source, date, or place given for Kim
Il-sung's speech).

10. *People's Korea* said in its February 13, 1982, edition that Kim Jong-il "proposed a
Three-Revolution-Team Movement and dispatched teams composed of party
activists and young intellectuals to various branches of the national economy."
Other North Korean sources, however, say that Kim Il-sung initiated the movement early in 1973 and Kim Jong-il only took charge of the effort later that year
when he was promoted to party secretary for organization and guidance.

11. Among the many analysts taking this view was Pusan National University Professor Lee Sang-min, in "The Personality in the North Korean Political Process
(I)," *Vantage Point* (August 1989): p. 7.

12. Interview February 17, 1994.

13. Yang Ho-min, "The Three Revolutions in North Korea," *Vantage Point* (June
1978): p. 8.

14. Interview March 15, 1995.

15. "P'yongyang's harshest attack on the Chinese appeared in an editorial of
Nodong Shinmun on September 15, 1966. . . . Ostensibly attacking 'Trotsky-
ism,' the KWP organ pointed out that the major departure and basis of the position of Trotsky's 'left-wing' opportunism was the theory of 'permanent
revolution.' . . . The Trotskyites categorically opposed any combination of violent and nonviolent methods in the revolutionary struggle, and favored only 'offensive and reckless rebellion.' The North Korean leaders were apparently
alarmed by the violence of China's Cultural Revolution, which they did not want
to follow. However, P'yongyang refrained from commenting on the Cultural
Revolution in explicit terms" (Chin O. Chung, *P'yongyang Between Peking and
Moscow: North Korea's Involvement in the Sino-Soviet Dispute, 1958–1975* [Tuscaloosa,
Ala.: The University of Alabama Press, 1978], p. 128).

16. *Kulloja* (Worker), no. 3, 1975, p. 16, cited in Yang Ho-min, "Three Revolutions
in North Korea," p. 11.

17. This former official insisted on anonymity.

18. Choe In Su, *Kim Jong Il,* vol. 2, pp. 28–30.

19. Kang Myong-do in *JoongAng Ilbo.*

20. Ibid.

21. "True Picture of North Korea" (see chap. 13, n. 21).

22. The country's Central Broadcasting Station announced that Kim Yong-ju had
attended a ceremony and a concert on July 26, 1993. His name was listed then

between the previously tenth- and eleventh-ranking officials, suggesting he had been rehabilitated (*Korea Times*, July 28, 1994).

23. Kim Myong Chol, "Biography of an Infant Prodigy" (see chap. 13, n. 4). Hahn Ho-suk, "American Nuclear Threats and North Korea's Counter Strategy," in *The US-DPRK Relations at the Close of the 20th Century and the Prospect for United Korea at the Dawn of the 21st Century*, described as an English abstract of an original paper posted in Korean on the Web site onekorea.org by the author, who directs the "Center for Korean Affairs" in Flushing, N.Y. (*Korea Web Weekly*, http://www.kimsoft.com/2000/hanho.htm).

24. Eric Cornell, *North Korea Under Communism: Report of an Envoy to Paradise* (see chap. 9, n. 3), p. 124.

25. Agency for National Security Planning, Seoul, "Questions and Answers at the Press Conference," http://www.fas.org/news/dprk/1997/bg152.html.

26. Lim Un says Kim Song-ae was pregnant with Pyong-il in January 1951, which means a 1951 birth date. However, Kang Myong-do, a distant relative of Kim Il-sung's, himself born in 1959, who grew up as a member of the Pyongyang elite, told me that Pyong-il was born around 1953. The 1951 pregnancy may have led to the birth of Pyong-il's elder sister.

27. Interview with Guenter Unterbeck, former East German diplomat, October 8, 1994.

28. Former bodyguard Pak Su-hyon told me, "Some people used to have lavish parties with Kim Pyong-il, but they were kicked out. Kim Il-sung said, 'I am the Great Leader. Why should you party with Kim Pyong-il?' Actually there are two kinds of bodyguards. The military bodyguards do the real work—I was in the military—while the civilian bodyguards lead relatively easy lives. But the civilian bodyguards don't see much of Kim Il-sung's and Kim Jong-il's private life. The military bodyguards can see more than the civilians and have more access to rumors."

29. Kim Jong-min, in Cho Kap-chae, "Interview of Former High-level Official" [see chap. 9, n. 37]).

30. By some accounts Kim Song-ae and Kim Il-sung had two additional sons, Song-il, an officer in the People's Army, and Kyong-il.

31. Hwang Jang-yop, *Problems of Human Rights (2)*.

32. Ibid.

33. Ibid.

34. Hwang Jang-yop, *Problems of Human Rights (3)*. Hwang does not say when this happened and he does not name the couple.

35. Bradley K. Martin, "Kim's Son Reported Likely Successor in North Korea," *Baltimore Sun*, March 6, 1980.

36. Bradley K. Martin, "Kim's Son Touted as Next North Korean Leader," *Baltimore Sun*, May 9, 1980.

37. "Can Kim Jong-il Maintain . . . ?"

38. Kim Jong-min, in Cho Kap-chae, "Interview of Former High-level Official."

39. Quoted in Bradley K. Martin, "Kim's Son Praised—Abroad—in Glowing Terms," *Baltimore Sun*, April 15, 1981.

40. "North Korean Politics: The Primacy of Regime Security," paper presented at the International Conference on Korean Unification, sponsored by Seoul Forum for International Affairs, November 13–14, 1992.

41. Hwang Jang-yop, *Problems of Human Rights (2)*.

16. Our Earthly Paradise Free from Oppression.

1. Hwang Jang-yop, *Problems of Human Rights (2)* (chap. 6, n. 104).
2. Choe Dong-chol, a former prisoner I interviewed in Seoul in August 1996, quoted the Great Leader in this way.
3. Hwang Jang-yop, interviewed by Olaf Jahn, in *Far Eastern Economic Review*, October 15, 1998, said each of ten areas for non-elite internal exiles housed approximately thirty thousand prisoners at a time. Former prisoners testified to frequent turnover as inmates died.
4. See David Hawk, *The Hidden Gulag: Exposing North Korea's Prison Camps – Prisoners' Testimonies and Satellite Photos*, U.S. Committee for Human Rights in North Korea, 2003, www.hrnk.org.
5. See Human Rights Without Frontiers International Secretariat, "Correctional Institutions in North Korea," October 16, 2001, http//www.hrwf.net.
6. Hwang Jang-yop, who became the party's ideology chief in 1958, writes about this purge in *Problems of Human Rights (3)* (see chap. 9, n. 25).
7. Kang and a French co-author have published a book: Kang Chol-hwan and Pierre Rigoulot, *The Acquariums of Pyongyang: Ten Years in a North Korean Gulag*, translated by Yair Reiner (New York: Basic Books, 2001).
8. Kang Chul-ho told me he had heard that the mining ultimately proved uneconomical and the site was turned into a regular prison camp in 1993, the political prisoners moved elsewhere.

17. Two Women.

1. Kim, *With the Century*, vol. 3 (see chap. 2, n. 2), pp. 304–305. One may guess that this anecdote was inserted into the senior Kim's memoirs at Kim Jong-il's behest, because it portrays the younger Kim in what the regime's propagandists evidently consider to be a positive light.
2. After the family's highly publicized defection, Pyongyang alleged that Yeo had misappropriated 100,000 *won*. Lee in my interview with her scoffed at that charge: "In North Korea if you had 100,000 you'd be among the wealthiest." If the charge were true "he would have been sent to jail."
3. Traditionally there would be no marriage between members of the same Korean clan, but Kang and his former wife were members of different Kang clans, the names represented by different Chinese characters. "My Kang character is 'comfort' Kang, the same as Kim Il-sung's mother. Prime Minister Kang's is 'swallow' Kang. The prime minister is not a relative of Kim Il-sung. But the prime minister's father was in the anti-Japanese resistance and died while protecting Kim Il-sung." Although it is well established that he married the prime minister's daughter and in that fashion became a fixture of Pyongyang café society, there have been allegations that Kang was not, as he claimed, a member of Kim Il-sung's extended family. A later defector who knew him told me on condition of anonymity that he had inquired of some of Kim Il-sung's Kang relatives at the time of Kang Myong-do's defection and had been told Kang Myong-do was not one of them as he claimed. This source spoke of sensing a competition among defectors to impress their South Korean hosts with high-level connections back home. I suppose such a factor could have worked either way. Kang Myong-do might have invented his lineage or his detractor might have tried to minimize Kang's value in order to build up his own. From Kim Jong-min,

a higher-ranking defector who knew Kim Jong-il and Kim Il-sung personally and whose information generally checked out, I heard that Kang Myong-do was indeed a "distant relative" on Kim's mother's side.

4. Kang told me that even Kim Yong-sun, a very high-level international affairs official in the 1990s and 2000s until his death in 2003, "doesn't have that much contact" with his boss. "If there's a very specific and important issue, he can get in to see Kim Jong-il. If someone else visited him once, it would be a lifelong memory. I saw Kim Jong-il a couple of times at Chilgol. The relatives didn't like him much—they said he had a 'cold expression.' After he came to power I met him with a friend of my grandfather in 1983 and in 1992 at the twentieth anniversary of the opening of his palace. In 1993 I saw him at the opening of a new product line in a factory producing food for the Kims."

5. Kang had not heard about selected thirteen-year-olds going straight to work.

6. His own first wife, whom he divorced before marrying Prime Minister Kang Song-san's daughter, was a "volunteer," "like a waitress," at one of Kim Jong-il's mansions, Kang said, and "even waitresses can be termed 'Happy Corps.'" But his marriage resulted from his infatuation with her, not from having been awarded her in a drawing.

7. Hwang Jang-yop, who worked closely with Kim Jong-il before his defection, has a slightly different version of how the women were married off: "The women who serve him get to choose their husbands, and the women are given as 'gifts' to the chosen men. By continuing to 'take care' of his harem in this way, he has full control over them and commands their loyalty" (Hwang Jang-yop, *Problems of Human Rights [3]* [see chap. 9, n. 25]).

18. Dazzling Ray of Guidance.

1. *People's Korea*, February 13, 1982. Propaganda for his father had played on similar themes. Recall the illnesses that afflicted the elder Kim during his guerrilla-fighting days. In addition, note the following passage from his official biography regarding his health in the late 1950s, when he was embroiled in a dispute over his emphasis on heavy industry over consumer goods. "In strained days Comrade Kim Il Sung . . . dropped in at Taisung-ri, Kangsu County, on his way to Nampo, South Pyungan Province, for on-the-spot guidance. A certain old woman whose son, a regiment commander of the People's Army, was killed in action, said to Comrade Kim Il Sung, grasping his hand with tears in her eyes, 'Premier, you look so pale, don't you? Don't worry. Whatever the factionalists may say, finding fault with the people's livelihood, we have no reason to worry. We are all living well'" (Baik II [see chap. 4, n. 24], p. 554).

2. Hwang Jang-yop, *Problems of Human Rights (3)* (see chap. 9, n. 25); Kim Young-song, *O, suryeongnim neomuhapnida* (Oh! Great Leader! This Is Too Much) (Seoul: Chosun Daily News Publishing Co., 1995).

3. Choe In Su, *Kim Jong Il*, vol. 2 (see chap. 10, n. 43), pp. 212–216.

4. *People's Korea*, February 13, 1982, citing Kim Il-sung, "Report on the Work of the Central Committee to the 6th Congress of the Workers' Party of Korea," October 10, 1980.

5. September 2, 1977, Radio Pyongyang broadcast cited in Yoo, "Rise of Kim Jong-il" (see chap. 5, n. 18), p. 6.

6. A version of the results, toned down in an attempt to make it palatable to foreigners, could be seen in an article in a Hong Kong magazine written by an informal spokesman for the regime, Kim Myong-chol: "Famous as an infant prodigy, the son proved himself a super-achiever: he finished all courses from primary school to university first on the list with full honors and captured first prizes in national student poetry, essay and painting contests. He was a voracious reader of the masterpieces of Korean and world literature, both classic and contemporary. Two episodes may be worth mentioning. When in kindergarten, he was not satisfied with a nurse's explanation that one and one make two. Citing clay lumps, he claimed the answer *could* be two, depending on circumstances. Later, one of his teachers, who had returned from a trip abroad, told his high-school class: 'Koreans are backward because they do not know how to use a knife and fork.' Kim Jong-il challenged him by retorting: 'Foreigners in Korea are clumsy when they use chopsticks. Are they backward?'" ("Biography of an Infant Prodigy," *Far Eastern Economic Review* [see chap. 13, n. 4]). Note that the second anecdote bears great similarity to Kim Il-sung's noodle-slurping story from his own school days. Both are calculated to massage the nationalistic Korean ego.

7. *The Problems of Human Rights in North Korea (3).* "Kim Il-sung went to the Soviet Union after 1940 to train in the 88th special brigade," Hwang wrote. "While serving as a captain in the Soviet army, he married Kim Jong-sook, who gave birth to Kim Jong-il. The boy's Russian name was 'Yura.' All these are historical facts, which at first Kim Il-sung did not deny."

8. "Great Achievements of Mr. Kim Jong Il," *People's Korea,* February 13, 1982.

9. "Kim's son praised—abroad—in glowing terms," *Baltimore Sun,* April 15, 1981; "Great Achievements of Mr. Kim Jong Il," *People's Korea.*

10. Kim Jong-min in "Interview of Former High-level Official" (see chap. 6, n. 88).

11. "Kim Jong Il has a morbid interest in terrorism and personally controls all terrorist attacks initiated by North Korea," Hwang wrote. "The Myanmar bombing may have been orchestrated as part of the so-called 'Class struggle' to assassinate important figures of the South Korean ruling class" (Hwang Jang-yop, *Problems of Human Rights [3]*).

12. Bradley K. Martin, "Dynasty (North Korean Style): A Tedious Two-Hour Special," *Wall Street Journal,* November 7, 1983, p. 27.

13. A Pyongyang-datelined Reuters story by Andrew Browne that appeared in Tokyo's *Daily Yomiuri* on June 3, 1991, said Kim was not recorded as having visited any other country except China. A German diplomat who asked to be anonymous told me that a photo showed Kim Jong-il in East Germany in 1984 when his father was visiting there and a sudden crisis came up—a flood in North Korea—that evidently required the younger Kim to travel and get his father's advice or orders. The diplomat said there was no official record of Kim Jong-il's presence in East Germany ever, so presumably he went under an assumed name.

14. Tak, Kim, and Pak, *Great Leader Kim Jong Il,* vol. 1, p. 179 (see chap. 5, n. 15). This was the "18th World Film Festival" in 1972.

15. Choi Eun-hi and Shin Sang-ok, *Chogukeul cheohaneul cheo meolli* (Pacific Palisades, Calif.: Pacific Artist Corporation, 1988).

16. Rhee Soomi translated for the author the excerpts quoted in this book from the cassette issued by *Wolgan Choson.*

17. Former official Kim Jong-min told me, "I think his English has improved. He watches a lot of foreign films. He's not good in English conversation but due to economic needs he had to know a little bit more about the West. After 1981 there was an order for everyone of higher official rank to study English one hour a day. That indicates Kim Jong-il is interested in English."

18. Cited in Martin, "Kim's son praised" (see chap. 15, n. 39).

19. Hwang Jang-yop, *Problems of Human Rights (2)* (see chap. 6, n. 104).

20. Kim Jong-min in "Interview of Former High-level Official."

21. Kim Myong Chol, "Biography of an infant prodigy."

22. Interview with Kim Jong-min, former president of Daeyang Trading Co. and brigadier general-level officer in the Ministry of Public Security (police).

19. A Story to Tell to the Nations.

1. Baik II, p. 161 (see chap. 4, n. 24); Kang Myong-do testimony in *JoongAng Ilbo* (see chap. 2, n. 7).

2. "The bombing of the Korean commercial plane is evidence of the perverted character of Kim Jong Il, who has little respect for human life and loves to terrorize people" (Hwang, *Problems of Human Rights [3]* [see chap. 9, n. 25]).

3. South Korean critics had argued since at least the 1970s that North Korean workers were exhausted from their hopped-up labors. "After the desperate struggle to strengthen the ruling system and to achieve economic growth through the system, North Korea must now work to meet the demands of the labor-exhausted people" (Chay Pyung-gil, "The Policy Directions of the North Korea Regime" *Vantage Point* [November 1978]: p. 12).

4. China's "official data seriously underestimate China's GDP (Gross Domestic Product) by a factor of three," said a report by the East Asia Analytical Unit of Australia's Department of Foreign Affairs and Trade, cited in a Reuters report on page 7 of *Korea Times*, December 18, 1992. Tripling China's official per capita GDP figure of $370 as the Australian analysts suggested would yield a sum in the range of most estimates of the North Korean per capita figure. The latter estimates, in turn, may have failed to reflect economic shrinkage.

5. Kim Il-sung rode in an American-made limousine.

6. A South Korean professor had predicted this bind in 1979: "In North Korea the mental character of a man is organized by means of formulating the official level of aspiration. The objects of the basic needs and desires of North Koreans are food, clothing and shelter. Their needs and desires beyond them are restrained and disapproved. They are trained to compare today's living standards with those of long past, thus inducing them to be content with the apparent and meager improvement in the misrepresented reality. . . . [N]orth Korea does not permit the generation of desires above a certain prescribed level. . . . Discovery of a new object of desire may prove a major impact. If North Koreans are exposed to household appliances and housing facilities used by people of better-off countries, they are bound to be impressed and feel discontented" (Prof. Koh Young-bok, "The Structure and Nature of North Korean Society," *Vantage Point* [December 1979], pp. 7–8).

7. North Korea walked out of rescheduling talks in 1987, whereupon two syndicates comprising 140 Japanese, Australian and European banks declared Pyongyang in default on the amount owing to them: $770 million.

8. Kim Il-sung himself voiced a similar complaint in his memoirs (*With the Century* [see chap. 2, n. 2], vol. 2, p. 99), in the remark I quote in chapter 3 that "[s]ome people say that communists are devoid of human feelings and know neither life nor love that is worthy of human beings. But such people are totally ignorant of what communists are like."

9. Official historian Baik Bong complains that, as a November 1946 election held to ratify nominations for the provincial, city, and county people's committees approached, "political enthusiasm increased among all the people, but at the same time, maneuverings by reactionaries assumed increasingly open proportions. Manipulated by the U.S. imperialists, the reactionaries pretended to be 'friends of believers' in an attempt to lead Christians to stay away from the election. They also spread slanderous and misleading statements such as 'The election has no meaning,' 'The election is certain to become a one-man show for one particular party,' and 'We will get land back for you.' They used all possible malicious tactics, including the instigation of what is called the 'black box' campaign. But all the subversive activities of the revolutionaries failed to deceive the people" (Baik II, p. 180). (Black box was for no votes, white for yes.)

10. Kim, *With the Century*, vol. 1, p. 362. Kim wrote, "Their immaculate religious faith was always associated with patriotism, and their desire to build a peaceful, harmonious and free paradise found expression invariably in their patriotic struggle for national liberation."

   Richard Read, a correspondent of *The Oregonian* who was in Pyongyang to cover the festival, visited the Catholic church and noticed churchgoers depositing their Kim Il-sung badges in a bowl as they entered, "telling me that something genuine or at least different was going on. A student from Kim Il-sung University interpreted my interview with the priest. The interpreter's English was good, and he seemed relatively sophisticated. The priest, it materialized, drove a Mercedes and made more money than the highest-ranking party member I'd been allowed to meet. Toward the end I asked: Who's more important to you, Kim Il-sung or God? The interpreter looked thoroughly confused for the first time in the interview. 'Who's God?' he asked" (e-mail to the author, May 31, 2003).

   Thomas J. Belke in *Juche: A Christian Study of North Korea's State Religion* (Bartlesville, Oklahoma: Living Sacrifice Book Company, 1999, p. 1) writes: "In fact, Juche's approximately 23 million adherents, who worship their current and former dictators, outnumber those of more well-known world religions such as Judaism, Sikhism, Jainism, Bahaism, and Zoroastrianism."

11. Hwang Jang-yop, *Problems of Human Rights (3)*.

12. Kang Myong-do, son-in-law of Premier Kang Son-san, told me in a 1995 interview that the Pochonbo band was part of the Happy Corps. The Pochonbo band members by 1989 were along in years, he noted; thus their appearance at more-or-less public performances such as the one I had attended. Kim Jong-il had a new band made up of yet younger women, the still-secret Hwangjae-san Band, the members of which were likewise Happy Corps members available to him for sex on demand, Kang said.

20. Wherever You Go in My Homeland.

1. Kim Jong-su did drop what, in retrospect, I recognize as hints that food might have been a problem. He told me of the traditional wedding custom of presenting

food to whoever might care to attend. "Now we have to train people not to be so lavish at weddings," he said. Later he said, "See how we're wasting food here? I tell my son, 'Think of the starving people in Africa. Don't waste food.'"

2. When I saw such soil I was reminded again of my home region of northwestern Georgia, these days considered largely unfit for agricultural uses more demanding than pasture or forest.

3. Director Kim said annual rice harvests were up from around seven metric tons per 10,000 square meters ten years before to 8.5 and corn production was up from 6.5 tons to eight tons per 10,000 square meters. The great leader's "precious teachings" played a key role in all this, the director said: Kim Il-sung had personally visited the farm eighteen times, giving such advice as "Use more fertilizer." I asked how the country's president had become such an expert on farming. "The Great Leader and the Dear Leader are political activists," farm director Kim explained patiently. "They are clear in economic fields, and the Great Leader in particular cultivated some crops himself to develop production power."

4. Tak, Kim, and Pak, *Great Leader Kim Jong Il,* vol. 1 (see chap. 5, n. 15), pp. 198–199.

5. Choe In Su, *Kim Jong Il,* vol. 2 (see chap. 10, n. 43), pp. 96–97.

6. Kim, *With the Century,* vol. 2, p. 172.

7. Foreign observers doubted it ever would be completed and considered it a white elephant.

8. That was Bruce Cumings, who recounts the story as follows: "In the mid-1980s, the American embassy in Seoul had the hallucination that my work was one cause of the incessantly anti-American student demonstrations of the period. This is pure nonsense, but it flew back into my face so many times that it may be pertinent to our story. The first volume of my Korean War study [see chap. 2, n. 25] circulated as an English-language *samizdat* in the early 1980s and then was translated (badly) by publishers who pirated the copyright, only to find the book banned by [South Korean dictator] Chun Doo Hwan. Nevertheless, it was usually available in the right bookstores.

"In 1987 and 1988 I kept getting calls from the Voice of America or the U.S. Information Agency, asking me for taped interviews that would then be broadcast in Korea. My work was being distorted by the students, they said, and I should clear the record. The American director of the Fulbright program told me that I ought to come out to Korea and disabuse the students of their false impressions. Other American historians were invited under these or other auspices to travel to Korea and set the record straight on the Korean War and other things; a couple of them did not hesitate to please the powers that be by denouncing me as a radical if not a pro–North Korean sympathizer.

"I never agreed to any of the official entreaties. Usually I would just not return their calls, but once or twice I opined that if Americans stopped backing dictators and began treating Koreans with dignity, the problem would go away and I would sink back into my ordinary obscurity" (Cumings, *Korea's Place in the Sun: A Modern History* [New York: W.W. Norton & Co., 1997], pp. 385–386).

Kim Chullbaum (*The Truth About the Korean War* [see chap. 5, n. 5], p. viii) describes the problem that many older South Koreans perceived: "[A]fter 1980, in our society, as far as the factional leaders who were pushed close to Marx-Leninism were concerned, the faction of young scholars who leaned toward the left wing and the radical students accepted the assertions of the revisionist scholars and, while calling for the war of national liberation promoted by Kim Il Sung, it is a fact that they aggravated the confusion of ideology and thought."

Historiographer James I. Matray in "Korea's Partition" (see chap. 4, n. 1) notes that Cumings and co-author Jon Halliday in *Korea: The Unknown War* (see chap. 4, n. 60) "insist that South Korea initiated the Korean War, contending that the 'Fierce Tiger' unit of the ROK's Seventeenth Regiment on the Ongjin Peninsula launched an assault northward at around 0200 on 25 June 1950. Reviving [I. F.] Stone's interpretation, Halliday and Cumings claim that Rhee set a trap for North Korea. The South Korean attack would provoke a communist invasion and bring US military intervention, thereby setting the stage for the ROK conquest of North Korea. Cumings presents a detailed explanation of this 'trap theory'—and much more—in the second volume of his *Origins of the Korean War*. Despite the testimony of former communist military leaders, the North Koreans always have maintained that the ROK attacked first and initiated the war."

While Western scholars' left-revisionism continued to inspire the anti-American left in South Korea, Matray says that in scholarly circles from around 1985 the movement had "peaked in popularity and begun to lose adherents." He notes that John Merrill (see chap. 4, n. 80) "observed in 1989 that the question of who started the Korean War no longer was a matter of debate. The size and scope of the North Korean offensive argued powerfully that Pyongyang planned the invasion in advance. William Stueck agrees, emphasizing the international dimensions of the conflict in the most recent full-length account of the Korean War." This last is a reference to Stueck, *The Korean War: An International History* (Princeton: Princeton University Press, 1995).

9. Hwang Jang-yop, *Problems of Human Rights (3)*.

10. "As Korean people we have this great Leader. But our compatriots in South Korea are undergoing all sorts of terrible suffering, under the colonial rule of the U.S. imperialists, and looking to our great Leader, they are enduring hardships and struggling valiantly, thinking of the days when they too will be able to live happily with the fatherland reunited" (Baik II [see chap. 4, n. 24], p. 4).

11. While a student in Jilin, Kim wrote in his memoirs, he and his comrades made a major alteration in communist doctrine. Instead of workers (and peasants) as the vanguard of the revolution, as Marxist-Leninist teachings had held, "we defined the young people and students as constituting the fully-fledged main force of the revolution." The correctness of this view is shown by the importance of young people and students in social and political movements since the March 1 (1919) uprising. And, added Kim, "Young people and students are the main force of the revolution in South Korea, too." He cited the April 19 uprising of 1960, the Kwangju uprising of 1980, and the popular protests that culminated in the 1987 government decision to resume free elections for president.

12. In North and South Korea certain important social indicators, as reported by their respective governments, were virtually identical in the 1980s. Life expectancy at birth, in 1985, was 68 in the North and 69 in the South. In 1986 about 65 percent of each population lived in urban areas. Adult literacy rates over 98 percent were recorded in both Koreas in 1988 (Byoung-lo Philo Kim, *Two Koreas in Development* [see chap. 1, n. 2], pp. 88–91).

13. Author's conversation with one of the group's American hosts, June 1989.

14. In view of his obvious intelligence and ability, it is interesting to speculate that Kim Jong-su might have been the otherwise unidentified elder son from a "previous marriage" referred to in the succession rumor, mentioned in chapter 15, that Swedish Ambassador Cornell (*North Korea Under Communism* [see chap. 9, n. 3], p. 124) heard from East European diplomats in Pyongyang in the mid-1970s. Although I was not aware of that rumor at the time I talked with my source, I did ask then whether Kim Jong-su was Kim Il-sung's firstborn. "There are probably a couple older than he is," the former official replied.

15. During his UN assignment Kim Jong-su did stay in touch with at least one other journalist-researcher, Selig Harrison — and in situations that suggested once again that Kim had access to top leadership in Pyongyang. After speaking with Kim Jong-su, Harrison was invited to his second meeting with Kim Il-sung (Harrison, *Korean End Game* [see chap. 8, n. 3], pp. 211–212 and 221–222).

21. If Your Brain Is Properly Oiled.

1. Cho Gap-jae, "Interview of Former High-level Official" (see chap. 9, n. 37).

2. "The average North Korean lives an incredibly simple and hardworking life but also has a secure and cheerful existence, and the comradeship between these highly collectivised people is moving to behold" (Andrew Holloway, *A Year in Pyongyang* [published in 2002 on the Internet Web site of Aidan Foster-Carter, http://www.aidanfc.net/a_year_in_pyongyang.html], chapter 3, p. 6).

3. "The claim of the Pyongyang regime to have attained the goal of 8 million–ton grain production is belied by the prevalence of pellagra victims caused largely by malnutrition throughout North Korea. A shortage of food grains that forces the North Korean population to eat large quantities of maize with little intake of animal protein makes North Koreans vulnerable to the disease" (Lee Won-joon, "Changes in North Korea's Agricultural and Fishery Policies," *Vantage Point* [July 1979]: pp. 7, 9). Researchers in the American South found in 1937 that the missing substance in the diets of pellagra victims is not protein, per se, but the vitamin niacin, which is "plentiful in red meat, fish, poultry, green leafy vegetables and, as it happens, brewer's yeast" (Howard Markel, "The New Yorker Who Changed the Diet of the South," *New York Times*, August 12, 2003, p. D5).

4. Testimony of Kang Myong-do (see chap. 1, n. 7).

5. This interview took place August 20, 1992, in Honolulu. Recall the story of Chong Ki-hae, the returnee from Japan whose new life in the North Korean "motherland" we chronicled in chapter 6. A reduction in the grain ration came in the early 1970s, Chong told me, confirming that part of Professor An's timeline. The cuts were described as "patriot rice" but explained as having been mandated by poor harvests. Farm districts had not been able to meet their harvest quotas, although they had *reported* having met or exceeded them, Chong told me.

6. I interviewed him on February 8, 1994, in Seoul. Ko told me he had been born on February 13, 1961, in Kimchaek City, an industrial city in North Hamgyong Province.

7. According to high-level defector Hwang Jang-yop, "As Kim Jong-il began to rise to power, North Korean leaders began to insist that the anti-Japanese partisan struggle led by Kim Il-sung took place over a wide area spanning Northeast China and the Korean peninsula rather than only in Northeast China

under the leadership of the Chinese Communist party. North Korean leaders claimed that proof of this could be found all over North Korea in the form of 'slogan trees'—trees on which Kim Il-sung wrote anti-Japanese slogans such as 'Down with Japanese imperialism' and 'Long live Korean independence.' The idea probably came from stories told by independence fighters who recalled that while hiding in the forest they had stripped the bark off the trees to write slogans such as 'Long live Korean independence.' But strangely, no such slogan trees were discovered in Northeast China, the main stage of the partisan struggle. The trees were discovered only in North Korea, and over 10,000 of them at that. Back then, the partisan fighters most probably sent only one or two spies to the Korean peninsula at a time. And they would not have sent spies to northern Korea just to strip the bark off trees and write slogans on them. The spies would have been busy avoiding the watchful eyes of the Japanese police as they engaged in secretive intelligence work, so where on earth would they have found the time to strip the bark off trees and make the ink to write slogans on the trees with brushes?" This fabrication "was probably done through the Party History Center, a bureau in the central party under the personal supervision of Kim Jong-il," wrote Hwang. He acknowledged that he himself from 1987 had been in a supervisory position over the Party History Center. However, he said, "I did not involve myself in the Research Center projects. My duties stopped at reviewing the documents and offering my opinion on current issues. Once I quietly asked a member of the Research Center, 'You say more than 700 slogan trees were discovered on the Moranbong in Pyongyang. But when we were schooling in Pyongyang we often climbed the Moranbong to have lunch, and we never saw any markings on the trees. Isn't the sudden discovery of hundreds of slogan trees going a bit too far?' To which the official answered, 'The slogan trees on Monanbong are different. The partisans did not strip the bark off them to write slogans with brushes but carved markings on them with knives as means of communicating with one another.' I was too flabbergasted to question him any further." Knowing that there were only about 60 Koreans in the Eighty-eighth Special Brigade, Hwang wrote, "helps us deduce the size of the armed rebellion against Japanese rule. So how could so many people have climbed Moranbong and left communication signals on hundreds of trees?" (Hwang Jang-yop, *Problems of Human Rights [I]* [see chap. 2, n. 1]).

8. I interviewed him on February 15, 1994, in Seoul.
9. See "Summing Up of the 1970s," p. 16: "As north Korea declares the attainment of the goals with no statistical backing, its agricultural situation is hard to figure out. A clue to answering the agricultural question came when President Kim addressed a meeting of county-level responsible secretaries of the Party in October 1979. He was quoted as having said: The Juche farming method is faced with a limit and we should cultivate more land to produce more grains."
10. I interviewed him on November 1, 1993. He told me he had been born on July 14, 1953, and had defected on May 2, 1991.
11. I interviewed him on February 17, 1994, in Seoul.

22. Logging In and Logging Out.
1. See, for example, Giles Whittell, "Kim Sells Workers to Gulags in Debt Deal" (London: *The Times*, Aug. 6, 2001).

2. See Anatoly Medetsky, "North Korea Seeks Closer Ties with Russian Far East," Vladivostok-datelined dispatch from the Associated Press, April 4, 2002; "North Korea Opens New Air Route to Russian Far East," Seoul-datelined Reuters dispatch, April 5, 2002; "North Koreans in Russian Far East," Khabarovsk-datelined article in *JoongAng Ilbo*, July 23, 2002.

23. Do You Remember That Time?

No notes.

24. Pickled Plum in a Lunch Box.

1. Hwang Jang-yop on July 3, 2003, told South Korea's National Assembly that he had heard about the testing directly from Kim Jong-il and Kim's aides. See "S. Korea Clears Top Defector for U.S. Visit," Reuters dispatch from Seoul, July 18, 2003. For an extensive chronology of the first nuclear crisis see "IAEA-North Korea: Nuclear Safeguards and Inspections" (Monterey, Calif.: Monterey Institute of International Studies, Center for Nuclear Studies, 2002), http://cns.miis.edu/research/korea/nuc/iaea7789.htm.

2. I heard this pungent description from Katsumi Sato, the editor of *Gendai Korea*.

3. Testimony of Kang Myong-do (see chap. 2, n.7). When I interviewed Kang after his remarks had been published in *JoongAng Ilbo*, I asked him how he had known about the nuclear program. He replied that a Yongbyon official had told him. "We knew each other for about ten years. He's a close friend of my elder brother. Lots of high officials didn't know for sure about the nuclear program, but we were always curious. So I just casually asked him. I guess he never thought I'd defect." At the time I spoke with Kang, his assertions were getting little support from the South Korean and U.S. governments. There seemed to be a tendency both in Seoul and in Washington to play down the sophistication and productivity of the North Korean nuclear program. The fear seemed to be that acknowledgment that the North was well along in its program, with a number of nuclear weapons probably completed, would force a major policy reappraisal. "The South Koreans were afraid I'd say it again," Kang told me. "In fact, I believe totally in what I said." Kang indicated that he and his information had received something of a cold shoulder from the Americans—because, he presumed, Washington had not thought it politic to come out and say that North Korea already had a functioning nuclear weapons program. Before defecting to South Korea he had made contact with U.S. officials, he said. "I went to the U.S. Embassy in Germany and turned over a letter I had written to President Bill Clinton, offering policy recommendations on the nuclear issue. But I had to wait a couple of days before someone in the U.S. government came to talk with me. Since the Americans were in talks with Pyongyang at the time, I thought maybe they were sending me back to North Korea. The U.S. wanted to say that the North did not have nuclear weapons at that time. I know that the Americans know better, know that there are in fact nuclear weapons in North Korea."

4. See "Nuclear Jitters," *Newsweek*, April 29, 1991.

5. Defector Ahn Hyuk, a former table tennis champion, noted in an interview that Kanemaru was taken to Kim Il-sung's most lavish villa, Hamneun Majeonho,

near the seaside. "There are a couple of buildings there, one for Kim Il-sung and one for his guest. About an hour before Kanemaru awoke each day, Kim Il-sung would go to the front of his building and walk around, waiting. Kanemaru was really snowed by Kim's eagerness." (Ahn asserted that Kanemaru was not the only foreign visitor of whom Kim made a fool. Billy Graham, the American evangelical preacher, "also succumbed to all that pampering. Kim Il-sung probably was being kind to him in order to get some Christian donations funneled to North Korea.") Kim Il-sung around that time was publishing his memoirs, laced with accounts of Japanese bad behavior. He recalled, for example, that when Koreans in 1930s Manchuria, faced with Japanese "punitive" campaigns, fled to the hills, even a baby's cry could give them away to the enemy. One woman hugged her baby too hard to keep it from crying; when the enemy withdrew, she found it was dead. "To avoid such accidents, some women used to dose their babies with opium to keep them fast asleep. Unable to endure the ceaseless atrocities perpetrated by the 'punitive' troops, some women even gave their beloved babies to strangers. . . . Bourgeois humanists may mock the maternal love of communists, asking how a woman could be so cruel towards her baby or be so irresponsible with its life. But they must not hold these women responsible for the deaths of their infants. If they knew how many bitter tears were shed as these women buried the soft bodies of their babies in dry leaves and left their babies in the care of strangers, they would condemn and hate the Japanese imperialist who sent their human butchers to Jiandao. The crime of trampling upon the maternal love of this country's women was committed by none other than the fiends of Japanese militarism. If she is to make amends for her past, Japan must repent of these crimes. . . . In demanding evidence of their past crimes, the rulers of Japan continue to mock the memory of millions of Koreans who were slaughtered by their army" (*With the Century,* vol. 3 [see chap. 2, n. 2], pp. 14–15).

6. While hardliners such as that official may have continued to hope for a quick collapse of the Kim regime, many other South Koreans had replaced that wish with caution born of observing the rocky road Germany had been treading. There seemed to be more South Koreans who would be happy enough to see a military government take over in North Korea and emulate the period of rapid economic development that the South had experienced under its own military government. That could bring the North more into the world that the South knew and reduce the ultimate burden to the South whenever the two might merge.

7. Japanese officials in two of those agencies confirmed that Americans briefed them but declined to comment on details including dates and who the briefers were.

8. Address by Korea University Professor (later South Korean foreign minister) Han Sung-joo at the Foreign Correspondents' Club of Japan, Tokyo, May 12, 1992.

9. See Don Oberdorfer, *The Two Koreas: A Contemporary History* (Reading, Mass.: Addison-Wesley, 1997), pp. 260–271. Oberdorfer, a former *Washington Post* diplomatic correspondent, offers in chapters 11, 12 and 13 a detailed account of diplomacy concerning the North's nuclear weapons, based on his interviews with participants and documents he obtained by invoking the Freedom of Information Act. A more recent work by three participants is Joel S. Wit, Daniel B. Poneman and Robert L. Gallucci, *Going Critical: The First North Korean Nuclear Crisis* (Washington, D.C.: Brookings Institution Press, 2004).

25. I Die, You Die.

1. "Seven N.K. Defectors Go Missing Over Two-Year Period: Daily," Yonhap news agency, February 15, 2002, FBIS document i.d. 0grscgs02ah5r9.

26. Yen for the Motherland.

1. The interview was conducted in April 1989.

27. Winds of Temptation May Blow.

1. Bradley K. Martin, "Why South Korea Favors Propping Up the North," *Global Finance* (July 1992): pp. 44–47.

2. *Korea Times* (Seoul), November 26, 1992, p. 9, citing a report by Korea Trade Promotion Corp. (KOTRA). North Korea does not release trade statistics. The KOTRA figures are compilations of two-way trade data from sixty-one countries. North Korea's global exports dropped 24.8 percent and imports 9.9 percent for 1991, according to a KOTRA report cited in *Korea Times* for November 20, 1992, p. 9.

3. Unnamed South Korean officials estimated that the North Korean economy had shrunk by 3.7 percent in 1990, 5.2 percent in 1991 and about 5 percent in 1992, according to a report in *Korea Times*, January 8, 1993, p. 9. More alarming still was a Kyodo News Service report (*Japan Times*, April 1, 1993) datelined Beijing, which indirectly quoted "reports compiled by East European and Russian diplomats in Pyongyang" as saying the shrinkage in 1992 might have amounted to 30 percent.

4. While North Korea claimed to have produced between eight and nine million tons of food grains in 1991, Russian experts estimated actual production at five million tons, according to Marina Trigubenko, director of the Asia Research Center at the Russian Academy of Sciences. At a seminar sponsored by Seoul's Korea Rural Economic Institute, Trigubenko said the North would have a hard time feeding its 21 million people even with its programs to control population growth and reclaim some 300,000 hectares for farming (*Korea Times*, October 30, 1992).

5. *Korea Times*, October 23, 1992.

6. Conversation with a European investor, 1992.

7. A South Korean analyst observed in 1987 that as older men were forced out of high military posts, their replacements tended to be Mangyongdae alumni, such as general staff chief Oh Guk-ryol; his deputy, Kim Gwang-hwan; navy chief of staff Kim Il-chol; Lieutenant Generals Choe Song-wuk and Li bong-won, party military commission members; and Kim Du-nam, director of the party military bureau. Other Mangyongdae alumni who did well as the junior Kim's power increased were Kim Hwan, who became a party politburo member; Paek Hak-rim, minister of public security; Pak Yong-suk, a party bureau director; Yun Gi-jong, party finance bureau director; and several provincial party chiefs (Yoo Sok-ryol, "The Rise of Kim Jong-il and the Heir-succession problem," pt. II, *Vantage Point* [December 1987]: p. 8).

8. Yoo Sok-ryol, *True Story of Kim Jong Il* (see chap. 3, n. 61), p. 11.

9. Ibid.

10. Han spoke at the Foreign Correspondents' Club of Japan on May 22, 1992. In 1978 South Korean scholar Chae Pyung-il had written, "(N)orth Korean

society, moving into the welfare-distribution era, cannot escape from the liberal movement — liberalism by Communist standards. The emergence of the new generation in high government posts as well as the growing number of technical-managerial specialists in production units is bringing about new organizational behavior in North Korean society. Many, though not all, of the new generation have become more realistic, often pragmatic" (Chay Pyung-gil, "The Policy Directions of the North Korea Regime," *Vantage Point* [November 1978]: p. 13).

11. Kim Dal-hyon was in charge of the External Economic Commission at the time of our visit. In a cabinet reshuffle on December 11, 1992, he retained his deputy premier's rank and was given the chair of the State Planning Commission. Premier Yon Hyon-muk was replaced by Kang Song-san, who had been premier once before, from 1984 to 1986. Viewed as a reformer, Kang had governed North Hamgyong Province as chief secretary in the interim following his first stint as premier and recently had pushed the plan for a special economic zone in the Tumen River area, which is part of that province (Reuters report, *Korea Herald*, December 12, 1992; Agence France-Presse and Yonhap reports, *Korea Times*, December 12, 1992).

12. I later heard that this sort of virtuoso show of memory and comprehensive thinking at a press conference had been highly thought of among officials in the former Soviet Union.

13. *Korea Times*, October 21, 1992.

14. *Korea Herald*, March 13, 1993.

15. In a lecture on "The Unified German Economy and Its Implications on a Unified Korean Economy" delivered at Seoul's Research Institute for National Unification, August 26, 1992, World Bank Chief Economist Lawrence H. Summers observed, "There is a political dynamic that was unfortunate for gradual reform in East Germany and is in North Korea. Namely, there was a reason for Poland to exist quite apart from its being communist. There was no reason for East Germany to exist except for its being communist. There is no reason for North Korea to exist except for the fact that it is communist. That is why East Germany stayed harder-line longer than Poland, Hungary, and Czechoslovakia despite the blandishments of significant amounts of financial assistance from West Germany and that is why I suspect North Korea is unlikely to make a move toward a market system."

16. Kim, *With the Century* (see chap. 2, n. 2), vol. 3, p. 221.

17. Pyongyang had long championed a federal system as a stage in reunification. The developments in Germany, if anything, hardened the North's demand that Korean reunification permit maintenance of separate political-economic-social systems in North and South.

18. It was picked up and rebroadcast on South Korea's KBS, October 23, 1992.

19. *International Herald Tribune*, January 29, 1993, p. 3. Aidan Foster-Carter ("Korea's Coming Reunification: Another East Asian Superpower?" published by The Economist Intelligence Unit, London, April 1992) estimated Seoul would need to come up with $9–$10 billion to invest in the merger each year for a decade, plus $6–$16 billion a year in subsidies.

20. Reported in *Korea Times*, Yonhap dispatch, August 18, 1991.

21. South Korean government estimates for 1991 are $6,498 and $1,064, respectively. *Korea Annual 1992* (Seoul: Yonhap News Agency), pp. 177, 276.

22. *Korea Times*, January 29, 1993.
23. In a campaign appearance December 3, Chung told a group of Korean journalists he would become a "unification" president, using the South's economic superiority to push inter-Korean exchange and, within five years, absorb the North into the South's free-market economy (*Korea Herald*, December 4, 1992, p. 2).
24. The South Korean press in January 1993 quoted an unnamed government source as saying North Korea was planning "investment fairs" in Minneapolis and other major American cities, targeted mainly at ethnic Korean investors (*Korea Times*, January 26, 1993).

28. Sea of Fire.
1. Kim, *With the Century*, vol. 1, p. 12 (see chap. 2, n. 2).
2. Kim Dong-hyeon, Choi Hong-yeol, and Lee Cheong, "Testimony of 1st Lt. Lim Yong-son, who had distributed anti–Kim Il-sung pamphlets and escaped from North Korea in August 1993," *Wolgan Choson*, 1993.
3. Hwang Jang-yop, *Problems of Human Rights (2)* (see chap. 6, n. 104).
4. Ibid.
5. *Korea Times*, February 3, 1993, p. 9.
6. Quote of unnamed participant provided by Pyongyang's official Korean Central News Agency, picked up by Agence France-Presse and carried in *Korea Times*, March 18, 1993.
7. Lee Chong-guk was interviewed also by the Japanese weekly *Shukan Post* for an article that appeared in the June 3, 1994, issue. When I interviewed him he confirmed the information in that article.
    A skeptical analysis of North Korea's chemical warfare ability may be found on pp. 129–130 of Selig Harrison's *Korean Endgame* (see chap. 8, n. 3).
8. Jon Halliday and Bruce Cumings, *Korea: The Unknown War* (see chap. 4, n. 60), pp. 214–217, sum up reasons why the North Koreans would feel themselves on the defensive.
9. Whether he did or not, "it's his game to win or lose," as Han Sung-joo, South Korea's foreign minister, said in an appearance at the Seoul Foreign Correspondents' Club on March 18, five days after the North's announcement.
10. Agence France-Presse dispatch, *Korea Times*, March 3, 1993.
11. Choe Pyong-gil, "Yu Song-chol's Testimony" (see chap. 2, n. 18).
12. In his March 18 appearance at the Seoul Foreign Correspondents' Club.
13. Reuters dispatch, *Japan Times*, April 1, 1993.
14. Kennedy discussed the concept in an interview reported in a Reuters article (*Korea Herald*, March 2, 1993) about his new book, *Preparing for the 21st Century*.
15. One diplomat from a former Soviet-bloc country told the author that Deputy Premier Kim Dal-hyon, a relative of the ruling family, had received his chemistry training in Romania—where, ironically, one of his teachers was Elena Ceausescu.
16. Associated Press dispatch from Tokyo quoting Korean Central News Agency, *Korea Times*, March 23, 1993.
17. Vladimir Ivanov, a Russian expert, cautioned in a July 1992 conversation that Washington would be mistaken to push for the collapse of the North Korean regime—a policy that he felt could invite a military response from Pyongyang. A fellow at Harvard's Center for International Affairs, Ivanov recommended

that American policy makers encourage the youthful, reformist elements in North Korea. He estimated that only about 10 percent of the elite were dyed-in-the-wool Kim Il-sung loyalists. Of the remaining 90 percent, half—the old—were irrelevant, he said. "A policy attacking the 10 percent fanatics hurts the 45 percent young elite," people who could be reformists, Ivanov said. One caveat is that Ivanov spoke from the perspective of someone who had lived through the fall of the Soviet Union. Cynicism among the Soviet elite had been rife.

18. See "Interview of Former High-level Official" (see chap. 6, n. 88) in which Kim Jong-min, interviewed under a pseudonym, said:

"North Korea's elite or economic experts view South Korea's economic development as the result of President Park Chung-hee's efforts. They view the Park period as being very significant."

Q. On what basis do they arrive at that conclusion?
A. "There is a publication in North Korea entitled 'Secret Communication' [pitongsin]. Cadre who receive this know most of what is going on concerning South Korean politics. 'Secret Communication' carries South Korean broadcasts or newspaper articles without any doctoring.

"Those who receive and read 'Secret Communication' range from cadre who are subject to ratification by the secretariat down to unit responsible persons. Provincial party level responsible secretaries are known to receive this publication as well. It is delivered daily, and is turned back in after being read. The contents are primarily South Korean top news stories as well as international political issues."

Q. Do experts analyze economic policies of the Park Chung-hee era?
A. "Of course, individually they interpret them as they like; however, no one dares talk about it in public. Even when I was in North Korea, there were some who individually liked President Park Chung-hee. They even listened to his speeches."

Q. What points do they like about Park?
A. "First, they felt that Park was a simple person, that he was straightforward and meticulous. Listening to his announcements on the South Korea–Japan talks or the Tokto issue [a dispute with Japan regarding sovereignty over an island], his position was quite clear. There was a feeling that these positions stemmed from nationalist points.

"We even felt a sort of pride when Park strongly criticized the United States at the time of the Chongwadae [Blue House] wire-tapping incident. At the same time, however, he could not issue a totally hostile statement no matter how much he opposed the United States. Seeing that, we sympathized with his position as a president of a small power."

The interviewer paraphrased Kim Jong-min's remarks, saying Kim had estimated that the number of people who were able to find out about South Korean events through either "Secret Communication" or the radio totaled 2 to 3 percent of the total population. Kim Jong-min, the interviewer said, did not feel firmly convinced that this small number of people with knowledge of other societies could guide serious reform in North Korea.

19. Kim, *With the Century,* vol. 3, p. 303.
20. Kim Dong-hyeon, Choi Hong-yeol, and Lee Cheong, "Testimony of 1st Lt. Lim Yong-son."
21. Hwang Jang-yop, *Problems of Human Rights (2).*
22. Kang testimony in *JoongAng Ilbo.* The detail about the Russian experts came out in the author's interview with Kang.
23. Letter to author, January 3, 1994.
24. The jamming of VOA began in early January 1993, according to a Reuters report (*Korea Times,* January 15, 1993, p. 3).
25. See chapter 20.
26. Since deceased, a true friend dearly missed.
27. Pyongyang's official Korean Central News Agency on March 30, 1993, carried a demand that the United States "promptly cancel" a proposed "Radio Free Asia" broadcasting project similar to Radio Free Europe. The broadcasts would carry news of communist countries such as China and North Korea to any of their own people capable of picking up the transmissions. "The United States is trying hard to stifle our socialism at any cost by sending the wind of 'liberalization' into our country," said the statement by an unnamed Foreign Ministry spokesman (*Asahi Evening News,* March 31, 1993). Not satisfied with saying it once, Pyongyang repeated the demand on April 3. *Japan Times* for April 4, 1993, carried a Reuters dispatch quoting the KCNA as saying, "While threatening by wielding the nuclear stick, the United States is foolishly attempting to destroy the socialist system of Korea by raising the wind of liberalization with black propaganda full of lies and deception, a method it used in the European region."
28. Selig Harrison's *Korean Endgame* (see chap. 8, n. 3) provides a thorough account of the diplomacy. As a Georgian I took a certain pride in Carter's diplomatic success. I first met him in Decatur, Georgia, in the 1960s when he had lost his first race for governor and was preparing for another. What struck me about him then was his hair, which suggested ambitions beyond our state. "What is a Georgia politician doing wearing a Kennedy hairdo?" I later asked the person who had introduced us.
29. Hwang, *Problems of Human Rights (2).*

29. Without You There Is No Country.

1. Kim Il Sung, *With the Century* (see chap. 2, n. 2), vol. 1, p. 15.
2. Hwang Jang-yop, *Problems of Human Rights (2)* (see chap. 6, n. 104).
3. Kim, *With the Century,* vol. 3, pp. 421–422.
4. Ibid., preface.
5. A frequent visitor to North Korea who requested confidentiality was my source for this. On the topic of food-supply corruption, wire-service reports in October 1992 quoted an unnamed visitor to North Korea as saying the problem had become so serious as to be the object of a government campaign. Following are excerpts from an Agence France-Press article as printed on page 4 of *Korea Times* for October 14, 1992:

    "Tokyo (AFP) — North Korea, allegedly hit by acute food shortages, has launched a campaign against widespread civilian looting and extortion of food by government officials, a recent visitor to Pyongyang said Tuesday.

"The visitor, a specialist on Korean affairs, told the Japanese Kyodo news agency that the Public Security Ministry in Pyongyang had posted notices in residential areas warning against food extortion.

" 'Severe punishment will be meted out to persons engaged in the illegal extortion of food,' the notices were quoted as reading. They also mentioned 'acts of plundering grain from state and collective warehouses,' the visitor told Kyodo in Beijing.

"The notices also said that 'hostile elements who have slipped into the leadership' were committing extortion and that food coupons for rice, oil, flour and noodles were often obtained under false pretenses, according to Kyodo.

"Corrupt officials offer to help citizens obtain spare parts, energy, fuel, metal and cement in exchange for food coupons, the notices said.

"They added that such officials also extorted food under the pretexts of 'receiving guests, earning foreign currency for the country, providing rations for the military and helping the state budget,' according to Kyodo.

"Offenders will be treated as anti-socialist elements, arrested and tried while their families will be deported to labor camps, the notices allegedly said."

6. Interview with an ethnic Korean who traveled to North Korea. The sentence for speaking ill of Kim Il-sung or Kim Jong-il was life imprisonment, according to this informant.

7. See, for example, "NK Bans Contact Wtih Chinese," *Korea Times*, January 28, 1993, p. 1. The Yonhap news agency report picked up from the Japanese wire service Kyodo quotes a Western source in Pyongyang as saying the ban extended even to reading the Chinese newspaper *People's Daily*.

8. See Bradley Martin, "Remaking Kim's Image," *Far Eastern Economic Review*, April 15, 1993, and the author's similar Korean-language article, "Revisionism in Pyongyang," *Newsweek Hankuk-pan*, April 1, 1993.

9. As Dae-Sook Suh notes, some of the others were Kim's seniors and equals (*Kim Il Sung* [see chap. 2, n. 35], pp. 1–54).

10. Kim, *With the Century*, vol. 3, p. 328.

11. Kang Myong-do series in *JoongAng Ilbo* (see chap. 2, n. 7). Kang described the economic situation during that period as follows: "Currently the North Korean economy is nearly collapsed, about 70 percent paralyzed. Food shortages have occurred since 1984. That was the year of flooding in South Korea, when the North gave rice to the South from northern reserves. Nineteen eighty-nine was worse, with the youth festival. That's when the North Korean economy really dived; 20,000 foreigners attended. The government did it all for free. From 1989 to 1993 the harvests were bad. In 1993 there were zero harvests in North and South Hamgyong [and two other] provinces. It was all frozen. Not even one kilogram was produced in those four provinces. Food rations stopped in 1992. Even in Pyongyang there was a three-month suspension of rations. The authorities would go house to house, see if anyone was dying of starvation. If so, they would give them a little food. In rural areas they got dried corn.

"The pears produced in Hwasong, North Hamgyong province, are famous. Prior to 1990, 100 percent were exported to the Soviet Union. In 1990, the Russians refused to import them. North Korea had to turn them into liquor or animal feed. From 1993, because the food shortage had become so serious, in North Hamgyong the party decided to ration pears instead of grain from August to October. As a result, many died of starvation. In October 1993 in a Chongjin Hospital I saw someone die. Those who got the pears boiled them. If they had any corn left, they would mix it with the pears. When it cooled, the mixture was really hard—almost impossible to digest. One man had indigestion and went to the hospital. They opened him up and found an indigestible lump. The man died during the operation.

"People cooperatively started pillaging state-run farms. So the authorities intensified the guards at farms. There were a lot of clashes between those guards and the people. The Workers' Party took it as a direct threat to the regime. . . .

"At Kim Chaek Steel Works, all three melting furnaces went out. After that, only one operated. Two remained idle. In 1993, even the one remaining furnace was out. They needed oil and coke from China, but the Chinese supplies were cut. In 1993, Choe Yong-lim, in charge of Kim Chaek Steel, rounded up people to collect coke around the factory area. He got oil from the military. After a month's delay, they got the furnace working again.

"The electrical power situation is horrible. Pukchang is the biggest power plant, with 8 turbines, of which only two operate now. In Pyongyang's power plant, only two of six turbines are working. Not all areas of Pyongyang are supplied electricity. In the rural areas, it's a long time since any power was available.

"Chongjin Chemical Complex, which employed 12,000 workers, has been closed for three years. There is no coal supply to fire the machinery. I estimate only about 30 percent of North Korean factories are operating now."

12. Oberdorfer, *The Two Koreas* (see chap. 24, n. 9), pp. 297–299. Andrew S. Natsios has more on Kim Il-sung's belated interest in reform and the rumored clash with his son on pp. 165–167 of *The Great North Korean Famine: Famine, Politics, and Foreign Policy* (Washington, D.C.: United States Institute of Peace Press, 2001).

13. Kang's remarks on the Kim Dal-hyon case are from the 1995 interviews in *JoongAng Ilbo* and my own interview on June 12, 1995. In my interview he gave further details on the personalities involved in the power struggle. "Kim Yongsun is not a relative of Kim Il-sung's," he said. "Kim Jong-u is not a relative of Kim Il-sung's despite what is said. Kim Jong-u is allied with Kim Guk-tae against Kim Dal-hyon. Kim Jong-u graduated from the People's Economic University and studied in East Germany. He's an economic expert and has visited the Middle East for trade—mainly Kuwait. He's 51 or 52, quite young. He's opposed to Kim Dal-hyon but the direct rivalry is between Kim Dal-hyon and Kim Guk-tae. Under them, Yi Song-dae is opposed to Kim Jong-u. Yi is now the chairman. Kim Jong-u is not very modest. That's why he has lots of enemies. Yi Song-dae right now doesn't have the backing. He's shrinking back. It's Kim Jong-u's world.

"There are some other bright and promising people. Kim Chung-il was a U.N. observer, now is in the propaganda department as vice-head—because Kim Jong-il specifically selected him to become the next foreign minister. He speaks English impeccably so he always interprets when Kim Jong-il meets foreigners. Yi Chol, ambassador to Switzerland, is important because of the bank accounts. Only the top elite know of those accounts. They are supposed to be for the country, but really they are for Kim Jong-il."

14. Kim Jong-il, "Abuses of Socialism Are Intolerable," *Kulloja*, March 1, 1993, cited in *Korea Times*, March 5, 1993.

15. July 11, 1994 (translated by Korean Central News Agency in *Korean News Semi-weekly*, July 12, 1994). The reference to Kim's leadership of this "20-year struggle" illustrates the escalation effect that sooner or later inflated so many claims advanced by or about Kim, no matter how immodest to begin with. But it would be especially difficult to justify this claim historically, since it has him leading the anti-Japanese struggle from 1925, the year he turned thirteen, all the way up to 1945.

16. Kenji Fujimoto is the pseudonym of the chef, who published his book *Kim Jong-il's Chef* in Japanese and Korean. See Yonhap dispatch from Tokyo, "NK Leader's Obsessed By A-Bombs: Ex-Chef," *Korea Times*, June 23, 2003.

17. Hwang Jang-yop, *Problems of Human Rights (3)* (see chap. 9, n. 25).

18. Hwang Jang-yop, *Problems of Human Rights (1)* (see chap. 2, n. 1).

19. Hwang Jang-yop, *Problems of Human Rights (2)*.

20. *Korea Times*, May 12, 1995.

21. The transcript first appeared in Korean in *Wolgan Choson*, which cited a Japanese intelligence agency concerned with North Korean matters as its source. It was translated into English and posted on *Korea Web Weekly* at http://www.kimsoft.com/2003/kji-tape.htm.

30. We Will Become Bullets and Bombs.

1. Kim, *With the Century*, vol. 3 (see chap. 2, n. 2), p. 27.

2. "On the 50th Anniversary of Kim Il-sung University," Dec. 7, 1996, speech to party officials reportedly taped by Hwang Jang-yop and taken south when he defected the following year, published in the April 1997 edition of *Wolgan Choson*, extracts translated on *Korea Web Weekly*, http://www.kimsoft.com/korea/kji-kisu.htm.

3. On this subject Kim Il-sung wrote, "It is now a matter of course that our People's Army contains neither those who insist on unprincipled equality and impartiality nor those who dispute their superiors' orders. The soldiers answer their superiors' orders only by saying, 'I understand!' Our People's Army is a collective of loyal soldiers who live in a spirit of unity of superiors and subordinates, unity of army and people, a spirit of constant self-reliance and fortitude from the day they take the oath of the military code of conduct to the moment they are discharged from the service. If anyone wants to know our soldiers' attitude towards democracy, he need only understand their militant slogan, 'When the Party decides, we do everything.' If he wants to see the genuine features of unity between superiors and subordinates manifested in the deeds of our soldiers, he need only learn of the last moments of Heroes Kim Kwang Chol and Han Yong Chol, who had sacrificed their lives for the sake of many of their comrades in arms" (*With the Century*, vol. 3, p. 220).

4. Party organs were introduced into the KPA after Kim Il-sung's 1959 speech in which he said the biggest problem in the Korean War had been "total lack of political training and revolutionary heroism." The party organs were needed to give soldiers firm ideas of what they were asked to fight for and reasons why, Kim said (Kiwon Chung, "The North Korean People's Army and the Party," in Scalapino,

ed., *North Korea Today* [see chap. 3, n. 11], p. 116). On page 118, citing a 1961 book by Kim Yon-hoe, Chung adds that political commandants' "responsibilities concentrate on supervising the training and promotion of the soldiers, ensuring their positive devotion to the Party, the preparation of political programmes and materials for use in classes, and supplying pamphlets and newspapers, pictorial exhibitions and films. Promotion for the soldier is almost completely dependent on the recommendation of the political commandants whom the rank-and-file soldiers fear more than the professional military commanders."

For a detailed description of the military's General Political Bureau see Joseph S. Bermudez Jr., *The Armed Forces of North Korea* (London: I. B. Tauris, 2001), pp. 28–33.

31. Neither Land nor People at Peace.

1. Kang Myong-do testimony in *JoongAng Ilbo,* June 8, 1995.
2. Hwang Jang-yop, *Problems of Human Rights (3)* (see chap. 9, n. 25).
3. His remarks appeared in *Chosun Ilbo,* October 12, 1995.
4. "S. Korean Agent Reports North Has Executed at Least 50 Officials in Purge," Seoul-datelined dispatch from Agence France-Presse, July 13, 1998.
5. "The enemy reporters claimed that an army unit mutinied and took over the Hwanghae Steel Mill," Kim told those visitors. "A Taiwan news organ went so far as to claim that the coup was led by the joint chief of staff. Moon Myong-ja [a Korean-American reporter] heard about the army 'coup' and rushed here to find out the truth. Miss Moon found that no such event had occurred. The enemy news organs seem to track every move made by the joint chief of staff. If he is not seen in public for several days, they wonder what he is up to. You comrades have families and know that family life goes through many events. Our joint chief of staff, too, has a family to take care of. The basic problem is that the Japanese and South Korean bastards have dark, shady motives and assume that we have dark, shady motives, too. They see the events here through their colored glasses. Those people from hostile nations who visit us are shocked when they see the real truth here."

The remarks apparently were taped by the visitors, officials of Chongryon. In 2003 Japanese intelligence leaked them and *Wolgan Choson* published them. For an English translation see "Kim Jong Il's Candid Talk Caught on Tape," *Korea Web Weekly,* http://www.kimsoft.com/2003/kji-tape.htm.

Western versions of what happened are in Oberdorfer, *The Two Koreas* (see chap. 24, n. 9), p. 375, and Bill Gertz, *Betrayal* (Washington, D.C.: Regnery Publishing, 1999), p. 264.

32. In a Ruined Country.

1. "Leader Kim Jong-il Wins Landslide in North Korea-style Elections," Seoul-datelined dispatch from Agence France-Presse, August 4, 2003.
2. A religious group, Buddhist Sharing, estimated two million to three million dead, but the methodology of the estimate was widely criticized. In its September 11, 2002, issue, however, a Seoul daily, *Chosun Ilbo,* citing refugee testimony, reported that a country-wide census the previous year had found that people "missing in

North Korea including those who starved to death in the six years from 1995, when the food crisis peaked, to early 2001 reached . . . 2 million to 2.5 million" (http://english.chosun.com/w21data/html/news/200209/200209110023.html).

3. According to Nicholas Eberstadt, North Korean seven-year-olds were twenty-two pounds lighter and eight inches shorter than South Korean seven-year-olds. See Eberstadt, "Disparities in Socioeconomic Development in Divided Korea: Indications and Implications," *Asian Survey* 406 (November/December 2000), pp. 875–876.

4. Specialists were beginning to address the question of causality. Nicholas Eberstadt the following year said that more information was needed on whether the North Korean famine resembled other twentieth-century communist famines in having followed quickly after major, closely related policy changes. See Eberstadt, *The End of North Korea* (Washington: The AEI Press, 1999), p. 65. In a later work, Andrew S. Natsios notes general agreement that the collapse of the North Korean public distribution system, which handled food rationing, followed long-term trends: "steadily declining agricultural production caused by poor agricultural practices, perverse economic incentives, a declining volume of inputs such as fertilizer and pesticides, and several years of natural disasters, beginning in 1995." A second factor, outside the immediate control of the Pyongyang regime, was "the precipitous decline in food subsidies from the Soviet Union and China." However, Natsios argues, the factors that "transformed a small, regionalized famine into a national catastrophe resulting in the massive death tolls of 1996 and 1997" were two very recent policy decisions by the Pyongyang regime. One was "cutting off food subsidies to the eastern coastal plain in 1994 and 1995" while the other was "the central government's decision to reduce farmers' per capita rations from 167 kilograms per year to 107 kilograms after the disastrous harvest of 1995. This decision ended the voluntary cooperation of the peasants in supplying their surplus to the urban and mining areas" (*The Great North Korean Famine* [see chap. 29, n. 12], p. 91).

5. Collins submitted the study to Seoul's Hanyang University as an academic thesis in 1996.

6. Kang Chul-hwan and his family, former Korean residents of Japan, spent ten years in a prison camp before relatives in Japan pressured and bribed officials to treat them better. Kang escaped to China in January 1992 with Ahn Hyuk, another former camp inmate, and they defected to South Korea in August 1992. "While I was there," Kang told me, "North Koreans were having two meals a day, sometimes rations of animal feed. That's what I got in the industrial city where I worked in the factory, a city with a big population and not enough food. In the camp, people like Ahn got around 300 grams a day. [Ahn himself said 360.] People like us, in the family complex, got around 500 grams a day. Corn and salt. The corn was uncooked. You had to cook it yourself."

7. *The End of North Korea,* p. 62.

8. "One source said that the Onsong riot occurred around October 11 and North Korean authorities brought in helicopters to control the riot, and conducted a massive search for the leaders and 'rebellious elements.' The source said that North Korean officials told him to quickly return to China since it was difficult to do business in North Korea at the moment. However, no specific reasons for or the current situation of the riot were uncovered.

"What is known, though, was that North Korea's so-called 'Special Unit' was mobilized to control events. This troop is known as the special forces that deals with riots and conducts espionage activities in the northeast region of China. The Onsong district is a mine area where criminals or people of bad 'character' are banished to, and the people there are known to have strong revulsion of North Korean society. Moreover, thanks to relationships with people in China, the people of the Onsong district are known to be fairly well-informed of the outside world" (Jee Hae-bom, "Riot Reported in North Korea," *Digital Chosun*, Nov. 1, 1999).

9. A catalog of camps may be found in David Hawk, *The Hidden Gulag* (see chap. 16, n. 4).

10. Ref. No. KN010, from AID/BHR/OFDA (Bureau for Humanitarian Responses, Office of U.S. Foreign Disaster Assistance, AID).

11. From around 2000 a few prominent defectors seemed to step into the pulpit to become specialists in single-minded condemnation of Pyongyang on behalf of human rights and religious organizations. Some of those in the 1990s had been among the defectors who gave me nuanced accounts of their experiences. While I had no doubt that they had good cause to take up activism, and likewise did not doubt that their passion was very real, I felt fortunate to have conducted my interviews with them earlier. Those interviews also occurred before the administration of President Kim Dae-jung, who took office in 1998, had begun in an obvious way to try to muzzle certain defectors to suit a new and diametrically opposite propaganda purpose: to keep their strongly negative views of the Pyongyang regime from derailing the "sunshine policy" of reaching out to find accommodation with the North.

12. Graisse of the WFP said, "Is the army better fed than the average citizen? The only answer you can give is: Show me one country where it's not."

13. See Natsios, *The Great North Korean Famine*, pp. 209–211.

14. "On the 50th Anniversary of Kim Il-sung University" (see chap. 30, n. 2).

15. For the citation to that 1998 speech see chap. 31, n. 5. Regarding the temporary nature of some measures, Natsios writes: "As the famine waned and the regime remained in power," top officials sought to restore "the highly centralized, totalitarian structure that existed before the catastrophe struck." For his examples, see *The Great North Korean Famine*, pp. 229–230.

16. "S. Korean Agent Reports North Has Executed at Least 50 Officials in Purge," Seoul-datelined dispatch from Agence France-Presse.

17. Suh, *Kim Il-sung* (see chap. 2, n. 35), p. 154.

18. Kim Kwang In, "NK Exhumes and Decapitates Body of 'Traitor,'" *Chosun Ilbo*, October 5, 2001. According to a report from a defector, Kim Man-kum was restored around January 2000 to the good graces of history ("Fallen Political Bureau Member Reinstated," *Chosun Ilbo*, September 4, 2002, http://english. chosun.com/w21data/html/news/200209/200209040029.html).

19. Speech before Unification Council of South Korea, Nov. 12, 1997, cited in Natsios, *The Great North Korean Famine*, p. 203.

20. One reported practice that might be termed genocide: forcing abortions and infanticides upon female political prisoners—including refugee women, impregnated while staying illegally in China, who had been captured, returned to North Korea and put into detention. See *The Hidden Gulag*, pp. 65–72. And

on p. 74 the report says that a group of former political prisoners feared that increased international publicity about the prison system might inspire the authorities "to 'massacre the prisoners' in order to destroy evidence of the camps."

21. "K., a North Korean in his 30s, was recruited at age 17 into an elite military unit working for the agency responsible for weapons production. He took an oath to work underground for the rest of his career and was assigned to a cave in remote Musan County in North Hamgyong province, about 15 miles from the Chinese border.

"'This is how we hide from our enemies. Everything in North Korea is underground,' said K., who described the cave on condition that he be quoted using only his first initial and that certain identifying details be kept vague.

"North Korea is riddled with caves like the one in which K. worked. Under its paranoid regime, virtually everything of military significance is manufactured underground, whether it's buttons for soldiers' uniforms or enriched uranium for nuclear weapons. A South Korean intelligence source estimates that North Korea has several hundred large underground factories and more than 10,000 smaller facilities. Joseph S. Bermudez, Jr., the author of three books on the North Korean military, puts the total number between 11,000 and 14,000" (Barbara Demick, "N. Korea's Ace in the Hole," *Los Angeles Times*, Nov. 14, 2003, p. 1).

33. Even the Traitors Who Live in Luxury.

1. Kang's remarks in this chapter are from my interview with him on June 12, 1995, and from his testimony in *JoongAng Ilbo* (see chap. 2, n. 7).

34. Though Alive, Worse Than Gutter Dogs.

1. Kim Kwang-in, "NK's 5 Concentration Camps House 200,000," *Digital Chosunilbo* (English Edition), December 5, 2002, http://english.chosun.com/cgi-bin/printNews?id=200212050035.

2. For eyewitness accounts of such executions see Kang Chul-hwan, "Public Executions Witnessed Personally," *Chosun Ilbo*, March 25, 2001.

3. Kang Chol-hwan and Pierre Rigoulot, *The Aquariums of Pyongyang: Ten Years in a North Korean Gulag,* translated by Yair Reiner (New York: Basic Books, 2001). Some other works by former political prisoners have yet to be translated from Korean into English.

4. I cannot rule out that he was referring to Chinese donations, which were given without conditions.

5. See, for example, Park Son-hee and Park Chun-shik, *Inochi no Tegami* (English title *River of Grief: The Ordeal of Two North Korean Children*), Japanese main text with English summary translation by Alexander Martin (Tokyo: The Massada, 1999). This brother and sister refugee pair had hidden in China until journalist Hideko Takayama helped them get to South Korea, as she related in "Could you take us to South Korea?"—part of a cover package entitled "Escape from Hell: The secret refugee trails from North Korea—and the story of the people who got out," *Newsweek International*, March 5, 2001.

Also see Médicins Sans Frontières, *North Korea: Testimonies of Famine—Refugee Interviews from the Sino-Korean Border, Special Report* (New York: Doctors Without Borders / Médicins Sans Frontières, August 1998), http://www.doctorswithoutborders.org/publications/reports/before1999/korea_1998.shtm.

6. One scholar who has continued to disparage defector testimony is Bruce Cumings. "Literally for half a century, the South Korean intelligence services have bamboozled one American reporter after another by parading their defectors (real and fake)," Cumings writes in his 2003 book. To back this harsh assessment he cites his own experience when he was a Peace Corps volunteer in the South in the 1960s. Crusading anti-communist defectors "used to come around the school where I taught, to tell all the assembled students that everyone was starving in the North, and no one owned a watch or leather shoes. One famous defector, Kim Sin-jo, was . . . an all-purpose source for exaggerated and inflamed propaganda about the North, as well as a well-known alcoholic. He later tried to re-defect back to the North" (*North Korea: Another Country* [see chap. 4, n. 25], pp. xii and 153). Moving forward in time, Cumings manages to turn around the message of defector Kang Chul-hwan's book on his gulag experiences, writing (p. 176): "*The Aquariums of Pyongyang* is an interesting and believable story, precisely because it does not, on the whole, make for the ghastly tale of totalitarian repression that its original publishers in France meant it to be; instead it suggests that a decade's incarceration with one's immediate family was survivable and not necessarily an obstacle to entering the elite status of residence in Pyongyang and entrance to college. Meanwhile, we have a long-standing, never-ending gulag full of black men in our prisons, incarcerating upward of 25 percent of all black youths. This doesn't excuse North Korea's police state, but perhaps it suggests that Americans should do something about the pathologies of our inner cities—say, in Houston—before pointing the finger."

7. Kang Chul-hwan, "Public Executions All But Gone," http://english.chosun.com/w21data/html/news/200210/200210300011.html.

35. Sun of the Twenty-First Century.

1. Yonhap news agency report carried in Seoul's *JoongAng Ilbo*, December 29, 1999.

2. For more on the issue of economic sanctions see Selig S. Harrison, *Korean Endgame: A Strategy for Reunification and U.S. Disengagement* (Princeton, N.J.: Princeton University Press, 2002), especially pp. 88–89; Marcus Noland, *Avoiding the Apocalypse: The Future of the Two Koreas* (Washington, D.C.: Institute for International Economics, 2000), especially pp. 107–110; Michael O'Hanlon & Mike Mochizuki, *Crisis on the Korean Peninsula: How to Deal With a Nuclear North Korea* (Washington: Brookings Institution, 2003), especially pp. 86–89; Victor D. Cha and David C. Kang, *Nuclear North Korea: A Debate on Engagement Strategies* (New York: Columbia University Press, 2003), especially pp. 90–92.

3. "Despair, Détente and Dollars," *Institutional Investor* (international edition—Asia), July 2000: pp. 64–67.

4. "NK Purges 'Liberals,'" *Digital Chosunilbo*, September 29, 1998.

5. An unofficial translation of the 1998 constitution appears on the Web site of the Chongryon's Tokyo-based English-language newspaper *The People's Korea* at http://www.korea-np.co.jp/pk/061st_issue/98091708.htm.

6. The transcript first appeared in Korean in *Wolgan Choson*, which cited a Japanese intelligence agency concerned with North Korean matters as its source. It is translated into English on *Korea Web Weekly* at http://www.kimsoft.com/2003/kji-tape.htm.

7. *JoongAng Ilbo*, December 29. 1999.

8. "Ex-Dictator's Daughter Receives Warm Welcome in North Korea," Agence France-Presse dispatch, May 12, 2002.

9. "Kim Jong Il is presiding over a process that might be called reform by stealth. He is tacitly encouraging change in the domestic economy without incurring the political costs of confronting the Old Guard in a formal doctrinal debate" (Harrison, *Korean Endgame*, p. 26).

10. Catherine Sung, "Kim Jong-il shows he has a lighter side," *Taipei Times*, June 15, 2000. Internet: http://taipeitimes.com/news/2000/06/15/print/0000040078.

11. Hwang Won-duk, "What we have achieved at the North-South Summit and the follow-up tasks," speech to Korean Veterans' Association conference, June 30, 2000, reprinted in Korean by *Wolgan Choson* and translated on *Korea Web Weekly* at http://www.kimsoft.com/2000/summitsk.htm.

12. A translation of the North-South Joint Declaration is on the Web site of *The People's Korea* at http://www.korea-np.co.jp/pk/142th_issue/2000061501.htm.

13. Laxmi Nakarmi, "Kim Jong Il's New Direction," *Asiaweek*, September 15, 2000. Hwang Won-duk speech.

14. *Time Asia*, December 25, 2000–Jan. 1, 2001.

15. Ruediger Frank, "North Korea: 'Gigantic Change' and a Gigantic Chance," The Nautilus Institute for Security and Sustainable Development, Policy Forum Online, May 9, 2003, http://nautilus.org/fora/security/0331_Frank.html.

16. Zhang Xinghua, "Kim Jong-il Visits Shanghai Secretly," *Global Times*, January 23, 2001, p. 2.

17. "Kim Jong-il Studies the Chinese Model," *Izvestia*, January 19, 2001, p. 6; Ruriko Kubota, "Kim Jong-il Aims to Build Shanghai-like High-Tech City," *Sankei Shimbun*, February 2, 2001.

18. Zhang, "Kim Jong-il Visits Shanghai Secretly."

19. Kubota, "Kim Jong-il Aims."

20. See, for example, "Kim Jong Il Has Inadvertently Thrown Down the Gauntlet," *Keys* (Seoul: Network for North Korean Democracy and Human Rights). Internet: http://www.nknet.org/en/keys/lastkeys/2002/10/01.php.

21. Sin Sok-ho, "Three Months After North Korea's Economic Reform: Street Vendors All Over P'yongyang—'Let us Sell More and Earn More,'" trans. FBIS, *Dong-A Ilbo*, October 8, 2002.

22. "U.S. Opposes N.Korea's Attendance at ADB," *Korea Herald*, April 18, 2002.

23. Yoo Choonsik, "Top Hyundai Executive Kills Self," *Bangkok Post* (Seoul-datelined Reuter dispatch), August 5, 2003; Vijay Joshi, "Six S. Koreans Convicted in Summit Probe," AP dispatch from Seoul, September 26, 2003; Kwon Kyung-bok, "North Condemns Cash-Summit Convictions," *Chosun Ilbo*, September 28, 2003.

36. Fear and Loathing.

1. The remarks of Prof. Kim Jae-soo appeared in an interview published in the New Year's 2000 issue of *Choson Shimpo*, the Korean-language paper of the pro-Pyongyang General Association of Koreans in Japan (Chongryon), and were quoted in the January 11 issue of Seoul's *JoongAng Ilbo*.

2. Madeleine Albright, with Bill Woodward, *Madame Secretary: A Memoir* (New York: Miramax Books, 2003), pp. 455–472.

3. James A. Kelly, "Ensuring a Korean Peninsula Free of Nuclear Weapons," transcript of remarks given at research conference organized by Korea Institute for International Economic Policy, Korea Economic Institute and American Enterprise Institute, Washington, D.C., February 13, 2004, on line at http://www. nautilus.org/DPRKBriefingBook/multilateralTalks/Kelly_ NKChanceforRedemption. html.

4. Jung Chul-geun and Ko Soo-suk, "Thinking Big, But Not Too Big," *JoongAng Ilbo* (Englsh Internet edition), November 10, 2002.

5. Kim Ho-song, "Wise Leadership for Improving Socialist Economic Management," *Nodong Shinmun*, February 1, 2003 (FBIS translation).

6. Frank, "North Korea: 'Gigantic Change' and a Gigantic Chance" (see chap. 35, n. 15).

7. Testimony of Stephen W. Linton, Ph.D., Chairman, Eugene Bell Foundation, before the Senate Subcommittee on East Asian and Pacific Affairs, June 5, 2003.

Linton said that, thanks to humanitarian aid programs, "North Koreans are far more relaxed in their dealings with foreigners today than they were only several years ago. Clearly, fear of people-to-people contacts is not the primary reason North Korea has not wholeheartedly embraced economic reforms." Instead, he concluded, the problem was that "North Korea's leadership has never believed in a world governed by fair play. Instead they believe that nature as well as history has created a world of natural 'haves' and 'have nots.' In this view, because the world's natural resources are unequally distributed in favor of larger nations, smaller nations have to rely on diplomacy and influence (pressure) to acquire what they need. Not surprisingly, all their energies are exerted in acquiring the leverage needed to force foreign powers to take them seriously." Linton implied that the North could not truly reform until U.S. and other sanctions were removed. "In the North Korean way of thinking, sanctions 'prove' that the economic playing field will never be level enough to permit their products to compete in the international arena," he wrote. "When seen from this perspective, North Korea's international and domestic policies are relatively easy to understand."

8. Alexander Boronchov (name as transliterated), "P'yongyang Residents Carry Cellular Phones," trans. FBIS *Dong-A Ilbo* (Internet version), July 17, 2003.

9. Kathi Zellweger, "Caritas and the North Korean Crisis: Concern for People in Need" (paper prepared for address to Evening Forum of the Korea Society in New York), October 19, 2003.

10. "North Korea May Have Devalued Its Currency," Reuters dispatch from Tokyo, October 5, 2003, quoting a report by *Asahi Shimbun*.

11. Ser Myo-ja, "North Issues Tax, Labor Codes for Gaesong," *JoongAng Ilbo*, October 1, 2003.

12. See Don Kirk, "86% Rise in Profit For Hyundai In Quarter," *The New York Times,* August 12, 2003, p. W1, and Kim So-Young, "Hyundai Feud May Stall N.K. Projects," *Korea Herald,* November 21, 2003.

13. Hans Greimel, "N. Korea Unveils Industrial Zone Rules," AP dispatch from Seoul, December 18, 2003.

14. Jeong Yong-soo, "Unification Minister Says Reform Afoot," *JoongAng Ilbo,* October 1, 2003.

15. "North Korea Wants Foreign Lawyers, Accountants," Reuters dispatch from Beijing, October 28, 2003.

16. "Ko Soo-suk, "North Expects Gains in Bank Mergers," *JoongAng Ilbo,* November 11, 2003.

17. Andrew Ward, "European Investors Move into N Korea," *Financial Times,* November 21, 2003, p. 5.

18. Hans Greimel, "EU Makes Economic Overture," AP dispatch from Seoul, January 13, 2004.

19. "ROK Official Says North Sees Tangible Accomplishments in IT Industry," Yonhap, January 8, 2004.

20. Peter Hayes, "Enemy to Friend: Providing Security Assurances to North Korea," *The DPRK Briefing Book,* Nautilus Institute, February 9, 2004, http://www.nautilus.org/DPRKBriefingBook/multilateralTalks/PHEnemytoFriend.html.

21. Richard Halloran, "New Warplan Calls for Invasion of North Korea," *Global Beat* (Internet), November 14, 1998.

22. Richard Halloran, "Plan targets Pyongyang's 'commandos,'" *The Washington Times,* February 25, 2003.

23. Jeong Yong-soo, "Unification Minister says Reform Afoot."

24. Ruediger Frank, "The End of Socialism and a Wedding Gift for the Groom? The True Meaning of the Military First Policy," *The DPRK Briefing Book,* Nautilus Institute, December 11, 2003, http://www.nautilus.org/DPRKBriefingBook/transition/Ruediger_Socialism.html. For a contrary view describing the military-first policy as a barrier to economic recovery, see Aidan Foster-Carter's "North Korea: Guns or Butter?" posted April 6, 2004, Northwest Asia Peace and Security Network, http://www.nautilus.org/fora/security/0418_FosterCarter.html.

25. George Wehrfritz, with B. J. Lee and Hideko Takayama, "The First Signs of Life: Will economic reforms in the Hermit Kingdom save Kim Jong Il's regime or hasten the fall?" February 2, 2004.

26. John W. Lewis, "Hope on N. Korea," *Washington Post* op-ed article, January 27, 2004.

27. Wehrfritz, Lee and Takayama, "The First Signs of Life." Like so much other fine material in the international editions, this extremely important article did not appear in the *Newsweek* edition circulated to U.S. readers. I am grateful to Hideko Takayama for sending a copy to me.

28. "North Korea is cutting the workforce of its government and ruling party by up to 30 percent in an effort to reduce bureaucracy and use the workers in more productive areas, a Japanese daily reported Tuesday. North Korean leader Kim Jong-il, who is also chairman of the National Defense Commission, recently ordered the reassignment of administration officials and members of the Rodong (Workers') Party to enhance the government's efficiency, the *Sankei Shimbun*

said. The glut of officials has slowed the regime's operations, it said" ("N. Korea to Cut 30 Percent of Gov't, Party Workforce: Report," Yonhap dispatch from Tokyo, January 27, 2004).

29. "When China began its reforms in 1979, more than 70 percent of the population was in the agricultural sector. (The same held true for Vietnam when it began reforming the following decade.) Debureaucratization of agriculture under these conditions permits rapid increases in productivity and the release of labor into the nascent nonstate-owned manufacturing sector. . . . In contrast, North Korea has about half that share employed in agriculture" (Marcus Noland, *Korea after Kim Jong-il* [Washington, D.C.: Institute for International Economics, 2004], pp. 48–49. Noland's study offers various scenarios for the country's future and assesses the prospects for successful reform).

30. See, for example, remarks by South Korea's foreign minister in Norimitsu Onishi, "Seoul Has Big Plans for North Korea (Nightmares, Too)," *The New York Times,* December 17, 2003.

31. "South Korea Emerging as N. Korea's No. 1 Export Market," Yonhap, December 9, 2003. From 1996 to August 2003 the South's cumulative private-sector investment in the North came to $1.15 billion. More than 80 percent of that was invested in the two light-water nuclear reactors that had been promised to North Korea in exchange for its 1994 nuclear freeze. But the total also included investments by Hyundai, the Unification Church and others ("South Korean Private Investment in North Amounts to 1.15 Billion Dollars," Yonhap, October 28, 2003).

32. Marcus Noland, "How Bush risks losing Korea," *Financial Times,* January 22, 2004.

33. "Food Aid Will Be Cut In North, Agency Says," *JoongAng Ilbo,* January 25, 2004.

34. Frank, " 'Gigantic Change' " (see chap. 35, n. 15).

35. Kim Jung Min, "Young People Struggle for Jobs in South Korea's Weak Economy," *The Wall Street Journal,* January 28, 2004, p. B28.

36. "N. Korea Threatens to Suspend Inter-Korean Tourism," *Asia Pulse,* February 5, 2004.

37. "North Korea Blasts Japan's Move to Stop Cash Transfers," Agence France-Presse, January 31, 2004. Japan insisted that the issue be on the agenda along with nuclear weapons in the six-party talks. See Richard Hanson, "Japan, North Korea stumble over abductions," *Asia Times Online,* February 16, 2004, http://www.atimes.com/atimes/Japan/FB16Dh01.html.

38. See Frank, "End of Socialism and a Wedding Gift for the Groom?"

39. See James Brooke, "Quietly, North Korea Opens Markets," *The New York Times,* November 19, 2003, p. W1.

40. Noland, "How Bush risks losing Korea."

41. Bill Gertz and Rowan Scarborough, "Notes from the Pentagon: North Korea split," *The Gertz File,* August 8, 2003, http://www.gertzfile.com/gertzfile/ring080803.html. On a trip to Iraq in January 2004 Wolfowitz was quoted as describing Saddam Hussein as being, in terms of evil, "in a class with very few others—Stalin, Hitler, Kim Jong-il" (Thomas E. Ricks, "Wolfowitz Stands His Ground on Iraq," *Washington Post National Weekly Edition,* January 12–18, 2004, p. 7).

42. "There is extensive evidence of a major coup attempt by elements of the VI Corps in 1995, which appears to have been crushed only with some difficulty,"

Foreign Service Officer Larry Robinson wrote in a secret cable to Washington from the U.S. Embassy in Seoul in 1998. Leaked to journalist Bill Gertz, the cable is reproduced in Gertz's book, *Betrayal: How the Clinton Administration Undermined American Security* (Washington, D.C.: Regnery Publishing, Inc., 1999), pp. 255–264.

43. Kang Myong-do, *pyeongyangeun mangmyeoneul kumgungda* (see chap. 13, n. 52).

44. Philip W. Yun, "North Korea—New Lessons Learned," *The DPRK Briefing Book*, Nautilus Institute, http://www.nautilus.org/DPRKBriefingBook/multilateralTalks/Yun.html.

45. See Cha and Kang, *Nuclear North Korea: A Debate on Engagement Strategies* (New York: Columbia University Press, 2003). For other recent takes on the policy issues, see a Brookings Institution study by Michael O'Hanlon and Mike Mochizuki, *Crisis on the Korean Peninsula: How to Deal with a Nuclear North Korea* (New York: McGraw Hill, 2003); and Gavan McCormack, *Target North Korea: Pushing North Korea to the Brink of Nuclear Catastrophe* (New York: Nation Books, 2004).

46. Kelly, "Ensuring a Korean Peninsula."

47. Ambassador Li Gun, "Requisites for Resolving the Nuclear Issue," Center for National Policy, republished by Nautilus Institute, *The DPRK Briefing Book*, February 6, 2004, http://www.nautilus.org/DPRKBriefingBook/multilateralTalks/Li-Gun-NukeIssue.pdf.

48. "This administration has made the world less safe because they were unwilling to continue that dialogue," the senator from Massachusetts said in a televised forum sponsored by CBS. "I would put all the issues of the peninsula on the table, not just the nuclear issue but the economic, the human rights, the deployment of forces," he said. "I believe that between China, Japan and South Korea and our own interests, and the state of the economy in North Korea and their own interests, there is a deal to be struck." See "Democrats Press for More-Direct Talks with Korea," Washington-datelined Agence France-Presse dispatch, March 1, 2004.

49. North Korea Raises Nuclear Tension," Seoul-datelined Associated Press dispatch, March 18, 2004. Also see George Gedda, "Newsview: U.S., N. Korea Decide to Wait," Washington-datelined Associated Press dispatch, March 10, 2004.

50. Kelly, "Ensuring a Korean Peninsula."

51. By way of analogy think of 1945 Japan. The people were so deeply indoctrinated in emperor worship that the U.S. conquerors decided it would be best for Emperor Hirohito to publicly confess his lack of divinity—and then stay on as a stabilizing influence.

52. John Harwood and Greg Hitt, "Bush and Kerry Frame Contrasts of Race Ahead; As Democrat Adds to Wins, President Defends Policies in Rare TV Appearance," *The Wall Street Journal*, February 9, 2004.

53. Boronchov, "P'yongyang Residents Carry Cellular Phones."

54. Vernon Loeb and Peter Slevin, "Overcoming North Korea's Tyranny of Proximity," *Washington Post*, January 20, 2003, p. A16, quoted in Cha and Kang, *Nuclear North Korea*, p. 6.

55. An article in March 2003 said that the United States and Asian countries had "begun to accept the idea" of a nuclear-armed North Korea. See Doug Struck and Glenn Kessler, "Foes Giving In To N. Korea's Nuclear Aims," *Washington*

Post, March 5, 2003, p. A1. However, in the year that followed the voices of agreement with such a notion seemed muted.

56. In what Marcus Noland calls the "neo-conservative's dream" scenario, "the global community puts the squeeze on the Kim Jong-il regime. Aid is cut off. Growth falls to its previous low of minus 6 percent. The inexpertly enacted July 2002 economic policy changes drive inflation up 300 percent, reputedly its rate over the course of the year since the introduction of the reforms. In the 'international embargo' scenario, North Korea's relations with the rest of the world deteriorate precipitously, perhaps under suspicion of exportation of nuclear weapons or materials, and all international trade is cut off." Noland's economic modeling showed that in the "neo-conservative's dream" scenario, "the likelihood of regime change rises to about a one in seven probability, growing thereafter, and in all probability, Kim Jong-il is out of power before George W. Bush. (Remember, in neo-conservative dreams, George W. Bush is in power until 2008.) In the final scenario, 'international embargo,' the likelihood of regime change is over 40 percent in the first year and the Kim Jong-il regime probably collapses within two years" (Noland, *Korea after Kim Jong-il*, pp. 40–41).

57. Proposed "North Korean Freedom Act of 2003," introduced by Senator Sam Brownback for himself and Senator Evan Bayh. Proposed "North Korea Human Rights Act of 2004," introduced by Representative James Leach.

58. The Senate bill was drafted by Michael Horowitz of the Hudson Institute, director of the Project for International Religious Liberty and the Project for Civil Justice Reform. See "The North Korea Freedom Act," *Korea Times*, February 27, 2004. Leading lobbyists for such legislation included religious leaders.

59. A statement on human trafficking by State Department spokesman Richard Boucher on September 10, 2003 (see http://www.usembassy.it/file2003_09/alia/a3091009.htm), said, "Burma, Cuba, Liberia, North Korea and Sudan still meet the Tier 3 standard, because their governments still fail to comply with the minimum standards, and fail to make significant efforts to do so. The President, acting on the recommendations of the Secretary determined that sanctions will be imposed on Burma, Cuba and North Korea. While Liberia and Sudan are also subject to sanctions, the President determined that certain multilateral assistance for these two countries would promote the purposes of the Act or is otherwise in the national interest of the United States. For Sudan, that assistance will be limited to that which may be necessary to implement a peace accord." Elisabeth Bumiller reported that religious lobbyists Charles W. Colson, the one-time Watergate criminal who found born-again Christianity in prison and went on to head a prison ministries organization, and Richard D. Land, an official of the Southern Baptist Convention, were behind President Bush's broad initiative on human trafficking. See "Evangelicals Sway White House on Human Rights Issues Abroad," *The New York Times*, October 26, 2003, p. 1.

60. See "North Korea," Human Rights Watch, pp. 12–16, www.hrw.org/asia/dprkorea.php. Also, "A Human Rights Report on the Trafficking of Persons, Especially Women and Children," The Protection Project, 2002, pp. 408–409, 209.190.246.239/ver2/cr/nk.pdf.

61. David Hawk, *The Hidden Gulag* (see chap. 16, n. 4), pp. 65–72.

62. See Jerrold M. Post, M.D., and Laurita M. Denny, M.A., "Kim Jong-il of North Korea: A Political Psychology Profile," computer printout. I found some lapses in the research. During the famine, Post and Denny stated without qualification, Kim cut off nearly all of the food supplies going to the country's four eastern provinces. The citation, however, was to a book whose author had prudently used such qualifying words as "appeared" and "suggests" to acknowledge that the evidence was not all in regarding his hypothesis. Also, the cited pages blame "the regime," making no mention of Kim as the one who would have taken the action. In the same paragraph of the draft profile appeared a claim that, according to eyewitness testimony, Kim had ordered systematic infanticide in the political prison camps. The citation in that case was to a newspaper article that said nothing at all about whether Kim Jong-il had given the orders. Although the infanticides themselves were documented, I knew of no one who claimed to have seen or heard Kim ordering that they be performed.

63. For example, in his 1996 speech marking the fiftieth anniversary of Kim Il-sung University, Kim Jong-il told of seeing hungry people search for food when he visited a steel mill. He said he had been told that "in other areas the roads, trains and train stations were full of such people"—a trend of events he described as "heartbreaking." To his 1998 visitors from Chongryon in Japan, he complained that the Pyongyang power plant "stops working often and the people of Pyongyang are freezing. I cannot bear watching them suffer like that." True, he continued to dine gourmet-fashion, like the king he was. True, he left to subordinates the task of doing something about the people's misery while he focused on the military. But to say that he did not feel *any* of his people's pain was a leap beyond what the evidence would justify.

64. Michael Breen, *Kim Jong-il: North Korea's Dear Leader* (Singapore: John Wiley & Sons [Asia] Pte Ltd, 2004), p. xiv. In a chapter entitled "Is Kim Jong-il Evil?" Breen offers his own, nonclinical analysis of Kim's personality, informed by the author's long and close association with Koreans. "As offensive as his regime may seem in the modern world, we should not assume that the leader of an undemocratic state is necessarily evil, any more than European kings were evil in the pre-democracy period," Breen writes. "Kim Jong-il is neither insane nor evil. But he benefits from being at the top of a system which . . . is both" (pp. 91, 110).

65. As a longtime, generally harsh critic of the leader and his regime, I could understand the impulse to pile on. Once, while working on this book, I offered to write an article for a magazine. As I tentatively proposed it, the article would answer the question of just how evil Kim Jong-il was by proving that he ranked right down there with Hitler and Saddam Hussein. Luckily the proposal was not accepted. Otherwise, imagine the editors' reaction some weeks later when I found I had to acknowledge that—bad as Kim Jong-il's tally was on the evil side of his ledger—my review of what I had learned about him revealed that there was something more to the man.

66. For the functionaries' gambits, see Chuck Downs, *Over the Line: North Korea's Negotiating Strategy* (Washington, D.C.: The AEI Press, 1999), and Scott Snyder, *Negotiating on the Edge: North Korean Negotiating Behavior* (Washington, D.C.: United States Institute of Peace Press, 1999).

67. Cha and Kang, *Nuclear North Korea,* p. 127.
68. Quoted in Ambassador Li Gun, "Prerequisites for Resolving the Nuclear Issue," *DPRK Briefing Book-Nautilus Institute,* February 6, 2004, http://www.nautilus.org/ DPRKBriefingBook/multilateralTalks /Li-Gun-NukeIssue.pdf.
69. Bill Gertz, "Kim Wants to Rule All Korea, Defector Warns," *The Washington Times,* November 4, 2003.

37. Sing of Our Leader's Favors for Thousands of Years.
1. Albright, *Madame Secretary* (see chap. 36, n. 3), p. 466.
2. "DPRK Hails Leader as Partisan's Son, Mentions Son-to-Grandson Succession," U.S. Foreign Broadcast Information Service translation of essay by Song Mi-ran: "Partisan's Son," *Nodong Shinmun,* October 6, 2002, p. 2. Article ID: KPP20021011000026,:document ID: 0h59iwg02ykiwf, insert date: 11/08/ 2002.
3. *Yomiuri,* May 4–5, and May 14, 2001; *Japan Times,* May 4–5, 2001; *Chosun Ilbo,* May 4, 2001; *Asia Times Online,* May 5, 2001; *The Guardian,* May 5, 2001.
4. "Kaleidoscope" column "A Strange Country," *Chosun Ilbo,* May 6, 2001, Internet version in English.
5. "Kim Jong-nam was Traveling with Wife Shin Jong-hui," Yonhap, May 15, 2001, FBIS document number FBIS-EAS-2001-0515; *Korea Herald,* May 9, 2001.
6. Kang Myong-do in *JoongAng Ilbo* (see chap. 2, n. 7).
7. "Will Kim Jong Nam Succeed His Father Kim Jong Il?" *Chosun Ilbo* Internet edition, January 14, 2001.
8. Lee Han-yong (pseudonym of Li Il-nam), *Heijou 15-gou kantei no nukeana* (The secret tunnel of Pyongyang No. 15 residence) (Tokyo: The Massada, 1996). I am grateful to Hideko Takayama for her translation of relevant parts of this book.
9. Article in *Women's JoongAng 21* summarized in *JoongAng Ilbo,* Internet version, November 23, 2000. FBIS article i.d. KPP20001124000008; Lee Han-yong, *Heijou 15-gou.*
10. Hwang Jang-yop, *The Problems of Human Rights in North Korea (3).* Seoul: 2000. Translation by Network for North Korean Democracy and Human Rights on the Web at http://nknet.org/en/keys/lastkeys/2002/9/04.php.
11. Lee Han-yong, *Heijou 15-gou.*
12. Ibid.
13. *Bungei Shunju,* February 1998. Translation/abstract by *Korea Web Weekly,* http://www.kimsoft.com/1997/nanok.htm.
14. Lee Han-yong, *Heijou 15-gou;* "Song-Yi Telephone Conversation Disclosed," trans. FBIS, *Joongang Ilbo,* Feb. 17, 1996, FBIS document i.d. 0dn7jom016u5eq.
15. Lee Kyo-kwan, "Signs of Kim Jong-nam's Preparations as Kim Jong-il's Successor Analyzed," trans. FBIS, *Chosun Ilbo* Internet version, January 14, 2001, FBIS document i.d. 0g7d33w01s3eel; *Bungei Shunju,* February 1998; "North Korea's 'Crown Prince' Shown by Japanese TV Organization," Agence France-Presse, February 15, 1999.
16. *Bungei Shunju,* February 1998.
17. Ibid.
18. Lee Han-yong, *Heijou 15-gou.*
19. *Bungei Shunju,* February 1998.

20. *JoongAng Ilbo,* April 21, 1995, p. 5.

21. "Kim Jong-il's Ex-Wife Reportedly Still in DPRK," Yonhap, March 30, 1998, FBIS document i.d. 0eqpsm100ruf3v.

22. "Song-Yi Telephone Conversation Disclosed," trans. FBIS, *Joongang Ilbo,* February 17, 1996, FBIS document i.d. 0dn7jom016u5eq.

23. Korean Broadcasting System KBS-1 radio network, "Defector Shot in Seoul; Police Assume DPRK Retaliation," 2100 GMT Feb. 15, 1997, FBIS translation document i.d. 0e9s3u002ex9dk.

24. See "Song-Yi Telephone Conversation Disclosed," trans. FBIS, *JoongAng Ilbo,* February 17, 1996, FBIS document i.d. 0dn7jom016u5eq.

25. "Kim Jong-il's Ex-Wife Reportedly Still in DPRK."

26. "Kim Jong-il's Daughter 'Sol-Song' Receives Training in Economy," *Chosun Ilbo* Internet version, October 18, 2001, FBIS translation document i.d. 0glgev9025f8zh; Yonhap, "Identity of DPRK Leader's Son Arrested in Japan," trans. FBIS, May 3, 2001, FBIS document i.d. 0gcyw5101oxg04.

27. "Son of DPRK's Kim Jong-il Said to Join Government," *Joongang Ilbo* Internet version, FBIS document i.d. 0flin2p01wxvxp; Lee Kyo-kwan, "Kim Jong Nam Being Groomed as Heir Apparent," *Chosun Ilbo* Internet version, May 13, 2001, http://English.chosun.com/cgi-bin/printNews?id=200105130135; Lee Kyo-kwan, "Is Kim Jong Nam NK's Heir Apparent?" *Chosun Ilbo* Internet version, February 26, 2002, http://english.chosun.com/w21data/html/news/200202/200202260259.html.

28. "Police Step Up Protection for DPRK Defectors After Threats," *Korea Times* Internet edition, July 17, 1997, FBIS document i.d. 0edjbsc013cm0b; for the claim that Kim Jong-nam was involved, see *Wolgan Choson,* February 2001.

29. See "ROK Paper Interviews Nephew Defector of Song Hye-rim," trans. FBIS, *Dong-A Ilbo,* February 14, 1996, FBIS document i.d. 0dmumu702tf940.

30. *Wolgan Choson,* February 2001.

31. *Joongang Ilbo* Internet version, FBIS document i.d. 0flin2p01wxvxp.

32. "Will Kim Jong Nam Succeed His Father Kim Jong Il?" *Chosun Ilbo* Internet edition, January 14, 2001.

33. George Wehrfritz and Hideko Takayama, "The Sun Also Surprises," *Newsweek International,* May 14, 2001. The magazine cited as its source Lee Young-hwa, a leading critic of Pyongyang among the Korean residents in Japan.

34. "Will Kim Jong Nam Succeed His Father Kim Jong Il?"

35. James Brooke, "China Called Likely to Oust 78 North Koreans," *The New York Times,* January 22, 2003, p. A5.

36. See "S. Korea Rejects Report Kim Jong Il in China," Seoul-datelined Agence France-Presse article, citing *JoongAng Ilbo, The Japan Times,* May 20, 2001. The Seoul newspaper cited an unnamed South Korean government source.

37. "DPRK Leader's Eldest Son Said To Remain in Russia," *Chosun Ilbo* Internet Version in English, September 22, 2002, WNC article I.D.: KPP20020924000074.

38. "Diplomatic Source 'Confirms' Kim Chong-il's Son Vacationed Often in Moscow," trans. FBIS, *Sankei Shimbun,* September 15, 2002, FBIS document i.d. 0h2qz7900k8j47.

39. "NK Leader's Ex-Wife Died in May," Yonhap dispatch in *Korea Times,* Internet edition, November 7, 2002, http://www.hankooki.com/kt_nation/200211/t2002110717351941110.htm.

40. A German diplomat who asked to remain anonymous told me that a photo showed Kim Jong-il in East Germany in 1984 when his father was visiting there and a sudden crisis came up—a flood in North Korea—that evidently required the younger Kim to travel and get his father's advice or orders. The diplomat said there was no official record of Kim Jong-il's presence in East Germany ever, so presumably he went under an assumed name.

41. Article in *Women's Joongang 21* summarized in *Joongang Ilbo,* Internet version, November 23, 2000. FBIS article i.d. KPP20001124000008, http://wnc.fedworld.gov.

42. *Yomiuri,* May 4, 2001; *Japan Times,* May 5, 2001.

43. "Kim's 'Son' Tried Japan's Soaplands," *japantoday.com,* July 15, 2002, a summary translation by Mark Schreiber of an article in *Shukan Shincho* for July 18, 2002.

44. I am grateful to Hideko Takayama for pointing out and translating these articles.

45. Yonhap, "Identity of DPRK Leader's Son Arrested in Japan," trans. FBIS, May 3, 2001, FBIS document i.d. 0gcyw5101oxg04.

46. Article in *Women's Joongang 21* summarized in *Joongang Ilbo,* Internet version, November 23, 2000. Translation by U.S. Foreign Broadcast Information Service, article i.d. KPP20001124000008, http://wnc.fedworld.gov.

47. Song Mi-ran, "Partisan's Son," *Nodong Shinmun,* October 6, 2002, trans. FBIS as "DPRK Hails Leader as Partisan's Son, Mentions Son-to-Grandson Succession," FBIS document i.d. 0h59iwg02ykiwf.

48. "DPRK Leader's Eldest Son Said to Remain in Russia," *Chosun Ilbo* Internet edition, September 22, 2002, FBIS document i.d. 0h32b5801gsbn8; Pak Min-son, "Kim Jong-chol Rises as Heir in the North," trans. FBIS, Yonhap (quoting *Aera*), April 17, 2002, FBIS document i.d. 0guzlkc02mpq4n; "Kim Jong-nam Is Scrambling for Power with His Brother," trans. FBIS, *Ming Pao,* May 4, 2001, FBIS translation, document i.d. 0gd0p3a01sdpha; "Kim Jong-il's Son Kim Hyon in Charge of WPK Propaganda Department," Jiji Press, August 31, 2002, FBIS document i.d. 0hlv9za018bge9; " 'Highest Ranking' DPRK Official Said Defected to ROK," trans. FBIS, *Kyonghyang Shinmun,* June 7, 1996, FBIS document i.d. 0dssz2200270jy.

49. Lee Han-yong, *Heijou 15-gou;* "Song-Yi Telephone Conversation Disclosed," trans. FBIS, *JoongAng Ilbo* article, February 17, 1996, FBIS document i.d. 0dn7jom016u5eq.

50. Based on the timing, it appears one of those two might have been become the mother of Kim Hyon.

51. "DPRK Leader's Eldest Son Said To Remain in Russia," *Chosun Ilbo* Internet version in English, September 22, 2002, WNC article I.D.: KPP20020924000074.

52. Under the pseudonym Kenji Fujimoto, he subsequently published a book, *Kim Jong-il's Chef,* in Japanese and Korean, in which he repeated that Kim Jong-il favored Kim Jong-un (sometimes rendered as Jong-woon or Jong-oon) as his heir.

53. See Kim Yeon-kwang, "Second Son Being Groomed as Heir Apparent," *Chosun Ilbo* (Internet English Edition) (Seoul), February 18, 2003, http://english.chosun.com/w21data/html/news/200302/200302180027.html; *Sankei Shimbun* (Tokyo), February 19, 2003; George Wehrfritz and Hideko Takayama with B.J. Lee, "Heirs to the Kingdom," *Newsweek International,* March 10, 2003; Wehrfritz,

Takayama, Lee, "North Korea: Mother Knows Best," *Newsweek* (U.S. edition), March 10, 2003.

54. Yi Kyo-kwan, "Kim Chong-il's Daughter 'Sol-song' Receives Training in Economy," *Chosun Ilbo* (Internet version) in Korean, October 18, 2001, FBIS document i.d. 0glgev9025f8zh.

55. In 2004 the ailing, eighty-one-year-old King Norodom Sihanouk of Cambodia seemed to go in this direction when he announced his abdication and named as his successor Prince Sihamoni, a fifty-one-year-old ballet dancer, professor, cinematographer, and choreographer who had been living in France. Unlike some of the prince's tougher-minded siblings, "Sihamoni is a neutral person and does not get involved with politics and is not partisan," the king said in making his surprise announcement. This possible precedent cannot have gone unnoticed in Pyongyang, as Sihanouk was a close friend of the late Kim Il-sung. Indeed, Sihamoni himself as a young man stayed in Pyongyang, where the Kims provided a villa for the Cambodian royal family. See Seth Mydans, "Cambodia's Next King: Apparently the Least Apparent Heir," *The New York Times*, October 12, 2004, p. A10.

56. Or how about Parental Leader? The Korean term that Pyongyang officially rendered as "fatherly leader" is better given as "parent leader," according to B. R. Myers, who prattles on and on about this translation issue in "Mother of All Mothers: The Leadership Secrets of Kim Jong Il," his review of this and three other North Korea books in *The Atlantic Monthly*, September 2004, pp. 133–142.

INDEX

infiltration
  into North, 99
  into South, 98, 129, 151, 535–542
    1996 submarine landing, 512
  tunnels, 139, 513
inheritance, 164
intellectuals, 159, 291
International Monetary Fund, 634
investment, external, 340, 347–348, 465–466,
      469–481, 639, 672
  laws, regulations concerning, 471,
      473–474
  from South Korea, 477–478
    rich migrants from North, specifically,
      480
  See also Japan: Korean residents of:
      investment, donations, remittances by
Iraq, lessons from, 483, 489, 513, 659
isolation
  related to subversion attempts, 125
  as U.S. policy, 495

Japan
  abducted citizens of, 637, 670, 697
  army of, 7
  collaborators with, 57, 60–61, 121, 231,
      238, 280, 448
  colonization by, 15, 174
    compensation for, 440–442, 476
  danger to, if South Korea communized,
      115
  desperate 1941 war decision, comparison,
      512
  earthquake, Tokyo area, 19
  emperor worship, imposed on Koreans, 8,
      330
  External Trade Organization (JETRO),
      183
  Hiroshima atomic bombing, 50
  investment, 475
  Korean residents of, 19, 100, 461–464,
      699–700
    discrimination against, 101, 263, 462
    investment, donations, remittances by,
      348, 461, 464, 471, 671, 700
    pachinko, 263, 297, 461, 462
    returnees to North Korea, 101–104,
      228–229, 263–265, 297–301, 311,
      313, 584, 699 (*see also* Chongryon)
  liberation from, 7, 50–51
  missiles negotiations, 635–637
  in nuclear weapons crisis, early 1990s,
      436, 439–441, 489
  sanctions threatened, 671
  trade, 181, 442, 475–476, 477
  unification and, 683

joblessness, as prima facie evidence of theft,
      531
Johnson, Lyndon B., 128, 129, 132
juche ideology
  definition and origin of term, 111, 123
  economic self-reliance in, 176–177, 644
    as impossible goal, 123–124, 338
    socialist barter system's collapse and,
      476
  medicine and, 175
  national culture and, 171
  promoted in *New York Times* ads, 138
  Sino-Soviet split and, 113, 123

Kanemaru, Shin, 439–441, 489
Kang Chul-ho (prison camp inmate;
      defector), 301–304, 567
Kang Chul-hwan (political prison camp
      inmate; South Korean journalist),
      298–301, 600–603, 631
Kang Myong-do (son-in-law of prime
      minister), 275, 277, 280, 281, 318,
      342, 386, 437, 439, 472, 503–505, 548
  on aid to Third World, 137
  on Chilgol Kangs' views of Kim Hyong-
      jik, 14
  on elite's fears, early 1990s, 494
  on foreign transactions, 181–182, 276
  on Mansions Special Volunteer Corps,
      315–316
  trading career of, 579–582
Kang Pang-sok (Kim Il-sung's mother), 14
  illness and death of, 32
  as laundress and seamstress, 22
Kang Ryang-uk, Rev. (Kim Il-sung's relative
      and teacher; vice president), 18, 56
Kang Song-san (prime minister), 491, 504,
      525, 580, 581
Kelly, James, 655, 659–660, 674, 675, 676
Kennedy, John F., 125, 129
Kerry, John, 675
Khrushchev, Nikita
  in Cuban Missile Crisis, 125
  on Korean War, 63, 82–83
  opposes Stalinism, 106–107, 292, 574
  and peaceful coexistence, 123
kidnapping, 535
  of defecting diplomat's son, 592–596,
      631–632
  of prospective foreign language teachers,
      328
  of South Korean movie director and
      actress, 326–339
  See also Japan: abducted citizens of
Kim Bo-hyon (Kim Il-sung's grandfather),
      205